W9-AVD-518

ai cari
Doug e Anna
con affetto
[signature]
25 marzo '88

MORGANTE

Translated by Joseph Tusiani

Introduction and Notes by
Edoardo A. Lèbano

Indiana
Masterpiece
Editions

MARK MUSA   EDITOR

LUIGI PULCI

MORGANTE

The Epic Adventures
 of
Orlando and His
Giant Friend
Morgante

Indiana
University
Press
BLOOMINGTON AND INDIANAPOLIS

This book is a publication of
INDIANA UNIVERSITY PRESS
601 North Morton Street
Bloomington, Indiana 47404-3797 USA

www.indiana.edu/~iupress

Telephone orders   800-842-6796
Fax orders   812-855-7931
Orders by email   iuporder@indiana.edu

Publication of this book is made possible in part with the assistance
of a Challenge Grant from the National Endowment for the
Humanities, a federal agency that supports research,
education, and public programming in the humanities.

© 1998 by Indiana University Press

All rights reserved

No part of this book may be reproduced or utilized in any form
or by any means, electronic or mechanical, including photocopying
and recording, or by any information storage and retrieval system,
without permission in writing from the publisher. The Association
of American University Presses' Resolution on Permissions
constitutes the only exception to this prohibition.

The paper used in this publication meets the minimum
requirements of American National Standard for Information
Sciences—Permanence of Paper for Printed
Library Materials, ANSI Z39.48-1984.

Manufactured in the United States

Library of Congress Cataloging-in-Publication Data

Pulci, Luigi, 1432–1484
Morgante : the epic adventures of Orlando
and his giant friend Morgante / Luigi Pulci ;
translated by Joseph Tusiani ;
introduction and notes by Edorado A. Lèbano.
p.   cm. — (Indiana masterpiece editions)
Includes bibliographical references and index.
ISBN 0-253-33399-7 (cloth : alk. paper)
I. Tusiani, Joseph, date.   II. Title.   III. Series.
PQ4631.M3E5   1998
851'.2—dc21   97-44991

1 2 3 4 5 03 02 01 00 99 98

To Michael Jr., Paula, and Pamela Tusiani
AND
To Alessandra S. Lèbano

CONTENTS

English Translation of Il Morgante
3

*Summary of Each Canto
with Notes and Commentary*
765

ACKNOWLEDGMENTS

We, the translator and the annotator, wish to express our deepest gratitude to Professor Emanuel J. Mickel for his careful reading of the entire text and for his valuable critical suggestions. We are also indebted to Ms. Jane Lyle of Indiana University Press for her attentive reading of the manuscript.

INTRODUCTION

Guglielmo Volpi begins his biographical study of Luigi Pulci, the first ever written on the author of *Morgante,* with these words: "A shroud of mystery surrounds Luigi Pulci; a fate of sorts looms over his head. While we have documented information for some of his fellow citizens, particularly in Florence's State Archives, very little has been found so far that can be used to illustrate his life."[1]

That our poet was not born under a propitious star, as Volpi intimates, is confirmed by those events in his life that are known to us and to which we find reference in his letters, his sonnets, his *Confessione,* and his other poetic writings. Perennially haunted by creditors while he was alive, soon after his death Pulci was denied not only the paternity of some of his minor works,[2] but even that of his masterpiece.[3]

After enjoying considerable renown in the literary circles of the fifteenth and sixteenth centuries,[4] *Morgante,* almost totally forgotten in the following century, was harshly criticized by the men of letters of the eighteenth century, who considered it to be an inferior burlesque poem, and accused its author of an immoderate lack of respect for religion.[5]

Pulci's masterpiece was well known outside Italy long before the end of the eighteenth century. The Florentine poet's work is credited, in fact, with having influenced Rabelais and Goethe,[6] as well as several English writers. In the introduction to his verse translation of canto I of *Morgante*—the most famous of the very few previous attempts to translate Pulci into English verse or prose—Lord Byron not only states that *Morgante* "divides with the *Orlando Innamorato* the honor of having informed and suggested the style of Ariosto," but also recognizes Pulci as the "founder" of the new style of poetry which was flourishing in England in his time.[7]

In the first decades of the nineteenth century, the moralistically motivated judgment of the preceding century gradually began to change. Critics of the Romantic age deserve the credit for affirming the need to research and collect "facts and documents capable of shedding further light on Pulci's life and the milieu in which he carried out his activities as a man and as an artist,"[8] and, last but not least, for investigating the impact of the Florentine poet on the development of the Italian language.

Educated people's growing interest in *Morgante,* which was hailed by Giosuè Carducci as the work of "the most independent poet of the Renaissance,"[9] was stimulated by the appearance in 1869 of an important essay by Pio Rajna, who maintained that in composing his *Morgante,* the Florentine poet had closely followed the text of an anonymous fifteenth-century *cantare popolare* (popular epic)—which he identified as *Orlando.*[10] Indeed, Rajna's study was a contributing factor in the publication, before the end of the century, of new, more accurate editions of several of Pulci's minor works.[11]

Early in the twentieth century, Attilio Momigliano's[12] and Carlo Pellegrini's[13] careful and perceptive readings of Pulci's masterpiece spurred a process of critical revaluation of the poem that Benedetto Croce had proclaimed to be "one of the most richly genial books of our literature."[14] Momigliano and Pellegrini were joined by a number of critics, including (to name only the most representative) Giuseppe Fatini,[15] who, like Guglielmo Volpi,[16] edited a valuable edition of *Morgante,* and later compiled an annotated bibliography on Pulci criticism; Carlo Curto,[17] who examined the presence and use of popular and traditional religious literature in *Morgante;* and the eminent German scholar Ernst Walser,[18] author of an extensive and thorough essay on the question of Pulci's religious beliefs. Significant contributions have also been made by Enrico Carrara,[19] Umberto Biscottini,[20] Illidio Bussani,[21] Guido di Pino,[22] and particularly Giovanni Getto,[23] whose study on *Morgante* is still regarded as one of the most sound critiques of Pulci's creative genius; Gaetano Mariani,[24] who, following Rajna's lead, probed the relationship between *Morgante* and the *cantari* that preceded it; and Riccardo Scrivano,[25] author of a detailed history on Pulci criticism from the late Quattrocento to 1955.

A place of preeminence is reserved for two distinguished Pulci scholars: the philologist Franca Ageno,[26] editor and commentator of the most authoritative edition of *Morgante,* and the literary critic Domenico De Robertis,[27] whose *Storia del 'Morgante'* remains essential reading for a critical appreciation of Pulci's poetic language. Of notable relevance as well are articles and books by Remo Ceserani, Ruggero Ruggieri, Raffaello Ramat, Angelo Gianni, and Salvatore Nigro, which deal with old and new Pulcian problems, such as the poet's imaginative reworking of *Orlando;* his seriousness, or lack of it, in matters of faith; his heated polemic with the philosopher Marsilio Ficino; the search for, and definition of, *Morgante'*s artistic unity; and the formulation of a reasonable explanation for the change in tone and spirit of the last five cantos of Pulci's masterpiece.[28]

One of the best-documented and most stimulating studies published in the last twenty years is Paolo Orvieto's complex and exhaustive *Pulci medievale,* which provides a comprehensive analysis of the Florentine poet's works, and whose main purpose is to demonstrate the medieval matrix of *Morgante,* a poem the author defines as "an inexhaustible reservoir of forms, an extreme ramification of medieval encyclopaedism."[29] Orvieto stresses, therefore, the necessity for the scholar to reconstruct the cultural and formal "prehistory" of

Pulci's masterpiece in order to better assess its historical and literary significance, as well as the poet's personal style. Orvieto's book also contains a direct challenge to Rajna's long-established and generally accepted thesis of *Morgante*'s derivation from *Orlando*, suggesting that the relation between the two poems ought to be reexamined, if not "overturned."[30] In a subsequent article, published in Germany, Orvieto elaborates on the statement made in his *Pulci medievale,* offering what he believes is plausible proof in support of his enticing as well as controversial theory. Maintaining that Rajna has failed to prove that *Orlando* was written before *Morgante,* the critic proposes that both poems drew their material from another poem, a certain *Cantare d'Orlando,* which has been lost.[31]

If it is true that this new and fascinating theory has not yet received all the attention it deserves—in his *Le Muse dei Pulci,* Stefano Carrai,[32] though acknowledging Orvieto's statement, nevertheless declares his unwillingness to discuss "the possibility of overturning" Rajna's traditional thesis—it is also true that it has had a notable impact on some scholars of the younger generation, such as Ruedi Ankli, author of *Morgante Iperbolico,*[33] the latest study on Pulci's poem.

Whether or not it can be unquestionably proven that Pulci did pattern his work on the anonymous *Orlando,* a comparison between the two texts clearly proves, as De Robertis has amply demonstrated in his book, that Pulci's poem is the product of a far greater linguistic and artistic genius.

To be sure, the studies, articles, reprints, and new editions of Pulci's works which have appeared in the last ten years[34] attest that the remarkable appeal which the Florentine poet has held for literary critics and people who love poetry has not faded with the passing of time.

Luigi Pulci, who in canto XXVIII, 140–141, declares that in writing his poem it was his intention "to please everyone," and expresses the hope that those who read *Morgante* will bless its author, would certainly be pleased to know that, in spite of having been born under a seemingly adverse star, he has accomplished exactly what he set out to do.

Called "Gigi" by friend and foe alike, Luigi Pulci was born in Florence in August of 1432.[35] He was one of nine children born to Iacopo Pulci and Brigida de' Bardi, both members of ancient and noble Florentine families. At the time of Luigi's birth, however, the traditionally Guelph Pulci family, believed to be of French descent, had lost almost all of its former wealth and political influence. In 1450, Iacopo, who had previously served the republic as a public official, was appointed *podestà,* but he was barred from taking office because his name was on the infamous list of those who had failed to pay off their debts to the Commune. When he died a year later, he left to his survivors—his wife, three sons (Luca, Luigi, and Bernardo), and two daughters (Lisa and Costanza)[36]—a house and some farmland, which his heirs had to sell to cover his debts. Lisa and Costanza were married in 1452 and 1453, respectively, and their husbands were added to the list of the family's creditors, since they had received only a portion of their wives' agreed-upon dowry.[37]

The Pulci brothers, who shared a common love for poetry,[38] therefore had to find ways to earn enough money to meet their pressing financial obligations and to support themselves and their mother. Luca moved to Rome, probably before 1458,[39] where he managed a not very successful banking business, while in 1459 Luigi entered into service as a trusted secretary and accountant[40] to Francesco Castellani, a wealthy Florentine gentleman and personal friend of Florence's ruling family. According to Pulci's biographers, Luigi's acquaintance with the Medicis probably dates from about 1460.[41] Castellani is also credited with having fostered Luigi Pulci's knowledge of the classics, lending him books and suggesting that he should attend the lectures on poetry which the humanist Bartolomeo Scala was then giving in Florence.[42]

As Salvatore Nigro points out, Cosimo de' Medici's court at that time was strongly bourgeois and patriarchal; in fact, "the union of Medicean politics with Ficinian platonism" had not yet taken place.[43] Luigi Pulci, though he could not be appointed to any public office because of his family's insolvency, became a frequent visitor at the Via Larga Palace, Cosimo's Florentine residence, where he must have felt quite welcome and at ease. Lucrezia Tornabuoni,[44] Lorenzo's mother and wife of Cosimo's oldest son, Piero, took a great liking to the young man,[45] who was already known as a poet of popular inspiration. Indeed, it was at her urging—as stated in *Morgante*[46]—that Luigi, either in 1460 (Pellegrini) or in the spring of 1461 (Ageno), began to work on his poem. Carlo Pellegrini convincingly argues that the main reason why Lucrezia made this request of such an unlikely candidate was that, being a very devout person, she wanted Pulci to write a poem which, by celebrating the figure of Charlemagne, would extol all the good deeds the emperor had done to defend and promote the faith. If the poem did not turn out as Lucrezia had originally envisioned, that was hardly, as Pellegrini further remarks, the fault of its author.[47]

When not in Florence, Pulci spent his time in the area of Mugello, just outside the city, where he owned some farmland and a mill, which was his major source of revenue.

While the humanistic influence was certainly noteworthy in Lorenzo the Magnificent, whose tutors Johannes Argyropoulos, Cristoforo Landino, and Marsilio Ficino also taught him to appreciate the great Tuscan poets, Pulci had the knowledge typical of a man who lives more on the fringes than at the center of culture. The *Vocabolista*, which Pulci compiled prior to 1465, was probably inspired by his desire not to seem out of place in the learned humanist circles of his native city. It is a work filled with classical names and affected diction, inspired by medieval manuals and lexicons and by his reading of the most popular Latin authors (Virgil, Ovid, Livy, and Cicero) and Italian writers (Dante, Petrarch, and Boccaccio). It was perhaps Pulci's only (and largely unsuccessful) attempt to be included among the Florentine literati. Indeed, this eccentric, sarcastic, popularizing poet showed no unusual interest in philological studies; nor did he share with his contemporaries the cult of forms and preoccupation with elegance of expression that are so much a part of Italian humanism.[48] Of the great men of letters of his time, Pulci admired and respected only Angelo Poliziano, whom he highly praises in his *Morgante,* together with two minor poets, Bernardo Bellincioni and Antonio di Guido, who were personal friends.[49]

Around 1465, after Cosimo's death,[50] Pulci, using his sonnets as a weapon, engaged in the first of several heated disputes with his fellow *cortigiani.* His attack on the humanist and magistrate Bartolomeo Scala, a former disciple of Ficino and a reader of Virgil, was short-lived however, and was also soon forgotten, mainly because Scala failed to answer Luigi's allegations. It appears to have been caused by a combination of personal jealousy[51] and a strong dislike on the part of Messer Gigi for this tiresome humanist who pretended to have something to teach even Poliziano.[52]

In the meantime, Luca, having gone bankrupt in Rome, returned to Florence, where he set up a new banking venture which resulted in his contracting even more debts. After Luca's ruthless creditors had dispossessed him of all that he owned, they went after his brothers, and even tried to have the Commune confiscate their properties. At the end of 1465 or immediately thereafter, Luigi and Bernardo, though innocent, were forced to leave Florence in order to avoid possible physical harm.[53]

Luigi's "exile," however, lasted only a few months. Because of Lorenzo de' Medici's personal intervention on the poet's behalf, he and his brother were given assurance of a safe return. From a letter, dated March 12, which he wrote to Lorenzo, who was then in Rome, we learn, in fact, that in early spring of 1466, Pulci was back in his native city.[54]

Their literary and linguistic importance notwithstanding, the fifty-two letters that Pulci wrote between 1465 and 1484—forty-seven of them addressed to Lorenzo de' Medici[55]—are valuable not only because they provide precious information on some otherwise obscure moments in his life, but also because in these letters, which are often characterized by a sense of urgency and spontaneity, the poet repeatedly voices his loyalty to Lorenzo, his unflinching desire to be kept in his younger friend's heart and mind.[56] Though Pulci may have counted upon Lorenzo's protection and personal concern (he knew, after all, that the support of Florence's powerful ruler had benefited many, including some less deserving than he), the sincerity of his affection for the Magnificent is a fact that most Pulci scholars do not question.[57] Can we say the same of Lorenzo's feelings for Luigi? While Pulci's familiarity with the Magnificent did have a beneficial influence on the poet's life, at least during the initial phase of their friendship, we tend to agree with Carlo Pellegrini, who, in spite of Pulci's protestations to the contrary, states that from what we know of Lorenzo's nature, "one is inclined to believe that he protected Pulci more because he liked his bizarre temperament, which amused him and provided a distraction from the affairs of state, than because he nourished a sincere and unselfish affection for him."[58]

In the course of 1467, Pulci attended an important meeting between

Lorenzo de' Medici and Galeazzo Maria Visconti, the duke of Milan (July 27), and was a frequent visitor at the Medicean villa in Cafaggiolo. Probably in that same year, he also made several trips to Pisa on Lorenzo's behalf, and it was there that he struck up a friendship with Benedetto Dei, a fellow Florentine of some distinction, with whom he corresponded, and whose name is also mentioned in *Morgante*.[59]

In 1469, the year of Piero de' Medici's death, just when Luigi Pulci, confident in Lorenzo's continued support, was hoping to "raise again"[60] his family's fortune, things took a bad turn. Because of his failure to pay his debts, Luca was thrown into Florence's Stinche prison, where he died in the spring of the following year. Consequently, Luigi and Bernardo inherited Luca's pregnant widow and their three children.

Between 1470 and 1474, Luigi was often away from Florence as Lorenzo de' Medici's personal representative. Before the end of 1470, he visited Giulio Cesare da Varano, the lord of Camerino, then spent the first few months of 1471 at the court of Alfonso of Aragon, son of Ferrante, the king of Naples.[61] Our poet accompanied Lorenzo's wife, Clarice Orsini, to Rome in May of 1472, taking her back to Florence sometime later. On August 31, 1473, the Magnificent sent Luigi to Bologna, where he was to meet with the able and valiant Neapolitan condottiere Roberto da Sanseverino, the count of Caiazzo. In the meantime Sanseverino had gone to Milan, so Pulci followed him there. Shortly thereafter, Luigi left Milan, going first to Bologna and then to Venice, on a special mission entrusted to him by Count Sanseverino.

After his return to Florence, at the urging of his brother Bernardo and the Magnificent, who lent him one hundred gold florins,[62] Pulci married, before the end of 1473, Lucrezia degli Albizzi,[63] who bore him four sons, whom he named Roberto (after Count Sanseverino), Iacopo (after his father), Luca (after his older brother), and Lorenzo (after the Magnificent).

The year 1474 marks the beginning of Pulci's quarrel with Matteo Franco,[64] a priest whom Bernardo Bellincioni accuses of caring too much for women and money and too little for God.[65] In contrast to Pulci's previous dispute with Bartolomeo Scala, it lasted many months[66] and was followed with a great deal of interest by Luigi's friends and foes alike. It soon degenerated into a heated exchange of obscene as well as defamatory sonnets.[67] The tone of these sonnets—most of which were written between 1474 and 1475—is so scurrilous that their early and later editors were prompted to warn readers that the two poets were actually good friends who insulted one another only in jest for the amusement of Lorenzo and his court. (This commercially inspired interpretation is also found in a Lucca printing of the *Sonetti,* edited in 1759 by the Marquis Filippo De Rossi.)

The Franco-Pulci polemic was definitely not fictitious, but rather sharply personal, probably because of some unknown conflict of economic interests. The dispute is also important insofar as it gives us valuable information concerning Pulci's life, character, and religious feelings. As Walser notes,[68] the one who brought religion into the dispute was most likely Pulci himself, who, in a sonnet (IV), had scolded Franco for being an unworthy priest. In his reply, Matteo, referring to the magic rituals which were held at the home of the Neroni family, where Luigi was often a welcome guest, accuses him not only of having committed a "great sin" (XV), but also of being a man who "makes war on God with his tongue and pen" (XXXIX). Though Franco's accusations must be taken *cum grano salis,* they should not be completely overlooked, since they do reflect what a number of Pulci's contemporaries thought of his religious beliefs.

In 1473, just prior to his quarrel with Franco, finally yielding to the urging of the pious Medici women—most probably Lorenzo's sister Nannina, Bernardo Rucellai's wife[69]—Luigi Pulci celebrated Easter by going to confession and taking communion.[70]

The sincerity of Pulci's sudden religious fervor is highly questionable. Most Pulci scholars, even those who deem it to be genuine, recognize that it was entirely momentary and superficial. It certainly did not convince Franco, who concludes in one of his later sonnets, commenting upon Pulci's confession, which he says was inspired by Salayè, that Luigi's repentance "did not last long."[71]

All things considered, Pulci's communion, an event that took place during a period in which the poet was still devoted to the study of the cabala and the supernatural, appears to have been merely the act of a *cortigiano* who consented to the occasional observance of a religious practice in order to retain the benevolence of the closest relatives of Florence's ruler.

In some respects, Pulci's dispute with Matteo Franco is related to the sharp attack the poet eventually launched against the philosopher Marsilio Ficino.

From a letter[72] written in February of 1474 and addressed by Luigi to Lorenzo to complain about the latest degrading sonnets Franco had composed against Pulci, it appears that until February 1474, Ficino had not overtly sided with Franco in the latter's quarrel with the author of *Morgante.* If, as some scholars maintain, Luigi's polemic with Marsilio originated because of the philosopher's alliance with Franco, then open hostilities between Pulci and Ficino must have taken place only after February 1474 or, presumably, in 1475.

In his remarkable study on Florence's Platonic Academy, Arnaldo della Torre, accepting some of Volpi's, Momigliano's, and Pellegrini's theses, ascribes the breaking off of good relations between Ficino and Pulci to the latter's bizarre temper and to his much overemphasized independence of judgment.[73]

All the reasons advanced by these critics—Pulci's so-called natural inclination to slander, his overstated broad-mindedness, his jealousy over the increasing number of favors Marsilio was receiving from the Medici, and, finally, the philosopher's open support for Franco—are not enough to fully explain the violent polemic (which continued long beyond 1477) in which Raymond Marcel, too, sees something much more serious than "a personal rivalry."[74]

Even taking into account the fact that Pulci was not one of the easiest persons to get along with, it is nevertheless erroneous to attribute his clash with Marsilio to his bad temper and his unusual spirit of independence; it is equally wrong to believe that our poet would risk losing the friendship and the protection of Lorenzo de' Medici, a lord he professed "to love, honor and fear,"[75] just to give vent to his feelings of jealousy and personal dislike for a man as learned and respected as Ficino.

When discussing the reasons for Pulci's sudden attack on the Tuscan philosopher, one should perhaps consider not only the poet's native intolerance of intellectual speculation, but also his position vis-à-vis the Church and Christian religion.

It is an established fact, as attested by the *Lettere* and *Morgante,* that in spite of his religious upbringing,[76] Luigi Pulci soon abandoned the observance of religious practices to dedicate himself, for a period that lasted about twenty years, to the study of the occult sciences,[77] which had experienced a remarkable revival in Florence toward the second half of the fifteenth century.

In seven letters,[78] written between 1466 and 1470 and all addressed to Lorenzo de' Medici,[79] Pulci talks about spirits, speaks of his growing familiarity with Salayè,[80] and announces his imminent trip to Norcia in order to visit the cave of the Sibyl.[81]

It is significant that while these letters reveal their author's acknowledged fondness for the occult, they contain no indication that the poet ever underwent any sort of a spiritual crisis. Indeed, the name of God frequently occurs in the *Lettere;* however, that can hardly be held as a sign of our poet's piety. Pulci, in fact, mentions the Almighty in the last paragraph of several of his letters when he asks God to watch over Lorenzo and his family. These invocations are similar in content and form to those we read in the closing stanzas of *Morgante.* Concerning this point, it should be noted that while Luigi invokes God's blessings on the members of the Medici family, when he refers to himself, he entrusts, with only one exception,[82] his welfare solely to Lorenzo.[83]

Just as it would be unwise to consider irreligious some of the phrases of the *Lettere,* it is also too simplistic to justify them as caused only by a momentary feeling of desperation. If Pulci was really a believer, as Carlo Pellegrini[84] and others maintain, would not these expressions sound strange coming from a man whose faith should presumably have been strengthened by life's adversity?

While prior to 1475 Luigi's attitude toward religion may have been a topic of discussion in the restricted Medici circle, the situation changed considerably when, in 1475, Pulci addressed to his friend Benedetto Dei a sonnet—"In principio era bujo, e bujo fia" (CXLIV)—in which he ridiculed the pilgrims going to Rome on the occasion of the jubilee year.[85]

As if this were not enough, during the course of the following year, Pulci declared war on Marsilio Ficino, who was lecturing in Florence on the immortality of the soul and the question of man's reward after death. It is assumed, as we have previously noted, that the poet's resentment against the philosopher, the principal exponent of the Neoplatonic doctrines then debated at the Accademia, was perhaps aggravated by the fact that, besides competing with Luigi to gain the favors of the Medici,[86] Ficino had lately sided against him in the latter's dispute with Matteo Franco.

Unable, because of his limited cultural background, to participate in theological and philosophical discussions, even if he had so desired, Pulci resorted once more to a sonnet—"Costor che fan sì gran disputazione" (CXLV)—to begin his attack on Ficino.

If one reads the sonnet against the pilgrims in the light of sonnet CXLV and the other sonnets written against Ficino and Neoplatonic philosophers, one will note that the motives that inspired sonnet CXLIV are repeated and intensified in the poems that followed it. First the pilgrims and then Ficino are the pretext for the poet's harsh invective against the intellectual achievements of a culture he does not fully understand and from which he feels totally estranged, as well as against the dogmas and the practices of a religion which he has no compunction to ridicule. In "Costor che fan sì gran disputazione," in fact, Pulci not only makes fun of the Neoplatonists' learned discussions on the immortality of the soul, he also denies the immortality of the soul itself and the existence of a divine reward for the just after death. All those who, following clergy and philosophers, believe in a better afterlife are surely deluding themselves. The afterlife, says Luigi, is nothing but a "baratro oscuro" (a huge, dark abyss).

Sonnet CXLV was immediately followed by a second sonnet, CXLVI,[87] in which Luigi—as if to leave no doubts in the minds of his readers—scorns and denies all the miracles of the Bible.

These last two sonnets caused a real scandal in Florence. The reaction was strong and immediate. Pulci (as is also attested by stanzas 42–43 of canto XXVIII of *Morgante*) was publicly censured from the pulpit by some preaching friars and was also promptly rebuked by several humanists who immediately intervened to defend Ficino, religion, and philosophical studies (we know of at least five answers, all in verse, one of which is attributed to Pandoldo Rucellai).[88]

Rather than being intimidated or silenced by such a reaction, Pulci undauntedly pursued his attack, this time addressing to Ficino at least three more sonnets, XCVI, XCVII, and XCVIII, in which the philosopher is called "Dio delle cicale" (God of the cicadas), "Viso d'allocco" (Fool's face), and "Venerabil gufo soriano" (Venerable Syrian owl).[89]

Poetry not being his forte, Marsilio replied to Luigi, although indirectly, with four Latin letters (all written before 1477), which he addressed to Bernardo Pulci, Bernardo Rucellai, and Lorenzo and Giuliano de' Medici.[90]

In the first of these four letters, Ficino states that a man who has offended Divine Majesty as much as Pulci has done is surely destined for damnation; in the second, he declares that trying to convince Luigi to make amends for his terrible and many sins is as useless a task as sowing in the sand;[91] in the third, the philosopher begs Lorenzo to make Pulci understand that the Medici will no longer tolerate his continuing to insult Christ and his faithful with impunity; and in the fourth and last, Marsilio reminds Giuliano de' Medici of the fact that Luigi has continually hurled insults at him, other learned men, and God, and asks him to put a stop to the poet's constant barking.[92]

Ficino's pleas finally obtained the desired effect. From a letter the philosopher wrote to his friend Giovanni Cavalcanti on January 1, 1477, we learn that Lorenzo and Giuliano had most severely reprimanded Luigi.[93]

Duly worried by the furor he had caused, and even more shaken by Lorenzo's wrath, Pulci desisted from attacking Ficino at least openly, and also decided to try to calm the storm raging around him (Walser even talks of a possible excommunication)[94] by performing a public act of repentance.[95] Most probably, as Ageno proposes,[96] the return of the lost sheep to the fold occurred in 1479, though some other scholars place it a few years later.[97] It is documented by a sonnet and a 337–line poem in *terza rima,* known as the *Confessione.*

In sonnet CVII, written on the occasion of the feast of the Annunciation—the only poetry he ever composed to celebrate a religious holiday—Luigi begs Gabriel to be as close to him as the angel was to Mary when he visited her, so that, with his protection, he may better fight against the devil. Though orthodox in tone, the sonnet strikes the reader as cold and unconvincing.

Considerably more significant is the *Confessione,* which is supposed to be Pulci's final profession of faith and his sincere retraction of all his preceding irreligious writings.

Addressing himself to Mary (1–18), the poet confesses to be a sinner (19–33), asks the Virgin to intercede for him with her Divine Son (34–54), tries to justify his sins by blaming nature for having endowed him with his irreverent "sonnets" (55–63), then proclaims to believe in the divine creation of the world, in the rebellion of Lucifer, in the coming of the Last Judgment, and in all the miracles of the Old and the New Testament, including the resurrection of Lazarus (64–210).[98] Having then recalled Christ's last days on earth (211–264), the poet regrets having waited so long to sing the praises of Mary, with whose intercession he hopes the Lord will again grant him acceptance into His fold (265–276). In lines 277–315, Pulci reveals the story of his conversion, which was performed by Friar Mariano da Gennazzano, an eloquent Augustinian preacher who was very dear to Lorenzo de' Medici, as well as highly respected in Florence as a holy and learned man. Pulci credits Friar Mariano's inspiring words,[99] which rekindled in his heart the extinguished flame of faith, for his decision to turn his life around and to retract all the irreverent rhymes he had previously written. The *Confessione* ends with a prayer to Christ's Mother, to whom the poet professes to belong entirely, and by whose guidance he hopes to soon join her in heaven (316–337).

The sincerity of Pulci's *Confessione* is a matter of speculation.[100] As Flamini pointed out,[101] confessions of the type written by Pulci were quite common in the literary production of the fourteenth and fifteenth centuries. In his own *Confessione,* Luigi appears to get his inspiration from Dante, as well as from religious poems of the Trecento and the first half of the Quattrocento, from which he derives phrases, words, and disposition of the subject matter.

That Pulci's conversion and confession may have been imposed upon him for reasons that were not essentially of a religious nature[102] is a possibility that should not be easily discarded. We must remember that Lorenzo and, in particular, the Medici women were not as lax in matters of faith as we have sometimes been led to believe. If it is true that humanistic society enjoyed a certain range of religious freedom, that it at times allowed expressions of more or less guarded skepticism, and that it even favored the centuries-old mockery of the sacred (be it persons or objects), it is nonetheless true that that same society would not permit or condone the clear-cut negation of Christian dogmas.

It is plausible, therefore, that, having finally realized that he had gone well beyond permissible limits, Pulci intended to show repentance for all his past irreverent and heretical pronouncements not only by repeatedly making hyperbolic professions of orthodoxy, but even by proclaiming as true articles of faith the sibylline prophecies of the pre-Christian era. Indeed, the fact that both in his *Confessione* and in his masterpiece the poet condemns his past irreligious sonnets (which he tries to excuse at the same time by saying that they were written "against hypocrites") may suggest that the accusations of his contemporaries were not totally unfounded.

As Momigliano correctly observes in commenting upon the *Confessione,* the overly pious tone of many verses; the poet's regret about having taken too long to sing Mary's praises, as if nothing better can be done to merit salvation; his blaming nature for his scandalous sonnets; the amusing transformation of Friar Mariano da Gennazzano into a seraph who urges Luigi to retract his poetry, thus "giving an external reason for a conversion which should be the result of an inner turmoil"—all these things "lend to his *Confessione* a tone of subtle irony against those who have made him do it."[103]

In his highly regarded essay on Pulci's culture and religious beliefs, Ernst Walser has shown that Luigi did not derive his sharply rationalistic, pantheistic, and tolerant ideas from the study of antiquity, but rather from his familiarity with Florentine Jews, from whom he also acquired his profound knowledge of the cabala. As Walser points out, the introduction of Averroistic doctrines into European thought was due mainly to Jewish scholars who translated Arabic texts and provided Latin commentaries of such texts throughout the Middle Ages.[104] For the distinguished German scholar, it is a serious mistake to consider the author of *Morgante* a materialist or an atheist. This is because in Luigi we can find not only negative but also positive elements which prove that his skepticism stemmed from "a harmonic view of life which, though opposing Christian elements, must nonetheless be called religious."[105] Answering his own questions—Was Pulci a heretic? Was he indifferent or even orthodox?—Walser finally asserts that Luigi was "ein wirklich religiöser Mensch" (a truly religious man), who dealt passionately "mit den Fragen des Glaubens" (with questions concerning the faith).[106]

If it is true that Walser's interpretation of Pulci as a religious individual but not necessarily a Christian is the one most frequently referred to by Pulci scholars, it is also true that his thesis is not acceptable to all because it reflects a modern perspective on what it means to be religious. In an article written about thirty years after the publication of Walser's book, in fact, Ulrich Leo states that "the question of Pulci's religiosity has not as yet been solved."[107] More recently, Remo Ceserani has suggested that with regard to the "delicate problems of Pulci's religiousness, the only thing that can be ascertainable, because it is based on facts, is the opinion that [Pulci's] contemporaries had of his orthodoxy."[108]

Toward the end of 1478, as the aftereffects of the Pulci-Ficino polemic were gradually dying out, appeared what is believed to have been the first twenty-three-canto edition of *Morgante,* of which, however, no extant copy remains. From this lost first edition probably derives the oldest known twenty-three-canto printing of the poem (called the "Ripolina"), published in 1481. It was followed early in 1482 by another edition, still in twenty-three cantos, published in Venice. The full twenty-eight-canto edition of the poem, bearing the title *Morgante Maggiore* (Greater Morgante), was published in Florence in February of 1483.[109]

In the aftermath of his dispute with Ficino, the friendship between Lorenzo and Luigi, which had already shown signs of strain at the time of Pulci's quarrel with Matteo Franco, became cooler and somewhat distant, a change that is also reflected in Pulci's correspondence with the Magnificent. The letters Luigi addressed to Lorenzo during the last period of his life are, in fact, less frequent (eight in the span of nine years) and shorter, and their tone is unusually businesslike. From these letters, and the two he addressed to his friend Benedetto Dei,[110] we learn that from 1475 to the early spring of 1483, Pulci spent most of his time in Florence or at his farm in Mugello, with frequent extended stays in Bologna and Milan in the service of Roberto da Sanseverino, who had replaced Lorenzo as his patron and employer.

Information concerning the last months of Pulci's life is scarce.[111] However, from his last two dated letters to Lorenzo,[112] we know that our poet in August of that year was in Bagnolo, not far from Ferrara, with Roberto da Sanseverino. According to Ageno,[113] it was Sanseverino's intention to appoint Pulci as his personal representative in Florence, with an annual stipend of fifty or sixty golden ducats; however, prior to formalizing the appointment, he requested that Luigi accompany him to Venice, where a great reception was planned in his honor. Just when it seemed that Pulci would finally land a job that could ensure him financial stability, the poet, having suddenly fallen ill while on his way to Venice, died in Padua sometime in October or November of 1484.[114]

Pulci's repentance and his repeated professions of orthodoxy apparently did not succeed in convincing his contemporaries, both in and outside Florence. When he died, at the age of fifty-two, the clergy of Padua refused him a religious funeral. The body of Luigi Pulci was therefore buried in nonconsecrated ground, outside the walls of the cemetery of Saint Thomas.[115] Thus, the adverse star under which our poet was born followed him also in death. As Carlo Pellegrini appropriately remarks,[116] Pulci was definitely right when he stated in *Morgante* (XXV, 276, 1–2): "We all know, more or less, where we were born / but do not know where we are bound to die."

In addition to the minor works already mentioned, Pulci authored *La Giostra di Lorenzo de' Medici,* a poem which describes, in 150 stanzas, a splendid tournament given in Florence by the Magnificent on February 7, 1469;[117] *La Beca da Dicomano,* a parody in twenty-three stanzas of the rustic love story that Lorenzo de' Medici narrates in his *La Nencia di Barberino;*[118] at least one novella,[119] several *rispetti* and *strambotti* (rustic love songs), and two *frottole* (popular songs).[120]

Morgante is a complex and multifaceted work, the product of the bizarre fantasy of a poet who defies any ready-made definition. As Ageno[121] aptly remarks, averse by nature to appreciate the lofty and noble ideals of the chivalric world—a world far removed from the bourgeois and mercantile Florentine society in which our poet lived—Pulci's creativity was essentially stimulated by an earthy, plebeian, and picaresque view of reality. Unable or perhaps unwilling to write the kind of work that was expected of him, Pulci revived the content and forms of the *cantari popolari* of the fourteenth and fifteenth centuries, of which he made quite an ingenious and often grotesque parody. A reading of Pulci's masterpiece based on a careful examination of its richly colorful and popularizing language, as well as of the spirit with which its author approaches and reworks the material at hand, demonstrates that *Morgante* belongs more to the medieval methods and ideas of the cultural tradition of the fourteenth century than to the humanistic tradition of the fifteenth.

The poem's major and minor characters, be they male or female, Christians or pagans, as well as the significant presence of the giant Morgante, the demigiant Margutte, and the devil-theologian Astarotte, have been analyzed in the notes and commentary to the cantos in which they appear. Special attention has been paid to the poet's treatment of religious matters (invocations, conversions, parody of sacred writs, persons, and objects), and to intertextual relationships between *Morgante* and other epics, namely *La Chanson de Roland, Orlando,* and *La Spagna.* While we have pointed out Pulci's frequent use of idiomatic expressions, Tuscan proverbs, and other linguistic rarities, we have also provided, whenever necessary or appropriate, the meanings of particularly difficult stanzas, as well as explanations for the translator's renditions of some almost untranslatable lines. In our commentary we have frequently quoted the critical opinions of leading Pulcian scholars, noting the often contrasting interpretations that a text as complex as *Morgante* generates.

We are confident that Joseph Tusiani's first complete translation of *Morgante*—an undertaking which has been declared to be a "Herculean labor of love"[122] and "a project of a magnitude that [would] tax the most ambitious scholar"[123]—will enable students and persons interested in epic literature, but not conversant enough with the particularly difficult language of Luigi Pulci, to appreciate fully the artistic beauty and literary relevance of this poem. We also hope that this annotated English edition, by remedying the long neglect that *Morgante* has heretofore suffered among scholars in English-speaking countries, will lead to a fair critical evaluation of the position that Pulci's singular masterpiece occupies in the history of epic literature in Europe, and also contribute to a reassessment of the Italian poet's influence on modern English literature, and particularly on Byron's *Don Juan*.

N O T E S

1. Guglielmo Volpi, "Luigi Pulci. Studio biografico," *Giornale storico della letteratura italiana* XXII (1893): 1.

2. For a discussion on the paternity of Pulci's works, see Carlo Pellegrini's *Luigi Pulci, l'uomo e l'artista* (Pisa: Nistri, 1912), 63–90.

3. See "Elogio di Messer Luigi Pulci," in *Elogj degli uomini illustri toscani,* tomo II (Lucca, 1772), 79.

4. Numerous references to Pulci and his *Morgante* are found in the works of several poets and writers, from Bernardo Bellincioni and Antonio di Guido (see notes, XXVIII, 143, 2–3 and 144, 1) to Leonardo and Tasso. Concerning da Vinci, who considered Pulci one of his favorite authors (see Edmondo Solmi, "Nuovi contributi alle fonti dei manoscritti di Leonardo da Vinci," *Giornale storico della letteratura italiana* LVIII [1911]: 328–352), Giovanni Getto links Leonardo with Luigi, stating that they shared "a certain affinity" (*Studio sul 'Morgante'* [Firenze: Olschki, 1967], 199–200).

5. See Mario Giovanni Crescimbeni, *L'istoria della volgar poesia* (Roma, 1968), 318; Gian Vincenzo Gravina, *Della ragion poetica,* Libro II (Venezia: presso Angiolo Geremia, 1731), 108–109; Gian Battista Quadrio, *Della storia e ragione di ogni poesia,* tomo IV, libro II (Milano, 1749), 526–563; Girolamo Tiraboschi, *Storia della letteratura italiana,* tomo VI, libro III (Napoli, 1781), 175. It is interesting to note that Ismaele Pedagucci, in the preface (p. 4) to his self-published 1732 edition of *Morgante Maggiore,* felt the need to state that "Pulci could have restrained himself from using ridicule and should definitely have refrained from abusing sacred things." (Unless otherwise noted, the translations of all quotations are mine.)

6. See Giovanni Tancredi, "Il Margutte del Pulci, il Cingar del Folengo e il Panurgo del Rabelais," *Atti del congresso internazionale di scienze storiche,* Roma IV (1904): 227–239; Vincenzo Jovine, "L'Astarotte di Luigi Pulci e il Mefistofele di W. Goethe," *Rendiconti della R. Accademia dei Lincei* 18 (1908): 482–517; B. F. Bart, "Aspects of the Comic in Pulci and Rabelais," *Modern Language Quarterly* 11 (1951): 156–163;

K. H. Hartley, "Rabelais and Pulci," *Australasian Universities Modern Language Association* 9 (November 1958): 71–78; and Marcel Tetel, "Pulci and Rabelais: A Revaluation," *Studi francesi* 9 (1965): 89–93.

The "historia" of Pulci's giant Morgante was certainly known also to Cervantes, who mentions him by name in the first chapter of Part I and Part II of his *Don Quijote de la Mancha*. We would be surprised had Cervantes ignored Pulci's poem, since *Morgante* was the first work ever to satirize chivalrous literature with a display of grotesque inventiveness, and thus was a canonical text for any author who undertook a similar task.

7. See Advertisement, in *The Works of Lord Byron*, 283–284, Poetry, vol. IV, ed. Ernest Hartley Coleridge (London: John Murray, 1901). In the same Advertisement, Byron explains that "he was induced to make the experiment partly by his love for, and partial intercourse with, the Italian language," which he compares to "a capricious beauty, who accords her smiles to all, her favours to few, and sometimes least to those who have courted her." Byron's literary debt to Pulci is examined by Peter Vassallo in his book *Byron: The Italian Literary Influence* (New York: St. Martin's Press, 1984), 140–165.

8. See page 208 of Giuseppe Fatini's "Rassegna della bibliografia pulciana (1811–1952)," in *Atti e memorie dell'Accademia toscana di scienze e lettere* "La Colombaria" 17, n.s. 3 (1951–52) (Firenze: Oslschki, 1952), 207–266.

9. See Giosuè Carducci, *Discorsi letterari e storici*, Edizione Nazionale delle Opere, vol. VII (Bologna: Zanichelli, 1945), 121.

10. See Pio Rajna, "La materia del *Morgante* in un ignoto poema cavalleresco del secolo XV," *Il Propugnatore* 2, 1 (1869): 7–35, 220–252, 353–384.

11. Such as *Lettere di Luigi Pulci a Lorenzo il Magnifico e ad altri*, Nuova edizione corretta e accresciuta a c. di Salvatore Bongi (Lucca: Giusti, 1886); *Strambotti di Luigi Pulci fiorentino*, a c. di Albino Zenatti (Firenze: Libreria Dante, 1887); *Il Driadeo d'amore di Luca Pulci al Magnifico Lorenzo de' Medici* (Napoli: Tipografia Trani, 1881). Concerning Luigi Pulci's participation in the composition of *Il Driadeo*, see P. G. Baccini, "I poeti fratelli Pulci in Mugello e *Il Driadeo d'amore*," *Giotto* 2 (1903): 352–363, 371–382, and *Giotto* 3 (1904): 405–411.

12. See Attilio Momigliano, *L'indole e il riso di Luigi Pulci* (Rocca San Casciano: Cappelli, 1907).

13. For the title of Pellegrini's study, see note 2.

14. See Benedetto Croce, *La letteratura italiana per saggi storicamente disposti*, a c. di Mario Sansone, vol. I (Bari: Laterza, 1957), 221. The same evaluation appears also in Croce's *Conversazioni critiche* (Bari: Laterza, 1932), 274–275, and in *Ariosto, Shakespeare, Corneille* (Bari: Laterza, 1961), 65.

15. The title of Fatini's bibliographical survey is given in note 8. His edition of *Morgante* (Torino: UTET), first published in 1927, has been reprinted several times, most recently in 1984.

16. See Luigi Pulci, *Il Morgante*, a c. di Guglielmo Volpi (Firenze: Sansoni, 1900–1904). In addition to his previously cited biographical essay, Volpi wrote articles of a critical and linguistic nature dealing with the relationship of *Morgante* to Dante's *Divine Comedy*, Pulci's humor, and some of the poet's minor works. For a more complete bibliography, see my "Cent'anni di bibliografia pulciana: 1883–1983," *Pulci & Boiardo, Annali d'Italianistica* 1 (1983): 55–79.

17. See Carlo Curto, *Le tradizioni popolari nel 'Morgante' di Luigi Pulci* (Casale: Tipografia Cooperativa Bellatore & Co., 1918). This study was followed by *Pulci*

(Torino: Paravia, 1932), and by a brief bibliographical article, "Gli studi sul Pulci nel dopoguerra: 1918–1932," *Rivista di sintesi letteraria* I (1934): 102–119.

18. See Ernst Walser, *Lebens- und Glaubensprobleme aus dem Zeitalter der Renaissance: Die Religion des Luigi Pulci, ihre Quellen und ihre Bedeutung* (Marburg: a. n. Lahme Envert, 1926).

19. See Enrico Carrara, *Da Rolando a Morgante* (Torino: Erma, 1932), 164–205.

20. See Umberto Biscottini, *L'anima e l'arte del 'Morgante'* (Livorno: Giusti, 1932).

21. See Illidio Bussani, *Luigi Pulci e il poema cavalleresco* (Torino: Fratelli Bocca Editori, 1933).

22. Of Guido di Pino, see his *Saggio sul 'Morgante'* (Bologna: Zanichelli, 1934) and the article "Novità del *Morgante*," in *Linguaggio della tragedia alfieriana e altri studi* (Firenze: La Nuova Italia, 1952), 51–59.

23. See Giovanni Getto, *Studio sul 'Morgante'* (Como-Milano: Marzorati, 1944). The edition I consulted was published by Olschki (Firenze, 1967).

24. See Gaetano Mariani, *Il Morgante e i cantari trecenteschi* (Firenze: Le Monnier, 1953).

25. See Riccardo Scrivano, "Luigi Pulci nella storia della critica," *Rassegna della letteratura italiana* 59, 4 (1955): 232–258.

26. See Luigi Pulci, *Morgante,* a c. di Franca Ageno (Milano-Napoli: Riccardo Ricciardi Editore, 1955).

27. See Domenico De Robertis, *Storia del 'Morgante'* (Firenze: Le Monnier, 1958).

28. See Remo Ceserani, "L'allegra fantasia di Luigi Pulci e il rifacimento dell'*Orlando*," *Giornale storico della letteratura italiana* 135 (1958): 171–214, and "Studi sul Pulci," *Giornale storico della letteratura italiana* 146 (1969): 412–435; Ruggero M. Ruggieri, "La serietà del *Morgante*" and "La polemica del *Morgante*," in *L'umanesimo cavalleresco italiano: da Dante al Pulci* (Roma: Edizioni dell'Ateneo, 1962), 199–223 and 225–251; Raffaello Ramat, "Storia di Luigi Pulci," in *Antologia della critica letteraria,* vol. II, a c. di Giuseppe Petronio (Bari: Laterza, 1964), 252–270; Angelo Gianni, *Pulci uno e due* (Firenze: La Nuova Italia, 1967), and Salvatore Nigro, *Pulci e la cultura medicea* (Bari: Editori Laterza, 1972).

29. See Paolo Orvieto, *Pulci medievale* (Roma: Salerno Editrice, 1978), 10.

30. Ibid., 1.

31. See "Sul rapporto *Morgante-Orlando Laurenziano*," in *Die Ritterpik der Renaissance,* Akten des Deutsch-Italienischen Kolloquiums, Berlin 30.3–2.4. 1987, a c. di Klaus W. Kempfer (Stuttgart: Franz Steiner Verlag, 1989), 145–153.

32. See Stefano Carrai, *Le muse dei Pulci,* Studi su Luca e Luigi Pulci (Napoli: Guida editori, 1985), 111.

33. See Ruedi Ankli, *Morgante Iperbolico,* L'Iperbole nel *Morgante* di Luigi Pulci (Firenze: Olschki, 1993).

34. See my latest bibliographical survey, "Un decennio di studi pulciani: 1984–1994," The Italian Epic & Its International Context, *Annali d'Italianistica* 12 (1994): 233–265.

35. There is even some confusion about the precise day of Luigi's birth. According to Volpi ("Studio biografico," 3) and Nigro (*Pulci e la cultura medicea,* 5), the poet was born on August 15; Ageno gives his birth date as August 16 (see the Introduzione to her edition of *Morgante,* vii). In the "Elogio di Messer Luigi Pulci," cited in note 3, the reported date is December 3, 1431. In the *Elogj degli uomini illustri toscani* (76), the Pulci family is said to have died out by the end of the year 1600.

36. In addition to the information given by Volpi in his biographical article, events

in Pulci's life and the poet's literary output are discussed at length on pages 9–60 of Carlo Pellegrini's book. On this same topic, see Carlo Carnesecchi, "Per la biografia di Luigi Pulci," *Archivio storico italiano* XVII (1896): 371–379, and Emilio Santini, "All'ombra del Magnifico," *Rivista d'Italia* XVI (1913): 513–533.

37. See Volpi, "Studio biografico," 5.

38. Luca (1431–1470), recognized as the author of most of the *Driadeo d'amore*, a mythological poem in *ottava rima* (see note 11), participated, at least in its initial phase, in the composition of the chivalric poem *Ciriffo Calvaneo* (for a discussion on the paternity of this work, see note, XXVIII, 118, 1–4). A translator of some of Virgil's "eclogues," his younger brother Bernardo (1438–1488) wrote Petrarchan sonnets and *canzoni,* as well as religious poems dealing with the passion of Christ and the life of the Virgin Mary. His religious drama *Barlaam e Iosafat* is generally considered to be his most notable work. His wife, Antonia Giannotti, herself a poet, was one of the best-known Florentine authors of religious plays in her time. *Santa Guglielma,* one of her several plays, was reprinted until the end of the seventeenth century. With regard to Antonia's writings, see Antonia Pulci, *Florentine Drama for Convent and Festival: Seven Sacred Plays,* trans. James Wyatt Cook, ed. James Wyatt Cook and Barbara Collier Cook (Chicago: University of Chicago Press, 1996).

39. See Volpi, "Studio biografico," 5–6.

40. See Pellegrini, 11–12.

41. Volpi believes that Luigi's familiarity with the Magnificent went back to the latter's youth ("Studio biografico," 9). Of the same opinion is Salvatore Nigro, who states that in 1461, when Pulci became a familiar face in the Medici palace, Lorenzo was only twelve years old (*Pulci e la cultura medicea,* 7).

42. See Pellegrini, 13.

43. See *Pulci e la cultura medicea,* 7.

44. On Lucrezia Tornabuoni, see notes, XXVIII, 2, 1–4; 131, 3–8; and 133, 1–8.

45. Stating that Lucrezia felt "an almost maternal love" for Pulci, Pellegrini argues that her affection for the young man must undoubtedly have been fostered "by the sad condition in which the poet found himself, his uncommon intellectual gifts, [and] the innate goodness of his soul" (*Luigi Pulci, l'uomo e l'artista,* 13).

46. See *Morgante,* I, 4, 1–2, and XXVIII, 131–136, 1–4.

47. See *Luigi Pulci, l'uomo e l'artista,* 14.

48. See Ageno, Introduzione, xxi. On this question, see also Giulio Vallese, "Il *Morgante* e l'antiumanesimo del Pulci," *Italica* 30 (1953): 81–85, and my article "Luigi Pulci and Late Fifteenth-Century Humanism in Florence," *The Renaissance Quarterly* 27, 4 (1974): 489–498.

49. See *Morgante,* XXVIII, 143–150.

50. Born in 1389, Cosimo, also known as Cosimo the Elder, died on August 1, 1464. His grateful fellow Florentines had the words *Pater Patriae* inscribed on his simple tomb in the Church of San Lorenzo. He was succeeded as Florence's unofficial ruler by his son Piero, who died in 1469. Lorenzo, who since boyhood had participated in affairs of state, was invited by Florence's leading men to take his father Piero's seat in the councils of the republic. Born on January 1, 1449, Lorenzo in 1466 married Clarice Orsini, whom his late father had chosen as his bride. Before dying in 1488, Clarice bore him six children. Lorenzo, who suffered from recurrent attacks of gout (a disease that afflicted many members of the Medici family), died on April 8, 1492.

51. A man of very humble origins, Bartolomeo Scala, a protégé of the Medicis,

was appointed to several public offices, from which Pulci was barred, being a debtor of the Commune.

52. See Pellegrini, 19–21.

53. In an undated letter that Pulci sent to Lorenzo de' Medici in Florence, probably written, according to De Robertis, in January of 1466, the sender says: "I am most sorry that in the highest moment of your friendship and benevolence I have been in such a fashion driven away [from Florence]; by now I am so entirely yours that this outrage is also an insult to you. . . . It seems as if I were a banished rogue, punished, guilty; but what have I done? No one in that city [Florence] . . . will ever be able to rightly blame me for owing something to someone. . . . I dislike unjustly paying for another person's punishment. . . . Like a hare and more wretched animals, I was born to fall prey to everyone" (see *Morgante e Lettere,* Lettera II, 938–939 and 1050–1051). In a subsequent, also undated letter addressed to the Magnificent (which De Robertis believes to have been written shortly after the letter quoted above), Pulci states that Luca's creditors are trying to get their hands on the farm and farm animals that belong to him and Bernardo without having any right to them. The properties the Pulci brothers had in Mugello belonged originally to their mother. While Luca's creditors could do whatever they wanted with his farm, the other two farms were his and Bernardo's alone. Then, angered and frustrated at being held responsible for Luca's insolvency, the poet exclaims: "If you will not be able to help us, nor will God or the devil, I promise you, since I am wrongly losing my fatherland and my possessions without having been heard, that I will at the same time lose my life and soul, and will perhaps do something that will astonish all" (Lettera III, 940–941 and 1051).

54. See Lettera V (*Morgante e Lettere,* 944).

55. As De Robertis notes in his edition of *Morgante e Lettere* (926), we know of only one letter addressed by Lorenzo de' Medici to Luigi Pulci. Its official tone does not allow the reader to deduce the writer's personal feelings.

56. Luigi Pulci was sixteen years and about five months older than Lorenzo.

57. Ageno (Introduzione, viii) even writes that Luigi "loved more than anyone else Lorenzo, whose benevolence he sought, but certainly not for personal gains."

58. See Pellegrini, 19.

59. See note, XXVII, 92, 6–8.

60. See Lettera XV, 959. Though undated, this letter is commonly believed to have been written in 1469, soon after Luca's imprisonment.

61. During this period, Pulci started a promising business as a cloth merchant in Foligno, which he handed over to Bernardo. However, because of his brother's total ineptitude in practical matters, Luigi was later forced to abandon this commercial venture.

62. See Salvatore Nigro's previously cited book, 6.

63. Originally hailing from Arezzo, the traditionally Guelph Albizzi family held a position of considerable power in Florence until the middle of the fifteenth century. Having made their money in the wool trade, the members of this large Florentine family played an active role in the economic and political life of their city. Because of their opposition to Cosimo de' Medici, they and their political party were sent into exile in 1434. Though later allowed by Lorenzo to return to Florence, the Albizzi never regained the social and political prestige they had once enjoyed.

64. Born in Florence (1447–1494) of humble origins, Matteo Franco was a parish priest and a poet who, following his admission to the Medici court in 1474, was able to obtain many benefits from Lorenzo, often by impudently requesting them in his

poetic writings. While for Guglielmo Volpi Franco was "either ardently loved or deeply hated" ("Un cortigiano di Lorenzo il Magnifico [Matteo Franco] e alcune sue lettere," *Giornale storico della letteratura italiana* XVII [1891]: 239), for Giuseppe Morpurgo this Florentine priest was "one of the least pleasant figures among all those who appeared on the scene of fifteenth-century Florence" ("Tre amici [Lorenzo de' Medici, Luigi Pulci, Angiolo Poliziano]," *Rivista d'Italia* XVII 1 [gennaio 1914]: 43). If on one hand Matteo Franco was a good friend of Poliziano, on the other hand Franco was a declared enemy of Bernardo Bellincioni, with whom he exchanged sonnets.

65. See sonnet CXLVIII in *Le rime di Bernardo Bellincioni*, Redatte e annotate da Piero Fanfani (Bologna: Presso Gaetano Romagnoli, 1876), 203–204.

66. Stefano Carrai maintains that the Franco-Pulci dispute originated sometime before the end of 1473, and that the hostilities between the two men continued at least through the summer of 1476 ("Schede per i sonetti di Luigi e del Franco," in *Le muse dei Pulci*, 78–84). In his *Marsile Ficin* (Paris: Société d'Edition "Les Belles Lettres," 1958, 424), Raymond Marcel states that the quarrel between Franco and Pulci "lasted at least three years."

67. In his sonnets Franco does not limit himself to hurling venomous insults at Pulci, calling him a most dissolute man and God's enemy (XVI) and making obscene remarks about Luigi's physical appearance and sexual ability (XVII), but he also slanders Pulci's wife (XV) and expresses the wish that Luigi will soon join his dead brother Luca, a "veritable thief," in hell (XXXVII). Though equally violent, Pulci's attack on Franco is definitely less varied, seems somewhat forced, and is believed to have had much less impact on Matteo, whom Luigi keeps accusing of being a bad minister of God, a Jew, of not knowing how to say Mass, of being the recipient of all vices (X, XXI, XXIII, XXV, XXIX, XXXI). Its extreme vulgarity notwithstanding, the most comically amusing of Pulci's sonnets against his adversary is sonnet XI, in which Franco is compared to a "fart."

68. See *Lebens- und Glaubensprobleme* . . . , 18.

69. A Florentine humanist, author of *Historia de bello pisano* and *De bello gallico*, Bernardo Rucellai (1448–1514) is also noted for having founded the *Orti Oricellari* (The Rucellai Gardens), where the city's leading writers convened to read and discuss their works.

70. The event is documented in a letter, dated April 18, 1473, which Nannina addressed to her mother, Lucrezia Tornabuoni. This letter, which Nannina dictated to Pulci, states, "This morning Luigi de' Pulci with great devotion took communion together with others." See *Carteggio Mediceo avanti il Principato*, Filza No. CXXXVII, doc. 335.

71. See sonnet XLVII.

72. The first sentence of this letter, somewhat freely rendered, reads as follows: "I wrote this letter with my hand shaking with fever because this morning some relatives brought me some sonnets which wounded me like a knife, since in them I was blamed and accused of things that I did not yet know; this aggrieved me so much that I became feverish while in the square" (Lettera XXXVI, 991).

On the basis of a possible attribution to Pulci of the sonnet beginning with the line "Sempre la pulcia muor, signore, a torto" (where the word *pulcia* not only means "flea" but can also stand for the poet's last name), Orvieto argues that Lettera XXXVI refers "not so much to the intense period of [Pulci's] rivalry with Franco (though it clearly alludes to it), but rather to the sharp period of his polemic with

Ficino and the members of the Platonic Academy, a polemic in which Franco actively participated as a close friend and confidant of Ficino" (*Pulci medievale*, 221).

73. See *Storia dell'Accademia Platonica di Firenze* (Firenze: Carnesecchi, 1902), 821.

74. See *Marsile Ficin*, 427.

75. See Lettera XLVI, 1001.

76. In his last will and testament, the poet's father requested that his heirs make "an annual offering to the monks of Saint Benedict" (see Volpi, "Studio biografico," 4–5). The piety of the Pulci family is also attested by Bernardo and his wife, Antonia, who both wrote religious poems and dramas (see note 38).

77. According to Ageno (see Introduzione, xii), Pulci's initiation into the practices of the occult sciences can be dated back to 1453.

78. In Lettera II, composed at the time of Luca's banishment from Florence, Luigi promises to send Lorenzo a few lines of his poetry from hell by means of some spirit. Lettera III, believed to have been written in January of 1466, ends with the phrase "Either God or Salayè will help us." In Lettera IV, part of which is in verse and part in prose (it is dated March 22, 1466), having stated that Lorenzo is as fond of poetry as he is of his spirits, Pulci declares once more his allegiance to Salayè. The poet's familiarity with this evil spirit is mentioned again in Lettera VII, dated August 23, 1466. Lettera VIII, written on November 4, 1466, contains the phrase "I can think of no one else but you and Salayè." A brief mention of some "spirits" is found also at the end of Lettera X (believed to have been written in the spring of 1467). In Lettera XVI, Luigi promises to send Lorenzo some more truffles after his return from Norcia, where he is about to go in order to visit the cave of the Sibyl (this letter is dated December 4, 1470). (See *Morgante e Lettere*, 939, 942, 949, 950, 951, 954, and 963.)

79. Note that Pulci's last dated letter to Lorenzo de' Medici was written in Verona on August 28, 1484, and was received in Florence on September 6 (*Morgante e Lettere*, 1005–1006 and 1077).

80. See also *Morgante*, XXI, 47, 8 through 49.

81. Pulci's visit to Norcia is also mentioned in *Morgante*, XXIV, 112.

82. See Lettera III, previously mentioned in note 78.

83. See Lettere V, VII, XIII, XVII, XVIII, XIX, XXX, XXXIII, XXXV, XXXVI, XXXVIII, XLVI, L, and LI.

84. Though Carlo Pellegrini recognizes that Pulci did not always have "clear, well-defined, and precise religious ideas," he nevertheless maintains that Luigi, a practicing Christian from his youth, remained essentially a believer even during the period in which his dedication to the study of the occult led him to neglect the practices of his faith (39–41).

85. Ernst Walser considers this sonnet to be either a very crude joke or the expression of the poet's personal indignation upon contemplating the less than edifying spectacle of many pilgrims (*Lebens- und Glaubensprobleme . . .* , 22). Definitely less convincing is Momigliano's opinion, according to which this sonnet is simply a satire against bigots, originating from the inner feelings of a poet who, though deprived of a very strong faith, shows himself to possess nevertheless "a very honest religious conscience" (*L'Indole e il riso di Luigi Pulci*, 52). Note that Pulci in a previous sonnet (CVI) defines a pilgrimage as "an exchange of lice."

86. According to Orvieto, if 1476 was the year in which Ficino consolidated his position of great influence in Florence, it was also the year of Pulci's definitive estrangement (240). (For a detailed discussion of the Pulci-Ficino dispute, see the chapter "Crisi e decadenza del Pulci" in *Pulci medievale*, 213–243.)

87. This sonnet, addressed to Bartolomeo Dell'Avveduto, begins with the line "Poich'io partij da voi, Bartolommeo."

88. These five sonnets against Pulci were published by Paul O. Kristeller in *Supplementum Ficinianum* II (Firenze, 1937), 287–289. While four of the five had previously been published by Volpi and Pellegrini (three by Volpi and three by Pellegrini, of which, however, only one had not been printed by Volpi), the fifth sonnet, beginning with the line "Parlando della cosa a te invisibile," was edited for the first time by Kristeller from a manuscript (cod. 119, fol. 3) in the Florentine Archives.

89. As Volpi, Pellegrini, Della Torre, and Kristeller point out in their already mentioned works, the name of Ficino was omitted in the first and later printings of the *Sonetti* (as in the 1759 Lucca edition of this work). In these editions sonnets XCVI, XCVII, and XCVIII appear to be directed to a "geometra," while the word "filosofia" becomes "geometria." The opening verse of sonnet XCVI, "Se Dio ti guardi, Marsilio Ficino" (codex Trivulziano, 965, fol. 15), is replaced in the printed edition by the line "Se Dio ti guardi, brutto ceffolino." The same occurs for the first line of sonnet XCVII, "Marsilio questa tua filosofia" (codex Trivulziano 965, fol. 16), which becomes "Viso d'allocco la tua geometria." It is generally believed that these changes were made at the suggestion, or perhaps the request, of Lorenzo de' Medici in order to protect Marsilio (and indirectly Luigi as well) by making it difficult to understand against whom the sonnets had originally been written.

90. See Marsilio Ficino, *Opera omnia*, I, 2, Riproduzione in fototipia dell'edizione di Basilea del 1576 a c. di M. Sancipriano con presentazione di Paul Oscar Kristeller (Torino: Bottega d'Erasmo, 1959), 661–725. The four letters are not dated. The first and the second, directed to Bernardo Pulci and Bernardo Rucellai, are preceded by the heading "Contra mendaces et impios detractores" (Against false and impious detractors). The third and the fourth, addressed to the Medici brothers, have the heading "Maledici contemnandi" (On the condemnation of a slanderer). It must be noted that Pulci's name does not appear in the printed version of Ficino's letters against the poet. In vol. 1 (p. 28) of his *Supplementum Ficinianum*, Kristeller reports that in some MSS letter 2 on page 661 contains the Latin name of Pulci as "Loisius Pulcius" or "Giges Pulcius." Kristeller, along with several other scholars, tends to believe that the poet's name was deleted (as in the case of Pulci's sonnets against Ficino) at the request of Lorenzo de' Medici. This would certainly prove that the Magnificent acted as arbitrator between the two rivals. It is difficult to prove whether Lorenzo's intervention and, later, the Medici brothers' "invectiva" (harsh reprimand) against Luigi did *de facto* put an end to the war between the poet and the philosopher. We know—as also alluded to by Pulci in *Morgante* (XXV, 116–117)—that the first printing of the poem, in only twenty-three cantos, was received with very sharp criticism on the part of several literati, some of whom, we can safely assume, were friends and followers of Ficino. Arnaldo Della Torre (289), basing his argument on the less aggressive tone of the poem's last five cantos, is inclined to believe in the cessation of hostilities between Luigi and Marsilio. We tend to agree, instead, with Raymond Marcel (432–433), who holds that even if the conflict between Pulci and Ficino became "more subtle and more impersonal" after the Medicis' reprimand to Luigi, it did continue and was not "less severe."

91. From the tone of this letter, one realizes that Ficino is no longer willing to tolerate the impious expressions of his adversary. As Marcel rightly remarks (429), Marsilio, "usually a tolerant and indulgent man," by condemning Luigi mainly as an enemy of God and the faith, shows that their dispute was not due to reasons of a

personal nature. The philosopher was, in fact, justly angered by Pulci's sacrilegious attack on the doctrines on the origin and destination of the souls, which Ficino had discussed in his *De Christiana Religione.*

92. Ficino's Latin phrase is "Canis ille continue contra me latret, quemadmodum contra bonos doctosque viros, animamque et Deum."

93. In his *Opera omnia* (731), Ficino writes: "Medices utrique paucis ante diebus in causa nostra adversus adversarius nostro non correptione tantum usi sunt, sed etiam invectiva," which, freely translated, means: "A few days ago the Medici brothers, acting on our behalf, with very strong words reprimanded our adversary."

94. See *Lebens- und Glaubensprobleme . . .* , 26.

95. Walser considers Pulci's change of mind too sudden to allow us to believe in his conversion (ibid. 28).

96. See *Introduzione*, xiv.

97. While Volpi and Nigro sustain that Pulci's "conversion" took place in 1481 (Volpi, "Studio biografico," 42, and Nigro, *Pulci e la cultura medicea*, 6), Stefano Carrai believes that it occurred "a few years later" than 1481 (*Le muse dei Pulci*, 175).

98. This miracle had been denied by Pulci in sonnet CXLVI, which is addressed to Bartolomeo Dell'Avveduto.

99. Stefano Carrai maintains that not only Friar Mariano da Gennazzano, but also the Dominican monk Girolamo Savonarola, who at that time was preaching in Florence, had something to do with Pulci's conversion ("La datazione della *Confessione* e le tracce della polemica tra Luigi e il Savonarola," in *Le muse dei Pulci*, 173–187).

100. Even Carlo Pellegrini, who states that "everything [Pulci] wrote against religion was caused by his personal dislike of friars and priests and was [directed] against all those who paid more attention to the external manifestations of the faith than to its true essence," when commenting upon this poem, which he considers important documentary evidence of Pulci's religious convictions, devotes no more than ten lines to it (*Luigi Pulci, l'uomo e l'artista*, 47–48).

101. See Francesco Flamini, *La lirica toscana del Rinascimento anteriore ai tempi del Magnifico* (Pisa: Nistri, 1891), 483.

102. Concerning the *Confessione*, Walser admits that he dares not decide "whether it may really be taken as completely honest or whether it stems from a momentary depression" (*Lebens- und Glaubensprobleme . . .* , 75–76).

103. See *L'indole e il riso di Luigi Pulci*, 65–66.

104. See *Lebens- und Glaubensprobleme . . .* , 64–71.

105. Ibid., 55.

106. Ibid., 75.

107. See "Luigi Pulci e il Diavolo," *Der Vergleich. Literatur- und Sprachwissenschaftliche Interpretationen. Festgabe für Hellmuth Petriconi zum 1. April 1955,* ed. Rudolf Grossmann, Walter Pabst, and Edmund Schramon, XII (1955): 127.

108. See "Studi sul Pulci," 431.

109. See Franca Ageno, "Le tre redazioni del *Morgante*," *Studi di filologia italiana* 9 (1951): 5–37, and Ernest H. Wilkins, "On the Dates of Composition of the *Morgante* of Luigi Pulci," *PMLA* 66 (1951): 244–250.

110. The letters to Lorenzo are letter XLI, dated June 16, 1475, from Bologna; letters XLIII and XLIV, dated March 28 and September 29, 1476, from Florence (Lorenzo was then in Pisa); letters XLV and XLVI, dated January 3, 1477, and May 14, 1479, from his farm in Mugello; and letter XLVII, dated October 15, 1479, from Milan. Of the two letters (XLVIII and XLIX) Luigi addressed to Benedetto Dei, who

was then in Milan, only the second is dated (November 28, 1481). From these last two letters we learn that Pulci's much-hoped-for appointment as *capitano di giustizia* (chief magistrate) of Val di Lugana, Sanseverino's fiefdom, did not materialize.

111. According to Lorenz Boninger, Pulci tried once more, but unsuccessfully, to find some sort of permanent employment in Milan ("Notes on the Last Years of Luigi Pulci [1477–1484]," *Rinascimento: Rivista dell'Istituto Nazionale di Studi sul Rinascimento* XXVII [1987]: 259–271).

112. The letters in question are Letter L, dated August 14, 1484, sent to Lorenzo from Bagnolo Mella, a small town in the province of Brescia, where the peace treaty between the Duchy of Ferrara and the Republic of Venice was signed; and letter LI, sent to Lorenzo from Verona on August 28, 1484.

113. See *Introduzione*, xv.

114. In his previously cited article, Lorenz Boninger, refusing the October–November period generally accepted by Pulci's biographers, states instead that while "an exact date for Pulci's death may never be established . . . September and early October 1484 is the only possible period" (268).

115. In Bernardino Scardeone's *De antiquitate urbis Patavii* (Basileae, 1560, 423) we read: ". . . quam eiusdem eloquentiae viro Aloysio Pulcio nobili Florentino: qui Patavii defunctus ob scripta prophana prophano in loco juxta coemeterium S. Thomae martyris prope puteum absque solitis sacris sepultus iacet" (also quoted by Volpi [28] and by Pellegrini [50]).

116. See *Luigi Pulci, l'uomo e l'artista*, 50.

117. For the text and a detailed discussion on the date of composition (between 1469 and 1475) and the paternity of *La Giostra* (Luca wrote only the beginning stanzas of this poem), see Paolo Orvieto, *Luigi Pulci. Opere minori*, 55–60 and 61–120. On *La Giostra*, see also Mark Davie, "Luigi Pulci's *Stanze per la Giostra*: Verse and Prose Accounts of a Florentine Joust of 1469," *Italian Studies* 44 (1989): 41–58.

118. Pulci composed *La Beca* before the end of 1470; Lorenzo wrote his poem during June–October 1470.

119. The short story known as the "Novella del besso senese" was probably written during Pulci's visit to Naples in January–February of 1471. Pulci refers to this novella in canto XIV, 53, 1–5 of his *Morgante* (see Stefano Carrai, "La novella di Luigi," in *Le muse dei Pulci*, 53–67). Pulci may also be the author of a second novella, in *ottava rima* (42 stanzas in all) (see Edoardo A. Lèbano and Paolo Orvieto, "Il 'Tractato del prete colle monache'," *Interpres* II [1979]: 282–294).

120. Of Pulci's two *frottole* ("Le galee per Quaracchi" and "Io vo' dire una frottola"), the first, a satire on female vanity, was written before 1472, while the second—believed by Volpi to have been written after 1481 because of its disconsolate tone (Pellegrini and Momigliano refer to it as the poet's "last will" and "De profundis," respectively; see Pellegrini [70] and Momigliano [73])—must be dated, according to Orvieto, to the earlier period of Luigi's banishment from Florence (1466) following Luca's disastrous bankruptcy (see *Luigi Pulci. Opere minori*, 17–20).

121. *Introduzione*, xvi.

122. See Kenneth John Atchity's article "Renaissance Epic in English," *Italica* 50, 3 (Autumn 1973): 436.

123. See Albert N. Mancini, "The English Face of Pulci," a foreword to Joseph Tusiani's "From Pulci's *Morgante*," *Forum Italicum* 18, 1 (Spring 1984): 121.

MORGANTE

ENGLISH TRANSLATION

OF

Il Morgante

CANTO I

In the beginning was the Word near God,   1
God was the Word, and so the Word was He:
this I believe, in the beginning was,
and nought without Him ever can be done.
Therefore, O Lord, who art so just and good,
of all Thy angels send one down to me,
so that, well guided, I recall and tell
an old and famous, worthy story well.

And you, O Virgin, daughter, mother, bride   2
of that same Lord Who handed you the key
to heaven and to hell and every thing
the day your Gabriel whispered to you "Hail!"
since those who serve you know your mercy still,
with pleasing rhymes and smooth and lovely style
aid to my verses most benignly lend,
and this my mind enlighten to the end.

It was the time when Philomel again   3
with her own sister so laments and cries
that, in recalling all her ancient pain,
she causes woodland nymphs to love anew;
when, not yet Phaëthon, still being trained,
but Phoebus drives his balanced chariot,
and, lo, appears on the horizon now
that, irked, Tithonus starts to scratch his brow.

'Twas then I launched my little vessel, first   4
to obey one my mind must e'er obey
by toil of prose and enterprise of rhyme,
and then to weep for Charles, my Emperor,
whose glory—this I know—by far exceeds
the praises of all those who penned its height:
yet badly understood and written worse
was the same story I now treat in verse.

Leonardo Aretino 'twas who wrote   5
that if a worthy writer he had found,
possessed of both intelligence and care,
the way he had an Urman and his Turpin,
Charles would be reckoned now a man divine,
for mighty victories and realms he won,
and surely did for Church and Faith achieve
far more than people mention and believe.

Saint Liberator's be a witness still—   6
the abbey that near Menappello stands
down in Abruzzi, in his honor built—
where Emperor Charles in bloody battle slew
a pagan king together with so many
of his infidel troops, and where, as all men know,
more bones can to this very time be seen
than will someday in Jehoshaphat convene.

But, blind and ignorant, the world does not   7
esteem his virtues as I'd like to see.
And yet some of his greatness you still own,
O Florence, and can yours forever be:
every good custom, all the courtesy
a man on earth could ever gain and keep
through wisdom or through treasure or through lance
has come out of the noble blood of France.

Within his court Charles lodged twelve paladins: 8
the wisest and most famous was Orlando,
whom treacherous Gan brought ultimately to death,
by ordering a treaty, in Roncesvalles,
there where he blew the horn so loud and strong
"after the dolorous defeat," as Dante
says in his *Comedy,* in which he placed
him up in heav'n with Charles, forever blest.

It was around the feast of Christmas Day,   9
and Charles in Paris held his entire court:
there with Orlando, whom I call the first,
were also Astolfo, Ansuigi, and the Dane.
What merriment and what triumphal things
on the occasion of Saint Denis's Day!
Angiolin of Bayonne, and Oliver,
and gentle Berlinghier were also there.

There were Avolio, Avìn, and Otho,   10
with Richard, paladin from Normandy,
wise Namo with the aging Salamon,
Walter of Mont Leon with Baldovin,
the very son of wicked Ganelon.
So glad and jubilant was Pepin's son
that more than once from happiness he cried,
seeing his paladins on either side.

But cautious Fortune there in ambush lay,   11
ever to ruin all our worthy efforts.
While Charles so rested, blissful and content,
in word and deed Orlando ruled the court,
including Charles himself and everything.
Bursting with envy, Gano, the accurst,
thus to King Charles began to speak one day:
"Must we forever your Orlando obey?

"A thousand times I've tried to make you see   12
Orlando's overbearing arrogance.
Here we are, you to serve, counts, kings, and dukes,
with Namo, Otho, Ogier, Salamon,
eager to honor and obey but you.
But this we cannot take—that he alone
should reap your every praise: so we've decided
by a mere child no longer to be guided.

"'Twas you who from the time in Aspromont   13
made him believe how valiant he had been
for doing near that fountain mighty deeds;
but had our brave Gherardo not been there,
Almontè would have had his victory.
Yet with his gaze upon the banner fixed,
he dreamed of being crowned that very day:
such is the man our Charles deserved, I say.

"If you recall the time in Gascony   14
when to your aid the Spanish troops arrived,
the Christian people would have been ashamed
if he had not his mighty power shown.
The time has come for me to tell the truth:
Know, Sire, then, that everyone complains.
As far as I'm concerned, I'll seek those mounts
that I have crossed with two and sixty counts.

CANTO I ❖ 5

"We want your greatness equally divided
so that each of us here may have his share.
Meanwhile the entire court is most displeased,
or do you deem Orlando a new Mars?"
Sitting one day alone, not far from there,
Orlando chanced to overhear these words:
for all that Gano spoke, much was he grieved,
but more for seeing him by Charles believed.

He would have murdered Gano with his sword,
but at that very moment Oliver,
snatching his Durlindana from his hand,
managed, as best he could, to free the two.
Orlando, angry most with Charlemagne,
hardly refrained from killing him instead.
Bursting with rage and maddened with disdain,
alone, embittered, he left Paris then.

From Ermellina, the Dane's lovely bride,
he took Cortana, and then took Rondel,
and so toward Brava he began to ride.
Alda the Fair, as soon as that she saw,
with arms outstretched most fondly ran to him.
But he, whose mind was wandering astray,
as soon as "Welcome, O my lord," she said,
brandished his sword to smite her on the head.

Heeding his own unbounded anger still,
Gano alone he seemed to find and fight.
Alda the Fair most apprehensive grew,
wherefore Orlando to his senses came.
Quickly his lady seized the bridle then,
and he dismounted from his steed at once.
Of things he told her till that moment passed
while resting with her a few days at last.

Then, driven by new fury, home he left,
determined now to cross all Pagandom.
But while from path to newer path he rode,
Gano the traitor he could not forget.
Aimlessly having ridden on and on,
an abbey in a desert place he saw
'mid dark and distant lands—the boundary
between Christian and pagan property.

15

16

17

18

19

The abbot's name was Clairmont, truly one   20
of the descendants of Anglante's blood.
Above the abbey a tall mountain rose,
on top of which some horrid giants dwelt,
of whom the first was Passamont, the second
fierce Alabaster, and the third Morgante.
With certain slings of theirs down rocks they threw,
and new assaults they managed each day new.

The frightened little monks dared not go out   21
at all, either for water or for wood.
Orlando knocked on the well-bolted door
until the abbot bade to open it.
After he entered, he began to say
that, having been baptized, a man was he
who worshiped and believed in Mary's Son,
and how to their old abbey he had run.

"You're welcome," said the abbot, "to our place,   22
and willingly we'll share all that we have
since you believe in Mary's Blessed Son;
and then, Sir Knight, the reason you will hear
why we have been so hesitant before,
lest you should blame as most uncivilized
that little monk who would not let you in.
Suspicion makes all courtesy grow thin.

"When hither to these mountains first I came   23
to spend my life, in spite of all the dark
you see around you, we were just as safe
as they were too, and with no fear we lived.
Wild animals alone we had to fight,
which more than once have made us wake in dread.
But now, if in this place we care to stay,
domestic beasts we have to fight each day.

"'Tis human beasts now keep us on the watch: 24
three most ferocious giants have appeared,
I know not from what region or what realm,
but surely savage are the three of them.
Force and ill will, with intellect conjoined,
achieve the worst, you know. We here are few.
Our prayers they disturb, so fierce and bold,
I know not what to do, unless so told.

"Our ancient fathers in the desert earned
  great merits for their service unto God,
  for just and holy all their actions were;
  and do not think they but on locusts lived.
Manna rained down from heaven, I am sure;
  but often in this place you eat and taste
  the rocks that from the mountain rain below,
  which Passamont and Alabaster throw.

Even more fierce, Morgante, who's the third,
  uproots pines, beeches, poplar trees, and oaks,
  and flings them—mind you—on this very roof.
  I nothing else can do but burst with rage."
While in the vestibule the two conversed,
  a rock fell down that nearly crushed Rondel:
  so strongly had the giants flung their stuff,
  Orlando with a leap sought out the roof.

"Come, come inside, Sir Knight, in heaven's name,"
  the abbot said; "the manna's raining down."
"My dear abbot," Orlando thus replied,
  "this fellow wants my horse no more to graze:
  he nearly healed him of his stubborness;
  from a good arm indeed this stone has come."
The holy father said, "I told you so:
  the mountain will someday fall down below."

Orlando left Rondel within their care,
  and begged them all to bring some food to eat.
"Abbot," he said soon after, "I must find
  the one who threw that boulder at my horse."
Replied the abbot, "Like a brother, I
  must not in anger give you any advice:
  Baron, refrain from such a promenade
  or you will lose your life, I am afraid.

"Passamont carries in his hand three darts,
  each equaling a mace, a club, a sling.
  Giants, you know, are stronger than we are
  for reasons that to them alone seem just.
  Be very careful, if you wish to go,
  for very mighty these three villains are.
"I'll soon find out," Orlando so replied,
  starting to move on foot into the wild.

The abbot signed a cross upon his brow,
saying, "Go, then! God bless you as I do!"
Orlando, as he reached the mountaintop,
went straight, just as the abbot had informed,
up to the cave where Passamont abode;
who, as he saw Orlando all alone,
stared at him more than once from head to toes,
then asked him if his service he would choose,

for which he promised great reward and fun.
Orlando said, "You crazy Saracen!
I've come to you, according to God's will,
to give you death, and not to serve as boy.
You have displeased His monks, and this is not,
you wretched dog, the manner to behave."
Instantly for his arms the giant ran,
so vilipended by the unknown man.

Soon he returned to where Orlando stood,
who by no means had left home base at all.
Swinging a rope at once, he suddenly
let a huge stone from such a sling fly down:
as swiftly rolling on Orlando's head,
it made the count's strong helmet strongly sound.
Fainting with pain, face to the ground he sped—
so wholly stunned that he indeed seemed dead.

Passamont, who believed him truly dead,
said to himself, "My arms I need no more.
Who did this idle cur mistake me for?"
But Christ abandons not His faithful men—
Orlando most of all—or He'd be wrong.
Just as the giant started to disarm,
Orlando most miraculously regained
both force and senses and, no longer faint,

"Where are you going, giant?" thus he spoke.
"Say, did you truly think Orlando dead?
Turn back, you bastard dog; fast wings you need
if you envision to escape my wrath.
Not you—your treachery has hurt me most."
Greatly surprised, the giant turned around,
but neither could he move nor sigh or groan:
only he stopped to grab a weighty stone.

30

31

32

33

34

Orlando, with his bare Cortana in hand,   35
aimed at his head; Cortana did the rest:
it quickly split the pagan skull in two,
and to the pavement Passamont fell dead.
As down he fell, the haughty villain cursed
Mahound devoutly: in this way he died.
But as that foe's harsh blasphemy was heard,
Orlando thanked the Father for the Word.

He prayed, "O Lord, forever I shall be   36
grateful to You for this my latest grace.
To You, and You alone, my life I owe,
who by this giant was here nearly slain.
Justly You balance all created things,
and empty is our might without Your aid.
This is my prayer then—that once again
I may return to fight for Charlemagne."

This whispered, down the mount he started out,   37
till Alabaster right below he found,
trying his very best, as he could see,
to root out of the ground another rock.
Approaching him, Orlando said out loud,
"What do you plan to do with such a stone?"
When Alabaster heard this warning ring,
immediately he swung his fatal sling.

So massive was the stone he quickly hurled,   38
our good Orlando shunned the peril fast,
for had that blow upon his shoulders come,
there was no need for medic anymore.
Mustering all his might, as swift as breath
he plunged his sword into the giant's breast:
thus one more heathen, dying on the ground,
did not forget to curse his own Mahound.

Blissfully all this time Morgante slept   39
in the deep mansion that with his own hand
he out of twigs and logs and mud had built:
there every night he shut himself and lay.
Orlando knocked, and kept on knocking till
the giant he awoke out of his sleep.
He comes to open—a pale ghost he seems,
for he has had the strangest of all dreams.

He had just dreamed that, having been bitten by
a poisonous snake, he had invoked Mahound,
but as Mahound could nothing for him do,
he therefore Blessèd Jesus' help invoked,
through which his life was presently restored.
All the while grumbling, to the door he came.
"Who's knocking there?" he asked, murmuring low.
Replied Orlando, "You will quickly know.

40

"I came so that you, too, like your two brothers,
of all your countless sins might now repent.
I have been sent by the good monks below,
or rather by God's providence above.
For all the ill you wrongly did to them,
Heaven Itself has passed this sentence on you.
Know, then, that just as cold as one pilaster,
I've left both Passamont and Alabaster."

41

"O kindly Cavalier," Morgante said,
spare me in Heaven's name such villainy.
Tell me, I beg you, who you really are—
and if you pray to Christ now let me know."
Replied Orlando, "If but this you crave,
I by my faith will sate your every wish.
Christ I adore, Who is the only Lord,
and Who should by you also be adored."

42

Submissively the Saracen replied,
"I have just dreamed the strangest of all dreams:
a most fierce serpent had just bitten me,
wherefore I first invoked Mahound in vain;
then, as my prayer reached this God of yours
Who was condemned to die upon a cross,
He aided me, and made me sound and free,
and so a Christian I would like to be."

43

"O baron just and good," Orlando said,
"if this true wish you keep within your heart,
your soul will soon possess that truthful god
who can alone bestow eternal grace;
and if you so desire, my friend you'll be,
and I'll to you with perfect love be bound.
False are your idols, and most vain indeed:
only the Christians' God is the true God.

44

"Our Lord and master with no sin was born   45
out of His Virgin Mother's holy womb.
Oh, if our blessèd Lord you only knew,
without Whose might no sun or star can shine,
you would renounce Mahomet instantly
together with his false and impious cult.
Turn to my God, if truly you repent."
Replied Morgante, "This is all I want."

Then to embrace Orlando out he came;   46
Orlando, too, embraced him joyously,
and said, "Now to the abbey you must come."
"Let's go at once," Morgante answered him,
"for with the monks I want full peace at last."
At this, Orlando was so glad within,
he said, "My dear good brother, 'tis your task
the abbot's full forgiveness now to ask,

"for, since my God has granted you His light,   47
and in His mercy has now welcomed you,
'tis only fit that you be humble too."
Morgante said, "Because you are so good,
now that your God will ever be my own,
tell me, I beg you, who you truly are,
and then you do with me all that you claim."
And so Orlando told him his true name.

The giant said, "May Jesus Christ be thanked   48
upon this earth a thousand times and more!
Excellent Baron, I have heard your name
mentioned in every season of my life;
once more I say I will remain forever
loyal to you for all your gallantry."
Of this and of much more conversed the two,
then toward the abbey they began to go.

Orlando and Morgante so departed   49
from the two giants lifeless on the ground.
"Let not their death afflict you in the least,
and since it is God's will, forgive me too.
Numberless wrongs to those poor monks they did,
and this is what our Scriptures clearly say:
'The good with good, the ill with ill restored.'
This is what suits our never-failing Lord.

"Because His love of justice is immense,   50
  He lets his faultless judgment ever bite
  all those who in the least against Him sin;
  thus is the good ever with good restored,
  or He would not be holy, if unjust.
  Therefore, you too be subject to His will,
  as every man must willingly obey
  whate'er our Lord expects, with no delay.

"Even our theologians are agreed,   51
  reaching the same conclusion all of them,
  that should the souls in heaven glorified
  allow the least compassion in their minds
  for their poor relatives now damned in hell,
  in great confusion and in great lament
  their blessedness would come to naught at all,
  or God's own justice to injustice fall.

"But they have placed in Jesus every hope,   52
  so that whate'er He likes they also like;
  they say that what He does is ever best,
  and never can He err in any way.
  So if their parents are in endless pain,
  this should not grieve or vex them in the least,
  for what their God desires they desire,
  just as is seen in the eternal choir."

"You do not have to waste more words with me,"   53
  Morgante said, "for you will soon observe
  if my two brothers make me shed one tear,
  and if I know the way your God to serve,
  Who, as you say, in heaven is obeyed.
  Who cares about the dead? Let's enjoy life.
  The hands of both of them I will cut off,
  and bring them to those holy monks as proof

"that they are dead, and so they all will live   54
  with no more terror henceforth, free to walk
  in safety through this desert as they please;
  thus I will, too, my good intentions show
  to this your Lord who gave His realm to me,
  and out of such thick darkness makes me go."
  Those hands he severed, as he said he would,
  and left the rest for beast and bird as food.

Together at the abbey they arrived, 55
where in great fear the abbot had remained.
The monks, who did not know what had occurred,
rushed to their abbot, frantic, out of breath,
asking in great anxiety and fright,
"Father, O Father, must this man come in?"
The abbot saw the giant, and he too
was sorely troubled by the sudden view.

Orlando, who could clearly see his grief, 56
said promptly to him, "Abbot, have no fear.
Christ he believes, and he's a Christian now,
who has renounced his faith in false Mahound."
Morgante showed the severed limbs as proof
that both the giants on the ground lay dead.
The abbot thereupon thanked God on high,
saying, "You're pleased, my Lord, and so am I."

Meanwhile he stared at him, and once and twice 57
measured Morgante's size from head to toes.
And then, "O famous giant," he began,
"know that I do not marvel anymore
that you could pluck and fling so many trees
now that I see how tall and strong you are.
A true and perfect friend of Christ you'll be,
who have until now been His enemy.

"Even one of our apostles (Saul's his name) 58
long persecuted the true faith of Christ;
but then one day the Holy Spirit made him
heed Christ's own words, 'Why do you fight me so?'
Thus he repented of his every sin,
and went all over preaching Jesus Christ:
of our true faith he's now the loudest sound,
which on the earth will evermore rebound.

"The very same, Morgante, you will do: 59
for—as our Gospel says—a sinner who
repents is feted more by God above
than ninety-nine just souls that ne'er have sinned.
One thing I tell you—from now on you must
devoutly raise your wishes to the Lord,
and in great joy you will forever dwell,
who had been lost and doomed to endless hell."

This said, the abbot to Morgante paid
great honor. Many months passed from that day.
One morn Morgante and Orlando, pleased,
went out together roaming here and there.
Meanwhile the abbot, in one room amassed,
had many a bow, many an armor hung.
Morgante liked one, took it, put it on,
not knowing how to use it—just for fun.

There was great want of water in that place;
therefore, like a true friend, Orlando said,
"I wish, my dear Morgante, you would go
for water right away." The other said,
"Whatever you command I do at once."
Upon his shoulders a big tub he placed
and started out toward a well-known fountain
where he was wont to drink below the mountain.

When at the fountain he arrived, he heard
out of the woods a mighty-sounding storm.
Soon from his quiver he removed a dart,
set it upon the bow, and raised his glance.
Look! A huge herd of boars was coming fast
with a great tempest of resounding steps:
rushing upon the fountain all so fast,
they nearly made our giant breathe his last.

Morgante shot an arrow randomly,
which pierced a boar most sharply in the ear
and on the other side went quickly through.
Dying, the beast was shaking to and fro.
Another, almost to avenge that wound,
with rage against the mighty giant came.
With hardly any time to shun this blow,
Morgante could not use once more his bow.

Seeing the boar suddenly on his back,
he gave him quite a punch right through the head:
two halves he made of it down to the bone,
and stretched him near the other on the ground.
The other boars, perceiving one more dead,
throughout the valley all began to flee.
Morgante lifted up the brimming tub,
and went his way without the faintest throb.

He balanced on one shoulder the full tub,
the boars upon the other. Back he came
gingerly to the abbey, spilling none
of all the precious drops he brought with him.
Seeing him back so soon with two dead boars,
and with that tub so filled, Orlando wondered
how he could be much stronger than before:
so thought the abbot; so was opened every door.

65

Seeing so much fresh water theirs to drink,
the monks rejoiced, but more for those two boars.
All animals are glad at feeding time,
and so they laid their breviaries to rest.
With no remorse they all began to toil
so that the precious meat would neither be
too salted nor too dry or maybe stale:
O fastings of their Lenten days, farewell!

66

All of their bellies almost burst at once:
they burped as if emerged out of the sea,
so much so that their dogs and cats complained,
finding the smallest bones too whistle-clean.
The abbot honored each and every one,
and to Morgante, after such a meal,
he gave a horse long kept in his own stable—
indeed a horse most beautiful and able.

67

Morgante to a meadow took that horse,
and wanted him to run and show his best.
Maybe he thought the steed was made of steel,
or he forgot he was not breaking eggs.
Crouching in pain, the horse fell to the ground,
and, bursting, lay forever dead and cold.
Morgante kept on saying, "Up, you cur!"
pricking him harder and harder with the spur.

68

Finally he decided to dismount,
and said, "Just like a feather I am light,
yet he has burst; well, how about it, Count?"
Replied Orlando, "You are like a ship's
tall mast, it seems to me. But let him be.
Fortune now signals you should come with me.
On foot together we must move ahead."
"And I will follow you," the giant said.

69

"When the right moment comes, you will find out   70
how I behave upon the battlefield."
Orlando said, "I swear that you will be
the strongest cavalier, so help me God.
But never will you see me sleep down there.
Ah, never mind this horse now. We should rather
bury him in some forest far away;
but how or where, I truly cannot say."

The giant said, "I'll carry him myself   71
since he refused to carry me instead:
so, as God does, I'll render good for ill.
Just help me, please, to lay him on my back."
"My dear Morgante," said Orlando then,
"if my advice you value, do not place
this dead horse on your back, or he will do
what you have done to him also to you.

"See that he does not take his quick revenge,   72
as Nessus did, although so dead and cold.
You must have heard his story, so I hope.
He'll make you—I am certain of it—burst."
Morgante said, "Just help me now with him,
and you will see what this my back can bear.
My dear Orlando, I am even able
to carry—bells and all—that very steeple.

The abbot said, "The steeple is still there,   73
but, for the bells, you've broken all of them."
Replied Morgante, "Let those two then pay,
who in those caverns now are lying dead."
He hoisted then the steed upon his back,
and said, "Orlando, you will see right now
if these two legs of mine have gout or force."
And so two leaps he jumped with all the horse.

Indeed, Morgante like a mountain stood: 74
no wonder he could do all this and more.
And yet Orlando somewhat blamed himself,
for, being now one of his family,
greatly he feared he might incur some harm.
So once again he warned him, "Put him down;
he's heavy, and his grave is still not near."
Morgante said, "'Tis nothing. Have no fear."

After he threw the horse into a deep ravine,   75
back to the abbey presently he came.
Orlando said, "Why do we linger here?
There's nothing, dear Morgante, here to do."
And so one day he shook the abbot's hand,
and said with all due reverence to him
that he was planning now to bid adieu,
and asked his pardon and his blessing too.

Wishing for an occasion to repay   76
all those good monks for all their kindnesses,
he said, "I long now only to retrace—
and right away—the days forever lost.
I planned to say goodbye some time ago,
but then, sweet Father, this my heart could not.
Nor can I all my inner feelings say,
who see you happy only if I stay.

"But I forever in my breast will keep   77
the abbot and the abbey and this place—
it took so short a while to love you so.
May the true God, the deathless Lord above,
reward you well for all you did for me—
He Whose great reign is ultimately yours.
We wait now till your blessings we are given,
and in your prayers remember us to Heaven."

When the old abbot Count Orlando heard,   78
great tenderness he felt down in his heart.
His breast inflamed with deep paternal love,
"My cavalier," said he, "all I have done
will never match the greatness of your worth;
but if our hospitality was not
in any way commensurate in this case,
blame our great ignorance and this poor place.

"We shall still honor you, oh much much more   79
with masses, sermons, praises, and 'Our Fathers,'
than with great suppers, dinners, or those things
that in a cloister have no right to be.
For all your countless noble virtues shown,
I've learned to love and cherish you so much
that now where'er you go I too shall be,
while, on the other hand, you'll stay with me.

"A contradiction sounds in these my words;   80
   but you, I know, are sensible and wise,
   and can by intuition read my thoughts.
May our good Lord, Who sent you to these woods,
   amply reward you for your pious deeds
   and for your generosity to us.
You made us free in this our solitude:
   to God and you we raise our gratitude.

"You saved our bodies and as well our souls: 81
   those giants had so long vexed all of us
   that we had lost the only way that leads
to Jesus Christ and all his other saints.
   It grieves us that you have to go away,
   and deep in sadness we shall here remain.
Of course we cannot keep you your life through,
   for surely this our cloth is not for you.

"You have to bear your armor and your spear,   82
   whereby you'll earn in heaven just as much
   as if you wore this cassock—so says God.
Because of you this giant takes his load
   to heaven above. In peace, therefore, depart,
   great cavalier, whoever you may be.
If asked about your name, I will insist
   that God once sent an angel in our midst.

"If a new armor now you wish to have,   83
   go to that room, take anything you like,
   and for this giant find a fitting suit."
Replied Orlando, "If there's anything
   I care to have before we leave this place,
   I will most gratefully accept only
something that to my friend may useful be."
   The abbot said, "Well, then, come in and see."

They went together to a little room,   84
   filled to capacity with ancient arms.
   The abbot said, "I give them all to you."
Morgante, rummaging through everything,
   finally found a hauberk he could use
   in spite of its all-broken, rusted mail.
He wondered how that thing was so precise,
   for never had he found one for his size.

It had a long, long time ago belonged
to an enormous giant, slain right there
by Milo of Anglante, who had also
come to the abbey, if the story's true.
The entire tale is frescoed on its walls—
how this great enemy was killed at last,
who on the monks had waged so long a war,
till Milo came and stretched him on the floor.

Gazing upon that story, Count Orlando
said to himself, "O God, Who know all things,
what providence or chance brought Milo here
so that he might destroy that horrid foe?"
Then certain words he read, and copious tears
welled in his eyes and wetted all his face,
as in my second Canto I'll reveal.
The King of Glory save you all from ill.

C A N T O I I

O just and holy and eternal King,
O highest Jove put on a cross for us,
You, Who closed tight the door through which one goes
down to the bottom of the dark abyss;
may You, Who gave my vessel a good start,
its pilot be, intent forevermore
on Your magnetic star: thus with Your aid
the present story will be wholly said.

The abbot, when he saw Orlando weep
(his eyes, just like a child's, became first red
and then surrendered to a tearful light),
could not but ask why such a thing should be.
Orlando finally controlled himself,
and the old man decided this to add:
"You must be overcome, so I assume,
by all the paintings frescoed in this room.

"From those illustrious people I descend: 3
if not a nephew, I'm a cousin of
that great Rinaldo, that most noble man
who was a mighty knight throughout the world.
Although my father, out of wedlock born,
much with his birth displeased our heavenly King,
from mount to mount spread Ansuigi's fame—
which makes Clairmont by lawful right my name.

"Oh, how I wish that Milon's son were here,   4
who was my father's brother, to be sure.
But gentle Baron, tell me, please, your name,
if this is what our blessèd Jesus wants."
His heart now burning with affection new,
Orlando burst into new tears, and said:
"Know then, o reverend abbot, cousin dear:
Orlando of your family is here."

Forward they rushed, each other to embrace,   5
and each for too much love openly wept.
All of their inner sweetness overflowed,
finally unrestrained, out of their hearts.
The abbot hugged and hugged him with great warmth,
each time more eager to embrace him more.
Orlando said, "What destiny or grace
has made me find you in this wilderness?

"But tell me now, dear Father, tell me why   6
you wanted to become a monk up here
instead of brandishing a spear like me
and like so many of our family."
"Because it simply was God's holy will,"
the abbot to Orlando fast replied;
"'tis He Who bids us through so many a road
finally enter His divine abode:

"one through the crosier, through the sword another,   7
for just as nature breeds different minds,
equally different these ladders are:
so long as men to their safe harbor come,
the first or the last ladder's just as good.
We all are pilgrims through unlikely realms,
and, dear Orlando, we're all bound for Rome,
yet not by the same road are going home.

"Thus soul and body evermore are vexed   8
because of the first sin of that old fruit.
I, book in hand, am here both day and night,
whereas you, brandishing a sword, ride on,
perspiring in the sunshine and the shade;
but touching home base is the game's sole end.
I mean to say we all must struggle here
to reach eventually our ancient sphere."

Morgante with the two had also wept,   9
as all this lofty reasoning he heard,
but for an armor he was searching still.
At last he found a big old hat of steel
that in a corner full of rust had lain.
Orlando, when he saw him try it on,
said, "You would make a lovely mushroom. Look
what a small cap upon so long a stalk!"

Morgante also found a big old sword,   10
which on his side he hung, and then he looked through
things in a corner where a broken bell,
long ago fallen, lay beneath the roof:
with all his strength he snatched its clapper out,
and showed it to Orlando finally:
"What do you think of this, my noble lord?"
"I say that for Morgante it's very good."

The giant added, "With this clapper here—   11
see for yourself how heavy, long, and thick—
would you not say I'd strike a lovely sound?
I want to smash both iron mail and bone:
I'm dying to begin my aiming game."
Orlando spoke to Clairmont in this way:
"I beg you, holy abbot, dear and kind,
to tell us where great action we may find.

"We are both looking, if God's will be pleased,   12
for any battle, any tournament."
The abbot so replied, "Of course I will,
and I believe your wish will be fulfilled.
First, O belovèd cousin, you should know
that nearby, in the East, a pagan king
lives safe within a mighty city's walls,
whom everyone King Caradoro calls.

"He has a daughter whose great beauty's matched   13
   by gentleness of heart and worth of mind,
   and yet there's no one beats her in a joust,
   for every knight's a coward in her eyes:
   ah, were she not a Saracen, indeed
   the noblest of all ladies she would be.
   But at the city's confines, all around,
   there, camped for war, more Saracens are found.

"A mighty king is monarch of them all—   14
   called Manfredonio by all of them.
   His breast is flaming for the lovely lass,
   and, just as Love commands, great deeds he does,
   and has now brought all Pagandom along
   to win this lovely lady at long last.
   They say there are from very distant lands
   one hundred forty thousand pagan hands.

"King Caradoro, instead, has maybe eighty   15
   thousand most valiant, dauntless Saracens.
   King Manfredonio, every passing day,
   boastfully shouts he'll have this girl or death,
   and builds new bombards and new catapults,
   moving each new day closer to the doors."
   Our Count Orlando, who such tidings heard,
   ask not with what desire was quickly stirred.

After he spoke of many other things,   16
   once more he begged permission to depart;
   he asked the holy abbot once again
   to recommend him ever in his prayer:
   among those warriors he wished to be,
   there in the land that he had spoken of,
   but with his blessing he desired to go.
   The abbot said, "It shall indeed be so:

"if you are happy, I am happy too.   17
   By now you know our monastery well,
   and I remain your ever-loyal host:
   whatever's here belongs to Milon's son,
   and there's no need even to mention this.
   To both of you I give my blessing then."
   Thus, thanking Clairmont with new tears and sobbing,
   Morgante and Orlando left the abbey.

Through desert regions they at random fared— 18
one on foot and the other on a horse.
Through forests and through plainlands on they rode,
with neither home nor obstacle in sight.
The darkness of the night was nearing fast
when, roused by doubtless joy, Morgante said,
laughing, to Count Orlando, "Can it be
I see a tavern right in front of me?"

No sooner had he spoken than—behold— 19
there in that desert a fair mansion stood.
Towards it rode Orlando right away
and, seeing the door open, fast jumped down.
No one was there to answer his *Hello.*
Into a hall they walked just to make sure:
many a table richly set they viewed,
and, spread upon them, every kind of food.

Each single hall was beautiful and bright, 20
frescoed with paintings exquisite and rare,
and there were costly beds in each of them,
all finely decked with draperies of gold
and deep-blue canopies replete with stars,
each worth a priceless treasure, to be sure.
Of gold and silver there was many a door,
and festive-looking was the dazzling floor.

Wondered Morgante, "Can it ever be 21
that no one's here to guard so rich a home?
Orlando, this room here seems good to me
for a full day of comfortable rest."
Orlando could not help but ponder this:
"Either a very clever Saracen
has set a trap to catch some Christian thugs
and lure us here by food like stupid frogs

"or there's a worse deceit beneath all this: 22
it doesn't seem quite natural to me."
Morgante said, "Who cares?" He had begun
to reason with the logic of his teeth.
"Our host will pay," he added soon, "not we:
meanwhile let's eat and make the most of it;
of what is left we'll later make a facile
bundle, for when I steal, I steal a castle."

Orlando said, "This medicine of yours   23
could purge the entire palace, I believe."
All over, through the kitchen too, they searched
with neither cook nor serving boy in sight.
Well then, back to those tables soon they went
and let their jaws begin their joyous work:
for one full day they'd eaten but in dream—
their hunger was therefore no simple whim.

And there were countless appetizing plates: 24
peacock and partridge, hare and pheasant, deer
and rabbit, and fat capon; there was wine
to drink, and water also for their hands.
Enormous morsels made Morgante yawn;
they both drank like sick men, and ate like healthy ones.
When to their hearts' content themselves they'd fed,
they rested in a most luxurious bed.

At the first gleam of daylight they arose,   25
thinking that, ermine-white, they'd walk right out.
They did not bother asking for the check,
or the innkeeper would have seen new coins.
Morgante, left and right, went through the house
but could not find an exit anywhere.
Orlando said, "Are we so drunk that we
can guess no longer where the door might be?

"If I see straight, this is the dining hall,   26
but all the tables—look—and all the plates
have disappeared. There was a staircase here . . .
During the night some people must have come,
who, like us, had a great and happy time . . .
But what is happening here? Where's everything?"
Around they wandered in their endless doubt,
but from the selfsame room were never out.

They could not see a window or a door.   27
Morgante said, "But how did we come in?
Orlando, we'll digest our dinner soon,
for we have fallen both into this trap,
and are now like a grub in its cocoon."
Orlando said, "We're buried here alive."
"To tell you the whole truth," Morgante said,
"this room must be by ghosts inhabited.

"Orlando, the whole house must haunted be,   28
just like the castle of the ancient days."
Orlando crossed himself a thousand times,
unable to explain how that could be.
He kept on saying, "Could this be a dream?"
Morgante, happy still for the free food,
said, "When I ate, I know I was awake;
who cares about the rest, for heaven's sake?

"What counts is that my meal was not a dream;   29
and even if it came from Satan's hand,
tell him to bring me in the future more."
For three full days they wandered all about,
ever unable to escape from there;
but on that third day, going farther down,
in a deep corridor themselves they found,
whence they could hear a low, sepulchral sound.

It said, "You're much mistaken, Christian knights,   30
if you believe you'll ever leave this place
unless you dare to duel with me first.
You have discovered now my stone, but here
you too will stay for all eternity."
When such a threat he heard, Morgante said,
"Orlando, did you hear the words of doom
spoken by someone hiding in that tomb?

"I want to go and open up that grave   31
from which the chilling menace seems to come,
ev'n if Cagnazzo and Farferello should
come out with Lustycock and Eviltail."
Praised by Orlando for his enterprise,
he soon proceeded toward the sepulcher.
"Show me," he said, "how many spirits dwell
right here, of those that from high heaven fell."

This said, Morgante lifted up the stone.   32
Blacker than coal—lo and behold—at once
a devil came out of that very tomb—
a bundle of proud bones shaped as a ghost,
naked and bare and with no flesh about.
Orlando said, "It must indeed be true:
this is the devil that I met before,"
and, in so saying, jumped on him therefore.

This devil grabbed and held him very tight.   33
They both fought hard. Morgante more than once
said to Orlando, "I will help you, wait!"
but Count Orlando needed not his help.
Yet by the devil he was shaken so,
upon his knees Orlando nearly fell,
but fast he rose and wrestled him again.
Closer and closer drew Morgante then,

dying his own strong battle to commence;   34
but when he saw Orlando's sorry plight,
he started with his clapper his great war,
saying, "In such a way we'll share the fight."
Ah, but that demon drove him to despair
with both his laugh and the gnashing of his teeth.
Morgante grabbed him by the armpits and—zoom—
laid him against his will down in his tomb.

As soon as he was in, out loud he cried,   35
"Close not the lid or you will not come out."
Whispered Orlando, "What are we to do?"
The other answered, "Let me tell you then.
You must baptize that giant right away,
and then you're free to go just as you please.
Make him a Christian: when you so have done,
resume your journey and go safely on.

"If you close not this lid upon my head,   36
I swear I'll never vex you anymore.
My word of honor: what I swear is true."
Orlando said, "With joy all this I'll do,
although your villainy deserves it not.
To leave this place, I'll do just as you say."
With water then the giant he baptized,
and with Morgante and Rondel came out at last.

No sooner had he left the mansion's site   37
than a great roar within its walls was heard.
He turned to look: the palace was not there.
"'Twas then the great deceit was better known:
there were no walls, there was no place at all.
Morgante said, "My heart is telling me
we could this moment go right into hell
and oust the fiends that in its bottom dwell.

"If only we could somewhere find the door   38
   (there are, they say, so many of them on earth
   all lit with fire, through one of which a man—
   what's his name?—used to find Eurydice),
   I'd fight with all the devils just like that.
   All those unhappy souls we would set free;
   I'd even cut right off Minos's tail
   if, like this one, those demons too were real;

"And Charon's beard I'll pluck hair after hair,   39
   and I'll unseat King Pluto from his throne;
   and then I'll take one sip from Phlegethon,
   and swallow Phlegyas, and with one punch
   kill Erichtho, Tisiphone, Alecto,
   Cerberus, and Megaera all at once;
   last, Beelzebub I'll make run fast as he can,
   swifter than a camel through the Syrian sand.

"Say, couldn't we dig a tiny tiny tunnel?   40
   You'll see the greatest running of your life
   if this my clapper I bring down with me;
   then match me with all devils if you wish."
   Replied Orlando, "There's no food down there,
   my dear Morgante, and we'd suffer most.
   Right at the entrance we could die ablaze:
   so let's forget the trip to such a place.

"If you, dear friend, can through a valley go,   41
   forget the steepness of the mountain road.
   Why put your head inside a lion's lair?
   Let's choose the easy way that we know best."
   And so the two upon a fountain came,
   where two apparent foes were fighting hard:
   they both were couriers with missives sent,
   now like two cats against each other bent.

Coming upon the spring, Orlando asked,   42
   "You over there, why do you quarrel so?
   Couriers you must be: Who sends you here,
   and what important letters do you bring?
   Are you from France or from some other place?
   Stop bludgeoning each other for a while.
   Tell me if you are Christians—so may God
   spare you a stronger and much rougher rod."

"I am a Christian," one of them replied,   43
"and not too long ago I came to live
in a fair castle known as Montalbàn.
Rinaldo, my true master, sent me here
in search of his dear cousin; Ganelon,
that traitor, still is scheming his defeat:
in fact, this very man Your Lordship sees
looks also for Orlando, if you please.

"By chance upon this spring we both arrived,   44
and, as the law of couriers demands,
we asked each other the same question: 'What
important brief or message do you bring?'
and, being weary, down to rest we lay.
'Twas then I learned this man has been sent here
by Gan to find Orlando—yes, to look
for him in the remotest pagan nook.

"And since Orlando I defended fast,   45
saying no word, he only raised his mace,
and so it was that we began to fight."
After he heard these words, Orlando said,
"O God, may You protect this life of mine
against the fraud and treason of that man.
I cannot find, wherever I may go,
a place where I'd be safe from such a foe."

Seeing his lord most visibly upset   46
and furious against old Ganelon,
Morgante was so moved and so incensed,
he grabbed the courier by the throat at once
(the one, I mean, that Ganelon had sent)
and, keeping him inside the fountain deep,
so loved with all his wrath to kick and pound him,
he broke his every bone and, last, he drowned him.

To the good courier Orlando said,   47
"I am the one you have been sent to find.
Tell our Rinaldo that in this far place
you've found his cousin, as you well can see.
Yes, I'm Orlando, faring in despair
from land to land, as Charlemagne decreed."
When the good courier heard he was Orlando,
down on his knees he fell in awe and wonder.

"Tell Charles for me," Orlando added then,
"that he should follow still old Gan's advice
while I go wandering throughout the world
as if, no more his friend, I were his foe.
And tell him where you saw me, how and when—
alone and poor and begging and forlorn;
and what I did for him to all is known,
except, O courier, to him alone.

48

"What a good action is, he does not know,
nor does he care that his own nephew, far
from France, no longer in his court abides.
So long as Gan be there to handle him,
he forces me to dwell in pagan lands
just as the fickle wheels of Fortune want.
And tell him that a giant's here with me—
he is a Christian, and Morgante's he—

49

"together with my horse and with my sword.
My armor is the only wealth I have,
and still I do not know to what new place,
or what new region, Fate may take me yet.
One thing is sure: for Barbary I'm bound,
or for whatever land despair suggests,
my death to find, which he so covets, but
never inside his court will I set foot.

50

"And say to my Rinaldo, Ammon's son,
that with great love I recommend to him
the warriors I left within his care,
since I am doomed in Pagandom to die.
My best to Namo, Astolfo, Salamon,
and Berlinghier, of whom I'm still so fond;
and tell sweet Oliver to take good care
of my dear bride, his sister—Alda the Fair.

51

"Inform the Dane, O kindly courier,
that for a while I won't return to France,
and tell him I have Cortana and the steed
lest some suspicion rise about their fate.
See how my overall is all adorned
with small Mahomets painted to and fro.
To him my very self I recommend—
Orlando, roaming lone from land to land.

52

"Now, if you please, reveal your name to me."
    The courier replied, "This is, my lord,
    a happy task: Chimento is my name.
    May Jesus Christ prevail upon your mind,
    for your strange answer fills my heart with grief:
    this is not what Rinaldo sent me for.
    May you, Orlando—I most humbly pray—
    listen to what I have come here to say.

53

"The very day from Montalban I went
    to Paris—right where I am coming from—
    the royal court looked like a frightened home:
    the Emperor, I say, was not himself;
    people were stunned, and helpless the whole realm.
    I'm sure your ears have oft been ringing here,
    for everybody still recalls your fame,
    and everybody mentions still your name.

54

"My lord awaits you most impatiently,
    and France and Paris curse this sorry deed.
    And now a little fable I must tell,
    for oft our minds a telling tale demand.
    Well—once upon a time a little ant
    began to roam the earth, as many do,
    until a horse's skull at last she found.
    Inspecting it, she crawlèd round and round,

55

till, having reached the region of the brain,
    this looked to her so beautiful a room
    that in her heart great happiness she felt,
    and kept on saying, simple and naive:
"Surely some mighty lord used to live here."
    Finally, after searching every cell,
    convinced that there was nothing there to find—
    no crumbs to eat nor food of any kind—

56

back to her little hole at last she went.
    I beg your pardon, sir, if I am wrong,
    and may you understand more than I say.
    I want you to believe my every word
    and back to your dear cousin go at once,
    or he will soon abandon every hope:
    he told me that his face I should not see
    unless, my lord, to France you come with me.

57

"It is great love that makes me utter this: 58
   do not forget your relatives and friends.
'Tis hard to roam the world the way you do!"
After the courier spoke, Orlando said,
"Chimento, a true friend you are indeed,"
   and more than once most bitterly he sighed.
Finally, from the man he walked away
   and, since he was in tears, did nothing say.

Ah, even from Chimento far away,   59
   Orlando kept on sighing the day long.
Sad and forlorn, the messenger returned,
   not knowing how to face his lord Rinaldo.
Meanwhile Morgante in good spirits walked
   with that hard, heavy clapper in his hand,
till from a hill the two saw, shimmering,
   the troops of Manfredòn, the pagan king,

with tents, pavilions, pennons everywhere;   60
   and a great din of instruments they heard—
kettledrums, horns and trumpets and small drums.
   And knights-at-arms all over they could see,
with helmets fair and dazzling in the sun.
   Watching most fixedly the plain below,
Orlando saw a pagan multitude—
   as large as the good abbot said he would.

This happy sight delighted him as much   61
   as did Morgante. Down the hill he rode
and before Manfredonio appeared,
   who, being generous and sweet and kind,
first marveled at Morgante silently,
   then, taking by the rein Orlando's steed,
said gently, "Welcome to my camp, dear count!
   Come to my tent, sir, after you dismount."

Leaving Rondello to Morgante, Orlando   62
   sought the pavilion of the pagan king.
There Manfredòn addressed him in this way:
   "Whether a Saracen or Christian knight,
no less than a dear brother you're to me,
   and lest you should have sought this place in vain,
I'll give you, if I may, a salary
   that totally will please Your Excellency."

To those kind words Orlando so replied: 63
"Your lovely speech has overwhelmed my heart.
I cannot ask a salary of you
unless you see how bravely I can fight."
Of this and many other things they spoke
until the pagan king said, "You should know
what you perhaps have never heard so far,
for wise and courteous knights you seem and are.

"I'll tell you first my story of distress,   64
and then you'll let me know what can be done.
Alas, alas, most madly I'm in love
with a sweet lass, and know not what to do.
Twice have I tried to beat her in a joust,
but twice she proved the better of the two,
so that most rightly scornful she has been,
and I no longer hope her hand to win.

"'Tis true, I have so many soldiers here   65
that make me hope to triumph in the end;
but this is not an honorable thing,
for with the spear alone must I prevail.
If one of you is now so strong a man
as both to face and beat so strong a girl,
all that I own on earth shall be his prize,
for in this lady my sole treasure lies."

Replied Orlando, "We shall try our best: 66
each will employ his most undaunted might,
and I believe we'll ultimately win,
unless this lady's not of flesh and bone."
The pagan said, "There's more that you should know.
Before the lass appears upon the field,
one of her brothers she sends there instead—
a very brave yet very gentle lad

"whose name is Lionetto. He's the son   67
of His Great Majesty, King Carador,
and, ah, to my dismay, there's none more brave
among all those who worship our Mahound.
His sister, yes, the one who, as I said,
keeps this my heart ablaze and makes me die,
is my sweet angel yet my cruel foe—
she's called Meridiana—and rightly so.

"For truly, as her name seems to reveal,   68
she looks as fulgent as the midday sun.
With this most gentle lass I fell in love
not for her face or for her words or deeds,
but only for her virtues fame has spread—
or was it Fate that wanted this to be?
I, from the day my heart began to burn,
have for her sake grown good and kind in turn.

"And now I beg you, O most famous knights,   69
to fill me with the pleasure of your names."
Orlando with most grateful words replied,
"To please you, I'll reveal them right away,
though we would like to give you greater gifts;
yet not to tell our names would wrong you much.
I in the East have spent many a year—
Brunoro is indeed my name; and here

is a great giant, a good friend of mine   70
whose strength and valor you will someday see:
he loves to hear himself called fierce Morgante,
and is much stronger than he seems to be.
He worships both Mahound and Trevigant."
Hearing these words, most graciously the king
answered, "Upon my honor, you will be
treated and honored as you wish by me."

Manfredòn honored them as best he knew,   71
joyously housed them in his royal tent,
and many things discussed with both of them.
But then, most unexpectedly one day,
brave Lionetto, charging once again,
straight toward the king's pavilion seemed to dash,
whereupon, just to reap much greater scorn,
Manfredòn bade the sounding of the horn.

Young Lionetto fought so fast and hard,   72
he scattered in great terror many a man.
Like a ferocious hungry wolf that swoops
down on a flock of most defenseless sheep
(the shepherd only shouts in helplessness),
he wounded some, felled others, causing countless
soldiers to die. All those who were not taken
prisoner ran for shelter, sorely shaken.

When Count Orlando heard that Lionetto   73
upon the field had rushed in such a way
that everybody shunned the daring lad,
he mounted his Rondèl immediately,
saying, "Morgante, come: I'll wait for you.
Of Lionetto have you ever heard?
Now you will see who's stronger—his Mahound
or Jesus Christ, in whom your hope is found."

Replied Morgante, "Never have I seen   74
Orlando in action; but the time has come.
Thanks be to God, who gives me such a chance."
Spurring his charger on, Orlando sped,
vanishing like an arrow in the air;
Morgante, too, was ready now to go:
clapper in hand, he would not miss the view
of what Orlando was about to do.

Orlando sought the thick of battling men,   75
and still Morgante kept him within sight,
for, ever very close behind Rondèl,
wherever went the charger, he went too.
Wielding a bloody spear, right at that time
brave Lionetto reached the battlefield.
Orlando lowered, seeing him, his lance,
but Lionetto raised one more at once.

Turning his horse, against Orlando fast   76
he charged: so greatly sounding was the clash,
both mighty spears into small fragments broke,
and Lionetto from his steed was thrown,
whereas Rondel like a true swallow fled.
Watching his lord and master, said Morgante,
"Surely Orlando is a perfect knight;
Mahomet's wrong, and Jesus Christ is right."

But Lionetto, rising from the ground,   77
jumped on his horse again. With piercing shouts
he called Mahomet more than once, and said,
"You traitor, whom I wrongly have adored,
this very moment I'm renouncing you
since you have brought me to this shameful end.
I beg you this my soul no more to bless:
not even Count Orlando could strike with such success."

Then, turning to Orlando, this he said:
"It was my charger's fault—remember that."
Smiling, Orlando thus replied to him,
"A tickling finger puts him soon to sleep."
Morgante then replied, "I don't think so;
now that you sit on this your horse again,
I think it is your duty, pagan lord,
to test your worth once more—but with a sword."

And Lionetto answered, "Suits me well:
let the sword bring an end to this our fight."
"Well, good for you, by God," Morgante said;
"you'll soon find out you've wrongly blamed your horse."
And now, Lord God, Whom I am glad to serve,
and Who can make both land and sky grow dark,
watch over us, instruct, save us from hell,
that I may sing this worthy story well.

C A N T O   I I I

1

Father, incomprehensible and just,
wholly enlighten, God, this heart of mine
so that of every sin it may be cleansed;
and though I have till now been negligent,
yet still my Father and my Lord You are,
as well as the one savior of mankind;
You are the very one that launched my boat,
promising You would help it to its port.

Orlando answered him, "Indeed we must,"
and so the sword was chosen for the fight.
Daring and young, brave Lionetto had
in the meantime thought out more plans than one
to do our Count Orlando lasting wrong;
thus, to make sure they would not futile be,
high with both hands his sword he lifted up:
at such a blow Orlando's horse would stop.

The pagan's fury our Orlando saw,   3
determined thus to shun its falling might;
but he could not, for on his horse's back
down came the sword: Rondel went down, and down
went Count Orlando, landing on the ground,
and saying, "God could not protect Himself
against His traitor; how can we?" But here
no treason is allowed to interfere.

Then to himself he said, "O Vegliantìn,   4
where are you?" The young foe could hear these words,
and reckoned, knowing what they clearly meant,
that his old father should be told at once.
Orlando saw himself half-recognized,
and "If this lad hears more about me, then
my full identity is known," he said;
"a better service he will do me dead."

With swords and arrows, javelins and picks,   5
Orlando went around the wrathful foe—
many a weapon 'gainst one sword alone;
yet he cut tuilles and brassarts everywhere,
and hauberks all about—a harvestful
of severed hands and quickly falling wrists:
yes, with his sword he fanned each pagan face,
of his true value leaving ample trace.

Seeing his Count Orlando in this sore   6
predicament, right there Morgante rushed,
flaunting as fast his clapper round and round,
letting them watch more fireflies than one sees
in August. Spears and arrows everywhere,
yet those who threw them did not dare advance;
so when he came where his great lord did shine,
he looked just like a bristly porcupine.

Orlando was intent, back on his steed,   7
on finding where his Lionetto stood;
but Lionetto, who knew now his name,
was riding toward the city at great speed,
avoiding out of cowardice the fight.
There was Orlando restless on Rondel,
spurring with such a vehemence his horse:
at last he reached Lionetto near the doors.

"Why, pagan lad," he shouted, "do you tremble so?"   8
But fearing for his life, the frightened prince
faster and faster to his safety ran.
Orlando with his sword pursued him yet,
until, despairing of the city's walls,
the young man was with massive fury pierced:
by now utterly blind, utterly mad,
Orlando severed from his trunk his head.

Back to the field, after his death, he went,   9
and there he found Morgante fighting still.
The giant learned of Lionetto's death
and with great joy toward the flag returned.
The news of what had happened was brought fast
to the fair lady brighter than the sky:
she scratched her cheeks and tore her golden hair,
and the whole court began to weep with her.

Soon the old father moaned, "My son, my son,   10
who killed you?" and his moans were sad and loud;
"Mahomet, a true god you cannot be
if his untimely death means nought to you.
Do you expect me now to honor you
and worship your great might within your mosque?"
Meridiana, weeping and distraught,
had in the meantime all her weapons brought.

A perfect suit of armor soon was placed   11
before the damsel's eyes, including jambs,
hauberk with plates withstanding any blow,
a fully tested cuirass, and with it
helmets and gauntlets, armlets, gorgets, all:
never had such a suit been seen before.
And what a sword—infallible indeed!
Armed in this manner, mounted she her steed.

She did not want her troops to follow her,   12
save for a squire with a second lance.
In such a fashion to the field she came
(unless the author of this tale is wrong),
and as she reached it, a fair horn she blew—
as fair as her own cheeks of ivory.
Orlando said to Manfredon, "To war
I'm rushing, since I hear the horn once more."

Meanwhile Morgante roused Rondel to fight.   13
While Count Orlando toward the damsel rode—
she wanted her dear brother to avenge—
close to his stirrup our Morgante walked.
Soon fair Meridiana sighted him,
and soon she thought Brunoro was the knight.
Orlando now addressed the lady first,
but she replied, "May you be ever cursed,

"if you're the one who Lionetto slew—   14
who was the pride and glory of the East.
May you by god Mahomet now be doomed,
by Trevigant and by Apollin, too!
I want you this to know: that famous lad
will never have his peer on this our earth."
Orlando said, "I say, in front of you,
I am the one who Lionetto slew."

The lady said, "Then talk to me no more: 15
here in this field I will avenge his death.
Cruel Mahomet, does your heart not bleed
for the extinction of your own strong race?
The sun will never see such knight again,
nor will the like rise ever on this earth."
Against Orlando then she spurred her horse,
and so against the lass he went of course.

Suddenly with their spears they met and clashed;   16
the lass's blow was valiant indeed,
for at the very start of such a fight,
Orlando felt the impact of her wrath.
The fragments of both spears went through the air
while, very bold and fast, Rondel passed by
together with its master, shaken up
by the great force that he had failed to stop.

Irate, Orlando wounded her at once: 17
right on the helmet's crest he hit her so,
the whole panache flew fast down to the ground:
her helmet fell, and down her tresses hung
as radiant as stars in a clear sky:
it was the hair of holy Venus—no,
of a fair lass, into a laurel turned:
it shone like silver—no, like gold it burned.

Turning to his Morgante, laughed the Count,
saying, "Let's go away from here at once.
I was convinced a truly noble knight
had come to fight, and not a royal dame:
we've not come east to play a game of love."
Meridiana, blushing, spoke no words
but quickly—her long tresses streaming down—
together with her squire rode back to town.

18

Manfredon asked Orlando right away,
"Pray tell me, Sir, how did the battle go?"
Orlando with a sneer replied to him,
"A woman came against me, dressed in mail:
as soon as I untied her helmet loose,
down on her shoulders her long tresses fell.
So, as I saw the knight was not a man,
to save her reputation here I ran."

Let's leave Orlando with the pagan king,
and go right back to Charlemagne in France.
Charles felt, indeed, most wretched and forlorn;
so did the Dane. Gano alone rejoiced,
not seeing Count Orlando at the court.
But most of all, the Lord of Montalban,
Astolfo, Avin, Avolio, and Oliver
in sadness wept—and so did Berlinghier.

20

The courier Chimento, then, one day,
back from his mission, knelt before the crown.
"Sire," he said, "how good to see you here,
whose mighty name and worth are so renowned."
Seeing the courier in grief, Rinaldo
said, "I can sense your tidings are not glad."
Chimento answered with a tearful sound,
"Your cousin Count Orlando I have found."

Much more he wished to say but, overcome
with great emotion, simply he could not:
he looked at every paladin around
and tried in vain to utter one more word
till, having mentioned but "departure," down,
as if now lifeless, to the floor he fell.
'Twas then that everyone surmised and sighed
that surely Count Orlando must have died.

22

Rinaldo said, "Dear cousin, cousin dear,   23
now that no longer on this earth you are,
what shall I do; how can I live alone?"
Bewildered, lost, Oliver also wept.
Trembling, astounded, for his nephew dear
Charles raised his humble requiem to God,
while in his spirit cursing the day when
he left his court without suppressing Gan.

The wise Duke Namo of Bavaria wept,   24
and Salamon made also great lament.
The tearful mourning lasted until dusk,
and every knight in great dejection lay.
Ganelon, too, pretended to feel grief.
But, coming to, Chimento finally
stood up, cheered up the paladins, and said
they should not weep: Orlando was not dead.

He added, "On the contrary, he's well,   25
and sends his very best to each of you.
In the Girfoglia desert by mere chance
I found him near a fountain where a fight
with one more courier I had begun
(right in that very spring the man then drowned),
whom treacherous Gan had sent to dig a tomb
for our Orlando, senator of Rome."

Shouted Rinaldo, "This accursèd man   26
with your permission, Charles, O foolish Charles,
is still destroying Clairmont's glorious race."
Shamelessly bold, thus Ganelon replied,
"In every way, Rinaldo, I'm by far
better than this your cousin, and you, too."
Out burst Rinaldo, "In your throat you're lying,
who're only good at cheating and at spying,"

and with his sword 'gainst Ganelon went fast.   27
But Gan, who knew him, faster disappeared.
Bernard of Pontier, Gan's captain, turned
to Lord Rinaldo and in anger said,
"Rinaldo, you're a villain, I must say."
He spoke too much. Upon him rushed Rinaldo
and from his neck his head cut off and sundered,
and then against every Maganzan thundered.

28

The poor Maganzans, who such fury saw,
left one by one the royal room at once.
"This insult is too grave!" Emperor Charles
shouted; "Rinaldo of my home makes havoc,
and by so doing hardly honors me."
Right at this moment all the knights came in
and begged irate Rinaldo, all of them,
to be still patient and to keep his calm.

Rinaldo still was fuming, "I'll prevent
this traitor from betraying any more.
O Charles! O Charles! With your own eyes you'll see
how this your Gan will hurt you someday soon."
King Charles replied, "Rinaldo, Ammon's son,
I have to swallow down this medicine
so that my every wish may be fulfilled."
Rinaldo asked, "To have Orlando killed?

30

"Do you still bear with him so that he may
destroy with you your kingdom and your court?
To find my cousin I must go at once."
Oliver added, "I will come with you,"
and Dudon begged Rinaldo, "Make me, too,
worthy of such an honor, such a grace."
Rinaldo answered, "Set at ease your mind:
I'd never leave my dear Dudon behind."

Calling Guicciardo, Ricciardetto, Alardo,
"Keep Montalban well guarded all around
until I find my noble cousin; go
to Montalban this very moment: I—
I, who can smell foul treason from afar—
know that this Gan is a born traitor: so
trust no one but each other's inmost hearts
and Malagigi's future-seeing charts."

32

Rinaldo with Dudon and Oliver
took leave of Charles, the Christian emperor.
In their departure the three cavaliers
quickly with all care donned three capes of green
with a vermilion band on which appeared
two lynxes painted: thus they started out,
bearing the emblem of a Saracen
descended from the race of Mambrin's men.

Testing their luck, this way the three began   33
their journey out of France that very day.
Through every Spanish valley on they rode,
traveling ever between south and west.
May God be with them. We shall leave them now
to introduce a mighty Saracen
who lived not far away from Barbary—
Brunoro, a true giant verily.

He was a rightful cousin of the great   34
Morgante, whom Orlando took along;
also of Passamont and Alabaster,
the one the count had in the desert slain
soon after he had met the holy monk,
the relative that made him so rejoice.
Brunoro, of his brothers so bereft,
in their revenge from Barbary had left

with maybe thirty thousand well-armed men,   35
all of them veterans of many wars.
Straight to the abbey went they to dislodge
the abbot and his monks. So fast they rode,
and were so weary when they reached its walls,
they stormed the abbey instantly, and such
was the new wrath with which they rushed right in,
there was no other obstacle to win.

First thing, they fast our reverend abbot threw   36
into a dungeon. Fierce Brunoro said,
"With a good, sounding whipping we should kill
this lazy glutton, but perhaps a jail,
for the time being, is the better thing:
'tis good to save him for a harsher goal.
He's, after all, the cause of our disaster—
the death of Passamont and Alabaster."

Right at this moment to the abbey came   37
Rinaldo with Dudon and Oliver.
Seeing the mighty troops of Saracens,
he soon inquired who their captain was.
Brunoro with great courtesy replied,
"I am the one; and now, if you so please,
may you reveal your name to me, Sir Knight."
Rinaldo said, "Your question is quite right.

"Here from the Sultan's regions we have come,
wandering knights in search of fight and fame.
For justice we fight, too, like Hercules,
but have till now much disappointment known;
and it so happened that, for being wrong,
we were defeated by prevailing might.
Of our beloved friends, we saw some die,
who fought, against their knowledge, for a lie."

38

Brunoro said, "I can't believe my eyes
that you are here alive. By God, I blush
in telling you what passes on my mind:
you're knights in dream alone and nothing more.
If with my family you wish to dine—
and maybe food is what you need now most—
down from your steeds alight, and you will see
greatness of meal and hospitality."

39

"Thank you," Rinaldo said, "for food and drink."
The monarch summoned then a Saracen,
and said, "These men are here for a good time:
they battle only for much bread and wine
and maybe—if within their reach—some meat.
We need not here provide them with a hook
or ladder, for they have strong, lengthy hands:
they're knights, they say, come from the Sultan's lands.

40

"If Lady Justice waits for these men's aid,
she'll be locked up inside a dungeon soon
ev'n if she has more gold and silver, more
lawyers and documents and witnesses
than August figs." Brunoro smiled again,
"That rogue compared himself to Hercules!
A courier, he, or Cavalier-of-Cat!"
Rinaldo heard and understood all that.

41

"Boy, for their breakfast see if you can find
rotted leftovers or some chicken bones.
Some capon's feet or heads will nicely do,
for swill and slops befit these people well.
You'll see how hard that glutton will begin
to lick each bone like the true dog he is.
Bring some dishwater, quick, and cast them off—
no, dump the swine inside their filthy trough."

42

Rinaldo still pretended not to hear   43
and not to understand Brunoro's speech.
He did not want the pagan king to know
the one he was, and played therefore the fool.
Lo and behold, a bucketfull of swill
was brought before him as before a swine,
with many bones that would delight a hound
and in Jehoshaphat would not be found.

Rinaldo started nibbling gingerly,   44
but first removed his helmet; Oliver
refused to do likewise; so did Dudon:
the two sat there suspicious, to be sure.
Seeing them eat but through the visor's hole,
Brunoro was amused and nearly laughed:
he ordered then and there one of his Moors
first to unbridle every warrior's horse,

and then to feed it with abundant hay.   45
"These men," he said, "will pay for it; if not,
they'll lay their weapons with great damage down:
ah, without paying they won't leave this place."
But "You don't know what's coming to you, man,"
Rinaldo thought, and started to devour.
To king and master paying sudden heed,
the stable boy fed Dudon's famished steed,

and afterward took care of Vegliantìn,   46
which the marquis had ridden to that region;
last, near Baiardo the poor pagan walked.
As he was reaching for the manger, fast
Baiardo, like a mastiff, snatched his arm
right off the shoulder, biting it so hard
he crushed it like a reed or bit of straw—
a most delicious mouthful sweet and raw.

The hapless servant to the ground collapsed   47
and in atrocious pain suddenly died.
Rinaldo said, "The battle has begun:
now you will pay, not we, so I believe.
See how man's projects oftentimes are wrong!"
When the sad tidings reached Brunoro's ear,
"God, what a horse" he soon was heard to say;
"I want it as a present right away."

Rinaldo, turning a deaf ear, said, "Sir, 48
the barley that you have seems very good."
Brunoro to his squire often said,
"This horse has to be mine—I like it so."
Back to his dinner our Rinaldo went
and like a ravenous wolf kept eating on.
Now, being famished too, a Saracen
went to sit down beside our Christian man.

After a while Rinaldo liked him not: 49
he sounded like a deluge as he ate
with all the soup cascading on his chest.
Rinaldo looked at him in full disgust,
and said, "Holy Mahound! You, Saracen,
are nothing but a swine or something like.
I swear to you: either you say goodbye
or for a show like yours I'll make you cry."

The pagan answered, "You must be a fool 50
for ordering me out of my own house."
Rinaldo said, "You'll see some final act!"
The Saracen refused to go away,
and plunged right back into his noisy trough.
Losing his patience then and there, Rinaldo
put his right gauntlet on and with it—whoop!—
made him digest and pre-digest his soup:

he landed on his head so fierce a blow, 51
he simply cracked and crushed it like a nut;
nor did he raise his hand to wipe his mouth:
into the cauldron, dead, he nearly fell,
thus making all that broth quite muddy-red.
Dudon was shouting, "Hurry up, Marquis!
Move on from there! Up here the fight is real."
Oliver at these words gave up his meal.

'Twas then an angry pack of pagan dogs 52
unleashed their fury 'gainst Dudon at once
by dint of hands and swords. Rinaldo saw
how the whole quarrel started and with joy
into the midst of all those pagans jumped;
and so did Oliver of Burgundy:
quickly unsheathing his bedazzling sword,
he stained and soiled it with fast-gushing blood

by cutting the first head he came across.
Dudon, in turn, killed a most daring foe.
Seeing the unexpected fight begun,
Brunoro, turning to Rinaldo, said,
"May God assist you, noble cavalier,
why have you been assailed, in heaven's name?"
and he commanded everyone to stop
and some of them come forward and speak up.

53

At such an order the whole battle ceased:
indeed, Brunoro wished to be informed.
Once again turning to Rinaldo, he said,
"Tell me, Sir Knight, why do you hurt me so
by hurting all my men so pitilessly?"
Rinaldo answered, "As your people know,
they should not vex me when I eat my food
or, like a mule, I'm in a kicking mood.

54

"One of your men came here to dine with me,
but did not want to leave when ordered so:
he ate and ate and so much food gulped down,
it looked as though he'd never dined before.
That's why I wanted, after such a meal,
to give him a delectable dessert."
While to the pagan king all this he told,
he wielded his Frusberta—bloody sword.

55

Brunoro said, "If what you spoke is true,
let us recall the incident no more.
And do not be so hasty with your sword.
I've done a favor to you: so now, if you don't mind,
let all committed sins forgiven be:
put all your swords away, if so you please."
All of them therefore put their swords away,
but something else Brunoro wished to say:

56

"If I've correctly understood your words,
Justice alone is what you're fighting for;
then something else you must explain to one
who your opinion holds in great esteem.
I'll tell you, first, the things that you should know,
and then this problem you will solve for me:
else of your charger you have seen the last—
the one that thanked my boy for his repast."

57

"I'm more than ready," our Rinaldo said.
  Brunoro started then to tell his tale:
"This abbey, as you see, has been assailed
  because two brothers that I dearly loved
  have with impunity been murdered here.
As soon as such a crime reached these my ears,
  I came for my revenge. I've apprehended
  the abbot, who my heart has so offended.

"If it is justice you are fighting for,
  to me—and me alone—you must give help;
instead, it seems you came to cause me pain:
  I honored you, who now dishonor me."
Rinaldo said, "Your reasoning is wrong.
  I will most clearly tell you now my thought:
  I badly plow if with one ox I toil;
  with two, instead, I furrow well the soil.

"Suppose I have two bells and you hear one—
  only one—ring: can anybody say
which of the two is better? There's your tale;
  but now I want to hear the abbot's, too."
"This is quite fair," Brunoro agreed with him.
  A rope around his neck, the abbot came:
  immediately the old man was untied
  so that the coin might show its other side.

Brunoro thus began, "I've told this knight
  of the enormous wrong done unto me:
I've told him how I have forever lost
  the ones who never should have trusted you.
Come, tell now your own version to this man,
  who seems to be both righteous and wise."
The abbot said, "My story I will tell,
  and then both versions you must ponder well.

"In peace I lived in all this wilderness
  till this man's brothers every day began
to hurt me with the utmost villainy,
  often uprooting rocks and beechen trees;
several times they even broke our bells,
  the fall of which killed monks to me so dear.
Long, to be sure, I bore their every wrong—
  I, weak and helpless 'gainst them all so strong.

58

59

60

61

62

"But finally, one day our heavenly Lord,   63
Who ever aids the innocent and right,
sent my dear cousin to this very place—
yes, Count Orlando, Milon's very son.
A truly honest paladin, he felt
so truly sorry for my grievous plight,
wasting no time, he reached the mountaintop
and, killing two of them, made those men stop.

"The third of them became a Christian soon,   64
and with his dear Orlando started out,
with all my blessings, toward the eastern lands—
and here I am, still sighing for them both."
When Lord Rinaldo heard this story, much
about Orlando he began to wonder:
for all he knew, he could not well conceive
how the old abbot was his relative.

He started to address the pagan thus: 65
"Now you will see how straight the furrow goes,
for we have heard the second bell at last.
You've been in all your words quite circumspect;
therefore, unless you prove the contrary,
my verdict is already written down:
if what the abbot said to us is true,
indeed he's right, and fully wrong are you.

"And I intend to prove all that I say   66
by fighting you on horseback or on foot,
for I and justice truly are good friends."
The pagan said, "He should be hanged with you;
so from this moment call yourself my foe,
O scoundrel that undoubtedly you are."
Rinaldo answered, "Well, if I am so,
you'll tell me better after the first blow."

Brunoro said, "Let's come to terms right now—   67
that if I beat you, I will have your horse.
Full well I know that, with our chessboard full,
I will checkmate you at the very start."
Rinaldo thus replied, "So let it be:
if I am beaten, take my horse indeed;
but ev'n if we play chess, you'll lose at once,
for it is I who'll tell you how to dance.

"But if you please, let's make another deal: 68
that if I beat you in a single fight,
the abbot will be left in peace and free,
and all your men will bother him no more.
Thus, if the duel proves that I was wrong,
I want this steed of mine, with all its mail,
to be forever yours; in short, I say
that if I lose, 'tis yours to take away."

The deal was soon agreed on, and the two   69
took as much field as each of them desired:
just as Brunoro turned his horse at once,
so did Rinaldo his Baiardo. Fast,
the Saracen laid down his spear to strike:
it hit Rinaldo's shield with such great might,
it pierced it through and broke it instantly.
Rinaldo wounded him so terribly,

his spear went through his shield and mail as well: 70
breaking and passing through the breast, it came
out from the other side, two feet away,
dripping with all the blood that it had drawn.
Upon the grass the hapless monarch fell,
and into hell his wretched spirit plunged.
Seeing their sire dead, the pagans then
against our Oliver with fury ran.

Rinaldo's lance, which was not broken yet,   71
passed through the breastplate and the belly, too,
of the first helpless pagan in its way;
then his Frusberta speeded up his hands.
Oliver, too, a paladin of France,
sliced all those Saracens like loaves of bread,
for he had jumped upon his Vegliantìn
and daringly defied number eighteen.

'Twas then Dudon fast to the abbot ran,   72
who had once more been fastened very tight:
he cut the rope and let his hands go free.
The abbot right away began to fight:
quickly he ripped a bar off a huge door
and plucked a pagan's head with it at once;
so deftly, then, could he his weapon mix
that he decapitated more than six.

And what about the other monks? They all
removed their tunics: with big rocks and sticks,
against the Saracens they all onrushed,
murdering many of the faithless throng.
Rinaldo sliced so many more that day,
and each one floated in a pond of blood:
he leveled here some brains and there some brows—
just as we see it in a slaughterhouse.

73

Oliver with his sword, named Durlindan,
performed such wonders you will never guess:
he made a boundless pool of pagan blood.
Dudon was braver than the bravest bull.
Thus the whole pagan throng was chased away,
for no one could withstand so great a wrong.
To make things worse, the abbot at the door
let on the fleeing men his anger pour.

74

They cleared the abbey in no time at all;
some even jumped out of the windows fast.
Into the desert they were soon dispersed,
where the wild beasts took care of each and all.
At last our happy monks closed every door
and could resume their interrupted soup.
After he rested, our Rinaldo walked
straight to the abbot, and to him so talked:

75

"If I have not misunderstood your words,
reverend abbot, you still claim to be
a cousin of Orlando, our great knight.
But make me happy now with your reply:
Where are you from, and for what reason—say—
have you become a monk in such a place?"
"If that is all," the abbot soon replied,
"you will, my son, be quickly satisfied.

76

"I am the son of one of Bernard's sons,
as Ansuigi known to everyone;
brother of Ammon (so unique and brave,
his fame in Paris is alive and high),
of Otho, and of Buovo, let me add.
Here I am clothed in gray, for it was God
Who blessed me with the grace of my vocation,
soon strengthened by Pope Leo's approbation."

77

Rinaldo, when he heard this story, ran
to kiss and hug him with unbounded joy,
and thanked the stars of the whole firmament,
saying, "Dear abbot, now that we have chased
the pagan throng away, I must reveal
my very name, so sweet is the delight
that overwhelms my heart in front of you:
like Count Orlando, I'm your cousin, too:

78

"Rinaldo—I'm Rinaldo, Ammon's son;
so I am your relation, like the count."
And as he spoke, out of great bliss he wept.
The reverend abbot, who had not foreseen
such unexpected pleasure, hugged Rinaldo,
saying, "O God of justice! After all
so many graces and so many a year,
I see in front of me Rinaldo dear,

79

"just as I saw my famous Count Orlando,
whose quick departure sorely saddened me.
God! *Nunc dimitte servum tuum;* take me,
dear Blessèd Lord, whenever You so wish."
Rinaldo, still in tears, then said to him,
"and this is Oliver, his brother-in-law;
and this is our Dudon, the Dane's true son."
With the marquis the abbot kissed Dudon.

80

All monks were happy and rejoiced out loud,
seeing the Saracens around no more
and grateful to the Lord Who let them know
that brave Rinaldo was their abbot's cousin.
But since for the third time I must now thank
the One that shows the road that lies ahead,
in the same manner I conclude my song:
May Christ deliver you from every wrong.

81

CANTO IV

Gloria in excelsis Deo, peace on earth,   1
Father and Son and Holy Spirit! We
benedicimus te, O Lord of truth,
laudamus te with humble song, O Lord,
Who have right now decided to console
our abbot with your most unbounded love,
and have so far escorted this my rhyme
so that it may be fruitful in due time.

It was the season when we fall in love   2
and butterflies with one another flirt:
the sun, by now beyond its final goal,
was from Morocco turning its bright face;
the moon was hardly showing half its horns;
the mountain's shadow covered every dell
when our Rinaldo begged the abbot not
to keep concealed from him the name he sought.

Thus he replied, "Clairmont is my true name,"   3
and more than this the abbot did not say.
Then days elapsed and, spurred by restlessness,
Rinaldo said to him, "Oh, in God's name,
give us permission to depart at once.
In Paris I have left all of my men,
and, so I fear, the day has not yet dawned
when we at last may find the man we want."

Being most wise and learned, answered so   4
the abbot: "Dear Rinaldo, I regret
you're soon to leave this place that's now your home;
yet what you wish is honorable most.
I saw you, and I'm happy for this grace;
although full well I know I am too old
to hope to see you once again, yet I
with all my blessings must now say goodbye.

"If your great wish is seeing Count Orlando,
go, my beloved cousin, go in peace.
May God be with you everywhere you go,
just as with young Tobias Raphael."
Rinaldo answered, "So I hope and pray.
We'll see each other in heaven near the One
Who gives all men their due after their death,
amply rewarding those who save the faith."

5

Rinaldo, like Dudòn and Oliver,
weeping and sighing, bade Clairmont farewell.
Through valleys and through mountains on their steeds,
in quest of Count Orlando so they went.
"When, O great knight, will the great day arise
I'll see your face at last?" Rinaldo sighed.
"If you I find and bring to Charles once more,
I do not mind my death for such a chore."

Rinaldo rode in front of his two friends,
Oliver and Dudòn, who followed him
through a most dark, thick forest loyally.
Suddenly a fierce dragon stood in sight,
with a strange-looking skin, half green half yellow,
fighting a mighty lion then and there.
The beast Rinaldo in the moonlight saw,
but that it was a dragon did not know.

7

Oliver more than once had uttered words
that those who ride at night quite often say:
"Below that hill a fire I can see:
people at last in all this wilderness."
It was, instead, that most accursèd snake
that often vomits flames out of his mouth:
he seemed in all that dark a furnace bright,
covering the whole forest with great light.

The lion, more than scuffling, seemed to be
tearing with claws and teeth the dragon's limbs,
biting his neck and breast most wrathfully.
Instead, the dragon had so wound his tail
around the beast, the more the lion tried
to free himself, the more he fastened him;
not even he, the lion, liked the game
of a mouth gushing out flame after flame.

9

Baiardo started neighing very loud   10
as soon as of the dragon he caught sight.
Oliver's Vegliantin soon wished to flee,
while Dudòn's charger often looked behind,
feeling the dragon's fiery breath so close.
But nonetheless Rinaldo forward rode,
saddened and sorry for the losing lion
who, close to death, had no one to rely on.

Thus not to see him by the dragon killed,   11
decided he to help him instantly.
Spurring Baiardo forward, so he ruled
his bit he made him stop right near the snake,
who, biting, rending still, had brought the beast
to such a plight that surely was his last;
but first he begged for help from Paradise
before he carried out his enterprise.

While prayers soared to God, he heard a voice   12
that said, "Fear not, O gentle, cautious knight,
the fierce and mighty serpent that you see:
he will right now be vanquished by your hand."
Rinaldo answered, "Thank You for such words,
O Lord Who died for us upon the cross,"
and with Frusberta so the dragon struck,
he did not hit the lion for sheer luck.

The lion seemed to sense that help had come   13
and, strengthened by the knight's appearance, tried
his very best to break the serpent's hold.
Frusberta could not pierce the dragon's back,
which, to be sure, was harder much than steel:
indeed he tried, but helpless was his sword—
the sword that used to sunder plate and mail
against that serpent's skin could not prevail.

Rinaldo said, "This dragon's hide must be   14
the very one that Satan calls his own
if my sword's sharpened point cannot go through
nor can its blade diminish it at all."
But in so saying, still he let Frusberta
fall deep and deeper, aiming at his bone.
O wondrous deed! Frusberta leaps and glows,
proud of its countless, ever-dauntless blows.

The lion seemed to hold the serpent tight
as if to say, "If I do not let go,
one of his blows will kill him finally."
But after all such blows Rinaldo knew
that that most cruel worm, had he by chance
gone one step closer, with his fiery breath
would much offend him: so, the spell to break,
his throat he severed like a rooster's neck.

15

Dudòn and Oliver had fled away,
borne by their steeds that could not bear so much.
As soon as the fierce dragon lifeless fell
after the last proud leaping of his head,
toward Rinaldo the saved lion came,
starting to lick his dauntless charger's mane:
Fondling and festively content, in such
a way he thanked Rinaldo very much.

Thus to the bridle he went forth with him.
Rinaldo said, "O Mary, full of grace,
since you have shown this marvel to my eyes,
I'm begging you, O Queen of Mercy, still
to let me see what way am I to go
through this horrendous, frightful forest till
I find my dear Dudòn and Oliver:
or let this grateful lion take me there."

17

The lion seemed to understand all this,
for he began to move as if to say,
"Very well, then: you come right after me."
And so Rinaldo let himself be guided,
the woodlands lying so untrodden still
that even one step further was no joy.
Thank God the lion knew each thoroughfare:
Rinaldo found Dudòn and Oliver.

Dismounted from his charger, Oliver
stood there forlorn and melancholy most;
so was Dudòn, still weeping in dismay:
he had gone back where his Rinaldo was,
hoping to succor the bright paladin.
Oliver in the meantime so had thought:
"I fear we're soon to see Rinaldo's fate
if we against the snake one minute wait."

19

They could not find their way back to the woods,
so many narrow valleys being there.
At last they saw the lion and Rinaldo,
who could not help but watch them in surprise.
Seeing Oliver without his Vegliantin,
he said, "Where have these men concealed their horses?
Maybe they met some wild beast in these woods,
because of which, I'm sure, they've lost their steeds."

Oliver, seeing his Rinaldo there,
was—should you ask?—the happiest of men.
He said, "I really thought—believe you me—
that you had left forever this our earth,"
but as beside him in the moonlit night
he saw the lion, terror-struck was he.
Rinaldo said, "Dear Oliver, this beast—
be not afraid—won't harm you in the least.

"Know that the cruel dragon is now dead,
and I have freed this happy friend of mine
that, as you see, gratefully follows me—
indeed a mighty bargain, I must say.
Before the moon conceals its face from us,
this frightful beast will save us, I am sure,
from the dark forest we've been wandering in.
But tell me: have you lost your Vegliantin?"

Oliver, most ashamed, apologized:
"As soon as with the dragon you began
to fight, our horses made us scratch as though
from scabies 'mid ravines and countless shrubs.
Each of us tried his best to help you most,
which was indeed the rightful thing to do;
but all our mighty efforts failed, and thus
you are most likely cross with all of us.

"We left our horses near a fountain spring
where for a sip of water they had stopped:
there, at the mountain's foot, we tied them both
and started then to ask what had ever come of you—
if you, that is, had smashed the serpent's head,
or if beneath his might you lifeless lay."
Rinaldo said, "Let's find your steed in haste,
and, Oliver, let's not one more word waste."

20

21

22

23

24

25

Each of them found his charger readily.
"But," then Rinaldo said, "we shall not find
anything to devour till we come out
of this dark wood or find some living soul.
I wish you knew this sorry plight of mine,
Emperor Charles, who caused me so to roam!
And this, O Ganelon, you should know now!
But, oh, expect much worse than this, I vow."

Thus, fearfully advancing on his steed,
greatly Rinaldo pitied his own self.
Meanwhile the lion right before him went,
showing the pathway to the three of them.
After they climbed a tiny hill, from there
they saw a light that seemed to be quite near:
there a tall giant lived in a low den,
whom a big fire had lit up right then.

27

A hut-shaped mound of branches he had heaped,
and on a spit of his had pinned a deer
that he had stripped completely of its skin.
As soon as hooves' and bridles' sound he heard,
he grabbed the very spit he had before,
not knowing what to do, what else to grab:
thus much more wildly than the wildest bear,
with it he dashed against our Oliver.

Poor Oliver, as soon as he could see
the giant's horrid club and evil mind,
began to flee, but he was hit at once
right on his chest so bitterly and hard
that, notwithstanding his enormous might,
he was dismounted from his Vegliantin.
Rinaldo, seeing Oliver aground,
could not but sigh with the most anguished sound.

29

"You scum," he said, "who merited the gallows
so many, many times! I'll tell you this:
before the moon you see goes down to bed,
you'll taste a sip of your own medicine."
The clumsy beast in his most clumsy way
replied, "And I will let you taste my slaps.
Say, did my venison lure you from afar?
Either a glutton or a thief you are."

Rinaldo, who had little patience left, 30
planted his gauntlet on the giant's face,
and, oh, so great and mighty was his fist
that he wiped off his mustache right away,
saying, "Not even God would patient be."
The giant, when his senses he regained,
against Rinaldo whirled and whirled his spit,
eager to make him feel some special heat.

But skillfully Rinaldo shunned the blow, 31
making Baiardo leap just like a cat:
combating giants was indeed his game,
for he had learned their every trick and ruse.
The giant's stick came out as from a bow,
but one more time Rinaldo used his fist:
so great a gauntlet did he land and place,
lifeless the giant fell upon his face.

But, to be sure, he was not wiser than 32
the dragon that has killed the elephant:
being so proud and foolish, the poor snake
does not foresee that the enormous beast
will crush him altogether as he falls.
Likewise, Rinaldo did not think of that:
therefore, when down that massive mountain fell,
he nearly crushed him with Baiardo as well.

Freeing himself was not an easy chore: 33
he even needed Dudòn's helping hand.
Rinaldo said, "I by no means foresaw
this giant would so quickly tumble down
as to chastise me with his very fall.
Venison, so he said, has brought me here:
so to his cottage let us quickly go,
wherefrom the fire sends such lively glow."

Down from their horses the three warriors leapt 34
and to the cottage walked most eagerly.
They saw the deer, and quickly said Dudòn,
"Believe you me, we are not late at all."
He grabbed a branch and made a spit of it.
Meanwhile Rinaldo found three loaves of bread
and a keg full of some strange-looking beer.
He said, "We'll eat a biscuit, not a deer."

The loaves loomed like the bottom of a tub,
so much so that I shiver as I speak.
Rinaldo asked, "If we have bread and wine,
what are we waiting for, Dudòn? All's burned."
Dudòn replied, "A little longer wait
till this whole bounty is well done and crisp."
Rinaldo said, "The beast is more than warm;
if overcooked, this deer will do us harm."

Dudòn continued, "Dear Rinaldo, what?
You are so starved your throat is tickling you:
if it's not finely cooked, at least it's warm."
Thus they began to tear the deer apart.
Rinaldo would have eaten all of it,
but it was shame that made him well behave.
Yet he devoured a full loaf and—I beg
your pardon—did not shun the waiting keg.

When dawn lit up the eastern firmament,
they left the tiny cottage. Said Dudòn,
"Our picnic, I must say, was excellent
with all this manna God has sent to us
as a reward for that strong giant's life.
See! Those who want to cheat are cheated first.
That stupid braggart, Oliver, by stealth
struck you, and now enjoys his early death."

Down to the plainland from the mount they came
with their proud lion walking right before.
Rinaldo said, "Most lucky we have been,"
and Oliver agreed most readily.
Out of a dismal forest came the three
into a place where people seemed to live:
in fact, they spotted houses in a dell
and heard the greeting sound of many a bell.

No sooner had they gone a mile ahead
than they saw shepherds near a river, not
too far from where they were. They also heard
right at that very moment shouts and screams.
Baiardo leapt, and so did Vegliantin.
'Twas then out of a valley a great throng
of men and women came in great dismay—
people from danger running still away.

While our Rinaldo begged God's helping grace,   40
one of those pagans walked right where he was.
Immediately Dudòn inquired, "Say:
what's going on in this so strange a place?
We've heard your noise from far away indeed.
Do not deny me this—please answer me."
The Saracen at once gave this reply,
"Soon you will know there is a reason why.

"I know that as I speak you'll pity me.   41
Because of one most dear and gentle girl,
an entire city's uninhabited:
a cruel monster poisons all of us.
Our King Corbante, a most righteous man,
has now decided that this horrid beast
should have for its repast his lovely daughter:
so Forisena is bound for her own slaughter.

"This beast has swallowed many of us here: 42
morning and evening, two of us he craves."
"Tell me," Rinaldo asked, "what I must know:
how far from here is this unlucky town?"
Replied the Saracen, "You soon will see
the most unhappy and most wretched land.
But for your life go back wherefrom you came!
It is quite near: Carrara is its name.

"For your own good I'm warning you right now   43
in the great name of our most blest Mahound:
you too will lose your life if there you go—
as your great restlessness reveals to me.
You'll find the entire city in distress,
and my great lord the king most sorely vexed
because of this accursed, ferocious beast
by which the lovely lass will soon be seized.

"With each new dawn he comes right to our doors: 44
if food is not presented instantly,
he kills us just as fast with his foul breath:
therefore we place a man there as his prey.
And now the royal maiden's turn has come,
and, as I said, her father has agreed.
All people scream; the beast so roars and calls,
everyone leaves in dread the city walls.

45

"I think we're being punished for our sins
because Corbante murdered his own brother—
who was the wisest, fairest, and most just
of all the knights our land has ever borne.
'Twas to his brother that the throne belonged,
yet we did nothing to impede his crime.
That's why the dragon came—to make us pay
for our enormous sin in such a way.

"And there are those amongst us who believe
that in this monstrous beast abides the soul
of the young murdered prince. Rinaldo said,
"I thank you for your kindness. May Mahound
save each and every one of you from this
most wicked monster you describe so fierce.
But, O most courteous Saracen, pray tell
if this girl's young and beautiful as well."

47

The pagan answered, "This you should not ask,
for no one ever saw a fairer face:
charm of behavior, most angelic ways,
a flag of beauty and great virtue—she
has barely passed her fifteenth birthday yet.
That's why the people try to save her life.
Brave cavalier, if such a beast you slew,
half of our kingdom would belong to you."

Replied Rinaldo, "Kingdoms I seek not:
seven of them I left in my own land.
But I delight in women, if I may:
so if you tell me that this maiden's such,
I certainly will cut the monster's scales."
Quickly he turned to the renowned marquis,
saying, "Let's go immediately. This lady,
the princess of this town, is ours already."

49

When the three knights to sad Carrara came,
everyone gazed upon them eagerly:
the Saracens were greatly comforted
and wondered at the lion, their true mate.
Rinaldo, as he reached the royal house,
greeted Corbante and his lass as well.
Replied Corbante, "Welcome to this town,
if you have come to strike the monster down."

"O King Corbante," out loud Rinaldo said,   50
I am the Lion's Warrior, and do
worship Apollin with our Trevigant.
Certainly, in the name of god Mahound,
I will no longer dream of going east
now that I know why you so greatly grieve."
And then he whispered to him one more word,
"Now that about your daughter I have heard."

Oliver fixed his eyes upon the girl   51
while in this manner our Rinaldo spoke.
He aimed at such a beauty then and there
and with his glance transfixed her instantly,
whispering to himself and deeply sighing,
"For heaven's sake, this is no flesh to give
for a fierce beast to eat or trample over:
it should be given to a gentle lover."

Meanwhile Corbante had these words to say: 52
"Whoever you may be, O famous knight,
I'm satisfied you worship our Mahound.
O gentle cavalier, if you believe
that you can kill this beast, I promise you
that half of this my kingdom shall be yours;
and if you even want the other half,
so be it, if you save me from this grief.

"As you can see, this land is barren most,   53
which used to be a lovely garden once.
And now my daughter's destiny has come:
though innocent and sinless, she must die."
Oliver in the meantime murmured so:
"This beast will not devour such fresh, white bread,
which, as I see, is only lover's food.
For such a dinner, die we surely would."

The poor king asked, "Oh tell me what to do   54
now that the cruel beast is near the walls:
I smell its awful breath no one can bear,
and so, I think, most probably do you."
Rinaldo said, "I for no kingdom fight
but only spurred by kindness and desire.
Thus for the love of your fair daughter, we
shall kill this monstrous dragon instantly."

Oliver was indeed a lovely lad,   55
and therefore he adored the lovely lass.
Rinaldo guessed the blowing wind at once
and in the Frankish tongue teased Oliver:
"The falcon has removed its leather hood:
partridge or woodcock it has seen at last,
but ths is clear to me: we are like two
mouths eager the same food at once to chew."

Oliver to Rinaldo nothing said: 56
he only lowered his transfixing glance.
Corbante issued a most urgent ban
ordering every man not to leave town—
it calmed the population, I should say.
Rinaldo went along with it, and also
for himself ordered a new gauntlet, wound
with sharpened iron edges all around.

Of King Corbante took he then farewell,   57
who kindly to the doors escorted him
with many other most revering men.
He said, "I can't escort you any more.
But let me of one thing remind you: Please,
take care of your dear life. In any way,
think of yourself, of your existence first,
before you give a thought to this our beast."

So lovely and so gentle were these words,   58
Rinaldo memorized them in his heart.
He said, "Oh, let me boast, O kindly lord,
that safe and sound I will return to you.
Give me your blessings with your gauntlet now
and comfort all your people for my love."
Corbante blessed him most paternally
and begged the skies for him devoutedly.

Oliver, too, begged Heaven's gracious aid: 59
to God he recommended his poor self.
Meanwhile the dauntless lion walked ahead—
the lion that knew well where else to go.
Rinaldo and Dudòn rode close behind.
The Saracens were watching, all of them—
some from the doors and some from the high wall—
wishing the death of the fierce animal.

Right at this point the princess sweet and fair   60
had bravely climbed into a bartizan.
Rinaldo said, "Your Forisena—look—
seems to feel sorry for you, Oliver:
'tis love that, just to see you, brings her here."
Oliver answered, "Here we go again:
you surely want to tease me, but the least
we now can do is to destroy this beast."

Rinaldo said, "Can you so cruel be   61
by watching not at all your charming lass?
Surely you are no lover, let me say.
What would you really do if such a girl
were in your arms for safeguard or for shield?
Whom would you kill—the beast or your sweet love?"
"You always like to tease," Oliver said,
"but there is more that I can guess, instead."

As soon as this he spoke, the lion showed   62
where the flame-vomiting great serpent lay.
Oliver said, "Our lady is right there,
and, dear Rinaldo, I am worried still."
Replied Rinaldo, "Oliver, you'll see
Venus and Mars here fighting." Thus he teased him.
The cruel dragon leapt with sudden ire,
vomiting poison and most horrid fire.

The land and the horizon seemed ablaze.   63
Rinaldo, like the others, had a sponge,
vinegar-soaked, to fight the stench away.
He said, "O ill-advised, ill-thinking beast,
do you believe we are your ready meal
simply for coming here against our wish?"
And, these words uttered, on the ground he came:
Dudòn and the marquis did quite the same.

No sooner had Rinaldo left Baiardo   64
than right against Dudòn the monster dashed:
he gave him such a fierce and fearsome bite,
he crushed his armor and his flesh and bone.
Dudòn was screaming, "God, how much I burn!
Oliver, help me. I bear no more."
Thus saying, as if lifeless down he fell—
won by the biting and the breath as well.

Oliver was too late to succor him 65
and could not even help his dear Dudòn.
The beast burned everyone who came against him,
leaving more room for biting others still.
Suddenly then the serpent shook his head
and grabbed—a stump of cabbage—Oliver,
biting and biting more into his thigh
so madly that he made him sorely sigh.

He felt his armor into pieces crushed 66
as never any dog had crushed a bone.
Finally by the arm the dragon grabbed him.
Oliver in the meantime used his hands,
armed with the gauntlet that Rinaldo had ordered made;
'twas not the time to shower bread on him,
or say that Saint Donnìn had set his teeth on edge:
a different kind of war he had to wage.

Incited by Rinaldo more and more, 67
into his throat he thrust both hand and gauntlet
until the serpent swallowed all of it.
Oliver held him tight, and with his sword
severed his head. The dying serpent's flame
as well as stench caused Oliver to faint
and senseless fall upon the ground; still tough,
the dragon's head, however, came not off:

just as he gave his last, in such a way 68
he clenched his teeth, Oliver's hand was trapped.
Rinaldo's face all over crimson grew,
for he had thought he'd free it in no time;
but he could not, though sad and overwhelmed
with sorrow for poor Oliver's strange plight.
And yet so oft he thrust his sword with wrath,
at last he freed that hand out of the serpent's mouth.

But that brave lion they had brought along 69
had all this time been watching everything,
for surely, had somebody cared to know,
he would have wished to tell the entire deed.
Dudòn meanwhile had finally risen up
while Oliver lay still upon the ground.
And so the Saracens walked through the door,
most merry for the beast that lived no more.

With many people King Corbante came
to see how this whole thing had come to pass.
He saw the dragon flattened on its face,
saw our Dudòn still bleeding from his wounds,
and then saw Oliver's much-scalded hand:
much more than stunned, dead he seemed to him;
the beast made the whole place appear quite burned,
which the whole story into horror turned.

70

At last he viewed the monstrous dragon's head,
which was indeed a horrid thing to see.
He saw Rinaldo and Dudòn perplexed
over poor Oliver still lying down,
and felt a great compassion in his heart.
Well he could see the young man's leg that bled,
but did not know if his compassionate mood
was great enough to show his gratitude.

71

In tears, at last Rinaldo he embraced,
and then Dudòn. "O worthy knights," he said,
"teach me a way to thank you as I should.
This grace was granted by Mahound himself,
who, as I see, has sent you to my land.
Very well, then, my kingdom and my life
are yours, and with my scepter and my crown
I at your feet my property lay down.

72

"But if this man is dead, I'll ever mourn
so gentle and magnificent a knight."
Rinaldo answered, "Noble king, rejoice!
The man you're mourning does not need your tears.
Your gentle words have eloquently proved
the greatness of your gratitude and mind.
We accept your crown and kingdom but with true
and proven friendship give them back to you."

73

No sooner had Rinaldo spoken so
than Oliver was seen to come to. When
his senses he regained, and saw the king
and such a throng around him, he was stunned
just like a man who sees about him things
that were not there a little while before.
But a few moments later he knew well
what had occurred, and all his stupor fell.

74

The news of what the paladins had done
spread through the city and astounded all.
With all the Saracens that wished to see them
came King Corbante's daughter—she who looked
like a bright sun at noon and was divine
in everything she ever did or said.
Oliver looked at her with such a gaze,
she did not know his heart was all ablaze.

Soon King Corbante bade his people bring
the dragon right inside the walls, and then,
taking Rinaldo by the hand, with all
his men back to his city started out.
Back in his royal court, he ordered that
so great an action be recorded for
all future generations; in its gore
he had the monster hung above the door.

A marble plaque with letters carved in gold
read, "In that year three paladins arrived
in this our town (the names were written down,
for they themselves had whispered them to him)
who freed its population from the terror
caused by this monster which at last they slew."
It said that from nowhere the beast had come
to give the people grief and martyrdom,

and that right on the day the lovely lass
was to be swallowed by the dragon's jaws,
the three brave knights upon their steeds appeared
and saved the princess from her horrid fate.
The marble plaque remained a long, long time;
so did the lifeless beast above the door:
it frightened with its lifeless, ghastly frame
all those who back into the city came.

Corbante took Rinaldo to his palace,
and gratefully and greatly honored him.
He sent for his physicians, bidding them
take care of both Dudòn and Oliver,
who needed medical attention for
a week or so, so sorely hurt were they.
Meanwhile our Forisena, sweet and shrewd,
Oliver's love had quickly understood.

And because Love unwillingly forgives
one who is loved and does not love in turn;
nor would his law in any way be just
should mercy be denied to one who pleads for it,
nor would a righteous lord a faithful liege forsake:
as soon as that fair lady grew aware
that the marquis now for her love was dying,
she by his love was kindled then and there.

80

Soon she began to gaze into his eyes,
returning Oliver's most ardent darts—
those darts which Cupid caused him to throw forth
so that one fire might consume two hearts.
One day, while a physician dressed his wound,
she came to visit him. With loving glance
she greeted him, and, though her words were cold,
her looks—so Love decreed—were warm and bold.

81

On hearing Forisena greeting him
with such timidity, Oliver felt
his old still grievous pain soon disappear,
for a new wound was making his heart bleed.
His soul was full of doubt yet full of hope,
but now he knew, most certainly he knew
that Forisena loved him. Love is such:
they very little talk who love too much.

82

When she came closer to him, he could see
how all her face grew suddenly aflame
as she began with brief and broken words
to tell how truly sorry she was still
for having been the cause of all his grief,
and bashfully she lowered then her gaze:
which gave the man his greatest hope of all
(lovers have always followed such a rule).

83

Thus she had said to him, "My cruel fate,
heaven itself, a very ruthless star
or some inexplicable will of God
had doomed me to the most horrendous death.
But you, O famous knight, came east in time,
surely sent here by the Eternal Court
to save me. 'Tis for you once more I live:
that's why so much for this your pain I grieve."

84

These were the words that filled Oliver's heart
with such delight, with sweetness so complete,
that he thanked Love a thousand times and one
for all the gracious kindness shown to him.
He would have gladly died before her eyes,
now that to live without her was dismay.
Groping for words, he almost did not speak;
finally, he replied, most shy and meek:

85

"Under the moon I never did a thing
that made me happier than I am now.
If I have saved you from so sad a fate,
I feel such sweetness for it in my heart
the like of which I never felt before.
I know you're truly sorry for my pain;
but from a different pain I wish I were released.
Oh, why was I not swallowed by that beast?"

86

The gentle lady understood those words
indeed too well, and wrote them in her heart
(how fast one learns at Love's important school!)
with many a sigh, thus saying to herself:
"Yes, for this different pain I also grieve.
'Twas for the best that you have not been killed.
Grateful to such a lover I will be
for there's a heart, and not a stone, in me."

87

Sighing, still sighing, Forisena left,
and suddenly poor Oliver grew sad,
mindful no longer of his aches and pains
now that a fiercer claw had wounded him.
Almost in tears, then, at Rinaldo he looked
but lowered soon his eyes. He said to him,
"No matter how immensely hard he tried,
love and a cough a man could never hide.

88

"Brother, dear brother, as you well can see,
Love finally has seized me in his claws:
this my unrest no more can I conceal.
I know not what to do or where to turn.
I curse the day I saw her the first time.
What shall I do? How would you handle it?"
Replied Rinaldo, "I will tell you how:
I'd leave this lady and this town right now.

89

"Oliver, dear marquis, forget this girl:
    we did not come here just to woo a lass,
    but hopefully to find the famous count."
And Dudòn, too, in the same fashion spoke:
"We'll go from place to place, search the whole world
    until we find Milon's illustrious son."
Oliver most unwillingly said yes, but the poor lad,
    so forced to leave his love, was desperately sad.

And so a few days afterward, when both
    Oliver and Dudòn were well and strong,
    the three decided they should leave Corbante,
    but first reveal to him their real names
so as to let him know who helped him thus;
    also, the three decided they should ask
    whether the monarch wished to be baptized
and, with his people, join the sons of Christ.

Meanwhile the king in honor of the three—
    he and his men—had ordered tournaments
    and jousts and dances in the Moorish style,
    thinking, each day, of something greater still
to please his noble guests before they left.
    But greater still Oliver's love became.
    At last on King Corbante called one day
    Rinaldo, who to him began to say:

"O Most Serene and Noble Sire, since
    we have been honored by Your Grace so much
    (Rinaldo addressed the king in Saracen),
    we shall forever keep you in our minds.
And since it surely is the will of God
    that our true names be now revealed to You,
    know that I am Rinaldo, Ammon's son,
    though as the Lion's Warrior I am known;

"and this most famous knight is Oliver,
    brother-in-law of Count Orlando himself;
    and here is, then, Dudòn, Ugier's son,
    who once was known to worship your Mahound.
Now to go back to what we wish to say,
    we're wandering most sadly through the world
    because our count has left the court, and we
    still do not know where our great knight may be.

90

91

92

93

94

"Somebody told us he has traveled east
to visit with an abbot dear to us,
and that he had a giant alongside:
and so in search of him we're going still.
But, King Corbante, there is something else:
because you all adore Mohammed here,
you're lost. There is one God—ours. It was He
who for your sins sent this calamity.

"Without permission of our mighty God,
this wicked monster could have not appeared
to claim and swallow the unfaithful throng.
But, being merciful and just and good,
our God has saved you from such bitter gall
so that you now renounce your false Mahound.
Show that you're grateful for the grace He sent
to spare yourself some harsher punishment.

"Leave your Apollin and your futile gods
and to our Blessèd Lord return at once.
Leave Belfagor with all his pharisees
and be baptized with all your men accursed.
Many a reason I would offer you,
but, being wise, you fully understand.
I know you know that that fierce animal
could not have come for no reason at all.

"Everything happened for your many sins:
a shepherd, over others you should watch:
as such, your subjects sinned far less than you.
Yet Christ has not forsaken you: in time,
as you can see, He sent us to your town
so that your daughter might still live for you.
Come back, therefore, to the most holy faith
of the true God who saved your girl from death."

It seemed that God himself inspired the king,
for, shedding tears, the pagan so replied:
"So then, you are the Lord of Montalban,
a man who has no equal in the world!
And this is Oliver, whose noble fame
has reached our ears. Of course it was your God—
not our Mahound—that sent you to this place,"
and the three men he wanted to embrace.

And for his sins most bitterly he wept,　　　　　　　　　　　100
saying, "I see that much too long have I
with all my people lived in horrid sin,
but in mysterious ways our deathless Savior
works to enlighten and awake the mind
of a poor sinner long in darkness trapped.
Thus often a great ill bears a great good:
'tis sin alone engenders servitude."

Corbante bade his Forisena come,　　　　　　　　　　　101
and told her who the three great warriors were
who had delivered her from all her grief.
And then he sent for all the courtiers,
and in no time the royal hall was filled,
and all-adorned with draperies of gold.
Last, from his throne a fervent speech he made,
and all his people to his side he swayed.

So, big and small, all people were baptized,　　　　　　　102
and his whole kingdom was, that very day,
ordered to heed the new religious law.
Thus everyone became a Christian, and
throughout the region spread the sounding fame
of the three knights who had right there arrived,
though their true names—Rinaldo so had willed—
from everyone Corbante kept concealed.

While our three knights retired for some rest,　　　　　　103
the entire populace with louder joy
still celebrated their true God's great might
with songs that thanked Him for His boundless grace,
as in the other Canto you will hear,
where, to be sure, our story will proceed.
But now the King of Glory I implore
to give you peace and rest and life forevermore.

CANTO V

O sinless Dove, full of humility,   1
onto whom God, eternal, just, and true,
came from the sacredness of heaven down
to take on human flesh and human be,
grant me, O most benevolent, the grace
that I may now resume this song of mine
in the name of Joseph, Joachim, and Ann,
and Him Who in a manger became man.

Rinaldo with Dudòn and the marquis   2
mingled with the new converts merrily.
Thus King Corbante's entire populace,
including his great chieftains, was baptized.
Musing on his kind lady, Oliver
was thinking stranger thoughts each passing day,
and many a joust and tournament and fight
he feigned to please her with his matchless might.

Warmly Rinaldo begged him to depart,   3
but there he was, still hesitant to go:
his lady held him so enthralled and bound
as ship by anchor fastened in a bay.
Concealment makes a fire burn more hot:
so Oliver's deep love much deeper grew.
The more Rinaldo bade him go away,
the more excuses found he there to stay.

Now he pretended he was not well yet,   4
and now he mentioned some new illness (yes,
his heart was wounded—so he did not lie),
and now he begged and now he promised so:
"My mind's made up—tomorrow we shall leave."
But let's, in Mary's name, leave here our knights
with Oliver so feverish and forlorn,
and to our Count Orlando let's return.

Meridiana, lady kind and fair,   5
sent him a messenger: she wished to know
if he'd accept a fight—just man to man.
Orlando answered, "Knights-at-armor never
fight with a female who is not worth even
a worthless medal or one small bezant."
Such a reply, plus Lionetto's fate,
made her in these harsh terms Mahound berate:

"You should at least deprive me now of life   6
since by that villain I am scorned so much:
never has until now a cavalier
refused to meet the power of my spear."
But at that moment to her place arrived
the fame of the great Lord of Montalbàn—
a mightly knight was in Corbante's court,
known as the Lion's Warrior in short:

he was, indeed, the very mighty man   7
who all alone had slain the cruel snake.
Meridiana bade her messenger
go at full speed to King Corbante's court,
and let the monarch know that everywhere
had in the meantime spread the joyous fame
of such a strong and mighty cavalier
as had so deigned his scepter to revere:

and that with treachery King Manfredon   8
had pitched all of his tents around her town,
thus keeping it by all his troops besieged;
and that, to vex her more, not even one
of all those soldiers cared to challenge her:
to help her in her plight, he should at once
send her this paladin so much renowned
for kindness and for lineage: around

each of the eastern regions his bright fame   9
had spread, as her request now surely proved.
The messenger departed instantly,
to King Corbante's presence came at last,
and wisely told him all he had to say.
So King Corbante told Rinaldo this:
King Carador was asking for his might
to save his daughter from so sad a plight.

"Sir, if you think," so King Corbante spoke,
"that you can end this sweet young lady's grief,
then with my blessing go to Carador.
I know King Manfredonio is wrong
for moving there his army and his court.
Maybe, if such a man you rightly slay,
King Carador will ask to be baptized,
just as I did, and henceforth worship Christ."

Rinaldo, who remembered that Orlando—
the abbot so had said—must have been there,
most gallantly replied, "This sword of mine
will quickly sever Manfredonio's head,
dear King Corbante: I'm at your command
for noble deeds of justice such as this."
"A relative of ours, Carador,"
replied the king, "knows well what friends are for."

Retorted our Rinaldo, "Tell this messenger
that, for your sake, most gladly I accept:
tell him I promise that I firmly hope
to save his people from without and from within,
for, willy-nilly, soon will Manfredon
fold all his tents and banners to the wind."
Corbante did his gratitude express
for words that brought him so much happiness.

Turning, then, to the Saracen envoy,
he said, "Now let King Caradoro know
that willingly this knight accepts his challenge.
Soon, very soon, Apollin's crowds will see
the greatness of his might, and wonder so
that none will dare oppose his winning path.
Even if Count Orlando were his foe,
he would not fear him: tell your princess so.

"Look at his lion, waiting for him still:
there is on earth no knight can halt his worth.
And look at those two men who are his friends:
they too believe in action, not in words."
The messenger departed in great haste:
he had been told to fly rather than trot.
Thus he was able to his king to say
three knights already were along the way,

and that the Lion's Warrior, to be sure,
looked like a brave and famous paladin;
and of Dudòn and Oliver he said,
"There's no one in your court, King Carador,
who ever could compare with these two knights.
Corbante bade me tell you to rejoice
because this Lion's Warrior, indeed,
would dare the very count upon his steed."

15

Of old Corbante taking then his leave,
Rinaldo countless times assured the king
that to his help he'd rush from everywhere.
With equal courtesy great King Corbante
replied to him; they kissed each other's hand,
and with each other's blessing said goodbye.
"Goodbye!" poor Oliver in great dismay
could with his tears to Forisena say.

16

Seeing her Oliver now leave her sight,
the princess with great firmness in her heart
decided that she'd follow him at once,
no longer able to conceal her love.
So that blindfolded archer—Love himself—
brought her to a high window whence she viewed
Oliver farther, even farther go,
until in grief she threw herself below.

17

Hearing such tidings, quick her father ran
to see his daughter, now already dead.
Much more than his own life she meant to him,
who finally was made to understand
it had been Love to make all this occur.
If men had not been there to comfort him—
somebody grabbed his hand, his arm some other—
he would have killed himself over his daughter.

18

Thus he was moaning, "Oh, how glad I was
the day I saw the horrid serpent slain!
And now I feel such anguish in my heart!
Will you, O Love, so torture an old man?
You've turned my entire sweetness into grief.
O world, how can I trust you anymore?
You've left me, fickle Fortune, here to grope
in my old age without one ray of hope."

19

After a Christian funeral he laid
his lovely Forisena in a grave
with letters carvèd by his very hand:
from all her grief his daughter had been saved
by three brave knights arrived from far away,
and then by Love himself she had at last
been brought to tragic fate the very day
she saw her dear belovèd go away.

20

No one can change what Heaven has decreed,
for sweet and bitter must on earth remain.
This girl, who was so wondrous and so rare,
had for excessive love most dearly paid.
Oliver in the meantime, unaware
of what would make him grieve, through woods rode on;
calling his Forisena night and day,
he with the other two went on his way.

21

Till at a crossroad, near a cliff, one day,
they saw an old man so distraught and strange,
so deeply grieving and so sad and lost
that neither man nor beast he seemed to be.
Rinaldo felt most sorry at that sight,
and "Who can this man be?" said to himself.
His most unkempt and all-white beard he saw,
and, shivering with horror, said hello.

22

In tears, and sobbing, the old man replied
(and made Rinaldo's pity deeper still):
"Oh, in the name of the Most Holy Ghost,
have pity on my life so full of woe!
Never from these dark woods will I escape
unless you help me (and more tears he shed):
so let me for a while rest on your steed,
and may God bless you for so good a deed."

23

"Of course, of course," Rinaldo then replied,
"for, dear old man, you look half-dead to me."
Down from his horse he jumped immediately
to let the poor old stranger mount and rest.
Dudòn and Oliver came right behind.
Rinaldo told them what had just occurred.
Dudòn replied, "You're very kind, no doubt,"
and from his steed leapt down to help him out.

24

Rinaldo led Baiardo by the rein
while Dudòn grabbed the old man by the hand.
Baiardo seemed to wonder at that sight,
shunning the old man as an ancient foe.
Rinaldo held the bridle faster yet,
giving Dudòn his help as to a friend.
Baiardo bit the rein then, uncontrolled,
shaking his head and kicking, mad and bold.

25

But, oh, as soon as the old man got hold
of the same bridle, like a tender leaf
he made the poor horse tremble and move fast,
making him run, whether he wished or not.
Rinaldo asked Dudòn, "What do you think?
I am afraid we'll dearly pay for this:
see how the old man runs, fatigued no more—
the very one who barely walked before.

26

"From Vegliantìn dismount, dear Oliver."
And Oliver dismounted right away.
Pursuing the old man with nimbleness,
Rinaldo kept repeating, scolding him,
"Stop! Stop, you bastard dog! Do you believe
that, doing this, you'll take my steed from me?"
But nothing seemed to stop him. Like the wind,
he disappeared, leaving the three behind.

27

Swift as an arrow, through the forest went
brave Vegliantìn, perspiring mightily.
Rinaldo said, "We've been betrayed, you'll see,
by this old man who's now developed wings:
I've been a fool, and the whole fault is mine,"
and, saying this, in vain he called and screamed.
Faster than any leopard, the old man,
astride Baiardo, ever forward ran.

28

But after, to his heart's content, he mocked
Rinaldo so, right at the forest's end
for him he waited and before him stood.
Vegliantìn moved his hooves so very fast,
he soon caught up with him. Rinaldo fumed.
Said Malagigi, "And what now, you rogue?"
As soon as our Rinaldo heard this, he
could tell whose voice it was immediately.

29

He said, "You're still behaving as you did:
you've made me think the worst, to say the least,
and have much troubled our poor Vegliantìn."
Then Malagigi in this way replied,
"Never, my dear Rinaldo, will you read—
unless I tell you—this mysterious text."
Dudòn and the marquis, back from their chase,
could recognize at once Malgigi's face.

Greatly the three brave paladins rejoiced,
seeing Malgigi in so strange a land.
The old man said, "From Paris I have come
to Montalban to weave my magic arts,
so much I wished to know your whereabouts.
Seeing you, then, in this most distant place,
I knew that such great woes you had incurred,
you surely needed my consoling word.

"Inside this forest where you're riding still,
no food or water will you ever find:
here you indeed would die, had I not come.
But take this root with you: such is its might
it will sate both your hunger and your thirst.
You must at times conceal it in your mouth."
And so some grass he gave them. "This you should,"
he said, "bring with you 'til you leave this wood."

Willingly the three knights ate of the grass
that Malagigi had described to them;
they even gave their horses some of it,
they too still being horribly athirst.
Said Malagigi, "All along these roads
keep always some with you, just to make sure.
Your steeds will find more grasses everywhere,
but just this one will of their thirst take care.

"And let no other thing perturb your minds.
The Roman senator Orlando is
with Manfredonio, as you soon will see."
So, after many other words, he made
through magic a most awesome steed come down,
so awesome it made everyone aghast.
They wanted to know more, but—oh, how weird—
a snowy horse before them had appeared.

Said Malagigi, "My dear brother, take
your brave Baiardo back; my charger's here."
Rinaldo watched in awe the handsome horse,
saying, "How could you do the thing you did?"
Our Malagigi promptly mounted it
and as an arrow vanished far from them;
but warmly first everyone's hand he shook
and in three days in Montalbàn was back:

35

in other words, as all our maps can show,
right from the place of his farewell he fared
two thousand and odd miles to Montalbàn.
Often Rinaldo called his brother back,
and, most afflicted, Jesus's name invoked,
imploring him to show the right way on.
Six days already he had been astray,
behind the lion that still showed the way.

36

On the sixth morning this undaunted knight
in a dark forest happened to arrive.
All of a sudden his Baiardo stopped,
and suddenly the lion, bristling up,
began to roll his eyes ferociously.
Vegliantìn also seemed assailed by fear,
while Dudòn's horse craved but to flee away:
soon he began to snort and paw and kick and neigh.

37

"My God!" Rinaldo said, "What can this be?
Our horses must have seen some shadow here."
Meanwhile they heard a horrid noise around,
which struck their minds with terror instantly.
Behold! A most wild-looking, savage man
was seen to run the mighty forest through—
a chilling sight that frightened all of them,
who'd seen no face so filthy and so grim.

38

Hairy and fierce, his head looked like a bear's;
his teeth were so horrendous and so sharp
they were like fangs that would have split a rock;
most scaly were his windpipes and his throat;
right at the center of his chest, one eye
was burning fire two spans long and wide,
and in one tangle hair and beard he showed,
with donkey's ears most visible and broad.

39

His arms were bristly, very long and weird,   40
and hirsute were his breast and all his limbs.
Instead of hands and feet he had sharp claws,
and, to be sure, no sandals did he wear—
that naked, barefoot, dog-like barking beast:
never on earth was such a horror seen.
Burnished and knotted, as a raven black,
he brandished in his hand a sorb-tree stick.

With it he'd dug a tunnel underneath,   41
which he had covered with a massive stone:
fully concealed in it, there lay the fool,
watching the pathway from a tiny hole
out of which darts and darts at ease he hurled
at everyone who happened there to pass.
He slaughtered many a man, I need not tell—
this fiend known as the monster out of hell.

On watching such a thing with his own eyes,   42
"Oliver, did you see?" Rinaldo asked;
"certainly a she-devil it must be."
Oliver answered, "May God help us all!
I think it is the Witch Epiphany
or maybe Beelzebub himself." Meanwhile
that breast and that wild face he saw before,
and that club ten arms long and even more.

Horribly shouting, forward came the beast   43
and, like a bear enraged by chasing hounds,
broke with that stick and with his hands and feet
branches and thorns and bushes in his way.
So asked Dudòn, "Can this be Death himself,
out to assail us in this wilderness?
A fire—look!—his footprint soon creates.
I'm sure he's one of Malagigi's mates."

Rinaldo answered, "Have no fear, Dudòn: 44
whether he's Death or Thirty Thousand Devils,
wait till this crazy beast comes closer: I
have exercised my hands on tougher threads."
Right at that point the monster raised his club
and dashed against Rinaldo wrathfully.
Rinaldo spurred Baiardo on each side,
his evil plan thus hoping to misguide:

down with a fawn-like leap he bent, and so
avoided the strong mace that fell in vain.
Ready Rinaldo in the meantime stood:
wasting no time, he forward launched his horse,
clashing against his breast with such a thrust
that upside down he made him quickly fall.
As the horrendous monster hit the ground,
he ululated like a wounded hound.

45

Seeing in the meantime the demon fall,
Dudòn told Oliver, "Let's jump on him
before he rises for a new assault."
Rinaldo said, "Move not, either of you:
stand back and see what I will do with him.
I'm not accustomed, friends, to others' aid."
Meanwhile the savage man rose and—behold—
whirled his long staff with fury uncontrolled.

46

So harsh a blow upon Rinaldo's head
he soon discharged that, had it landed there,
never would he have feared a future blow,
never would he have minded heat or cold.
But our Rinaldo shunned the fatal threat,
like true quicksilver most alert and straight:
leap here and there he made his brave Baiàrd,
ever remaining cautiously on guard.

47

Nimbly and neatly jumping here and there,
he seemed a little lion cub at play;
though he unleashed from time to time a blow,
back to his leaping like a hound he went.
The morning was already three hours old
when Dudòn said to Oliver, "Let's hope
Rinaldo won't get tired of the chase,
or he will soon be bruised by the long mace."

48

Not one pistachio did the demon care
if brave Frusberta shaved some of his hairs:
ever more wrathfully he whirled his club,
but still the prince's sword soared to the sky.
May God in all His mercy spare this mace
on those who in His gospel still believe!
It was a club so hard and gnarled and deep,
it looked like the tall mast of a big ship.

49

It was the afternoon's third hour, and still   50
Rinaldo with that magic demon fought;
but oh, he made a milkshake of the beast,
whose blood turned soon a pool upon the ground
with brave Frusberta whistling happy tunes.
But unexpectedly the club came down,
and our Rinaldo—'twas his sorry luck—
happening to be under it, was struck:

fearing the mighty blow, our warrior fast   51
raised his Frusberta to protect his head.
Down fell the club, which, as somebody thought,
partially cut Rinaldo then and there,
the rest of it soon breaking at the blow;
others proclaim he did it all alone.
Many have spoken, many more will speak
about what truly happened to that stick.

It takes a good grammarian to state   52
whether he sundered the whole mace or half.
That savage, cursed, wild man, more bitter than
a sorb tree kept by hoarfrost still unripe,
brandished his trunk with greater expertise:
he gave Rinaldo such a maddened blow,
it made him fall before he fled like wind;
but Oliver, who followed right behind,

unsheathed his sword, that much more splendid shone   53
than any ray of star was ever seen,
and pierced with it the leather of his skin.
But fast that wicked, fierce, felonious beast
vanished as badgers vanish to their holes.
Oliver, on his saddle standing still,
quickly returned where our Rinaldo, faint
and fuming, now his senses had regained.

Rinaldo asked, "Say: have you ever seen   54
a thrush so strongly hit by such a bough?
He would have cured my deafness for all time
had he been more successful with his plan."
Dudòn replied, "The more I think of it,
the more that awful bludgeon makes me shiver.
Oliver, did you let him out of sight?
You chased him on your charger—am I right?"

Oliver answered, "He must be a crab,   55
for fast he disappeared into a hole
beneath a rock to shun my lifted sword,
rejoining Satan in his very hell."
Meanwhile the monster, brandishing a bow,
out of his quiver took a poisoned dart,
and from the narrow hole was quick to shoot,
thus wounding Vegliantìn right on a foot,

and if that arrow had not come to land   56
inside the deadened matter of its hoof,
goodbye veterinarian or bath!
Rinaldo said, "Poor horse, do not be cross!
There's something good to gain from crazy fools.
Not even this my lion's a good guide."
But seeing not from where the dart had come,
each of the three was stupefied and dumb.

"Now take me, Oliver," Rinaldo said,   57
"right to the rock where you saw him last.
Let's see if this wild monster, still unchained,
can fall into our trap once and for all.
One thing I know: he'll have his rich dessert
ev'n if I have to set his home on fire."
He mounted his Baiardo, and the two
rode forward. When the rock was within view,

the monster, peeping through his tiny hole,   58
lifted his weapon, ready to let go:
he hurled an arrow at Rinaldo's chest
so hard he thought he'd break all of his ribs;
thank God, his breastplate saved him from sure death!
Promptly Rinaldo from the cave withdrew,
saying, "At last your hiding place I see;
but I will smash it, porphyry though it be.

"Because you dared attack me with your dart   59
and with your mace, thus causing me to fall
as hard as never in this way before—
I swear by Jesus—you shall pay for it."
Suddenly turned into a storm of wrath,
he lifted up Frusberta with both hands.
Straight in the stirrups, quick he whirled it round,
and like a water snake soon made it sound.

The sky and the whole earth re-echoed high: 60
meanwhile a feeble, broken sound was heard
as of a stone relinquished by a sling:
a blow that could have sundered even steel.
it fell upon the cover of the cave,
cutting it instantly like still-warm cheese:
from head to toes, the monstrous body he split—
the story says, and let's have faith in it.

Just as expected, splinters of that stone   61
leapt by the thousands here and then leapt there,
and the whole firmament was bright with sparks.
Dudòn commented, "God! Not even Hector
or well-renowned Achilles could compare
with this man here, who beats them both in strength."
So deep into the hole Frusberta went,
Baiardo on his knee suddenly bent.

Indeed, Rinaldo had to toil and sweat   62
to take his sunken sword out of the rock.
He said, "And so, cheap highwayman, you thought
that a deep cave would save your hardened skin!
He who delights in quarrel and deceit
must in this fashion ultimately end:
so for your sins you now have paid at last.
That's how I handle every maddened beast."

Watching in horror through the cavern's hole,   63
Dudòn could see that glutton wholly split,
from his head down to both his legs and toes.
Looking no further, he could only say:
"Merciful God, have pity on us all!
This, I am sure, has for a reason come;
something in this You want us to discern:
from this wild monster's end all men should learn."

Then with the point of his own sword he wrote: 64
"The Lord of Montalbàn on such a day
by chance came here ... " with all the rest of it:
how in that stone the weirdest creature hid,
and how Rinaldo pierced him through and through.
Those very letters carved by Dudòn's hand—
or rather by the point of his brave sword—
one still can see along that very road.

"The Woods of Hell" that place is called today.   65
  Pilgrims who travel to Mount Sinai must
  in wintertime that very forest pass
  if they want not to cross the Balai River.
  Those letters are still there, and one still reads
  how brave Rinaldo slew that fiend from hell.
  Deep in that cave one still can see the bones,
  and hear throughout the night blood-curdling moans.

  The three knights left, and once again the lion   66
  kept showing them the way that lay ahead.
  It was already dark. Rinaldo thought
  that they should tarry in those woods no more—
  which made both Oliver and Dudòn grieve,
  for much too weary to ride on were they.
  Cautiously, then, they rode throughout the night
  'til in the sky they saw the eastern light.

  As soon as God Apollo left the sea,   67
  they found themselves quite near a lovely hill.
  They climbed it; then they climbed another knoll
  which rose in front of a high mountain: there
  at once they went, and from its summit saw
  a little valley with a little stream,
  tents and pavilions and, spread in groups,
  various people and armed knights and troops.

  'Twas there King Manfredonio was camped,   68
  languishing for Meridiana's love.
  All of his men were there, ready for war.
  The girl, whom he alone thought most unkind,
  had sent to King Corbante a messenger
  to let him know that she had been besieged
  by Manfredonio, who until that day
  wanted her virtue in a forceful way;

  and that the Lion's Warrior alone,   69
  whom she awaited, could now save her life;
  and that she spent in prayer day and night
  and begged her people's sacrifice and plea.
  Humbly with them to her Mahound she prayed
  to keep her dear virginity unsoiled,
  as in the coming Canto tell I must
  with the assistance of the Holy Ghost.

CANTO   VI

Our Father, Who in all Thy heavens art,   1
not circumscribed, but through the greater love
Thou hast for wonders that were first to start,
praised be Thy name and Thy unending worth,
and grant me so much grace as may suffice
to let me, free of error, tell our tale:
therefore, O Father, being good and kind,
with Thy own help sustain this weary mind.

The sun, I say, had risen in the East   2
and, having dabbed some rouge upon her cheeks,
Dawn to her ancient spouse had said goodbye;
Jupiter's daughter could be seen no more—
that amorous and most refulgent star
which often vexes lovers much too much—
when down Rinaldo came from the high mount,
looking for his Orlando, the great count.

As soon as the new city was in view,   3
he told Dudòn, "You now can see the land
that such a beauteous lady calls her home.
It proves that King Corbante was not wrong.
I see a mighty throng of infidels:
here with his troops King Manfredon must be."
Oliver, after these few words he said,
could recognize Orlando on his steed.

He saw him with Morgante at his side   4
just as he was arraying all those men
for the great battle that was soon to start,
and had already made the bugles sound.
It was the giant, though, who raised his awe.
Showing him to Rinaldo, so he spoke:
"That man's Morgante, and beside him—can't you tell?—
rides Count Orlando; look at his Rondél."

As soon as his dear cousin he could see,   5
great sweetness overwhelmed Rinaldo's heart.
"Now that I've seen the paladin," he said,
not even sudden death would frighten me.
Well, then, our journey let us soon conclude:
our promise was to reach King Carador.
In a short while we must Orlando face
together with these dogs or pagan race."

No sooner had they crossed the city walls   6
than they inquired of the ruling king.
"Soldiers of fortune," so they said, "we are,
by King Corbante sent right here to serve."
Seeing that lion, every citizen,
instead of answering, ran fast away.
But farther into town Rinaldo rode,
up to the square where rose the king's abode.

As soon as the three knights were sighted there,   7
the news of their arrival crossed the doors
of the great palace of King Carador.
Meanwhile Rinaldo from his horse alighted
with Oliver and Dudòn, just as fast.
From street to street the news had quickly sped.
"This man must be the knight," said everyone,
"who as the Lion's Warrior is known."

Right from the window where she chanced to be,   8
Meridiana, mistress of delight
and gentle virtues, for her maidens sent.
So winsome and so simple and so shy,
and yet so prompt was she in welcoming
our knights, one never could have asked for more
of one of the fair nymphs of Pallas or Diana:
so lovely was indeed our sweet Meridiana.

Rinaldo, when he saw the damsel there,   9
wanted to kiss her as all Frenchmen do.
He in that language said to Oliver,
"Never such beauty have I seen before."
And Oliver replied, "Compared to her,
the sky's most shining star is dark as night."
Rinaldo added fast, "You'd better stop:
a fire's quenched, another's lighting up.

"Maybe no more, as until now you've done,   10
will you, throughout the night, throughout the day,
sing Forisena's endless worth in rhymes:
a headache's cured by a much stronger ache.
Well I can see she's conquered all your thoughts,
and that new fetters fasten now your heart."
Oliver said, "Were I to live forever,
nothing from Forisena would me sever."

Already the long staircase they had climbed,   11
and with great honor she had welcomed them
right at the middle of the polished ramp
where she had kindly come to greet the knights.
With all his barons, Carador meanwhile
had also walked into the royal hall.
Rinaldo and the others kissed his hand
just as with pagan monarchs rules demand.

The king had many platters soon brought in,   12
and bade their steeds be fed with hay and straw.
Throughout the city their great fame spread fast,
and many came to catch a glimpse of them.
Dinner was served, and what a feast it was!
Oliver at the lass was gazing still.
After their dinner, Caradoro then
wished to say something to them, and began:

"Now let me tell you, famous cavaliers,   13
what this my heart from each of you desires.
Throughout our country, through the entire East
has spread the reputation of your might,
as well as of your still-unbeaten steeds:
and this is why you have been sent to me.
Here every plainland, as you well can see,
is full of men that give us misery;

"and there's with them an old and famous king   14
who, with my daughter being still in love,
not only wants her hand and this my throne,
but even has some of my subjects slain.
Every new day a newer scheme's devised
whereby he terrorizes my whole field.
But now by chance or fate a wandering knight
has brought a giant of enormous might.

"This giant with a clapper in his hand   15
makes ashes of whichever spear he meets;
several of my pagans he has smashed
or freed from further fasting on this earth.
Wherever he arrives, at once he strikes;
no priest on earth can save us from such harm.
One day, I saw him crush a poor man's head
as if it were a music box instead.

"If with that knight you're brave enough to fight,   16
and also with that giant hand to hand
(this is the only fashion known to them),
I'm sure my men will ultimately win.
And in the name of my great Lord and God
I swear that, if you beat either of them,
whatever you will wish to ask me—even
my lovely daughter's hand—you will be given."

Right there, Meridiana heard all this.   17
She wore a very elegant rich dress,
richly embroidered in the pagan style,
all over strewn with flowers white and red
that matched her face of orange and of milk—
such as would spur an icy heart to love;
enamel, pearls, and gold were on her breast,
with a most priceless ruby in the midst.

Right in her hair she wore a diamond   18
that turned the darkest night into bright day.
Her face, so dear and heavenly and pure,
shone like a truer sun over man's earth.
It was this wondrous face made Oliver,
who only looked at her in blissful awe,
say to himself, "A victory you'll reap
if all your promises, O King, you keep."

Rinaldo saw that Oliver once more   19
had fallen deep and hopelessly in love,
and sighed, "As I can see, he's caught again."
He noticed that his face had lost its hue
and recognized the sighing lover's look.
A well-known adage he in French repeated:
"Just as a donkey knows a potter's floor,
we'll hang a wreath on top of every door.

"This time, however, you don't seem to swoon   20
as in Corbante's court you used to do,
for, while you like this lady's face and hair,
she seems to like a lover for his sword—
and sword and lass are differently tamed.
Nowhere is love so merry as in the East!"
Oliver heaved a sigh as if to say,
"Never have I enjoyed such regal play."

And he recalled his Forisena then,   21
who still had keys to lock, unlock his heart,
but was not yet aware of his new ache.
And so he said, "Let Heaven strike me dead
if I should ever wish to free my heart
from the sweet chains I must be buried with.
And if the gods permit love after death,
her, her alone I'll love with all my breath.

"No, Love does not part company so fast—   22
Love that is willed by our consenting stars.
Whether we travel east or travel west,
I'll always love my lovely Forisena.
Yes, ever mighty is man's primal love,
and that first dart is in my breath so deep
that I believe not even death can free
my flesh and bones of all its misery."

But for a while let's leave these two at table.   23
King Manfredòn had spread his spies around,
for he was one whose every thought was aimed
at being told whatever happened there.
A man in love—moreover—night and day
thinks but of how to yank love's piercing drill.
No one can tell a lover's countless ways
to search and find his lady's faintest trace.

So he was told how three great paladins   24
had come that day to see King Carador:
surely they looked well armed and very brave,
but no one could yet tell their real names.
However, this was sure: the three of them
had boasted they would make his people grieve;
they also had the biggest and most fair
horses a man could look for anywhere.

Orlando paid attention to the words,   25
"Could this man be Rinaldo, Ammon's son?"
but to himself he said, "It cannot be:
Rinaldo owns no lion, as they say."
He added, "I will send a messenger,
and soon my every doubt will disappear.
To Carador he will announce, in short,
I'll fight the three knights lodging at his court."

King Manfredonio liked Orlando's words,   26
and so a messenger was quickly sent.
As with the king the three were speaking still,
King Caradoro to Rinaldo turned,
and asked, "Brave cavalier, what's your reply?"
Rinaldo was ecstatic at the thought
of seeing his Orlando finally.
"Sire, I am at your command," said he.

After Rinaldo, Oliver replied,   27
"Each of us three will come to the sweet game,
and this is what we ask you to report."
(Ah, Oliver, by love made now so brave!)
"And tell him to show up whene'er he pleases."
Bearing the news, the messenger returned
and said to Manfredonio, "Glad and bold,
in no esteem you or your men they hold.

"Judging by the expression on each face,   28
they seemed to be so happy at the news,
with one another—I'm convinced—they vied
for the great honor of this single fight."
Replied Orlando, "In no time at all
I'll make them speak a different tongue, I swear."
To this, Morgante chimed, "And as for me,
I'll make an easy bundle of the three,

"and leave them hanging from this belt of mine;   29
but first my metal I will make them taste,
for this my clapper's dying to resound.
Why, do they think they're coming to a dance?
Very well, then, with this my instrument
I'll see to it that they miss not one step."
By now Rinaldo, soon in full array,
with Caradoro's blessing walked away.

In that same square such prowess had he shown, 30
the entire population stood in awe:
with shield and breastplate, from the ground he leapt
right on his charger, grabbing fast its reins.
Carador said, "From a good stock he comes."
Meridiana at those words rejoiced,
she who had come outside for sheer delight,
eager to see him mounted for the fight.

A while before, she had made Oliver 31
happy by helping him put on his suit:
ecstatic, on his horse he jumped and, right
before her eyes, showed his equestrian skill
better than any knight would ever do.
Dudòn as quickly was on horseback too.
Each of the three jumped neatly on his steed,
and the whole population cheered indeed.

Three times Baiardo gamboled in midair, 32
each time a hundred feet, as people saw,
so proud and bold and strong and fierce was he.
And Oliver, to please the princess, made
his Vegliantìn just like a leopard leap.
Dudòn, too, strongly spurred his horse's flanks.
Thus from King Caradoro finally
trotted away our knights and seemed to flee.

Out of the city's door they came and rode 33
straight to the bars that girded the hostile camp.
In utter joy Rinaldo took a horn
and sounded it as a sure sign of glee.
The news was brought to Manfredon at once.
Eager, Orlando and Morgante rushed
to see and meet the three awaiting men:
they greeted one another in perfect Saracen.

Orlando failed to recognize his cousin 34
because Baiardo was completely draped
and he, Rinaldo, spoke the pagan tongue.
Seeing the lion, he berated him:
"A perfect knight-at-arms would never think
of taking that wild animal along;
I say that you should not have brought him here,
and I speak out of charity, not fear."

"You'd make a perfect friar," said Rinaldo,   35
"since so much charity is in your heart.
But banish so much terror from your soul:
your words, good Sir, belie your cowardice.
If you but knew the reason why I take
this lion with me, or how meek he is,
never would you have spoken as you've done:
know that this gentle lion hurts no one,

"save those who wrongfully oppose my views   36
or those who're only traitors at their best."
The count could not but wonder deep within,
but only answered, "Facts, not words, good sir!
If you now choose a single combat, with
no help and hand to hand, en garde therefore!
With different kinds of fight I do not bother:
I'll treat you as I treated many another."

"Maybe you are mistaken," said Dudòn.   37
To him the giant in this way replied,
"You answered as you did, kind sir, because
you do not know who my great master is.
I am not armed, Your Excellency, like you,
but I can fight you any time you say."
Our Dudòn lost his patience then and there
(I wish that he had not) and even dared

lower with flaming arrogance his spear   38
and strike Morgante on the shoulder with it,
thinking he'd fell him flat upon the grass.
Morgante called it but a butterfly,
and soon regaled Dudòn with such a blow,
he made him sway and totter on his horse;
and as he saw him stagger, firm and grim,
closer he went and fast unseated him.

The giant carried him to the great tent   39
and gave him as a gift to Manfredon.
Out loud the monarch laughed and, laughing, swore
that, by Mahound, that captive he would hang.
Morgante walked right back to join Orlando,
who on the field awaited his return.
Wrathful Rinaldo soon was heard to say,
"For what you have just done I'll make you pay.

"Wait here, if so you please, until I find   40
something to fasten this my lion to,
and then we'll test the worth of spear and sword
for what your wicked giant has just done."
Replied Orlando then, "Do as you wish:
on horseback or on foot, with sword or spear."
Down jumped Rinaldo, tied the beast, and then,
turning to Count Orlando, spoke again:

"You will not blame my lion anymore;   41
so, let us see who owns the better spear,
and if you're just as brave as all your words:
a biting dog—that is—barks not in vain."
This said, he turned his steed to wound him more.
Likewise Orlando, turning his Rondél,
took to the field and, furious and fast,
faced young Rinaldo with his lance in rest.

Ask not what, meanwhile, brave Baiardo did,   42
under his hooves annulling the whole plain.
Even Rondel that day was nimble most—
he, better yet, resembled Vegliantìn.
Rinaldo 'gainst his cousin used his spear
in such a way that it would cause no harm;
but well he knew his cousin was so strong,
no one could ever do him fatal wrong.

His lance struck hard the middle of his chest,   43
and Count Orlando did the same to him:
both spears went up in pieces through the air,
with neither party gaining in the least;
both chargers, on the contrary, fell down,
after the mighty blow, upon the ground,
and from the saddle the two knights were both
unseated: so they raised their swords with wrath.

So fierce a duel the two knights began,   44
no battle ever can compare with it.
Frusberta and Cortana deeply cut,
and their respective lords so wielded them,
of plates and mails they made all useless things.
On the count's helmet, hewn of tempered steel
(to Saracen Almonte it had belonged before),
Rinaldo with his sword struck fiercely more and more.

But now he had to think of his dear life,   45
seeing Orlando flaming with new rage:
how well he knew what great disasters came
when his dear cousin was by anger swayed.
But Christ performed a miracle right then
to save from tragic error the two knights:
remembering at once which friends to choose,
the dauntless lion broke his tether loose,

and joined Rinaldo. Count Orlando said,   46
"By God, good baron, you amaze me most:
this is what I would call sheer villainy.
But you this time have used poor judgment, sir,
for of your madness I will cure you both.
To his regret, Rinaldo looked behind:
so saddened was he by the lion's sight
that he could only shyly say, "Sir knight,

"bear with me still, that I may finally   47
secure this lion in the city walls.
Believe me, my intention when I came
was to fight here without this gentle beast."
Replied Orlando, "I know not your mind,
but the deceiver is deceived at last.
But if it were my wish to wreck your lion,
look at what clapper can my friend rely on.

Rinaldo answered, "We shall then return—   48
I to the city, and you to your king.
Tomorrow, with the darting of the day,
my word I give you that I will be here,
and once again I'll call you with my horn.
We then shall see the greater of the two:
that's all, O gracious knight, I ask and plead."
And Count Orlando happily agreed.

Back to his tent he afterward returned,   49
complaining with Morgante 'long the way:
"Curse on that lion! If I had with me,
instead of this Rondél, my Vegliantìn,
this knight would not have had his chance to leave:
he would by now have known my power's seal
if I had here with me my Durlindana,"
and was too sad for having but Cortana.

Oliver and the Lord of Montalbàn   50
back toward the city were now riding still.
But now let us return to treacherous Gan,
who had to many places sent his spies.
A messenger arrived right at this time
to Carador with letters fully sealed.
'Twas chance that brought him right to our marquis,
to whom he said, "I beg you, answer me:

"May God so comfort you, what is the name   51
of this your land, and also of your king?
I am afraid I've spent my days in vain,
coming so far and reaching the wrong port."
Our most renowned marquis so answered him,
"Your question, sir, deserves a kind reply:
this region's name to me is still unknown,
but I can tell you who sits on the throne.

"The king who rules this land is Carador,   52
who has a daughter named Meridiana:
it is because of her we are besieged
by those you see along the river camped."
The spy replied, "May our Mahound protect
your life forever from horrendous fate,"
and to the royal mansion soon he sped,
where to King Caradoro this he said:

"May our Mohammed give you joyous days.   53
Gan of Maganza sent me to your court:
this most important brief he gave to me
the day I left his presence to come here.
Look at the seal that he has pressed on it
so that you may give credence to the deed."
King Carador that seal soon recognized—
it came from wicked Gan, the count despised.

That brief he opened and quite understood   54
its message. "My dear sir," the letter said,
"noble King Carador, full well you know
that treacherous Rinaldo has set foot
already in your land and lovely town
(Your Majesty, I warn you out of love),
and Oliver is with him—a born hero—
and Dudòn, also, known as the Mace-bearer.

"Orlando is in Manfredonio's camp,   55
    and surely one knows where the other is.
Both of them—this I know—are striving hard
    to give you boundless anguish, Carador.
To ruin you, they both have sought your place,
    and in due time you'll judge it for yourself.
But Charles, our emperor, dislikes all treason,
    and for my writing this is the sole reason.

"Orlando has a giant at his side,   56
    who, if he one day comes closer to your walls,
will make them all from their foundation shake.
    Of both your kingdom and your men take care:
they're Christians and you are an infidel.
    Be not afraid and save yourself from harm,
which, as I know, in many ways will come.
    The world is large, and you are wise, not dumb."

The king was full of lofty gentleness   57
    and therefore guessed quite well what Gano wrote:
at once he had the messenger in chains.
    'Twas at this time Rinaldo reached the court
and was informed of all that had occurred.
    He read the letter handed out to him,
and so did, in his presence, Oliver:
    a proof of the king's heart, deep and sincere.

When our Rinaldo understood the brief,   58
    he thanked his Jesus with profoundest love;
turning, then, anguished most, to Oliver,
    he said to him, "You saw what Gano wrote."
Meridiana was all eyes and ears:
    as soon as she found out her lover's name
was Oliver, the very famous knight,
    you can imagine her immense delight.

At once Rinaldo sent a messenger   59
    to Count Orlando with these very words:
"Since we have both agreed on this our truce
    so as to let no treachery ensue,
I beg you to come safely to this town
    where I expect you: you will soon hear things
that you will be most happy to have heard;
    but please, come quickly, and of this no word."

The messenger went soon to Count Orlando,   60
who as Brunoro in the camp was known,
and handed him the letter secretly.
Orlando read it and without delay
showed it to Manfredonio, the king.
Manfredon said, "Who knows, King Carador
is plotting something very strange and new,
which now that knight wants to reveal to you.

The truce is on, and therefore safely go.   61
Let's find out who the Lion's Warrior is.
Many strange people travel on this earth . . .
O noble count, I think that you should go."
Morgante, who was present all this time,
said, "Let us hope he's not deceiving you:
I do not understand why just today
such secret things he's willing to convey.

"I to the city want to come with you   62
lest there should be a double treason there:
besides, I'll be too glad to die with you.
But first you'll hear my clapper in that camp
if there is ever need to use its might.
If I put one and one together, truce
and now this invitation seem to me
a sign of some forthcoming treachery."

So to the city finally they went.   63
Rinaldo, knowing they were on the way,
walked forth to meet his mighty cousin soon.
When he drew near, he greeted him in French.
Most courteously Orlando answered him
as he believed he should; but nonetheless
he answered in most perfect Saracen,
not knowing his dear cousin even then.

Rinaldo said, "Let's go to Carador,   64
if you do not dislike it, gentle knight."
Orlando said, "We'll do just as you say,
for pleasing you will ever be my joy."
Morgante added, "Go, then; I'll come later."
So to the manor house went the two knights.
Rinaldo introduced the count to Carador,
eager to have all things brought to the fore.

On seeing Count Orlando, Carador
stood up in his own throne. Orlando wished
to kiss the monarch's foot, but Carador,
grabbing him by the hand, most promptly said,
"May our Mohammed amply bless and keep you!
For this your coming I am grateful most,
who now can see the greatest thing on earth—
the joyous wonder of Brunoro's worth."

65

Meridiana, when she was at last
before Orlando, very deeply sighed.
Orlando, seized by sudden pangs of fear,
turned to the maiden and so said to her,
"Madam, have I perhaps offended you
to make you sigh so deeply? Tell me, please."
Fully aware of Lionetto's fate,
Orlando somewhat seemed to hesitate.

66

"I've been in love with you," the princess said,
"from the day you and I our lances threw.
At the first stroke my helmet you removed
(the very thought now makes me blush anew)
and, like a perfect paladin of France,
caused this my hair to fall in disarray.
And then 'Go back to town' you said to me:
'fighter of females I wish not to be.'

67

"That seemed so delicate a deed to me,
it only from Orlando could have come.
Ah, you despised a woman of no worth,
and this is what has made me deeply sigh."
Orlando, ever shrewd as one could be,
by those sweet words was not at all perturbed.
He said to Carador, "After such praises
something will come of which I'll seek the traces."

68

"You'll soon know everything," said Carador,
"from the brave warrior who has called you here,"
and, turning to Rinaldo, begged him so,
"Tell him the reason you have sent for him."
But You, O Lord, Who rule the deathless rays
and govern thus the beauteous starry sky,
grant that in my next Canto I may say
the story that I interrupt today.

69

CANTO VII

Hosanna, King of the eternal realm,
Who ever on Thy subjects keepest watch,
and even pardoned him who for his doom
tasted the tree forbidden by Thy word:
help me and, as Thou canst, until the end
sustain my intellect so that I may
resume my story of so much delight,
looking to Thee as to my guiding light.

On Count Orlando our Rinaldo gazed,   2
and he who was so gazed at did not know.
Oliver often sneered, unrecognized:
their helmets did not make their faces known.
'Twas then Rinaldo thus began to speak,
"Not long ago, in a dark wood we came
across three Christian knights most wild and bold:
and all of them we left there, dead and cold.

"Because they dared offend us, each of us   3
started a single fight with each of them:
our swords began to whirl, and soon our might
by far proved much superior to theirs.
Dead in that wood we left the three of them,
for hungry wolves to find. But, let me add,
the three looked like true knights with sword and lance,
come to these regions from the reign of France."

As soon as Count Orlando heard these words,   4
"You were so right," he hastily replied;
"they all are thieves whose fate I do not mourn:
I also more than once have punished them,
as we should do with all our enemies.
But nonetheless, brave knight, tell me their names,
and I will tell you if I ever knew
any of those that in the woods you slew."

Rinaldo said, "The first was Oliver,
who, as all people say, was a marquis;
the other was the Lord of Montalbàn,
the knight whose braveness was all over known;
and I believe the third was a knight, too—
Dudòn, the very son of the great Dane."
Orlando, hearing this, began to wonder,
but then it was the lion made him ponder.

5

Elaborating further on his tale,
Rinaldo added, "Soon their steeds you'll see."
Orlando said, "I never heard their names,
but show their horses anyway to me."
They went to see them. Count Orlando looked
and was full overcome with boundless fright
as soon as Vegliantìn he saw beside,
and thought, "This pagan surely has not lied."

6

Never in his existence had he felt
so overwhelmed with grief: he nearly fell.
Oliver, seeing him so anguish-struck,
behind his helmet laughed. Then to the hall
they all returned. The famous paladin
was in the meantime brooding on revenge.
He said, "Unless some more you wish to talk,
to Manfredonio's camp I must go back."

7

Rinaldo said, "A little longer stay,"
and Count Orlando led into a room.
After he put all of his weapons down,
and down his armor suit, he thus laid bare
the emblem with a lion and the bars.
Their helmets he and Oliver took off.
Seeing Rinaldo right before his eyes,
Orlando almost swooned: oh, sweet surprise!

8

Hugging his cousin countless times, and hugging
his dear brother-in-law, our Oliver,
Orlando said, "Merciful God in Heaven!
What grace is this! I've found you at long last!"
Soon he inquired about the other knight,
"And where's Dudòn, of whom you spoke before?"
"Dudòn," Rinaldo answered, "is the one
brought to the king's pavilion by your man."

9

Morgante, seeing all that hugging, asked
of Count Orlando, "May you be so kind
as to reveal to me who these men are,
whom with such tenderness you have embraced?"
And when he heard the names of Oliver
and Lord Rinaldo, overcome with joy
he fell upon his knees and reverently
wanted to touch Rinaldo and the marquis,

and broke into great tears of happiness.
King Caradoro to their room had come.
Rinaldo said, "O cousin bold and brave,
allow me now to warn you: I believe
you should not go back to the camp. I fear
King Manfredon, like Carador, by now
has read what Gano wrote concerning you.
But of our poor Dudòn what shall we do?"

11

Answered Morgante, "I'll take care of that:
bodily to the tent I carried him,
and like a candle here I'll bring him back."
Orlando said, "Morgante, I am glad:
this is the time we sorely need your help."
Morgante a while longer did not wait.
"It's up to me to win this fight," he said,
"but I will let my clapper work instead."

To Manfredon most cautiously he went,
and there the giant by mere chance arrived
when, in the presence of the king, who had
ordered his hanging right before his tent,
Dudon was humbly begging for his life.
'Twas at that moment our Morgante appeared
and said to Manfredon, "What is your plan?"
The king replied, "I want to hang this man."

13

"Don't hang him," our Morgante added fast:
"Brunoro wants him to the city brought,
and surely he must know the reason why
just as you know he's always right and true."
King Manfredon replied, "No! Bring the noose!
He'll hang according to our martial laws.
So shall it be, whatever the reaction:
Morgante, this will give me satisfaction."

Morgante said, "You're hurting but yourself, 15
for, by so doing, you'll offend Brunoro:
if such a knight you lose, you'll also lose
me and your kingdom and your court with him.
Believe me, I myself will take him there.
If I'm not wrong, King Carador wants peace,
and maybe you will have his daughter's hand
as I could overhear and understand."

Manfredon snorted, "By our god Mahound 16
I swore the other day to hang this man
right here before my tent, as you can see,
and god Mahound forgives no perjury."
Hearing such words, Dudon implored his Christ
not to forsake him in so dire a plight.
'Twas such an answer made Morgante walk
closer to Manfredon after such talk:

he looked the whole pavilion round and round, 17
and saw it was most worthy of a dream.
At first he thought a gentle uppercut
would make the king more reasonably converse,
but then, "This is too childish," he agreed:
"some other ointment must be here employed."
Grabbing the whole tent from the top, he broke
all its support and every tightening rope,

giving it such a fierce, horrendous shake, 18
it would have made a castle crumble down:
had Pietrapana such a shock received,
just like that tent it would have fast collapsed.
Morgante, one-two-three, forced all things down,
and made a bundle of the crumbled mass:
Dudon and Manfredon he wrapped up tight,
and with his clapper vanished out of sight.

With the great bundle on his shoulders poised, 19
and his brave clapper ready in his hand,
he neatly plucked the head of every man
who tried to stop him through the pagan camp.
And oft so fiercely on the legs he cut them,
none of them dared draw closer to their foe:
full heads and legs and arms leapt in midair
with endless wrath and moaning everywhere.

Chaos had meanwhile seized the whole wide camp
where, just like madmen, all the soldiers ran.
Morgante soiled his clapper red with blood,
making his way among the crowd with it,
and breaking shoulders here, and eyebrows there.
As best he could, King Manfredon splashed through,
shaking and shouting for deliverance,
by Dudon scratched and bitten more than once.

20

Morgante with great caution going forth,
in spite of all the pagans crossed the stream
with the big bundle on his shoulder still,
thanks to the clapper so adroitly used.
But, wrapped up as he was and nearly choking,
Dudon cried out, "Now that those dogs are gone,
please lay me down for I am close to death:
by God, Morgante, let me catch my breath."

21

Morgante laid the mighty bundle down
and, seeing no more pagans all around,
quickly consoled Dudon and made him breathe.
But suddenly he thought of Manfredon,
enmeshed as liver ready for the roast.
Seeing him look as lifeless as could be,
"No! I won't bring you to the town," he said;
"the war is over soon if you are dead."

22

"Into the river dump him," said Dudon.
Morgante dumped him, uttering no sound.
But the king's spirits suddenly revived,
for following its nature, water soon
refreshed him with its all-reviving waves.
And as King Manfredon was coming to,
a group of infidels to him ran fast
and luckily could fish him out at last.

23

On went Morgante with his dear Dudon,
whom to Rinaldo and Orlando he brought.
He told them right away how he had dumped
the pagan monarch down into the stream,
and that by now the king was surely dead,
and what of his pavilion he had done.
Ask not what sounding laughs those tidings raised
while tenderly Dudon the count embraced.

24

Orlando understood everything well, 25
and that they were by Gano still tracked down.
Full of resentment, Manfredon walked back
to his own camp, where he had time to brood
on the great daring by the giant shown.
His luck in being rescued from the stream
and everything that had occurred to him—
yes, everything looked like a horrid dream.

'Twas then a messenger from Gano came, 26
to tell him that by now King Carador
lodged in his court the Lord of Montalban
with both Dudon and Oliver; and that
the Roman senator was also there:
they all were seeking nothing but his death.
Their double treason was at last well known:
they wished to kill two pigeons with one stone.

"Ah," said King Manfredon, "ah, now I know 27
why Count Orlando to the city went.
That captive must have been Dudon, I guess.
Now all their falsehood is quite clear to me.
I've been betrayed, and here my rope will end:
how true it is that all roads lead to Rome.
Yet never, never could I have believed
that by Clairmont's own blood was I to be deceived.

"Now, even if we win this lady's hand 28
and vanquish under siege King Carador,
these paladins are men of such great fame,
I truly do not see what aid to seek.
It was that giant plotted the whole scheme
by making me first wonder and believe
that each of them was but an Afric knight,
no Christian being of gigantic height."

So very frantic now grew Manfredon, 29
he thought of fleeing in the dead of night;
and then he said, "We are so near the walls,
we cannot jump in safety out of here.
'Tis better, then, to put the armor on
and wait the onslaught of the enemy.
At daybreak, both Rinaldo and the count
will, to be sure, descend here from the mount,

"and soon make havoc of my entire camp.   30
Also, Dudon will come for his revenge,
and with his clapper that most fearsome fiend
will give my people more than they can bear.
Yet, though we are the target, here we'll stay,
and may Mahound protect us with his hand."
Thus spoke the king, and, after that, in short
he bade all of his barons to his court.

All of them soon agreed they should remain.   31
The night long with suspicion they stood guard.
Morgante, who was warm with pent-up might,
the night before had to Orlando said,
"Sir, now that wicked Manfredon is dead,
while darkness is still with us let me go
with this my clapper there. I warmly long
to be alone amid that pagan throng,

"and burn their huts and sheds and all their tents: 32
with this my broom I want to sweep them clean.
You'll see some lovely smoke from every roof
and the whole camp in all directions run:
and fun indeed they'll have—those lazy louts.
'Tis fire makes all bees leave fast the hive:
fire and clapper I will have with me,
and what a blind man's fury you will see!

"With the head gone, how can the tail be well?   33
Therefore, undoubtedly the whole back's sore.
I'll make their latest soup spurt from their mouths,
and then I'll crush their every nerve and bone
by letting this my clapper strongly fall.
Many at first, I know, will rush against me,
but in the end you'll see them quickly run."
Nearly by laughter vanquished and undone,

Orlando said, "Then go; I am most pleased,"   34
and looking now where Caradoro stood,
added, "I know that all the words he said
will sound to you like idle evening chat—
words that the wind will scatter just like smoke
or the sun melt like either wax or snow.
One thing, King Carador, I want to know:
what this whole camp and pagan troops will do.

"If they decide to leave by their free will,   35
  oh, let them go and take the safest way,
  for there is always danger in a fight,
  and God alone knows what the future brings.
  Eager to see what they decide to do,
  we shall remain inside these very walls;
  but if they don't before the day is through,
  we will attack so as to rescue you.

"Your blessing you will give us in the end,   36
  and so the East much better we'll explore."
  Rinaldo and Dudon and Oliver
  agreed with him; Morgante wasn't there.
  And so with such a plan they went to bed,
  having already supped a while ago.
  With a most cheerful heart, King Carador
  honored with a great feast the mighty four.

Morgante ate the supper he had wished—   37
  a big, fat lamb well-roasted then and there.
  Before the usual time he went to sleep
  for, as he said, much work lay still ahead.
  No sooner had the morning sun appeared
  up in the east than down from bed he jumped:
  he grabbed his clapper and some flaming hemp
  and started walking toward the pagan camp.

He found the infidels already armed,   38
  yet could set fire to the corner where
  all of their horses under boughs were still,
  thus killing many of them in the flames.
  But soon his stratagem was known to all,
  and he was circled by a thousand foes.
  The whole camp most disdainfully arose,
  and all against him dashed with mighty blows.

Around him they a tarantella made,   39
  so as to make him sing in German soon:
  that was the bridge of Paris, to be sure,
  and with those pagans all around—goodbye!
  Lances and rocks against his chest they hurled,
  most fearful of that clapper, all of them;
  but when so many more against him went,
  Morgante seemed to need a helping friend.

Thicker and thicker grew the pagan throng. 40
The giant was so husky and so huge,
he never missed a single blow indeed.
Many dead soldiers lay in front of him
for, if his clapper touched one even once,
from head to toes he smashed an infidel:
oft in a circle went his clapper by,
and there a hundred heads leapt to the sky,

making that circle wider than before. 41
At times he used such heavy-piercing fists,
he made you hear the sound of breastplates crushed
with lungs and livers thinly pulverized;
of every suit of armor he made ash,
of every leg he made two chunky stumps.
So blasting was the giant's bellowing noise,
they all were deafened by his dreadful voice.

Bellowing, blowing as he was, he looked 42
like Christ, who asked *Quem Quaeritis* and made
at such a question all around him fall.
There were so many corpses all about,
no one dared fight too close; from far away
they started throwing all their spears and darts,
and, as if sucking eggs, Morgante there
still blew and bellowed, like a wounded bear.

He was the straw-stack, and the pitchforks they; 43
indeed, he was as punctured as a sieve;
and yet, fast as a spindle, he attacked
the Saracens despite their thrashing game.
He never slew less than two men at once
when, not so rapid, down his clapper came;
more than five thousand people he had killed,
although so battered, on the battlefield.

In countless rivulets all over him 44
his blood flowed down out of his many holes—
deeper than gadflies' bitings, I should say.
Some struck him with a mace or with an ax,
some pierced his breast, and some, both of his legs;
and some hurled rocks that made their weight soon felt:
all of those people like a deluge were
pushing the giant to his sepulcher.

So loud a din was in the pagan camp,   45
its echo reached the city instantly.
The sentinels on guard near every door,
seeing Morgante now so close to death,
with one great roar the alarm signal gave.
Orlando said, "A good one this will be:
King Manfredon will unmolested go
while that dear fool gives all his men such woe.

"So deep into the woods the lame goat went,   46
it must perforce have met a pack of wolves.
At times his ardent wrath is uncontrolled:
it was quite foolish of him to believe
a bit of hemp could burn the entire camp
just as a broom would chase small mice away:
this time, I am afraid, he is the mouse
for crumbs of cheese now trapped inside the house."

He asked his three dear friends at once to arm,   47
and so of all his men did Carador:
they had to save Morgante from those pagans
who were now giving him such bitter fruits.
This is what happens to a man who wants to
trot in the mud instead of walking slowly
on a dry road. Orlando bade his men
saddle his horse, his own brave Vegliantin,

and Durlindana took from Oliver,   48
to whom he gave Cortana and Rondel.
Oliver, like a loving page, in turn,
now helped his fair Meridiana arm.
Down to the pagan camp so fast they went,
each of them seemed a bird. Morgante saw
that help was coming to him at long last,
and used his clapper, much more bold and fast.

And he began to chide those infidels   49
by fast unsaddling many of them: down
went severed heads and arms, shoulders and hands.
He touched, retouched, sounded, resounded, killing
more and more Saracens like so many dogs.
A foot or so the bulging brains were high;
standing on corpses, he could still employ
against the living his still-whirling toy.

And every time he swept a fly away,
he smoothed a cheek by shaving it all off,
and where he thought he saw some ugly stain,
he fast removed it with his iron piece.
The very air looked bleak and bloody most,
so often did the giant strike and wound:
pieces of mail and armor could be viewed
like shards around a person chopping wood.

Often a head that he had severed fell
with such a weight upon some hapless man
it split, in turn, a second head, which dropped
lifeless forever to the ground below.
Thousands that day down into hell he plunged.
Ditches were filled with corpses all about.
King Manfredon, now from his drowning healed,
with many people came upon the field.

Orlando, too, showed up on the other side
together with the Lord of Montalban,
who, even uninvited, bravely fought.
The latter made at once Baiardo leap
into the throng right where the giant bled:
upon those men most recklessly he jumped,
into the thick of infidels, now lost
and pretty soon quite dead and decomposed.

As soon as our Morgante saw that leap,
also his heart seemed to leap up in bliss:
more than ten feet Baiardo sprang up high
before his hooves reached solid ground anew.
And so commenced the frightening assault.
Rinaldo his Frusberta soon unsheathed—
the sword that pierced through that fiend from hell—
now to take care of infidels as well.

With points and backhands and with right and left
hits of the sword, which ever heavy fell,
then with backhanded and upsurging strokes
he killed full twenty pagans with ten blows:
down through the saddle some of them he split,
others from head to chest or teeth at least:
their entrails soared up high; never before
had people witnessed such a cruel war.

Our Count Orlando spurred his Vegliantìn:
as right into that wicked throng he leapt,
he made a hundred foes fall on their faces
before he even let the tocsin ring:
caring for neither sleeve nor wrist, he made
of all those Saracens a slaughterhouse.
"Morgante," so he shouted, "have no fear:
Caesar's with you when Count Orlando's here."

55

These very words brought so much fear amongst
the infidels, too many of them ran.
Happy were those who had already fled,
with so much wrath our knights now chased them all,
making both jam and gelatin of them.
Little by little the whole crowd was slain.
Oliver and Dudon joined the assault
with shouts that sounded like a thunderbolt.

56

Right on the field he met and recognized
King Manfredon, and lowered soon his spear.
The king at the same moment spurred his horse
and, striking Oliver right on the shield,
up to his breastplate landed such a blow,
he utterly unhorsed him then and there:
so heavy and so mighty was that blow,
Oliver was unseated by his foe.

57

Meridiana, who with all her men
had come unto the field, saw everything,
and could not help but laugh at such a show.
Oliver, like a lion, turned aflame
and, feeling his heart breaking in his breast,
murmured, "What a mistake at the wrong time!
Before my lady's eyes I've fallen down,
thus losing both her love and my renown.

58

"At the right moment, ah, the trap has snapped!"
Nothing could now console him anymore:
Fortune, who ever every target hits,
up to the very threshold teases us.
Ask not if that mishap tormented him.
But out of kindness the young lady rode
straight to him and, "O Oliver," she said,
"do you need help to mount again your steed?"

59

60

Now it was this that doubled all his shame;
his face, already crimson, seemed on fire:
he would have wished to die that very hour.
Meridiana, grabbing then his reins,
said, "O my handsome knight, please ride again!"
These other words so utterly confused
our Oliver that, ah, the poor young man
doubted that he could rise and ride again.

With his own eyes Morgante saw quite well
how Oliver at the first stroke of the spear
hurled by King Manfredonio had been felled
before Meridiana's very eyes.
He said, "Now let me see—indeed I must—
if I can glue this clapper on his head,
thus to avenge unlucky Oliver,"
and dashed against the monarch then and there.

62

Meridiana, seeing him advance,
shouted, "Morgante, please go back, go back!"
and, this said, ran to fight King Manfredon:
she too wished to avenge the man she loved.
Morgante still was rushing toward the king,
eager to wound him. "Are you here," he said,
"Majesty—king of *scopa* or of chess?
Your cloak with this my clapper I must press."

Meridiana said, "The fight is mine:
if Count Orlando happened to be here,
you would not dare inflict such wrong on me.
Go back at once or you will feel my sword.
With all his troops that man came here for me,
eager to take my fame and land away."
Morgante now was turning back already,
obeying that magnificent young lady.

64

He saw Dudon's most dire predicament:
the hapless lad was desperately trying
to save himself from the encircling spears.
So he began most savagely to fight,
many a helmet breaking here and there
and making all of them resound like bells
as soon as he laid down his savory stalk:
rather, on each he struck as on a clock.

No matter where he smote, a mark remained: 65
all those who by his clapper thus were touched
had no more time to reach their wounded cheeks,
for quickly all of them like nuts were cracked.
At times he whirled his clapper round and round,
and seven soldiers' voices soon were stilled;
he crushed all helmets just like pits of peaches,
and head and arms and shoulders filled more ditches.

And so he helped Dudon back on his horse.   66
Dudon was shouting, "Bastard Syrians,
I'll make you pay for what occurred today
and yesterday, when I was almost hanged!"
Right at that moment famous Oliver
had reached the field with his uplifted sword,
just where the king was having his own fight
with the young lady of so much delight.

An hour and more the two had bravely fought,   67
with no victorious blow on either side.
There, right before his lady's lovely eyes,
Oliver blushed just as all lovers do,
saying, "My lady, stop the grievous fight,
and let me here avenge my injured fame.
Ah, truly, when I fell, I wished to die,
having so much displeased your very eye.

"All my life, never had I fallen down;   68
there is a start for everything, I guess."
The lady answered, "You will fall again
and still again if countless times you fight;
and this is just what happens, as you see,
to any knight who's worthy of this name.
In war one is unseated more than once:
he never is unhorsed who always runs.

"I fight King Manfredon—if you allow   69
this duel mine and mine alone to be—
not to avenge one insult but a thousand:
that man must pay for his deceit and fraud."
Said Oliver, "If this is what you crave,
more than allow—I highly praise your deed."
King Manfredon all this most clearly heard;
turning to the Marquis, he spoke this word:

"By God, I beg you, knight of high renown,
here let me, like a faithful lover, lose
my lady and my life at the same time,
if this is what my cruel Fate decrees.
I have been seeking what a lover seeks,
but poison and not honey I have found.
Since everyone my death seems to demand,
I mind not dying by her very hand.

70

"I know that to my court I'll not return,
I know I'll see my Syria no more,
I know that Fate despised me, yet unborn,
I know that all my troops will soon be slain,
I know I was not worthy of such love,
I know one cannot have what one desires,
I know no force wins love or ever will,
I know that, even dead, I'll love her still."

Meridiana at these words could not
but feel great pity for the lovelorn king.
She said, "In such a way a lover ends.
If even I could kill him countless times,
I would not want him by this hand to die:
he has already doomed himself to death."
She even wept and felt so sad that she
still so ungrateful did not wish to be.

72

She now remembered how in previous fights
he more than once had looked at her, entranced,
and said then to herself, "Why am I still
so ruthless and so wrathful 'gainst this man?
As I can see, he did all that he did
simply because he loved and loves me still:
never was woman praised for being foe
to one who such great loyalty can show.

"God, I am sure, wants not so base a thing."
Not knowing what to do, Meridiana
addressed the king. "O Manfredon," she said,
"you wish to die, so I must not be rude.
If you now care to follow my advice:
to save yourself and all your pagan troops,
order your horns right now to sound fall-in,
and presently your journey east begin.

74

"It is your wicked fate that I must not   75
be yours as you still want and warmly yearn:
why, then, rebel against Apollin's will?
I see your ship amid a myriad reefs:
with all your Saracens go back at once,
and free yourself of this your forceful love."
Manfredon answered with each sighing breath,
"I will be freed by nothing else but death."

Then the young lady wished these words to add: 76
"I feel so sorry for you, Manfredon,"
and gave him a most precious diamond ring:
"Keep it as a remembrance of your love,
your very faithful and enduring love;
and now, please, leave, and follow my advice.
If presently you leave with all your men,
you'll have my father's blessing only then.

"Through sweetness everything can be achieved,   77
whereas excessive force can break the bow—
even a Syrian one. 'Tis time alone
all human things to their fruition brings.
And for your kindness' sake I beg you now
to check and soothe your loving torment so
that you may go in happiness away
and, safe and sound, among the living stay.

"Because there is no time to waste (I see   78
all of your people at this moment die),
let's say goodbye right now and leave at once,
for Heaven cannot grant us more than this.
Keep in your eastern land the ring I gave you
as an undying souvenir of me;
and if you're not yet dear to God and Fate,
a better star or fortune still await."

Manfredon listened to the lady's words,   79
but, ah, her final phrase so carved his heart
as if through jasper it had firmly cut.
He wished so much to say but could not talk;
finally through his tears these words he spoke:
"A better star or fortune still await! . . .
'Tis Heaven sends you to your Syrian home! . . .
By all your kindness I am overcome.

"When will that day arise? When will that be?   80
I must not want what I cannot obtain.
Not to displease you more, I will go back.
Only remember me: no more I ask.
I see so many dead here on this field,
but with those men that death so far has spared,
devoid of any hope, back I will go
to my own throne, if Fortune wishes so.

"And for your love I'll keep your precious ring;   81
I'll always wear it on my very breast.
if I—a wretched man—have ever sinned
against your father and against my lord,
ah, blame me not: blame Love for all my wrongs—
Love that has brought me where his whims dictate.
This luckless man at any rate forgive,
and for your love I will be glad to live."

Turning to Oliver, he asked forgiveness   82
for that most vicious blow which caused his fall.
The kind marquis forgave him willingly,
for his departure made his heart rejoice:
they were two gluttons eyeing the same dish.
Oliver had with great attention heard
all that Meridiana said till then,
and in his very heart had wished *Amen*.

After more sighing, after some more tears,   83
King Manfredon said finally goodbye.
Sighing and weeping too, the damsel then
replied "Goodbye!" and dearly shook his hand
(of course they had removed their gauntlets first).
Oliver saw the count soon afterward
and told him what he had right then decreed—
which pleased Orlando and Rinaldo indeed.

Now by mere chance King Carador arrived   84
and soon was told of the agreement made.
Morgante, seeing all of them together,
with lifted clapper walked into their midst
and wanted to know what was going on,
keeping his weapon idle for a while.
Orlando said, "Morgante, fight no more!"
but he was fighting harder than before.

"King Manfredon together with his troops   85
has now agreed to leave Meridiana,
and go right back to Syria," said the count.
'Twas then Morgante laid the clapper down,
saying, "Orlando, this was on its way,"
and struck another man with a great blow;
another still, just like a waxen taper,
he flattened with his unexpected clapper.

Orlando ordered, "Put the clapper down!   86
We've killed already many men today."
King Manfredon bade with the sounding horn
all of his grieving men back to their tents.
And so the bloody battle of that day
ended in such a way or, better still,
just as in my next Canto I will tell.
May Christ's assistance ever with you dwell.

C A N T O   V I I I

O Holy Virgin, Mother of my Jesus,   1
Mother of every grieving mortal man,
because of whom our humankind was saved,
so much you love us, and so great you are,
that here I beg for so much grace and worth
as may allow me to rejoin our knights
who wished now to go back into the city
while Manfredon departed with great pity.

With every further step, death he implored,   2
sighing, "My love, Meridiana dear,
you could have been the source of all my bliss,
and yet—unhappy me!—I'm leaving you."
He would have made the coldest granite weep
with all the loving words he still could speak.
But all his troops he nonetheless arrayed,
preparing for his trip—forlorn and sad.

If you had seen the weeping and the woe   3
of all his people ordered to depart,
I'm sure you would be sorry for their plight.
At the last moment some of them could see
a father or a son dead on the field,
and therefore mourned them with most bitter tears:
someone a brother, some a friend embraced,
and someone struck his face, someone his breast.

Someone removed the helmet of a son   4
or of a father or father-in-law,
and then, with fond affection kissing him,
could only say, "Alas, you will no more
go back to Syria with these our troops.
To your sad mother what shall we report?
What can we ever say to comfort her?
You too have in this place your sepulcher."

On their way home, still others pondered so,   5
"Wrong, they were wrong in bringing such a crowd
to such a distant region helplessly.
That princess, to be sure, was by no means
worth the high price that we are paying still.
Is, Manfredon, Meridiana yours?
Look at your people who, outcast and sad,
have lost, except their lives, all that they had.

"You to this land have brought all Pagandom,   6
as if for Helen you had gone to Troy:
well, is your wicked lust now satisfied?
So many dead must on your conscience be."
Back to his Syria went King Manfredon,
disconsolate, in tears, and most confused:
and so all men who to their passion bend,
reason no more and suffer in the end.

Orlando with Rinaldo and Oliver,   7
and with Morgante and Dudon, returned,
followed by Carador and all his knights
with flags a-flutter in the winning wind.
The entire crowd of Africa, indeed,
mightily cheered our Christian paladins:
drums, horns, and trumpets sounded everywhere
with dances on the walls, flames in the air.

After the easy rest of many a day,   8
at last the princess sent for the marquis.
Into a little room she welcomed him,
and it was there that, suddenly aflame,
all of her sighs she finally revealed:
she begged him thus to be a perfect knight—
not to deny his love to one whose heart
had been the target of too many a dart.

"I cannot do it," Oliver replied;   9
"I am a Christian, you're a Saracen.
My God would curse me—this I surely know;
therefore you'd better kill me with your hand."
And she replied, "If you can prove to me
that our Mohammed is a useless god,
for this your love a Christian I will be,
and I will bless your lordship over me."

Oliver then explained the Trinity—   10
one substance and three persons all in one—
also its power and its deity;
and then this clear analogy he made:
"If you still doubt that one and three are one,
you have a great example in the fact
that by one candle countless ones are lit
while that first candle loses nought for it."

He spoke then of the miracles that were,   11
how from the graveyard Lazarus was raised,
how Christ was crucified and, after death,
to hell descended, many a soul to save.
The lady said, "I have no more to ask,"
and with much happiness was then baptized.
And then to Confirmation soon they went,
breaking and thus forgetting even Lent.

Discreetly more than once our Oliver   12
the merriest of dances danced with her
(no longer on his mind was Forisena,
who had until now filled his every thought)
until the lovely maiden, sweet and dear,
was finally with child and, in due time,
gave birth to a baby boy, who, says the story,
one day gave Charlemagne his greatest glory.

Out of a room the lady came one day: 13
Rinaldo, seeing that, most secretly
took Oliver aside and said to him,
"What are you doing? You must be a fool."
Oliver then revealed all things to him—
that she had been baptized, and how and why.
"If she's a Christian now," Rinaldo said,
"the news at least—be careful—do not spread."

But now let Oliver complete his dance;   14
let him and all the others rest awhile.
To the Maganzan lord we shall go back—
the ever-restless Gan of Pontier.
He in the meantime had received bad news—
King Carador had hanged his messenger,
wasting no time; so he had every reason
to worry and suspect another treason.

Being a perfect master in that field,   15
suddenly he recalled a mighty king—
the Saracen Erminion, an old
enemy of Rinaldo's from the day
the Christian paladin had injured him
by giving death to King Mambrino, brother
of the woman he had wedded finally—
the wise and lovely Lady Clemency.

As women with their husbands ever do,   16
that noble lady had entreated him
several times to avenge her brother's death.
A very prudent man, Erminion,
awaiting the right time and the right place,
had until now been hesitant to act.
Gan of Pontier had at his fingertips
the secrets of all stratagems and tricks:

if he could sow some discord anywhere,   17
no charity or conscience halted him:
most ruthlessly he acted out his plans.
Aware of Lady Clemency's design,
he wrote a brief. After a long preamble,
Rinaldo's violent outrage he recalled,
and in this fashion told Erminion
he should no longer his revenge postpone:

"To you, O mighty King Erminion,   18
  Count Ganelon sends greetings numberless:
  forever at your service, Majesty,
  humbly he recommends himself to you.
  I do believe that everything you know:
  the town where now Rinaldo can be found—
  the very one who King Mambrino slew
  and is still banished from the court he knew.

"Now as a highwayman the earth he roams.   19
  Orlando is with him and, by mere chance,
  Oliver and Dudon are with him, too.
  But by no means should you now fear these men.
  Your kingdom and your country leave at once
  and come to Montalban's ill-guarded walls:
  Alard and Ricciardetto guard the castle,
  whom still our Charlemagne hates with a passion.

"If with your people right away you come,   20
  I know that you will seize it in no time:
  there's hardly any food or army left.
  In such a way you'll take your fine revenge:
  too great a treason he is guilty of
  for having slaughtered him just as he did.
  Out of old love and loyalty I write,
  knowing the very things that would delight

"our emperor: he would be glad to see   21
  Clairmont's descendants from the earth erased,
  but can a man of honor do so much?
  Now he has banned Rinaldo and the count,
  hoping that some grave perils take their lives.
  So if you come with all your troops to fight,
  no one will blame our Charles if Montalban
  is quickly vanquished by another man."

He sealed the brief and told his messenger   22
never to rest a moment, day or night;
on his return he would receive from Gan
one hundred talents for a job well done.
'Twas to his own advantage soon to leave:
the messenger picked up his purse and horn
and, after an unpleasant, long, long road,
up to the mighty Saracen he showed.

Erminion knew treacherous Gan too well,   23
yet most attentively he read the brief,
and every reason persuaded him;
most jubilant was Lady Clemency.
Finally they decreed the sudden draft
(there was no time to waste, announced the king)
of many a brave and dauntless Saracen—
under one flag one hundred thousand men.

When all those soldiers were in full array,   24
an admiral, whose name was Lionfant,
arrived with thirty thousand daring men,
armed, every one of them, with Syrian bows.
His coat-of-arms two gilded lions showed—
both rampant—in the midst of a blue field.
Not drafted, he had come with volunteers:
you can imagine, then, Erminion's cheers.

He gathered from the coming of these troops   25
a truthful omen of his victory.
Noble and great Erminion's coat of arms
showed a white eagle in a sanguine field.
There was one more identifying mark:
a very tiny rose on its left wing.
He called for Fieramont, his handsome brother,
and then for Salincorno. To the latter

he said, "O Salincorno, you will come   26
to France, the lovely land; you, Fieramont,
will in the meantime wear my regal crown,
so deeply your bright virtues do I trust.
You will not leave this throne for any reason
until you see me cross that mountain there:
all of my kingdom I commend to you,
and you to justice be forever true."

So full of joy was Lady Clemency,   27
she gave Gan's messenger, before he left,
a most stupendous charger as a gift;
one hundred bezants in his hand she placed,
and also let him have a splendid cloak
of the most precious and enchanting silk,
saying, "This token of my love please take,
and countless times thank Gano for my sake."

Erminion also gave him many gifts—
delicate objects in the Moorish style.
Wasting no time, the happy messenger
left with their answer from a job well done.
Such a reply would gladden Gano's heart,
for—not the pit—he soon would have the peach:
one hundred thirty thousand men would be
marching on Montalban immediately.

28

In a few days the messenger was back
and sought the presence of his Ganelon,
who, most ecstatic, read the answer that
announced one hundred thirty thousand men.
The courier said, "Lord of Pontier,
now keep the promise you've already made.
Erminion treated me most royally,"
and showed the lavish presents readily.

29

All he had promised Gano gave to him,
for he was full of happiness that day.
He wrote then to Guicciardo in Montalban,
to tell him that his brother and the count
were coming back and would in France be soon.
Such was that cursèd traitor's stratagem:
to have those men feel safe at last and, hence,
keep town and castle quite without defense.

30

Meanwhile Erminion in earnest toiled:
he put together an impressive fleet,
and when the first propitious breezes blew,
he bade their sails unfurled. Both day and night,
onward most restlessly the vessels went.
With such dexterity was the large fleet
piloted onward that in a few days
all ships were safe and sound in Spanish bays.

31

News to Marsilius was soon dispatched
that a great army had arrived in Spain:
he wondered why so large a fleet had come,
and could not help but panic then and there.
He summoned all his counselors to court,
and they decided that a messenger
be sent to King Erminion at once,
to know the reason for his bold advance.

32

Wise as he was, Erminion replied   33
that with his army he was seeking France,
eager an ancient outrage to avenge;
permission he was asking to go through,
and would in no way harm his territory.
Marsilius praised and cheered his enterprise.
The dismal news reached Charlemagne at once:
thousands of pagan troops were bound for France.

So dismal was the news to Carlo's ears,   34
never in all his life had he so grieved.
He called Turpino, Namo, Salamon,
and shared with them the news he had received,
saying, "Orlando won't be here to fight;
Rinaldo's not with us (my heart beats fast),
nor is here Oliver, so brave and true:
Namo, Turpino dear, what shall we do?

"Now we all know who my dear nephew was;   35
who was Rinaldo; who the great marquis."
Turpino and the others all agreed
that they should think of their defense at once,
and in this way they comforted their Charles.
Namo it was who spoke for all of them.
"Our cities," so he said, "we shall defend,
and for help someone to the Pontiff send."

To cities and to castles and to forts   36
all over France they soon dispatched supplies,
and bade a messenger go fast to Rome
to bring the evil tidings to the Pope.
Meanwhile Erminion with all his flags
and all his horsemen was near Paris's walls:
they stormed the mountain and they stormed the plain,
and a great terror seized the entire reign.

Throughout the country ran the infidels,   37
stealing and burning, taking prisoners
and sacking and ransacking all they found:
wherever those hard criminals arrived,
havoc in every corner there remained.
Out of his barons King Erminion
selected Lionfante as the man
who would besiege and vanquish Montalban.

He with his people in the plain would camp, 38
from Paris City a few leagues away.
To Charlemagne he sent a messenger
to let him know that he was fighting him
just to avenge Mambrin, a worthy pagan,
and vanquish Montalban and St. Denis:
the chosen messenger was Mattafol,
a pagan king who knew no fear at all.

In front of Charlemagne this Mattafol, 39
behaving like the maddened fool he was,
after he clearly said why he had come,
began to threaten him most savagely.
Intimidated, Charles most humbly answered,
which made Astolfo, no more patient, take
his sword out of its sheath in great disdain,
ready to flatten Mattafolle's brain.

But he could not, for Namo grabbed his hand, 40
saying, "'Tis chivalry forbids this deed,
or we would injure an ambassador.
Let him behave as he has always done,
thus saving his own king from any blame."
Mattafol promptly interrupted him,
saying, "Astolfo, on the battlefield
this pride of yours I'll make most likely yield."

Enraged, he walked from Charlemagne away, 41
despite Duke Namo's prompt apologies.
Back to the great Erminion he went,
and said, "I brought your message to the king,
but by Astolfo I've so gravely been
offended that I beg you, if I ever
meant anything to you, to let me fight—
tomorrow morn—with every Christian knight."

Erminion replied, "You still don't know 42
the worth of all these paladins of France:
this is the reason why so many a man
has had his belly punctured oftentimes.
Know, then, that Charlemagne keeps not one knight
that has not shown great prowess with his spear.
If so you wish, tomorrow you may try,
but see that in the end you do not cry.

"Rinaldo and Oliver are not with them,
   neither is strong Orlando in their midst;
   yet they have still the brave and great Ugièr,
   who massacred so many Saracens;
   the worthy and most famous Berlinghier;
   Otto and other knights right at the court.
   I warn you, to their camp, ah, do not go;
   but you are free to act, if you think so."

All, all alone, Astolfo the night long
   spurred his brave charger on toward Montalban:
   Rinaldo was not there; how could Alardo,
   Guicciardo, and Ricciardetto keep the fort?
   But as he reached the camp, into the hands
   of certain infidels at once he fell:
   he soon was taken to the admiral,
   as ruthless Lionfantè known to all.

Soon Lionfantè asked him all he knew
   of Charlemagne, his people and his might;
   and told him the true reason they had come
   to Montalban: to avenge—it was their hope—
   the death of their most noble King Mambrin,
   slain by Rinaldo so disgracefully,
   so proditoriously, so wickedly,
   he broke the simplest rules of chivalry.

That was the reason for so great a war—
   the vindication of an ancient sin.
   The Lord of England thus replied to him,
   "Listen, O Lionfant, to these my words.
   In Jesus' name, the one who said so, lied:
   Rinaldo killed him as an enemy,
   without a shade of treason, face to face,
   and of dishonesty there was no trace."

He told him the whole truth in such a way
   that Lionfante with great patience spoke.
   "Now that I know what truly has occurred,"
   he so replied to him, "I do regret
   having my banner to this region brought:
   I wish I were in Syria with my men.
   Since he was not so treacherously slain—
   by god!—Erminion's wrong, I so maintain.

43

44

45

46

47

"In Spain I met your Lord Rinaldo once,   48
and he was such a gentleman, I swear,
that he could never smear his noble soul
with such an act of despicable treason.
He, on the contrary, looked like a great
and free and strong and just and gallant knight.
I'm truly sorry he is not yet here;
therefore I will not harm him—have no fear.

"By fair Mohammed, even if I could,   49
no longer would I conquer Montalban;
rather, its lord should be at once informed
that, with his cousin, he is needed here.
But tell me, prisoner I'm speaking to:
Are you perhaps a paladin or knight?"
As soon as our Astolfo told his name,
kind Lionfante praised him for his fame,

and, being a most honorable man,   50
had him escorted back to town: he sent
many armed soldiers with him to the walls,
and felt relieved when all of them came back.
Astolfo found the city's doors still locked,
but they were opened to him with great joy.
As soon as Ricciardetto heard the rest,
he felt as if a load was off his chest.

At once he asked if he had any news   51
of his dear brother, telling him that Gan
had written him a letter to announce
Rinaldo's quick return to Montalban.
Immediately Astolfo understood
Ganelon's trick, and wrote to Charlemagne
that surely it was Gano—he could swear—
who had invited all those pagans there.

During those days, Ganelon seemed to be   52
more saddened by that siege than any man.
Often appeared he on the verge of tears,
saying, "I see, dear emperor, no way
to save our Montalban; that's why I grieve.
I fear the castle will be vanquished soon,"
but then at night he'd let Erminion
know what in Carlo's camp was going on.

CANTO VIII ❖ 129

By chance one day, Emperor Carlo saw

the messenger he had sent to the pagan king

wearing a certain cloak of reddish silk—

a present from Erminion himself.

Often he wondered, "I cannot surmise

who else could give him such a lavish gift,"

until he questioned Gan himself one day

to know if he had seen that strange array.

53

Gano replied to him, "Not long ago,

I sent him to that country to find out

about Orlando. Nothing came of it,

and so I did not tell you. Coming back,

the messenger, interrogated, said

that he had met a pagan in some wood;

and also added that that man he slew,

and robbed him of the suit that's baffling you.

"'Tis true that, a few days ago, I wrote

to Ricciardetto, just to cheer him up:

'Know that Rinaldo and his famous friends

will be on this French soil most presently.'

I sent that message, knowing that he still

believed him dead and lost forevermore.

As each detail in Carlo's mind was clear,

he saw Astolfo's messenger appear.

55

Astolfo's message he did not believe

because it coincided with Gan's words;

therefore he answered, asking him if maybe

he was just dreaming when he wrote that brief

accusing Gan of prodding King Erminion:

Fortune was making fun of Charlemagne,

or maybe Heaven granted that—forsooth—

what Gano said should sound like gospel truth.

Now let's go back to Mattafol awhile.

Against Astolfo he was so incensed,

he did not deem his hurt a light offense.

As the new day arose, he armed himself,

his anger adding fuel to his fire.

And, ultimately starting out alone,

he stopped below the wall of Paris, where

St. Denis's Church was sited. It was there

he blew a horn that he had brought along,   58
calling Astolfo and bidding him show up
if he was not afraid to duel him.
Emperor Charles consulted Salamon
as well as Namo, asking what to do
or whether to give in to Mattafol;
and this was his decision in the end—
the mighty Dane against him should be sent.

With mighty wrath the Dane soon armed himself,   59
and harnessed then his charger with hard steel.
He asked permission of his emperor,
and fast from him and all the others sped.
Clearly he saw where, standing as a lord,
Mattafol once again now blew his horn:
he was amazed to find him all alone—
a man who ne'er had the least terror known.

As soon as bold Ugièr reached Mattafol,   60
with great civility he greeted him.
"Have you, O noble cavalier," he said,
"come here to duel with a Christian knight?
Throughout the country of the Saracens
I've fared, and never have I been unhorsed.
Do you intend, either with sword or lance,
to build your reputation here in France?

"I'm the most cowardly paladin of all,   61
yet deem you worth much less than a bezant.
If you're so dauntless as you think you are,
take, Afric baron, as much field as you wish."
The Saracen replied, "I'm not too sure
if here before me stands that brazen knight
who at the court insulted me one day:
then you're the one that I must kill today."

The Dane retorted, "Our good emperor   62
has been too patient with you, I should say;
had you not come as an ambassador,
you would have paid already for your sin.
The one who almost punished you that day
is Count Astolfo, mighty Lord of England.
I'm known to everyone here as the Dane."
Some field was taken by the Saracen.

63

As far as a bow's throw he rode away,
and then he turned and stopped his horse right there.
The valiant paladin, on the other side,
rode as far back, then turned, awaiting him.
Right in the middle of the field they clashed,
and one spear met the other faultlessly.
The Dane's broke hard on the opposing shield,
at which the pagan for a moment reeled.

With greater violence the Saracen
struck on the shield the mighty Christian knight:
he pierced it through and, through the plate's defense,
went down and tore the jacket underneath.
From windward soon to leeward bent Ugièr,
who from his charger ultimately fell.
King Mattafollè, seeing him unseated,
could not believe his eyes, and said, conceited

and loudly laughing, "Now you'll boast no more
that in no battle have you been unhorsed.
You said that you had fought with everyone,
but you had not, Sir Knight, tried Mattafol.
You see that neither Christ nor all your saints
could have prevented this your sudden fall.
So, as you must, surrender now to me."
The Dane replied, "You're right; this then must be."

66

So by the point he handed soon his sword
to the strong foe who had defeated him.
Straight to St. Denis's Church the Saracen
took him, and said, "Upon your honor, wait."
"O Pepin's son," out loud he then commenced,
"know that Ugièr was from his saddle thrown
and is my captive in St. Denis's Church:
then for another knight you'd better search."

When Carlo heard the horn the second time,
he felt as if his life had reached its end:
he looked and looked around in the vast hall
where he had summoned his bewildered men.
Duke Namo and the others counseled him
that, since the pagan challenged them anew,
their only choice was to send one more knight,
lest they should look like cowards in his sight.

Namo was picked unanimously. He went,   68
happy to do the will of all his peers.
On reaching Mattafol, most grouchy still,
he greeted him and said from where he was,
"Take as much field as you wish, and let us fight:
I am a man who does not like to talk."
Full understanding what he meant by that,
the Saracen rode back, then turned to fight.

Duke Namo also turned so furiously,   69
he seemed about to swallow Mattafol:
he landed on his shield so great a blow,
his spear, unable thus to pierce it, broke,
and yet the strong and daring Saracen
remained, not the least shaken, on his horse:
instead, he grabbed Duke Namo by the chest
and neatly dumped him from the saddle fast.

Seeing himself defeated on the ground,   70
wise Namo said, "I now believe your words:
having unseated me, you must no doubt
be braver than the other Saracens."
This said, his sword unsheathed he handed him,
adding, "I am your captive." Said the pagan,
"And now, if what I ask saves me from blame,
Sir Knight, I want you to reveal your name."

Namo replied, "Your question brings no blame.   71
Know, then, that I am the Bavarian duke."
"Oh, by Mahound," the pagan said, "cheer up:
you will be honored here among my troops."
He took him, then, right to St. Denis's door,
where our Ugièr, the Dane, was prisoner.
Back on the field, he let his horn resound,
despising Carlo and his holy crown.

A most pathetic sight was Carlo's face,   72
surrounded by his terror-stricken knights:
in Paris everyone was now afraid.
On hearing the new horn, our Berlinghier
wanted his armor brought to him at once,
and, eager, mounted his most mighty steed.
(Carlo was seated on his fatal throne,
comforted by the knights he called his own.)

He brandished his long spear of cypress wood,
and girded his dagger and his sword as well.
Spurring his charger on, by leaps and bounds
(a hound he seemed) he reached his pagan foe,
and said, "Are you the uncouth cavalier
who dared insult our famous emperor?
If you just knew who's fighting thus concealed,
you'd ask forgiveness on this very field.

73

"If you remain alive, you'll be the first,
so many have I slain with this my sword:
ask not if I can shear the thinnest hair;
such is the way my razor operates.
The pagan said, "I, by Mahound, despise
a man who in the night but gathers dew.
Send for a priest and light some tapers soon,
for, although wearing boots, you're a baboon."

74

Mad as a devil, Berlinghier replied
to the insulting Saracen, "You beast:
are you accustomed to eat bran and cabbage
with fools escorting the triumphal coach?
Mahound or his grandfather or Apollin
could never stay my arm from harming you."
After much laughing asked the foe, "Since when
have you acquired the face of a new man?"

75

Berlinghier answered, "No more empty words:
soon I will seem a giant to your eyes.
Much laughing is, in general, a sign
of a knight lacking in both worth and wisdom.
I know not what you mean by sun or dew,
and, although wearing boots, I'm no baboon.
My sword's sharp point, Sir Baron—this I say
and this I know—will take your life away.

76

"Are you perhaps Rinaldo or the much-
renowned marquis or Count Orlando himself?"
the pagan asked. "Or can you beat the Dane—
you, who can boast of a death-laden sword?
Then, if you care to, tell me who you are."
Threatening, Berlinghier replied to him,
"I'm not Rinaldo, Orlando, or Oliver:
I'm kind and brave and loyal Berlinghier."

77

On hearing such a name, the Saracen
answered, "May god Mahound's great name be praised!
So, you are one of Carlo's paladins:
I have been told he lodges in his court
no paladin whose worth has not been tried.
I more than once have looked you up and down
to see how far away you should be thrown
onto this field or landed on this lawn.

78

"Take all the field you want. Make me not laugh,
thinking, dear knight, of what you have just said—
that you can kill me on your first onslaught:
Mohammed cannot do it, nor can you.
If you pay not some men your work to share,
or if you're not too fast to fly from me,
I swear I'll take you, cavalier of France,
right to St. Denis on my pointed lance."

79

Berlinghier so replied, "I have chastised,
all of my life, buffoons such as you are;
now it's your turn. Let's move to action soon,
for all your words sound foolish to my ears."
The pagan answered, "Then these are my terms:
of my ten fingers only two leave loose,
and put into a sack the rest of me:
you're but a baby, you will quickly see."

80

"Well, if a sack you want," said Berlinghier,
"take now the field, and in a sack you'll be."
And suddenly he turned his steed around,
adding, "O Mattafol, you're tiring me:
you are what your name says; then, let's not cast
more precious pearls to the devouring swine."
The Saracen advanced, turned then and there,
and with his aiming spear faced Berlinghier.

81

Berlinghier like a pigeon forward came,
and like a falcon came the Saracen;
from everywhere resounded the great din
of the two steeds that like two swallows flew.
Then the two fighters laid their lances low,
at last in the position to attack.
The Christian's spear, although of cypress wood,
breaking at once, not in the least withstood.

82

The pagan wounded so our Berlinghier   83
upon the shield that, as if made of wax,
it was pierced through; his sharp and naked sword
hit then the thorax and the cuirass too.
Deep to the flesh the heavy blow descended,
and, the lance being very thick and green,
it fell embittered, and with such dismay
brave Berlinghier upon the meadow lay.

Mattafol with his sword more than ten feet   84
lifted the broken shield, then threw it down,
saying, "Who travels with a threat of war,
oft he returns with a peace treaty home."
So harshly taunted, Berlinghier drew sword,
eager to start his duel once again:
fast from the ground he rose with but one goal—
unleashing his revenge on Mattafol.

"Ah," said the Saracen, "you're much mistaken: 85
'tis a tradition among truthful knights
that if one is unseated at first clash,
one first surrenders sword and then oneself.
Now that I've won and smashed and crippled you,
justice itself you're fighting. Do you wish
to show me how a fencer should begin?
But this does not become a paladin.

"Among all other truly virile knights,   86
I often heard you mentioned as a man
incapable of making any error—
an honest, wise, and kind and faultless man.
But now you've fully disappointed me:
your action is indeed uncivilized."
To Mattafolle Berlinghier replied,
"Dagger and sword you'll have—but on your hide."

Losing his patience, Mattafol retorted,   87
"You've made an unforgivable mistake,
for which you will be punished right away."
This said, he spurred his charger on both sides,
and struck the Christian knight with such a blow
right on the helmet that, the author says,
Berlinghier genuflected on the grass,
utterly unaware of where he was.

"And so, do you surrender now to me?"   88
the Saracen demanded. "Oui," most promptly
the paladin replied, handing his sword
to the pagan by the point. There is another
writer who says—and this detail can still
in all the ancient chronicles be found—
that Mattafol commanded him to be
down on his knees as long as wanted he,

saying, "This is the way to expiate   89
your sin of purring so prodigiously."
After he grabbed the sword, not by the point—
which, being poisoned, would have meant his death—
but by the pommel whereby it was handed,
he laid it down beyond the holy doors
of St. Denis. Poor Namo, seeing his helpless son
taken away as captive, could only weep and moan.

Endowed with all good qualities and ways,   90
Berlinghier stood above all other men.
He was a spring—a stream of gentleness
at the right time and place, as one should be;
in fact, he's mentioned in more books than one.
Style and reality at times conflict,
but this he knew: that gentleness is wasted
on one who gentleness has never tasted.

Mattafol was to him a maddened fool,   91
just as his very name most aptly told,
and therefore one unworthy of his honor:
wise men excused our Berlinghier for this.
Besides, had he succeeded with his plan,
he would have freed King Charles and all his men.
Combating for the faith makes every scheme
legal; so blind is one who still accuses him.

Emperor Carlo, when he heard the horn,   92
said, "Ah, this sound is not a joyful sign.
Fallen is Berlinghier, the perfect man,
and I know not who'll beat this Mattafol—
this infidel accurst who came to France
to kill my people and to seize my throne."
Meanwhile Avino did not hesitate
to arm himself to avenge his brother's fate.

But soon Avino saw himself unhorsed.   93
By Otho he was followed on the field—
the valorous and famous English lord:
he too was taken captive instantly.
The Saracen defeated all of them.
Turpino came, Gualtier of Mulion,
Salamon of Brittany, and good Avòlio,
and all fell prisoners, as smooth as oil.

Richard, the mighty Lord of Normandy,   94
entered the field and, much to his regret,
down like a coward went at the first blow.
Then Angiolin of Gascony appeared,
eager to test the power of his arm:
he, like the others, ended up in shame.
King Carlo sat dejected and annoyed,
seeing his people, one by one, destroyed.

Gano the traitor was the one man left: 95
Charles did not want him to go out and fight.
Thus Mattafol returned to Montalban,
right near the city where his lord had camped,
and showed the captives to the pagan king.
Erminion paid homage to them all,
welcoming them into his royal tent.
May Christ in heaven all of you defend.

C A N T O   I X

O happy spirit full of every grace,   1
unshaken column and most gracious hope,
O Holy Virgin, humble Nazarene,
who up in heaven are the bride of God,
to the conclusion lead me with your hand
and let me tell all that my fancy holds
so that—thanks to your love, great and divine—
all those who hear may like this song of mine.

Already Phoebus's face was in the sea,   2
wetting his golden locks down in the waves;
he had already from our hemisphere
removed his splendor, leaving far behind
the laurel tree that had rejected him;
it was the time of Taurus's hottest rage
when in the tent of the great King Erminion
our captives and the Dane had their reunion.

There was a celebration in the camp—   3
which seemed a good beginning to the king.
And, to his satisfaction, Mattafol
a large throng of armed men had there with him:
he wore a cloak on which all eyes could see
a god Mohammed in pure silver hewn;
most proudly through the camp he loved to walk
while everybody of his prowess spoke.

Mattafol's one regret was that Astolfo   4
was not among his many captives there;
thus he was threatening in the midst of all
(a phoenix on his helmet could be seen).
Astolfo would have come or, better, flown,
dismounting from his charger as he pleased;
but knowing well his tendency to fall,
our Ricciardetto kept him from coming out at all.

Bellowing, howling through the royal hall,   5
like an enraged and famished lion, Charles
advanced with Ganelon, who was indeed
jumping with joy, though hiding his great bliss.
Therefore he said: "Alas, your fame grows dim!
If only our Rinaldo had returned!
Oh, if the count and Oliver were here,
I would not be so overcome with fear."

Maybe that traitor was telling the truth,   6
for surely if Rinaldo had been there,
the man who never could take white for black
would soon have killed him like the knave he was.
Carlo was moaning, "Very well I see
our empire's lost its natural old warmth:
the one who was its heart is here no more—
I mean Orlando; much I grieve, therefore."

Let's leave these men—some anguished and some glad—   7
and let's go back now to the newly christened
who had their lodgings with King Carador,
and nothing knew of their abandoned lands
or of the recent war against them waged.
Happily with the pagan king they'd lived
quite a long time; but now they wished to go away,
and this is what they told King Carador one day:

"A long, long time we have lived here with you,   8
immensely honored by your entire court:
give us your blessing, then, King Carador,
and we shall leave you, where you are, in peace.
For all lost time we want now to make up—
and better late than never, to be sure.
Some other country we must seek and see
before in France we settle finally."

King Carador permitted their departure   9
and, thanking them with an appropriate speech,
said, "O most worthy, O most noble knights,
my kingdom and my life are yours forever."
And then he bade his gracious daughter come,
and gave the cavaliers most precious gifts.
The princess called her Oliver aside,
and in his presence much she sobbed and cried.

At last she said, "What have I done, my love—   10
my gentle love—that you should leave me so?
Why are you leaving this so grievous heart?
You used to swear forever to be mine,
and now you're going far away from me—
and whether east or west I do not know.
This is the grief by which I'm most undone—
the fate of our unlucky little son.

"Pregnant and all alone I'm left behind,   11
bereft of hope to see you once again:
that's why here in your arms I'm weeping so.
But grant, at least, this only grace to me:
that, since my mind is so distressed with pain,
wherever you may wander I come, too:
whichever country where you still may roam,
I, your most loyal servant, will call home."

Comforting his sweet princess, Oliver   12
replied, "My lady, as soon as I return
to France—the lovely land—with all my heart
I will come back most joyously to you.
So banish from your spirit all dismay,
for I am bound, and not unbound, to you.
Therefore, our little son—when time is due—
for my love's sake I recommend to you."

Oliver left Meridiana then,   13
surely with many sighs and many tears,
and—I'm afraid—with a most futile hope.
King Carador with great magnificence
and pagan dignitaries all around
(indeed he tried his best to make them stay)
the Christian knights escorted out of town,
walking ten miles with them—if not eleven.

Finally, then, he shook their hands, and even   14
promised them as much help as he could give.
Through a strange country thus they went away,
and as they reached a desert to be crossed,
the savage lion that had been with them
suddenly disappeared and, to be sure,
turning his back to each and every one,
into a lightless vale was seen to run.

Rinaldo said, "Dear cousin, did you see   15
how fast the lion vanished out of sight?
God through this miracle is telling us
that there must be a reason for his flight.
Our Lord in heaven, ever good and true,
has let this happen for a happy end."
Replied Orlando, "If I've heard you well,
you're quite religious now, as I can tell.

"With all our blessings let him go in peace,   16
for I am glad to know him far from here,
since oft he scared the devil out of me."
Thus many a day upon their steeds they rode
until, at a long plainland's very end,
they finally arrived in Danismarche,
the country ruled by King Erminion,
who with his troops was now at Montalban.

They climbed a mountain from whose top they saw   17
armies of Infidels full-armed for war.
When they were closer to them, they were told
by all those soldiers that their master's name
was Fieramonte, who had brought along
four thousand men with fighting expertise,
and now was on his way to visit one
of several cities that he called his own.

He was the man Erminion had named,   18
on his departure, ruler of his reign.
This Fieramonte liked Baiardo at once,
and soon great plans were seething in his mind.
Thus to Rinaldo in this way he spoke,
"O bright and worthy knight, please tell me: who
gave you this horse, so beautiful and brave?"
and asked him if Baiardo he could have.

Rinaldo answered, "Many wanted him,   19
but he is not a horse to give away."
The pagan said, "If this you cannot do,
oh, let me ride him for a little while."
Rinaldo understood the hidden ruse,
and said, "O Saracen, there is a tale
that you should know before my steed you borrow—
that of a fox and a rooster: here's the story.

"A fox was going for a walk one day,   20
for she was hungry and could nothing find.
She spotted a fat rooster on a tree
and, acting like a simple little girl,
begged him to come much closer, so that she
might hear and treasure his sweet song much more.
From branch to branch the rooster came down quick,
and soon the fox devised a newer trick.

'Your voice,' she said, 'sounds feeble to my ears.   21
How to sing better let me teach you now:
if you, while singing, close your eyes a bit,
you'll soon find out how sweet your voice can be.'
The rooster thought it an amusing thing,
and said, 'So many thanks for teaching me!'
and closed his eyes and then began to sing
just to entrance the fox's listening.

"While the naive and simple little beast   22
was singing with eyes closed, as madmen do,
the fox, astute and deadly as she is,
under that pretext grabbed him all at once
and swallowed him, unsalted as he was.
This happens to all those who little know;
this is what you would do if I paid heed:
I'd be a fool to let you ride my steed.

"I'm at your service if you want a joust: 23
if either with your spear or with your sword
you honorably unseat me on this grass,
the horse is yours and the whole case is closed."
Rebuking him, thus Fieramonte spoke,
"What are you saying, despicable knave?
How dare you, roguish fool, so boldly preach?
The Sultan would not dare make such a speech.

"If you but knew whom you are talking to,   24
you would not talk so irresponsibly;
but I have always taken care of fools.
My brother, the great King Erminion,
would fight not one but seven Charlemagnes
with all of France, just as he's doing now.
He has besieged already Montalban,
and now King Charles is helpless—the poor man.

"Numberless troops and giants are with him   25
to avenge the death of noble King Mambrin,
murdered by the most famous of all traitors—
Rinaldo, fleeing still from land to land,
eager to unbaptize all the baptized."
Rinaldo said, "You beastly Saracen!
You're lying in your throat, for in no way
and never did Rinaldo thus betray.

"Like it or not, take as much field as you wish,   26
and in Rinaldo's name I'll pick this fight.
Of such a noble family is he
that neither trick nor treason can he know."
This said, he turned the bridle. Seeing him
so madly fuming, asked the Saracen,
"Could this man be a demon out of hell?
Never was I belied so fast and well."

He turned his horse and, burning with new rage,
took ample field, then stopped and turned again.
Rinaldo, aiming at the helmet, thrust
his iron-pointed spear so deep and low,
he made poor Fieramonte gasp his last:
piercing him from the scruff, he plunged his spear,
which through the eyes then ended on the forehead—
thus on the ground bold Fieramont fell dead.

27

Witnessing such a deed, the Saracens
felt on themselves the terror of the blow,
and, like an army with no general,
began to flee at random on the field.
But there was, right in Fieramonte's troops,
a shrewd knight who, on seeing his lord dead,
came to Rinaldo, fell upon his knees,
and said, "You have avenged me, sir. But please,

28

"allow me now to tell you the whole truth
about the traitor that you have just killed,
O gracious and most gentle cavalier.
His brother, the true monarch of this country,
had left him in his place to rule the land,
for he's at war with Charles the emperor
and, as he said, is now at Montalban,
where he will do, to win, the best he can.

29

"Seeing himself as the sole ruler here,
against all justice he began to sin,
stealing from citizens and foreigners,
flaunting his wickedness in many a way,
and trampling on the people's every right.
To show the utmost baseness of his soul
to those who were still doubting and agape,
all of our women he began to rape.

30

"If any man in any way rebelled,
he had him secretly suppressed at once;
in spite of his outrageous violence,
terror commanded silence in the end.
But now you've made him pay for all his sins,
and all our population will rejoice.
My very sister, who refused his lust,
into a dungeon wrathfully was thrust.

31

"If you're a knight of any influence   32
(judging by what I've witnessed, you must be),
take now his charger and his cloak as well;
then we shall walk behind you into town,
where every happy citizen will cheer.
We all are knights of excellence and worth:
without one stroke of sword or other fight,
to you we'll give the entire land outright.

"Friends we have here as well as relatives;   33
if in our city you decide to stop,
you'll see parades and tournaments and jousts:
meanwhile we'll tell our bravest knights to don
their armor, and most happy they will be.
And you will make that maddened crowd behave:
so each of us will play our grandest game.
Now, if I may, Faburro is my name."

And this is the reply Rinaldo gave: 34
"Even before I answer you, Faburro,
or while I'm still consulting with my friends,
it seems to me you can control that crowd:
see, just like birds they're flying, one by one.
They are already a half mile away,
and with them vanished we can nothing do."
Replied Faburro, "I agree with you,"

and started thus to spur a colt he had.   35
Rinaldo called Orlando and Dudòn
and Oliver, and told them the whole tale.
Orlando listened to Rinaldo's words
and, weighing what the pagan had just said,
commented, "Surely it must be God's plan
that we have landed in so strange a region—
to make us spread the faith and Christ's religion."

But his Morgante was not there with them—   36
which saddened him. Morgante had been left
with King Carador's daughter by Oliver,
and had remained most willingly behind,
awaiting the return of all of them.
Oliver thought the giant should be there
lest Carador should think of giving death
to his dear son the moment of his birth.

Meridiana had begged Oliver   37
to leave Morgante as his pledge of love:
thus of her only love she'd ever think
from the first day she saw him ride away.
And Oliver had begged Morgante so:
"Here you can stay where this my heart will be.
To you with Count Orlando I'll be back:
watch over son and mother for my sake."

Indeed, Orlando missed him very much.   38
He said, "If my Morgante now were here,
so savage and so strong he truly is
that he would make the whole world crumble down
with a few blows—not only walls or doors.
How many people's cheeks would soon turn red!
We shall soon be in a predicament
where his great clapper would be heaven-sent."

Faburro in the meantime had returned   39
and ordered soon the necessary things.
Rinaldo had removed from Fieramonte
the cloak and all the arms that had been his;
he had then seized and mounted his brave steed,
fully resembling the dead pagan knight.
Finally toward the city rode each man,
thus following Faburro's very plan.

Greatly the population honored him,   40
who was Lord Fieramonte—so they thought.
Rinaldo let the pagans in the square
continue with their festive tournaments.
Meanwhile Faburro frantically around
looked everywhere for relatives and friends,
telling them that their tyrant lived no more,
and things would be quite different therefore:

free, they would soon be free, completely free.   41
And he made many soldiers take up arms,
and each and every one of them was glad
to fight and save his fatherland at last.
While in the square a tournament took place
and everyone was having a good time,
with many armed men Faburro then and there
arrived and soon surrounded the whole square.

The Saracens who were around Rinaldo   42
began to make their swords all red with blood:
some people died, and some for mercy begged.
Throughout the city they began to run
with a great tumult and loud-thundering wrath.
The streets were full of men who, unaware
of what had been minutely prearranged,
said, "Fieramonte's mentally deranged."

Fast ran Rinaldo to the royal house   43
where was the queen together with her sons.
Atop the staircase he arrived, and heard
the lady ask, "Why are our people so
perturbed, and why such havoc suddenly?
Dear Fieramonte, this cannot be you.
What's happening? Who's fighting in our town?
Why is the entire city upside down?"

With only one of his Frusberta's strokes,   44
so hard he hit her that he cut her head;
and then he killed her children one by one.
The Saracens were asking, "What's all this?"
The entire city finally he seized
with all the people that were still in it.
And then he found Faburro's weeping sister,
and from her dungeon instantly released her.

For a few days they in the city dwelt,   45
and to Faburro each revealed his name,
his true identity thus making known.
The population understood all things,
and everyone was christened joyously
that he might render thanks to Jesus Christ,
Who to the land had brought at last salvation
and now had made of them a Christian nation.

Then with Faburro, who had been informed,   46
our knights discussed the foe near Paris camped,
as well as Gan, who had intrigued and schemed,
awaiting the right time to start that war
and checkmate Charlemagne ultimately;
also, how they could help St. Denis soon.
With all of them Faburro then agreed
that they should go to Paris at great speed.

Orlando said, "My one regret is this— 47
to leave our mighty giant in the hands
of Carador, which makes me truly sad."
Dudon replied, "If so you wish, dear count,
a flying falcon, I will go to him,
and shortly your Morgante will be here."
Everyone liked that he should be the one,
and take Baiardo, faster thus to run.

So it was done. Dudon was on the road, 48
and so our noble, valiant baron flew
that, in no time, upon Baiardo's back
he reached the famous pagan Carador.
Our paladin at once was recognized.
"If I am not mistaken," said the king,
"Dudon has come to visit us anew,
and look, Rinaldo's charger is here, too."

Meridiana recognized him, too. 49
Down the long staircase running to embrace him,
she said, "I am so happy, dear Dudòn.
I recognized you by the horse at once.
What happened to my Oliver? Oh, please,
do tell me all you know about my love."
And Dudon answered, "Oliver on his part
sends with his many greetings all his heart."

If one had only seen the gentle lass 50
like a fresh rose turn crimson in the face
as soon as from afar Dudon she saw,
and run to hug him, and at once inquire
where her beloved Oliver might be,
one would have had no doubt about her love.
"How is Rinaldo, O my noble hero?
My poor Dudon, you now must be so weary . . .

"And how's Orlando, the renowned and great 51
paladin that no other knight can match?
I'm dying to know all and each of them."
King Caradoro, who was present, soon
greeted Dudon with Moorish courtesy
before he asked about the other knights.
"Far, far away," Dudon began to tell,
"in Danismarche they are safe and well.

"This is my reason for returning here: 52
I have been sent by Count Orlando and
by Ammon's son; our Charlemagne needs help—
and needs it now, for King Erminion
with all his armies and with all his flags
keeps Montalban surrounded and besieged.
I need Morgante and I need your men."
Forward our mighty giant walked right then.

Oh, to embrace Dudòn how fast he ran!   53
He asked about Orlando countless times.
The count, Dudon informed him, wished to leave
for France, but now invited him to go
to Danismarche and stay with him awhile.
At last the four to this agreement came—
that they should rally every pagan throng
and leave for Montalbano before long.

Many a squadron in no time at all   54
was ready now for action there in France.
Meridiana said, "O father dear,
oh, please, do not deny this grace to me:
on the French battlefield I want to test
my valor, even if I have to die.
Oh, if my happiness you care to see,
let me the captain of our armies be."

So eager was King Carador to show   55
Rinaldo and the other Christian knights
how grateful he was still for all their help,
he thus replied, "I, too, agree with you;
therefore I bid you, in God's name, farewell.
A real friend Rinaldo's been to us;
his help he gave us when we needed it;
and now we won't forget his benefit.

"Oliver and Orlando treated us   56
like friends indeed, as my whole kingdom knows,
in the most dire of adversities:
so Dudon's plea is a most worthy one.
Let's not forget who has befriended us:
Heaven abhors ingratitude on earth."
Meridiana heaved a happy sigh,
not knowing how her father would reply.

Then, turning to Morgante, this she said:
"And you, O giant dear, will come with me."
Morgante answered, "Of one thing be sure:
I'll never let you go far from my sight:
I give my word of honor and I swear."
The lady said, "My heart is overjoyed.
I cannot wait to see the count anew,
and at his side dauntless Rinaldo, too."

57

The lady said all this with but her lips,
though with her heart she murmured "Oliver."
Morgante, who knew well their whole romance,
replied, "But why omit your lover's name?
I know he mentions yours each day and night.
Have you so soon forgotten all his love?"
The lady said, "His name I mentioned not,
for Oliver is in my every thought."

Quickly they rallied forty thousand men,
and ten full-armed divisions thus were formed.
King Carador himself dismissed them all
as every flag grew restless in the wind.
They were provided with all kinds of arms,
as all true cavaliers indeed must be:
horses and scimitars of Moorish make
and shields and bows and many a plate or plaque.

59

Meridiana rode a steed so stout
and so immense, a mountain was as high.
Whatever he was given—hay or barley—
had to be wetted in cool water first.
No, he was not a steed; though, as a horse,
he was as perfect as a horse could be:
nimble and strong and with a serpent's head,
he did not simply run—he rather sped.

This beast in a deep forest lived one day,
born of a serpent and an Arab mare;
he blew and bellowed like a raging bull—
so strange a beast had not been seen before.
The one who caught him gave him to the king,
who to Meridiana gave him then.
She always led her "horse" from war to war,
and so her fame began to spread and soar.

61

The ten most brave divisions rode and rode   62
until they came to Danismarche at last.
When the good tidings reached Rinaldo's ears,
one morning, at the very break of dawn,
he called Orlando and the great marquis;
all that was happening at once they knew:
from far away they spotted, proud and tall,
the giant with his clapper coming in front of all.

Orlando shouted, "Our Morgante's there,   63
bringing so many mighty pagans here.
King Carador is proving now to us
that for our friendship he is grateful still."
Oliver said, "If your Morgante's he,
my fair Meridiana—where is she?
So much I long to see her that I perish,
and even this illusion now I cherish."

As they drew closer, Oliver could see   64
his lady riding faster than before:
he recognized her by the horse she rode,
or was it Love who opened so his eyes?
Meridiana, seeing him, in turn,
just like a star turned flaming in the face,
and from her charger down at last she came:
Oliver, naturally, did quite the same.

He kissed her first, just as a Frenchman would,   65
and then embraced her with great gentleness.
The gentle lass could hardly say hello,
such tenderness inflamed her all at once.
Oliver felt such sweetness in his heart,
his whispered greetings were not even heard;
but he kept saying, "Welcome, welcome she
who to my eyes the only star will be!"

Christians and infidels rejoiced together,   66
and then together praised King Carador,
who, far away and after a long time,
remembered still the benefits of yore.
Faburro said, "O sovereign cavaliers,
an ancient proverb I have often heard,
that's in my mind still green and lively most:
a charitable deed is never lost."

They rested in the city several days.   67
New Christians in the meantime armed themselves—
an army of four thousand, all of them.
Faburro said, "Now that Morgante's here,
let's march; but, dear Orlando, if for me
you care at all, oh, grant me this one grace—
that I the captain of my people be,
and soon in France my valor you will see."

Replied Orlando, "Mighty friend Faburro,   68
I never have denied you anything."
Faburro rallied all his people then,
and after they were ready for the march,
as his own coat of arms he chose the moon,
richly embroidered on his flowing cloak
of snowy silk and gold, so beautiful,
it looked like the two sharp horns of a bull.

Now we shall leave this throng of Saracens   69
already out of Danismarche, and go,
wasting no time, to Pepin's son, in tears
and moaning, "I can't bear it anymore.
Neither Rinaldo nor his cousin's here,
and the whole world is crumbling down on me.
In court, I did not much appreciate them;
but now I do, and grieve, and still await them."

Gano, his glances riveted on him,   70
comforted him with false, treacherous words,
feigning a smile with sadness overcast:
"O Carlo, this your grief now grieves me most:
why still so many tears upon your face?"
He rallied thirty thousand of his men
and (ah, the traitor!) said, "I want to bring
new help to Montalban, O noble king."

He made them march right past the emperor,   71
and chose Magagna as their captain; then,
"With this so great a company," he said,
"I will assail the pagan admiral;
and Lionfante—this I know—will fall:
in his own web the spider will be caught."
He colored so his tinsel—shrewd and bold—
that Charlemagne mistook it for true gold.

With this deceit to Montalban he went,   72
scheming to seize it with impunity.
With all his men he saw the admiral,
and said, "By treason I shall give you all
your enemies and the city they are in:
this very night I'll put you right in there."
But Lionfante, being honest, knew
exactly what a man like him would do,

and said, "I know a fable you should hear.   73
So, once upon a time there was a fox.
One day, she was so thirsty that, to drink,
she jumped into a bucket but fell down
into the well. A wolf by chance came by,
and asked her what mishap had brought her there.
The fox said, "Feel not sorry, friend, for me:
who wants big fish must at the bottom be.

"'The carp I catch, my friend, are one pound each;   74
if you were here with me, what fun you'd have:
meanwhile I am enjoying my big meal.'
The wolf replied, 'Why don't you share your feast
with one that could become your bosom friend?
Remember: you invited me before.'
Replied the fox, shrewdly awaiting it,
'Very well, then: just in the bucket sit.'

"The wolf did not have time for second thoughts: 75
eagerly in the bucket down he sat,
and smoothly to the bottom went with it.
Meeting, midway, the fox fast coming up,
'Where are you going?' he naively asked;
'Shall we not fish some more? Wait, friend, for me.'
'The world's a ladder,' she was heard to chime:
'my friend: some men go down, some others climb.'

"The wolf was at the bottom of the well,   76
and the fox ran by chance into a dog.
She told him she had killed his enemy.
The dog said that the news delighted him
but he detested traitors just the same:
therefore he jumped and grabbed her by the neck,
and shrewdness he chastised by killing her:
justice was then restored, my noble sir.

77

"If you've committed treason in your life
a thousand times, you won't succeed today:
this time you will not leave this place alive
by any means, you wicked traitor. Now
you have to pay for all your ancient crimes.
I, too, detest a traitor, to be sure.
So let me wind around your neck this rope."
He grabbed him, and his men then tied him up.

Immediately he sent a messenger
to Montalban, to let Astolfo know
that, though he was a Saracen and not
a Christian, his nobility of blood
did not allow him to betray a foe
in any way; that Gan was in his hands,
and he, with his consent, would make him swing:
and thus he told Astolfo everything.

The messenger arrived and told Astolfo
all that his lord had ordered him to tell,
thus baring the whole treason in detail.
Astolfo honored first the messenger,
then called Guicciardo and the other knights
and told them of the traitor's latest deed.
What should he do now? He asked everyone
to know how they should deal with wicked Gan.

80

Frankly, his personal opinion was
that they should answer, "Make him swing at once."
But they agreed 'twas not the thing to do:
that circumstances were against their wish,
and that, though Gan deserved the final rope,
all of his people would rebel at once.
And so they thanked the noble pagan and
begged him that Gan alive away be sent.

Astolfo gave the messenger a steed,
saying, "Forever keep it for my sake."
And in a flash the messenger returned
and told his lord Astolfo's only wish.
A man of boundless kindness, Lionfante
replied, "As he desires, so do I,"
and, much against his will, set Gano free.
Gano to Paris went immediately,

and, being the old traitor that he was,   82
told Carlo he had thought of a new plan
to capture by deceit Erminion,
but he himself had been betrayed, and so
had fallen captive into pagan hands.
So well he hid his own iniquity,
he said, "He gave a treacherous double word
that like a thunderbolt you must have heard."

Carlo believed him (and he told the truth: 83
the double treason he had planned was true).
Astolfo at this moment wrote to him,
informing him of Ganelon's deceit,
but Carlo's faith in Gan was just as blind,
for it was preordained it should be so.
He sought that man's advice as in the past,
and just as warmly placed in him his trust.

Closer to Montalban in the meantime   84
Erminion drew with all his noble troops.
'Twas Easter Sunday when, most terrified
and out of breath, a messenger arrived
who, in his state of shock, could hardly speak.
Finally, still bewildered, he began:
"Grim news, Erminion, I bear to you:
this I can say—you and your men are through,

"and your own brother Fieramonte's dead: 85
a Christian knight with whom he wished to fight
pierced with his spear his helmet and his brow—
he says he is the Lord of Montalban,
who has with him the famous Count Orlando,
who makes both mount and plainland shake with fear.
Your city has been seized with all your land,
and all your people are now dead or banned.

"Faburro is the one who so betrayed you.   86
He ordered all his friends to be baptized,
and placed your entire realm in Christian hands.
Thousands of pagans have been maimed or killed
most cruelly, most mercilessly, sir.
I saw those Christians butcher them like dogs,
and with these eyes I saw the one who slew
your helpless wife and all your children, too.

"And now I want to tell you they'll be here
against you—forty thousand cavaliers,
already marching when I started out.
Faburro is the one who leads them all:
'tis he who rallied all his fighting men
and from afar is coming now with them."
When King Erminion heard this cruel sound,
most loudly he blasphemed his god Mahound,

saying, "You treacherous and evil god!
I swear that I will worship you no more.
Satan will from now on be my one god—
if not some darker denizen of hell.
What have I done to you? Where is my brother,
left safe and sound upon my very throne?
Where is my wife, entrusted to your care?
And where are all my prayed-for children—where?

"What shall I do now that Orlando's back,
now that Rinaldo, my great foe, is here?
The time at last is come I'll make this man
pay for the brutal death of old Mambrìn."
His brother Salincorno, who was there,
said, weeping, "Listen, brother, to my words.
Where did your fame and all your valor go?
Which have you lost—your kingdom or your life?

"Man's wisdom is assayed in times of strife,
for it is hard to see, when all goes well,
if you are better than your fellow man:
I hope you understand what all this means.
Though Fieramonte's dead, and though our poor
and wretched city's totally destroyed,
you've here so many men of your own faith,
it will be easy to avenge their death."

Infuriated, King Erminion
had the bound captives to his presence brought,
and then to Charlemagne this message sent:
that he would make them die a horrid death—
a shameful and most novel martyrdom—
unless (so he concluded) instantly
Paris, his crown, and land he gave to him;
the Dane would first be quartered limb from limb

for having—he, who was a pagan once—
repudiated his own god Mahound.
The messenger found quickly Charlemagne
and King Erminion's letter handed him.
Nearly insane and desperate, King Charles
to that request gave no reply at all.
The messenger returned at once and said
that he could swear the emperor was mad.

92

Our Carlo, when the messenger was gone,
stood at a balcony, alone and grieved,
not knowing what to do in his despair.
But would his Jesus now abandon him?
Right at that moment Count Orlando came
with his dear cousin and with pagan troops,
as in the following Canto I will write.
May Christ forever be your saving light.

93

C A N T O   X

Te Deum laudamus, High Creator;
Thee we proclaim our just and truthful Lord.
Praised be Thy Mother full of grace and love,
and grant me, Lord, if Thou desirest so,
that I may bring to Paris all my troops
and thus aid Charles in his predicament.
Let me resume my poem, as I must,
ever inspired by the Holy Ghost.

1

Leading his people, but three miles away
from Paris, was Faburro when King Charles,
who eagerly was waiting for some help,
saw all those troops and heard their sounds of war.
Not knowing who they were or on whose side,
he for himself felt sorry even more;
back to his people went he in dismay,
begging Gan to do something right away.

2

Promptly, to his own Captain Magagna, "Go,"   3
Ganelon ordered, "to the door at once,
for still more armies from the plainland come.
Now it's the time to show how brave you are,
for if you stay indoors, you nothing gain."
Meanwhile in Paris many men were armed.
The sad news made them frantic and, therefore,
kept everybody watching from the door.

Dauntless and daring on his mighty steed,   4
Faburro in the meantime had arrived.
His lance he lowered, and a Christian knight
that very moment to the ground fell dead.
Gan of Maganza faced the foe and said,
"Treacherous little vassal, now take this,"
and, lowering his lance, hit soon his shield,
but brave Faburro did not budge or yield.

His sword instead hit Ganelon so hard,   5
it made him find the plainland straightaway;
so many more were forced to hit the ground
that all the others in great terror fled.
Wasting no time at all, Gano got up,
eager once more to test his worth or luck.
He did as best he could—the wicked traitor,
but the new people came an instant later.

The alarm signal through all Paris went,   6
and Carlo mounted his brave steed at once.
When, out of breath and sad, he reached the door,
clearly Orlando's banners he could see,
his own dear nephew, and his horse as well,
which showed its master's emblem to all men.
'Twas then Faburro right before him stopped,
dismounted, and saluted him, and said:

"Emperor Charles, at last: I'm very glad   7
to meet the one I ever wished to meet.
Fear not, and wipe your tears once and for all:
I do assure you that Orlando's here."
Carlo removed his gauntlet, overjoyed,
and said, "Courageous baron, welcome here,"
and after this Faburro's hand he shook.
Right then the Lord of Montalbano—look!—

arrived, dismounted his Baiardo, knelt.   8
And—look!—Oliver, too, did just the same.
If he was dreaming, Carlo did not know,
such was the happiness that filled his heart.
The two undaunted knights were kneeling still
when Carlo's nephew on his horse arrived.
From Vegliantìn he fast jumped down, and soon
he too was kneeling before Pepin's son.

Carlo embraced them all with equal love,   9
blessing them, blessing them a thousand times.
And then Meridiana also came:
she too dismounted, and, like them, she too
knelt in the presence of the Christian king.
Oliver said, "In Jesus she believes,
and never has her worth been matched before:
she came to meet you, gracious emperor.

"The daughter of a mighty pagan king,   10
she from her land has brought here many men
who only wish to help you, Charlemagne."
Joyously Charlemagne stretched both his arms,
took the most winsome lady by the hand,
and thanked her for her most auspicious deed;
and with all lavishness he honored, then,
Meridiana and her pagan men.

Oliver said to his most gentle lass,   11
"What think you, lady, of our emperor?"
And the fair, gracious lady thus replied,
"Worthy of endless glory, endless praise.
Surely all those who highly speak of him
cannot be wrong, as I can clearly see.
His reputation, his magnificence
are somewhat smaller than his very presence."

Carlo permitted her to ride in front,   12
and close behind her rode her Oliver.
Bearing his clapper—look—Morgante appeared.
Charlemagne looked at that enormous man,
saying, "Such giants I have never seen,"
and truly was astounded and in awe.
Morgante, even kneeling, seemed to stand
higher than Charlemagne, who shook his hand.

Charles toward his royal palace started out,   13
far happier than he had ever been.
Catching Orlando's sight, Ganelon thought
that his appearance meant his very death.
He called his dear Magagna in despair
and even then devised a treason new,
saying, "These crazy men from everywhere
have entered here; so let's defend the square;

"let's shout that Carlo has betrayed his own   14
people by giving Paris to the foe,
and that some of these pagans are disguised,
thus passing for Orlando and other officers."
The entire population so he roused,
and to the square with other soldiers ran.
All the Parisians sided soon with Gan,
calling King Carlo a deceitful man.

Because they had their helmets on, Orlando   15
and all the others were still known to few.
As soon as the Maganzans seized the square,
Emperor Carlo finally was told
he had against him every man in town—
an omen of disaster, so he thought.
Quick, to the barricades Rinaldo ran
with the scimitars of many a Saracen:

quickly the bars were broken, and wherever   16
the passage had been blocked by Ganelon,
Meridiana with her soldiers fought,
in that sad hour performing miracles.
With his brigades Orlando came at last,
and with his whirling clapper came Morgante;
Oliver, too, before his lady's eyes
gave blows galore to win her love as prize.

Surrounded as he was by those Maganzans,   17
Rinaldo whirled Frusberta as he could,
here cutting armlets, cutting breastplates there,
and sending many a man dead to the ground;
others were maimed; and captive others fell.
But look, Magagna himself is coming now:
Rinaldo such a blow right on his forehead threw,
he split his head like a tench made ready for the stew.

They all began to flee when on the field   18
they recognized Rinaldo's flaming wrath
right in the midst of other Christian knights.
He bade the entire square at once be cleared,
shouting, "Where is that despicable traitor—
Gan of Pontier?" But Gan was fleeing; he
dared not inside the walls with other men assemble:
Rinaldo's very name immensely made him tremble.

Thus in no time was all that fury stilled.   19
Our warriors at last were recognized
and warmly hugged and kissed by everyone:
the entire population greeted them.
They all apologized to Charlemagne
while Gano's men were nowhere to be seen.
Then right before the royal house they went,
followed by shouts of joy and merriment.

Alda the Fair had in the meantime come   20
to see her spouse, Orlando, once again.
Rinaldo to this lady gave a rich,
beautiful crown with a fair ruby set
which, in itself, was two great castles' worth.
Alda the Fair with charming tenderness
welcomed her husband first, and then the other,
and then our Oliver, her darling brother.

After our heroes rested for a while,   21
thus to the emperor Rinaldo spoke:
"Carlo, I've looked around but have not seen
Ugier or Namo or the other knights.
Where are they? Did you kill and bury them?
Or are they captive in some pagan land?
Charles to Rinaldo said, "They're all alive,
and shortly you will see them here arrive."

And so he told him how the war was going,   22
and what had happened after he was gone:
Erminion had besieged his Montalban
and was still threatening his knights with death;
Astolfo was inside the city still,
and Ricciardetto more than ever brave.
This to Rinaldo and friends was quite a blow—
that Montalban and knights were threatened so.

Orlando said, "Immediately we must,   23
my dear Rinaldo, free our paladins.
Tomorrow morning we shall take a ride
and pay a visit to the Saracens—
their camp is only thirty miles away."
Meridiana had this much to add:
"With you allow me, gentlemen, to be,
and I will take Morgante along with me."

Oliver and Faburro wished to go.   24
"First we must see what in that camp goes on,"
Orlando answered. All agreed with him.
Thus each of them had his own armor brought.
Finally, in their mail and breastplate clad,
on the next morning they the city left—
right at the start of the new-rising day—
and soon to Montalban were on their way.

Nearly eight leagues they had been riding when   25
they spotted the pavilion of the king
where Berlinghier and Salamon and Namo,
the Dane, and other knights had been tied up.
Had it not been that King Erminion knew
already that Orlando had returned
and would now pay him (he was sure) a call,
he would have quartered them or hanged them all.

But now he did not know what he should do.   26
He pondered, "If we execute these men,
both punishment and shame may come of it.
Surely Orlando, to avenge their death,
will be most quick to pillory us all
or give us some strange martyrdom at once.
Instead, if they're alive, we can arrange,
at the very least, a prisoners' exchange."

Orlando saw pavilions and tents,   27
horses full-covered with most dazzling arms,
and he heard sound of trumpets and old horns;
throughout the camp, cats, crickets, falcons, and
other war instruments were being built
for the last fight to capture Montalban.
To all his friends he said, "It is quite easy
to guess why King Erminion is so busy."

Meridiana said to Count Orlando,   28
"O my dear Lord, oh, may you grant me now
the grace I am about to ask of you.
On this my steed I want to go right through
that pagan camp from end to end, and leave,
so doing, vestiges of wrath and death,
and crown with glory my entire existence."
Thus the sweet lady begged with dear insistence,

adding, "but let Morgante come with me,   29
should I be ever looking for his help.
Maybe I'll bring a souvenir to you—
one of their flags; but I am sure I will."
Replied Orlando, "Noble is your wish
to raid the pagan field in such a way.
In safety go and come, and, have no fear,
our strong Morgante will be always near."

Meridiana brandished then her spear,   30
mounted her charger with a serpent's head,
and shouted, "Long live Charles and long live France!"
At the right time she put her lance in rest,
clashed with a pagan, and with sounding storm
into his belly let her weapon sink;
she then unsheathed her shining sword with wrath,
opening thus throughout the camp a path.

As soon as that first infidel was slain,   31
this news was brought to Salincorn: a knight,
a treacherous knight, into their camp had come
and with his sword assailed and felled their men.
Instantly Salincorno armed himself,
most ready and most eager for revenge.
And so this gentle, wise, and kind young man
quickly behind Meridiana ran,

rebuking thus his people still in flight: 32
"Go back! Are you afraid of but one knight?
Or has this man the arms of Hercules?"
And very plainly they replied to him,
"It is the devil slaughtering your men.
If you do not believe, just come and see.
He fights and quickly fells each man he meets—
which seems to us the highest of all feats."

So answered Salincorn, "I want to see
with my own eyes who this daredevil is,
who has come here to rout all of our troops.
Orlando himself could not have done all this."
Meridiana turned her horse at once
now that she knew that Salincorn was there.
But he his lance had lowered as he spoke,
and hit the lady's shield with his first stroke:

in countless bits the spear went in midair.
"Cowardly knight," the lady taunted him,
"do you so little care for your own fame?
A valiant man acts not the way you do:
he would not use a spear against a man
who fights with sword alone. You break all rules.
But since you've hit me, turn and look at me:
I still am on my charger, as you see."

34

And Salincorno, feeling most ashamed,
went back, most eager to apologize.
He said, "I had not noticed if your spear
was broken or in perfect function still."
Promptly Meridiana answered him,
"Do you behave in Danismarche this way?
Are these Erminion's soldiers? Tell me, sir.
I only know you're nothing but a cur.

"But at the court of Charles it is not so,
for every fair tradition prospers there.
But let us see how strong a knight you are,
and if, this time, your eyes make no mistake.
Draw sword at once, I challenge you to death,
and a more bitter fruit I'll make you taste."
His sword poor Salincorno brandished then,
eager his wounded honor to regain.

36

After they both exchanged some of their blows,
with neither gain nor luck on either side,
all of a sudden Salincorno tried
to wound the gentle lass, and spurred his steed.
Much was he blamed by those who were around,
for he could only cut the serpent's head:
the lady fell upon the grassy field—
an act that all his reputation killed.

Ready to crush the pagan's head at once,							38
Morgante raised his clapper very high,
but, "Don't," Meridiana shouted, "don't!
With my own hand I will avenge my fall."
Desperate as he was for what he did,
now Salincorno had to grieve and pay.
The Saracens around Morgante made
a circle—ah, too many, I'm afraid.

Fast they surrounded him and the young lass,						39
and the most horrid battle thus began:
that clapper horrified a hundred men,
and many more it cut and broke and smashed.
Rinaldo said, "Why are we in the shade?
In Jesus' name, this is no time to rest.
I see unseated there Meridiana,
with all those pagan lances lifted on her."

Orlando spurred his charger right away,							40
turning the bridle toward the camp at once.
Oliver did the same at the same time,
commencing thus to rout the enemy.
Erminion heard the coming of those knights
and saw the wonder of their new advance.
He said but this: "You, treacherous Mahound!
Rinaldo and Orlando, safe and sound,

"have both returned to spite me even more.						41
I do not know of other knights so bold
as to come here and risk their very lives."
Ordering many men to stop them both,
he said, "I do believe this is the time
I too should arm." His suit of armor came;
he had his horse, all draped in steel, brought by:
he was resolved to win or else to die.

Orlando rode into Erminion's men;							42
his spear he lowered, and so hard he hit
the first shield he could see, the plate and breast
of the poor man behind it were pierced through.
He then unsheathed his Durlindana bright,
and like a hammer it broke weapons down:
a slaughterhouse in a short while he made;
Rinaldo, too, could boast of many dead.

Oliver did what he had always done, 43
but still his eyes were fixed upon the one
who guided him as sunlight guides the blind;
desperate, wicked blows around he whirled,
eager his lovely lady to defend.
Where'er he turned, he made the *Agnus Dei,*
his glance forever riveted on her,
and drawing closer to his lady fair.

He through the crowd could not yet force his way, 44
for still more men he saw against him come;
yet forward, ever forward still he rode,
like a fierce lion leaping here and there:
his sword—a ruthless scythe—cut many a head
within that evil and accursèd throng.
Poor those who were in Altachiara's way!
Dearly with their own lives they had to pay.

Morgante, in the midst of the whole fight, 45
made with his clapper a resounding din.
Meridiana was in great distress,
her female body being bruised and weak.
She by no means could walk from there away—
she would have had to fly to do just that.
And yet Morgante, who was growing bolder
with every man he killed, dearly consoled her.

He was completely pierced by spears and darts 46
and still more darts and spears and spits and pikes;
so copiously all over was he bleeding,
each of his wounds looked like a water pipe,
emitting from both ends unceasingly.
He had a hundred arrows on his head.
But he had killed so many all about,
from all those corpses he could not get out.

One on the other he had made them fall, 47
horsemen and horses mingled in one heap:
it would have been a miracle to know
the exact number of the soldiers slain.
Five hours or more he had already fought;
so you are free to guess how many men
he crushed—so many he could hardly touch
the other pagans not within his reach.

Meridiana fought most strenuously,
trying to shun the darts against her hurled:
her face was flaming like a bright new fire.
No longer could her shield now cover her:
it was so heavy just as she was weary;
nor could she from that circle save herself:
yet, wounded and on foot, she'd rather die, indeed,
than to the foe surrender or just for mercy plead.

48

But she was trusting in Morgante still,
and said, "You're dearly paying for my fall:
I am afraid these men will murder you."
Rinaldo—look—right at that moment came
toward that circle with so loud a shout,
all of those pagans quickly stood aside:
"Make room! Make room, you savage beasts, unable
to fight two on the ground! Move, dirty rabble!

49

"Get back!" And his Frusberta did the rest;
"You wicked Saracens will all be dead."
Meridiana, as she heard his voice,
was suddenly revived with hope and joy.
Rinaldo doubled every mighty blow,
avenging thus her countless suffered wrongs;
then, of a sudden like a leopard, deep
into the midst he made Baiardo leap.

50

He told Meridiana, "On my horse!"
and from the ground, fast as a cat, she leapt—
limping and weak, apparently, no more:
Rinaldo from the circle dashed away,
galloping with the lady through the camp.
All those who witnessed such a feat were stunned.
"That was Rinaldo, Anglante's mighty lord,"
they said, and so the giant was ignored.

51

Back to his tent many a pagan went,
having seen things that nature could not do.
"'Twas at this moment Salincorno came:
by chance Meridiana sighted him.
But our Rinaldo, gentle cavalier,
whose sword was not yet hanging from his belt,
right on the helmet wounded him so fast,
he landed his Frusberta in his chest.

52

On the ground, lifeless, Salincorno fell,   53
and thus the lovely lady was avenged.
Rinaldo by the bridle checked his steed
to help Meridiana on the saddle:
swifter than lightning, there at once she leapt.
Oliver said, when his sweet girl he saw,
"I wanted to bring help, my love, to you,
but I have not been able to get through."

Orlando and Faburro and Oliver   54
had slaughtered countless infidels that day,
and were still putting others soon to waste.
The Saracens had not surrendered yet,
but our brave paladins had stained their swords
with so much blood of all those rabid dogs,
these were now fleeing, terror-struck and dumb—
most of them bleeding—to their tents or home.

Seeing them running still from everywhere,   55
"Who's chasing you?" Erminion asked out loud.
And to their threatening king they so replied,
"Furious Mars himself is chasing us:
there's no one so determined or so brave
that may rely on either skill or might.
New Hectors have come here and are our foes:
we cannot save ourselves from all their blows.

"Rinaldo—or his cousin—we have seen   56
leap with his horse into a ring of men:
there—all the fighting Saracens were there,
and yet we could not stop him in the least.
Upon his steed he took another knight,
who was surrounded; out of there he jumped,
and safely went away in spite of us.
We never saw a man so valorous.

"And he has killed your brother Salincorn."   57
Erminion was torn by boundless grief,
and said, "Now that poor Salincorn is dead—
he was the proudest pagan at my court—
'twas barbarous Rinaldo, I am sure
(or maybe his cousin), slew him treacherously."
"Not treacherously," it was their answer then;
"but he who killed your brother could kill a hundred men."

"Curse be upon thee, wicked god Mahound!"   58
   several times Erminion repeated,
   swearing that he would soon avenge his brother
   even if he should die a thousand times.
   Wrathfully jumping where Rinaldo was,
   he placed in rest a lance he chanced to have,
   and, recognizing our Rinaldo at last,
   he greeted him in this strange fashion fast.

"May God unbless you," said Erminion,   59
"if you're indeed the Lord of Montalban—
   the one whose emblem is a lion in a cage:
   even your lion with this hand I'll kill."
   Hearing so strange a sermon, soon to him
   Rinaldo answered, "Knight uncivilized,
   O king of butterflies or bees, what do you say?
   For all your numberless old wrongs you now must pay."

Erminion replied, "I must avenge   60
   my relatives you murdered long ago.
   'Tis you who through the vilest act of treason
   slew King Mambrino like a wicked foe."
   Rinaldo added, "Listen now to me.
   You're lying in your throat, Erminion.
   'Tis you who like a traitor have come here
   to siege my city while I was not near.

"But I have crossed the mountain and the plain   61
   in time to make your flight a hopeless thing.
   "'Twas I who killed your brother Fieramont
   and gave the men the martyrdom they earned;
   'twas I who split your Salincorno's brow,
   and with this sword will make you join him now."
   Hearing himself rebuked in such a fashion,
   upon his horse the pagan with a passion

struck his own helmet many a time, blasphemed   62
   his deity Mohammed with devotion,
   and with his gauntlet pounded on his chest:
   he would have wished to die right then and there.
   He so replied, "For all your spiteful wrongs,
   this very day you will be sorry most,"
   and, like a man in a most hopeless plight,
   shouted, "En garde! I challenge you to fight."

He added then, "Since you've offended me 63
unjustly so, let us now make this deal—
you'll give me Montalban if I defeat you;
but if you win me, rest assured that I
will give you back your prisoners at once,
for none of them have I yet harmed or killed;
and that there be a month-long armistice,
past which let either side do as they please."

Rinaldo said, "So be it: I accept." 64
And then Baiardo suddenly he turned,
saying, "If ever you were bold and brave,
this is the time to show your highest worth,"
and thus he started like a thunderbolt.
Erminion was also valiant most,
so that when the two clashed, the very earth
seemed to be opening in fear beneath.

With his stout lance, Erminion hit soon 65
upon the shield the paladin of France:
the spear broke, but unruffled stood the knight.
Now brave Rinaldo gave the Saracen
so fierce a blow that, all his strength despite,
he found himself sprawled out upon the grass,
saying, "O God, who rule both sun and moon,
did Fortune want to vanquish me so soon?

"Then what all people say on earth is true: 66
this is, of famous knights, the first and best."
Soon to his feet he rose and said, "Great knight,
for all my sins I have been punished now,
and can no more, as I have said before,
by any means avenge my relatives.
I everything have lost at the same time:
this is the end of all my glory and fame.

"Oh yes, my relatives will be avenged. 67
Oh yes, I will avenge my Fieramont
with Salincorno and the other men ...
But those who take revenge with their own shame
truly, in my opinion, are fools
and must perforce be broken by defeat.
I've followed Lady Clemency's advice,
and now I'm paying with my own disgrace.

Rulers who heed a woman's counseling   68
foredoom themselves to rapid ruination:
a woman's mind knows not its own true goals.
Then is there any wonder I am finished?
My bestial plan is known to all at last;
everything is detected in the end.
Oh, now I know how one must laugh at such
simpletons who trust Fortune very much.

"I'll keep my entire promise, gentle knight,   69
for I am still an honorable king:
all of your prisoners will be returned.
To my pavilion let us go at once.
Sir, of your promise I remind you now."
Rinaldo said, "By the great God we Christians
together with our Charlemagne proclaim,
all of the things you want I'll let you name."

They started out toward the pavilion then.   70
Erminion, who was a noble man,
bade the retreat be sounded in his camp
since Fortune had so crushed him utterly.
All of his troops seemed stunned and in dismay,
just as in fast calamities occurs.
The captives were untied and, finally,
with all their weapons and their steeds, set free.

Had you been there to witness the great joy   71
and jubilation of our mighty knights,
you would have been so moved that I am sure
tears would have gushed out of your gentle hearts.
"Your daring, dear Rinaldo," Ugier said,
"has saved us all from these most savage claws,
or else this time our very skin, I guess,
we would have sold for four bezants or less.

"So furious a din throughout the camp   72
we heard today, we thought the entire world
had crumbled down or was about to end,
and that Charles's throne had to the bottom sunk.
And everybody was afraid of death
because that fierce and red-cheeked Saracen
most solemnly had sworn to hang us all:
we were so desperate in our close call."

And Namo said, "'Tis Jesus, our good Lord,   73
has sent you here to rescue us today;
and so, thanks to your valor, we are free—
delivered from our grief and fear at last."
Orlando said, "Let's talk of it no more.
Let's leave these pagan armies instantly.
Charles does not know what we have done today:
so let's to Paris soon be on our way."

They left Erminion in his distress   74
and went to Charlemagne—our paladins.
A hundred times and then a hundred more
Carlo embraced them. Anguish turned to bliss,
and the whole city shouted victory.
Gano alone was bitterly dismayed:
in boundless terror he had left his tent,
most eager to escape his punishment.

After some days of rest with all his friends,   75
Rinaldo finally told Charlemagne
'twas his intention now to say goodbye
and leave the court, and go to Montalban
and spend some time there with his lovely bride.
Grateful and happy, Carlo shook his hand.
Rinaldo then departed before long,
and took only Orlando's squire along:

his name was Ruinatto, and he was   76
Terigi's friend. After he rode awhile,
maybe six leagues from Paris, he could see
a white-haired, sweet old man upon the grass
(he was our Malagigi, so disguised
that Lord Rinaldo failed to recognize him):
upon a river bank and resting near a grotto,
the old man had with him a barrel full of water.

Rinaldo greeted him most courteously.   77
The old man so replied, "Oh, welcome, sir.
If you are thirsty, O most mighty knight,
I am inviting you to taste a beer
that I am sure you very much will like."
Rinaldo answered, "Thirst is killing me,
for when I travel, even though undone,
water of ditch or stagnant pond I shun."

After Rinaldo, to his heart's content,
quenched all his thirst, he let his squire drink,
and said, "Good pilgrim, thank you very much."
His Ruinatto also drank like him,
quite unaware of Malagigi's trick.
So Malagigi took his barrel back.
No sooner had the two resumed their trip
than, very tired, fast they fell asleep,

78

and on the ground in great oblivion lay.
Shrewd Malagigi, who had come behind,
burst into laughter seeing what his drink—
his magic potion—had so quickly done.
Rinaldo's sword and charger quick he stole,
and fast toward Paris started out at once:
he put Frusberta, the most sovereign sword,
back in the sheath where Durlindana stood;

79

and so Baiàrd where Vegliantìn had been.
Thus he returned where Lord Rinaldo slept,
and laid beside him both his cousin's horse
and sword before he vanished soon away.
Also, beneath his head he placed an herb
that would awaken him. He soon woke up
and, mindless of all else, himself ignored,
failing to see his charger and his sword.

80

Turning to Ruinatto, soon he asked,
"A lazy good-for-nothing you must be.
Where's my Baiàrd? What have you done with him?
This is the steed of Milon's very son."
Baffled, his squire so replied to him,
"Yes, like a good-for-nothing I have slept,
for I was overcome with sleep like you,
and surely could not vanish out of view."

81

Seeing more clearly, thus Rinaldo spoke:
"I swear it is Orlando did all this:
eager to make eternal fun of me,
he had Baiàrdo and my sword exchanged."
Fire and wrath possessed him all at once,
and so he swore, "You'll dearly pay for this."
Toward Montalban he started out in ire,
and back sent Ruinatto, his own squire.

82

He wrote to Count Orlando, "While I slept 83
along the road, you took away from me
my charger and my sword; you treat me still
like a big fool, and always laugh at me.
Many a time you fooled me, but today
I do rebel against your thankless act.
Send back my sword at once, send back my steed,
or this will cost you very much indeed."

Orlando in the meantime had by chance 84
recovered Lord Rinaldo's sword and horse,
and, being very angry with himself
and furious and fuming, so he said,
"Just like a little child I've been deceived:
a scoundrel's expert hand in this I see;
more than the deed, the way displeases me."
And so our man could not but restless be.

And so it was that Ruinatto brought 85
the letter that his cousin wrote to him.
Surely Orlando wondered very much,
before to Ruinatto this he spoke:
"What do you really know about this thing?
What happened—tell me—all along the road?"
And Ruinatto quickly answered so:
"Sir, I can only tell you what I know."

And so he told how the old man was there, 86
and how the two of them lay down to sleep.
Orlando listened most attentively,
and soon possessed of great astonishment.
But to himself he said, "According as he speaks,
Rinaldo thinks of me as a small, tottering chick,"
and so he sent a letter just to let
Rinaldo know he laughed at all his threat.

Surely, the day he left King Carlo's court 87
he was under the influence of wine—
the reason for exchanging sword and steed,
and having to lie down for sleep along the road.
And with these words, the letter he concluded,
"Because you are my cousin, dear Rinaldo,
I do not like to fight you; so, my lord,
I'm sending you your charger and your sword.

"But if you do not send my horse to me,   88
   I'll prove to you that I am deeply hurt;
   and if once more you want to quarrel with me,
   you know that I like actions more than words.
   And nothing would you gain from fighting me,
   for there's beneath the sun no man I fear.
   You're wise, and what I mean you know of course:
   so please send back to me my sword and horse."

To Montalbano Ruinatto came   89
   with the reply of his beloved lord,
   and placed the sword into his very hand,
   and handed him Baiardo, his brave steed.
   Like a wild lion our Rinaldo roared,
   reading the Roman senator's reply.
   So with this answer he sent back to him
   a squire—Tesoretto was his name.

No, he refused to send his sword to him,   90
   as well as Vegliantìn, unless he swore
   to fight a duel with him on the field.
   Full well he knew he did not fear his threats.
   And he concluded that their fight should be
   right on the plainland under Montalban.
   So Tesoretto reached Orlando fast
   and made Rinaldo's message manifest.

Orlando, who was gentle and discreet,   91
   but if he lost his temper very proud—
   so proud and wrathful, the whole world he scorned—
   told everything to Charles the emperor:
   that he had sent a courteous missive, hoping
   to pacify Rinaldo in the end;
   but, having noticed then his arrogance,
   he now would go to Montalban at once:

never had he refused a fight before,   92
   and did not wish to lose his honor now.
   Charlemagne said, "You'll do just as you please.
   If things are as you say, then fight you must."
   Orlando said to Tesoretto, "Go
   back to your prince, and ask him if he's dreaming;
   but if he truly wants to shed his blood,
   tomorrow I'll be there, so help me God.

"Tell him to wait for me right in the plain,   93
at a short distance from the pagan field."
To Montalbano Tesoretto sped,
and gave Orlando's answer to his lord.
With his own nephew Carlo armed himself,
seeing Orlando eager for the fight.
Charles loved Orlando very dearly—hence,
much he detested, deep within, the prince.

Carlo—to tell the truth—would have been glad   94
to have Rinaldo out of sight forever;
so, knowing his Orlando's matchless might,
he said to him, "This is the only way."
Rinaldo was a restless, bold young man
whom he—the emperor—could never trust
for all his crazy youthfulness or madness:
ah, he had caused him a great deal of sadness:

He had removed his crown right off his head . . .   95
Of course he had forgiven all his pranks,
yet he recalled them all most vividly:
thus the two things balanced each other well.
Now Carlo, seeing Orlando's wrath alit,
thought (and so hoped) Rinaldo's time had come.
Orlando took Rondello and Cortana,
not having Vegliantìn nor Durlindana.

Meridiana and Morgante went   96
with Carlo and Orlando, just to see.
The emperor was begged by all his knights
not to allow the Lord of Montalban
to fight a duel with his famous cousin,
but they could not oppose their sovereign king,
who was most strongly blamed by every man,
though much he tried to justify his plan.

So the whole court behind King Carlo went   97
to witness the great fight of the two knights.
Morgante, who was full of common sense,
had tried to stop his master but in vain.
Gano, who was informed, rejoiced and said,
"I'm sure Orlando finally will kill
Rinaldo of Ammon, prince of all treason,
of all my troubles the sole cause and reason."

Some of the courtiers had this to say: 98
"Carlo is losing (so it seems) his mind.
If the count wins and Lord Rinaldo dies,
he will regret his death a thousand times;
but if Orlando by the prince is slain,
never will Carlo live a happy man.
Both of them have arrived from distant lands
to save us, yesterday, from pagan hands;

one still can hear the population's cheers,   99
and suddenly all things are sad and grim.
With all his wicked troops, Erminion
is hardly gone: how happy he will be!"
Such were the various comments everywhere,
for no one liked the deed that was to be.
And, above all, it was the pagan men
who with Meridiana dared complain.

All of them said to her, "Our noble queen,   100
oh, such an error let them not commit.
Use all your power, all your influence
with Count Orlando and the emperor.
Though we are Saracens by law and faith,
this sore predicament breaks all our hearts."
With tactful words Meridiana made
a brave attempt the two to dissuade.

Listening to no words and to no one,   101
Orlando said, "Once and for all I'll show
that I'm Orlando, and he was most wrong
in taking both my charger and my sword.
I do not want to kill him: I just want
him to admit that he alone is wrong."
And so at last they rode in such a way
they were near Montalban the second day.

Rinaldo in his fort was more than praying   102
to test Orlando's valor on the field
(well you can see what kind of man he was;
well you can see what tempered mail was his).
"If on his steed I see him," so he said,
"soon we shall prove how the two swords can cut."
Thus when he saw Orlando in the plain,
armed, he at once came down from Montalban.

He took both Durlindana and Vegliantìn,   103
and thought, "If I am beaten by Orlando,
he'll have his sword, he'll have his charger back."
Erminion had waited all this time
for Pepin's son eventually to come:
indeed, he sent a messenger to him,
whereby inquiring if it was all right
for him to witness the important fight.

Most kindly Charlemagne replied to him   104
he'd gladly welcome King Erminion.
Therefore he came but, out of gentleness,
very few people he did take along.
Carlo was truly glad to welcome him,
and therefore always at his left side rode:
the pagan king accepted hesitantly,
but Charles insisted with great courtesy.

Rinaldo came. His Ricciardetto was   105
beside him with the noble British lord,
who very much had begged him all this time
no more to wage against Orlando war.
Astolfo hugged Orlando very tight,
and then Morgante and his Oliver.
Before Meridiana he did bow,
whom he had not yet noticed until now,

and said, "O Charlemagne, dear emperor,   106
how could you let such a mistake occur?
Nothing, I tell you, will you gain from this,
but you will lose your honor, to be sure.
If your great paladin Rinaldo dies,
his death will be the very end of you;
but if you lose your nephew, then your sorrow
will make you, torment-torn, wish for no morrow.

"But what is this? Will the brief anger caused   107
by just two words still unforgiven be?
O Charles, our bright and worthy emperor,
this is unjust, unworthy of your fame:
by God, you're trespassing your reason's bounds."
But meanwhile Charlemagne said to himself,
"No more will he remove my crown from me,"
and steadfast in his counseling was he.

Closer Orlando in the meantime came,
and to Rinaldo said, "Dear cousin, still
are you resolved to fight me? Take the field,
and let the two of us thus challenged be."
Rinaldo's only answer was to turn
his very horse and wait for him to charge.
Charlemagne whispered, "I don't like all this,"
but deep within he was so full of bliss.

108

Never was bird or wandering falcon seen
to turn so nimbly or so vehemently
as Vegliantìn by Lord Rinaldo spurred
or as Rondel by Count Orlando pricked.
The Saracen great king was most amazed
at that magnificent, astounding start.
Rinaldo unbridled Vegliantìn at once;
so did the count, as eager to advance.

A full half-mile each from the other rode,
and then towards each other rode right back.
Stunned by their valor, said the Saracens,
"Surely lightning with less speed comes down:
if these two knights on the whole earth are known,
we now can see why Carlo loves them both."
With open eyes Erminion seemed to ponder
all that he saw, replete with awe and wonder.

110

But that great God Who rules the world and skies
showed that of justice He's the only source,
and that He loves His faithful servants still.
While Vegliantìn against the count advanced,
he seemed to bristle up, and then and there
turned toward Rinaldo suddenly his head
as if he recognized his lawful master
and wanted to protect him from disaster.

Rinaldo shouted, "What the hell is this?
Turn back! Turn back! What are you doing, horse?"
Orlando let his lance at once depart.
But—look—a lion on the bank appeared.
As soon as all the people saw him there,
indeed they were amazed and wonder-struck:
right near Orlando the fierce lion was seen to stop,
with one of his horrendous paws now lifted up.

A written letter could be seen in it,
which Malagigi to Orlando sent.
With his right hand Orlando picked it up,
and, having read it, much he sneered and grinned.
Meanwhile Rinaldo, wrathful and yet sad,
dismounted from his Vegliantìn at once.
How strange! He saw the lion at his feet,
and then Orlando, reading from a sheet.

Deeply surprised, closer to him he went.
Orlando then began to tell him that
shrewd Malagigi had deceived them both—
and so he quickly told him everything.
Ah, through their folly, one of them was close,
indeed, to paying a most costly price.
Rinaldo read the brief and, in conclusion,
of both his horse and sword made restitution.

114

He even thanked his just, eternal God
Who had performed this miracle for him.
He said, "Oh, please forgive me, cousin dear,
for having sinned so much 'gainst Charles and all.
But our Lord Jesus, merciful and good,
has with His grace enlightened me at last."
Wondering if the lion there would stay,
they saw he had already gone away.

Carlo and all his knights had seen all this,
and understood that Malagigi himself—
the one who wrote—was the white-haired old man
who had exchanged our cavaliers' brave steeds.
Indeed, he thanked our God our two brave knights
did not inflict upon each other harm.
Erminion, who saw everything well,
thought that he had just seen a miracle,

and therefore started to blaspheme his god,
saying, "Indeed you're false, my god Mahound.
The one who sent that lion truly is
Father Omnipotent and truthful God.
If ever I prayed or sacrificed to you
in my past days, I most regret it now.
I want to worship Christ from this day on."
In tears he turned to Carlo, and began:

"O lucky Charles, O Charles we call our own,   118
all graces, I am sure, come down to you
from Jesus Christ, as I can plainly tell.
I see that He rewards His faithful servants,
for a great miracle He has performed.
False is Mahound and he who worships him.
Yes, from this day on, noble Charlemagne,
let me baptism from your hand obtain."

With great affection Charlemagne embraced   119
the pagan king, whose face appeared so changed,
and who by true repentance seemed so moved.
He said, "O Christ, forevermore be praised!
If by my hand you wish to be baptized,
let's go, Erminion, to the nearby stream."
So to the stream they traveled, where, at last,
according to their rite he was baptized.

Baptized the pagan king was finally;   120
so also was the famous admiral
who had besiegèd Montalban—the one
whose name was Lionfante, as I said.
The Saracens who did not wish to be
christened returned to their far eastern homes.
But with great pomp King Charles went back to Paris,
where with his knights he dwells in his great palace.

But wicked Ganelon, who had escaped   121
from Paris and was hiding far away,
as soon as he was told how things turned out,
felt a most grievous anguish in his heart.
Wondering how he could betray his Charles,
no rest he ever found both day and night:
he heard that in his court there was great feast—
which was the thing that most his mind displeased.

He thought and thought and deeply thought again   122
where he could devilishly land his tail,
where he could cast and haul his net at once:
Oh, what great wrath and fury maddened him!
At long last he could then control himself,
and came to this conclusion in the end—
that maybe he should try King Carador,
and some new scandal bring, thus, to the fore.

These were the words the wicked traitor wrote: 123
"I'm sorry, Carador, for you, who sent
to France your daughter fairer than the sun
and now a vile and pregnant prostitute.
I'm truly sorry you've allowed such shame
to mar the honor of your regal home.
How could you send a girl so fair and young
amid an alien and lawless throng?

"Throughout the land of France they speak of this—   124
your daughter has become Oliver's mistress—
Oliver's whore, to be far more precise.
So where is all your fame, so widely spread?
Where is your worth, and where your honored name,
O king, who have so sullied your own race?
What I have said about your daughter's true,
and if you're wise, you know what you must do."

He gave his letter to a messenger,   125
who went to Carador immediately.
He covered the whole distance in no time
and handed out his message to the king.
As soon as of his daughter's shame he read,
his grief was such he had not known the like;
and the poor queen was so dismayed and sad,
she utterly believed herself betrayed.

Her luckless daughter she bemoaned, and said,   126
"O my poor child, why did I let you go?
Why is your shame now known to everyone?
While you were here, I apprehensive grew,
for well I was aware of stratagems
and traps around you cast; but could not think
that all those men could so ungrateful be.
Ah, those who quickly err, repent as they see fit.

"O my good Carador, full well you know—   127
so I don't have to tell you—all the toil
and sacrifices we have had to bear
to raise our girl from her sweet infancy.
And then you give her to your enemy—
those Christians full of treachery and fraud.
Your lovely daughter you will see no more,
or they will send her back to you—a whore."

These words were swords that pierced a father's heart.   128
He knew not what to do—poor Carador—
in his most hopeless plight: how to regain
his daughter and the honor of his name.
Finally, after many sighs and tears,
he and his wife to this conclusion came—
giant Vegurto should at once be sent,
their suffered wrong and grievances to vent.

If Carlo was an honest emperor,   129
he soon should send his daughter back to him,
and put therefore an end to his disgrace,
which was by now well known through all of France—
how Oliver kept his daughter as a wench;
and so he sent that giant in his name
to fetch Meridiana right away,
and tell him that no more his troops should stay;

finally, if he thought of some revenge,   130
it was all right with him, but, being wise,
they had to wait for the right time and place.
The proud fierce giant restlessly prepared
an Arab horse for his impending trip
and in no time was out of Pagandom;
a sling he took with things that he might need,
and reached King Carlo's Paris at top speed.

The entire population came outside   131
to see this giant, measureless indeed
(Morgante would have looked but like his squire).
Into the royal hall he walked at once,
and with most arrogant, ferocious words
in this strange fashion greeted Charlemagne:
"May you be punished by Mohammed's ire,
treacherous and unjust and lawless sire.

"My lord has sent me here, big foolish Charlie,   132
commanding you to give his daughter back
and, with her, all the people of Mahound
who are still with you, saying not one word!
Also, with these my very hands I must
hang Oliver, that traitor, by the neck.
And I will do as I've been told, at once,
and make him pay for all his arrogance.

"O Charles, O Charles, O Charles (he shook his head),   133
   letters have reached King Carador about
   what in your court is going on and, ah,
   about his daughter he heard horrid tales.
   In a most shameful way you've treated him.
   Everyone knows what I am telling you:
   Oliver as a mistress of no worth
   still keeps a Saracen of noble birth.

"This is not what my king expected of you,   134
   this is not what French gallantry should be,
   this is not what his worthiness deserves,
   this is not how an emperor should rule,
   this is not what one's duty ought to be,
   this is not what true friendship ought to reap:
   no longer can she be our daughter, then,
   one who has slept with any of your men.

"Surely the count did not have this in mind   135
   when with the other knights he left my king."
   While speaking, many a time he shook his head,
   so filled with fury and disdain was he.
   Hearing himself accused of all those crimes,
   "Worthy and great ambassador," said Charles,
   "by the great God we Christians all adore,
   nothing of what you said I knew before.

"I've thought of everything beneath the sun,   136
   and yet your words I fail to understand.
   But, to begin with, let me tell you this,
   despite the fact that all is new to me:
   I deem your famous and most noble king,
   indeed, to be a loyal and true friend.
   His daughter has been treated with great honor,
   and regal care I have bestowed upon her.

"Oliver, to my knowledge, did no wrong   137
   either before man's eyes or secretly.
   Or I would be displeased and sorely hurt
   by such a villainous ignoble deed.
   Oliver could not bear such insolence.
   "My King," he shouted, "you have heard too much.
   What is this wicked traitor's lying claim?"
   The Dane and Lord Rinaldo echoed him.

Meridiana, who was in their midst,   138
   could not but turn vermilion and afire
   as soon as she heard mention of her sin,
   which she believed no mortal ever knew.
"May my dear father's majesty," she said,
"forgive me, but he's talking like a fool.
   As long as in this palace I have been,
   Oliver, more than others, treated me like a queen.

"King Carador's request, to say the least,   139
   is strange indeed and takes me by surprise."
"Why should we bear all this?" said Oliver,
   unsheathing Altachiara as he spoke.
   Wise Namo grabbed his arm, and said to him,
"My friend, you're not too prudent, I'm afraid;
   this giant's just as fierce as he was born:
   that's why he spoke with arrogance and scorn.

"Oliver, not in scorn or arrogance   140
   must we compare our nature with this man's:
   the measure of it would uneven be
   and therefore so would greatness, to be sure.
   A messenger must speak and be unharmed,
   and must be treated with great gentleness."
   Vegurto lost his patience then and there,
   and wanted soon to harm our Oliver.

Fierce as a dragon jumped he on our knight,   141
   with such a blow of his uplifted ax,
   he surely would have broken flesh and bone.
   But Oliver so quickly threw himself
   down on the other side, poor Charles fell off his chair.
   Mighty Morgante intervened to help:
   he ran and held the giant very tight,
   although Vegurto was of boundless might.

In turn, Vegurto grabbed him by the arms.   142
   Now every man who gazed on these two giants
   facing each other for the coming fight
   surely had wonder written in his eyes.
   But—look—Morgante threw him on the ground,
   making all those around him loudly laugh:
   for when he laid him down upon the floor,
   'twas like a tower falling with a roar.

As he was falling down, he struck the Dane   143
in such a way he fell right under him.
Orlando and the marquis burst into laughter.
But Namo counseled Carlo that he should
erase those accusations right away.
Quickly Vegurto from the pavement rose,
and as he stood, his shouts were loud and cruel:
each knight he challenged to a deadly duel.

Oliver taunted him, "Could you be Briareus   144
or Jupiter or famous Ephialtes
or that proud Capaneus of long ago?
Well, then, great giant, I do challenge you
even if you're Anteus in disguise.
With my most glorious emperor's permission,
I want to fight, this very hour, with you,
and do me then the worst that you can do.

Ah, Oliver, 'tis Love inflames your breast—   145
Love that makes men in love forever brave.
Not even Mars himself would frighten you
if your sweet lady were to see you fight.
Vegurto answered, "By my god Mahound,
there's nothing on this earth I covet more."
To arm himself our Oliver now ran,
eager to fight and beat that massive man.

Morgante could not bear it anymore,   146
and said to Charles, "Dear emperor, I'll burst
if I don't make this man die with these hands.
Please, let me play my clapper from both ends:
with the first blow I'll make him reel so fast,
he'll look as if he'd drunk some poppies' juice."
Carlo's reply was by nobody heard,
for every heart was by great anger stirred.

No leash could now still hold Morgante back: 147
without awaiting Charlemagne's reply,
he began bringing his brave clapper down
against Vegurto, starting to advance.
Had you been there to judge that sounding game,
it would not have been easy not to laugh:
one with a clapper and the other with an ax,
unripe peaches they smashed on their opposite backs.

In no way could the giant use his sling;   148
an echoing bang from time to time was heard:
it was Morgante's clapper sinking fast
upon Vegurto, trembling in his knees:
the royal hall resounded all about.
But every time it fell, Vegurto's ax
tore off Morgante's flesh in many a shred,
the mighty giant being grim and mad.

Oliver had returned into the hall,   149
full-armed, and with Vegurto wished to fight;
but when he saw Morgante bringing down
his heavy clapper on the pagan foe,
aside he waited most impatiently,
for that was not the moment to go near.
Vegurto's and Morgante's threats were loud:
their very voices sent chills through the whole crowd.

Never were lions heard to roar so wild   150
or seen to fight each other with such wrath,
and never were two dragons so incensed.
The clapper or the ax was ever high.
Very few times the blows had fallen void,
and opened a great ditch into the floor.
Two hours they clubbed each other—even longer,
and yet Morgante's clapper sounded stronger.

Although Vegurto was much taller than   151
our great Morgante, stronger he was not.
They were already red with blood all over,
and the whole court was witnessing their fight.
Morgante struck Vegurto finally,
determined now to give him death at last.
He sank his clapper right into his head:
down fell Vegurto to his ruin—dead.

And as that tall, enormous tower fell,   152
it sounded like a ship's down-crumbling mast:
the mighty fellow made the whole earth tremble,
so massively he crumbled in the hall.
There where he landed, with his weight he broke
enamel, brick, and the sustaining wood:
down went the royal box with every broken beam,
and many Christian knights fell right on top of him.

So died the fierce and proud ambassador,   153
and therefore no reply could be brought back.
Meridiana grieved because of it,
but Oliver was greatly overjoyed.
Emperor Charles was much displeased and sad,
although he did not show it on his face:
they had just killed a true ambassador,
and been ungrateful to King Carador.

A long, long time King Carador awaited   154
his lovely daughter from the Christian camp.
But let us leave them all, and go right back
to Ganelon, whose plan did not succeed,
just as he soon informed our emperor,
as in the coming Canto I will say.
Much have I bored my reader, I'm afraid.
May Christ be his salvation and his aid.

CANTO   XI

O holy pelican, who with your blood   1
delivered us from the ferocious snake's
pestiferous poison, and who, for love of us,
willingly tasted vinegar with gall
before your grieving mother's very eyes:
Archangel Michael to my rescue send,
so that, victorious, I may not fail
to keep on telling this my worthy tale.

Gan in this fashion wrote to Charlemagne,   2
"Emperor Charles, what have I done to you?
If I am guilty of no fraud or treason,
why do you keep me banished from your court?
My having ever served you makes me glad,
whereas you seem ungrateful for my deeds,
allowing, without listening to me,
my every foe to scorn me cruelly.

"The day I conquered the Parisian square,   3
  was I supposed to know who was inside,
  or if it harbored men of a new race
  with whom Orlando had come fully disguised?
  To remedy or check that crazy wrath,
  I did my duty—to the square I ran.
  How could I know that they had let you down,
  and that there was conspiracy in town?

"Rinaldo did not listen to my words,   4
  but, most infuriated and incensed,
  he even threatened me with sudden death:
  'twas then, to save my life, I ran away.
  You're happy there, and here I live in grief:
  after so many years spent at your court
  as your most trusted counselor and knight,
  I am an exile, banished from your sight."

Being so very fond of Ganelon,   5
  Charles read his letter, bursting into tears.
  Believing everything that he had read,
  promptly he sent his answer back to him.
  He wrote, "By leaving, you have saddened me,
  and very much your absence grieves my heart.
  Resume your place, and be—this I implore—
  my trusted friend as you have been before."

As Carlo wanted, Ganelon returned.   6
  The emperor was glad to see him back,
  and ran to hug him as he saw him come:
  "Welcome! Oh, welcome back, Gan of Pontier!"
  Gan-Judas kissed the emperor on the brow.
  Rinaldo said, addressing the marquis,
  "Charles has allowed him to return. You'll see:
  things, from now on, just as they were, will be.

"I swear I'll let our Carlo cut my head   7
  if Gan was not the very one who wrote
  and sent a messenger to Carador:
  how can he now look Carlo in the eyes?
  Ah, he will give him so much trouble still,
  one of these days he'll really make him cry."
  Oliver and Orlando agreed; in short,
  there was ill feeling in the entire court.

But since it is Dame Fortune's great delight   8
to look at things that change before her eyes,
for she herself keeps changing like the moon,
while Carlo seemed to feel at ease at last,
and thought that, with no fear of anything,
he would enjoy the rose without its thorn,
among the many a joust and tournament
with which he wished to see his knights content,

one day, our Oliver of Burgundy   9
challenged Rinaldo to a game of chess.
They argued as they played, and both of them
grew so incensed and spoke so heatedly,
Oliver told Rinaldo, "At times your brain
is smaller than a goose's. When you shout,
you are more wrong than ever. Don't behave
as if I were your squire or your slave."

Rinaldo answered, "Say: do you believe   10
that I should bow to you simply because
Meridiana's here?" And from then on
their words became so villainous and harsh,
Oliver raised his fist, ready to strike,
but the young princess grabbed his hand in time.
Rinaldo right away was on his feet,
and Oliver one second did not wait:

faster than lightning for his arms he ran,   11
and, back to Lord Rinaldo, drew his sword
(Rinaldo did not have his own on him).
Orlando threw himself between the two
while like a leaf Meridiana shook.
'Twas then King Carlo thus rebuked Rinaldo:
"There's not one day you do not rouse a brawl;
you're always wrong, and please me not at all."

Rinaldo at the peak of all his wrath   12
replied to Charlemagne, "You're lying, Sire:
'tis he is wrong for having threatened me."
King Carlo shouted to his men around,
"See that this man is placed under arrest,
or I will punish each and every one."
Rinaldo said, "Beware: If you come close,
you'll sooner chase off flies than these my blows."

Seeing his cousin in so dire a plight,　　　　　　　13
Orlando said to him, "Make up your mind:
go back to Montalban, as I suggest.
Carlo, I see, is much too furious
to ponder which of you is right or wrong."
Rinaldo mounted his Baiardo at once
and, thus to Count Orlando paying heed,
toward Montalbano spurred his eager steed.

Carlo complained to Count Orlando, who　　　　　14
had helped Rinaldo to escape his wrath:
"Did you see how that traitor treated me?
Each passing day he dares give me the lie.
One of these days he'll get what he deserves."
He bade all of his counselors convene,
and in most simple terms told everyone
how he had planned to deal with Ammon's son.

Orlando said, "Please follow my advice:　　　　　15
let the young daring lord cool off awhile,
and you will see him on his knees before you,
asking to be forgiven by his king."
Carlo replied, "Impossible! I won't
give him another chance to call me liar.
I want to chase him to his dying day,
farther and farther from my court away."

Duke Namo in the end gave this advice—　　　　16
that the young lord be banished from the court
in order that no peril might ensue
from such a grave and sorry precedent.
He said, "The entire populace is restless,
in fear of a new Saracen attack.
They might rebel and cause some awful woe,
for the whole city loves him, as you know."

Astolfo was against the banishment:　　　　　　17
he was in favor of full pardon, and,
on hearing Oliver against him speak,
felt much disdain and anger in his heart.
The banishment was finally decreed
by Charlemagne, who heeded Namo's word.
Treacherous Gan had dared only this phrase to speak:
"Has he called you a liar? Then hang him by the neck!"

Astolfo, seeing he had lost his case 18
and that Rinaldo's exile had been signed,
departed from the court immediately,
eager to reach Rinaldo in Montalban
to let him know that he'd be soon besieged
and they had all agreed to banish him,
and also to inform him of the word
that from the lips of Gano he had heard.

A thousand times and one Rinaldo swore 19
that he would never rest until the day
he'd take that evil traitor's evil life
and quench his thirst for vengeance in his blood.
"Dear cousin," to Astolfo then he said,
"because you love me, listen now to me:
let us both rob and ransack all these regions
and to the bandit's code pay full allegiance.

"Whoever's in our way—Saint Peter, too— 20
we'll mug and rob and execute by sword;
our Ricciardetto's bandit number three."
Astolfo said, "What are we waiting for?
I'll rob my dear old father for one cent.
Our highwaymen's career begins at dawn:
no friend or relative we'll ever spare,
and then our gain and plunder let us share.

"And if we run into Saint Ursula, 21
escorted by the Angel Gabriel,
who announced Christ's coming to the Virgin Mary,
we'll take their cloaks and rob them just as well."
Rinaldo said, "Dear brother, I can swear
that God Himself has sent you here to me:
you are so wise, therefore so dear and true.
I cannot wait to reach the woods with you."

And Malagigi, who was there, agreed 22
that they should quickly do as they had planned.
Rinaldo gathered people of all kinds,
granting asylum to all banished men,
and welcoming to Montalban all those
who had escaped the hangman's well-earned noose:
he fed them, clothed them with a lavish hand;
thus in one month he rallied a good band.

He kept the entire country in great fear,   23
and every day some frightful news was heard:
"So-and-so in a deep forest has been killed
for twenty bezants; someone else for a hundred"—
with echoes reaching Paris's very walls.
Ask not if Ganelon was overjoyed:
he more than ever urged the emperor
soon to declare against Rinaldo war,

and under siege place Montalban at once.   24
To make Rinaldo's wrath more flaming still,
he said to Carlo, "Idle is our court
because of this one knight turned highwayman.
I'm firm in this opinion of mine—
that we should now announce and have a joust,
the people and the court this way to entertain,
and also tell Rinaldo he threatens us in vain."

Carlo liked Gan's suggestion very much,   25
and to the entire town therefore announced
that there would be a joust on such a day,
and welcome were all those who wished to come.
The court was much delighted, to be sure.
Eager to finish what he had begun,
most zealous Gan decided to incite
Grifon of Altafoglia to the fight:

he was a man of the Maganzan race   26
(Orlando, by the way, had left the court).
"Mighty Grifon," thus Gano spoke to him,
"now that Rinaldo, banished, is not here,
do not turn down this chance to prove your worth
(Orlando, too, is gone we know not where)."
And to his worthy master readily
Grifon replied, "I'll make you proud of me."

The exact moment of the joust arrived,   27
and to the knight that would deserve it most,
the emperor would give a diamond ring
wondrously set upon a stem of gold—
a token of his honor and respect.
From all his kingdom many a throng had come,
and for the joust was ready many a shield:
it was Grifon that entered first the field.

One day, Rinaldo, as he was feeding his falcon,   28
saw cousin Malagigi coming near.
Finally in his presence, into laughter
he burst, and said, "In Paris—don't you know?—
they're jousting merrily. You must go there
unknown and garbed in the bizarrest way.
Listen: A beard of grass will so disguise you
that no one in the least will recognize you."

Rinaldo's heart was all lit up with joy;   29
and everything he needed soon he took—
cloak, suit of armor, and his fiery horse.
He said, "I want to take both Ricciardetto
and the bright British lord along with me.
Just to make sure, Alardo will stay here."
The three knights armed themselves and the next day,
disguised, toward Paris went from Montalban away.

They, in the good old days, used to dismount   30
right at the inn of their beloved friend
Gualtieri, better known as Don Simón;
but not too far from Paris, now they found
a new innkeeper—a poor beggar—there.
The three, dismounted, put their steeds indoors,
most eager any treason to eschew;
the new innkeeper was Bartholomew.

Rinaldo sent Ricciardo into town   31
to spy on what was going on in there.
Ricciardo on his cloak and on his horse
had tied a flowing band that ran across;
he also wore a gentle wreath of flowers
that nearly altogether hid his chest;
truly a cloak of spotless silk had he,
indeed most rare and beautiful to see.

There was a garland in the crownpiece, too,   32
and still another on his horse's back—
a springtime wreath of many a colored bloom;
the coverlet was yellow, all of it.
He noticed that the joust had but begun,
and could not help but join in the sweet dance.
Soon he unhorsed the first he met and, swift,
unhorsed the second, third, and fourth, and fifth.

This done, back to his brother he returned, 33
and told him of his prowess on the field.
Rinaldo, who was armed as well as he,
and Duke Astolfo both went rapidly.
The entire population looked at him,
who seemed, indeed, so skillful and so brave.
Oliver then and there had joined the fight,
eager to use his spear and show its might.

As he arrived, Rinaldo spurred his horse— 34
nimble Baiardo—on both flanks at once.
Against him came the valiant marquis,
for the two knights each other did not know.
Right in the midst of their great fight, the two
great champions hit each other ruthlessly:
up in midair both spears broke into pieces—such
was the hard blow—but neither champion was hurt much.

But both their horses on their knees fell down, 35
and in the fall Oliver's helmet broke
its laces and immediately laid bare
the features of the valorous marquis.
On seeing him, Rinaldo truly thought
of killing him and running then away,
but he allowed his prudence to prevail.
Oliver rose, bewildered still and pale.

Right then, Rinaldo grabbed another spear, 36
and made, astride his charger, a full turn.
But at that moment a Maganzan foe,
known as Frasmondo, was assailing him:
upon his shield the mighty lance fell down,
unseating him and then a second man—
Grifon, who had been sent by Gano there,
and whose great strength was said beyond compare.

The lord from England on that field fought, too, 37
grounding now one and then another man:
many a foe unseated he that day.
Rinaldo looked around for Gan alone:
at last he recognized him, and at once
against the wicked traitor spurred Baiardo;
he reached him and, at once to do him in,
straight at his visor aimed his javelin.

Writhing in pain, Gan trembled on his steed;   38
Rinaldo's spear most vehemently broke.
Mattafellón, Gano's undaunted horse,
suddenly crouched—if Turpin tells the truth.
As Ganelon fell down, immediately
many Maganzans to his rescue ran;
many Maganzans hastened at full speed
and quickly helped him back upon his steed.

Down to the ground that day Rinaldo flung   39
whichever fighter passed within his reach.
Alda the Fair had in the meantime kept
her glances fixed upon the handsome knight
who still was making all the hostile spears
look like soft stalks of fennel all about.
He even caught the eyes of Gallerana,
who was with Alda and Meridiana.

The joust completed, good Rinaldo had   40
the public cheers that he so well deserved.
Alda the Fair to that most worthy knight
donated a most precious diamond ring,
saying, "Forever wear it for my love."
One of her rubies Gallerana gave
to him who had just proved so great to be.
Rinaldo accepted them most courteously.

Rinaldo with Astolfo and his brother   41
returned to the innkeeper out of town.
Gano, who in the fight had been so shamed
and now felt vilipended, in his heart
resolved that with his people he would so
surround the paladin he'd give him death,
so that he would not boast, when far away,
of having won such mighty men that day.

So they together out of Paris ran,   42
and found our Lord Rinaldo at the inn.
They grabbed him, scratched him, bit him, all of them
trying to push him down while still unarmed;
but such was his resistance, such his fight,
they left him and then seized Astolfo instead.
Barely Rinaldo made his saving flight,
with Ricciardetto following within sight.

Gan bade his men remove Astolfo's helmet,   43
resolved to give him death soon afterward.
But first he wanted to extract from him
all that he knew about his valiant friend.
He recognized him, though, and said to him,
"Are you that traitor who has ever spoken
ill of our court and our great Charlemagne,
and turned a highwayman at Montalban?

"Your many crimes have brought you at long last   44
to your well-earned last hour. Now, if you look
back on your life, you'll know you have to pay
for all your deeds with equal grief and woe."
Pain did not make Astolfo say a word.
Gan of Maganza back to Paris went
and to King Carlo with a devilish glee
surrendered Duke Astolfo secretly.

His fear had been that, if along the road   45
someone had recognized the captive knight,
he might be helped and taken from his hands.
He said, "O Charlemagne, O Lofty Crown,
hang him, and thus your duty you will do.
Not even one good action has he done
all of his life. If you recall his days,
he's earned his gallows in a thousand ways."

King Carlo had him in a dungeon thrown,   46
and ordered, too, that justice soon be done.
But while Big Charlie such instructions gave
and Ganelon in ecstasy rejoiced,
Rinaldo, anguish-torn, felt in his heart
great pity for Astolfo, dearest friend.
He thought what he could do to help him out;
"Carlo," he said, "will hang him—there's no doubt."

That very day Orlando, who had been   47
through many a land and wanted now to see
his cousin once again, reached Montalban.
He found Rinaldo and Ricciardetto in great
anxiety. Astolfo's story made
the count, who did not know it, greatly sad:
in Agrismont he had been Buovo's guest,
ignorant of the joust and all the rest.

He too with his Rinaldo soon agreed
that Carlo would not spare Astolfo's life.
Why, even Malagigi had lost hope,
Charles having placed a consecrated host
upon him, fearing all his magic arts.
Also, the emperor had bidden many
powerful guards around the prison sit,
that neither trick nor ghost might open it.

48

"As far as I'm concerned," Orlando said,
"I want to go and with Astolfo die."
"And so do I," Rinaldo said; "let's hurry,
for, to be sure, this is no time to sleep."
As soon as the sun plunged into the sea,
they had their armor brought and donned it fast.
They took Ricciardo along for company,
and through the night till daybreak rode the three.

Still early in the morning they arrived
outside the doors of Paris. No one knew
(and they saw to it) who they really were;
inside St. Denis they remained concealed.
Some pilgrims happened to pass by, and soon
Orlando sent Terigi in their midst
to ask if they could tell him what was new
with Carlo and the knights, his retinue.

50

They so replied to him, "We nothing know,
but we have heard this rumor nonetheless—
that Charlemagne, this very morn, will hang
one of his knights for something wrong he did:
from this road here the gallows we can see.
While in the city nothing else we heard."
Back to the count our good Terigi sped,
and the last news from Paris soon he said.

Rinaldo sighed, "The emperor's not joking.
That wicked Gan must be a happy man . . ."
Orlando added, "If you follow me,
I'll prove to you, dear cousin, you are wrong."
Replied Rinaldo, "I would die with you;
but first I'd rather kill Emperor Charles
than see Astolfo—this is Gano's aim—
die in such undeserved disgrace and shame.

52

"Yea, Gano's heart I'll sever from his breast   53
rather than bear the sight of so much grief.
All this, Orlando, I do swear to you:
with you I'll come where thickest is the fight—
I, banished as I am, and fearless, even
if I shall be the only one to die."
Together the two cousins swore in faith
that they would risk and challenge even death.

There on the watch with eager glance they stood   54
to see if anyone came out of town;
meanwhile Orlando's squire, Terigi, had
his eyes on every road surrounding it.
Each of them kept his horse ready to go,
each of them felt the sharpness of his sword.
Orlando told Terigi, "Climb up there,
and watch from that high steeple everywhere;

"then signal to us here; but first be sure   55
to look all over, and be not deceived.
If you should see some banners soon appear
or any person toward the gallows move,
tell us at once, lest we should have no time
to free Astolfo from the hangman's noose,
though Ganelon will try—it seems to me—
to hang him in the utmost secrecy."

Quite early in the morning Gan arose   56
and ordered all the necessary things.
He even bade the hangman come to him:
ask not if he implored him to be quick.
Each of the knights begged Charles to reconsider,
but Carlo threatened those who begged him so:
the execution before everything,
and no one dare still contradict his king:

Even the admiral who had been baptized   57
together with Erminion begged the king—
that is, that widely famous Lionfant
who had besieged Astolfo in Montalban;
Meridiana and Morgante begged him,
but all their begging, too, was most in vain.
Gan of Pontier entered the hall meanwhile,
saying to Carlo, "All is ready, Sire."

He interrupted those who begged him still,
saying, "If there's no justice, Emperor,
soon every city in great chaos rots.
Both Troy and Rome regret not having punished
their wicked subjects and their wickedness:
'tis justice saves from ruin every throne.
Your sentence must be carried out, My Lord,
and see that you do not recant your word."

58

Carlo replied, "O Gan, do what you must:
let justice run its course and be well served.
I want you now to think of all details."
"Sire, it shall be done," Gano replied;
"so have no fear, but set your mind at ease.
If you, before I take Astolfo out
of jail, should wish to see him just for sheer
amusement, I will gladly bring him here."

Carlo replied, "Yes, bring Astolfo here."
At once Astolfo before Charles was brought.
The wrathful emperor began to say,
seeing the paladin before him kneel,
"How could you be so bold, so very bold,
Astolfo, as to come to this my court
with that young knave who for three months or so
has ransacked my whole kingdom to and fro?

60

"When I decreed Rinaldo's banishment,
I did not doubt your loyalty to me;
but you escaped with him to Montalban,
and turned into a wicked murderer.
Now it is time you paid for this your sin:
after the sweet the bitter always comes.
Your death and wickedness mean nought to me:
I'm sorry for your father's misery."

In grief, poor Otho out of Paris had
already gone. He did not wish to see—
the wretched and afflicted poor old man—
his dear son die so ignominiously.
With tears upon his face, Astolfo then
replied amid much sighing and distress.
Most humbly thus he spoke, "My Emperor,
I've sinned, and I admit my guilt therefore:

"no, I cannot deny I have offended,   63
   together with my cousin, the High Crown.
   But if I, in the past, have served you well
   while, O King Charles, I was your paladin,
   forgive me in the name of Jesus, Who
   one day forgave Longinus from the Cross,
   and of my father, faithful still and dear
   for all his loyalty of yesteryear.

"Forgive me for your loving nephew's sake—   64
   the worthy count; for what I did in Spain
   with you, for what I did in Aspramont,
   and for your famous and most mighty Crown.
   And if I have to die in infamy,
   oh, do not let that traitor worse than Judas
   and Trojan Sinon touch me; but command
   that I be hanged by someone else's hand."

"What difference does it make?" King Carlo asked.   65
   Ganelon's gauntlet was about to strike,
   but soon Duke Namo made him change his mind.
   Astolfo, now by the Maganzans seized,
   was taken to the scaffold near the door:
   the entire population was in tears.
   Ugier was often tempted to untie
   Astolfo and, instead, make Gano die;

he was afraid to go against his king,   66
   and was not even sure he would succeed.
   Close to each other the Maganzans walked,
   fearful of the surrounding paladins
   and of the people clamoring around.
   Treacherous Gan, to spite Astolfo more,
   called him a bandit and a thievish cur,
   prodding meanwhile the executioner.

Namo and Salamon had begged the king   67
   to free the wretched knight and let him go.
   Avolio, Avin, Gualtier of Mulion,
   and also Berlinghier begged for his life,
   saying, "Have pity, Charles, on poor old Otho,
   who for so long has served your crown so well!"
   The whole court for Astolfo begged and sighed,
   but the awaited pardon Charles denied.

Finally Ganelon had in his hands   68
the man whose life he wanted so to take.
Right in the midst of the Parisian shouts,
he had ordered Astolf fastened to a cart,
and round his head had bound the traitor's crown,
and on his back the jacket of brocade;
a gilded noose around his neck was thrust—
which was the thing that grieved Astolfo most.

Around all Paris on his death-cart, after   69
clamoring trumpets and high flags went he,
'mid threats and shouts that branded him a thief.
But more than ever, Ganelon the traitor
feared that Orlando or Rinaldo might
at once appear: he almost saw them come.
Terigi looked at what was going on
and, to report the news, began to run.

Orlando mounted fast his Vegliantin   70
while our Rinaldo on the watch remained
just like a falcon ready to be launched.
To be more sure of seizing Ganelon,
he gave him time to leave the city and reach
the bottom of the gallows. Thus he spoke:
"The farther from the town he walks away,
the sooner he will be our easy prey:

"so let them closer to the scaffold come,   71
for if we charge a moment sooner, they
back into town most easily will run;
instead, we must make sure we grab that man.
Astolfo must by any means not die:
we will be there before the roast is served.
And if, to watch the show, our king is there,
with these my hands his heart right out I'll tear.

"All the Maganzans will begin to flee   72
as soon as they behold Orlando's sign
together with the lion in a cage."
And so our warriors agreed on this,
and waited there like hounds with pricked-up ears,
ready to stalk a hapless hare or doe.
Treacherous Ganelon with boundless spite
led poor Astolfo to the gallows' site.

I could not tell you how the British lord
was mocked and jeered by the surrounding throng.
With his eyes closed (he nothing wished to see),
like a poor, frightened lamb he forward came—
he who had been a noble paladin
at court as well as on the battlefield,
and had saved Carlo from defeat and woes,
killing with his own hand a thousand foes.

73

Emperor Charles, how thankless you can be!
Don't you know God abhors ingratitude?
Have you not read this is the very sin
that dries God's mercy in His heaven above?
That, mixed with that of pride, it was this sin
from the high north wind into Judecca plunged
Lucifer with his many followers?
Than this pestiferous sin no sin is worse.

74

You also must have heard that Scipio,
quite old in wisdom while still young in age,
robbed Hannibal of all the boundless fame
that he had reaped and amply earned at Cannae;
unjustly thankless were the Romans then,
and, consequently, years of grief ensued.
This very sin afflicts each continent,
and ruins every kingdom in the end.

75

This is the sin that chases justice out
(and with no justice can the world endure?).
This is the sin that nurtures every fraud,
this is the sin that has no equal yet.
Because of it Jerusalem collapsed.
This sin sent Judas to his deepest hell;
this sin before our God so loudly cries,
because of it His mercy He denies.

76

Though you refuse to hear me, you know well
the things this paladin has done for you.
I know you praised him more than other knights
while, fighting infidels, he was away.
O Pepin's son, have you forgotten all
he did for you? Your tears will come too late.
Even if he has done something quite infamous
and wicked, will you now forget that from his cross

77

Jesus forgave the men who nailed Him there, 78
begging His Father's pardon for them all?
Behold! Astolfo's kneeling at your feet,
begging forgiveness in humility;
and since no rightful prayer moves your heart,
he in the end is asking for the grace
of dying not by wicked Gano's hand;
but even this you still refuse to grant.

I wish you knew, big Charlie, you big fool, 79
that he who leads Astolfo to his death
is leading you and all your knights as well.
Yes, keep on trusting this most wicked man,
and in due time your Gan will take you, too,
out of your city to the selfsame spot.
It is his ill advice made you ungrateful
and cruel to the one who was to you most faithful.

Seeing himself right at the gallows' foot, 80
and seeing no one coming to his rescue,
Astolfo burst into most bitter weeping
when stepping on the first horrendous rung.
As the Maganzans pushed him from behind,
he said, "O God, is all compassion dead?
Will You from heaven no more mercy give
to those who in Your Gospel still believe?

"If, desperate and full of righteous wrath, 81
I for three months have been a highwayman,
must I for this be sentenced now to death?
Against the pagan kingdom I have fought,
and with this sword killed many a man for you,
enough to win your mercy at this hour:
instead I'm dying like a common thief,
hanged by Gan's hand—which doubles this my grief.

"'Tis Gano who betrayed you countless times, 82
and countless times attempted on your life,
and has already murdered many a knight.
What happened to your mercy, once so vast?
Is it your wish that I should die this way?
By your divinity, above so dear,
by your most glorious and holy Mother,
have pity on my poor and wretched father—

"Oh, not for me, if I deserve it not,   83
    but for his just and ever noble deeds.
Oh, you remember well how in the past
    both in the West and East I fought for you,
so that I thought most truly I deserved
    a different crown, a different chariot,
and a completely different, glorious banner:
    now Gano's noose I'm wearing in this manner."

Avin had come to watch with his own eyes   84
    a show he did not want at all to see.
It was great love that brought him there, and now,
    in all his anguish into tears he burst.
Against his will Astolfo looked above,
    and saw the gallows and its steep ascent.
He tried his best no single step to climb,
    to stay his fate and give himself more time,

but the Maganzans, spitting in his face,   85
    did to him as the Pharisees to Christ.
Laughing and mocking, some thus taunted him:
    "At last you're paying for your wicked sins.
Remember me when you're in Paradise."
    And others, like the Jews, said this to him,
striking him fiercely on both cheeks: "Now guess:
    which of us here has struck you on the face?

"O noble warrior, you should know it well,   86
    well you should recognize the striking hand
if you are prophet or astrologer.
    What are you looking for? For Pepin's son
or for the Roman senator to save you?
    Whom do you want—the Lord of Montalban?
He'll come as the Messiah to a Jew;
    right from the cross Christ called Elijah, too."

It broke one's heart to see Astolfo there.   87
    His hangman pulled him by the winding noose,
saying, "Come up! Come up of your own will,"
    and treacherous Gano echoed, "Hurry up!"
But poor Astolfo was afraid of death,
    being not even eighteen years of age:
hoping, still hoping for some rescuing knight,
    longer he tarried on the scaffold's height:

right on the ladder on both knees he fell,   88
but, quick, the hangman pushed him with a jolt.
Others with arrows pricked him on both legs,
but with great patience he endured their blows.
Finally, willy-nilly up he stood,
and one could hear a creak in all his bones.
Pulled from above and pushed from underneath,
he reached the third rung, closer to his death.

Ganelon said, "You're in for a surprise.   89
Hurry, you wicked traitor, hurry up,
and soon our streets and highways will be free."
And it was this that pierced Astolfo's heart.
"I've never been a traitor," he replied;
"you are the traitor and the murderer:
well you deserve what you now do to me.
But I no more can fight my destiny.

"I fail to understand why under you   90
the earth is still, and sun and moon still shine,
now that ill luck has placed me in your hands,
O wicked traitor, master of deceit.
O sinless Crucified of Nazareth,
is there in heaven no defense for me?
By this I am most wounded and appalled—
by Judas I have been a traitor called.

"Where is Your justice, O my God and Lord?   91
Is there nobody speaking up for me?
O merciful, eternal God, let not
this despicable traitor take my life
and with his wicked tongue insult me still."
So much disdain abounded in his heart
that with the vigor that was not yet dead,
against the ladder now he banged his head.

But more and more the hangman pierced the lad,   92
beating him with his foot or with his fist
now in the face and now in both his ears.
Wretched Astolfo crouched as best he could,
trying in the meantime to wind both legs
around a rung or any wooden pin.
As he was deafened by the shouting throng,
the hangman shook the rope in such a strong

and ruthless way, he nearly choked to death:
maybe Astolfo was a second Job?
All of a sudden down below he looked,
and saw his dear Avin among the crowd.
It was as if a spear had pierced his heart:
bending in grief his shoulders even more,
to him he recommended, more than other
things, his beloved bride and his old father.

93

At times he looked at Paris up above,
at times toward Montalban: he did not know
that from St. Denis soon his help would come.
Gano, to taunt him, at that moment said,
"What are you looking for—your Malagigi?
He'll soon be here; he is not far away
(why, then, Astolfo, are you cross with me?)
and soon will make his phantoms set you free."

Nevertheless, as I have said before,
with his own hand he'd sewn a sacred host
right on Astolfo's back while still in jail,
fearing that Malagigi might arrive
and save the knight from death. Astolfo moaned,
"Alas, alas, no longer can I tell you,
O evil traitor, it is you—not I—
who for your numberless past crimes should die."

95

Ganelon with new insults pierced him more
while ordering the hangman to be quick:
the hangman kept on pulling with his strength.
Astolfo finally made up his mind:
he was determined now to rise and climb
and meet his fate, and get it over with.
Puffing new jeers with many a louder sound,
stood the Maganzans ruthlessly around.

Seeing Astolfo on the scaffold high,
Orlando said, "There's no more time to waste:
do you not hear all those tumultuous cries?"
And something similar Rinaldo said:
"I see the hangman ready now to start:
he's fixing—look—the noose around his neck.
Let us impede right now a greater harm."
Out of St. Denis dashed they in a storm.

97

Fast, on both flanks Rinaldo spurred Baiardo,   98
a charger that allowed no nimble deer
even to run or follow neck to neck.
Orlando and Ricciardo did the same:
no leopard or no lion was so fast.
The count's own squire, Terigi, rode behind.
Rinaldo showed to all his cagèd lion,
and so Orlando flaunted too his sign.

In his last hour Astolfo was all ears,   99
hoping for rescue with his dying breath.
He saw his friends arrive as fast as wind,
faster than arrows and faster than birds.
So nimbly broke the wolves into the flock,
nobody was even aware of them.
Orlando and Rinaldo! He saw the two,
and all his anguish suddenly was through.

Like a swift cloud of dust the two appeared;   100
lightning and thunderbolt arrived at once.
Meanwhile the hangman had already begged
Astolfo to forgive him for the deed
he was about to do; at the same time
Astolfo, now resigned to yield his life,
had begged, in turn, his hangman that his noose
be knotted not too tight and not too loose

for faster running. To what sore extreme   101
had Fortune brought so brave a paladin!
Look—with a rope around his neck, he now
was so resigned to death he spoke no more.
He who had reaped so many a victory
was now imploring but one grace alone—
that, ah, the noose be fixed about his neck
so as to make its knot run smooth and quick.

Soon in the midst of the Maganzan foes,   102
out loud Orlando cried, "You treacherous race!"
brandishing Durlindana, his brave sword.
"Death! Death to all!" shouted Rinaldo, going
closer and closer to the gallows; there
he soon unsheathed Frusberta; with one blow,
he cut the ropes: the entire ladder fell,
and the whole scaffold crumbled down as well.

Never had such a blow on earth been seen,   103
such was the strength, the fury, and the wrath.
Light as a little bird Astolfo fell,
but suddenly regained all of his might;
falling, his hangman split his head and died.
Gan of Pontier, the traitor, ran away.
Avin, who saw him, fast behind him rode,
but they could not break through the massive crowd.

Still in the midst of the Maganzan mob,   104
Orlando now in front, now in the back
let Durlindana do its wonted best:
those who were touched, to heaven took a trip.
And Ricciardetto, too—quite strong was he—
killed a great number with his weighty sword.
Roared like a famished lion every man
while, faster, Ganelon to Paris ran.

All the Maganzans suddenly were seen,   105
utterly routed, running to and fro,
intent only on saving now their lives.
At this, Rinaldo threw a random blow:
soon with no life a poor Maganzan fell.
He took the dead man's armor and his horse
and gave them to Astolfo, British lord;
finally toward the city they all rode,

chasing the stunned Maganzans more and more   106
as wolves a flock of frightened little sheep,
cutting now this and that and then one more,
and making arms and brains writhe on the ground.
Up to the city's walls they chased them, doubling
their blows and slicing jaws with dauntless swords.
Down to their saddle-bows some had been slaughtered,
down to their breasts and heels some others had been quartered.

Astolfo mounted his new steed at once   107
and into the Maganzans leapt with ire,
shouting, "O renegade and ruthless race,
people accursed and bestial and base,
for this your latest crime you now must pay."
And with his sword he started his revenge
by killing many of those men, before
they had a chance to reach the city's door.

Still after Ganelon, our Ricciardetto 108
faster and faster at full gallop went,
his glance still riveted on him alone—
the traitor he must grab and not let go.
As soon as our great barons entered Paris,
the entire population was dismayed,
and when the news of what had happened spread,
each paladin was quickly on his steed.

When Charles was told how things had just turned out, 109
and that Rinaldo and the count were there
in Paris, and Astolfo had escaped,
in grief he struck his forehead with both hands.
Seeing himself now come to such an end,
he ran away from his own boundless shame:
first he removed the crown from off his hair,
and then his regal cloak began to tear.

Rinaldo was already in the square 110
with Count Orlando, stirring up the crowd
that soon felt sorry for Astolfo's plight.
Now everybody wanted Carlo's death
for his undying trust in Ganelon
with such a bitter fruit as all could see.
They seized the square and to the palace ran,
most eager to arrest King Charlemagne.

Shouted Rinaldo, "Leave this chore to me: 111
I mean to do with Charlie what I must.
As soon as I lay down my hands on him,
stand back and be prepared to see the show.
I first of all will grab him by the arm
and throw him down from his most lofty throne;
then from his head I will remove his crown,
pluck off his hair and beard, and, finally,

I'll put a miter back upon his head 112
and send him then, right in Astolfo's cart,
throughout the city like a sentenced thief.
And I'll have Gano lashed so thoroughly
that he will be tattooed from head to toes.
At last he will be quartered limb from limb
together with our crazy, senile sire."
And toward the palace ran he, mad with ire.

But Charlemagne had left his royal hall,
knowing Rinaldo's temper very well.
Seeing the empty throne, Rinaldo came
out of the palace, wasting no more time;
throughout the city he searched for him alone,
threatening those who sheltered Charlemagne
or knew where he had gone and did not speak:
his punishment would be most fierce and quick.

113

Charles out of fright had gone for refuge right
to Count Orlando's home, the very moment
he had been told Rinaldo was in town.
Alda the Fair had hidden him away
(by chance she had arrived that very day).
Oh, how the lovely lady shook with fear
lest all that angry crowd force down the door
and kill the old and trembling emperor.

114

Still chased by Ricciardetto, Gano ran:
but when the felon could no longer flee
and saw Rinaldo right in front of him,
his sword he soon surrendered to the count.
"I'll take it," Count Orlando thus replied,
"later to do with you as justice wants."
"O Count Orlando," Ganelon implored,
"do as you please, but spare my life, my lord."

115

As soon as that most wicked man was seized,
everyone shouted, "Give him now his due!"
Eager to slash him with Frusberta at last,
Rinaldo was unable to stand still:
he was just like a panting, restless hound
that finally has seen the hunted hare.
Orlando told him, "Let's find Carlo first
so that the two on the same cart be placed."

116

Throughout the city for the entire day
they searched for Charlemagne; at sunset, then,
with empty hands back to the court they went,
where now the count was royal deputy.
Alda the Fair of the enchanting face
during the night went secretly to him,
and to her husband finally revealed
how their poor emperor she had concealed.

117

Orlando told her, "Keep him hidden there   118
until the fury of the crowd abates,
and do your utmost so that all the time
our emperor has everything he needs
and suffers no discomfort in the least:
he's old, and as a father dear to me.
But let nobody see him—promise me."
Orlando was so wise, as you can see.

Feeling immensely sorry for King Charles,   119
and fearing lest Rinaldo's flaming wrath
should to their king prove fatal in the end,
most unabashedly he even wept:
Carlo was old, and was his uncle still,
and with him dead the whole court would die, too.
For a few days they rested and, meanwhile,
Gano's surviving friends they did exile.

Then back to his one topic came Rinaldo—   120
that Gano should be tortured and then killed,
as he deserved no lesser punishment,
and that he should be given such a task.
Astolfo, too, begged for that privilege
as compensation for his damages:
most gladly he'd take care of everything.
Orlando said they should arrest the king

first, and then deal with both so ruthlessly   121
that everybody would at last rejoice.
Deep in his heart, treacherous Gano grieved
and, being the most guilty man he was,
expected the most horrid punishment.
Orlando, who was wiser than all knights
and knew Rinaldo's character too well,
was biding time, his temper thus to quell.

At the right moment, after a few days,   122
in such a manner he addressed his friend:
"What do you think has happened to our Charles?
Maybe despair has brought him to his death.
He probably has taken his own life.
Nobody saw him out of Paris go.
But this is what renews my misery:
last night he in a dream appeared to me.

"As soon as I could see his face, I knew   123
   that wholly sad and sorrowful was he:
   he had the color of a buried man,
   his bloodied beard encrusted on his chest,
   and all his hair disheveled on his head;
   but in the sternest, most disdainful way,
   a crucifix held firmly in his hand
   seemed to me—and me alone—to reprimand.

"Therefore I have been crying the day long . . .   124
   As soon as I awoke, the vision fled.
   In fear I soon arose, and prayed at once
   to our most Blessed Virgin Mary, to
   the Father and the Son and the Holy Ghost,
   to let me know the meaning of my dream.
   And so I knew that I had been apprised
   that Carlo's dead, and we've offended Christ.

"Oh, no! We never should have wished him dead.   125
   For a long time he'd worn the mighty crown,
   and all of us can very clearly see
   how much God loved His pious progeny:
   he was, indeed, the only king on earth
   to take his banner from God's very hand.
   Alas, we have offended Jesus, both
   for his great virtues and for his noble worth.

"And I believe it is most worthwhile still   126
   to send a crier through the streets of Paris:
   'Let anyone come forward who may know
   where Carlo can be found, alive or dead.'
   To honor, then, so great an emperor,
   let us now think of a most worthy tomb,
   or else a sign will soon to us be given
   of the just anger of resentful Heaven."

After he heard such words of grief and woe,   127
   Rinaldo grew all of a sudden pale.
   Blaming himself for all that had occurred,
   he said, "I did not want all this to pass."
   His heart ablaze with pity and remorse,
   his eyes all-swelling and now full of tears,
"Orlando," he added, "what you said to me
   is hard to bear and grieves me terribly.

"Never could I suspect that so much ill
would come of this my action; but, alas,
it's easy to be wise after the deed.
It is most likely that he killed himself
for, being of a royal family,
he must have thought that taking his own life
was better than, killed by some other, to fall,
as you and I have read of Hannibal.

"Let the town crier to all men announce
they should come forth and with no fear reveal
if they have hidden, or still hide, their king.
My heart is broken with remorse and grief,
and in God's name I want to honor him
as a most perfect emperor should be.
For this my sin my tears will e'er abound;
I'll kiss his tomb as soon as he is found.

"To honor him as he should honored be,
all of his counselors should soon convene
and order that his sepulcher be carved,
oh, not in bronze or marble but in gold,
with a great crown upon a mighty steed
as the old Romans praised some of their men,
and with strong letters graved forevermore
to bring his worth and glory to the fore,

"and let men know of his God-given flag,
which was far more victorious on earth
than the high bird Camillus brought to Rome
after the falling of the Capitol."
As a wise man Orlando heeded him,
then ordered the announcement to be made.
And as the ban was echoing everywhere,
to Count Orlando came Alda the Fair.

She told him that the king was in her house,
and that much grief had made him pale as death.
The entire court rejoiced at the great news,
for they had thought their king had long been dead.
Rinaldo was the happiest of men,
who called himself responsible for that.
Emperor Charles amid much honor shown
was brought back to his home, back to his throne.

128

129

130

131

132

Astolfo begged forgiveness of King Charles,
and Carlo begged Astolfo's pardon, too,
blaming the treacherous Maganzan count,
and saying, "I have been so ill-advised."
For a few days they did as people do—
they all apologized for what had been,
as I will tell you in my coming verse.
May God deliver you from ill and worse.

133

C A N T O   X I I

O fountainhead of mercy and of grace,
mother of sinners and our advocate,
whose blessedness in heaven this my mind
with never-sated ecstasy proclaims,
you ended our disgrace the very day
on earth you heeded God's Annunciation:
oh, leave me not, O Virgin of high glory,
so that I still may weave the present story.

1

It would be much too long to tell in rhyme
the many phrases of so many a knight;
and there are things unworthy of report.
Rinaldo wanted treacherous Gan to die,
but Carlo wished to pardon him—a grace
that deeply disappointed everyone.
His life was spared on one condition—that
the felon never more stay at the court.

2

Fully displeased and hurt, Rinaldo went
with Ricciardetto back to Montalbàn.
But wicked Ganelon, who could not stop
weaving new schemes and treason in his mind,
immediately put out his horns again.
Rinaldo wasn't there, so he felt safe;
and Carlo, who had spared his life, could not
be strong enough to keep him from the court.

3

So once again he thought of still new ways   4
to make Charles trust him as in the old days
and thus destroy his kingdom in the end.
So Charlemagne became his friend once more,
and what was white he once again called black.
Ganelon said to him, "Listen to me:
if you don't want in endless shame to crawl,
Rinaldo you must crush, once and for all."

"I heartily agree," Carlo replied,   5
"for well you know what he has done to me.
But how to go about it, I know not,
for many a thought is warring in my mind."
That traitor full of every fraud said then,
"I am convinced this time I'll help you well.
Pretending to be exiled by your ban,
I in disguise will go to Montalbàn.

"From there I'll send you letters that will seem   6
as genuine as if in Mecca mailed:
I'll tell you that my men are sorely vexed
and that by now all of their sins are punished;
things of this kind I'll write and send to you:
in short, I'll beg your friendship once again
(*peccavi, Domine, miserere mei*),
your pardon for my sins of yesterday.

"To all you'll show the letters you receive.   7
Rinaldo will believe that, being far
away, I will no longer here return.
Thus, the first day he leaves his Montalbàn,
we shall combine our efforts, you and I,
and with this very hand I'll give him death.
As soon as he is dead, you can be sure
that, safe at last, your kingdom will endure."

Emperor Charles liked his advice too well,   8
and made believe he banished Ganelon.
Resorting to his old astuteness, Gan
most humbly knelt and pleaded for himself,
while with the sternest glance the emperor
showed that he wished to see him there no more,
and that he'd better try his luck elsewhere,
and leave his very presence then and there.

In the utmost secrecy the traitor left
and went to live, disguised, in Montalbàn.
He wrote to Charlemagne that, with his men,
he had set foot in Pagandom at last;
in great humility he begged him, too,
all of his sins most kindly to forgive.
His answers Carlo showed to every man
before he sent them on to Montalbàn.

9

One day, Rinaldo left his citadel
to spend time with a falcon that he had,
and Ruinatto, just to please his lord,
had also gone with him toward Agrismont.
And Ricciardetto, too, had gone, one day,
down to the river's bank where Ganelon
was hiding in a forest near a rill,
in a small valley down a lovely hill.

10

As Ricciardetto walked about in ease,
Gano mistook him for Rinaldo: so
out of the wood with a great din he came
and, fast, assailed him with his company
so that he was surrounded in that place.
During the night to Paris then he went
and handed Ricciardetto to the king,
and they decreed that he should die by hanging.

11

Orlando, quickly given the sad news,
with much entreating begged the emperor
to set the captive free and let him go
without dishonor and outrageous shame.
Burning with anger, Charlemagne replied,
"I want to hang him like a traitor: he
obstructed justice in Astolfo's case,
and therefore death together they must face."

12

Orlando said, "But Carlo, the old fire
could quickly burst into a blaze anew.
You will displease me if you kill this man,
and fast Rinaldo's vengeance will arrive.
You know that Gano is a traitor, yet
you cannot live without him one short hour."
Charlemagne answered, "Never, never was he such
as you described him, no! He loves me very much.

13

"But you, you and Rinaldo, have, instead,   14
hated him all the time, simply because
he's faithful to me and, both day and night,
thinks of destroying all my enemies."
Orlando left, after a while returned,
and said, "O Carlo, by the Holy Gospel
I swear that if you kill my cousin, I
will make you, too, at the same moment die."

This said, he took his Durlindana out,   15
drew soon a cross upon the ground with it,
and on the very cross placed then his hand:
and so he left the city and the king.
But Gallerana, wise and gentle queen,
with Oliver, the Dane, the British lord,
and the duke Namo, begged the king in many ways
at least to have his death postponed by thirty days.

On the Seine River, Carlo had the gallows   16
quickly put up with every needed thing.
Treacherous Gano was a happy man,
thinking of the success of his own scheme.
But the whole court was full of great disdain.
Rinaldo, in the meantime, with his squire
returned to Montalbàn, and did not see
his Ricciardetto there: where could he be?

He wrote a letter to Astolfo, asking   17
for more details, also assuring him
he'd waste no time in gathering more troops,
and thus bring help to Ricciardetto at once.
Astolfo told him everything he knew,
and that King Charles had granted him one full month
before the hanging; it was quite a pity
Orlando was no longer in the city.

Indeed, it was a pity—agreed Rinaldo—   18
that Count Orlando was not there: no rescue
mission was wholly sure without his help.
Yet he was busy rallying his men.
Queen Gallerana, who much grieved for it,
begged her imperial husband every day
to set the captive, Ricciardetto, free,
and welcome back Orlando finally.

She warned him not to tempt fate recklessly
by placing all his trust in Ganelon,
and, oh, one grace she now was begging of him—
to place young Ricciardetto in her hands.
But no, not even she in any way
could sway King Carlo from his ruthless plan.
Alerted for whatever circumstance,
Rinaldo's troops were ready to advance.

19

The date that had been set by now was near,
and, heeding Carlo's order, Smeriglión
and Vivian of Maganza soon appeared.
So devilishly bold was Ganelon,
he threatened those who tried to soften him:
the emperor had given him such power
that nothing could Duke Namo there detain:
back to Bavaria went he in disdain.

20

Likewise, Avino, Otho, Berlinghier,
Salamon, and Avolio had left
along with Baldovin, son of the Dane,
unable Gano's arrogance to bear.
Erminion, the converted Saracen
who still was Carlo's guest, was much perturbed:
and so was Lionfant, Astolfo's friend—
the admiral so kind and prominent.

21

Morgante was still there with the young princess
Meridiana and her retinue:
of Ricciardetto everybody spoke,
unjustly sent by Carlo to his death.
The time arrived, and Gano of Pontier
summoned his soldiers and to all of them
gave these instructions—at once to hang
poor Ricciardetto on the river's bank.

22

Called by Astolfo's letter, with his men
Rinaldo had arrived, and there was he,
waiting for his dear brother to appear.
At last he saw some banners in the wind,
preceding Ricciardetto, coming forth
'tween his two hangmen—Smeriglión, who seemed
of his known skill quite proud and happy rather,
and the good Vivian, who was the other.

23

He did not wait, as in Astolfo's case,   24
until his brother reached the gallows' foot,
lest he should bear so ignominious an act
as even someone spitting in his face.
Fast, toward the city door at once he dashed,
and with one blow struck three Maganzans down:
and so his Ricciardetto he set loose,
who, like Astolfo, wore the fatal noose.

Fast, with Baiardo here and there he leapt,   25
and with Frusberta did so much that day
that no one would believe the telling tongue.
As soon as the news traveled, everyone
began to flee. In the meantime, Alardo
caught Smeriglione with his head uncovered:
there with his sword so fierce a blow he threw,
he split his skull with all his brains in two.

Then with a mighty storm he turned against   26
Vivian of Pontier, who was nearby,
and with his sword he struck him on the head:
helmet and ruff he slashed down to the chin.
Then it was Gano our Rinaldo wanted,
and so against him he began to fight:
he struck him on an arm, and so the wound
was wide that Ganelon, soon on the ground,

was carried like a lifeless man away.   27
Young Ricciardetto mounted, then and there,
the steed that Smeriglión had left unmanned,
and started to assail the selfsame foe:
such blows he threw, such mighty things did he,
I will not bore my reader with a list.
Carlo had reached the city door right then,
and saw Rinaldo and many slaughtered men.

Thus to himself he said, "I have done wrong: 28
my people are against me once again,"
and ran out of the city straightaway.
Rinaldo entered Paris at this point,
shouting, "O crazy cowards that you are,
how could you bear so much outrageous shame?
Death! Death!—I tell you. Burn and sack the town!"
And he turned all of Paris upside down.

He set on fire a small village first,   29
and pillaged every store and every home:
thus the Parisians knew it was no joke
and he meant business, sparing not a one.
Little by little the mad fury grew,
till but few people in their homes remained.
Hearing such screams as "Fire!" "Death!" in fright
they opened fast their doors and came outside.

There was not one Maganzan to be seen   30
that was not fleeing faster than he could,
and many desperate tears were heard around.
But suddenly Queen Gallerana came
right in the midst of all that fighting throng,
and, being wise and merciful and kind,
implored Rinaldo, making him agree
to put the fire out immediately.

Rinaldo had by now heard everything—   31
how much the worthy and most glorious queen
had done to save poor Ricciardettos's life;
therefore he sent a crier through the town
to tell the people that, to please their queen,
they should stop fighting and put out all fires.
And so with ease that day he conquered Paris,
escorted Gallerana to her palace,

and was crowned king by everybody there,   32
with no one daring contradict him.
On Carlo's very throne at last he sat;
a diadem was placed around his head,
and a rich, regal mantle on his back.
Everyone spoke with wonder of his might,
for he had done that day things of such worth
as very seldom happen on this earth.

Gano to his Maganza thus returned   33
(or, to be more precise, was carried there
like a dead man by his escorting men).
Old Gallerana suffered not one wrong,
for all about her treated her as queen.
It was Rinaldo who soon ordered that
the queen be fully honored on her own
as if Emperor Charles were on his throne.

'Tis true, however, that somebody wrote   34
that Malagigi ran to Paris fast,
and with him brought there Lady Beatrice—
Rinaldo's mother—who most ardently
wanted to wear the empress's diadem.
But Gallerana was the empress still,
for still the prince recalled it had been she
who always wanted Ricciardetto free.

Namo and Salamon returned to Paris   35
with famous Berlinghier and Baldovin,
who was the son of Scaglion's very lord.
Back to the court Avino, too, returned,
together with brave Otho and Gualtier
and the entire populace of Paris.
Of all Maganzans was the door swept clean,
so that no seed or leaf of them was seen.

Throughout the city there were jousts and games,   36
dances and festive fireworks all around.
All the most gentle ladies came right out
to meet as many gentle men in love.
Romances, ballads, rustic songs were sung
until the singers' voices became hoarse;
whistles and drums were heard both near and far
with lute and harp, harmonica, guitar.

Our Lord Rinaldo, by all men revered,   37
was, to be sure, as happy as could be;
yet there was sorrow in his deepest heart
because Orlando was not there with him.
Orlando and Terigi on their steeds
for days and days had ridden through the lands
of the forbidding pagans: Charlemagne
he was determined not to see again.

Weeping in sadness, Ricciardetto moaned,   38
"I am afraid King Carlo killed the count,
and so much grief in this my breast I feel
that never will I find surcease or rest.
Treacherous Gan, to spite me, must have been
the first to carry out so bloody a deed."
Saying the same, a sigh Terigi heaved,
and for his Ricciardetto much he grieved.

The count had ridden a full month and more,   39
and now had come to Persia finally.
As soon as he set foot on that far land,
he heard that a great war was to be fought,
and then, one day, down from a mountain he
could see a famous town whose Admiral
appeared to be besieged by the defiant
Great Sultan with a most horrendous giant.

The Admiral had a daughter, lovely so,   40
she beat the splendor of the morning star.
Her name was Chiariella: such delight
and such entrancing worthiness had she
that for her love the Sultan grabbed a steed,
and marched, together with his Saracens,
such beauty, if he could, at last to win.
His giant's restlessness by all was seen

(his name was Marcovaldo). He had come   41
from faraway Morocco's countryside.
A person of great wisdom and great might,
he was in love and, like a silly boy,
felt nothing but the heat of Cupid's flame;
he who had always checkmated all men
was much in love and suffered now such fits
of passion, he had wholly lost his wits.

He mounted an enormous Arab mare   42
with blackish mane and stars upon her brow:
she had but one defect—she did not feel
the bit, and mistook mountains for low plains.
She would have run and run the whole day long,
such was the ready power of her limbs.
Milon's great son and his Terigi went
right where the mighty giant had his tent,

which was made out of serpents' hardened skin   43
with many small Mohammeds carved in gold,
many a ruby, just as Turpin says,
and many a sapphire—a most precious stone.
Keenly Orlando watched the pavilion
where the great giant dwelt: on each detail
he had his eager glance so firmly cast
as to annoy great Marcovaldo at last.

In the tradition of a mighty lord,   44
he at that moment was still playing chess.
He turned, and said to an attending boy,
"Who is that knave, holding the candle there?
Chase him away, for surely he's a fool.
Where has this lemon come from, anyway?"
Vegliantin's bride was seized by a pagan hand
while still Orlando watched the decorated tent.

Terigi, when he saw the Saracen   45
grabbing the rein of Count Orlando's steed,
being the faithful squire that he was,
struck with his sword the pagan on the head,
and made him upside down fall to the ground,
with his brains leaping in the meantime forth.
"Terigi," said Orlando, "beautiful!
How right you were in punishing this fool."

As Marcovaldo saw his servant fall,   46
he wondered, for Terigi—so it seemed—
had hardly touched him. "Lazy knave!" he shouted.
"You crazy fool that should in fetters be!"
Then, turning to another servant, "Bring
that man in here immediately," he said;
"one of my men was killed before my eyes,
and so that man I quickly must chastise."

Orlando took his Durlindana out,   47
for it was time to tarry there no more.
Against the pagan throng at once he went
(Terigi in the meantime whirled his sword),
killing as many men as blocked his path
until no one was there in front of him:
on those who could not run or were not quick,
Orlando's sword impressed the master's trick.

On seeing Count Orlando do all this   48
in a brief moment right before his eyes,
the mighty giant wondered very much,
and in this manner to himself he spoke:
"Only Angrante's noble lord—the one
whose glorious name is known throughout the world—
could have done what this man did my crowd."
These words made Count Orlando laugh out loud.

Out loud the giant ordered, "Bring my arms,   49
for I am much intrigued by what I see.
I want to test my valor with this knight
who has come here to rout all of my men,
as we shall see if me he wants to fight."
He took his charger by the rein at once
and with a spear against Orlando ran.
But good Terigi saw the wicked plan,

and from a pagan grabbed another spear,   50
saying, "Take this, dear count! Take this at once!
The courtesies of France are dead down here.
Look at the giant eager to advance!
His cheeks have never known a blushing flame,
for here he's coming like a mountain peak—
you with a sword and he with lance in rest.
To him this must be chivalry at its best."

Replied Orlando, "Let him be himself,   51
for I don't give a hoot for what he is.
Quite true, he is so huge my spear will reach
his belly button, and this grieves me most,
but just as ever this my sword is sharp.
With it I'll treat him as I treat a foe."
Terigi was there watching with delight
while Vegliantìn looked like a hawk in flight.

Orlando lowered suddenly his lance   52
and eagerly against the pagan went.
He struck him on the bottom of his shield,
which like a leaf was pierced and torn to bits.
He also pierced his hauberk and his plate,
thus giving Marcovaldo boundless pain.
His spear broke on the breastplate of the count,
which made the giant soon blaspheme Mahound.

The Arab mare, much frightened by that blow   53
which almost seemed of superhuman might,
was, as I said, insensitive to the bit;
so, unrestrained and unresponsive, fast
out of that plainland she began to flee.
But eagerly the count stayed in the dance:
he and his squire Terigi, fast and bold,
spurred their brave horses, chasing Marcovald.

After she crossed the entire plain, the mare   54
right at the foot of a high mountain came.
'Twas there the giant finally succeeded
in stopping her (his brow was full of sweat).
Orlando shouted, "Ill-bred Saracen,
across the entire plain I've followed you
to tell you that this is your final day:
turn back! It's useless now to run away."

Hearing himself addressed in such a way,   55
the pagan turned and, with his sword unsheathed,
said, "On this earth no man will ever boast
that he has made me out of terror flee.
But this I want to tell you: in no way
can this my charger's boundless wrath be stopped
as soon as in her mouth she feels the bit:
up here she flew, and you're aware of it.

"But where I wanted you, you've come at last,   56
together with your man who killed my boy.
If I am still the Marcovald I know,
I'll quickly cut your every nerve and bone:
I have deflated seven persons' pride,
and with my foes I follow but one rule—
I do not care to use my lance with skill:
I will with this my sword go for the kill."

Orlando said, "You're talking out of shame: 57
you've labored hard to break a stalk of fennel,
and now you feel obliged to make excuses.
Though next to you I look but like a frog,
I know that with my sword I scratched your itch
and made your blood fall much below your knee.
If only you'd be seen by your sweet dame!"
(And here he mentioned Chiariella's name.)

The pagan said, "Where have you learned the name   58
of her who holds the keys to this my heart?
She, for your information, many a time
has seen me fell fighters dead to the ground,
and never has she been not proud of me.
And yet, to make her happy—if I knew
that this new gift of mine would give her joy—
I'd send her soon your head as her new toy."

Replied Orlando, "Your much bigger head
will make, O giant, a much better gift.
Very well, then, let's see how brave you are,
and what to Chiariella you will send."
He raised his Durlindana suddenly,
saying, "Now start invoking your Mahound!"
and gave him such a blow on the right shoulder,
it made the giant seem a shaking boulder.

59

He made the giant's shoulderpiece send sparks,
and yet it could withstand the cutting sword.
At once the Saracen avenged himself
by letting a great blow fall on the count.
Orlando tried to shun it with his shield,
but the enormous sword soon cut it through,
making two halves of it, one of which fell
down to the ground, according to our tale.

60

Seized by unbounded wrath, Orlando fast
threw in the giant's snout the other half;
brandishing, then, his Durlindana well,
he struck the pagan's arm with such a blow
that, although strong and with perfection wrought,
the weapon seemed of either wax or ice:
the arm he severed where the hand is joined,
and mightily the giant roared and groaned

61

as he could see both sword and hand fall down:
down from his mare he with much pain fell, too,
saying, "I now surrender as I must,
for nothing can Mohammed do for me.
But out of kindness tell me, cavalier,
if you perchance are of the Christian faith—
you who have brought me to untimely fate:
never so strong a pagan have I met."

62

Orlando said, "Since out of kindness you
want me to speak, in kindness I'll reply.
I am Orlando, and the man you see
here in my company is my good squire.
You'll die and will be damned in hell forever
if you do not believe in Mary's Son:
become a Christian now, the Gospel take,
and send your soul to heaven, for God's sake.

63

"Mohammed is awaiting you in hell
with all the other fools that follow him;
there in eternal fire you will burn,
down in the dark and dolorous abyss."
The pagan said, "May Jesus Christ be praised
with all His saints for all eternity!
I want you to baptize me instantly,
Orlando, and a Christian I will be.

64

"Your God I'm thanking, for I have been slain
by the most famous man upon the earth;
if I were sorry, I would be most wrong.
Baptize me, for God's sake, O gentle knight:
such peace already in my heart I feel,
I seem to have been cleansed of every sin."
Orlando saw a river, rushed there rather,
removed his helmet, filled it all with water,

65

and then baptized the giant with great zeal.
As soon as he was dead, Orlando heard
a song, and saw so many angels come
and to the holy kingdom take his soul.
Oh, but he grieved for having killed the man,
and with Terigi shed most copious tears.
Together, then, they dug a big, dark grave,
and to that man a decent burial gave.

66

Before he died, the giant had expressed
his final wish to Count Orlando: if,
by any chance, he should one of these days
talk to the lady he still loved so much,
would he be kind enough to let her know
all that had happened till the very end,
and also that, until his last and dying breath,
he swore to Chiariella his great, undying faith.

67

Oh, to reward him for such boundless love,
would that she might at times come to the place
harboring his forgotten, lonely grave,
and in this manner call him: "Chiariella,
my dear, poor Marcovald, is here in tears—
the one you called the fairest on this earth."
He hoped that if he heard such call from her,
his soul would rise out of his sepulcher,

68

and he would do as much as Pyramus,
called by his Thisbe in his dying hour
under the black mulberry tree. Orlando
comforted him most dearly, telling him,
"I know I'll do so, long before I die,
for surely I will go where she is still."
This, in due time and place, Orlando did,
who always kept the promises he made.

69

Terigi, too, had seen the giant's soul
with many holy angels rise to God
amid sweet songs of everlasting bliss.
Almost bewildered, with an ashen face,
he heard those angels sing "Ave Maria"
in a sublime, most heavenly delight,
and therefore, turning to the count, he said,
"Oh, how I wish I had been killed instead!

70

"Among the pagans let us go at once,
for to be here alive means nought to me.
I want to die, O Jesus, for your faith,
now that I've seen that blessèd soul depart."
"Back to the camp let's go," Orlando said,
before these latest tidings reach men's ears.
Let us go there unknown, and say no word
of what to Marcovaldo has occurred."

71

Thus the two Christians crossed the pagan camp,
fully and by all means unrecognized;
then they proceeded toward the city where
the great, crowned Admiral had deigned to stay.
They asked where they could find the royal palace,
and spurred their horses onward as they knew.
And so arrived they, in no time at all,
right at the mansion of the Admiral.

72

There at a window stood the Admiral.
Dear Chiariella, fresher than a new-
burgeoning rose, our Count Orlando saw
and, to know more, just fixed her glance on him.
Addressing, then, her father, "Did you see,"
she said, "these fighters on their horses come?
Judging by how one rode, so proud and light,
I am convinced he is a famous knight.

73

"I hope he is Orlando, the renowned
 Christian who looks exactly like this man:
 the plainland would not be so full of flags,
 the camp would not be now so close to us,
 nor would the Sultan keep us under siege."
 Orlando heard all that she said, and smiled.
 The Admiral addressed him with great cheer,
 "O mighty cavalier, you're welcome here!

74

"May our Mahound protect you every day!
 If you are wishing to be hired by me
 (and you can clearly see my grievous plight),
 I willingly will hire both of you.
 The men you see have come to do me harm:
 here is the Sultan with his countless flags,
 who from far Egypt came with all his hordes
 to fill our mounts and valleys with their swords.

75

He has brought all the eastern nations here,
 and seeks my lovely daughter forcibly.
 With him, by chance, a giant also came,
 who terrifies my entire family:
 he owns a mare that chases everyone,
 and, being deaf to bits, runs uncontrolled;
 some of my men she has already killed,
 and now is wasting every ripened field."

76

Orlando thus replied, "Now rest assured!
 This giant will no longer mount his mare:
 he'll injure you no more, I promise that,
 nor will he see his throne and land again.
 Below the mountain right in front of you,
 I have just killed him with this sword of mine.
 Sire, I bid you set your mind at ease:
 the mighty giant's resting now in peace."

77

Unable to believe what he had heard,
 the Admiral was eager for details:
 "What? Did you truly slay so fierce a man?"
 And soon he hugged him with much happiness,
 saying, "I nothing care about the rest."
 And the young lady with great tenderness
 ran to embrace Orlando instantly,
 who liked that very much, believe you me.

78

Rinaldo would have liked it just as much.   79
But "Oh, where are you, Lord of Montalbàn?"
Orlando said. "You surely would not move
if I a little farther stretched my hand."
The princess asked, "Then is it true, great knight,
that you have killed the giant Marcovald?
Blessèd the womb that carried such a man!"
and countless times she thanked Mohammed then.

Already Chiariella was in love   80
with Count Orlando, whom she liked so well;
Cupid already had transfixed her heart.
But to the Sultan let us now go back:
he knew that Marcovaldo had been slain,
and greatly wept for him—which was but right.
With tears on one and on the other cheek,
he was still looking toward the mountain peak.

He had not yet been told the slayer's name.   81
He had been murdered by a passerby—
'twas all he heard—which seemed unlikely most,
for well he knew how fierce the giant was.
Luckily, in his camp there was an old
and very wise and subtle necromancer.
To him he said, "Let all your ghosts or stars
reveal to me the man who killed our Mars."

Most eager to obey, the necromancer,   82
who was a teacher of unbounded knowledge,
thanks to his magic arts, before him summoned
all that he needed for his exercises;
thus he found out a Christian murdered him—
a Christian knight disguised as a Saracen,
who was now with the mighty Admiral:
the giant's killer thus was known to all.

When the Great Sultan heard this oracle,   83
he felt a grievous anguish in his heart,
and said, "O you, Mohammed, mindless god,
to your amusement you have ruined me."
Then in this manner to the Admiral
he wrote, "O King of Persia, you should know
that he who gave the pagan giant death
is in your tent—and of the Christian faith:

"You will most surely his next victim be.   84
From this day on, if this can please your mind,
I want great Marcovaldo to avenge,
and fully bow to all your terms of peace."
He sealed and sent the letter instantly.
The Admiral was grieved by what he read
about his Christian guest; an instant later,
he called the count a grim and wicked traitor,

and to the Sultan soon this answer sent—   85
that by all means he wanted peace and truce,
and to give this Christian what he most deserved:
and thus the peace between the two was signed.
One day he took Orlando by the hand
and told him, "Cavalier, this you must know:
with the Great Sultan I have signed a treaty
because of which the scum will leave my city."

Orlando could not think of treason yet,   86
and simply said that he was very glad
and much rejoiced at the exciting news.
He added, "I was sorry for your plight,
but now my heart feels suddenly relieved."
The Admiral then bade the Sultan come:
he came immediately upon his horse,
even to watch his lovely girl, of course.

They signed the treaty very secretly: 87
that they should both arrest the Christian knight
when, in his bed, he could not call for help.
On such a stratagem they both agreed.
So came the night, and they all went to bed.
Orlando, too, retired to his room
and, thinking he was safe, disarmed, and there
lay of his future troubles unaware.

During the night, when he was sound asleep,   88
a group of full-armed pagans seized his room;
one of them opened forcibly the door,
and like mad dogs they all upon him dashed.
Orlando, alas, did not wake up in time,
and so those rabid wolves bound both his hands.
Thus he was taken suddenly to prison,
and was not told upon what charge or reason.

And after him Terigi, too, was seized,
and thrown down to the bottom of a tower.
Orlando still was stunned and in a daze:
he could not understand what had occurred
to make the Admiral betray him so.
He said, "He wants to kill me, I'm afraid,"
just as in my next Canto you'll be told.
You may God's angel by the forelocks hold.

C A N T O   X I I I

O Holy Virgin, full of mercy, Mother
of Him we mortals sing Hosanna to;
O Virgin imperturbable and pure,
your daily manna ever give to me;
with your hand lead me to the very end
of this my tale, for time deceives us all—
and so do life and death on this blind earth—
so that all men along with me may hear.

1

The lovely princess to her father dear
spoke with the sweetest and most prudent words,
tenderly saying, "With such firmness we
must ever punish every wicked man:
so in this case I'm grieving not at all.
Give me the keys and grant me now to use them
in locking and unlocking as I say,
so that no one may henceforth dare betray."

2

The Admiral was glad to hear all this—
that his young girl should take so great a role—
and so entrusted her with all the keys
(the very thing the princess wanted most).
To Count Orlando's prison soon she went,
and very, very softly called his name,
saying, "Sir knight, I'm sorry as can be:
tell me what I must do to set you free."

3

Thanking her as he could, Orlando said,   4
"First: do you know the reason why your father
is torturing me still in such a way,
here in this dungeon where he threw me fast?
In heaven's name, oh, set my mind at ease:
save me from this bewilderment and doubt.
And if you cannot free me from this tower,
save me at least from death's imminent hour."

And Chiariella to the knight replied,   5
"The reason why my father keeps you here
is that a necromancer told the Sultan
that you're indeed a Christian, though you try
to pass for one of us—a Saracen.
Because the giant's death has hurt him much,
he's signed a treaty with the Sultan: he is sure
this was the way to avenge his Marcovaldo's death.

"According to our law, a Christian man   6
who kills a Saracen must quickly die.
Since it was you who took the giant's life,
our law requires that you, too, should die.
Yet since I love you very much, and feel
most sorry for you, here I have the keys.
Of course you will not die—oh, ban all doubt!
But you are free, and will soon walk right out.

"So many, many wonders I have heard   7
about the knight who bears Orlando's name
that with his worth I deeply fell in love—
the very love that won't abandon you.
As far as your own name (why don't you trust me?),
say it to me, and I'll be grateful most."
Orlando answered, "Lady, full of wonder,
I am the one the world knows as Orlando.

"Look where my luck has brought me: you yourself   8
hardly believe I am the man I am.
I left, but of my people not a one
I wanted with me save my squire alone.
Both night and day incessantly I rode,
and now by force your father keeps me here.
If I had thought of treason, certainly—
I swear to God—still here I would not be.

"To you I recommend myself, still here,
    as you can see. See that my horse is fed
    just as he should, and then to you I give
    whatever's in my power—my heart and soul.
    And something else I'm asking now of you:
    see if you can at least my squire free,
    so that my trusted man can go to France,
    and therefore beg for Carlo's help at once."

Convinced it was Orlando speaking so,
    the lovely princess needed no more proof.
    Excessive sweetness almost made her heart
    explode, and so with happy tears she said,
"I do believe Mahound has sent you to me
    because I love you, but I do not know
    how or when. Always have I loved you, dear,
    but in a different way I'd want you here.

"If even with this very hand I have
    to kill my father, you'll be saved from death:
    Cupid commands—and blindly I obey—
    that you be safe, and safe you so shall be.
    At the right moment I will let you escape,
    and you will have your horse, and happy be:
    your squire will be also free for such
    a trip to France—a trip I cherish much."

That was the way sweet Chiariella spoke.
    She left Orlando and sought her father soon.
    She said to him, "That servant—oh, poor man—
    will surely die, determined as he is
    no more to eat. He, like a madman, threw
    all that I placed in front of him away;
    and guilty he is not in any way,
    for what his lord commands he must obey."

The Admiral replied, "Send him away:
    if he should die, we would be blamed for it.
    But have the other man well guarded, though:
    nothing but trouble he will give to us."
    The lady said, "I'm giving you my word,
    whether he dreams or raves I cannot tell.
    I ask him questions and he stares at me,
    and, answering not, seems in a daze to be."

9

10

11

12

13

Then, laughing, to the dungeon she went back,   14
and told Orlando all that she had done.
Orlando, talking to Terigi, said,
"This is my plan: to Carlo you must go,
and take, I beg you, Vegliantìn with you;
and tell the king that I have been betrayed
by the Admiral, and am now in his prison;
and tell him, too, what seems to be the reason.

"Say to my dear Rinaldo everything;   15
also, to Oliver and the whole court:
tell them to help me while there is still time,
if later they don't want to mourn my death."
Terigi left immediately: his horse
he saddled and was out of town at once.
Riding through many a mount and many a plain,
he reached the city left by Charlemagne.

He did not know the emperor had left Paris,   16
and was with his dear Gano in Pontier.
He heard that Lord Rinaldo was now Charles,
and so to him and Oliver he went.
As soon as Lord Rinaldo saw him coming,
a sad presentiment assailed his mind:
weeping, and almost in a state of shock,
our poor Terigi could not even talk.

Rinaldo asked, "What happened to my cousin?   17
I am afraid you're bringing here bad news."
Wretched Terigi with great effort spoke,
addressing, finally, Rinaldo so:
"The Saracen who's Persia's admiral
keeps him imprisoned; Chiariella, though—
his daughter, so refined and full of charm—
has sworn to save the count from fatal harm.

"All this because he killed big Marcovaldo.   18
The Sultan had a necromancer there,
and thus found out the giant had been slain
by a Christian knight. He signed a treaty with
the Admiral—that treacherous, wicked man—
to have our good Lord of Anglant arrested.
During the night we both were seized and bound
and thrown into a dungeon underground.

"Orlando's asking help from Charlemagne,
  from you, Rinaldo, now Your Majesty,
  and from his friend and dear brother-in-law,
  while there is still some time to save his life.
  I'm all perspired as you well can see:
  I have not ridden, I have rather flown,
  doing, to reach you soon, my very best:
  now you are wise and understand the rest."

Never in all his life had Lord Rinaldo
  been so distressed and sad as he was now.
  Sighing, he said, "Duke Namo, speak for me,
  for I am not myself in all this grief."
  The wise old man replied, "One thing is clear,
  if I have understood Terigi well:
  that we must help Orlando right away.
  And now I'd like to tell you in what way.

"Only the emperor and Oliver
  can lend effective help in this our plight,
  for power and great love are here involved.
  So I suggest we send for Charlemagne,
  and he return as emperor again
  for the salvation of his Christian people:
  thus he'll be glad to grant you what you ask,
  and you will leave for Persia with your task.

"Astolfo will be named Gonfalonier,
  and this should please our Carlo, after all
  he did to him as well as to Ricciardo.
  And Gano shall be banished once again."
  As soon as the wise Namo spoke these words,
  Rinaldo said, "Agreed: the case is closed,"
  and then and there, in writing he expressed
  to Charlemagne the paladins' request:

"Sire, you're old, and therefore I respect you;
  it grieves me that you are now so senile
  as still to trust your wicked Ganelon,
  who has betrayed you myriads of times
  and yet is for his crimes unpunished still:
  because of him you banished me from court
  and, heeding his advice, you tried to kill
  my Ricciardetto and Astolfo as well.

19

20

21

22

23

"'Tis you who should be banished from this court;   24
    however, since you are my lord and king,
    I do forgive you, and make peace with you,
    and give you back your just and holy reign,
    and, if you care to have it, your old crown,
    all of your retinue, your regal cloak,
    your noble, ancient scepter, and your throne,
    and on your past I hereby put a stone.

"Know that Orlando's in a pagan jail.   25
    Come, then, to Paris with no fear at all.
    Both Oliver and I wish there to go,
    and with our people rescue him at once.
    Astolfo shall be here Gonfalonier.
    And tell that traitor not to show his face.
    Your Gallerana, reconfirmed as queen,
    is loved by all as she has always been."

The letter sealed, he sent the courier,   26
    who was in Carlo's presence in no time.
    Carlo rejoiced, most eager to go back
    (what boundless grief tormented Gano's heart!).
    To Paris he returned, and the whole court
    went out to meet him, glad to welcome him.
    They all embraced the monarch tearfully,
    bemoaning Count Orlando unanimously.

Oliver was in tears, for he despaired   27
    of ever seeing his brother-in-law again.
    Valorous Ugier and Astolfo wept,
    and Salamon appeared as in a daze.
    Berlinghier, Baldovino also wept,
    and wise Duke Namo tried to comfort all.
    Bowing, Rinaldo placed the emperor
    with due respect upon his throne once more.

He harnessed, quick, his charger afterward;   28
    Oliver, too, wanted to leave with him.
    Ready to go, Terigi was there also
    when Ricciardetto said, "I will come, too."
    Gladly Rinaldo told his brother, "Come!"
    All of them wanted now to leave, but he
    took no one else together with those few,
    and so they bade their Charlemagne adieu.

Wearing their cloaks of varied shapes and hues,   29
they left. While crossing Spain upon their steeds,
down in a lovely dell they met one day,
amid some of his horsemen, King Marsilius.
With flowering, sweet words, in Saracen,
they greeted him as soon as they came near.
Marsilius told the prince, "Your horse would be
the greatest gift that you could give to me.

"This very day, at dawn, a dream I had   30
told me that such a horse will soon be mine.
If you just give him to me, by Mahound,
you will relieve me of a troubling thought—
that is, of having now to fight with you.
Therefore, behave like a most gentle knight,
for if you turn down what I have proposed,
for him I'll fight, and you'll be sorry most."

Rinaldo answered, "Gone are those old days   31
when one would own a horse seen in a dream,
and he who owned whatever you desired
had to respect the wishes of a dream.
Hear! Once upon a time, a villager
(his name is not important) dreamed of two
oxen, which were his neighbor's property
and he would have much liked to have for free—

"or buy with just the money of his dreams.   32
The owner said, 'I had to pay for them,
and so I do believe that you must, too:
or with no oxen you can go right home.'
While he addressed his neighbor in this way,
many a person gathered round the two.
Not knowing how to solve the problem, soon
they both agreed to go to Solomon.

"Solomon, being the wise man he was,   33
went with both litigants upon a bridge
and there made the two oxen go across;
then with a cheerful countenance he turned
to him who had just seen them in his dream,
and said, 'Look in the water: can you see
their reflection?' (Very limpid was the sight
of the two oxen dreamed of in the night.)

"The dreamer said, 'They look exactly like
the oxen that I saw.' 'Well, take them, then,'
said Solomon, 'for what you dreamed is yours.
But he who paid for them has this advantage—
he does not have to dream of what he owns.
So you are even, both of you, I say.'
Regarding this my horse, I tell you then,
O pagan king, that you have dreamed in vain.

34

"And now, if more you want, take then the field:
this horse will to the better fighter go."
Amazed at such an answer, King Marsilius
thought, "He must be a fool out of some woods:
I cannot find among my horsemen here
or through the whole of Spain so brave a man
as this, who also looks like a strong knight."
And then he answered, "To the death let's fight."

35

Rinaldo wasted not one word; instead,
he shook the rein and, turning thus his steed,
returned against the king to punish him:
he made the earth and the whole sky now tremble,
for his Baiardo did not limp a bit.
Astonished, some of the onlookers said,
"Can this young paladin a Christian be,
who challenges Marsilius recklessly?"

36

When King Marsilius saw the cavalier,
to himself he said, "Oh, help me, god Mahound!"
But our Rinaldo's might was such that neither
Plato nor Trismegistus could have helped.
His lance he lowered and his horse he spurred:
Rinaldo's breastplate in the midst he hit
with such a cruel and most bitter stroke,
at once the spear into small fragments broke.

37

Rinaldo hit him on the visor fast,
and made so many sudden sparks arise
as never out of Aetna have been viewed.
That blow would have destroyed a thousand men:
his helmet sounded and his brain rebounded.
Well, without other such explaining words,
headlong Marsilius fell off his horse:
his was no vision but a dream of course.

38

"Now as a loyal cavalier," he said,   39
"please tell me who you are. Upon this earth
I've never seen so strong a man as you."
Replied Rinaldo, "By this head of mine,
and with no fear I'll tell you who I am,
despite the fact I am in Pagandom—
let come what may. O worthy Saracen,
I am the very Lord of Montalban."

His helmet's visor thus he lifted up   40
to show that by no means was he afraid.
The pagan king replied, "By god Mahound,
Nature outdid herself in making you."
Rinaldo said, "And this is Ricciardetto;
in search of venture we're both traveling.
This is Terigi, Orlando's faithful squire,
and this is our most famous Oliver."

Looking at all of them, Marsilius said,   41
"You are so well disguised, you look to me
like four poor servant boys. You're so well armed,
however, that I failed to recognize you.
Great champions such as you can safely go
and make many more fall into their trap,
just as I have. But tell me now: am I
the very first to whom you gave the lie?"

Rinaldo said, "The very first, I swear;   42
since you have asked me, I must then reply:
it's good to start with such a mighty king,
but someone else will soon the second be.
If you still want the horse I gave you not,
because of your widely resounding name
my horse is yours, Your Noble Majesty,
and so is this my sword and all of me."

Marsilius was a wise, generous man,   43
and, being wise, most wisely he replied,
"I'm no teenager that may follow you.
If I accept so great a gift, I will
offend a man whose worth I have today
so well assayed. By giving him to me,
you are now making that my dream come true,
though I dreamed not that I'd be felled by you.

"And now, Rinaldo, grant me one more grace—   44
with these your friends, oh, come and stay with me
in Saragossa. Please, do not say no.
Our town will look uncivilized to you,
and with your Paris cannot be compared—
the city where all courtesy is found;
and yet for a few days I'll do my best
to make you—by Mahound—a happy guest."

Rinaldo answered, "In no way, O king,   45
will I decline so affable an offer.
And if upon the field I've done you wrong,
I am most sorry for it, and most grieved;
and if I now admit my foolishness,
it is because my conduct is not such.
I knew not who you were, in Jesus' name."
"Let's speak of it no more," the king exclaimed.

"Do not apologize for what you did: 46
a knight must always show his noble worth,
but it's not always possible to be even.
Although it was your might that brought me down,
the time had come I wanted to dismount."
Before such kindness our Rinaldo laughed,
and "Such a kind reply can only add
new splendor to your crown," Rinaldo said.

Then King Marsilius mounted once again;   47
so did Rinaldo, who had first come down
to honor thus a man of higher rank.
Finally King Marsilius held his hand,
and wanted also to hold Oliver's,
but most politely Oliver refused.
So, after many a courtly compliment,
to Saragossa they together went.

Right at the royal palace they dismounted,   48
Marsilius still holding young Rinaldo's
hand on the stairs and also in the halls.
His lovely daughter Luciana, one
who beat in beauty every maiden born,
most affably and kindly met them both:
she greeted first the king and then each guest
with winsomeness and graciousness and zest.

As soon as Lord Rinaldo looked at her,   49
he felt as though his heart had then and there
been pierced by a sharp arrow, and he said,
"A goddess here in Saragossa lives,
and you, O Love, have brought me here to see her:
more than the sun she is bedazzling me."
Then he was greeted by that gentle beauty,
which he acknowledged with chivalric duty.

For a few days there in great bliss they lodged.   50
Ask not if Cupid trotted here and there
in all his ever-novel, subtle ways.
There the young lady waited on Rinaldo
most faithfully, and more than once her fair
and most enchanting, limpid eyes met his:
which was the very sulphur or the tinder
needed to make his fire bigger, higher.

While they were resting in such blissfulness,   51
a messenger arrived, who suddenly,
in King's Marsilius's presence, on his knees,
something most terrible announced to him—
that a big steed with feathers and with teeth
had killed five hundred men and even more:
it was Gisberto's horse, so out of hand
it seemed a demon in a desert land.

"We were five hundred mighty cavaliers,"   52
the courier said, "and when we reached the mountain,
we were assailed by this ferocious beast.
Into the plainland we could not escape,
for in the midst of all your men he hid.
Never was there a ravenous wolf or hound
biting, devouring, poisoning in such a wise;
and his kicks, too, were numerous as flies.

"O King Marsilius, with these my eyes   53
I saw him fall upon a Saracen
and with his forelegs furiously kick:
did you expect him to caress his face
or to remove two tufts of all his hair?
He crushed his entire helmet and his brains,
and ten feet far his head suddenly flew.
Imagine now what his hind legs must do.

"With but a pair of kicks into that wall,   54
  he'd make this entire palace crumble down.
  I packed my things and ran immediately,
  for, being there, I felt uncomfortable:
  there are no weapons that can halt that beast,
  so proud and wicked and so wild is he:
  a pitiless Breusse he seemed to me.
  Amid so many blows I could but flee.

"I am afraid not even one survived,   55
  and I have also seen your nephew die—
  poor boy—in such a sad and horrid way."
  When King Marsilius heard the tragic news—
  that in so sad a way so many men
  had lost their lives—"O god Mahound," he said,
  "why have you such a monstrous deed allowed—
  the full destruction of your faithful crowd?

"Mahound, they were your pagans—all of them,   56
  and now they all are dead, just as you wished.
  Have you a treaty with the Christians signed?
  But if you have, what will become of you
  after we all, like wretched dogs, are dead?
  You will have sent your only friends to death,
  and cruelty will be your sole distinction
  if you bring all your faithful to extinction."

Rinaldo saw his Luciana fair,   57
  moaning with sweet and very tender words.
  To King Marsilius he turned and said,
  "One of your horsemen send right now with me,
  to show me where this savage beast abides.
  Grieve not for what has happened yesterday.
  Those who are dead, may God now make them whole!
  With these my hands I'll kill this animal.

"If there are fools and beasts, I'll be one too,   58
  for there are also beasts with but two legs,
  and maybe one will be less crazy then."
  The king gave his permission right away,
  although he thought that maybe he was wrong
  (Rinaldo had become so dear to him):
  he gave him a young page, but Oliver
  and Ricciardetto wanted to go, too.

Marsilius would have liked to escort him, but   59
Rinaldo said, "I'll take no one along";
Terigi insisted that he, too, must go,
his duty being to be next to him.
They all could see how Lord Rinaldo glowed,
just as the one who's painted blind had wished.
Marsilius said, "Our god I do implore
to help you, dear Rinaldo, evermore."

Rinaldo toward the desert started out,   60
and soon the messenger showed where he thought
(he wasn't very sure) the steed might be.
Rinaldo from Baiardo jumped right down,
and at that very moment the great horse,
which had heard noises in the woods, appeared.
The pagan, upon seeing such a beast,
thought that to watch him from a tree was best,

and therefore climbed one to the very top.   61
Oliver said, "By God, you're practical:
this is the safest way to catch a beast."
The pagan said, "He is a lunatic,
and well I know what one small kick can do.
A sage and a philosopher behaves
just as I did: I've climbed up here, in short,
to give my king an accurate report."

Seeing the Saracen who like a squirrel   62
had taken soon possession of the tree,
said Ricciardetto, "I hope a little bear
detects your hiding place up where you are."
The pagan answered, "Mind your own affairs:
the game of playing safe is dear to all.
I do not want to learn when it's too late.
Is mine but shame? But shame is my old mate."

Baiardo saw the savage horse and grew   63
so restless that no ropes could keep him still:
more than a battle, wanted he that beast.
He ran on top of him and, kicking, biting,
they both had soon their forelegs in midair;
they both revealed the selfsame bloody thirst.
They neighed, they snorted, they each other blasted,
and longer than two hours their battle lasted.

Rinaldo from a distance watched awhile;   64
but, seeing that the fight was going on,
and that with kicks and bitings the brave steed
gave his Baiardo devastating pain,
decided he to act the way he pleased:
so while Baiardo was still battling, he
between the ears a gauntletful released—
and one was quite enough—upon the beast.

Fast, as though lifeless, the wild horse fell down.   65
Baiardo, suddenly afraid, jumped back.
Stunned, a long time he lay upon the ground;
then he regained his senses, looked around.
Immediately Rinaldo went to him,
opened his mouth by holding his hard jaw,
and placed a bit in it, which did the trick:
all of a sudden the wild horse grew meek.

Terigi and the marquis were much amazed.   66
Rinaldo mounted on Baiardo's back,
not bothering to bridle the wild steed,
which came behind him like a little lamb.
From the high tree the Saracen came down,
and hardly could believe what he had seen:
upon that horse he gazed, fearful and diffident,
while watching Lord Rinaldo in awe and wonderment.

In Saragossa everybody ran   67
as soon as our Rinaldo reached the door:
and yet that horse still meekly came behind.
The news was brought to King Marsilius,
who came right down to look; and in her heart
fair Luciana coveted that steed;
and such a present so she seemed to woo,
she begged Rinaldo and her father, too.

Rinaldo, who had given her his heart,   68
was more than glad to give her such a gift.
Soon the right harness for the steed they found,
and when Rinaldo placed the saddle on him,
he let his master treat him like a small
and timid sheep milked by the shepherd's hand.
He mounted him and, turning but his bridle,
wondrously proved the beast was far from idle.

Another day they stayed together, bound   69
by Cupid more than ever all the time,
and then our knights bade the great king goodbye.
On hearing of Orlando's sorry plight,
Marsilius permitted them to go,
and truly gave them everything he owned.
Before her father the young princess sighed
awhile, and then quite openly she cried.

Day after day, most secretly she wept,   70
for with Rinaldo she was deep in love.
Full twenty thousand soldiers she had placed
at his disposal, thus to save his life.
Rinaldo deeply thanked her, and revealed
his love to her before he went away.
"I'll send for them when the time comes," said he,
"but meanwhile let my heart your servant be."

They crossed the whole of Spain, until one day   71
at an enormous forest they arrived,
and they found people in great sadness there.
Rinaldo said, "Not even one I know,"
and called a worthy, bearded vavasor
who seemed to be perturbed and rather grim.
He asked him, "Kindly sir, I'd like to know
the reason why you seem so full of woe."

The bearded man replied, "I'll tell you why   72
there is such lamentation in this place.
We all are from the town that you can see
from here—not even twenty miles away.
Its name is Arma, let me tell you soon.
Alas, we have been chased from our own homes,
and there is nothing that can comfort us
save that we share the same unending loss.

"Vergante is the name of our lord king,   73
maybe the cruelest man that ever lived:
both Christ and Trevigant he still denies.
This wicked man of boundless tyranny
has seized all of our daughters, one by one,
to rape them, and has banished us away;
and every day into his jails are thrust
all those who don't surrender to his lust."

Rinaldo did not like so sad a tale;   74
he left and went right on along his road,
leaving the bearded man in great despair
and all the others in their hopeless grief.
But in the evening toward that town he went.
He turned his horse's bridle toward its door,
and said, "Let's go and look into this matter:
who knows, some fortune we may reap and gather."

Once in the city, to an inn they went,   75
and the innkeeper looked so sad and wan.
They asked him why he was so full of woe,
and he, too, told them of his king's deceit,
so that they all began to wonder why
such a fierce tyrant was still ruling there.
Supper was served and, as one could expect,
they and their steeds were treated with respect.

The good innkeeper seemed an honest man,   76
and much Rinaldo grieved when he was told
that King Vergante kept his daughter still.
He said, "Innkeeper, would you wonder if
I were to give your King Vergant his due,
and dry the tears of every man in town?"
And somewhat our innkeeper was consoled
as in the coming Canto you'll be told.

CANTO   XIV

Father in heaven, King of the Universe,   1
against Whose will no leaf stirs in the air,
allow me not to fall precipitously
while still my spirit's quick and eager most.
From line to line Your song has taken me
midway the threshold: therefore with Your hand
me in soft breezes till the end escort,
taking me safe and sound into the port.

Th' innkeeper thus replied, "I'll call a saint   2
whoever carries out my own revenge."
"Wait till tomorrow," Lord Rinaldo said,
"and in the meantime let's go all to rest.
At daybreak, place our steeds in readiness,
and you will see I mean all that I say."
Rinaldo went to bed; there our young man
thought out a beautiful, successful plan.

Quite early in the morning he arose.   3
The horses had been harnessed by a grateful
innkeeper who, refusing to be paid,
offered, though very poor, all that he had.
At Oliver and Rinaldo, now full-armed,
he looked with boundless admiration: proud
and most invincible they seemed to be,
Baiard and Vegliantìn especially.

Rinaldo toward the palace started out.   4
Yes, looking for the king our hero went,
followed by everybody's eager glance.
There he could hear the sorrowful laments
of the young women. Arrogant and wrathful,
the king caught sight of them and soon inquired,
"Who are you, foolish knights who so much dare?"
This question he had asked of Oliver;

but thus Rinaldo answered soon to him,   5
"I'll give you the reply that you expect,"
and, saying this, drew closer to the throne.
He said, "You are so famous, to be sure,
I cannot understand why God's so slow
in giving you to Beelzebub as food;
treacherous dog, your stinking tyranny
ten leagues away has nauseated me."

The royal hall was full of pagan men,   6
who, laden with disdain, uttered no word:
like hounds they would have gladly torn to bits
that wicked master, worthy but of death.
Rinaldo added, "All alone I want
to punish you, Vergante, with my hands:
I am a pagan, sent by the good grace
of our Mohammed to this very place.

"Brazen, adulterous, infamous knave,   7
   cruel, iniquitous, murderous tyrant
   born of most wicked and excessive heat,
   Heaven no more can bear so grave a sin
   in which so deeply rooted you remain,
   shameless and lustful and most filthy pig,
   cheap, lazy blockhead who should lie and dine
   out of a trough with your companion swine!

"Do you still wear a crown on this your head?   8
   The gallows' miter you should wear instead,
   hater of every just and goodly law,
   hater of God and all created things.
   The lightning with the thunder will arrive,
   though not on Saturday Mahound does pay:
   you the eternal fire will engulf,
   evil and ravenous, perfidious wolf.

"Have you forgotten Heaven is still just,   9
   disgraceful rapist, miserable thief,
   you, fornicator full of every fraud,
   impious cuckold, ruffian of no worth?
   Not even Echo's voice could in the least
   excuse one word of all your wickedness:
   keeping the noble female Saracens—
   once untouched virgins—as your concubines!

"And beating them so harshly every day—   10
   if one of them resisted your desire—
   that I know no one who grieves not for them,
   nor why the deep abysses keep you out."
   Out of his mind Vergante seemed to be
   while on Rinaldo every glance was fixed.
"Heaven has sent him here," some men agreed,
"for what he says is gospel truth indeed."

Vergante did not know what to reply.   11
   The fury and the tempest grew so hard
   that suddenly Rinaldo grabbed the king,
   snatched his most awesome diadem off his head,
   and tore to countless bits his regal clock:
   all men were happy such a feast to see.
   Among that maddened crowd he then and there
   hurlèd the monarch down into the square.

All those who saw so great a feat occur 12
most furiously emptied the great hall,
saying, "It was Mahound allowed all this."
Blessèd all those who could an exit find!
Rinaldo, a most wise and skillful man
able to prove his actions and his words,
all of a sudden with great daring went
where he had heard the women's sad lament.

'Twas there he saw them naked, with their backs 13
all over streaked with vestiges of blood.
He left; out of the palace he could see
the entire population proud of him,
and everybody honoring his worth
and bowing to his most resounding fame.
Closer he drew to all the noblemen,
and so his speech he in this way began:

"The one true God Who first created Adam, 14
and wanted then to die to cleanse his sin,
knowing that all of us were doomed to hell
(and surely He was right and we were wrong),
after a pagan told me of your king,
has made me come to this your very town
to rescue all your daughters from their foe,
and tell you how to Him you all may go.

"Long have you been from His true home away; 15
thus for a long, long time, after your death,
you'll stay acquainted with your false Mahound.
But my good Jesus, just and pitying god,
Whose mercy is forever infinite,
in all His worth and everlasting grace
has sent you here a glimpse of what is true,
and in His timeless kingdom waits for you.

"He could no longer bear the outrage of 16
your wicked lord who so unjustly hurt you:
every wise man must understand from this
a token of His might—my having killed
your king before the presence of his knights.
From Him alone my aid and comfort came,
for it was He so helped in this endeavor
as to preclude any resistance ever.

"'Twas He inspired you—oh, rest assured—   17
in the great course of justice to believe,
for long had He endured him; and right now,
to save you all from the eternal fire,
He wants me to reveal most frankly to you
the error that has slowly grown with you.
Therefore, I beg you all, return to Christ,
for no one goes to heaven unbaptized."

After he spoke, the entire populace   18
began to shout in perfect unison,
"Praised be the man who finally has slain
a king who tortured his own subjects so!
And, since a greater good had to ensue,
let's worship Him who died upon a cross.
Tell us your name, we all most humbly pray,
and with your hand baptize us all today.

"Now that the wicked traitor you have killed,   19
we will, in everlasting memory,
build you a monument of solid gold
and carve upon it this immortal tale."
The prince replied to all, "I am Rinaldo
of Montalban, who gave you victory,
and of my Jesus, Whom you will adore,
the olive and the peace to you I bore."

Concordantly all people shouted then,   20
"Long live Rinaldo!" and "Love live your Jesus!
Everyone here has heard your famous name
and all your deeds a thousand times and more."
And so Rinaldo started to baptize
some of those noblemen with his own hand:
each of them knelt before him in great haste,
fervently wishing to be christened first.

In a few days they all were thus baptized.   21
The innkeeper at whose inn the Christians lodged
did all he could to thank them with his heart.
The joyous tidings reached the vavasor
and all the others whom Rinaldo had met:
wasting no time, they to the city came.
The vavasor, to all known as Balante,
was happy for the death of King Vergante.

If one were now to see those sweet young girls,   22
advancing piously to be baptized
and looking so entranced and beautiful,
he'd surely fall in love with all of them.
The first stars in the sky they seemed to be:
their mothers and their fathers watched in bliss.
There was throughout the town great jubilation—
throughout the castles, too, throughout the nation.

The vavasor of the unbounded forest   23
said to the prince, "I'm grateful most to you,
who came to break that wicked traitor's head.
Know that I am of noble lineage:
you can now have whatever's in my power."
Rinaldo answered, "I would like to know
how many men here in this town might be,
that I could arm and take to war with me."

The vavasor replied, "This land has five   24
other big cities under its dominion:
one hundred thousand pagans can be armed,
not counting all the villages and castles.
I know that I am accurate in this,
and soon you'll see these throngs ready to fight."
Rinaldo, who was quickly so apprised,
expressed his gratitude to Jesus Christ.

Most merrily Rinaldo and his friends   25
for a few days enjoyed their well-earned rest.
The population wished to crown him king,
but this Rinaldo did not want at all.
He said, "In freedom I will leave you soon,
and from now on let Christ be your great Lord."
Then, when the right time came, as he saw fit,
he bade all people in the manor meet,

for there he wished to speak to all of them.   26
He said, "Now that on you I can rely,
I want you all to know the reason why
I have abandoned Paris to come here,
and why I bear such anguish in my heart,
under a burden that destroys my life:
the Admiral of Persia keeps in prison
a man known as Orlando, my dear cousin.

"I wish that you may keep me company   27
until I make Orlando free again."
At the conclusion of his speech, Balante
was chosen as their spokesman by them all:
he in the name of all those barons pledged
that what Rinaldo wanted, he should have.
Therefore Balante, truly a wise man,
stood up and in this fashion he began:

"Rinaldo, don't you know that, having been   28
freed from Mahound, Vergante, and from hell,
we have become, and shall most gladly be,
your slaves and servants for eternity?
Whatever you desire you shall have—
today and ever, if you ever live.
To such an enterprise we'll come with you,
for such a sorry plight now grieves us, too."

Rinaldo thanked them all with all his heart.   29
To every city messengers were sent
immediately, and in no time at all
many a throng was quickly armed for war
and came before Rinaldo at the court:
in less than one short month, before his eyes
full ninety thousand soldiers there convened,
ready for battle and well disciplined.

Two fierce, horrendous giants also came,   30
bringing ten thousand troops, all on their steeds
and all equipped with necessary arms:
both of them had renounced their god Mahound,
and willingly had come to serve Rinaldo.
Of these two giants—rather mighty towers—
the first was known to all men as Corante,
whereas the second's name was Liorgante.

The latter, who once loved his master much,   31
seeing Rinaldo who had killed him, grew
suddenly sad within his heart, and spoke
thus to Balante: "He unjustly died,
and since I was his servant and his friend,
this outrage I cannot easily bear,
for my disdain is surely deep and true.
By my new faith, I cannot come with you."

Rinaldo said, "Maybe you spoke the truth,
if, as you say, you will not come with me.
O mighty giant, you'll remain here dead:
in Christ you don't believe nor in Mahound."
Fickle and proud, the giant then replied,
"Wait till I grab you by your hairlock, man,
and I will teach you a gigantic lesson
once and for all, Vergante's loose assassin."

Rinaldo's little patience, to be sure,
collided with the giant's very well.
Rinaldo then and there unsheathed his sword
and thrust its pointed edge so fiercely deep
into the giant's breast, he passed him through
and in his loins then let his weapon land:
poor Liorgante could not use his mattock, stricken
and falling dead at once like a small chicken—

no, like a mighty tower he fell down.
At such a roaring din all people ran,
asking each other, "What has happened?" and,
when they were told the thing that had occurred,
all of them said, "This we cannot deny:
that traitor loved Vergante very much,
and even said he had been wrongly killed."
Rinaldo then was cheered by the whole field.

Following wise Balante's good advice,
Rinaldo sent a messenger at once
to Saragossa to inform the fair
and famous Luciana of his wish:
he very warmly begged her to advance
with all her men and in all secrecy;
he begged her all her promises to keep.
Few days were needed for the courier's trip.

Joyously Luciana welcomed him,
and told her father what the prince had written.
Marsilius said to her, "Let all your knights
and all your regiments be ready soon.
In all my thoughts I shall forever hold
our dear Rinaldo and his wondrous deeds,
for by his kindness I was deeply charmed."
Thus in no time at all, all troops were armed.

32

33

34

35

36

Sweet Luciana said, "This grace I ask— 37
that you allow me, sir, to go with them,
and if I fail to honor your great blood,
command me nevermore to wear a sword.
This is the time your race will bloom anew."
Marsilius said, "Do as you wish, provided
we fully please our dear Rinaldo. See,
I'm much more eager than you seem to be."

To Balugante the fair damsel spoke: 38
"O Balugante, come along with me
and with the men I'm leading to the East
to give this enterprise a brighter light."
And he so answered, "By my Trevigant,
under your flag I willingly will come."
Thus twenty thousand horsemen were all ready
at the command of this most brave young lady.

The princess bade Marsilius farewell 39
and with her full-armed horsemen left at last.
As emblem on her flag there were two hearts
by the same chain each to the other bound.
A rich pavilion she also brought,
that would arouse the envy of all men—
a tapestry so fine, so rich and rare,
the like of which was never seen elsewhere.

The news that Luciana had arrived 40
reached, after a few days, Rinaldo's ear.
Many a baron suddenly he called,
and with the highest of them on their steeds
was on his way to meet the lady fair.
As soon as he could see her dazzling light,
Rinaldo said, "Jesus is born anew
if such a star here in the East I view."

Dismounted, there she was before his eyes— 41
which made Rinaldo very sorely grieve,
seeing himself in chivalry surpassed.
Quickly he, too, dismounted, uttering words
of apology, and gazing on her face
just as an eagle gazed upon the sun.
The princess greeted him, naturally,
and "Welcome, lovely lady," answered he.

Back on their horses, all of them went then   42
into the city with great feast and cheers.
Before the mighty palace down they jumped,
and thus the lady spoke: "O my dear lord,
a rich pavilion I have brought to you—
a token of my everlasting love:
your Luciana wrought it with her hands
with threads of gold and Syrian silken strands."

She had it then displayed before his eyes.   43
When Lord Rinaldo that pavilion saw,
he marveled at its excellence, and said,
"Surely I fail to understand what goddess
could ever such magnificence achieve
if not Athena," and profusely thanked her,
adding, "What reason orders, I will do—
keep it as token of my love for you."

In the main hall the rich pavilion then   44
was soon displayed. It was divided into
four equal parts, each representing one
of the four elements. The first of them
was so red-bright, and with such art achieved,
indeed it looked like a true fire lit—
so radiant, so sparkling, so ablaze,
it fully dazzled the onlooker's gaze.

Rubies, carbuncles had been set on it,   45
with the main color blended perfectly;
garnets and balases were there, so fine
they radiated splendor all about.
And there were cherubim and seraphim
as in the fire of eternal love.
There was the salamander still aflame,
utterly happy in its festive game.

The second part portrayed the cloudless air,   46
all blue, and the whole sky with every star,
the moon, the sun, Venus and Mercury,
with Jove nearby and Vulcan hammering hard;
Saturn and Mars with features most severe,
and the twelve signs and many more fair things—
so many there's no time to list them, though.
Many a bird was seen to fly below.

An eagle, widely veering, flew above,   47
fixing the sun, as she is wont to do,
so keenly that the sun her feathers burnt,
making her headlong fall into the sea;
but with new feathers there she decked herself,
resuming thus her youthfulness once more:
and the new phoenix, as she's ever done,
laid her new nest above, much closer to the sun;

but myrrh and incense she had taken first,   48
cassia, amomum, balsam, spikenard,
till she was burnt and on the top reborn.
There was the tame, there was the savage hawk—
one obviously the foe of every dove,
the other plunging with the heron down.
The goshawk with the pheasant was in sight,
also the tercel studying the partridge's flight.

There was the falcon and there was the magpie,   49
apparently most eager high to prance,
and while she flew, a mighty din she made;
there was the little skylark whirling by,
with her own murderous enemy close behind;
the merganser was seen to dash from sky
to earth, preceded by the nimble swallow,
though neither seemed in any way to follow.

Many a crane closely together flew,   50
and the preceding ones seemed loud to cry;
also the geese after their leader went,
docilely following behind his wings.
The little springtime turtledove was there,
but did not seem to nest among green boughs:
unhappy most, of mates no longer fond,
she bathed—it seemed—inside a muddy pond.

With blood from his own breast, the pelican   51
fed his own little ones and gave them life.
There were the wader, the gray partridge, fearing
lest any bird who saw them do them ill;
closing the claws of every buzzing fly,
the kite was basking in his own delight;
many a vulture there was seen to hover,
and there the kestrel loved the wind—his mover.

Even the glede was hovering up high,   52
while festively the jay was screaming near;
down the kingfisher with much clamor came,
seeking the plainland in a stormy roar;
wagging her tail, the wagtail too was there,
and, also there, the hoopoe raised his crest;
the fly-hawk, too, was seen to feed on fable,
than his own brother being much less able.

With many a jolt there the woodpecker flew   53
(not long ago, a fool bought one of them—
thinking it was a parrot—for three *lire,*
and sent it as a gift to Corsignano,
thus making Siena blush until this day).
The oriole was there with the fig-sparrow,
and genuine parrots could also be seen,
one black, one white, one scarlet, and one green.

Close to each other, many starlings went,   54
bearing an olive twig within their beaks;
the crows made a great tumult in the air,
and there the sparrow, full of malice, flew,
seemingly proud of all her wicked deeds.
There was the raven, come from Noah's Ark,
and so the owl, and so the rook appeared,
cawing and croaking after every bird.

Proud and self-loving, there the peacock stood,   55
crying when fixing on the ground his gaze.
Heron and duck and turkey were still there;
so was the quail, which seemed so weary flying
from region to far region; and there was
the swan that crosses every lengthy sea,
the white duck and the cormorant—oh, look—
seemed to fly down to bathe within a brook.

The palmiped, the woodcock, and the stork,   56
the many-colored-feathered little hen,
the Holy-Mary's bird, the plunging martin
were also there, with a white swan that slept
upon a stream and, being close to death,
seemed to be singing his accustomed song.
With both their goiter and their sharp long beak,
there was the ostrich and there was the drake.

Teals and wild ducks and water hens were seen   57
with other water birds I could not name;
some little birds that are as halcyons known
and make the sea aware of their loud nests;
other large birds that are bee-eaters called,
so many that I cannot list them all:
they live on river and on lake and marsh,
all of them fond of water and of fish.

The ocean- and the tree- and the rock-thrush,   58
the blackbird and the blackbird of the rills,
the missel and the hawfinch and the linnet,
the nightingale of the melodious throat,
the mountain linnet, crossbill, bobolink,
the shrike, the wryneck, and the meadowlark—
they all were there with the red-breasted bird
and with the siskin I have never heard.

The wood lark and the goldfinch, too, were there;   59
the bullfinch that is wholly red and black,
the chaffinch and the greenfinch bright as gold,
the beccafico and the ortolan;
even the little monarch of the bush,
the titmouse and the warbler and the blackcap,
the pipit with the tail both long and red,
and a strange bird that is by mushrooms fed.

House martins, swallows hovered in midair,   60
and in a distant corner, all alone,
the solitary, pensive sparrow sat,
forever glad to be but by herself,
unmindful and mistrustful of all else.
In her small wickedness the cuckoo stood—
the bird that her own eggs both lays and matches
with those that her wet nurse, not knowing, hatches.

Also, the bat was weirdly flitting by   61
with many other night birds lost in darkness:
the owl, the barn owl, and the hornèd owl
with all their many most unhappy kin:
all of the birds accounted for by Noah
were reproduced on that pavilion.
The last of all was the chameleon—
the griffon, he, according to someone.

Beaming and fair, right in the midst of it,   62
crowned Juno was embroidered on her throne,
with Deiopeia and the other nymphs
surrounding her and honoring her worth.
Aeolus seemed another storm to rouse,
knocking upon the heavy-bolted door:
Notus and Aquilon at once came out,
and suddenly Orion, tempest-fraught.

Daedalus could be seen, who, having lost   63
his son, was sadly pounding at his brow
(ah, why had he not heeded his advice?).
Phaëthon could control his coach no more
and was already in the Scorpio's claws,
and as he fell precipitously down
and the scorched earth opened its mouth, athirst,
by Jove's great lightning he was struck and cursed.

The third part of the work portrayed the sea.   64
One could most easily detect the whale
that can make often many a vessel sink,
and one could hear the Siren's lulling song
that in old days made seamen fall asleep.
There was the dolphin in the act of showing
his back above the waves, thus to inform
the mariners about the coming storm.

The sea cow could be sighted coming out;   65
also the flying gurnard could be seen,
while the sea-thrush was standing idly by.
Ready to trap the oyster was the crab:
a little straw right in his mouth he showed,
and when he saw her open up, at once
he laid it in the slightly opened shell,
sneaked right inside, and swallowed her as well.

The turbot and the ray, the shark were there,   66
the salmon, the red mullet, and the spider,
with the sea scorpion, sharp and wicked most.
Lobster and sole, dory and sturgeon, too,
and the weird-looking, ugly octopus;
the mullet and the trout and carp were seen,
the shrimp, the mussel, and the cuttlefish,
moray and mackerel—any kind you wish.

Long schools of tuna there were being caught,   67
and there were lampreys and there were sardines,
with other fish of such varieties
one cannot list them in a hundred tongues—
fish from all streams and lakes and different ponds,
and as we know, there are more fish than stars:
eels, pikes, and tenches, species now extinct
upon that great pavilion had been limned.

There was the barbel and there was the roach,   68
and the anchovy there was quite distinct:
deep in the water he was much alive,
but seemed to be quite lifeless out of it.
The falling manna could be sighted there
with the fish waiting for it right beneath;
there was the fisherman with bait and net,
sweating and trying many a new deceit.

Then one could see god Neptune with his trident   69
gazing with admiration and suspicion
on the ship *Argo* crossing his domain
and steered by Tiphys toward the Colchis land.
Scylla was heard to bark most cruelly,
and her companion monsters showed their snouts.
One could see Thetis, one could see Ulysses,
who sailed beyond the pillars of Hercules.

Cymothoe and Triton calmed the storm,   70
and, sweetly floating, Glaucus soon appeared.
Searching for his Hesperia, Aesacus
sadly below the water tried to go.
Oft Galatea emerged to show her face,
thus making Polyphemus fall in love.
The Trojan ships, transmuted into nymphs,
were swimming with both hands across the sea.

And ships and vessels in large quantity   71
one could see there, with boats of every shape:
whalers and galleons and galleasses
and brigantines and caravels and trawlers,
lugsails, sagittae, pitch-smeared gondolas,
and cutters forward brought by rowing hands;
fishing boats, dinghies, skiffs, and boats of many a size,
carrying various things and men and merchandise.

The last part of the work portrayed the earth.   72
All herbs and plants were represented there,
and one could see the globe contract and close
with all the famous cities drawn on it,
with all the animals, some of which roamed
in western and then some in eastern lands;
and other creatures, tame and wild as well,
both in the south and north were seen to dwell.

Massive, indeed, the elephant appeared,   73
hardened and black and all one piece in front:
downward he spread his very ample ears
and stretched his long proboscis to pick up,
according to his nature, all his food;
only a Moor could touch him—no one else.
Two tusks out of his mouth one could well see—
full six spans long and made of ivory.

The lion and the jackal came behind.   74
There was the famous horse that bore no reins
together with the donkey, the meek ox,
and the most vicious and most stubborn mule.
The beaver could be seen that, very wise,
chooses the lesser evil to survive:
he cuts and leaves his genitals behind
for the pursuing hunter soon to find.

The leopard there appeared full of disdain   75
for having leapt three times to catch his prey.
Sweetly asleep, the unicorn was seen
upon a maiden's lap: by her alone
he wanted to be both caressed and combed;
he did not trust the water, so it seemed:
he had to test it first with his horn in,
and watched it if it was all soiled or clean.

Bizarre and very savage was the bear;   76
the wolf, out of the woods shamefully driven,
was cursed by men and torn to bits by dogs.
There was the pig, utterly grimed with mud;
there was the roebuck that had run for miles
and, out of breath, was now about to drink;
the singing shepherd had entranced the deer
in order to transfix it with his spear.

There was the buffalo, which can be caught   77
by the nose only, with the little goat
and the meek sheep already milked and sheared.
The very wretched and most frightened hare
seemed still to run from peril fast away.
There was the dromedary with the camel
that on his knees, most affable and meek,
accepts upon his hump the heavy yoke.

Replete with every malice was the fox,   78
while ever-faithful still the dog appeared.
There was the rabbit playing in full bliss,
and with sharp senses there the boar was seen.
Look at the doe, and now look at the lynx,
able to see his prey beyond the mountain.
All families of badger still were there,
sleeping inside a hole, inside a lair.

The thorny, feathered hedgehog, too, was there,   79
and, waiting with painstaking patience over
the mouse's little hole, the cat was sure
of the success of his insidiousness.
The beaver and the dormouse, lost and sleepy,
the skunk and the beech-marten and the squirrel,
there was the otter thirsty for new slaughter
and therefore jumping in and off the water.

Cercopithecus, Barbary ape, baboon,   80
wild sheep, chamois, and musk deer and sable,
the little weasel and the spotless ermine
looking so white, immaculate and pure;
southern and northern martens were there, too;
also, the chipmunk far away from all,
and every sucking beast so white and nice
together with the others full of vice.

There was the spotted leopard and the panther,   81
the dragon that had slain the elephant
and afterward most stupidly was killed
by the same beast that fell upon him dead,
for he had not foreseen his own quick end.
There was the arrogant, conceited serpent,
exhaling lively flames out of his mouth
and poisoning all he touchèd with his breath.

Full of deceit and fraud, the crocodile
had killed a man and now was mourning him;
there was the asp that, having seen his charmer,
in order not to hear his uttered words,
kept one ear lowered to the ground below
and one completely covered with his tail.
There was the basilisk who, looking grim,
killed with his hissing those who looked at him.

The seven-headed hydra, the cerastes,
the viper that explodes when giving birth,
the reptile that's so clever and so wise
in shedding off his skin 'tween stone and stone,
the heedless asp much colder than a slab
and eager to wound people with his tail:
the water snake and the green lizard, too,
with others I won't list were there in view.

One could see the hyena, cold and fierce,
dig every corpse out of its sepulcher:
those who know well her habits say of her
that she can imitate the human voice;
chelydri with their dark and horrid looks,
jaculi ever running nimble most,
and then phareans but in Libya found,
and, last of all, the mole deep in the ground.

Forlorn and wretched, Ceres then was seen
in her still-grievous quest throughout the earth:
wherever she arrived, she seemed to ask
if anyone had seen her Proserpine,
saying, "I've lost her, and do not know when."
Meanwhile, out for a walk, the lovely girl,
embroidered on the canvas right beneath,
of violets and roses wove a wreath,

and Pluto then was seen abducting her.
The whole pavilion was thus adorned:
the gems and the carbuncles studded on it
transmuted into daylight a dark night—
a work of art in Syria never seen.
It spread around three hundred feet and more,
and all the ropes and strings it was tied on
were silk and gold, much brighter than the sun.

82

83

84

85

86

Rinaldo could not feast his eyes enough   87
upon that marvel, saying, "I am sure
in heaven Luciana did all this,
not Philomela in a desert place.
Never will this my heart abandon her.
I know I don't deserve so great a gift,
yet anything of lesser excellence
would not become your great magnificence.

"This I will keep forever for your love,   88
this I will keep as the most worthy thing,
this I will keep with everlasting pride,
this I will keep as proof of your great skill,
this I will keep forever in my heart,
this I will keep—a token of your own,
this I will keep as long as here I dwell,
this I will keep in heaven or in hell."

The princess said, "Now listen to my words.   89
The very sun I'd give you as a gift,
but that would not suffice for such a friend.
Just as in ancient days your noble heart
appears magnanimous and great today.
Now let me tell the truth about this work.
Not Luciana—I must make amends—
'twas Love who did all this with his own hands."

Now is there any heart made of such steel   90
or porphyry or jasper or the like
as would not open up and quickly change?
Not only all the arrows that he had—
Love hurled his quiver and his bow as well.
Rinaldo (now his voice began to choke)
wished to the lovely princess to reply,
but he could not—his voice had said goodbye.

The wise young lady, noticing it was   91
excessive love had made him speechless, said,
"Am I so wild a woman as to be
unworthy of a lover such as you
until a better time and better place?
And who would not do anything for you,
provided fame and honor she recover?
Ungrateful she who does not love a lover!"

Although a thousand darts were in his heart,
Rinaldo finally profusely thanked
the lovely lady for her cherished words,
and most especially for her last phrase.
Praised by all people, the pavilion was
brought to a chamber in the royal palace.
There many wonders started to unfold,
which in the coming Canto will be told.

92

C A N T O   X V

Benevolent Majesty, Celestial Life,
with light endowing both our hemispheres,
the source of every holy, endless thing,
grant me the grace that in Your lawful reign
right at Your holy feet my soul may know
the difference between the false and true:
I beg You, if my prayer You commend,
to guide my feeble mind until the end.

1

Rinaldo and Balante both agreed
that all the Christian troops should march at once,
and soon wage war upon the Admiral,
for this was also Luciana's wish.
In no time the news reached the Persian land
that a mighty pagan multitude was coming,
but no one to the Admiral had said
whose troops they were, and that Vergant was dead.

2

Therefore one hundred twenty thousand brave
and proud and great and ever-dauntless men
(according to our author's private list)
with Luciana's Spanish troops advanced.
They did not move—believe me—in single file:
they covered every mountain, every field,
till to the Persian region they all went
and round the city pitched their every tent.

3

Rinaldo, who was restless night and day,
his cousin's freedom ever on his mind,
when all his mighty men were safely lodged,
sent Ricciardetto to the Admiral,
saying, "Go quick to him, and here come back
with his reply: convince him that he must,
either in single fight or open war,
wasting no precious time, come to the fore."

4

And Ricciardetto, as he had been told,
went to the Admiral with his request.
Most arrogant, the Admiral replied
that he knew not who all these soldiers were,
and was by the whole matter much amazed.
His crown, forever honored everywhere,
was not accustomed in the East to fight
any plebeian, cheap, and worthless knight:

5

he first should find another king like him,
and only then would he reply to him—
that is, prove in a duel his own worth.
He would not hear of any open war
without a plausible or lawful cause.
These very words he even added then:
"If you were not an envoy duly sent,
I would have hanged you with this very hand.

6

"Shame—not compassion—made me change my mind.
To him who sent you, then, bring this reply:
ask him if he's awake or dreaming still,
for his proposal is a foolish one.
There's no more reason why you should be here:
therefore I beg you to depart at once."
But Ricciardetto could not patient be,
and therefore answered most disdainfully:

7

"If you knew well the man who sent me here,
you would not deem him worthless, to be sure,
nor would you call his fair proposal foolish;
but now your inner cowardice I see.
Know, then, that if down here you're known as king
(even if I could bear such haughtiness,
O Admiral, O proud and stupid man),
Morocco has become my lord's domain.

8

"He's also king of both Carrara and Arma,   9
and owns many more kingdoms on this earth.
Why, Mars himself would by no one be blamed
should he resolve to fight with such a man."
The Admiral, who saw him so incensed,
answered, "Then in this way I will reply:
Go to the lord who sent you here, and say
I'll delegate a champion right away."

Fast Ricciardetto to his camp returned   10
and told what had occurred—in other words,
all that the Admiral had had to say.
But now we'll let these people rest awhile,
musing upon the messenger's report,
and to the Admiral retrace our steps.
Frightened, he was in such a sorry state,
he felt upon his heart a mighty weight.

Seeing him so dismayed, said Chiariella,   11
"A most effective remedy I know.
You know Orlando is the greatest man
that ever mounted horse—and this is all
I have to say to you who see yourself
reduced to such a siege here in this place.
Know, then, the man you keep here in your dungeon
is Count Orlando, Milon's very son.

"He for my love will do—this I believe—   12
all that I ask, for he himself has so
promised me countless times: I am the one
who, since he was arrested, honored him."
The Admiral, rejoicing at such news,
replied, "By god Mahound, is he the one?
I'm glad that all this kindness you have shown
to one whom Heaven made one of our own.

"But he must promise me he will return   13
right back to prison when the fight is done,
lest the Great Sultan should be cross with me,
for well you know I took him for his sake.
After all this, we must devise a way
whereby to make his freedom possible."
Thus Chiariella to Orlando went,
eager on every detail to comment.

"If for my love, Orlando, you accept
    to fight the man who's come for action here,
    your favor I will carve in this my heart
    forevermore until Mahound allows.
    My life and honor I commend to you,
    and therefore give you a full-harnessed steed."
    Orlando then replied, "So be it! Listen—
    to die is better than to rot in prison."

"Ah," Chiariella said, "is this the thing
    that I have promised you a thousand times?
    You with a knife have pierced this heart of mine,
    and now I'm here to open up these doors
    just as you wish, O my most lovely lord.
    But only to impede a mighty fire,
    I have been waiting until Charles came here
    to make the deed more obvious appear.

"Forget the promise that you must return
    right back to prison, as my father wants.
    By god Mahound, I'll come to free you, long
    before the sun for many a day comes down.
    I'll keep your steed and armor yours to take."
    Such were the words that Chiariella spoke,
    and Count Orlando, out of prison, free,
    was taken now the Admiral to see.

The Admiral embraced him cordially,
    and most profusely then apologized:
    much he regretted having done him wrong,
    and placed on the Great Sultan all the blame:
    he sold himself for peace at any cost,
    as often men for their own profit do:
    he used all means of stratagem and strife—
    to save his kingdom and to save his life.

Wise as he was, Orlando much rejoiced,
    saying, "Your daughter's love will make me do
    all that I can and must, to please your heart:
    'tis Chiariella that inspires me.
    This much I know: without her I'd be dead;
    it is a miracle I'm still alive."
    He armed himself before the pagan king,
    and Chiariella helped him in this thing.

Utterly armed, he jumped up on his steed,   19
and, also armed, sweet Chiariella with
three hundred horsemen kept him company.
Thus of the Admiral he took his leave,
and forward marched against the enemy.
As soon as Lord Rinaldo, himself armed
and vigilant in his tent, saw him advance,
gladly his charger mounted he at once.

He had been armed by Luciana dear,   20
who also lent the horse he'd given her
in Saragossa, and had come with him
bringing along as many horsemen (thus
making the game as even as could be).
Rinaldo toward Orlando rode, and soon
greeted the count with boundless courtesy—
and his reply could not but equal be.

Indeed, each of them tried his very best   21
to make his voice unrecognizable
so as to bring his action to success.
After his greetings, thus Rinaldo spoke:
"I do believe, O knight, you took the field
to prove that you are what a knight should be:
very well, then, let's prove each other's worth."
So one of them rode south, the other, north.

With so much skill Orlando at this point   22
shook, in departing, his own charger's rein,
no one had ever seen such chivalry.
Sweet Luciana most intently watched
what seemed to her an act of mighty skill,
while Chiariella spoke so to herself:
"This is the knight the world acclaims as one
of the most clever and best heroes known."

Rinaldo was the first to turn his horse,   23
and, as he used to, started to assail.
Thinking that he had not yet turned around,
Orlando turned at once and faced him fast.
But neither prose nor rhyme can here describe
the very worth each of the two displayed:
Marcello one, and Hannibal the other;
one flew, and one a nimble bird was rather.

Much dust and lively sparks one only saw.
I do not know whether, beneath great Troy,
Achilles won high Hector in renown,
each showing signs of daring past belief.
But is there any need of footnotes here
in order to convince the blind and deaf?
Are they not both great paladins of France,
the most undaunted knights to wield a lance?

24

At the same time their lances both broke down
upon their shields while both their steeds went forth
as lightning comes in a most fleeting glow.
Against each other came they with their swords
while everyone drew closer just to watch,
and it was then the horrid fight resumed.
The giant, named Corante, came to see—
with Luciana—what the end would be.

Just like a solid tower there he stood,
watching the mighty tempest of the two.
On her Rinaldo Luciana herself
had placed a cloak that was a joy to see;
but, furious and flaming, now the count
had with his Durlindana imprinted it.
Grieving, poor Luciana, pale and wan,
sighed, "Never have I seen so strong a man."

26

So flaming and so furious were they—
Rinaldo and our Count Orlando—that
they hardly saw each other in their wrath.
There was no vantage point on either side.
Wounding each other with their sparkling swords,
each told the other with each falling blow,
"Here, bastard dog! Now save yourself from this!"
and words were followed by the weapon's hiss.

With his Frusberta, suddenly Rinaldo
struck Count Orlando on his helmet's crest
so very hard, it soon came whistling down.
All his life never had he felt such pain:
utterly bending on his horse's back,
"O God," he said, "don't make me die, and you,
O Holy Virgin Mary, see my plight!"
But, although shaken, he returned to fight.

28

He drew his Durlindana with such wrath, 29
he landed it upon the prince's helmet,
which instantly resounded like a bell,
hardly withstanding the horrendous blow.
With her own eyes sweet Luciana saw
everything, and that blow she did not like:
Rinaldo, staggering, on his horse's neck
bent down and with great difficulty rose back.

With two more blows like that one, to be sure, 30
he would have quickly wandered far afield;
he came to, and was quite himself again.
But the sword landed on the charger's mane,
splitting his neck into two equal parts:
Rinaldo and his horse fell down at once.
"You traitor!" to the count Rinaldo said,
"'twas out of cowardice you killed my steed."

Orlando thus replied, "In all my life, 31
never have I been called a traitor; I
instead have always been a gentle knight.
Now if I hit your charger with my blow,
I'm sorry for it, and apologize.
But long before you leave my sight, I will
compel you to retract the word you've said."
This spoken, jumped he quickly from his steed.

And so they started the most bitter fight 32
that was between two heroes ever fought.
Each tore the other's shield to countless bits:
dragons they seemed to be, and knights no more.
Breastplate and hauberk well withstood all blows,
but the two fighters oft were on their knees,
each of them blowing, roaring, wrath-obsessed—
a lion or some other savage beast.

They hit each other now with cutting blows, 33
now with backhand and now with tip of sword;
each other's teeth beneath their helmets sounded,
and so with piercing weapons they both searched
each other's flesh as if to drive out fish.
The better and the faster to succeed,
each of them doubled every falling blow,
making clouds tremble with the earth below.

Rinaldo raised his great Frusberta now
to punish Count Orlando on the head;
Orlando stepped aside, causing the sword
to miss him and fall down with boundless storm:
much deeper than a foot it pierced the ground.
Imagine what that weapon would have done!
So mighty and so blinding was his wrath,
he hardly could remove it from the earth.

34

Hurling himself against Rinaldo then,
thus Count Orlando shouted, "Well I could,
as you can see, now pierce you to the bone
since you have pierced the earth instead of me,
but this I want to stress—that well I could—
but, being not a traitor, I will not."
"You are quite right," Rinaldo said; "therefore
a traitor I won't call you anymore."

It was already evening, and the sun
plunged in the Spanish sea its golden mane.
Gracious and ever-regal Chiariella
with boundless kindness spoke to both of them:
"Since the whole field's already growing dark,
please put an end to such a cruel fight.
And if you love me, then do this for me:
a truce of twenty days I want to see."

36

They both agreed, and both were satisfied.
And Chiariella added, "I admit
I never saw two braver knights than you,
nor will I ever see them in my days.
All over I'm still trembling when I think
of all your bravery and dauntless blows:
so that such worth be spared and seen anew,
I want my truce honored by both of you."

Rinaldo with Balante went right back
to the pavilion, where his Luciana
helped him disarm as she had helped him arm.
Back to the pagan city went Orlando,
where Chiariella told the Admiral
that what Orlando had done before her eyes
no other mortal man could ever do,
adding and sighing, "Love him as I do."

38

Orlando wanted to return to jail,
therefore surrendered Durlindan and armor,
and spoke to Chiariella a bit more.
Let's now go back to the field in the plain.
The day before, Corante had armed himself,
saying, "I want to fight and try my luck."
Below the city walls he came, and, quite
ready—a ban announced—he was to fight.

In front of full five hundred chosen men—
the best of his whole camp—he had appeared;
now mounted on a steed of grayish mane
born of an Arab mare, he proudly rode,
and, hurling insults at the Admiral,
shouted, "From me you cannot save yourself,
nor can you hope for truce or any treaty,
being a man deserving of no pity."

Several pagans had already come
out of the city, challenging the giant,
but soon he slaughtered them like helpless dogs,
here severing a shoulder, there a head,
and wielding blows so brutal and so fierce,
nobody any longer dared advance
ten feet or even less toward such a club—
a necessary prudence in that mob.

Soon Chiariella heard that the Saracen
had crushed already many heads like eggs,
and made in terror all her people run.
Fast to Orlando's jail she went, and said
to him, "Now more than ever, paladin,
I need your help or I am wholly lost:
I came to tell you that a giant's here
who slaughters every person coming near.

"You are my only refuge; here I am
begging you not to leave me so dismayed.
I think the man must be a little mad:
he frightens all, and fears not even God.
Wasting no time, you must come out with me,
for all our population shakes with fear,
and by that mattock more than terrified,
all of my men have locked themselves inside.

39

40

41

42

43

"He has already clubbed a hundred men,
and now is grinding other nerves and bones."
Orlando answered, "Chiariella dear,
I am already where you bid me go.
I know that if your people wait for me
down on the field, they will be rescued soon."
He asked for both his armor and his horse,
and Chiariella helped him up, of course.

She also bade several soldiers arm,
although Orlando asked for but a few,
saying that of the giant he'd take care.
And quickly Chiariella armed herself
and, like Orlando, jumped up on her steed
with admirable nimbleness and skill.
Her brother, a young man of valiant frame,
went out with her (Copardo was his name).

The giant at the door was waiting still:
as soon as them he saw, he forward moved.
But just as Chiariella saw him ride,
"I want to fight this man," she bravely said,
"if you, Orlando, grant this grace to me."
Orlando answered that he was quite pleased.
The princess, then, against the pagan went,
and he awaited her with spear in hand.

Quick, Chiariella lowered then her lance
and broke it on the giant's very chest,
but, being strong and mountainous, he budged
upon his charger's saddle not at all;
instead he hit the princess's shield so hard
with his ferocious and most valiant spear,
he made her, then and there, fall from her steed—
which deeply saddened Milon's son, indeed.

Corante thought he'd grab her by the arm
and, like a wolf, now snatch her fast away.
Orlando said, "Don't touch her! If you do,
by everything I do believe, I swear
that I will thrust my sword into your breast.
Move on, you stupid, cowardly buffoon!
I pity you your cowardice—God knows—
but all wild grass—'tis certain—also grows.

Are you not yet ashamed, you lustful dog,
who thought you could abduct so great a lady?
In all the regions ruled by the great sun,
no one deserves more genuine reverence.
Think not it was your valor made her fall,
but rest assured it was her charger's fault."
The giant said, "By god Mahound, that's true!
My prisoner I'll give as gift to you."

49

Orlando answered, "A wise man you are,
who give as gift what you could never sell.
If you could only gaze upon her eyes
you'd say, 'This is no food for one like me—
a most uncouth and rough and savage man.'
Partridge is much too good for teeth like yours."
Copardo, to avenge his sister then,
all of a sudden dashed upon the man.

50

Each of them, brandishing a spear, at once
challenged the other with concordant will;
but poor Copardo to the ground fell soon,
and was the giant's helpless prisoner.
'Twas then Corante to Orlando said,
"I hope you understand this man is mine."
And so, surrendering to justice, went
Copardo to the giant's very tent.

51

"Well, this young lady, too," the giant said,
"should be my prisoner, but since I threw
her from her horse, I claim her now no more.
If so I wanted, I would let you have her,
for you have said I've given you as gift
the very one that I have failed to sell."
"So be it then," Orlando quickly said;
"with arms, not words, the lady's to be had."

52

Replied the giant, "Then I challenge you,
who took my very prey away from me,
and are now threatening and calling me
a coward for a gift I'm giving you:
out of my courtesy to you I gave
this lady, and you still believe me not."
Orlando let his horse's bridle go,
and took as much field as an arrow's throw.

53

The giant had well earned his tip, and so   54
Orlando turned and met his lowered lance.
Our count put his into his belly fast,
and pierced his breast, his heart, his kidneys too,
letting it go two feet the other side:
and it was then a mountain crumbled down.
Corante—look! quite loose his bridles hang—
falls to the ground with a resounding bang.

In his pavilion Rinaldo said,   55
as young Copardo fell a prisoner,
that just for fun he would go back to fight,
sorry to see so brave a youngster bound,
who by his god Mahound had sworn to him
that, from the giant had he not been freed,
he would most gladly do all that he willed;
and therefore he inspected the whole field.

Right at this time the sudden news arrived—   56
Corante, thrown from horse, had quickly died,
pierced by the iron spear from side to side.
Rinaldo was much saddened by the news,
and wanted to hear well the killer's name,
eager so vile a murder to avenge.
He swore that he would cut and maim and rend
as soon as the sworn truce came to an end.

Copardo in the camp had understood   57
that, oh, Orlando's cousin was right there.
Seeing, therefore, Rinaldo so incensed,
he said, "Will you forgive me, paladin?
Judging by what I heard from your own men,
with little wine we'll celebrate our peace.
Things I will tell you that will please you most,
and put an end to such a holocaust.

"I want to tell you that the very man   58
you fought is Count Orlando, now in jail:
I'll take him here to you, and this I swear
by the god worshiped in my native land."
Remembering the man who fought with him,
Rinaldo was still marveling at his prowess:
now he was sure Orlando was the knight—
the only one to go through such a fight.

"And if my sister," so Copardo said,   59
"were not so very deeply still in love
 with all his fame and matchless bravery,
 today he would no longer be alive,
 because my father did not know the man.
 But when she saw her city all besieged,
 'twas Chiariella who proposed one remedy—
 that he might chase the foe, should Orlando be free.

Yet, fearing the Great Sultan, he detained   60
 the count without permission to depart.
 But here, you now are here, armed as you are:
 I'll put the entire town at your command,
 so sad have I been made by the sad plight
 of such an excellent and worthy man.
 So much my sister loves him that, therefore,
 she would by treason open any door."

Rinaldo, with his heart now overwhelmed   61
 by tender sweetness, hugged Copardo soon,
 and said, "My cousin I so greatly love,
 I feel already overcome with joy.
 I know that perfect truth has moved your words
 if I have understood your report well;
 and Chiariella, so I swear, will be
 lauded forever for her courtesy.

"I think that to the town you should return,   62
 and say to Chiariella everything.
 Then, in due time, inform me. I am sure
 that this my plan will finally succeed.
 Implicitly I trust your loyalty
 and therefore make no other deal with you."
 He gave him, then, his armor and his steed,
 and soon before his father he appeared.

"Who sent you to me?" asked the Admiral.   63
 Copardo answered, "I have run away."
 The Admiral replied, "Then you did wrong,"
 but added, "Maybe all is for the good
 I did not let you swing some time ago."
 To his dear Chiariella went Copardo,
 and everything at once with her discussed:
 needless to say, the girl was happy most.

Back to his dungeon had Orlando gone   64
the very day he felled Corante slain.
To this conclusion the young lady came—
she should betray both land and Admiral,
and at the same time her Mahound renounce:
now you can see what faithful love can do.
She left Copardo and quickly found her way
to her Orlando, who in prison lay.

To him she said, "What would you think, Sir Knight,   65
if your Rinaldo suddenly came here
to free you from the jail in which you lie,
and, told you are the one who fought with him
and even dared to kill his running steed,
by consequence refused to give you help?
If one should ask you, would you not agree
you were ungrateful to his loyalty?

"Very well, then, I'll tell you everything,   66
and bring you happy tidings finally,
for I can see how wretched you are here.
Well, then, your dear Rinaldo's here at last
to free you from the darkness of this jail,
being the man who greatly loves you still.
That's why he's fighting now the Admiral,
and for your love the city is at war.

"Copardo on his return reported this,   67
and now because I gave you all my love,
my soul, my heart, and all the rest of me,
I even wish my father's total end
to put the city in your cousin's hands;
thus you will see the fruit of this my love.
Enough, therefore, with empty leaf and sprout:
I only want you of this prison out."

After he heard his Chiariella speak,   68
Orlando answered, "I believe you are
the darling angel Heaven sent to me
the very day I in this jail was bound,
and from that moment you have been the star
that like a magnet has attracted me.
What merit or what fate has made me such
as to be loved by you, my dear, so much?

"Here, Chiariella, are my heart and soul—
the keys to this my life to you I give
so as to let our love immortal be.
You're bringing me the olive and the palm,
and you alone are saving me from hell,
and thus transmute my tempest into calm."
Orlando at this point could not express
his overwhelming inner tenderness.

69

Thus Chiariella saw Copardo again,
and bade him tell Rinaldo to advance
the following night; in the meantime she let,
discreetly, Count Orlando out of jail.
She sent a written message to Rinaldo,
telling him to come forward with no fear;
but this postscript she had also added there:
"After you read the message, hang the messenger."

70

Rinaldo, who had been awaiting this,
had in the meantime armed all of his men.
He followed her instructions to the letter:
he ordered for the messenger some food,
and saw him later kicking in midair.
Against the city's door he started out.
Copardo, Orlando, and Chiariella at once
were armed and mounted, ready to advance.

71

After they stormed the door, they wildly roared:
"Ransack the city! Death to everyone!
Death to the wicked Admiral, and death
to all his followers and all his court!"
In that commotion everyone arose:
seeing the enemy already there,
some ran in terror, some ran for a sword,
some hid, and some for help most loudly called.

72

The Admiral, awakened, shook with fear,
and hearing shouts and seeing all those men,
some of his servants he addressed at once:
"What's happening? And why all of these screams?"
Soon out of bed he jumped, and armed himself
as best he could. Like a blind man he ran,
not knowing where to go, what place to find—
a person with no refuge and no mind.

73

At last he went where the great battle was, 74
and it was there he saw our Oliver
right in the midst of the horrendous fight:
there with his sword he struck his helmet's crest,
whereby removing rust and mold from it,
not hard enough to ground him in the least.
Oliver recognized the pagan lord
and paid him homage with his cutting sword.

The night before, the Admiral had gone 75
to bed with a tight-fitting leather cap;
Oliver went beneath it with his sword,
splitting the pagan's head and neck as well,
and causing him to fall down from his horse.
Soon every man around the Saracen
began to flee in terror, full of dread,
just as it happens when the captain's dead.

When Lord Rinaldo saw the pagan fall, 76
"Forever blest," he shouted, "be the hand
that has so sundered that mad dog's mad brains!
Surely you are a knight of Charlemagne."
And thus the mighty slaughter had begun.
A pagan giant at this point arrived,
known as the fierce Grandono. Blindly then
he threw himself among those fighting men.

That cursèd Saracen met Oliver 77
and forcibly unsaddled him at once,
so unrelenting was his winning blow;
then into a new dance he threw himself,
and in the thickest throng still fighting there,
he never missed one of his falling blows:
often in blindness his own men he hit,
for night and madness don't agree a bit.

And while the giant was so busy at work, 78
'twas fate that brought sweet Luciana there.
Horrid Grandono, running into her,
struck her so rudely and so wickedly
(he was a madman blindly wounding all)
that then and there he sent her to the ground:
coldness or heat she would have felt no more
had not Rinaldo jumped into that war.

He helped her back upon her horse, and did   79
the same with the marquis, of whom he asked
who had unseated him. Oliver said,
"A mighty giant, who ran fast away."
While all these things were happening here, Orlando
ran into Ricciardetto and, since he failed
in that thick fight to recognize the lad,
sent him aground together with his steed.

And then Terigi, his own squire, he saw   80
and struck upon the helmet with his sword,
making him headlong fall down from his horse,
although the helmet was unbroken still.
Seeing himself so helpless on the ground,
Terigi moaned, "Where are you now, Orlando?
If you were here, on horse I still would be,
and, fallen, now your vengeance I would see."

Orlando recognized him by his voice,   81
dismounted fast and, asking for forgiveness,
said, "I'm so sorry for my sad mistake.
But there's no time to waste: back on your horse!
Such are the things that happen in the dark."
Orlando asked, "Where are the others now?
Oliver, Ricciardetto—are they here?
Have you not seen them? Much for them I fear."

Replied Terigi, "I saw Oliver   82
a while ago, fighting a pagan throng,
but Ricciardetto's lying on the ground—
and it was you who did it with your hand.
I am afraid he has not long to live:
these hunting dogs will soon finish him off."
Orlando Ricciardetto saw at last—
on foot and whirling his sword very fast.

He shouted, "Ricciardetto, fear no more!   83
Here is Orlando: so you cannot die.
I am invincible, as you know well.
Listen! The man who threw you from your horse
was a dear friend of yours—O sorry luck!"
As soon as Ricciardetto heard these words,
he said, "To be quite honest, I thought so,
for both my steed and I fell at one blow.

"So to myself I said, 'Could any pagan   84
in such a place have been so bold and strong?'"
'Twas then Orlando, brandishing his sword,
threw himself deep into the gory fight,
shouting, "O wicked traitors, evil mob,
whose glory is to fight against one man,
rabble and swine and Saracens, behind—I say:
no, you will never take my Ricciardetto away."

Back Ricciardetto jumped upon his horse,   85
and looking for Rinaldo they all went.
Orlando and Rinaldo met at last
and, joining forces, doubled they the fight.
Now Chiariella for her sin was paying,
finding herself in danger more than once:
by her Copardo and the others no more seen,
she managed in the end barely to save her skin.

Throughout the night Christians and pagans fought   86
until, most weary and with broken bones,
the entire population asked for peace
lest all of them should quickly be undone.
There were amongst them several prudent men.
On these conditions they would all surrender—
that their own town be left unharmed and free,
their men be spared with all their property.

The day was lighting up the eastern sky   87
when Chiariella to Rinaldo came,
saying, "O gentle, most courageous knight,
all is in perfect order, as I see."
To the great palace they together went;
Rinaldo held Copardo by the hand,
and many, many things with him he talked;
next to Orlando Chiariella walked.

Throughout the morning all the people came,   88
homage to pay to the victorious knights.
With boundless wisdom then Rinaldo spoke,
"O Chiariella, how you make me fall in love!
I want you to be queen of this your land:
for all the benefits and honors shown,
I now want to behave most gratefully,
and let Copardo a crowned monarch be."

He then gave orders that the Admiral's   89
body be found for decent burial,
and in the city reestablished peace.
Orlando trusted him with all he did,
while he and Chiariella sweetly cooed.
While she and he took rides outside the walls
in their delightful daily rendezvous,
Rinaldo in the palace ruled anew.

But all these people we must leave awhile.   90
The Sultan had returned to Bambillona,
for he had signed the peace and placed Orlando
where he was certain he would lose his life.
Having now heard of a new fire lit,
and that His Majesty the Admiral
had lost both crown and life, and land therefore,
he thought that there would be another war.

Thinking things over, he decided to   91
go back to Persia with his entire army.
Not many leagues away he pitched his tents,
eager to know what truly had occurred.
He to the city sent a messenger
to say he mourned the Admiral's demise,
and that no matter what had come to be,
their land's new lawful lord was none but he;

and if Rinaldo did not leave that land,   92
he must defend it in an open war,
and see what grief is now in store for him;
last, Chiariella he most deeply blamed,
Orlando's mistress—harlot, to be sure:
so grave a treason she alone had planned.
A man he'd send as his ambassador—
a most revered and loyal vavasor.

Right at the palace where all people were,   93
the vavasor arrived, and freely spoke:
"May the Mahound that each of us adores
bring to a sudden end these baptized men,
and may he keep and save my lawful lord,
still on the field, together with his daughter
of the enchanted spear—Antea named;
and may he also," so the man proclaimed,

"protect and cherish all the Saracens,   94
and most especially the Sultan's men.
Long live our Trevigant, long live Apollin,
and may all faithful Christians be destroyed,
and most especially the knight Orlando
and the great, haughty Lord of Montalban,
Astolfo and the Dane and Oliver
and Charles and France and every soldier there!"

Rinaldo could no longer bear the pride   95
of that insane and beastly Saracen
who seemed to deem their worth much less than tares,
and to Orlando said, "Now watch how well
I can chastise a madman when I want to:
we now shall see how fast this man can jump
or whether nature made him lithe of limb,"
and from a window down into the square he threw him.

Such tidings reached the Sultan in a flash,   96
and very bitterly he therefore grieved,
threatening soon to arm all of his troops
and then besiege the city with his men.
Seeing him so distressed and anguish-torn,
his daughter said, "The reason seems quite clear:
the vavasor you sent, as you recall,
did by no means respect their protocol.

"As I've been told, he said the strangest things.   97
Now, if you really want those Christian knights
to hear the message that you wish to send,
no letter and no messenger you need:
send me, instead, and in my speech I will
employ the best diplomacy and art.
I'm sure I will return with a reply."
"Very well," said the Sultan: "go, and try."

Too many times in Syria this girl   98
had heard Rinaldo's far-resounding name,
and, being an admirer of man's valor,
she was in love with his heroic worth.
To those who ask how she was called—although
the vavasor already mentioned it—
we'll say that, yes, Antea was her name:
a goddess's face and hers were just the same.

Her golden locks seemed Daphne's very own,   99
and she resembled Venus in her mien;
her eyes were stars of the eternal realm,
her nose was a most perfect copy of Juno's,
her teeth were but celestial ivory,
her chin was round and shapely and well chiseled;
her throat and both her shoulders were so white,
they seemed from Pallas stolen in the night.

Her arms were agile, delicate, and lithe,   100
and both her hands were long and purely white
but brave enough to hold the hunting bow—
Diana she resembled in all this.
So truly perfect, truly great was she,
she did not seem a woman of this earth:
of perfect measurement was her round breast;
also, she had Proserpina's thin waist,

and Deiopeia's hips, and very well   101
could wear a heavy quiver full of darts.
Her dainty little feet were oh so white.
In other words, her body's every inch
was such that there was nothing that she lacked.
Such is the stuff that stars are fashioned with.
Oh, tell the nymphs to run away and hide!
They would be ugly, this young girl beside.

She had such lovely ways, such tender smiles,   102
such wonderful and winsome habitudes,
she could have thrown six paradises open
and made a river seek its mountain source;
and not one Joseph—hundreds of Narcissuses
she would have caused to pine for her alone.
She looked like Rachel in both gait and gown,
her words were honey and sugar dripping down.

She was all gentleness and courtesy,   103
honest and wise, bashful and innocent,
forever virile in her promises,
and not too often capable of scorn,
though even then in a most regal way
that showed her height of lineage and life:
in her, so many virtues were combined,
heaven or earth had no more grace to find.

She was conversant with the liberal arts,   104
had oft the hunting falcon on her arm,
and wounded boars and lions in her chase;
and when she jumped up on her nimble colt,
she made him more than run—she gave him wings:
she turned him left and right so easily
that anyone who could have watched her worth
would soon have sworn that she was Mars on earth.

It was the horse the Sultan had received   105
from the Almansor of far Barbary:
born in Arabia, the steed surpassed
in strength and beauty every horse on earth.
The Sultan had donated him to her,
for very much she longed for that one gift.
His coat appeared of gray and yellow sheen,
such as in Syria no more is seen.

Judging by all his perfect features, he   106
was quite a charger, as you all will hear,
although from Clairmont he did not descend.
He had a little head but a large mouth,
a lively glance, a star between his eyes,
wide nostrils, and an often curled-up lip,
short ears but a most vigorous, long neck—
so light it hardly gave the rein a shake.

Most beautiful he was for these new reasons: 107
the width of his whole belly was three spans;
his back was narrow, well-proportioned; big
were his four legs and with short, matchless joints;
his hooves were wide and tall and wholly dry.
Ever of happy and vivacious mood,
his tail he closes, and he digs and neighs,
behind and onward kicking, kicking always.

The very day Antea wished to ride him,   108
there in the square of Bambillona he gave
a wonderful performance with no fault.
And when she saw the worth of such a horse
and the most rare perfection of his breed,
she wanted to wear plate upon her breast,
and from that day she armed and was most eager
to test in jousts and tournaments her vigor.

Then like Camilla or Penthesileia,   109
she started to appear armed on the field;
hers was a magic armor that no blade
could ever cut or in the least offend.
It had been forged there in Damascus, steeped
in gold so bright it made the sun less fair.
Thus she unhorsed with it whichever knight
wanted to dare her to a single fight.

They came from every region of the East,   110
from Persia, from Phoenicia and Egypt;
and famous wandering knights there also came:
she felled and vanquished each and all of them.
Whichever rival came in front of her
was quickly by her lance thrown to the ground.
Thus her fame reached the firmament's last border;
Bambillon and the Sultan both adored her.

And they were right, indeed, in doing so,   111
for everything she did seemed most divine
and far above all ordinary ways,
especially among those pagan men,
accustomed—such as Baal, such as Ninus—
to countless ancient idols and false gods:
they ended up believing that this woman,
conceived and born in heaven, was not human.

And many other wondrous things could be   112
said of this maiden's everlasting worth;
but since time's running out, we must go on
and try to bring our story to an end.
Enchanting though a certain song may be,
'tis good to hear some music that is new.
The coming Canto will so sweetly sound
that it will soothe and comfort every mind.

CANTO XVI

O David's glorious daughter, who illumine   1
both hemispheres and make the heavens fair,
and through whom many a grieving soul was saved
when Gabriel announced his *Hail* to you,
my story has been painted heretofore
with color, art, and brush utterly yours:
I with your grace am past the midway mark;
so do not leave my mind in shade or dark.

Antea was most eager now to see   2
Rinaldo, Count Orlando, Oliver,
and Ricciardetto, the young daring knight;
therefore she was preparing for the fight.
Three squadrons of her men she rallied soon,
equipped with armor and with lance and sword.
Thus she bade leave of the Great Sultan and
went quickly riding toward the Persian land.

As soon as at the city she arrived,   3
indomitably fierce, she took a lance
and, spurring her steed on, put it in rest
and broke it with great chivalry on the ground.
Her charger was most furious and bold,
but she could tame him with more skillfulness
than brave and dauntless Hector could have done,
onto the scene attracting everyone.

Rinaldo, from a window watching still,   4
could not but marvel at the feat he saw,
and said, "I never saw so great a lady,
and never such a wonder have I viewed:
she's the most clever teacher of us all."
Orlando, too, was mystified by it.
Such a great lady they all wished to view,
with Luciana and Chiariella, too.

The gentle pagan maiden they approached,
and greeted her with mighty reverence.
She soon replied to them in Syrian,
uttering words that melted all their hearts.
Then Chiariella and Luciana brought her
to the great regal hall right in their midst;
there on a lavish throne she soon was placed,
wherefrom she made her purpose manifest:

5

"That God Who first created sky and earth
with nature and all stars and sun and moon,
and opens up and closes each abyss,
thus bringing, as He wishes, day and night;
He who, most good and just, is never wrong—
though men upon this earth blame Fortune still—
may He protect my father the Sultan evermore,
gentle Rinaldo and the Roman senator,

"and also Oliver and Ricciardetto,
Terigi, and the men who are with you,
Saint Denis's Church and Charles your emperor.
The reason why the Sultan sent me here
is not that I should look for war or fight:
therefore my mission I believe you guess.
He only wants what common sense demands—
full jurisdiction over all his lands.

7

"This city and the towns from the extreme
corners of Persia, and of Syria,
and the entire eastern continent,
are subjects to our kingdom, all of them;
therefore, now that the Admiral is dead,
my father's their sole ruler once again:
in other words, as you can clearly see,
this land is by all means our property.

"No, I cannot believe you are so wrong
as not to know the one this crown belongs to.
The Roman senator, instead, has acted
out of revenge and vehement disdain:
within his noble heart, such strength has he
that he allows his reason to be won.
The Sultan did the same (now hear, Rinaldo!)
just to avenge the death of Marcovaldo.

9

"My father will be pleased if you agree   10
 to leave the city peacefully at once:
 thus to your native lands you will return.
 If you do not comply, let God decide.
 We'll prove to you how sharp our swords can be,
 and so I tell you, in my father's name,
 to give this city to us, free once more,
 else I have come and have declared new war.

"A wise man does not need more than one word."   11
"O poor Copardo!" she continued then,
"Dear Chiariella, you were so mistaken!
 O Heaven's anger, why are you so slow?
 But may you be forgiven for one thing
 (if I can judge correctly with these eyes)—
 for having freed from darkness and brought here
 so gentle and renowned a cavalier."

She turned to Count Orlando with a smile,   12
with words and ways of such sweet gentleness
that made one see God's heaven open wide,
and, standing still, both sun and moon enrapt.
But Chiariella's face became at once
the color of sweet-smelling violets;
Copardo's too; with shame they both were won
for what against their father they had done.

Antea spoke again, "I have so far   13
told you the thing my father wants from you;
now I must tell you what is in my heart:
is this the knight whose universal fame
is not diminished in his very presence?
Are you the one the entire world acclaims
the very best who ever lowered lance,
honor and pride of Charlemagne and France?

"Are you my handsome, widely known Rinaldo?   14
 Are you the man who dwells in Montalbàn?
 Are you Orlando's very dear first cousin?
 Are you the bright descendant of Clairmont?
 Are you the one who Chiariello slew?
 Are you the brave who Brunamonte killed?
 Are you Gan of Maganza's enemy? Are you
 the greatest hero the world ever knew?"

"Rinaldo, gentle lady, is my name,   15
and, as you said, from Clairmont I descend."
And then the lady added, "The whole world
echoes your fame, which greatly pleases me;
but there are men who're saying this of you—
you're not a cavalier. As you know well,
ambassadors should from all harm be free,
whate'er they say, whoever they may be.

"'Twas you who murdered our ambassador.   16
I do not care which of the two was wrong:
I only know that killing a man sent
by such a lord as my great father is
has hurt your honor just as it has mine.
That very man I hope now to avenge,
and so I won't go home without a fight:
I'm challenging you now. If by your might

I am unhorsed and vanquished, everything   17
you have until now conquered shall be yours.
My father will be pleased—of this I'm sure.
But if, instead, I throw you from your horse,
then you'll unfold your banners to the wind
and go with all your people back to France:
thus you will leave in peace and no more bother,
by coming here again, my noble father."

To the famed maiden so replied Rinaldo,   18
"Because, I swear, I'm neither deaf nor dumb,
I'll keep, forever carved in this my heart,
each syllable you have so clearly spoken.
But something you have mentioned at the end
in which we both most totally concur:
the sword alone is the best referee
to solve our problem—and it so shall be.

"But there's one favor I would ask of you   19
before we, armed with sword, go to the field.
Orlando, my dear cousin, begs you, too—
he who just happens to be here today.
I feel my heart is wounded, and know not
how I was caught, or with what bait, by you.
Astride my horse I'll come, on the third day,
armed to the field, just as you wish and say."

Quickly Antea to his words replied, 20
"I much am pleased by what so pleases you,"
but as she answered in so sweet a way,
she blushed—oh, what a flame over her face—
it was one fire burning up two hearts.
How easily a gentle soul is seized!
Both lovers had been wounded by that dart
which ever vanquished the most hardened heart.

Fixedly more than ever, so they kept 21
gazing and gazing at each other then.
Gazing upon her avidly, Rinaldo
could not believe there was a better sky,
and the young lady suddenly was sure
even Narcissus's face was not so fair.
Each on the other fixed the ardent gaze,
for Love had set both of their hearts ablaze.

So great a dinner was meanwhile prepared, 22
the like of which had never yet been seen.
To his dear friend Rinaldo spoke these words:
"Dear Oliver, I need your help right now.
For Persia and my gain I care no more.
I want you to take care of all details,
and I want, also, nobody but you
to wait on her as I myself would do.

"And if I ever helped you in your love 23
with Forisena and Meridiana,
please see to it that not a thing is missed
to honor this dear pagan worthily."
Oliver said, "This is how Fortune goes:
dear Luciana, find another love!
Of course you'll have no friend more prompt or keener."
Thus he began to order the big dinner.

They served the best and most delicious food 24
that ever in that region could be found,
with precious wines and sweets and varied fruit.
The city's gentlest ladies were invited—
and they were not the ugliest, of course.
Oliver waited on them all; Antea,
especially, was served by the marquis
with plate and knife and food and courtesy.

The dinner over, the musicians came   25
to make the ended day less sorrowful:
small and big trumpets, castanets and flutes,
cymbals and bagpipes for the dancing bouts,
horns, drums and tambourines, wind instruments
and many others used in Moorish lands,
with lutes and citterns, harps and decachords,
and clowns and games and many pleasant words.

And so they passed the day in merriment.   26
But when the sun drew to Granada close,
the gentle lady said with charming voice
that, much to her regret and deepest grief,
she absolutely had to go right back
to the Great Sultan, waiting for an answer;
but on the third day, just as she had said,
armed she would be upon the open field.

The feast was then concluded with a dance,   27
and so the famous lady went away.
Rinaldo on his horse escorted her
as far as where the Sultan's mansion rose.
He felt so wretched—oh, he felt like dying
when he departed from so fair a face:
his tears—believe me—he could hardly check
until to his pavilion he went back.

The Sultan asked his gentle daughter what   28
she'd done in Persia with the Christian knights.
She told him of the challenge and the deal—
that on the third day she'd return to fight,
hoping to teach Rinaldo on the field
a lesson that he never would forget,
and take right back the lands that he had seized.
On hearing this, the Sultan was much pleased,

for very much indeed he trusted her.   29
Now let's go back to comfort poor Rinaldo,
lying in bed in such a sorry state,
he seemed to be neither alive nor dead.
Sighing, Antea's name he ever called,
and "Wretched me!" he said. "You've done me wrong,
giving and taking my whole heart away."
And it was Love he blamed for his dismay:

"Why did you make her steal me from myself?
In such a way she stole me from myself
that she has changed me into what she is,
so that I am no more the man I was.
She took all of my thoughts away from me,
and this is not what you have promised me.
Ah, do not boast if through such gentle eyes
you've caught me with your arrow by surprise!

30

"Europa would have never been deceived,
nor would Jove have disguised himself as a bull
or changed his own true features in the least
to abduct poor Ganymede up to his sky,
if they had only seen so fair a face.
And Daphne would not be a laurel tree
had Phoebus seen Antea on the day
he begged the nymph to wait for him and stay.

"He would not have become Admetus's slave,
nor would have Jacob, had he seen Antea,
served Rachel for so long so loyally,
being the prudent person that he was.
Surely her face would in an instant tame
the most ferocious tigers in the woods;
she'd make the wind and sea no longer stir
and, absolutely still, just look at her.

32

"And Perseus would not have had to free
Andromeda, cut off Medusa's head,
and afterward turn Phineus into stone.
Hippolytus would not have made excuses,
nor would Orpheus have wooed Eurydice,
nor would Arethusa be now a spring
had fair Antea on the earth lived then—
she who entrances all departed men.

"There would have been no need for goddess Venus
to teach Hippomenes how to defeat
fast Atalanta with some golden apples
thrown right before the swift-approaching steps,
nor would Acontius have writ 'Cydippe,'
seeing her lovely face and lovely hair.
No banquet would have been disturbed a bit
by a golden apple thrown right into it:

34

"Paris would not have given it to Venus,   35
    there would have been no quarrel over it,
    Troy would not have become a heap of ashes
    and all of Greece would not have come to war
    if they had seen the bare and tender limbs
    that pierced my heart and set my soul aflame.
    Nor, had his eyes been by such beauty sated,
    would have Narcissus his own life truncated.

"And as, O Cupid, you know well, Leander   36
    of Abydos, so wretched and forlorn,
    would not have had to be by a dolphin brought
    ashore to his belovèd lady's feet
    if he had seen Antea, whom I love,
    nor would have Polyphemus from the shore
    called with his reed, of Galatea in quest,
    jealous of Acis dreaming on her breast.

"You would have never married, Theseus,   37
    Hippolyte, the queen of Amazons,
    nor would you have abandoned Ariadne,
    so much in love, upon that little isle.
    Palaemon and Arcita would have never
    contended for Emilia in Athens,
    nor would Pyramus and other lovers have died—
    there is not time to list so many men—

"if such a lady had existed then.   38
    Never have I so fair a daughter seen—
    so fair that, when I see her shining face
    so perfectly resembling Venus's own,
    and when upon that face, wholly divine,
    I watch those eyes, those eyebrows' perfect arches,
    when I recall her ways, her words of cheer,
    truly the *Hail!* once more I seem to hear.

"You've every right to wound me, cruel Love,   39
    and boast of having wholly vanquished me.
    Why, do you think I may my armor wear
    to pierce with this my spear the very heart
    that can, in turn, both wound and make me whole
    like Peleus, not like you, treacherous god?"
    All these and many other words he spoke;
    then he began Antea to invoke:

"Where are you? Why have you forsaken me?   40
  Could you not spend at least one day with me?
  And can you think I'll come against you armed?
  Oh no, that day I will not sound the horn!
  So wholly have you caught and fettered me
  that I will see my king and France no more.
  Neither in Bambillona can I be
  with you, nor with myself can here I be.

"What shall I do? How will my kingdom fare?   41
  Where will this wretched heart ever find peace?"
  Orlando with specific plans in mind
  found, the next morning, his Rinaldo in bed.
  With keen attention he began to say,
"O my dear cousin, are you maybe ill?"
  Rinaldo feigned a rather curious dream
  that he had had, to hide the truth from him.

Replied Orlando, "We are those two monks   42
  who ate a pudding, and one burned his tongue:
  one saw the other's eyes wide open, dazed,
  and asked the reason for that sudden change.
  The other answered, 'Just the two of us
  are left to eat; the others are all dead.
  Surely you know that we were thirty-three,
  and so I'm mourning them, as you can see.'

"The other, well aware of his deceit,   43
  pretended he was weeping out of grief,
  and told the one who wanted to know why,
'See, I'm crying, too; my heart is broken,
  for but the two of us are still alive.'
  Thus one deceived the other. This is how
  we seemed to deal now with each other. But
  why don't you say the pudding was too hot?

"Although this is a different kind of heat."   44
  Rinaldo, still in self-defense, replied,
"Cousin, I swear to you I have just dreamed
  of a big lion jumping fast on me:
  calling for help, I desperately screamed,
  and with Frusberta tried to wound the beast.
  Maybe I cried out loud in this my plight,
  and so you came to wake me from my fright.

"Therefore, for this I'm much obliged to you;   45
    I was indeed so terrified and lost,
    I really feel you have delivered me
    out of the very jaws of that wild beast."
    Orlando answered, "Cousin, foolish cousin,
    I wish that what you've told me were a dream!
    Ah, Mistress Moon is very far away!
    Did you in this your dream, oh, maybe, say:

"'O fair Antea, have I done you wrong?   46
    Where did you leave me? Did you swear in vain?
    Where are you now, and when will you come back?
    And will you never, never pity me,
    who gave you all my heart, as you know well,
    and, as god Love can see, am now your slave?
    Often of me you wanted this to know,
    'Are you the very one that I love so?'

"'You are the fairest of the fair,   47
    you are the treasure of nobility,
    you are the one who makes me bold and brave,
    you are the light of the eternal sky,
    you are the one who filled my heart with hope,
    you are the one who makes me live and die,
    you are the fountain of all grace and art,
    you are my very soul, my very heart.'

"Cousin, you are not dreaming—you're awake;   48
    then do not try to hide the truth from me:
    if this is what you want, I'm not your man.
    So, you have come to Persia just to woo
    a pagan lady? You should be ashamed,
    for this means almost to renounce your faith.
    Tell me: have you become totally blind?
    Christ's punishment may not be far behind.

"Where is, Rinaldo, all your bravery?   49
    Where is, Rinaldo, your unbeaten might?
    Where is, Rinaldo, every prudent thought?
    Where is, Rinaldo, your foreseeing vision?
    Where is, Rinaldo, your most noble dream?
    Where is, Rinaldo, either sword or steed?
    Where is, Rinaldo, your untarnished fame?
    Where is your heart? You gave it to a dame.

"Do you believe this is the time for women?   50
  Do you believe this is the time for love?
  Do you believe we've tarried long enough?
  Do you believe we have to waste more time?
  Do you believe this idleness is good?
  Do you believe simply in having fun?
  Do you believe a girl is worth your lance?
  Do you believe you'll not return to France?

"This is the way to give our kingdom peace.   51
  This is the way for you to win your crown.
  This is the way to conquer your Antea.
  This is the way to enter Bambillona.
  This is the way to spread the Christian faith.
  This is the way to win the world's acclaim.
  This is the way to show that you are wise.
  Alas! Alas! My every pleasure dies.

"Banish these foolish and unworthy thoughts,   52
  and think of but your armor right away,
  for our Lord Christ is partisan, you know,
  and maybe your behavior does not like.
  You see, the Sultan is assailing us:
  if you are lucky to defeat Antea,
  this entire kingdom and its neighboring lands,
  using no sword, we'll have in these our hands."

As our Rinaldo could no more pretend   53
  to hide what was so wholly manifest,
"I clearly see," he answered with a sigh,
"I have offended very much our God,
  and now, indeed, deserve great punishment.
  But, then, if either Jove or fiery Mars
  has fought again so great a love in vain,
  why use my power or my art or brain?

"As I have promised, to the field I'll go,   54
  wearing my sword and brandishing my spear.
  But how, how could I ever wound myself,
  winning the one who has already won?
  I am completely blind—this I admit—
  as blind as painters paint my cruel lord;
  a sightless guide is leading me: therefore,
  in vain, O man, you're knocking on this door.

"I cannot want because I do not want to;
I cannot—do not want to—leave this woman.
I'm not the cousin that I used to be,
for this my ill is in my very bones.
If I could cure myself of this disease,
Solomon would have been a stupid man—
so Aristotle, Plato, Socrates.
Then, cousin, let's not quarrel over this.

"I won't discuss astrology with one
who does not know the meaning of the star,
nor will I speak of surgery to one
who uses only hammer, mill, and plow.
I will not, consequently, speak of love
to one who knows only Alda the Fair.
I wish only that Love would find a way
to make you, too, experience what I say."

Orlando fully disconcerted stood
after his cousin told him all he did,
knowing that more than obstinate was he.
Therefore, to Oliver and Ricciardetto
he said, "Our dear Rinaldo is all-armed:
he wants to fight Antea in his bed,"
and thus he told them all that he had heard,
and the two men were very much dismayed.

But Oliver to Count Orlando said,
"If I get mad, I'll make him hear my bell."
"Be silent," Count Orlando fast replied;
"'Mind your own love' he soon would say to you.
He even silenced *me,* not in the least
accusable of any such intrigues.
Go, disentangle the minutest thread,
and you'll be paid with thicker wool instead.

"From such a scandal you must run away
as fast as that old lady abbess did,
who, by mistake, instead of her own wimple,
put on her head the abbot's underwear;
because of which the youthful nun in sin
said, 'Madam Abbess, something's in your hair:
oh, please tie up your wimple on your head.'
And to her holy abbott soon she sped.

55

56

57

58

59

"It is our task to see what must be done—   60
   we'll go, tomorrow, armed onto the field:
   I'll be the first, and you will follow me
   in challenging Antea as we must.
   I know I'll kill her, follow then what may,
   and if the Sultan fights us, we shall soon
   defend ourselves and, with God's help, then save
   my cousin from becoming a woman's slave.

"But maybe he would quickly change his mind   61
   if through my error or my evil luck
   I by this lady should be thrown from horse
   (though I believe he would most likely laugh).
   But our Lord Christ will give me might and strength
   and with his help sustain me in the fight.
   We'll let Rinaldo rest in bed until
   he wakes up fully, of his own free will."

Oliver did not answer to all this.   62
   Ten thousand horsemen were alerted soon.
   So the next morning all of them were armed,
   and marched against the Sultan's waiting troops.
   Rinaldo, uninvited, marched there, too,
   telling Orlando, "Blow the horn: you know
   this is an art for which I have no fame:
   so, then, call on Antea in my name."

"What do you know?" then Count Orlando said.   63
   "Being the fool I am, I'll do just that,
   for I am glad to please you all the way."
   And so he placed the horn right in his mouth
   and blew with such great power into it
   that the first sound that mightily came out
   reached sweet Antea's ear immediately.
   So struck with grief and overcome was she,

she said, "My reputation I have lost: 64
   maybe they think that out of cowardice
   I was in my pavilion still asleep."
   Her arms she wanted, mounting fast her horse.
   As soon as Lord Rinaldo saw the lady,
   it was as if the falcon's cap were off:
   on his Baiardo he sat up indeed,
   here and there jumping with his valiant steed.

As soon as she arrived, she greeted him   65
with gentleness that echoed in his heart,
and when she paid Orlando his due homage,
confused, Orlando lowered soon his glance.
The lady said, "You must have thought I lay
still sleepy and most idle in my bed
while all of you were waiting for me here:
your military chivalry is clear.

"You, first, Rinaldo darling, take the field,   66
who have been greatly yearning for this fight:
and by my God, the promise that I made
I will today most scrupulously keep."
Rinaldo said, "I've come to fight, but wish
I could a weapon use that did not cut."
He turned his charger, and the maiden hers.
Oliver said, "Nothing will come of this."

It seemed to him that fair Antea laughed   67
the moment that she turned her Arab steed.
Turning, Rinaldo laid his lance in rest,
making Baiardo do a Moorish dance;
then, as he seemed about to assail the lady,
the very fine Arabic shield he had,
quickly behind his shoulders he withdrew,
and far away his spear discarded, too.

Being the courteous lady that she was,   68
Antea, seeing this, turned her shield, too,
not to seem villainous or cowardly.
Grieved by all this, Orlando sighed and said,
"Tinder and flint attract each other fast.
Antea, may you be forever cursed!
We must do something. Ricciardetto, look!
It's time, it is high time our arms we took,

"for when I heard Antea make so many   69
promises, should Rinaldo win the joust,
I said, 'All of our problems then are solved,
and this our land is free from danger now.'
But seeing that Rinaldo's such a fool,
now I'm afraid we're ruined. Look at him—
out of his mind that man just seems to be."
And Ricciardetto echoed, "I agree."

Then toward Rinaldo Count Orlando rode, 70
and said, "Where did you learn to joust so well?
I did not know you were so good at this,
and a few lessons I would gladly take.
The fire in you works so well, I see,
this is the day you'll be forever shamed."
The lady said, "'Tis Love who so decrees.
Why don't you take, sweet gentleman, his place?"

Oliver then began thus to implore, 71
"Brother-in-law, I beg you for this grace—
against this lady let me test my worth."
Replied Orlando, "I am more than pleased;
rather than beg, you even may command."
Oliver turned his charger instantly
and, when he saw fit, charged for a good aim;
'gainst the marquis the lady did the same.

Oliver clashed into the maiden hard, 72
and broke his spear, but on her saddle she
felt not the blow and did not move an inch;
instead, so hard she struck him on the shield,
she caused him thus to fall down from his horse:
and so her prisoner he had to be.
Good Ricciardetto kept him company,
sharing along the way his misery.

Toward her pavilion they started out. 73
Rinaldo laughed at his own brother's fate.
Orlando said to him, "I do believe
your sins have made you lose your intellect.
But those who are in heaven blest and crowned
await the moment of your punishment."
Rinaldo, whose whole heart for love was pawned,
refused on purpose even to respond.

This angered so Orlando that he said, 74
"By our Lord Jesus, I now swear that if
your evil is not punished in some way,
I will not anymore believe in Him,
and I will see to it you leave the game
and play with your Antea no more jousts,
for I will kill her right before your glance,
and make your penance in this way commence."

And to Antea he said, "*You* take the field. 75
Rinaldo is responsible for your death,
for I will make you feel—unless I trip—
a heat quite different from that of love."
The lady answered, "There's no obstacle:
even if you are stronger than a wall,
I'll make you, Orlando, willy-nilly fall.
With such a promise, here I challenge you."

Raging with wrath, Orlando turned his horse— 76
bellowing, fuming like a maddened bull.
And suddenly the maiden took the field,
and neither of them wasted any time.
She aimed and struck on Count Orlando's shield,
thinking to make him grieve once and for all:
she broke her lance, but did not shake that wall,
as she had said before—strong, hard, and tall.

Utterly stunned by this, the lady said, 77
"A very strange illusion mine has been—
that I could fast unseat so great a man."
Even Orlando broke his lance in vain,
because her shield was magical. The two
undauntedly drew sword immediately:
their duel started then, so fierce and weird
that for Antea her Rinaldo feared.

So much was he in love, he wished to see 78
the ground all-reddened with his cousin's blood,
for when Orlando gave his wicked blow,
the sound of it had echoed in his heart,
causing his whole breast to reverberate
as in a sick man seized by sudden cough:
and for it all he blamed our Jesus Christ,
saying the prayer of the atheist.

Seeing at times Antea with a slight 79
advantage over Orlando, much he sighed
and prayed that she might soon unhorse the count,
and would have gladly helped her with his hand.
See how completely Love had blinded him!
He had arrived from France a while ago:
to free him from his dungeon he had come,
and now he wished his ruin and his doom.

May this example be a lesson then.   80
Orlando and Antea with their swords
worked miracles: she did the best she could,
knowing his weapon's magic nature, and
gave him a bit of his own medicine;
but she could not accomplish very much
because Orlando's armor was so hard,
it well withstood the fury of her sword.

The duel lasted the entire day   81
with not a vantage point on either side,
as neither sword would break or even cut.
The sun already in the west had fallen,
and since the wicked fight continued still,
Orlando to the lovely lady said,
"The time has come to stop, it seems to me,
for not to do so would be villainy.

"In being still unbeaten there's no shame;   82
and so our fight is over for today."
The lady said, "You're wrong: I feel great shame
in having not yet killed you on this field;
very well, then, you safely may depart."
Soon afterward they left the open field:
returned our Count Orlando to his tent,
and to her father's place the maiden went.

Their word they gave each other to resume   83
their fight on the third day as rules demanded.
But now another story we must tell.
Gan of Maganza the whole world had roamed
in search of Lord Rinaldo, and had not
been able to find out where he might be.
'Twas fate that brought him to this Sultan's field,
to whom he his identity revealed.

He said he had been banished from the court,   84
and blamed Rinaldo for his many a woe—
the one he had so long been looking for,
throughout the world, to strip of flesh and bones.
The Sultan had been told who Gano was—
a man far shrewder than the shrewdest fox,
and more than Judas treacherous and grim:
and yet, as best he could, he honored him.

He told him what had happened there in Persia—
that Count Orlando had already seized it,
and Chiariella had betrayed her father:
that's why he had begun that enterprise—
the kingdom legally belonged to him.
To win it back, he had to declare war,
determined to prolong the fight and strife
till he would save from them both land and life.

85

He told him that Rinaldo, Oliver,
and Count Orlando had been on the field,
and that without a single blow of sword,
both Ricciardetto and Oliver had fallen:
his daughter had unseated both of them,
who both were captives now at her command.
At such news Gano was the happiest man,
already brooding on his evil plan.

He thought and thought about it; then he said,
"O mighty Sultan, this is my advice:
fighting Orlando is a futile thing,
for in the end he'll free your prisoners.
If I were you, I'd hide them far away
to keep them both forever in your claws,
and on this field I'd waste my time no more:
with them to Bambillona I'd go therefore.

87

"I know Rinaldo loves his brother dearly,
and Count Orlando loves his brother-in-law:
thus you will get all that you want from them
if they are given these two warriors back.
I would unfold my banners to the wind,
for this is not the place where my thoughts dwell."
The Sultan he was able so to sway
that he agreed to move his troops away.

Rinaldo with Orlando had returned
to Persia after their resounding feud.
Orlando, still enraged, had said to him,
"I thought that you were praying on your knees
to be by that young lady caught and bound;
then, seeing that your hopes could not be helped
by any alchemy or other scheme,
you could, alas, do nothing but blaspheme."

And he had guessed correctly, to be sure.
Thus in the evening they went both to rest—
the angry cousins who had rashly fought.
At break of dawn Rinaldo soon arose:
high from a window he looked down below,
and saw the Saracen camp no longer there.
He was amazed, and felt much grief and fear,
thinking that he no more would see Antea.

He did not think of Ricciardetto at all,
and not of Oliver, still prisoners—
the very ones he used to love so well.
Such was love's fire raging in his breast!
To Orlando, still in bed, he quickly went,
and said, "Have you not heard the latest news?
High from my window I've just watched below:
where did the Sultan and his army go?"

91

"Oh, no! It cannot be," Orlando said.
"How could our God—and He alone—allow
that man to go so suddenly away?
O Oliver, O Ricciardetto dear,
I see already 'round your necks a noose.
So, foolish cousin, are you happy now?
Now we must pay for all the Sultan's ills,
but him I'll slaughter if those two he kills.

"We must immediately do something here.
This is no more the time to be in love."
Finally in agreement, the two knights
bade Chiariella marry her Balante,
whom they entrusted with the kingdom's care.
To Saragossa with her Balugante
Luciana now should go, and to Marsilius bring
their warmest gratitude for everything.

93

Most clearly Luciana was aware
that in Rinaldo's heart she lived no more.
So you can guess how glad she must have been
to go away. "Ungrateful Love," she sighed,
"do you reward my faith in such a way?
This is what happens when you trust a man."
Back she went sadly to her father, then,
with Balugante and their fighting men.

With peace now reestablished in the city,   95
Rinaldo, Orlando, and Terigi left:
ever from place to place in quest they went,
eager to see the Sultan's flags once more.
One morn, into a forest they arrived,
following a most weird and barren path,
with many a slope and grotto and ravine
where only goats with solid hoofs are seen.

When in that desolate forest they arrived,   96
they saw five murderous giants lurking there:
they had so ransacked all the neighboring land,
there was not one inhabitant in sight.
Down in a safe and fully covered cave
they all convened and hid like highwaymen.
A poor young maiden whom the five had seized
was, terrified and weeping, in their midst.

From King Costanzo they had stolen her,   97
who was Bellamarina's mighty lord.
The wicked men had tied her in their cave,
where she was spending in much grief her days.
As soon as our small group was near their place,
one of the giants toward Rinaldo walked
and asked for his Baiardo at any cost:
if he did not dismount, his life was lost.

He added, "If you wish, you'll stay with me,   98
and I will take you with me where I go:
you'll help me carry all my booty home,
for we sweep clean these highways every day."
Rinaldo said, "Oh, did you really mean
I'll be with you when you go out to steal?
Dear giant, quite naive you seem to me:
your humble servant I could never be."

This said, he turned Baiardo away from him,   99
wounding him with a spur in doing so:
he made him leap three times much higher than
a cricket or grasshopper ever could.
With lowered lance he struck the giant then:
right in mid-chest he landed so his spear,
the wicked giant's heart he thoroughly split,
and let Baiardo smash him with his feet.

One of the others met Orlando soon,   100
and on his helmet landed such a blow
that, had his spear not lessened all it might,
he would have quickly plucked his head right off.
Orlando was so stunned that he could not,
in spite of all his strength, but crouch and cower:
utterly in a daze, he seemed to waddle.
The horrid giant grabbed him from the saddle,

and a half-mile he brought him bodily,   101
wishing to dump him down outside the road.
'Twas then Orlando to his senses came:
seeing himself so seized, he drew his sword
and pierced with it the giant in the eye,
making him lifeless in an instant fall:
the sword reached through the ear the other side,
and at so great a blow the giant died.

Terigi had been always close behind.   102
But let's go back to Lord Rinaldo, still
surrounded by the other savage three:
surely, indeed, they would have split his head
had it not been for his emboldened steed,
biting and kicking with so fierce a storm
that none of them dared move close to his kick.
One of the giants, then, began to speak:

"Christian or Saracen, whoe'er you be,   103
it seems to me there's nothing you can gain:
so this is my advice: go on your road,
for this your horse is better than a friend."
Rinaldo started out while Vegliantìn
was for his mighty master looking still:
Orlando saw him, mounted him, and, fast,
of his Rinaldo went about in quest.

Rinaldo, instead, was looking for his cousin: 104
too far apart, they did not find each other.
Each of them tried to leave that forest soon.
Orlando heard a sound within those woods:
behold, that girl in front of him appeared.
She knelt before him and implored his help;
she told him that away she fast had run
as soon as that loud scuffle had begun:

would he not, please, deliver her from death?   105
Orlando asked about Rinaldo first.
The lady said, "I know he is alive,
but know not where he went or from which way.
But in God's name, let's hide and save ourselves."
'Twas then Orlando placed his hopes in God.
Throughout the day, throughout the night, they rode
ever through slopes and ditches in that wood.

Up on a cliff Rinaldo stood at dawn   106
and saw a peopled countryside at last.
He saw a shepherd sitting in his hut
and eating certain rustic meal of his:
he went to him and ate his breakfast there.
After he ate, he very sleepy felt,
having not slept the night. Unable to foretell
any betrayal, soon asleep Rinaldo fell.

The shepherd saw Rinaldo sound asleep,   107
and right away on his Baiardo jumped.
Rinaldo saw his horse was there no more
(he had awakened from a frightful dream
in which he'd been by a big lion grabbed)
and said, "Most surely I am ruined now."
As best he could, he went, alone, on foot,
with neither shepherd nor Baiardo in sight.

The shepherd rode right to the city where   108
the Sultan had amassed all of his wealth.
Soon the chief hangman, who was living there,
saw such a simpleton on such a steed,
and asked him for how much he wished to sell him.
"Three hundred gold doubloons," he soon replied.
"But try him for me," was the hangman's word;
most eager to comply, the shepherd spurred

Baiardo, who could feel who'd mounted him: 109
quickly, therefore, into midair he leapt.
The shepherd, who knew not the art of riding,
fast found himself upon the barren ground
with two ribs broken. Seeing him so jump,
the hangman to the shepherd simply said,
"This has occurred to teach you some remorse,
for I know well this is a stolen horse."

He paid him with three hundred sounding coins.   110
Now to Rinaldo let's return. He still
was walking, walking, though not knowing where,
calling for Ricciardetto and Oliver,
"Is this the way I'm coming to your rescue?"
Then, thinking of Orlando, thus he moaned,
"Where, O beloved cousin, are you stranded—
where in this wood? And I—where have I landed?

"O Charlemagne, how thrilled you now must be!   111
O Gano, you must be the happiest man!
O my Clairmont, your bloom is wholly dry!
O Montalbàn, you soon will crumble down!
O brave Guicciardo, where is now your worth?
O lady mine, where is your gentleness?
And what will you now do, Astolfo dear?
Rinaldo, how will you get out of here?"

Thus moaning and lamenting, he arrived   112
through many a winding way in Bambillona.
He met a pagan near the city wall
and asked him how that very town was called.
Seeing him in so pitiful a state,
the pagan ridiculed him with a laugh.
"Spurs with no horse?" he soon was heard to say.
"You much have gambled, man, along the way."

Rinaldo lost his patience and replied,   113
"I swear by God that you will pay for this."
He grabbed him by the cloak and by the rein,
and said, "Now you will give your horse to me,
and you will be the fool with only spurs."
With no more words he drew Frusberta forth,
and in the French style such a blow he threw,
he split him, in the Turkish style, in two.

When he fell dead, another man appeared,   114
who looked like a good person, to be sure.
Rinaldo asked him, "Tell me, please, the name
of this big city right before my eyes."
The man replied to him with courtesy,
"This city, sir, is the great Bambillona;
the Greater Bambillona, indeed, is called—
the Sultan of Mecca is its lord.

"The Sultan has a daughter who is now   115
  spending her every day in loneliness:
  she deeply loves a Christian paladin,
  who left her without bidding her goodbye.
  I heard he is a man from Montalbàn.
  Missing him still, in much dismay she lives,
  and wants to see nobody. She's so sad,
  who used to make the entire city glad.

"I know I've told you more than you have asked,   116
  but tell me if there's more you wish to know.
  I will be happy to reply to you,
  who seem to be a very courteous man."
  Rinaldo said, "In great delight I'll go
  if you're so kind as to reveal your name."
  The pagan said, "To please you is my aim,
  and nothing else: Gualtieri is my name.

"And now, if so you wish, oh, let me come   117
  with you where'er you go. I'm a poor man,
  and have no wealth or business here to share;
  eternal loyalty I swear to you."
  After Rinaldo heard such words, he said,
"Gualtieri, as a brother welcome be!"
  as in the coming Canto you will know.
  Christ's peace and comfort keep you all from woe.

            C A N T O   X V I I

Virgin, before and after you gave birth,   1
Virgin so pure, O Virgin wholly blest,
Virgin who up in heaven see your Son,
Virgin so worthy, Virgin so revered,
Virgin, who rule and counsel everything,
Virgin, who before Jesus plead for us,
Virgin so full of grace, so full of glory,
Virgin eternal, help me with my story.

"Know, then, I am the very one who makes   2
the Sultan's daughter in your town still sigh;
but Fortune, who is ever wheeling fast,
has brought me here with these my spurs in hand,
after she made of me men's laughingstock.
Now take this horse of mine, O Saracen
(for my Baiardo, my brave steed, I've lost
together with my cousin, valiant most),

"and to the city go and find her soon;   3
tell her Rinaldo's waiting on the field,
though not astride, yet eager still to fight
and thus avenge the captives in her hand:
you'll see these tidings will delight her most."
Up on that Arab mare Gualtieri jumped;
he entered Bambillona, found Antea,
and made Rinaldo's wish to her quite clear.

Antea said, "Has Fortune this allowed—   4
that my Rinaldo has come back alone,
with neither steed nor other company?"
She ran to Oliver and Ricciardetto,
and said to them, "Fear nothing anymore."
Knowing full well that in great fear they lived,
to comfort them she did all that she could do:
much, for Rinaldo's sake, she loved them, too.

She'd treated Ricciardetto in such a way   5
that no discomfort had he suffered there—
such was the loving knot that held her bound.
Having done this, she to the Sultan went,
and "You don't know," she told him, "what I know;
therefore I'll tell you what I have just heard:
Rinaldo waits for me, alone on foot,
outside the walls and in his armor suit."

The Sultan said, "I find it very strange   6
that so distinguished and renowned a knight
should have been left alone and with no horse."
He said, "What do you think, Gan of Maganza,
you, vessel of all knowledge and all worth?
You are familiar with Rinaldo's might,
and so I've no desire to tempt fate.
Your counsel, then, I would appreciate."

Ganelon had foreseen that this would be,
having so many a treason on his mind.
Being, therefore, prepared for a reply,
"My Sultan, if you heed my word," he said,
more on the rest of it we shall not bet
than on a worthier thing—Antea's life.
There's nothing this Rinaldo would not start,
to win the lady that has won his heart.

7

"Not far from here that wicked, cursed Old Man
lives on the tallest peak of Aspracort—
the very one who keeps your land in fear.
Let, then, your daughter with enticing words
force her Rinaldo to agree to this—
that if he should give death to the Old Man,
he'll have the captives held in this your city,
and you will honor the whole Persian treaty.

8

The Sultan, a most shrewd and clever man,
knew he was planning a disaster for him,
and thought, "Here is the wickedest of men!
Here is the finest traitor of them all!"
He answered, "Much I praise what you suggest;
other alternatives would foolish be."
Thus his own daughter soon he begged to ask
of her Rinaldo such a daring task.

9

She told the Sultan that she was quite ready,
and started soon to make herself more fair:
she donned a rich and very lovely dress—
an azure field studded with some gold-flaming
bright stars—all woven out of precious silk.
Thus on her steed she mounted, followed by
two squires, but, of course, not armed at all.
She met Rinaldo, then, outside the wall.

10

Rinaldo saw his sweet Antea come,
and felt a sudden shudder in his heart,
which, willy-nilly, opened up at once.
"Here is the sun," he said, "among the stars."
The one that made him suffer then drew near,
and saw that he was sitting in the shade
beneath a mulberry tree close to the road,
leaning upon the hilt of his own sword.

11

She said, "Rinaldo, countless greetings to you!
What evil fate or fortune brings you here
in such a heat, on foot and all alone?"
As soon as Lord Rinaldo heard those words,
he felt a great explosion in his breast,
and said, "Oh, welcome, my most shining sun!
What grace has sent you here to comfort me?
Your suit of armor, though, I do not see."

12

The maiden so replied, "You darling fool!
For what we need here, every weapon's good,
for, to abate my anguish, I should go,
as Thisbe did, right out of Bambillona,
since we are both beneath a mulberry tree
the fame of which is known. Heaven itself
maybe would in some way reveal to you
how my most worthy loyalty is true.

13

"I have come here because my father wants
me to reveal to you what you know not:
that if you kill a fierce old foe of ours,
you'll soon be given your two captives back
with all that I have promised you in Persia.
I do not know if you have heard of him,
but very mighty is, indeed, his fame:
the Old Man of the Mountain is his name.

14

"My word of honor I am giving you
if you will do, Rinaldo, what I say.
But tell me how you lost your horse, and why
your friend Orlando is not here with you.
Oh, please take this my steed! If you do not,
an enemy of mine you soon will be."
"In a thick forest," thus Rinaldo said,
"I lost Orlando and someone stole my steed.

15

"As best I could, I managed to come here,
strengthened by my great love for dear Antea;
instead of trotting, I've come here on foot,
and never shall I ride another horse
until my brave Baiardo I can find.
Now since you can command me, tell me about
this Old Man of the Mount—or of the wood—
because I do not know all that I should.

16

"If this old monster has a head of iron,
two pieces for your love I'll make of it:
knowing I'm never wrong, so do I swear.
And with regard to what you promised me
after I kill him, utterly I trust you."
Antea replied, "One of my Mamelukes
I will command to come along with you,
and lead you to this dog's detested view.

17

"Back to the city I shall now return,
for here at this late hour I cannot stay.
Your two beloved captives shall not want,
for I have honored them both night and day.
However, they will both be free as soon
as you, Rinaldo, from your task come back.
Mahound be with you!" Thus her steed she turned,
so as to hide how in her heart she burned.

18

Back to the city with a sigh she rode,
and told the mighty Sultan everything.
Ask not how happy Gano must have felt:
his happiness he hardly could contain.
So that his treason be a double one,
he said, "You will not prick your hand at all
if, as you must, in time you pluck the rose:
one more alternative I will disclose.

19

"Rinaldo stands no chance with the Old Man;
let, then, your daughter go to Montalban
and place it under siege immediately:
but thirty thousand soldiers will suffice
while this propitious fire burns still hot.
Orlando is not there for its defense:
what can Guicciardo, Alardo, and Malagigi do?
If Montalban you seize, seized will be Paris, too.

20

"This Ricciardetto and this Oliver
are two of Charlemagne's most valiant knights.
Charles has been left in Paris all alone,
and out of fear will nothing do but watch.
Your victory is sure, the game is yours,
provided that, my lord, you act at once."
The Sultan was so pleased with what he heard,
and was so persuaded and so stirred

21

by Gano's words, he told his daughter, more
than once, that was her chance to win some fame.
At first the girl denied it could be done,
for with Rinaldo she was much in love:
she told her father very prudently
that honor meant much more than fame to her,
and that for Lord Rinaldo she would wait
and keep the promises that she had made.

Her father answered, "Long before he's back
from the Old Man—if ever he can kill him—
many a day will have meanwhile elapsed.
In the meantime you'll be at Montalban
with all your banners and your dauntless troops.
Besides, Orlando is not there; nor are
Rinaldo, Ricciardetto, and Oliver:
therefore, while still the iron's hot, go there.

"As soon as your Rinaldo is back here
(for I have noticed that you love him so),
you'll keep the promise you have made to him,
and I will do my best to honor him
till he returns, of his own will, to Persia;
meanwhile he will stay here—a welcome lord.
We'll say that you have gone to Mecca and
will be back shortly: he will understand."

Gano insisted with effective words
that were a master traitor's masterpiece.
At last the Sultan gave his orders, and
Antea said that she would do his will.
As customary, banners were prepared
and tools to use in crossing savage woods;
pavilions and tents were readied fast,
and all old-fashioned weapons were amassed.

I am convinced that never on Mount Aetna
did Vulcan, the great smith, hammer so hard
as people did in all of Bambillona.
Some of them quickly took their Syrian bows,
others filled quivers with well-sharpened darts,
some very keenly watched their scimitars
to see if they cut quickly as they should,
and others stirrups, saddles, reins renewed.

22

23

24

25

26

Ready in a few days they were to go. 27
The Sultan gave his blessing to his daughter
and then wished all his troops a happy march.
Thus to the wind were all the flags unfurled.
Antea watched her horsemen with great pride
and heartened all of them upon their steeds.
"Christendom," thus she said, "I soon will see,
castles, and villas, cities finally;

"and shores and woods and mountain peaks and plains, 28
and the fair castle Malagigi guards—
my dear Rinaldo's home, called Montalban.
I'll see the lovely church of Saint Denis,
I'll see the Dane, Astolfo, Charlemagne
as soon as I reach Paris in my fight,
and if Rinaldo's citadel I seize,
I will obtain from him all that I please.

"I'll have my chance to fight with paladins; 29
Rinaldo will be back, and so Orlando,
and it will be my luck to fight them, too:
my reputation to the sky will soar."
With all these very things she fell in love
as on she rode, absorbed in all her thoughts:
she was a maiden now in search of fame,
a maiden with a heart that nought could tame.

Riding beside her and escorting her, 30
Gano along the way was talkative.
"We'll do all this," he answered more than once,
exciting and inciting the young girl.
"I swear," he added, "that Rinaldo's fate
means little to me. In two months or less
you will have conquered the whole realm of France
without a single blow of sword or lance.

"Everywhere friends and relatives have I, 31
while Charlemagne has not one trusted town
where I may fail a plan of mine to start
as soon as they see a new war begun."
Antea said, "Behold the stubborn man!
Who called him traitor, he was more than right,
for if all that I think is quite correct,
never did I so great a knave detect."

So all of them round Montalban convened. 32
But to its lord let us now all return.
Rinaldo and the Sultan's mameluke
proceeded in the Old Man's savage quest.
Rinaldo to his pagan squire said,
"Now, if you love me, mount this Arab mare,
for never, till my well-known horse is found,
will I—I swear—another charger mount."

Reverence made the pagan hesitate; 33
reverence also caused him to accept.
They started out discussing the great might
of that horrendous and accursèd man.
The mameluke so warned him, "See to it
that never do you fall beneath his claws."
Rinaldo answered, "You will laugh at this—
I am a fiercer monster than he is."

As soon as they were deep in a great wood, 34
they saw, right in the midst, a great ravine—
wholly deserted, tenebrous and bleak.
The pagan said, "That is the palace where
the mad dog's living; even from this far
I recognize him: at the window he is now."
Rinaldo saw that at the window he stood,
watching from there all over down the wood.

Out loud he cried from there just as he saw 35
Rinaldo appear, "What people can these be?
What are you looking for around here—death?"
Down to the door he came with raging storm.
Rinaldo answered, "Through the sunless wood
we, unaccompanied, have come to you,
and I am here to give you what you said,
to spite and shame Mahound, your helpless god.

"I know you are the mighty Sultan's foe, 36
and I have come to make you pay at last
for all the wrongs you did him till this day,
for many a crime against him you've committed."
The Old Man said, "I ever was his friend,
and to the whole wide world this fact is known.
But since an honest knight you seem to me,
hear how this rumor may have come to be.

"As sound asleep he lay, this Sultan saw
    a vision right before the morning rose:
    he saw a mountain tumbling down on him,
    armed for the battle on his horse's back.
    Because of such a dream, he is convinced
    I am that mountain; he's already sent
    Antea to challenge me, but from my sight
    departed she—the loser of the fight.

"The same suspicion makes him hunt me still,
    and more and more he tries to take my life,
    heedless of any terms or any truce.
    But if it's Heaven's preordained decree
    that this should come to pass, then I am sure
    that this event must ultimately be.
    So there you are, arrived to challenge me:
    wait till I take my weapons instantly."

Rinaldo said, "I'll give you ample time
    to don your suit of armor as you wish,
    this being the one way I choose to fight.
    You'll see how good it is to face my sword.
    Maybe I'll teach you how to halt your pride
    and make the Sultan tremble nevermore."
    The Old Man armed himself, as fast as a dart,
    with a snake's skin which boiling had made hard,

and for a sword he brandished, fast, a club—
    a weighty, knotty, massive iron club
    with three big leaden balls attached to it.
    Quick to Rinaldo he returned and said,
    "I'll make you change your mind immediately
    as soon as you can feel my blows; and if
    of these three leaden balls you taste but one,
    its echo will resound in Bambillon.

"But if you do not mind, reveal your name
    to me, and if a pagan knight you are,
    since you have spoken with such arrogance,
    and wish the mighty Sultan to avenge."
    Rinaldo answered, "Mind it? I do not.
    I am the famous Lord of Montalban,
    come here to kill you for Antea's sake:
    this I will do before my leave I take.

37

38

39

40

41

"I know, Old Man, you're lying in your throat,
saying you beat the lady in the fight:
seven like you could not have done so much.
On her behalf I'm challenging you now:
more than a thousand times I swore to her
that I will not go back without your head.
From the rich dress she wore, before I left,
this lovely star she gave me as a gift,

42

and in return I soon will give to her,
O traitor I despise, your severed head."
As soon as the Old Man heard who he was,
a cloud of doom descended on his brow,
and if departing had been honorable,
he would have left at once, such fear had he.
Instead he raised his mighty club, and then
his duel with Rinaldo soon began.

43

Rinaldo looked at those three leaden balls,
which, had they been successful only once,
would have made both his cheeks a yellow splash.
Yet some of them he had a bit to taste,
unable to avoid them all the time—
which made his helmet more than once resound:
therefore, he had to muster all his skill,
using his shield, using his sword as well.

44

Each time the club came down, as best he could
he pricked him with his sword, now on the legs,
now on the gorget, with his other arm
handling the shield to shun his every blow:
in such a manner he could save himself—
a master in the art of self-defense;
but, being not always successful, he
faltered and often fell upon one knee.

45

After they dueled for an hour and more,
Rinaldo lifted his Frusberta high
to show what he could do by such a blow:
the big old helmet that the Old Man wore—
so cruel was the throw—fell down at once,
and down with it the Old Man also fell—
a helpless thrush so staggering, so stunned,
he lay a while as lifeless on the ground.

46

Hurt in his pride, "O cavalier," he said,   47
"I call myself your prisoner right now:
  you could have killed me while I senseless lay.
  So from now on do with me, famous knight,
  according as you wish." Rinaldo said,
"Most willingly I take you as my friend.
  I want a man so noble and sincere
  to come with me where'er I go from here."

The Old Man so replied, "I'll be most proud   48
  to follow such a kindly paladin.
  Meanwhile may you accept and ever like
  this palace and whate'er I own on earth—
  and if there are new ways to please you, tell me."
  Rinaldo said, "I want only one thing—
  something for breakfast: we'd be easy prey
  to anyone who gave us food today.

"We have been traveling through desert lands   49
  where neither bread nor flour can be found;
  my friend is starving, who has come on horse:
  imagine one who came so far on foot!
  We've fasted when no fasting was prescribed,
  having been on our way since yesterdawn."
  The Old Man had much food brought in at once,
  and showed to them the utmost reverence.

Together, then, they rested in great ease.   50
  Now let's go back to where I left Antea,
  in the vicinity of Montalban.
  She came one day below its very walls,
  and with her people there she pitched her tents.
  As Gano had suggested, right away
  she to the castle sent a messenger,
  where good Guicciardo and his brother were.

The envoy brought her missive in no time   51
  and let them know how with her fighting men
  the Sultan's daughter finally had come.
  They should not be surprised by this at all,
  this being her revenge against the wrongs
  done by their brother to her family:
  therefore, they'd better send her down the keys
  or battle lest their castle soon she seize.

Guicciardo to that message so replied—   52
that neither cause nor vengeance did he know
that might have spurred Antea to her deed,
and was therefore astonished by the news.
The keys that she had asked for, he himself
would bring them down to her upon his steed,
and hand them to her on the tip of his lance,
according to the lore and laws of France.

The messenger returned with this reply,   53
which made Antea smile. The following dawn,
Guicciardo with Alardo and his troops
readily donned their armor for the fight.
The entire citadel was reinforced,
and every street was barricaded tight.
Armed on their steeds, the Christian warriors came
down to the field where stood the gentle dame.

On seeing them advance, she forward rode   54
to meet them with the utmost courtesy,
to herself saying, "Surely they can prove
they have Rinaldo's blood inside their veins,
so bold and dauntless on their steeds are they:
their features and their manners speak for them."
Missing her dear Rinaldo nonetheless,
she greeted them with lovely gentleness,

saying, "There is no need to tell your name,   55
gentleman whom these eyes have noticed first:
you are Guicciardo, that most gentle knight
in whose heart gentleness itself is reared.
Alardo is the other cavalier
in whom the ancient valor is reborn.
But kindly tell me: Where did you conceal the keys
that on the tip of your spear you'd promised to release?"

Guicciardo answered her, "I do not know,   56
young lady, what has brought you to this deed,
but, things already being as they are,
here to the field in self-defense I came,
although I much regret having to fight
so beautiful a woman as you are.
If any member of my family
has hurt you, deeply it distresses me,

and I would be most grateful if I knew   57
which of them so offended you and where,
before surrendering the city's keys
to you, who look like Mars himself to me.
Only my own dear brother and a cousin—
indeed an expert in the fighting art—
I mean, Orlando and Rinaldo of Ammon—
better than you astride a charger have I known."

The lady to Guicciardo so replied,   58
"In gentleness, and not in enmity,
only to win renown by fighting you,
have I come here your castle to besiege."
"O gentle lady," said Guicciardo then,
"what you have mentioned, in your Syrian land
is maybe known as perfect chivalry,
but in our France it is but villainy.

"Yet, if you seek renown by fighting me,   59
I am most pleased—on this condition, though:
that, if I beat you, you return at once
to Bambillona with your fighting men;
the castle, if you beat me, shall be yours."
Antea said, "By Mahound, I accept.
Gentle Guicciardo, turn your horse right now:
I want to see if you are brave, and how."

They took the field and laid their spears in rest.   60
Wounding, they came against each other soon
in a great storm: their horses strongly clashed,
and good Guicciardo broke his mighty lance,
letting its many splinters pierce the air.
But the young lady, wholly unimpressed,
punctured and gave Guicciardo such a wound,
he had no other choice but reach the ground.

"You are my captive," said the lady then,   61
"and now the other gentleman I'll fight."
She bade Guicciardo taken to her tent,
and, 'gainst Alardo riding right away,
"It is, O baron, now your turn," she said,
"since your Guicciardo's been so fast unhorsed."
Alardo took the field, ready to go,
and spurred his charger 'gainst his daring foe.

Swifter than birds and swifter than two darts   62
hurled from a strong ballista or a good bow,
they charged, each placing a great spear in rest
right at the selfsame moment. Thus they clashed,
and when they were together in one grip,
the whole earth shook with sudden mighty fear,
so loudly did Antea shout and spur
the steed that like a dragon carried her.

Alardo left upon the lady's shield   63
the iron vestige of his rending spear,
but, if I'm not mistaken, its great tip,
though very sharp indeed, could not go through
what was much heavier than leaf of oak.
So the young man unseated was at last,
for he could not withstand the woman's blow:
he, like the other, also had to go,

in fetters, to the selfsame tent away.   64
There Ganelon was waiting. 'Twas to him
the lady said, "Have you already thought
about these two men's fate? I'd like to know."
That traitor, who this question had foreseen,
did not have long to pause for this reply:
"Lady, if we're not cautious, trouble follows:
if I were you, I'd send them to the gallows."

The Sultan's daughter so replied to him,   65
"You should not doubt Antea, paladin.
The very man whose Montalban you hold
has fought with me, and very well I know
he could have killed me with his brandished spear,
yet, loving me too greatly, he did not:
it is my turn his love now to reward—
which will leave Ganelon surprised and cold.

"In Persia I have fought your Oliver,   66
and beat him; Ricciardetto I have, too,
though much against my will I did a thing
for which I am—I swear—most sorry still.
I left them captive in my father's hands
and now, because of it, I fear for them.
Rinaldo left for what to him was best—
the Old Man of the Mountain to arrest.

"When he will have accomplished such a feat,   67
    my father will return both prisoners,
    and so they all will shortly join us here—
    something that is so dear to this my heart,
    which never will have peace inside my breast
    until they all are back, as my God knows.
    Thus Gan, this treacherous, accursèd knave,
    will dearly pay for the advice he gave."

So she gave orders to four mamelukes   68
    dearly to sound their clubs upon his back:
    never did alarm bell more clearly ring
    than all those echoing, down-falling blows.
    Guicciardo and his brother were in bliss;
    after he was well beaten up, those friends
    raised him up straight with many a scorning laugh,
    all saying to him, *"Nasserì bizeffe!"*

Gan did not know the meaning of those words;   69
    Antea soon translated them for him:
"These mamelukes desire as their reward
    one *nasseri* for every blow they give
    the wicked culprit they are bludgeoning.
    The thing is very simple, Ganelon:
    to many people treason can be fun,
    but traitors are despised by everyone."

In such a way, but only partially,   70
    Ganelon paid for all his countless sins;
    thus in divine and most mysterious ways
    are our grave errors very often purged:
    therefore with patience we must bear them all,
    but not despair just as Iscariot did.
    Man ultimately pays for every crime,
    and we are vindicated in due time.

Guicciardo expressed his boundless gratitude   71
    to the young lady for her gentle deed,
    but out of grief still pounded at his chest,
    thinking of Oliver and Ricciardetto
    still prisoners: tears streaming down his cheeks,
    he feared the Sultan might forget his deal.
    Antea gave her reassuring word
    that neither knight would in the least be hurt.

Guicciardo and his brother begged her then,   72
"May you, Antea, be so kind to us
as to select Rinaldo's very castle,
until his journey's over, as your home.
No more have you to fight to win it: we
put everything we have now in your hands."
Antea at those words was overjoyed,
while Ganelon in jail was most annoyed.

Now let us leave Antea, blissfully   73
awaiting her Rinaldo in Montalban,
where all those Christians did the best they could
so great a dame to honor and respect.
Meanwhile Orlando most dejectedly
on and on traveled with the luckless girl
who, just to save herself, as we have said,
had from the giants desperately fled.

"Where are you, O dear cousin?" so he moaned,   74
"Where did you leave me so dismayed and sad?
Where are you now? Why am I not with you?
Where are you taking me, good Vegliantin?
Where shall we soon end up? God only knows.
Where are we going—to what alien land?
Where through this forest am I taking this
poor girl? Where will they tell me who she is?

"I curse the wickedness of my own fate,   75
I curse both Persia and its Admiral,
I curse this misadventure of my life,
I curse all Africa and all its men,
I curse the Sultan of the Syrian land,
I curse Antea looking for a man,
I curse god Love that made everything start,
I curse our Ganelon with all my heart."

Hearing Orlando in this way lament,   76
the girl felt deeply sorry for the count,
and said, "Do not despair, I beg you, sir,
but recommend yourself to God, good Lord,
that He may not forsake us in our plight."
Orlando answered, "Lady, for my love
ride with Terigi a bit ahead of me,
for now alone awhile I wish to be."

The squire and the girl did as he wished.   77
The count dismounted then from Vegliantin,
and in the middle of the road knelt down.
Raising his arms to heaven piously,
humbly as ever he adored his Jesus,
praying to Him as well as to His mother
that he might safely leave that wilderness.
Such was his fervent prayer more or less:

"O just and highest and almighty Father,   78
O Virgin in whom ever I have hoped,
O great Redeemer of the Christian world,
never will I from this bare ground arise
if first You don't enlighten this my mind,
that I may see my cousin's whereabouts—
whether he's dead or in some dungeon bound,
and where he, ill or healthy, may be found.

"I beg you in the name of Gabriel,   79
the angel who received your special blessing
when our redemption came he to announce,
that you may lead me where my cousin is;
and since I'm traveling untrodden ways,
send Raphael to me as to Tobias,
and may he take me where I still may see his face,
if this my humble plea is worthy of your grace.

"For all the love that you to Adam showed,   80
for the offering of Abraham unto you,
for every prophecy we're reading still,
for David and for Moses, dear to you,
for the Most Holy Cross that saved us all,
for Jacob and for Noah, ancient fathers,
for the laments of Prophet Jeremias,
for Joachim, and Joseph, Zacharias,

"for all the miracles you have performed,   81
bestow upon your faithful so much grace
as may reveal where my dear cousin is:
I beg you in the name of our Holy Gospels."
Right at that moment a sweet voice was heard,
so sweet it seemed to have come down from heaven.
It told him, "On this road go straight ahead,
and to your safe Rinaldo you'll be led.

"You'll also find the horse that he has lost   82
and a most mighty giant now has bought."
At once the lightning that had struck his eyes
together with the voice fled fast away.
Orlando jumped up on his horse as fast,
thanking the Holy Powers up above.
Terigi and the girl once more he joined:
ahead they had been riding till that point.

Out of the forest finally they came,   83
and reached a mighty city where King Falcon
was ruler. They dismounted at the inn.
While waiting for their breakfast to be served,
they saw two noble youths just then arrived.
Suddenly happy, the young lady ran
out to the door to see them then and there,
but one of them soon grabbed her by the hair.

He was King Falcon's nephew, and his name   84
was Prince Calandro. When this young man saw
her lovely cheeks and her long-streaming hair,
he wanted soon to take the girl away.
As loudly as she could, she screamed and screamed,
and at those piercing shouts Terigi ran
and tried to save her from the pagan's clutch;
but by that villain he was given such

a blow, he soon fell senseless to the ground.   85
With the innkeeper there Orlando ran,
brandishing Durlindana with such ire
as never roused a tiger or a bear.
Such a backhanded slap he gave Calandro,
he split him in two pieces like a stump:
fast he invoked Mahommed as he fell,
and so he had to bid the girl farewell.

There were a few armed regiments with him: 86
they all on top of Count Orlando jumped,
but as they tasted some of his brave blows,
one after another they forcibly withdrew.
The news was quickly to King Falcon brought:
to the innkeeper he came fast and asked,
"What's happening? Who killed Calandro? Why?"
"Sir, he deserved it," was the man's reply.

Wisely Orlando thus addressed the king: 87
"'Twas I who killed your nephew, Holy Crown.
A girl of a most noble family—
honest and good and pure—was here with me,
but that young wicked fool had come to seize
the helpless lass and do her injury,
and he was carrying her against her will.
The rest you guess: to you I then appeal.

"I know you care for safety on your roads,   88
and want no man to travel yet in fear:
safe you want all of us both day and night."
King Falcon then replied, "I'm glad for it.
Put, O great knight, your sword back in its sheath,
for I am greatly thankful for your deed.
Above all other things I cherish justice:
she is my everything—bride, daughter, niece.

"I want you now to come into my city   89
so that I may repay you for this wrong."
See what a gentle man this monarch was,
see what a wise and humble king was he.
Replied Orlando, "Each of us will come,
but since we all are knights along our way,
I ask for one more act of gentleness—
that the innkeeper is being paid for us."

King Falcon answered, "But of course, of course!"   90
He bade his treasurer be there at once,
and with his money the innkeeper paid.
So then each one was on his charger's back—
Orlando and his squire and the girl.
King Falcon paid due homage to them all.
But in the middle of their banqueting
an envoy came, who wished to see the king.

A pagan man was he, black as a crow,   91
most villainous and proud, most odd and dark,
all dressed and mantled with a dragon's skin.
Soon in a fierce and most discourteous way
he told the king, "May you be soon destroyed
by both Mahound and Jove, who rules the world.
'Tis time you know the time has come that you
must give my monarch what to him is due."

Bewildered and perturbed, King Falcon said,
"O my poor daughter, daughter of my grief,
how great it would have been if you had died
instead of coming into this bad world!"
Orlando begged him to reveal to him
the meaning of that missive right away.
King Falcon then replied, "You soon will hear,
and will, I'm certain, share my many a tear.

92

"There is an island in the sandy sea
with eight big giants, brothers all of them.
Each of them has the arrogance and wrath
now shown by this bold man, who's one of them.
For our eternal punishment they want,
out of our sad and frightened populace,
a little girl to be assigned to them;
and, ah, this year my daughter's turn has come."

Such was his grief he could no longer speak.
The messenger repeated his demand,
and poor King Falcon his dear girl embraced.
Orlando asked, "Can I reveal to him
what I have come to think of this whole thing?
I can't hold back my tears—believe you me—
so much dismayed am I for her and you."
The king replied, "Tell everything—please do."

94

To the proud giant then Orlando said,
"I know not what your lord is asking now,
but a fierce, cruel man you seem to me.
Your missive so much threatens and commands
that no one but the Sultan could have sent it.
Tell me your name and who has sent you here,
and then my final answer I will say—
I mean, in what a measure we shall pay."

The pagan said, "If really you wish
to know my name, Don Bruno here I am:
and Salicorno's king of this whole land."
Orlando answered, "What a man's sword earns
is most undoubtedly legitimate.
Do you agree with me? Therefore I'm one
whose sword will make you very quickly see
whether this girl belongs to you or me."

96

Don Brun replied, "By God, 'tis what I want.   97
Let's go; we'll give the city quite a show,
and if you beat me, I'll forgive you, too."
Orlando, already with his breastplate on,
said to King Falcon, "It will now be good
to punish this low rabble finally."
He rose and put the helmet on his head,
saying, "Let's go, you pagan, where you said."

Soon to the square all of the people rushed,   98
the banquet being most abruptly stopped.
Don Brun had mounted a great steed of his,
and Count Orlando charged his Vegliantìn.
Much of the population there convened;
also, the lovely lass, so fair to watch,
the duel of her fate had come to see,
praying for her Orlando's victory—

praying, that is, in her own Moorish style.   99
She begged her own Mahound to heed her plea
and keep her dear virginity unsoiled,
saving her from that giant whose desire
was menacing her fresh, still-blooming prime.
At this, the fighting knights their lances lowered
while a great shiver seized the entire square
as Vegliantìn threw flames into the air.

Everyone marveled at that mighty horse.   100
Orlando in the belly pricked Don Brun,
whose shield, however, could withstand his blow.
Twisting all over, the accursèd pagan
easily tore his lance like a bit of straw,
pinning it to the border of the shield:
his spear into a thousand splinters broke,
whereas Orlando's shield withstood each stroke.

Don Bruno took one of his scimitars,   101
which had a magic might, somebody says,
although our author does not mention this:
it had been strongly tempered, I suppose.
Against the sky blaspheming with loud shouts,
he gave Orlando a horrendous blow.
"If you're good, save yourself from this!" he yelled,
and made two halves of the protecting shield

with which the Christian knight had saved himself. 102
Orlando, with the half still in his hand,
answered Don Brun in a resounding way:
he landed it upon the pagan's snout
and in one second made three teeth fly out:
fainting, he crumbled on the ground below.
Everyone marveled—astonished, aghast—
that such a tower could go down so fast:

"Who else but Count Orlando could do this? 103
He would have felled a castle with that blow."
The Saracen at last came slowly to,
and, rising, put his hand fast to his mouth,
searching for those three fangs no longer there:
blood was still flooding down upon his chest.
He uttered an extremely painful sound,
and was most eager to blashpheme Mahound.

To Count Orlando then he said, "Much more 104
than my three teeth, I mourn my honor lost.
But one must always keep one's given word:
so tell me what you want me now to do."
Orlando answered, "But two words I need—
you shall exact no tribute from King Falcon,
and that whenever you sit down to eat,
this very promise you do not forget.

"I also want your wound attended to 105
before to Salincorno you return;
meanwhile for a few days stay here and rest."
And so Don Bruno rested a few days,
and every time he asked for food to eat,
his servants, all around him, asked themselves:
"With all his missing teeth, what will he do?
Yet Gramolazzo's seat he'd gladly chew."

Before he left, he gave his word of honor 106
that never to King Falcon would he give,
as he had done, annoyance in the least,
for with the duel he had also lost
the right to any tribute; so he went
back to his region. Thus King Falcon felt
relieved; his gratitude was so complete,
he laid his kingdom at Orlando's feet.

Don Bruno came at last where sand and wind 107
made a most stormy tumult in the air,
and it was there that, heaving many a sigh,
he saddened Salincorno with his tale.
Wrathful beyond belief, and stuttering,
he said, "Whenever I sit down to eat,
I must recall the teeth I failed to keep.
Now, Salincorn, 'tis you must take the trip

"and ask for the old tribute." Salincorno 108
replied, "Mahound or not, I surely will.
Who is the knight who has so treated you?
He cannot be one of King Falcon's men."
Don Bruno answered, "Through the desert land
of Barbary no mighty lion roams,
nor elephant nor Libyan snake you'll see,
that would not lose its fangs or teeth like me.

"I am not sure I know the warrior's name: 109
I only know he's a good herbalist
who also knows how to extract one's teeth.
This is my tribute, then, and my May wreath;
now, if you want to go, you must be told
that several of your teeth you too will lose.
No tribute must be asked, to him I swore;
it's up to you to force the king once more.

"As far as I'm concerned, no more will I 110
go back, lest I a traitor should be called."
But Salincorno was so eloquent,
he finally convinced Don Brun to go.
Five hundred men he kept on the alert,
ready to march with him at once; and so
in a few days he to King Falcon came—
a bestial man without a bit of shame.

Heedless of law or faith or any pact, 111
with all these people he besieged the town,
to which he sent a messenger at once.
The messenger appeared before the king
and briefly said all that he had to say,
according as his lord had asked him to—
that he should send to fight the very foe
who had offended his dear brother so.

Upon a mare, he sounded soon his horn,   112
threatening sky and nature with its din.
Orlando, hearing Salincorno's name,
bade his Terigi bring his armor suit.
The king's fair daughter, who around him stood,
said, "O dear count, may God now give you luck;
may He today give victory to you
since Fortune's here to threaten me anew."

"Fear not, young lady," then Orlando said,   113
"for we shall win in spite of everything.
Unlike his brother, who has lost his teeth,
this Salincorno will soon lose his jaw."
He and Terigi jumped up on their steeds,
but, followed by her escorts, the young lady
wanted to ride with him down to the plain—
thus she refused without him to remain.

The giant said, "Are you that pagan knight   114
who dared offend my Bruno shamelessly?
Say, ruffian, is this woman your cheap whore?"
Orlando answered, "By my very head,
chivalry is but rudeness in your case.
Thus I will treat you as I did the first,
but what I did to him is less than nothing,
and so I'll give your mouth no time for frothing.

"This girl's great father has a hundred servants,   115
and never would he call you one of them.
How dare you claim as tribute her fair limbs—
the tribute that's obsessing still your mind?
With these your soldiers you have now come here,
and call me ruffian, too; but clean your feet,
for if this thing you covet, your desire
for whores and concubines will soon expire."

The giant answered, "As you know quite well,   116
we are not always equal in our strength.
My teeth, which are as strong as any boar's,
are not Don Bruno's, as you soon will see.
There are eight giants in our family:
five of them watch over Malpruno's valley,
and here to fight you have remained but three,
here where the sand is churning like the sea."

Replied Orlando, "Five have, then, been spared
from boiling in this stew—you can be sure.
With this my sword I made one of them die;
the other by my cousin has been slain.
From King Costanzo in a desert land
they dared abduct a little lass one day:
with me is she of the most splendent brow,
and I must give her to her father now.

117

If ever to that region I return,
and in the deepest forest find those three,
I will not be so kind as I have been,
for I will sever their three heads at once."
Now Salincorno was so full of wrath,
he started to behave most stormily,
as soon as all these mentioned crimes he heard,
and how two of his brothers were interred.

118

"You fierce assassin, wicked traitor you,
take now the field!" he shouted instantly.
Orlando bade his Vegliantìn take wing,
suddenly turned, and lowered fast his lance,
which was, when he departed from his town,
as stout and solid as a trunk of fir.
So with his massive spear he punctured him
right through his chest—indeed, a fatal beam.

119

He shouted, "By Mahound, what's this to me?
It is, as I can see, a sailing mast."
Because it was too hard and thick and dry,
the spear was able to withstand the blow,
but the most wicked Saracen could not,
nor could his mare, though massive and robust:
down fell the blow with vehemence and speed,
and down fell Salincorno with his steed.

120

The princess, who had witnessed such a thing,
said to herself, "A miracle I've seen."
The fierce and great ferocious giant said
to Count Orlando, "I'm not beaten yet.
I have not been unhorsed, as you can see,"
and, saying this, he from his steed jumped down;
"it is quite clear 't has been my charger's fault—
also, your spear's most villainous assault."

121

Orlando answered, "If I'm not too clear,   122
I can explain things better with my sword—
the only way to settle this our feud."
The pagan said, "By god, if I come near,
I'll let you dearly pay for this your blow."
And Count Orlando answered, "So you will."
Quickly he drew his Durlindana's blade
while valiant Salincorn his iron mace up-laid.

Here nones and vespers were most quickly heard,   123
here the most doleful notes at once began,
here the third hour before the matins rang,
here not a single fly was seen to rest,
here without lightning the whole heaven roared,
here Salincorn was paying for his sins,
here the far better fighter would be seen,
here Durlindana would be cutting clean.

Whirling his mattock oft, the Saracen   124
said, "Wait for this to wipe and clean your snout."
"You crazy beast!" the paladin replied.
"What will you say if this my sword avoids it?"
The pagan's breastplate soon he found with it
in such a state he made the man grimace;
he could not reach his helmet: next to him,
less than a little hanging flask he seemed.

It was his very height made Salincorn   125
miss with his falling mattock more than once;
so fierce and vain a blow did he release,
he ruinously fell upon his face.
Quickly Orlando showed his gentleness.
"Stand up," he said. The Saracen stood up,
and asked, "O knight-at-arms, please tell me: Why
did you not kill me as you saw me lie?

"Surely a gentle person you must be,   126
of noble blood—which you cannot deny.
You did not want to strike me cowardly:
so if my question, sir, you do not mind,
please tell me who you are." Most humbly, then,
Orlando answered, "I'm King Carlo's nephew,
Orlando, Milon's son, Lord of Angrant,
enemy of Apollin and Trevigant."

As soon as Salincorno heard "Orlando,"   127
his heart began to shake; so did his hands.
He said, "But why and when and in what way,
paladin, have you come to such a place?
With you I must not handle club or sword
for well I know my strength would be in vain.
Our fight is over now, and you have won:
so, as you wish, do with me from now on.

"I heard you are the noblest Christian knight,   128
and with great magic power you were born.
Then I would rather come across and fight
your cousin, a great enemy of mine,
and make him pay for many a suffered wrong.
And as a friend, you must now promise me
that when you meet Rinaldo face to face,
you'll find a way to let me know the place,

"because I am resolved to smash the head   129
of one who'll be my foe eternally.
If he is a descendant of Clairmont,
the Salinferno blood runs in my veins;
therefore, such grievous shame I cannot bear.
Even the one whose name forever rings—
Mambrin of Ulivant, revered and splendid—
from this my very blood he too descended.

Orlando said, "Where now Rinaldo is,   130
I do not know; but if I find him, I
will send a messenger to you at once.
On this condition now I let you go—
that our King Falcon you no more annoy.
Somewhat unwillingly I let you go,
but soon you'll fall into another net
if with Rinaldo you just try to fight."

The Saracen then promised to release   131
the king from any tribute whatsoever,
and bade his camp removed from there at once.
Orlando to King Falcon went right back
into the city, bringing him the news
that he was safe and all his men were free.
Then after a few days his court he left,
leaving that monarch of all joy bereft.

Through many winding avenues he rode,   132
never and never resting day or night,
from country to new country asking where
the monarch of Bellamarina lived.
Finally in that city he arrived,
and there at last that poor, wandering girl
he could bring back to her afflicted father,
who long had thought her dead, and to her mother.

The entire city was in mourning clad—   133
so was the king with all his courtiers.
No longer from high steeples did the voice
of the muezzin ring and call for prayer.
In the mosques, where the news had not yet come,
rites were performed in the accustomed way:
the luckless princess had been lost so long,
they now were singing her funereal song.

In great excitement the great tidings reached   134
our King Costanzo: his dear daughter was
in town, alive! His heart leapt up with joy,
and with his family he ran to meet her.
The entire city at that news came out,
as always happens with a wondrous thing:
to hug the girl each wanted to be first.
You can imagine her own father's feast.

"Father," she told him, "this is Count Orlando."   135
And so she said to him how he had found
and saved her from the giants, in what way
they had succeeded in kidnapping her,
how most unhappy her long days had been,
and with what great respect along the road
Orlando had treated her until that moment.
Astonished, King Costanzo made this comment:

"Is this the one who saved you from sure death?   136
Is this the one who made you free again?
Is this the one who was so strong and bold?
Is this the one who makes all men less known?
Is this the one who's gladdening my court?
Is this the one who saved you from your tomb?
Is this the one who killed the horrid giant?
Is this the one who's known as Lord of Angrant?

"No better baron ever mounted horse,   137
no better horseman ever helmet wore.
No better champion ever brandished sword,
no better paladin put lance in rest,
and never has a gentler man donned spurs."
He hugged and hugged Orlando with great feast
while, showing to the count their gratitude,
the queen and everyone around him stood.

Now let us leave them all in their great bliss,   138
and go once more to Bambillona, where
the Sultan seemed to have forgotten all
that His High Crown had promised to Antea,
concerning the two prisoners. In fact,
he now was planning to have both men killed
before Rinaldo from the Mount's Old Man—
mission accomplished—came to town again.

And so that traitor for the hangman sent,   139
and even wrote a brief to King Costanzo
congratulating him and, as a sign
of his delight and love, invited him
to come and see that execution: "Sire,
they're being punished for more crimes than one,"
as in the following beautiful Canto I will tell.
May you be ever guarded by Angel Raphael.

CANTO   XVIII

Magnificent, O Lord, with Your salvation   1
render my spirit and my very soul,
and you, to whom *Ave Maria* was said,
and who for virtue and for grace are praised,
O glorious Mother. O benevolent Virgin,
among the other graces granted me,
to this our story still your favor lend
until I bring it to its very end.

I said the Sultan had already written
to King Costanzo, asking him to come
to see the execution he had planned.
The very while the messenger appeared,
the monarch read the letter eagerly,
and understood the traitor's mind at once.
He placed that letter in Orlando's hands,
saying, "Here's what your Sultan recommends."

When Count Orlando clearly saw all things,
he turned to King Costanzo in dismay,
saying, "May God and you be now my friends!
See how the Sultan has betrayed me now:
this time I'm truly begging for your help."
Replied the king, "Believe me, you've not served,
my dear Orlando, an ungrateful man:
you'll have, by God, all my assistance then.

"I'll draft a hundred thousand men at once,
and twice as many should the need arise,
to make with them another Round Table.
My crown has wealth and multitudes of men;
so do not doubt, you will be more than pleased,
for much I long to see that rogue exposed."
Many a messenger was heard and seen,
bidding all men to arm and at the court convene.

In a few days they were up on their steeds
with flags and pennons ready for the march.
The king's own flag was black and yellow; never
had such an army been arrayed before.
He wrote to the great Sultan that he would,
without a doubt, pay him a visit soon:
therefore the execution he should stay,
waiting for him already on his way.

Orlando, who had personally reviewed
every battalion, had a joyful heart,
and once again was watching those armed men
who seemed to him as dauntless as could be.
Now the young princess with her winsome words
let Count Orlando know how glad she was
at last to have him compensated so;
and the young lady wished with him to go.

And even King Costanzo went along.   7
So day and night upon their steeds they rode
until at last they came to Bambillona,
around whose walls they pitched all of their tents.
Pretending to be still good, perfect friends,
both King Costanzo and Orlando went
to see the Sultan, and were followed by
many important chiefs whose rank was high.

The Sultan saw all of those men appear,   8
and still so many in the plainland camped;
he heard war instruments and neighing steeds
and, growing soon suspicious and afraid,
at this most sound conclusion he arrived:
"There are too many men around my walls."
Yet, being wise, he hid his discontent,
and fast to Salincorn a message sent—

yes, to the one who had already fought   9
Orlando, and now wished to dare Rinaldo—
that he should come down there with many a troop.
And Salincorno did not rest until
he armed ten thousand men to help him soon:
and since they hailed from torrid regions, all
were black of skin and of imposing height,
and clubs instead of swords wore in the fight.

With all of these he to the Sultan came;   10
but to Rinaldo let's go back, who had
defeated the Old Man. One day, the pagan
who first had sent Antea along with him
saw a great crowd appearing in the plain,
and to Rinaldo and the Old Man was saying,
"Who can they be—these men now coming here?
I cannot tell; their flags are not too clear."

As soon as they a little closer drew,   11
Rinaldo forward walked and asked a squire,
"Who are those men, and where are you all going?"
"He's the chief executioner," said he,
"going to do his duty in Bambillona,
where the two Christians wait for him in jail:
A sultan's daughter brought them to captivity,
and one of the two knights is a marquis."

As Lord Rinaldo had this question asked,   12
astride Baiardo came the executioner.
As soon as he caught sight of his own steed,
Rinaldo like a dauntless lion jumped,
holding the executioner by the reins.
Shouted the pagan, "Were it not that I
intend to spare the beast you seem to be,
I'd teach you not to hold my reins and me."

To hit him, fast Rinaldo raised Frusberta,   13
but lest he hit Baiardo, too, he stopped.
'Twas then the Old Man, who had seen them start,
ran to Rinaldo's aid immediately:
eager to separate them, so he used
his mace, the pagan could not shun its wrath:
with but one blow so hard his head he split,
down like a half-pear fell it to his feet.

Upon Baiardo leapt Rinaldo then.   14
And, mounted as he was upon his horse,
he raised Frusberta then and there so high,
he hit a pagan soldier on the head,
which with its blood enameled soon the ground
as he fell lifeless at his charger's feet.
Just as he saw him falling, with great speed
the Old Man jumped upon the pagan's steed,

and right into the pagan crowd he rushed,   15
commended by Rinaldo heartily:
whoever by his novel mace is reached
must willy-nilly to the ground fall dead.
The mameluke who had the magic mare,
he also worked, for there was much to do:
all of those men were routed out of ken—
I should say scum and rabble, and not men.

And still the Old Man with his iron mace—   16
harder than any oak or any elm—
retouched and sounded, hammered and harassed,
killing at times full twenty with one blow.
Rinaldo like a savage boar leapt on
whichever groups of pagans he could see,
and smashed and pushed and tore and cut and ground
any opposing force his valor found.

He who first vanished, took the best along,   17
for upon all Frusberta left a sign,
and every time the Old Man used his mace,
to many he would say while blessing them,
"This way I wake a sleepy person up,"
and, saying this, he held his club aloft,
because of which they fled or—better still—
they disappeared as lightning ever will.

Thus to the Old Man spoke Rinaldo then,   18
"Let's go at once to Bambillona, where
the Sultan is about to kill those two."
"I am your servant," answered the Old Man;
"your task is to command, mine to obey.
One thing I want—that we together stay:
where'er you go, there I will also be.
Just nod or simply whisper, 'Follow me.'"

At once the three of them were on their way—   19
the mameluke, Rinaldo, and the Old Man.
As soon as he caught glimpses of the camp,
Rinaldo said, "If still my vision's good,
down there I see as many Saracens
as lived beneath Nebuchadnezzar's rule.
The plain is filled with banners and with tents:
I wonder if they are the Sultan's friends.

"Surely the men besieging mighty Troy   20
were only half this multitude and throng,
such is the ground with tents and tents galore.
Perhaps the Sultan wants, this very day,
those two to taste their last and bitter meal;
but in the name of God, I'll make him weep."
This is what in his heart Rinaldo said,
and, full of fury, rashly went ahead.

One day Orlando said to Spinellón,   21
by King Costanzo held as a great knight,
"I think that we should see our prisoners.
We'll go, and beg him just to show them to us
inside their dungeon, not outside of it."
The pagan said, "Forever I obey,
and if it is a prudent thing to do,
we should invite there King Costanzo too,

for very much indeed he would enjoy   22
seeing two knights of such esteem and fame."
Replied Orlando, "This will please me most."
So Spinellón invited King Costanzo.
They walked into the city, and (why make
this story any longer uselessly?)
the Sultan gave permission to them and
even put the keys in King Costanzo's hand.

Thus to the jail our men went right away.   23
On hearing the door open, Oliver
told Ricciardetto, "Here they're bringing us
something that does not taste as sweet as cake:
I'm sure this is our final suffering,"
and a great sadness therefore seized the two.
Speechless Orlando stood when finally
Oliver and Ricciardetto he could see.

Said King Costanzo, "Listen now to me: 24
if you decide to worship our Mahound,
out of this dungeon you will soon walk free;
if not, you will—I give you both my word—
tomorrow morning kick and kick the wind."
Soon Ricciardetto to those words replied,
"If we are given by your Sultan death,
we're glad to die for Jesus and our faith.

"But if Rinaldo, my beloved brother,   25
or Count Orlando, his cousin, now were here,
we would not be in this predicament.
At least I hope that, after we have died,
they'll make this wicked, cruel tyrant pay
for such a wrong. Avenged we both shall be,
and Bambillona, all of it, will moan,
by their strong hands reduced to stone on stone.

"Oh, but it grieves me not to see again,   26
before I die, my brother and my cousin,
and yet, as if inspired by my God,
I think I hear their voices presently."
Orlando could no longer bear all this,
eager and eager to embrace the youth;
and so, no sooner had Ricciardo stopped
than, with the visor of his helmet up,

he said, "How right you are! Orlando's here,
who never, never has abandoned you."
Oliver looked and said, "Of course it's he,"
and Ricciardetto recognized him too.
Around his neck he threw his arms at once,
and Oliver hugged his dear brother-in-law.
Joy made them greatly weep, and with no shame:
the king and Spinellón did just the same.

27

Together, then, they spoke of this and that.
Orlando told them not to doubt at all,
for he had taken care of everything:
cheer up, then, everyone, and worry not!
So to the Sultan they together went,
and gave him back his keys to avoid suspicion:
they thanked His Lordship for the courtesy
that he had granted them so graciously.

28

Not even once Orlando had removed
his helmet; so the Sultan asked one day,
"Tell me, Sir Knight, who ever stay concealed,
why do you keep your helmet always on?
This is a fact I fail to comprehend,
and if I grow suspicious, 'tis your fault.
At any rate I bid you tell me why,
or I'll believe some fraud in this may lie."

29

Replied Orlando, "Certain enmity
is forcing me to keep this helmet on,
so that no man may so malicious be
as, ah, to do me in, one of these days."
The Sultan said, "Some scheme is hidden here:
the compass does not reach its radius well.
A man who always travels in disguise
either is afraid or about something lies.

30

"I must, this moment, look upon your face;
if not, some sudden ill you may incur."
Orlando said, "In this I cannot please you,
but am your servant in all other things."
The Sultan added, "I must soon find out,"
and, this said, placed his hand upon his face.
Orlando's slap was then so hard and thick,
it left his hand imprinted on his cheek.

31

Enraged and furious, the Sultan rose,   32
scolding his mamelukes, "You lazy scum!"
Orlando did not flash his sword up high,
to keep it hidden from the watching knights.
'Gainst all of them he turned most wrathfully,
with many a punch defending soon himself:
he made them many a pitless peach then eat,
which savoring, they hastened to retreat.

Ispinellón, a loyal friend indeed,   33
suddenly laid his hand upon his sword
and, letting not one blow fall down in vain,
he opened quite a rivulet of blood.
Seeing that there would be no gain for him,
the Sultan ran into a room somewhere
and kept himself, for terror, out of view.
Orlando, too, to safety then withdrew,

with Spinellón and King Costanzo around   34
and close to him: they all at last came out
of Bambillona, and sought their camp again.
The barons of the Sultan, in dismay,
some here, some there in great confusion fled,
marveling at the boldness of those knights:
and through the city soon the news was heard
of what had just to their own lord occurred.

After the Sultan was quite reassured,   35
he bade all barons to his presence fast.
Up in his chair he rose, and there was never
a finer speech delivered anywhere.
Quickly he started with these very words:
"Never before was this my person struck,
yet everything I am prepared to do:
so I forgive, if this is best for you.

"As you can see, this King Costanzo leads   36
all of these men that cover mount and plain;
I do not know what thoughts are in his mind,
but to avoid suspicion and more harm,
I've feigned to welcome him most willingly.
Now, with regard to him who struck my brow,
I think it will be better to let go,
to shun a possible far greater woe.

"But I will see that justice be upheld   37
by executing the two captive knights:
finally King Costanzo and Spinellón
will with their men return to their own lands.
Once these two knights, our prisoners, are dead,
by fewer men shall we be hurt or harmed:
if King Costanzo I make my enemy,
no advantage whatsoever I foresee.

"In the meantime, as Gano has advised,   38
Antea could siege and conquer Montalbàn.
I'm sure Rinaldo never will return:
the Old Man, I believe, has murdered him.
At the right time and place I will reveal
to King Costanzo all the wrong he did:
I do not seek revenge that soon backfires,
but time I bide, as prudence now requires."

'Twas Salincorno who continued thus: 39
"No! No! While it is hot, must iron be struck.
Why want an explanation or a truce?
With these my very hands I'll seek revenge
before the sun returns a few more times.
As far as the execution is concerned,
good! Speed it up! And in great haste proceed!"
And on this issue all of them agreed.

A spy was quickly sent to King Costanzo   40
to tell him what the Sultan had decreed.
In turn, Costanzo let Orlando know.
Orlando said, "Let us start out at once
so that no harm may come to our two knights."
And they were eager right away to march.
Meanwhile the Sultan had the hangman called,
bidding all things be ready for the scaffold.

Heralds throughout the city then he sent,   41
inviting every man with arms or steed
to come and on the very day announced—
rain or shine—see and witness justice done.
Now, upon hearing this, a brave young man,
named Mariotto, answered right away:
he was a lad of great nobility,
and of their emperor the son was he.

This Mariotto thirty thousand men   42
brought to the Sultan, who therefore rejoiced,
all of them in hard leather oddly clad.
One hundred thousand horsemen thus convened,
fully equipped and in their fashion armed,
to order the procession of the court;
the hangman came with many men around,
went to the jail, and the two barons found.

In their full armor they were bound anew   43
upon the saddle each of his own horse—
a thing that made the Sultan thus exclaim,
"It seems to me you're taking them full-armed,"
to which the hangman, who dared not object,
replied, "I thought it was the thing to do."
You know that the real hangman has been slain,
as I've already said, by the Old Man.

A second spy was promptly on his way   44
to tell that the procession was to start.
Ispinellón and Count Orlando soon
and in great haste did rally all their men.
And King Costanzo to the count so spoke:
"It will be hard, my lord, to save those two:
no sword or lance will make us now prevail,
so tilted at this moment is the scale."

Oh, what a sad, pitiful sight it was   45
to see the two knights in lament and tears:
"O Count Orlando, O Ammón's Rinaldo,
where is your power of so much renown?
Oh, wait no longer, come in all your pomp,
for we are birds already caught and lost."
And with these words a doleful sound they made,
for each was terribly of death afraid.

Already every flag was now in view,   46
with Mariotto marshaling the parade:
outside the city they had come by now.
There was, of course, the Sultan, overjoyed,
and scorning 'long the way the Christian knights,
"You rogues! You traitors! You perfidious foes!"
But Ricciardetto, in spite of all his crying,
to him retorted, "In the throat you're lying:

"one is the rogue and traitor—you alone.   47
Oh, but somehow Rinaldo will be here
and with his hand will rip your heart right off:
for it was you who promised and agreed,
O wicked man, to give us back to him."
Replied the Sultan, "Round your neck a noose
will make your throat most silent before long,
but in the meantime they will cut your tongue."

Orlando and King Costanzo clearly saw—   48
and so did Spinellón—the sad parade
in which the very Sultan was involved.
Each of them held his spear upon his thigh,
then they advanced; then clever Spinellón
to Mariotto said, "This is not good.
I tell you that this hanging is not good,
for very gravely it offends our God.

"Besides, the Sultan—this is what I heard—   49
had promised to await Rinaldo's sight.
Now he is therefore greatly to be blamed
for the great haste with which he's doing this.
And there is something else: as soon as Charles
receives the news, he will against you rush.
Rinaldo and his cousin will come too,
and make you pay for what today you do.

"And even if nobody were to come,   50
do you not blame the Sultan for his deed?
What happened to the oath sworn by the crown
that seems to hold all of this world in thrall?
Go back to Bambillona, Mariotto,
so that no scandal may come out of it."
Concluded Spinellone with a sting,
"Costanzo's much displeased by such a thing."

And Mariotto so replied, "You're wrong.   51
If Charlemagne were at this moment here,
or even Orlando and his mentioned cousin,
along with Hector, the great man of Troy,
and with his ax mighty Burrato, too,
the Sultan would not be afraid at all;
and if what I believe you disregard,
I, Spinellón, am daring you: en garde!"

Ispinellón refrained from further talk: 52
he backed up on his horse immediately
and then, advancing with his lowered spear,
pierced every rib of Mariotto's chest,
so furious and mighty was his blow.
The crowd that was around moved soon away
as Spinellón brandished his sword at last,
but the king and Orlando moved as fast.

Orlando spurred his Vegliantín so well   53
that quickly with a push and then his spear
he felled the first opposing Saracen;
and up he raised now his almighty sword,
and none of all his blows fell empty down:
let all who stand before him run away!
And King Costanzo, too, is in the fight:
the Sultan's camp is presently in flight.

When all that uproar reached the Sultan's ears,   54
he quickly said, "I am afraid my thoughts
have told the truth, for I have been betrayed
by King Costanzo, as my doubts foretold."
He saw all of his people in dismay,
which made him greatly worry even more;
but forward yet he came, and with his sword
gave every captain an uplifting word.

Throwing himself now here, now there, Orlando   55
was in the middle of the thickest crowds:
right there, and there alone, he wished to be,
making far ampler circles of his sword:
wretched were those by Durlindana touched,
for soon they felt the sharpness of its edge!
Indeed, all those who lingered in its way
received a shaving good for Judgment Day.

About Rinaldo let's now say a word.   56
As soon as he was near the camp, he saw it
ready for battle, and to himself he said,
"Ricciardo, dear, you're done for, I'm afraid.
But, Sultan, do you keep your promise so?"
"I've been betrayed," he said to the Old Man;
"the things I see indeed look very bad:
therefore, fast as we can, let's move ahead."

These, too, in no time at all were in the fight.   57
Rinaldo did not know what to do first,
and so he begged a Saracen to tell him
the reason why the camp had come to blows.
The man replied, "The Sultan called us here
for the two knights condemned to hang today;
but King Costanzo wants no execution:
that's why the camp's in such a great commotion."

Meanwhile our Spinellón, who'd fallen down   58
after the giant hit him with a blow,
seeing Rinaldo at that moment come
(quite unaware of things he seemed to be),
said, "O my lord, just as you have been told,
you see here, topsy-turvy, the whole East
for these two Christians by the Sultan sent
this very day to death, though innocent.

"But my lord, King Costanzo, is against it: 59
therefore, to save the two, we are all here,
for very much we're sorry for those knights,
one of whom is Rinaldo's brother Ammon,
and there (to keep you in suspense no more),
there in the thickest fight is Milon's son:
he's doing mighty things to save those two,
and here, you see, on foot I'm fighting too.

"I've not been able yet to mount my horse   60
from which a certain Salincorno threw me.
All those who wear a yellow uniform
are fighting for my lord this very day."
Rinaldo said, "O kindly baron, I
most certainly would like to know your name."
"My name is Spinellón," thus answered he,
"and very much Orlando and his Rinaldo are dear to me."

'Twas then Rinaldo shouted, "Saracen,   61
I am Rinaldo, and have come down here
in search of Count Orlando, my dear cousin.
Mount, quick!" And quick the man was on his steed.
"Now take me where the paladin is fighting!"
All of a sudden reassured and glad,
Spinellón said, "And now we'll surely win:
let's go where Count Orlando I have seen."

CANTO XVIII ❖ 353

They went together through the entire camp   62
until they reached the spot where, blood-besmeared
and breathing hard, the count was fighting still.
Rinaldo said, "Put down your sword awhile,
and give me, cousin, news of the two knights."
Orlando recognized Rinaldo at once
and, weeping, hugged him with great tenderness,
then told him of the Sultan's wickedness.

"We'll celebrate our great reunion later,"   63
he said. "Now let us help the prisoners."
No lion ever roams the forest deep
as our Rinaldo started with a roar:
the head of this and that one soon he split,
thus forcing the thick crowd to open wide.
The Old Man, Spinellón, and Count Orlando
are with him, and the four make but one thunder.

As soon as they were in the thick of troops   64
and there began to rout all of those men,
they were four wolves onrushing on a flock;
and those who did not flee were sorry fast
as like a strong wind they destroyed all things.
Wasting no time and with great fury still,
they dashed upon the tent where the Sultan stood,
and it was there their swords got soaked with blood.

The Sultan sat upon a blackish steed,   65
protected by his private mamelukes,
when at that moment came the four like one,
shouting, "To the accursèd Sultan death!"
As soon as the Old Man could see his face,
he took a spear and raised it shoulder-high,
saying, "Now this is what I want to see—
if fate or fortune for your death chose *me*."

Seeing that spear now lowered suddenly,   66
the Sultan, too, moved his own steed at once,
and, seeing that he meant much more than chatter,
'twas he who could hit first the Old Man's shield:
belly and brassart he had wished to pierce,
but the spear broke, as Heaven willed: in countless
fragments it went to lodge high in the air.
No man can alter what's decreed up there.

And so the prophecy was then fulfilled
of a high mountain falling down upon him:
for as the Sultan hit the Old Man's shield,
despite its thickness, so he pierced it through,
and with it breastplate, hauberk, and, though padded
with floss, the jacket, and then flesh and bones;
and then so hard he with his charger clashed,
the Old Man's steed upon the Sultan crashed.

67

But fast the Old Man's horse was up again,
whereas the Sultan's with its lord stayed still,
both of them lying dead upon the ground:
which proves that Heaven's will is never wrong,
for this had been decreed and preordained.
The Sultan dead, his men were horrified
by such a death and sought the nearest door:
and so this almost ended that harsh war.

68

Seeing the Sultan fall, Rinaldo said
to the Old Man, "Upon my faith I swear
that he was not a fool for fearing so.
Prophecies do not lie, as you can see.
Well, then, now that his routed troops are fleeing,
let us, too, show them what brave knights we are."
And so they roamed about, with violence
pursuing the withdrawing Saracens.

69

With one of his Frusberta's blows, Rinaldo
unsaddled first the hangman—a dead man.
He said to him, "You have offended me:
my good deeds don't deserve such recompense,
for to the captives I brought help and solace."
Rinaldo answered, "Show me where they are,
and you'll be able in this way to live;
or from my sight alive you'll never leave."

70

The executioner led Rinaldo then
to where the captives in a corner lay
in anguish and in sorrow and in tears:
ah, they had cried so much that very day
that one could hardly recognize them now.
"Tell me how much you'd pay," Rinaldo asked
the two sad Christians, "if I set you free?"
Oliver, ever silent, looked at him silently.

71

But "Nothing," Ricciardetto soon replied;   72
"we have no money here nor anything;
as our misfortune wished, we've been brought here
most wretchedly and, ah, most hopelessly.
But if Rinaldo were, this moment, here,
nothing on earth would make us now afraid.
Alas, not even Count Orlando arrives—
he who had promised us to save our lives."

"Are you Christians?" Rinaldo asked of them.   73
And Ricciardetto answered, "Sir, we are,
and we were even high and sovereign knights."
Rinaldo could not bear it anymore.
He placed his hand upon his visor fast
so as to make them look upon his face:
they recognized him soon, and were astounded,
but they could not embrace him, being bound.

Rinaldo then unbound and hugged them both,   74
saying, "But don't you know Orlando's here,
here in this camp, still routing all these men,
in order to deliver you from death?
I beg you now to follow my advice
so that you finally may get some rest:
go with your executioner at once
to the pavilion of King Costanzo."

The three of them to the pavilion went.   75
But the strong giant at that very hour
killed King Costanzo mounted on his horse—
and much Orlando wept for such a death.
He also with one blow felled Spinellón,
and there, by chance or fate, Orlando came,
and did so much, he gave himself to Christ,
and by Orlando's hand was then baptized.

How wonderful, how wonderful the words   76
that Spinellón pronounced before he died!
Grace had already opened heaven's door,
through which his soul was in a while to pass.
Keeping his glance fixed on that place up there,
he seemed to hear all of its angels sing.
"Orlando," he told the count, "with these my eyes
I see, all open for me, Paradise."

"Can you, too, see up there the things I see?   77
Who is the one all men revere and dread,
crowned on a throne, and just and merciful,
amid myriad lights and diadems?"
Replied the count, "Jesus our God, Who feeds
on happiness and hope all men on earth,
and is by faithful Christians worshipèd."
At this the dying pagan bowed his head.

"Who is the lady sitting next to him,   78
who seems the fairest of all women born,
and has a lovely angel at her side?"
"She is his Virgin Mother, Nazarene,
and th' angel at her side is Gabriel,
who greeted her with *Ave, gratia plena.*"
At this the Saracen was seen to be
raising his arms before her piously.

And he went on, "Around her now I see   79
twelve men, all of them crowned upon their thrones."
Replied the count, "This little company
are her apostles duly glorified."
"And who's the one who holds a lovely cross
and most intently seems to gaze on Jesus,
ever more eager to behold His face?"
"He is the Baptist, His dear cousin," says

Orlando. "And those three so near the Lord—   80
who are those ladies?" "They are the three Marys
who with much love went to his sepulcher
on the third day after his crucifixion."
"And who's the one who looks upon his Maker
as if to tell Him, 'I will not obey'?"
Replied the count, "Our Adam he must be,
whose sin has damned us all in misery."

"Who is that dear old man with so much faith   81
who wants to sing Hosanna more and more
and seems so blessèd down at Mary's feet?"
"The one who in the manger was with her."
"And who is the old man who sits beside
his wife?" "He's Joachim," replied Orlando,
"with Anna; he is Holy Mary's father,
and she's her glorious and pious mother."

"And do you know who all those people are,   82
   so just and wise, with big books in their hands?"
Replied Orlando, "They must be the prophets
   who her Annunciation could foretell;
David is one of all those blissful men,
   with Moses, the lawgiver, and Jeremiah."
"And what are those numberless crowns I see?"
"All holy men and women they must be,"

Orlando answered, "martyrs, patriarchs,   83
   confessors." "And those other lovely things?"
"Heavenly splendors," so replied the count,
   "such as the planets, sun and moon, and stars."
"And that sweet bliss, those balmy fragrances,
   all those sweet harmonies and twinkling lights?"
Orlando said, "'Tis God's beatitude,
   our everlasting Lord's ultimate good."

"And those who seem on fire as they sing   84
   with wings outspread around and near the chair?"
Replied Orlando, "But now rest awhile.
   They are but different kinds of heavenly beings,
and each of them has been assigned a place:
   the first are Cherubim and Seraphim;
the others, Thrones, who stand so near the chair,
   and these three groups form the first choir up there.

"The other hierarchies after this   85
   of Seraphim and Cherubim and Thrones
are called Virtues and Powers, but before
   these two, the Dominations are up there;
then Princes and Archangels are with them,
   and Angels, too, who sing in unison.
The pagan said, "In Paradise I see
   all of them just as you described to me."

"Ah," said Orlando, "up in heaven's light   86
   you'll see them better in a little while.
So with pure love and zeal to heaven lift
   all of your thoughts, your very mind and eyes,
and then be sorry for me, left behind,
   chained to the heat and frost of this blind world."
And so he gave his blessing to the man,
   and Spinellone's soul to heaven ran.

Orlando, full of overwhelming joy
for Spinellone's sweet and happy end,
with all his spirit was in ecstasy
so that he seemed Saint Paul to heaven raised,
who then called dead poor mankind still on earth.
But in the meantime Salincorno came,
pushing all those who tried to stop his speed.
Swiftly Orlando mounted on his steed,

shouting, "Come back, you good-for-nothing riffraff!
Or will you let one pagan rout you all?"
And they replied, "A giant's on the field
who seems to threaten Jupiter himself:
rather than wounding or cutting, he swallows us,
and this is why we all are fleeing fast."
Orlando scolded them with cries of shame,
but at that moment there Rinaldo came.

88

Already Salincorn had asked the count,
"Where is Rinaldo? I'd love to meet the man."
Seeing his cousin near, Orlando said,
"O Salincorno, you can meet that man:
here is the one you threatened wrathfully—
Rinaldo is the one I'm talking to."
And, turning to Rinaldo, to him announced the count,
"To have a fight with you, this giant came around."

The giant gave Rinaldo but one look,
and saw he was a very dauntless man,
and for a moment marveled, standing still;
once more he looked at him and at Baiardo,
and he who was so warm cooled off at once,
saying, "Sir Knight, if I see well, I never
beheld a finer soldier 'neath the sun;
yet of all traitors you are number one.

90

"'Tis you who 'mongst my relatives have killed
that Chiariello who was so renowned;
two of my brothers you have also slain,
and you killed Brunamonte, as you know,
'mid countless wrongs and treasons; Mambrin, too,
the one who from this very blood was born,
and Costantino you betrayed and slew,
so that a thousand nooses wait for you.

CANTO XVIII ❖ 359

"We are six brothers, still upon this earth,
but I alone will, traitor, punish you."
Jut like a tercel waiting for its flight,
Rinaldo longed to jump upon the man.
He asked, "Well, then, if you can do so much,
why did you let my brother throw you down?
How dare you call Rinaldo a traitor—you,
the greatest rogue and ruffian I knew?"

The giant said, "Orlando, if you please,
know that our nature cannot bear all this;
this man knows very little of us giants:
if I just start, he will regret it fast,
for I will clean his snout with this my mace."
Rinaldo, who knew not where his fear went,
wished with a gauntlet his moustache to charm,
but just in time Orlando grabbed his arm,

saying, "Why don't you start a lawful fight?"
"I," Salincorno answered, "the day long
have fought already, and much damage done,
felling Costanzo and also Spinellón;
I therefore should not have to fight this man
either in single combat or any other way.
But on the field we'll both tomorrow be,
and we shall both play dice most profitably."

94

Happy, Rinaldo agreed; so Salincorno
made his way back to Bambillona's walls
while all our knights to their own tents returned.
The Old Man said, "Until the new day dawns,
I won't, Rinaldo, take my armor off;
and I hope greatly that this pleases you."
"Such a suggestion's wise," Orlando says,
and so they do not bother to undress.

Wise as he was, the Old Man all that night
held vigil with some soldiers fully armed.
Now, thinking that the camp was all asleep,
out of the city Salincorno came.
Toward Rinaldo straightaway he went,
believing he would catch him unaware;
but soon he met the troops of the wise Old Man,
and so the battle suddenly began,

with many people wounded on both sides
and a great din now spreading through the camp.
Still Lord Rinaldo was too sound asleep.
Baiardo, wide awake the whole night through,
next to Rinaldo started loud to neigh
till, yet unheeded, he his reins broke loose
and, though unsaddled and unharnessed, ran
to kick against the shield of the young man.

'Twas then Rinaldo finally awoke,
and Ricciardetto and Oliver woke up:
still half asleep, they armed themselves at once.
Orlando leapt up on his charger fast,
and where the Old Man was now fighting sped,
followed by the whole camp immediately.
Well Salincorno saw that things would go awry,
sorry for having put his finger in the pie.

To duel with Rinaldo yet he asked,
and so Rinaldo told him: "Take the field!"
They seemed to eye each other with great wrath
as readily their spears were lowered down.
The pagan rabble that had come to watch
thought that the world was quickly crumbling down
when Lord Rinaldo the great giant found,
such was the tremor of the verdant ground.

The first to break a spear was Salincorn;
Rinaldo followed. The two horses crossed
each other, and the blows were almost even.
Each fighter grabbed another spear, and each
against the other rapidly came back.
Salincorn hit Rinaldo's crest: at once
his helmet by that blow was all unstrung,
and, cut clean off, its plume away was flung.

But now Rinaldo on Salincorno's shield
lands such a blow, it would unsaddle all
of his six brothers, were they here with him:
thrown from his mare, the giant's on the ground.
Shouts Salincorno, "Never have I been,
in all my life, in such a manner scorned.
You, O Mahound, you dirty dog, I curse
for having called your friend this man's wet nurse.

97

98

99

100

101

"I think you're doing business with the Christians."

The saddlebow, as best he can, he reaches,

and with both hands gets hold of his strong mace.

Walking against Rinaldo angrily,

he shouts, "You will soon join the other dogs

unless this mace springs loose from this my hand;

but if, this very night, you are not slain,

I do not wish to see my caves again."

With such a blow he hits him on the side,

Rinaldo's helmet trembles on his head,

and though our paladin is strong and brave,

so terrible and mighty is the blow

he for a minute seems about to faint,

and surely does not want a second one.

Frusberta, too, has fallen from his hand,

but luckily remains to him still chained,

and even his helmet now has fallen down.

Against him swoops the Saracen meanwhile,

thinking that he by now is a dead man.

Orlando, who has closely watched the fight,

now shouts, "O pagan, have you lost your mind?

He has no helmet and no sword in hand,

yet with your mace you charge him like the cur

and cowardly traitor that you always were."

And suddenly he hits him with his sword.

Seeing Orlando's fury, this is what

the giant thinks: "I'd better stop right now,

for this sword even breaks hard porphyry."

Rinaldo, who has seen all this occur,

feels his heart shrinking from remorse and shame:

he is once more the man he was and, eager,

goes 'gainst the giant with new wrath and vigor.

With his sword brandished, in the stirrups high,

'tis Salincorno's helmet he finds first,

and by such wrath is he possessed and spurred,

he cuts it as a knife cuts into milk.

Ah, do not ask what fury pushes him:

he breaks his hardened skull and then his brains,

and of his neck and chest he makes two parts

with more precision than a tailor cuts.

102

103

104

105

106

Thrown from his mare, the giant hits the ground   107
with such a roar as when a mountaineer
strikes with his hatchet the tallest beech down.
The Saracens that are around the fight
are scattered through the ditches here and there,
each of them dashing to the nearest door
after they see their Salincorno fall—
and if he's not been seen, he's heard by all.

They keep on fighting through the entire night   108
by lantern light and boughs of pine tree lit,
till many of them in these ditches fall,
some dead, some wounded, and some maimed for life.
Our Christians kill as many Saracens
as they can put their eyes on. Lucky those
who are the first to reach the nearest door!
Those who are last—goodbye!—will live no more.

After the few who made it are inside,   109
the city's walls are in great haste shut tight,
and straightaway men meet to ponder how
they can protect these very walls: indeed,
they dread the thought of going out again.
But let us leave these men and these armed knights:
we should go back to Charlemagne a bit,
for dear old Charlie we must not forget.

Emperor Charles, now back in Paris, wanted   110
to send Meridiana back to Carador,
who was so eagerly expecting her.
But she herself wished not to stay in France
since her beloved Oliver had left.
Morgante offered to escort her: so
the day arrived when, wasting time no more,
at last he left her with King Carador.

There, at her court, but a few days he stayed,   111
for much he longed to go toward Syria,
where Count Orlando was. He said goodbye,
and all alone his lonely way he went.
Meridiana very much had begged him
to write to her about her Oliver,
and to return and visit her someday,
who there remained in sadness and dismay.

One day, Morgante to a crossroad came
out of a valley into a thick wood.
Dimly he saw, still far away, a man
coming towards him, looking tough and grim.
He with his clapper knocked the ground and said,
"Surely this thing I've never seen before."
So down he sat upon a stone to see,
when he got there, who that strange man could be.

112

Morgante looked him over once and twice,
and then twice more, from head to toes, and all
his limbs looked horrid, odd, and ugly to him.
"Tell me, wayfarer," soon he said, "your name."
The man replied, "Margutte is my name;
I too a giant wanted once to be;
midway I then was forced my dream to quit:
I tell you, I span more than thirteen feet."

Morgante said to him, "You're welcome here.
I'll have at last a little flask with me,
since I've not had a drop for two full days;
and if you care to keep me company,
along the road I'll treat you as I must.
But tell me more: I have not asked you yet
if you're a Christian or a Saracen,
if you believe in Christ or Apollín."

114

Margutte so replied, "In one-two-three,
I less believe in what is black or blue
than in a capon—boil or roast, who cares?
And often I believe in butter, too,
in beer and—every time I find it—must,
which should be strong and genuine, not weak;
yes, above all, I in good wine believe,
for those who drink eternal life achieve.

"I believe also in the cake and pie—
the mother, one; the other is her son;
the true *Our Father* is a liver stew,
which makes three dishes, two, or only one,
from the same liver generated all.
And since a bucket I could use for glass,
Mohammed, who forbids and censures wine,
is—I believe—a ghost, a dream of mine;

"just as Apollin must some madness be,
  and Trivigant—who knows—a witches' ball.
  Faith does to men what tickling does to one:
  I know you've grasped already what I mean.
  Now you can think of me as heretic;
  but, not to make you waste your words, I'll say
  that I'm a true descendant of my folks:
  so try to plant no vineyard on these rocks.

117

"This faith is just as man has fashioned it.
  Now do you care to see what faith is mine?
  I was, in Turkey, born of a Greek nun
  and of a holy pope from Bursia.
  I learned to play the rebec as a child,
  for I was dreaming that I would someday
  Troy, Hector, and Achilles sing in rhyme,
  and, oh, not once but many a thousand times.

118

"But I grew weary fast of my guitar,
  and bow and quiver I began to wear.
  One day, after a quarrel in a mosque
  wherein my own dear aged pope I slew,
  across my back I laid this scimitar
  and took a stroll around the whole wide world:
  and my companion friends have been but these—
  all of my sins from Turkey and from Greece—

119

"or, better yet, as many as are in hell.
  My mortal sins are seventy and seven,
  which—winter, summer—never leave my sight.
  My venial ones? You count them if you can!
  If even this our world should endless be,
  no one, I swear, commits as many sins
  as I did in this life of mine commit:
  I know my trade just like the alphabet.

120

"But if you kindly listen to me more,
  in its right order I will tell the list.
  While I have money and I am at play,
  whoever wants to join me is my friend.
  I play at any time and anywhere
  until I pawn my property and fame,
  and even the hair of my own beard I gamble:
  how's that for but a prelude or preamble?

121

"And ask me not what with a die I do—
if I draw flame or cross, or head or cat,
or a push only; we're one family,
all made of the same hair and the same hide.
And do you think it bothers me to cheat,
or I'm not good in feigning now and then,
or better cheats and thieves on earth exist?
In this I am the shrewdest specialist.

"Gluttony is the second of my arts.
Here your discernment you must use: indeed,
you must the page of every secret know,
concerning pheasants, partridges, and capons,
and all the delicacies in each detail,
in search of the most succulent delight:
none of my words would ever fail in this—
to keep your palate wet and full of bliss.

"Why, if I told you with what art I baste,
or if you saw how daintily I stir,
you would most surely call me a gourmet.
Of a blood pudding every stage I know:
it has to be well cooked but never burned,
not very hot nor even icy cold,
but done just right—well oiled but never greasy,
not too high nor too low (does it sound easy?).

"Of the soft liver let's not even talk.
Five stages (you can count them) it requires:
first, see to it that all of it be round
so that the flame will reach it equally;
and this remember, too: let not one drop
fall of the juice that ever keeps it soft.
Therefore, the first part let's divide in two—
to both of which is great attention due.

"Then, as the ancient proverb says, it must
be small, but with sufficient wrapping veil—
which is, I tell you, an important rule.
Not overcooked, then—always see to it—
for if you bite it when it's just half done,
like a sweet fig it melts right in your mouth.
It must be hot, and then, as if playing castanets,
you're free to sprinkle spices, orange peel, and fragrant bits.

Hundreds of perfect recipes I know,   127
but the most subtle art—believe you me—
is how to bake a cake and cook fish tarts.
I'd scare you if I told you all the ways
one can prepare a tasty lamprey stew.
All those who hear admit that I am right:
gluttony's chapters are seventy-two,
excluding those that represent my view.

"If you forget but one, farewell, cuisine!   128
Not even God can later right your wrong.
If I start now, until tomorrow morn
I'll keep on telling you secrets of this art.
I in Aegina was innkeeper once,
and many a lecture gave about these things.
But after this, I hope I won't displease or hurt you
if I reveal one more cardinal virtue.

"What I've been saying reaches only 'F':   129
imagine when I'm down to letter 'Z'!
I'm telling you no lie, sir: I can plow
with camels and with donkeys and with oxen,
and have deserved, for this and now for that,
dungeon and stake a thousand times and more.
I fling my tail where my head doesn't fit,
but most of all, I like to speak of it.

"Try me at dinner, try me at a dance—   130
I do my duty with my hands and feet.
I am presumptuous, demanding, bold,
and relatives and strangers I love not.
Long have I parted company with shame,
and, chased away, I like a dog come back.
I magnify my actions seven times,
to which I add a thousand extra rhymes.

"How many geese I've kept in pasturage . . .   131
ah, do not ask me that—I won't reply.
If I should say a thousand more or less,
be sure I would not be far from the mark.
If I by chance into a convent go,
out of five nuns I can drag six outside:
in such a way I make them flirt and swoon,
servants and novices for me fall soon.

"These are, therefore, the three cardinal virtues,
  mentioned so far: gluttony, dice, and arse.
  Now listen to the fourth, which is the first,
  and you will see the barrel's last drops out.
  What these my hands can reach, you can be sure,
  needs no support of ladders or of hooks.
  Several times, with papal miters crowned
  and brooms upon my back I walked around.

"I can make drills and bolts and noiseless files,
  gimlets and picklocks of whatever kind,
  ladders—it matters not—of wood or ropes,
  and sliding bars, and heavy socks of felt
  that keep my walk concealed from every ear:
  with these my hands all this nice work I do—
  also a flame that not by itself can glow,
  but only with my spit when I say so.

"If you could see me in a church alone,
  I am more eager to undress an altar
  than town hall clerks are to sequester pots;
  then to the poor box in a dash I go.
  But my first flight is to the sacristy:
  I cherish the cross and chalice I can find,
  and all the crucifixes I strip clean,
  with all the saints and Marys I have seen.

"Maybe I have swept out one chicken coop;
  and if you saw me take the laundry out to dry,
  no housewife—you'd admit—nor anyone
  could ever fold it better than I do.
  Morgante, even if it is a twig,
  where'er I set my foot, there steal I must;
  for what is yours, also belongs to me:
  everything came from God originally.

"But long before I robbed in secrecy,
  I for some time a highwayman had been:
  if there are saints in heaven, for one cent
  I would have mugged the greatest of them all.
  Then, for some rest and for my peace of mind,
  I wished to be a murderer no more—
  oh, not because I'd lost my inclination,
  but for the perils of the occupation.

132

133

134

135

136

"What's left? The virtues of theology.   137
  God knows if I can forge an entire book!
  So well I change an 'X' into an 'F,'
  no compass could design a better one:
  I tear all pages out, and each of them
  with letters and with rubrics then I match,
  and I can change—and you could never tell—
  title and jacket, marks and name as well.

"Perjuries and false oaths along my tongue   138
  most easily can slide into my mouth,
  just like Saint Peter's sweetly ripened figs,
  or like lasagna or something of that kind.
  And never, ever think that I may care
  whose toes I step on: let the loser pay!
  Chaos and scandals I have caused galore,
  and so the skein's thread gets tangled even more.

"I pick up arguments as ready cash.   139
  As for blaspheming, no dividing line
  I make between a human or a saint,
  and on my calendar I mark them all.
  For telling lies, let no one boast as much:
  if I say something, something else I mean.
  I'd like to see more fire than land or water,
  and earth and sky with famine, plague, and slaughter.

"And charity and alms and fast and prayers—   140
  perish the thought!—are none of what I do.
  Not to seem stubborn, every man I beg,
  and always say the things that hurt one most.
  I'm proud and envious and troublesome—
  but this is written in my life's first page,
  for of grave sins I knew a multitude
  with every vice and extra turpitude.

"That's why I now can go throughout the world   141
  just as I please, pride written o'er my face.
  I'm clean and polished like a pantry board,
  and leave my imprint everywhere I stay,
  just like a snail, and am most proud of it;
  and I change faith and laws and friends and skin
  from land to land, as I see fit, of course:
  Even in my mother's womb I was perverse.

CANTO XVIII ❖ 369

142

"I have omitted an important chapter
of other thousands of my random sins,
for if I only cared to read each title,
ah, what a mighty mess at once you'd see!
Besides, if I start now, I will stop winding
this thread at the beginning of July.
But let me tell you at the very end:
never, never have I betrayed a friend."

Attentive and immobile for an hour,
Morgante listened to his every word,
and so he answered him: "Except for treason,
judging by what, Margutte dear, I've heard,
there is no more completely wicked man;
and you have not yet told me everything.
I don't believe that, if she tried again
to make you, Nature could create a man

so perfect and so suited to my taste:
together we'll be well as on one leash.
As far as treason, though, watch out! Or soon
in this my clapper—see?—you will believe,
since you do not believe in God in heaven:
I know how to tame beasts inside a fence.
As for the rest, just be as you have been:
saints are in heaven, gluttons at the inn.

145

"I beg you, then, Margutte, come with me,
and bosom friends we two shall ever be.
I know the way to every place on earth.
We do not have much money, it is true,
but to innkeepers, when they bring the check,
I'm wont to give my money as I leave:
so far, wherever a good meal I found,
I've paid them with a beating strong and sound."

Margutte said, "I like you very much;
but are you ever pleased with that alone?
I always steal whatever I can grab,
even if I have to take a useless pot;
and when I leave, I'm deaf and dumb, not lame.
Even if but a spindle you can rob,
where'er you go, there's something, if you will:
and there is nothing that I would not steal.

"Through many a country I have traveled far,   147
and I have even crossed the entire sea:
I've always stolen all that I have spent.
Therefore, Morgante, take me where you wish."
So their belongings on their backs they laid,
down for his clapper our Morgante bent,
and with his friend and with a joyous shout,
towards the Syrian land he started out.

Clad in a pilgrim's gown, Margutte wore   148
a three-sliced cap as in the Moorish style,
except that those three slices were of bone—
certainly not the slices of a peach—
and it was very heavy, very big,
so much so that it often bothered him;
he wore boots iron-pronged and spurred and yellow,
and looked more like a rooster than a fellow.

Gazing upon them, so Morgante said,   149
"Are you, by any chance, of the roostery race?
For, look, your feet have spurs!" At this, he smiled.
"I wear them out of prudence, to be sure,"
replied Margutte; "utterly unaware,
someone soon felt them at his own expense:
many a peril thus I have withstood,
for many to this trap got stuck and glued."

The whole day through, they to each other spoke,   150
and then at evening to an inn they came.
There, the innkeeper suddenly was asked,
"Say: would you have some food and drink for us?
We'll pay you now or later, as you wish."
Th' innkeeper answered, "A grand time you'll have:
I have a capon left that's big and fat."
Margutte said, "And nothing more than that?

"Here you must give us all that you can find,   151
for we are men who welcome many a dish.
Can you not see how huge my friend is here?
A capon's nothing but one acid pill."
Th' innkeeper answered, "Acorns let him eat.
Where do I go for something else? It's dark."
His tone of voice was full of arrogance:
Morgante lost his patience all at once.

His clapper he began to use on him,
and the innkeeper did not like it much.
Margutte said, "Ah, stop it for awhile!
I will go through the house and search each room.
A buffalo I saw as I came in:
you'd better build a mighty fire, sir,
and heed my every whistle, my dear host,
until that buffalo becomes our roast."

'Twas fear that built the fire readily.   153
Margutte tore a beam of the roof down,
and to the mumbling host had this to say:
"Surely you bid the clapper crush your skull:
what do you want, to roast that entire beast—
the handle of a shovel? If you please,
of this our dinner I'll myself take care."
The buffalo was roasted then and there.

And do you think he bothered skinning it?   154
He only split its body right in two.
Like an old broom he made himself at home:
he ordered, shouted, everywhere was heard.
Somewhere he found a rather lengthy board,
and there the table instantly was set.
On it he placed some bread and wine and meat,
for in the inn Morgante did not fit.

And so they ate the buffalo entire,   155
three basketfuls of bread and even more,
and drank enormously. Margutte said
to the innkeeper, "Tell me: would you have
some cheese and fruit that you can bring to us?
All this has been too little for two men.
Well, something else will do. . . ." Now, if you please,
I'll let you know the story of the cheese.

Th' innkeeper brought a cheese then to the table,   156
which could have weighed only five pounds at most;
a quarter of a basketful of apples
th' innkeeper found for his two famished guests.
Margutte looked at everything, and said
then to his host, "You wild and stupid beast!
Once more we'll use the clapper on your hide
unless much more than this you can provide.

"What will my big friend do with but an ounce?   157
Stay here a tiny bit till I come back.
Meanwhile, you wait on him most generously!
See that this giant never asks for wine,
or he will straighten up your crooked bones.
So let me now be like a little mouse:
I'll find what's to be found and—you will see—
I'll make more food rain down abundantly."

Margutte searched all corners of the house,   158
tearing and pulling every closet down,
breaking and wasting pots and pans around:
he smashed all things that he could touch and see
until not one of them was still in sight.
Of cheese and fruit he a big bundle found,
and brought them to Morgante in a sack:
voraciously they started the attack.

Th' innkeeper and his servants, terror-struck,   159
all of them waited promptly on the two.
The owner thought, "The only thing to do
is not to lodge such bandits anymore.
Tomorrow they will pay me with the sound
of that big clapper—ah, what sounding cash!
So much they ate, for thirty days to come
for all this town there will be not a crumb."

After he ate quite well, Morgante said   160
to the innkeeper, "Now we'll go to sleep.
Tomorrow morning, as I always do
when traveling, we'll both prepare the bill:
you will be fully paid for everything,
and in this way we'll be forever friends."
"Pay," said the host, "as you see fit or fair,"
praying to God he'd soon be out of there.

Morgante went to find a rick of straw,   161
and leaned against it like an elephant.
Margutte said, "My money here I spend;
so, my dear host, unlike the giant, I
want not my ears to whistle in the wind.
Maybe I'm practical or ignorant,
but surely an astronomer I'm not:
like you, I want indoors a cozy spot.

"But first, before we put the candles out,
      I wish you would most kindly bring more wine:
for I at night can never fall asleep
unless, at table still, I take a sip
so as to rinse my teeth a little bit.
In peace we'll sing together a small tune:
      a quick nightcap between the two of us
      now that the giant cannot swallow us.

162

"Say: have you ever," added then Margutte,
"seen a more handsome and imposing man
who like a deluge eats and drinks as much?
Nature, I so believe, made only one.
When to an inn he comes, he wants to be
treated by the innkeeper royally;
      but when he has to pay, you'll never see
      a man who pays and tips more generously."

Some more wine came, and they spoke on and on,
and the innkeeper less suspicious grew.
Right out Margutte came with a small tune,
and then he asked about the road ahead,
saying he was for Bambillona bound.
The host replied that not for thirty miles
      around would they see any house or manger—
      a three-day journey not devoid of danger.

164

Margutte was not deaf and, hearing this,
thought out a plan of wickedness at once.
He so replied, "I'm glad you told me that—
that this our road ahead is not too safe.
But now, to bed! I tell you in advance
that it's my habit not to pay in goods:
      for all the food we ate I'll pay in cash,
      and you will tell me the amount you wish.

"I always carry a well pressed-down purse.
      But tell me: do you have by any chance
      a camel, all unharnessed, in your stable?
      If I am not mistaken, I saw one,
      but with no saddle and no yoke, it seemed."
      And the innkeeper so replied to him,
"The saddle I put on her when I ride,
      under the mattress in my room I hide.

166

"I'm sure you understand the reason why:
you know how many strangers here arrive
for supper and for dinner and for snacks."
Margutte said, "I very much would like
to see this saddle, if you do not mind,
while we are here, still talking and still drinking:
besides, the nights are long like a blind beggar's tune."
Th' innkeeper said, "I'll show it to you soon."

167

The simpleton brought then the saddle down,
and soon Margutte's stratagem was born—
he would take care of the whole bill with it.
"I like your shrewdness," to the host he said;
"this saddle as a pillow I will use,
as on this very board I rest and sleep.
I know you do not have a bed for me
where I may fit and stretch out comfortably.

168

"But now I much would like to know your name."
Th' innkeeper said, "You'll know it right away:
my name is Sleep, and I am known as such."
"Then do as your name says," Margutte said;
and to himself he added, "You'll wake up
when it's too late and when the saddle's far.
But . . . have you company or children rather?"
Th' innkeeper said, "Only my wife; no other."

169

And then Margutte asked, "How much a week,
say, can you total in this inn of yours?
And would you have enough to change for us
some doubles we may spend along the road?"
Th' innkeeper said, "I won't be here much longer:
these past four months—I swear to you by God—
scarce twenty ducats I have made at best,
which I keep hidden in that little chest."

170

Margutte said, "Well, then, we'll make you earn
more money now than you have earned so far.
But aren't you afraid to keep it there?
Someone may steal it." "It was never stolen."
Margutte closed an eye maliciously,
and murmured, "But this time you will find out."
For the completion of his stratagem,
another bit of malice dawned on him.

171

He said to the innkeeper, "Since you've been
so nice a person, and so kind to me,
I'll introduce myself: Pilfer's my name;
and now we know each other and are friends.
I have been suffering a bit from ringworm,
and 'neath this cap I hide my malady.
Say, would you, for another coin or two,
bring me some butter? As ointment it would do."

172

The host replied, "I won't accept a coin;
therefore, feel free to tell me what you need,
for in these things my kindness is well-known."
Margutte answered him, "I'm so ashamed . . .
never, my friend, do I undress at night
because . . . I tell you . . . in my sleep I walk.
Bring me a pair of ropes, and I'll be able
to tie myself this evening to this table.

"But keep your chamber fastened with a bolt
lest I should give you some resounding punch;
and if, alas, I should untie myself,
and freely then parade from room to room,
do not come out!" And Sleep at once replied,
"Forget it! I'll stay crouching in my bed.
And I will warn this entire family
to save themselves from some calamity."

174

Th' innkeeper brought Margutte ropes and butter,
and let his servants know his malady:
they should not fall into a blind abyss,
and therefore not sneak out of their own beds.
The rogue! Now learn this newest Greek deceit!
Alone, Margutte, by the candlelight,
pretended, then, to tie himself most tight,
and Mr. Sleep bade finally good night.

Margutte, hearing everybody snore,
took everything he found around the house:
he went then for the money in the chest,
and everything put on the camel's back;
when opening a closet or a door,
he smeared with butter each resisting lock;
then, having stolen to his heart's desire,
he set a massive heap of straw on fire.

176

Now, rushing to Morgante, "Sleep no more,   177
my friend," he says; "you have slept long enough;
didn't you say you wanted to go east?
I have been there and back, as you will see.
Quick, let's get out of here; begin to move,
or you'll be most annoyed by all the smoke."
Morgante said as he awoke: "What's this?
You have been faster than I thought, God knows."

They started out at once, somewhat afraid: 178
there was around the inn full many a home
with men that would wake up at the first noise.
Margutte said, "I've left to our good host
so little, it would make policemen blush:
I'll never learn to overfill a sack,
but where I went I always tried to be
considerate of others' property."

While they were going rapidly away,   179
little by little the whole inn caught fire,
and before Sleep could see the damage done,
the flames had seized already the whole house:
it did not dawn on him it was deceit.
·People began to come from everywhere:
he and his wife escaped, but as a rule
such are the things that happen to a fool.

When it was day, and dawn was dimly seen,   180
Morgante spotted a cheese grater, too,
and to himself he said, "Less wicked men
go to the gallows and the stake each day:
but look at all the rubbish of this man!
By God, his noose has waited long enough."
Margutte said, "I stole the bucket, too;
cheer up! This is an art I always knew.

"We now must travel through a certain land   181
where only those with money can survive;
and surely we'll go shopping even there."
And so he told him the whole tale about
the chest with all the money; how he set
the house aflame and took the camel out,
how Mr. Sleep had wanted to retire,
doubtless by now awakened by the fire.

Splitting his sides with laughter at his words   182
(and how he laughed when some details he heard!),
Morgante kept on saying, "Luckless gallows,
what a ripe peach and luscious bit you're missing!
Be patient if some more you have to wait.
At least this rogue spares no one as he works.
Orlando will be pleased to meet this man—
if ever I will see him once again."

Margutte said, "In business this is the highest gain—   183
to leave your man as stripped as possible.
Where will you ever find a friend like me,
so wicked and so deft in everything?
If steal you must, no predatory hawk
or gypsy or Arab you need, other than me.
For all you ever steal, be grateful never!
For the first time you see me, man, so clever.

"I even asked for butter, telling him   184
I needed it for a ringworm of mine:
instead I smeared with it the bolts and hinges
of every door, to let nobody hear
until I took the loaded camel out.
There is no malice that is not my mate.
I do my very best to shun a bruise,
and then the red with yellow I confuse."

"Margutte dear, I like you even more,"   185
Morgante said. Meanwhile a passerby,
seeing the camel, said, "That poor humpèd beast
surely belongs to Mr. Sleep of the inn."
"I must be Mr. Sleep," replied Margutte;
"can you not see, you dunce, that we are moving
to that new inn near where that castle is?
You are a bigger animal than this."

The whole day long, and then the next, the two   186
fared in a land familiar to them;
but on the third they entered a deep wood
that to wild beasts was habitat and home.
Because of the long journey they were very
hungry, but neither wine nor bread had they.
Morgante asked, "And now what shall we do?
You see, Margutte, nothing is in view.

"Let us at least below that mountain go,   187
    looking for any brook that might be there,
    for if a rill or fountain we can find,
    at least our thirst will quickly go away:
    My words do not come out as quick and clear
    unless I wet my mouth a little bit.
    It seems a place where water can be found."
Margutte agreed that his advice was sound.

So much they searched, they finally could see   188
    a very cool and limpid fountain there:
    and there they rested for a while at last
    after a walk that made them weary most.
    But look! From far away a unicorn
    appeared, in search of rills to slake his thirst.
    Margutte said, "Look there! Look there! I think
    that unicorn is coming here to drink.

"He will soon be our meal: he seems so eager—   189
    the way he comes—to fall into the trap.
    Hide and stay hidden till he gets down here
    and quenches with his thirst our hunger, too."
    The unicorn was sorely thirsty indeed,
    but of the hidden trap most unaware:
    he came and in the waves his horn immersed,
    in his own fashion slaking his big thirst,

when from the side where he was hiding, fast   190
    Morgante flung the clapper in his hand:
    he hit him with a blow so gracefully,
    the unicorn fell heavily at once,
    his senses and his pulses still forever;
    so savage and so novel was that blow,
    on the rebound the clapper hit a rock,
    which instantly caught fire as it was struck.

Seeing that light, Margutte said to him,   191
    "Morgante, look! How handy is that flame!
    Maybe we'll eat him roasted after all.
    Judging by how that stone has answered you,
    we'll force it to give out a lovely fire."
    Morgante said, "Each rock becomes a flint
    where'er Morgante with his clapper goes:
    I always use my weapons as I choose.

"But you, who are so clever, and have taken   192
all of that stuff along, Margutte dear,
why don't you carry tinder and flint with you?"
Margutte answered, "You will never find
among my malices a gentle thing,
but only fraud and wickedness galore."
Morgante said, "Now fetch me some dry hay,
and come right here." Margutte said, "Okay."

So to that rock they went, and there Morgante   193
hammered so hard, he would have heated ice;
so hard, indeed, Margutte's ears were hurt,
so that he dropped the hay he had picked up.
Laughing, Morgante spoke again and said,
"Look here, and tell me if I can draw sparks."
Shamed, poor Margutte gathered the dropped hay,
and held it high till fire lit its prey.

His pilgrim's gown he afterward took off,   194
unloaded then the camel, which had knelt,
and a whole kitchen suddenly appeared.
Set was the table (long live the innkeeper!),
for he had stolen the saltcellar, too,
with drinking glasses and with other cups;
the unicorn he burned and shaved a bit,
and of a huge pear tree he made a spit.

The beast was cooked, and they sat down to sup.   195
Morgante gulped down nearly all of it,
so that Margutte hardly tasted it.
Therefore, he said, "What a great fool I am!
By God, you could devour an entire whale!
This throat of yours is never sated, eh?
In everything I want you as a mate
except when we sit down before a plate."

Morgante so replied, "I in the air   196
saw hunger like a water-laden cloud;
and I could have devoured an entire whale
with all its hide most unreservedly,
or a whole unicorn, horn and all.
You make me laugh, who's licking but the spoon."
Margutte said, "You're laughing, I am weeping,
for all my hunger in me I'm still keeping."

Added Morgante, "But you have my word:
next time, by God, I'll give you much to eat."
Margutte said, "I will do better then:
I'll just tear off a portion good for me,
and then put what is left in front of you,
so that our friendship may for long endure.
In all the other things revered you'll be,
but I'm impatient in my gluttony.

197

Who takes my food away, he's not my friend,
but one who with each morsel rips an eye.
So let me tell you now, once and for all:
I want my share, down to a fennel stalk,
even if I have to split a fig with you,
or but a chestnut or a mouse or frog."
Morgante answered, "You can so unfold
your thoughts, you're now becoming pure as gold.

198

But now, just poke the fire, which is dead."
Margutte chopped some wood from many a tree,
lit up a fire, and then pitched a tent.
Morgante said, "If this your fire can last
throughout the night, I will be proud of you.
You've done so far a thousand worthy things,
you are the teacher of all those who know."
And so right there they spent the night, and so

199

in the meantime the camel grazed around.
But as soon as Aurora showed her face,
Margutte told Morgante, "It is day:
let us get up, and soon be on our way."
So everything they put in order quick.
Now, since each song contests a previous one,
what followed next will be in my next rhyme:
Our Father we shall praise in the meantime.

200

CANTO XIX

O lovely little children, praise your Lord,   1
our Lord's most sacred name forever praise!
May our King's name be blessed forevermore,
from this day onward till the end of time!
Now You, Who until now have led our way,
oh, take me out of this my labyrinth,
so that I may resume Morgante's feats,
thanks to the might of all Your holy deeds.

Taking their chance, our two companions left: 2
through unfamiliar, lonely lands they went,
with neither vale nor plainland e'er in sight,
with no dog barking and no rooster's song.
Into a dark place finally they came,
where most distinctly they at last could hear—
from far away, from very far away—
laments that seemed of men in great dismay.

Morgante asked Margutte, "Do you hear   3
what I hear—the sad sound, from time to time,
of voices that now seem to soar up high,
and now subside? I think it's not too far."
Margutte listened once, and listened twice,
and then replied, "Yes, I can hear them, too.
It must be bandits eager most to prey
on helpless passersby who come this way.

Morgante said, "Be careful as you go: 4
let's see what this thing is, and who weeps so!
I think the voice is coming from down there:
therefore, this is the way we too must go.
Whoever he may be, he seems so sad,
though we hear not the sorry words he says;
but if they're scoundrels, you will have great fun,
for I have often punished more than one."

When down they came from a most dangerous cliff,   5
they heard those voices clearer than before,
with a lament that now much higher soared;
finally a young maiden they could see,
barefoot, disheveled, and in great despair,
who could not even cover her fair limbs,
so torn appeared her gown most wretchedly,
and with a heavy chain so bound was she.

A lion crouched beside her, guarding her;   6
and as the wild beast heard the two men come,
quickly against them with great wrath he went.
Against Morgante furiously he sprang,
with his jaws open wide, and eager most
to use all of his claws and teeth as well.
But such a heavy blow Morgante shed
with his big clapper that he crushed his head.

"What were you trying, crazy beast, to do?"   7
he said; "a crab presumes to bite a whale!"
And toward the maiden went he soon in haste,
and found her to be noble, wise, and good.
He asked her what her trouble seemed to be,
and why to such despair had she been brought.
She kept on crying, and Morgante asked her why,
and finally the maiden gave him this reply:

"Forgive me, sir, and try to understand   8
the reason why I've hesitated so:
great is the grief that overwhelms my soul.
But if my tears have moved your heart, I now
will tell you what has caused my grievous pain,
which makes the sun eclipse before your eyes.
For seven years, as you can clearly see,
I have been here in woe and misery.

"My father owns a castle, called Belfiòr,   9
not very distant from the river Nile
(and Filomeno is my father's name).
One day, I took a stroll outside the walls:
with its most balmy, lovely weather, spring
had just come back, and meadows were in bloom:
alone and carefree, out I went, and with
a great desire to cull a lovely wreath.

"The sun, already near the Spanish shore,   10
  was warming up Granada and Morocco,
  there where it sinks into the ocean fast.
  I was pursuing still my childish whim;
  from bough to bough a nightingale was singing
  such a sweet song, it conquered soon my heart
  and made me think of Philomela meanwhile,
  as I was treading still the sand of the Nile.

"Along the bank as I was walking still,   11
  the nightingale into a valley flew,
  and I behind him ever walked and walked,
  gathering red and yellow flowerets.
  But then the bird into a small wood went,
  and I—my lovely hair loose on my back—
  decided to sit down upon the grass,
  enchanted with its singing loveliness.

"With flowers on my lap like Proserpine,   12
  I, young and beautiful and glad and fair,
  was heeding the sweet song most blissfully
  when that sweet music into weeping turned:
  alas, alas, out of the wood I saw
  a savage man appear and come my way!
  Flowers and nightingale I soon forgot,
  and started running, wretched and distraught.

"I would have gotten, I am sure, away   13
  had not, alas, my lovely tress been caught
  in a small branch that quickly stopped my flight:
  the man arrived and disentangled it,
  and then by force he grabbed me and, alas,
  stole me from my dear father in this way.
  With violence he dragged me to this den,
  where, as you see, I have remained since then.

"This entire forest is resounding still,   14
  through which I passed as that most wicked man
  was dragging helpless me up to this tomb;
  and if some pitying satyr wanders here,
  and justice still can strike men with its bow,
  I'm sure this wickedness has wrenched his heart.
  Alas, my face was snatched by many a thorn,
  and Echo echoes still my every moan.

"I beg you to imagine how, all torn   15
   and shredded into bits, my lovely hair
   was left in woods and shrubs, for wolves and snakes—
   unlucky like the hair of Absalom.
   Alas, I feel as if my heart is snatched!
   Alas, these cheeks that were so rosy and fair
   (I hope that you believe me) were, that day,
   to every bush a proud and happy prey!

"My gold-embroidered mantle and my dress,   16
   which but a speck would soon have soiled and cheapened,
   I saw them in the mud and in the mire,
   and torn by stones and trees through countless crags.
   Ah, do not think that these my eyes were dry—
   unhappy me!—when I my ill luck knew:
   where'er I passed, amid a thousand fears,
   they left behind two rivulets of tears.

"Yet in my prime these very eyes have been   17
   solace and light to many a loving man,
   who could have sworn and in all truth affirm
   they were much brighter, fairer than the sun.
   How many times—so gallant were they all—
   men came at night with serenade and song!
   But above all they praised these eyes of mine,
   that with much grace and virtue used to shine,

"and, as you see, are now so lusterless.   18
   Ah, now, if one of those young men could look
   into my eyes again, he would not be
   so pitiless and harsh as not to weep
   now and forever, all his future years,
   remembering how beautiful they were.
   Ah, but in the whole world I will not find
   a single person pitying and kind.

"My father must have died of grief already,   19
   long having waited for me but in vain,
   and, inconsolable, my mother now
   knows not my hardship in this savage place;
   nor does she know that every passing day
   a giant hurts and strikes me with his hand,
   and keeps a lion that before me lies,
   so that myself no more I recognize.

"Father and mother, O brothers and sisters,   20
   O my sweet friends and relatives and mates,
   O my poor body, so distressed and sick,
   O life, so anguished and so full of ills,
   O crazy world, O wicked, cruel stars,
   O fate, so truly hostile and unjust,
   O death, O solace of each mortal woe,
   who still detains you? and why tarry so?

"Is this the very land where I was born?   21
   Is this my palace, and my castle's site?
   Is this the nest where for some time I lay?
   Is this my father, this my brother dear?
   Is this the crowd that dearly cherished me?
   Is this the kingdom, just and old and fair?
   Is this the haven of my happiness?
   This, the reward of all my virtuousness?

"Where are now all my richly gilded gowns?   22
   Where are now all my jewels, all my wealth?
   Where are now all the parties of my nights?
   Where are now all my dainty delicacies?
   Where are now all my loyal lady friends?
   Where are now all my pleasures and delights?
   Where are now all my maids, so sweet and dear?
   Where are they all? Alas, they are not here.

"Where are now all my suitors, so refined?   23
   Where are now my harmonicas and lyres?
   Where are now all my banquets and my balls?
   Where are now my romances and love tales?
   Where are now all my husbands-yet-to-be?
   Where are now all my other countless joys?
   Where can harsh woods and wolves and bears be found—
   dragons and tigers? Right here and all around.

"What's going on now in my father's court?   24
   What's new in all the mosques and all the squares?
   Beautiful dames are feted everywhere,
   new spears are tested and new countless breeds
   of horses by the troops of knights-at-arms,
   and everyone is happy and amused;
   and, even if some people wept for me,
   after so long their grief has ceased to be.

"Oh, wretched me! How new my life is now!   25
    Each night they used to help me to take off
    my purple clothing of unmeasured worth
    and far more dazzling than the risen sun:
    and now my dresses' tatters hardly hold!
    How many maids I at my bidding had!
    How many precious stones my head once wore
    'mid songs and parties and delights galore!

"But now, as you can see, I've come to this—   26
    no longer will I see a living soul,
    and, ah, my royal palace is this cave
    where in the moonlight every night I sleep.
    Let those who deem themselves at times too happy
    now learn from one whose luck has quickly changed!
    All roses fade, and but their thorns remain:
    until the end has come, you judge in vain.

"I was as happy as my heart desired,   27
    and now I would exchange my woes with Job,
    for this ferocious giant every day
    lashes me with a bundle of iron chains,
    and for what reason I will never know:
    maybe because, whenever he returns
    from hunting lions and dragons and serpents,
    on me the smart of all his wounds he vents.

"And snakes and vipers I am forced to eat,   28
    and the strange meat that from his hunt he brings—
    I, who the tastiest partridge once abhorred;
    but so he strikes me, so he threatens me,
    against my will those things I have to eat.
    At times he even kills some human beings,
    and then he roasts and eats them all, together
    with one Sperante, who's his very brother.

"The giant's named Beltramo. Both of them   29
    like robbers roam these forests every day,
    and many a time they brought me for my play—
    unmindful of the anguish of my thoughts—
    some little newborn serpents; other times,
    some very odd and playful little bears,
    and, lest somebody try to set me free,
    they used to keep that lion close to me.

"So I have lost a lovely paradise,   30
   and ended up down here, in these dark caves.
   Burrato came and with his hatchet tried
   to save my life, but failed, and struggled hard
   to leave this place alive. Full well I know
   how grievous all his terror must have been;
   yet, sorry for me, he did all he could,
   and even said he'd seek once more this wood.

"That's why, as soon as I could see you here,   31
   I said with boundless joy within my heart,
   'I'm sure this is Burrato, a man who does not lie,
   and ever keeps the promises he makes.'
   To free me from this horrid martyrdom,
   and also for my love, more wandering knights
   have fought these giants; but all those who tried
   have only tried in vain, for they all died.

"Now, if you too are here to set me free,   32
   my father—if by chance he's still alive,
   still hoping that I may at last be found—
   would give you the whole kingdom of his land,
   so longingly waits he for my return.
   But if not even this can move you, then
   you with my heart and soul I do implore."
   Crying and sighing, then she spoke no more.

Morgante wanted to console her, but—   33
   so sad was he—he failed to utter a word.
   The maiden was still talking when—behold—
   Beltramo, who was coming with a boar,
   from far away began to threaten her.
   Right on his back he carried the wild beast,
   and a bear, too, with his right hand dragged he,
   bleeding from bites and scratches copiously.

Seeing the strangers, soon he shook his head,   34
   as if to tell her, "You will pay for this."
   Sperantè, too, was coming back with him,
   dragging a fearful dragon by the tail:
   he was a bigger and more clever brute—
   and much more evil—than his brother was.
   Close to Morgante, they began to shout
   so loudly, the woods echoed all about.

Morgante gazed on the unseemly shape   35
of the two brothers, and then greeted them,
for sudden terror made him shudder first;
and both of them replied to his hello
in the sole fashion natural to them.
'Twas then Beltramo in this way began,
"Down here what are you doing with your friend?
Maybe you now have come to your own end.

"I want to know which of you killed my lion."   36
"I killed your lion," said Morgante soon;
"he was about to wrong me, giant dear."
Shouted Beltramo, "In the name of God,
you will pay dearly for it—be assured!
So, you are faring through this land of mine,
and I know well that you my lion slew
to do with her whatever pleases you."

Replied Morgante, "Giants we are both;   37
there's little difference between us two.
We are but knights who wander through the world,
and fight for love in every land we reach:
therefore, this maiden that before me stands
I wish from her hard servitude to free.
Let's see, then, who can boast a stronger race:
I will now test my clapper, you your mace."

Sperante lost his temper then and there: 38
harder he grabbed the dragon by the tail
and gave Morgante such a dragonful,
saying, "You braggart filthy with your soup!
You're wandering indeed, but with your mind,
if you came here in search of praise and fame.
Our prey are snakes and lions; must we now
before two gluttons in great terror bow?

"Well, well, you're threatening us, villainous fool!   39
Here other men have come and left their bones."
Morgante shouted with a savage shout
as soon as by the dragon he was hit:
quick to his face he brought his hand in pain,
for both his cheeks had suddenly turned red.
Away he threw his clapper, blind with ire,
and dashed in fury 'gainst the savage liar.

So these enormous fellows hugged each other 40
exactly just as snakes and lions do,
tearing each other with their fangs and claws.
Morgante with his teeth bit off his nose,
and then two morsels made of both his ears,
saying, "You don't deserve better treatment."
Beltramo jumped upon Margutte quick,
placing his ribs in order with a stick.

Ask not if he located all of them, 41
and ironed them like coats' and jackets' pleats:
he touched and retouched and mishandled Margutte,
making him spin just as a spindle spins,
with ever bitter fruits in store for him,
perspiring even though 'twas January:
to flee, he would have jumped the highest bar,
but only helped himself with his scimitar.

Beltramo was so towering and fierce 42
that when he brought his fatal mattock down,
each time he bent and broke it on the ground;
but every time Margutte like a cat
jumped in the air not to be caught by him,
in this way shunning that horrendous curse.
Yet fast, unable to prevent all that,
he saw himself down, flattened like a mat:

so ruthless was the blow that made him fall, 43
he was just like a headlong-fallen owl,
stretched on the ground and emptily kicking the air.
But even down, more bruises fell on him,
for still the club resounded like a bell.
Poor pilgrim's gown, carded and combed so well!
After those nones and vespers sung and said,
Beltram bent down, ready to pluck his head.

Margutte, seeing himself so nearly lost, 44
suddenly put his hands upon the ground
to land but two of his masterly kicks:
he reached him with a spur beneath the chin
and drove that most horrendous giant's tongue
into his palate. Wondering and stunned,
Beltramo stood and for a while withdrew:
Margutte fast was on his feet anew.

He saw Beltramo fumbling for his mouth   45
with all the blood that gushed in rivulets:
right then he placed his head between his legs
and from the ground most quickly lifted him;
suddenly, then, he dropped him: the big tower
fell in this way precipitously down,
and, as it fell, destroyed and tore and struck
whate'er it found, like a collapsing rock.

Our little rooster jumped upon him fast,   46
so that he seemed a chicken on a stack:
Margutte, then, was saved by his own spurs.
'Twas easy now to take Beltramo's head:
the scimitar began to cut its bone.
The giant did not shiver in the least,
for when Margutte dropped him on the ground,
all of his limbs were broken with a sound.

How happy was the maiden at that sight!   47
But while Beltramo went to meet his death,
Morgante with the other did not joke.
Desirous to avenge that dragonful,
he'd not been able to defeat him yet,
much though he writhed and twisted on the ground:
they reached at last the edge of a ravine
and, to each other fastened, fell right in;

with a loud noise and a resounding din,   48
into that gorge they both immensely fell
as when a landslip or a massive boulder
boomingly falls down from a mountaintop:
no bush or thorn or even stone remained
where this enormous, heavy faggot passed:
cleaned was the ground of its minutest stalks
as with one bang they hit it with two backs.

Bottom they hit, and only then they stopped,   49
but our Morgante stayed on top of him:
with a round rock he struck Sperante's head
so many times until he saw him dead.
Thus through the clean-swept forest back he climbed,
and to Margutte, much rejoicing, said,
"Thank God you're still alive, Margutte dear!
I thought that I would find you murdered here.

"Fighting, into a precipice we fell,   50
    where for a while I thought I'd leave my brains,
    banging my head and shoulders heavily."
    Then to the maiden turned he. With her cheeks
    pale and discolored still, she seemed to be
    shaking all over, apprehensive still,
    not knowing of the passing of Sperante;
    but she was reassured by our Morgante:

"Now fear no more and never doubt again!   51
    Rejoice, dear girl, and set your mind at ease!
    With these my hands the giant I have slain,
    and dead he lies now, to wild beasts a meal.
    Now to your father you will soon return,
    for you are free now, as you longed to be:
    justice, you see, has triumphed finally."
    And so the three rejoiced most happily.

He then cut loose the maiden's chains, and said,   52
"Now, lovely lady, let us go away."
    The lovely lady, happy as a lark,
    still hoped to find her father on this earth.
    Morgante always led her by the hand,
    for she was still confused and in a daze,
    and very weak from all the woes and fears
    that she had suffered for so many years.

Margutte said, "That bastard dog has so   53
    well ironed all my ribs, he could have been
    an expert tailor, let me tell you that:
    I feel my back all broken, to be sure."
    Replied Morgante, "If I'm not mistaken,
    you have just paid for what was overdue:
    I clearly heard your jacket being pestled
    while with his brother down that cliff I wrestled."

So that day long they through the desert went   54
    always together, talking in this way;
    but as they could not find a thing to eat,
    each of them was as hungry as could be.
    Looking from far away, Margutte saw
    (the luster of the moon was white and wide)
    a turtle that to him seemed like a hill.
    What could it be? He looked and looked, and still

was not too sure it was a living thing   55
or just a simple figment of his fancy:
therefore, not trusting what he thought he saw,
he did not dare to let Morgante know.
But to Morgante, when he neared the beast,
he jubilantly said, "Can you not see
this mighty fellow crawling now before you?
I thought it was a mountain, I assure you."

"It's nothing but a turtle," said Morgante,   56
"and yet I too believed it was a hill."
This said, he with his clapper then began
to brush its dust away, and break its brain.
Ask not if he mishandled its tough hide!
The maiden, seeing that, was all aglow.
After the scales were broken bit by bit,
he asked Margutte that a fire be lit,

and, as he always used to do, he struck   57
a stone so hard that he drew sparks from it.
And our Margutte soon got busy, saying,
"All of my life the kitchen was my art."
The camel he unloaded once again,
and soon the table was before them set;
then he went looking for a boundless tree,
shaved it all clean, and a great spit made he.

After the roast was ready for the flame,   58
stuffed with some galls and acorns he could find,
he told Morgante, "Wine we do not have;
now you, who are so big, sit here and turn:
I'll go and see if water I can find
while you take care of what is here to eat."
Down sat immense Morgante with a laugh,
waiting for him to bring something to quaff.

No sooner had Margutte left the road   59
than from afar a pattering he heard.
He walked ahead to see what it could be,
and heard a beast and people talk at once.
So fast he dashed against them that they fled,
eager to shun his sudden violence:
they left the beast with two barrels of wine—
poor men, who in the woods had lost their way!

Margutte grabbed those barrels (what a play!)   60
and let the beast immediately go free.
When he came back, Morgante was aglow,
for by the smell he knew when wine was near.
They both began to taste the turtle, and
Margutte said that it was overdone.
How they were dying all that wine to taste!
So on the table soon they brought the roast.

As soon as they sat down to start their meal,   61
to the sweet maiden with a heavenly face
Morgante gave a chalice full of wine,
such as would be sufficient for her supper;
and then, faster than lightning, down he drank—
like a raw egg—all that was left of it,
for though Margutte with attention looked,
the two full casks he in one moment sucked.

Margutte shouted, "I don't like the thing   62
I see; you're gulping down instead of drinking,
Morgante; do you think I am a fool?
You're making fun of me with every game.
Say, were you waiting for the fennel stalk?
Another would have waited countless years.
You're too dishonest, but I swear by the sky
that we shall soon part company, you and I.

"If all the buzzing flies were just like you,   63
there would be need for neither cask nor tub.
Why, do you think your sippings are too small?
But what I have to say means more than wine—
you're not a man to have as friend and mate:
you do not leave a drop to anyone.
The unicorn you ate, and gave me bones;
and now you've drunk two barrels all at once."

Morgante liked Margutte very much,   64
and very much he liked to tease him, too.
Well then Margutte without drinking ate,
and even the sweet girl laughed teasingly.
Margutte said, "Many a luscious pear
this man has had," and stealthily he winked,
laughing at everything she wished to say;
but angry with Morgante he still would stay.

After the supper round the fire they sat   65
on leafy boughs and on a bit of hay,
and blissfully they fell asleep, awaiting
the fresh arrival of another day.
They loaded, then, the camel the next morn,
and started out on their new journey fast,
with still no food and still no roof in sight,
so that the maiden told them, full of fright,

"This wood, Morgante, is so thick and wild,   66
I dare not even look ahead of me."
Right then Margutte said, "Listen, what's that?
It seems just like a whistle far away."
When to the turning of the path they came—
behold!—a basilisk before them stood,
with his eyes dazzling bright and open wide.
Quickly Morgante pushed the girl aside.

Against the beast he threw his clapper fast,   67
and luckily he hit him on the neck:
as if made out of wax, his head he cut,
which landed more than twenty feet away.
There went Margutte, picked it up, and brought it
back to Morgante. Then most carefully
they measured that foul serpent: full twelve feet
of perfidy and poison and deceit.

They asked each other, "Should we roast him, too?"   68
The maiden answered, "I was forced to eat
tiger and dragon and crocodile's meat,
but neither head nor tail I cared to touch."
Margutte said, "Why argue? This to me
will be the most delicious morsel ever:
I'll but remove the tail, if you insist,
and then we'll roast him, and let's have a feast!"

And so the animal was roasted whole,   69
together with the skin he had been born with;
and he was swallowed without bread or salt—
by everybody deemed a delicacy.
They could have eaten Lucifer as well.
There was some water in the wood nearby:
they all went running there to slake their thirst;
but so Margutte spoke, full of mistrust,

"Oh no, this time I will not leave home base,   70
for I won't trust you even with a pawn,
Morgante, from now on—I swear to God—
for you'd still take advantage of me now;
you'd take the whole roast as you did the wine:
oh no, this time I will not leave home base."
Morgante laughed, and the fair maiden, too,
so loud, her teeth seemed falling two by two.

As they had always done, they slept that night,   71
and started out with the new-risen day
through savage forests and through sunless caves,
not knowing ever where to rest awhile.
Many a time the maiden had to stop,
most sorely weary from the grievous road.
But our Morgante thought it most unwise
in such a dismal place to rest their eyes,

and said, "I do not see any place yet   72
where we may stop to drink or eat or sleep:
unless we want our evil luck to send
some wild, ferocious beast to kill us all."
Under the shining moon they walked and walked
all of that night with anguish and distress;
and once again another dawn was bright,
and yet no food or water was in sight.

The three were thirsty, and were famished most,   73
worn-out and weary after miles and miles.
But at one point Margutte blinked his eyes—
surely he was a winking devil, he!
Morgante said, "What are you staring at?
Well I can see that you are blinking still.
Have you by any chance our supper spied?"
"What do you think! That's it," Margutte soon replied.

"Leaning against a tree, right there, right there,   74
I see, Morgante, a strange creature. Look!
He seems asleep, and does not move his feet:
you will not make one mouthful of this one!"
Morgante looked: it was an elephant,
most soundly sleeping to his heart's content:
'twas dusk already, and against a tree
there he was leaning, snoring blissfully.

Promptly Morgante said, "Margutte, quick,   75
give me your scimitar!" This said, he drew—
slowly, so very slowly—near the tree;
the beast would not have heard a cart go by,
so sound and solid was his heavy sleep.
Morgante opened finally his arms
and cut the whole tree underneath the beast,
which on its back fell down, utterly dazed,

starting to roar so loudly that the whole   76
region re-echoed for long miles around.
Morgante quickly fastened with two ropes
his legs and lengthy nose; he grabbed him then,
and with his sword he gave him instant death,
so that upon the ground the beast sprawled fast.
"This is a mighty beast," Margutte gloated;
"tonight I too will eat till I am bloated,"

and started, then, to cook most readily.   77
Meanwhile Morgante built another fire,
and the girl helped him in his every need,
because she too saw hunger in the air.
Margutte now was searching for a spit:
he saw two pine trees not too far away,
which from the selfsame trunk had sprouted out.
Morgante said, "A gift from God, no doubt!"

and with a single blow split one of them,   78
adding, "You now with this will make a spit;
of the other we shall make a chandelier
to place upon the trunk throughout our meal."
He raised his sword, cut all the branches down
until the entire leafage was removed;
the trunk, then, in four sections he did chop,
and finally on fire he set the top.

Margutte said, "A triumph this will be!   79
Tonight we'll have a gala, I can see,
with this our dinner here by candlelight.
Our dining hall around this pine will be,
and underneath this luster we shall dine.
But since atop a ladder I can't reach
where you, Morgante, stand without your sandals,
it is your job tonight to light the candles."

Replied Morgante, "In the name of God,   80
Margutte dear, wait till the meat is cooked,
and I'll attend to what I have to do."
Margutte fixed the roast immediately,
and said, "You turn now! Water we all need:
so let me see if there's some reservoir.
This is a meal you won't gulp down, I bet;
you'll share it with me, much to your regret."

Morgante nonchalantly said, "Go, then;   81
"I promise I will wait till you come back,
and the whole elephant you'll find still here."
He did not say "In this my stomach," though.
Margutte up and down, and here and there,
to find some water did the best he could,
until he saw the shadow of a rill
from which his cap alone he then could fill.

Margutte had not even left the fire   82
when, plucking a piece of the elephant,
Morgante tasted it, and said, "'Tis roasted well,"
and then and there he ate it all, half done.
"My appetite," he to the maiden said,
"is not accustomed to more suffering."
With great politeness and without discussion,
of course he gave the hungry girl her portion.

Returned Margutte, only to find out   83
that the whole elephant, down to its bones,
had been already eaten; there he sat,
Morgante, picking with the spit his teeth:
with the same spit as with a fennel stalk
he rummaged through his gums. Of the whole beast
nothing was left except the head and paws—
everything else had served to please his jaws.

Margutte asked, "Where is the elephant   84
you promised not to touch till I came back?"
"He's not too far," Morgante answered him,
and the girl said, "He's telling you the truth:
from head to toes he swallowed all of it—
according to his saying, nothing much."
Morgante told him, "Every word is true,
Margutte: in my stomach I saved it all for you.

"You have not studied logic, I can tell: 85
  you fail to grasp the truth I have revealed."
  Stunned, and as if still dreaming, said Margutte,
"Perhaps I understand what you have done:
  say, could it be that you have gulped it down?
  I'm sure you would have eaten me as well.
  Maybe I'm better off I wasn't there,
  and saved myself from all your mad despair.

"One of these days you'll eat me like a whale.   86
  But this has been a very monstrous thing;
  what your horrendous gullet did is only
  the action of a glutton and a swine.
  Have you not understood how much I seethe,
  bearing with you and all your wicked ways?
  Or do you think I will make gelatin
  if only head and legs I now put in?

"Like this, Morgante, we cannot go on: 87
  let us part company right here and now
  unless you change the rules of this your game."
  Splitting his sides with laughter still, Morgante
  a bit of water sipped, and sought the fire.
  Upon that head Margutte fixed his eyes,
  and, eager more than ever for some food,
  he gnawed it, like a dog, as best he could.

Then, ever mumbling, he lay down to sleep;   88
  so did Morgante, till up in the east
  the sun appeared, and with the sun the day.
  'Twas then they started out, together still.
  Margutte wished to go away alone,
  but the girl made him patient once again.
"Don't leave us in these woods," so begged him she,
"at least until a living soul we see."

Replied Margutte, "I have heard it said   89
  that never should we make fun of each other:
  instead, while I was feeling hurt and scorned,
  this man was placidly picking his teeth
  as if he'd not offended me at all.
  Now this is something I cannot forget:
  he could have done a hundred things but one—
  sneeringly pick his teeth with so much fun.

"But this he did to spite me even more,   90
rebuking me for having touched no food
as if not he, but I, were to be blamed.
And—mind you—he had said he'd wait for me."
The maiden said, "Instead, I promise you
that if you take me to my father's home,
I will reward you with a lavish dinner."
Margutte calmed himself, believing in her.

And so for several more days they went,   91
seeing no houses and no living souls.
But finally one day they heard a sound
of horns and trumpets, but saw no one yet.
At last some homes like bakeries came in view,
with a small villa that looked really great,
right at the exit of that wilderness:
Filomen was the ruler of that place.

As soon as the young maiden heard that sound,   92
suddenly to the sky she raised her arms,
starting to thank Mahound with all her heart:
she knew that all that sound not far away
was surely made by some inhabitants:
of pagan customs she was well aware.
She kept on saying, "Blessèd be Mahound!
A way out of this hell we now have found."

Morgante, too, rejoiced with her: at last   93
he to her father would now give the girl
for whom he felt so sorry; and at last
he now could hope to see Orlando again.
Little by little they the forest left,
and saw a peopled country finally.
Finally they arrived at the first home,
from where the sound that they'd just heard had come.

The maiden did not know that was the place   94
of which her father was the king and lord.
A poor and old innkeeper first they saw,
but, oh, no food had he to give Morgante.
Margutte said, "Let's use this camel here!"
and, giving for his meal the beast away,
with all his expertise began to roast it,
and then in front of big Morgante thrust it.

Morgante sank his teeth into the hump   95
and with one morsel swallowed all of it.
Margutte, sternly looking at him, said,
"Now you are proving that you are a scoundrel,
and every time you pay me with a sneer:
so long as you can fill that throat of yours,
you can, indeed, afford the role of a big clown,
and say no word whene'er at table you sit down."

A quarter of that camel soon he plucked,   96
saying, "This time I'm taking what is mine:
see here if, like a tailor, I can cut!
Ah, not so fast! I see a soldier move . . .
But I won't leave this chess game, if you please,
for well I know you'll nothing leave but bones.
It is not wise to dine with you—a rotten,
most villainous, and most dishonest glutton."

Both the innkeeper and the maiden laughed.   97
Margutte, wicked from his mother's womb,
under the table touched her with his foot
while in the others' presence winking at her.
Morgante noticed that, and said to him,
"With whores you have been dealing all your life!"
At this, the pure and virtuous girl said nothing,
but blushed and nearly shrank in her poor clothing.

Morgante said, "Just as you told me, you   98
are wicked both in actions and in words.
I do believe, Margutte, that you have
quicksilver in your socks and in your boots;
but, ah, tonight, when to the inn we come,
so that you won't repeat this turpitude,
both of your feet inside a tub I'll bind,
and that will fix whatever's on your mind."

Margutte said, "With all my mortal sins,   99
did you not know I'm wicked as could be,
so wicked that if tested in the fire,
I am as pure as eighteen-carat gold?
As soon as I could sneak out of the egg,
I was the number one of wicked men
and, better yet, the scum of all the knaves.
So what if this my foot just misbehaves?"

"Margutte," said Morgante, "couldn't you see
how much I honored her along the road
to bring her to her father who is king?
See that this deed of yours occurs no more!"
"Every sinner," Margutte answered him,
"is lawfully forgiven the first time;
if I have sinned, forgiveness I implore:
I know that I will sin worse than before."

Hastened Morgante, "And much worse you'll get.
See that my clapper I don't use on you,
for only then, Margutte, will you see
if I can iron all your ribs at once."
Replied Margutte, "Keep me on the leash,
forever fastened just as I should be,
or you, Morgante, will find out that I,
even before you, may my clapper try."

"Very well, then, behave the way you please,"
Morgante, full of anger, said to him;
"I know my clapper will more solid be,
and there will be no need for leash or curb."
But it was then the maiden said, "I heard
that someone here remembers Filomeno.
Innkeeper, do you know who he may be,
or in what town he rules in sovereignty?"

So the innkeeper said, "I know the man:
he's Filomeno, King of Belfior.
And something else I want you soon to know—
Lord Filomeno's master of this town,
and we are all his faithful subjects, bound
by ancient love and loyalty to him;
and since most wise and just our monarch is,
his people have tranquillity and peace.

"Alas, for a long time he's been in tears,
for a dear daughter they have snatched from him—
no one knows who. It was so long ago,
I wonder if we'll ever see her again.
In vain, for many years he searched for her,
and then in mourning he and all were clad.
No more does our muezzin shout his prayers,
and from that day have passed full seven years."

Our maiden's face was suddenly lit up   105
with an enchanting hue of happiness:
she felt her heart being torn within her breast,
and almost cried, so boundless was her joy.
She said, "Now I am back in paradise,
where once my youth was carefree and content."
She felt like fainting from her sudden mirth,
hearing that Filomèn was still on earth.

The news made our Morgante very glad.   106
"Tonight I am so happy," so he said,
"I would not even mind it if I died.
Margutte, quite a dinner we'll have soon,
and I thank God I forced you to behave."
Margutte, still in a bad mood, replied,
"Well, if your conscience is so delicate,
keep your mouth shut and let me have your plate."

The maiden did not introduce herself,   107
but asked about her mother and her friends.
Of everything she wanted to make sure—
of brothers, sisters, her whole family.
Right in that place they rested the whole night,
and, happy then, they left their host at dawn.
Margutte thought 'twas not the time to steal,
lest he should soon Morgante's clapper feel.

Th' innkeeper showed them the way to take   108
if in Belfior they wanted soon to be:
if they remained along the Nile's bank,
never would they the wrong direction fare.
While big Morgante treaded still the sand,
out of the stream a crocodile appeared—
jaws open wide and ready him to swallow.
Margutte said, "What now, you croco-fellow?

"This man's too big a morsel for your mouth."   109
Morgante thrust the clapper in those jaws:
the crocodile got hold of it with wrath,
with so much wrath he sank his teeth in it.
'Twas then Morgante, pulling, pulling hard,
twisted his clapper still inside his mouth,
broke all his teeth—lower and upper row—
and hurled him fast over the Nile—oh, what a throw!

One mile and more over the stream away   110
he threw him—writes a certain author—fast,
and had he grabbed him by the neck, I'm sure
he somewhere in mid-Egypt would have plunged.
The crocodile without a shake fell dead,
and the big clapper showed his marking teeth.
"He truly looked for it," Margutte said;
"for he was surely dying to be dead."

At sunset they were near the very wood   111
where the young girl's abduction had occurred.
"I recognize," she to Morgante said,
"the place where, like a silly child, I came,
not thinking there's no rose without a thorn.
Ah, so end those who only seek their fun!
Who after every pleasure wants to go,
he ultimately weeps, and rightly so.

"O most unhappy, most accursèd place!   112
Morgante, here I heard the nightingale,
and here, little by little, I began
to follow all its flights and all its song.
So fair a game it seemed to hear it sing!
But now you know what boundless grief ensued.
You I now thank for bringing me back here,
and henceforth I'll be careful—have no fear.

"And that I am no ingrate you will see,   113
for, written in my heart, I'll ever bear
the memory of how you rescued me,
and with what honesty and tender care
you then escorted me along the road—
which was, indeed, a greater service still:
not like a lover you behaved, but rather,
generous, gentle giant, like a brother.

"Just like Beltràm, you could have done with me,   114
but this you did not do; I love you, then,
as a dear brother, as you love me too.
So in my castle you'll be known as such;
Margutte, too, we'll treat in the same way,
though he was oft as naughty as could be."
Margutte said, "I have done wrong, I know—
but let me tell you—with no malice, though."

And now they're close to Filomeno's walls,   115
and now—lo and behold—they are inside.
Everyone sees the giant's horrid height,
and is afraid of staring at it more,
but soon the maiden reassures them all.
How happy will her father shortly be!
An unforeseen delight so makes us live
as unexpected sorrow makes us grieve.

Filomen heard that, with a girl, a giant   116
had come to town together with a friend,
and to the palace now was on his way,
and looked imposing and of great renown.
Right at that time Morgante forward came.
"May God protect us!" Filomeno said;
"who is this man, and who can this girl be?
But dressèd still in mourning I will be

"until I have my daughter in my arms."   117
This to himself he said, not knowing her.
He wondered why she'd traveled all alone,
saying, "This is the weirdest company."
His eyes then stopped where his desire had flown:
"This is my Florinetta!" shouted he.
And as she heard these words, the maiden ran
with loving open arms to Filomèn.

Think now, just think how happy, at that moment,   118
and how consoled that wretched father was!
Out came her mother, running at that shout,
and although Florinetta's face and limbs
had lost the grace and beauty of before,
she recognized the maiden at first sight,
and her sweet baby with such love embraced,
she nearly seemed out of her mind, and dazed.

The entire populace came forth in bliss,   119
for much was Filomeno loved by all:
in a short while the entire hall was filled.
Morgante, who, in turn, was overjoyed,
to Filomeno spoke then in this way:
"Here is your daughter that I bring to you,
and more than ever, I'm a happy man."
And to embrace him Filomeno ran.

Beside her father Florinetta sat,   120
and, having somewhat rested, said to him,
"O Filomèn, I'm sure you want to know
about all these long years away from you,
in what sad place and how I've lived so far,
and why it took so long to come back home.
All my vicissitudes you now shall hear,
the very thought of which renews my fear."

She started from the day when, all alone,   121
out of the city walls she'd wished to go;
and told the tale of how, forlorn and sad,
she was abducted and soon dragged away,
and of her life, so full of grief and woe,
with all those chains that ever kept her bound,
watched over by a lion all those years:
and those who heard her speak were all in tears.

There was not one who did not marvel most: 122
to god Mahound all of them raised their arms.
Mother and Father and all relatives
trembled with horror as that tale was told.
But the fair maiden still had more to say.
Turning to her Morgante, thus the rest
of her long story she told everyone—
what her Morgante for her sake had done:

how first of all he bravely rescued her   123
from that horrendous giant in the cave,
and how, along the journey, ceaselessly
he had much honored and respected her,
taking her ever by the hand, just like
a father or a brother or a cousin—
so honest and so loyal and so true—
yet nothing of him but the name she knew.

So highly of Morgante did she speak,   124
the entire population vyingly
embraced him and bent down to kiss his feet;
and Filomeno grew so fond of him,
he begged the giant by all means to stay
and live in sovereignty until his death.
Morgante thanked King Filomeno much,
saying, "I am your servant, and as such,

"alive or dead, I'd stay forever here,
with soul and body, if all this could be;
but I must go to Bambillona soon—
this is the reason why from France I came—
or Count Orlando I would gravely wrong.
But you, where'er I am, just send for me!
And now, if Florinetta's love is true,
here I will spend two entire days with you."

126

Sweet Florinetta said, "At least a year
you must remain with me, Morgante dear."
And everybody greatly honored him,
and he was worshiped even like a god.
She and Margutte knew what pleased him most;
obliging Florinetta therefore told
Margutte, "You shall be the cook, and see
that, day and night, well stocked the kitchen be."

127

Ask not if our Margutte, soon at work,
more than a cat had made himself at home.
"Belly of mine," he said, "become a tub,
and all your wrinkles I will fast undo.
Manna from heaven—see—is raining here."
Just like a crazy man he leapt with joy,
and, ever fat and fatter, smeared all over,
gluttony's every point could rediscover.

128

"While I was in Aegina," so he said,
"this used to be my occupation—right?
I wish my concubine were here with me!
Surely some tidbits I would save for her.
A cook who leaves his kitchen is a man
who leaves his very intellect behind:
here shall Margutte live, therefore, or he
will soon a fish out of its water be."

129

In short, he most painstakingly provided
each dinner with all things delectable.
Of every kind of food to table brought,
he always made the first and last assay,
and for himself saved some especial bites
which, being wise, within himself he stored;
at times he would most furtively sneak out
and the wine cellar test from spout to spout.

He knew about it countless stratagems: 130
whatever in the house he found misplaced,
he put together with his odds and ends
inside a sack he had somewhere concealed.
In a few days a hundred knaveries . . .
and had they longer stayed, a thousand new!
With money and with flatteries, and more,
defiled he female slaves and Moors galore.

Everything ended in his net unseen,   131
and everything he did the Moorish way.
At night he kept a barrel near his bed
with bread and meat for his debauch and spree;
then for a while he stirred his nightingale,
and then he counted, waiting for his sleep,
all of his sins from first to last degree,
but glass and die still in his hand had he.

Or some fat slop like a fat pig he quaffed;   132
then he would thrust a feather in his throat
so as to throw up when the sack was full;
he filled it, then, and tickled it again.
Finally, weary of this double deal,
and with both nostrils overflowed with foam,
into the mattress hammered he his head,
besmeared and greasy like deep-larded bread.

Worse than a filthy drunk he stank of wine   133
(just think how much Margutte could gulp down!),
but when he was dead drunk as a milord,
easily he was worth twelve chattering magpies;
and then he kissed the barrel once again
and numbered all the chapters of his life:
the lies he told came out so mightily,
seven full cartloads could have carried three.

The time had come Morgante wished to leave,   134
and although Florinetta begged him much,
he went to Filomeno asking him
permission to depart, for Count Orlando
he was most eager to behold once more.
A lavish farewell dinner was decreed
to extend to great Morgante once again,
before he left, the thanks of every man.

After they all had dined in merriment,   135
and much conversed about so many a thing,
and after Florinetta gave Morgante
jewels and rings and many precious stones,
and Filomeno thanked him even more,
wisely Morgante answered both of them,
saying that he accepted their gifts most gratefully,
to be reminded of them where'er he chanced to be.

Margutte, when he heard those very words,   136
said, "Let me now do something for myself!"
He went to grab a spit and then a pan,
blackened his face and, so disguised and clumsy,
ran where the maiden sat; there he began
to act as scoundrels impudently do,
and said, "If you don't tip your cook, dear lady,
that cheek of yours imagine smeared already!"

From her tiara Florinetta took   137
a precious stone and dropped it in the pan.
Margutte seized it with his nimble hand,
saying, "I'll take it, for I hate to beg."
Morgante would have smashed him then and there
had he had something in his hand to use:
he said, ashamed of the ignoble deed,
"Clearly I see now who you are, indeed."

'Twas then Margutte to the kitchen sped,   138
where he began to put in order fast
the sack with all that he had robbed and hid—
the one he used to place on camel's back;
and when he saw Morgante about to leave,
he even thought of what he had to store
deep in his belly, and thus had a feast
of dainties that would last two days at least.

He ate and drank and stored for two milords,   139
saying, "I won't find thrushes, nicely cooked,
when I'll see trees and trees, nothing but trees."
Meanwhile Morgante announced that he would leave,
and Florinetta, even closer to him,
made sure that he would always think of her:
she begged him to come back as soon as he could,
and not to leave until he said he would.

Morgante answered that most happily   140
and by all means he would return someday,
and even swore a hundred times and more.
Unable, though, to tell how grieved he was,
a hundred times and more he hugged and kissed
the lovely girl, and no one would believe
the soothing tenderness that he felt then,
and all the love now felt by Filomèn.

Margutte simply said to them, "Goodbye":   141
he surely was like meat more raw than cooked.
As soon as they had left the castle, said
Morgante to Margutte, "Save yourself,
for now at last I'll tell you what you are—
you bum and beast and brat, yet dear to me.
How did God make you so debauched and low?
You've shamed me, you've embarrassed me, you know.

"You have committed all your shameful sins.   142
Of course I knew that you were wicked most,
a glutton and a thief and fount of lies,
but never had I seen what I just saw:
'tween miter and a scaffold you were born,
like Christ between a donkey and an ox."
Margutte answered, "Yes, 'tween rope and broom!
This is the truth, as rightly you presume.

"I thought, Morgante, you already knew   143
the multitude of all my mortal sins:
the day I met you, I confessed them all
to you with letters big as druggists' signs.
Can you now blame me for what's known to you?
These are but childish, venial, little sins.
Let me just prove myself in some big action:
you'll know me better, to your satisfaction."

Morgante finally agreed with him   144
that they had better laugh at what had been,
and on their journey so they started out.
They found themselves in a dark wood one day,
and, being weary most from the long road,
Morgante near a fountain stopped at last.
Margutte, with his stomach well replete,
fell asleep, weary, at Morgante's feet.

Morgante, when he saw him lying down,   145
delicately from his feet removed his boots,
and hid them, somewhat far away from him,
just to have fun the moment he awoke.
Margutte snored, and he still looked at him;
but, just to tease him, then he woke him up.
Margutte stood right up and was aware
that his boots—damn it!—were no longer there.

He said, "Morgante, you're a trustless man: 146
I well can see you took my boots away,
being the vile and gross man that you are."
Morgante said, "Now guess where I have hid them:
they cannot be too far from where we are.
With this I'll let you pay for countless wrongs."
Searching for them, Margutte looked in vain,
and, ever mumbling, yet he searched again.

Morgante laughed still more, the more he fumed.   147
Margutte finally could see his boots:
a little monkey had got hold of them,
and had already tried them on and off.
Ask not if then he laughed! He laughed so hard,
his eyes began to swell and, swollen so,
seemed just about to burst out of his head—
yet at that play he looked, amused and glad.

Excited more and more by such a play,   148
he kept on laughing, and his laughter grew
so loud, his chest, which needed some relief,
could not at all some respite ever find,
so much impeded and constrained and blocked.
The little monkey tried them on again:
Margutte's laughter reached such a commotion,
there was right in the end a great explosion,

which soon rebounded like a cannon blast,   149
such was the mighty thunder all around.
Morgante ran to see what had occurred,
gazed on Margutte whence that sound had come,
and was so sorry for the trick he played
when on the ground he saw him lying still;
and when he saw the monkey right beside,
he knew that from much laughter he had died.

He did not want to cry, but cry he did,   150
seeing himself so lost and lone without him
that nothing he would do would matter now.
He with his clapper dug the earth at once,
and buried his Margutte in a cave
so that no wild beast would his body eat;
and on a stone the story he described—
how he from laughter in that place had died.

He only from him took the precious stone   151
he had received from Florinetta at last:
with him he put his bundle in the grave,
and then departed from it, still in tears.
For days and days, as in a daze he walked,
mourning so dear a brother lost forever,
whom he was leaving in the wild and wet,
before Orlando such a man could meet.

There is an author, at this point, who says   152
that he rejoined Orlando finally,
and that from Bambillona then he left,
and all these other things occurred to him
until he came to his untimely death.
On this they all seem to agree, but when—
whether before or later—we're not sure,
and many doubts and arguments endure.

This is the reason I will go right on,   153
for nowhere in *Orlando's Song* is found
the vaguest mention of Margutte at all—
a new addition, therefore, to the tale.
A certain book in Egypt can be read,
which our Margutte's story praises most:
the author's name is one Alfamenonne,
and the book's title is *Statuti delle Donne*.

First written in the Persian tongue, it was   154
translated into Arabic and Chaldean,
then into Syrian, and then again
into Greek, into Hebrew, and then, next,
into the ancient, famous Roman tongue;
finally it became our vulgar speech:
therefore, through Nimrod's very tower it passed
till it became our Florentine at last.

Well, then, Margutte knew all wickedness,   155
and reached the worst of it when still a child,
for it was then that he began to crave
for all the food he saw and could not have;
he therefore lived so wickedly and worse
that still his name's notorious in the world:
in sum, he in his actions and mistakes
resembled less a lion than a fox.

Now this poor fellow let us leave in peace,   156
for justice always triumphs in the end.
Morgante, faring through a lengthy plain,
little by little came to Bambillona,
the very walls of which he now could see.
Like sulphur in the fire, once again
his Count Orlando there he wished to see—
but did not know when this would ever be.

He was just a few miles far from the camp   157
when this big fellow finally was seen
like the imposing mast of a big sail,
which made the entire camp soon marvel most.
But when our Count Orlando looked at him,
"By god Mahound," he said, "this is Morgante,
judging by his whole body I can tell;
and then his clapper, too, I know quite well."

He bade his Vegliantino soon be brought,   158
but nonetheless he grabbed his spear at once
lest he should be a giant Saracen:
one's eyes can play a trick from far away.
Morgante, as he saw the paladin,
did not forget to greet him right away:
aloft he threw his clapper then and there,
and jumping, then, he grabbed it in midair.

To Count Orlando as he closer drew,   159
upon his knees he fell immediately.
Orlando came right down and went to him,
his arms wide open to embrace the man
whose great and faithful love he clearly knew.
"Stand up," he said, "Morgante, please stand up!"
And soon his arms around his neck he threw,
and him he kissed a thousand times and two.

Welcoming his Morgante more and more,   160
and with his arms around his neck still bound,
he said, "Oh, joy! Oh, joy! Is this, then, true?
Oh, now that you are here, Morgante dear,
no more afraid of cliffs and storms am I:
now Bambillona's walls begin to shake,
and I can hear both earth and heaven quiver,
and finished is the war, once and forever.

"I would not come to terms with Alexander,   161
or Hannibal or Caesar or Marcellus,
regarding peace or truce or any gain,
now that, dear brother, you are here with me—
you, the best friend and mate I ever chose.
All Babylon I'd conquer with you near me,
and Troy once more, and even Rome of old.
But first, so many things I must be told.

"What happened to Astolfo, Arnald, and Ugier,   162
to Angiol of Baiona, to my Namo,
and to my dear and gentle Berlinghier?
What about Salamon I love so much?
What about Otho, Avolio, Avin, and Walter?
What know you of Guicciardo and Alardo,
my cherished brothers left in Montalbàn?
Whatever happened to that traitor—Gan?

"When did you see our royal Carlo last?   163
Tell me if Gan is back in Paris now,
and if, as usual, our emperor
is forced to follow what he says and does
until he reaches his disastrous end.
With all his magic arts, has Malagigi
told you the place where I was to be found,
and how my lordship here is great and sound,

"and how with so much hardship and great woe   164
I conquered Persia and the Admiral?"
Morgante rose, and answered, then, to him
that Charles and all his paladins were well,
and Malagigi, through his magic arts,
had told him everything he had to know—
namely, that Gan had been exiled once more,
and Carlo's council fired him therefore;

too, that the Sultan's daughter, named Antea—
the famous princess everybody knew—
was with Guicciardo now in Montalbàn,
much honored by all its inhabitants;
and that she had duped Gano cleverly—
which made Orlando laugh most heartily.
Toward the pavilion they began to walk,
and, till the day was over, still they spoke.

165

Rinaldo, Ricciardetto, and Oliver
their dear Morgante could embrace right there.
Morgante gave them news from France, and then
about Margutte lengthily conversed—
how the poor fellow from great laughter died,
and all that they had done before his death.
To all he mentioned every pleasant whim,
and, while narrating, still he wept for him.

166

A meeting soon was held: they all agreed
that, with Morgante with them, they should now
attack and seize the city. War was near,
and now their preparation all could see.
The entire city strengthened every wall,
ordering what was necessary most;
so a relentless battle was begun,
which for two hours most wrathfully went on.

167

Morgante's aim was soon to reach the door,
which, being all of iron, was too strong.
Each of the Saracens was hurling down
a storm of stones and darts to give him death,
but the fierce giant walked so close to it
that with his clapper he could knock it down;
but though his clapper nothing could resist,
he could not smash that portal in the least.

168

Yet more and more he struck and hammered it
until, aware that he could nothing do,
he grabbed the bell that was attached to it
and with his power pounded on the door
while heavy stones rained down upon his cap
and all his brains rebounded from their shock:
each sounding boulder he most bravely bore,
pounding and pounding harder than before.

169

Above the door there was a boundless tower   170
of massive rock that a long time withstood;
but when Morgante shook it with his might,
no earthquake could have shaken it so hard
as not to make it tremble from its base:
in several parts it quickly broke—a tower
that had been held unconquerable by all,
who marveled now at him who made it fall.

Orlando, too, was most amazed to see   171
how he at times would gather all his strength,
such as would make Mount Aetna crumble down.
At last, the giant shook the tower so fast
(the whole camp came to see this mighty feat),
not even Samson could have done as much:
from top to bottom thus he made it crash,
and never did men hear so loud a clash,

or see such dust rise darkly to the stars.   172
Morgante raised the door over his head,
as if it were a shield, to save himself
from all the stones that still were falling down.
Above the walls the people—wretched souls!—
some were already dead, some wounded lay,
some with no arms, some with their heads split open,
some by the new debris utterly covered,

some with no boots, some kicking in the air,   173
some buried in the ruins upside down,
some caught between two boulders helplessly
and soon thrown down as if already dead,
some bleeding from the nose and from the eyes,
some limping and some others badly maimed:
ah, in those ruins the dead men were seen
as an immensely spread-out gelatin.

Those who were stationed to defend the walls—   174
all of them ran in great bewilderment,
so terror-stricken, they seemed wandering ghosts;
our Christians, too, came forward—all of them.
Each of them said, "Can nature do so much?"
Morgante, looking casual as ever,
although no obstacle was seen or left,
some corners with his clapper smashed or cleft.

He shouted to Orlando, "Let's go in!   175
Follow me, all of you, and fear no more,
for Bambillona's safely in our hands,
to god Mahound's enormous spite and shame."
Frightened, the Saracens were fleeing still
away from that cursed devil out of hell.
Orlando and the others then and there
entered the city, riding toward the square.

Right at the entrance there was once a large   176
section of houses built of mud and wood:
one after the other, Morgante smashed them all,
until not even one was seen to stand.
Now think of all the pagan heads he crushed
before he razed those outskirts to the ground!
He whirled his mace about him like a fiend,
and where he passed, there everything he cleaned.

Ultimately all the citizens agreed   177
to let their town with no more fighting fall,
lest they all perish, by Morgante killed.
So Bambillona in this way was seized,
and so much slaughter came to a quick end,
for still the giant was aflame with wrath,
and had the pagans dared one moment to remain,
by clapper or by fire they all would have been slain.

Orlando to the palace, shoulder-high,   178
was brought, and with respect placed on a throne,
and then and there by everyone was crowned
sultan and king of Bambillona Town.
He wished to honor his Old Man right then,
for very fond of him he had become:
he named him governor of Syria,
to every ruling chief superior.

One day, as they were walking in the town,   179
a good muezzin, in the Moorish style,
had just climbed to the top of a big tower.
Morgante said, "Ah, hear that big old crow!
After the theft he came to bolt the door,
and now is even thanking his Mahound.
No, do not ask me what I now will do
to make him come right down without a bow!"

This said, he hurled his clapper in the sky,   180
aiming precisely at his head: up there,
the big old crow was shouting, shouting still,
when, like a tempest, the big clapper came:
just as Morgante had devised and aimed,
it struck his head amid the eyes at once,
and, crushing it together with his prayer,
made it a hundred feet soar in the air.

Now let us leave these men in Bambillona,   181
and go awhile to Montalbàn again.
Antea was still there, she who had made
Gano her prisoner, as we have said.
But so that we may better tell this tale,
may God forever keep his hand upon us.
In the next Canto we shall sing again.
May Joseph's sinless Son protect you until then!

C   A   N   T   O   X   X

My soul now sings the praises of the Lord,   1
and His salvation makes my spirit glad
because of that one Good all men desire.
Of all my merits that eternally
He has foreseen, He has rewarded most
His little maiden's great humility.
Because of this humility that ever was in you,
and with your highest mercy, now deign to help me, too.

So fully conquered this my mind has been   2
by what I've sung till now, I've somewhat veered
off the familiar pathway of my tale:
I much regret the error I have made.
O Blessèd Virgin, you I praise again,
you in whose grace this story I began;
with the same grace to me your help still send,
and do not leave me till the very end.

To Malagigi Gano wrote one day,   3
begging to beg Antea for his freedom.
To Paris he no longer could go back,
having been banished by the emperor.
He also knew Rinaldo was at war,
and out of love desired to help him fast;
and even if his life he were to lose,
he would at last return with some good news.

After he read the letter, Malagigi   4
tore it at once and with the utmost scorn;
then he felt sorry for the man who had
long in a dungeon lain, and begged Antea
to deign to set poor Gano free at last.
Out of her gentle heart Antea agreed:
thus wicked Ganelon was once more free,
and out toward Pagandom soon started he.

From land to land he traveled, eager most   5
to hear about Orlando's whereabouts.
Orlando and his friends were all intent
on honoring poor Spinellon's remains,
which, properly embalmed, were finally
sent with rich vestments to his native land:
so in a hearse by four white horses driven,
to his awaiting sister they were given.

And King Costanzo, too, did just the same,   6
still grateful for the favors once received:
greatly he honored all his men, and gave
employment to all those who wanted it.
Right at this time that execrable traitor,
father of every wickedness and shame,
was traveling from town to pagan town,
unable still to track Orlando down.

For several months through many an unknown land   7
he went, bemoaning his own bitter luck.
One day he found himself in a dark vale
where he could see some pagan shepherds, all
in tears and sorry for their luckless fate:
like dogs they were mistreated, all of them,
by a wealthy shepherd who, of his own accord,
had made himself their one and only lord.

Gano inquired who that shepherd was;
and so they answered, "One who became rich,
and often proves to be a wicked mate.
Once he betrayed a Christian knight: he stole
his horse while he was sleeping, and what's worse—
he sold it, then, to our chief hangman, who
for such a precious steed paid him so much
that now this wealthy man no one can touch.

8

"The steed belonged to a certain knight Rinaldo,
one of King Carlo's paladins from France.
This wicked man invited him to dinner,
and robbed him later with no qualms or shame.
Hot in his hands is all that money still—
so much as we would need to buy the man,
and hang him." Gano heard attentively,
and wished to know where might this shepherd be.

9

Quickly they pointed out his house to him.
And Gano said, "You will all come with me.
Say, is it possible to find a noose?
Help me, and I myself will hang this man."
One of the shepherds promptly answered him,
"We'll use the best and strongest rope we have."
And so they found the shepherd a bit later.
Ganelon threatened him and called him traitor.

10

"Never was I a traitor," he replied;
"am I perhaps Gan of Maganza? No!
What have I done to you? Why are you here?
Never do I betray one of my own."
"Well, you will see it," Ganelon replied,
"you, who can speak with so much arrogance:
you are the very one who stole the horse,
and you will have no time now for remorse.

11

"To the chief hangman, then, you sold the steed."
"This I do not deny," the shepherd said;
"that horse I raised from when he was a colt,"
and many such good reasons he brought up.
But by two shepherds Gano had him bound,
put finally the noose around his neck,
hanged him from a cork tree, and left him there,
from that tall branch now kicking in the air.

12

Spurring his own Mattafellonè, thus   13
on the main road returned he once again.
In a big valley he some giants met,
who would have liked to take his sword from him.
Gan moved, and one of those huge fellows said,
"We want to know where you are headed, and
if you're a Christian or a Saracen."
And so his true name Gano told them then.

One of those giants quickly answered him,   14
"Of all the traitors you are number one:
so many shameful things you've done so far,
it will be merciful to make you pay
for all your sins." Gan grabbed his spear at once,
seemingly spurred and heartened by disdain:
the first of those few giants was so hit,
lifeless he fell after a little bit.

The others jump upon him with their clubs,   15
and Gano with his sword protects himself,
and cuts with it one's nose down to the bone.
But one of them could grab him from behind,
and from the saddle brought him to the ground:
Gano surrendered, helplessly, to him,
who to a palace brought him bodily,
where they would torture him more easily.

All of them said, "You must now tell the truth: 16
it was Rinaldo sent you here to spy;
but as you well can see, his plan has failed.
Now you had better tell us where he is,
for as he rode along this thoroughfare,
one of our brothers brutally he wronged,
and even slew, most cruelly indeed.
Now that you're here, you'll pay for him instead."

Malicious as he was, Gano replied,   17
"I am, I am his mortal enemy,
and long have I been searching for the man
who made King Carlo be my friend no more.
I persecute him just as Paul did Christ,
for we are bound by ancient hate and wrath:
so, much I grieve for what he did to you,
and more for your dear brother whom he slew.

"If self-defense is quite legitimate,   18
  it also must be judged in a new light:
  so when I saw my path unjustly blocked,
  in self-defense I acted as I did."
And such a web he spun in such a way,
  he made them altogether change their minds:
  thus they decided they should take him, rather,
  to a castle that was home to their own mother.

Creonta was the giants' mother's name,   19
  and to her presence Ganelon was brought.
He told her what exactly had occurred,
  and how he had been forced to kill her son.
But as he was narrating all those things,
  a certain shepherd happened to come by—
  the one who'd lent the noose some time before:
  Gano was quickly recognized therefore.

He overheard what soon was to be done—   20
  that Gano should be placed in custody—
  and knowing that the count in Bambillona dwelt,
  as best he could, to Ganelon drew near,
  and said, "I'm here to save your life. Orlando
  is now in Bambillona; I will shortly
  be on my way, and I will see him soon.
I am the one who helped you hang that man."

Gano pretended he had nothing heard,   21
  and no one else had listened to those words.
Bodily he was taken to his jail,
  the lady still not knowing whether she
  should have him executed or in chains.
The shepherd, that whole night and the next day,
  ran fast to Bambillona, where he found
  Orlando, and about Gano told the count.

He to Rinaldo said, "It is your duty—   22
  so I believe—that you should bring your help,
  for, thanks to me, he fought the very man
  who dared to steal your horse some time ago;
  I too, because I love you, gave a hand,
  and he and I could hang him finally;
  he also killed one of these giants, foes
  of yours, as everybody here well knows.

"For many reasons common sense demands   23
that you should not allow this man to die:
he seems to be a knight of great renown,
and so much daring has already shown."
Most cleverly the shepherd wove his plot,
although accustomed but to grazing sheep
and watching over many a pig and bull;
but nature's talents no one can annul.

The Christian knights were pleased with what he said,   24
and welcomed him most joyously indeed:
with other gifts a horse they gave to him,
and, best of all, a very charming gown.
They asked him to return now to his pens,
and there announce that troops would soon arrive:
Gano should then be cheerful now that he
was shortly to be glad and safe and free.

In parliament they soon discussed the way   25
they all should march and Ganelon set free;
full order they restored within the city
and chose one who should meanwhile govern it.
Look at them all, now ready on their steeds!
Since it was best—they thought—to go by sea,
toward the seashore they began to ride,
with big Morgante walking right beside.

On all their flags and everything they wore,   26
a lion loose in a black field was seen:
it was Rinaldo who suggested this,
adopting thus the customs of the land.
At last they reached a foreign port, and saw
a ship that had been anchored there a month:
her captain, being wise, refused to sail
if first he did not see some wind prevail.

Scirocco was one of the steersmen's name;   27
the other was named Greco, most refined.
The latter was so sweet and ever kind,
whereas the former looked most tough and grim.
To this one came Rinaldo, asking him,
"Tell us how much, and take us all on board."
He did not even want to hear of it;
"The weather," said he, "is not good a bit."

To the *salvum me fac* at last he came,   28
and to the last cent wanted to be paid.
Morgante answered him, "I'll pay you cash
by plundering your ship and you as well."
Scirocco about such words could not care less;
but then the other—Mister Goody-Goody—
advised him so: "Please, take them all on board!
They are good knights; please listen to my word."

Our big Morgante almost sank the ship   29
as he set foot on one of her two sides,
so weighty and so measureless was he.
Scirocco said to him, "You are too big;
we need at least ten planks to take you on."
Replied Morgante, "Wait till dinnertime:
what will you say when I sit down to eat?
See that with goods your stow is well replete!"

As soon as the sun hid beneath the ocean,   30
Scirocco noticed a good wind was blowing,
and so at last the ship began her sailing
with Greco at the rudder. Like a candle
up in the firmament, the moon was shining
with not a hint of cloud on the horizon:
throughout the night they went delightfully,
not yet aware of what was soon to be.

The morning came, and the treacherous wind   31
suddenly blew against the vessel's prow:
they hauled to windward fast, most furiously,
and for an hour or two vaulted about.
But with new vigor now the wind was blowing,
and soon the sea began to flaunt its wrath:
eddies and lightning flash and thunderbolt
and air and sky now tangled in one knot.

The sea is swelling, rising with its waves,   32
each mounting fast upon the other's crest,
until the water rises to the deck
and whirls and jumps and leaps from prow to poop.
The ship is old, the waves dismantle it,
so that the caulking soon is coming down;
both men and sea make one resounding shout,
and still Morgante pumps the water out.

Frantic, some here, some there, the seamen dash: 33
this is no time to lie in idleness.
While in this way the ship is tossed about,
loudly our knights to Saint Erasmus pray,
all of them hoping to be saved by prayer—
the only shield against the raging storm;
but neither saint nor devil is in sight,
for—look!—the foremast shakes and falls outright.

Scirocco shouts, "Now help us all, Mahound!"   34
and lifts the spare lateen yard instantly,
attaching at half-mast a small spare sail,
the lateen yard now serving as a foremast.
Meanwhile a blow has wrenched the helm right off,
striking the steersman in the chest, and hurling
the poor man down away from the helpless ship—
a lifeless body floating in the deep.

The small spare sail has hardly been hauled up   35
when a new storm arrives to smash all things,
wrathfully bringing even that sail down,
though only raised at half-mast. Right away
two massive bundles are thrown down astern,
but still the sea upsurges and surmounts:
the steersman's whistle is not listened to—
which of all grave emergencies is true.

What a horrid vision is the angry sea!   36
Often it rises like a mountain peak
eager to reach the altitude of clouds.
The ship is seen to stand right up, and soon
plunge with her prow beneath the gaping waves,
and one of these can strike her with such wrath,
you can now hear her keel to pieces crumble
with all the rest that seems to hiss and mumble,

painfully moaning like a sickly man;   37
but the sea roars more fiercely: dolphins rise
and show at times their backs; the entire main
is like a meadow with so many sheep.
Morgante more and more pumps water out,
afraid of neither thunderbolt nor lightning:
he won't surrender to the ocean's whim,
sure that the sky can never injure him.

CANTO   XX   ❖   425

Orlando is already on his knees,   38
Rinaldo and Oliver are loudly crying;
the Old Man and Ricciardo make a vow—
that if such cruel fate will spare their lives,
they'll seek the Holy Sepulcher at once.
Meanwhile they all are scowling at their death,
and vows and prayers are of no avail:
the ship is stricken more, the waves prevail.

Scirocco hears this *Holy Mary,* said   39
by all our paladins with folded hands,
and with a foul obscenity tells Greco,
"Well, I can see we've Christians here on board.
I know now why this storm will not abate
so long as these mad dogs are here on deck:
thanks to Mahound, this portent we have seen—
how ignorant and stupid we have been."

And what will happen now? Just do not ask.   40
Rinaldo hears these words, and fumes and itches.
He grabs him, saying, "Do not move from here!
We'll see now, scoundrel that you are, who wins—
if Christ or Apollìn or this Mahound.
I hope you're like a dolphin and can swim:
jump by your own accord if so you wish,
or I will throw you headlong to the fish."

Scirocco says, "This ship belongs to me."   41
Morgante tells Rinaldo, "Go ahead!
This man is mad and needs some medicine:
I'll throw him down myself if you do not."
Rinaldo—well—becomes bizarre again,
and with his knuckles strikes him on the head
so nicely, he flies fast into the sea,
and, oh, the tempest weakens instantly.

No seaman—not a soul—is now so bold   42
as to behold Rinaldo in the face:
even the sea seems to obey in fear,
all of a sudden tranquil and becalmed.
There, standing at the bow where the foremast is,
Morgante makes a sail of both his arms
to keep the lower studding sail still tight,
and he succeeds, so steady is his might.

Greco begins to laugh on seeing this,   43
and promptly comes, still laughing, to the prow
to see if everything is now all right.
"We need no other sails," he says; "then why
are you so eager still to lend your help?"
Even the count bursts into laughter, saying,
"Let others bring spare masts and sails galore!
With such a mast and sail, we need no more:

"nobody dies where our Morgante stands."   44
Morgante for so long displays his sail
(the wind is good, and eager to oblige)
that he succeeds in steering the old ship
as far as they can sight a port at last.
Of course, he has to rest once in a while.
Finally, everyone (thank God!) is saved,
for wind and sea have very well behaved.

But Fortune, ever envious of us,   45
while our Morgante brings at last to safety
the ship and all her passengers and crew,
sends up a whale against them suddenly:
toward the ship most angrily he comes
and starts to toss her with his back at once:
he nearly turns her over for the worst,
but luckily Morgante kills him first.

Some of the seamen throw against him darts,   46
but do not see how they can save themselves.
"The ship is turning over," Greco shouts,
and there is nothing we can do, I fear."
Meanwhile the mammal gives another shake,
so strong, they do not know what else to do,
seeing the ship uplifted in the air:
Morgante jumps upon him then and there,

and, by now being closer to the port,   47
says, "I have brought the ship so far, and now—
well—even if I have to lose my life,
I'll see that she's not smashed so near the shore."
Rinaldo hands him at this point his clapper;
Morgante treads his back by leaps and bounds
and with the clapper pounds him on the head,
leaving as many marks as he has said.

So harder is he pounding still his head,   48
he breaks and altogether crushes it:
the mammal at this moment swims away,
gasps like a barbel half-alive and stunned,
gives a few shakes, and upside down falls dead.
Morgante now decides that it is best
to jump into the waves and reach the shore,
for now the water covers him no more.

So Greco lands and drops the ferry bridge.   49
Politely Count Orlando pays him well,
so well that Greco's not displeased at all.
A few days later, wasting no more time,
the ship goes back with other merchandise.
Mighty Morgante in the meantime walks,
still very slowly, closer to the shore,
troubled by all those pressing fish no more.

But he cannot escape his evil fate.   50
To kill the whale, he had removed his boots,
and now, so near the shore, a little crab
bites him right on the heel. Out of the water
he comes, and sees that, yes, 't has been a crab:
he gives no thought to it, but his pain grows.
He starts to laugh about it with Orlando,
saying, "I bet a crab has killed Morgante,

maybe determined to avenge the whale,   51
according to some ancient fear I had."
Ah, look where Fortune leads this man at last!
It worsens but he takes no care of it;
the pain grows, therefore, sharper every day,
because the tendon of the nerve grows stiff:
such is, indeed, the lancinating pain,
alas, by a tiny crab Morgante's slain.

So, powerful Morgante is no more!   52
And Count Orlando is so sorely grieved,
he nothing does but weep Morgante dear.
He to Rinaldo says, "You saw a man
who made the East once tremble with great fear;
but could you ever in the least foresee
that he would die so quick and strange a death?"
"I can't believe it yet," Rinaldo saith.

"How I recall that day in Montalbàn   53
   when we defeated King Erminion!
So many things he with his clapper dared,
   no one could ever think them possible.
And we are laughing still at Manfredón,
   who came to chain Dudone as his man:
this one he wrapped, and Manfredonio, too,
right in the tent, as liver for his stew.

"And then the day he helped Meridiana,   54
   I saw so many men around him dead,
it did not seem a human sight at all.
   And tell me, did you see in Bambillona,
right at the door, such a portentous thing?
   Who could believe his life was, ah, so short?
He made me think of Jove, the day he had to fight
those ancient giants, eager to prove their human might,

"and so I said, 'Had here Morgante been,   55
   you, my dear Jove, would still with Bacchus be
in Egypt, well disguised as some new beast,
   for this man surely would have vanquished you.'
Never in future years will any man
   believe that such a feat could ever be:
I, who have seen him, now completely fail
to believe this—that he has killed a whale.

"May such a fate ever accursèd be!   56
   O man's existence, transient and weak!"
Thus every knight bemoans Morgante's death,
   and Count Orlando more than anyone.
'Til he who orders that he buried be
   (hoping his soul has found in Heaven peace):
he wants his body shipped to Bambillòn,
the necessary full embalming done.

The owner of the inn where they have lodged   57
   these past few days has promised all his best
to find for him the ointment he will need
   to have Morgante's body all-embalmed:
this in all secrecy is quickly done,
   and costs the count a hundred ducats: so
at the right time, and praised by everyone,
Morgante's great remains reach Bambillòn.

Mònaca was the name of the seaport   58
where for some days the Christian knights remained.
Th' innkeeper told Orlando, "Quite a fleet
for one dead man can in this place be seen!
The truth is that he was unjustly wronged,
but I believe he will be soon avenged.
The Emperor of Mezza rules the city,
and we are all in mourning out of pity.

"One of his children, Mariotto named,   59
had left to aid the Sultan, but as soon
as he arrived in Bambillona Town,
great Spinellòn, a pagan, murdered him,
who very greatly was bemoaned by all.
'Tis true that the great Lord of Montalbàn,
Orlando, and all Christian knights were there:
that's why to see them punished is our prayer."

While the innkeeper all these things divulged,   60
right there the captain of the fleet arrived:
Can di Gattaia was his name. "Who are
all of these warriors?" the young man asked.
And Count Orlando soon to Can replied
that they were desperate men from Persia
with not one friend or mate upon the earth,
ever in search of action and of wealth.

"Tell me," Can asked, "how much do you demand?"   61
Rinaldo answered, "Each of us is worth
a hundred barons, if that pleases you."
"A hundred mighty loafers!" Can replied.
"You look just like five ordinary thieves.
By God, the sum you ask would be too high
even for a Rinaldo or a count,
who are the noblest heroes of Clairmont!"

Rinaldo said, "Then hire those you like,"   62
and with the mistress of the inn, a lovely
and most seductive lady, he once more
began to flirt until he was most pleased.
He had one of the flags unfolded then,
on which appeared the lion that I said.
Truly that lion soon they saw; therefore,
quickly such tidings reached the emperor:

"Right at a certain Chiarione's inn   63
    five wanderers have come to lodge and stay;
    they have a lion printed on their flag:
    we do not know if they are Saracens."
    The emperor told some of his own men,
"Arrest and bring the five of them right here;
    and if anyone dare resist arrest,
    bring him here bodily, if so you must."

These pagan men went quickly to the inn,   64
    thinking that they would bind five little lambs,
    and take them just like little lambs or sheep
    with but the weapon of a tiny string.
    One of them grabbed Rinaldo by the hair,
    thinking he was a falcon to be capped:
    Rinaldo moved his arms and with one neat,
    great fist sent him down lifeless to his feet.

The other had a club within his hand,   65
    and with it struck Rinaldo in the face,
    saying, "Who do you think you are, you cur?
    So, then, you crazy fool! Do you believe
    you won't obey our pagan emperor?"
    Rinaldo turned against that man at once,
    by the throat grabbed him and, without a word,
    did not let go till he no longer stirred.

Another even dared to put his hands   66
    on Count Orlando, who just looked at him,
    and, walking, then, one step aside, with such
    a slap caressed his cheeks, he burned the flesh
    down to the bone, and made him soon find out
    whether the inn's floor was paved with plank or bricks.
    Oliver and Ricciardo, seeing what
    was happening, unsheathed their swords at that.

The Old Man with his mace did not break bones—   67
    he smashed and pulverized them thoroughly.
    The count unsheathed his Durlindana at last,
    and those who felt it very sorely wept:
    on top of one another they fell dead,
    and blessèd he who could but show his heels!
    They all were cut and sliced like leaves of broccoli,
    and corpses filled the whole room to full capacity.

CANTO XX ❖ 431

The emperor was told how things had gone,   68
and, well escorted, came in person down.
Meanwhile Rinaldo had returned to fight
while Count Orlando leaned against the door.
Being but slightly wounded, our Rinaldo
seemed to be seized with mighty wrath and shame:
a Christian was no man to prattle with!
That's why he fumed and threatened all with death.

Escorted, then, the emperor arrived,   69
and from the door the count budged not at all.
One of the pagans whispered to the king,
"This is the person who has killed your men."
Orlando gazed upon the Saracen
but with a look so twisted and so grim,
his frown, his presence, and his very stature—all
convinced the king that man was supernatural,

and therefore at that moment changed his mind   70
(still Count Orlando had so strange a gaze,
there are some authors who have even said
that, in all truth, he was a bit squint-eyed).
He greeted him, and "O sir knight," he said,
"what fancy or what whim has brought you here
to kill some of my men in such a way,
and the most sovereign king to disobey?

"If you, as you have said, are here from Persia,   71
I am afraid that you have come to spy;
or, rather, you must be a Christian knight,
as I can sense and more than vaguely feel.
You could have been rewarded with much gold
had you obeyed, and I would have been pleased.
If you have come to us as an enemy,
the harm will all be yours ultimately.

"What you have done has hurt me very much,   72
and maybe I shall punish your mistake—
the death you gave to some of my own guards."
Orlando so replied, "O famous lord,
we all would have come to your royal court
to do our duty and to honor you
by witnessing your great magnificence,
if you had only had a bit of patience.

"Instead you sent your men here to the inn   73
   to seize us, just like thieves caught in the act,
   and hardly gave us two full days of rest
   since we have landed in this port of yours.
   Had god Mahound himself done this to us,
   we would have killed him with our teeth and nails
   rather than to your court be brought like thieves,
   handcuffed amid full twenty foolish knaves.

"That we are Persians, you can rest assured;   74
   we go in search of action everywhere,
   and know not where to find it—whether here
   or in some garden or on desert sand.
   We have already great discomfort known,
   and take only the road God shows to us,
   and no one on this earth do we betray.
   Now I will let your crown judge what I say."

Of all the wise men he had ever heard,   75
   Orlando was the one who pleased him most.
   So said the emperor, "I have been rash,
   but while you go in search of praise and fame,
   here I am only seeking grief and woe,
   hoping no longer to be glad again:
   I have forever lost my only joy,
   for—'tis some time now—they have killed my boy.

"And though the entire world is gathering here,   76
   as you can see, to fight for my revenge
   (well you can count the ships now being armed
   and all the troops all ready now for war),
   with all my money and with all my men,
   never will I regain what I have lost,
   and evermore I will be clad in black
   as I am now; my joy will not come back,

"unless I am so lucky as to be   77
   able to snatch Orlando's heart right off:
   oh, I will shred it in so many bits
   that every sinner will soon learn from it—
   if only our Mahound can grant me this.
   I have just heard the traitor lives today
   in Bambillona, triumphing in gladness,
   while, still in mourning, here I weep in sadness.

C A N T O   X X   ❖   433

"But let's not speak of it. If you can come,   78
together with your people, to my court,
where you can stay until the day you leave,
I will—by god Mahound—well honor you,
and what I own will by all means be yours:
maybe your action—and your fame—is here."
Orlando thanked him very, very much for all
he said, and on Rinaldo and Ricciardetto went to call.

One of th' innkeeper's lovely daughters had   79
meanwhile attended to Rinaldo's wound;
and since she was so gentle and so fair,
Rinaldo told her he would marry her.
From day to day the fleet was growing fast:
Morocco's king had also come with all
his savage men in suits of floss and cloth,
and he just looked like Minos in great wrath.

From Càvery a brutish admiral   80
was there, with a big crowd and bigger rabble:
as Leopantè he was known to all.
All of his fighting men wore uniforms
made out of heavy tusks of elephants—
much harder than the hardest plate or mail.
A frightful lion loose in a black field
he had, just like Rinaldo, on his shield.

Now by some chance he happened to pass by   81
Chiarion's inn, right where Orlando lodged;
somebody else arrived before he did,
playing some instrument the Moorish way:
he gazed upon Rinaldo's flag, and asked
whose flag and emblem it could ever be;
and he was riding in a chariot driven
by four black horses, each as black as raven.

He said, "O Chiarion, tell me the name   82
of the audacious man who stole my flag."
Orlando answered him, "If it is yours,
and if you're brave, you now will have it back."
The pagan said, "You have offended me:
it is diplomacy to notice all
these little things; and then, upon your honor,
you know how each of us defends his banner.

"I want to know who gave you this my flag.
If you have well deserved it, you indeed
can bear it, for it is most surely yours;
but you to me look like the very man
who'd rather steal than fight for it at all."
Orlando said, "In Persia I have won it.
And now I want you one more thing to note—
I'm not a thief, and you are lying in your throat."

83

So answered Leopante, "I reply
that you're a thief, and I am not a liar;
I am, instead, a worthy admiral,
better than you a hundredfold by far,
and by neither Mahound nor the whole world
will you display my banner to the wind.
I'd want you to deserve it with your lance
if you were now a paladin of France."

84

Our Count Orlando did not fear the sky,
nor Jupiter himself when wrath prevailed.
He answered, "It is more than gospel truth—
fools such as you find room up in the cart.
Who bites me, let him pay for biting me,
and let him find my teeth the second time.
So leave the cart, and mount the horse like me,
and soon the lion's owner we shall see."

85

With great disdain the chariot he left,
and quickly jumped up on a mighty steed.
Orlando bade his Vegliantin be saddled,
and waited for no rein to hold him down:
instead our knight leapt fast on top of him
in front of everybody come to watch,
and Leopante greatly was amazed
as they both laid their heavy spears in rest.

86

Oliver, and Rinaldo, and Ricciardo,
and the Old Man, are all by now full-armed.
Everyone came to watch these warriors,
and stood as if half-dreaming and in awe.
The admiral and Count Orlando now
faced one another with their dauntless steeds:
like clarinets of glass their lances broke,
and so his sword each mighty baron took.

87

These words the emperor did overhear   88
and, just to see these people duel, came.
He had just mounted a superb young colt,
which did not run—so fast he beat his wings.
Orlando wounded Leopante soon,
and often gave him a resounding shock;
but Leopante stopped the pagan lord
many a time, replying with his sword.

Being a devil out of hell unleashed,   89
Rinaldo wished horrendous things to see,
and kept on saying, "Count Orlando, you
are not yet angry, or seem not to care."
Orlando, highly stung by this, began
to do such things no man could e'er believe,
storming against the Frank with so much force,
he even struck and reached him on his horse.

Let Leopante watch now for his life!   90
He does not know that sword, named Durlindana,
has killed already many a pagan man.
Suddenly he regretted his mad deed
and, after many a futile, empty blow,
wanted to test the flatness of the road:
among his people fell and there he died,
and so the lion's riddle was untied.

Thus power overcame somebody's right,   91
which it is futile ever to defend:
wise is that person who evades the issue,
and fair to try to understand the world.
So Leopante kept his lion still—
he who had wished to wield a spear for it:
the spear breaks down, and with his life he pays—
who looks for trouble, trouble he will face.

There was great weeping 'mong the Saracens,   92
who saw their master perish in that way.
They buried him, but from that sad cortege
a very valorous young man came out
and then and there to all the mourners said,
"A faithful servant I have been to him;
now, since nobody dares lift up a sword,
I—I alone will now avenge my lord.

"'Twas you who killed him, and I challenge you."   93
Orlando said, "Your challenge I accept;
but not with me, much older, must you fight—
with one instead who is as young as you,
though I believe you could unsaddle me."
"Come forward, Ricciardetto," added he,
and Ricciardetto, eager most, of course,
saying no word at all, soon turned his horse.

As soon as they against each other went,   94
down from his saddle Ricciardetto fell,
unable to avoid the dauntless blow
that very strongly struck him on the shield.
Loudly the pagans cheered, but Oliver
covered his face as if to blot that sight,
and, to avenge poor Ricciardetto, ran
to challenge this indomitable young man.

But soon he too left his Rondello's back.   95
The Old Man of the Mountain armed himself,
went with his spear to clash with the brave lad,
and gained only an honorable death:
so faultlessly the Saracen had aimed,
his weapon passed as through a flimsy web.
Ah, so infallible a blow he threw,
the celebrated Grand Old Man he slew.

Rinaldo, seeing his beloved old friend—   96
the man he loved so dearly—quickly fall,
felt his own heart fall too inside his chest.
The Old Man's soul was wedded back to God,
but Count Orlando grieved so very much,
for many a day he was bewildered, stunned.
The Old Man's body, like Morgante's, soon
was sent for burial in Bambillòn.

At once Rinaldo challenged the brave lad   97
who had so quickly caused the Old Man's death,
with such disdain and such horrendous spite,
he swore that he would kill the young man soon.
Their lances broke upon each other's breast;
therefore they found each other with their swords:
a mighty crowd had gathered there to watch
with great attention such a bitter match.

The pagan lad was very brave indeed: 98
he struck Rinaldo on the helmet so,
he fell at once upon Baiardo's neck,
still on the saddle by a miracle.
Orlando, who had watched that horrid blow,
coldly perspired at the thought of it.
Rinaldo finally stood up again,
blaspheming Heaven like a pious man.

With so much anger he unsheathed Frusberta   99
that had the pagan failed to lift his shield
the very moment he beheld the sword
with all that fury being raised aloft,
Rinaldo would have split his head in two:
instead he found his shield, and cut it clean.
Just like a bagpipe, then, his helmet sounded
as, nearly lifeless, the young man was grounded.

A cry of horror shook the Saracens.   100
Rinaldo, when his mighty wrath was spent,
felt very sorry for the hapless lad
who had appeared to be so strong and brave,
and now—so he believed—lay dead before him.
He suddenly dismounted from his horse.
"Be kind to him!" loudly the monarch said.
"Touch not a man who is already dead."

Rinaldo answered, "By the god Mahound,   101
I am so sorry this young man is dead:
never will any man in Pagandom
with greater skill and valor mount a steed.
I wish that there were something I could do—
something at all, right now—to save his life."
He knelt, and hugged him on the ground, and then
carried him in his arms inside the inn.

The entire population praised his deed.   102
There, at the inn, he laid him on a bed,
and stroked him over to revive his pulse;
and so did the marquis and Ricciardetto,
until, little by little, the young lad
woke up, with all around him, finally.
He came to, hugged Rinaldo joyously,
and then they kissed each other merrily,

asking each other's pardon tenderly.
Orlando looked, attentive, at his sword
(this is what noble soldiers ever do),
examining its sharpness and its weight:
it was the sword—he thought—of a great man.
Curiously, then, he wanted to observe
its handle, and some letters there he saw,
which he read quickly with delight and awe.

103

Those letters said that the young lad was born
from Clairmont's very blood; and that is why
the count went back to the young man in bed,
and with great tenderness and reverence
asked him if his ancestors he recalled,
just as those letters seemed to indicate.
Would he, for his own good—if such a prayer
was honest—let him know, then, who they were?

104

He so replied to them, "O gentle knights,
my mother's very name is Rosaspina,
and mine is Aldighieri. I was born—
so Mother tells me—close to the seashore.
About my father I do not know much,
for he was not a Saracen by birth.
According to the tale I heard from Mother,
Gerard of Rossiglione was my father.

105

"I do not want to know the reason why
you care to know; you look so kind to me
that I, to please you, do not find it hard
to heed your prayer and grant you your request.
I'm a descendant of Clairmont's old race;
therefore, a noble blood flows in my veins—
maybe the best that on this earth could be,
and keeps in France still royal sovereignty.

106

"Rinaldo, the great lord from Montalbàn,
has the same blood, and so the famous count
whom Charlemagne holds in such high esteem
that the whole world still echoes with its sound.
Long have I roamed in search of these two knights,
and I'm still looking for them, but in vain;
but so will I all over search and try
that I will see them both before I die.

107

"And if one of the two had been right here   108
when from my charger you unsaddled me,
I know that I would have been soon avenged."
Orlando could not bear to listen more,
so overwhelmed with tenderness was he.
Everyone started hugging him with joy.
Seeing himself embraced, the young man thought
that he was dreaming still—but he was not.

"Tell me," he said, "please tell me, all of you,   109
why you are hugging me with such delight."
Orlando was the first to answer him,
"O Aldighieri, what delight indeed!
Oh, what great peace repays my every grief!
What boundless sweetness in my breast I feel!
The two you have been looking for are here:
I am Orlando; and this, Rinaldo dear,

"and this is Oliver, our relative,   110
and this is Ricciardetto, your own cousin."
When Aldighieri heard those happy words,
he thought and said, "What grace or destiny
grants me that I should find these people here?"
He hugged Orlando, worthy paladin,
and Oliver, Rinaldo, Ricciardetto,
and jumped right out of bed in merriment.

About King Carlo he began to talk,   111
and also about the mighty, dauntless Dane
whom he had known still in his pagan days;
and he began to talk of his Gerard,
saying, "A Christian I intend to be,
and utterly renounce our false Mahound;
and then to lovely France I'll come with you,
and there forever live my whole life through.

"Under my flag ten thousand men are here—   112
ten thousand horsemen of the troops you see.
An entire army by the king is armed,
who wants to vindicate his murdered son,
and all his anger vent against you soon.
I, when I heard you were in Bambillona,
came from my kingdom, with my men, to be
ever united with you finally.

"And secret letters I have sent to you   113
   to tell you of such preparations here
   (I do not know if ever you received them
   or if at least the news has reached your ears):
   these people, as you see, are threatening you
   as though you were already doomed and won.
   This city will be conquered, if we fight,
   both by my armies and your matchless might.

"You and Rinaldo in all Pagandom   114
   are very highly feared and highly praised,
   so that as soon as your two names are heard,
   all crowds will, terror-stricken, flee away.
   These men are rabble—not true warriors:
   at first they boast that of all Christian knights
   they finally will make a sauce for stew,
   then pass the buck and soon are out of view."

Rinaldo liked his thinking very much,   115
   and Aldighieri rallied all his men.
   Right at this time a messenger arrived:
   the king had ordered—so his herald said—
   that all the troops be in the square reviewed;
   and all his men indeed had armed for war,
   as from the coming Canto you will know.
   May Blessèd Jesus save you all from woe.

CANTO   XXI

God ever greet you, Mary, full of grace,   1
   and may the Lord forever be with you.
   O Holy Nazarene, O Mary, blessed
   amongst all other women on the earth!
   My little sail without you runs aground;
   sustain and aid, therefore, our fantasy,
   which you so far have kept on its high flight,
   and leave me not until the shore I sight.

The foreigners and all the citizens
quickly assembled in the square. It was
a half-inspiring and half-crazy show
seeing such a multitude of pagan men:
never before had such a crowd been seen
of diverse tongues and every novel race.
Rinaldo said, "Let's go now to the square,
and rout all of those people out of there."

2

They readied all their arms and all their steeds.
Meanwhile the emperor was telling them,
"If any one of you, my noble knights,
avenges me for my great suffered wrong,
he will inherit towns as vast as empires,
and rule these regions in full sovereignty;
from countless men and boundless wealth aside,
also my daughter he will have as bride."

3

Up stood Can di Gattaia, mighty man,
and said, "I am, Your Majesty, the one!
If first I have to kill a thousand men,
I—I alone will snatch Orlando's heart."
All of them boasted and most loudly barked,
each swearing he would slay the treacherous count.
With words they made the blood rise two feet tall,
and those who trembled most, spoke most of all.

4

Rinaldo was the first to reach the square.
Can di Gattaia, when he saw him, said,
"O baron, if you are the man I know
(I've recognized you by your coat of arms),
by god Mahound, I feel like laughing still,
thinking you really thought you'd be believed
when cash you wanted for four rascals such as you,
so much of it no weight of bran or coal would do.

5

Rinaldo said, "One hundred I demanded,
but you must double now the sum I asked;
and if what many people say is true,
right now you'll be the first of all who boast
to prove that all your feats are smoke and wind:
come forward, then, if me you want to fight!"
Can di Gattaia, as those words he heard,
a mighty spear against Rinaldo hurled

6

with all the wrath that soon had lit his soul.
Rinaldo moved against that rabid foe,
aiming at nothing but his gorget: there
landed his lance, and pierced the whole neck through,
and through the gullet, there the soul expired.
The emperor was angered by that sight,
and said, "You have offended me many a time,
but very soon you will regret your every crime."

Replied Rinaldo, "Let me tell you now:
I am Rinaldo, of the Clairmont race,
come here to harm you and besiege your town;
and this is the most famous Count Orlando,
against whose might you never could prevail;
and this in front of you is Oliver,
and this is Ricciardetto, my own brother dear,
and Aldighier, our cousin—behold—is also here.

"Soon, pretty soon now, you will all be dead."
No sooner had Rinaldo spoken so
than all those madmen started on their flight.
The emperor, on seeing such a thing,
in great astonishment and quickly said,
"Can luck or god Mahound have done all this?
Take, like a foe, the field, then, right away;
for many an ancient sin I'll make you pay."

Rinaldo, full of anger, turned his horse,
and, turning back with greater anger still,
clashed with the above-mentioned emperor,
now caring for no empire and no life,
and with a spear transfixed his heart at once,
making him join great Can inside a grave.
Now ran and scampered every pagan man,
and a most cruel battle soon began.

Aldighier fought together with his men
while Count Orlando did unheard-of things.
Oliver did not keep his worth concealed,
and Ricciardetto all his daring showed.
But the great fury in a while was spent:
the pagans, seeing all those bloodied arms
and hearing the count's name—and Oliver's
and Prince Rinaldo's—started to disperse.

7

8

9

10

11

Add that Orlando had already slain   12
Morocco's mighty king in the same battle:
this was the blow that most decisively
made all those silly, beastly pagans flee.
Everyone reached his vessel at the port,
and waited for no north- or southeast wind.
And so that war was ended in this manner,
and o'er the city flew the Christian banner.

To the imperial palace went Rinaldo   13
together with the count and Aldighier;
and there went Ricciardetto and Oliver
together with Rinaldo's gentle squire
(Rinieri was his name), who was baptized
with Aldighieri. When the christening
was over, all of them agreed, therefore,
that Aldighier be known as emperor,

though much against his will. Chiarion, too,   14
the good innkeeper, was baptized by them
together with his lovely daughter (she
with loving care had healed Rinaldo's wound,
and now Rinaldo wanted to repay her).
By chance, then, Greco, captain of their ship—
the one who was refined and learned, and
had brought them there—had happened there to land.

As soon as from his vessel he came down,   15
he heard the news that they were in command,
and had the empire's keys within their hands.
How glad was he who had been kind to them!
With great devotion and with reverence,
humbly he paid a visit to them soon,
saying—for very good and wise was he—
that he rejoiced in their prosperity.

And he was hugged by all so heartily   16
as if he were a brother to them all.
Something flashed quickly in Rinaldo's mind—
to give th' innkeeper's daughter to this man.
He said to her, "O maiden sweet and fair,
now listen well to what I have to say.
I know I promised that I'd marry you,
but this is something I could never do,

for I have left another wife in France.   17
But Greco here will now your bridegroom be,
and such a dowry I will give to you,
and such a gift, that you will both be pleased."
The gentle maiden's cheeks turned somewhat red,
and blushingly she then replied to him
that she by his decision would abide,
and finally became she Greco's bride;

but first, of course, he had to be baptized.   18
Rinaldo gave the man such property
(for his good service he had earned it well)
that never would he have to sail again.
This proves how true the ancient proverb is—
that the least favor by no means is lost,
and that, past much ingratitude and pain,
one soon forgets a thousand thankless men.

Chiarion they appointed governor   19
of the whole kingdom, for they all recalled
how he, though very poor, had honored them.
In Mònaca they rested a few days,
and then, to help their traitor Ganelòn,
they said to the new governor goodbye:
no tongue could tell you, and no pen could write,
the sadness of that parting and their plight.

In tears was the good captain, so depressed,   20
in tears was the fair maiden, sorely grieved,
in tears was the innkeeper, sorry most,
in tears were all the town's inhabitants,
in tears (would you believe it?) was Rinaldo,
in tears Orlando and the great marquis,
in tears both Ricciardetto and Aldighieri,
in tears even the squire, poor Rinieri.

But here some authors disagree with me: 21
some say that Greco was named governor,
some others say that Chiarion and Greco
governed together in great harmony.
But Chiarion, not Greco, I believe,
was left to rule: Rinaldo recompensed,
thus, each of them; besides, he had been born right there,
and was of every use and custom well aware.

Orlando and his friends together rode   22
until they saw Castelfalconè near.
They met two shepherds not too far from there,
one of whom was the one by Gano sent
to Bambillona. They were glad to see them,
and asked if Gan was still alive in jail
or if he'd died, and what had since occurred;
they wished to know whatever they had heard.

The shepherd said Gan was alive and well,   23
though troubled by the hardships of the jail.
This said, he grabbed Orlando's charger's rein,
and led them to the cottage where once lived
the shepherd that by Gano had been hanged,
saying, "This was the house of the great thief
who stole Rinaldo's horse; we moved right in
after he hanged and paid for his great sin."

Then all the Christian knights dismounted there.   24
The shepherds killed some tender kids for them,
and other sucklings put they on a spit;
and there was milk to drink and milk to spill.
As much as they, their horses, too, were spoiled
with bales of barley and with heaps of hay.
Rinaldo said, "To mine give barley and straw, of course,
for they alone—the proverb says—make a war-horse."

So there they ate and rested a few days.   25
Orlando asked those shepherds in what way
they could assault that castle in the meantime,
and soon the shepherds told him that the fortress
was very strongly guarded from four sides,
and had six doors through which to enter in,
but for its great protection, every door
by a wild-roaring lion was watched o'er.

Creonta was the giants' mother. Long   26
were all her nails, and, like a dragon's, sharp;
bearded, squint-eyed, malicious, quick was she,
and at her bidding haunting wraiths she had,
and was forever full of wrath and scorn,
and dreadful to whoever looked at her;
hirsute and black, all wrinkled and most dire,
she on her head had horns, in her eyes fire.

Never before had filthier shapes been seen.   27
She was the witches' queen, so foul and fierce,
Satan himself was most afraid of her;
so were Tisiphone, Alecto, and Megaera.
It nearly was impossible to enter
because of such a monstrous, horrid beast.
And of the giants everything they said—
what were their habits, and what arms they had.

All this was music to Rinaldo's ears,   28
eager to hear the worst and weirdest tales.
If there was ever a new fight to start,
he felt like going to a wedding feast.
Ask not if now his heart leapt up with joy!
He said, "Unless somebody cut these hands,
of her a stump of cabbage I will do:
let's see which is the bigger devil of us two."

He left his meal and saddled his Baiardo.   29
Orlando and the others did the same.
Quickly, determined, then, Rinaldo went
in the direction of a castle's door:
against him dashed a mighty lion soon,
thinking that he would bite a little lamb.
Rinaldo and his friends jumped down with speed,
entrusting to Rinieri every steed.

The lion from the ground took then a leap,   30
and, landing on Rinaldo, his sharp claws
savagely sank into his shield at once,
shaking his head and opening his mouth.
Rinaldo thrust a blow down to his paws,
and cut the flesh and every nerve and bone:
the lion with his mouth instantly hit
the ground, and instantly Rinaldo split

the head with a new blow right on its neck: 31
dead on the threshold the fierce lion lay.
Said Aldighieri, "Hear me, all of you:
I want to be the one to kill the other beast."
Rinaldo answered, "Kill him right away,
or he may give you some distress and woe."
Our Aldighieri, uttering no word,
suddenly put into his throat a sword,

which from the loins as suddenly came out. 32
Orlando said, "And I will kill the third."
Lo and behold, towards him came the lion,
and, meek and mild, before him sweetly knelt.
Orlando stopped his Durlindana fast,
saying, "This is a miracle of God.
Follow me! Heaven's opening the door;
the other beasts won't harm us anymore."

And he was right. The lion then stood up 33
and, while the others soon made room for them,
as if their guide began to walk ahead.
Orlando went where all the giants dwelt:
they marveled at him, and one of them said,
"Who are these men, and how have they come in?
Can Heaven be so mighty as to keep
a pride of lions deaf and sound asleep?

"This looks to me the strangest thing of all." 34
Out of their palace instantly they came.
The noseless one came forth and, like a fool,
toward Rinaldo walked. His beard was long,
and there was not a hair left on his head.
Rinaldo gazed upon that livid face,
which seemed to him unlike a man's or ass's,
and said to him, "How do you wear your glasses?

"And how in springtime can you smell a rose? 35
A most exotic beast you seem to me."
The giant to Rinaldo so replied,
"I'll tell you, filthy glutton, pretty soon."
So forcibly Rinaldo struck that pate,
he would have split the hardest pear in two;
right through his eyes he then Frusberta thrust,
and made the man fall dead into the dust.

As soon as that big bundle hit the ground, 36
on Aldighieri one more giant rushed,
eager to make him feel his knotted club;
but Aldighieri, leaping like a hound,
shunned the great blow, and hit him on the arm
as if to teach him how to fence; that arm
he cut so clean as though it were a melon:
down fell both arm and club, and soon the felon

followed with a gigantic, horrid pain.   37
Seeing him on the ground, our Aldighieri,
wasting no time, let a great blow fall down:
right on the giant's neck the cutting sword
descended, and split open every vein.
The other brother, witnessing the deed,
rushed upon Oliver, irate and grim,
grabbed him and, now more wrathful, lifted him,

taking him as a wolf would a small lamb.   38
But our good shepherd, Count Orlando, saved him.
"Stop, Saracen," he said, "and put him down!
It never dawned on you that you must steal,
together with his dog, the watchman too."
Great anger made the giant bite his lips:
he gladly would have drunk Oliver's blood,
but out of terror dropped him with a thud.

Oliver from the ground stood up at once,   39
and with his Altachiara hit him hard:
right in the pagan's belly landed she,
and he said, "Now you drink your bitter death!"
And with that blow he killed him, and the man
could nothing do but find his casket soon.
Three were already dead; now one was left—
the fiercest, the most dismal and most deft.

Orlando said, "The battle now is mine,   40
for this remaining man belongs to me."
The savage giant, foolish and bizarre,
hit Count Orlando with a mace of his,
so hard indeed it almost made him fall.
Shouted Rinaldo, "Let this blow be yours,
just like the fight! Orlando are you not?
Or has your sword become too dull to cut?"

Hearing his cousin speak in such a way,   41
Orlando dropped his shield and, then and there,
the handle of his sword laid on his chest.
He hurled himself against the Saracen,
eager to pierce him through from side to side:
the point found soon the navel by the doublet,
which was of iron; it pierced all things through—
belly and entrails, spleen, and liver too—

CANTO   XXI   ❖   449

and on the other side the sword came out,
a foot or two, completely red with blood;
thus the pilaster ruinously fell,
and would have hit Orlando in its fall
had not the count most nimbly stepped aside:
the whole earth seemed to tremble and rebound.
But now, by boundless anger all possessed,
the sorceress Creonta tore her breast.

42

At that great din the giants' mother ran
where Aldighieri stood, and with her nails
began to scratch him like a maddened beast,
her mouth wide open and her eyes wild-rolling:
Erichto's fury never was so great.
Rinaldo tried to help him with Frusberta,
but as his sword was hesitant to cut,
Rinaldo moved to grab her by the throat.

43

So strongly had our Aldighier been seized,
he would have much preferred a little bear.
As she began to carry him away,
Orlando grabbed her by the hair, but such
was still her hold, no one could break that knot.
Poor Aldighieri to his friends was shouting,
"Satan himself, alas, has taken me,
and now to hell transports me bodily."

44

Orlando then his Durlindana used,
but, though so strong and sharp, his sword came back
as if refusing such a fiend to strike.
Laughing, the pagan woman said to them,
"If me you want to strike, your blows instead
strike but the wind and dew; in vain you try.
Never will you get hold of this my skin,
nor will you leave this castle once you're in."

45

A sudden horror overwhelmed the count,
seeing that she was telling him the truth,
and everybody's hair stood then on end
there in the presence of so fierce a demon
with her so ugly and smoke-burnished face:
no devil can be ever feigned so black
as this Creonta's skin and woolly hair;
her voice far more than old Smahèl could scare.

46

She saw before her all her children slain: 47
you can imagine her great ache and anguish.
How could the wretched woman bear all that,
now that their murderers were in her hands?
A thousand other wrongs against her sons
she also could recall with greater wrath:
she was like Salayè, who, when he heard
his fall but mentioned, by new wrath was stirred.

Lo! Gentler than Niello she became,   48
and looked no more like Salyass or Berith
or Squarciaferro. Very meek she turned;
she stuttered not like Bocco, rest assured,
but just like Nillo very clearly spoke;
unlike Sottìn, who spoke in pseudo-French,
or Obysìn, she spoke more clearly than
the one who stole but jewels—Rugiadàn.

Her speech did not resemble that of Bileth,   49
who broke the almandàl with certain snails,
or that of Astaroth, who from his horse
threw underneath a fool so many a drop,
or that of Oratàs, who gave us doves—
so well she seemed to let her words flow loose.
Releasing Aldighieri finally,
she thus began to speak most civilly:

"I do forgive you, and but ask for peace,   50
so pleased am I by all your gallantry.
If so you wish, let Gano now be free,
for I no longer want your harm or woe.
About my children's death much though I grieve,
no further vengeance want I to occur,
since from this castle out you'll never go;
so, all of you, keep doing what you know."

Stunned by the sudden change, and most amazed,   51
they freed their Gano from his jail at once:
imprisoned in a cistern he had lain,
immersed in water and in darkness deep.
As soon as from his dungeon he was free,
Gano unsheathed his sword immediately,
and wanted by all means Creonta's death,
but, to his great surprise, he saw her laugh.

Oliver and Orlando and the others   52
tried once and twice and thrice to give her death,
hitting the woman with their many blows:
she kept on laughing at their every plan.
They even more than once ran to the door,
which was by no one guarded anymore:
Look! By itself, as someone near it came,
it opened and then closèd every time.

Thus in the castle they were forced to stay,   53
by all that magic each of them confused.
In the meantime their brother Malagigi,
looking, one day, at his old magic charts,
at last could see, and very clearly learn,
why his Rinaldo was so held and trapped:
it was, no doubt, by dint of sorcery.
So to Guicciardo spoke he instantly,

and sent a letter to Astolfo in Paris,   54
begging him to come soon to Montalbàn.
Astolfo started on his way at once,
and reached his Malagigi in no time.
Of everything he soon was made aware,
and soon they both agreed on what to do—
Guicciardo and Alardo had to go;
with them Antea wanted to go, too.

She said, "My dear Rinaldo I will see."   55
Many a day had gone, or rather flown—
such is desire's ever-prompting wish—
when they could see three pagan cavaliers,
whom they saluted in the name of God.
As soon as they drew closer, one of them
stared at Astolfo's steed, and, not a bit
ashamed, decided just to ask for it.

Saracen Liombruno was his name, and he   56
was nephew of Marsilius, king of Spain.
He said, "I never saw so fine a horse
as could not have at least one fault with him.
But I have seen today so great a steed
that all my life I wished him mine to be."
Astolfo said, "In vain you speak, of course:
the more you talk, the more I like my horse."

Everyone would have loved that horse to own. 57
"So, you are deaf," Liombrun said to him.
 Replied Astolfo, "Who would understand?"
 The pagan answered, "He who'll throw you down."
 Astolfo said, "Can one do more than I?"
"If you refuse to gamble him right now,
 then try to have him with your readied spear:
 take now the field," the pagan said; "I'm here."

Saying no more, their horses turned to fight, 58
 they lowered both their lances speedily;
 but so that his bad luck would ever win,
 Astolfo found himself upon the grass
 'mid countless fragrant red and yellow blooms.
 Alardo, seeing this, could murmur only,
"Astolfo, cursèd be your cowardliness!
 Never before you fell, as I can guess."

Liombrun wanted now that horse much more. 59
 Alardo said, "I know how much you want him,
 but there is still a stony road ahead.
 If you were not a duck, you'd simply peck.
 But you will have to fight with me some more:
 if you defeat me, then the horse is yours;
 but I am sure I will not fall before
 I ask of the innkeeper what's in store."

Said Liombrun, "You are offending me, 60
 but I'm not hurt, for you mean nought to me.
 I want to see how you can reach the inn:
 there, if I let you not, you'll never go.
 Take, then, the field—I challenge you right now,
 knowing full well who will your charger own."
 Alardo turned, so swift and deft and tall—
 he seemed Rinaldo's brother after all.

Antea said, "How well we can discern 61
 the daring valor of Clairmont's old blood!"
 Forward came Liombrun right at this moment,
 and so the two with their two lances met;
 but our Alardo failed to shun a blow
 that would have even pierced a mountain through:
 the spear transfixed his heart with its sharp blade,
 and dead he joined the petals in the shade.

One soldier told another, seeing this,   62
"This for the Christian knights is much too much;
there's absolutely nothing we can gain:
we must admit they are no Saracens.
Let us now show them that our heels are fast,
and to our country now return at once!"
No sooner were these sad words spoken than
they all grabbed what they could and quickly ran.

Astolfo felt humiliated most,   63
because Antea was in front of him.
He tried his best to minimize his fall,
saying, "This horse I have been riding on
has recently become recalcitrant;
the very while I thought my spear would run,
he threw me down because his back jumped so
that down I let myself in anguish go."

Replied Antea, "No excuses, please.   64
Have I perhaps not seen what has occurred?
Even if you had fallen, that can happen."
Guicciardo, who so far had nothing said,
could not refrain from opening his mouth,
and said, "You never fell, Astolfo dear,
but we should hang this horse for all his crimes:
'twas he who made you fall a thousand times."

Now Malagigi interrupted them.   65
Astolfo mounted his brave horse again,
and so both with the moon and sun they rode
until Creonta's castle they could see.
Malgigi, ever ready with his art,
through some enchantment made them go right in,
and walked ahead of them as their one guide:
wher'er he went, each portal opened wide.

They reached the square, and many men they hugged: 66
Malgigi did not know our Aldighieri.
They told him how they met the brave young lad,
whom now to Paris wanted they to take;
and then about Creonta much they spoke.
Malgigi gazed upon her ugly face;
she looked at him, quite sad and anguished rather—
it takes a devil just to know another.

"I was in Montalbàn," Malgigi said,   67
"but I could see you in great danger here:
  this is the reason why I called Astolfo,
  with whom I soon discussed the ways to help."
Meanwhile Rinaldo held Antea's hand—
  her face was all-vermilion as she felt
  now sweet and bitter, and both warm and cold,
  eager her dear Rinaldo to behold.

Malgigi then went on, "Now listen well!   68
There's still much work to do, as says the one
  who shod, instead of oxen, only geese,
  and had the buttrice ready in his hand.
This woman with a magic all her own
  (let us speak low: I see her listening)
  and with her expertise that nothing lacks
  has made a certain image out of wax,

"which in some corner of her home she keeps   69
  with a fierce dragon watching over it—
  a dragon far more savage than she is.
This wicked woman we must seize at once,
  and hold her here until I have the time
  to find that image and destroy it fast;
  and as that gruesome image I undo,
  terrible things she'll do right in your view.

"Only Rinaldo will now come with me,   70
  for it is well I take a friend along,
  who will then kill the dragon with his sword.
Let's go, and let's not waste any more time!"
Slowly Orlando toward Creonta walked,
  who started to roll wildly her red eyes
  and on the ground mysterious signs to write:
  Oliver and the others grabbed her tight.

It took all of their strength to hold her there: 71
  at times she uttered certain shouts and screams
  that seemed to come from nowhere else but hell.
Meanwhile Malgigi took Rinaldo where
  the dragon vomited but flames and poison,
  and told him to get rid of him at once.
Rinaldo, uttering no other word,
  walked near the dragon with his lifted sword.

Ask not how soon that dragon writhed in wrath
and, as he saw Rinaldo, stood right up.
Rinaldo flung Frusberta on his neck
in such a way, he made that wrath subside:
only a shred of skin was yet uncut,
and the tail wriggled a few seconds more:
Rinaldo killed the dragon and, therefore,
opened a pool of poison and of gore.

72

Closer Malgigi to the image drew:
it had been made out of the fair and purest
wax of young bees, assembled artfully
under the constellation of some star,
meticulously complete in all its limbs;
the figure seemed to stand on its right foot,
and showed, transversely lifted, its left leg:
it was a weird, and twisted, horrid hag,

73

her face the most horrendous part of all.
Malgigi, who knew well that magic game,
using his magic art—most truly his—
made a great flash of fire soon appear,
which suddenly adhered to all that wax,
little by little melting it away.
And while the wax diminished bit by bit,
both earth and air were trembling over it.

74

Rinaldo more than once then shook himself,
such was the fear that overwhelmed his heart.
Malgigi made some signs all over him,
saying, "Be not afraid of what you see,
but do not move at all: be still, right here,
until you see all this mighty fury end."
But as the image was disintegrating,
the woman went through more and more gyrating:

75

she crouched and curled up, twirled and twisted; then,
just like a serpent, on the ground she stretched,
and then again she coiled herself up whole,
and scratched and struck herself and loudly screeched:
all of a sudden all the air got soaked
with rain and winds and squeaking thunderbolts,
and hail and storm and devastating fire
started appearing with portentous ire.

76

Though overwhelmed with terror, Count Orlando,   77
Oliver, and the others held her tight:
strongly the woman was consumed with thirst,
which very slowly led her to her death.
Just as the image was melting away
(they were about to open every door),
the woman's soul was slowly snatched in turn,
and, just like Meleager's, seen to burn;

and, dead at last, upon the ground she stretched   78
the very while the image was no more.
Out of the palace Malagigi came,
and the whole sky was limpid once again.
Delivered from their terror and dismay,
they all thanked Malagigi, who had put
an end to such a horrid, evil threat.
And a few days they rested after that.

One day, Alardo could no longer keep   79
the secret to himself, and therefore spoke
about Astolfo, who now looked so brave.
Rinaldo, when he heard the tale, began
to taunt him, charging him with cowardice.
Astolfo could not bear such ridicule,
and dashed, full of disdain and wrath and spite,
against Rinaldo, eager for a fight.

Seeing that sword, Rinaldo stepped aside,   80
saying, "You fool! What now? As I have done
many a time, I'll let you go unharmed;
but never, from now on, repeat this deed."
Orlando did not like the thing he saw,
and to Rinaldo said, "You've lost your mind.
By God! Astolfo loves us like a brother,
and always did. Rinaldo, what's the matter?"

And they were on the verge—the two of them—   81
of starting a new fight; but soon Rinaldo
calmed himself, knowing very well indeed
the valor of the count when wrath prevailed.
Astolfo, still aflame, went to and fro,
like a wild lion willing to assault:
during the night he left most suddenly,
putting their every plan in jeopardy.

Let us therefore not make any design   82
lest Fortune quickly make another one:
she always hits the target, to be sure,
with neither truth nor justice all the time.
She is against the good, whom she detests,
until not even one is left; today,
she makes fools wise, and wise men fools; tomorrow,
those who would like to lend are forced to borrow.

Along a desert land Astolfo went,   83
aimlessly, like a man by anger seized.
It was deep night when he perceived a light
coming from where three holy hermits lived,
who long had known privations on this earth
to earn the everlasting banquetings.
Astolfo, as that flickering light he saw,
in that direction soon began to go.

The hermits' door he pounded, and was soon   84
welcomed into their holy hermitage.
During the night some Saracens arrived,
who gagged and robbed them all, and when they saw
what meager booty they had come to reap,
they even took Astolfo's steed with them.
When he awoke, Astolfo saw, alas,
what in the deep of night had come to pass.

Soon the three hermits he ungagged and freed,   85
and asked them if they knew which way those thieves,
who had mistreated them, could ever go.
One of them answered to Astolfo thus:
"Ah, let them go! They will be punished soon
for all their sins and all their evil crimes
by our Eternal Lord, Who has decreed
the punishment of every wicked deed

"and the reward of good ones. They are thieves   86
who stalk these woods, and beastly are they all;
we have been robbed a few more times before.
But our celestial bread we still can eat,
and it repays us of all suffered wrongs.
If you should look for them, you could be harmed:
so let them go, and leave it to the Lord,
Who to His servants gives their just reward."

Replied Astolfo, "Such a recompense   87
does not apply—I'm certain—to my horse,
for I without him would be forced to walk,
and your good Lord would only watch me go.
This hope and faith of yours has always failed
to give me anything to eat or drink:
so I intend to find my horse at once,
and make them pay for all their arrogance."

Out on his search he went, and finally   88
he saw the bandits in an open field,
cozily resting in the pleasant shade,
and, saddled still, his horse was grazing there.
Axes and spears and swords he also saw.
Closer to one of them Astolfo walked,
shouting, "You, wicked traitors, highwaymen!"
and quickly placed his sword beneath his chin.

With a small spear the other soon replied.   89
Astolfo saw the sharp point come his way,
and in the middle cut it with a blow,
then with a new one gave him sudden death.
Against the other highwaymen he rushed,
catching and stunning each and every one:
he murdered four; the six that still remained
he soon handcuffed and by the neck then chained.

Back on his charger mounted he again,   90
and toward the hermitage began to ride.
When the three hermits saw the highwaymen,
they marveled at Astolfo very much,
and with their hearts thanked God of Nazareth.
And to those hermits then Astolfo said,
"Of all these men the hangmen you shall be,
for they are full of all iniquity."

Replied the hermits to him, "Brother, dear,   91
God does not want us such a thing to do:
therefore, it is your duty and your task."
Astolfo said, "I don't believe that God
welcomes my justice more than your *Our Father*,
if it is true that evil He abhors.
Bring, then, their hooded cloaks, and hurry up,
and quickly hang them all from the same rope."

Those hermits, ah, were squeamish, all of them,   92
and seemed to be most horrified and shocked.
Astolfo, who was spiteful and irate,
as if they were three donkeys cudgeled them,
saying, "Then let your mincing buttocks pay!"
As in a flash, out their own cords they brought,
and, feeling Brother Stick upon their rears,
they seemed to have the skill of a hundred years.

All, all alone, Astolfo rode ahead   93
inside that forest, with no goal in mind,
but going only where the pathway went.
But let him with his guardian angel go!
Still fuming over what had just occurred,
Orlando walked out of his home one night
and, seen by no one, wanted, all alone,
to see where his Astolfo might have gone.

Never in all his life had our Rinaldo   94
felt so discomforted as he was now.
Antea said, "What are we doing here?
Our every hope is gone, as I can see.
I in your Jesus' hands leave all of you,
and will to Bambillona shortly go."
Rinaldo and the others instantly
said that they wished to keep her company.

The count's departure everyone bemoaned;   95
even the well-known traitor Ganelon
seemed to be sorry most. In tears he said,
"O my dear lord, oh, where, oh, where are you?"
And so, with their Orlando in their hearts,
upon their horses night and day they rode,
to Bambillona taking their Antea,
who wept much more, the city seeing near.

Her wretched father she could find no more   96
(he was so happy when she left him there!),
nor could she see her most familiar troops,
and her laments broke everybody's heart.
Rinaldo with most comforting, good words
said, "Queen and empress of your ancient land,
I'll leave you here, believe me, and I know
that Count Orlando would have told you so."

Antea in Bambillona thus remained,   97
and the whole population came to see her:
I could not tell you with what feast and joy
she was by all her people welcomed home.
At last she wore her regal crown again,
and the whole town was living a new life.
Rinaldo stayed with her a day or two,
and then all of them bade Antea adieu.

With many a sigh through Pagandom they went,   98
looking for Count Orlando all the time,
and still not knowing what new place to search.
To Mònaca they all together came,
where Chiarion and Greco they could see.
They asked them if they knew about the count,
and Prince Rinaldo told them that his cousin
out of disdain had left one night the castle.

Greco and Chiariòn were sorely grieved;   99
so was the maiden, now his happy bride.
They all bade many people search at once
through castles and through towns and cottages
so as to know where Milon's son could be.
They nothing did but talk about the count;
Greco and Chiariòn, meanwhile, did all their best
to make Rinaldo and friends feel right at home and rest.

Now let us leave these knights in Mònaca,   100
resting awhile in Chiarion's abode.
From place to place Astolfo still was roaming,
by any means not knowing where to go,
just like a hawk that, of its own accord,
begins its random flight from land to land,
determined not to heed its lord again,
as it can happen out of quick disdain.

In the same fashion acted our Astolfo,   101
who by this time had come to Barbary,
into the city of a Saracen
who had a new religion newly found.
In neither Christ nor Apollìn this man
believed, nor in Mahound or Trivigant:
he called himself a god—this haughty giant
named Chiaristantè, pompous and defiant.

Corniglia was the name of this new town,   102
and Filiberta was the giant's wife.
Their portraits had been hung inside a mosque,
and out of fear the entire populace
went to that mosque to worship both as gods.
Ready to satisfy his every whim,
a virgin every day he took to bed,
and dumped her, then, where still good wine was sold.

So cruel and so wicked was the man   103
that his whole kingdom coveted his death.
When to this city our Astolfo came,
right on the outskirts at an inn he stopped,
and the innkeeper told him the whole truth
about this lord who governed from his court
with such injustice and outrageous lust.
Astolfo rested—rest he needed most.

Let's not abandon now our count forever.   104
Orlando had just left Creonta's place,
and at the hermitage by chance arrived,
where someone for his gluttony had paid.
One of the hermits told him the whole tale—
which he had memorized—of all those thieves
they hanged with their own hands, forced by a knight
whose charger had been stolen in the night.

Ah, but their backs were broken still, and bruised,   105
for all the beating of Astolfo's stick
that somewhat had pressed down their hermits' gowns;
but they were glad those highwaymen had paid,
and for his goodness warmly thanked the knight.
Orlando rested there with them that night,
and the good hermits in the name of God
with Count Orlando shared their little food.

When everybody was still sound asleep,   106
God's angel in a vision then appeared
to one of the three hermits. Greeting him,
these words he spoke: "The knight whom you have lodged
is Count Orlando. Highly honor him,
for our great champion he most truly is.
The one who hanged those bandits is his cousin,
another brave and worthy paladin."

And to Orlando the same angel said   107
as he appeared to him, "What will you do,
Orlando? Your Astolfo, yes, was here,
and very soon you'll find him safe and sound—
within the sixth day from this moment on.
Tomorrow morning you will leave this place.
So, kindly baron, banish grief from you
lest you displease your God with such a view."

As soon as he awoke the coming dawn,   108
Orlando saddled his brave Vegliantìn.
Meanwhile the hermit came to him to tell
about the thing God's angel had revealed
in a most awesome vision in the night
as in his cell he was still sound asleep,
and with great reverence he bowed and paid him homage.
Embracing him, the count left soon the hermitage.

Toward an enormous vale he started out,   109
where a most frightful serpent he could see,
which at that moment with a griffin fought.
Orlando stopped, their quarrel to observe,
amused and wondering how it would end.
The griffin was about to lose the fight
because the snake had flung its tail around
his neck, which more and more was being bound.

So beautiful the griffin seemed to be   110
(never had our Orlando seen the like)
that he decided soon to help that bird.
Quick, with a leafy bough of a beech tree
he hit the serpent, which fell dead at once,
and saved the frightened griffin in this way:
once more the bird arose and in great freedom flew
while, lone and sad, the count was on his way anew.

A little farther on, Orlando saw   111
four mighty lions: Vegliantìn got skittish
when those big fellows right before he viewed.
One of them came against Orlando straight
with his mouth open and his claws outstretched.
Orlando thrust his Durlindana fast
into his loins, except her hilt and pommel.
The others did not wait to jump upon him.

Finding himself in that predicament,   112
Orlando measured every blow he threw.
But—look!—the griffin from the sky came down
with such a fury, no one could discern
if it was but the wind or a winged bird:
he jumped upon the lion, now so close
to Count Orlando, and so much he hurt
his eyes with his sharp claws, out they did squirt.

That lion soon abandoned, then, his fight.   113
Orlando killed another with his sword.
To help the count still more, the griffin jumped
on the fourth lion, hissing from midair.
He sank all of his claws into his head
and did not let go till he saw him dead:
down to his brains he let his claws descend,
thus proving that he was a grateful friend.

And so no favor done is ever lost.   114
Help anyone, although unknown to you—
the proverb says; but if you hurt a man,
be sure that vengeance in due time will come.
Sow, therefore, even among stones and shrubs,
for kindness in the end will sprout and bloom;
and Aesop's fable let us all rely on:
a mouse's help was needed by a lion.

It pays to rescue even animals,   115
for they at times reward us for our help,
just as the *Detti de' Morali* says:
the one who has been helped becomes your slave.
The greater man you are, the more you help,
and help received lights up man's breast with love.
A noble heart that to another gives,
always, in turn, a hundredfold receives.

Neither the griffin nor Orlando killed   116
the blinded lion out of gentleness:
with his wide wings outstretched, the bird at last
resumed his ample flight up in the air.
And so Orlando started out again
in search of his Astolfo day and night.
And night and day (to make the story short)
he rode to reach at last Corniglia's port.

A pagan was the owner of the inn   117
where he dismounted, to take care at once
of Vegliantìn, who had through mounts and plains
learned how to fast for days and days and days.
Let him now rest quite safe and happy here.
We must return to our Astolfo now,
who in the suburbs of the city wandered,
and many a thing with his innkeeper pondered.

One day he saw him terribly perturbed,   118
and wanted soon to know what saddened him.
Wasting no time, th' innkeeper answered him,
"I have to give my daughter to our king:
else he will take my inn away from me,
my daughter, and my life, and all I own;
but let me tell you, I will sooner die
than with so dire an order now comply;

"I'll rather kill my daughter with these hands   119
than suffer such a shame as tears my heart
with all this anguish and this great dismay."
Astolfo said, "It will not come to this;
maybe you'll laugh about it in the end.
Let's ask of Chiaristante if he dreams,
and if new messengers should come to you,
I want to see them, knowing what to do."

Of course King Chiaristante soon replied   120
by sending a new messenger at once.
Th' innkeeper said, "The messenger is here."
Answered Astolfo, "Let me do the talking."
The lovely girl—the messenger announced—
had to be sent to the king's court at once.
Astolfo then drew close to him, and said,
"To the king's court bring my reply instead.

"To Chiaristante say exactly this: 121
all of his men have had enough of him,
but if he keeps on doing what he does,
he will be punished soon for all his crimes.
Throughout the East all nations talk about
this wicked, horrid man—and him alone.
And now he is so brazen and so awful,
he wants this newest crime to look most lawful."

The messenger, astounded, raised his arms,   122
saying, "Now I am sure you are a fool."
Astolfo once again replied to him,
"Go to the court, and just relate my words."
Th' innkeeper did not say a word at all.
The messenger commented, "Crazy world!
This loafer dares offend our lord and master.
When I go back, he'll know his own disaster."

Back to his lord like a burned cat he went.   123
Soon on his knees, the frightened youth related
everything he had heard. His lord asked then,
"Who can this miserable glutton be?
Surely he is a madman on the loose.
And what did the innkeeper have to say?"
The sergeant said, "He, too, seemed to agree;
but, sire, that man looks like no fool to me."

And Chiaristante answered, "Go right back;   124
and tell them that I want to see them both.
But I am sure this man is here no more."
The messenger assured him, "He replied
in such a way, I tell you he's still here."
Astolfo was most cautious and full-armed,
and desperately looking for some war.
The messenger returned to him once more,

and said, "Eh, you, who gave me that reply!   125
My lord bids you and your innkeeper come
with me, this very moment, to his court.
Move!" and he tried to push—or brush—them out.
Replied Astolfo, "Not to waste his time,
go tell your lord to meet me out of town,
if me he wants to fight; and tell your man—
in case he cares to know—I'm Galliàn;

"and tell him I'll be there to make him pay   126
for these your words more than he can afford."
With a sad face the messenger went back
and said, "Upon his horse he will come here
to make things clear; his name is Galliàn,
and much he scared me as I looked at him.
If you—he told me—want the maiden still,
upon the field you have to prove your skill."

To Chiaristante such a thing seemed strange. 127
He said, "Then tell this Galliàn to come
and meet me—as he pleases—in the square,
with lance or sword or even with a mace.
We soon shall see who this mad idler is,
and for his madness he will dearly pay."
Thus the new message to the inn was sent.
Full-armed, Astolfo to the city went.

Deeming Astolfo an honorable man, 128
th' innkeeper thought, "God must have sent him here.
Whoever he may be, I'd rather die
from the king's vengeance than be forced to this."
And he said, "Go! And may Mahound be with you!"
Astolfo was already in the square,
and all men ran to see the jousting knight
while Chiaristante armed himself to fight.

Orlando had already heard the news 129
about a knight now waiting in the square,
ready to challenge to a fight the king.
He armed himself, and wanted to be there.
But his innkeeper hated being cheated
and wanted more than words to pay for food;
his charger he demanded as a token,
but seeing him on foot, he was heartbroken,

and said, "Now take your horse, and then come back, 130
just like the honest man you seem to be."
Both grief and sadness tore Orlando's heart,
for money he had not with which to pay,
and his poor Vegliantìn could hardly stand;
he did not say a word: 'twas not the time
to tell th' innkeeper he refused to pay.
"By God, I'll pay you," he could only say.

He paid innkeepers with his sword and mace 131
whenever he had run short of his cash.
While Count Orlando through the city rode,
the children made uproarious fun of him,
for Vegliantino fell at every step.
Loud were their laughs each time, until he reached
the square, and everywhere these words were heard:
"Who is this awful, big, and plucked old bird?

"This horse should rest not only on May first,
but for at least a year, and not one month."
Orlando kept on going toward the square,
able to understand all that they said,
for every tongue and dialect he knew.
A Saracen now grabbed him by the bridle,
like one who liked to hurt and inflict pain,
unbuckling Vegliantino's curb and chain,

and pulling then the bridle in contempt.
Orlando could no longer bear all this,
and smashed his cheeks and eyebrows with a fist,
shattering down his nose and both his eyes.
Greatly astonished, those who saw it gasped,
for never had so great a blow been seen.
The count dismounted then, still in a fit,
and placed in order Vegliantino's bit.

The man with now one-third left of his face
unsheathed his sword, quite ready at his side,
convinced by now that this had been no joke.
Orlando gave him some more punches still;
just think: if he had had his gauntlet there,
with but two slugs he would have murdered him.
He hit him on the temple once again,
and from his mouth came out all of his brain.

Using no stirrups, with his armor on,
he mounted on his steed immediately,
and everybody looked, astounded still,
and out of terror moved aside at once.
Meanwhile King Chiaristante came to dance,
and now we'll see if he can neatly waltz.
Astolfo shamed and threatened his new foe,
and, turning, took the field, ready to go.

And each of them began to spur his horse.
Now with Astolfo clashed the Saracen.
Though very strong, his spear could not withstand;
Astolfo's, on the contrary, stood still,
and on the pagan's breast so loudly rang,
his shield by any means could nothing do.
Down went the pagan and his steed as well,
his foot out of one stirrup as he fell.

132

133

134

135

136

But soon he rose together with his horse.   137
"You are my captive now," Astolfo said.
The pagan answered, "It would not be fair:
it was the fault of this my clumsy steed."
Astolfo added, "Who will be the judge?"
"The one who killed a man with but a punch,"
answered the pagan, who had watched Orlando
do what he did with great delight and wonder.

Astolfo answered, "Let this pugilist   138
be, then, the judge." Orlando gave his verdict:
the king was wrong. "You German, smeared with lard,"
the pagan said, "I've not observed you well:
surely you drink more wine than sponges water.
As I can see, you're watching me asquint:
a squint-eyed man cannot but wicked be—
still with your helmet on, I know you thoroughly."

Replied Orlando, "My opinion, sire,   139
you wished to know; should I have lied to you?
No longer in the stirrup was your foot;
anyone else, then, would have judged like me.
But if, O Saracen, you did not fall
through any fault of yours, and wish to fall again,
wicked and squint-eyed as you say I am,
I'll test you, by Mahound, in a new game.

"This horse of mine, as anyone can see,   140
is very thin and weak, and often falls;
but we can fight on foot and use our swords."
Astolfo answered, "It sounds good to me,"
not knowing that Orlando was that knight.
Orlando instead had recognized him well,
but since the count was speaking Saracen,
no one knew either him or Vegliantìn.

"Sir, if you care to borrow this my horse,"   141
Astolfo said, "you'll please me very much."
The Saracen replied, "If you agree,
we shall now put your daring to a test,
since I've been challenged by a lowly cur—
I, who am worth a hundred men like you."
Replied Orlando, "Only one will do."
And so the field was taken by the two.

King Chiaristante thought he now would fight   142
a man of straw that anyone could strip,
such was the wrath with which he charged the count,
but soon his lance against a tower broke.
Orlando pierced his breastplate and his mail
with such a blow as Hector never knew:
a long giraffe he would have fast dismembered,
and so the stirrup was no more remembered.

As soon as Chiaristante hit the ground,   143
these words he spoke: "I beg you, kindly knight,
to tell me now your name, and whether you
are of the Christian or the Afric faith.
From a great ruler of this eastern realm—
his name was Greco—a refined, wise man
who on the sea has wandered ever since—
I took this town away with violence.

"Maybe I'm dying for this sin of mine,   144
for this is what God's justice now demands.
Surely Mahound himself has sent you here
to punish this with all my other crimes."
Orlando from his charger had come down
(around him all the people sang with joy)
and, bending, whispered to the Saracen,
"I am Orlando, Christian paladin."

Lord Chiaristante answered, "I forgive you,   145
for since Mohammed wanted me to die,
by the world's greatest knight I have been slain . . . "
and not another syllable said he.
Unanimously, all the people rose,
as soon as he was dead, to spit upon his corpse,
and their exultance did not seem complete
till havoc everybody made of it.

Some of them bit an arm, and some a hand;   146
some plucked his hair, some others tore his breast:
he seemed a little hare 'mid many a dog,
such as in hunting games at times we see.
In the same way those pagans bit their lord,
treading upon him, spitting on his face,
and saying, "Treacherous man, at last, at last,
you've paid for all your wicked, sinful past.

"So you have not been able to enjoy   147
  the kingdom that you stole from our good lord,
  who for so many a year with but one ship
  has roamed the seas, alone and destitute."
Now see how mighty just disdain can be!
Let any lord beware of hostile subjects,
forever over him like a dangerous roof!
Let what we have narrated be the proof.

A cry of jubilation then arose,   148
  and Count Orlando, taken from his horse,
  was lifted by them all, and called their king.
  Orlando felt quite mortified, and said,
"I am not worthy of this reverence.
This is, instead, the knight who fought for you,
the one who on the field was first to call,
and even lent his horse to save you all.

"I would not even be his worthy squire."   149
  So Duke Astolfo was now lifted up,
  brought to the palace, and proclaimed their king.
  He wanted Count Orlando at his side
forever. Everyone was mad with joy,
and everybody loved Astolfo dearly.
Next time, a cruel tyrant he'll be styled
by everyone, and nearly crucified.

Futile it is to analyze the crowd,   150
  for out of fury many things are done.
  Astolfo now could rest, compelled no more
  to wander through deep-hidden thorny woods.
From Count Orlando more and more he wished
to know about his lofty, noble feats,
and yet he did not know his real name,
though often to converse with him he came.

"Sir, in the name of courtesy," Orlando   151
  asked him one day, "reveal your name to me,
  and tell me if you are a Saracen." Astolfo
  answered, "I, known to all as Galliàn,
was born of noble blood in Barbary.
Mountains and valleys, the whole world I roamed
with not much luck till now; but now, you see,
all of these things have happened here to me."

Speaking of this and that, the count at last   152
touched on the topic he was driving at.
He started to disparage then himself,
saying, "There is no man beneath the sun
I long to catch and wreck and ruin more."
Astolfo by those words was much perturbed,
and came to this decision instantly—
that he should leave the court immediately.

Orlando kept on talking as before   153
until Astolfo was in all his rage.
'Twas then Orlando took his helmet off,
and, oh, Astolfo wept great tears of joy.
They told each other all they did not know,
from when Astolfo quarreled with his friends,
and how and when at last they reached this shore;
Astolfo kissed Orlando a thousand times and more.

Orlando sent for the innkeeper then,   154
who had most kindly let him use his steed,
and paid him with King Chiaristante's horse.
To his innkeeper and his daughter, too,
Astolfo gave great properties as gifts,
for they had honored him most heartily;
and all of them were grateful and most glad,
for Chiaristante, once their lord, was dead.

Astolfo was munificent to all.   155
But let us leave Astolfo with his cousin,
and for a while return to Filiberta,
who had found refuge in a certain castle.
One day, one of its doors being wide open,
two pilgrims reached the place and entered it:
they said that to pay homage they had come,
and Filiberta wished at once to see.

"Lady," they said to her, "we trust you'll be   156
attentive to the words we have to say,
and wise enough to lose not one of them.
Everyone grieves for all your boundless sorrow,
and men, and even beasts, weep everywhere;
but weeping cannot alter your dismay.
In order not to bore you with all this,
we've thought of the one remedy there is.

"Rinaldo, the great, famous Christian knight,   157
with Oliver, Alardo, and Ricciardo,
with Ganelon, the traitor all men know,
Guicciardo, Malagigi, and a squire,
happens to be (the reason is not known,
but what we say is true) in Mònaca.
They wander aimlessly, and well you know how strong
they are when they decide to right a wrong.

"Perhaps they know this man called Galliàn.   158
I'd go to see Rinaldo, and on my knees
would gladly place this city in his hands
if here he came to punish this big cur.
So kind is he, and gentle, and humane
(and on the side of justice all the time)
that with the squadrons that he calls his own
he'll come to give you back your lawful throne.

"And if you have to, even play a trick   159
on both Mahound and Apollìn. There is
a reason why we came with our advice—
for nothing can occur without God's will.
Squires or pilgrims—ask not who we are.
We are old friends of your great royal race,
maybe just Arabs headed for their Mecca—
and let this be enough. *Salamelecca!*"

And so they left—they vanished, better yet.   160
Astonished, Filiberta pondered over
their strange advice, and found it to be sound.
For Mònaca, therefore, she left at once.
Having abandoned every hope, she saw
maybe some good in her despair alone.
Never forget, therefore, to use your mind:
sleep, and you'll only dream; search, and you'll find.

As says a proverb known to everyone,   161
willingly Fortune ever helps the bold,
and scorns and shuns the hesitant and shy.
Dame Filiberta to Rinaldo went,
and was most affably received by him.
She then narrated her calamities
to Prince Rinaldo, and so shocked was he,
he wanted the new fight much more than she.

CANTO   XXI   ❖   473

As soon as Greco gazed upon her face,   162
he recognized that Filiberta at once,
and shouted, "Wretched woman, now you see,
the realm you stole from me is yours no more.
Nor could your Chiaristante keep it long.
With my one little ship I roamed the seas
through many a strife and storm, since I was banned
from my beloved, lovely fatherland.

"But justice had to triumph finally.   163
Your husband did not think he would remain
inside my kingdom for so short a time,
for when he stole it, surely he believed
he would rule over earth and air and fire
and every shore forever with his pride.
He even dared to call himself divine,
and in a mosque placed his own painted sign.

He thought that he could do as Baal did,   164
he thought that he would be a god forever,
he thought he would dethrone Jove in the sky,
he thought he was a new Prometheus,
he thought he could control both heat and frost,
he thought he'd conquer Capaneus's fame,
he thought he could beat Fortune, too, and soon
make the sun tremble, and with it the moon.

"But Heaven's sword, you see, is sharp, and cuts,   165
at the right time and place and evenly:
all earthly things are leveled in the sky.
'Twas I who yesterday bemoaned my fate,
but 'tis your ship that Fortune shakes today:
nothing is ever certain on this earth.
Let therefore every mortal cause no grief,
considering that life is, ah, so brief.

"God's justice never fails—it follows you   166
wherever you may ultimately go.
Never could you have run away from it.
Where is your scepter now? Where is your crown?"
Rinaldo listened to all this in awe,
with great astonishment in all his heart.
To Greco Filiberta could not at all reply,
but for her ancient sin she now began to cry.

Never had until then Rinaldo heard   167
that Greco was Corniglia's lawful lord.
He did not interrupt him as he spoke
so that he could give vent to all his grief;
but then he said to Greco, "Tell me, who
could hurt you so, as to renew such pain?"
And Greco answered, "Sir, now hear me well,
and I am sure you'll weep at what I tell."

From the beginning the whole truth he told.   168
"But why," Rinaldo asked, "did you not say
all this to me the day we met?" Said Greco,
"I did not want such havoc to recall,
to steal from my perfidious wicked Fortune
the joy of her last laugh at wretched me."
Rinaldo said, "Now that all this I know,
more willingly to this new war I'll go.

"You've not degenerated, as you see,   169
for one's own ways and mores are never lost.
One still can tell man's honesty and worth
though Fortune rakes his property away,
but not those things to which she has no keys,
nor can the wind extinguish that true light:
in countless ways, in everything we do,
a soul's nobility shines ever through."

He answered Filiberta then and there   170
that to Corniglia he would shortly come,
and she would have a chance to praise him more.
He met with Gano and the other knights,
and all agreed that they should leave at once.
So every bridle quickly was in place,
and, fully armed, each was upon his steed,
and all together left then with great speed.

They rode and rode and rode (et cetera)   171
until they reached Corniglia one day.
With all their threats they sent a messenger
to Duke Astolfo: they had come to put
Dame Filiberta on her rightful throne,
just as they had officially been asked;
they had one thousand horsemen there with them,
and, even by force, that town had come to claim.

Astolfo and Orlando soon replied
that they were not afraid of anyone;
they were the rightful rulers of the town,
and willingly would come outside the walls
to challenge each of them, and prove to all
they cared for neither threats nor gloomy looks.
And so, for my next Canto I expect you.
May He Who lives close to the Word protect you.

172

CANTO   XXII

Forever praise the Son of Israel,
creator of sky, earth, and moon, and sun!
He then sent down His Gabriel on earth,
so sorry was He for this human race;
eternally around Him flieth Michael,
singing together with th' eternal choirs:
and so, Eternal Father of all men—
You, just and holy—my new song sustain.

1

The chariot of Phoebus was already
deep in mid-ocean, bound for other lands—
if this is so, when he from us departs—
and far into the east the night had spread,
when I left our Astolfo, who with wrath
answered Rinaldo's messenger at once—
or maybe only feigned just to have fun.
To bed he and Orlando then had gone.

2

The following morn, Astolfo armed himself,
and to Orlando said, "Let's take a stroll
right where Rinaldo pitched all of his tents.
It will be good to break four spears with them."
Orlando said, "My steed is saddled now:
I'm dying our Rinaldo to behold."
Outside the city, fully armed they went,
where all their friends had pitched their every tent.

3

To his dear Aldighier Rinaldo said,   4
"The one who walks in front is Galliàn;
  but I don't know the other one who has
  so thin a steed. But let us meet them both."
And so they went—Alardo, Oliver,
Guicciardo, Malagigi, Greco, Gan.
In greeting them, they chose in French to speak:
Astolfo and the count replied in Arabic.

It was Rinaldo who began to speak,   5
"If, as I reckon, you are Galliàn,
  the very one who Chiaristante slew
  (I am the first to speak, the first to ask),
what reasons do you have to justify
(you may begin this anywhere you wish)
that Chiaristante has been rightly killed?
Or has your guilt already been revealed?

"But let's forget about it. It is you   6
who make poor Filiberta beg on earth;
  but tell me, has she done so great an ill?
Before you ask, I want you this to know:
this town, with all its castles all around—
unless you do object to what she owns—
belongs to this man who is here with me,
for what you look at is his property.

"You cannot seize this town from every part—   7
justice would be against you, to be sure;
  and though I am a Christian, out of duty—
much though I grieve—I start this enterprise.
Take, to your heart's content, the field you wish,
and let our conversation have an end."
Astolfo answered him, "Oh, wait a little:
do not depart so quickly from our riddle.

"Do not men say the other coin means much?   8
Rinaldo, maybe little touches you,
  or else you look on things with clever eyes—
but can you understand this Galliàn?
A spear means more, much more than playing cards.
I do not know what pity touches you,
unless a dame to you is very dear:
is this the reason why you have come here?

"Christian or Saracen, you like all dames,
and Filiberta's eyes can lure you most:
she has been always easy to approach,
and, if you want, agrees with what you say.
Though you pretend to be so rough and rude,
we do not fear the rascals you call yours.
The one who murdered Chiaristante—see?—
has come to fight you—have you faith in me?"

9

Replied Orlando, "As far as I'm concerned,
I'd leave my hot bed even at midnight.
Too many words do not break many spears:
do you not think I know Rinaldo well,
and all the men that he has brought up here?
In Mònaca he rallied all its thieves;
besides, with Filiberta he did flirt,
and now he wants to show he's not been hurt."

10

If you could have but seen Rinaldo now,
wrath almost made him burst out of his armor:
in fury more than once he turned against them
just like a hawk that sees its blackbird gone.
Saying no word, he turned his brave Baiardo,
so mad, his eyes were almost spurting out:
he could not talk, so hurt he thought he'd been.
Meanwhile Orlando spurred his Vegliantìn.

11

Again they hit each other with their spears.
Ask not with what enormous wrath Rinaldo
was fighting. Both of them aimed at their shields,
but, oh, to whose advantage do not ask.
All of them broke, and both their steeds leapt up.
Rinaldo could not vent all of his ire
using his spear; and so his sword he took,
and 'gainst Orlando rapidly came back.

12

Unsheathing Durlindana, cried Orlando,
"Is god Mahound so great that you, dear cousin,
should murder me for Filiberta's love?"
Hearing the well-known voice, Rinaldo stopped
his sharp Frusberta; he had also seen
great Durlindana at her best before him.
They ran to hug each other instantly
while still Rinaldo said, "How can this be?"

13

They all together to the city went.
Astolfo led them to his palace soon,
and many things together they discussed,
pondering what remained still to be done.
Several days in such a way elapsed
when unexpectedly Dudòn arrived,
who made all of them marvel then and there;
"Dudòn," they asked, "what tidings do you bear?"

Dudòn replied, "My tidings are not good."
And down he sat; in tears he added then,
"O Count Orlando, from the day you left
the royal court, with clear and hidden tricks
Fortune has persecuted until now
our good King Charles, your emperor and mine,
and now the trap she set is very near;
but there are many things that you should hear.

"The great Calavrion, Lord of the Mountain,
brother of the Old Man, who has been killed,
passing through Spain, has now reached France at last.
He says his brother has been wrongly slain
by one who is now fighting under you,
but will avenge his death one of these days.
One hundred forty thousand fighting men
have come right here to fight with him, and then

"he took one of his brothers here along,
whom Archilagio everybody calls—
a man who in his land is most renowned.
Carlo himself is quite afraid of him;
therefore, just like a bird you have to fly.
We also have to help our Montalbàn:
full sixty thousand cavaliers are there,
all of them from Maganza and Pontier.

"The captain of all men in Montalbàn
is Grifonetto—if you please, Rinaldo."
"Scot free at my expense," Rinaldo said,
"O wicked Gano, you got off this time."
Dudòn commented, "Vivian is there."
Answered Rinaldo, "Ricciardetto is not."
Dudòn replied, "The valiant Dane's with him."
Ganelon at this news grew pale and grim,

14

15

16

17

18

and answered, "Here you lie, Rinaldo dear,
for I was not aware of these new things:
have I, in fact, been out of prison long?"
Rinaldo said, "I'm not a fool, you know.
Much you would like, I know, one of these days
to swallow—what a feat!—my Montalbàn.
But, oh, whatever comes, remember this—
I'm living just to be your Nemesis.

19

"More than a dinner I now want to bet—
Calavrionè has descended here
because this felon has arranged all things,
and this pertains to Montalbàn and Grifon."
Orlando said, "Your speech is much too rash:
you name a felon much too easily.
You still don't know how things are really,
and yet till now we've made one company."

20

Now clinging to the words he had just heard,
Ganelon said, "Rinaldo, you're a man
I've not been able to know well as yet;
but you'll be tamed by time, as others were.
As far as what you have just said against me,
I would not give a heap of grass for it:
I know you speak only what you know not,
but I am honest in my every thought.

21

"When the Maganzans are in Montalbàn,
I'll be the first to punish all of them;
if Grifonetto has betrayed you, I
with these my hands shall tear his heart to shreds,
for such a shame I can no longer bear:
I want to be a loyal friend to you
all of my life, until the day I die,
for well you know how grateful still am I.

22

"I am no more the Ganelon I was,
for so has time now clipped my wings that I
have now begun to yield to all its might,
aware of my mortality each day:
besides, what do we have out of this life
if not the evil or the good we do?
Time teaches but one lesson—'tis not good
the fruit that does not ripen when it should.

23

"So long as I'm on earth," the felon said,   24
"I want to live my life in traveling:
I have to see the Sepulcher, Saint James,
and I must visit other holy shrines,
according to a vow I made in jail.
Full well I know I have offended Christ,
and a great deal of penance I must do
to rid my conscience of its shame anew."

Rinaldo said, "Your shame I well can see;   25
but there's a question I must ask you now:
Is shame a thing you have been dreaming of?
Your face—oh, don't you see it?—is all red.
Ah, do not waste so many words with me!
You take me for a big, thick-headed fool—
and this is how you've treated me till now;
I know you well, dear Mister I-Know-How.

"I know your vices like the alphabet.   26
Look at the man who's meowing to me!
I do not need to be so buttered up,
for of your butter not one ounce I'd buy.
And yet some other ointment you prepare:
what will you show me now—the mandrake root?
You are a great snake charmer, but I'd rather
charm a vine-shoot. So let's not fool each other."

"Gano, I don't believe you," said Astolfo,   27
"for you were born a traitor, to be sure:
soprano and contralto do not blend,
and worse, your tenor voice is out of tune.
To catch a liar and a sinner, just
let one talk on and on, and there's your man.
So here's the one who is ashamed of shame,
and knows he and a sewer are the same.

"He has, of course, the conscience of a Joseph,   28
of Abraham, of Isaac and Jacob.
He has so much betrayed and hurt our king,
of our poor Charles he's made another Job,
and now that he's about to shake his dice,
he even says Rinaldo he never knew.
For what you are you should be recognized,
evil destroyer of the faith of Christ.

CANTO XXII ❖ 481

"Many more times than Judas you betrayed him: 29
so here's the man who wants to seem so good!
I do not give a darn about old Charlie,
who's so senile as to confide in you,
and does not realize he's scorned and duped
so long as on his head he wears his crown,
and does not know that when he hears a snap,
he'll be that crumb of cheese inside the trap.

"But I feel sorry for the count, my cousin, 30
also for Oliver, who both believe
that now the wolf is on a pilgrimage,
according to the vow you say you made.
If you should find a little lamb astray,
say, would you pick it up? To break your fast!
So help you God, as much as I believe you!
Were you the *Creed* itself, I'd not believe you.

"May you be cut to pieces just as thin 31
as all the thoughts with which you schemed this trick—
oh, not your first, but possibly your last.
You say that now you're not the man you were . . .
You were a rotten traitor the first day
you saw this earth. If you're not satisfied
with your last deed, this is the only reason—
if you are there, you'll spin a hundred webs of treason.

"Did I say a hundred? A hundred thousand more! 32
And don't you think this is a well-planned scheme?
But if new threads are needed for your web,
your pocket and your doublet have them all;
besides, your mind can weave new threads galore
until you sing your song to its last note.
But one more thing I'll say: let's go to France,
and there—you'll see—I'll punish you at once.

"There I will hang you, wicked renegade, 33
just as one day you wanted to hang me."
Orlando, who had listened to all this,
said to Astolfo, "Everything's been said,
and now the awful load is off your chest;
but let this argument now end right here."
Gano could not believe what he had heard:
the fire in his breast had just been stirred.

They all agreed that they should leave at once.   34
Dame Filiberta—so Rinaldo wished—
should still be queen, by everyone obeyed,
and be in power till the day she died;
and Greco should return after her death.
Quite pleased with the decision, Greco left
with all his men, and Filiberta stayed
with still her husband's crown upon her head.

Never in his whole life had Prince Rinaldo   35
felt so bewildered as he felt this time.
Ganelon had betrayed him—so he said—
sure that without Orlando he'd succeed.
And so they all agreed unanimously
to leave for Paris. On their steeds at once,
they rode, and took a shortcut, night and day,
and not, as you may think, the trodden way.

They went through woods and forests, left and right,   36
to make the road as short as possible,
the way a grieving cow is seen to do
when from afar she hears her little calf:
she treads on boughs and thorns and everything,
lowing and lowing till she sees him near.
In such a way through mounts and plains they ran,
forever calling traitor wicked Gan.

But none of them had guessed that with all that   37
their Mister Know-It-All had nought to do,
as Malagigi very clearly said.
But let them get to Roncesvalles, and Charles
(although that treason was the last to come,
and would be followed by great harm and woe),
Charles, good three times and three more times unwise,
will at last open—a dead man—his eyes.

Then his dear nephew he will mourn too late,   38
and, scratching both his cheeks, he will, alas,
regret he'd always trusted Ganelon:
but what will his regret accomplish then?
So let the one who sees all things in heaven
turn, and still turn, her ever-mobile wheels!
She'll make even this traitor in due time
finally pay for every wicked crime.

They saw a city then, called Villafranca,
which looked to them quite beautiful indeed.
'Twas on their left; they came to it at last,
and rode through it. The people that they saw
seemed very generous and valiant men,
and Diliante was their ruler's name.
As soon as in the square he sighted them,
kindly to dinner he invited them,

39

for some important knights they seemed to be.
Rinaldo did not want to lose that chance,
and so they all were caught in that new web,
as they replied to him right in his hall.
The nephew of the Old Man of the Mountain
he was—a man who'd proved his worth all over.
Acknowledging their greetings, with great cheer
he said to all of them, "You're welcome here.

40

"Who are you, gentlemen? Where are you from?"
Orlando so replied, "O Worthy Crown,
we have been banished from our land away
after the Sultan died in Bambillona.
We were his warriors, and now we go
with nothing left but honor and our arms."
And Diliante said, "I grieve for you,
but let us be resigned when nothing we can do."

41

And so at table they together sat.
A youthful little silly clown was there,
who wanted to make fun of our Rinaldo.
Rinaldo did not mind that idiot
and kept on gulping down the food he found
(the master laughed at his young jester's pranks).
Passing from joke to joke, at last the fool
demanded, then and there, Rinaldo's bowl.

42

Rinaldo, who refused to part with it,
said to Orlando, "What a stupid thing!
Whenever we arrive at a fine place,
we always find these clowns as our dessert."
Addressing Diliante then, he said,
but watching still his bowl with both his eyes,
"Germans don't quarrel when they eat their meal;
so after dinner, with this fool I'll deal."

43

Rinaldo ate a bowl of truffles, stewed   44
in the most wonderful, delicious way,
and did not think that he would snatch it from him;
but the voracious fool did quickly that,
and by all means refused to give it back:
he gulped it down, and spilled some on his chest.
Rinaldo, angry with that idiot
who took his food away and should have not,

against him rushed like an immense gorilla,   45
saying, "I'll make your soup squirt from your nose:
you are a wicked madman, not a clown."
He gave him such a peach right on the head,
he stretched him flat, face downward, at his feet,
an ear and one of the two temples plucked.
Enraged, the king stood up before his eyes,
impatient now, although he was most wise,

and said, "You crazy glutton, what is this?   46
How dare you strike one of my family?
Is this the way a worthy knight behaves?
Are you repaying thus my courtesy?"
Rinaldo said, "I gave him what he asked for."
Orlando told his cousin angry words.
Rinaldo's hand was nearly coming down
to strike the king as he had struck his clown.

But Diliante calmed himself at last,   47
and said to him, "Let us now eat in peace;
but after dinner, if you so agree,
since you have shown me little reverence,
we'll test each other's valor in the square,
and so we'll take this madness off our minds."
Rinaldo answered, "Very well—the spear!
What are we waiting for—a rotten pear?"

Replied the pagan, "Any time you say,   48
provided you accept to joust with me—
and that will be our roast and our dessert.
I want a good conclusion of our meal,
considering the trouble I went through."
Orlando said, "A joust sounds good to me,
for, sire, you are great and strong, but in the end,
I'll guarantee you that you'll also like my friend."

After they ate their dinner, Diliante   49
soon to a squire beckoned for his arms,
and so his armor suit was brought to him;
and when he saw himself armed at his best,
he jumped up on a savage steed of his,
saying, "If I get plucked, I asked for it."
Mounted on his Baiàrd, Rinaldo, full of wrath,
was ready for a duel to the death.

They took their field and, quickly turning back,   50
Rinaldo and Diliante braced themselves.
They hit each other with undoubted skill
but, overbearing, Lord Rinaldo's might
soon to the pagan fighter tasted sour
as vinegar—and worse: he found himself
back to front on his steed, and more than once
the monarch was about to lose his balance.

Rinaldo's left foot lost its stirrup, and   51
the spears broke into pieces in the air;
passing each other like two crossbow shots,
the horses showed they knew their art too well.
Finally Diliante, straightened up,
was quick to realize his sudden luck,
and, turning to Rinaldo suddenly,
said, "Baron, Mars himself you may well be:

"I've never seen a spear so deftly thrown,   52
and never have I seen so strong a man:
a better blow was never seen in France.
Please be so kind as to reveal your name,
for if you now decide to strike my cheek,
I'll offer you the other willingly.
In love I've fallen with your worth; therefore,
the feud that's been between us let's ignore."

Rinaldo said, "Most joyously I will.   53
I am Rinaldo, and this man's Orlando;
these are Guicciardo, Alardo, and Oliver,
and this is Ricciardetto, if you please;
and this is Mister Traitor Ganelon
(at times I can a perfect title find);
this is Dudòn; this, Malagigi; and, see,
this is Astolfo: Paris-bound are we.

"And this young man's my cousin, who's become   54
    a Christian recently. I am afraid
    you never met him: a Saracen was he."
    (He did not mention Aldighieri's name.)
    Treacherous Gano put his eyes on him,
    and thought of a new treason then and there.
    Now Diliante said, "At any rate,
    I'm very honored that with me you ate.

"But if I'm not mistaken, are you not   55
    the one who killed my uncle, Grand Old Man?"
    Rinaldo answered, "I was sent to him
    by the great Sultan, but, may God be praised,
    I did not kill him, but became his friend:
    I then baptized him, and avenged him, too,
    by murdering the man who gave him death.
    You, Diliante, did not know the truth."

And Diliante answered, "I'm so sorry   56
    that this event has been so ill-reported
    with all the consequences that I see:
    because of this, all France is now on fire,
    and I'm afraid this fire will still grow.
    Calavrion is angry with you still,
    and, with his people fully armed for war, is
    by now, as you have heard, not far from Paris."

Right at this moment a great din was heard,   57
    which turned the entire city upside down,
    making the frightened population run.
    Orlando asked, "What's happening? What's this?"
    The pagan answered, "Do not be afraid!
    Often a lion comes, and acts this way:
    he has devoured too many men before,
    for oft he even crosses many a door.

"And, oh, I am responsible for this,   58
    so much so that I'm hated by my own.
    A long, long time ago, I raised a lion,
    all-white and meek, and gentle as could be.
    One day he ran away—and that is why
    he slays my people now, and wrecks my life:
    my men are being, day by day, destroyed,
    and I myself have by the beast been clawed."

Rinaldo boasted, "I will kill this beast."   59
He was so sorry to see people run.
The pagan said, "If you can do so much,
this town will worship you as a true god."
Rinaldo said again, "I'll do it now,
or I will never mount a horse again."
Into the forest whence he'd come to stalk,
meanwhile the sated lion had gone back.

Right to that forest then Rinaldo went,   60
with many people coming right behind;
but when the roaring lion out of his den appeared,
everyone, like Zacchaeus, found refuge in a tree.
Rinaldo saw the wild and fiery beast
and rushed on him, to give him sudden pain.
His sword aloft, Rinaldo jumped at once,
and went against the lion's vehemence.

The lion jumped upon Baiàrd instead;   61
Rinaldo tried to help his horse right then,
but, not at all expecting that great blow,
the beast was seen to leap high in the air,
and fall then on Rinaldo with such wrath,
hugged as he was, he could not use his sword:
his brave Frusberta he could not rely on,
and so Rinaldo wrestled with the lion.

Each shook the other in that wild embrace.   62
The lion at this moment brought him down,
and started at his suit to bite and scratch.
But suddenly the prince was on the beast
and held the lion strongly by the throat.
All of the pagan men had come to watch,
and—let me tell you—every shrub and tree
swarming with crows and starlings seemed to be.

Rinaldo with the lion came to blows,   63
but after tossing, turning, turning, tossing,
with such a punch Rinaldo hit the beast,
his gauntlet fell to pieces in his hand
(think if a buzzing fly could e'er survive!),
but of the lion's head made minute ash:
sprawled on the ground, and lifeless, lay the beast,
and everyone came down as to a feast.

Back to the city Prince Rinaldo went,   64
with a huge crowd of pagans right behind,
and even women treading on their knees.
"Oh, blessèd, blessèd hands!" they all were saying.
The streets were full of people everywhere:
as a new David, killer of Goliath,
he was adored by all the population.
The lion dead, there was great jubilation.

King Diliante thanked the paladin,   65
saying, "I'll be your slave eternally:
may god Apollin bless you evermore!
But now," the wise King Diliante said,
"I must go back to what I was just saying
the very moment that great din was heard—
that I am sorry there is war in France
because of Calavrione's ignorance.

"Calavrion believes that it was you   66
who killed his brother, or helped others do it;
therefore he is still thinking of revenge,
not knowing that already you've avenged him.
If I should write to him, my words would be
rhetorical; therefore this is my plan:
full thirty thousand soldiers will I yield,
well armed and ready for the battlefield.

"'Tis all I have besides the man you see.   67
But there's another plan you now should know:
in Bambillona King Costanzo died,
and to his daughter he has left his reign.
Many men under his own crown he ruled,
who have disdainfully from Bambillona
gone back to their own land, feeling mistreated
since Queen Antea in that town was seated;

and well I know they're looking to be hired.   68
Uliva is, indeed, my relative.
I know they all will do as I suggest;
and if you have no cash to hire knights,
I've so much money that I can afford
to pay at least one hundred thousand men.
To King Costanzo you were close, I know,
because the Sultan was your common foe."

Rinaldo savored every spoken word,
for well he heeded what the king revealed.
"O Diliant," he said, "you're so humane,
I have to wait until the sun goes down
to thank you as I should; and much I grieve.
What you have told me seems quite true to me:
to all your promises at last we bow,
but send a message to Uliva now."

69

Orlando said to Diliante then,
"This girl you call Uliva—I believe—
remembers, most distinctly, all of us.
Maybe you do not know she was one day
forcibly taken from her town away:
some giants dared abduct her, but we soon
gave death to them, and thus, at last, could free
the maiden who had known such misery.

"And to her father we restored her then.
And King Costanzo came, because of this,
to Bambillona with his entire army,
just as you know, who heard the rest of it.
The whole world is aware—I so believe—
of the great boldness of his every deed.
More than Uliva, for his death I wept,
and all I did for him unsaid I kept.

71

"With a great funeral I sent his body,
embalmed, as I had done with Spinellon's.
I'm grateful to my benefactor still,
and it was I who killed the monstrous man
by whom he had been slain, avenging him.
Your plan is good: to Uliva we shall send
a messenger as promptly as we can."
Rinaldo answered, "I will be that man.

"Meanwhile, you will array your squadrons here;
and you, Orlando, leave for Paris soon,
and see that Gano's every web is smashed."
Replied Orlando, "Do then what you must,
but it is prudent to go there by sea."
"Take me along," said Aldighieri then.
"I need only Guicciardo and Alardo,
of course with Ricciardetto," said Rinaldo.

73

And toward the sea in full array he rode. 74
And may God give him favorable winds!
Meanwhile Orlando all his skill employed
for the quick execution of their plan:
fast, he assembled all those pagan troops
and set the date for their beginning march.
But Gano's mind worked just as fast: the traitor
was planning just the thing he would do later.

One day—Rinaldo had already left— 75
taking advantage of Orlando's absence,
he saw the field wide open and quite free
for all his treason that could fill a sea.
To Diliante's chamber right away
he went, and flooded with sweet words the king.
"Sire," he said, "whoever's kind to me,
betrayed or disappointed will not be."

"Therefore, because your kindness I have known, 76
gratefully now I'll tell you what is true;
but so that you may know my every thought,
a bit out of resentment I will speak.
First, then, your word of honor I expect
if you want me to tell you the whole truth.
Swear, by Mahound, no soul shall know from you!"
And Diliante said, "And swear I do."

"Now, Diliante, heed my every word! 77
Calavrion has left for France in haste,
and West and East are in a great uproar,
most eager to avenge your dear Old Man
(Trevigant knows how close I was to him!)
and look for something they already have.
Because of this, some men—I do believe—
when the whole tale they hear, will weep and grieve.

"The man who killed him drinks from your own glass, 78
and eats, and sleeps, and speaks with you today,
and—a new Judas—at your table sits,
and eats from your own dish; but you are blind.
I thought you just pretended not to know.
The young knight Count Orlando took along—
do you know who he is? Why has his true
name not been mentioned by the prince to you?

"Rinaldo introduced them all to you,   79
except this one, whom he presented just
as 'a dear cousin that you do not know'
and, saying this, forbade you to ask more.
It breaks my heart to see you so betrayed—
and even being played as ball or bagpipe—
and that in this Rinaldo you believe,
blind to the art with which he can deceive.

"Know, then, that Aldighieri is his name.   80
He went to Mònaca one day to joust,
and there he killed our so renowned Old Man.
He was Orlando's relative, he said,
and then they staged the silliest of shows—
they started reading letters on his sword,
which said—they all were carved in Saracen—
Orlando and Rinaldo are cousins of this man.

"Well, I believe this is the entire truth,   81
and you have been most wickedly deceived.
This man was then baptized and made a king.
Missives they had already sent to all,
pretending they were coming to bring help,
and thus avenge poor Mariotto's death;
but they'd already planned the stratagem
whereby your Old Man lost his life to them.

"This shrewd Rinaldo first sent to the joust   82
his brother and then Oliver, who both
pretended to have been thrown from their steeds—
and they are knights accustomed to no fall.
The Grand Old Man was caught then in their web,
for he was challenged by this Aldighier.
He hardly answered, seeing but a youth;
but he was murdered by him—that's the truth.

"Rinaldo, wicked from his infancy,   83
had tried to kill him with his very hand
at the request of a loose whore of his—
Antea—whom he left in Bambillona
when he could see no other easy gain
(look on whose head the Sultan's crown is now!);
but the Old Man could not be sacrificed
because he wanted soon to be baptized.

"Our law does not allow by any means
    to kill a man who makes it known to us
    that he would like to be by us baptized.
    Unable, therefore, to get rid of him—
    as I was saying—in a knightly way,
    and wishing his Antea still to please,
    he brought him to that joust and that deceit.
    In Mònaca they're all aware of it.

"I am amazed—I must confess to you—
    that such a gross mistake you could have made,
    believing what Rinaldo said to you.
    Now I do not presume to teach my lord—
    now that he has his foe locked in a cage.
    This I advise: keep honoring them all,
    but on this matter ever silent be:
    this is a secret between you and me."

So the accursèd traitor went away,
    to himself saying, "If I am no fool,
    I'm sure the barrel gave him its last drop."
    King Diliante was perplexed and stunned,
    already scheming with his every thought
    what he should do, or in what way behave,
    so as to catch the otter in the net:
    yes, he could see the truth of all that Gan had said.

One night, at supper, very casually
    but with malicious innocence he asked,
"Dear Count Orlando, what's this baron's name?
    Or is he still, perhaps, a Saracen?"
    And these new weighty words he added then,
"Did not your Christ at His last supper say,
    'One who breaks bread with me will in the end
    betray me, yet pretends to be my friend'?"

"What do you mean by this?" the count replied.
    The pagan said, "I've pondered what I said.
    He does not sleep who much has on his mind:
    about his foe he wants to find out more.
    Full well I knew the man who came right here,
    for I have friends in Mònaca and in Corniglia, too—
    the one who murdered the Old Man, the giant
    who's not much taller than King Diliant.

84

85

86

87

88

"Ah, did you think I did not have, Orlando,   89
    my secret reasons to invite you here,
    and that I really trust Rinaldo's words?
    Even if you had not passed through my land,
    for all of you the trap had been set there.
    With your own feet you walked into your cage:
    and through these doors you'll never walk away
    if first all of my men you do not slay.

"I know that Gano is among all those   90
    who dared betray the Old Man of the Mountain;
    but even if I let some thrush go free,
    if they're too many, well, they break the net.
    Let some of them escape, as did Rinaldo;
    but one of you I'll keep arrested here—
    the Aldighieri who my uncle slew.
    I also know that Gan did all that he could do,

"being a man who in his entire life   91
    mastered not one, but every treason well;
    but to his lard the cat so often goes,
    this is the penance he cannot escape."
    Look what a clever man he seemed to be,
    and what a perfect web could Gano weave!
    Orlando was perplexed when he heard this,
    and thought immediately of Gano's malice.

He would have answered to the Saracen,   92
    but Aldighieri soon preceded him,
    saying, "Because I have been singled out,
    sire, by all you said, I am the one
    who killed your uncle; but if so you wish,
    I'll prove to you a traitor I was not:
    I killed him with my spear, and lawfully—
    a liar's he who states the contrary.

"My dear King Diliante, from now on,   93
    just as in Mònaca with the Old Man
    (God knows that through no fraud I took his life),
    I want to joust with you, if you accept."
    King Diliante answered, "So do I;
    and if you beat me, you will soon be free,
    all of you from my town in peace will go,
    and take along all of my people, too."

"Ah," said Orlando, "this is what I like!
  But I cannot believe you might have thought
  of harming us in any other way:
  it would be most unworthy of your lineage.
  This is the manner we can reach our peace,
  and like a wise man you have spoken, sire;
  'twas Aldighier who killed the Old Man—right,
  but there was never a more honest fight,

94

"nor was there any treason or deceit,
  and, by Mahound, he has been fully avenged!"
  Said Aldighier, "And how! I have been told
  that I was placed as dead upon a bed."
"So, Diliante, be content to do
  as you have said," Orlando said to him,
  and you'll be always praised for doing so:
  much honor to the Grand Old Man we owe.

95

"He rests in peace in Bambillona now,
  where he was buried as a man of worth,
  and his sad death I here am mourning still.
  I've wandered through the kingdoms of the world,
  on land and sea, and often I have left
  my armor suit as pawn, for want of cash;
  but never will you hear a person say
  I've cheated or betrayed in any way.

96

"Treason is not a common thing in France:
  what Aldighieri said is really true,
  and he but dreams and blabs who says the opposite.
  This man came as a stranger to this land;
  he knew him not, and killed him with his spear,
  and man to man, just as good fighters do;
  your uncle was a Christian, he of the pagan cult:
  not Aldighieri's, then, nor was it Gano's fault.

97

"Tomorrow morning, test your weapons, both,
  and see which of the two has rust on it."
  The Saracen replied, "I wish I were
  down on the field this moment, spear in hand!
  All of my feelings I'll release this way."
  Shaking his head, threatening Gano said,
"A traitor you have called me; let it be!
  But maybe afterward you'll joust with me."

98

The pagan said, "And with you, too, I'll fight;   99
I heard Rinaldo give you such a name."
Threatening still, Ganelon shook his head:
how well that ribald knew how to pretend!
That evening, each of them went, then, to bed,
and their agreement was once more spelled out;
but when the knights were in their room alone,
wasting no time, they jumped on Ganelon.

Orlando asked, "How has this man been able   100
to learn this secret in such great detail?
He knows the entire book from A to Z.
A wolf from our own pack has gone to him!
Astolfo, very cautious we must be:
let all of us sleep with our weapons on—
one eye right on the pot, one on the cat:
there is a trap here—I am sure of that."

Astolfo answered, "Why such mystery?   101
Why don't you say 'twas Gan informed him well?
Why do you give us wine, sip after sip?
You should have tapped the barrel all at once."
Gano replied, "Your head is full of crickets,
and you were always crazy and uncurbed."
Astolfo said to Malagigi then,
"Please make this hare come out into the open!"

Malgigi did not want to use his art,   102
most scrupulous about it as he was;
nor could he use it indiscriminately.
He had to be concerned with many things—
the proper holy vestments, certain charts
that needed deftly practiced exorcisms,
pentacles, instruments, and seals and tapers,
and swords and blood and pots, and aromatic vapors.

This is what I believe; for one may ask: 103
"Well, then, if Malagigi was with them,
he should have told them what was going on:
'Here one does this; in Paris Charles does that.'"
Our Malagigi, then, would be like God
if he knew everybody's deeds and thoughts.
Seldom do necromancers probe the low,
nor do they always tell us what they know.

In a bad mood they grumbled the whole night: 104
each would have made of Gano gelatin;
Astolfo would have loved to be the first.
King Diliante the next morning rose
and in full armor in the square appeared;
and just as you have guessed, our Aldighier
came also to the field: they did not greet each other,
but as the lad arrived, they turned their horses, rather.

Orlando and his friends, full-armed, were there.   105
King Diliante turned his steed again,
which like a newborn fawn he forced to leap—
and one could see his spurs all stained with blood.
As soon as they against each other clashed,
each looked undoubtedly like Mars himself:
the pagan's mighty spear broke then and there,
Aldighier's went to pieces in the air.

They used the sword, then, for their second round: 106
they were not joking, you can rest assured.
Many a notch remained on both their shields,
but neither fighter seemed to mind the blow.
They kept on fighting for two hours and more.
Orlando said, "Astolfo, until now
the scale has not yet tipped—it is quite clear—
whether you put the sword or else the spear.

"I well could swear each of them was Achilles: 107
listen how Aldighieri's sword is whistling,
and look how Diliante's sword is sparkling!"
But now the battle much too long has lasted:
Aldighier with a blow, well worth a thousand
(for cruel Fortune does not like to jag),
so cleanly split the pagan's head in two,
no pitch would have been able it to glue.

And so, King Diliante, you are dead!   108
Better it would have been had you believed Rinaldo,
who told you that a giant had murdered the Old Man,
and had thrown Ganelon out of your court.
Like all young men, you were quite ignorant
and bold, and now you had to pay for it.
For your revenge, right time and place should have come first:
no great accomplishment was ever born of haste.

The citizens consulted one another,   109
and soon at this conclusion they arrived:
"Because, O Christian knights, you are the men
who freed us from the wild and haughty lion
that had devoured so many of us here,
and now delivered us from Pharaoh's hand—
from Diliant—our gratitude's immense:
so all of us with you shall come to France."

And, finally, the troops in a few days   110
were all arrayed, and with Orlando went;
a lion could be seen on their white flags
which they to Bambillona brought with them.
Soon, very soon, they were about to see
Calavrion and all his men; meanwhile,
he made, quite unaware, all Paris tremble, and
believed that he could tame the sky, the sea, the land.

Orlando from a mountain peak could see   111
already the enormous pagan field
covering every slope and every plain
with all the tents along the plainland pitched.
And this is what Orlando told his friends:
"With all these men we have to fight right now."
Near Paris Aldighier was satisfied:
imagine when he would set foot inside!

The night before, Emperor Charles had dreamed   112
that a big lion into town had come,
passing through one and through another door,
to rout his entire field in sudden fright.
Orlando was already near the walls.
Carlo was sorely grieved when he was told
that still new troops against him came to fight:
he knew not where he was, such was his plight.

He told his Namo, "This I cannot bear;   113
this time I know that I am all alone;
the entire world will fall upon us now."
Right at that moment Count Orlando showed
his own headquarters' colors—white and red—
and everybody recognized him soon.
With joy the entire population ran
to meet him; in the town remained no man.

Emperor Carlo with his entire court   114
went out to meet Orlando, barely seen:
judging by all that haste and all that noise,
'twas like that day when everybody ran
to see Christ entering Jerusalem.
Ah, people, in no time perverse and thankless!
But shouted everyone with joy that day,
"Be not afraid! Orlando's here to stay!"

As knights would do, in great humility   115
Orlando knelt before King Charlemagne;
soon they embraced each other and then walked
with the whole crowd into the royal hall.
The emperor was watching Aldighier,
and asked who the lad was, and from what land.
Orlando said he was Gherardo's son,
and that he was as brave as anyone.

About Rinaldo, then, the king inquired.   116
Orlando let him know that, as a knight
most eager to be part of the new battle,
he'd soon be there with more recruited men.
Then about wicked Gan the king inquired.
Orlando said, "He has just disappeared:
he said he wants to go to Montalbàn,
soon to make Captain Grifonetto run."

"It was the right decision," said the king,   117
"for Grifonetto, maybe, misbehaves."
Astolfo interrupted him, and said,
"You make me still so sick, you'll make me die,
O Carlo, if you still believe that Gano
has ceased to be the traitor that he is:
well, keep believing in him till you die,
and banish now Orlando from your eye.

"Let me define that wicked man for you!   118
Well, here's my definition: he's a cur,
able to make himself at once despised
by citizens, by brothers, and by friends.
Carlo, you're not a man who should be king,
for like a little donkey you behave:
his tail he seems to know and recognize
the moment it is bitten by new flies.

"No sooner has your nephew reached your court   119
than you devise new plans to chase him out,
but when he's far from here, you scratch your face.
Instead you should adore that man, and know
how much he loves you, and how strong he is.
At least in this believe me, Carlo dear:
if we had had within our midst the count,
these pagan men would not have crossed the mount."

While everybody spoke of this and that,   120
down in his camp Calavrion had heard
about the count in Paris at the court:
Heaven he soon blasphemed, aflame with wrath.
He had envisioned Carlo in his hands,
and now had heard the town resound with arms:
around the camp he strengthened the defense;
called Archilagio to a conference.

No more was Archilagio boasting now   121
as he had always done, each passing day—
that he would seize the king right in his home.
Now everybody was a different man,
and started to behave most cautiously,
thinking of Count Orlando with great fear.
Who captures lions seated in his house,
he will be frightened by a living mouse.

A different man was Archilagio now.   122
But let's go back to our Orlando in Paris.
Orlando said, "O Carlo, here we must
plan everything immediately: 'tis time
to act, and not to waste in empty words.
This Aldighier is looking for his father:
to Montalbàn with a thousand men he'll go,
and Berlinghier the road to him will show.

"You're saying that Gherardo is right there."   123
Young Aldighieri was ready to go,
and very glad that he was going there;
and gentle Berlinghieri left with him.
But you must know that Gano of Pontier
had planned another treason in no time:
ahead to Montalbano dashed he then,
with maybe twenty thousand trusted men.

Unrecognized, he went with all of them: 124
there was Beltramo, from Maganza, too,
and also from Lausanne Count Pulidor.
It was his hope to conquer Montalbàn,
and catch Gherardo fully unawares,
the Dane and Vivian in a friendly snare.
But Berlinghier the falcon's emblem saw,
and from a distance recognized the foe.

He guessed at once (he was no simpleton,   125
and wicked Gano's schemes had learned by heart)
that the foul traitor had designed to go,
for some of his new plots, to Montalbàn;
and therefore he so hastened on the road
that in a plainland Gano's troops he reached.
He asked at once about that strange brigade,
who was the captain that those men obeyed,

if Gano was with them, and where they went.   126
Beltramo gave a rather strange reply:
"Not knowing who they are, these men don't talk;
because the road is easy, they still go."
But now they recognized their Ganelon,
who, like a mummy, shriveled in their sight.
Aldighier shouted, "If my eyes don't lie,
are you not Ganelon, the thievish spy?

"Traitor, O wicked traitor, rabid dog,   127
traitor, the head and father of all ills,
traitor, born only to betray Rinaldo,
traitor, most fraudulent and murderous,
traitor, most worthy of eternal fire,
traitor, disloyal and iniquitous,
traitor, whom Carlo justly did discard,
traitor, I'm here to challenge you: en garde!"

Aldighier lowered in great haste his spear.   128
"You're lying, Aldighier," Gano replied;
"you are the traitor, you with all your race;
you always were, with all your family."
Beltramo and Count Pulidor came forth,
and with their cutting swords the three of them
pierced Aldighieri's breast at once. How sad!
Three wicked, savage men against one lad!

Beneath him, they his charger killed right then.   129
But Berlinghier had lowered now his lance,
and as he saw Beltramo come against him
upon his horse, he pierced his plate and heart.
When Pulidor caught sight of his friend falling
heavily on the ground like a huge rock,
he bent on Aldighier and pierced his side,
knowing Beltramo had already died.

Though on the ground—poor lad—our Aldighieri   130
then thrust his spear with all its lengthy steel,
and made Pulidor fall dead on the field.
But gentle Berlinghier did not stand still:
hit by his blows, each helmet seemed of ice,
and soon with corpses the whole field was filled.
His sword was always stained with blood; no wonder:
everyone thought that he was Count Orlando.

I do believe our Berlinghieri felt   131
so very much ashamed—and shame was all
the spur he needed (though no gentle heart
is e'er in need of it) the day he fought
with Mattafol, who made him itch and scratch;
this time, instead, he made all heroes dim:
all those he touched, fast at his feet fell slain,
for never did he raise his sword in vain.

What Hannibal, what Caesar, what Marcellus,   132
what African, what Paul, and what Camillus,
what Hector even could compare with him?
All those he pricked seemed bitten by horseflies;
he made a pool of blood, such a slaughterhouse
of horsemen, I still blush to mention it:
where'er the lightning flashed, the thunder burst,
his newer fury fiercer than the first.

This time, he seemed to be the pilgrim falcon,   133
and not the frightened dove of long ago,
for every man he wounded with his claw
fell, at that very instant, lifeless down;
at times he closed himself in, like a swift,
whirling his sword and routing all around him;
just like a lion in a flock, with threat
he killed, and every mail became a net—

or, better still, a cobweb. Pagan men,   134
beware of his all-reaching, faultless sword!
The strongest plate seemed softer than lasagna.
Watch out! Let not this awful bee now sting you,
but let your heels be the one shield and sword,
for magic art or ointment help you not.
Poor little frogs, away! The snake behold!
Loudly he whistles when he whirls his sword.

Alone, like once Horatius at the bridge,   135
our Berlinghier held the whole fight that day,
and no one could relate the mound of corpses
lying around, in front, and everywhere.
As far as I'm concerned, I'd never tire
to sing the praises of this wondrous knight,
so fond am I, and will forever be,
of all his feats of shining chivalry.

While Berlinghier was doing all these things,   136
Gherardo and the Dane and Vivian
arrived—behold them—with three thousand men,
coming from Montalbàn the three of them.
Still Grifonetto had the fort besieged,
and they were bound for Paris, help to seek.
Gherardo recognized his Berlinghier,
and asked him what had caused such anguish there.

Berlinghier told Gherardo everything,   137
and how that traitor had deceived them still.
The Lord of Rossiglione said, "I see
the one who killed so many men around him:
a valiant knight he seems, though with no steed."
Berlinghier answered, "Now let us think only
of routing all these men, and also slay
the traitor who deceived us in this way."

Gherardo, then, the Dane and Vivian   138
lowered their lances all together fast:
so with their help the fight was reinforced.
But sensing how the game would quickly end,
and seeing Ugier among them, Gano
soon understood that to retreat was best:
with all his people he began to flee
in great confusion, most disorderly.

When the Maganzans were no longer seen,   139
a feeble sound from Aldighieri came.
God! Was he still alive? To Berlinghier
feebly he said, "My side is all pierced through . . .
help me, dear brother . . . help me." More than once
Gherardo asked, "Who is this Frankish lad?"
Berlinghier, with much grief and anguish-won,
answered, "He's Aldighieri, sir—your son."

Gherardo, when he heard these words, dismounted   140
fast from his horse, and walked toward the lad.
Aldighier, who had heard Berlinghier speak,
with his last effort, wounded as he was,
rose on his knees, removed his helmet, and
embraced his father—his old, grieving father—
tenderly kissed his brow over and over,
and made with all his tears a flowing river.

Gherardo, too, was moved to sudden tears.   141
He asked about his mother, Rosaspina,
and Aldighieri told him, "She's still queen
among the Saracens in her own land . . .
Ganelon wounded me—this you must know . . .
My soul is soaring . . . soaring . . . to its realm."
And, other phrases failing to complete,
down he fell lifeless at his father's feet.

O father, now forever desolate!   142
O father, whom nobody can console!
O father, first in heaven, then in hell!
O father, how you longed to see your son!
O father, and you've lost him now forever!
O father, here's the son you found at last!
O father, who will know no peace or joy,
dead at your feet you see your little boy!

Never will you be happy in your life.   143
Gherardo fainted as he saw the soul
of his beloved son so soon depart.
When he came to, and saw this earth again,
he seemed bewildered, dazed, as if astray—
a man out of his mind, out of his wits.
As best they could, Ugier and Vivian
with pitying words comforted the poor man.

They set upon four horses then a bier, 144
placed the beloved, sad remains in it,
and so to Paris took they Aldighier.
His father, sorrow-stricken and in tears,
had the dear body brought before the king,
and everybody came to see him there.
"This is," Gherardo said to Charlemagne,
"my Aldighieri, by your Gano slain."

And there King Carlo wept most bitterly, 145
and there his entire court shed tears of grief,
and there was poor Gherardo, unconsoled,
and there the common folk bemoaned his fate,
and there they would have quartered wicked Gan,
and there they cursed such cruel, horrid luck,
and there they planned the wake and funeral,
and there the Council of the King came all.

In the imperial palace Aldighier 146
was richly dressèd in a purple cloak
with hems of gold and fringes of Douai.
Calavrion was given the sad news
right in his camp, and also Archilagio
sincerely mourned the youth's untimely death:
he knew him to be brave and valiant,
for he had met him once in Pagan Land.

He did not know he'd killed the Grand Old Man; 147
but from that day he had been fond of him.
(What am I saying? Had he known that, too,
he still would have admired his foe's great worth.)
He wrote to Charlemagne to let him know
he much would like to see dead Aldighier,
and asked for a safe-conduct. Thus for the last time
he'd say goodbye to one he'd loved while in his prime.

Most graciously King Carlo soon replied 148
that he and all his troops could come at once,
for well he knew his honesty and fame,
and his true greatness worthy of a king.
Calavrion, with sadness o'er his face,
escorted by his army's highest chiefs
and by his trusted Archilagio, entered
Paris, where a great welcome he was tendered.

There much he wept, and comforted Gherardo, 149
and said of Aldighieri, praising him,
that had the young man lived, no knight on earth
would ever be more brave or more renowned
(I do not know if such a praise was true:
Risa Riccieri's praised with the same words).
Pagans and Christians Aldighieri mourned,
who was with worth and virtue so adorned.

Carlo was deeply shaken by such loss: 150
each passing day, he shed more copious tears.
The poor old father kept on mumbling words
that could have made wild beasts and mountains weep
and, out of pity, stop both sun and moon.
No heart was there so hard as not to break,
so pitiful a scene was it to see
that poor old man in all his misery.

They buried with full honors the brave lad; 151
not even Trojan Hector was praised as much as he.
Then in his palace the great emperor
led always by the hand Calavrion,
and even would have liked so great a lord
to walk on his right side; the pagan, though,
such a great honor by all means declined,
for he was gentle, well-behaved, and kind.

After they all were seated, Count Orlando 152
addressed them first with a most worthy speech;
so pertinent and wise were all his words
that soon Calavrion became his friend
and, as a wise man does when heeding reason,
utterly changed his mind and his old plan.
Truth, and the whole truth, he made manifest,
and, peace restored, each other they embraced.

Why bother, then, Arpino's orator, 153
Demosthenes, Quintilian, or others,
teaching our count the diplomatic art?
Ganelon was condemned by all of them.
Calavrion placed all his Saracens
at their disposal, and they swore an oath
to avenge immediately poor Aldighier
by marching and besieging Pontier.

They all approved the military move.   154
As soon as Gano heard the news—the felon—
breathlessly toward his city soon he rode,
and took Grifone out of Montalbàn
to reinforce his Pontier at once.
Carlo, arriving with Calavrion,
was told that Gano was already there,
with food and weapons gathered with great care.

The city was besieged by all these men,   155
most skillfully deployed outside each door.
They occupied each mountain, plain, and hill,
eager to catch the traitor finally.
They were like dogs forever on the watch,
sniffing the traces of the hunted hare;
but they had seen the hare right in its hole,
and now no longer needed hound or pole.

Let's leave them here with Gano so besieged.   156
Rinaldo was still traveling by sea.
One day, because of an approaching storm,
the captain, seeing a strange land nearby,
announced, "We are off course by one full day,
but we must choose now between ill and worse.
Under the sign of Mars we seem to sail,
where seamen's deftness is of no avail.

"We'll either soon be sinking with the ship   157
or else we must be headed for this port;
but if we land, as soon as we are seen,
by its ferocious lord we'll all be killed.
I do not think he'll treat us differently.
He lives on rape and theft and violence,
on shipwreckings and every other shame,
and Arpalista is the felon's name.

"The town is Saliscaglia; up north   158
of the same town a castle can be seen,
which houses women fully trained for war,
and all of them obeying such a lord.
They, like the ancient Amazons, wear mail,
and are by nature horridly hirsute—
ugly and hairy, very harsh and queer,
but when they start to fight, they know no fear."

Rinaldo answered, "You are tickling me,   159
dear captain; on the spot I like it most,
for I can cure a madman of his madness.
Oh, how I wish I were already there!
There are some men who are like heretics—
they don't believe until at last they see.
Let us avoid the storm, and land, instead,
and captain, of the rest be not afraid!

"The sea is angry only when we fear it,   160
for fear itself cannot be overcome;
but if I have to fight and use my arms
against this murderous and cruel lord,
why, I will make him leap from his high walls,
and see if with no wings he still can fly."
He to the captain spoke so vehemently,
he landed and cast anchor finally.

The city was located on a mountain   161
that very high rose up above sea level,
so full of cliffs and rocks, so thick with shrubs,
not even goats could ever wander there.
The captain's heart was seized with sudden fright.
Rinaldo said, "Be not afraid! I want
to enter Saliscaglia as its lord,
and bring down here great merchandise and food.

"Give me some seamen to escort me there."   162
The captain said, "I like it very much;
a couple of my men will come with you."
Rinaldo entered soon the town, and there
stole from a kitchen first, then from a mill,
and, sneaking out, to safety then he sped;
but to come out, his sword was the one key
until he reached the vessel finally.

He said, "If I can wet my lips a bit,   163
through marshes and through woods I safely go;
Mount Sinai I can carry on my back
if with my lips I wet my chin and throat:
well, I intend to die filled to the brim."
His gullets then he started to caress
and, wooing a big barrel to a feast,
he ate a dinner worthy of a priest.

The news was brought to Arpalista soon: 164
a stranger had arrived and sacked his town.
He bade all of his ladies arm at once,
and ordered them to guard the city's door.
The lady captain of that female throng
was one to all known as Arcàlida.
Now back in town, Rinaldo, to be sure,
exhaled wine through the visor's aperture.

Arcàlida appeared outside the door,   165
saying, "Where are you going, cavalier,
still of yourself so sure though all alone?"
Rinaldo answered, "I will let you know.
Wait till I pierce you through, and you'll be dead."
Meanwhile Alardo spurred his horse and pierced
another damsel with no further battle,
placing her on the ground down from the saddle.

Guicciardo found another damsel then;   166
rushing against her with his lance in rest,
he wounded her beneath one of her breasts
and, like Alardo, overturned her fast.
Ricciardo pricked another on the back,
and sword and distaff she could hold no more.
Among these damsels there, the Christians had
battles quite different from those in bed.

With our Guicciardo fought Arcàlida,   167
who finally was seen on top of him:
maybe she wished to see how strong he was,
considering she did not hurt him much;
but soon Alardo rushed upon the dame
and sent her to some other land at once,
so hard he hit her right beneath her breast,
piercing a plate that could not pass the test.

All doors were quickly closed around the town,   168
and they kept fighting in the utmost dark:
there, one by one, the damsels then were seized
and placed, flat on their backs, upon the ground
where many a door was forced and opened wide,
and many a street was run and soon rerun.
Rinaldo was quite happy, then, to see
those dames fall on their backs so readily.

At Ricciardetto and Guicciard he winked,   169
saying, "It took you an eternity
to overcome four females—who knows why!"
Alardo answered, "Why did you not try?
Maybe you do not know one cannot judge
a woodcock by its long beak all the time.
Nor do you know how they resisted us,
kicking and pushing as God only knows.

"They're so well trained for any single fight,   170
we had to come with water, water still,
before we could extinguish all that fire.
Thank God we all withdrew from them alive!
If you just tried a bit, you would, I'm sure,
prefer a spear with a much lower flag:
just one of them would so engage your might,
you'd have no strength anyone else to fight."

But Arpalista, who had heard all this,   171
his cousin Archilesse sent right there;
and so this madman, just as he arrived,
shouted, "Mahound confound you everywhere!"
and dared Guicciardo to a single fight.
Guicciardo to his Jesus prayed for help:
he needed it, and did not pray in vain—
ah, from the top he soon was in the plain.

And like a wolf that to his wood speeds back   172
ran Archilesse, dragging him away.
As soon as Prince Rinaldo saw this thing,
"Wait," he said, "his defender is right here,"
and Archilesse finally he reached,
and with Frusberta threatened him at once.
"You do me wrong," out loud the pagan said,
and, leaving then Guicciardo, he challenged him instead.

They used the lances but both lances broke,   173
and so with swords they both returned to fight,
giving each other most barbaric blows.
Seeing himself in such a desperate plight,
the Saracen tried then to kill Baiardo:
he gave him such a bitter, bitter blow
that, had it fallen closer to the neck,
he would have cured him of each future shake.

"My poor Baiardo!" shouted then Rinaldo;   174
  "much better it would be to fight those dames
  than this most wicked, cruel Saracen
  who has so badly carded your fine coat.
  But I'll avenge you, in the name of God."
  Baiardo seized his breastplate with his teeth,
  and soon Rinaldo made such an incision
  on the pagan's head, he split it with precision.

But look who's coming—Arpalist himself!   175
  He came in his full armor, and he donned
  a silken cloak that like a comet shone
  or like the sun amid so many stars.
  Rinaldo, when he saw so many fireflies,
  said to himself, "This man looks very nice:
  how kind of him to bring that robe to me!
  A great gift to my captain it will be."

To Arpalista he said then, "I came   176
  to punish you for all your wicked past,
  for tyranny has been your daily life.
  I have been told how you have always preyed
  on the poor ships that break against these shores,
  as I was sailing where Uliva lives.
  But at this very place I landed then
  to punish so unjust a Saracen.

"I know that mine will be a famous feat,   177
  of which Mahound in heaven will be proud."
  The pagan listened most attentively
  and said, "You cur! I've had enough of you:
  I would have done a meritorious deed
  by hanging you at once as you deserve,
  and as I do with pirates of your kind
  who rob and steal and ransack all they find."

"I never was a pirate," said Rinaldo,   178
  and, saying this, he spurred his horse at once.
  They rode and took the field and then turned back,
  to wound each other, with two lengthy spears.
  The Arpalist had brought a tall fir tree.
  "This spear," he said, "wakes up all sleepy bums:
  many of them I wakened, I must say,
  and you will be the last this very day."

So to the Saracen replied Rinaldo: 179
"That spear of yours seems much too big to me.
You should have some consideration, sir,
for this poor spear of mine that's but a beam;
if you decide to place your lance in rest,
I will come back to you with my ship's mast."
But when he saw the pagan did not stop,
a spear just like it quickly he took up.

With these enormous spears they hit each other   180
so hard, their shields resounded at the blow:
each fighter on his saddle shook a bit,
because the lances did not even bend
and such a blow could hardly be withstood;
yes, it is true that neither of them fell,
but—look—the pagan at this sudden stroke
found himself turned upon his charger's back.

Rinaldo, bending over and all shaken,   181
with his left foot out of the stirrup, ran
the risk of falling from his horse's back,
but he held on, and on the saddle stayed.
Quickly he wielded his Frusberta then,
and so the Saracen unsheathed his sword:
for a full hour and more they battled close,
but Arpalista braved Rinaldo's taunting blows.

Then in the end, he raised his shield aloft   182
to shun a new blow falling on his head;
Rinaldo grabbed the unexpected chance,
seeing his hand exposed and fully bare:
right on that hand he let a blow fall down,
and cut it cleanly, lifted shield withal.
The Saracen gave out a roaring sound,
seeing his severed hand now on the ground;

then said, "I do surrender; spare my life!   183
I have lost everything with this your blow.
You've wounded me, and maimed my body, too,
but since it was my fault, myself I blame.
So make your name, great knight, now known to me,
now that I do confess my sins to you.
I am as good as dead, your prisoner,
and since to you I yield, now spare me, sir."

Rinaldo said, "I'm Count Orlando's cousin,   184
and I am certain you have heard his name:
I am Rinaldo, son of great Clairmont."
Hearing that name, the Arpalista struck
his forehead with his other hand, and said,
"O god Mahound, you now can laugh at me:
why did you, filthy dog, why did you, cruel
traitor, now force me to this luckless duel?

"Cursed be the day I first believed in you!   185
Cursed be your deity forevermore!
Cursed be all those who ever pleased your will!
Cursed be all those who still may worship you!
Cursed be your heaven, which I now abhor!
Cursed be your wickedness now and forever!
Cursed be the man who honors still your name!
Cursed be the day into this world I came!

"Cursed be my own bad luck, for making me   186
not know you, O Rinaldo, long before
perverse and truculent and impious Fortune
could dump me to the bottom from the top!
I place my entire country in your hands,
and you can do with me just as you please.
From here, now poor and lonely, let me fare,
for I must search for death some other where:

"no, I won't give Mahound his last delight—   187
I will not die inside his pagan realm."
Rinaldo said, "I shall not keep you here
against your will, by force or in disdain;
I want you to surrender, as you must,
to my great, noble cousin, Count Orlando:
if you do this, and this you swear to me,
this very moment you can go—you're free."

Answered the Arpalista, "So I swear: 188
I always had a great desire to see him—
so you can rest assured I so will do."
And so the poor and wretched fellow went,
and you can guess how grieved he was to go.
Rinaldo seized the castle and the town;
its former master traveled, most forlorn,
in search of the great count, as he had sworn.

This is what divine justice had decreed,   189
and this is how all human things must go
for those who feed on wickedness and theft.
The night before, toward dawn, this man had dreamed
of his own fall and future misery,
just as we also do at times: a snake
had entered Saliscaglia, and made
him leave at once, for his own life afraid.

In search of death this Arpalista went,   190
and finally in Paris he arrived.
King Carlo was not there, nor could he find the count,
and so at last he rode to Pontier.
Gano was there, who asked him right away,
"Tell me your name, and I'll recruit you soon."
He told him then about his cruel fate,
and how he looked for death, being desperate.

Gano replied, "Perhaps you have been sent   191
by Carlo or the count to spy on us;
and since I am more desperate than you,
let one despair now with another fight:
take, then, the field, and here at last you'll find
the death you have till now been looking for."
He turned Mattafellone with a cry,
and threatened him, and called him still a spy.

The Arpalist was happy as a lark   192
for having found a man he now could fight:
wasting no time, with so much wrath he rushed
that Ganelon could not defend himself
and from his steed fell suddenly, so stunned
he did not seem to know he had been felled:
the Arpalist had hit so very hard,
the spear left on his visor many a shard.

Ganelon's many men, all in the square,   193
pointed their lances at the Saracen;
but coming of a staunch and valiant stock,
so well and strongly with his stump he fought,
many a breastplate he around him smashed.
Soon, after he recovered consciousness,
Ganelon gave an order to his men
no more to fight against the Saracen.

Being the wicked man he was, he thought   194
  that he could use the pagan for his schemes.
  Suddenly kind, he begged the Arpalist
  (who much rejoiced) to join him in his palace,
  saying he wished to talk to him at ease.
  And in this manner he began his speech:
"Sir, who you are, or wherefrom, I know not,
  nor if King Charles has sent you with a plot.

"A strong and honest man you seem to be: 195
  therefore I trust you most implicitly.
  You told me it is death you're looking for,
  but you are after something else, I know.
  'Twas Carlo's wish to banish me from court,
  and, as you see, I'm forced to camp right here.
  Ingratitude was ever round a throne,
  and envy makes all of its victims known.

"Had it not been for me, he would not reign,   196
  but all I did for Charles has been in vain.
  Because one of my plans did not succeed,
  I have been called a traitor and a fool,
  and out of envy he's still hating me
  and furtively his courtiers strike still.
  Because I loved him more than I can say,
  just like a rebel I was sent away—

"unjustly. There are gossips round his throne   197
  who think only of setting traps against me—
  people who want to grab all for themselves.
  Such are his faithful men, such are his sons—
  chatterboxes, flattering nincompoops—
  they should be limned on vases and on walls,
  and such are those who rule King Charles, while I
  am called a thief, a traitor, and a spy.

"Now like a baby they have brought him here,   198
  and, heeding their advice, he's followed them
  just like a sheep a crumb of salted bread.
  Of all his 'children,' only one is wise—
  'tis true: he's Count Orlando, noble knight;
  and yet for his advice he little cares
  and many a time has banished him like me,
  so that he roams the world continually.

"I am a man with truth upon my lips   199
    and, I'm afraid, at times more than I should:
    and truth I speak, whoever may be hurt—
    and very well you know that truth can hurt.
    Ah, do not ask if envy overbrims,
    and more than once has aimed its darts at me.
    But of myself I'll tell you so much more
    as if I'd told you nothing heretofore.

"You know that when somebody likes you not,   200
    you'll never please him with whate'er you do:
    you tell the truth, he says you flatter him;
    you flatter him, he says you threaten him,
    and 'Kill him! Kill him!' all his puppies bark.
    This is what hunting dogs are seen to do:
    hit one of them; as soon as you have hit,
    the whole pack quickly runs on top of it,

"and they all do it, loyal just to seem,   201
    and he who's bitten most is first to come
    right back to you with hairs still in his mouth.
    I cannot hope to find excuse or help
    with these most pitiless, unfaithful men,
    as numerous as geese upon one stump—
    men who, if fatter chances they could see,
    willingly would desert you instantly.

"I mean that all the good I ever do   202
    is always misinterpreted, alas,
    and often I unjustly pay for it.
    Well you can see what hate and envy bring!
    Just a few days ago, one Aldighier
    assailed me on my way to Montalbàn,
    and said, "I know you, though disguised you are,"
    as if my face he'd ever seen before;

"and wanted me to hear a tale about   203
    a certain Diliant along the road,
    a tale that he repeated more than once
    as if I did not know. 'Twas an excuse:
    high from his horse, he lowered then the spear.
    When suddenly I saw him come against me
    (you know that death is dreaded by all men),
    I slew the man who wanted to be slain.

"There is no animal that wants to die.
   And this is why King Charles besieges me,
   and why so many troops are camping here.
   But, Saracen, I'll bother you no more.
   I think it was God's will has sent you here
   to help me in my sore predicament.
   Go to the emperor, I humbly plead,
   to do a good and just and holy deed—

"and I will always owe my life to you.
   Tell him that I am ready to go back
   upon my knees, the noose around my neck,
   and beg forgiveness for my childish acts;
   and if I ever pleased him in the past,
   would he remove these men and end this siege?
   And if he only spares this life of mine,
   never inside his court will I be seen."

After the traitor ended his fine speech,
   the Arpalista thought that he was right,
   and was so eager to behold King Charles
   that every second seemed an hour to him.
   He saddled then his charger right away.
   And Gano said, "A wise man always knows—
   only a wise man it is safe to trust.
   To Count Orlando give my very best.

"You'll see how far superior he is
   to other men. He's honorable, good,
   discreet, a worthy heir of his great race—
   a man without whom Carlo could not reign;
   and I am his stepfather—mind my word."
   See how astutely such a man could work!
   He wanted to make sure his words would reach
   Orlando's ears and his good heart beseech.

Fully instructed, left the Arpalist,
   so glad he was beside himself with joy.
   He genuflected before Charlemagne
   and told him then that Gano placed himself
   most humbly in his hands, and all the rest,
   and how he thought that Evil Claws had grabbed him;
   and, last, for the success of his whole plan,
   told how Orlando was described by Gan.

204

205

206

207

208

So charmingly he played his violin,
Carlo forgave both Gano and the count,
on one condition—that Rinaldo, too,
should pardon him; he, rather, should be found
so that he might in person come to him.
The Arpalista, then, narrated how
he'd been Rinaldo's captive, and that he
had sent him to Orlando finally;

209

he told him everything, and showed his stump,
which greatly moved to pity all of them.
At last to Gano he returned with speed.
Gano came back to court, and on his knees,
and weeping, spoke these words to Charlemagne:
"Before I die, I will Rinaldo find,
and all disdain and shame I'll remedy
so that the count and you, Charles, pardon me.

210

"If even I must search the whole wide world,
I will find out where Prince Rinaldo lives."
Thus he was freed and totally absolved.
Calavrion, who heard about this deal,
to Carlo said, "I will not say a word;
but I will punish you, one-handed cur,
who have come here to bring the holy news,
but should instead have round your neck a noose.

211

"Having made peace with Count Orlando at last,
I came from Paris—better yet, I flew—
with all my people and with all my zest
(with hands uplifted I was thanking God)
to join in punishing that wicked traitor.
Now, take the field, you sinful Saracen,
captive and slave and monster with no shame!
Your other arm I'll mutilate and maim."

212

The Arpalista lowered soon a spear.
Now see what wonder Fortune could perform!
Each on his horse beside the other passed,
each very quickly found the other's shield,
each struck the other's breastplate in a flash,
each from his saddle ruinously fell,
each of them died at the same moment, for
never had such a blow been seen before.

213

Calavrion, then, paid in heavy cash—   214
alas—for something he should not have bought:
here is how final justice punished him.
Arpalist found what he'd been looking for:
this time the board was cut exactly as
the carpenter had traced with his red chalk.
And Archilagio resolved at last
to take his men back to his region fast.

Carlo returned to Paris with his court,   215
and Gano started out to search the world.
Wherever he would hear a sound of war
or quarreling, he said, "Rinaldo's here,"
and, following that clue, looked for him there.
But to Rinaldo let's go back. He brought
to Saliscaglia the cult of Christ,
for all renounced Mahound and were baptized.

Yes, all the Saracens were soon baptized,   216
and greatly he was honored by them all.
He had already lived some time with them
when, in a vision, in the deep of night,
an angel from the Choir of Cherubim
said, "Here, Rinaldo, you must stay no more.
Because somebody blocks our pilgrims' road,
they cannot reach the Sepulcher's abode.

"All you have done so far is dear to God,   217
but be as brave in this new enterprise.
A greedy, wicked man—this you must know—
in Caprafolle Desert lives today,
who does not let our pilgrims go in peace.
From hill to hill on foot you now must go
until you find this cruel madman, known
as Fuligatto there to everyone."

When in the morning he awoke, Rinaldo   218
to Ricciardetto and the others said
that he had seen God's angel in his dream,
who told him what to do and where to go.
They all were startled by the sudden news:
they did not say God should not be obeyed,
but much they grieved as soon as they did know
the angel bade him all alone to go.

As best he could, Rinaldo cheered them up,
saying, "Take care of this our town for me,
and always right with justice every wrong.
I recommend Baiardo to you all.
Unless I'm killed, I shortly will return:
God to obey sets this my heart on fire.
Justice to all of you I recommend,
and keep in peace and opulence this land."

219

He bade the ship be readied in no time:
at his disposal still was the same captain,
eager to sail where'er he wished to go.
By chance some pilgrims at that time arrived,
and so, though the departure grieved him most,
Rinaldo traveled in their company. On the lips
they kissed each other, and they swore, for better
or worse, forever to remain together.

220

And on the open sea at last he was,
keeping his armor utterly concealed.
He, like the others, donned a pilgrim's gown,
but with Frusberta always at his side.
On sailed the ship with favorable wind
until they saw the coast of Barbary.
Towards a town they started out with speed,
wherefrom on foot they inland would proceed.

221

As soon as they came into port, Rinaldo
said to the captain, bidding him goodbye,
"A month from now, I think it will be well
for you to bring your ship back to this shore;
by then my pilgrimage will over be.
May Christ be with you and your compass, too,
which is as valuable as pitch and tow!"
The captain wept with him, and spoke then so:

222

"When the day comes that I shall be interred,
my heart's great anguish will be half as much—
I mean the day my soul will leave this body.
Go, then, in peace wherever you must go!
May your God help you if you go to war,
may Mary full of grace be at your side!
Quite soon I'll bring my vessel to this bay."
And other words the captain failed to say.

223

He genuflected then, and kissed his feet. 224
And so Rinaldo with the pilgrims walked
into the town where lived the Admiral.
There was a feast with jousts inside the square,
and there a maiden's lover did so well
that everybody stopped to see him joust;
the maiden was blond-haired and very fair;
also her sister, a brunette, was there,

who, being such, was rightly called Brunetta 225
(a most becoming and appropriate name);
the blonde instead looked like an angel fair,
and was that day among all maidens blest
because her lover threw everyone down.
She teased her sister, saying, "No one breaks
a stump of fennel in your honor here;
my lover breaks all lances with his spear."

And poor Brunetta with these words replied, 226
"Is it my fault or nature's if, alas,
I was not born as fortunate and fair?
If I had been allowed myself to make,
in such a way I would have shaped my limbs,
sculptured or painted beauty I would dim.
Be thankful for the lovers you have found,
and may you ever have them all around.

"Very well, lovers, go ahead and joust, 227
and may somebody of Brunetta think!
I'm just reminding each and all of you
that victory's achieved by worth of spear,
and giants in the joust are often seen.
Thus every maiden of her man is proud,
and even Lady Prudish is impressed
by one who rightly lays his lance in rest."

She then a falcon toward Rinaldo threw, 228
who looked so handsome and so brave to her;
and she recalled a dream that she had had—
about a pilgrim newly come to town
who in the joust unsaddled every man.
So in her heart she said, "He is the one."
Her tutor now was sent most quick to him:
"Say to that pilgrim I must speak to him."

Not knowing the whole tale, Rinaldo went.
Skillfully she revealed her dream to him
and why to him so much she wished to talk.
He told her he would please her every wish:
to serve a lady in the name of love
is kindness to be governed by forever.
So he would arm himself in secrecy
to please a lady of such courtesy.

229

Brunetta knew where he could arm himself
and asked her tutor to provide a steed.
Her sister taunted her with ridicule,
saying, "Do you expect this man to joust?"
She laughed and with her laughter seemed to say,
"This man will bring you some of his *Our Fathers*
if from his pilgrimage he comes this route."
But there's Rinaldo in his armor suit.

The fairer maiden's lover said to her,
"Say, have you seen a clumsier bird than this?
What will you say if I unsaddle him?
At the first blow down on the ground he'll be."
And wretched, poor Brunetta answered him,
"Yes, if you think he is a man of snow."
Rinaldo heard the words that man had said,
and with disdain and anger he turned red.

231

He challenged the smart aleck then and there.
The lovely blonde cheered up her loving man;
so did Brunetta her Rinaldo, too.
Both fighters' shields resounded, quickly struck,
but at the mighty blow the Saracen
lifted his legs and fell on his behind,
which bare was sighted to his utmost shame:
how true, how true was poor Brunetta's dream!

Around the square resounding shouts were heard,
and you can guess Brunetta's joy and pride.
Scornfully to her sister now she said,
"Sprinkle your face with water and wake up!
Mine was a dream right at the break of day."
Seeing her lover with a broken arm,
the blonde felt cheated and humiliated,
and much Brunetta, her own sister, hated.

233

To fight Rinaldo, others forward came,
but everyone was quickly on the ground.
The maidens' father in full armor came
onto the field, by all unrecognized:
Rinaldo felled him, too, and as he fell
he lost his helmet and by all was seen.
As soon as that big feast came to an end,
he with Rinaldo to his palace went,

    234

still wondering about his boundless might.
He also invited there all of his friends,
and a most solemn banquet then began,
with lovely girls who waited on them all.
Both maidens on Rinaldo gazed in awe,
enamored of the greatness of his worth.
Then, after dinner, to a room they went,
where the two sisters had an argument,

    235

each saying that she was the lovelier,
and both agreeing that Rinaldo should
ultimately be their sole and final judge.
"Brunetta!" said Rinaldo then and there,
to whom he gave already all his love.
So deeply hurt and grieved her sister was
that from a window of a room of hers,
ah, with a silken noose she hanged herself.

    236

The entire town lamented the sad case.
Rinaldo with his pilgrims later left,
and poor Brunetta, so discomforted,
said, "May Mahound show the whole road ahead!
And may you, pilgrim, evermore remember
Brunetta, who forever will be yours."
She gave him then a brooch with a sweet sigh,
to be—poor, little girl!—remembered by.

    237

But his true name she wanted first to know,
and when she heard he was Rinaldo, such
was the delight that kindled all her heart,
its warmth would never leave her all her life:
never was she to see her knight again,
yet in her breast her love would never die.
Thus our Rinaldo, more than ever burning
to punish Fuligat, resumed his journey.

    238

He was already through the desert faring 239
when a full-armèd cavalier he saw.
His horse was covered utterly with plate,
and on the shield a hawk was visible.
Rinaldo recognized the cavalier:
'twas Ganelon, who found him finally.
He knelt and asked forgiveness and with great
tears spoke of Aldighieri's cruel fate.

Rinaldo mourned his Aldighier so much 240
that he could not forgive him for his death.
He did not answer, deep in grievous thoughts.
The pilgrims at that moment begged him so,
"O kindly knight, his weeping you can see:
may pity, then, and mercy bend your heart!
Oh, do forgive him in the name of God—
that God who wants you pilgrim on this road."

Rinaldo thus forgave him in the end, 241
and where he came from Ganelon went back.
A mighty din re-echoed in the air:
people were seen to run, screaming for help.
A knight in armor came ahead of them,
who, when he saw Rinaldo, shouted so:
"Pilgrim, go back at once! Go all away!
It is forbidden on this road to stay.

"All of us here have hardly come alive 242
out of the hands of that accursèd demon;
riding in front, I am a Christian man
and bear an open wound within my heart."
"O sovereign cavalier," Rinaldo asked,
"who is this demon you were speaking of?"
"'Tis Fuligatto. If you farther go,"
he answered, "I'm afraid you'll clearly know.

"Too many horrid things he's done so far. 243
Under his plate he wears a serpent's hide
and has a sword he handles with both hands,
and a shield made of bone—this evil man,
and so barbaric are his wicked blows,
one of our pilgrims he's already slain;
the club he wears looks like a beam, and weighs
thirty-five pounds, as everybody says."

A few more words he said; he fainted then,
and to the ground like a dead body fell.
Rinaldo mounted the man's horse at once,
sensing that he would be a valiant steed,
and to his friends said, "What are we to do?
I see a city not too far from here:
let us go there, and we shall soon find out
this most ferocious demon's whereabouts."

244

That city was Sardonia; a stream
ran all about it with a lovely grace.
Rinaldo came beneath one of its doors,
and when he raised his glance to view the walls,
he saw a man from every merlon hung.
The prince decided finally to knock.
A girl replied; she saw the horse and swore
that Fuligatto was outside the door:

245

"Are you that Fuligatto, thief and cur?
Are you that Fuligatto, murderer?
Are you the man who slaughters all of us?
Are you the one who causes so much grief?
Are you the wolf that every lamb devours?
Are you the one who waylays all who pass?
Are you that traitor mounted on that steed?
Are you now here to fatten him with blood?"

246

Rinaldo answered, "No, I'm not the one.
Can you not see that we are pilgrims here?
You should have learned by now you cannot see
a wolf that walks along with little lambs.
Open the door, young lady, right away,
for we are weary of our long, long road."
The maiden, reassured by such a call,
came to the door and opened it to all.

247

She said, "O pilgrim, may God give you peace
and save you from this tyrant's greedy hands—
so greedy and rapacious that—you see—
these men are hanging lifeless from the walls.
If you are willing, come and see the queen!"
While through the city's streets our pilgrims walked,
nothing but women in it they could see,
and so they asked the girl, naturally,

248

"Where are your husbands and your brothers? Where   249
  the fathers, servants, sons, and other men?"
She said, "Must I now show them all to you?
Just look up there, and you will see them all.
Our husbands and our brothers are up there,
hung with our fathers, sons, and relatives:
there they will be for all eternity,
killed by that fiend of hell, as you can see.

"Ah, do not ask me what I cannot tell—   250
  how fierce a monster Fuligatto is.
The very name 'Fuligatto' scares us.
I cannot tell you all that he has done,
for you would not believe me if I did.
He has destroyed this land: he seized our town,
and hanged, as soon as here he did arrive,
as many men as he could catch alive.

"With these my eyes I saw him grab a youth   251
  as handsome as the best by nature made,
and tear his heart right out with his bare hand;
then on the walls he had his body hung.
Ah, look at my poor husband hanging there!
I am afraid to look at him again.
Here I have seen the blood reach a man's height,
so that the stream became vermilion bright.

"When I recall such boundless cruelty—   252
  the weeping and the keening and the screaming
of girls and women with disheveled hair,
striking and scratching with lament their cheeks,
or others lying dead or dragged away,
I feel my poor heart break within my breast.
Ah, what a dreadful sight it was to see
the city turned to blood and misery!"

While still the girl was speaking, they at last   253
  came to the square. A statue there they saw
of a man in full armor, made of bronze:
upon his full-draped horse he seemed alive,
and showed a spear in rest upon a thigh.
Rinaldo asked her who that horseman was.
The maiden answered, "The inscription's clear:
this town was happy when this man was here—

"the cavalier and ruler of Clairmont."   254
    Rinaldo read th' inscription, and it said,
"This man's Orlando, who some time ago
    delivered us from mighty Galigant,
    whose emblem was a lynx in a gilded field;
    in memory of all his sacred deeds,
    to him who killed a foe so fierce and crude
    this monument was raised in gratitude."

    Gazing upon Orlando, wept Rinaldo   255
    most tenderly, and him he so addressed:
"Wherever in the world I roam and go,
    there your great fame and reputation rings."
    And still in tears he went away from him.
    Before the queen he finally appeared.
    Before the young and beauteous queen he came,
    and Filisetta was her lovely name.

    She looked at him; she greeted him, and asked   256
    what road he had been treading until then:
    though in his pilgrim's gown, he seemed to her
    a valorous and noble gentleman.
    Rinaldo mentioned to the queen the reason
    why he had come that far, and from what land,
    and that he was Rinaldo he also let her know,
    and how an angel from above had told him, "Go!"

    Queen Filisetta knew about his worth,   257
    but, seeing him in person, was amazed
    by his demeanor and majestic gait,
    and said, "Orlando well resembles you.
    King Galigante had to drop his rein,
    as you can see, because of this great man
    (I know you saw the statue in the square,
    and read the letters that are carven there).

"It was his valor that has freed this town,   258
    and in eternal memory of him
    we raised his sculptured image in the square—
    our everlasting homage to your race.
    But Fuligatto, after him, is worse:
    he's making havoc of this entire land.
    We cannot even bring those corpses down
    (amongst them is my man, who wore the crown).

"If I could only bury him, I would   259
forgive this Fuligatto everything.
He's made my people die atrociously:
ah, don't be such a fool to meet this man!"
Rinaldo answered, "Vex yourself no more,
and go ahead, take your dead husband down.
Meanwhile my friends will all stay here with you,
and then you'll see how things will soon be new.

"So doubt no more, for what God wills on high   260
can never fail through accident or fate.
Queen Filisetta, we would like to eat,
for all of us are famished, to be sure.
Then, when I go, I'll leave my friends with you
for you to take good care of, for my love."
Soon with a happy heart and full of zest,
the queen paid homage to her every guest.

Only one day Rinaldo rested there,   261
and from his pilgrims he departed then,
not without copious tears. He had to go
and thus obey God's will before all else;
and through the desert all alone he went.
But Filisetta, generous and kind,
gave him the spear her husband used to wield,
and with it a most fine and lovely shield.

She said to him, "Oh, wear it for my love,   262
since it could not be worn by one who's still
among so many lifeless bodies hung.
God with His angels be beside you ever,
and may this hope forever comfort you!"
And now along his road we'll let him go.
I'll tell you what he did in my next song:
God save you all from Fuligatto's wrong!

Deus, in adiutorium meum intende,   1
Who carried for us all the heavy cross
that gives us back Your kingdom and Your grace,
oh, leave me not so very near the port,
for we can nearly see all tents removed;
with a low, humble voice You I implore,
for if well ended, all our deeds are praised:
so to the harbor bring my sail at last.

Rinaldo through the desert still went on.   2
The sun had covered all the ample sea,
and then the moon appeared in its full light,
which made the previous sundials futile, when
Rinaldo in the deep of night at last
came where fierce Fuligatto dwelt alone—
a very strange, frightening home. He knocked,
and knocked again, until that traitor talked:

"Who are you, man? What are you looking for?"   3
Rinaldo said, "I have been sent to you."
Threatening, Fuligatto let him in,
saying, "If you are seeking your God's pardon,
I'll bless you with the cross of this my sword."
Rinaldo said, "I always tell the truth:
know then that this your home I will not leave
by any means till death to you I give.

"I have come here to test your strength with mine."   4
So answered Fuligatto: "You'll soon leave
if I but let you taste one of my blows.
So here it is—the snake that I have dreamed of,
which seemed to wrap himself around my limbs—
because of which I soon arose in fear.
It seemed I could not snatch him from my side . . .
So you're the serpent that still wants to hide."

Rinaldo answered, "Quite the contrary: 5
you are the serpent and I am the hedgehog.
One day the hedgehog, being most naive,
allowed the snake to rest inside his hole,
but as the wretched hedgehog tossed and turned,
the serpent wanted very much to oust him;
'twas then he answered him, "In short, I say:
if you're uncomfortable, then go away."

Most baffled and amazed, said Fuligat,   6
"Who can this madman be, and what is this?"
He twisted soon the bridle of his steed
and blindly hit Rinaldo on the head.
Feeling so crude a knocking, soon Rinaldo
leapt on the saddle of his waiting horse:
he gave him such a punch he snarled his ear,
and his blood made Fucecchio Lake appear.

Stunned, Fuligatto dashed down to the ground.   7
Rinaldo touched him not till he was up.
As soon as he could stand, still dazed he said,
"I think you are a devil that through magic
has come to earth out of his dark abyss:
your blow was such, I'm still out of my wits.
Let's rest for the remainder of the night:
tomorrow morning we'll resume our fight,

"and think of neither treason nor deceit."   8
Rinaldo said, "'Tis you who should not fear."
Throughout the night they at each other scowled.
Then as the day arose up in the east,
in their full armor to the field they went.
The challenge was renewed, and with the swords
they took the field as freely as they yearned,
then with their spears against each other turned.

They met and clashed, and their two lances broke   9
to pieces in the air: Rinaldo's horse
could not withstand the blow: his hind legs failed;
Rinaldo on the saddle tried to stay
but hit the ground together with his steed.
Aflame with anger, now Rinaldo said,
"Dismount at once, or you'll come down, of course,
after I strike and kill right now your horse."

Dismounted Fuligatto then and there.   10
How masterly the blows on either side!
One of them was so mighty that Rinaldo
hit now the ground and knelt on his left knee;
but up he stood at once. To Fuligatto
he seemed the nimblest man he'd ever seen,
and for his countless fierce and savage blows,
he saw himself to certain death so close

that, after long enduring such a fight,   11
he said, "Kind baron, one of us must die.
Tell me your name, so that I now may know
the knight by whose strong hand I may be slain."
Rinaldo said, "I owe this much to you:
I am Rinaldo, Lord of Montalbàn."
"Ah," Fuligatto said, "are you the one
who to the entire world is so well known?

"I know that you are from the Clairmont race,   12
I know you have three brothers of renown,
I know that you have murdered Fieramont,
I know you are the greatest knight on earth,
I know you're Buovo d'Agrismonte's nephew,
I know you win in battle every foe,
I know your sword is called Frusberta, and, oh,
I know you're cousin of the great Orlando.

"I am in love with your unending fame."   13
And so he spoke that Prince Rinaldo went
as friend and brother and a sworn ally
into the palace with him amiably.
Then they agreed to change both place and fate:
so Fuligatto set his home on fire,
saying, "Let this my place by none be seen,
where such a great and worthy knight has been.

"Let's go now where you say and where we must."   14
Right at this moment a great serpent, feeling
the heat beneath, out of his hiding place
appeared and fastened on Fuligatto's neck,
so that the man from terror nearly died.
The serpent to unwind and chase away,
Rinaldo with his sword most ably fought,
and flesh as well as bone he had to cut,

till with his tail the snake was seen to writhe.   15
Now Fuligatto looked like a dead man,
and our Rinaldo thought with grief and wrath
that he'd be left alone, but he was wrong,
for Fuligatto came to finally
and, standing up, was glad to be alive.
So, thanking all the saints in heaven, they
through the great desert soon resumed their way.

They had been riding a long time together   16
when in a savage place they saw two lions
dead at the very center of the road.
Rinaldo said, "What can this ever mean?
Who do you think has killed these lions so?"
But Fuligatto knew and therefore said,
"Spinardo most undoubtedly did this:
half-man, half-horse all people say he is.

"Atop Mount Perilous he's known to dwell   17
(I am convinced we are not far from there)
and always has a sling and three darts handy."
Rinaldo said, "Then he must be the one.
But is it possible to find this beast?"
And Fuligatto said, "He often comes
to wander in these woods in search of food."
But—look!—not far from them a flag they viewed,

a flag with strange Mahounds all over it,   18
and so they started quickening their pace.
Spinardo, like a badger or a bear,
was hiding in his cave when suddenly
he heard the trotting of both steed and mare:
he put a stone into the sling at once,
then grabbed his darts, and jumped on the two, full
of anger, roaring, blowing like a bull.

His roaring startled with great fright the mare,   19
which Fuligatto hardly could control;
but finally he calmed his beast, and said,
"Rinaldo, a favor I must ask of you:
if I do kill this monster, promise me
that you will then believe in my Mahound,
and if you kill him, I'll believe in Christ;
but this I beg of you: let me try first."

Rinaldo told him that he fully agreed;   20
but everything they said Spinardo heard,
and, laughing at their strange agreement, let
one of his darts 'gainst Fuligatto fly:
it landed deep inside his arm and stayed.
Rinaldo from the top of Belvedere
saw Fuligatto, wholly dazed and stunned,
fall nearly lifeless quickly to the ground.

He shouted, "Wicked man, what have you done?   21
A traitor and a beast you are for sure;
but, by my God, if Fuligatto dies,
with these my hands I will tear out your heart."
Spinardo did not answer him at all;
with anger he released a second dart,
which through Rinaldo's legs passed, fierce and fleet,
and thinly hissing like a snake in heat.

Rinaldo shouted, "My revenge will come;   22
if you are crazy, I'm no Solomon."
Dart number three Spinardo quickly hurled.
Rinaldo answered with a mighty blow
that cut his dart and with enormous speed
flew then towards the foe, just like a hawk
that has caught sight of partridges or doves,
or like a lion looking for his game.

Rinaldo's sword with such a tempest came,   23
it would have pierced a slab of porphyry:
with fury and with anger still at work,
he split Spinardo's head immediately
and, since Frusberta seemed more eager still,
he also cut his neck and his whole trunk
right at the point where beast and man are bound,
and made him lifeless fall upon the ground.

Falling, with bitter wrath Spinardo shouted,   24
"O god Mahound, if I am not avenged,
Lucifer has a place for you in hell!"
Rinaldo then to Fuligat went back
and healed his open wound with certain herbs
that God in heaven told him where to cull.
But Fuligat, as soon as he was healed,
behaved just like a blind man in a field:

he like a madman 'gainst Rinaldo ran   25
and with his lifted sword let down a blow
that for his kindness would have thanked him best.
Rinaldo saw he was delirious still
and, shunning that and many another blow,
let him do as he pleased to vent his wrath.
But Fuligat regained his senses soon,
and asked forgiveness for the thing he'd done.

Rinaldo said, "Forgiveness you must ask   26
of the great Lord Who deigned to save your life."
And he began to preach the Faith to him,
and Fuligatto heard him with great joy,
saying that he believed in Jesus Christ
and, just as he had promised, kept his word.
Rinaldo near a fountain christened him,
and challenged theologians at his whim.

He spoke of the Triune, Father and Son and Word,   27
and how the Holy Spirit then took flesh—
yes, flesh and bone and strength like all of us—
died on a cross and down to Limbo went,
to free us from the ignominious sin
of our first father—the forbidden fruit;
of Joseph and of Mary preachèd he,
a fountainhead of all theology.

Then back on steed and mare the two were soon.   28
Some people, incidentally, believe
that, unaware of his own strength, Rinaldo
could not control his hand, and pushed the man
into the fountain for his christening;
but on this point my thought is not too clear.
Well Fuligatto more than one drop gulped
and by Rinaldo himself had to be helped.

But let them leave and ride along their road.   29
They traveled up a mountain through the night;
then, as the morning light appeared, they saw
many a pagan in the plainland fare.
Rinaldo asked, "O God, so just and holy,
who can these huge and savage people be?
I'll test you, Fuligatto, brother dear:
in such a plight, ah, do not leave me here."

He answered, "Leave you? Never say this thing!   30
Death—only death—can sever me from you;
I'll be beside you everywhere you go.
Now let us move and these newcomers fight,
for they to me mean less than worthless crabs."
The leader of those men came forward fast,
and our two Christians also forward came
to greet him; and the pagan did the same.

The Christians wished to know the pagan's name.   31
"I am Pilagi d'Ulivant," said he.
"In Saliscaglia I want soon to be:
Rinaldo and his wicked brothers have
offended me far more than I can say,
giving us trouble and distress and death,
and now they take our women out for a walk . . .
but my revenge will soon down here be heard.

"By god Mahound! Too much I like your steed."   32
Rinaldo said, "And I like yours as much."
The pagan said, "Let's test them in a fight."
Rinaldo said, "You play, and I will dance."
"I'll go to Saliscaglia on your steed."
"But you'll develop calluses before."
"I will be there for my revenge, don't worry!"
Rinaldo said, "You are in such a hurry."

"He's always been a traitor and a cur."   33
Rinaldo said, "I'm truly most amazed,
for I have heard men speak of his great worth:
Pilagi, he'd not want you even as a slave."
"So, will you fight, then, for Rinaldo's love?"
Rinaldo said, "Yes, for his love I'll fight."
"Take then the field," the pagan soon replied,
turning his black horse with white feet aside.

Rinaldo did not think of fireflies then: 34
he turned and made his steed leap in the air
to give the Saracen far more than nuts;
but as he reached the point of the onslaught—
whether his horse had stumbled or slid down—
he and his steed were on the ground together,
and when he saw him slow to rise, the beast
most angrily he killed with but one fist.

"Cursed be," he said, "you good-for-nothing horse!   35
Cursed be the barley that I gave to you!
Cursed be the hay you ate, you lazy beast!
Cursed be this hand of mine that combed your coat!
Cursed be the person that has owned you first!
Cursed be the beast that ever suckled you!
Cursed be the grass you have been grazing! Cursed,
forever cursed the day I saw you first!"

Loudly was Fuligatto shouting now,   36
coming with lance in rest against the foe,
for he had dared Pilagi to the death,
and he was forward spurring now his mare;
and so, as fate or fortune had decreed,
he made his spear pass through from side to side,
and dead upon the ground soon fell the man,
because of which a total war began.

Pilagi had ten thousand fighting men,   37
all of whom now 'gainst Fuligatto turned.
Grinding his teeth and mad with ire, Rinaldo
jumped on Pilagi's black horse with white feet
and, like a wrathful bear inside a flock,
untied the sack of all his stormy wrath:
never fought he so bravely and so hard!
But how he missed, that day, his own Baiàrd!

"Where are you, my Baiardo?" so he said,   38
whirling and wheeling his Frusberta fast.
Just like a blind man he his weapon whirled,
and woe to those who waited for its alms!
Men's arms and heads were leaping everywhere,
and the whole ground was in a moment filled
with the ground flesh of many a Saracen—
such as was good for jam or gelatin.

Leaping on all of them, he cut them down: 39
never were beasts with such great fury slaughtered;
their blood rose high and reached the saddle's belt,
but our Rinaldo was not sated yet.
Hills seemed but plainlands to all those who fled,
but he left little room to all of them.
Strong Fuligatto, too, killed many a man:
they all were dead or in great terror ran.

The battle soon was over. Fuligatto   40
noticed the gown that dead Pilagi wore
(with a black lion limned in a white field)
and put it on. Rinaldo liked it, too,
so much he would have wanted one himself.
They left so many people dead or dying,
they left this site of misery and death,
and soon once more they were on their right path.

The whole day through, they rode and rode and rode   41
through forests and through marshes and ravines,
and they had nothing in their stomach put:
they would have leapt to catch a loaf of bread,
for like a rainbow their great hunger loomed.
But now they heard two bells ring in the distance,
and saw a hermitage, still far away,
where laurel wreaths adorned each holiday,

and, better still, much bread and cheese and meat.   42
There was a river there: so there were fish.
Towards that hermitage they hastened quick,
who from much hunger could see straight no more:
better than partridge all those fish would taste!
They knocked, then, on the hermitage's door.
A hermit came and said, *"Ave Maria."*
Rinaldo asked, "Is there any bread here?

"If not, praised be the angel of black hell!"   43
The hermit asked of them, "But are you Christians?"
Rinaldo said, "You can be sure of that,
but would you have at least some bread for us,
dear hermit, for God's sake? We've lost our road
wandering through these woods so wild and strange."
The hermit said to him, "Oh, how I wish
I had some bread; but I have only fish."

And from his shoulders he removed a net,   44
saying, "While I go fishing, you rest here,
and in the meantime build a nice big fire.
I can assure you I will fill this net,
and you will have as much as you can eat,
and for your horses there'll be something, too."
Dismounting both, they to their horses bore
some twigs as hard as coral—even more.

The hermit caught so many fish, he filled   45
a bucket and a sack. Meanwhile Rinaldo
and Fuligatto built a lovely fire.
The hermit came, and went to fetch some wine.
But—look!—an angel from above descended
and to the hermit said, "Bring to Rinaldo,
bring to the paladin this food of mine,
and tell him Jesus sends it from his home divine."

The hermit came and gave to both his guests   46
that food replete with every sweet delight,
saying it had been sent by God himself.
What gladness overcame their hearts at once!
How sure they felt of the eternal choir!
See, then, how Christ rewards his faithful men!
"I hope you'll feel at home," the hermit said,
"but you won't like this place, I am afraid."

The house to oglers ugly seemed, and seedy,   47
wind-worn; and the reed's rattle and the night
distilled the stars down through the gaping roof;
the hermit with a crust and crumb of bread
had pairs of pears and some leftover fruit;
he tipped and tapped a barrel most bartenderly,
and then for fish some fishy scales he caught:
but, oh, not bad, the bed with shoots was wrought.

Let's leave them like two worms upon some twigs,   48
let's leave Rinaldo and Fuligatto here
till morning: they'll digest the many scales
and all the wine they drank the night before.
Another fancy's flashing in my mind:
from far away a horn is calling me,
and he who blows it does the best he can,
for here the sad and doleful notes begin.

Where did I leave you, Ricciardetto dear?   49
You do not know yet what your future holds.
Alas, I see the world in darkness wrapped!
A serpent from the bottom of the earth
comes out, with seven mouths: it vomits fire
and with its flames devours an entire throng:
it will soon make the walls of Paris sound,
with Montalbàn, where Malagigi's found.

Do not believe the Old Man was avenged!
Soon a descendant of his noble race
will come, and make so many people die
that everyone will sate himself with blood;
all Pagandom will topsy-turvy go.
I can already hear the sound of the sad end,
which will be heard as far as Acheron,
for many a mountain will be leveled soon.

50

The trumpet in Jehoshaphat will say,
"Come, all of you! To your Last Judgment come!
Out, all of you, out of your tombs and biers!
And show the book of all your good and ill!"
Alas, that sound re-echoes in my ears.
I see all buildings ruinously crumble
with not a single stone ever in sight—
ah, Jove himself seems now so full of fright.

51

Lions I see come out of every lair,
with tigers and wild beasts all mad with rage;
and I see spears in pieces through the air,
disheveled weeping women all around,
demons released from their infernal caves,
and from the dark abyss the ill-born souls.
How will you, poor Jerusalem, have peace
if Sion sinks into a precipice?

52

I see all Bambillona armed for war
and every banner to the wind unfurled:
Antea is not happy about the crown,
nor is her father's great disdain yet spent;
the entire camp is up, the trumpets sound.
O Carlo, you'll be soon in great dismay.
O God, the earth is trembling; hell is, too:
I think you're being crucified anew.

53

I see the moon eclipsed; I see the sun
stopping again as once for Joshua.
Oh, what a throng is gathering in France!
The River Seine will be a stream of blood.
Fortune is having finally her feast day,
crumpling on earth and sea more masks than one.
In my next Canto this I'll tell you, solely
if aided by the Holy, Holy, Holy.

54

CANTO XXIV

Merciful Father, in Your Holy Gospel   1
'tis written: those who start win no praise yet;
so out of Egypt You must lead me now,
into a land where all salvation's born.
The Christian people will be soon in tears;
You, You alone can aid Your faithful troops:
alas, I now can only dip and fill
into the bloody Seine my very quill;

and though unwillingly I write the truth,   2
yet I must write it just as others did,
not to repeat the Grecian tale's mistakes.
Homer has praised Ulysses' wanderings
too much; I even wonder if the truth
was said about the goddess's famous son:
but one who's wise deduces one's true glory.
And let us now continue with our story.

Rinaldo, Fuligatto, Ricciardetto,   3
Guicciardo, and Alàrd will meet again
(I know not when; I have not said it yet):
along so many a road they'll roam the world together.
But this was not my goal when I began;
therefore they will return to Montalbàn,
where they, alas, will ultimately die;
and if they don't go back, well then, goodbye!

Will Fuligatto reach our Montalbàn?   4
Who knows! He'll maybe die along the way.
But my song started with King Charlemagne.
So let this song of mine now reach its end,
and let me punish wicked Ganelon
for a new treason that, alas, I can
as in a mirror finally behold;
for Charles I'm sorry, who is now too old.

O Carlo, soon to be in heaven blest,
you still must suffer on this earth so much,
the very thought of it congeals my heart.
Gano went back, and day and night worked hard:
a traitor, ah, cannot betray himself.
And Charles of course believes (or does not know)
that by this time the traitor has grown sterile,
incapable of any fraud or peril.

The Old Man, mighty Master of the Mountain,
left on this earth a son, named Buiaforte,
who, out of fear, found refuge there in Spain,
where King Marsilius welcomed him to court,
because Antea, great and lofty queen,
wanted to give him death, and with her troops
had fiercely been pursuing him of late,
remembering her father's ancient hate.

Most valorous in war this man became,
but he was also proud and arrogant,
and in no time his reputation grew
for all he did to spread the pagan faith.
He wore a hard and very solid club
and boasted of gigantic limbs as well;
to King Marsilius he was very dear,
as later I'll endeavor to make clear.

Meanwhile throughout the world the mighty fame
of great and glorious Queen Antea spread:
in Bambillona Town she was adored
just like Semiramis in ancient times.
She held the crown and scepter of the East
but in her heart bemoaned her father's death:
so she was biding time, eager to weave
her cruel vengeance round the Christian field.

Wherever she sat down to eat, her bread
was always placed before her upside down—
just to remind her of the Sultan's wrong
and of the hatred buried in her breast.
The proverb is: now glad, tomorrow sad.
At last she let her foolish thought prevail,
for hate is strong within a female's heart;
Ganelon added, then, his wicked art.

As I have said, Ganelon had come back,   10
and had already written many letters
just to arouse the Sultan's dormant hate,
and to remind him that Rinaldo was
in Egypt still; that Charlemagne was old
and by now victim of his grievous age;
that it was time to send his flag to France
and therefore with his squadrons soon advance.

Antea held a great and awesome court   11
(who deems himself the strongest, he falls first):
some said one thing and some said something else,
whether she should against the Christians fight.
Each wanted to remind her of the day
when big Morgante came to waste her land,
and of Orlando who besieged her field,
and of the reason why their lord was killed.

So came the day when they to council came,   12
in which the noble queen and they all spoke.
Unanimous decision: to Marsilius
they wrote that he should come to France at once
with all his men and all his readied fleet,
and from the Spanish side attack the foe:
Antea would seize Paris before long,
and there avenge at last each suffered wrong.

In Saragossa such a plan seemed good,   13
and since King Bianciardino at the time
was their ambassador to France, and tried
to bring Marsilius and Charles together,
as soon as they adopted this new plan,
because of it he was recalled with wrath,
and told to leave the court most speedily:
so empty-handed back to them came he.

Thus King Marsilius on land and sea   14
drafted a massive throng of Saracens.
Wise Bianciardino, upon his return,
tried to discourage such an expedition:
of many incidents since Pepin's times
he wanted to remind his king, to show
the heavy risks and perils of a war:
thus he advised that they should wait therefore.

Equally wise was King Marsilius,   15
who was convinced by Bianciardino's words;
he heeded reason and cooled off, and let
Antea know that time had not yet come:
from Bianciardino he had heard that Carlo
had good intentions, and therefore believed
that there would soon be peace with Charlemagne,
who consequently would surrender Spain.

Carlo had taken all of Spain again   16
because he wished to crown his nephew king
of Aragona and Granada as well;
Ferraù on the bridge had lost his life.
But since this story is well known to all
because of lengthy books that deal with it,
we shall return to Queen Antea, who
wrote soon to King Marsilius anew.

After her letters were unsealed and read   17
to the Assembly of the Counselors,
wise King Marsilius gave his reply—
a masterpiece of tact and dignity
which the entire session soon approved.
As Diomed to Turnus, he replied
that he regretted all that time gone by,
having so little gained from Charlemagne.

Therefore the queen to Gano wrote again,   18
urging him now to sharpen all his darts,
for King Marsilius's hopes were all in vain
and Bianciardino was quite wrong, in turn,
believing that King Charles would give up Spain
(he had been by appearances deceived):
he to the king should write and press for aid,
for time was more than ever on their side.

Now he who wants to teach this traitor how   19
to weave another scandal, a new fraud,
is like one who to a good tailor tells
the way to wear a thimble or to thread.
Gano, impenitent as ever, wrote
to King Marsilius precisely so:
"Greetings to the great lord and King of Spain
from his devoted, humble servant Gan!

"Marsilius, you seem to act like one   20
   who, playing chess, thinks hard of a good move,
   but as he finds it, a much better one
   he looks for, not resigned to checkmate yet.
   The wolf wants to make peace now with the lamb
   and—black on white—demands that he must have
   with every sheepdog every single ram:
   of course you and your pagans are the lamb.

"This is poor logic as all people see,   21
   except Ambassador King Bianciardin,
   who maybe in your land has brain to sell
   but came down here with none that would suffice.
   I do not know on what he's harping now,
   but since you recommended him to me,
   I did far more than I was asked by you,
   divulging secrets that no person knew—

"ah, most unethically. I also told him   22
   not to believe the Duke of Brittany,
   nor Namo, both maneuvering in the dark.
   He has returned with Spain all in his hand,
   but here—I'm sorry—we are laughing still,
   for shortly such a peace will make you flee:
   Charlemagne's nephew, the most famous count,
   with our complete approval will be crowned.

"Such a long time have you with Carlo fought   23
   that you by now should very clearly know
   that he expects heaven itself to serve him
   since his Fiovus got his flag from it.
   Or maybe Bianciardin is very shrewd
   and does not let you see what you should see;
   but if you like to keep a wise man close,
   why don't you think, then, as a wise man does?

"I cannot think your Bianciardin so gross   24
   as to believe that Spain is yours again:
   I therefore in all honesty admit
   I cannot disentangle such a web.
   One thing I know: Orlando will soon jump
   upon you, for down here he's been assured
   that by whatever means he'll wear the crown
   of Spain, Granada, and of Aragon.

"'Tis true, I heard, a little while ago,   25
   something that made me judge you more than wise:
   that Queen Antea, such a famous queen,
   with many troops of hers was passing by,
   and that you thought the ripest time had come
   to pluck the rose as at the prime of May.
   You too would hear the thunder, I believe;
   now think what your alliance would achieve!

"The truth is that King Charles was glad no more,   26
   and I believe Orlando panicked, too,
   though, being wise, he knows how to pretend,
   and in the meantime seeks all remedies.
   Must I reveal all secrets, then, to you?
   Well, then, the walls of Paris shake with fear,
   and all men tremble. Hannibal has come—
   it seems—with new barbarity to Rome.

"Therefore, a wise man does not need advice.   27
   I know you know already, Charlemagnet:
   you lodged him in your court just like a son,
   but have warmed up a snake right on your breast.
   I see your kingdom in great peril: soon—
   this I must tell you—you will come to grips
   with a most savage and voracious lion:
   this is what Spain and peace have to rely on.

"Now tell your Bianciardin, if so you please: 28
   I know not if he counsels you, or dreams—
   please do not send a different reply.
   Write to Antea, as I think you should,
   and think that, if Orlando comes your way,
   his crown will mean your infamy and shame,
   and exiled all your people I can see.
   Marsilius, you've heard the truth from me."

In Saragossa King Marsilius   29
   received this letter from a messenger,
   who, kneeling on the floor, kissed soon the hand
   he would have rather seen cut off at once.
   Marsilius acknowledged the true seal,
   read it, and strangled fast the messenger,
   for, being wise, he wanted to comply
   with that "Send not a different reply."

He wrote to Bambillona, to the queen,   30
announcing to her he had changed his mind;
therefore, beneath his flag he had already
rallied all of his fighting Saracens:
a number of them would come soon by sea,
and a full hundred thousand on their steeds,
and Balugante would their captain be.
Gan's letter he did send for her to see.

"Ah," said Antea, "Ganelon, you are   31
the master of deceit! But I'll be back
in France, and put a noose around your neck."
All of her men were ready now to fight:
besides the cavalry, her archers, all
from Persia and all of Syria, were
two hundred thousand men and even more—
a choice and valiant company at war.

Of her Rinaldo Antea thought no more: 32
she knew he had grown old in Egypt now—
forever gone was all her burning flame,
and so she minded only her new plan.
Wicked and obstinate, Gan in the meantime
was very eager to perceive all things
and always doubted what would reach his ear,
for where a traitor is, there's also fear.

He ordered every day new feasts and jousts   33
so that all men would ever merry be,
and he, amongst them all, seemed to be first
to show delight about Orlando's crown.
"He is the champion of our Christian faith,"
he (what a hypocrite!) to Carlo said,
and what he uttered Carlo's bosom reached
as if he had Saint Matthew's gospel preached—

and even Luke and John and Christ himself.   34
Ah, wicked traitor, you Iscariot!
You have betrayed your king much more than Judas Christ!
But there's an adage that befits you well:
the mills of God grind slowly, but they do!
There'll be no coin, then, unaccounted for.
Your time of reckoning has yet to dawn,
but it will come, and God alone knows when.

Carlo in Paris lived, content and carefree:
he was already old now, and gray-haired.
He thought that Ganelon's bad seed was dry,
and that, if not yet sated, he was weary;
instead he had an ointment for each wound
and, ever at his side, a poisoned knife.
Rather than leave his vice, he would die first:
the last of all man's vices is the worst.

35

Meanwhile the news had come that many troops
had been arrayed by King Marsilius,
and many ships were seen upon the sea,
in wartime operation all of them;
nobody knew yet Gano's stratagem,
no one as yet suspected anything.
But Bianciardin's departure, unsuspected,
left every wise man doubtful, as expected.

36

To a plenary session Carlo called
all of his counselors; Gan was the first
who fiddled skillfully before the king:
all of his schemes he wove in such a way
that once again King Carlo was deceived.
'Twas then wise Turpin broke the dirty game,
saying, "Keep talking, Gano, as you please,
but with your words your action disagrees."

37

Namo it was who took the floor to speak:
for a long time he beat around the bush,
but then he came where he was driving at,
and let him know all that he thought of him.
Our Duke Astolfo was the man he was:
he waited for no clue, and said to him,
"You as a liar have the greatest fame,
but, Gano, think of this, then—lies are lame,

38

"and therefore truth is known, compared to them."
After Astolfo Count Orlando said,
"Gano, I know this ermine will turn black.
You should have died the day that you were born,
rather than set your foot in this our realm!
What evil, what great wars, what horrid feuds
you have aroused, O monster stained with blood,
our age's infamy and foe to God!"

39

CANTO XXIV ❖ 547

The Lord of Brittany had counseled first,   40
"It seems to me that, wasting no more time,
and without weighing each and every fraud,
we should hang Ganelon, unless we all
decide to fall into his very trap
like starlings into some well-hidden net."
They did not understand these words, I bet:
in Roncesvalles the trap would soon be set.

Gano had raised his hand then in protest,   41
but after Salomon, Alvin said, "Wait!
Have I not seen you talk to Bianciardin
down in the garden, and even flirt with him?
Say, were you saying psalms or matin prayers?
Go! Put a noose around your neck yourself,
and let me see what happens to your feet!
Are you not sated yet with your deceit?"

The Dane so added, "Gano, hear me too!   42
The day when Bianciardino told you 'Hush!'
and shook your hand (I saw you with these eyes)—
tell me—were you discussing peace with him?
I'm sorry you deceive our Charlemagne,
who is still unaware of Judas's kiss:
lanterns and clubs I can already see,
for traitor you have been and will still be."

But Ganelon replied then to the Dane,   43
"I am the butt of everybody's hate,
and all interpret me the way they please.
Let not my lord rebuke me with his wrath!
With Bianciardin I spoke of many a thing.
Words! From one subject jumping to another,
we spoke of nothing, just of this and that—
and you heard what you wished to hear, I bet.

"One day—'tis true—as I was in the garden,   44
where Alvin saw me 'flirt,' he spoke to me
about some personal and private problems
just as a friend who seeks advice would do;
besides, but a few minutes we stayed there.
An honest person never doubts another,
but he who has a guilty conscience sees
two for one, and mistakes small flies for cranes.

"Carlo, I'm used to suffering such wrongs,   45
   and have developed perfect taste and hearing;
   but when a lie has gone around for long,
   as in a mirror then the truth appears.
   I wish my life had ended on the day
   I came to this your court, where I grew old!
   I've left my land and kingdoms of my own,
   and only hate and thanklessness have known.

"Old as I am, back to Maganza I'll go;   46
   and this I know: one day, after my death,
   the world will be aware of the disdain
   that countless times has wrongly wounded me.
   Much freedom you have given to these men,
   O Carlo! Carlo! and I pay the price.
   But let these dogs forever rabid be:
   their evil will not soil my honesty."

"You, wicked and perverse!" said Oliver.   47
"O Carlo, let me speak or I'll explode.
   We all can see Rinaldo is not here,
   or he would oil this rotten spindle well."
   No longer could he then control his wrath,
   for he left furiously his seat at once,
   and such a slap on Gano's cheek he landed,
   it left his face and heart for long imprinted.

Ah, Oliver, someday you'll weep for this   48
   in Roncesvalles, where you'll regret it most!
   This is the day when Magdalen adores
   and wets with precious ointment Jesus' feet.
   And this your slap is fire being lit,
   which copious blood of Christians will put out:
   it will make Gan so wrathful and so dark,
   even in heaven it will leave its mark.

Oliver was at times quite bold and rash;   49
   so Ganelon put up with him and said,
"Go to your seat now! I'll remember this.
   Under your very eyes he hit me, Charles,"
   and, uttering no other word, he left.
   Carlo was shouting, "Where is your respect?
   You proud and arrogant and beastly fool!
   I'll give you what you want, once and for all."

Oliver said, "How I would like to make 50
that arse of yours quite red from all my blows!
But no—I'd make your faithful Gano do it,
who like a fool has always treated you."
At this, King Carlo stood upon his throne
and took his dagger out to silence him;
but, fast, Orlando made the Viennese marquis,
with but a wink, avoid the royal enmity.

Then to King Carlo he expressed his view— 51
that they should now not waste their precious time;
they should instead all ponder what to do
lest every remedy should come too late:
therefore, another meeting they should call
on the next day as early as could be,
since it was night now, and such wrath prevailed:
prudence and wrath together ever failed.

Many an author wrote that Oliver 52
slapped Ganelon when he was chosen to
escort King Bianciardino; but to me
such an opinion seems quite strange indeed—
that is, that out of spite and anger they
should choose a traitor such as Ganelon
for a peace treaty with the King of Spain;
they mistook Bianciardin for Falseròn.

Right at this time, tossed by a storm, a ship 53
arrived in the near harbor of Marseilles.
They mentioned an ill-fated, somber eve
of some sad holiday without its fasting,
and how Antea had in Bambillona
three hundred thousand men with more to come,
and how they'd sworn to bring their war to France,
and were by now most ready to advance.

That is why Carlo called a meeting soon, 54
and questioned every knight on what to do.
They all agreed—and it was so decided—
that they should quickly send the Dane to Spain,
for there he once had worshiped god Mahound
and knew every tradition of the land;
and that with him he also should take there
Astolfo, Sansonet, and Berlinghier.

Orlando ordered that through all of France,   55
cities and fortresses and castles be
as far as the seashore soon reinforced,
so as to keep the nation well prepared;
he also sent the herald everywhere
to order every horseman back to service,
and bade all archers be—but right away—
before King Carlo on Saint Denis's Day.

And troops were so recruited in no time   56
out of the Frankish County, Normandy,
Holland and Seeland with their many isles,
from Rossiglion, Navarra, Piccardy—
a hundred thousand men and even more.
Of many languages and many lands,
these men their way to Paris quickly found—
many a prince and duke, marquis and count.

But long before our Christians were arrayed,   57
in many ports the Saracens were seen;
after they landed in so great a number,
the entire littoral they seemed to own.
Under the banner of their lofty queen,
toward Paris all of them began to march,
covering mountains, every plain and coast,
and ransacking the villages they crossed.

Two giants had been hired by Antea   58
out of their distant, native sandy sea—
so huge, a taller man had ne'er been seen.
Their shoulders spanned twelve feet in width; just think
what the remainder of them must have been!
They brought with them two skeletons of whales:
with these, wherever they were seen to pass,
they smashed to pieces every arm like glass.

These horrid giants were—one, Cattabriga;   59
the other, Fallalbacchio. Next to them,
normal men looked like mannequins of wax,
and woe to those on whom their mattock fell!
They could have killed a fly on every face,
and crushed on every helmet every crest:
they were the leaders of the entire horde,
and underneath their feet the whole earth roared.

Toward Paris these two giants also marched,   60
robbing and razing to the ground all things—
setting on fire castles, towns, and homes,
raping all women as they always did,
and killing men and children and all beasts.
Orlando was not happy when he heard
about their savage, bestial infamy,
and rallied, then, his soldiers instantly.

Ganelon said, "Am I this time the one   61
who's brought about this treason and this woe?
Do always good and let your conscience judge!"
(Ah, wicked man, you're lying, and you know it!)
The closest ever to the emperor,
he said to him, "Dear king, why do you fear?
Fear not! Orlando's here; so, what's the matter?"
He looked more honest than our best *Our Father.*

The Saracens were now four leagues away   62
or even less: the giants were there, too.
In front of them, sure of himself and bold,
advanced their captain, Sicumoro named.
Upon their banners a white field was seen
with, gilded on the top, a god Mahound.
Antea came in front of all her men,
eager to see Orlando once again.

During those days throughout the town of Paris,   63
strange things and most weird omens had occurred—
it even had rained blood in every street,
and day and night all dogs were heard to bark.
Malgigi came to Montalbàn this time,
and saw the danger of the Christian men;
he to Orlando came and through his magic
explained why things appeared that looked so tragic.

They both agreed that it was Ganelon   64
who even now, as he had always done,
was thinking of another slaughterhouse;
but they should not antagonize him yet.
Antea now appeared, and her two giants
towered above the navels of her men:
they could be seen above each flag and star,
for they looked like two mountains from afar.

Orlando, seeing those two giants, said,   65
"Can nature make so powerful a thing?
By God, Malgigi, make them disappear,
for they are not as common men should be."
Malgigi said, "What am I now to do?
Be not afraid of giants, I advise.
What will you say to me if with my special glue
I catch them, and the whole camp laughs at such a view?

"Send Oliver this moment to the queen   66
to know from her why she has come so far,
and why she's brought to France so many men—
all of her Saracens—to make them die
(this is what this my magic art reveals—
she won't be able to return at ease).
But you, Orlando, do as I suggest:
upon his horse send Oliver in haste."

As Count Orlando said, Oliver went   67
to see Antea. From Rondèl dismounted,
he knelt before her, greeting her most humbly;
and the high queen replied to him as kindly.
When he stood up, she hugged him heartily
(he looked more handsome and more kind to her)
and, his hand shaking, said most affably,
"Welcome, oh, welcome here, my kind marquis!

"O Oliver, you are as young as ever: 68
you look just like a picture painted now!
Don't you remember when I left you sad
in Bambillona, a long time ago?
Oh, I have sighed so many a time for you,
although the Sultan lost his royal crown
and kept on fighting, as you recollect,
till all our land was by Morgante wrecked.

"This is, dear Oliver, how the world goes.   69
Now it appears legitimate and just
that I should such a mighty lord avenge.
For justice and for lawful love I fight,
I fight for God and for my pagan faith,
and to seek fame and honor in the end;
to emulate Semiramis I try,
whom the whole world still praises to the sky.

"But let's not talk of this. How's our Orlando?   70
Dear Oliver, I'm longing for the day
when I'll be able to address the count,
so much in love with all his worth am I.
I've heard Rinaldo is still wandering
through Egypt—which still sorely grieves my heart.
If I had found him back in France, right here,
no more would he have thrown his able spear

"just as he did the day you were displeased   71
and Milon's son was likewise ill at ease.
Now, if this kingdom I can conquer back,
I'll do it; it is reason urges me
(of course I'll leave King Carlo on his throne
with all his titles and his haughty fame);
but for all this no praise should come to me:
it is, dear Oliver, God's high decree.

"Before we are allowed down here to fight,   72
our war has been decreed in heaven first—
I mean the struggle between our two gods—
up there, where simultaneously the past
meets with the future ever faultlessly.
And I—God be my witness—much am grieved
for having caused such harm along my road;
but you know well no war is without blood.

"So many men from diverse lands have I,   73
not even Hannibal could count on such
a number when he came to plunge on Rome:
I hear around me every eastern tongue,
which makes these men like dogs ignore each other.
But if, dear Oliver, right now Morgante
were here, these fellows he would bravely fight—
they with their whales, he with his clapper's might."

And since he was such a good friend of hers,   74
she bade her men then shake Oliver's hand;
he was, besides, a famous Christian knight,
one of King Carlo's greatest paladins.
But both her savage giants looked at him
with a most frightening, forbidding glance:
proud and conceited, they did hardly bend
to shake, in all their clumsiness, his hand.

Oliver laughed and at Antea looked,   75
raising his hand as high as he could reach,
so that big Fallalbacchio would not have
to bend down to his chin or further down.
Seeing the giants' mouths as large as ovens,
he said, "Antea, giants I have fought,
but here these two are such enormous monsters,
they do not teach theology in cloisters.

"Had they been there, there would have been no need   76
for Nimrod to erect a tower to heaven:
on top of one another, they could do it,
if such a thing were possible (I doubt
that any winch could ever lift them up).
But since we two have much to talk about,
if I may say so, send them out of here,
for they are cattle not to have so near."

After much more was said between the two,   77
and when the giants were in sight no more,
said the marquis, "If I have heard you well,
you're here the mighty Sultan to avenge.
I wish that I could say, 'He asked for it'
(the truth is widely known to the whole world).
I for his death was very deeply sorry,
but he was wrong, and this is the true story.

"Believe me, Ricciardetto and I myself   78
barely escaped, though innocent, great woe:
while you were here in Montalbàn at play,
we both were in a dungeon and in chains
with no more hope, in a deep sunless place
where bolts of lightning were our only light—
a deed unworthy of the Sultan, since
we both were Carlo's noble paladins.

"And I won't mention Marcovaldo's story   79
and the high treason of the Admiral,
for you know very well how in the night
he seized and captured your beloved count.
Thank God, Rinaldo came, his cousin dear.
Now, if you say that Heaven's holy might
has preordained the wars that come to us,
equally preordained the Sultan's exit was.

"The Old Man was your enemy, you know.   80
  Rinaldo for your love went there to kill him,
  but since he gave himself to Christ, could not;
  and also, as the world already knows,
  the Sultan had been fated to be slain
  by both a mountain and a horseman. So,
  if he was destined thus his life to lose,
  you for his death should fate and God accuse.

"Yet if you're still determined to avenge   81
  your father, many chances you still have
  to test the valor of the Christian knights;
  and if you want to fight Orlando again,
  I'll let you know (for this I can arrange)
  on what day you may come to challenge him;
  your greetings to the count I will convey,
  and I will go away when so you say."

Antea answered, "By all means I want   82
  to test my prowess with the count again
  (knowing that I will lose as oft I do)
  and thus avenge the Sultan. I know not
  if I am right or wrong in grieving so;
  however that may be, it seems it is
  my duty now to break for him a spear
  since I have brought so many men down here.

"So to your lord and master now return,   83
  and my best greetings give to all of them,
  specially to Orlando, who, I'm sure,
  will choose the day: and we'll be there to fight."
  And so they hugged each other once again.
  But just as they were leaving, the two giants
  threatened the Christians with their wrathful malice,
  saying that they would shortly level Paris.

With his reply our Oliver returned   84
  and to the count related everything,
  how, as he chose, Antea wished to fight him.
  About the giants he informed him, too,
  each brandishing the skeleton of a whale,
  and full of threats as they were leaving. Nature,
  it seemed, had still some matter to release
  when she created those monstrosities.

When he heard everything from Oliver,   85
Orlando called on Malagigi fast.
Said Malagigi, "On the given date,
see that the troops of Paris be prepared,
and fight this duel, as you did before,
right on the grounds of our Saint Denis's field;
I'm sure Antea and her pagan men
will want to pitch their tents along the Seine.

"As for those two giants, you will laugh   86
the moment you will see them caught like birds—
a show that you have never seen before.
Remind me of it when we see those two,
and I am certain you'll be most amazed.
But there is something else you must remember:
to Gan you must say nothing of all this,
lest he devise another trick of his."

Saint Denis's field was chosen as the site,   87
and on the day the fight was to take place,
forward Antea with her giants came:
they terrified all men and Mars himself.
King Carlo crossed himself and said in fear,
"Who could have thought that Nature could do this?
These monsters are so savage and so odd,
no man on earth can help us here but God."

And Salomon to Namo also said,   88
"Satan, I am convinced, has sent them here.
Take my advice: let us go in right now
before they slaughter every man in sight.
Let us explain to Count Orlando this—
that if they let those clubs of theirs fall down,
nobody will survive so strange a stick,
even if he were Atlas or even Tambernic."

Carlo had Count Orlando called at once,   89
and said, "Of those two giants have you thought?
If I but look at them, they seem to me
two haunted bodies from another world."
Replied Orlando, "Sire, do not fear!
Not once but twice, Malgigi said to me
that with those giants he alone will bother:
it takes one devil to chastise another."

But at those giants Charles was gazing still,   90
and back to Paris would have gladly sped.
In terror everyone seemed to withdraw
as soon as on Saint Denis's field they came,
leading Antea's pagan multitude.
Close to Malgigi soon Orlando drew,
and saw him, mumbling words, about to start
against those savage fiends his magic art.

Malgigi said, "Orlando, wait awhile—   91
stand back!" Orlando stepped aside at once.
Malgigi then began to circle down
letters and seals, and to prepare and use
his instruments and pentacles. But when
the ghosts that he had exorcized appeared,
like a most violent wind the whole earth shook,
and in one instant the whole sky turned black.

Lo! In the middle of the field there was   92
a man much stranger than Margutte—lame,
hunchbacked, cross-eyed, all-twisted and ill-shaped,
but of gigantic size, save for his head,
which had two pairs of horns for all to see:
jumping like magpies to and fro, he laughed
and joked and made a lively carousel
as Fracurrado or Arrigobel;

he also played a flageolet and pipe.   93
Dancing, to those two giants he went near,
and there, grimacing like a silly clown,
around them danced the strangest saraband,
now somersaulting like a big baboon,
now often pirouetting apishly:
Christians and pagans watched the merry deed,
each quite amused and idle on his steed.

After a while that nonsense and that dance   94
began to bother the two massive heights,
for that small man was like a firefly seen
now here, now there, as when a wick goes out:
their heads began to spin, and they were not
at all amused by so much foolish play.
All those around them split their sides with laughter,
not guessing what that little man was after.

Have you by any chance seen how a dog,   95
baffled and scorned, pursues a cawing crow?
She stops a bit, then flies and caws anew.
Likewise, the two could not get hold of him
(Malgigi will be most successful soon):
whene'er they tried to put their hands on him,
he wriggled or away he vanished fast,
making the giants furious at last.

But when Antea looked at this, she soon   96
said to herself, "Those stupid fools don't see
the trap concealed beneath that clownish act:
this is, I'm sure, one of Malgigi's tricks,
and it will quickly wreck my entire plan."
Meanwhile the little man made fun of them,
and then, to try their patience, finally
he showed his arse full naked (pardon me).

Look how our Marguttino cared to play!   97
To spite them more, he through their legs then slid,
bothersome like a gadfly. But look now!
A round and lovely little wood appeared
with branches bird-slimed like a fowling place.
Oh, no, it was no magic—it was real,
with natural twigs and birdlime, with the owl,
the screeching thrushes, and the whistle—all.

The midget-giant leapt into that wood   98
as oft a thrush or other birds would do;
from there he sneered and jeered and laughed at them
with oral and with anal noisiness.
The giants, angered by his ridicule,
just like two falcons jumped and closed him in:
through the small wood they tossed and turned around
until with birdlimed twigs they got all bound.

Like two enormous oak trees soon they looked,   99
with boughs around them broken by the wind.
Now is the time to say "Shame shame!" to them,
so quickly and so beautifully smeared!
They wanted now to wield their boundless clubs
but, tangled as they were, could nothing do:
they deafened, as they fiercely yelled and roared,
the Christian soldiers and the pagan horde.

Malgigi said, "Now jump upon them fast!　　　　　　　100
I with my art can do no more than this."
Orlando was the first to move, and soon
behind him came many more Christian knights.
Close to the thick and heavy bush they walked
with spears and darts, and rummaged through it all,
each of them most intent to find and pierce;
but meanwhile they had better stop their ears.

The entire city had come out to watch,　　　　　　　101
aroused and startled by the sudden noise;
but our Terigi did not wait to see
the giants fall; like a wise man, instead,
he ran and walked into Saint Denis's Church,
without dismounting from his horse pulled down
a lamp, and with a taper that he saw
he lit it up, till it was all aglow.

If you had heard those giants shout and roar,　　　　102
you would have sworn—such was their wrath and pain—
that all the demons out of hell were there.
But when Terigi in a flash came back
with his lamp all lit up, they all made room.
As with a heap of brushwood one would do,
he threw those flames upon the giants, and
together into smoke the giants went.

It seems to me they were not like those two—　　　　103
Shadrach and Meshach—in Nebuchadnezzar's time.
Their buttocks (so God willed) were promptly spared
by the great fire that would have surely made
all bucketfuls of water futile most.
Terigi was the hero of the day:
had the two giants fallen down, they would
have crushed beneath them quite a multitude.

Right at this point I very much would like　　　　　　104
to quote, in my defense, the Poet's lines:
"To that truth which resembles falsehood, always
a man must close his lips, so far as he is able,
for, although blameless, he incurs reproach."
But if, unlike Cassandra, I've not cheated
love's planet, I believe I have the right
to ask to be believed for what I write.

The eyes of this my mind can clearly see   105
these giants, and I know I've well described
their features and their actions in detail,
using no allegory and no fiction.
Now let all those who have objections speak,
for my reply will satisfy them all.
"Whatever comes out of this author's lips,"
they'll say, "re-echoes the *Apocalypse.*"

Someone may say, "Why don't you answer this?   106
If Malagigi knew his art too well,
together with the wood he could have made
the fire, too, and melted those men like wax."
My answer is: the magic art obeys
manner and time and place; were it not so,
I'd be a necromancer of success,
and rule from West to East in happiness.

But the same God Who's King Above All Kings   107
to all has given limit, order, measure,
forbidding us to cross the ornaments,
and taking care of everything Himself:
therefore, no witchcraft, sorcery, or omen
can do what nature is denied to do.
Brittle as ice is every further norm,
for he alone showed strength within his arm.

And if Saint Paul could see *arcana Dei,*   108
there was a purpose for so great a grace—
so that he could confound the Pharisees
with all his holy doctrine; but the wicked
and ever-cursèd denizens of hell
have been deprived of every godly worth;
however, many secrets they still know,
and so, by natural force, they much can do.

Different kinds of spirit elves in droves   109
fly in the air above us: they are those
who fought neither against God nor for him
the day when he established the Elect.
Maybe on this my dear Palmieri's wrong—
in placing them from bodies into new ones,
because of which too much he needles us
by making of Pythagoras first a Euphorbius.

And maybe Thyaneus is also wrong,   110
who'd been a pirate in his previous life,
and, hired by a far worse buccaneer,
replied and very kindly treated him.
Now you could mention Asmodeus here;
but I reply 'tis but a metaphor,
there in the Bible, where it is revealed
how Sarah's husbands one by one he killed.

Malgigi and the other necromancers   111
can tempt us with their magic art, therefore;
but with his art he could not kill the giants
nor bid the demons set those two on fire.
Yes, he could make the wood appear before them,
but they were free to enter it or not:
they too had been endowed with that free will
which God has kindly granted to us all.

At best the demons could have brought the fire,   112
but did not have the power to light one spark.
Little by little I discover, then,
that I have visited the Sibyl's cave,
which I had once considered but a joke:
and still within my breast some spark remains,
for those enchanted waves I'd like once more to see,
which Cecco d'Ascoli has made so dear to me.

Moco and Scarbo, then, and Màrmores,   113
and the bifurcate bone that closed at last—
such things I longed for as a man in love:
here were my Muses: my Parnassus, here.
I do admit my fault, and will someday
ask mighty Minos's pardon, recognizing
the truth with all those men who err from ignorance—
pyromancers, hydromancers, geomancers.

Now let's go back to all those pagan men   114
who, most astounded, looked upon that scene.
Antea asked, "Where did the giants go?"
(The smoke had raised a curtain round the fire.)
"Could those two mountains disappear so fast?"
And of their sudden death she could not have
any news brought to her with great precision;
still on Malgigi fell her first suspicion.

But when she saw th' headquarters' very flag   115
and realized it was Orlando's sign;
when she could see his helmet and his crest,
with all her people forward came the queen.
Soon from her horse dismounting, she embraced
the knight according to the protocol;
he too dismounted from his Vegliantin
and, with his visor up, could now be seen.

With skillful words Antea said to him,   116
"How very strange is my two giants' case!
Malgigi can perform all miracles
(is he in Paris or in Montalbàn?):
the sun and planets he could even stop;
but this does little honor to King Charles.
To fight the knights of France I have come here,
but only with the sword and with the spear.

"I have not come, Orlando, to fight ghosts   117
just like your Angel Michael in the sky.
If you've decided to destroy us all
with the infernal flames, one thing is left
for me to do—weigh anchor and sail on;
but on King Carlo's head you are not placing
a crown of bay or myrtle leaf, I swear:
a far more glorious crown he now should wear."

Orlando said, "The Viennese marquis   118
has brought me, madam, your most kind regards,
and also mentioned that you have returned
to reap much honor and new fame in France
by making the Seine's waters red with blood.
Let's see if the right reason called you here.
I mourned the Sultan's death, and still am mourning now,
but to the will of God we finally must bow.

"You know I took you back to Bambillona,   119
put in your hand your father's scepter, and
with this my hand upon your head the crown
that had been promised to the very one
who should with all his valor win it back.
Brittle as glass your reasons seem to be,
for, yes, you're queen, but you were crowned by me,
who thought that grateful you would therefore be.

"If Malagigi with his necromancy   120
   has killed your Fallalbacchio and Cattabriga,
   he could have also killed them in the East
   had they caused there the trouble they have here,
   and had they not been born so measureless:
   it takes a madman to chastise another.
   Surely it was his only way to play:
   to let some devils other devils slay.

"I'll tell you now what Oliver has said—   121
   you want to end this war by fighting me,
   and that in heaven, too, Christ and Mahound
   will also fight before we clash on earth;
   well, I am ready, and I swear to you—
   by the one God Who's just and never errs—
   that if I am defeated by your lance,
   you will have conquered the whole realm of France."

Antea answered, "And I swear to you   122
   that I'll return to Bambillona at once
   if me you beat. My dear Orlando, God
   in Heaven knows how greatly I have longed
   for such a day, to test your worth at last!"
   And so they both were on their steeds again,
   and afterward they shook the reins a bit,
   and each took as much field as he saw fit.

Surely Antea's valor was not spent,   123
   but also Orlando's fierceness was no less.
   They now had turned their horses, and at once
   each broke a spear upon the other's shield:
   they both looked like two towers that defied
   not only human might but sky itself.
   With such dexterity was each spear driven
   that the two fighters were by all judged even.

Now they unsheathed their swords and brilliantly   124
   pounded a thousand times their armor suits:
   nobody ever saw so many sparks
   rise from both sides up to the throne of Jove.
   Achilles and the Trojan seemed to duel,
   for neither of them budged upon his horse.
   Quite even was the fight and, in all truth,
   wonderful and praiseworthy they were both.

But at this point both camps were in a brawl,   125
and on both sides a fiercer war began;
Antea and the count soon left the field,
seeing their people fighting all around.
Orlando dashed into the pagan camp,
cutting and smashing every Saracen,
until they turned their backs—their buttocks, rather—
all feeling their knees knock and turn to water.

After she left the count, Antea, too,   126
entered the battle and met Oliver,
with whom she wanted eagerly to fight.
One does not always from one's horse fall down:
so then, in spite of his enchanted weapon,
most willingly he from that fight sneaked out.
Gano he saw, and moved against him forward,
but Gan was still a dog and still a coward,

and therefore let himself fall to the ground.   127
A prestidigitator he could be,
or—look at him—a sorcerer's trained snake!
But on his saddle he was soon helped back.
Walter of Mulion, Avolio, and Arnaldo,
with Angiolìn, pounded the pagan backs;
the Lord of Brittany, and Otho and Avìn,
starting a bloodbath each of them was seen.

And who would ever have believed that Charles—   128
that weak old man—could not still idle be?
Maybe by God himself he was inspired:
with his Gioiosa—so his sword was called—
high from his steed he cut so many heads,
he bloodied up himself and the whole ground;
and from that day on, the old emperor
was fated to unsheath his sword no more.

Until then Charles had been a worthy man: 129
nature had given boundless worth to him
with a great fortitude and a great mind;
many a thing he had already seen,
and held a mighty realm for his great race;
but his deeds were not fully recognized:
had Carlo been in Lucan's sounding line,
just like another Rome he now would shine.

Most bravely the Bavarian duke fought, too,   130
whose final day had come and now was nigh.
Being with all his worth so near the end,
he flickered as the morning star would do,
and broke and smashed and routed every throng;
even His Excellency Archbishop Turpin
killed those in front of him, and hurt them all,
but with his sword, not with his pastoral.

After he left Antea, Count Orlando   131
had made so many pagans so much bleed
that now their blood was flowing toward the Seine:
he killed so many of that crazy horde,
and still his sword was ever seen aloft.
The entire field with corpses now was strewn,
and Vegliantin with many a leap and bound
was kicking, sending others to the ground.

This is that Vegliantino (let all those   132
who hear me understand the entire truth)
who proved to be Almont's most worthy steed;
in the same manner, when at times we mention
Baiardo's name, my praise is also true:
until they die, they with their lords will stay.
Thank God! For Heaven still His favor sends
on him who still His Gospel here defends.

But on that day, many a feat was done   133
by Sicumoro, the great captain who
towered above the other officers.
He shouted to his Saracens, "Be brave!
Give back to them death, blood, revenge, and flesh!
Come on, and banish cowardice away!
Cut all these Christian bastards limb from limb!"
Thus were the Saracens cheered up by him.

So many reddened swords were seen up high   134
that the whole sky seemed of a sudden red;
and just as in a field the whole wheat bends
to the most mighty wind and, if this ends,
soon to the other side once more it sways,
so seemed that fight from side to side to go:
but though the battle was so wild and wide,
Fortune until now favored neither side.

The pagans launched then such a fierce assault,   135
the Christians could not bear it anymore:
the blood rose two feet high, and Charlemagne,
alas, was felled, and saw himself, alas,
upon the ground, in all that blood immersed;
up to the Christian flags the pagans ran,
and there the fight seemed to begin anew,
with endless devastation now in view.

Baldwin, the son of Ganelon, meanwhile,   136
attentively had watched how things were faring:
as soon as he saw Charles thrown from his horse,
and on the ground the Christian gonfalon,
he looked around in search of Milon's son
and asked if someone knew where he could be;
most frantically along the field he trotted
until the count right in the fight he spotted.

From far away he shouted then to him,   137
"Do something for your Christian paladins,
or take us right away inside the doors!
Here we are being massacred like dogs,
and everybody's running fast from death;
the pagans are for Paris heading now,
and all our flags are on the bloodied floor:
with Carlo fallen, we have lost the war."

No sooner does a savage lion leap   138
on seeing a new flock than Count Orlando
into the thickest of the battle jumped,
moving like wind towards the fallen flag.
Now we shall see how Durlindana cuts,
making all ointments futile at their best!
The Christian knights lay scattered on the floor,
unrecognizable in all that gore.

Sicumor had already in his hand   139
our lovely flag, and was about to flee;
Orlando cut his hand with but one blow,
so hard, the Saracen felt close to death
and found himself sprawled down upon the earth,
so that Zacchaeus could have climbed on him.
Against those crazy Saracens turned he,
soon after, making the whole plainland free.

This I believe—that Mars told Jove that day, 140
"You did not have this dauntless paladin
when those fierce giants tried their last assault:
your realm and throne would not have trembled so!"
Orlando then asked Baldwin, "Where, but where
did you see Pepin's son?" And Baldwin led him
where for a while their emperor had lain,
and they both helped him on his horse again.

Oliver in the meantime saw himself 141
surrounded by a throng of mamelukes:
but woe to those who could not imitate
the owl that with his glance moves here and there!
He cut and threw one man upon the other.
One swims in blood, not in the Serchio, here.
So cleverly he used his wondrous might,
hundreds of beards he made vermilion bright.

Orlando helped back on their horses Namo 142
and many others, who had fallen down
and, with no squires near, were lying still.
The pagans, routed so, began to flee
like birds caught in the air by wind or hail
or lightning flash and thunderbolt. "Let's go,"
they did not say, nor any other words,
for fear, indeed, had turned them into birds.

Orlando's help was so immense and quick 143
that soon our Christians' vehemence and wrath
allowed them to reorder all their troops
and rouse their ancient worth in all of them,
so that the pagans scampered everywhere.
Often Antea saw herself quite trapped.
In short, I tell you, many a pagan beast
fattened the gadflies and all flies increased.

And if—thank God!—the night had not arrived, 144
no pagan slaughter would have been so great.
Their squadrons had been routed one by one.
Orlando with his special company
transfixed them in the ditches and the caves.
But now the sun lit up the other hemisphere:
so they were forced to let the trumpet blast
and on both sides announce the end at last.

Antea begged Orlando for a truce—   145
twenty full days—to bury all her dead;
but smarter she would be to burn them all
or give them to the devil or the stream.
Very well, then—to make the story short—
Orlando then withdrew inside the doors.
Gano was overjoyed for this one reason—
he wished to plan a more successful treason.

Now, anyone who had been there to watch   146
this horrid battle near the River Seine—
unless a beast or a cold-hearted man—
would have felt his heart shake, as I my pen.
All men were buried in their very blood.
Is this, Antea, your great gift to France?
All of your men have died because of you,
nor do you know what you will soon go through!

But now in Paris let us leave the count,   147
and go to King Marsilius in Spain.
After the Dane had come to him—he knew
the greatness of his valor and his worth—
he thought the wind had come to wreck and break
the entire web's minutest filaments:
meanwhile he was awaiting news from France—
if his Antea had used well her lance.

Knowing his delicate predicament,   148
Ganelon sent a messenger to him:
that birdlime of Orlando—so he said—
was not afraid of rain or thunderstorm;
the giants had been easily deceived,
and now Antea showed her back full bare:
she was, indeed, a thrush now fallen down,
dying and stunned, exposed upon the ground.

A new ambassador he sent to France   149
to try a new peace treaty with King Charles,
and tell him that his Bianciardin was right
when he came back, but did not mention why.
He sent there Falseron, a generous man,
prudent and also very eloquent.
He came to Paris, and to Charlemagne
to speak in such a manner he began:

"That mighty God, Whom each of us adores,   150
and Who created the angelic beings
that turn above us all the moving spheres,
protect and save the lofty majesty
of Charles and those who honor so his crown—
Orlando and the others—happily!
My lord Marsilius has granted me
the honor to salute Your Majesty.

"The reason why he sent me here to you,   151
O Pepin's most illustrious son and heir,
from whom you have not gone astray a bit,
is that he thinks that you were most amazed
when our King Bianciardino suddenly
returned to us, departing from your court,
without informing why he left your city
when he appeared so close to a peace treaty.

"Your wisdom I implore, Your Majesty.   152
Bianciardin left for valid reasons which
are secret and cannot be now revealed—
they would not even be quite pertinent.
At the right time and place, to please you most,
they all will be in great detail divulged.
You know that things must have a beginning and a norm,
and matter must forever agree with its right form.

"But this, as I have said, some other time   153
will by somebody else be said to you:
put off your mind his quick departure, then,
for everything will soon be known to you.
So here I am, to say, *Quod scripsi, scripsi,*
just as my lord commanded me to say,
and to renew with Your Great Majesty
our peaceful efforts with sincerity.

"'Tis useless now to speak of Spain again,   154
for King Marsilius believes and says
that Charles will keep his promise and therefore
confirm all that he said within Ida's Woods.
One hundred thousand horsemen, to remind you,
had been arrayed with massive infantry
to come and help your holy, lofty crown,
against the sudden wrath of Bambillon.

"But in the meantime when Marsilius heard
　　that Sansonetto had arrived in Spain
　　together with the great and mighty Dane,
　　Astolfo, Berlinghier, as if for fun,
　　each of us understood the reason why.
　　The count alone, indeed, would have sufficed,
　　and (between you and me let this remain)
　　Antea was ill-advised by her own men.

"I want you now to know that Buiaforte,
　　the son of the late Old Man of the Mountain,
　　is at Marsilius's court in Saragossa,
　　and truly much complains about Antea;
　　because although his father killed the Sultan,
　　he killed him with his spear in open field
　　as in th' eternal spheres it had been writ:
　　therefore, why blame your nephew—or why him—for it?

"But let's not speak of this. If you, King Charles,
　　being the noble emperor that you are,
　　want to return Marsilius's true love,
　　let the first peace now happen in your heart;
　　and if some rancor should still linger there,
　　let each of you soon banish it away.
　　All I have said, believe me, is most true:
　　his very words I now repeat to you.

"Better King Bianciardino, I am sure,
　　would have related than this Falseron;
　　but—God is my sole witness—all I said
　　has been dictated by profoundest love.
　　Besides, you know that I have lost my son
　　(although he did not like a coward die
　　but with his sword uplifted on the bridge)—
　　yet I forgive the count, and hold no grudge."

And he could say no more: in tears he rose
　　and, although overcome with sudden grief,
　　he hugged and hugged Orlando tenderly—
　　were his tears false? I really do not know.
　　Carlo's expression changed immediately,
　　won as he was by gestures and wise words.
　　Orlando to his knees fell readily,
　　begging his pardon with humility.

155

156

157

158

159

King Carlo answered, "Kind ambassador,   160
for many reasons, then, be welcome here!
I do accept your King Marsilius's love,
and for his greetings I am grateful most.
As for Bianciardin, if to obey
he had to leave, his duty he performed;
on his departure I decline my comment,
which would not be quite honest at this moment.

"Well I remember what we have discussed—   161
and I believe that you recall it, too—
our peace and Spain; and Namo here can tell
that I do not forget all that is just.
He left and you have come. With Count Orlando
and all the other knights we all agree
that all the Spanish kingdoms should be yours—
but Christians you must be, no longer Moors.

"The reason why the Dane was sent to you   162
is neither Queen Antea nor mistrust;
someday the entire truth will be made known
together with King Bianciardino's case.
Your King Marsilius—I also know—
will always help my enterprises well:
for the salvation of both Spain and France
can be achieved through peace and not through lance.

"If it is necessary, I will send   163
to Saragossa my own nephew or Gan.
Orlando's willing to surrender Spain,
although (I know you are aware of this)
he deems this action rather strange indeed,
since all your land he conquered all alone;
to King Marsilius, who cared for me
while at his court, a brother I must be.

"Of Queen Antea I will not speak now: 164
the end will let her know what she began,
and all in Bambillona will then weep
for having been so foolishly advised.
Everyone born onto this earth must die;
so, if her father in a battle died,
'twas Heaven willed his death, as you have said; in short,
Antea should now cease threatening Buiafort.

"I felt most sorry for poor Ferraù,   165
    and, just as much as you, I'm grieving still;
    but let me comfort you at least by saying
    that visibly his soul was brought to heaven
    by countless angels with a thousand songs,
    and, as you said, a hero's death he died.
    Let's talk no more of things that grieve us still;
    let's ultimately do Marsilius's will.

"Go now and rest awhile in Gano's home,   166
    and you and I shall speak of this again.
    We can adjourn our meeting now; it seems
    that we shall come to an agreement soon."
    He had the man accompanied by all.
    O Carlo! Carlo! I'm afraid that someone
    will say this time, *"Amice, ad quid venisti?"*
    Remember, *"Ovem lupo commisisti."*

Orlando and the other paladins   167
    escorted Falseron, a worthy man,
    as far as Gano's palace; Charles himself
    walked with him kindly, holding still his hand.
    And feasts and tournaments that day were held
    in honor of that man before he left;
    all knights were pleased to honor him, therefore,
    to show the glory of their emperor.

Ask not, dear reader, if our Ganelon   168
    was at this point the happiest of men,
    and swam contented in his own delight:
    to your imagination this I leave.
    His cheek was hurting still, and was still red,
    but when he wants to bite, a dog barks not:
    that slap the scoundrel never mentioned, but
    about Rinaldo mumbled randomly.

Our Malagigi through his magic art   169
    (once more he used it) knew what Gano said,
    and spoke thus to Orlando: "Charle-mad!
    (we can no longer call him Charlemagne),
    you and your men will be most sorry soon."
    When its last day was near, to Troy's empire
    the same disaster in this way occurred,
    when they despised Cassandra's truthful word.

Orlando in his heart felt great disdain,   170
for Carlo countless times had promised him
to crown him and to give him reign and state;
but, Gano being ever after him,
all of his plans were soon to nothing brought
or did not seem to matter anymore:
Malgigi's divination is superfluous,
for it is Heaven governs all of us.

Falseron said one day to Count Orlando   171
that much he wished to see Antea again,
and her whole camp, while still in the French land;
and that he had already weighed the thought
that it was proper that he come along,
and also take with them, if he concurred,
Gano and Oliver. They both agreed,
and so they rode toward Antea's field.

As soon as Queen Antea heard the news   172
(Falseron was a most important man),
forward she came, dismounted from her steed,
and greeted him; then, on her horse again,
she greeted Gan, Orlando, and the marquis
most reverently; then she escorted them
throughout the camp and to their hearts' content,
until they stopped to see a precious tent.

It was a truly great pavilion: 173
inside it was all painted with the tale
of the Old Man—how the whole mountain fell
upon her father with his horse as well;
how Bambillona was complaining still;
how big Morgante had arrived and used
his clapper to destroy and waste the land;
and how Orlando battled in the end.

Antea tried her best, thus, to remind herself   174
that she still had her father to avenge.
But Falseron, who's false far more than she,
after he watched those paintings carefully,
said to her, "If you cared for my opinion,
I'd tell you you're not honored in the least.
First of all—if I'm not completely blind—
you carry, Antea, your own shame behind,

"but you have covered it with silk and gold;   175
   now see that your revenge is painted here
   if ever your revenge will come to be.
   But, as we say, make hay while the sun shines!
   Yet seldom does lack of reflection bring
   a thought that we may have to any height.
   But you must not seek honor anywhere,
   since this your shame can seem to you so fair."

I wonder if they understood the words   176
   that wicked Falseron so shrewdly spoke.
   On the one hand, he both rebuked the queen
   and seemed to push her closer to revenge,
   and on the other, with his chattering
   he meant that he was offering his service
   (for his own gain) to treat for her the peace—
   but I am now digressing with all this.

Quite mortified, Antea stood before him,   177
   and with her silence answered all he said.
   As one remembers only what one must,
   she thought he had just told her what to do.
   And since she was magnanimous of heart,
   and gentle souls most willingly forgive,
   she wanted to make peace with Charles as soon
   as possible, and leave for Bambillòn.

Falseron spoke again, but I know not   178
   if, as he said, he truly wanted peace
   or if, instead, he was as false as ever.
   The truth is that, before she left, Antea
   to Paris went, and did as she had planned.
   Charlemagne blessed her with his hand, and all
   his paladins were happy for the peace;
   she then unfurled her banners to the breeze.

Speedily, then (diminishing her fame   179
   a little), I will let Antea leave
   Paris forever. I must weave so thin
   a web, each thread will seem to be too thick.
   Since Falseron is eager to return,
   trumpets to Saragossa call me back,
   as from the next sad Canto you will know,
   where all our Christians weep in bitter woe.

CANTO XXV

Lord, Your right hand has heretofore sufficed 1
to take me, with no other thread or ruse,
out of all labyrinths; but now I enter
so very dark a place, all of Your light
is needed in its fullest radiance
to tell me how to color this my tale:
Your mercy on Your Christians I do implore and call,
and on Your champion, Count Orlando, most of all.

O Carlo, have you then made up your mind 2
disdainfully to send to your own foe
a man who has betrayed you every day?
Do you not know what an old vice can do
deep in a heart forever obstinate?
You think you'll make Marsilius your friend:
but peace will come from bloodshed and from lance,
and there'll be weeping in the realm of France.

Already Falseron had asked to leave, 3
and Ganelon was to depart with him.
Before the majesty of Charlemagne
he knelt and asked what else he wished to say.
Carlo said, "On your wisdom I rely,
and I am sure I never will be wrong.
You know the adage—and you know it best:
a wise man choose, and let him do the rest."

And so that traitor even hugged Orlando, 4
and begged him, if he had more things to add
concerning that peace treaty, that he write
to him; and he was panting and perspiring,
repeating all his huggings wickedly;
he even kissed, like Judas, Oliver,
to whom he said, as sticky as a leech,
"Now I am sure at last our peace we'll reach."

Smiling, the knight from Burgundy replied,   5
"O Rabbi, hail! I know that you are lying."
Duke Namo and clear-thinking Salomon,
Otho and all the others seemed displeased,
convinced now more than ever that new treasons
Ganelon was devising in his mind:
they all had gone to Charles to let him know
they did not think that he should let him go.

But although no one favored Gano's trip,   6
Emperor Carlo listened to no one:
an old mistake, deep-rooted in long years,
takes on a force that no one can control,
and he who in a mirror sees himself
is ever most deceived by what he sees.
Foretold by Malagigi, now had come
the time of sadness and of martyrdom.

Carlo believed 'twas in his interest   7
to push a man like Gano into deals
that, being hard and tedious, required
a master of hypocrisy and lies;
and yet our traitor wanted to be coaxed,
pretending that the trip demanded much
of one now old and in poor health as well—
so his excuse appeared quite reasonable.

He said, "Why don't you send now Milon's son   8
to deal with matters that relate to Spain?
Marsilius believes in him much more."
Ah, but he did not say what he had schemed:
that Count Orlando was a special thrush
not to catch quickly in a birdlimed web—
a captive not to let easily loose:
showing the owl, then, was part of his ruse.

Ganelon thought, "If I can catch this man,   9
Marsilius will have just what he wants
without resorting to another spear,
and will admit that this is his good chance."
Having seen Falserone also plot,
he well could tell an ear of wheat from its own beard:
amply relying, then, on his own fraud,
Carlo he begged to send the count instead,

saying to him, "Marsilius already   10
knows that Orlando cannot be too glad
about this deal: 'twas he who conquered Spain
and killed both Serpentìn and Ferraù.
I'll tell you the whole truth: if I were you
I'd send him, and would think no more of it.
I know you know what's on my mind; then send him,
or we'll have later some misunderstanding."

And as he left he said to Count Orlando,   11
"I'm sure one of these days my lord will send you
a lovely race horse, for on my departure
he had already promised that to me."
And so for many a day the cursèd traitor
with Falserone traveled on his horse,
his bow and his small club ever at hand;
and how he wished to talk you'll understand.

Falseron asked him more than once how well   12
he knew the count and also the marquis;
but when he thought he had him in his trap,
the fog came down, and wind and air he caught,
for Gano wished to bring to Saragossa
all of his plans, and every time said, "What?"
thus from the Arno jumping into the Bacchillòn;
and he who did the asking was quite a simpleton.

But Falseron a simpleton was not: 13
he understood that Ganelon's intention
was to speak only to Marsilius,
and was still machinating God knows what;
therefore, he deemed it wise no more to talk,
seeing the sorb was not yet ripe to fall:
of Oliver's reply he'd made a note,
sensing the kiss of that Iscariot.

He wrote to King Marsilius at once,   14
to let him know Maganza's lord was coming,
bearing the olive and the palm, to him;
that he should dine and wine him more than ever,
thus hoping to extract his inmost thoughts:
yes, he had reasons to believe he could
if he just went about it prudently;
he would explain the rest personally.

As soon as King Marsilius heard the news—   15
that treacherous Gan was being sent to him—
to honor him, he called his pagan chiefs
and bade his court be ready for the feast.
Crossing another hill, another plain,
to Saragossa Ganelon was close;
in person, then, Marsilius came down
with everybody following the crown.

Full fifteen miles out of the city came   16
Marsilius to meet our Ganelon,
with all his men, instructed to dismount,
as soon as he was sighted, from their steeds.
He ordered many jousts and tournaments,
and even practiced Cicero a bit.
So down he came as soon as Gan was seen;
but Gano was the fox that he had always been,

and said, "O King Marsilius, oh, please!   17
I won't allow my noble lord to honor
a humble servant who can but obey."
Down from his horse dismounted he with speed
and at Marsilius's feet most humbly knelt;
but the king said, "Your emperor has sent you:
so of your kneeling I do not approve."
They hugged each other with sincerest love.

Soon every baron, as instructed, knelt   18
and then hugged Ganelon most joyously.
When all of them were back up on their steeds,
Marsilius removed his cloak, with many
falcons embroidered on it, and right then
put it on Gano's shoulders with his hands—
an open gesture of magnificence
that signified his great benevolence.

Questions he asked of him along the way: 19
"How's Carlo? How's Duke Namo? Oliver?
And how is my beloved Count Orlando?
So here is Gano, whom I love so dearly,
and here's your Bianciardino!" As he rode,
with every word he tried to set a trap.
The traitor winked with sudden radiance
and hugged his Bianciardino more than once.

When they all came close to the city's door,
the noble queen and many damsels, too,
who had come out to meet him, welcomed him
most warmly, from their steeds dismounting all.
And Mister Know-It-All, our Gano, said,
"So many stars have fallen from the sky,
or here are all the nymphs of fair Diana."
The queen inquired, "How is Gallerana?"

20

Count Ganelon replied, "O mighty queen,
our Gallerana has this message for you:
although she is now a Parisienne,
never has she forgotten her own land,
and maybe unexpectedly someday
in Saragossa you will see her here;
indeed, all birds their enemy detest,
and long to see their native, ancient nest.

21

"This ring she bade me give you as I left,
but she herself will bring you greater gifts."
Promptly the noble queen replied to him,
"Our Gallerana will certainly do her best
to see her brother and her fatherland;
her brother—this I know—will die content.
This ring will be most cherished in my home—
so will the man I have received it from."

22

In all of Saragossa balls were held,
with games and mime shows, country dance, and fireworks,
with men who could outrun the fastest horse,
and with buffoons and clowns in pirouettes;
the dames from windowsills and balconies
threw white and yellow blooms upon their knights,
and every Moorish urchin more than once
shouted, "Montjoie! Saint Denis! Charles! and France!"

23

It truly seemed that day that Furius
had to his worthy town come back at last,
for everybody ran outdoors to watch,
and with palm branches nearly paved the streets.
Ah, pretty soon this town will sorely grieve
with all these citizens who seem today so blest,
and call bad Ganelon their savior, thinking
that in his hand their hoped-for peace he's bringing.

24

King Bianciardino's palace was not far 25
from King Marsilius' most lofty court;
'twas there the king and all his Saracens
escorted Ganelon: it was his hope
that that old devil, very good at tempting,
might soon tempt Gan, who was himself temptation:
so thieves with thieves forever meet and err,
since a new devil tempts now Lucifer.

The following day, the king convened the council, 26
and had a chair brought up next to his own,
the right and left side of them both conjoined,
as a clear token of equality.
Gano was led to it 'mid great applause,
and everyone had come to hear the man—
th' ambassador from France who there had brought
tidings of peace—so everybody thought.

So King Marsilius and Gan were seated, 27
and there were Falseron and Balugant,
with Bianciardino near them, Gallerana
and Arcaliffa and some admirals.
After he looked at all that pagan throng,
the traitor, who knew malice in and out,
turning to King Marsilius, bowed, and then
his very noble speech thus he began:

"May that true God Who, after making nature, 28
gave first of all to the angelic legions
motion and measure, form and place, and then
in the Damascus Plain made our first father,
who thus was not created a mere creature
(and therefore our first mother damned us all),
save and maintain the fair and worthy banner
of King Marsilius in great, sovereign honor!

"My lord and master's high and mighty crown 29
has sent me, famous Saracen, to you
to sign the peace and give you back your Spain
as with your Bianciardino was agreed.
Let your land be therefore beneath your flag.
To you he swears, by Pepin's sacred bones,
that he, as much as you, wants only this—
a true and final, everlasting peace.

"But since you Saracens descend from Sarah,
  who did not heed the law of your Mahound,
  as our respective Bibles clearly teach,
  he wants you to have jurisdiction here—
  to rule, that is, to punish and command—
  but there is now no reason anymore
  why you should all remain still unbaptized
  and thus continue to offend our Christ.

"And since our Count Orlando had been promised
  that he would be crowned monarch of this land,
  know, then, that he has been the very first
  (to me he opened all his heart and soul)
  to ask me to assure you it is you
  he wants as king; forget, then, that he swore
  to the marquis he would not take Alda the Fair
  along, unless as queen the throne with him she'll share.

"Therefore, Marsilius, do not regret
  having once nourished here King Charlemagnet,
  who well remembers—as indeed he should—
  how much in this your court you honored him,
  and is so sad for having fought against you;
  he keeps repeating, "We have both grown old
  with dignity, and time has gone so fast!"
  and is convinced that all was for the best.

"Marsilius, from any point you wish,
  I'll prove that Charles still loves and holds you dear,
  not only for your help, so timely now,
  but also for the reason I have mentioned—
  that like a son you raised him at your court.
  And even if you should victorious be
  out of this battle between France and Spain,
  he'd understand, with his own loss, your gain.

"Instead, you on both sides will amply gain—
  experience, I mean. Our emperor
  in all the ancient writings is well versed,
  and Alcuin, the founder of his study,
  lectures on every discipline and art.
  Therefore, I'll quote a sentence of my own—
  no fame is reached without travail and sweat,
  for human virtues are not separate.

30

31

32

33

34

"This is the reason Scipio advised   35
    that Carthage be forever kept alive,
    so that his Rome would have opposing force
    on land as well as perils on the sea,
    to let no man in idleness remain
    should one like Hannibal arise anew:
    idleness tames all virtues, he knew well,
    and 'twas through idleness Rome later fell.

"I'm saying that your fight or rivalry   36
    with Charles has made you both most worthy men:
    a man by fighting and by living learns,
    and honor, kingdom, glory thus he earns.
    Therefore, your greatness is so dear to him,
    for it is part and parcel of his plan:
    peace to the realm of France—it is quite clear—
    is more convenient than use of the spear.

"And since our Falseron had said to us   37
    that you already had arrayed your men
    for war, as soon as of Antea you heard,
    and why you then refrained from using them,
    everyone understood about the Dane.
    Carlo is thanking now Your Majesty,
    and offers to you, if the need there be,
    the help of France, Brittany, and Burgundy.

"From England, Flanders, with their mighty worth,   38
    the paladins and Carlo's entire court,
    and my Maganza's military power,
    and me—as two souls living in one body—
    alliance, peace, friendship, and brotherhood
    which only death may sever or annul!
    Alter alterius onera portando,
    is also the one wish of Count Orlando."

Ganelon said so many other things   39
    that kept all those who listened to him spellbound.
    He seemed Demosthenes come back to earth
    as he narrated all the wars and feuds
    and the first cause and roots of all of them.
    His entire speech was later written down,
    and he was praised as one who with such vein
    had dipped his tongue into the monarch's brain.

He even taught Marsilius religion,   40
saying, "One thing alone you're lacking now
so as to keep your soul from going down
into that hell where Malabranca lives:
you must acknowledge the True Father and His Son."
(Look what an outdoor demagogue he was!)
"For if you should confess the Gospel that is true,
you would be happy here, and then in heaven, too."

The traitor was an artist in all things,   41
and even cared to be believed a saint.
Marsilius, as he touched upon that subject,
seemed very clearly sensible, and said,
"Let every man interpret his own charts,"
for Gano's words and thoughts he knew quite well.
His answer was magnanimous and sane,
regarding Charles and peace and his own Spain.

And then he improvised this little tale: 42
"Near Saragossa, in a forest deep—
judging from what I heard once in Toledo,
where necromancers seem to congregate—
there is a cavern, narrow at its mouth,
but soon becoming very wide below:
six mighty columns there can still be seen,
watched over by kind ghosts of various mien.

"They say that the first column is of gold;   43
of silver, copper, iron are three more;
another is of pure and simple tin;
the last is—if I am correct—of lead.
I for some time did not believe those men,
for with my mind I like to reach the truth;
yet friends I sent to probe that precipice;
when they returned, to me they all said this:

"'These columns signify the six religions: 44
the one of gold is just the first of them;
according to their quality, the others
diminish by degrees, are less esteemed.
Here are the magic letters written down,
which are imprinted on each human soul,
which must in turn choose in this cave its faith
before into man's flesh it comes as breath.

"The spirits that protect this very place   45
  beg every human soul that passes near;
  like random birds, men's souls go flitting by
  and seek the one that kindles their desire;
  little they know, so simple and so pure,
  yet they are driven by their own free will:
  the one they choose is their religion called;
  blessèd are those who choose the one of gold!

"I speak in parables to those who hear,   46
  and I know well you are that Gan of old
  with whom I cannot barter white for black,
  for it is hard to mistake figs for dates.
  But above all, I'm kindled by true love,
  for a true friend I now can see again,
  and him I thank who sent you here to me—
  I know not whether Charles or God's decree."

After their conversation ended, and   47
  all the important Saracens departed,
  and after Gano, well escorted, reached
  King Bianciardino's fair, palatial home,
  Marsilius in the garden the next day
  ordered a banquet of great elegance.
  Gano attended, and that cloak he wore
  which he had gotten just the day before.

But in his mind a thought was restlessly   48
  at work—a bitter, dark, and gloomy thought,
  which said, "What shall I do? Must I withdraw?
  The more I think of this my sin, the graver
  it seems to me; and yet the day is near."
  But poison had already filled his soul,
  and once the limit of His mercy's crossed,
  friendship with God is absolutely lost.

O cursèd company, O place accursed,   49
  where such a boundless evil was conceived!
  So came the food and feast and tournament
  that such a solemn banquet brought along—
  and all that I could say would little be.
  Our murderous and cruel traitor seemed—
  though deep within tormented by his wrong—
  the happiest of people all day long.

Marsilius had learned from Falseron   50
what Gan had said and done along the road,
and that he could not make much of his words,
except that he had clearly understood
that he was hesitant, and seemed confused,
and did not want to bare his inmost thoughts,
but wished only to say at last to him
whatever in his mind was still so dim.

Bianciardin, most familiar with Gan,   51
had tried whatever instruments he had
to see what plaque had formed around his tooth
in order to extract it, but in vain.
Marsilius, therefore, was still confused,
unable to interpret Gano's thoughts:
that there was strain and fraud he had no doubt;
he had to try, alone, to sound him out.

After so much delight of fun and dance,   52
and songs and games and fireworks in their style;
after a race of leopards, deer, and steeds
in honor of Maganza's welcome lord,
Marsilius, before the final dance,
wanted to see some servants in the hall;
feigning some tiredness, he began to yawn
and bade everyone walk out on the lawn.

Marsilius and Gan were all alone;   53
so, turning to him with a happy face,
the monarch took him by the hand and said,
"You know the adage, dear ambassador:
'At morning it is good to see a mountain,
and it is good at eve to see a fountain.'"
It was already now late afternoon;
so toward a fountain both of them went soon.

They sat and looked around a bit; then Gano   54
much praised that fountain which he liked so well,
the whole place being utterly surrounded
with fruit trees, and the water cool and clear
(ah, but it could not quench the savage fire
that kindled so much evil in his heart!).
'Twas then, as an old friend, Marsilius started
talking with Gan of all the days departed.

He reminisced about young Charlemagnet, 55
how Gallerana fell in love with him
while he was at his court—a lovely lad,
so nimble and so handsome, wise and dear;
and how he grew aware that in the hearts
of those two youthful lovers Aetna burned,
and how, out of sheer kindness, he did not
disclose the truth by which he was distraught.

He thought he had been raising in his home— 56
like Zambugeri, his own flesh and blood—
another son, another part of him,
for willingly he held him in his court,
where in great honor he remained awhile,
favored and feasted in a thousand ways;
but, ah, as soon as he was king of France,
he turned against him his uplifted lance.

He spoke about the battles of the past, 57
and with great caution mentioned every wrong
he had received from Carlo; then he said,
"I feel secure, confiding now in you."
Though skillful and well pondered, every word
disclosed a rancor gnawing at his heart
as he recalled the ancient time he should
have reaped great love, and not ingratitude.

Three times he had seized Spain away from him, 58
and wanted Count Orlando to be king;
and he narrated to Maganza's sire
(Maganza's liar, rather) every wrong.
To ascertain Marsilius's complaint,
down on the fountain's water Gano looked,
but he, unlike Narcissus, wished to gaze
not at himself but at Marsilius's face.

Gano appeared so pensive at this point 59
that, hoping once again, Marsilius
hoisted his sail according to the wind
and quickly changed the rhythm of his dance:
he told him that his valor was not dead,
and might and money were still his to use,
and with Orlando dead, how glad he'd be
to prove to Charles his wrongs and treachery.

Most cautiously he said all this to Gan   60
to see what trap was being set for him
by that horrendous and most wicked traitor
who seemed to care but little for King Charles;
but as the king touched on that subject, Gano
needed no more to be cajoled or coaxed:
lest someone's hand his tail should grab and break,
he lifted up his head—the evil snake.

This final conversation was the key   61
that, sweetly turning, with a thousand ruses
could ultimately open Gano's heart.
Many a time the traitor sighed, like one
who wishes to reveal some grievous thing;
he said then, "O you tempter wise and sly,
who sit, to know my faults, right at my back!
We are, I see, two foxes in one sack.

"You'd like to see Orlando dead (*amen!*),   62
and also Oliver; you know about the slap
he gave me right at court, and that I bear
its imprint on my face and in my heart;
how Falseron has tried along the road
to make me talk, and Bianciardin has here
played the same tune: you lodged me in his palace
to have me tempted to reveal some malice.

"And most profusely Falseron in France   63
embraced Orlando, thus forgiving him
even the slaying of his Ferraù
(whether it was lip service I know not,
for well I know how shrewd you all can be);
and countless times he all his cunning used,
trying his best to bring Orlando here, and this is
the reason why he smothered him with kisses.

"But he's a clever ant that will not leave its hole   64
at any sound of hammer or of ax,
and, sire, you could still await your crow,
though well aware how bad a bird it is.
He's full of rancor and such bitterness,
never would he come here to Saragossa:
he feels the anguish of the Spanish sting,
for of this land he wanted to be king.

"But what if I should bring the count to Roncesvalles?   65
  For silver coins, like Judas, I ask not,
  but these are things that need much pondering,
  and not once—countless times—have to be weighed:
  this is too heavy a load on this my back.
  Mine is no treason—it is only vengeance:
  Oliver's sign is still upon my cheek.
  Hate legalizes everything we seek."

When King Marsilius saw that Ganelon   66
  was on the right track, heeding vestiges,
  he thought the time had come for the main sail
  and now to use the Latin oars no more.
  He called on Bianciardin and Falseron,
  using a garden's secret exit, and
  would soon return where Gan, the wicked count,
  was waiting for him, seated at the fount.

Because he kept no secrets from those two,   67
  he told them what he had just heard from Gano,
  how he had opened heart and soul to him,
  and at such news the two were overjoyed.
  Ah, traitor, wicked and perfidious man,
  with no more fear of God or of His law!
  Gano said, "Christ, I've so offended you,
  You will forgive me the last thing I do.

"I think the place where this my soul will go   68
  has been decreed already, and no way
  can it avoid or shun its written doom.
  Oliver has so often hurt my name,
  I do not care whether I live or die
  if first I do not give him what I must;
  and if no more I drag this shame behind,
  the world I'll roam, a happy man, though blind."

Gano was born a traitor, and therefore   69
  predestined more than the Iscariot;
  but let no man hurt man without the fear
  of vengeance, and recall the adage well;
  for, driven by despair, he feels so sure
  as to dare say, "If fickle fortune now
  tangles and spoils my plan, what's so peculiar?
  I'll die—so what? A fly dies in Apulia."

Ganelon had devised this treason then—   70
that Count Orlando come to Roncesvalles
in order to receive a gift as token
of what would then a lasting tribute be;
at Piè di Porto Charlemagne should wait,
where peace was to be made and ratified:
Marsilius would go there personally
and genuflect before His Majesty.

He had to feign he wished to kiss his feet,   71
and make a true and lasting peace with him;
seeing his dear Charlemagnet again,
like Simeon he'd say to him, "O Lord,
now take my soul, if it so pleases You,"
with all the other things that in the meantime
were to be weighed, digested, part by part,
with endless caution and most subtle art.

Orlando, then, should come to Roncesvalles   72
and meet with King Marsilius at once;
their ancient hatred would appear forgotten,
and he would soon accept his tribute then—
Fray Alberigo's last and bitter fruit.
But just as Gano mentioned such details,
the throne where King Marsilius was seated fell,
and, oh, the reason why no one would see or tell.

What Heaven wants is not a miracle.   73
Many a portent at that moment came:
at once up in the sky the sun grew dim,
and dark clouds, impregnated with much rain,
began to thunder, just as Jupiter
is wont to do when his disdain is high;
and wrathful wind and hail and storm appeared
all of a sudden. God! It was so weird!

While everybody in great terror stood,   74
a lightning bolt just very near them fell:
it struck the summit of a laurel tree,
burned it, and severed it down to its roots.
O holy Phoebus, why did you allow
that golden leafage to be struck like that?
Does, then, your laurel lose its privilege,
which used to seem so green at every age?

Marsilius said, "Mahound, what can this mean? 75
Surely there is a meaning in all this.
O Bianciardino, I can tell you now
that this is a bad omen for our realm."
A massive earthquake at this moment came
and made both hemispheres suddenly tremble:
with panic Falseron visibly shook,
and Bianciardin too happy did not look.

Terror had frozen each and every one. 76
Right at this moment over all of them
a flash appeared that looked like real fire,
and all the fountain's water overbrimmed
and, turning soon vermilion, spurted out,
burning whatever it would fall upon,
until the grasses all around were burned
by all the boiling waves that now to blood had turned.

Above the fountain rose a carob tree 77
(the tree that for his hanging Judas picked)
that, oozing and perspiring now with blood,
terrified Gano more than other things;
then suddenly its twigs and trunk dried up,
losing its leafage and its former shape;
and then a carob fell on Gano's head
that made his gray hair stand on end in dread.

The beasts that roamed in the surrounding park 78
among themselves began to howl and roar;
then, fighting snout to snout, all of them clashed
against each other with unheard-of wrath.
Watching those things, for a long time the king
and all the others stood perplexed and awed,
and no one seemed to know what else to do,
so much God's anger threatened them anew.

But though these portents in the garden were 79
before their eyes, they were not seen at all
by other courtly knights or citizens—
which made Marsilius frightened all the more.
Then, when this awful storm came to an end
and everyone was still confused and stunned,
Bianciardin words of comfort tried to say,
interpreting the signs in his own way.

With all his art and skill he tried to prove   80
that those weird apparitions signified
the conflagration and the fast collapse
and all the blood the Christians were to shed.
But Gan's interpretation differed much:
all of those meanings he dismissed as vain,
and through the night until the coming dawn,
his mind by diverse things was preyed upon.

With common sense his reason battled hard,   81
but in the end his wicked nature won.
On the next morning King Marsilius,
greatly perturbed and in great agitation,
for all the sages of Toledo sent:
wasting no time, they all to him should come.
On this he did not trust his Bianciardin,
whose text and clause had most discordant been.

To Saragossa all those sages came   82
to give that matter their respected views—
astrologers, magicians, necromancers,
interpreters, diviners—all of them
(and they were many) valiant and well known.
Marsilius narrated everything:
the truth, he ordered, they to him should tell,
as to Nebuchadnezzar Daniel.

So all those experts quickly were convened,   83
and after a long dispute, they agreed
that all that blood and all those things could be
interpreted by Carlo and his knights
against Marsilius and his pagan men;
concerning some particulars they were
in disagreement and in great confusion,
but in the end they reached the same conclusion:

the lightning that had hit the laurel tree   84
could be interpreted quite easily:
caesars and poets—never vulgar men—
were wont in ancient days to wear its crown;
therefore an empire was to be erased.
Then a wise elder in their very midst
said that the carob's case so strange he found,
only by Gano it could be unwound.

Hearing his own name mentioned terrified   85
Gano much more than the event itself:
I do not know if by coincidence,
as often it occurs, the old diviner
mentioned that name; or did he know Gan well?
Ganelon answered, "'Tis your business, man,
to give your explanation to the king—
unless you much prefer to lose your tongue."

Marsilius rebuked the necromancer   86
and gave them all permission to withdraw.
The general consensus was that they
should plan the treason with great diligence,
and that the nations of the pagan faith
should now prepare for war with all their might:
they in the meantime were in great turmoil
while still the Dane remained on Spanish soil.

Ganelon wrote to Charlemagne at once   87
how he had made things ready for the peace:
one thing was needed now—that Count Orlando
come with his fighting troops to Roncesvalles.
He wrote about the tribute and the rest,
reiterating the whole rigmarole;
to Piè di Porto he should come immediately,
where King Marsilius would welcome him worthily.

He wrote: "Marsilius is sending you   88
a present Jove himself would be proud of—
a precious crown, a garland shining bright
with a carbuncle never seen elsewhere,
which in the night from every angle shines
in dark and rainy weather; and with it,
a necklace, too, of many a precious stone,
for Gallerana both to wear and own.

"He's sending her a veil superbly spun   89
with gold and silk, which whitens in the fire:
because of this, they call it salamander
(about which several authors are quite wrong);
a very lengthy tusk of elephant,
a dragon's horn together with its claws,
two savage lions of such size and height
to frighten everybody with their sight;

"and for your park many a nimble leopard   90
   that with few leaps can overrun all beasts;
   tigers and apes and bisons of much strength,
   and crocodiles and panthers and giraffes;
   he's sending many steenboks, and then bows,
   quivers, and arrows of all kinds, and hoods
   and belts and many leather-strengthened cloaks,
   many Great Danes and families of hawks.

"After his camels were all loaded with   91
   the richest merchandise and various tools,
   with Barbary apes and also with baboons,
   Marsilius then filled a dromedary
   with countless bags of jewelry—a treasure
   not even Darius was known to have,
   which, to believe, you have to wait and see—
   and this will, then, your yearly tribute be.

"He's also sending you two spirit elves,   92
   Farès and Floro; you will talk to them
   right in a mirror where they're both consigned,
   and worthy things from Floro you will hear;
   also, one hundred all-white steeds, one hundred
   colts, all with saddles and with reins of gold
   for Count Orlando, and a caravan
   of drapes and tools and objects Syrian.

"To Oliver he's sending a rich gown,   93
   embroidered, all of it, with precious stones,
   and worth ten thousand serafs—even more.
   After the peace has been made known to all,
   in Saragossa there are feasts and fireworks,
   and now Granada's mighty lords and princes
   are coming here, Marsilius to revere,
   and "Peace!" and "Long live Charles!" they're shouting here.

"How I thank God, Who granted me the grace   94
   to see such happiness before I die!
   The place where you should come, which, as I said,
   is Piè di Porto of Saint John, to me
   seems the ideal site for what we need.
   But I shall be with you before you think;
   meanwhile your court with opulence adorn,
   and with a letter bid the Dane return."

This was the letter Charlemagne received,   95
and never was a happier man seen.
He showed it to his council in full session
and called his Gano a great diplomat.
But Namo did not join in his delight;
nor did the others, who, deep in their hearts,
thought that the net which Ganelon had cast
doubtless this time would hit rock bottom fast.

Tired of staying at the Paris court,   96
Orlando with the Duke of Burgundy
had gone to Gascony, where he was now.
Charles wrote to him that he should go at once
to Roncesvalles, where he was to meet
with King Marsilius, and accept his tribute:
he should discard all rancor and disdain,
and finally in his new kingdom reign.

And he enclosed the letter he'd received   97
from Gan, and on his very crown he swore
that—at the end of all those bitter fights,
now that Antea was back in Bambillona,
though with his blessings she had left French soil—
he gladly would have seized, personally,
Persia and Syria, Bambillona too,
to make him the sole ruler of it all;

and since he truly was champion of Christ,   98
he wanted him to watch over His Tomb,
which he had taken from the foes of Christ;
therefore, to Roncesvalles he now should go,
and, learning from th' humility of Christ,
before Marsilius he, too, should kneel
(see how, as usual, he was blind and wrong!)
and Count Anselmo he should take along.

This is that Count Anselmo known to all   99
as he who worked in Roncesvalles great wonders
before his happy soul flew back to God.
Orlando placed that letter in his hand.
Oliver was against this sudden march
but then, to follow Count Orlando, yielded:
his brother-in-law was he, after all,
and with him had replied to many a call.

And so Orlando left for Roncesvalles,
as ever to obey King Charlemagne.
Will Angel Raphael be with him there?
He should not leave him now: so maybe yes;
and maybe not. He will, more likely, take him,
with other angels, up to paradise,
where his most blessèd, justice-loving soul
will soon receive the martyr's aureole.

100

Emperor Charles replied to Ganelon
that, as advised, he had prepared all things:
on such a day, from Paris they would leave;
meanwhile, he praised his great diplomacy.
Now, when our traitor finished reading this,
his leave from King Marsilius he took
and, in so doing, waited for the hour
when, lo, the rose would ultimately flower.

101

Gan thought so highly of Orlando's might
that he believed his vanguard should comprise
at least one hundred thousand pagan men;
two hundred thousand more should follow next;
then twice as many men he would deploy
along the rear guard. He was sure of this—
that should they reach the third day of the fight,
they'd still be frightened by Orlando's sight.

102

He said, "Your Majesty, now hear me well!
This is one detail you must bear in mind—
fate has decreed since time's first origin
that on the third day, no one can withstand him,
and he makes havoc of all enemies;
this was confirmed by Carlo many times:
he was so fated, too, in Aspramont
under King Agolant and King Almont;

103

"Archangel Michael with his very hand
gave him the sword that's Durlindana called,
and dubbed him faithfully Cavalier of God,
lasting defender of the Christian faith
(though, much more sugary than honey, some
affirm it was Saint George or Fate Morgana).
Action has proved what I am telling you;
so something of this fable must be true.

104

"Orlando's one who would not be afraid   105
  of Mars himself, should he come down to fight,
  and on that day will as a god perform,
  for in his heart the soul of Caesar dwells.
  Even of Oliver we must take care,
  for I believe he will come down with him;
  and Count Anselmo, too, may join them there,
  and there's no better warrior anywhere.

"Therefore, you need six hundred thousand men—   106
  the very best your Spain can now provide;
  and let nobody tell you otherwise,
  or you will be defeated by the count.
  This is the time to think of countless things
  (this is by no means a vision or a dream):
  if we intend Orlando's men to seize,
  wine we must use, just as we do with bees.

"Therefore we'll send ahead many a camel   107
  loaded with casks of wine and bags of food:
  as soon as they warm up a little bit,
  they will come out victorious at first
  and cut some of your vanguard pagans down;
  then, from fierce lions, lambs they will become:
  they may still rout your second line of men,
  but not the third one; you will beat them then.

"But let them be in Roncesvalles on time   108
  before the Christians put their breastplates on:
  they must not give them time to arm themselves,
  and they'll digest, then, dates and raisins well;
  if all is done at the established time,
  they'll have no weapons yet—they'll be like kites:
  Orlando and his knights, of course, will do
  things that, when written, will be thought untrue."

Gano concluded, "One more thing I'll say.   109
  Baldwin, my son, I recommend to you:
  with all the other Christian knights he'll come,
  for with the count he always wants to be."
  Marsilius said, "Bring this my cape to him,
  and tell him it's my gift; but for my love
  he'll always wear it, and—the king so orders—
  in Roncesvalles still have it on his shoulders."

Treason was ready to be carried out.   110
On both the Bible and the Koran now
each of them made the other swear an oath,
and Ganelon from Saragossa left.
Marsilius had offered gold and silver,
but Gan did not put out his hand to get it—
a good deed on his part, his first and last:
blood money he refused! And then so fast

the traitor left and on his charger rode   111
that he reached Paris after a few days.
To the imperial court he went at once.
Carlo embraced him on the verge of tears,
such was the tenderness that filled his heart,
and Gano hugged, in turn, some men around:
he looked like one come on some holy mission,
and the whole court went mad with jubilation.

Think, my dear reader, how the traitor now   112
assembled all his lies and bagatelles—
serpents and mandrake roots and wooden boxes,
powders and paper bags and magic stunts—
and how each little sack he then untied!
He opened his tin can of treacle, too,
but did not show (so well he hid his trick!)
the toxic acids and the arsenic.

With Gallerana Gano chattered then   113
and told her how Queen Blanda hoped and prayed
to see her soon in Saragossa, and
therefore refrained from sending her more gifts.
But more and more he urged the emperor,
reminding him to think of his own honor,
and that he had to go with all his noblemen;
also, Orlando's case he then brought up again.

Carlo got down to business breathlessly,   114
instead of asking his Iscariot,
"*Ad quid venisti?*" Gan had brought the Gospels
(the holographs of the Evangelists),
and so he did not think of so much gall
until the day they told him, "*Dirupisti:*
Orlando's dead, his men are smoldering bones,
and your Belle France is but a heap of stones."

It was my thought to shorten up this story,   115
unable to foresee if our Rinaldo
might bring his help to Roncesvalles on time;
but from the sky an angel showed to me
Arnaldo's text (an author worth consulting),
saying, "Luigi, wait! Why all this haste?
Maybe Rinaldo will arrive on time."
His version, then, I'll follow in my rhyme.

How well I know that I must go on straight,   116
most careful the least falsehood to avoid,
because this story is a truthful one.
If I but take a single step awry,
they croak at me, rebuke and reprimand,
each of them showing his own foolish mind:
therefore, I now prefer to live alone,
far from the endless number of such men.

Gymnasium and Academy to me   117
have been my walks within my lovely woods,
where Africa and Asia I see well:
with all their little baskets come the nymphs,
bringing narcissi and all fragrant blooms.
And so the city's countless spites I shun,
and to your areopaguses I will
come back no more, O crowd so fond of speaking ill.

When Malagigi saw King Charlemagne   118
led by the nose by Gano, like an ox
along the traced-out furrow, in an outburst
of spiteful anger, he left Paris soon.
In Montalbàn he hastened to resort
to his old art, to know in what far land
Rinaldo and his brothers might be seen,
for with no news of them he long had been.

There is a spirit known as Astaroth—   119
a very wise yet fierce and savage one
that lives in the profoundest caves of hell:
he's far more black than any spirit elf.
This is the one Malgigi exorcised
one night. "Tell me the truth about Rinaldo,"
he said, "and then you'll know what you must do for me;
but stop, I tell you, staring at me so menacingly.

"If you do this for me, I promise you   120
   that never 'gainst your will shall I evoke you,
   and on my death I'll burn a book of mine
   that tells me how to call you from each place,
   and so you won't be captive anymore."
At this, the spirit, after some resistance,
   stared with a look that threatened but disaster
   to see if he could still defy his master;

but when he saw Malgigi frown with wrath   121
   and now about to use the magic ring
   that would have thrown him into some dark tomb,
   he wished no longer his last card to play,
   and said, "I am expecting your command."
And Malagigi asked, "To find Rinaldo
   and Ricciardetto, tell me where to go,
   and all about their actions let me know."

This demon so replied to him, "Rinaldo   122
   has gone to see the pyramids of Egypt,
   and if you want to know all he has done,
   so many are the things I must report
   that you will have no time to go to sleep."
Malgigi said, "The most important things,
   then, kindly tell me, and the others skip;
   but speak more loudly lest I fall asleep."

"Rinaldo was with Fuligatto," said   123
   Astaroth then, "and I've already told you
   what he had done until that very day.
   Guicciardo, Ricciardetto, and Alardo
   wanted to see the entire land of Greece,
   and later cross the Straits of Hellespont
   because they knew, from its great fame of old,
   about the lofty peak, Olympus called.

"For three full days upon their steeds they rode   124
   (the steepness of the climbing made them sweat),
   when on that mountain, as they slept one night,
   a phantom came and murdered Fuligat.
   Maybe they were so weary from the road
   that his hard breathing caused his blood to stop
   around the heart in such a poor condition,
   and so he could not end his expedition.

"Rinaldo buried him as best he could,
    and then resolved to climb up to the top;
    from there he saw so many clouds below,
    and clearly read the letters time had written
    and carved upon the sand so long before,
    not yet—it seemed—by wind or rain erased.
    But then, as he was coming down the mountain,
    a strange chimera found he near a fountain.

"He killed her, and this was a wondrous deed,
    for no one else had climbed so high before:
    that monster was so fierce, her very sight
    would in a flash have slain another man.
    Toward Cairo, then, he rode and, finally,
    toward Damascus. When he came to Jaffa,
    he wished to see the Sepulcher of Christ."
    (The devil did not mention the word "Christ"

but said, instead, "the Tomb of Calvary.")
    "Their horses they left there, and took, instead,
    either a camel or a dromedary
    because they wished to see Mount Sinai;
    but such a hostile wind began to blow,
    all of them ran the risk of dying there,
    floundering in that heavy sea of sand
    which with great labor crossed they in the end.

"They climbed Mount Sinai and then came down
    from where the mighty stream is seen to run;
    many another land they wished to see,
    even the place where Nimrod's tower rose.
    When they returned, back on their steeds again,
    they climbed Mount Tabor first, and on they went,
    through Indian lands, as far as Prester John,
    and there they combated more years than one,

"till not a single lord was left around
    who still refused to be baptized and yield
    to Thomas's faith. When in that place no more
    they wished to stay, Rinaldo finally
    went toward the regions of the setting sun
    and wanted mighty Atlas to surpass,
    minding no toil nor frost, eager to try—
    maybe—to snatch from off his back the sky.

125

126

127

128

129

"At last he saw the signs that Hercules 130
put down to warn all mariners against
sailing beyond; and many other things
he saw, through all those ports meandering,
and the more beautiful they were, the more
solaced and comforted he ever felt,
and above all, he praised Ulysses for
sailing beyond, a new world to explore.

"To Egypt then he finally went back, 131
where many provinces he soon baptized.
I think he is determined to return
to these your Christian cities nevermore.
I even know he wrote you more than once
(although his letters never were received)
that, had he had with him Orlando's hand,
half of the world would be at his command."

With great attention Malagigi heard, 132
for three full hours, all that the devil spoke,
until he said, "Enough! or I will fall asleep.
For this sole reason I have called you here:
that you go to Rinaldo right away,
and bring him, fast, along with Ricciardetto,
to Roncesvalles, where Count Orlando is;
I know you understand; then hurry, please!"

Astaroth said, "But me they will not trust." 133
Replied Malgigi, "Enter soon Baiardo:
on him Rinaldo and Ricciardo will
willingly jump (forget about Guicciardo
and also Alàrd; to Montalbàn they'll go).
But listen to me: do your best to spare
Rinaldo any ache along the way:
in Roncesvalles he must appear on the third day!

"And one more thing I now must say to you 134
(I'm baffled and bewildered by a thought
that keeps my mind befuddled even now):
you know that Carlo is in France no more;
tell me, then, what will happen on his journey
now that Orlando's been betrayed in Roncesvalles,
and Gan in Saragossa has discussed
his treason with the king, his pagan host."

Astaroth said, "The mystery's so dark,   135
I'd have to think about it the night through;
and still my judgment would imperfect be,
for heaven's avenues are closed to us.
We see the future as astrologers,
just as among you learned people do;
humans and beasts would both of life be stripped
if our demonic wings had not been clipped.

"Here I could quote you the Old Testament   136
and all that has occurred in the long past;
but there are things that do not reach our ears,
for the First only is omnipotent;
in Him, as in a mirror, everything—
future and past—is present endlessly:
He Who made all, knows all—and He alone;
and there are things to His own Son unknown.

"Therefore, unless I think, I cannot tell   137
what is about to happen to King Charles.
Spirits, believe me, fill this entire sky,
each one with an astrolabe in his hand,
a calculation and an almanac.
Heaven is menacing some weird events—
treason and blood and war and slaughter, because Mars
is in an angular position within Scorpio;

"and so that you may better understand,   138
Saturn is in ascendancy with them,
in such a great and potent revolution
that Turnus's battles did not see the like.
This sign forbodes the massacre of men
and the most dreadful things that ever were,
with states and lofty kingdoms changed and shaken;
and never were—or are—these signs mistaken.

"I wonder if you have, these past few days,   139
seen those two comets passing through the sky—
Veru and Dominus Ascone called.
Treason and wars and feuds they signify,
and death of princes and of potentates:
never before have they been proven wrong.
Judging by what I hear and see, 'tis clear
that what I say, and worse, will soon be here.

"What Gano has discussed with King Marsilius   140
I do not know; my mind was not with them.
But he's the traitor he has always been:
may I be spared the toil of finding out.
I know there is a seat awaiting him,
and if I heard the truth about his life,
for all eternity his wicked soul
will soon bemoan its sinfulness in hell."

Malgigi answered, "You have said a phrase   141
that keeps my mind in great confusion still—
the Son, that is, does not know everything.
I fail to understand so dark a speech."
Said Astaroth, "You have not read the Bible,
and do not seem familiar with it:
questioned about the Final Day, the Son
replied that only to His Father it was known.

"Now, Malagigi, listen well to me,   142
if my solution you still care to know,
and then your theologians go and ask.
'Three persons in one essence,' so you say—
that is, 'one substance'; and we demons say,
'a pure and simple act without commixtion';
this of necessity must be, therefore,
the One that here on earth you all adore—

"a mover whence all other motion starts,   143
an order whereby every order's made,
a cause that other causes antecedes,
a power whence all other power comes,
a fire that gives life to every glow,
and a beginning of beginnings new,
a knowledge to all knowledge uppermost,
a good by which all other goods are caused:

"this is that Father and that ancient Sire   144
Who made all things, and all things therefore knows;
the order that I mentioned cannot change,
or you would see both heaven and earth collapse.
Now, since I'm not, as long ago, his friend,
I can no longer in that mirror see
where maybe now your worries are also evident;
though of the future I was always ignorant.

"If Lucifer had known the future, he   145
would not have had so much presumption, and
would not have fallen to the center down—
he who was eager on the winds to sit;
but he had not—could not—have seen all things,
and our damnation was its consequence;
and since he was the very first to sin,
he was the first Judecca swallowed in.

"And we would not have tempted all those men   146
who now enjoy Heaven's beatitude,
but, as I have already said, we all
have our minds covered with a darkening veil;
nor would have Satan, as your Gospel says,
tempted the mighty Saintest of All Saints
by bringing Him up to a pinnacle
where He acknowledged, then, His miracle.

"And since He with perfection does all things,   147
and circumscribed and preordained all things,
and all He made is ever present to Him
insofar as with justice it was made,
this Lord cannot regret what He has made;
and if somebody speaks of any change,
falsehood, I say, is here for truth mistaken,
for the first order still remains unshaken."

"But tell me something else," said Malagigi,   148
"(a rather learned angel you must be):
if that Prime Mover everyone adores
already knew your downfall, deep in Him,
and saw as present both its time and instant,
then His decree appears to be unjust,
and there is no more mercy in creation
if being born already means damnation,

"and if we are predestined to sin and imperfection;   149
but now you say that He's so good and just,
and yet we cannot change from what we are:
it seems to me that God is surely partial
to all those angels who up there remained,
and could distinguish truth from ill and falsehood,
and, knowing not what end was to ensue,
refused to follow Lucifer, like you."

Furious like a devil, Astaroth   150
replied, "That just and holy Sabaoth
did not love Michael more than Lucifer,
nor did He create Cain less good than Abel.
If one of them is more than Nimrod proud,
and one the opposite of Gabriel,
if they do not repent, and both exclaim 'Osanna,'
it is free will that dooms, ultimately, either one—

"just as it was free will that damned us all.   151
And, being merciful, for a long time—
and not to make our ugliness much greater—
until our end of penance, patiently
He bore with us, who can no more be brought
back to His grace, having been justly doomed;
and His foreknowledge did not take away our time,
His grace to do good deeds having come e'er on time.

"Just are the Father and the Son, and just   152
the Word; His justice and great mercy are one,
just as the malice and the sin of men
were just as great ingratitude and pride.
Our thankless soul does not repent because
that which has its beginning from the will,
having discovered truth, first, on its own,
and by none tempted, never was condoned.

"Your Adam did not know his own first sin: 153
therefore his failing was forgiven soon,
the serpent having tempted him: but still,
his disobedience, in itself, hurt God;
that is why out of Eden he was thrown,
although the grace of penance he was granted,
and with it, too, forgiveness of his sin,
and mercy's ointment, ever his to win.

"But the angelic nature, now corrupt,   154
cannot be sound and perfect anymore,
and, having sinned as conscious nature, feels—
this is the very reason—great despair.
For if that Sage refused to answer Pilate,
who wanted to know from him what truth is,
it was because he had it right in front,
and so his ignorance was soon condoned.

"Unfortunately, he did not persevere   155
   in his good actions when he washed his hands.
   Judas himself would not be damned today,
   for he repented; but he had lost hope,
   and with no hope no man can e'er be saved;
   nor does Origen's sentence save him yet;
   and may no other theory elude us:
   in diebus illis salvabitur Iudas.

"So, an omniscient First in heaven dwells,   156
   by Whom all things were made, and Who is not
   unjust when He creates and when He damns,
   but made all things with justice and in truth;
   future and past are ever present to Him,
   for, as I mentioned, by necessity
   all things He made before that Mover stand,
   whence all informing virtues then descend.

"And now that, as my master, you have forced me   157
   to tell the cause of all my misery,
   you'd also like to know the reason why
   He even bothered making us at first,
   knowing that He would damn us in the end.
   Well, then, this is a rubric known only
   to that most joyful Ruler of the Sky;
   I know it not, and so I won't reply.

"This I have said, oh, not to make you doubt,   158
   but only for the reason that I see
   mankind enwrapped in error round this subject,
   eager to know (and nothing at all they know)
   not only where the Danube comes from—also the Nile.
   Let this suffice: all things were justly made
   by that most just and truthful Lord above,
   as in each sentence psalms and psalmist prove.

"Poets, philosophers, and theologians   159
   do not know well what I am telling you,
   yet mortal man's presumption wants to know
   about the hierarchies and their state.
   I was among the highest seraphim,
   and did not know what had been said down here
   by Dionysius and Gregory: no man
   heaven from earth should dare presume to scan.

"About this subject, above all, you must   160
   never believe what spirit elves suggest;
   nothing but lies they tell you, and succeed
   only in filling with new doubts your mind,
   hurting much more than bringing you new shame.
   Such elves, as you should know, cannot be caught
   in water or in mirrors: in the air
   they live, and falsehood and deceit they bear.

"Later, among themselves they ever boast   161
   that they can make the non-existent seem:
   some of them take delight in duping men,
   some take their pleasure in philosophizing,
   some in revealing hidden treasure chests,
   and some in telling lies about the future;
   so now you know a notebook dear to me:
   even in hell there's kindness, as you see."

"Enough of this," now Malagigi said;   162
"but tell me what Marsilius is doing."
   Said Astaroth, "I'll tell you right away.
   In Saragossa he has called a meeting
   of the whole populace: I clearly see
   many great armies and a massive fleet;
   he looks quite cheerful and allows no man
   around him to suspect his secret plan."

"Could you now tell me any word at all   163
   'tween Falserone and King Bianciardin?"
   Astaroth answered, "Let this one suffice—
   that I suspect a treason going on."
"Enough, enough!" said Malagigi; "Fly,
   and, wasting no more time, Rinaldo find;
   bring him to Roncesvalles with Ricciardetto,
   as I have said to you—the sooner the better."

The devil said, "Ricciardo has with him,   164
   as far as I can see, a lovely steed
   which he received from the Greek emperor
   and does not want to leave to anyone;
   so if I take him on Baiardo's back,
   this charger could not follow him, and thus
   would cause some problem to us. But for you—
   to serve you better—this is what I'll do.

"I will tell Rubicante in your name—   165
or maybe Farferello—that he must
take Ricciardetto to the eastern land
where there's a man they're trying to baptize.
You are a necromancer of such fame
that, just to please you, with no book or ring,
most willingly Beelzebub, our prince,
would come on earth from the infernal dens."

"If he's not forced by oath," Malgigi said,   166
"this spirit, to deceive and spite me, may
throw Ricciardetto down into a stream:
Astaroth, tell me, now, if I should trust him."
"Be not suspicious!" answered Astaroth.
"There is no need for magic art this time;
remember this: a man with common sense
uses against himself no violence.

"Yes, you could throw him into some dark tomb;   167
but you won't have to, for he thinks of you
highly, and loves you, such is your great fame
down there amongst us; see? it's good to have
friends and renown all over." He left fast,
like a stone hurled and whistling in the air
or, better yet, a lightning bolt in the blue;
and the earth trembled when away he flew.

Let Astaroth now fly up in the air,   168
for our Rinaldo he will find tonight.
Our story is so varied and adorned
that I cannot stay always in one place;
and please discard contrasting theories,
for there's much beauty in Arnaldo's text:
he makes you touch the truth of the whole matter,
and the least falsehood never does he utter.

And here I wish to thank dear Angiolino,   169
without whose help I would have toiled in vain—
a cherub I should say, or seraphim,
Montepulciano's glory and renown;
'twas he enlightened me on Charlemagne
by pointing out Arnald and Alcuin:
deep in a wood I was, unknown to me,
but now the rightful path I clearly see.

Rinaldo by all means had to be called,   170
or there was no salvation for King Charles:
had he been not enabled by his might
to hold on and prolong the savage fight,
with all his flags Marsilius would have come
and finally besieged Port of Saint John,
where Carlo had descended to abide,
and maybe Ganelon would not have died.

Astolfo, Sansonet, and Berlinghier,   171
together with the Dane, had come from Spain.
At Piè di Porto, Charlemagne they found
and spoke about Marsilius at length:
how he had feasted Ganelon so much
as to arouse suspicion in their minds;
the banquet in the park they mentioned, too,
and everybody said all that they knew.

But Carlo did not change his mind, and so   172
Astolfo, Sansonet, and Berlinghier
left him: they still could see his Ganelon
forever at his side and at his ear.
The traitor, who his wicked trade knew well,
wanted his own son, Baldwin, to go with them,
but sin and guilt to tinsel and conceal:
tell me if this was not a fox's deal!

On his son's shoulders, as he left, he placed   173
the cape Marsilius had given him,
saying, "Let this be now your uniform—
the gift of a most worthy, valiant man,
and wear it—promise me—in war and peace.
My greetings to Orlando and his troops,
and tell the count to do Marsilius honor,
for this is what will please our emperor."

Now King Marsilius with all his men   174
was marching, Count Orlando soon to meet.
Boastingly, each of them along the road
threatened that he would shortly kill the foe.
And one Arlotto from the Syrian land
said, "King Marsilius, I swear to you
that I will bring you soon Oliver's head:
you know how much that man I hate and dread."

Falseron also swore to kill the count—   175
that Count Orlando who had killed his son:
the traitor had forgotten that in France,
with tears of joy, he had embraced him warmly.
Marsilius, who longed for fame and honor,
arrayed his troops exactly in the order
devised by Ganelon: he very well
remembered each suggestion, each detail.

The vanguard line—one hundred thousand men—   176
was under the command of Falseron,
and, being the good strategist that he was,
with them a row of satraps he displayed—
all men of noble status and great worth;
he also placed there, inconspicuously,
a monarch of great bravery and fame—
that King Arlotto I've already named;

Turchion, Fidasso, and black Finadust,   177
who was seven feet tall and always bore
a very fierce and strong and ruthless club
that broke whichever arm was in its way:
one cemetery a day was not enough,
so many were the men killed by his wrath;
Maldue of Frasse and King Malprimo, too,
among this vanguard squadron were in view.

Of this Malducco I'm not fully sure,   178
for Turpin places him in the third army;
this I must say to silence all those men
eager to blame me for a straw they find,
and make me thus the butt of ridicule.
But in King Bianciardino's throng were placed
two hundred thousand horsemen armed for war
by King Marsilius, and maybe more.

There also was a king from Portugal,   179
King Chiariello, King Margheriton,
Balsamin, Fieramonte, King Fiorello,
Buiafort, and the great King Syrion,
and in one squadron many other lords,
far more than those whom Ilium had seen.
King Balugante led the rear guard throng
with all the others following along.

Let Turpin be my witness once again: 180
in the third army were three hundred thousand men.
The Arcàlif was there with King Grandonio,
bearing, just like a whip, a boundless club
with certain balls; like a black demon, he
whirled his great club, and never seemed to joke:
whoever saw him with no helmet on,
"This man," he said, "blasphemes and makes all people run."

To Roncesvalles Orlando had come down   181
with the brigade that he had always led:
he was awaiting now Marsilius and his tribute—
the wretched tribute he was soon to have.
The Christian camp was carefree everywhere,
with people scattered and all over free.
Even Orlando often, for delight,
with Sansonetto strolled, just to enjoy the sight.

Son of the Sultan, Sansonetto was   182
of Count Orlando very fond indeed:
he had become a Christian for his love
the day the noble count to Mecca came,
and then had followed him through mounts and plains,
oft to the very Sultan's great surprise.
But Oliver alone felt ill at ease
and urged the camp to arm in all that peace.

Already King Marsilius had sent   183
camels with wine and ample food ahead;
King Bianciardino had arrived with them
exactly on the day before the battle,
and spoken soon of peace to Count Orlando,
informing him about the latest things,
and begging him to take Marsilius as friend,
to put, once and for all, to their old hate an end.

Using some wicked ruses of his own,   184
he told him, then, he had to go to Charles;
instead, just like the Magi, he changed route
and to his King Marsilius went back,
to tell about Orlando and his camp—
that he was lodged with scarcity of guards,
and therefore unprotected were all tents
and things around: there was not even a fence.

Marsilius delivered a fine speech,   185
the night before, to all his camping troops.
Thus he began: "May god Mahound be praised!
His name I ever honor, call, exalt.
Before we start our battle with the Christians,
it is my duty to reveal the reason
why I have brought these armies to this fort;
much I would like to say, but time is running short.

"Everyone knows how long my war has been   186
with Charlemagne and all his Christian knights:
old and gray-haired in the meantime I grew,
and pagan blood was in abundance shed.
But on the field not even once was I
able Count Orlando to confront:
I would not have to face now the long plight
about to start, with victory or defeat.

"Three times, as you all know, he roused against me   187
my entire Spain and part of Aragon:
of all my kingdom, Saragossa's left.
Now he would also like to wear the crown
of all my realms as well as of Granada;
but he has come to Roncesvalles at last,
and I believe Mahound has sent him here—
and may his faith protect us all from fear.

"Seeing my own destruction overhead,   188
I pleaded soon for peace, and sent to France
King Bianciardino and then Falseron;
but God, I know, did not approve of it.
The answer Carlo sent through Ganelon
was, as you know, most arrogant and proud:
from Pagandom he wanted to save Spain,
and those who are baptized baptize again.

"To one who asked him whether, *iusiurando,*   189
it is legitimate to break an oath—
a solemn promise made—Caesar replied:
'Only to hold a throne or for revenge.'
Then with no scruples I betray Orlando,
exactly as the little widow did—
the one who killed by treason and, one night,
brought Holophernes' head by lantern light.

"I do not know if any of you recalls   190
the miracle that happened at the Mec
and brought the anger of our God on us:
'twas, I believe, in May—the first *alec*—
when in the air a lively flash appeared,
which soon was heard to say *'Salamalec'*;
the Holy Ark then sweaated blood: if this
was not a truly mighty sign, what is?

"Now here I am, not knowing what to do,   191
since our Mahound in heaven is so cross
as to allow our things to worsen yet;
so narrow is the space now left to me
that I have hardly room to place the throne
that once above all others was revered,
and well I know that both the Ark and this my throne
will be—I am convinced—seized by the Christians soon.

"Through many a foreign land I led you all,   192
through countless wanderings and toils and woes;
we all have come into this world to die,
but here you are to honor these last years,
and reap in heaven your immense reward,
for our Mahound rewards his Moslem well
and has in store for all his faithful men
fountains and streams of milk and honey. Then,

"dear soldiers, if once more you prove to be   193
the brave that I have known for a long time,
this is the day of your great victory.
Instead, Orlando will receive his tribute
in blood: he is awaiting it—you know—
in Roncesvalles, as if we were his slaves.
But if still sharp all of our swords are now,
to us all Christianity will bow.

"We shall seize France as well as Burgundy,   194
England, and Flanders, and then Brittany,
Normandy and Navarre and Gascony,
Piccardy and Provence and Germany.
I for myself will take just what I need—
my ancient and most celebrated throne;
kingdoms and empires, yours the rest shall be,
for I am nothing if you're not with me.

"Then I will send King Bianciardin to Rome   195
  to order the great Pope to come right here
  to Saragossa, lest his head be cut;
  if not, I'll go with all my banners there,
  right to Saint Peter's altar ('tis its name),
  and, to reveal how greater my might is,
  and that Mahound is the true prophet, there
  I'll feed my horses, to his great despair.

"So then, put on your helmets, all of you,   196
  brandish your spears and follow your own flags.
  Have I forgotten anything? Oh, yes:
  during the fight look carefully around,
  and do your best to spot my royal cape
  worn by a brave and very valiant lad:
  of all the Christian knights, spare him alone,
  for that young man, I say, is Gano's son."

As soon as he concluded his great speech,   197
  the king instructed all his officers
  and mounted each upon his horse. At once
  all pagan banners, raised aloft, appeared.
  The vanguard troops were led by Falseron,
  and all his men were fully armed for war:
  on all his banners Belfagor was sealed,
  utterly black within a grayish field.

King Bianciardin was in the second army,   198
  which occupied a mountain all around,
  for he had brought with him from all of Spain
  a multitude of fighting Saracens;
  on his rich, mighty flag, entirely blue,
  now waving in the wind, was Apollin
  (there is, about this, many a variant,
  and someone says that it was Trevigant).

Next, Balugant commanded the third army: 199
  upon his steed like a new Mars he looked.
  Many an admiral was also there,
  and King Marsilius was one of them:
  his banner was in front of everyone
  with a Mahound painted on it, with
  two golden wings in a vermilion field.
  In such a way the pagans were arrayed.

Now I must leave Marsilius, already   200
marching with all his men on Roncesvalles,
for Astaroth had his wings, too, and had
somewhere in Egypt our Rinaldo found:
he needed no eyeglasses, after all,
to read Malgigi's written indications.
Rinaldo asked who such a man could be,
who traveled all that road so speedily.

After he saw him right in front of him,   201
despite the sternness of his fixed glance,
he smiled and said, "Oh, welcome, welcome here!"
And soon he called Guicciardo and Alardo
and asked if they had guessed who that man was.
But Farferel, quite inconsiderate,
in such a terrifying shape appeared,
all of a sudden all those present feared.

Ricciardo was not there; he was away,   202
viewing a certain pyramid which showed
a ring of gold, purposely build by Chemmis,
through which the entire firmament was seen.
Those built by Mucerin, Armeus, and Amasus
he found less beautiful and less imposing;
the first, built by twelve satraps, seemed to him
ugly, and also altogether grim.

But when Rinaldo told him everything,   203
how glad he was to see the count again!
And so they all agreed on what to do:
Guicciardo and Alardo on their steeds,
through different lands, should go to Montalbàn.
And then Rinaldo questioned Astaroth,
"Now tell me, Astaroth: would it be possible
to make this journey utterly invisible?"

Said Astaroth, "Of course! Wait till I send   204
someone as far as Ethiopia:
a spirit will come back with a small herb
that, like the heliotrope, can do just that.
You only have to wear it on yourself
and it will do the rest, as nature bids.
When reason and all science fail, then let
every wise person on experience bet."

And then a certain squire he addressed,   205
saying, "Milusse, go and find this herb!"
Rinaldo looked but could not see the one
that he had spoken to, and grew afraid.
Astaroth said, "I understand your silence:
I would not call if no one were around.
Well, then, a thousand demons are around me,
who, ever faithful, night and day surround me."

Rinaldo said, "Then in the devil's claws,   206
alas, I am! But here we are: what now?"
Astaroth answered, "Devil that you are,
along the road they'll be good friends of yours;
some lavish banquet you will see each day,
and ever find an inn with great supplies,
where you yourself will order wine and meat:
better than acorns I will make you eat.

"A prince and leader down in hell we have,   207
like you on earth; Beelzebub is first.
Some of us do one thing, and some another,
and everybody to his task attends;
but 'tis Beelzebub commands us all,
for Lucifer, the very last of us,
is ever in the lowest pit immersed
because up there he wanted to be first.

"And if you care to know the truth right now,   208
even on oath trust no one of us ever,
because our nature is inimical
to yours by dint of envy and disdain.
Because of you I came right here to toil—
I, once a seraph, worthier than you;
as Malagigi wished, I must behave,
and as you see, I serve him like a slave.

"But since I know you'll make a slaughterhouse   209
in Roncesvalles, I'll carry you with pleasure;
and Farferel will carry Ricciardetto.
I'm sure I'll see too many people dead
and blood all over in great torrents run;
you know full well the wretched find some solace
in seeing others wretched equally:
so out of Egypt I will take you willingly."

Milùs returned and brought with him the herb,   210
which he gave to Rinaldo in a pouch,
saying, "It comes from the Antipodes."
"Give it to Ricciardetto," Astaroth said.
Rinaldo looked but could not see his friend.
"The truth," he said, "you told me, Astaroth;
so let us go!" Upon Baiardo he jumped,
who from now on will seem more brave and prompt.

When good Baiardo felt the devil in him   211
(for he had lodged that tenant once before),
he understood at once how things were going,
and like a dragon he began to blow;
the other horse, too, neighing, pawing, jumping,
was eagermost to go, and with much wrath
he and the devil Astaroth leapt out,
both ignorant at once of any gout.

After they left the pyramids, they had   212
to cross the long and ample marsh of Moeris;
there Astaroth to our Rinaldo said,
"What do you want me now to do?" "Just jump!"
Rinaldo answered. Astaroth did that.
But Ricciardetto shut his eyes, afraid
to see how high his horse would leap and dash.
Well, with one leap they crossed the mighty marsh.

After he entered Libya, trotting still,   213
he reached the stream—maybe a swamp or lake—
which is Tritonia after Triton called,
and farther on, past Carthage, to the right,
he reached the river called Mejerdah, where
Atilius had killed that snake or dragon,
the fame of which is still as it has been—
of how he sent to Rome the serpent's skin.

But shall we let Rinaldo still ride on   214
without a stop for breakfast in the midst
of all this trotting and despite the haste?
Of course not: it would not be right at all.
Astaroth said, "Let's all dismount right here!
And pitch a tent that we may all call home!"
Rinaldo said, "Let's have something to drink
and eat first; then we'll go as well as sing."

At this, upon a meadow soon appeared—   215
look—a pavilion gleaming like true gold,
and since they were not joking all of them,
dinner they ordered, wasting no more time.
Tables were set at once, and all around them
waiters began to serve, so neatly dressed,
with such respectful bows, so many a "please,"
they all resembled nuptial maître d's.

Some brought them napkins for their necks, and others   216
brought orange-scented water for their hands.
As soon as they were seated, a small dish
of warblers and fat ortolans was served.
In ancient days, you see, the ortolan
existed even far from Tuscany!
We do not think so now, and envy not, therefore,
Jove's nectar and ambrosia anymore;

for the mere mention of an ortolan   217
still makes th' inhabitants of Prato gloat;
that's why one day Pastor Arlotto said
that on this subject he had pondered much,
knowing there was some mystery beneath,
till he discovered what it was at last—
that is, to Magdalene Christ wanted to appear
disguised as *ortolano* of good cheer.

So many firsts and seconds, then, were brought,   218
never was a more solemn banquet seen.
Down in their stomachs everything they stored—
even a peacock served with its own feathers.
Barley and hay was given to the steeds.
Laughing uproariously, Rinaldo said,
"These are true miracles, it seems to me:
let's build six tabernacles here, not three!"

And Ricciardetto said, "It seems to me,   219
brother, that we have found our greatest inn:
besides a good innkeeper, we have here
the greatest dishes and the daintiest wines."
Astaroth was around, with Farferel,
both with an apron on: as if they were
th' innkeeper, they seemed sweetly to be pleasing:
"I beg your pardon, sir: anything missing?"

Rinaldo said, "Innkeeper, wait a minute: 220
who cares if all these dishes come from hell?
I only wanted but to eat and drink:
if of myself I fail to take good care,
I won't be trotting as indeed I should."
In other words, they had the greatest meal.
They asked their host from where he had obtained
all they had eaten to their hearts' content.

The devil said to them, "This breakfast and   221
all that up to this moment you've been served
has been prepared by King Marsilius;
when you're in Roncesvalles you'll understand;
your waiters, too, would like to be informed.
In the meantime, if you prefer to taste
your emperor's most special beef or roast,
just order it and I'll oblige as host."

"Let us resume our journey right away,"   222
Rinaldo said, "for very much, indeed,
I long to see my cousin once again.
Everything has been great, dear Astaroth."
But as the knight was speaking, not a trace
of that pavilion or those men was left,
and so they mounted each upon his horse;
the day had passed the middle of its course.

Because of recent downpours, the Mejerdah,   223
a river of importance, into seven
branches had swollen, spreading through the land,
until it looked now like an ample sea.
There Ricciardetto to Rinaldo said,
"For our digestion this one spot is best."
Rinaldo answered, "We must go ahead."
"Let's jump and go then," Ricciardetto said.

And then Rinaldo, "O my kind Baiardo,   224
never were you ashamed of your performance,
but now I know how better you will be.
O Astaroth, we have now to proceed
by leaps and bounds as nimble leopards do,
and write new wonders that will read like lies."
Said Astaroth, "Rinaldo, fear no wrong:
just hold on to your saddle and be strong!"

Baiardo was by nature fierce and proud: 225
even if Astaroth had not been in him,
he would have leapt and with no fear at all
trodden the air like a light-floating bird.
While still on solid ground, just like a crane
or any other bird, he started rising,
galloping; closely, then, began to trot,
and went and went, and lame he sure was not.

Say, reader: did you ever see a fish   226
leap in the sea to shun a waiting net?
This horse did just the same, but higher went,
saying, "Phaëthon's chariot went lower,"
and, before touching ground once more, believed
that he had reached the sources of the blue.
Juno herself, I say, was fearful most,
thinking her reign and scepter nearly lost.

After they crossed the above-named Mejerdah,   227
they reached Gibraltar's Strait, where long ago
the Grecian hero set his solid marks—
Calpe and Abila—to warn all men
(not on account of cliffs or hostile wind,
but for the fact that the earth's globe declines)
that those are wrong who sail beyond, and go
down to the bottom of the world below.

Rinaldo, then, who recognized the place   228
that he had seen with his own eyes before,
asked Astaroth, "But can you tell me why
he thought of planting such a landmark here?"
Astaroth answered, "A long, feeble tale,
which many centuries could not correct,
calls such a place 'Hercules' Pillars' still,
where many a man has perished 'gainst his will.

"Listen to me: that old belief is wrong,   229
for it is possible to sail beyond;
the water's flat and level everywhere,
although our earth is shaped just like a wheel.
Mankind was in those days so ignorant,
Hercules of himself should be ashamed
for having set his ancient pillars there;
yonder our ships shall definitely fare.

"The other hemisphere can, yes, be reached,   230
    because all things to their own center fall:
    thus through a divine mystery the earth
    sublimely hangs among all other stars,
    and castles, towns, and reigns are on that shore;
    but those old people to all this were blind.
    Look how the sun would like to speed from here
    down to the other waiting hemisphere!

"As soon as in the East a sign is high,   231
    with wondrous art another falls right down,
    just as in this our western world we see,
    because the sky divides with justice all.
    Antipodes those people there are called;
    the sun they worship, Jupiter and Mars;
    and they have beasts and forests just as you,
    and 'gainst each other mighty battles do."

Rinaldo said, "Since we have come to this,   232
    one more thing tell me, Astaroth, I beg you:
    if these men, too, from Adam's race descend,
    can they, who only futile things adore,
    attain salvation as we Christians do?"
    Astaroth answered, "Tempt me now no more:
    I can no longer tell you what I scan,
    and you ask questions like a stupid man.

"Why should your Redeemer have been so partial   233
    to this one speck of the whole universe
    as to create your Adam here for you
    and have Himself for your love crucified?
    Through the Cross everybody has been saved,
    and maybe, after a long error, you
    will the same truth in unity adore,
    and mercy thus obtain forevermore.

"One thing is necessary—that your faith   234
    be solid, and the Virgin up in heaven
    be glorified. The door is always open—
    remember this—until it will be shut
    on Judgment Day; if what you offer comes
    from a pure heart, it will be welcome most,
    for Heaven cherishes obedience,
    observance of the law, fear, reverence.

"So long as the old Romans reverently   235
    kept their devoted rituals alive,
    despite the fact they worshiped Jupiter
    and Mars and all the other futile gods,
    Heaven was not displeased by their religion,
    which differentiated beasts from men,
    and made them for some time rise high and shine,
    whereas the lack of it meant their decline.

"In other words, those people who adore   236
    the planets think that they adore the best;
    and justice, as you know, remunerates
    the good and gives the bad their punishment:
    so those who honestly observe their laws
    should not despair of reaping their reward.
    You're either saved or damned by your own thought,
    if too much ignorance deceives you not.

"Remember that some ignorance is too   237
    obtuse and gross and lazy, bad and slow,
    if, keeping the door shut onto your sight,
    it makes the soul and all its vision vain;
    this is the kind that God cannot forgive:
    'Noluit intelligere' the psalmist says
    of one who is so foolish and so blind
    that, not to do what's good, keeps closed his mind.

"Those who observe their own religious laws   238
    can all obtain redemption, as we read
    of all our Patriarchs to Limbo sent:
    for nothing was without a reason made
    by the First Father Who over all reigns:
    therefore He did not without people make
    that world where downward go those starlit rings,
    planets and signs and many lovely things.

"That hemisphere was not at random made,   239
    nor does the sun endure such toil in vain,
    from sunset on to sunset, night and day:
    the highest Jove would not so care for it
    if there were only empty lands down there.
    Also remember: the angelic nature—
    since deeper into this you like to enter—
    from that part down was doomed to the earth's center.

"The true religion is the Christian faith,   240
    and holy, just, well-founded is its law;
    your doctors are quite clear about all this,
    and so is what the Holy Scripture sings;
    the pagans, then, and the perfidious Jews,
    unless the heavenly grace cloaks all of them,
    with all their laws are in damnation's clutch—
    their Talmud and their Koran and all such.

"You know how loudly all the prophets spoke   241
    about the Virgin and the high Emmanuel,
    and how they all are silent from the time
    the Holy Word became just one with him;
    and many Sibyls, and your poets, too,
    bespoke the beauty of the future age;
    read *Eritrea,* where of Jesus it is said
    that on a manger's hay he would be laid.

"And if in false belief some foolish men   242
    await a different Messiah still,
    while still acknowledging His miracles—
    how He told Lazarus 'Come forth!' and healed
    the deaf and dumb, the blind, the paralyzed
    (which cannot be denied)—they do not know
    that He delivered every creature born
    by virtue of the Tetragrammaton.

"No more have you to argue with the Jews   243
    about Elijah and Elisha; if,
    regarding this, he had announced a lie—
    that is, that He alone was the Messiah
    sent by the Father, who desires truth,
    being Himself the life and truth and way,
    He would not, as a liar, have the might
    to make the wondrous things He brought to light.

"For all the words that I have said to you,   244
    maybe Malgigi takes me now to task,
    but many things are to the Son unknown
    because of the new nature He took on—
    of His humanity, I mean to say.
    But when His divine nature is conjoined,
    only the Highest Mind can all things know,
    things being present *ab initio.*"

Rinaldo said, "Come now! Let's find Orlando!   245
You have just told me there is war down there,
and so I want to reach all of those lands
and cross this sea where Hercules was wrong,
for one must always learn while living still.
We now should cross Gibraltar, I believe;
but briefly let me down from this my horse."
Dismounted he, and started this brief prayer:

"Lord, if it is your will that I must fare   246
to Roncesvalles, have mercy now on me,
borne by your enemies to bring my aid
to Count Orlando and your holy faith!
Remember that you opened once the sea
ahead of Moses, all your men to save:
breathe into me what I don't understand, oh:
in manus tuas me valde commendo."

Baiardo, as he came upon the shore,   247
seemed altogether rutilant with fire:
he jumped and started riding in the air;
not even crickets jump and leap so high.
Signs of the cross were not appropriate,
for these are signs the demon could not bear.
Powerful Heav'n! If this is your decree,
no wonder they can leap over this sea!

Ricciardo shuddered with new sudden fear,   248
seeing himself so high so suddenly
upon his Farferel now in the shade;
he was afraid, for he could see the sun
beneath, as if he were 'tween sun and sky:
he at this moment thinks of Icarus,
who trusted, ah, too much his waxen wings;
and with great effort to his saddle clings.

Much with that leap Rinaldo would have liked   249
to go as far as the sun's shining hair,
but he could not, for higher he was now,
and down beneath the sea the sun was falling.
Baiardo, finally on the ground again,
showed all his vigor wondrously untamed:
as though he had not jumped or climbed at all,
upon the earth he like a cat could fall.

To Farferello Ricciardetto said,
down on the other shore, "I must confess
that I have not been a good bird this time:
the sun no longer looked the same to me
when I could see myself fly over it—
maybe I was too near the Zodiac.
Well, I have jumped so high, I do believe
I'll boast of no more jumpings while I live."

250

'Twas at this moment Ricciardetto's horse
was heard to neigh as if he meant to laugh,
because that devil greatly was amused
by the man's phrases of discouragement,
and therefore said to him, "Your guide is good;
so, Ricciardetto, have no fear at all!"
Rinaldo said, "Let's make a deal: let's be
in Roncesvalles with one leap, instantly!"

251

Ricciardo answered, "Wait a minute now!
Be careful, Farferel, as you go on.
Whether this game ends well or badly, you
could not care less, and then would laugh at us.
I am still speechless from my recent fear
and am all over trembling, so much so
I think that these my clothes are upside down
and I'm still falling 'mong the fish to drown."

252

It was just the beginning of the night
when our wayfarers beyond Calpe went.
They soon reached Spanish Baetica, and then,
with every plainland, every mountain crossed,
till, following Granada's coast, they found
themselves in total darkness, just like moles.
They surely could have used a wink of sleep,
but it was prudent wide awake to keep.

253

So in a moment at the Baetis River
they all arrived, near ancient Cordova,
where—poets and historians maintain—
was born, with Avicenna, even that
Averroës, who Aristotle's inmost
secrets possessed, and the great comment made.
But such a leap was to both steeds, I bet,
just like a little step of minuet.

254

They were determined now to jump, and so   255
we too shall jump over the Guadian land,
over another river still to cross—
known as the Anas in the ancient times—
where they could see the city of Cazlona,
a pagan town of great importance then;
and next they jumped over the Tagus, too,
close to Toledo, when the day was new.

Reader, what will you say? Right in Toledo   256
a necromancer had by chance invoked
that spirit with the name of Rubicant,
who somewhere down in Egypt had remained
to tempt a certain lord or admiral;
commanded by his master to reveal
all that Marsilius was doing, he
said many things about him readily.

As he was talking to his master still,   257
he saw Rinaldo and Ricciardo pass
outside the city and, because he knew
where they were going, wanted this to add:
"Marsilius sad tidings will receive,
so sad, indeed, that for his realm I fear:
someone is passing, while I speak to you,
who's the best knight the world today can view.

"His gentle brother I can see with him,   258
named Ricciardetto; and the two are borne
by Astaroth and Farferello, both
obeying Malagigi's one command.
Rinaldo is the knight I'm speaking of,
to Roncesvalles now going at great speed:
he'll give the pagans so much death and sorrow
that hell will triumph mightily tomorrow."

Toledo was a town where necromancy   259
was studied even in a public school,
where there were lectures on the magic art,
and pyromancy publicly was taught.
Many a geomancer gathered there,
and hydromancy was experimented
with other great stupidities and lies,
such as witchcraft and flickering of eyes.

That necromancer said, "But are you sure
this paladin's the Lord of Montalbàn?
If he's the one, there's nothing can be done."
The spirit said, "He's crossing now the plain,
for those two devils are in their two steeds,
and go from place to new and stranger place
flying like a lightning flash, it seems to me:
in Roncesvalles tomorrow they will be."

260

The master said, "Are you in any way
aware of any obstacle that may
impede their trip or bring them some delay?"
Rubicant answered, "I can only guess
that both their horses will in a short while
be seized with thirst upon a certain pass,
where they will be compelled to cross a mountain
on top of which they'll find at last a fountain.

261

"There I believe they'll stop awhile to rest,
and, being very famished, they will soon
be looking for something to eat and drink.
This I may do—convince them it is time
to let their horses drink; and if they drink,
you'll nearly see them then proceed on foot,
and they won't be in Roncesvalles on time,
the battle starting with the morning's prime.

262

"One day, the saint Galicia venerates
happened to come and at this fountain stop
utterly out of breath (as they will be);
he rested there and washed and cooled his brow.
Not knowing who he was, a goatherd, who
upon that mountain watched over his goats,
said to him, "Pilgrim, yours was a bad trip
if from this fountain you have had a sip.

263

"Whoever drinks here—let me tell you this—
soon by a devil he becomes possessed:
so, if you drank, you have him now in you."
The saint replied, "I give you now my word
that you are wrong and cannot guess the truth,
for I will make the opposite be true:
all the possessed who happen to drink here
will see their demons quickly disappear;

264

"so to your cave go back, you beast, and stay!"   265
    and Heaven then he thanked not once but twice.
    I'll quickly send a friend of mine up there
    before they come and reach the mountain's top—
    Squarciafer is this clever spirit's name.
    We'll see if they will be such stupid fools
    as to be duped by how he's dressed and what he'll tell.
"It surely pays to try," you know the proverb well.

    The necromancer answered, "Close the stitch,   266
    and think that everyone can be as shrewd:
    this Astaroth, for one, knows the whole tale
    about the fount and the Galician saint;
    be careful not to fall into a trap,
    for there is wickedness galore up there:
    grater and grater do not trust each other,
    and so a different cheese would be much better."

"What Astaroth or Farferel may do   267
    or say, I do not know," Rubicant answered;
"but often you believe still closed a latch
    you have not tried to open with much force
    when, in reality, the bolt's not nailed:
    so if the rubric you refuse to read,
    your lack of diligence must pay for it:
    the stitch is lost if you forget its knot.

"One is the thing that tilts the balance here: 268
    if this Rinaldo goes to Roncesvalles,
    many a pagan in one day will die,
    and there will be a mighty feast in hell
    (down there, most likely, all of them will go),
    and to Beelzebub, not to be blamed,
    this Astaroth has much to answer for,
    having to pay for wicked deeds of yore.

"You have just heard the truth of everything;   269
    so to my business let me now attend,
    for I cannot explain his thought to you:
    his will already knows how things will be.
    But, look, a gentle messenger is here;
    let me remind you—time is running out."
    And there (to shorten this our tale a bit)
    was Squarciaferro, whom they wished to meet.

"Very well, then, dear Squarciaferro! Here   270
all of your cunning you must promptly use,"
the master said, "and tell some lie as well.
I can reward you in a thousand ways.
I know you know what this my heart wants most,
so I don't have to tell you what I told;
yet there is something more I'll say to you—
a friend I'll be, forever good and true."

Rinaldo had already reached the peak,   271
and both their horses now were breathing hard;
just at this time the messenger appeared
next to the fountain, and you could have sworn
he was a pilgrim, holy and devout,
wearing his staff, emaciated most,
bearded, and mumbling his *Our Fathers*. Brother
Wolf's hide he wore, but like a meek lamb he seemed rather.

Next to the fountain he was seen to sit,   272
mumbling and whispering and sighing still
as if he had just finished Miserere
or had from Vespers only then come back.
And he was heard to say, "Be welcome, sir!
I must remind you, in the name of God,
to slake your thirst do not go farther, for
you won't find other fountains anymore.

"This water is the best in the whole world,   273
and never hurts a human soul or beast;
these horses look so thirsty, both of them:
stop here awhile, and here refresh yourselves!"
And so our Brother Clever Simpleton
walked to the stream as if to start a prayer,
and, like a happy duckling splashing it,
whistled and lured the steeds to drink a bit.

Enjoy now, reader, what I'm going to say: 274
it would be good to have, where'er we went,
according to our means and needs a friend,
for we know not where we may chance to be.
This hermit looked so old and innocent,
Rinaldo would have blindly trusted him,
the more so, for he thought 'twas holiness
that made him see him in his human dress,

he being, as I said, invisible;   275
let me remind you, then, my listener,
that Astaroth was not obliged to tell
Rinaldo anything about all this;
and may nobody who has reached the peak
of his good fortune so self-centered be
as to reduce himself to the extreme:
he should, instead, all men and things esteem.

We all know, more or less, where we were born,   276
but do not know where we are bound to die.
Happy are they who died in swaddling clothes,
considering the woes they could have had!
How many men are fed, then killed, by hope!
How many vessels between stream and sea
have till now perished, as the Poet wrote,
although by flame or iron virtue is not hurt!

Lost in a forest, one may save oneself   277
thanks to one little match or little tinder;
and often, too, a begging, poor old man—
if sorry for your plight—can save your life.
Being a devil, Astaroth therefore
could have allowed Baiàrd to go for his cool drink;
but since he liked Rinaldo very much,
that water soon he told him not to touch,

saying, "O Squarciaferro, never mind!   278
You do not have to splash the water so,
for you know well I know how shrewd you are;
and Malagigi, who your shrewdness reads,
will surely bind your tail to some old tree.
But if you want to come to Roncesvalles,
come, then, with me: we'll see some mighty snow;
if not, back to your silly master go,

and tell him I was wicked back in heaven;   279
let him imagine, then, how I improved in hell!
He thought I was so stupid and naive
as to believe that his deceit would work.
And you, too, thought that your disguise would fool me,
and that Baiardo would your whistle heed:
rascal and rascal share an equal right.
So come in person to observe this fight!"

Rinaldo stopped upon his horse at once   280
when, most perturbed, he heard all of those words.
He from the fountain was one foot away,
and said, "Now tell me what you mean by this,
O Astaroth; this time I'm full of doubt,
and understand no book or commentary;
and since I am aware in both I err,
I'd like to know who is this Squarciafer."

Astaroth said, "Are you confessing all?   281
Well, then, he is a holy hermit come
here to remind you, as you well can see,
about your thirst; and his so pious garb
surely is not our tailors' artifact."
Rinaldo looked at him from head to toes
and said to him, "You're one of us, sweet brother.
Who would not love you, hearing your *Our Father?*"

After he knew the things he wished to know,   282
he said, "O Astaroth, you are my friend,
and therefore I to you am grateful most,
and in all truth can this affirm and say:
if ever such a grace should granted be
that God Himself would change His old decree,
His judgment and His sentence and His law,
I'll hold your benefit in grateful awe.

"I cannot offer more than this right now;   283
my soul belongs to Him Who gave it to me,
and well you know the rest is bound to die.
O highest love! Ultimate courtesy!"
(As you can see now, everyone may take
this phrase as being a Petrarchan line;
instead it was Rinaldo said it first;
and may all those who do not steal be cursed.)

Astaroth said, "I value your good will.   284
As far as we're concerned, the keys are lost:
grave is the sin when majesty is hurt.
O happy Christians, cleansed if you can say,
striking your chest and shedding but a tear,
'O Lord, my Lord, *tibi soli peccavi.*'
We sinned but once, and yet, as you can tell,
we all are relegated down in hell.

"Oh, if we could after a million and
    a thousand centuries behold again
    the least and faintest spark of that first Love,
    the load we bear would suddenly be light!
    But why are we still asking all these questions?
    If one cannot, one should not ask at all;
    this I can only tell you: be content
    if we discuss another argument."

"Now, holy father," said Rinaldo then,
    "you do not have to blush more than you should."
    Squarciafer answered, altogether shamed,
    "What would you do if I had duped you so?"
    Astaroth said, "Either Malgigi will,
    one of these coming days, pillory you,
    or else through Roncesvalles we all shall pass,
    and meet in hell soon after, all of us.

"And well I know you'll have to work too hard
    in view of all these paladins' great worth;
    if you're a Moor, a footman try to be,
    and next to Prince Rinaldo find yourself."
    Squarciafer answered, "You will see it soon,"
    and suddenly his hair became all black
    and curly, and his eyes with fire lit;
    and he became a pagan, bit by bit.

Looking upon Rinaldo, then he said,
"And now let's go! I am an Indian, not
    that fake and lying hermit that you said;
    we're even now," and so he shook his hand.
    At this, Rinaldo his Baiardo turned,
    and plains and mountains were one even thing:
    they rode and rode until the peep of day,
    till Saragossa shone along their way.

When Prince Rinaldo Saragossa saw,
    and the River Iber, he was much amazed
    that the whole journey had been shortened so;
    and he recalled his Luciana then
    (he wondered what she looked like at this time);
    but as he came upon that stream he said,
"Dear Astaroth, I beg you, since we're pretty
    close, I'd be very glad to cross the city,

285

286

287

288

289

"and see how strong it is from every side;   290
I hope you will say yes to my request.
I'm also begging you to tell me now
all that Queen Blanda's doing, all you know."
Astaroth said, "Her dinner's being served,
and if you now desire to dine with her,
there we can go and sit right at her table:
don't ask me if to triumph we'll be able."

"You've sharpened so my appetite and sight,"   291
Rinaldo said, "my hunger I can see,
and surely more than fennel stalks I need.
Also, we'll stay a little with the dames,
and rub our knees with theirs a little bit,
and maybe we shall hear some lovely tales
of Roncesvalles, and whisperings of treason."
Astaroth said, "You're right: 'tis a good reason."

As soon as they set foot in Saragossa,   292
they saw no animals nor living souls:
some Moorish children had been left behind,
and not a single witness was still there,
for King Marsilius had drafted all
to fight upon the field in Roncesvalles.
So they dismounted near the royal room,
and first they wanted their two steeds to groom.

Like a good servant, Farferello gave   293
barley and hay galore to the two steeds,
so that the footman to some helpers said,
"Say, who is he who's doing here so much?"
And they replied he was unknown to them.
But with his yellow and vermilion eyes
Farferel frowned upon him, causing fright
by brandishing a club of fearful height.

"Bagdad's arch-braggart—look—has come right here,"   294
he said, "to pay a visit to Madame.
But if I glue it to your back, this club
will make you speak a different tongue at once,"
and he was hesitant to do the rest,
thus leaving the poor footman in despair;
and, not to let a man out of his shell,
he brandished at the door his club quite well.

Rinaldo, Ricciardetto, and Astaroth,   295
in the meantime, appearèd in the room;
not seen nor heard, into the room they walked,
where a great gala was still going on—
was, rather, at its peak, with chattering
of people and with merriment of sound;
and, seated, Luciana could be seen,
beautiful still, beside the lofty queen.

Right at the table's end they all sat down.   296
Here came a dish, which Astaroth soon grabbed;
the one who brought it to a squire turned
and, blaming him for it, began to fight.
While they were quarreling in such a way,
the queen had raised a cup, about to drink:
close drew Ricciardo very quietly
and took it from her hand most daintily.

Meanwhile Rinaldo gulped everything down,   297
for himself snatching a good portion of
whate'er the chef was sending to the hall:
the waiters from whose hands the food was snatched
among themselves began to quarrel fast.
'Twas then Queen Blanda shouted angrily,
"What's happening? What happened to my cup?
Am I being waited on by madmen? Stop!"

Everyone to the queen apologized   298
till she herself was most amazed indeed.
Rinaldo did not want to waste his time
and kept on grabbing from Luciana's dish;
and Luciana somewhat seemed confused:
turning her baffled glance now left now right,
she sat, not knowing what to think or say,
seeing her portions vanish soon away.

The day before, they all had seen a wolf   299
enter the city, following a crowd—
which was believed to be foreboding ill,
for no wolf enters without cause a town;
even the queen, the night before, had dreamed
of a big lion ransacking her home:
she did not know yet, she was not aware,
Rinaldo's lion was already there.

And she had spoken of this dream of hers;   300
and, seeing now all those strange things around,
she was perplexed and deeply grieved, and said,
"'Tis a bad omen for our pagan troops;
I'm certain that a spirit elf has come—
since with Orlando they have come to blows—
to bring into this dining hall bad news."
And she was sad and even more confused.

But look at Squarciaferro! Just for fun   301
he through the dining room runs up and down,
tripping and making this and that one fall,
spilling things, breaking crystal cups and vases;
and poor Queen Blanda noticed everything
and saw new omens of adversity,
and, like her, all the paladins around her
by all those happenings were most confounded.

Rinaldo snatched a strange fruit, called banana,   302
out of the hands of a jester he disliked,
and forced it in his mouth to shut it up;
turning around, the ignorant buffoon
blamed Luciana and the queen for it,
but Ricciardetto placed upon his head
so nice a bump, the clown fell like a pear.
But suddenly a sneeze came from nowhere.

Tables were being cleared after the meal   303
when Ricciardetto, holding it no more,
let out his sneeze—and once and twice and thrice.
Nobody in the dining hall had sneezed,
but certainly a sneezing had been heard:
in great confusion 'neath their chairs they looked,
the entire room was emptied instantly,
and blessed were those who could the staircase see.

Rinaldo thought the time at last had come   304
to show himself to Luciana, now
just like the others running, but refrained
from doing so, lest he should frighten her.
Feeling by someone grabbed at once, she screamed
and wanted to get out, but she could not:
Rinaldo kissed her twice as Frenchmen do,
each time watering roses out of view.

Their horses now were ready for the ride,   305
and soon the footman was a Moor again.
Rinaldo and Ricciardo mounted them
and, after all that fun, began to move,
leaving those people in great terror still
and on each other trampling, last on first:
the royal palace—all of them agreed—
was surely full of demons—yes, indeed!

Along the road Rinaldo thought and said,   306
"My Luciana is still beautiful.
Astaroth, I remember the first day
I fell in love with her—I then was young—
having to Saragossa come by chance:
she for some time was my one shining star
and came as far as Persia, just for me,
with Balugant and full-armed cavalry.

"A rich pavilion she brought to me,   307
so fair that for her love I keep it still;
it is indeed a wondrous piece of art.
First, there is fire figured on one side;
the sky with every bird is on the other;
then on the earth all families of beasts,
and in the sea all fish; you know, of course,
that there are schools of them unknown to us."

Astaroth answered, "This pavilion   308
I see so well as if it were right here,
for neither wall nor mountain can impede
our sight: a spirit truly is a mind
that sees all things on which it turns its will;
you've wandered through the East and through the West:
and so my mental eye can ascertain
the very things you're seeing now again.

"But you have said one can behold on it   309
all animals of both the earth and sky:
not true: some of the most important ones
are missing, which your hemisphere contains:
so with your glasses look at it anew.
But with no glasses Astaroth can tell you
that this pavilion is in Montalbàn,
right in your room—and it's a pretty one."

Rinaldo said, "With such sweet nettle-sting,   310
dear Astaroth, you've pricked this heart of mine
that I want you to tell me what mistakes
my Luciana made about this work;
and I will add what's missing for her love,
for I still feel my ancient flame in me.
Speaking of lovely things makes one forget
the bumpy road, and shortens it, I bet."

Astaroth said, "There are in Libya   311
many beasts never seen by human eyes,
and one of them is amphisbaena called:
backward and forward all these serpents crawl,
with their backs growing right between two heads;
others have in their mouths three rows of teeth—
they are the manticores with human mien;
and horned and wingèd pegasi are seen:

"Pegasus's Fountain after them is named.   312
Another one is called rhinoceros,
which uses in its fight its nose's horn
and to the elephant is mortal foe:
so if by any chance the two should meet,
I can assure you, one of them must die;
there is the *rufium* with spotted back,
and the *crocuta,* then, half-wolf, half-dog.

"*Leucrocuta* is another beast: 313
he has a deer's back and a lion's neck
and breast and tail and most voracious mouth,
which he can open wide up to his ears;
often he imitates the human voice
whenever fraud or malice tells him so;
axis another animal is called,
with spots of white, most horrible and bold.

"And there's a serpent known as *catoblepe,*   314
which, being lazy, with its head and mouth
moves on the ground, and glides with all the rest:
it dries up crops and grass and all it touches,
and from its breath such venomous heat exhales,
it makes the hardest boulder crack and burst;
with its horrendous look it kills a man,
but is, in turn, by a small weasel slain.

"There's the ichneumon, very little known,   315
    who fights the asp and makes his armor strong
    by plunging and replunging into mud;
    when he perceives the crocodile asleep,
    who naturally keeps his mouth wide open,
    at the right moment into it he flies
    as into an empty vase, and so he's then
    into sleep tickled by a little wren.

"Known as the *eale,* there is another beast   316
    with his back altogether black and yellow,
    with tooth of boar and tail of elephant;
    in all the rest he's almost like a horse;
    he has two horns, but—most incredibly—
    just as he wishes, either one can bend,
    as other beasts are seen to prick their ears,
    or often bend them, out of wrath or fear.

"The hippopotamus, a clever beast,   317
    just like a horse of rivers or of seas,
    enters a field, most shrewdly, with his back,
    and if he thinks he has excessive blood,
    he walks around in search of a canebrake,
    pricks there a vein, and, as his nature prompts,
    in this way rids himself of his unhealthy blood;
    and then he heals his open wound with mud.

"And do not think it strange that we have learned   318
    the practice of phlebotomy from him,
    for, being a benevolent, dear mother,
    Nature was kind enough to teach us everything.
    His hide is, then, so hard and thick, no one
    can pierce it, unless it's wet and dampened first;
    he fights with fangs that look like a wild boar's,
    and with his bifid tongue he neighs and roars.

"And hardly known is the *leontofawn,*   319
    whose meat is poison to a lion's meal;
    bearded like goats is the *tragelaphus;*
    there is the jackal, in the summer bare,
    and wholly hirsute, then, in wintertime;
    well known as wolves are also the *lycaions;*
    and there are other animals called elks,
    wild horses that deliver mighty kicks.

"Then there are bisons, savage oxen, too,   320
widespread in Scythia and Germany;
and then a serpent that is known as boa;
a beast that (like sheer madness this will sound)
can by no means articulate its joints;
and so, while sleeping, it is trapped and caught,
for it is wont to sleep leaning on trees:
you cut the tree down and the beast you seize.

"And there's a breed of weird, strange-looking apes   321
born in the lands of Ethiopia;
they all have legs behind and hands in front,
and are exactly similar to men.
Rome saw these beasts in the Pompeian games
for the first time, and there they multiplied.
Just a few days ago, to Charlemagne Gan wrote,
promising one of these—but truthful he was not.

"And there's a beast known as chameleon,   322
who, where she lies, takes on the very hue
of all the things she is surrounded by,
becoming thus most difficult to view;
another serpent called the *salpiga*,
batting no eye, can hurt one fatally;
and *spectafici, arunduci,* and many a snake
Medusa with her blood could never make.

"There are *celidri*, celebrated serpents,   323
dipsas, haemorrhois, and *cafezacus,*
scaura and *prester,* full of poison, all;
and there's a dragon never seen before,
with other unknown animals concealed
deep in the sea or down in swamps or lakes;
and many new strange basilisks are found
with many a strange effect and hissing sound;

"*dracopodes* and *armena* and *calcatrix,*   324
irundo, alsordius, arachs, altynanyti,
centupeda and *cornuta* and *rimatrix;*
the ever-lonely, ever-fierce *naderos,*
berus and *boa, phareas* and *natrix,*
which Luciana never heard about;
andrius, ahedysymon, alhartraf,
and she did now remember the giraffe.

"There is the ibis looking like a stork,   325
    which feeds on serpents' eggs and, when she must—
    at the right time—she gives herself an enema
    with salty water, placing (as men saw)
    her beak, just like a bagpipe, in her rear;
    and so, in such a manner, Mother Nature,
    whose wisdom and sagacity are ample,
    taught our physicians through this bird's example.

"Th' *agothylex,* known also as *caprimulgus,*   326
    sucks the goat so, till all her milk is dried;
    the *kythes,* then, a bird unknown to you,
    his aged parents feeds with his own beak;
    another one is *cynamulgus* called,
    whose meat, once tasted, makes you lick your fingers;
    this is a bird a glutton need not split,
    for only fragrant spices he can eat.

"Then the *memnonides* are famous birds   327
    that make what has been written credible:
    every five years they fly as far as Egypt,
    all of them seeking Memnon's sepulcher;
    and there they fight (O fair and wondrous tale!),
    showing such sadness, shedding such true tears
    as if attending a true funeral;
    and to their native land, then, back fly all.

"The *ardea* resembles, then, the heron   328
    that flies above the clouds to shun a storm;
    then the *coredulus* that eats the heart
    of all he grabs, and leaves the rest untouched;
    then the *carista,* that (O lovely thing!)
    can fly through fire and is never burned.
    And the *choretes,* maybe, you don't know—
    a bird—such is its name—that fights the crow.

"And there's a bird that's in the summer seen   329
    after the rain: it is *dryacha* called,
    which nature has created without feet;
    the *athylon,* which, crying, can pursue
    a fox, but, if it sees a donkey, starts
    following him instead like an old friend;
    but the *bistarda*—and you all know this—
    is a vile bird that feeds on carcasses.

"And have you heard of the *caladrius?*   330
If, when laid close to a sick man, this bird
looks somewhere else, it means that man must die;
but if it looks at him, the man will live.
The *ibor's* heard to neigh just like a horse;
and the *lucidia,* a most splendent bird,
shines like a ruby and appears so bright
that it can show man's pathway in the night.

"Th' *incendula* fights always with the owl: 331
she wins during the day, the owl at night.
But above all, *porfirion* I praise,
a bird that surely does not limp from gout:
whate'er he grabs, he eats by drinking it,
barrel and kneading trough are close to him;
one foot is anserine, for he swims oft;
the other, which he eats with, is all chopped.

"Now if I wanted all the fish to count,   332
and tell you all their great varieties,
'twould be like counting in Apulia
all fireflies and mosquitoes and all flies.
I see the battle now about to start,
and we won't be in Roncesvalles on time."
Let us leave here, conversing still, our men.
Christ save our Count Orlando, if He can!

CANTO   XXVI

Benevolent Father, let Your boundless mercy   1
this time be at my side more than before;
send Your archangel with his company
and let angelic swords be reddened, too:
in Roncesvalles the blood will rise so high,
it will then flow through ditches and in streams,
for, ah, the dismal final day is near,
Malgigi has predicted with great fear.

O Charles, alas, how wretched you will be
when you witness the tragic new events,
and see your knight, your dear young nephew, dead!
O my own sad and sorely keening rhymes!
O King Marsilius, treacherous Saracen,
your fraud is soon to bear its fruit at last!
Shortly, O Gano, you'll be glad to see
your treason carried out ultimately!

2

The one who still bemoans Prometheus's theft
on the horizon, stained with blood and fire,
had shown his head; the Ganges, therefore, seemed
the Christians' future weeping to foretell.
The pagan troops of King Marsilius
already were in front and very near,
and on a mountain could be sighted, then,
little by little, all the troops of Spain.

3

Could you have seen those banners in the wind,
vermilion, black, and yellow, white and blue,
and on them serpents, leopards, lions, deer;
could you have heard the neighing of the steeds,
made more tumultuous by trumpets' blast,
you would have been astounded, terror-struck,
so many a signal and so many a gong
was seen and heard amid the pagan throng.

4

But Guottibuoffi, a renowned old man
from Burgundy, was most afraid of this,
and every day reminded Count Orlando
that they should think of something right away
and keep the camp on the lookout and armed.
Who knows for what strange reason, but this time
Orlando did not seem at all to care,
of any fear and danger unaware.

5

Oliver had announced, the day before,
that he had had a very frightful dream
which had aroused so many doubts in him
a Daniel was needed to explain.
Orlando said, "If but one glass can do
so very much, what will a barrel bring?"
What he had told him, frankly, was a sign
that he had dreamed under the spell of wine.

6

Maybe Orlando, being old and wise,   7
already knew his own impending fate,
but did not show what lay deep in his heart;
he was awaiting now his crown of thorns—
the tribute and the homage of all Spain.
Ah, all our knowledge is of no avail,
for, when a grievous peril is in view,
'tis hard to tell ourselves what we should do.

That morning, very early, Oliver   8
had climbed a mountain in the company
of Guottibuoffi, who each evening told
the guards to be most cautious in the night.
Meanwhile, as I have mentioned, had appeared
the vanguard troops of King Marsilius.
Oliver understood the treason then,
seeing the pagans walking toward the plain.

He said, "O Guottibuoffi, this indeed   9
is the last day of Carlo's glorious reign.
And never has our count believed your words—
that we should have been ready for the fight.
Here is Marsilius, treacherous and shrewd,
paying the count a visit full of fraud:
judging by what I see, there is no sign
of peace at all in all these arms that shine.

"Once and for all Malgigi's prophecies,   10
this time, I am afraid, have all come true!
I can hear Paris tremble far away.
O Ganelon, how well you now have aimed,
and thanked for all his favors Charlemagne!"
This said, he spurred his charger then and there
and, galloping, at once came down the mount
and reached the tent where he had left the count.

Our Count Orlando was in a bad mood   11
that morning; so as he saw Oliver
coming toward him, running on his horse,
from far away he shouted, "What is this?"
Oliver said, "Bad news, upon my word!
Last night you did not even want to hear me.
Marsilius has his tribute for you—war;
and he has brought the world, to give you more."

All of a sudden, round Orlando came   12
all Christian paladins, all of them urging
that the alarm be sounded with the horn.
Orlando jumped up on his horse at once
and sought the mountain; so did Sansonetto.
There, from the summit, all around he looked,
and clearly King Marsilius could see,
bringing as tribute future misery.

'Twas then he turned to Roncesvalles and said,   13
bemoaning the sad fate of all his men,
"O luckless valley, full of grief and woe,
today you will be bloodied for all time!"
Others had joined him, and were right behind,
and all suggested but one thing to do,
since what had happened could not be undone—
to call for help by sounding now the horn.

On the same mountain Berlinghier had come   14
with Avin and Astolfo right away;
each of them looking down upon the plain
could see the countless hordes of Saracens.
"O paladin of France," all of them said,
"have mercy on your honorable men!
Go now, and blow the horn with all your breath,
for nothing is more terrible than death!"

Orlando said, "If even I saw here   15
Scipio, Caesar, Hannibal, Marcellus,
Darius, Xerxes, Alexander, and
Nebuchadnezzar with his entire army;
if even I saw Death in front of me
with his well-sharpened scythe or with a knife,
I'd not ask Charles to help me out of this:
I never blew the horn for cowardice."

Orlando with his people then came down   16
and bade the entire camp be armed in haste:
through all of Roncesvalles the herald went,
ordering every man to mount his steed,
and Turpin with his cross blessed everyone,
comforting all and telling them to go
to battle and die willingly for Christ,
remembering the holy death of Christ.

If you had seen the camp arm in such haste, 17
surely great pity would have seized your heart,
for when you expect the contrary, all things
seem to bring double ecstasy or fear.
Many a trumpet through all Roncesvalles
resounded with reverberating din:
it seemed to call the dead out of each tomb
down in Jehoshaphat, the Day of Doom.

You can imagine with what speed each man 18
saddled his horse and gathered all his arms:
some shouted and some struck their squires, some
ordered their servants to be ready soon,
some others donned their armor the wrong way,
and others still, mistaking words for deeds,
as is the case in moments of great fear,
shouted, "Arms! Arms! Our enemy is near!"

Around Orlando all the paladins 19
had gathered very closely to discuss
the battle everybody seemed to fear—
that is, how all their troops should be arrayed.
Sighing and moaning out of grief, Orlando
was still so stunned, he could not even talk:
to Roncesvalles he'd taken all his men,
alas, to die so wretchedly! 'Twas then

Oliver said, "Brother-in-law, my dear, 20
you would have done much better to believe me.
It's a long time now I have preached to you
that I had reasons to believe Marsilius
a wicked traitor since his very birth;
and you still thought his tribute he would bring!
Carlo his mummies is awaiting still,
and known to all is Ganelon's ill will,

"but not to Charles, who still believes in him, 21
and has brought all of us to such a death.
But that Marsilius, as soon as he's ignored,
among his foul and execrable vices
has envy in his bones, which gnaws at him
and can be seen now by the fruit it bears:
I see as in a mirror his true picture—
a wicked hypocrite, a vile old creature.

"Malgigi is the one who knows him well,   22
and countless times he told you so himself;
I told you that the camp should have been armed,
I yelled so much, I even was afraid;
but I was not believed. The time has come now,
foreboded by so many dismal signs;
forgive me, but you'll soon wear on your head,
oh, not a king's, a martyr's crown instead."

Orlando did not answer Oliver,   23
for in no way can one reply to truth;
even if he had thought of a reply,
he would have found no words to utter it.
The camp was, meanwhile, at its best arrayed,
and to Orlando all the troops drew close,
obeying soon his order of fall-in.
This was the count's last speech to all his men:

"If I could e'er have thought Marsilius   24
would come to visit me in such a treacherous way—
just like the sinful traitor that he is—
I would have long prepared both hearts and arms;
but since I always loved him loyally,
I thought he loved me, too, as loyally,
and that we both had buried our old rancor,
for one is often a true friend once more.

"Oh, but not he, who cowardly forgives   25
but keeps his mind in bitterness and hate.
So, then, excusing Ganelon and Judas,
I crown him with the traitors' diadem:
I cannot find anything good in him—
a hawk that in the wood can change at once:
for granted its great loyalty you take,
but once you let it go, it won't come back.

"Here is the faith, then, of Melchizedek,   26
a man who speaks more tongues than Babel did,
who's worth *Alec-salam Salam-alec*
just as another Cain inviting Abel.
But maybe I shall be a new Lamech,
and he the spirit of Ahithophel,
or Marsyas, who in newer bodies hides,
forever running from Apollo's sight.

"He who betrays mankind betrays himself,
  and let no one from his own self conceal,
  for 'tis himself he ultimately dooms.
  If you will all be faithful unto death,
  your Lord with his sweet manna will restore you
  of all the bitter gall you will have known;
  and if today your bread has grief for leaven,
  this very evening you will dine in heaven—

(as that Greek leader said, in ancient days,
  happy to his own men; he said 'in hell,' though).
"Look with what fortitude Saint Lawrence bears
  his fiery grate for that eternal bliss:
  'Now to the other side!' O burning love,
  he did not feel the pain of other fire!
  How sweet and dear is willingly to die
  when, strong and pure, the soul to God can fly!

"As far as I'm concerned, like a meek lamb
  I'll go, like Isaac, to my sacrifice,
  although I see the knife already raised:
  to that eternal judgment I feel close,
  where both the wicked and the good are judged;
  that solemn operation will soon be:
  Venite, benedicti patris mei,
  and into hell the wicked will be thrown away.

"And yet, while still some life is left to us—
  because it is the end that crowns all things—
  let every knight display his greatest might
  so that the body—it alone—may die;
  against all hope be brave, for I myself
  know not what else, if ever, may ensue:
  often, I say, when remedy is rare,
  there is salvation only in despair.

"I deeply grieve for Charles: in his old age
  he'll maybe see the end, forever come,
  of the Belle France and every gentleness,
  for he has been a worthy emperor.
  But what goes up must finally come down:
  toward the same goal all mortal things proceed:
  while one ascends, the other must descend;
  and so the Christian world will also see its end.

"And for Rinaldo, too, my cousin dear,   32
   I deeply grieve: how gladly I would die
   if I could see him punish this vile traitor!
   Is my imagination now so strong
   that I cannot envision other things?
   A most consoling thought is in my mind,
   which seems to tell me, 'Your Rinaldo's near!'
   and so I look at you to see if he is here.

"The reason why I did not blow my horn   33
   is that I want to see what Fortune brings;
   also, I want no one ever to boast
   I had to blow it out of cowardice:
   the stars above will sooner be extinct,
   the sun will sooner by the moon be lit,
   and I Marsilius's pride will maybe mortify;
   and with this thought alone I wish to die.

"Aside from it, this place does not allow it: 34
   there's so much distance between Charles and us
   that all his help would not arrive on time.
   I will let Ganelon finally gloat.
   Ah, but before we're forced to leave this game,
   we'll make so vast a massacre of them,
   we'll teach a lasting lesson to the earth—
   never was Count Orlando afraid of death.

"Death or departure must be feared only   35
   when, with the body, the soul also dies;
   but if we join God's countless diadems,
   going from the finite up to the infinite,
   death is the start of a far better life.
   So raise your last and perfect hope to Christ,
   and life and death commend to Him Who chose
   to rescue Daniel from the lions' jaws.

"An old philosopher named Thales thanked   36
   God, first of all, for having made him man,
   not animal; because if you and I
   had been created animals, not men,
   we would be mortal as a consequence;
   so I believe it is man's task to love
   as much as possible this fleeting world,
   but above all to love his lovely Lord.

"Remember each of those good Decii   37
  who worked such wonders for their fatherland,
  and many other famous Greeks and Romans
  who thus left their small glory in the world;
  but their renown I little cared and care for,
  next to that holy realm where is the One
  Who shed His guiltless blood upon a cross
  to save from the foul serpent all of us.

"Do not believe your names will be as bright   38
  as those of Curtius or Horatius;
  yet, while they gave salvation to the world,
  their souls were not rewarded in the sky.
  Instead, as I am speaking now to you,
  I see already heaven open up,
  where angels are preparing, eager most,
  the seats by faithless spirits ever lost.

"I see a little cloud up in the air,   39
  a halo coming down from Paradise;
  a hem of Michael's mantle I can see,
  so bright I cannot view the rest of him;
  you I can see, triumphant on the lap
  of that high Love, applauding with a smile,
  just like those patriarchs with Abraham;
  I see us all, at last to heaven come.

"I give my blessing, then, to all of you;   40
  Archbishop Turpin will absolve you now,
  and so you'll be absolved in heaven, too."
  After these words he took his Vegliantìn
  and from the ground upon the saddle leapt,
  saying, "Let's go against the Saracens!"
  Upon his charger wept he bitterly
  as soon as he once more his men could see,

  and said again, "O valley full of grief   41
  that soon from our sad luck and misery
  will draw renown for centuries to come,
  such blood I will be forced to pour on you,
  you'll be remembered in both prose and rhymes.
  But if our mortal prayer was ever just,
  O Holy Virgin, I commend to thee
  your servants; do not look at sinful me!"

In the meantime the good archbishop blessed   42
all of those people with his holy cross,
saying, "I do absolve you," and each one
he urged to die most willingly for Christ.
So one another they embraced in tears,
and then they laid their lances at their side;
before them was the banner of Almont,
which had been conquered once in Aspramont.

Behold the mighty horde of pagan men   43
Falseron had amassed beneath his flags,
already to the plainland now come down!
He said, "These men from France and Piccardy,
as soon as on the battlefield we are,
we'll see if they are truly strong and brave!
Today at last I will avenge my son!"
And he was menacing the count alone.

"I have already told you, cavaliers   44
(and what I told you, firmly bear in mind),
that when you see Orlando on the field,
out of my way you must withdraw at once:
I want to be the one to snatch his heart—
get out, and let revenge be mine alone!
My Ferraù, if I am not deranged,
was more than worthy thus to be avenged."

One could have heard the strangest kettledrums,   45
and many bugles, many Moorish horns
re-echo through those valleys all around—
and out of hell that music seemed to come.
And then those pennons and strange-looking plumes,
those uniforms and newest rhythmic marches,
they were most horrible to watch. No wonder:
they would have frightened even Alexander.

The neighing of the horses and the murmur   46
of all the pagans coming forth with threats
(each of them wanted to devour the Christians,
and Falseron, Orlando most of all)
seemed louder than the roaring of the sea
when Scylla and Charybdis bark at monsters;
and the whole sky above was full of dust
like desert sand by sudden tempest tossed.

Arabs and Syrians were there, and Gypsies,   47
Egyptians, Indians, Ethiopians,
and above all, numberless atheists
with no religion of their own, arrived
from Barbary and other distant lands;
and there were also men from Gascony,
as author Alcuin writes with precision:
you can envision, then, their first division.

The weirdest suits of armor could be seen,   48
the oddest and most horrible big hats;
also, upon their backs the thickest hides
of serpents, and of crocodiles and fish,
and clubs and maces, scimitars and axes:
with many blows those men assailed the wind,
with darts and bows, with arrows and with picks,
with catapults uprooting more than sticks.

Facing each other, the two camps appeared,   49
and on both sides the shouting reached the sky:
some wished to roast Mahound, some wished him boiled;
each wanted to make pies of his own foe.
So to the battle we shall come right now,
not to keep Death still waiting—Death already
threatening with his scythe and telling me
to speed up scale and quill accordingly.

Orlando had already told his men,   50
"Let everybody in this fight be free:
there is room only for the perfect knight;
and now may Michael be your company!"
Astolfo was the first man to advance;
Arlotto, King of Syria, replied.
Each of them lowered instantly his lance,
and one cried "Saragossa!" One cried "France!"

Astolfo, now be careful, shame us not!   51
Behave like a true paladin: hold on
most firmly to your saddle and, if need be,
hug it, just as you would your little babe!
Arlotto, coming from the pagan camp,
surely was not a dreaming cavalier,
and I must add (please bear with me, therefore)
Astolfo was somewhat inferior;

so much so that as soon as Oliver 52
saw him with his spear down, he told Orlando,
"Astolfo's in for quite a feast today!"
In fact, that very moment, with such wrath
the pagan struck Astolfo on the shield,
he nearly with that single blow this time
took care forever of the young marquis;
thank God the spear descended crookedly!

But dexterously Astolfo wounded him, 53
landing his lance upon his visor fast,
and so immensely strong was his one blow,
nearly two spans of steel went through his eyes:
he plunged his soul among the damned in hell,
and his dead body from the saddle threw.
Astolfo did his duty after all:
this time not he—the pagan had to fall.

Angiolin of Bayonne, the Frankish knight, 54
said then, "Orlando, give me the next blow."
Forward, at this, he spurred his nimble steed,
braver than which no other was on earth.
A very cruel and bloodthirsty man—
Malducco, monarch of the reign of Frasse—
out of the pagan camp at once came forward,
and the two spears were at the same time lowered.

Each tried to catch the other unprepared, 55
but they were equal masters of attack.
Angiolin, shaken by Malducco's blow,
was seen to totter on his horse's left side,
but nonetheless, his valor was not spent:
his answer to the pagan was so prompt,
he saw his helmet touch the horse's back
so strongly that both crest and laces broke,

and had his steed not carried him away, 56
feeling his man's panache upon his back
and trying, as he went, to lift him straight,
the string that held the arrow would have snapped.
It was Avìn who joined now in the dance:
his spear he lowered and his steed he spurred;
"Who wants to challenge me," he said with wrath,
"let him come forward, and he'll soon find death!"

Out of the pagan throng came forward soon   57
King Mazzarigi, a most pompous man,
who had converted to the Christian faith
and then had abjured Christ and Word and Father.
Wasting no time, they passed to action fast:
the pagan's blow was mercilessly hard;
Avin replied most promptly with his spear,
but Death, so loudly promised, did not hear.

Unable any longer to stay there,   58
Oliver forward came on his Rondel,
and King Malprimo, as he saw him move,
began to gallop from the other side.
There is no need for thinner brushes here:
the spears began to turn all red with blood,
and every cuirass, every plate and shield,
and every harness soon grew purple-red.

Strongly the Saracen hit the marquis,   59
leaving his spear well planted in his shield,
with its point coming through the other side
and bruising on his chest one of his ribs,
by breastplate and by jacket ill-defended;
but in the end the spear shook off and fell,
and Oliver then let himself fall down
and many a time upon the ground turned round.

But no, his vigor and his pride could not,   60
even in that predicament, be hid:
with his unbreakable, unbending spear
he split the pagan's shield wide open fast,
and found his breastplate softer than a net:
Malprimo saw himself utterly lost
as in his heart he felt Oliver's lance,
showing the prowess of a knight of France.

As soon as Falseron saw such a champion   61
fall lifeless from his horse upon the ground,
his heart was overcome with sudden fear.
"This is," he said, "a miracle, no doubt;
here they're not playing domino or dice.
O god Mahound, how did you let him fall?"
This sad occurrence left him most depressed
because Malprimo was the first and best.

Oliver did not jump into the midst   62
of all the pagans, bruised as he was still.
Turpin had, in the meantime, lowered lance,
and now was leaping like a frisky lamb,
for that was not the time to sing his Mass.
Against him came accursèd Turchion
with lifted lance and with great pride and wrath,
most eager to avenge Malprimo's death.

He hit him in the strappings of the shield,   63
which he then shattered like a mirror glass,
leaving his chest relieved of such a load.
But Turpin, although old, knew his art well
and, as he saw the pagan lift his head,
let his spear fly and harbor in his ear,
and head and helmet crushed so thoroughly,
he cured him of his deafness instantly.

Our Count Orlando had in his brigade   64
that mighty man, Richard of Normandy,
and Guottibuoffi, and that Count Anselmo
who was to be so glorious that day,
Avin, Avolio, Berlinghier, his brother,
Sansonet, and the good Duke Egibard,
and all the other paladins of France,
a master, each, at brandishing a lance.

Now when Orlando and his troops advanced,   65
I leave it to the reader to imagine
how all that thundering din resembled Vulcan's
smithy: its echo reached high Jupiter,
and Mars himself up in the sky awoke;
so many spears in fragments hit the ground
that a strong wind seemed everything to fell,
including heaven and the world and hell.

Falseron, who so much had longed to come   66
to blows with Count Orlando finally,
all of a sudden changed his mind, as soon
as he could see him come with so much wrath
as to resemble Lucifer unbound.
"Have mercy on me, Apollìn," he said;
"oh, do not let me perish here so soon,
but let me, let me first avenge my son!"

But as the count drew close to Falseron, 67
"Traitor," he shouted wildly from afar,
"so this is what you promised—that you had
forgiven me for killing Ferraù!
Clearly I see now what a traitor is
your King Marsilius with all his court;
he should right now be hanged along with you!
Is this the tribute to our Carlo due?

"Say, are you not ashamed of kissing me 68
like Judas Iscariot, the day
you took your leave from Charlemagne and France?"
No one had ever seen Orlando so
angry and vanquished as he was that day.
At this, he let his spear at once depart—
which in the chest of Falserone broke—
shouting, "And now your dog Mahound invoke!"

The wonder of it was—I do believe— 69
Orlando's spear could pierce, as God decreed,
a shield made of the hide of some strange fish,
and, too, its lower plate, quite hard and thick;
and since King Falseron, instantly dead,
did not fall lifeless from his saddle down,
nobody of his death was yet aware.
Orlando with his charger moved elsewhere,

but soon came back, most curious to see 70
what had indeed occurred to Falseron,
having not seen him fall as he passed by;
he touched him with his sword, and he at once
among the other dead fell on the earth.
The greatest wonder was not that he fell,
but that as soon as he did hit the ground,
they say his body was not seen or found.

So, Falseron, you've had your full revenge— 71
you, who have brought to Saragossa Gan!
Upon the scene all of his soldiers sped,
dismounted soon, stretched out their hands, and found
only his weapons there: 'twas like a shell
left empty by the crab that disappeared.
O wonder, O new portent, O strange lesson,
proving how God in heaven abhors treason!

When all the pagans saw Falseron dead,   72
each would have run and swept the plainland clean,
such was their terror and discouragement;
but from all sides the trap had well been set,
for to see better, King Marsilius
had reached the summit of the lofty mount:
he saw the Christians were surrounded well,
and their retreat was now impossible.

With a big mattock that was heavy most,   73
forth at this moment came that old black crow,
as Finadusto known to all of them:
exactly seven feet the man was tall.
Berlinghier saw the ugly taper come
and, caring neither for his height nor for
his mattock, which was solid and cob-shaped,
with his spear raised, soon up against him stepped.

The scoundrel had a boundless turtle shell   74
which he had fashioned in the way he chose
and was now wearing on his chest as a shield:
thick as it was, the spear went through it fast,
and so horrendous was its sharpened point,
it opened every knot of his whole plate,
together with the triple leather jacket
which he had thought no man could ever break.

He thrust into his chest half of the stake,   75
and though it was not fatal, still the blow
left Finadusto shuddering with fear,
and had his charger not spread wings at once,
no longer would he have felt heat or cold:
no arrow ever from its holding string
flies in the air with such enormous speed
as Finadusto on his charger fled.

With many people Gallerano now   76
had meanwhile come; Fidasso was with him.
Soon more vermilion the plain became,
more spears in fragments on the ground rained down,
and every valiant captain forward came.
Orlando like a tempest ever worked,
and had with him brave Count Anselmo, who
made several helmets now and then ring true.

Oliver held his Altachiara close, 77
come to the thickest battle once again.
Walter of Mulion threw himself in,
and Baldwin, too, just like a lion leapt.
Avin, Avolio, Otho, everyone
sliced scummy Saracens like broccoli;
Angiolin of Belland and Guottibuoff,
delivering ripe blows, were also rough.

Both Mark and Matthew of Saint Michael's Plain 78
(but I, for one, say of Saint Michael's Mount)
with sword in hand all over Roncesvalles
had scarred already many people's brows.
Our duke Astolfo was not idle either,
while Turpin to the mountain chased the sheep.
Of all our knights, Angiolin of Bordeaux
had died—ah, killed by a deceitful foe.

Let's leave the battlefield so closely held. 79
But now, shall we not let Rinaldo come
with his dear Ricciardetto to the fight?
With such a burning longing he was coming
that he would ask, with each new step he took,
what wicked King Marsilius was doing,
and seeing from afar the battlefield,
Astaroth to him everything revealed.

Ricciardo, too, was wearing himself out 80
on hearing how the fight was getting thick,
and highly praised the count and Oliver
for making still the pagan camp decline;
yes, he was happy for it, but he wished
the time would fly so that he would at last
show all his worth and might in that melee,
and so he threw Milusse's grass away.

As soon as they were close to Roncesvalles, 81
down on the plainland from the Pyrenees,
from which the battle's thunder could be heard,
with sound of weapons and of men's laments,
Rinaldo said, "I think it would be great
(I'm only saying what I'd like to do)
to dash right now upon each Saracen,
down there, where I might find King Bianciardin."

Astaroth answered, "Bianciardin's the one
who rides all over in that cape of his.
Now to a steeple Farferel and I
will climb, and ring all of its bells in joy,
seeing the slaughter you're about to make;
and at your service here is Squarciafer
(*rogatus rogo,* then, pay heed to me),
who wants in everything your friend to be.

82

"Never believe that there's no kindness even
in hell, amongst us; there's an adage, here
on earth, that tells that every plant somehow
keeps something in it of its ancient root,
although its fruit is now degenerate.
Ah, let's not speak now of that happy time . . .
There is Marsilius; here Orlando fights close by.
Think of me sometime; go in peace! Goodbye!"

83

Rinaldo did not know how to reply,
unable to find words after that speech;
and yet he wished to thank his Astaroth
along with Squarciafer and Farferel,
and so he said, "As if you were my brother,
O Astaroth, I grieve to see you go;
yes, I believe you: even down in hell
friendship and gentleness and kindness dwell.

84

"And if you are allowed to heed my plea,
from time to time come back to visit me,
with Squarciafer and Farferello, too,
for I would love to give you some delight;
and I will pray—if praying's any good—
to the same Lord my Christian faith adores
that you repent, and He may pardon you;
else to repay you, there is nothing I can do."

85

Astaroth answered, "If you care to know,
there is a grace I ask and you can grant,
and then you can dismiss me happily:
tell Malagigi to deliver me,
and recommend me to him as you can;
then ever at your bidding I'll remain,
for serving you will be no toil at all:
just whisper 'Astaroth,' my name just call,

86

"and I will hear you from the depth of hell,   87
  and for my love my Farferel will send."
"I will be grateful for eternity,"
  Rinaldo answered, "and my brother, too;
  and not a letter—a full notebook I
  will write with the best ink to Malagigi,
  and he will do just as you wish and say.
  Oh, let me serve you in some other way!

"The messenger I'll send to him will fly,   88
  and I will write about your courtesy;
  and I will ask Orlando to write, too,
  so sweet your company has been to me."
  Astaroth said, "Remember me," and fast,
  with his companions, vanished out of view—
  as fast as lightning fleeting in the blue,
  while the earth seemed to open down below.

There was in Roncesvalles there at that time   89
  a certain little church that had two bells:
  up there the Christians stood on the lookout
  to see and grab some of those pagan souls,
  like hawks awaiting between bough and bough;
  they had to use their hands most actively,
  and beat, the entire day, their wings as well
  to introduce them to the judges of hell.

Great Minos, Rhadamanthys, and Aeacus   90
  were busy flinging, all day long, their tails;
  and think how happy Satan must have been,
  and how delighted Charon in his boat
  sang as he rearranged his oars and bound
  all of his sails with more enduring twine.
  There was great pandemonium in hell,
  with many a dance and Moorish tarantel!

Instead, in heaven, with celestial manna   91
  ambrosia and nectar were made ready,
  and at the door Saint Peter, old and weary,
  was, as I reckon, out of breath that day;
  thank God his hearing was still good, so loud
  was the *Osanna* of so many souls
  borne up to heaven by the angels blest!
  His perspiration flooded beard and breast.

Now to Rinaldo let's go back! As soon   92
as he assailed the camp right in the midst,
all of that mortar turned incarnadine;
and his move proved to be a clever one,
for, not aware yet of the damage done,
Marsilius suspected treason: maybe
there'd been among them some conspiracy
(wisdom and haste together cannot be).

Marsilius had perfectly arrayed   93
his pagan camp; he even had devised
which knights had to be killed, one by one.
Rinaldo, who had also thought of it,
knew in what danger every captain was,
and dreaded lest his order be obeyed;
because we know from past experience
a battle is no more than mere obedience:

"Leave not the post till I come back to you: 94
see that I find you here, alive or dead!"
"Stay like the North Star at Ursa Minor's end,
or like a ship new-anchored in a port!"
And, many having disobeyed already,
each captain, wise and wary, realized
how treacherous the enemy would be,
and wisely changed his plan accordingly.

It seemed to King Marsilius, watching still,   95
that now his pagans against pagans fought;
about Rinaldo he could not have known,
so he decided to come down and see;
there were no Christian arms or flags in sight,
and yet he saw a great scuffle going on.
"Gano," he said, "is a malicious cat,
and Bianciardino did—I wonder what."

He was afraid he had been double-crossed—   96
that Bianciardino, while in France with Charles,
had thought of bringing home some opium
whereby to put Marsilius to sleep;
and so convinced, deep in his mind, was he
that there was treason in his very camp,
he thought that it would soon explode: 'twas then
he wrathfully came down among his men.

Rinaldo, when Marsilius he saw, 97
told Ricciardetto, "Look, the mountain's down!
Staying here longer would be most in vain:
the time has come Orlando we must find,"
and since he was surrounded and hard-pressed
from every side by countless Saracens,
Ricciardo, ever cutting with his sword,
routed, by leaps and bounds, that pagan horde.

Rinaldo a new circle longed to see 98
and, seeing it already formed around him,
suddenly turned Baiardo and, inspired
to try some action to his heart's content,
he played so swift a backhand with his sword
that—if the author is correct—quite cleanly
he severed head from neck of more than twenty,
and all their trunks fell down with blood aplenty.

Seeing so many lifeless people fall, 99
everyone stepped aside in wonderment
and, raising up the visor, asked in awe,
"Who is this man who everything upsets?"
Rinaldo, wishing still to see Orlando,
turned at this point the bridle toward the camp
where the French knights were fighting; coming near,
from someone in his way he snatched a spear.

Orlando, when he saw him with such wrath 100
coming toward him closer, could have sworn—
judging from both his boldness and his horse—
that he was certain (and indeed he was)
it was Rinaldo. He saw then the lion,
and all his joy was uncontrollable;
with so much happiness his heart did swell
that from his charger down he nearly fell.

And Ricciardetto, too, his emblem showed. 101
Oliver, in the meantime, had arrived
and, recognizing both immediately,
felt deep within such happiness at once
that through the heart, already open and
ridden of blood through all its arteries,
his vital spirits from his body nearly spilled:
for often by much joy a person can be killed.

When he composed himself, Orlando gave   102
a hearty welcome to his cousin dear,
and asked him many questions, and Rinaldo
spoke of his lengthy journey to that place,
and of the things by Malagigi done.
Oliver, too, controlled himself at last,
but half-astonished yet, half-dazed and dumb,
he looked like Lazarus out of the tomb.

The pagan camp had shifted, for our knights,   103
after much damage to it, had by now
closed up decisively: the damage done
made each of them some reinforcement fear.
A thousand times Orlando hugged Rinaldo
over and over, smarting from delight,
and, watching there his cousin, still so brave,
all of his people he still hoped to save.

He ordered that the camp now freshen up   104
and reassemble—there was need for it.
Then to Rinaldo, called aside, he said,
"O cousin dear, I yearned to see you so
that, after gazing on you for some time,
I still feel dreaming as I speak to you.
There's nothing else I ask of God, for I
have seen you once again before I die.

"From distant Egypt you've returned to me,   105
who wish you could have found me less perturbed;
yet I'm so glad to see you once again
that every gloomy thought seems fast to flee.
I am not grieving now, but do not praise
that fact that for so long you did not write.
Oh, but a double joy I now derive—
I thought you dead; instead, you are alive."

"But I have sent you many letters," said   106
Rinaldo then, "and so has Ricciardetto;
to their right address they have not been brought,
and that good demon told me everything.
But let's not say unnecessary words
now that I see the entire world against you.
So tell me, cousin, what you want me now to do:
the storm is full of threats, and now our hours are few."

"That traitor—I mean not Maganza's man,   107
but King Marsilius—Iscariot—,"
Orlando answered him, "made us believe
he wanted peace; but there was fraud beneath.
And so, with this quite small security,
poor simple Charles is waiting at Saint John,
and for a certain tribute I came here—
and how this tribute's coming 'tis now clear.

"It seems that since the day you left me here,   108
heaven is venting all its wrath on me;
the weirdest cases have befallen me,
so many of them that not even Fortune,
who turns in many a way, can e'er devise.
Therefore, my soul is sighing endlessly,
for I am haunted by a past grave error
which for some time has made me live in terror.

"Ah, from the day I took Don Chiaro's life,   109
no good has ever come my way again
(and do not think I liked the thing I did,
but I could never disobey my king):
maybe that innocent, illustrious blood
is crying out for vengeance before God,
who now is holding Carlo in disdain,
who had been granted a great fame and reign.

"Rinaldo dear, unless I now am wrong,   110
I think that in this valley we'll all die;
but first so many pagans will die here
that Roncesvalles will be forever known."
Rinaldo answered, "Vex yourself no more!
Here at your shoulders is Marsilius
with all the men of Xerxes and of Darius:
there's no more time to talk and be so serious."

Marsilius had said to Bianciardin   111
when to the valley with his men he came,
"O Bianciardin, you made me doubt your word.
So strange a case I fail to understand:
Against my men Orlando's fighting there,
and I've been told Rinaldo is abroad,
in Egypt, with his brother Ricciardetto—
this is what Gano wrote me in his letter."

Bianciardin answered, "Two full-armed and mighty   112
knights have come here; with all our strength we fought them
from every corner and for a long time,
but forcibly among our troops they passed
and vanished, and no more could they be seen.
I think they are two haunted devils, for
they both to me seemed quite invisible
as they did things that one would call unfeasible.

"One thing we could see well—their arms aloft   113
and all their blows that thickened as they fell,
echoing like two bells together ringing.
I saw a circle made around the two,
and then things followed that looked like no man's:
a sword was heard to whistle suddenly
in a backhand that with a whirling violence
severed the heads of twenty men at once."

And this is how Marsilius replied: 114
"They are two demons by Malgigi sent.
Our army seems to me not ably led,
for these Parisians have made some gain:
I see my people running in retreat."
King Mazzarigi now appeared, shouting,
"Help! Help! And quickly! Things look very bad:
our camp is routed; Falseron is dead!"

As soon as King Marsilius heard this,   115
he rode toward Mazzarigi in a dash.
Bemoaning most sincerely Falseron,
he asked, "What is the meaning of all this?"
And Mazzarigi answered, "'Tis the will
of our Mahound, this time a wicked god;
I fled and, to make a long story short,
to death alone, sir, can we now resort.

"It was Orlando murdered Falseron,   116
and Ricciardetto with Rinaldo is here,
breaking all weapons, smashing nerves and bones:
how could we ever stop our soldiers' flight?
So all our people in great terror fled."
Said then Marsilius, "You filthy dog,
O god Mahound, most cruel and untrue,
be ever cursed with all who still believe in you!

"In Pagandom I'll worship you no more,   117
    you fountainhead of falsehood, treacherous scum!
    Rinaldo's here? How could you let this be?
    Through every land you led him here yourself,
    like that Tobias. What a lovely way
    this is to have our Spain back in our hands!
    And surely Ferraù will be avenged today!
    Cursed be Rinaldo, you, and all your sky, I say!"

    Marsilius was a man who in his heart   118
    believed more in the devil than in God;
    a great blasphemer, he blasphemed in private,
    but this one time he wanted to be heard.
    Yes, he could also be a gentle man,
    as in a previous Canto I have said,
    and I repeat it now and say it straight:
    one virtue does not change an evil trait.

    He also knew how to pretend and fake,   119
    most sanctimoniously, chaste piety,
    and in so fine a manner paint his life
    as to be most revered by all his men.
    But since the battle is now pressing hard,
    I'll say only that he grieved for Falseron
    and blasphemed God with his religious word,
    but very loudly, eager to be heard:

"The day be cursed when wicked Ganelon,   120
    the treacherous count, to Saragossa came,
    pretending to put heaven in my hand
    till I believed I with no wings could fly!
    Charles—so he said—was giving Spain to me,
    in peace and full accord! How many times
    that ancient adage proves quite true to be—
    in his own gain man finds an enemy!

"O Bianciardin, the day I saw the fountain   121
    strangely disturbed, you often said to me
    that I should find some solace at that sight,
    for only it could mean, and thus foretell,
    the final weeping of the Christian knights;
    you said it meant the blood that from their hearts
    was soon to spurt and be forever shed:
    but now I see Saracen blood instead!

"And like a foolish child I was naive,   122
   discarding all those gloomy presages
   by which some kind and pious deity
   wanted to warn me 'gainst my future woes
   without my having to resort to vials
   or necromancers to explain dark signs!
   As in a mirror the whole truth was clear,
   but to my wishful thinking I gave ear!

"Now by the Evil Claws I have been seized,   123
   and Falseron is dead, and I am lost.
   My camp was routed at the first onslaught,
   and Charles, I fear, is rushing wrathfully
   now that he hears this treason's thundering sound:
   soon, very soon, the Iber will turn red,
   and Saragossa I can clearly see
   filthy with blood, in tears and misery."

Meanwhile, in tumult, all the Christian men   124
   were slaughtering and chasing Saracens,
   running in front of them haphazardly
   as before lions flocks are seen to do
   or often in a park Great Danes and deer:
   up to the clouds their awful shouting soared.
   Rinaldo, above all, made quite a slaughter:
   while killing one, he threatened yet another.

When King Marsilius could see his camp   125
   so hopelessly and miserably shrunk,
   out of despair he suddenly grew bold
   and, pushing all his men in front of him,
   said, "I know well that I must die today,
   but I will make some other people weep."
   So the two armies clashed, and then and there
   a din of weapons echoed everywhere.

When our Rinaldo leapt into the fight,   126
   he seemed to be with cherubs up in heaven,
   'mid caroling and singing and delight.
   Those pagan dogs he threatened, shouting so:
   "You riffraff, you! I'll slaughter everyone!"
   And he began to cut them into stumps
   and stubs and countless mannequins, and oft
   he made of them two halves precisely cleft.

But with Marsilius to the pagan camp
many important generals had come,
so worthy and so valiant, all of them,
as not to grant the Christians any gain.
They'll sing good alto, say, to their soprano,
and to the French will teach romances, too—
even the sol-fa of the final rope
in which their lives will altogether stop.

Bianciardin under him had Chiariello
of Portugal, a strong and famous king,
with King Fiorello, Fieramont of Balzia,
and Balsamin, much worse than death itself,
who to the Christians will be mortal scourge;
and—have I said it?—there was Buiafort,
son of the famous late Old Man, who should,
perhaps, have stayed right home for his own good.

There were Brusbacca, King Margheriton,
and Mattafirro, a ferocious Moor,
who to the Christians gave a greater pain
than old Actaeon suffered long ago;
and let us not forget strong Syrion
with his fierce mace forever in his hand:
all these, under one flag, formed a militia
in their King Bianciardin's second division.

Then, in the third division, forward came,
beneath the flag of god Mahound himself,
Grandonio, Arcalif, and Balugant,
together with their King Marsilius,
and Zambuger, who, although very small,
wanted to test his worth upon the field,
and other chiefs from every Spanish region—
in short, a vast and most impressive legion.

Many and many spears could there be seen
lowered in less than one swift lightning flash,
and the earth seemed to shake beneath the steeds,
so many men at the same time advanced.
Let those who mentioned Trasimene or Cannae
be quiet: Mars himself knew fear that day,
and Jupiter, I'm certain, felt the need—
to save his peak—of several darts indeed.

Orlando said, "With King Marsilius
I—no one else—must fight; I want to treat him
just as I treated his dear Falseron,
and so for all his sins I'll make him pay:
not even in Mahound does he believe,
who has long abjured every god in heaven,
thus as a renegade making himself well known."
In search of him he went, in search of him alone.

132

Into the battle Baldwin, Gano's son,
had entered with his sword uplifted high,
and randomly so charged the Saracens
that they made room for him, who therefore found
himself alone upon the pagan field;
at this he marveled very much, not knowing
how to interpret that most baffling text:
he knew his own small worth, and was perplexed.

133

If you that day had Count Anselmo seen,
you would have witnessed most uncommon things:
always around him there were pagan men,
and the next moment they were all in hell.
Our Sansonetto, too, made his name bright
with wondrous actions in the thickest fight,
and those who had escaped Orlando were
by his Terigi punctured here and there.

134

Oliver made the stricken helmets sound
like basinets and bagpipes all around,
and all those Saracens that were too close
were destined not to keep their brains with them,
for they jumped out of their split-open heads:
soon there were horses more than horsemen there,
and these all shunned the Viennese marquis
whose sword that day kept working seriously.

135

The valorous and dauntless Duke of England
that day alone accomplished what so many
masters of war could do in many years:
so many Saracens he sent to hell!
Unopposed, he broke open many a throng:
never were beasts in such a number killed.
Berlinghier once again saw Finadust,
whirling his club, still solid and robust,

136

and, though he was much smaller than his foe,   137
remembered still his ancient excellence;
he hardly reached his shield and could therefore
not strike him on the helmet with his sword:
well, to his gorget, then, he raised it up,
and if you want to hear the truth, dear reader,
you will soon know that the whole truth I speak:
he plucked his head right off just like a leek.

Up to one's knees the blood was seen to rise   138
before it flowed throughout the dismal vale.
Ricciardo with his sword did more than drum:
many a time he with an ample whirl
plucked pagan heads as if they were but cobs
of millet or of sorghum; he could not
by any means inactive ever stay.
Imagine what Rinaldo did that day!

Matthew of Mount Saint Michael laid his spear   139
on King Fiorello's visor, hitting him
exactly where a birthmark was concealed:
piercing his brains, out of the nape it came.
Antaeus, too, would have been felled by it;
so you can guess how hard he hit the ground.
Each blow was always better than the first,
and many other heads were to be pierced.

Next to him, always Count Anselmo had,   140
throughout the day, his friend Duke Egibard,
who like a blind man struck all those he met
and, often running toward the pagan flag,
said, "Do you bet I'll bring it to you now?"
He did it, and was highly praised for it.
The pagans saw it, and were frightened all,
and each ran fast like a wild animal.

Where'er he fought, Orlando could be seen,   141
just as we see a hatchet chopping wood
raised in midair before we hear the sound
of its blow when the ax is high again.
And Turpin was not blessing with his hand—
he was impressing foreheads with his sword:
'twas not the time to show the cross, but rather
to pierce a Saracen instead of each *Our Father.*

Walter of Mulion looked like a dragon,   142
and Guottibuoffi did not want to flee,
but with his sword he made the red pool rise,
eagerly looking for a way to die.
Much more than gadflies thirsted they for blood,
and so horrendous was the battle's havoc,
I'm sure you won't forget that line—or will you?
"For blood you craved and here with blood I fill you."

Angiolin of Bayonne and of Belland   143
both wounded people with great ease and skill;
Otho all over ran the camp across;
Avin refused to let his sword hang idle;
to Astaroth Rinaldo sent more men,
his breathlessness and weariness despite;
and mighty Richard, Mark, Avolius,
each of them proved how brave and strong he was.

Thicker and thicker now the battle grew,   144
and Death was looming fierce on every side.
While fighting here and there, it was by chance
Orlando, face to face, met Buiafort:
he struck him on the helmet with his sword
but, made of tempered steel and maybe haunted
by sorcery, the helmet withstood its violence
but from the pagan's head fell to the ground at once.

Orlando grabbed him by the hair and said,   145
"If for your life you care, tell me right now
about this treason everything you know;
I promise not to kill you if you talk;
and tell me first your name!" The Saracen
answered with a great shout, "I'll tell you, wait!
I'm Buiaforte, son of your Old Man—
he of the Mountain—who was once your friend."

As soon as the lad's name he heard, Orlando   146
saw the resemblance to the Grand Old Man,
and, letting go his hair, most tenderly
hugged him, and kissed him with his helmet on,
saying, "O Buiafort, you've told the truth:
he was my dear Old Man." Aside he took him;
"About this treason tell me everything,
since Fortune brought me to this suffering.

"But let me tell you first, upon my faith,   147
    your fight against my people is quite wrong;
    and your dead father, wherever he may be,
    cannot forgive you for it—this I know."
Young Buiaforte, now in tears, replied,
"My dear Orlando, set your mind at ease!
    Against my will my lord has sent me here,
    and those who rule we always must revere.

"When I was banished from my fatherland   148
    to his great court, Marsilius welcomed me,
    promising to restore me to my throne.
    I go in search of counseling and help,
    abandoned as I am by everyone:
    and this is why I wanted to come here.
    It seems to you some skirmishing I've done,
    but in this battle I have killed no one.

"Throughout the world I heard your fame resound,   149
    and ever in my heart I kept your name;
    knowing my father's ancient love for you,
    at your command forever here I am.
    About this treason you can surely guess:
    the traitors are Marsilius and Gan;
    and, being wise, you know what's so well known—
    that all these people want your death alone.

"Baldwin is wearing still Marsilius's cape—   150
    so has your Ganelon instructed him.
    Look! No one dares against him lift a spear,
    for so we have been ordered by our king."
Orlando said, "Put back your helmet on
    and to the fight return as usual. What
    will be, will be; but this remember till the end—
    like the Old Man you will forever be my friend."

And soon he added, "Wait! Watch out, I say!   151
    There's a strange poison ivy on the field—
    I mean Rinaldo in the thickest fight.
    Be careful not to tell him who you are,
    lest in a fit of temper he should say,
    'Why with the pagans are you fighting then?'
    Be cautious and avoid the blows! Pay heed:
    Argus's eyes throughout this fight you need."

Buiafort answered, "What you say is true.   152
If this hard battle ends as you desire,
I'll prove to you I am your perfect friend
as once my father was—thank God for it!"
But for so many things time is too short;
so we must pause before we can resume
this subject matter soaked with many a tear,
as with God's help in my next song you'll hear.

C A N T O   X X V I I

How can I think of singing my new rhymes,   1
Lord, Who have led me to describe such things
as seem to make the very sun shed tears,
now that its rays have turned already dim?
All of Your Christians scattered You will see,
and spears and swords all stained with blood—so many
that, unless greater help comes down to me,
this tale of ours will soon be tragedy.

And yet I had first thought that I would write   2
about my Charlemagne a comedy,
by Alcuin encouraged to this end;
but at the present time this cruel fight,
which threatens to become so rash and ill,
is filling with sad doubting this my mind,
and doubting makes my reason, too, despair,
because Orlando's life I cannot spare.

Rinaldo and Ricciardo, yes, have come,   3
and yet I fear for all the Christian knights,
unable as I am to judge serenely,
all absolute opinions being wrong.
Marsilius is such a wicked man
that he'll resort to all his sails and oars,
for he, this time, must either win or die
lest after all his loss in shame he cry.

Orlando, after leaving Buiafort,   4
in search of Baldwin went most eagerly.
Baldwin, still longing for his death in vain,
finally spotted Vegliantin, his steed,
and on the battlefield ran furiously
to where Orlando was, wretchedly saying,
"Sir, let me tell you that my duty I have done,
and yet so far I have been challenged by no one.

"Many a pagan I have caused to die,   5
but this I fail to understand—why all
of them are fleeing fast away from me."
Replied Orlando, "You pretend to marvel
at such a thing! If this you want to know,
take off your back the cape that you are wearing:
you'll see that Gano, once you take it off,
has sold us all as slaves to King Marsilius."

Baldwin replied, "Alas, if my own father   6
has so betrayed us as to lead us here,
if I am still alive today, by God,
with this my sword I want to pierce his heart!
But I, Orlando, am no traitor—I,
who always followed you with perfect love.
By none could I have been offended more."
And from his shoulders off that cape he tore,

saying, "Into the battle I'll return,   7
since I a traitor have been thought by you.
Oh no, God help me! Traitor I am not!
May I today be seen by you—but dead."
And back into the pagan horde he leapt,
ever repeating, "You have done me wrong."
The count regretted being blunt and bare,
seeing the lad then in such great despair.

Throughout the fight, Baldwin was running still   8
when cruel Mazzarigi there he met.
"Saracen dog," he said, "have you come here
to destroy Paris and its citizens?
You dirty renegade! You Patarine!
Down in the lowest Styx you will be soon."
And Baldwin with his sword went right ahead,
sending him quickly to the place he said.

Marsilius, as clever as could be,   9
had rallied a small troop of Saracens,
all of them most indomitable men.
They started closing all the Christians in,
thus taking on the battlefield the lead.
The most important generals were there,
and one—a man infernal and felonious—
as I have said before, was named Grandonius.

By chance he found before him Sansonetto,   10
who until then had fought beside the count.
From off his helmet he removed the mold,
like a cucumber splitting clean his head.
As the poor lad was falling to the ground,
Walter of Mulion arrived to fight,
eagerly wishing to avenge his death;
but he could not, being of lesser worth.

With Altachiara Oliver drew near   11
and landed blows upon the Saracen,
who with his club annulled them all, and had
already bruised and broken Walter's back,
and such a bitter pain poor Walter felt
that he saw night long before sunset come.
Looking like Hercules, who Cacus slew,
many a man Grandonio made new.

Orlando, who was fighting somewhere else,   12
did not yet know of Sansonetto's fate.
Oliver finally could rise again,
but with somebody else's help this time,
his Altachiara being powerless.
'Twas at this moment King Marsilius came:
wrathfully spurring his brave charger on,
he clashed against the Master of Bayonne.

Angiolin did not have his spear in rest;   13
therefore, the king with such a frightful blow
struck on his shield, he pierced his belly, too.
Orlando, who'd been riding everywhere
bringing his help to all his men from France,
could not see Sansonetto at his side,
and asked Terigi where he might be found,
not knowing he lay dead upon the ground.

Terigi said, "A while ago I saw him   14
fighting right there, inside that ring of men."
Forward Orlando spurred his Vegliantin,
leaping into the group, where the marquis
was at the very end of his endurance:
right there with speed and fury had arrived
Marsilius, Arcalif, and Zambuger,
and all were now surrounding Oliver.

Orlando, seeing Oliver alone,   15
wondered how he could still defend himself;
but Vegliantin got skittish then and there,
refusing to go on, lest he should tread
on Sansonetto's body lying there.
Orlando recognized him, and, "O luck!"
he shouted. "O so cruel and unfair!"
"This scoundrel murdered him," said Oliver.

Hearing these words, Grandonio began,   16
fleeter than any fleeting wind, to run;
the king and all the others left the marquis at once,
of Count Orlando all of them afraid.
Orlando from his horse dismounted and
deeply bemoaned his Sansonetto dear;
from all those corpses he removed him then
and told Terigi, "Bring him to my tent!"

Across the battlefield Astolfo went,   17
and with King Balsamin finally clashed:
they wounded soon each other, but that bastard
Saracen dog then caught him unawares
with such a violent second thrust, his sword
passed through Astolfo's gorget and was seen
to come right out from the nape of his head,
sending him to the ditch instantly dead.

Then the same cursèd bastard Saracen   18
met on the field Angiolin of Belland:
with but one blow he made his helmet ring
and flung him nearly lifeless to the ground.
To Ricciardetto, at that moment there,
Angiolin turned for help (so stunned and breathless
appeared he still that he could hardly talk);
Ricciardo placed him on his horse's back.

Orlando had already given death   19
to Chiariello, King of Portugal,
and Fieramonte, who escorted him;
now he turned his steed to the other side,
where Duke Astolfo, lovely lad, lay dead.
Avin, as soon as he beheld him fall,
came to avenge him and to right that wrong,
but could not cut his way throughout that throng.

Orlando could. Most wrathfully he came   20
and made Saracen blood stagnate in pools,
for Durlindana every time threw sparks
such as could have ignited sulphur fast.
Like a ferocious goaded bull he charged
when his Astolfo on the ground he saw,
for he had always loved him when alive,
and wondered how could such an end arrive,

when he was told that Balsamin was he   21
who brutally had slain the Duke of England.
At this point forward came the Saracen,
landing in such a way his pointed sword,
he could have pierced the hardest marble through;
but his intention wholly failed this time,
for Durlindana clashed with it halfway
and robbed it of its sharpness right away.

Cheiron had failed to teach the Saracen   22
that good intentions do not hit the mark.
Orlando, most attentive to all things,
decided then and there to cut his hand;
so measureless was soon the sudden blow,
Balsamin found his hand instantly maimed:
all of his fingers were cut off save one—
the thumb—on which the *ut* could still be seen.

No longer—even if he wanted to—   23
could he from that day on point more than one,
or signal seven in a morra game,
or hide any small straws within his hand.
Avin arrived and landed on his helmet
such an experienced blow with his brave sword,
his head just like a poppy he did sever,
and sent him to the ground—one more cadaver.

Rinaldo chanced to meet that Buiafort,   24
who, as it seems to me, did all he could
to find his death upon the battlefield.
He spoke to him of King Marsilius
and of his court, where he had also been,
until Rinaldo in a fury said,
"Who's not with me, he is against me, man!"
and started drumming on his helmet then,

until, with ever-soaring madness, he   25
let his sword fall from right to left three times,
and four, and five, and six; the Saracen
did not have time to plead for mercy: dead
he fell without a moan. Thus ended Buiafort,
and when his soul out of his body fled,
with all his pharisees our Squarciaferro, quick,
grabbed it the way a falcon grabs a chick.

Next to Rinaldo Ricciardetto fought,   26
and it is hard to tell his every feat:
wherever there was new renown to gain,
there he was stalking like a bird of prey,
though every partridge to the gauntlet came.
Archbishop Turpin, too, leapt like a cat:
he would have freed himself out of a hundred ropes
just to cut noses, hands, and legs, and lobes.

Grandonius had started a fine game: 27
he had a club that as a beam was huge,
compared to which all weapons lost their worth.
Now those who tarried, made by nature slow,
were made to sing such vespers, they grew hoarse
and deaf and dumb, and ever out of tune.
But, ah, no longer was he free to wander,
for he was spotted by our Count Orlando,

who shouted, "Rabble that you are, beware!   28
You'll soon be dead and will no longer boast
of my best friend's—my Sansonetto's—death.
You will narrate the entire tale in hell.
Ah, you could not have done me graver wrong!
But you'll be sorry, dog, son of a bitch!
Thinking of running from me? Turn this way,
you miserable scum, for you must die today."

After he saw the count, Grandonius   29
wanted to run indeed, for he felt lost,
and fear had made his pride collapse in him.
But who could run from Vegliantin away?
Leopards and tigers and the nimblest bird
this time would not have made it had they tried.
Vegliantin seemed to sense his master's wrath
in wanting to avenge his Sansonetto's death.

Even if Mars himself, armed on his horse   30
and on both sides escorted by his men,
had come to earth to help Grandonius,
he could not have protected him at all
through either art or skill or deity.
His hand upon his sword, Orlando was
so fuming over Sansonetto's fate,
he was still shouting at him, "Bastard, wait!"

Then, as the pagan stopped and turned to him,   31
he raised his sword as high as his arm rose,
and landed it across the helmet so,
it went down further, severed both his cheeks,
and then his chest and then the rest of him,
till his soul sped; the sword cut through the saddle,
and the steed, too, into two halves it split.
But Vegliantin now misbehaved a bit.

Orlando's sword had come so strongly down   32
that to his knees he too was forced to fall
(he almost broke his back because of it)
and could not stand on his four legs again,
for Durlindana, being firmly stuck
down in a rock concealed beneath the ground,
nearly two feet down, kept him motionless—
poor Vegliantin!—just like a brooding hen.

Orlando pulled it out with effort then,   33
shouting, "O Vegliantin, what have you done?"
The poor steed seemed to be somewhat ashamed,
and like a cat stood fast on all his four.
'Twas Heaven, I believe, helped Count Orlando
with one more grace, as often in the past:
God always helps the good, whene'er in need they are;
therefore, call not a lie what I have said so far.

From dead Grandonius Orlando went 34
back to the battle, very deeply sighing,
for, ah, his death could not restore his dear,
dear Sansonetto back to life again.
He was like a mother bear that, chased by dogs,
uproots all boughs, breaks loose all binding ropes,
and all things ruins out of spite and wrath:
thus he avenged his Sansonetto's death.

He chanced to see Marsilius at last 35
and, grabbing from a Saracen a spear,
wanted to pierce his heart with it at once;
but at that moment someone else passed by,
and the spear landed in his chest instead,
and, coming through his back, with its prongs hit
still one more pagan's abdomen and spleen:
so two transfixions with one blow were seen.

He told Marsilius, "The time has come 36
to punish you for all your thievish deeds,
for in your mother's womb you were predestined
to wear a well-greased noose around your neck."
Now Zambuger, foreseeing his next move,
covered his father with his shield at once,
but Durlindana treated it like ice,
cutting the shield and the man's arm likewise.

Zambuger hit the ground in sudden pain 37
and—ah, poor boy!—was later trampled on:
a young recruit, he made a big mistake,
for he was like a little simple lamb
by a wild lion crushed most easily.
Marsilius soon vanished like a bird,
or like a deer by hunters terrified;
and Zambuger on earth no longer played.

Marsilius ordered that the arm be found 38
so that in all the mosques it could be shown
as a religious relic everywhere
(I hope all of my readers keep this detail in mind);
and Fortune now he started to blaspheme,
who in his favor did not turn her wheel,
and on gods Apollin and Belfagor
he wished to wage his most vindictive war.

But tell me, how could he avenge his son   39
if, the day long, he hardly left home base,
so much he dreaded Count Orlando still?
Rather, I think, he needed (this advice
Thraso gave Gnatho long ago) a sling
whereby to hurl a stone from far away,
for the more vile and low his cowardice,
the subtler and more keen a traitor is.

Just as we use the figure of a circle   40
to understand the entire firmament,
so those who wish this story to know well
must think of something, something else to guess.
We're not pretending, singing, dreaming here,
nor is this time for mental speculation:
my little boat will have the Lethe River crossed,
and you will still be sailing off the Misenus Coast.

But since there are cicadas of first class,   41
which I'm comparing to the Indian ones,
singing in every season noisily,
you, who are reading things that sound so strange,
look for a literal meaning all the time,
and you will find it on an easy road:
I do not understand your anagogical
or moral sense, or trope so tropological.

Well, then, not even King Margheriton   42
was joking with his able scimitar.
He had with him that mighty Syrion
whose club made people run at the third blow.
Our Christians were so frightened by its sight,
they looked like dogs before the sounding whip:
on all their helmets many a ball and chain
made, the whole day, a notable refrain.

Angiolin of Belland was killed by him   43
with such a cruel and resounding blow,
his head was, like an acorn, crushed at once;
and so were Mark of Mount Saint Michael and
his brother. But right there Rinaldo came
to bring his help to all his faithful friends.
Seeing that man, who many Christians still
continued with his whirling club to kill,

he shouted, "Saracen, what's on your mind?   44
Have you with your antenna come down here
to make all of our people feel its weight?
Turn this way! Death is pointing now at you."
At this, Frusberta he relieved at once,
and broke his helmet, found his scalp, and split
his skull, his neck, his shoulders: like a melon
he neatly cut in two the pagan felon.

Margheriton with fury threw himself   45
upon his prince, thinking of shielding him:
Rinaldo split his head right in the midst
exactly as a walnut husk is split;
lowering, then, his sword most rapidly,
he found the horse's head and cut it, too:
together with his master fell the horse.
Frusberta did not cut; better, it shaved, of course.

Bianciardin forward with more people came—   46
Fidasso, Mattafirro, Galleran,
the famous Arcalif and Balugant,
and King Brusbacca and Maldue of Frasse,
and other generals and admirals.
And such a deafening din was heard around,
it looked like the Tower of Babel 'bout to fall,
and soon in that direction hurried all.

Hearing that shouting and enormous din,   47
Orlando ran and found poor Baldwin there,
his chest transfixed by two horrendous spears,
and come to the last minute of his life.
"I'm not a traitor, as you see," he said,
and, saying this, down to the ground fell dead.
Loudly Orlando mourned him, sorry most,
blaming himself his death for having caused.

He told Terigi, "Bring him to my tent,"   48
and rushed soon afterward where he could see
Rinaldo working wonders with his sword,
and where the pagans' loudest cries were heard
and now the fight was at its bloody peak
(the Christian army was not laughing either):
some shouted, "Flesh!" and some, "Revenge and blood!"
and toward that tumult ran a multitude.

And there came also good Duke Egibard,   49
Avin, Anselmo, Guottibuoff, Avolio,
and Berlinghier with Richard and with Otho,
each coveting his share of all those blows.
So valiant and brave was Ricciardetto,
he made the bravest champions look clumsy;
above all, Turpin, the good priest from Reims,
as if they were but bricks, leveled the Saracens.

So many swords, so many hands were seen,   50
so many spears collapsing on their rests;
also, so many screams, strange sounds were heard,
one could but think of a most angry sea.
Throughout the day bells rang, and no one knew
whom they were cheering or for whom they tolled;
deafening thunder, flashes in the blue,
and Echo answering each forest through.

The fight was heard on earth and in the air,   51
for Astaroth—I will not tell you how—
along with Farferel caught every soul;
they always had a new bunch by the hair,
and how they scuffled, hanging from their hands!
Often the devils heard somebody's name:
"Leave that to me! To Satan I'll bring him down myself!"
and asked the other, "Is Marsilius not dead yet?

"Before he dies, he'll make us pine and sweat.   52
Has not Rinaldo furbished yet his snout
so that we can bring down both soul and hide?"
You, too, O Heaven, seem confused this time!
O cruel fight, like that of Rome or Troy!
This is unlike all battles here on earth.
A sanguine fire seemed to gird the sun,
and a bleak color the whole sky had won.

Hell was that day more beautiful to see   53
than what was happening in Roncesvalles.
The Saracens were dropping down like pears,
and Squarciaferro carried them in sacks;
quickly they filled every infernal storm
and every rock and every crooked path,
all mosques and ramparts and each precipice;
and what a feast throughout the City of Dis!

Lucifer had so many mouths wide open, 54
he seemed that day a nest of little birds
awaiting mother's beak: those pagan souls,
fast raining down, he swallowed by the tufts;
it was like grayish snow falling in flakes,
just like feed given to the little fish.
Ask not how many flakes he gulped down and enveloped
or if, just like a duck, a goiter he developed!

All the Carinthian balls were held in hell, 55
so that all I have said is but an inkling
(a feast there does not last till the next morn
or the day after and afterer-and-afterest,
as Roman women in the vineyards knew);
some played the drum, and some the castanets,
guitars and whistles—an instrumentation
that made steps change in great coordination.

All Roncesvalles looked like a saucepan filled 56
with an enormous omelet stuffed with blood,
with heads and little feet and other bones—
a special boiling and reboiling mess
that looked exactly like the blood-red stream
which Nessus down in hell was seeing still;
and it was blood the wind raised from the ground
in splashes, and in knots and clots yet bound.

The battle was a wholly purple sight— 57
it was like the Red Sea by tempest swollen
in which those still alive were seen to dabble;
you could have dipped a plummet anywhere,
such was the blood in which all people splashed,
and then, as admirals or steersmen do,
look at the sounding line brought up anew;
for the whole valley overbrimmed with blood.

Mars, I believe, this time could call himself 58
quite satisfied and sated with men's blood;
Rinaldo was the hero of them all,
for with his sword he did all that he pleased.
Orlando in the meantime found Malducco,
who had killed Otho and our Berlinghier;
ah, for these deaths he would no longer laugh,
for Durlindana made of him a half.

And Oliver with King Brusbacca clashed,   59
and crushed the head and helmet of the man
who had been fighting bravely 'mid his troops,
but did not know he, too, was close to death.
The Arcalif of Bagdad—was it chance
or cruel fate?—caught up with him right then,
and dipped his sword, unseen, into his side;
yes, like a traitor! Oliver so died.

But, bold, unvanquished, Oliver had turned   60
and seen the traitor who had wounded him
so proditoriously. He said to him,
shouting, "By treason, O most cruel sinner,
you have been able to transfix my side,
and gain new fame the only way you know how:
may this your treason be the lasting praise
of King Marsilius and his wicked race!"

And with such rage he Altachiara drew,   61
he broke his helmet and his brains as well,
splitting him further to the saddle down,
so that the Saracen exhaled his last;
then like a blind man through the field he roamed,
striking and hammering with his sword still,
not knowing whether he struck friend or foe.
Ah, but Orlando happened soon to know.

Orlando, like a hound, had hastened to   62
the cries of the marquis which he had heard.
Oliver, meanwhile, so much blood had lost,
he did not know where in the world he was;
he even struck Orlando on the helmet
with such a blow the count had never felt.
"Brother-in-law, what's wrong?" Orlando said;
"Have you renounced our Christian faith and God?"

Oliver said, "O my dear lord Orlando,   63
forgive me, sir, if I have wounded you.
Know that I see no daylight anymore,
and cannot tell where this my sword will fall:
for all the blood I've lost and am still losing,
I am delirious and close to death;
the Arcalif has wounded me—that traitor,
but with this very hand I killed him later."

Great was Orlando's weeping over this,   64
for very fond of Oliver was he.
The battle was already lost, and so
the pagan traitor cursed he in his heart.
And blinded Oliver was saying now,
"If, as you always did, you love me still,
once again lead me where the fight is high,
for unavenged I do not want to die."

Orlando so replied: "I do not want   65
to live what's left of this my life without you;
I all my boldness, all my pride have lost,
so that no longer any hope have I;
but since, my Oliver, I love you still,
come now with me all of your might to show—
one death, one faith, one will." Into the thick
of the still-raging fight he led him, quick.

Oliver, now once more amongst the foe,   66
as he had done before, chased back the throng,
looking like one who mows the lawn, around him
cutting all grasses with his sickle down.
A desperate man, he bravely fought his last,
severing heads, ripping to pieces, pruning:
of every place he made an empty square,
whirling his sword still blindly everywhere.

Oliver and Orlando, now together,   67
hit all they met upon the field so hard,
many a pagan fell flat on his face.
But Oliver was very close to death now.
After they reached the tent, Orlando said,
"Rest now, my Oliver, and cheerful be!
And do not move! Just wait till I return!
I want to climb that hill and blow the horn."

Oliver said, "There's no more need for it: 68
my soul is willing to depart from me,
for to its Lord it's eager to go back."
He could not clearly say his final words,
like one who mumbles phrases in his dream,
and with great effort all he wished to say
Orlando guessed: that to Alda the Fair
he sent his last love—to his sister dear.

Oliver's breathing stopped, and so alone   69
our Count Orlando at that moment felt
that he resolved to blow the horn at last
to make his Carlo of his case aware:
so hard he blew, the sound reached Carlo's ears;
but through his mouth and nose his blood came out—
Turpin has said—and the horn cracked and split
the third time that the count blew into it.

Wasting no time at all, Oliver's steed   70
back to the field among the pagans ran
as if he wished his master to avenge:
biting like three wolves and six dogs in one,
he also felled so many with his kicks,
using his hooves as if to drive the flies away.
But Ricciardetto, seeing this, grew sullen:
he understood that Oliver had fallen.

Rinaldo, all alone, still held the fight.   71
Balugant and Marsilius had fled,
and very fast the king began to flee
as soon as Count Orlando's horn he heard.
He deep within was gnawing at himself,
for of his Zambuger he nothing knew:
he looked just like a lion in a cage,
and his right punishment was just his rage.

The Saracens so greatly feared Orlando   72
that many of them had already fled
through all the forests and the woods around
until they heard the horn's terrific sound.
Our Turpin says that as they heard that thunder,
many a bird up in the air was stunned;
not only Carlo heard it, but—oh, wonder!—
he even thought the earth seemed to go under.

Now, what Rinaldo did in his last hours,   73
my pen's not bold enough here to narrate;
truly he seemed an angry snake in heat,
judging by how he flayed this man and that,
and how he drove those rebel pagans back
(nothing he knew of Oliver as yet):
he broke and weakened, rent, unraveled, tore,
pushing the pagans with great wrath before.

Baiardo raised his hoofs menacingly   74
and, like a bear that chases dogs away,
now grabbed an arm and now bit off a thigh,
smashing to pieces all those pagans' bones
like loaves of bread fresh from the oven.
Hyrcanian tigers never were so cruel;
so much he bit and tore all men to bits,
he looked like Hecuba out of her wits.

And now our author hardly can believe   75
all of the wonders Ricciardetto did.
He of the battlefield had made a pool,
and blessèd those who could command their feet!
He did not kill—he rather swallowed down:
never were beasts so hunted or tracked down
as he could slaughter Saracens that day,
so much so that all people fled away.

Now here, as some historians suggest,   76
Rinaldo and Baiàrd and Ricciardetto
killed thirty thousand Saracens that day:
if false or true, I have reported it.
The count alone killed a long row, and so did
Anselmo, Sansonet, and Oliver.
But right now Heaven's sword I must bring out
so that no one the truth may wrongly doubt.

Who knows if Michael, still unrecognized,   77
as in the old days near Jerusalem,
killed in one day as many as he wished,
so as to sign an *M* for myriad?
Maybe he came to help the Christian men,
sent by the Lord God born in Bethlehem,
Who always takes good care of every friend—
and Heaven's might, we all know, knows no end.

'Twas up to God now to take care of things: 78
but twenty thousand and six hundred Christians
against six hundred thousand Saracens!
I have been able this my tale to base
on worthy, simple, and reliable
authors who do not like to waste their words;
Turpin and Urman—as I always knew—
write only what they know and what is true.

And if somebody says that Turpin died
in Roncesvalles, well—in his throat he lies,
for I can prove the contrary: he lived,
that is, until Charles conquered Saragossa,
and it was he who wrote this very tale;
Alcuin also quite agrees with him,
who up to Carlo's disappearance wrote,
and honor to his memory has brought.

79

After him came the famous Arnald, who
about this matter wrote most diligently,
and did research about Rinaldo's feats
and all the wonders he in Egypt did;
following the thin trace of his red chalk,
never does he go off the patterned thread:
(since he was gifted as his life began,
no lie could you expect from such a man).

80

Wholly bewildered, Count Orlando went
back to the fight when Oliver was dead,
like one who from a funeral returns
to comfort his bereaving family;
or, rather, like a ship that with no hopes
has, after a great peril, come to port,
he much complained about his bitter luck,
but more about the ship the tempest took.

81

He saw no longer good Duke Egibard,
and Guottibuoff upon the ground lay dead,
with Avin and Avolius, with Richard and with Walter;
and therefore seized and overwhelmed with grief,
but more than ever valorous and great,
he said, "This is the last of all my fights:
until the end, Lord, give me strength and breath,
and I'll be faithful to You unto death."

82

Anselm and Ricciardetto still remained
with Turpin and Rinaldo; great, instead,
was still the pagan throng that fought for life
though every trumpet had announced a stop.
Orlando Durlindana then unsheathed,
and I know not if this was the last time
(but I will say so, lest you all be bored)
he was to brandish this most honored sword.

83

Now the few Christians left upon the field   84
loudly bemoaned the death of Oliver
and vented on the pagans all their wrath
by working mighty wonders in the end:
those impious wretches ran in terror still,
finding no mercy ever, no way out.
They had no time to tell their buttocks, "Run,"
because the fight was nearing its *amen*.

So many people's brains were seen to fall   85
that every crow was having now its day;
those whose intestines were less sorely pierced
presented bellies looking like cheese graters
or like pans good for roasting chestnuts
but not so very good for cooking tripe.
Orlando's boundless rage exploded so,
fury and strength were doubled 'gainst the foe.

In front of him he chased those pagan hordes,   86
resembling a wild lion in the woods
that with his roar and footprints scared all beasts.
Shouting, "Beware, all of you pagans! This
is my last fight," he wakened those who slept
or, rather, put those still awake to sleep.
About his life he did no longer care
with Oliver and Sansonetto no more there.

Caesar in Thessaly he would have won that day,   87
and even Hannibal at Trasimene or Cannae;
throughout the battle he was heard to roar
like a wild boar that bites all men he meets
and arms and heads and hands throws in the air:
he wished to end with honor his last hours.
If time was short, his will was yet immense,
and sweet it is to avenge a just offense.

Wherever he saw people, there he went,   88
and, like a gentle eagle closing in,
routed and scattered every regiment,
casting all of its banners to the ground.
Now think, good reader, if the field grew red!
The war was following a Turkish style:
Orlando pushed and felled and broke and tore apart;
those hoped to live who ran as fast as a dart.

Now to the right, now to the left the fight   89
was seen to wave in all its grievous pain;
the Christian side resisted valiantly,
such was Orlando's valor and great work.
He was like lightning dimming other lights:
whene'er he let his noble sword fall down,
the master's skill at once was printed there,
and few were those his hand would ever spare.

Surely that day she was not deaf nor blind—   90
that old, horrendous hag who more than once
sharpened her bleak and bloody scythe, and then
felt with her nail its edge, at the same time
staring at Count Orlando; often, too,
she stood behind Rinaldo, feeling brave,
for fast he ran wherever there was gain;
and Ricciardetto was not there in vain.

Simply by chance, I think, Rinaldo gave   91
the loveliest stump to cruel Galleran,
who until then to every Christian man
had looked like a ferocious werewolf loose:
he with Frusberta stopped his hand at once,
haunting it with the illness of the pine tree
and fir and beech, and rendering it soon
to future whitlows then and there immune.

And though the Saracens were briskly fleeing,   92
he made a pulp of all those Philistines,
for every time he let Frusberta down,
no fewer than six of them fell to the ground,
and several tombs were opened all at once,
because—to quote here Benedetto Dei—
they all were plunged into some awkward pit
to hear the lowest sprouting of the wheat.

Though anguished most and weary, Count Anselmo   93
was showing his indomitable worth;
but Mattafirro reached him from the side
and let a hatchet fall upon his horse,
making it drop upon the ground at once,
and therefore running after him with wrath:
he struck upon his helmet right away
and in this way could Count Anselmo slay.

Back on his steed was Mattafir anew,   94
and strong and desperate blows once more he thrust.
Rinaldo shouted like an angry guard,
rebuking him, "Your fame you can achieve
like Pyrrhus or Marcellus: you are one
who kills dead men without their helmets on,"
and with a stroke that made a master clear,
he severed then his head from ear to ear.

And then Fidasso in the fight he met,   95
who squatted like a midget and a hare
among the troops, and with his lowered head
went through the battle splashing in the blood
because he heard Rinaldo's awful din,
which sounded like a Libyan dragon's fight;
Fidasso then trusted himself too much,
and there he was forever made to crouch.

For Ricciardetto's horse rose on his hooves   96
so that he had to fall right back at once,
and in so doing landed on his chest;
with spears and darts the pagans searched beneath
as if still fishing; surely Ricciardetto
would have died instantly without a sound
if Count Orlando had not cut both reins and steed
with one strong blow, thus helping up the lad.

He shouted, "Ricciardetto, are you afraid?   97
There are too many horses here: take one!"
And Ricciardetto then, as every knight
used to do, tried to jump up on a steed
already fully harnessed for the fight.
But, ah, his worth was now devoid of hope
(his generous heart was beating still with pride),
for all the Christians had already died.

By Turpin and Rinaldo still pursued,   98
very few Saracens were on the field.
Ah, dear old Turpin! Turpin, dear old friend!
Nobody at this moment spoke of truce!
Bianciardin like a thunderbolt had fled,
Balugant and Marsilius had gone,
roaming the field to find a shortcut in it,
leading to Saragossa in a minute.

But, look there! Poor Terigi had one foot   99
caught in a certain trap upon the ground.
Orlando could not see him: in his blood
he was still writhing, kicking, looking like
a lamprey ready for a special stew;
thank God the cursèd pagan multitude,
as I have said, no longer was around!
So there he could remain, quite safe and sound.

Orlando, now so weary, now so weak,   100
the helmet on his head could bear no more,
so much had he throughout the long day fought.
Tormented now by thirst, he could recall
the fountain where he had the last time drunk,
and started looking for it at all costs:
at last he found it right below the mountain,
and drank and bathed and rested at that fountain.

As soon as he dismounted, Vegliantin   101
in front of his dear master lifeless fell,
but first he knelt and begged his leave to go,
and seemed to say, "I've brought you safely here."
Quickly Orlando sprinkled water on him,
trying to cheer him up, to keep him there;
but when he saw his charger did not budge,
in such a manner he began his dirge:

"O Vegliantin, you served me very well.   102
O Vegliantin, where is your boldness now?
O Vegliantin, let no one else now boast.
O Vegliantin, your final hour has come.
O Vegliantin, you've doubled all my tears.
O Vegliantin, you need no bridle now.
O Vegliantin, if I offended thee,
even if thou art dead, oh, pardon me."

Turpin has written (and I marvel still)   103
that as Orlando murmured "Pardon me,"
the horse was seen to open soon his eyes
and with the motion of his head say yes;
so much so, that Orlando shook the rein,
believing that he had come back to life:
as Pyramus and Thisbe once had been,
now were Orlando and his Vegliantin.

Seeing himself alone, Orlando turned
and looked upon the plainland right below
(Rinaldo and Ricciardo were not there),
and all those corpses filled him with great fear,
for all the blood had now stagnated there
and Roncesvalles was a most gloomy thing.
I let my readers try to think how sad
he was in front of all those people dead.

He said, *"O terque, o quaterque beati"*
(as once the famous Trojan hero said),
"and wretched those who still remain alive,
as I am now, until the final hour!
If still our bodies are full-armed on earth,
our souls are where Lord Jesus is adored.
O happy Oliver, you live, I say:
oh, for our fatherland, all of you, pray!

"Now we shall all remember Malagigi,
now all of France will put on mourning dress,
now Paris will be weeping in great woe,
now my poor bride will be most desolate,
now Saint Denis will almost be despised,
now all the Christian epos will be spent,
now Charles and all his realm will be destroyed,
now wicked Gano will be overjoyed."

But now he saw Terigi coming near:
like a thrush, he at last had freed himself,
and for his master had so keenly searched
until he found him finally down there.
Orlando asked him where on earth he'd been
and if of Prince Rinaldo he had news.
Terigi said, "I did not pay attention,"
and so his own bad luck he had to mention.

The story says that Count Orlando struck
his lovely Durlindana on a stone
several times with all his mighty strength:
the sword not only did not break or bend—
it split the stone as if it were a chip;
and all the pious pilgrims who return
from far Galicia the same story tell:
they've seen that stone and the split horn as well.

104

105

106

107

108

"Strong Durlindana," Count Orlando said,
    if I before had known your might so well
    as at this hour of my death I know,
    I would have held the world in no esteem
    and now would not be here in such a plight.
    O worthy sword, so sharp in all your deeds,
    not fully knowing all your inborn might,
    I used you with respect in every fight."

Now to Rinaldo let's go back. In chasing
    the Saracens no obstacles he found,
    and so, the hunting over, he returned,
    like a hound called by its own master back,
    and breathless now, and limping, weak and weary,
    retracing every step. Upon his horse
    he galloped back, exhausted, full of sweat,
    till he Orlando near the fountain met.

How happy was the count to see his cousin!
    He asked him soon how the whole thing had gone.
    Still out of breath, Rinaldo said to him
    that all the pagan multitude had fled.
    Turpin and Ricciardetto also came,
    and to make this our story more precise,
    Turpin informs that on Saint Michael's Day
    that cruel fight took place—the eighth of May.

'Twas the year of the Lord eight hundred six,
    ruled by the planet that wants only war;
    surely a half leap year it had to be,
    for on the earth one more natural day
    the sun remained; as far as I'm concerned,
    I know not if astronomers are wrong
    (not the whole earth, but just our hemisphere
    I mention, for white ink is not good here).

I do not know if readers will believe
    that in that fight so many people died;
    but firmly on my mind are still those words,
    "And Michael there will be your company."
    Nor can I in the least believe the count
    capable of concocting such a lie.
    The Blessed Champion, then, must have been there.
    But I insist 'twas in the month of May.

109

110

111

112

113

"We're not of May," this is what people say;   114
nor do they say it of the other months:
it is in May every bird chirps and talks,
and leisurely and long all donkeys bray;
'tis advantageous to repeat this thing.
To every proverb this does not apply,
such as "At table one grows never old,"
though if one eats too much, one's days are tolled.

But true or false, accept the number then,   115
and to my subject matter let's go back:
if Michael came, he is most welcome here;
if he did not, they died—and that's enough.
To write a story or a comedy,
one must be faithful to what has been written
already on it, what he hears and reads
whether in modern or in ancient deeds.

Now here the most heart-rending notes begin!   116
Orlando, kneeling on the naked earth
and with tears warmly streaming down his face,
begged Turpin to absolve him of his sins,
and with most humble words began to tell,
as though he were confessing now to him,
all of his faults, especially the three
that weighed upon his conscience heavily.

"What is the first?" Archbishop Turpin asked.   117
Orlando answered, "*Maiestatis laesae,*
idest in Carlo verba iniuriosa.
The second is that I have failed to treat
Oliver's sister as my wedded wife:
these are the first offenses to my God;
the other is a sin that gives me bitter pain,
as everybody knows—Don Chiaro I have slain."

Turpin said then, "But you were ordered to,   118
and blind obedience is dear to God,
who therefore pardons you most willingly.
As for your lack of homage to King Charles,
well, this I know—he asks for what he gets.
As far as Alda, if your conscience tells you
that chaste in thought and actions you have been,
I think our Lord won't see it as a sin.

"Do you remember any other sin?"   119
  Orlando so replied, "We are all human,
  proud, envious, irascible and greedy,
  slothful and gluttonous, vainglorious,
  quick to win, blind and deaf to do what's good;
  and so against my neighbor I have sinned:
  through carelessness or laziness—poor me!—
  I did not do my acts of charity.

"And other mortal sins I don't recall."   120
  Turpin said, "One *Our Father* now will do,
  and say the Miserere up to the word *Peccavi,*
  and I absolve you by th' authority
  of the great Cephas, owner of the keys
  that soon will place you in the lasting realm,"
  and, blessing him, he gave him absolution.
  Orlando said this prayer in conclusion:

"O Great Redeemer of all wretched mortals,   121
  Who for our love did humble so Yourself
  as to become flesh in that Virgin rare
  the day Your Gabriel unfolded wings,
  and, utterly unmindful of our faults,
  ransomed our human nature lovingly:
  now bid your servant go, if so You please,
  and, dear Lord, let me come to You in peace.

"Yes, I say peace, after so long a war,   122
  for I am weak and wearied by my years.
  Give to the earth at last this wretched body,
  which You can see already old and gray,
  while reason's not yet faltering in me,
  while still my soul in my weak flesh is strong:
  so that in time You welcome me to You
  (many are called, but the chosen are few).

"You know—I do not have to tell You, Lord—   123
  that I have always battled for Your faith
  while I have lived in this my world below;
  but now this fight I can endure no more:
  so, as I must, I give You back Your sword,
  but You, have mercy, Lord, on my gray hair!
  'Tis time that I Your glory only eyed,
  and now forever laid these arms aside!

"Lord, to Your servant lend your kindly hand,   124
out of this labyrinth deliver me,
for unto us You are the Pelican
that prayed for those who nailed him on the cross;
for I have known the vanities of life
(*vanitas vanitatum!*) and its faults,
and, oh, upon this earth, for all my toils,
sins and more sins have been my only spoils.

"At least I always walked within Your grace,   125
having long battled for Your holy faith:
therefore I hope to find Your mercy now.
Myself I blame still for Don Chiaro's death,
and maybe he for my damnation prays;
but You, and You alone, can pardon me;
to Turpin, on my knees, I told my sin; to You,
O Lord of mercy, I confess it now anew.

"O Lord, the day You first created us,   126
because You're so magnanimous and good,
You estimated—this I do believe—
that we upon this earth are all God's children.
If with his silent zeal the serpent tempted
Adam, You paid the penalty of it,
but did not have to, being Lord and King,
the very One Whose hand had molded him.

"And by forgiving our first father, You   127
forgave mankind in its totality;
You even deigned to make Yourself its creature
when You selected on this earth a mother
(maybe I'm entering too dark a vale):
the Christian fighters are your army then.
I have defended them with this my sword;
now You, in turn, help me, my gracious Lord.

"The ten commandments that in ancient days   128
You gave to Moses on Mount Sinai,
up to this day I have obeyed them all,
and Your most true religion I have kept;
therefore, O Lord of justice, if You must,
deal with me justly but with mercy too,
for to a Lord of justice one must turn
and only for just causes plead and yearn.

"Do not, O Lord, start quarreling with me,   129
    for in Your presence nobody can ever
    be justified if You desire it not,
    for we were born in sin and misery,
    and whatsoever comes unto this world is blind,
    save You alone, Whose birth occurred in light.
    On this old age of mine have pity, and
    deny me not to reach salvation's land.

"Alda the Fair I now commend to You: 130
    ah, she will soon be dressed in mourning for me!
    If she is yet to marry when I'm gone,
    may better fortune smile upon her days.
    And since, O Lord, I'm asking for too much,
    if You allow me one more grace to plead for,
    remember Your good Charles, that dear old man,
    and these Your faithful servants in whom myself I scan."

As soon as Count Orlando spoke these words   131
    with many bitter tears and sighs, three rays
    like three long strings seemed to descend at once
    down from the sun, as though by rainbow brought.
    Rinaldo and the others stood around
    like people watching a dear parent die,
    so grieving and so sad, yet so ecstatic,
    each of them looked like Francis the Stigmatic.

At the same time, with all that flashing light,   132
    a sweet and tender music like a breeze
    was heard to come right down upon the earth—
    so sweet and tender, light, ethereal!
    Orlando looked transfigured in his grief,
    and there the angel who told Mary *Ave*
    was right before him, sent by God in heaven.
    He said to them, *"O Viri Galilei!"* then

he took on human shape and, in midair,   133
    in front of Count Orlando, on his knees
    he said these final blessed words to him:
    "God sent me here as messenger to you,
    and I am he who came to Nazareth
    the day your Jesus took on man's own flesh
    in the Most Holy Virgin, who's your great
    and ever mighty heavenly advocate.

"And since I love your human kind too well,			134
as He who made that planet wants me to,
up there I'll take you, far beyond that sun,
wherein your soul will be forever glad,
and you will hear all our sweet carols sung:
because you are God's athlete in the world,
true champion, and the perfect archimandrite
of His flock, lost without you in the night.

"Know that in heaven your devout and pious,			135
adoring prayer has been heeded well;
all saints and angels liked it very much,
for you're a citizen of that land, too;
and since you have brought honor to its flag,
and nearly chased idolatry from earth,
God will reward the merits you've amassed,
for in His eyes is written the whole past.

"God saw you, still a little lad, at Sutri,			136
where more than once with great delight you stirred
the court of your beloved Charlemagne;
and saw all that you did in Aspramont,
and then in France and Spain; the many men,
like Sansonetto, all by you baptized
in Mecca; you have brought to Mary's son
Persia, Jerusalem, and Syria;

"and after Carlo had for a long time			137
kept under siege Pamplona but in vain,
you came: your presence was much needed there
(as it had been predicted by the charts),
and, as in Troy Achilles, you are still talked about;
then, when Macarius betrayed him, Charles,
following your advice, went back to France,
where he regained his bride and realm at once.

"Haughty Troiano, too, and Pantalisse,			138
all that you did and met since you were born,
Serpentin, Ferraù, and all the others—
all's written in God's eyes; Adastro, the great foe;
all you accomplished on th' Egyptian field
fighting like God's most brave and perfect friend,
while still Morgante was there in your company—
who is perhaps in spirit now present here with me.

"In heaven he will keep you company   139
   as here on earth your giant used to do,
   for it was you who placed him on the road
   that led him to his present happy state.
   And since I read your thoughts now that I mentioned
   Morgante's name, I want to tell you this:
   about that rogue Margutte you also wish to know:
   he's been appointed herald to Satan down below,

"and is still laughing, and will laugh forever   140
   as here on earth (but you have never met him):
   he is the only fun allowed in hell.
   Now you have asked of God the grace of death
   just as those ancient holy martyrs did;
   but I know not how deeply felt your grief is:
   to see if all your patience is still true,
   for the last time He has now tempted you.

"One before God must bend his loaded back,   141
   and say to Him like Job, "Give me the strength,
   O my dear Lord, to bear all suffering
   and do Your will alone until I die."
   As soon as Job could see the will of God,
   he bore his every trial with great joy,
   till none of his possessions was still his
   when his home, too, sank into the abyss;

"and to his wife, who much complained and grieved,   142
   he said, 'Dear woman, listen now to me:
   Dominus dedit (he had given it),
   Dominus abstulit (he took it back);
   sicut Domino placuit, in ea
   factum est: and this time 'tis truly so;
   and then he said, '*Sit nomen Domini*'
   (may the Lord's name be praised eternally).

"So if you want to stay on this earth still,   143
   God will new people place at your command,
   and you will make both land and sea still fear you.
   But since our Master does not change His mind,
   those who are dead cannot come back to life,
   for they're already mingling up in heaven
   with all the saints and the angelic sect,
   in the sweet number now of the Elect.

"No, you must not believe that those in heaven   144
  ever desire to return down here
  and give their limbs to sun and frost anew:
  only up there is peace with no more war,
  and hair is not discolored by the years.
  However, that good Lord Whose will is right
  will grant your wish, and death to you will send
  as soon as I back to His court ascend.

"Alda the Fair you in your prayer commended: 145
  one day you'll see her happy in the sky,
  seated in glory near that holy bride
  who's venerated on Mount Sinai still,
  and crowned with lilies and with roses, such
  as Aries and Flora cannot make;
  on her gray tunic she will wear a veil
  till she in heaven be your wedded bride again.

"For all his well-deserved and pious merits,   146
  Charles in the corner of the Cross will be,
  with Joshua and all its strong defenders,
  who sing in heaven, all in unison;
  and there you'll treat him still as you did here.
  Look at the sun, which seemed to run so fast!
  Now not so fast it's entering the sea,
  awaiting, twenty hours, your sovereign eagerly.

"And since your Charles will presently be here,   147
  all of your warriors will be interred;
  he has already left Saint John of Port,
  having been reached by your rebounding sound.
  Forgive the traitor who has killed your men,
  for he'll be rightly punished very soon;
  and now, to have God's blessing, for your sake,
  a bit of earth, your ancient mother, take:

"because God fashioned Adam out of it,   148
  as your communion it will serve you well.
  Rinaldo, when you're gone, will still be here,
  ever to raise the gonfalon of Christ,
  and soon above the angels will rejoice,
  welcoming there your Turpin, the dear man;
  and my Lord loves young Ricciardetto, too.
  And now, God's servants, live in peace! Adieu!"

And so, after he spoke these holy words, 149
the holy messenger returned to God.
They all were weeping, moaning for the count.
Orlando now stood up in copious tears
and hugged Rinaldo countless times, and then
Turpin and all the others. Then he prayed
so fervently, like Saint Jerome he truly looked,
so often with his hand his breast he deeply struck.

Indeed, it was a venerable sight! 150
He murmured *Nunc dimittis* to himself,
as in the temple the old man one day:
"O my dear Lord, when shall I be with You?
My soul's a prison of confusion: so,
from this blind world, O Lord, deliver me,
not through my worth—through grace's supplement:
into Your hands my spirit I commend."

Rinaldo had entreated him to stay, 151
with Turpin, Ricciardetto, and Terigi,
saying, "I have just come from Egypt: why
do you, dear cousin, leave me here alone?"
But since their praying was but wasted time,
remembering what Gabriel had said,
in reverence and awe they spoke no more:
what God decrees, all faithful men adore.

The count fixed Durlindana in the ground, 152
and then, embracing it, he said, "My Lord,
now make me see the road that leads to You;
this is in place of that most holy cross
on which Your sinless human body bled,
so that both earth and heaven gave a sign
when, not without a lofty mystery,
You shouted in your grief, '*Eli! Eli!*'

Wholly seraphic, looking at the sky, 153
he seemed a man transfigured all about,
addressing his Lord Jesus Crucified.
O happy end! O well-created soul!
Blessèd old man, who lived on earth so well!
Finally, then, Orlando bent his head,
and as he took the earth—so had the angel said—
out of his noble breast at last his spirit fled.

But first he placed his sword upon his chest   154
and gently on its pommel crossed his arms.
Thunder soon was heard, and the whole sky
seemed then to open wide most suddenly;
and like a little cloud ascending high,
a choir of angels sang *In exitu*
Israel de Egypto solemnly;
the trembling of their wings all men could see.

And many other lovely things were viewed   155
because that holy nimbus, bit by bit,
broke into newer lights and newer sparks
so that the firmament seemed all alit
with beams aplenty falling from the stars;
then, a most sweet and tremulous music brought
upon the earth a harmony so dear,
as though angelic instruments were near.

Turpin and all the others were enrapt   156
in such delight, they seemed elsewhere to be:
because that fire of eternal love,
when through God's grace it hovers over us,
warms up and comforts heart and soul so much,
we have the strength no more ourselves to know;
try to imagine, reader, with what love
they saw Orlando's spirit borne above.

After a sweet and lengthy psalmody,   157
voices they heard that very loudly sang,
Te Deum, Virgo alma Maria, Salve
Regina; and they looked up, like Elisha
who saw Elijah's chariot ascend,
or just as much astounded as was Moses
before the fiery bush upon the mount
when other things soon vanished all around,

until another thunderbolt was heard,   158
which sounded like a portal being shut.
And then they heard the whistle of a sling:
it was a butterfly from far away—
oh no, it was a dove as white as snow,
which—look!—on Turpin's shoulder, on Rinaldo,
Terigi, and Ricciardo, came to rest:
oh, what delight filled everybody's breast!

Turpin's opinion is that he believed   159
it was Orlando's very soul: he saw it
enter his mouth with all its wings and feathers—
most veritably so, as he that day
confessed to Charles, arrived in Roncesvalles
to ask for Count Orlando's honored sword:
surely Orlando, then, was still alive,
and so he knelt before him with a smile.

After Rinaldo and the others, left   160
so sad and lonely, long bemoaned and wept,
they all decided that they should inform
King Charles about their loss and tragedy.
Carlo was on his way, but poor Terigi—
such was his grief—looked more dead than alive;
he rested and then jumped upon his horse at once,
counseled by all to bring the dismal news to France.

Terigi, so, departed from his friends,   161
leaving his lifeless master there with them.
Now, not to seem so dazed, I'll take you back
to Carlo and his men at John of Port.
As soon as the resounding horn he heard,
he seemed to realize his own defeat,
and said to Namo and all those around,
"Did you, too, hear that horn's horrendous sound?"

All of them listened when they heard those words.   162
Ganelon seemed to hear, and was perturbed.
Orlando blew the horn the second time,
and Carlo said, "But what can all this mean?"
Gano replied, "'Tis sounding the retreat
now that the hunting's coming to an end.
Am I the only one to speak while, speechless, all men stare?
What think you—that the world is ending over there?

"It seems you do not know Orlando well,   163
sowing the sad suspicion in our minds
that he goes hunting through those woods all day
with Sansonetto and his Oliver.
We all remember that old time when he,
still a young man in Agrismont, each day,
pursuing bears, his hunting skill would show,
or chasing savage boar or deer or doe."

But when Orlando for the third time blew 164
with so much wrath and vehemence his horn,
and everybody listened thunderstruck,
Carlo, as usual composed and wise,
finally said, "That horn is echoing
deep in my heart and soul, and shakes my mind,
and 'tis no hunting sound it brings to me:
too late I recognize my misery."

And "From a horrid dream I just awoke, 165
O Gano, Gano, Gan," he said three times.
"I am ashamed of no one but myself
for not believing that this thing might be.
Now we need help and counseling at once,
for the most sorry fight is soon to come.
You're clean, but not you all; and yet the time
has come to apprehend the culprit of this crime.

"Arrest this traitor right away! Arrest him! 166
'Twas better for him never to be born.
O wicked, O most cruel sinner! And
O wretched, wretched me, who've lived so long!
Oh, how deep-rooted is an ancient vice!
O Malagigi, I should have believed you!
Your every warning was a true prognostic;
that's why my pain is now so much more caustic."

The Dane said then, "How many times, O Charles, 167
I told you—so did Salamon and Namo—
to Saragossa not to send that man,
for we could almost see the hook laid bare!
And when I saw him kiss our Oliver,
I said, 'We know you, Judas, very well!
O shame of every man and the whole nature,
some day you'll lead us to our sepulture.'

"But you did not accept the sound advice 168
we on such a serious matter offered you
because you at the time were obstinate."
Ganelon found himself without his nose,
being, like a fox by dogs, to pieces torn:
his hair and eyebrows were already shorn,
tufts of his beard were snatched off from each side,
and "Crucify the traitor!" all men cried.

But finally they all agreed that he   169
should soon be chained and in a dungeon kept
inside a tower in spirals going down—
a gloomy labyrinth with no escape.
And since no longer could they tarry there,
with all his barons Carlo left at once
(having been robbed, he bolted fast his door),
proceeding all toward Roncesvalles therefore.

He was aware that King Marsilius   170
had come with all his armies, fully armed,
as Ganelon had ordered him to do,
and that his men were in grave danger there;
never Orlando would have blown the horn
unless compelled by dire necessity
within a distance that its sound could travel through:
this was the signal of distress between the two.

The sun had crossed the middle of the day,   171
and toward Morocco now was falling down,
when Carlo heard Orlando's horn resound
for the third time, and left immediately
as Namo and the others had advised,
unanimous in thoughts at such a plight;
and when the shortened daylight he discerned,
to Christ, as usual, the monarch turned:

"Lord Crucified, Who from Your cross one day   172
bade, against nature, the bright sun grown dim,
with humble voice, O Lord, I'm begging You
that, till I reach that valley of dismay,
You may slow down its fleeting course today
so that I give my people burial:
oh, let it not so soon down in the ocean rest,
and leave me not so hopeless and distressed!

"Not through my merits, Lord, which are not such   173
as may obtain what Joshua obtained,
but since I have no wings wherewith to fly,
so that I may in Roncesvalles be soon!
May the most mighty prayers of the just
(so that Your power may by all be seen)
stop the command to th' eternal wheels assigned
until my cherished nephew there I find!"

And the sun stopped, which was already dim   174
throughout the firmament, in every land,
in grief for all the Christian people slain;
and someone says (but it's superfluous,
even if a most worthy author speaks)
that all the mountains turned to level plain—
the miracle that Carlo prayed for next!
But I condemn the author and his text:

I will be faithful to my common sense   175
and to the selfsame destination go,
for if an author builds his tale on lies,
his reputation in no time grows dark,
and he remains by candlelight, alone,
lazily sitting near the fire at night:
these people are so bold—have always been—
that Marsyas (one of them) has lost his skin.

Let it suffice to say that Carlo prayed,   176
and that his wish was granted right away:
the lovely planet, *ab aeterno* made,
its wonted order stopped observing soon.
O Heaven's mercy, you can halt the sun
for your beloved Charles! O boundless Love!
O clear example, showing in what ways,
to what extent, God loves our human race!

From mountain on to mountain rode Terigi   177
upon his horse, bemoaning still and sad,
shaking his head in disbelief and woe.
Charles recognized him as he saw him come
and, "O my noble knight!" he thought at once;
"Before he even speaks, his bearing tells me
he's bringing dismal news about the battle!"
(He seemed a waxen figure on his saddle!)

Before King Carlo good Terigi knelt,   178
saying to him, "My lord, *tarde venisti;*
Orlando's dead, we can go on no more,
and dead are all your champions, alas."
Hearing such tidings, Carlo scratched his face.
Terigi said to him, "If you had seen
the angels that to heaven brought his soul,
you would not scratch or touch your face at all.

"'Twas he who for the grace of death begged God,   179
    and such was his contrition as he died
    that Gabriel, the holy messenger,
    coming from heaven, answered soon his prayer,
    and everything they told each other then
    we, kneeling there, could very clearly hear.
    And there we saw—just think with what elation!—
    the angel who said *Hail!* for our salvation.

"Rinaldo and Ricciardetto, back from Egypt,   180
    have done today so many wondrous deeds,
    they made Marsilius, defeated, flee.
    In Roncesvalles you'll see your wretched men,
    all of them lying in a pool of blood,
    for it is blood that covers every shore.
    Nobody without weeping can see this,
    and tears are shed by stones and grass and trees.

"I saw Astolf and Sansonetto dead.   181
    So brave was Sansonetto (you would have
    been proud of him) that, to avenge his death,
    wrathful Orlando threw all banners down.
    Poor Oliver is also dead, and so
    is your Anselmo, brave Duke Egibard,
    Walter of Mulion, Avolius, Avin;
    and of the three, survives no Angiolin.

"The Arcalif of Bagdad, wicked man,   182
    most treacherously murdered Oliver
    after a slaughter of your Christian men
    which very deeply frightened all of us.
    Richard from sheer exhaustion fell down dead,
    and dead are also Guottibuoff and Otho,
    Matthew and Mark of Mount Saint Michael, too:
    so fierce a battle no one ever knew.

"Baldwin was seen to wear a certain cape   183
    as on the field with all his strength he fought,
    but when that cape he from his back took off,
    quickly a pagan soldier gave him death.
    Orlando then removed the helmet from
    the face of Buiafort, the Old Man's son,
    and heard from him the truth a moment later—
    that none but Gano is our wicked traitor.

"Turpin, Rinald, and Ricciardetto are,   184
of all your people, those who have survived
(yes, all the other warriors are dead),
and I have left them there in Roncesvalles.
Here I have come, or better yet have flown,
to bear the tidings of so much distress:
I wish that there had been, in my dismay,
a spear to pierce this heart of mine today,

"for, ah, with these my eyes I saw my master dead!   185
Now you cannot protect your Ganelon—
you, who committed your most grievous sin
when to Marsilius you sent that man.
So, Carlo, if you want to placate God,
have him soon quartered! But I feel death's chill
all over me as I am talking still to you,"
Terigi said; and then his soul to heaven flew.

Carlo, who heard that sad report and now   186
could see Terigi lifeless at his feet,
in his great anguish nearly from his horse
fell down, and said, "Let no one comfort me!
O battle, so inhuman and so gloomy!
O King Marsilius, you've done me wrong:
for as the emperor, I, on my part,
had made peace with you with a sincere heart.

"Never could I have thought a king like you—   187
of so much fame and of so great a realm—
(an adage speaks of loving those who love)
would dim his glory and his banner so.
O Ganelon, who ordered such a plot
whereby you led my worthy nephew there
in Roncesvalles to die; man with no shame,
I curse the day when to my court you came!

"What shall we do, dear Salamon, dear Namo?   188
O my bad luck, where will you take me now?
Shall we now go to Roncesvalles like poor,
blind men without a guide, without a goal?
O death, come quick to me—I'm calling you;
and if you do not come, you're cruelty itself.
Come, death! If on my life you now descend,
you will be called my one consoling friend."

Namo said then (and Salamon agreed),   189
"We must not marvel at Orlando's death:
on such condition God made Adam out
of mud: therefore, no wrong has here been done.
A ship will cross the lengthy sea until
she reaches finally a cliff or port:
before our very birth, the truth we learn—
death is the end of everything that's born.

"In this brief time that is allotted us,   190
let's do the things we are obliged to do,
such as our God himself expects of us,
for we were all created to act well,
as every sage has written and advised.
You know that I have lost four sons in action:
must now their bodies by the wind be driven?
Certainly such a thing would not please Heaven."

Added the Dane, "To Roncesvalles we'll go,   191
to find our Count Orlando first of all,
and give all our dead soldiers burial
so that they will not feed the roving beasts;
then we shall seek Rinaldo's sound advice."
Thus they consoled poor Charlemagne a bit;
but as they went, most nimbly galloping,
they found another unexpected thing.

As several books of history report,   192
in previous years our Count Orlando had
freed and regained the Sepulcher of Christ;
and there with many people he had left
young, noble Ansuigi to defend it;
and for ten years he kept the Tomb, until
the pagans took it back by force of war:
to France he was returning now, therefore,

and on his way he met his emperor.   193
Charlemagne, seeing all those people come,
felt in his heart that maybe King Marsilius
was marching to assail him once again;
but not long in such doubt did he remain,
for very clearly now he saw their flag—
a black cross looming on a snowy field;
which a poor victory to him revealed.

CANTO   XXVII   ❖   711

In short, as closer Ansuigi came,   194
he told him how from Mecca, in the night,
the Saracens had seized Jerusalem,
climbing its walls, with no *Salamalec;*
so he was forced to leave the Sepulcher
to guardians other than Melchizedek;
he was convinced, as he could understand,
that such a raid had been by Gano planned.

Charlemagne said, "O God, avenge Yourself,   195
if they in such a way can steal Your tomb!
Is this the day the world is waiting for,
when that horrendous bugle will be heard?"
And he recalled poor Hecuba, that sad
and most disconsolate old lady who,
after her many griefs and woes galore,
mourned at the very end her Polydorus,

and, like another Job, but "Patience!" said.   196
"Well, then, let's go to Roncesvalles at once!"
Carlo could see that it was sound advice—
they should not inconvenience the sun,
which was, that day, eccentric, and was not
following its old orbit, just to please
its own Creator and for Carlo's sake
(whate'er He makes, God also can unmake).

But since we want to go to Roncesvalles,   197
and, as I've said, the sun was waiting still,
let's go right to that fountain where Orlando
was being mourned by Turpin and Rinaldo
and Ricciardetto, weeping and in woe,
and waking round that blessed body still.
To Roncesvalles King Carlo came at last,
and there he felt his heart stop in his breast.

He looked upon his warriors, full-armed,   198
one on the other, on the blood-stained ground,
men and their horses piled up in one heap.
Others had fallen into some deep ditch,
and in the dirt were seen now, deeply stuck;
some seemed to stare at their own bleeding wounds,
some had their heads four feet from them away—
quite difficult to find on Judgment Day;

and some were quartered, rent to pieces, maimed,   199
with all their brains or their intestines out:
all those who once were men were shards and sticks
most weirdly hanging from their saddles still;
shields on the ground and spears on trunks were seen—
O what a slaughter of poor, hapless men!
O anguish and despair of many a father!
O weeping and laments of many a mother!

Carlo was weeping in bewilderment,   200
his heart atremble and his hair on end;
Salamon rubbed his eyes in disbelief,
Ugier and Namo both were horrified:
they all could see the all-vermilion earth
with trees and boulders dripping still with blood;
burnished and bloodied was all vegetation—
a spectacle of total desolation.

After he looked at every single thing,   201
Charlemagne turned to Roncesvalles and said,
"Now that the glow of every glory's spent,
valley of sorrow, be forever cursed!
May no seed in you bear any more fruit,
valley surrounded by still lofty peaks!
But may God's wrath forever on you rain,
infernal bolgia namèd after Cain!"

Then to the mountain's foot at last he came,   202
right at that fountain where Rinaldo waited.
Into more bitter tears he burst, and let
himself as lifeless from his charger fall.
Orlando he embraced and, sobbing still,
he said, "O blessed and most righteous soul,
oh, heed from heaven what I have to say:
I, after all, was your good king one day.

"I bless the very day that you were born,   203
I bless the happy splendor of your prime,
I bless the honesty of your advice,
I bless your never-failing gentleness,
I bless all the great wonders you performed,
I bless your most heroic worthiness,
I bless your every high and charming deed,
I bless and bless and bless your father's seed.

"And if I have to, I your pardon beg: 204
   you know that I did write to you from France
   when you, in Gascony, were cross with me
   for sending you to King Marsilius,
   in Roncesvalles, with Count Anselmo and
   the Lord of Burgundy. Who could have thought you'd die?
   Alas, I my just punishment have had:
   you are alive, and I am worse than dead.

"But tell me, O my son, where is the faith   205
   that we exchanged in our old happy days?
   Oh, much beloved soul, if you for me
   still care in heaven as you did on earth,
   give now to me, if God allows you to,
   your sacred, honored sword with your glad smile,
   just as you swore you would in Aspramont,
   there where I dubbed you cavalier and count."

As God decreed, Orlando heard those words,   206
   and, smiling, to his feet he rose at once
   and, with the reverence of bygone days,
   before his king he was on bended knee
   (let no one wonder, knowing that the sun
   stopped, for his sake, its course up in the sky)
   and, stretching out his hand, still smilingly,
   gave Durlindana to His Majesty.

Charlemagne at that moment felt his limbs   207
   with wonder and affection overcome,
   and, trembling, in his gauntlet took the sword.
   Before his lord, Orlando knelt again,
   and to God's holy kingdom flew his soul.
   Carlo felt sure of his salvation then,
   for had he not been certain, Turpin says
   he would have known the last of all his days.

There all the barons, kneeling on the ground,   208
   were shuddering with horror and with fear
   when they could see Orlando standing up,
   as is the case with all things supernatural:
   for there he could still be partially armed
   and with a stern and awe-inspiring mien;
   but when before the king they saw him kneel,
   quite reassured they all began to feel.

Rinaldo, then, and Ricciardetto hugged 209
King Carlo and the others tearfully,
and in detail discussed with all of them
the battle and the way it had been fought;
and, finally, agreed on where the dead
should be interred or shipped for burial.
But Charles himself seemed wan and agonized,
and hardly could, alas, be recognized.

He said, "Among the many graces, Lord, 210
that you have until now bestowed on me,
grant me that, through some sign or in some way,
I recognize my men that here lie dead
(I know not who I am or where I come from):
gather, as in Jehoshaphat, all bones—
hands with hands, feet with feet—and from on high
show me with love where our dead people lie."

They entered, then, the valley, where they found 211
all Christian soldiers with their limbs attached
and with their faces all to heaven turned,
for they were Adam's well-predestined seed.
Dear God, how many miracles You showed!
Happy the men who place their hope in You!
The bodies of the Saracens were found
scattered and maimed and facing all the ground.

Devoutly Charlemagne gave thanks to God, 212
who had so many graces granted him.
And now began a highly heaving sea
of grief and weeping no one could believe:
some looked for a dead father, a dead son,
some for a friend and brother; then, embracing
the recognized dear ones, their helmets they unlaced
and on their faces countless kisses placed.

King Carlo covered with his hand his eyes 213
as soon as dead Astolfo there he saw;
why was he not a pelican who revives
with his own blood the birds the serpent slew?
Ah, with his human blood he'd give him life!
Throughout the camp in such a way they cried.
Rinaldo wept and Ricciardetto moaned,
and Namo—the poor father!—was there, stunned.

But now with this our tale we must speed up,   214
for not much longer can we hold the sun,
still tarrying to please its highest Lord.
"O gentle faith! The man who worships God
(this is a noble line our Petrarch wrote)
with simple words can stop the firmament!"
Christians, be sure! That faith revealed to you,
all of these things, and even more, can do.

I think that those Antipodes below   215
several times that day kept wondering—
seeing the lovely planet not yet there—
whether the order of the sky was broken
or whether it had finished its last race
and was returning to its ancient mansion
before the mighty chaos opened here;
and in great doubt remained that hemisphere.

But to that far horizon went the sun   216
after the end of one more natural day;
the whole earth, maybe, thought that Phaëthon
had seized the chariot the second time.
On that same mountain Carlo and his men
remained that night until the morning rose;
and then he ordered that the Christian men,
or most of them, be brought to Aachen.

Several bodies were that day embalmed,   217
especially the paladins'; of them,
some were then shipped to Paris, others still
to other towns of France and foreign lands.
How many fathers were disconsolate!
How many screaming mothers tore their hair!
What scenes! What sorrow! Such laments before
had ne'er been heard on Greek or Afric shore.

Alda the Fair more than the others wept,   218
calling herself the wretchedest on earth,
mourning Orlando and her Oliver.
"Alas!" she cried, "For only a short time
was I the happy bride of the best knight
that ever mounted horse! And now, poor me,
I do not envy now his lucky death,
but I will weep and mourn till my last breath.

"O my sweet husband, my dear lord and father,   219
never will I behold you, great and bold,
ride fully armed among the Christian knights!
Oh, do not think that I may wed again!
But, rather, on your dear and handsome limbs
(in Aachen you're buried, I've been told),
as Dido once, your Alda, too, will swear."
And this is what she did—Alda the Fair.

Charles for his nephew built a sepulcher   220
in Aachen, and there his body brought;
and he decreed the greatest honors for him
before to Saragossa he moved on,
where the most doleful notes would soon begin;
and on the tomb he had some letters carved
with this phrase in the Latin idiom:
"One God and one Orlando and one Rome."

All France bemoaned her greatest champion dead,   221
especially the citizens of Paris
(Rome did not mourn her Scipio so much).
The funeral was held in Saint Denis's,
with every mourner fully garbed in black
(in ancient times, instead, the gray was used
as Pericles commanded all Athenians),
for wearing black announced forthcoming pains.

Astolfo's body was to England sent,   222
and he was greatly honored in his land
(Otho, his father—so they say—had died).
And they did not forget young Sansonetto:
a rich tomb, on the contrary, was built
for him by Carlo in Saint John of Port.
With his three brothers, even Berlinghier
was buried in a splendid sepulcher.

Oliver was interred in Burgundy,   223
where hoarse from weeping all the people grew.
But since we have many more things to say,
let us go back awhile to Balugant,
who for more trouble somewhere else is looking:
but will he know how to put up with it?
All of his men he gathered and arrayed,
who had in fear to woods and mountains fled,

and, knowing not about Orlando's death,   224
decided to return to Roncesvalles,
eager to bury all his other men.
As soon as on the mountain he was seen
about to come down to the valley, Charles
heard wise and shrewd Rinaldo say to him,
"Look! Balugant is coming here, I see.
His flags are most familiar to me.

"I think the time has come to call your men,   225
for God is granting us at last the grace
to start our great revenge against the foe."
At this, Charlemagne ordered everyone
most speedily to arm and wait for action.
Dawn had appeared in fringes in the sky
when all those pagan troops were well in sight,
on the third day after the famous fight.

Salamon, at that moment, and Duke Namo,   226
with Turpin, Ricciardetto, and the Dane,
gave this advice: "O Charles, since we are here,
and since a noble cause is dear to God,
let's chase this Balugant and all his men
until this evening's early flames are lit,
and Saragossa we'll then raze and take,
and hang its King Marsilius by the neck.

"And, as Vespasian and Titus did,   227
we'll sell as slaves those heathen Saracens
to buccaneers and pirates in some port,
for they are worse than pigs and worse than dogs."
Their resolution was adopted fast;
and so they clashed with all those pagan hordes
and started shouting Death! and Death! once more,
slaughtering them with ecstasy galore.

Rinaldo was the first to lower lance.   228
At Balugant he shouted, "Traitor, you!
The glory of France is not extinguished yet,"
and lifeless to the ground he would have sent him;
but skimming just his cheeks, the pointed spear
met another sinful pagan in its way:
it found his eyes and wholly pierced them through,
and fast therefore that Saracen it slew.

With Durlindana in his hand that day,   229
Charles wanted to avenge Orlando with her.
"Although, O famous sword," he said, "my strength,
compared to your great master's, is but nil,
do not forgive these pagan men today:
we must avenge Orlando, you and I;
he with a smile has given you to me—
so for a reason, this has come to be."

O glory of an ancient century,   230
O light and mirror, O most sacred Charles,
O old defender of the Christian faith!
The right heir of your noble progeny,
you're ready to cut Malchus's other ear!
He who believes in Jesus, acts like you,
and I believe that you were born for this—
to free us once again from the abyss.

Balugant rode into the Christian camp,   231
forcibly driven by his charger there.
Charlemagne saw him and with both his hands
raised soon his sword, with anger and disdain
shouting at him, "You'll join the other dogs!"
And, like a dead thing, Balugant was felled,
and as the helpless pagan hit the ground,
a hundred swords were quickly seen around.

Never in Rome, at the Testaccia Feast,   232
were swords in such a frightful number seen
around some bull that, from the cart let loose,
runs wildly all about before it falls.
Finally, one unlaced his helmet and
unmercifully plucked his hair and beard;
and one who wished to snatch his heart could not,
so furious was he, and so distraught.

As soon as pagan Balugant was dead,   233
his men began to flee from every side.
Have I forgotten up to now to mention
our valorous Arnaldo of Belland?
Many a Saracen he sent that day
down to Capernaum—I mean, to hell.
Balugant's battle hurt no Christian man—
'twas nothing but a small flash in the pan.

All of those pagans in no time were killed   234
or through the woods and forests fled in fear:
thus Balugant at last had plucked a fruit
that soon revealed itself a prickly pear!
When Carlo saw that they had been destroyed,
soon he resolved to cross the mountains: thus
toward Saragossa on their steeds they went,
and towns and villages they razed and rent,

pillaging, burning, killing, preying, routing: 235
women and girls and every Moorish child
(where could they ever find a place to hide?)
they slew, and in their cradles even babes.
Carlo gave orders to destroy all things,
thus to wipe out Marsilius from the earth.
Throughout their march they smashed whate'er they met before,
as landed pirates who raze and destroy the shore.

Did you see ever some poor shepherd run   236
with all his little sheep before a storm?
In the same manner all those routed men
tried—wretched things!—to shun impending death.
Both night and day they on their saddles sat,
restless as far as Saragossa's walls;
mountains and shores they crossed, and every hill and ridge,
and everywhere behind them destroyed they every bridge.

Spain was then partially a Christian nation;   237
so when Marsilius's treason became known
along with that of the Granada Moors,
many important lords were horrified,
and Saragossa was a nearly empty town.
Marsilius was there with a few men;
in Roncesvalles the others had been slain.
So at its doors arrived King Charlemagne.

King Bianciardino heard the news and said   238
to King Marsilius, "Rinaldo's here!"
For they could not by any means imagine
that Christian Carlo had arrived so soon,
and had brought there so many men along;
but what would prove more tragic to them was
that they knew nothing yet of Balugant,
who had, along the road, been left behind.

They started soon to reinforce the walls.   239
Rinaldo set one of the doors on fire,
and panic spread throughout the city fast,
and every person shut himself indoors.
The night was very cloudy, very dark
(how perfect for our Christians, reader dear!),
with gusty winds and a torrential rain
that filled with terror all those sleepless men.

The fire had spread out to many streets,   240
the wind was raising flames up to the sky,
roofs unexpectedly were crumbling down,
each mosque and everything was burning fast,
and many a flashing sword was seen around:
all Saragossa was a dreadful hell.
Marsilius knew not what he could do:
surely his plans and dreams had not come true.

When he heard people shouting "Long live France!"   241
and "Long live Charles!" it seemed to him a knife
or, much worse yet, a spear had pierced his heart,
such was the fear that overwhelmed his breast:
as in a flash upon a scale he saw
his kingdom and his honor and his life,
and understood that foxy Bianciardin
this time would pay for every wicked sin.

Now from the top of certain minarets   242
some old muezzins very loudly screamed
as if to say, "Come quick! Come quick! Come quick!
Help, god Mahound, your faithful Saracens!"
But all their words were only wasted breath,
for things were seen to fare from bad to worse,
and shouts and cries were echoing everywhere
with weeping and with wailing of despair.

Rinaldo had invaded now the city.   243
Women and little girls, disheveled, ran
from street to street, made by great terror mad,
and some of them were trampled on and crushed.
The Christians shouted, "Kill, and kill, and kill
these renegade and rebel Saracens!"
And all of them were one in heart and mind—
resolved to leave all mercy far behind.

Followed by a full squadron, Charlemagne,   244
brandishing bloodied Durlindana still,
ran to the palace of Marsilius,
shouting, "Where is the wicked traitor hiding?"
and, soon dismounting on the first step, climbed
the staircase, boldly fighting to the top,
and, like Horatius, a throng he tamed
until into the royal hall he came.

Dawn was just peeping in the firmament   245
when King Marsilius's home was entered into,
but no one yet could find the traitor there;
but since the flames were raging all about,
he in the end was forced to come right out
and was to Charlemagne brought bodily.
Enraged as he was, Carlo then and there
seized him and threw him down into the square.

Almost on top of Ricciardetto he fell,   246
and Ricciardetto, seeing him on the ground,
shouted, "You scoundrel!" grabbed him by the hair
and, placing then a foot upon his throat,
wanted to butcher him like a small lamb;
but the king said, "Have mercy on me! Mercy!
I want to tell King Charles, when he comes down,
the hiding place where Bianciardin has run."

Now, to describe what that sad town looked like,   247
with all that looting and those flames that night,
one has to think of an infernal smithy
down in the darkest cavern of the earth.
They all were rabid dogs in search of blood
thus to relieve their hydrophobia.
Justice of God, there—You were there! And You,
Heavenly Father, a stern judge are, too.

Turpin alone—I am not lying—killed   248
two hundred, even more, with his bare hands:
think what a bath he took in all that blood!
More florid and more vigorous he looked
than those who wore cuirass and uniform:
that night—it seemed—had made him young again,
just as the teasel makes the wool more bright.
No bridle ever could control his might.

Forward Queen Blanda at this time was dragged
along with Luciana by some knights.
Wearing her golden diadem no more,
fury personified she seemed to be,
screaming and letting everybody know
that like a queen she wanted to be killed:
treating her so was the most blatant shame
they gave an emperor of such great fame.

249

Indeed, she seemed Erichto in her wrath:
fully disheveled was her hair, and all
her purple garments and most precious cloaks
were strewn in great disorder on the floor.
Than many other ladies luckier,
she'd reached the end of all her misery!
And her example—it is my belief—
portrays exactly old Jocasta's grief.

250

Rinaldo, in the royal home by now,
as soon as he saw lovely Luciana,
furious as Coroebus at the sight
of his Cassandra dragged in the dark night,
commanded that she be released at once
and, stretching out his hand to her, from all
those wrathful binding arms delivered her:
"Do not dare touch her, soldiers! Do not dare!"

251

After they all released her and withdrew,
"Carlo," Rinaldo said, "if I have ever
for any favor to your presence come,
now, only for your greatest glory (though
to such a mighty monarch as you are
a woman seems a negligible prey),
I beg you that the queen and Luciana be
from now on free forever, placed in my custody."

252

Carlo replied, "O my beloved son,
could I refuse so noble a request?
I wish my action could precede your words.
Love, I can see, compels and rules you still."
Well, my dear reader, the conclusion is
that only those two ladies there were spared
of all that entire city's population:
the rest to sword and fire's ruination!

253

Like Sodom and Gomorrah, Saragossa   254
was burning down throughout that dismal night,
and every avenue was soiled with blood,
which then, in one stream, toward the river flowed
(for with French vigor men were murdered still);
so, like a forest of dead plants and bushes
burning beneath a blowing wind, a town
that once was happy to its roots burned down.

Oft from a flame another one was seen   255
suddenly to depart (as it is said
of the two Thebans placed upon one pyre)
and from one roof upon another leap
as though its fire had been preordained;
Megaera, Alecto, and Tisiphone
seemed to be there with big dog Cerberus,
there to avenge the Christians' every loss.

One could already see homes all around,   256
already burned or right then tumbling down,
until no stone on stone was there to watch.
What opulence, what riches gone forever!
What columns fell from capital to base
in ashes down! And all the people trapped
under the ruins looked, throughout the night,
like quickly roasted frogs—oh, fearful sight!

At times I marvel at what Turpin writes   257
(but then on second thought and second reading
I realize he always tells the truth):
several mothers their own children threw
into the Iber River, against hope
maybe still hoping in that maddening night:
madness or fury was their only guide,
and shouts were the one sound on every side;

but in the fire other mothers cast   258
their babes to save them from the Christian hands,
or into wells or sewers, anywhere;
still others killed their children with their hands.
God's awesome vengeance! I am almost tempted
here to compare so many women's wailing
to that of those beneath the Trojan doors
when Sinon lied about the mighty horse.

Unless I am mistaken, I am sure   259
that neither Titus nor Vespasian
made so much havoc of the Jews as they
made of those Saracens. Turpin himself—
just think—was quite a swordsman. Like Sagunto,
or Scipio's Carthage, the whole town was razed
by rain and iron and fire (of the three,
select the one that caused the greatest misery!).

And if some wretched pagan tried to flee,   260
he met with death whichever way he turned,
for Ricciardetto, Turpin, and the Dane,
and Ansuigi, galloped everywhere.
At last the Christians found King Bianciardin,
who had been hiding in a sack of tow.
Rinaldo thought of a most lovely trick—
with his own hand to set that sack on fire;

but, "No! His punishment must be more dire,"   261
Charlemagne said. Meanwhile Marsilius,
chained like a dog, was fastened to the throne
on which, by all revered, he once had sat.
Nobody could escape in any way:
the entire palace was well guarded, so
that neither man nor thing would sneak out stealthily:
all had to be destroyed—people and property!

Charles had with him a huge and strong-limbed fellow—   262
a slave, named Orco, in his court well known—
who, the night long—the scoundrel that he was—
had wallowed in the blood just like a swine.
Now, standing at the door with a big mace
that he had fashioned out of some forked bough,
he beat whoever tried to leave his post:
indeed, they had to reckon with their host!

They could not say as old Biantes said,   263
"All my possessions I will take with me";
they could have taken but one thing with them—
their own backs broken by that filthy mace;
and if somebody ran away from him,
you could have said in Greek *kalós kalós,*
for no one ever made it, unless one
leapt from a window, eager most to run.

CANTO XXVII ❖ 725

Anything reached by those unhealthy blows 264
ended like glass or ice, and nothing more.
About this horrid scoundrel someone wrote
that in the night he roasted Moorish babes,
which one by one he strung along his mace
and then like roasted sucking-pigs devoured;
oh, weird detail! So horrible it is,
Carlo, I'm sure, knew nothing of all this.

And so that doleful city in no time 265
was seized and utterly destroyed by fire,
and now the sight of ruins and dead men
was the most nauseous and ugly thing.
One should not wonder how in but one night
a town could be so totally destroyed:
for down, in clusters, mosques were crumbling in the end,
such was the wrath of God that did from heav'n descend.

Charles, in the past, had sent to King Marsilius 266
Anselm and Chiron as ambassadors;
the former of the two was wounded, and
the latter, killed on his way back to France:
whereupon Charles had thundered with this threat,
shouting, "Jerusalem! Jerusalem!
Thou'll weep, O Saragossa, bitterly,
for I will leave no stone on stone in thee!"

Behold now, before Charles, Marsilius! 267
The crowd was shouting, "Crucify him now!"
Others were yelling, "He should be impaled!"
Each wished to kill him in his own new way.
But Carlo answered that he wished to hang him
(a traitor is rewarded with a noose),
like the Iscariot, from that carob tree
from which he started his conspiracy.

He said, "Marsilius, you now must die 268
right where your treacherous command began;
and Bianciardin, that father of all lies,
next to you hanged, will make the winds lament."
"I want to be their hangman," Turpin said;
and Carlo answered, "I am deeply pleased:
the execution of two dogs and fiends
will be the holy deed of holy hands."

And then, after they were inside the park,   269
as soon as Charles around that fountain saw
the earth and all the trees and bushes burned,
he marveled most and suddenly grew pale.
"O Bianciardin," he said, "how many sins
you have committed with your malice here!
O wicked monster of iniquity,
O horrid shame of this our century!"

And when he saw that withered carob and,   270
nearby, the heaven-stricken laurel tree,
he felt his heart transfixed by a sharp stick
and of a sudden his hair stand on end.
"O treacherous Marsilius," he said,
"here is where you committed your great crime!
O cruel earth, oh, why, instead of this,
did you not swallow them like Curtius?

"Now that these footprints are so clear to me,   271
let no one with his cunning cover them,
for divine justice never falls asleep,
and 'tis the end that crowns man's every deed.
May, then, those who do evil not forget
that Heaven's sword hangs always over them,
and if for some time something they can hide,
nihil occultum, all is open wide.

"O Falseron, I in this place at last   272
have seen with these my eyes your vestiges:
maybe your soul repents of all your sins,
so many signs and prodigies are here!
Most fraudulent you were when, on the eve
of your departure from my Paris's court,
alas, you dared embrace my nephew dear,
and kiss him on the cheeks with seeming cheer.

"No more preambles, Bianciardin, you need: 273
the time has come now for the rope and noose,
and it's too late for mercy, to be sure;
and it is right that, just as you together
around this fountain planned your treacherous act
(a double malice calls for double justice),
you should, together still, soon kick the air
before you enter hell, still as a pair."

Seeing himself being taken to the scene
of his last crime—the place of his own choice—
and being now beneath that carob tree,
Marsilius recalled his own sad end,
which a wise necromancer had foreseen,
and a far greater sadness filled his heart;
the man had said, "Do not cut down that tree,
for it one day your last support will be!"

274

And then he begged—a wicked man was he—
that his last wish be granted before death:
he wanted to convert to the true God.
But Turpin said, "You're lying in your throat,
you scoundrel! I've been waiting for your words."
Rinaldo answered, "Not a chance, old man!
Oh, no! You shall not have this final satisfaction—
of cheating God in life and death with such an action.

275

"Water—you know—is wasted in five ways:
first, when you wash a donkey's head with it;
then, if you try to clean a putrid thing;
third, when it falls and stays within the sea;
fourth, when you use it to remove the grease
from off a table where a German dined;
and, last, it's that which I would vainly lose
in Christening you Saracens or Jews.

276

"I do believe the entire Jordan's waves,
in which our Holy Jesus was baptized,
could never make a Christian out of you;
nor could the water of this fountain, turned
as black as ink, and even blacker still,
by one of God's most warning miracles.
Have you—say—set one more malicious trap,
thinking your execution we would stop?"

277

"With Bianciardin and with your Falseron
deep down in hell you will be soon baptized,"
said Charlemagne, "in Charon's flowing stream,
which you are soon to cross inside his boat.
And I will send you also Ganelon,
with whom you'll plan another treason yet
so as to keep alive your wicked art,
for you have tricks—I know—still to impart.

278

"And since our God has kept for you aside   279
this dried and burned-down tree in front of us,
from which Judas Iscariot hung first,
you'll show us from up there your swinging feet."
Marsilius replied, "I've just remembered
what an old necromancer had foreseen
and now makes sense to me—that, ah, this tree,
one of these days, my last support would be.

"Let me confess to you that in the past   280
I have betrayed your trust more times than one;
but having reached the end of all my crimes,
there is one grace that I implore of you,
for it is kindness ever to fulfill
a dying wicked enemy's last wish:
have mercy on my poor and grieving wife!
Death cancels every hatred, every strife.

"When you were still a lad here at my court,   281
and with my dearest sister fell in love,
Galafro, my own father, was against it;
but my poor Blanda pleaded for you, saying,
'Sire, what will you do with Charlemagnet?
Is it his fault if your own daughter's fair,
and if, when jousting, he can beat all men?
You know he loves our Gallerana, then;

"'I, too, have noticed it in countless things: 282
he is, indeed, so much in love with her,
he can no longer curb the flames of love
which in his breast the gods above have lit.'
She always pleaded for you, so much so
that I believe you are obliged to her;
why, while you were at court—in truth I say—
she even saved your life in many a way.

"A thousand times Galafro had in mind   283
to punish you for all your faults; but she,
using her wiles and ingenuity,
always succeeded in restraining him.
Being a gentle and most worthy king,
you will—I know—not stain your soul with sin.
Then, for the crown that on your head I view,
Blanda and Gallerana I recommend to you.

"Do with my body as you wish; my soul,   284
I know, will be forever damned in hell."
"Why all this chattering?" our Turpin said;
"Yours was a never-ending litany."
And so he started to prepare the noose
by rolling up his tunic and his cape;
then he walked gladly to that carob tree
and hanged him by the neck most piously.

Master of Ceremonies for the day,   285
he fixed the noose round Bianciardino's neck,
and, looking for a gibbet, found and chose
a medlar tree not from the fountain far:
and so both men were swinging in the wind.
They left Marsilius on his carob tree,
and on his medlar Bianciardin, whose feet
had been deprived by Turpin of their seat.

Then Carlo ordered that Queen Blanda be   286
brought to her father's home; along with her,
who from the kingdom of Granada came,
he sent several more as company.
And now, since Saragossa from all sides
was nothing but a heap of smoldering ash,
the Dane took care of camp and men at once
before he started marching back to France.

Through all of Aragon and through the towns   287
and villages of Spain, the tidings spread
of the French knights' immense and high revenge,
and everybody praised Charles's lofty crown;
and not a prince was there who did not come
to pay a visit to the emperor:
they spoke of the results with boundless praise
while still condemning what had taken place.

Full many dignitaries came to meet   288
Emperor Charlemagne on his way home,
and, swearing full allegiance to his crown,
upon their horses joined in his cortège.
Now, not to bore my reader in the least
(for too much singing may be bothersome),
for God's most holy help once more I long,
to end with the next Canto all my song.

Success is counted by the end result,   1
and so, my kindly Lord, this final grace
do not deny me, for before its time,
a fruit is not yet ripe and is still sour:
that I may look to death like a white swan
tenderly singing in its final ache,
till Carlo's body to the earth be given
in peace, and then my soul to You in heaven.

A lady is up there, who may be listening: 2
'twas she who first commissioned this my tale.
Now that her soul, free of its worldly weight,
is up in heaven so much more revered,
I know that with my singing rhymes I'll go,
changing my route, in this small boat of mine,
till I reach port, as I have promised her,
who on this sea is still my guiding star.

I heretofore have neither asked, my Lord,   3
nor am I asking, for Parnassus's help
or for the Muses' or Pegasus's sisters',
known as Calliope or Clio still;
but this one Canto that still lies ahead
spurs all my mind and heart so ardently
that while I tell my seamen to prevail,
I reinforce with one more sheet my sail.

The town burned down and every loss avenged,   4
from Saragossa Charlemagne departed;
Marsilius, the traitor, had been punished
right at the fountain of his grievous sin.
Riding from shore to shore, in many a place
he ordered the rebuilding of each bridge
that he had wanted by his men destroyed
so as to leave the foe no open road.

And to Saint John of Port he then returned,   5
by no means wishing once again to pass
through Roncesvalles, where his dear nephew died.
Sighing and sobbing still, he kept repeating,
"Is there a man who can console me now?"
and he made every person weep with him.
"Why is this soul of mine still in my breast?
My life is only torment and unrest."

Somebody even wrote that Ganelon,   6
released from prison through some ruse of his,
as soon as he was free, saw such dark mist
around him, and was so confused and dazed,
that to his dungeon he went back at once,
led there by his remorse and by his sin;
I'm just reporting such a theory,
for every author well informed should be.

Meanwhile Rinaldo comforted his Charles   7
when the whole court unanimously shouted
that they should torture Gano right away
and give him soon the most horrendous death.
Some thought he should be quartered; others thought
that he deserved a more atrocious end—
the wheel, the cross, and every kind of shame,
collar and cap and broom and gallows at one time.

After a big discussion, Ganelon   8
'mid thunderous shouts was brought into the hall,
chained like a rabid dog; around him were
so many maddened pharisees intent
on snatching, each of them, a bit of him;
and as he thought of begging Charles for mercy,
hoping the emperor might still believe him,
Rinaldo to those angry people gave him.

Carlo was there to watch that hunting game: 9
the fox was now surrounded by the dogs,
and each of them was holding, ripping it.
Some of them hit him, others wrenched his hands,
others kept spitting in his face in spite,
others were very weirdly punching him,
and others of his throat got such a hold
that cheese to him would always taste like mold.

Some hit him with a hand, some with a foot,　　　10
some struck, some pushed, some pinched him all at once,
some with his fingernails made his cheeks thin,
some ripped off both his ears and swallowed them,
some deafened him by thundering around,
some had prepared the fire and the cart,
some ripped out both his eyes, and some were fond
of skinning him like a frog out of a pond.

As soon as wicked Gan was on the cart,　　　11
all those around it shouted "Death!" and "Death!"
Fire was ready for the branding iron,
and do not ask me what a great tattoo
the hangman gave him: not an ounce of flesh
was left yet unembroidered on his body:
he was, indeed, in hands professional,
his hangman being skillful and sensational.

Around his neck he wore the gilded noose,　　　12
and on his head the crown of the condemned.
Rinaldo was not satisfied as yet
while the mob shouted like a roaring storm.
Some threw a dead cat or a hen at him,
hitting the mark precisely as they wished:
from head to toes he looked far uglier
than in his deepest hell does Lucifer.

Around all Paris went the cart of doom,　　　13
through a crowd flinging shoes and slippers at him
and eager to behold the traitor cut
to shreds and made unrecognizable.
The tumult and the shouting and the din
were echoing as far as the last stars,
and "Crucify him! Crucify him!" went
(Gan was still aimed at) to the firmament.

When to the court the cart of death returned,　　　14
Charles had already ordered the four steeds.
As soon as to those horses Gan was tied,
their footmen started lashing them at once,
and so they sped and quartered Ganelon.
Rinaldo ordered his four pieces thrown
through briars and through mountains, bush and wood,
to wolves and dogs and deer and crows as food.

Such was the end of cursèd Ganelon,   15
for God's eternal justice is still near
when you may think it far away from us.
Now, reader, you will ask me what on earth
made Carlo so believe in Ganelon.
I will reply that it was preordained:
one of the two was born just to deceive,
the other but to trust and to believe.

Remember: Carlo was a holy man   16
who for a long time kept, right at his court,
a learned scholar, known as Alcuin,
from whom he learned Latin and Greek; he also
had built the University of Paris.
Yet mentally he seems so totally blind
that, to avoid this issue, many a prudent writer
has never even mentioned this Ganelon the traitor.

In spite of my research on all his life,   17
I too cannot but wonder how he could
have made so great a blunder for so long.
But even divine nature was betrayed
(and such a mystery was willed in heaven),
although its knowledge was still infinite:
for God allows—this is my firm belief—
not only man's good deeds—also his mischief.

A man of great experience, King Carlo   18
knew very much undoubtedly (we know
that Prudence is the product of old age:
that's why she's by three mirrors symbolized).
A man of science he was, too; and yet,
whene'er that traitor whispered in his ear,
soon he believed whatever that man said,
and so I cannot solve this puzzle yet.

It happens many a time and far too often   19
that if you love a friend like your own brother,
you deem whate'er he does indeed well done—
done to perfection with the finest brush;
and so does the first bond unite the two
that, should some other time another deed
displease or anger you in many ways,
with you that first impression ever stays.

For a long time Emperor Carlo had
kept Gano of Maganza at his court;
and, furthermore, he saw his own advantage,
for Gano was a person of great power
who proved at times to be a valiant mate;
and since old habits grow too powerful,
the habit of his many errors could
also make Carlo's love a habitude.

20

But others now may ask, "But wait a bit!
If Ganelon knew well what he had done,
and that the traitor's fire would be lit,
why then did he not leave the court at once
so as to make his treason fully work—
he, who was such a shrewd and wicked man?"
In other Cantos I have said to you
that it is spite that moves the things we do.

21

When Oliver struck Gano on the face,
I quickly said that Ganelon had sworn
revenge at once (a traitor though he was,
he thought that slap most inappropriate).
Of Lampognano I remind you, reader,
and pay attention to no ancient author:
use your fear always as your own defense,
for desperate men think only of offense.

22

Gano was maybe hoping that he would
quite cover up his treason with King Charles;
he from Maganza had so many troops
that he still dreamed that, with Orlando dead,
and always trusting in his own great might,
he would unfurl his banners to the wind
and, with Marsilius's great help, advance
and sit, a crowned king, on the throne of France.

23

Now let us leave this traitor, strewn through woods,
as I have said, through mountains and low ditches.
My mind is overcast with gloomy thoughts:
there is no steersman who may guide my boat,
and 'tis now up to me to sight the land
from the high sea in which I'm sailing still,
and check the port not with the plummet, which
is often stuck, but with the sounding stick.

24

Turpin is dead and buried with much weeping,　　　　　25
and now I fear that, dazed as I am still,
I may not make it out of this one route
unless I change the pilot of my ship.
A newer lyre for my song I need,
but since from changing course new gain may come,
maybe I will succeed in reaching port
with this full-loaded, riches-bearing boat.

Thus my renowned Arnaldo I implore　　　　　26
that he may guide me to the very end
till quietly Rinaldo disembarks
(I deeply trust his right hand on the helm).
After he saw Ganelon quartered, he
was like a bird that savors his last prey:
he cleans his claws, refurbishes his beak,
and, fully pleased, seems nothing more to seek.

He was in love with Luciana still,　　　　　27
and so he sent her, not alone, to Paris,
for she was Gallerana's niece; and there
she was baptized inside Saint Denis's Church
and with the Christian faith was reconciled;
and gentle Ansuigi liked her so
that, being still so young and charming, she
became his lovely bride ultimately.

To please Rinaldo, Ricciardetto went　　　　　28
along with her, to keep her company,
and our Rinaldo also gave her back
the precious present she had given him,
so that she might be of the past repaid
thus with his gentleness rewarding hers;
she kept it on her bed as a souvenir.
And now enough of Ricciardetto and her.

Rinaldo told Emperor Charles one day　　　　　29
he had made up his mind to leave his court
and, like Ulysses, novel lands explore.
Suddenly shaken, Carlo felt like dying,
but he gave his wanted blessing finally,
after no one could make him change his plans:
having avenged Orlando, our brave lord
wanted to leave and roam throughout the world.

Many a tear was shed in Carlo's court,   30
and Charles himself now felt so lone and lost
that he would always have him in his thoughts.
It was the last affliction of his life,
and nevermore he wished to hear his name,
just like a father who had lost his son;
and all France wept in sadness and dismay,
seeing so great a champion go away.

I do believe things were exactly so.   31
I, who have written many rhymes about
this man and all his prowess, feel as sad
and as disconsolate as they all felt,
and am now like a pilgrim left behind,
but who must not abandon his right path,
and so with all my mind and all my heart
from our Rinaldo never do I part.

And if I felt that I should even more   32
please my own fatherland and those who read
(so much can someone's fame enamor us),
this is the story that would make me grieve,
for those who treat it do not know it well;
but if my rhymes have power to survive,
to the whole world our hero will be known
till on this earth the last day's glimmers dawn.

The above-mentioned author, whom I trust,   33
seems to believe (and I believe he's right)
that though Rinaldo was well on in years,
his spirit was indomitably strong.
And he recalled what Astaroth had told him
about the other distant hemisphere
with wars and kingdoms, monarchies and laws:
Hercules' pillars, then, he wished to cross.

Besides, it was an angel said of him,   34
"All things are possible if God so wills."
Now, if he wanted to convert those throngs
that worshiped planets and vain fables still,
and, safe and sound, at last one day he reached
the other hemisphere where the sun rises
(there have been other miracles before),
what then? He less believes who knows much more.

The same is said of the Evangelist,   35
though this comparison may sound quite blasphemous.
But where the mystery or point abides
He only knows, Who made both earth and sky.
Our limited, imperfect, mortal sight,
bandaged forever with a darkening veil,
often a falsehood for the truth mistakes,
and, still half-dreaming, up a person wakes.

And someone says the Dane is still alive   36
(He who made nature, everything can do);
others, not I in this my tale at all.
They say he lives in a dark sunken cave,
out of which, fully armed upon his steed,
he often comes and frightens those who see him;
should their opinion be ignored, or not?
The same of Durlindana has been thought—

that Carlo threw it down into the sea,   37
and on the battle's anniversaries,
it rises up and floats upon the waves,
more bloodied than it ever was on earth;
and if somebody tries to pick it up,
under the water once again it hides.
Well, it may even be, but with my pen
I cannot demonstrate what happened then.

I think that in the age of those old knights,   38
so that the Christian faith might reach the lands
where still the Saracens were fierce and strong,
Christ let strange things occur to that good end;
because if Charles had not gone there—to those
quite distant lands—to fight for this our faith
(*ergo, Carole, in tempore venisti*),
maybe Mohammed we would still adore.

Francis and Dominic, and Charles, therefore,   39
have worked such wonders for the Christian faith,
through both their doctrine and their Frankish might,
that, thanks to them, still our religion lives,
or in a sorry plight we would be now:
for God His faithful servants ever aids:
He everything foresees, and at the hour
of need makes His great help upon them shower.

I thoroughly agree with Dante, who,   40
for a good reason, placed in heaven both
Charles and Orlando in that Holy Cross
(he understood and wrote intelligently);
but I must blame the ignorant, dark age
that, while King Carlo lived, could not produce
a Livy or a Sallust or a Justin, who might sing
in Greek or Latin all the wonders of this king.

But since at the beginning of my tale   41
I have already mentioned this great lack,
it is perhaps now better not to speak.
In such great glory I've already placed
Charles and Orlando that I here conclude:
I do not want to judge God's mysteries—
that is, how great in heaven is their gain—
lest I be called conceited or else vain.

Those who mean well are rent to pieces first: 42
I will no longer here discuss our faith,
not to fall into these our friars' mouths,
where also luscious lampreys often go,
nor to be told by lazy bigots, "Look!
There goes a man who talks without believing!"
and thus spread fast the greatest calumny:
if there was dark at first, let dark still be!

In the beginning God made heav'n and earth,   42
according to His high intelligence,
and darkness was the one dividing veil;
but I know not what in the end will be
in the rotation of that mighty axis:
it is the Mind that judges everything!
And if but futile things one day I wrote,
contra hypocritas tantum, pater, I wrote.

Not from the pulpit, then, not from the pew   44
must you rebuke a sinner, but instead
when he's not there and in your room you sit:
climb, then, up there with lead upon your feet!
My Christian faith is just as white as yours,
and I can say two Credos, not just one.
Go! To the Gospel every nation win,
helped by the doctrine of your Augustin;

and if some fool dares prompt you, once again   45
I tell you that like Thomas you must be:
judge with your hands, not merely with your eyes,
as the old fable of the thrush suggests.
And let nobody touch me anymore,
else I will play my monochord so well
that more than sol-fa they will recognize:
whether 'tis black or gray, I treat them both likewise.

All your deductions, all your syllogisms,   46
so many teachers and young bachelors
with all their logic and their sophistries
will never make a bitter lupin sweet.
And do not mention barbarisms here,
for I'll provide most clear and modern texts.
Well, I just wished to warn you out of love,
and let's forget what we discussed above.

As you remember, in Saint John of Port   47
we left our Carlo still in great distress;
but since the goal of those who go to sea
is always to reach port ultimately,
we now shall try to take a shortcut there,
lest in one hour a hundred hours we bear:
for man's desire is indeed most keen
when his last goal is very closely seen.

After he punished Gano—better yet,   48
after he sent a demon back to hell—
the one who long had tempted and betrayed him—
Carlo behaved as all wise men behave
when they have to adjust to newest things:
he moved his entire court and government
to Aachen, and there he lived some more,
and waged, before he died, many a war.

Death, who forgives no mortal, could not spare   49
even so great and bright an emperor:
so after forty-seven years of reign
in which he brought great honor to his crown,
King Carlo's soul departed from this world
and to its happy Maker thus returned—
to Him Who there the good and just rewards,
according to the Holy Gospel's words.

Though in his early life he did so much,   50
which neither Turpin nor Urman has treated,
we'll leave it now to Alcuin to sing
all of his praises on his newest lyre:
he now will sing the most noteworthy things
(omitting Pepin and his early years),
just as in ancient epochs poets did
when singing the high praises of the dead.

Great obsequies were celebrated soon,   51
and nearly the whole world was clad in black—
especially all Christendom on earth—
and nevermore would France be glad again.
Now, having left so many things unsaid,
so that I may his entire story tell,
and please and let all learned persons follow,
this is the time I must invoke Apollo.

For Delos and for Delphi and for Cynthus   52
may you now tune your lyre, I implore;
for Hyacinthus and your Daphne fair,
breathe into me with that your might once felt
by Ismara, Cyrrha, Pindus, Aracynthus,
so that both Marsyas and rash Thamyris
may envy this our lyre, while I show
that Carlo's fame does on this earth still glow.

In Aachen there lived upon that time   53
a citharist by name Lactantius,
who was a gentle artist of renown.
Highly he was esteemed by everyone
for having said so much in just one book
about King Carlo's life, which he knew well;
he, before Alcuin, had sung and treated
what Turpin then and Urman, too, repeated.

His story he began with youthful Charles,   54
who, from his kingdom having been thrown out
after his father Pepin's tragic death,
was forced to wear a shepherd's simple garb;
then King Calafro welcomed him to court,
where he was known to all as Charlemagnet:
he had been brought there by a foster father
by name Morando; it was there, soon after,

that Gallerana fell in love with him   55
and then became his wedded wife; and he
finally took her back to France with him,
and there he showed all of his inborn worth
by soon regaining his own fatherland
and wearing on his head the glorious crown:
his father Pepin had been treacherously
murdered by Oldorigi. Subsequently,

the citharist introduces Agolant,   56
who came to Italy with massive troops
for having heeded a buffoon of his;
and mentioned all the battles that he fought,
and how, as Charles was losing with Almont,
arrived Orlando, at that time a boy,
who finally killed this Almonte, near
a fountain, with the stump of a big spear.

Of Gerard and Don Buoso and Don Chiaro,   57
and of Riccier di Risa he sang, too;
and how, when they returned to France (for Spain
several times had dared rebel against them),
their loss was very bitter that last time;
in fact, as soon as that new war began,
young Ferraù was killed upon the bridge,
and Lazzera, up the mount, surrendered to the siege.

And then at Stella, Serpentino came   58
forward to fight a duel with Orlando
and—ah, poor man!—was left dead on the ground,
so that, pursuing, then, his enterprise,
Carlo once more was for Navarra bound,
and in Pamplona finally arrived;
there was a merciless and lengthy war
around that city, still besieged; therefore,

in anger and disdain, Orlando left   59
and went to Mecca, where he met the Sultan.
We read about the flight of Machidant,
of Sansonetto's baptism in our faith.
Orlando then went to Jerusalem
and with his hand regained the Sepulcher,
and recognized Ugòn as his own brother,
and then, with Sansonetto and the other,

returned to his King Carlo in Pamplona,   60
where he had kept his camp for many a year;
'twas there he heard Macarius had seized
his crown as well as his wife most treacherously,
because of which King Carlo had to go
in person to regain his royal throne—
and it was Malachel who brought him finally
where bold Macarius wept instantly.

Thus he, his sovereignty regained in full,   61
back to Pamplona, fast as wind, returned;
and after Desiderius of Pavia
arrived and seized the town ingeniously,
he sent ambassadors to King Marsilius,
and Chiron, one of them, was killed by treason,
whereupon with his men King Carlo swore
against Marsilius revenge and war;

but then, to reestablish peace between them,   62
Gano, the wicked traitor, soon was sent
to Saragossa, where instead he planned
and ordered his foul treason in detail,
and God revealed by miracles His wrath;
and to Saint John he ultimately went,
while Count Orlando came to Roncesvalles
for the great fight I have described before.

What I in my *Morgante* heretofore   63
have written, by Lactantius already
had solemnly been said—how Persia turned,
with all of Egypt, to the faith of Christ,
and very faithfully I followed him,
not knowing if at times he went too far:
I do not want the man who this *Morgante* wrote
to be in this accused of even one false note.

He wrote about the Dane, who turned to Christ,   64
and, too, about his steed named Durafort:
after he killed Carlotto wrathfully,
King Carlo kept him in a prison chained
until that horrid Bravieri came,
who vanquished all the courtly paladins;
and of the March he also was the lord;
nothing at all that writer has ignored.

He also wrote about Rinaldo's youth: 65
how with three brothers he was sent to Charles—
with Guicciard, Ricciardetto, and Alardo—
and how King Carlo welcomed him to court,
but for his many pranks many a time
the king expelled him from his royal home;
and how through Malagigi's magic art
dark devils made his Montalbano start.

In short, he wrote so many wondrous things,   66
he kept all people wondering in awe;
but even he then laid his lyre down,
unable to describe, as he had wished,
the lofty fame of all his epic deeds.
But to his story we must say goodbye,
for Alcuin, after Lactantius,
lyre in hand, has sung all things for us.

The entire population was in tears   67
(and truly I excuse, this time, all those
who weep for something that should make one weep)
when Alcuin, according to an ancient
custom, from a high podium he'd climbed
looked down and, seeing all that grieving crowd
still so disconsolate and in such dire
affliction, sadly started with his lyre.

As a preamble, be began to praise   68
all that Lactantius had sung before:
"Out of so many singers I was chosen,
though all of them more nobly sing than I;
therefore, if I in any way should fail,
be kind to me, my people, and just think
that I have come to you, like Philomel,
to sing of things no human tongue can tell.

"I'll sing the life of the great emperor,   69
and then, with you, I'll also mourn his death.
He was a father and a lord to me,
who at his court for a long time was raised,
where I was fortunate to share with him
the bitter bread of sorrow and lament;
but since I am obliged to life, to death
I must be loyal till my final breath.

"Pepin, his famous and most worthy sire,
  held first the scepter and the regal name,
  and sat upon his throne for fifteen years.
  Before him, to the Prefect of the Council
  a king's name and insignia sufficed;
  but Pepin, as I have already said—
  he who the next prefect was to be became
  the first to wear a crown and earn great fame.

"When, fifteen years after his coronation,
  King Pepin died, he was survived by Charles,
  later called Charlemagne, and Carloman,
  his brother; but I'm here to praise my lord,
  and not to tell how the two brothers ruled,
  at first, the kingdom they inherited:
  I'll tell you of that excellence alone,
  which with these very eyes I've seen and known.

"He fought against the Aquitanians first."
  (Dear reader, Aquitania is Guyenne,
  if you allow me to explain some lines
  that may need some explaining now and then.)
  "Pepin had laid his hands first on that land,
  as other pens have written until now;
  Charles stayed till the conclusion of the war,
  from which the victor's flowered palm he bore.

"I know I'm not expected to retell
  events you all remember very well—
  how Hunold had to flee to Gascony,
  and how a double victory he won
  by bringing to the pillory his foe:
  for Lupus, Duke of Gascony, was wise
  and—to his greatest glory—willingly
  with Hunold gave himself up to the king.

"Meanwhile the beautiful Hesperian land
  was being conquered by the Lombard wrath
  under the banners of King Desiderius—
  by ignorant and fierce yet valiant men
  who, under their king's flag, ruled Italy
  for twenty-four long years; and no one would
  have chased them out if Carlo in the end
  had not redeemed the fair Italian land.

70

71

72

73

74

CANTO XXVIII ❖ 745

"From lands across the ocean this indomitable   75
army had come at the request of Narses,
the eunuch captain; whereupon the pontiff,
who at that time was famous Hadrian,
seeing himself in danger and oppressed,
to Charlemagne sent envoys right away,
begging him soon to reach Italy's shore
as Pepin and Martel had done before.

"Urged by such just and holy praying, Charles   76
with all his paladins left France at once,
and had to cross the steep and narrow places
Hannibal with his Barcans had once crossed,
because those valiant men controlled the ridges
and passages of all the Apennines;
bridges and bars he smashed at any cost,
and so those mountains finally he crossed.

"Envoys he sent, for the first thing to those   77
who were in Desiderius's army still,
bidding them leave with all their troops at once:
he had been called to Italy to chase
and route the enemies of the Church away;
they'd better now recall that in the past,
at their expense they had known before
how mighty France's arms behaved in war.

"And so he finally began to fight   78
in the Vercelli plainland, I believe;
unable to withstand the Frankish might,
soon from Pavia Desiderius fled,
where Carlo had besieged him for some time;
and, having tamed his pride, with all his men
our king resolved to go to Rome, to see
and visit with the pontiff finally.

"Our Highest Holy Father, deeply pleased   79
at such a visit, welcomed Charles with honor.
He thus could have all of his regions back,
with Benevento and Spoleto, too.
Charlemagne for some time remained in Rome,
thus making Hadrian still happier;
then, having proved his Christian piety,
with his great blessing left he finally.

"But he had left, as I've already said,   80
King Desiderius in that town besieged;
so, fast as lightning, he retraced his steps
and made his siege so narrower and hard
that to surrender he was shortly forced:
and so that war could ultimately end,
and Carlo brought triumphal spoils to France—
the vanquished monarch with his wife and sons.

"Beautiful Italy was free at last—   81
the land that had been occupied before
by Goths and Vandals, Huns and Heruli—
a very cruel, fierce, and beastly horde.
So after he rebuilt the Church of God,
Charles with his holy flag returned to France
and, to its famous lilies' greater fame,
with Carloman's own children there he came.

"Many a worthy and egregious deed   82
I must omit, for I cannot recall
the many places where his banners went
nor follow him in all his victories;
but if untimely death does not blow out
the light I need this story to reveal,
with newer style, with more resounding verse,
I'll make it known to the whole universe.

"Now, as it happens to a generous man   83
who, even sleeping, dreams of lofty feats,
so too our emperor, as soon as he
conquered both Aquitaine and Gascony,
and freed the Church and its great Shepherd, marched
against the heretics of Saxony,
much more than any other land, a region
swayed by the devil from our true religion.

"This war engaged him more than previous ones,   84
simply because he had to deal with strange
and very bellicose and cruel men
who, by vain idols utterly deceived,
found our faith most demanding and therefore
fought and condemned the Christians' every law.
Charles led his army with great vehemence
just to avenge his Jesus' great offense.

"Several times, after our emperor
destroyed their sacrilegious idols, they
renounced the faith to which they had been brought
and into their old errors fell again;
but in the end, baptized en masse, they all
welcomed and recognized the true Redeemer,
renouncing their idolatry as wrong.
And so that war was thirty-three years long.

"Being most wise, Carlo demanded then
ten thousand men as hostage, and the rest,
obeying his specific order, went
to live in different towns through all of France,
as well as on Seeland's and Holland's shores:
so their perfidiousness, at last uprooted
like an untenable, fallacious law,
made with new throngs his population grow.

"Protector of good Chephas on this earth,
O great defender of the Christian legions,
O holy sword, chastising those who err,
O Moses, father of God's family,
O famous on the field, Papirius Cursor,
O Scipio, the friend of valorous actions,
O trusted mirror where our good we see,
O fame, O glory of our century!

"At that time also, all of Spain was stained
with still another wicked heresy
when Charlemagne's so high and noble crown
arrayed an army and a fleet at once
and started crossing mountains, hills, and streams
under the Heaven-given holy flag,
till every region, every town and shore,
trembled, all over Spain, at the new war.

"So Charles descended on the battlefield
with all his knights, whose fame can still be heard,
and Spain could not withstand all of their might.
Augusta and Pamplona were still left
to tame and convert to the Christian faith:
our king went there in person, and at last,
after a lengthy siege and a hard fight,
they both surrendered to his wondrous might.

85

86

87

88

89

"And so Pamplona, too, was finally   90
    conquered with a long battle and much blood,
    and the whole Spanish nation was baptized
    and abjured its false gods with their Mahound.
    'Twas then, with his brigade, King Carlo saw
    and crossed the Pyrenees the second time,
    and, soon inflicting damage to their shame,
    against the foes in Gascony he came.

"This was the bloody battle where Anselmo   91
    along with his beloved nephew died,
    in Roncesvalles, still famous to this day;
    but with these things you're all familiar,
    for victory was not a glorious one
    where treason could achieve all it had planned;
    Carlo, awaiting the right time and the right manner,
    cruelly, as you know, avenged his every banner.

"So Gascony's perfidiousness was punished,   92
    and Spain was—more importantly—baptized.
    There was a war against the Britons next.
    Soon after, having tamed all Brittany,
    toward Italy he turned his gonfalons
    because Araysus was oppressing Rome:
    the lord of Benevento's newer threat
    had made the Pontiff and the Church afraid.

"As soon as he arrived in Italy,   93
    he made that foolish leader bow to him
    and also to the pontiff, now a friend,
    and many men as hostage brought to France.
    Oh, countless are the things I will not say!
    Just like the sun that shines on every land,
    his flags unfurled appeared in every place
    for greater deeds and for a greater praise.

"Like good Camillus, having more than once   94
    saved Rome and her empire, he returned
    to France. Meanwhile, the great Bavarian duke,
    Taxillo, Desiderius's son-in-law,
    had drafted and amassed his fighting men,
    joining the Huns in a conspiracy,
    spurred by his wife's incautious instigation:
    in short, he planned his future ruination.

"Full-armed already, then, the emperor,   95
without awaiting the Bavarian flags,
marched with his own against the enemy
up to the stream that marks and separates
Germany from Bavarian provinces;
and so Taxillo, too, had soon to bow
and give to Charles all that to Charles was due—
an oath of bondage and a tribute, too.

"The Velatabi and the Abroditi   96
gave him some nuisance as confederates,
but they were quickly punished by our king.
At the same time a war was being planned
against our Charles by the Hungarians,
tribes known in ancient days as Scythians,
peoples who to Pannonia had come
from the most distant regions of the earth.

"This new war lasted for about eight years,   97
but Carlo finally defeated them,
not without heavy casualties and loss,
and all the treasury and boundless wealth,
which they themselves by treachery and force
had looted previously in other lands,
he took to his Belle France, with fame and victory,
thus adding a new glow to his most glorious tree.

"After that mighty war came to its end,   98
and Hungary was placed under the lilies
of France, with both Bohemia and Normandy,
vanquished and tamed by Carlo, his first son,
Pope Leo, banished from his Holy See
and living in great peril and dismay,
sent messengers to Charlemagne in France,
bidding him come and rescue him at once.

"So for the third time Charlemagne returned   99
to Italy, and to his holy throne,
whence he had been removed, he soon brought back
the Holy Pontiff in his papal mantle.
The Highest Shepherd, not a thankless man,
remembering how much the king had done
for his great predecessor years before,
bestowed on him the crown of emperor.

"Thus Charles was Charlemagne and Emperor   100
  of the Whole Universe and King of Rome,
  and added on his flag—for greater fame—
  the noble eagle that's the bird of Jove.
  After the pontiff gave him leave to go—
  every rebellion having been subdued—
  on his way back, with high munificence,
  he renovated and rebuilt great Florence,

"where he raised temples that bespoke his name,   101
  and left most regal gifts and privileges.
  And so our king of kings went back to France
  in all his glory and triumphal light.
  And that was not the final victory
  that made his crown so rich and luminous:
  so many other things our lord did still,
  I've neither breath nor word, nor ink nor quill.

"I cannot sing my lines while weeping still,   102
  so most conflicting are the two extremes;
  yet I must let my heart shed all its tears,
  constrained as it is still by such just ache.
  For many a year and many an alien land,
  Charles for the Gospel and the faith of Christ
  has done much more than I have here revealed:
  but up in heaven all is writ and sealed.

"Up there all of his merits will be known,   103
  up there the holy face will make all clear,
  up there he'll reap the fruit of his good deeds,
  up there he'll be received by his good Jesus,
  up there all weeping into song will turn,
  up there his regal throne will always be,
  up there he'll eat the ever-pleasing bread,
  up there he'll share with us the peace we need."

Alcuin, I am sure, wished to say more—   104
  about the Holy Sepulcher regained,
  about his trip to Constantine of Greece;
  but he could not: the sobbing and the tears
  of all that crowd, so sad and lonesome still,
  drowned every line and every lyre's chord;
  both arm and bow grew weak ultimately,
  so down the podium at last came he.

CANTO XXVIII ❖ 751

As soon as the great sage stepped down, the crowd,   105
which until then had most attentive been,
resumed its weeping loudly, audibly,
like fire that at times looks wholly spent
and, though with no more flame, remains still lit,
showing itself again when the wind blows:
this happened when that lovely song was through,
and openly those people wept anew.

There, all disheveled still, all maidens were,   106
there every matron wore a mourning cloak,
there the entire city loudly wept,
there all the people tore their black-hued gowns,
there all those splendid actions were retold,
there Carlo's worthy life by all was praised,
there, too, some hands were clapping in the crowd,
there "Holy, holy, holy!" those people cried aloud.

O fortunate old man, who lived so well!   107
O happy, righteous man all people love!
O mirror and bright model of good deeds!
O glorious fame no envy ever mars!
O Heaven, to his merits lend Your ears!
O men, still weeping for their lifeless lord!
O kindly shepherd, watchful and alert!
As great as thy own reign, O king, thou wert!

In Aachen the biggest church, which bore   108
the Holy Virgin's name, had been already
built by the happy, lofty emperor;
precisely in that church—and rightly so—
with boundless honor and all-sounding praise
his sepulcher was placed; and over it
an arch of gold was raised, a little higher,
within that holy Temple of the Choir.

To keep his features in the world alive,   109
the population, with a noble thought,
wanted his face engraven on the tomb,
bearing this short and simple epitaph:
"Here lies the body of our Charlemagne,
the Roman world's Most Christian Emperor."
Just notice, in so brief an idiom,
"Most Christian," "Charlemagne," and "King of Rome."

It was the year eight hundred and fifteen   110
of our Lord Jesus' Saving Incarnation.
Seventy-two full years our Charles had lived,
and was then in his forty-seventh year
as king; and for the past ten years and five
he'd worn the crown Pope Leo had bestowed.
He died the twenty-fourth of January,
the month to Janus dear originally.

Many a sign before his death occurred: 111
Lightning struck a beautiful bell tower,
which, crumbling, spread its ruins all about;
a portico of the cathedral fell,
and near Magontia a bridge burned down;
but to all those who bear such things in mind,
as about Caesar once, God gave a sign
about a worthier monarch here on earth.

He made his will, for he was very wise: 112
he split and shared his wealth with many lands,
and left all of his servants quite content
after they split so many things amongst them.
He had three silver tablets, marvelously
inlaid, and one of gold, all of them wrought
with admirable artistry: away
as gifts he gave them in the following way.

The first, on which Byzantium, the mighty   113
city, appeared in its entirety,
he destined for Saint Peter's holy altar;
the second, where great Rome had been engraved,
he wanted to Ravenna sent as gift.
O noble present of great wealth and weight!
O gift, bespeaking a munificence
just like the giver, noble and immense!

The third one, much more exquisitely done,   114
on which a map of the whole earth was seen,
and also the fourth tablet of pure gold
he gave to Ludwig, his beloved son,
the one remaining heir to the great throne
after the death of Carlo, the first born,
and Pepin, second (Ludwig, the third son,
alone succeeded to his father's crown).

And now that Carlo, dead and buried, basks   115
in that high ecstasy and total bliss
that is enjoyed by those who reach at last
the port of their salvation and their peace,
lest I do history a grave disservice
I hasten here to add a codicil,
that he who reads my book may praise and bless
the last result of this my thoroughness.

From history we have most clearly learned   116
that Ludwig, Carlo's sole surviving son,
inherited large reigns and many lands,
thanks to his father's excellence, I say,
for many years and various events;
he even made the Persian king his friend,
who was attracted not by him, but rather
by the magnetic actions of his father.

France and Guyenne and all of Burgundy,   117
Navarra, Aragon with all of Spain,
Flanders and England and all Gascony,
Dacia and Germany and Brittany,
Pannonia, Bohemia, Saxony,
and many other German provinces,
Dalmatia, Istria, and Lombardy,
they all remained under his monarchy.

And in all honesty and truth, this son   118
was not unworthy of his noble sire;
but since I plan to honor him elsewhere
in a new booklet I have just begun,
I now return to our first emperor
for certain things that I have not yet said
about the mores and ways of such a man,
to let my story come to its Amen.

Several authors wrote about his nature   119
and qualities, and if I understood
correctly, he was of most handsome height,
large of both chest and shoulders, dignified
in both his bearing and his ways of looking,
gracious in every word, grave in his mien,
long-bearded, with a well-proportioned nose,
majestic in his aspect and his pose.

Most affable and placable and great,								120
most wise, most virile, all the time discreet;
a friend, a servant, a good mate and parent,
he let all people leave his presence pleased,
for no one ever said, "My lord's unjust."
All of his laws and his decrees were just;
he cherished humble people's company
and gave example of humility.

He practiced his religion piously.								121
In every land, in every town he built
some noble palaces of dazzling worth,
so many abbeys, hospitals, and churches
that I believe no one has numbered yet;
and, being ever fond of dauntless deeds,
cities and castles he made strong and fast,
as he had done with Florence in the past.

As I have said, over the Rhine he built								122
a bridge that spanned five hundred feet in length:
it, too, before his death made the whole world
aware of how nobility must fall.
He under every circumstance revealed
prudence and temperance and fortitude—
three graces seldom God upon us showers
for the salvation of the Church or ours.

He often took delight in hunting games,								123
for, being wise, he idleness abhorred,
and, even old and weary, did not fear
cold weather or discomfort of wild land:
so that when he, too, reached that final goal
beyond which every man is bound to fall,
for nature does not have the strength of yore,
praying, he hastened his own death therefore.

He also took as much delight in bathing:								124
there he would often gather many friends,
maybe compelled to do so by the place
located on some very rigid mountain.
O blessèd king! O just and kindly lord!
How happy was that age! Never again
will your France know such beauty and such joy
through course of stars or planet in the sky!

All nations thought that it was God who sent   125
so great a lord upon man's earth to show
what justice, charity, and zeal should be;
and had the old idolatry not died,
he, just like Baal, would have been adored
with all the ancient reverence and love;
and maybe he's not wrong—that author who recorded
the detail of a cross ingrown upon his shoulder.

He had his children—boys and girls—instructed   126
in every subject, in all liberal arts,
nor did they at that time need other school
than the Academy of Paris there.
He wanted all his children at his side
if—dawn or evening—went he for a ride.
Often his daughters, laziness to fight,
were seen to use the spindle day or night.

With dutiful and tender love he loved   127
his mother, known to us as Bertha still,
practicing that commandment, in this way,
which Moses, our first Teacher, gave to us.
She was from Greece, born of most noble blood,
the daughter of great Emperor Heraclius.
In short, my reader, this I wish to tell—
that he who fears the Lord does all things well.

So my King Carlo's life was truly just   128
and righteous and inspiring. He therefore
held both his crown and empire as a truly
magnificent and happy monarch would.
But now a trumpet's blasting somewhere else
whose sound is echoing all over still:
so I must end my tale, despite its worth,
for everything must finish on this earth.

If I have failed with both my mind and verse   129
to celebrate King Charles as he deserves,
I cannot stretch my bow more than I have
without transgressing my intended aim.
Maybe my only fault is that I plan
to say much more of him in my next song,
in my *Ciriffo Calvaneo,* where
his worthy son his divine fame will share.

My vessel I have brought now into port: 130
no longer will I try Gibraltar's Strait
(my steersman does not dare sail farther on
lest, like a mole, he into darkness plunge
or run the risk of those in Noah's Ark)
till once again the mountains or the Alps
on the dark sky I finally may see
or sight the raven coming back to me.

Not that I want to stay forever anchored;   131
for if much farther than Ulysses I
should wish to sail, a Lady is in heaven
who will protect me (never had I thought
she'd die before the end of this my tale!).
Her blessed soul that now can see all things
will be my star. She showed me first the sea,
and once again she will remember me.

With Carlo's so renowned and holy life   132
this newer subject matter would go well—
a parallel biography of my
Lucretia Torna-*buona* (*perfect,* rather),
who sits now in the chair long kept for her
by our eternal Blessed Mother, who
is finally applauding her good servant
(and holy is her praise, and truly fervent).

Here we still read her book about her Mary—   133
a book we keep forever open—and
one dealing with Esdras, Tobias, Judith;
but only there true merit is rewarded,
there is appreciated the high fancy
with which she could describe John in the desert,
and there the angels now her lines recite,
there where the truth of everything is bright.

Nature achieved what she intended to—   134
a famous Lady, in our century,
whose merits rise above all women so
that there's no pen or ink, all this to write.
Though her true worth to all mankind was shown,
this blind and foolish world has known her not,
certainly not the way the Lord, who keeps her now above,
knows her, or it, too, would have given her worship and love.

Oh, how much good she did! And how much wrong   135
she righted while she was upon this earth!
Because of her so boundless charity,
right on the day when Gabriel flew down,
in the pure whiteness of her nuptial gown
her soul was wedded unto God again:
I beg her that me, too, up there she may accept
among her servants in the number of th' Elect.

If I have in the end fulfilled her wish,   136
that is enough for me, and I am glad:
no other prize or honor do I want,
happy to savor such great bliss within.
I know that my Morgante is in heaven,
and if I hear of some malicious man,
he'll use once more his clapper from up there
(he'll find a way) and comb all of his hair.

Let some foul birds bear in their beaks a stone,   137
like those geese on the summit of Mount Taurus,
in order not to croak before the hawk!
Or I will make them spin just like a top
with this my whip I'm keeping right before me:
even before Morgante, I was bad!
If you have teeth, beware of whom you bite,
I also say; the proverb says it right.

I am not asking for the laurel wreath   138
the Greek and Latin bards much coveted;
nor am I asking for a golden style
to sing of Aganippe and Helicon;
simple and pure, throughout my woods I go
with this my humble bagpipe sounding still:
Damoetas I meet there, and also Thyrsis,
and, among shepherds, there I sing my verses.

And never have I been presumptuous   139
like that most foolish citharist of old
who was by god Apollo flayed alive;
I'm no such satyr as I seem to be.
Let others, better artists than I am,
come with new style and song, with better lyres;
'mid beeches I will stay with uncouth men and others,
like them, who like the muse of all the Pulci brothers.

I in my little vessel will go only   140
as far as a small ship can ever fare,
and, then, aside from what my fancy dreams,
'tis my intention everyone to please;
but different things will always be on earth,
as different as men's intellects and miens:
some like the white, and some the black, and those
who like a poem may not cherish prose.

Maybe the ones who'll read will from so small   141
a spark, as from brief tinder, soon light up
their minds and thus be able to go near
Parnassus's summit or the Sibyl's cave;
and if from my flowers some honey drips,
like bees the learned men will gather it;
if I can please still others with the rest,
I, as an author, shall feel doubly blest.

I know that often, as Morgante did,   142
I maybe whirled my club a bit too much;
but a good judge will tell that what is fit
for private rooms is also fit for alleys;
besides, if with a giant long you stay,
you're bound to learn a tiny bit from him:
a different clapper I have had to wield,
now playing blindman's buff or striking shield.

Give not my verse to Varius or Tucca: 143
let it be read and praised by Bellincion,
who judges as a friend and does not goad.
Meanwhile I'll tread on ice with well-nailed shoes,
and on my shoulders keep, securely fastened,
my pumpkin so that I may float in water.
And I will act as wise men act: I, too,
will pardon those who know not what they do.

And then it will be read by my Antonio,   144
who makes our lyre gloriously sound
with our Ausonian sweet native verse
(though he who may bear witness to true light
in Vallombrosa is now living still).
I know one always finds what to condemn,
but if detractors are dark fiends from hell
or swans or ravens, this I cannot tell.

Meanwhile, I wait neither for canopies   145
nor for umbrellas with a whistle called;
I do not wish to write names in red
just as some authors in their booklets do.
I, when I see my Serafin again,
will maybe quote it all from memory,
already checked by Angiolino's hand
(Montepulciano is his lucky land).

He is that famous and divine Alcaeus   146
to whom alone the golden plectrum goes.
He envies not Amphion or Musaeus,
but in a laurel tree's most famous shade
he sits and, like the Thracian Orpheus,
moves mountains, has Parnassus's choir around him,
stops rivers, forces rocks, turns over glebes,
and could, if willing, give new walls to Thebes.

His celebrated lyre I will follow,   147
his sweet, harmonious, sonorous lyre
that like a magnet draws all of my heart,
until together we shall Pallas find;
and if, together still, we'll share one pyre,
its glow will tell our never-ending love,
and our commingled flames will narrate both
one death, one sepulcher, one epitaph.

Along Eurote's still so famous banks   148
we'll roam and up the Cynthus's lofty crags,
where Grecian and Ausonian muses bring him
some fair narcissi, some bright hyacinths;
there I will hear sublime, heavenly songs
which Pindus never heard, nor Aracynthus;
Pallas I'll lead to Delphi and to Delos;
then, like Quirinus, he will reach the sky.

This man will be like Pollio in Rome,   149
and he will be Maecenas, the great one
whom every muse for centuries will crown.
So, noble spirits, all of you wake up,
for he will make this tongue of ours rebloom,
so will the fame of all his writings glow:
a worthy subject is in front of you,
which by itself inspires praises new.

Now all the Graces one by one I see,   150
and all the fairest nymphs I also view;
and I see Pallas now, right in their midst,
singing with them the praises of this man;
and by no means can Fortune halt all this,
for a great poet wins the brightest stars:
even the grace of God gives many a sign
he is the light that in our age will shine.

Out of a fresh and precious laurel tree   151
so many gentle boughs and twigs are sprung,
from Indus down to Maurus I can hear
new harps, new Mercuries and new Apollos,
rejuvenating soon that golden age
which was about to give its final gasp:
those blessèd ancient days are back again,
when good old Saturn had his happy reign.

Oh, good and lovely centuries of yore!   152
All of you therefore tune your lyres fast,
for this my fantasy cannot stand still,
just like a wheel that, stopped, wants more to turn.
Who would deny now Gallus writing verse?
Pro re, pauca dixi, compared to my great wish.
And let this be the end of our poetic matter
with peace and joy and in the name of God, our Father.

Salve, Regina, glorious mother, O
life so delightful, hope so nourishing,
to you, because of Eve's old sinful flaw,
weeping and sighing, Ave still we sing
in this our valley full of tears and woe:
the keys you own for our last entering:
so in our exile, may you watch and please us
by showing us, sweet Mary, your son Jesus.

If just, O Holy Virgin, is my plea,
oh, make me worthy now to praise but you;
grant virtue, intellect, and grace to me,
so that against your foes I may stand true;
and since my ship you anchored finally,
my thanks, O Blessed Virgin, I renew:
I with your blessing have commenced my story,
and with your blessing you will give me glory.

And in your grace, O Virgin Mary, keep
that great and truthful soul forevermore—
your pious, good Mona Lucretia—
in your true peace and perfect charity;
oh, grant her all for which she yet may pray,
for what you like, she'll ask eternally:
and may her virtue and your intercession
obtain for me the grace of my salvation.

Summary

OF EACH CANTO
WITH
NOTES AND COMMENTARY

SUMMARY: Invocation (1–2). Angered by Gano's slanderous accusations, Orlando, having spent a few days with Alda, his betrothed, leaves the court of the Emperor Charlemagne (3–18). Determined to "cross all Pagandom," he arrives at a faraway abbey, where he is cordially received by Clairmont, the abbot. Clairmont tells the paladin that he and his monks live in constant fear of the giants Passamont, Alabaster, and Morgante, who renew their daily attacks as the abbot speaks (19–27). Stanzas 28–59 contain the central episode of the canto, which is the mortal duel that Orlando wages with the giants Passamont and Alabaster, brothers of Morgante, and the conversion of the latter, after whom the poem is titled. After a few days' rest at the abbey, Morgante, at Orlando's request, goes to fetch water, bringing back with him also two huge boars, which the monks immediately cook and happily devour (60–67). As a token of his gratitude, the abbot then gives Morgante a horse, which falls dead to the ground when the giant attempts to ride it. Disappointed, Morgante carries the carcass away, finally dumping it in a ravine (68–75). Having decided that it is time to leave, Orlando bids farewell to Clairmont, who takes Orlando and Morgante to a room in the abbey filled with ancient arms. Here Morgante finds a hauberk which fits him like a glove. From the frescoes painted on the walls of the room, Orlando learns that the hauberk once belonged to a huge giant killed by Milo of Anglante a long time ago (75–86).

All the cantos of *Morgante* open with a religious invocation. A similar, though considerably shorter, request for God's further assistance or blessing for the help already received can be found also in the last stanza of twenty-four of the twenty-eight cantos of the poem (a closing invocation is missing in cantos XIII–XV and XXIV). It must be noted that Pulci (as he himself states in canto III, vv. 5–8) was thereby following the tradition already established in the *cantari popolari* of the fourteenth and fifteenth centuries, such as *La Spagna* and *Orlando,* in which an invocation to God, Christ, the Virgin, or a saint replaces the appeal to the Muse of classical poetry.

La Spagna. Poema cavalleresco del secolo XIV was edited by Michele Catalano, who attributed it to the relatively unknown Florentine poet Sostegno di Zanobi, who possibly composed it between 1350 and 1360 (Bologna: Commissione per i testi di lingua, 1939, vols. I–III). The text of the anonymous *Orlando* is contained in the Mediceo-Palatino N. F. 78 in the

Laurenziana Library in Florence. It was first studied by Pio Rajna, who, comparing it with Pulci's masterpiece, concluded that *Morgante* derives from *Orlando* (see "La materia del *Morgante* in un ignoto poema cavalleresco del secolo XV," *Il Propugnatore* 2, 1 [1869]: 7–35, 220–252, 353–384). The manuscript of *Orlando* was later published by the German philologist Johannes Hübscher, who pointed out extensive textual similarities between the stanzas of *Orlando* and those of *Morgante* (see *Ausgaben und Abhandlungen aus dem Gebiete der Romanischen Philologie LX. "ORLANDO" Die Vorlage zu Pulci's "MORGANTE"* [Marburg: N. G. Elwert'sche Verlagsbuchhandlung, 1886], 1–264). Both *La Spagna* and *Orlando* have been the object of an exhaustive comparative study by the eminent Pulci scholar Domenico De Robertis (*Storia del Morgante* [Firenze: Le Monnier, 1958]). While most scholars believe that Pulci closely followed these two sources in the composition of his poem, more recently Paolo Orvieto has cast serious doubt upon Rajna's thesis. Maintaining that Rajna has failed to prove that *Orlando* was written before *Morgante,* Orvieto suggests that both works derive from another poem, a certain *Cantare d'Orlando,* which has been lost (see *Pulci medievale* [Roma: Salerno Editrice, 1978] and, more specifically, "Sul rapporto *Morgante-Orlando Laurenziano." Die Ritterepik der Renaissance,* Akten des Deutsch-Italienischen Kolloquiums, Berlin 30.3.–2.4. 1987, a c. di Klaus W. Hempfer [Stuttgart: Franz Steiner Verlag, 1989], 145–53).

The conventional nature of the invocations of *Morgante* is also proven by their formal similarity to those in *Orlando,* which Pulci seems to mechanically repeat, though freely inverting their order. These invocations, often contrasting with the content of the cantos they introduce, should not be considered a reflection of Luigi Pulci's true religious beliefs, as scholars such as Ulrich Leo and Carlo Pellegrini believe (see U. Leo, "Luigi Pulci e il Diavolo," *Der Vergleich Literatur- und Sprachwissenschaftliche Interpretationen. Festgabe für Hellmuth Petriconi zum 1 April 1955,* ed. Rudolf Grassmann, Walter Pabst, and Edmund Schramon, vol. 42, 1955, 126; and C. Pellegrini, *Luigi Pulci: l'uomo e l'artista* [Pisa: Nistri, 1912], 42). With regard to the question of religion, the difference between Luigi Pulci and the anonymous author of *Orlando,* as well as other authors of *cantari popolari,* is substantially one of attitude and tone. Whereas these authors quote from the sacred texts with the utmost respect, Pulci, as Gaetano Mariani also points out, does not hesitate to poke fun at religion and to parody the sacred texts (*Il Morgante e i cantari trecenteschi* [Firenze: Le Monnier, 1953], 48–50).

1, 1–4. The invocation is a free adaptation of the first three verses of the Gospel according to John (1:1–3).

2, 1–4. In this stanza are to be found the same concepts, derived from Dante and Petrarch, which Pulci had expressed in the first eighteen verses of his *Confessione,* a 337–line poem in *terza rima,* the sincerity of which is questionable (see Introduction). For the reference to Gabriel's greeting in line 4, see Dante's *Paradiso,* XVI, 34.

3, 1–4. Here the poet makes reference to the mythical sisters Philomela and Procne, daughters of Pandion, king of Attica. According to Greek and Roman mythology, Tereus, king of Thrace and husband of Procne, forcibly seduced Philomela and then cut out her tongue so that she could not tell anyone that he had raped her. Eventually Procne learned the truth and, wishing to avenge Philomela, killed Itys, the only son she had borne Tereus, and served the king a meal made out of the flesh of their own child. Upon discovering what Procne had done, Tereus wanted to kill both his wife and her sister, but the gods, moved to pity by the prayers of the two women, intervened, changing Procne into a swallow, Philomela into a nightingale, and Tereus into a hoopoe. (See Ovid, *Metamorphoses*, trans. Rolfe Humphries [Bloomington: Indiana University Press, 1983], "Story of Tereus, Procne and Philomela," 143–151.)

3, 5–6. Before the fifth century B.C., Helios was the sun god who, rising at dawn from the sea, brought light to the world while driving his great chariot across the sky. Helios had a son, Phaëthon, by the nymph Clymene. Beginning with the fifth century B.C., Helios was often confused with Phoebus Apollo. This is why several times in *Morgante* (IX, 2; XVI, 31; XXII, 2; and XXV, 74) Phoebus replaces Helios as the sun god and the father of Phaëthon. (See Ovid, *Metamorphoses*, "Story of Phaethon," 28–40.)

3, 8. Tithonus, son of Laomedon, king of Troy and brother of Priam, was chosen by Eos, the dawn goddess, as her husband. She was able to convince Zeus to grant Tithonus immortality, but forgot to obtain for him the gift of eternal youth. Once Tithonus became old and no longer attractive, Eos left him. (See Edward Tripp, *The Meridian Handbook of Classical Mythology* [New York: New American Library, 1970], 579–580.)

4, 1–3. The "one" at whose request Pulci started writing *Morgante* is Lucrezia Tornabuoni, Lorenzo de' Medici's mother (see note, XXVIII, 2, 1–4).

5, 1–2. The humanist Leonardo Bruni, also known as Leonardo Aretino, wrote several works, including the lives of Dante and Petrarch and the very important *Historiae Florentini populi,* which is considered the first "true" history of Florence. From 1427 until his death, he served as chancellor of Florence.

5, 3. According to Franca Ageno, editor and commentator of the authoritative edition of *Morgante,* Andrea da Barberino (1370–1431) quotes Urman of Paris as one of the sources for his *I reali di Francia,* which was for centuries one of the most popular tales of chivalry in Italy (*Morgante,* ed. Franca Ageno [Milano-Napoli: Ricciardi, 1955], 5). Based on Carolingian legends, this romance traces the history of the royal house of France from Fiovo, son of Constantine, to the time of Charlemagne. Ageno believes that Urman is probably a product of Barberino's imagination. In the Oxford version of the *Chanson de Roland* (2077–2245), Turpin, Archbishop of Reims, is the last of the Christian knights to die before Roland expires. In *Morgante,* instead, Turpin hears the confession of the dying Orlando (XXVII, 120–130) and survives the massacre, as do Rinaldo and Ricciardetto (XXVII, 184, v. 1).

As Ageno further notes, Pulci attributes to Turpin the paternity of the *Historia Karoli Magni et Rotholandi ou Cronique du Pseudo-Turpin* (ed. C. Meredith-Jones [Paris, 1936]), a work which the authors of romances of chivalry and epic poems often quote as the authoritative source, even when they relate events that are not narrated in the above-mentioned Latin chronicle.

6, 1–3. The abbey of Saint Liberatore still stands today in Maiella, near Manoppello, in the province of Pescara, in the Abruzzo region. According to tradition, which Pulci seems to accept, Charlemagne fought a fierce battle in this locality against a Saracen army.

6, 7–8. A reference to the valley of Jehoshaphat, where the Last Judgment is to take place (Joel 3:2).

7, 1–8. In this stanza Pulci states that Florence derived most of its greatness from French blood (see also canto XXVIII, 100, 1–8, in which the alleged rebuilding and rebirth of his city is attributed to Charlemagne, who stopped in Florence after his coronation in Rome). It must be added that Pulci believed, with other noble Florentines, that his family was of French origin (see Guglielmo Volpi, "Luigi Pulci. Studio Biografico," *Giornale storico della letteratura italiana* XXII, 64–65 [1893]: 2).

8, 3. As recounted in the *Chanson de Roland,* the defeat of Charlemagne's rear guard at Roncesvalles and the death of Roland and his paladins were caused by Gano's betrayal of his king's trust and friendship. For this despicable act, Gano (also called Gan and Ganelon) came to epitomize treason, and was therefore linked to the lineage of Doon de Mayence, patriarch of the rebellious vassal cycle, hence typologically related to Judas and his betrayal of Christ. In the Italian tradition, all persons belonging to the House of Maganza were considered potential traitors. (See also the early-fourteenth-century Franco-Venetian popular epics *Entrée d'Espagne* and *La Prise de Pampelune,* in *Poemi Cavallereschi del Trecento,* ed. Giuseppe Guido Ferrero [Torino: UTET, 1965].) It is interesting to note that Dante places Gano in the same circle of hell where another famous traitor, Count Ugolino, is punished (*Inferno,* XXXII, 122).

8, 5–6. The two verses closely follow Dante's tercet "After the tragic rout when Charlemagne / lost all his faithful, holy paladins, / the sound of Roland's horn was not so ominous" (*Inferno,* XXXI, 16–18; this and all other quotations in this commentary are taken from Mark Musa's translation of Dante's *Inferno* [Bloomington: Indiana University Press, 1971]).

8, 7–8. Dante places Orlando and Charlemagne in the heavenly spheres among the blessed souls of those who fought in defense of the Christian faith (*Paradiso,* VXIII, 43). It was not uncommon for authors of early *cantari popolari* and of later epics to quote from Dante. This practice was particularly observed by Pulci, who, as we have seen in stanza 8, felt free to borrow from the poem, with which he had considerable familiarity (see Guglielmo Volpi, "*La Divina Commedia* nel *Morgante* di Luigi Pulci," *Giornale Dantesco* XII [1903]: 170–174, and Gaetano Mariani, *Il Morgante e i cantari trecenteschi,* 56–64). According to Volpi, the importance of the presence of the *Divine Comedy* in

Morgante resides mainly in the fact that it gives us an idea of the type of knowledge the man of average culture of the second half of the fifteenth century had of Dante's poem. For Mariani, instead, when quoting from Dante, Pulci differs substantially from the authors of the *cantari popolari*. While these poets merely insert Dante's poetry into their works, Pulci often adapts Dante's tercets, "transforming them into the rhythm of his own verse, exactly as he does with the Gospel and the other sacred texts."

9–10. Charles I, better known as Charlemagne (742–814), was the first-born son of Pepin, king of the Franks, whom he succeeded in 768. In 773, at the request of Pope Hadrian I, he waged a victorious war against the Lombards of northern Italy, then mounted a largely unsuccessful campaign into Spain in 778, and engaged in numerous campaigns against the heathen Saxons. Because of his exploits, people all over Europe considered Charlemagne a true champion of the Christian faith. Soon after his death, legends began to flourish extolling his heroic deeds as well as those of his beloved paladins. Eventually, between the eleventh and twelfth centuries, these legends gave life to popular epics or *chansons de geste,* of which the Oxford version of the *Chanson de Roland* (a 4,002–line poem composed in the late eleventh or twelfth century) is the best-known and the most beautiful.

In traditional Italian chivalric literature, Orlando, Christendom's best-known legendary knight, is the son of Milo (or Milon) of Anglante (or Angrante) and of Bertha, sister of Charlemagne. He plays a significant role in the final stanzas of this canto when Morgante receives the rusted armor of another giant, who had ravaged those parts and had been killed by Milo. Orlando, who belongs to the House of Clairmont, is Rinaldo of Montauban's (Montalban throughout this translation) first cousin, since their respective fathers, Milo and Ammon, were both fathered by Bernard of Clairmont. Other sons of Bernard of Clairmont were Ottone (Otho), king of England and father of Astolfo, and Gherardo of Rossiglione, father of Ansuigi. Thus Orlando, Rinaldo, Astolfo, and Ansuigi were cousins, and they all belonged to the Clairmont clan. Bernard, as we are told in cantos II, 3 and III, 77, also had an illegitimate son, named Ansuigi, father of the abbot Clairmont (whom Orlando meets in canto I, 20ff.). This makes the abbot a cousin of the four knights named above. From Rinaldo we learn (IV, 94, 3–4) that Ugier the Dane, another of Charlemagne's twelve paladins, is a former Saracen warrior who has converted to Christianity. (In the Oxford French text Ugier is not one of the twelve peers.) Ansuigi and Ugier will not take part in the Battle of Roncesvalles (XXVII, 167 and 191–194). Saint Denis, the patron saint of Paris, was the city's first bishop. The Church of Saint Denis was, and still is, located near the city walls (VIII, 57, 8). Oliver of Burgundy is the brother of Alda "the Fair," Orlando's betrothed. Berlinghier, Avolio, Avin, and Otho are the sons of Namo, the old duke of Bavaria, Charlemagne's lifelong adviser. Angiolin of Bayonne, Richard of Normandy, Salamon, duke of Brittany, and Walter of Mont Leon play a very secondary role in the poem, where they appear only sporadically.

10, 4–5. Baldwin, Gano's son, must not be confused with Baldwin, son of Ugier the Dane. Gano's son reappears in the poem's last five cantos.

11–12. In Pulci's poem, Charlemagne becomes almost a puppet in Gano's hands. It is in fact the emperor's continued belief in Gano's false accusations that drives Orlando away from Paris and gradually deprives him of the respect of his paladins. It appears that old age has rendered Charlemagne utterly unreasonable and easily irritable. Only in the last five cantos of *Morgante,* particularly after Roncesvalles, will the emperor regain his former wisdom and leadership, as well as some of the almost sacred aura that surrounds him in the *Chanson de Roland.* For a discussion of the figure of Charlemagne in traditional epics, see Angelo Gianni, *Pulci uno e due* (Firenze: La Nuova Italia, 1967), 40–46.

13, 1–8. Aspromont, in the southernmost section of Calabria, where it was said that Orlando, fighting in Charlemagne's army, demonstrated his valor by killing Almont(e), son of the Saracen king Agolant(e), thus gaining exclusive possession of the famous sword Durlindana—the Durendal of the *Chanson de Roland*—as well as the horse Vegliantin(o). The sources for this belief were, according to Ageno, Andrea da Barberino's *Aspramonte* and the *Chanson d'Aspremont* (Ageno, 9). The Gherardo mentioned in line 4 is Gherardo of Fratta, Marquis of Vienna, in Burgundy, and Oliver's uncle; he is not to beconfused with Gherardo of Rossiglione.

16–17. Orlando reveals here his hot-tempered nature, which often brings him to the point of losing his self-control, thus making him appear even comical. Ermellina, Namo's daughter, is the wife of Ugier, whose sword, Cortana, and whose horse, Rondel, the raging Orlando appropriates before leaving the court. Brava (or Blaive) is the city of which Orlando was count and in which he and Alda were buried.

25, 1–4. The reference to "our ancient fathers" derives from Mark 1:7 and Matthew 3:4. The source for verse 5 is John 4:31.

27, 1–2. These lines contain an amusing reference to the food that was miraculously supplied to the children of Israel in the wilderness (Exodus 16:14–36).

28, 7. In *Morgante,* as in *La Spagna* and other *cantari popolari,* the title "baron" (*barone*) is used when addressing persons of noble bearing, be they Christians or Muslims. In fact, in stanza 44, 1, Orlando addresses Morgante, who has just decided to convert, with the words "baron just and good." At times the Italian "barone" is translated into English as "count" (for example, II, 61, 7). In medieval Italian texts (as in Boccaccio's *Decameron*), saints are also often called "baroni."

35, 6. Mahound (also called Mahomet) was considered the God of the Muslims and not Allah's prophet.

43–54. It is a known fact that religious conversions, be they individual or collective, are a customary *topos* in chivalric literature. It must be noted, however, that those we encounter in *Morgante* differ considerably, in spite of their conventionality, from those we read in other *cantari,* whose authors, regardless of how sincere their faith may be, do treat religious matters in a serious manner. Certainly Pulci's conversions are all too sudden, incredible, and often ludicrous. Even Carlo Pellegrini, who considers them to be an important indication of Pulci's religiosity, recognizes that they are "at times a bit too quick" (*Luigi Pulci. L'uomo e l'artista*, 42). Clearly Morgante's conversion, the first of many in the poem, can hardly be attributed to a spiritual crisis. The giant, in fact, declares his intention to embrace Christianity (43, 8) even before Orlando—who has tried to console him on the loss of his two brothers with an amusingly ironic explanation (49)—begins to impart his religious instruction (50–52). In response to Orlando's doctrinal considerations, Morgante, who does not feel any need for additional explanations, first proclaims his newly acquired Christian credo: "Who cares about the dead? Let's enjoy life" (53, 6), then, to demonstrate "his good intentions" and to reassure the "holy monks" whom he has terrorized for so long, he happily cuts off the hands of his two dead brothers.

Pulci's mocking attitude transpires in stanzas 20–28, where he has skillfully portrayed the mood of the friars as well as the lazy and hypocritical nature of their abbot. In line 1 of stanza 21, the words "little monks" have been used to render the noun *monachetti* of the original Italian text. In this specific instance, English cannot render all the nuances in meaning of the Italian diminutive *monachetti*. With the ironic use of this diminutive, Pulci stresses the fear that dominates the cowardly monks. It is clear that what interests the poet is the mental and spiritual portrait of Clairmont's friars (their fear and lack of faith), rather than their physical description. When later on in the canto (66–67) they reappear finally freed of the fear that had previously governed their daily life, the word *monachetti* is no longer used. And how could Pulci refer to them as "little monks" when we see them eating and drinking to the point of bursting and even depriving their cats and dogs of the leavings on small bones! The tremendous quantity of food that they are able to devour in such a short time elicits the poet's sarcastic remark "All animals are glad at feeding time" (66, 3). The episode gives Pulci the opportunity to make fun of the traditional reputation for gluttony of monks and clerics found in satirical literature. Clairmont—whose gastronomic preoccupation is revealed when, referring to the rocks thrown at the abbey by Alabaster and Passamont, he uses such verbs as "eat" and "taste" (25, 6–8)—is no less cowardly than his monks and clearly doubts the ascetic virtues of the "ancient fathers in the desert" (25, 1–5). Smarter than they are, however, he is able to hide his total lack of a spiritual life, frequently quoting from the Gospel and delivering an edifying as much as useless little sermon (57, 7–8 and 58–59). Quite revealing as well is the farewell speech/confession that the materialistic Clairmont delivers to Orlando (79–81 and 82, 1–3), who is about to leave the abbey with Morgante.

In the anonymous *Orlando,* Morgante's conversion takes place in canto II, 3–7, which correspond to stanzas 41–45 in canto I of *Morgante.* An examination of the two texts shows that while the content of the cantos in question is similar, the manner in which the two authors tell their story is substantially different. In *Orlando,* Morgante decides to convert only after Orlando's doctrinal lecturing; in addition, the giant severs the hands of his brothers only to please Orlando, who has expressed the desire to bring the monks unquestionable proof of Passamont's and Alabaster's death. Contrary to what we have noted in the first canto of *Morgante,* the author of *Orlando* neither reveals any parodic intention nor shares with Luigi Pulci the latter's sharp satire against the gluttony of the clergy. (For a more detailed discussion, see my article "Due esempi di satira antifratesca nel *Morgante,*" in *Studies in Honor of Tatiana Fotich* [Washington, D.C.: The Catholic University of America Press, 1972], 203–209.)

59, 3–4. Orlando is quoting from Luke 15:7.

71, 1–4. Here Morgante, who has just become a Christian, shows that he is well acquainted with Matthew 5:44.

72, 2. Nessus was a centaur who took travelers across the river Evenus. One day he was asked by Hercules to take Deïaneira, Hercules' woman, across the river on his boat. Having fallen suddenly in love with her, Nessus tried to rape the girl, who resisted him and called out for help. Hercules, who had meanwhile swum to the other bank of the river, mortally wounded the centaur with an arrow. Before dying, however, Nessus found a way to avenge himself. He told Deïaneira to soak a piece of cloth in his blood and make a tunic with it. She was then advised to give it to Hercules in order to keep his love should he abandon her for another woman. Eventually the jealous Deïaneira sent the poisonous tunic to Hercules, who wore it and died a very painful death. (See *The Meridian Book of Classical Mythology,* 395–396.)

CANTO II

SUMMARY: Invocation (1). While Orlando and the abbot discover that they are cousins, Morgante chooses as his main weapon the clapper of a huge bell (2–11). Clairmont then informs Orlando that Caradoro's kingdom is being besieged by Manfredonio, who is hopelessly in love with Meridiana, the king's daughter (11–15). Spurred on by the abbot's words, Orlando and Morgante leave the monastery, soon to end up as prisoners in an enchanted castle. Here they fight with a devil, eventually regaining their freedom, but only after Orlando has baptized his gigantic squire (16–36). Upon resuming their travels, Orlando and Morgante see two men engaged in a duel near a spring. They learn that the two are couriers and that they have been sent by Rinaldo and Gano, respectively, to find Orlando. Gano's messenger is expeditiously killed by Morgante, while Orlando sends Rinaldo's courier back to Paris with a message for the emperor and his cousin (37–58). The last stanzas of the canto (59–79) retell the duel which Orlando, an honored guest in Manfredonio's camp, wages with Lionetto, son of King Caradoro.

1, 1–8. In the invocation the poet asks Christ to steer his ship (*Morgante*), keeping his eyes fixed on the North Star. In the Italian text, reference is also made to the needle of the compass.

3, 1–8. As already noted, the Ansuigi who fathered the abbot is Bernard of Clairmont's illegitimate son. He must not be confused with Ansuigi, son of Gherardo of Rossiglione and grandson of Bernard of Clairmont.

5, 1–4. All knights in the epic tradition, be they Christians or pagans, are easily moved to tears and feel no compulsion to hide their emotions.

6, 5–8; and 7–8. In these stanzas Pulci completes the portrait of the abbot. Questioned by Orlando as to why he decided to become a monk instead of "brandishing a spear" as so many members of the Clairmont clan choose to do, the abbot promptly declares that he did so in order to follow the will of God. Clairmont's answer, no matter how orthodox his solemn words may sound, is in reality an amusing parody of priestly oratory. The author's satirical intention is, in fact, emphasized by the evident contrast between the decisively cowardly nature of the man and the sublime mission he claims to have been called to by God Himself. In his irreverent sonnet "In principio era bujo, e bujo fia" (*Sonetti di Matteo Franco e di Luigi Pulci, insieme con la Confessione. Stanze in lode della Beca ed altre rime del medesimo Pulci* [Lucca, 1759], 144), Pulci makes fun of the pilgrims going to Rome on the occasion of the jubilee year. It is interesting to note that in stanza 7, 2 the poet not only repeats a baffling concept of his controversial *Confessione* (see *Sonetti,* 153), but also has Clairmont compare life to a pilgrimage whose goal is the Eternal City (7, 6–8). Certainly the amusing verse "but touching home base is the game's sole end" (8, 6) sounds more like an abrupt conclusion than the logical completion of Clairmont's speech. As frequently happens throughout the poem, when Pulci, tired of a character or topic, wishes to go on with his story, he suddenly resorts to a proverb or a religious invocation. Such is the case in stanza 8, where a proverbial expression which originated from a popular children's game is used.

10, 5. From this moment on, the clapper becomes an integral part of Morgante, inseparable from the giant and at times becoming one with him. "Without the clapper," writes Attilio Momigliano, "Morgante is like Hercules without his club" (*L'indole e il riso di Luigi Pulci* [Rocca San Casciano: Cappelli, 1907], 276). In the *Guillaume d'Orange* cycle (known also as the second cycle of old French epic poems), a curious giant of Saracen origin becomes a companion of the protagonist, Guillaume d'Orange. In the epic *Aliscans,* Guillaume escapes from the field of battle and makes his way to King Louis, seeking the monarch's help. He takes with him a giant figure named Rainouart, a Saracen purchased from a merchant. This gigantic, naive youth, who has been working in King Louis's kitchen, turns out to be the brother of Guillaume's converted Saracen wife, Guibourc (formerly named Orable). This burlesque character, much concerned with satisfying his own bodily needs, owns a sword so small as to be nearly worthless. Therefore he takes a large tree trunk, which he uses as a battle club, and comes to be known as Rainouart au Tinel (Rainouart with the Club). This humorous personage became so popular that several epic poems were written about him, burlesquing the traditional chivalric figure, including *Moniage Rainouart,* a comic epic that traces the great warrior's withdrawal to a monastery.

Morgante's clapper and his parodic imitation of a chivalric tradition in which reason no longer governs the senses may stem from this popular twelfth- and thirteenth-century French epic tradition (see Jean Frappier, *Les Chansons de Geste du Cycle de Guillaume d'Orange* [Paris: Société d'édition d'enseignement supérieur, 1955], 276). Morgante is not an original Pulci invention. Absent from *La Spagna,* the giant first appears in stanza 6, canto I of *Orlando* (p. 1), corresponding to stanzas 25–26, canto I of *Morgante.* In stanza 12, canto III of *Orlando* (p. 9)—which corresponds to stanzas 10–11, canto II of Pulci's poem—Morgante, having found the clapper of a broken bell, declares to Orlando: "Since I have this clapper, I don't care about the world any more than I do about garlic." To be sure, the similarities between the two Morgantes are essentially superficial. While the anonymous author of *Orlando* assigns to Morgante a more or less walk-on part (he acts mostly as Orlando's servant), in Pulci's masterpiece the giant achieves a protagonist's status. This happens because throughout the poem Morgante has a life of his own. As Carlo Pellegrini acutely observes, the truly "lively and artistic character" of Morgante must be considered, notwithstanding its derivation from *Orlando,* essentially the product of Luigi Pulci's creative imagination (*Luigi Pulci,* 107–109).

20, 1–8. In this stanza, as in several other stanzas of *Morgante,* Pulci describes with some pleasure the beautiful objects, such as carved furnishings, precious fabrics, and shining fixtures, which decorate the rooms in the palaces and castles of the poem. The same can be said when the poet depicts the elaborate jewels and colorful apparel worn by the poem's major characters. (See Giovanni Getto, *Studio sul 'Morgante'* [Firenze: Olschki, 1967], 50–52.)

21, 6–8; and 22–24. Blessed with tremendous brute strength, coupled with a perpetual voracity proportionate only to his size, Morgante is definitely one of the poem's most aggressive and comical characters. His actions and reactions to internal as well as external stimuli are not the result of a thinking process—the outcome of a meditative effort. For this reason it can be said that the giant's inability to experience meaningful spiritual changes (his conversion, as previously pointed out, is a purely formal act, brought about by the dream he had in canto I, 43, 1–8) is equal to his almost congenital incapacity to consider the consequences of his actions. To quote Carlo Pellegrini again, "Morgante, aware of his own strength, immediately accomplishes whatever strikes his fancy; but deprived as he is of thinking powers, his audacity knows no limits; he believes himself capable of doing anything" (*Luigi Pulci,* 104). One of the humorous themes throughout *Morgante* is the presentation of chivalric man ungoverned by reason, a primeval force acting according to its own self-interest and appetites. It is the same device used in the *Roman de Renart,* where the world-upside-down motif dominates the entire work as time and again animals satirize humans by suggesting that men often act on motives that are less governed by reason than we think. Morgante's comical side shines in stanzas 34–40, where the giant, emboldened by having helped Orlando to defeat the devil, in a paroxysm of joyful excitement threatens to drive Beelzebub and all his demons out of hell. The comic quality of the episode resides less in Morgante's bragging (he is capable, after all, of the most curious and seemingly impossible deeds) than in his sudden loss of interest in performing the exploits he had declared himself ready to do, once Orlando wittily remarks that there is no food in hell.

31, 3–4. The four demons named by Morgante are the product of Dante's fertile imagination. They are to be found in canto XXI of *Inferno,* where the first to appear is Eviltail (76), who heads the devils of the fifth bolgia; the other three, Cagnazzo, Lustycock, and Farferello, are presented in lines 119, 121, and 123 respectively. For Farferello, see also note, XXV, 165, 2.

38, 4. Reference is made here to the story of Orpheus and Eurydice, with which Morgante is also acquainted (as he appears to be with the *Divine Comedy*). According to classical mythology, Orpheus, inconsolable over the death of his wife Eurydice, who was killed by the bite of a poisonous snake, descended into the world of the dead to rescue her. Thanks to the beautifully sorrowful sound of his lyre, he was able to move the gods of the underworld to pity. They allowed Eurydice to follow her husband back to earth, provided he would not look at her until they had reached the light of day. Just as the couple was about to emerge into the world of the living, Orpheus, unable to control his desire to look at Eurydice, turned back and lost her forever (for the story of Orpheus and Eurydice, see Ovid's *Metamorphoses,* 234–236). Given the reference here and the references in stanza 39, one cannot but wonder if Pulci was not aware of the standard glosses of the first six books of Virgil's *Aeneid* by Fulgentius (sixth c.), Bernardus Silvestris (twelfth c.), and Cristoforo Landino (fifteenth c.). All of these commentaries interpret Virgil's epic in Platonic terms as the acquisition, nourishment, and perfection of wisdom. In the commentaries Orpheus symbolizes the virtuous, wise, contemplative man who meditates on mundane things in order to avoid them. Eurydice is the natural appetite that wanders through earthly, temporal pleasures leading to the underworld. Orpheus can return that appetite to a love of the good only if he can keep from looking back (at the temporal). It is both amusing and fascinating that Morgante, the man driven only by appetite and physical strength, recalls the story of Orpheus and Eurydice but cannot remember the name of Orpheus, symbol of the contemplative soul and all that the giant lacks. According to well-known commentaries, Orpheus used wisdom and eloquence, his lyre, to defeat the creatures of the underworld. Morgante would retrieve his Eurydice by driving off all those devils with brute force.

38, 7–8. Morgante mentions here and in the following stanza several well-known mythological figures. Franca Ageno (44) is inclined to believe that Pulci's source for most of these figures was Dante. While Virgil in his *Aeneid* depicts Minos, the wise king of Crete, as the supreme judge of the dead (VI, 432–433), Dante transforms him into a grotesque and quasi-bestial judge of hell, who, by the number of times he wraps his tail around his body, indicates the circle where each soul must go (*Inferno,* V, 4–12).

39, 1. Charon, the ferryman of dead souls in classical mythology, becomes in Dante's *Inferno* (V, 4–12) a violent, demonic figure.

39, 2. Pluto, known also by the name of Hades or Dis, was god of the Underworld.

39, 3. Phlegethon, found also in *Inferno* (XVI, 116), was a river that was believed to cross the underworld.

39, 4. Phlegyas is another mythical character, whom Dante transforms into the raging boatman of the river Styx (*Inferno,* VIII, 17–24).

39, 5–6. Tisiphone, Alecto, and Megaera were known as the Erinnyes by the Greeks, and as the Furies by the Romans. They were thought to be malignant creatures who dwelt in the deepest regions of the underworld; they were feared for their unrelenting pursuit of those who had committed unpunished crimes. In Dante's poem, the Furies become symbols of eternal remorse (see *Inferno,* IX, 45–48). Cerberus, the ravenous three-headed dog of hell, and the sorceress Erichto are also portrayed in Dante's *Inferno* (VI, 13–18 and IX, 23–24).

39, 7. Beelzebub is the name given to the prince of the devils (Luke 11:15, Mark 3:22, and Matthew 12:24–27). Dante refers to Lucifer as Beelzebub only in one of the last lines of *Inferno* (XXXIV, 127). Franca Ageno (44) rightly points out that Beelzebub was one of the names by which the devil was known in traditional popular culture.

48, 49, and 50, 1–4. In Orlando's words, spoken to the courier but addressed to Charlemagne, one can detect a slight note of sadness and longing. Such feelings, though not the prevailing note in the poem, do occasionally occur.

50, 5. Barbary was the name given to the entire northwestern African region extending from Egypt to Morocco.

52, 1. The Dane mentioned here is Ugier, the Dane of canto I (9, 4).

55, 3–8; 56; and 57, 1. This brief fable of the ant is the first of the several singular animal tales we encounter in *Morgante.*

60, 4–5. Commenting on these lines, Giovanni Getto writes that "Pulci lives in our memory above all as a fine painter of flags waving in the wind and/ or armed camps" (*Studio sul 'Morgante,'* 41).

61, 5. Contrasting with the abbot's "troubled" reaction at the sight of Morgante (I, 55, 7–8), here Manfredonio shows great surprise rather than fear. All those who meet the giant for the first time react either like Clairmont or like Manfredonio.

61, 7. See note, canto I, 28, 7.

67, 8. More recent editions of *Morgante* give Merediana as the name of Caradoro's daughter. Since Tusiani's translation follows Ageno's edition of *Morgante,* the name Meridiana is used throughout this text and the notes.

70, 5. In *Morgante,* as in *La Spagna* and in other popular Italian and French epics and romances, Mahound or Mahomet, Trevigant, and Apollino appear, often mentioned together, as three pagan gods. They constitute, to a certain extent, the Muslim counterpart of the Christian Trinity.

76, 7–8; and 77. As it frequently happens in chivalric literature, when a Christian knight, in this case Orlando, fights a pagan warrior, here Lionetto, the latter's defeat is deemed to be incontestable proof of Christ's superiority over Mohammed. It is equally interesting to note that non-Christian knights such as Lionetto are prompt to attribute their defeat in a duel or battle to a betrayal on the part of their own god, whom they do not hesitate to deny and/or to address with the most offensive epithets.

78, 1–4. In this particularly amusing stanza, Orlando, sure of his own superior strength, pokes fun at Lionetto's flimsy attempt to explain his fall from the saddle as due to his horse and not to the powerful blow of the count's spear.

C A N T O   I I I

SUMMARY: Invocation (1). Lionetto, recognizing the true identity of the knight with whom he is battling, attempts to flee. Orlando follows and kills him (2–8). Meridiana, wishing to avenge her brother's death, duels with Orlando, who, upon discovering that his opponent is a woman, leaves the field and returns to Manfredonio's camp (9–19). Chimento, having reached Paris, informs Charlemagne and his court that Orlando is alive and reveals Gano's treacherous plans against the count (20–25). Rinaldo kills one of Gano's men, then, accompanied only by Oliver and Dudon (26–33, 1–4), takes leave from the emperor to go in search of Orlando. In the meanwhile, Morgante's cousin Brunoro, angered by the death of Alabaster and Passamont, has forcefully taken possession of Clairmont's abbey, imprisoning the abbot (33, 5–8 through 36).

When the famished Rinaldo, Oliver, and Dudon arrive at the abbey, Brunoro serves them an offensive meal (37–45). First Baiardo, Rinaldo's horse, bites the servant who is about to groom it, killing him; then, with a tremendous blow of his fist, Rinaldo cracks open the skull of the Saracen soldier who had vexed him while he was eating (46–51, 1–5). The ensuing general fight is promptly stopped by Brunoro, who, having told Rinaldo the reasons for his occupation of the abbey and the imprisonment of its abbot, asks the knight to pass judgment on his actions (51, 6–8 through 59, 1–4). Rinaldo, who had wanted also to hear the abbot's version of the story, finds Brunoro at fault and kills him in the duel that follows (59, 5–8 through 70, 1–6). Aided by Clairmont and his monks, Rinaldo and his fellow paladins succeed in freeing the abbey of all Saracens (70, 7–8 through 75, 1–6). The canto ends happily with the discovery that Rinaldo and the abbot Clairmont are cousins (75, 7–8 through 81).

4, 1–3. Vegliantin(o) is the name of Orlando's most famous horse. It is first mentioned, as Veillantif, in the *Chanson de Roland*. As told in canto I,

16–17, in his haste to leave Paris, Orlando took with him Ugier's horse Rondel and sword Cortana, leaving behind Vegliantin and Durlindana, which Oliver had snatched from his hands to prevent him from killing Gano.

5. In this stanza (and again in stanza 11, as well as in other cantos of the poem) are listed the different pieces of armor and the weapons used by Christians and Saracens. Noting that it is rare to find such precise technical terminology in other writers, Getto is of the opinion that Pulci discloses here more than a mere desire to show off his knowledge of the military vocabulary concerning war and chivalry (*Studio sul 'Morgante,'* 156).

6, 4. The expression "letting them watch fireflies" vividly illustrates the remarkable effects of Morgante's clapper on Saracen heads. As noted elsewhere throughout this commentary, popular expressions and proverbs are frequently employed in *Morgante*.

12, 4. One of the poet's many ironic, bizarre, or amusing comments. In this instance, Pulci may allude not to himself, but to the anonymous author of *Orlando*.

17, 6–7. An indirect reference to the beautiful long-haired nymph Daphne, who eluded Apollo's advances by becoming, at her request, transformed into a laurel tree (see Ovid, *Metamorphoses,* 16–20).

20, 5. The Lord of Montalban is Orlando's cousin Rinaldo.

21–24, 1–4. Angelo Gianni maintains that this is one of the most "genuinely touching episodes" in the twenty-eight cantos of *Morgante*. According to this critic, even though these episodes may be amusing or may provoke a smile, they are nevertheless "sustained by a very evident epic and narrative tension" (*Pulci uno e due,* 4–5).

25, 8. Ageno (64) reports that Orlando's legendary elevation to the Roman senate is mentioned in Andrea da Barberino's chivalric tale *Aspramonte*. In addition to the previously mentioned *I Reali di Francia* and *Aspramonte,* Barberino also authored the popular romances *Guerrin Meschino, Storie nerbonesi, Ugone d'Alvernia, Aiolfo del Barbicane,* and *Rambaldo.*

26–30. Rinaldo, first mentioned in canto II by Clairmont (3, 3) and a little later by Chimento (43, 4), makes in these stanzas his formal, forceful entrance on the stage of *Morgante*. To quote Carlo Pellegrini (123), "Among the paladins he is the one who possesses more than any other a personality of his own, and who more frequently performs under our eyes" (*Luigi Pulci,* 123). A side of Rinaldo's character that comes to light in this episode is his irascibility, his natural inclination to violence. After his few sorrowful words for Orlando, whom he believes to be dead (III, 23, 1–3), the paladin's reaction to Chimento's announcement of Gano's treachery is swift and spares no one. In his rage, he first loudly and contemptuously denounces Charlemagne's foolishly blind trust in the Lord of Maganza; then, unable to hit Gano, who has meanwhile promptly fled from the scene, he beheads, with a cutting blow of Cortana, Bernard of Pontier, who had dared to call him a "villain." Commenting on this episode, Pellegrini (124) states that the continued loss in dignity that the figure of Charles undergoes in *Morgante* is greatly due to

Rinaldo. Angelo Gianni (29–43) maintains instead that the deterioration taking place with regard to the presentation of the figure of the emperor and his knights is a topic "as ancient as chivalric literature." Surely the "diminutio capitis" referred to by Pellegrini and Gianni is already detectable in *Orlando,* and considerably more noticeable in *La Spagna.*

30, 8. With regard to Dudon(e), most Pulci commentators, Ageno among them (66), note that he is the son of Ugier the Dane. Believing that Pulci derived this character from *Orlando,* whose author, however, had not invented it, Marco Boni has been able to establish, as a result of exhaustive research, that the literary source used by the anonymous *canterino* was a poem or a romance composed before the end of the fourteenth century. This work, which Boni hopes will be found one day in some forgotten library holdings, was unquestionably written by an Italian, whose name has remained anonymous. It told the story of Dudon, second son of Ugier the Dane and brother of Baldovino (Baldwin), who, armed with a club, fought alongside Charlemagne, Orlando, Rinaldo, Ugier, and Oliver. (See "A proposito di un personaggio del *Morgante* ['Dodone, il Figliuol del Danese']," *Atti della Accademia delle Scienze dell'Istituto di Bologna, Rendiconti,* vol. LXXIII [1984–85] [Bologna: Tipografia Compositori, 1986], 97–113.)

31, 1. Guicciardo, Alardo, and Ricciardetto are Rinaldo's brothers.

31, 2. Montalban is the name of Rinaldo's castle.

31, 8. Ageno (66) establishes that Pulci's Malagigi (at times Malgigi) derives from Maugis, a thief who appears in the French *chanson de geste Renaus* or *Quatre fils Aymon.* In the Italian chivalric tradition, Malagigi is transformed into a good wizard who, through his powerful magic, is capable of foreseeing the future and of knowing the occult. If he wishes, he can even call on demons for assistance. Malagigi is also Orlando and Rinaldo's first cousin. He is in fact the son of Buovo of Agrismont(e), whom Clairmont mentions in stanza 77, 5. Buovo is the brother of Ammon, Rinaldo's father, and of Milo, Orlando's father.

32, 8. Mambrino is a character who appears in the Italian epics that narrate the adventures of Rinaldo and his brothers, who become highway robbers after having been banished by Charlemagne (see Ageno, 66–67).

34, 1. It must be pointed out that in the original Italian text, Pulci states that Brunoro is either Morgante's first cousin, *cugin carnale,* or his brother, *fratello.* The actual family relationship between Morgante and Brunoro is not made any clearer when Brunoro declares (stanza 34, 7) that he has come to the abbey to avenge the killing of his brothers Alabaster and Passamont, the two giants who in canto I are said to be Morgante's brothers. Obviously, Pulci often employs the terms "brother" and "cousin" interchangeably (as he does in canto V, 35, 1 and 36, 4).

35, 8. This seemingly matter-of-fact comment emphasizes Pulci's underlying irony. How could the abbot and his few frightened monks defend themselves against Mambrino and his army of 30,000!

36, 4. A term of gastronomic inspiration, "glutton" (*ghiotto* and its augmentative form *ghiotton[e]*) is one of the attributes the poet most frequently employs in the poem with regard to both Christian and non-Christian characters. This word occurs also in several *cantari popolari,* such as *L'Entrée d'Espagne* and *La Spagna.* (For a detailed discussion on the language of *Morgante* [e.g., the meaning and frequency of adjectives, verbs, and nouns], see Giovanni Getto's *Studio sul 'Morgante,'* 133–181.)

37–43, 4. Rinaldo's sudden arrival at the abbey, and his tragicomic encounter with Brunoro and his men, constitutes one of the poem's most memorable and hilarious pages. These stanzas are also important because they reveal another significant aspect of Rinaldo's character: his insatiable hunger and unquenchable thirst. His voracity, in fact, makes him second only to Morgante and the half-giant Margutte of canto XVIII, with whom he forms, to borrow Illidio Bussani's fitting definition, "the holy trinity of the religion of the stomach" (*Il romanzo cavalleresco in Luigi Pulci* [Torino: Fratelli Bocca Editori, 1933], 34). The contrast between the initially shrewd and humble behavior of the famished Rinaldo and the insultingly superior attitude of the mocking Brunoro gives the entire episode unquestionable comic force. If it is true, as Momigliano writes (179), that Brunoro's characterization of Rinaldo and his companions as men looking "for a good time" and capable only of battling "for much food and wine" (stanza 4, 3–4) may well apply to all the warriors in the poem, it is equally true that the sneering Brunoro makes a fatal mistake in assuming that Rinaldo's pretended meekness is his true nature. Hunger often exerts a determining influence on a person's behavior. This is precisely why Rinaldo, who is otherwise easily inflamed by the slightest affront to his dignity, now tolerates, pretending not to hear, Brunoro's openly offensive remarks (41–42). In order not to be recognized by his laughing host, he even lowers himself to the point of playing the fool (43, 4).

43, 8. See note, I, 6, 7–8.

46, 1–8. In the Italian *Storie di Rinaldo,* Baiardo is the magic horse given to Rinaldo by Malagigi the day the Lord of Montalban was knighted by Charlemagne (Ageno, 71 and 820). For the horse Vegliantino, see note, I, 13, 1–8.

48, 7–8 through 51, 1–5. Rinaldo, wishing to fill his empty stomach, has temporarily allowed Brunoro to ridicule him, but he will not suffer to share his meal with anyone. As the paladin happily proclaims (54, 7–8), after Brunoro's foolish soldier has paid for his arrogance with his life, he doesn't like to be bothered while he is eating! (In stanza 54, 8, the colorful English expression "to kick like a mule" beautifully renders the idiom *stare in cagnesco come un cavallo* [to be on the alert like a horse] of the Italian text.)

55, 8. Frusberta, in French *Froberge,* is the name of Rinaldo's sword.

57–70. Stanzas 57 through 70 constitute a most interesting burlesque of the judicial duel as it was idealized in the epic literature, and as it was practiced in France up through the twelfth century and even later. In earlier medieval law, conflicting testimony was always resolved by some form of proof stipulated by the court. Here Pulci's own experience in a more modern court setting allows him to play off the rational testimony of witnesses against the older irrational proof by ordeal or judicial duel. Thus we have the humor of Brunoro treating Rinaldo as if he had confidence in him as a man wanting justice (57), and Rinaldo using the image of the two bells to illustrate the need for hearing both sides of an argument (60).

In stanza 65, Rinaldo points out to Brunoro that the original offense was against Clairmont, kin of Orlando, unless he can "prove" otherwise. Here is where the humorous shift from modern rational proof to the older irrational proof takes place. Brunoro's pretense of being interested in rational proof is just that. What he really wants is to have his own way by force. However, Brunoro is a pagan and would not realize that God gives victory to the just in a *judicium dei* combat. Hilariously, Brunoro, who seemed willing to accept testimony and judgment based on it, now declares (66) that the abbot and Rinaldo "should be hanged" and that the Lord of Montalban is his "foe." It is curious and symptomatic of the lateness of the text that Pulci feels the need to describe what any medieval reader would have taken for granted, but an urban audience might understand only in contractual form: it is agreed that Brunoro will have Rinaldo's horse if he wins (presumably also the death of the abbot, though this is not stated); if he loses, the abbot will be left in peace. Note that Rinaldo offers to fight either on horseback or on foot (66). A medieval knight would have fought exclusively on horseback after about 1100; combat on foot was a form for ordinary people not skilled in horsemanship. As we shall see, Pulci does not always respect medieval chivalric conventions, nor, given the particular nature of *Morgante,* can we expect him to do so.

59, 5–8 through 60, 1–4. Rinaldo's answer to Brunoro, whose attitude toward the paladin has in the meantime drastically changed, proves again that he is not the fool he wanted Brunoro to believe.

67, 3–4. These two verses contain an expression taken directly from the game of chess. The popularity of this game long before Pulci's time is attested by one of Franco Sacchetti's short stories included in his major narrative work *Trecento novelle,* composed mostly between 1385 and 1392. In novella CLXXXIV, Sacchetti tells the story of an inveterate chess player, the parish priest of San Giovanni di Susana, near Florence, who would ring the bells of his church so that the townsfolk would come and witness his victory whenever he was successful in checkmating his frequent opponent, a gentleman of the Giandonati family. He did this so often, however, that when his home caught fire and he rang the bells, no one showed up to help him, and his house nearly burned to the ground. Interestingly, in his verses Pulci repeats almost verbatim the same words used by Sacchetti in his novella (see *Trecento novelle,* ed. Antonio Lanza [Firenze: Sansoni, 1984], 411–413).

71, 6 (and again 73, 5). Two of the poem's many amusing metaphors relating to food. Visually effective, they frequently recur in *Morgante,* particularly during the description of scenes of battle.

71, 8. As Ageno (79) explains, 18 was the highest number a player could achieve using three dice. Given the extreme difficulty of obtaining the required 6–6–6 combination, this expression, which derived from this game, was used to indicate a person's great courage in facing danger.

72–75, 1–6. The portrait that Pulci has drawn of Clairmont in cantos I and II is by no means that of a brave man. Nevertheless, the poet has depicted him as a very clever individual. The simple yet eloquent words that the abbot has chosen to recount Orlando's deeds after his arrival at the abbey (II, 62–64) provide further evidence of the monk's keenness of mind. It is, however, at this point in canto III that a different Clairmont is introduced. No sooner has Dudon cut him free of the ropes that tied his hands than, brandishing a huge bar, Clairmont throws himself in the midst of the fight, killing at least six Saracens. It is as if the man, maybe spurred on by a sudden impulse to emulate Rinaldo, or maybe unable to control his long-repressed rage, has finally found the courage he never felt before. Clairmont's change, however, does not appear to be a lasting one. Stanzas 77; 79, 6–8; and 80, 1–4 reveal, in fact, that after all of Brunoro's remaining troops have been driven away from the monastery, the abbot is once more the man he was. Equally unexpected is Clairmont's monks' participation in the fight (73, 1–4), a detail that adds a further comic touch to the entire episode. Notwithstanding the brief, tumultuous intervention of these monks in the melee, it is still difficult for the reader to dissociate them from the frightened *monachetti* of canto I. Pulci's caustic remark in stanza 75, 6 seems definitely to suggest that they too, like Clairmont, are incapable of substantial changes.

77, 6. The wearing of a gray-colored robe may indicate a monastic status (as in the case of the abbot Clairmont).

77, 8. In *I Reali di Francia,* the cardinal who eventually became Pope Leo is said to be one of the sons of Bernard of Clairmont (see Andrea da Barberino, *I Reali di Francia,* Parte VI, 40).

80, 3. Clairmont repeats here the words uttered by Simeon while holding the infant Jesus in his arms (Luke 2:29).

C A N T O   I V

SUMMARY: Invocation (1). Once Clairmont has revealed his name, Rinaldo, Dudon, and Oliver leave the abbey to resume their search for Orlando (2–6). In the midst of a dark wood, the paladins see a lion fighting with a dragon. Rinaldo kills the dragon, and the grateful lion becomes their guide (7–25). Soon after, Rinaldo kills a giant, and the three are able to satisfy their hunger by eating a deer the giant had hunted and was about to cook for himself (26–36). The lion takes them near Carrara, where they learn that Forisena, King Corbante's beautiful daughter, is going to be sacrificed to a huge monster (37–48). Having entered the city, Rinaldo tells the king that he and his companions will face the monster to save the girl's life (49–58). After a fierce fight, Oliver, aided by Rinaldo and Dudon, succeeds in killing the fire-breathing beast before losing consciousness (59–70). Amid the general rejoicing, Corbante takes Rinaldo, Dudon, and the still-unconscious Oliver back to his palace, where Forisena realizes that she has fallen in love with Oliver (71–79). Forisena and Oliver reveal their love for each other (80–87); nevertheless Oliver, solicited by Rinaldo and Dudon, begrudgingly consents to leave Forisena and Carrara, after the three paladins have revealed to Corbante their true identity (88–92). Exhorted by Rinaldo, Corbante embraces Christianity and, having called his subjects together, has all of them baptized (93–103).

1, 1–4. From Luke 2:14 and 20.

2, 1–6. This description of spring as the season of love has been appropriately placed at the beginning of the canto that tells of the nascent love between Oliver and Forisena.

5, 4. After his brief outburst of violence in canto III, Clairmont, having regained his composure (Pulci defines him, tongue in cheek, as a "wise and learned" man), resumes his frequent quoting from the Sacred Writ. The "young Tobias" named by Clairmont appears in the Book of Tobias, which, being a deuterocanonical book, is not included in the King James version of the Bible. This text tells of the trip that Tobias, son of Tobias the Elder, made to the faraway city of Rages in the country called Media. Tobias's travel companion was the angel Raphael, who safely brought the young man back to his father's home. (For the story of Tobias, see the Roman Catholic version of the Bible, Tobias V–XI.)

7–22. In these stanzas Pulci introduces the first of several seemingly miraculous animals that come to life in the pages of *Morgante*. The sight of the lion about to be killed by the dragon (10, 7–8) suddenly moves Rinaldo to pity, a feeling usually foreign to him. His decision to intervene in order to save the lion's life not only appears to have the approval of Heaven, but also receives the Lord's assurance as to the paladin's victorious outcome in his fight against this monstrous beast (12, 1–6). In the Italian text, as in its English rendering, the dragon in question is also called "snake" and "serpent." Equally referred to as "dragon" and "serpent" is the huge monster that makes its appearance later on in the canto. With regard to this matter, it must be observed that in many parts of the world, dragons are usually represented as fire-breathing, snakelike creatures. In Western culture, however, where dragons are often also portrayed as being fought by saints, their malignant disposition and their physical appearance may be linked to the evil snake of the Garden of Eden.

The prodigious nature of the lion is underscored by the animal's understanding of both Rinaldo's good intentions on its behalf (13, 1–3) and his prayer to the Virgin (17, 2–8 and 18, 1). Thus, this curious beast (whose disappearance occurs in IX, 14) now becomes Rinaldo's reliable guide and faithful companion, helping him to find the bewildered Oliver and Dudon, who have become lost in the woods. It is likely that Pulci knew Chrétien's *Yvain ou le chevalier au lion* or a version of the tale. Yvain also saves a lion locked in a deadly struggle with a serpent. The grateful lion then accompanies and serves the French knight, thus giving him the well-known epithet and the name of the romance. (The lion's frequent association with Christ has caused many a critic to interpret *Yvain* in allegorical and religious terms. See Julian Harris, "The Role of the Lion in Chrétien de Troyes' *Yvain*," *PMLA* 64 [1949]: 1143–1163. For a discussion of the relationships between *Morgante* and other medieval texts, including *Yvain,* see Paolo Orvieto, *Pulci medievale,* 95–102.) A careful reading of this episode, in which sacred, profane, epic, and grotesque elements are wonderfully interwoven, reveals an underlying subtle comic vein, a comicity that at times comes to the surface, as can be noted in stanzas 12, 8; 16, 5–8; 18, 7; and even more in 69, 1–4, when the poet, in a cunningly innocent tone, explains that the lion limited itself to watching the fight with the dragon, instead of coming to the rescue of its Christian friends, because it preferred to "tell the entire deed," "had somebody cared to know"!

23, 3–4. Here the poet makes use of another very common metaphor, derived from a contagious skin disease known as scabies. This disease, which causes intense scratching and normally occurs in sheep and cattle, was in Pulci's time quite widespread among humans as well.

25, 1–8. Rinaldo reaffirms his recurrent preoccupation with eating, expresses his sharp complaint against the emperor, and vows to make Gano pay for all his misdeeds.

26, 7–8 through 33. The figure we encounter in these stanzas is the poem's fifth giant, and the second one with whom Rinaldo fights after Brunoro. This is a natural thing for Rinaldo to do since, as Pulci jokingly tells the reader, "combating giants was indeed his game" (31, 3). Though this giant's name is never mentioned, he remains impressed in our memory as "the giant of the deer." He is a primitive creature who acts by instinct, arrogantly confident in his own brute strength. When Rinaldo, Dudon, and Oliver, following the lion, happen to arrive at his den, the giant asks no questions but, grabbing the first weapon he can find—the spit he was about to use to cook the deer he had just skinned—charges at the intruders like a wild bear. The words *matto* (mad) and *bestia* (beast), which characterize him in the Italian text (27, 5 and 8), clearly emphasize both his lack of cognitive qualities and his beastly strength. In stanza 29, 1 and 8, we also find the terms "scum" and "glutton." Their recurrence seems particularly appropriate at this point since they can be interpreted figuratively as well as literally. The reason for this farcical, though bloody, confrontation is, after all, the deer that the giant has killed, and which he is determined to keep for himself. Ironically, when he accuses Rinaldo of being "either a glutton or a thief," he is unknowingly right on the mark, since the paladin, depending on the occasion, can be both. What we witness in stanzas 30–31 is not a duel, like the one Rinaldo has fought with Brunoro in canto III, but rather something that resembles a grotesque fistfight, at the end of which the paladin, fighting on horseback, risks being crushed by the huge body of his falling opponent (32). If it is true that the embarrassing situation in which Rinaldo has found himself (33, 1–2) does compel him to offer a plausible explanation for it (33, 3–5), it is equally true that the accident seems to have no effect on the Lord of Montalban, whose very sensitive nostrils have meanwhile smelled the dead deer (33, 6–8).

34 through 36. The giant's hut, where Rinaldo has gone with his famished companions, is the scene of another amusingly vivid display of Rinaldo's overwhelming appetite. Having found in the hut three large loaves of bread and a keg of beer, Rinaldo is now ready to put his teeth to work, and would not mind beginning to eat the venison even if it is still quite raw. After telling Dudon that the meat is as cooked as a hard biscuit (34, 8), and a little later that it's "all burnt" (35, 4), to persuade his friend that the venison is now ready, Rinaldo in a convincing tone warns him that it is harmful to humans to eat overcooked meat (35, 8). Even though Dudon is not fooled by this newly established gastronomic rule (36, 1–2), realizing Rinaldo's growing impatience, he finally takes the meat off the fire, declaring, "if it's not finely cooked, at least it's warm" (36, 3). The episode ends with Rinaldo forcing himself, purely out of shame, to devour only one of the three loaves, while not shunning the "waiting keg" (36, 5–8).

37, 4. For the reference to the "manna," see I, 25, 5.

37, 6. The verse "Those who want to cheat are cheated first" reproduces a common proverbial expression of Tuscan origin.

42, 8. The city mentioned in this verse is not, obviously, the city of Carrara that is known all over the world for its nearby marble quarries, and which is located less than eighty miles northwest of Florence.

46, 6–8 through 52. Up to this point—and the content of lines 4–6 attests to it—Rinaldo has not expressed any intention to fight the monster and free Carrara from this terrible scourge. His curiosity, however, has definitely been aroused. The question he further asks the shepherd (46, 7–8) begins to disclose the paladin's easily awakened romantic inclination, an aspect of his character that has earned him Momigliano's definition as "the greatest woman-chaser in *Morgante*" (227). Once he has been assured that Forisena meets his requirements (she is only fifteen and very beautiful—47, 1–5), Rinaldo promptly declares that he will "cut the monster's scales." He clarifies, however, that he is going to perform the deed not because of Corbante's rewards, but simply because he "delights in women" (48, 1–5). The tone of his words may sound humble and lighthearted, but the paladin's high opinion of himself knows no limits (he has left behind not one but seven kingdoms!). It is in stanza 50 that Rinaldo gives a true measure of his consummate acting skills. The first three things he says aloud to Corbante are all lies; then he tells the truth, but only in a whisper. Rinaldo the actor is winking at the audience. The humor, which the reader has perceived since the beginning of the episode, elicits here an open, appreciative smile.

51; 53, 5–8; and 55. Contrary to what one might have expected, it is Oliver, and not Rinaldo, the first paladin, who falls in love in the poem. Pulci tells us, in fact, that while the Lord of Montalban was doing all the talking, that "lovely lad" Oliver was staring at Forisena, silently admiring her beauty. Interestingly, what first comes to Oliver's mind is that the girl's body must not serve as food for the dragon, but should become instead the object of a man's love. This thought, coupled with his resolve to prevent the beast from devouring "such fresh, white bread," which is worthy only of a lover, gives further evidence of the importance that Pulci's paladins always give to food and, to a lesser extent, to love or, more appropriately, sex. A further reference to Forisena as food occurs in stanza 55, one of the more colorful in the canto. Rinaldo, talking now to Oliver in French, their own tongue, first compares the marquis to a falcon who is about to dive on his prey (Forisena), then, alluding to both men's interest in the girl, states that they "are like two mouths" eager to eat the same food. If Rinaldo's knowingly unbefitting comparison of Oliver with a bird of prey shows his desire to poke fun at his friend, it nevertheless underscores, by contrast, the more sentimental and gentle nature of the marquis' love. For most characters in the poem, and definitely for Rinaldo, love is a fleeting moment, a passion that stirs the senses but only rarely touches the heart.

60, 3–8; and 61–62. Suggesting sarcastically that Forisena, who has appeared at the top of a tower, has gone there to get a better look at her beloved Oliver, Rinaldo continues to tease the marquis by making overt allusions to his manliness. Oliver, seemingly unruffled by Rinaldo's remarks, replies by reminding his loquacious companion that the only thing that concerns them now is the terribly fierce dragon they are about to face. It must be noted that the verse "but there is more that I can guess, instead" (61, 8) is a free rendition of the Italian *qua sa d'altro già che melarance,* which, had it been translated literally ("there is no smell of sweet oranges here"), would have made little if any sense. Pulci's audience had no trouble understanding that what Oliver meant to say was that the situation confronting him and his companions was definitely not a game. As Ageno explains (100), the reference to "sweet oranges" probably derives from a custom, observed from the thirteenth to the fifteenth centuries, that allowed members of the two sexes to throw oranges at one another during banquets and other festivities. The critic also adds that at Carnival time, people standing on carts engaged in the throwing of oranges with men and women who leaned out the windows or balconies of their homes.

66, 6–8. Before his martyrdom, Saint Donnin(o) was said to have saved from certain death a man who had been bitten by a rabid dog. Because of this fact, it was believed that the saint would grant his faithful immunity against hydrophobia. This information is again provided by Ageno, who quotes as her source Guglielmo Volpi (202).

72, 4–5. Note the promptness with which Corbante attributes to Mahound the demise of the dragon at the hands of those whom he believes to be fellow Muslims. Ironically, it is the same god who, according to the shepherd who talked with the paladins in stanza 45, has sent the dragon to Carrara as punishment for Corbante's crime as well as for his people's acquiescence to it.

79, 7–8 through 88. In these stanzas Pulci indulges in a brief psychological analysis of Oliver's and Forisena's love, which ends with the latter's suicide in canto V. Oliver's instant attraction to Corbante's daughter—an attraction that initially manifests itself through the paladin's "transfixed" stares, his frequent sighing, his silence, or the lowering of his eyes when someone speaks to him about her—rapidly becomes a truly ardent passion. An otherwise accomplished and fearless knight, Oliver appears to be a timid lover, a man torn by doubt and hope (82, 6), incapable of openly expressing his feelings to the woman he loves. Forisena, instead, is the more direct of the two lovers, and the one more apt to take action. Once the "sweet and shrewd" girl realizes Oliver's love for her (79, 7–8), she immediately falls in love with him (80, 7–8) and does her best to communicate her feelings to the marquis (81, 1–4). Having gone one day to pay a visit to the still-convalescent knight, she assures Oliver through her ardent glances ("though her words were cold") and her sudden blushing that she returns his love (81, 5–8; and 82–83). Oliver, though now sure of her love, has to make a real effort to reply to the girl, who has voiced her sorrow for being the cause of his suffering (84, 5–8). In his last words to Corbante's daughter, the marquis can allude only to a new pain which is now ailing him (85–86). Forisena, who has perfectly understood what Oliver meant to say, remains silent. Her unspoken answer, which she sighs only to herself, is undoubtedly revealing: "Yes, for this different pain I also grieve. . . . Grateful to such a lover I will be for there's a heart, and not a stone, in me" (87, 5 and 7–8). In her so human and touching attempt to find a reasonable excuse for loving Oliver (how could she not feel love for him whose pain she has twice caused, first for saving her life and then for loving her?), Forisena attains real character status by showing her vulnerability. In the preceding stanzas Pulci has also introduced several maxims and pronouncements concerning love, some of which are reminiscent of well-known lines in Dante's and Petrarch's works. (For verses 1–2, 80, see *Inferno,* V, 103; for verse 8, 82, see Petrarch's *Canzoniere,* sonnet CLXX, 14.)

94, 4. According to Ageno (109), French epics do not mention Ugier the Dane's conversion to Christianity.

95, 5–8; and 96–102. Of course Corbante's conversion, and consequently his baptism and that of his daughter and his people (everyone in the kingdom is ordered to "heed the new religious law" [102, 2–3]), has nothing to do with a sincere spiritual crisis. It is, in a few words, the logical consequence of Corbante's basic belief (and in this he does not differ from Morgante) that the god of the victor is always the true god. For the same reason that the king had previously thanked Mahound for sending the presumably Saracen warriors Rinaldo, Dudon, and Oliver to kill the dragon, now that the paladins have revealed their true identity, he cannot but renounce his false god and accept theirs. Worthy also of mention is the fact that the episode of Corbante's conversion, which takes less than two stanzas in *Orlando* (VIII, 39–40, p. 35), is the longest and also the most seriously treated in *Morgante.* It is nevertheless possible to perceive behind Rinaldo's sermonizing words the mischievous smile of the poet, somewhat amused for having given Rinaldo, one of the poem's most violent, rebelliously independent, frivolous, and at times even blasphemous personages, a role which so profoundly contrasts with the true nature of the man.

97, 2. Note that when urging Corbante to return to "our blessed Lord at once," Rinaldo is voicing a medieval belief that Islam was not an autonomous religion but a heretical Christian doctrine.

97, 3. As noted by Davide Puccini (133), Belfagor is an ancient Oriental god, eventually transformed into an evil spirit (see *Morgante,* Introduzione, note e indici di Davide Puccini, 2 vols. [Firenze: Garzanti, 1989]). Note also that here, and occasionally elsewhere in the poem, the term "pharisees" has lost much of its biblical meaning. As a matter of fact, Pulci uses it in place of the word "devils." To be sure, "pharisees" appears also in the *Ciriffo Calvaneo* (IV, 23, 2–3), where the pharisees are said to be very strange beings devoid of a true human form (*Ciriffo Calvaneo,* Composto per Luca De' Pulci a petizione del Magnifico Lorenzo De' Medici, con Osservazioni Bibliografico-Letterarie di S.L.G.E. Audin [Firenze: Tipografia Arcivescovile, 1834]).

C A N T O   V

SUMMARY: Invocation (1). Because of his growing love for Forisena, Oliver finds numerous excuses to delay his departure from Carrara (2–4). Following Orlando's refusal to duel with her, Meridiana sends a messenger to Corbante requesting the king's assistance in convincing the Lion's Warrior to free her city from Manfredonio's siege (5–15). Rinaldo, Dudon, and Oliver take leave from Corbante, and Forisena, distraught over Oliver's departure, kills herself (16–21). On their way to Caradoro's kingdom, the three knights meet Malagigi, who, disguised as a frail old man, takes Baiardo away from Rinaldo and flees. The Lord of Montalban, mounting Vegliantino, unsuccessfully gives chase (22–28). Pleased with the joke he has played on his cousin, Malagigi, still in the guise of an old man, suddenly reappears, but this time Rinaldo, Dudon, and Oliver recognize him by the sound of his voice. Malagigi first gives them an herb that can satisfy both their hunger and their thirst, then leaves for Montalban riding on a white horse that he has materialized by means of his magical powers (29–36, 1–3). Six days later, the paladins come face to face with a strange monster, whom Rinaldo kills after a long struggle (36, 4–8 through 65). Having resumed their journey, one morning Rinaldo, Dudon, and Oliver see the tents of Manfredonio's camp rising near a river (66–69).

1, 7. Joseph of Galilee was Mary's husband. Joachim and Ann are believed to have been Mary's parents (see "The Infancy Gospel of James: Protevangelium Jacobi," in *The Other Bible,* ed. Willis Barnstone [San Francisco: Harper Collins Publishers, 1992], 385–392).

5,5. The bezant was a small gold coin of the Byzantine Empire. "To be worth a bezant" was a proverbial expression used to indicate a person's or an object's lack of substantial value.

5, 1–8. Meridiana, wishing to fight Orlando "just man to man," is offended by the paladin's scornful refusal to accept her challenge on the battlefield. Like her brother Lionetto and many other characters in the poem, particularly those who are Muslims, she blames Mahound for her failures in combat.

11–12. Rinaldo's immediate acceptance of Meridiana's and Corbante's request is determined by several reasons: his desire to go where Clairmont has told him Orlando may be (III, 64, 3); the opportunity to finally take Oliver away from Forisena (IV, 90, 1–3 and V, 3, 1); his natural inclination to engage in new, difficult exploits; and, last but not least, his hope (previously voiced by Corbante in 10, 7–8) that as a result of Manfredonio's defeat, Caradoro and his people may also convert to Christianity. This last motivation may be expressed in verse 4 of stanza 12, where Rinaldo promises to save Caradoro's people from the enemy "without" (Manfredonio's army) as well as from the enemy "within" (their belief in a false god). Stanzas 11 and 12 are additional evidence of the paladin's shrewdness. It is true, as we have already noted, that Rinaldo can appear quite boastful to the modern reader. It is equally true, however, that the deeds he declares himself ready to undertake are always converted into actions. The same certainly cannot be said of some of his fellow knights and other characters in the poem, who often promise much and deliver little.

17, 1–8. Forisena, whose passion for the marquis has become ever more intense while his indecision about formally declaring his love has remained constant, cannot cope with Oliver's abrupt departure. The paladin, we are told, barely has sufficient time to bid her goodbye. Having decided to follow her beloved, once again the girl climbs a tower in her father's castle. What prompts hapless Forisena to act now, however, is not the cheerful curiosity she felt in stanza 60 (1–2) of canto IV, but her romantic love for Oliver. Upon seeing him moving farther and farther away from her, overcome with grief, she jumps from a balcony. Her death is really a statement, the public revelation of a love she was no longer able or willing to conceal (17, 4). The pathetic suicide of sweet Forisena cannot but call to mind the more poignantly tragic death of the wife of Guglielmo Rossiglione in Boccaccio's *Decameron* (IV, 9). The entire episode of Oliver's painful departure and Forisena's desperate act is solely a Pulci invention. In the corresponding canto of *Orlando,* we read only that the young princess "sheds bitter tears" when "the three barons" leave her father's castle (IX, 17, 7–8). Commenting on Forisena's sudden death (in particular lines 6–8 of stanza 17), Carlo Pellegrini (140) writes instead, "Comical is the way in which the poet tells the story . . . the matter appears to be the simplest thing in the world, and he at once goes on to another subject."

22–35. The appearance of the "distraught," "strange," and "grieving" old man who resembles "neither man nor beast" has the same effect on Rinaldo as the sight of the lion fighting a losing battle with a dragon in canto IV (6–

15). Interestingly, Rinaldo is moved to pity by two "beings" that approach him and his companions showing a friendly countenance. It may be said that both the lion and the old man enjoy quasi-supernatural powers: the lion because of the somewhat miraculous role it plays in the poem; Malagigi because he resorts to his magic in order to help the good to fight against evil. In the physical description of the wizard, who appears here as a "sad and lost" soul, Momigliano (164–165) perceives Pulci's attempt to make a caricature of Malagigi, who, "rather than moving us to compassion as a result of the conditions in which he finds himself, makes us smile." We are more inclined to believe that the *vis comica* that transpires from this episode is generated by the contrast between the predominantly serious and somber mood of stanzas 22–25 (when Rinaldo, Dudon, and Oliver rush to the aid of the old man) and the loud and frenetic tone of stanzas 26–28 (where Rinaldo, upon seeing the presumably "half-dead" old man run away "like the wind" mounted on his horse, rapidly moves from sheer surprise to raging fury).

This event seems to have offered Pulci the opportunity to introduce Malagigi at this point in the poem, to whose "future-seeing charts" he had briefly made reference in canto III, 31, 8. In *Morgante* the poet has further developed the personality of the good wizard, emphasizing also his traditional mocking disposition. Stanza 30, 1–2 demonstrates, in fact, that Malagigi's habitual inclination to pull a prank is well known to Rinaldo (the wizard will play yet another joke on Rinaldo and Orlando in canto X). Malagigi's answer to Rinaldo in stanza 30, 5–8 seems obscure. What he intends to say here is that the paladins do not yet know the reasons for his sudden appearance. The disparity between the burlesque fashion in which Malagigi has staged his entrance in the canto, and the seriousness of the message he now delivers should not be overlooked. It definitely contributes to creating the whimsically strange atmosphere, in which the comic is mixed with the magic, that surrounds the entire episode. It must also be noted that in stanzas 35, 1 and 36, 4, Malagigi addresses Rinaldo, who in turn refers to Malagigi not as "cousin" but as "brother" (for this, see note, III, 34, 1).

37–44, 1–4. The canto reserves yet another surprise for Rinaldo, Dudon, and Oliver. They now face one of the most horrid figures they encounter in their travels (39–40). This canto also contains one of the most detailed descriptions of a monster (the resemblance of which to man consists solely in his brandishing in one hand a ten-foot-long limb of a sorb tree) that we read in the poem. In stanza 41 we are also told that the monster, hiding in a tunnel he has dug under a large stone, enjoys killing all passersby, hurling darts at them from a "tiny hole" he has made in the stone. This additionally facetious detail and the fact that Pulci refers to the monster as a "crazy beast" clearly render humorous an episode which otherwise would be horrifying. It cannot be said that the paladins, least of all Rinaldo, appear overly terrified by the monster. Not even Oliver's comparing him with Beelzebub or "the Witch Epiphany," and Dudon's with "one of Malagigi's mates," suffices to indicate the presence of an overwhelming fear. With regard to the words "Witch Epiphany," translating the Italian *Befania* (42, 5), it must be pointed out that Ageno (123) states that *Befania* derives from the Latin *Epiphania,* and in this context means "bugaboo." From *Befania* comes also *befana,* a word Italians traditionally give to the old and good witch who on January 6 brings gifts to deserving children. "Thirty thousand devils" (44, 2) is a common popular expression which occurs frequently in Pulci's works. In one of his letters to Lorenzo de' Medici, the poet threatens to give himself to the "three hundred thousand devils" should the Magnificent fail to come to his aid (see Luigi Pulci, *Morgante e Lettere,* ed. Giuseppe De Robertis [Firenze: Sansoni, 1962], 943). The expression "thirty thousand devils" here stands for "infernal monster."

44, 5–8 through 62. The lengthy fight that Rinaldo wages with the monster is characterized by the swift and rapid movements of the paladin (45, 1 and 4; 47, 7; and 48, 1–4), who, while trying his best to avoid the terrible club of his adversary (47, 5–6 and 8), succeeds in wounding him time and time again (50, 3–5). Rinaldo's coolness and agility contrast with the uncontrolled rage of the screaming monster. The episode is also punctuated by some amusing ways of referring to death (47, 4 and 56, 3), the use of popular colorful expressions (49, 1; 57, 5; and 54, 1–4), Pulci's hilarious comments on the story (51, 2–8; 52, 1–2; and 60, 8), and Rinaldo's comically sympathetic exhortation to Vegliantino (56, 4–5), whose hoof has been hit by a dart hurled by the monster, who is obviously ignorant of all chivalric rules. Stanzas 58, 6–8 through 62 describe in hyperbolic terms the prodigious final blow of Rinaldo's sword, Frusberta, and the ensuing demise of the "maddened beast" (62, 8).

CANTO VI

SUMMARY: Invocation (1). After having seen from afar Orlando and Morgante in the midst of Manfredonio's troops, Rinaldo, Oliver, and Dudon enter Caradoro's city (2–6). In the king's castle, the three paladins are graciously met first by Meridiana and then by her father. Caradoro hopes they will fight the "wandering knight" and the giant, who have recently joined forces with Manfredonio (7–16). Oliver, who begins to fall in love with Meridiana, is teased again by Rinaldo (17–22). Manfredonio, at Orlando's request, sends a messenger to Caradoro to challenge the three knights to a duel with Orlando, who is known to all as Brunoro (23–26, 1–2). Rinaldo, Oliver, and Dudon, after having paraded fully armed in front of Caradoro's people, leave for Manfredonio's camp (26, 3–8 through 33, 1–2). Answering the call of Rinaldo's horn, Orlando and Morgante go to meet their challengers, whom Orlando fails to recognize (33, 3–8 through 36). Morgante easily unhorses Dudon, handing him as his prisoner to Manfredonio (37–39, 1–6). Having tied the lion to a tree, Rinaldo starts dueling with Orlando (39, 7–8 through 44). Their fierce clash is interrupted by the lion, which has miraculously become untied. At this point Rinaldo proposes to suspend the duel and resume it early the next morning; Orlando begrudgingly agrees (45–50, 1–2). Meanwhile Caradoro is informed by one of Gano's messengers of the true identity of Rinaldo, Dudon, and Oliver, as well as that of Orlando, alias Brunoro. The noble king first orders the arrest of the messenger, then gives Gano's letter to Rinaldo. The paladin immediately sends a messenger to Orlando, inviting him to secretly come to Caradoro's castle (50, 3–8 through 59). With Manfredonio's knowledge and approval, Orlando and Morgante leave for Caradoro's court, where Rinaldo introduces Orlando to Caradoro and his daughter (60–69).

1, 1–8. The first four verses of this invocation are taken verbatim from canto XI, 1–4 of Dante's *Purgatorio.* In this specific instance, one cannot fail to note a striking disparity between Dante's moving choral prayer, reflecting the profound faith that inspires the *Commedia,* and Pulci's conventional and pedestrian request for God's help in continuing his story. Conversely, the contrast observed in stanza 1 of canto VI of *Morgante* is totally absent in the corresponding invocation of canto X of *Orlando* (40), whose anonymous author simply quotes verses 1–6 of canto XI of *Purgatorio,* though somewhat inverting their order, and does not call on God for assistance.

2, 4–6. The "star" mentioned here is Venus, no longer visible in the sky at the first appearance of daylight.

9, 2. In a "French kiss," the cheeks of the person to be kissed were held between the index and middle fingers of each hand (Ageno, 134).

9, 3–8; and 10. Meridiana's demure countenance and her most gracious reception immediately affect both Rinaldo and Oliver, but in ways that are indicative of their different personalities. While the materialistic and capricious Rinaldo is tempted to externalize his attraction to the girl with a kiss, the romantic and sentimental Oliver expresses his admiration with a poetic metaphor. Thus the comment of our marquis offers the Lord of Montalban, who is well acquainted with the peculiarities of his friend's character, a new opportunity to tease him for his inconstant behavior in matters of the heart. Oliver's pledge of undying love for Corbante's daughter (11, 7–8) may well have been dictated by his desire to silence Rinaldo. It may also be one of the paladin's several useless attempts to recall the image of Forisena, which seems to have become increasingly overshadowed by Meridiana's appearance on the scene.

17–18, 1–4. Meridiana, first introduced at the beginning of canto III dressed in armor and ready to do battle with Orlando to avenge the death of her brother Lionetto, becomes here the poem's second female character upon whose physical description Pulci dwells with obvious aesthetic pleasure. While in stanza 8 the author had stressed Meridiana's "gentle virtues," he now depicts her strikingly womanly graces, guiding Oliver's admiring eyes, as well as those of the reader, to her colorful dress, her splendent complexion, her breasts, and her hair, to rest them finally on the girl's glowing face.

18, 5–7. In stanza 16, 5–8, Caradoro had publicly promised to give his daughter to the one of the three knights who could defeat Orlando and Morgante. Oliver's whispered comments constitute the highest homage he (and the poet) can pay to Meridiana's loveliness. The power of a woman's beauty knows no limits. It is the best weapon King Caradoro has to attain victory over his enemies. In lines 5–7 one may already perceive Oliver's intention, if not yet his resolve, to fight on behalf of Meridiana.

19–20. The brief dialogue that takes place in these stanzas between the marquis and the Lord of Montalban shows that nothing escapes Rinaldo's observant eye, that he likes to speak in metaphors, and that mocking Oliver has become for him almost a daily pastime. It is particularly humorous that Rinaldo, who, as the poet reminds the reader, is talking to the marquis in French, uses a typically Tuscan expression (19, 7–8) to define his companion's inclination to fall for every beautiful woman he sees. Referring, in fact, to the custom among Florentine men of hanging a small branch of a tree on their beloved's door on May first of each year, Rinaldo compares the marquis to a donkey who, attracted by the branch, stops in front of every door (Ageno, 137). Rinaldo may commit the sin of cynicism, but his assessment of the situation is definitely on target.

21–22. Rinaldo's mention of Corbante and his court has the effect of making Oliver remember Forisena (stanzas 21–22). This causes his new declaration of eternal love for the girl. Oliver's insistence on affirming that not even death could ever weaken his passion for Forisena (a love, he adds, that was willed by the stars) appears to be his last attempt at self-deception. In stanza 21, verse 3, it is stated, seemingly in passing, that Oliver did not know that Forisena had taken her life. Made at this particular point, the abovementioned statement is significant because it reveals Pulci's almost undetected ironic intervention in the canto. It seems to authorize the reader, who is aware of Oliver's volatile romantic nature, to ask himself or herself what the marquis would have done had he known that Forisena's death had left him free to love Meridiana.

27, 1–5. As Giovanni Getto (80) appropriately observes, Pulci cannot refrain from intervening again in the story. The poet stresses the fact that Oliver's boldness is caused here by his new love.

28, 5–8; and 29, 1–6. Morgante's actions in canto VII demonstrate that his natural disposition to brag often causes incredible deeds to occur. Amusingly expressive is the metaphor of the dance the giant uses in verses 4–6 of stanza 29.

30, 6–8; and 31–32. As Rinaldo has suggested in stanza 20, Meridiana is not only a beautiful woman, but also a clever and resourceful individual, perfectly aware of the influence that her presence exerts on men. Oliver, whom she has helped to put on his suit of armor, desiring to show off his equestrian prowess, jumps on his horse and makes it leap "just like a leopard." Dudon and Rinaldo do likewise, and the paladins' acrobatics are cheered by all.

34, 1–4; and 35–48. In stanza 25 we read that the thought that the Lion's

Warrior might be Rinaldo did cross Orlando's mind. The count, however, promptly dismissed it because he had never known his cousin to associate with such animals. Pulci here pointedly explains that Orlando cannot recognize Rinaldo's horse because of the fact that Baiardo's body is completely draped. Moreover, the Lord of Montalban talks like a Saracen. Rinaldo, who knows his opponent's true identity, seems to enjoy, at least at first, this lack of recognition (33, 1–2). Nevertheless, during his ensuing duel with Orlando, precipitated by Dudon's humiliating unhorsing by Morgante (37–38), he is particularly careful to use his spear (42, 5–6) and his sword (44, 6–8) in such a manner as not to seriously harm his cousin. Eventually Rinaldo, whose initial smile has been wiped from his lips by the increasingly furious attacks of Orlando, finds himself worrying about his own safety (45, 1–4). It is at this point that Christ, in order to avoid a tragic mistake, is forced to perform a miracle (45, 5–8). As a consequence of the lion's sudden reappearance at Rinaldo's side, the duel is postponed to the following morning (48). Note that in stanza 41, verse 4, Pulci makes unusual use of the proverb "A barking dog does not bite."

The modern reader may wonder why Rinaldo, Dudon, and Oliver did not immediately reveal themselves to Orlando, thus avoiding fighting him as well as Morgante. It is plausible that the paladins' behavior was dictated by the pledge they made to Corbante in canto V to save Meridiana from the danger of having to marry a man she despised, while at the same time freeing Caradoro's kingdom from Manfredonio's relentless siege. A failure to face Orlando on the battlefield, as a consequence of their discovery that the count had apparently taken up Manfredonio's cause, would certainly have constituted a dishonoring breach of promise. On the other hand, an explanation of the real reasons for their refusal to fight would have forced them to reveal their identity, and no one could foresee how Caradoro and Manfredonio would react to such news. The reason for the episode, which is found also in *Orlando* (X, 9–11, p. 41, and 19–33, pp. 42–46), probably is that duels among blood-related knights occur quite frequently in chivalric literature. Moreover, they provide an unfailing element of suspense and allow the author to develop unexpected situations and complicate, at will, the plot of the story. Obviously, had Rinaldo's and his companions' true identity been made public, Pulci would not have been able to bring Gano back into the picture in the following stanzas of this canto. Concerning Almont, mentioned in 44, 7, see note, I, 13, 1–8.

50, 3–8; 51–56. Gano exerts such an influential role in the texture of the narrative that one is at times inclined to think of him as the poem's *deus ex machina*. His plotting mind is never at rest. When, in fact, one of his plans fails, as happened in canto II, where Orlando learned of Gano's plot from Rinaldo's courier, he immediately devises a better one. The letter he sends to Caradoro, explaining why he is informing him of the true identity of the four Christian knights (stanzas 54–56), can be considered unquestionable proof of his consummate diplomatic skills. If this new plan also fails, it will be primarily because of Gano's prejudice against Saracens (56, 5), the reason why he has underestimated the nobility of Caradoro's character (57, 1–8). It must be pointed out that the king appears to have no previous knowledge of Gano's treacherous nature. In stanza 53, 7, the reader is told only that Caradoro recognizes the seal of the Lord of Maganza. The explicatory remark in line 8 of the same stanza is made by the narrator of the story and not by Caradoro.

58, 5–8. These verses are additional evidence of Meridiana's mental and physical alertness.

61, 5–8; 62. Morgante is portrayed here in an unusually pensive, meditative mood. He has been observing things, and his suspicion has been aroused. There is a brain in his head after all.

66–68, 1–4. Once Meridiana, who has been flirting all along with Oliver, comes face to face with Orlando (alias Brunoro), first she sighs, then, questioned by the count, she surprisingly reveals that she fell in love with him when he declined to fight against her. His refusal to duel with her, she adds, showed in him a nobility worthy of the great Orlando. Since Meridiana knows that Brunoro and Orlando are one and the same, her deliberately flattering compliment betrays a calculating and frivolous attitude.

68, 5–8. Suspicious by nature, Orlando is not easily taken in by flattery, even when it comes from a beautiful woman. It must be noted that in line 5 of the Italian text, we read the phrase *Orlando è corbacchion di campanile*. Ageno (151) explains that *corbacchion di campanile* (a belltower raven) originally meant that birds accustomed to living atop a belltower were not scared by the sound of its bells. When used in reference to a person, the expression came to indicate a man who did not easily react to anything said about or around him. This phrase, which exemplifies the remarkable difficulties presented by Pulci's text, has been rendered with the verse "Orlando, ever shrewd as one could be."

C A N T O V I I

SUMMARY: Invocation (1). After telling Orlando that he and his companions have killed Rinaldo, Oliver, and Dudon, the Lord of Montalban and the marquis take off their helmets, and Orlando recognizes the two knights as his cousin and his brother-in-law (2–9). Morgante offers to return to Manfredonio's camp in order to free Dudon and bring him back to Caradoro's palace (10–12). Unable to persuade Manfredonio to release Dudon, the giant makes a bundle of the royal pavilion and, with the king and the paladin wrapped in it, carries it on his shoulders, advancing through the Saracen camp with the help of his clapper. Along the way Morgante, at Dudon's suggestion, dumps Manfredonio in a river, since they both believe him to be dead (13–25). Having returned safely among his people, Manfredonio receives a message from Gano. Aware of Orlando's and Rinaldo's true identities, the king decides to wait for their next move (26 through 31, 1–2). Convinced of Manfredonio's death, Morgante attacks the Saracen camp, burning many tents and killing more than five thousand pagans. When, however, Morgante, surrounded by the enemy, risks being killed, Orlando, Rinaldo, Oliver, and Dudon join him on the battlefield (31, 3–8 through 56). Meridiana, who has followed them, first helps Oliver, who has been unhorsed by Manfredonio, to get back on his mount, then faces the pagan king alone, convincing him to leave her kingdom with all his remaining troops (57–86).

2–10. The explanation that Pulci deems it necessary to give in line 4 of stanza 2 underscores the lighthearted, comic tone of this episode. Clearly the seemingly cruel game that Rinaldo and Oliver enjoy playing at this time could not have taken place had their faces not been concealed by their helmets. With Oliver looking on sneering (2, verse 3), the brazen Rinaldo proceeds to tell Orlando the story he has concocted, at the end of which, as unquestionable proof of its veracity, he shows the count the paladins' horses. Upon seeing Vegliantino, Orlando, who has tried all along to appear indifferent and in full control of his emotions, almost falls to the ground overcome by grief, while Oliver quietly laughs behind his helmet (6, 7–8 and 7, 1–4). Interestingly, when Rinaldo and Oliver reveal themselves to Orlando, the rejoicing paladin does not show any resentment about the trick that has been played on him (8, 7–8 and 9, 1–4). To be sure, Orlando, one of the poem's most serious characters (only on rare occasions do his actions or his person become the object of laughter), has, in contrast to his cousin Rinaldo, little appreciation for what appears to be amusing or comical. This scene parodies the famous moment in the *Chanson de Roland* when Olivier explains that he did not know whom he was hitting, and that he meant no harm to the count. As here, the anguished Roland is immediately reconciled and appeased.

10, 7–8. Morgante, wishing to honor Rinaldo and Oliver, falls on his knees before the two knights. According to Attilio Momigliano (171) "here, as elsewhere, the poet forgets Morgante's size in order to show us a grotesque picture, such as that of a giant who humbles himself by genuflecting." The critic correctly remarks that under normal circumstances, the person doing the kneeling necessarily appears shorter than the one before whom such an act takes place. The grotesque element of the situation is caused here by the giant's inability to make himself physically smaller in order to demonstrate his respect for the two knights.

But how tall is Morgante? Throughout *Morgante,* Pulci often hints at but never precisely states the height of this character. The only references the poet makes to Morgante's physical dimensions prior to canto VII are found in canto I. In stanza 26 (1–3) the abbot Clairmont, talking to Orlando, singles out the giant's enormous strength as his most distinctive feature. In stanza 46 (1–2) we are then told that the giant rushes to embrace Orlando, who hugs him back. Morgante's behavior, however, seems so natural that the reader, overlooking the fact that the former is a giant and the latter a man, almost fails to grasp the absurdity of the act. In order for Morgante to embrace Orlando, he must literally lift the paladin up to his own height; otherwise he would be embracing an empty space, while Orlando would end up hugging the giant's legs. In stanza 55, 1–6, Clairmont's monks, frightened by the size of Morgante, wonder how he will manage to enter the abbey's walls. In stanza 57, 1–6, the abbot stares admiringly at the giant, measuring his size several times from head to toe. Stanzas 69, 4–5 and 74, 1 provide two more detailed indications of Morgante's height. In stanza 69, Orlando compares him to "a ship's tall mast"; in stanza 74 we are informed that "Morgante like a mountain stood." Surely Morgante's height must equal that of several men, one standing on top of the other. Momigliano (170–171) argues that he must be "at least forty meters tall." With all this information in mind, the reader cannot but wonder how the giant can gain access to the "little room, filled to capacity with ancient arms" (84, 1–2) where the abbot takes him and Orlando at the end of canto I. It is probable that Pulci did not intentionally want to be consistent in his presentation of this gigantic figure. Though the grotesque element that Momigliano talks about is also present in those instances in which the poet has reduced Morgante to human proportions, it increases greatly when the giant's huge physical dimensions are ostensibly emphasized. It may be that this alleged inconsistency in depicting Morgante is a device that Pulci uses at will to create a particular comic effect.

12, 3. Morgante's amusing comparison of Dudon to "a candle" derives from the traditional wax-covered candle-like structure, made of wood and paper, which on June 24 Florentines offered to St. John the Baptist, their city's patron saint (Ageno, 155).

18, 3. Pietrapana is the name of one of the mountains in the Apuanian Alps. This mountain range, rich in marble quarries, runs along the Tyrrhenian coast of Tuscany between the Magra and Serchio rivers.

18–19. With regard to Morgante's action in these two stanzas, Giovanni Getto (115) writes that it is "a strange exploit . . . resembling a real ogre's flight." When one considers how the giant's mind works, and the fact that he is strong enough to uproot even the tallest of trees, the deed in question appears to be not only amusing, but also consistent with his mental as well as physical capabilities.

20–21. Particularly funny is the description of the scene that takes place inside the tent, with Manfredonio trying to free himself while Dudon is scratching and biting him.

22, 5. Note that Pulci uses another gastronomic image here.

26, 8. The "two pigeons" of the common Italian proverbial expression are, according to Gano, Caradoro and Manfredonio.

27, 6. In the original Italian text, we read the line *e vassi pure a Roma per più strade* ("and one still goes to Rome by means of different roads"), which has been translated as "all roads lead to Rome." As already noted, Pulci often gives his own personal version of frequently used proverbial phrases, at times inverting their meaning.

28, 8. Just as Orlando's unusual association with Morgante is blamed for

Manfredonio's mistake, Rinaldo's association with the lion is sufficient reason for Orlando's dismissing the thought that the Lion's Warrior might be his cousin.

34, 1–6. Accustomed to Morgante's bragging, Orlando has not taken seriously Morgante's cheerfully expressed intention to wage war alone against the enemy camp (31–33). Thus, turning to Caradoro and laughing, the count tells him that the giant's talk was nothing but "idle evening chat." As noted by Ageno (161), the phrase "evening chat" originates from the old Tuscan proverb *Parole da sera, il vento se le mena*—"Evening chats are scattered by the wind."

39, 2. The phrase "sing in German" probably alludes to Morgante's use of profanities and blasphemy, certainly not to his knowledge of the German language.

39, 3. Ageno (163) reports that the Bridge of Paris, known as the *Grand Pont,* was the scene of many a battle.

39–44. Pulci gives a very vivid description of the rapidity of Morgante's movements and the devastating effects that the blows of his clapper have on the heads, arms, and legs of Manfredonio's soldiers. The Latin phrase *Quem quaeritis* is taken from John 18:4–6.

46, 1–2. Note the use of another Tuscan proverb, used here by the smiling Orlando with reference to the "dear fool" who is finally getting what he has been asking for (for a detailed explanation of this proverb, see Ageno, 165).

55, 7–8. Pulci clearly had in mind the well-known anecdote about the fisherman who was said to have transported Julius Caesar on his boat to Italy from Epirus. According to the story, the Roman general told the boatman, who was frightened by a raging storm, not to fear, because he was carrying Caesar and his fortune (Ageno, 168).

56, 5. A further use of culinary terms.

57–69. Here it is Pulci who mercilessly makes fun of Oliver, the frequent object of Rinaldo's teasing. After his very noisy arrival on the battle scene accompanied by Dudon, the marquis is immediately and effortlessly thrown from his horse by Manfredonio (as had happened to Dudon, who at least was defeated by a giant, Morgante). What makes Oliver's fall amusing is that it takes place before the smiling eyes of the very woman the paladin wanted to impress the most. The brief philosophical comment contained in stanza 59 (2–5) reveals Pulci's personal satisfaction about the humiliating blow that has been inflicted on the paladin's male ego. The burlesque aspect of the situation in which Oliver finds himself reaches its climax when Meridiana kindly offers to help him get back on his horse. The marquis, who has sensed in her seemingly concerned words a cheerful tone of derision (59, 7–8 and 60, 5), becomes so confused that he finds it difficult to "rise and ride again." Meridiana then adds insult to injury when she orders Morgante to step aside, claiming for herself the honor of dueling with Manfredonio in order to avenge Oliver and punish the king for having invaded her fatherland. One cannot help but wonder here if Pulci is not drawing this upside-down humor motif from the French *Aucassin et Nicolette,* in which women go to battle and men give birth in the land of Torelore. While Morgante runs to help Dudon, who, mounted again on his horse, has resumed shouting vain threats at the enemy, Meridiana fights for about one hour with the Syrian king. It is at this point that Oliver, having somewhat regained his composure, begs Meridiana to let him duel with Manfredonio. Displaying a remarkable sense of humor, the paladin proffers as a curious explanation for his disgraceful fall the fact that he has never fallen before, and that there is always a first time for everything (68, 1–2). Meridiana's prompt reply—that only the knight who avoids a fight does not fall from his horse (68, 3–8)—voices, in spite of her seemingly consoling words, her somewhat low opinion of Oliver's military prowess. Realizing this, the paladin no longer insists and tells her that she may do what she wants (69, 5–6). The episode further shows how shrewd the otherwise sweet Meridiana can be. To quote Attilio Momigliano again (233), "Female malice, which is so characteristic in its almost imperceptible but penetrating sharpness, is sufficiently well represented in stanzas 60, 67–69."

62, 7. Note that *scopa* (literally "broom") is an old card game still very popular in Italy. It replaces here the word *naibi* (a card game played in Tuscany during Pulci's time), which is used in the original Italian text.

70–71 and 72–81. This is the second time (the first was noted in canto II, 48–50) that, as Giovanni Getto (89) writes, "a delicate shade of gentle humanity comes true in the poem." The elegiac tone of the episode is recognized also by Angelo Gianni (8–10), for whom these stanzas, which are missing in *Orlando,* are among the most pathetic in *Morgante.* Moved by Manfredonio's request that he be allowed to die by the hand of the woman he loves, Meridiana, who no longer desires his death, urges him to return safely to his fatherland. Her suitor's desperation deeply touches the girl, who first gives him a diamond ring to remember her by, and then expresses the hope that "a better star or fortune" awaits him (78, 8). Meridiana's last words to the king, though dictated only by pity and kindness, have a profoundly consoling effect on Manfredonio, who, at least for a moment, feels entitled to dream of an impossible future (80, 1).

82–86. There is a sharp contrast, a definite lowering of tone, between stanzas 70–81 and the few remaining lines of the canto. In stanza 82, 5, Oliver is said to rejoice at the king's departure, since he and Manfredonio are "two gluttons eyeing the same dish." The gastronomic metaphor that Pulci employs here to define, in rather crude terms, the rivalry between the two men brings the episode to an abrupt conclusion. Interestingly, the proverbial expression noted in stanza 82 was also used in canto IV, 55, 8, where Pulci talks about Rinaldo's and Oliver's attraction to Forisena. In this canto, however, the expression in question appears after Forisena's beautiful body has been thought of as and compared to food. In contrast to canto VII, the main feature of the episode of canto IV is its amusingly earthy quality. Pulci's desire to resume the burlesque tone so characteristic of his poetry is also attested to by the witty remark in line 5 of stanza 83 and by the content of stanzas 84–86, where Morgante, ordered by Orlando to stop fighting, uses his clapper to kill at least two more pagan soldiers, with the preposterous explanation that this last blow "was on its way" (85, 5). "The facetious poet," as Momigliano defines Pulci (227), "cannot be sentimental for long, either because he does not wish to become sad, or because being sentimental appears to him to be a ridiculous weakness."

CANTO VIII

SUMMARY: Invocation (1). Manfredonio and his troops begin their return trip home (2–6). Meridiana, converted and baptized by Oliver, makes love to him (7–14, 1–3). Gano sends a messenger to the Saracen king Erminion urging him to attack Montalban to avenge the death of his brother-in-law Mambrino, who has been killed by Rinaldo (14, 4–8 through 21). Erminion quickly assembles an army of 100,000 soldiers, then, together with Lionfant and his 30,000 men, sails for Spain (22–31). Marsilio, having been informed of Erminion's intention to bring war on Charlemagne, allows his army free passage through his lands. Meanwhile, in Paris the French decide to defend their cities (32–37). Erminion, having reached Paris, dispatches Mattafol as his ambassador to Charlemagne. Incensed by the threats of Erminion's envoy, Astolfo publicly insults him, whereupon Mattafol returns to the Saracen camp, pledging to make the paladin pay for the affront to his honor (38–43). While on his way to Montalban, Astolfo is taken prisoner by Lionfant, who, having learned that Rinaldo killed Mambrino in a fair hand-to-hand combat, releases the paladin and has him escorted to Montalban by his men (44–50, 1–4). Gano, accused by Astolfo, again succeeds in dispelling Charlemagne's suspicions (50, 5–8 through 56). In a series of duels, Mattafol defeats Ugier, Namo, Berlinghier, and several other Christian knights (57–95).

3–6. Stanzas 3–6 constitute yet another of the poem's moving moments. Here is voiced the sad and tender lament of some of Manfredonio's men upon leaving behind so many of their dead relatives and friends, and the rightful condemnation by others of the wasteful war waged by their king. Note that the comment in verses 7–8 is expressed by the poet himself, who, by stating a truth that men often forget, underlines Manfredonio's irresponsible behavior, which has caused much suffering both for him and for his people.

7, 1–8. Giovanni Getto (54) considers these lines, which so vividly depict a festive scene of collective merriment, to be among the most "unforgettable" in *Morgante*.

8–14, 1–2. The story of Meridiana's conversion provides Pulci with an excellent opportunity to exercise his natural inclination for the burlesque.

When Meridiana, meeting Oliver in "a little room," asks him not to deny her his love, the marquis, suddenly overwhelmed by religious scruples he has never felt before, replies that he cannot satisfy her wishes because they profess a different faith. The solution to the problem, however, is quickly found by Meridiana, who in stanza 9, 5–8 requests the paladin to demonstrate to her that "Mohammed is a useless god." It takes Oliver only four lines (10, 5–8) to explain the mystery of the Trinity (an explanation that Franca Ageno [180] does not deem to be "really very clear"). Interestingly, in stanza 10 of the original Italian text, Oliver, who always addresses Meridiana with the singular pronominal *tu* form of the verb, suddenly uses the plural form *voi*. This strange change has prompted Ernst Walser to suggest that in this particular instance the poet is addressing his readers, and not Meridiana.

According to the German scholar, between verse 5 and verse 6 there seems to be a leap in thought. This would indicate that something, perhaps an entire verse, is missing from the text. Walser maintains that the missing line was omitted by Pulci in a later "pious revision" of the poem (see *Lebens- und Glaubensprobleme aus dem Zeitalter der Renaissance: Die Religion des Luigi Pulci, ihre Quellen und ihre Bedeutung* [Marburg: a. n. Lahme Envert, 1926], 49). Oliver needs only four additional lines (11, 1–4) to complete Meridiana's "instant" religious indoctrination. The princess, in fact, declares herself ready to be baptized; consequently the lovers can indulge in the consummation of the sexual act (11, 7–8), which comes as the logical, though irreverently comical, conclusion of Meridiana's newly acquired faith.

In line 2 of stanza 11 we find a reference to Lazarus's miracle. With regard to this miracle, it is relevant to point out that Pulci, in a sonnet to Bartolomeo dell'Avveduto (CXLVI), denies that the miracle ever took place; then in his *Confessione* (201–203) he states instead that he firmly believes in its historical occurrence (see the previously cited *Sonetti di Matteo Franco e di Luigi Pulci, assieme con la Confessione,* 146–147 and 158–159). In the episode of Meridiana's conversion, the transition from sacred to profane love is so rapid as to make it appear a mere pretext to legitimize Oliver's and Meridiana's sexual intimacy. And if this were not enough, the reader is finally told (12, 5–8) that from this union, which is not blessed by the Church, a baby boy is going to be born who "will give Charlemagne his greatest glory." Oliver's quickness in silencing moral scruples, as well as Rinaldo's blatantly double-standard reaction when he discovers his friend's affair with Meridiana (13, 1–8), provides additional support to the thesis that in stanzas 8–13 Pulci may have intentionally created a burlesque parody of religious and chivalric ideals.

To be sure, the love of Meridiana and Oliver is narrated also in cantos XII and XIII of *Orlando*; Pulci, however, has transformed the figure of Oliver into a caricature of the knight in love, whose major exploit is having impregnated the just-converted Meridiana. Worth mentioning is the fact that in stanzas 9–15 of canto XII of *Orlando* (which correspond more or less to stanzas 8–13 of *Morgante*), the episode acquires a different tone and color. The anonymous author does not make the crude, mocking remarks one reads in lines 7–8 of stanza 11 of *Morgante,* and the religious explanation that Oliver gives Meridiana is expressed in a few simple words, totally devoid of the purposefully learned tone of Pulci's Oliver. The marquis of the *cantare popolare* mentions neither the miracle of Lazarus nor the crucifixion of Christ and His descent into hell, but speaks only about God, Christ, and the Holy Spirit as the creator of the universe, assuring Meridiana that all will be clear to her once she has renounced her false gods. Contrasting with Pulci's Meridiana, who does not utter a single word during Oliver's theological explanation, *Orlando's* Meridiana shows her interest in what her lover is telling her by asking him to explain the mystery of the Trinity. Another important difference is that in *Orlando,* during the conversation between Oliver and Rinaldo, the marquis is the one who, in defense of his actions, tells his companions that he baptized the girl before making love to her. In the text of the *canterino,* Rinaldo's reaction differs considerably from that of the Lord of Montalban in Pulci's poem: should Oliver's secret affair with Meridiana be discovered, he tells the marquis, his sword Frusberta would keep the word from spreading. Commenting on the story of Meridiana's conversion, Umberto Biscottini writes, "It is perhaps the most diabolically skeptical and the most wildly ludicrous in the poem" (*L'anima e l'arte del 'Morgante'* [Livorno: Giusti, 1932], 88).

15, 6. Regarding Mambrino, see note, III, 32, 8.

16, 7–8; and 17–22. Past failures do not affect the "ever-restless" and extremely well-informed Gano. He masterfully composes another treacherous letter and entrusts it to a courier, who, because of the high monetary reward Gano has promised him, performs his task as speedily as humanly possible. The letter he writes to Guicciardetto following the courier's return from his mission (30, 3–8) shows that he has again tried to cover all the angles.

23–28. Pulci presents Erminion as a very prudent man who does not let his wife's constant urging to avenge her brother Mambrino's death influence his good judgment, but wisely waits for the right moment to act (16, 1–6). Though not trusting Gano, he can still recognize a good opportunity when he sees it. The measures he takes before leaving his kingdom (26) are a further indication of his cautious nature. Fieramont(e) and Salincorno enjoy a short life in the poem. Rinaldo, in fact, kills the former in canto IX and the latter in canto X. Erminion's brother Salincorno must not be confused with the giant of the same name who makes his appearance in canto XVII. As noted by Ageno (184), the word *amirante* (24, 2 in the Italian text) may mean both "admiral" and "military commander."

28, 6. In the original Italian text, Pulci uses another proverbial expression containing a gastronomic metaphor.

34–35. The reaction of Charlemagne (here also called Carlo) to the news of Erminion's invasion is, as usual, one of fear, self-pity, and indecision. Ironically, the call to arms does not come from him, but from Turpin (also called Turpino) and Namo, two of the emperor's older knights. Charlemagne's image does not improve in stanzas 67, 1–4; 72, 1–8; 92, 1–6; and 94, 7–8.

38, 6. See note, I, 9–10. The Church of Saint Denis, the patron saint of Paris, mentioned several times in this canto (57, 66, 71, 79, and 89), is also referred to in cantos IX, XI, XVI, XVII, XXIV, XXV, XXVII, and XXVIII.

39–40. As Getto (171–172) keenly points out, the names that Pulci has given to some of his personages (particularly women, giants, devils, and innkeepers) "appear in reality to drip with happy and whimsical humor." One of the characters having a most appropriate name is definitely the Saracen knight Mattafol (called also Mattafolle). If it is true that, because of his inability to control his rage, he is thought to be a "maddened fool" (39, 2)— this opinion is to some extent shared by Erminion (42)—it is equally true that his remarkable exploits during his brief appearance in stanzas 57–91 (he exits from the poem at the beginning of canto IX) prove that he is a fearless, proud warrior, gifted with an earthy sense of humor, and capable at times of truly chivalrous behavior. He is a minor character not to be easily forgotten. Also in stanzas 39–40, Astolfo—just barely mentioned in cantos I, 9, 4; II, 51, 5; and III, 20, 7—makes his first close-up entrance onto the stage of *Morgante*. The paladin, whom Namo prevents from hitting Mattafol's head with his sword, gives here a demonstration of his excessive impetuosity, which is one of the main features of his character.

57–95. Like an unstoppable avalanche, Mattafol, in a long series of fierce but bloodless duels, defeats all of Charlemagne's knights present at his court. Ironically enough, the only one not allowed to fight by order of the emperor is Gano. Time and time again the Saracen presents himself before the city walls and, sounding his horn, challenges the enemy. The first to fall is Ugier the Dane, who gracefully accepts his defeat and is taken prisoner in the Church of Saint Denis. He is soon followed, after a similar though not monotonous repetition of attacks and exchange of blows, by Namo, Berlinghier, Otto, Turpin, and several other Christian knights.

With regard to the long duel fought by Mattafol with Berlinghier (73–88), Ageno (178) reports that Pulci may have had in mind Ferrau's duel against Oliver and Ugier in cantos II and III of *La Spagna*. This interesting and amusing armed confrontation evinces the substantially contrasting personalities of the two knights: on the one side the arrogant, boasting Christian knight whom Momigliano (259) appropriately calls "the most shameless and skillful braggart of the paladins"; on the other side the much calmer and far brighter Mattafol, capable from the very beginning of detecting his opponent's character flaws. The attitude of superiority that Berlinghier flaunts in stanza 73 provokes the Saracen's sarcastic reply in stanza 74, 5–8. Their "verbal" duel, consisting of a fast-moving exchange of colorful epithets, lasts for several stanzas (74–81). What is significant, however, is that while Berlinghier is utterly infuriated and vows to kill the Saracen in the same way he has killed so many other valiant men before him, Mattafol, who does not appear to take his threats seriously, laughs in his face. Concerning 75, 3–4, Ageno (197) clarifies that in Pulci's time insane people were customarily branded; they were taken by cart to the place where the branding was to occur, and during the trip were whipped at will. The reference to the cart and to the eating of "bran and cabbage" indicates Berlinghier's intention to insult Mattafol by calling him "mad and a pig."

When the real duel finally takes place, its outcome is already anticipated in the first two lines of stanza 82, where Berlinghier is compared to a "pigeon" and Mattafol to a "falcon." Not only is the Christian knight defeated, but he is also taught a lesson in chivalric etiquette by a pagan (85, 2–8). Because of his behavior during, and even more at the very end of, the duel (86), Berlinghier covers himself with ridicule, thus fully deserving to be laughed at by Mattafol as well as by the reader. Certainly Pulci's tongue-in-cheek attempt to excuse the paladin's foolish and ineffectual performance in combat, while alluding at the same time to his many "good qualities" and his "stream of gentleness" (90–91), sounds like a final practical joke. Note that Gualtier of Mulion, mentioned in stanza 93, 6, and Walter of Mont Leon (I, 10, 4) are one and the same.

C A N T O   I X

SUMMARY: Invocation (1). While outside Paris Erminion and his troops rejoice in Mattafol's victorious exploits, Charlemagne loudly laments the absence of Orlando and his fellow paladins (2–6). Orlando, Rinaldo, Dudon, and Oliver take leave of Caradoro to begin their return trip to France. It is at this point that the lion, until now their traveling companion, suddenly vanishes (7–16). Upon the paladins' arrival near Danismarche, Rinaldo kills Fieramont(e), the arrogant brother of King Erminion, who had wanted to take Baiardo away from him (17–27). Following the ruse plan devised by Faburro, one of Fieramonte's knights, the paladins succeed in capturing the city, whose entire population is soon baptized (28–45). Before resuming their voyage, Orlando dispatches Dudon to Caradoro to fetch Morgante, whom Oliver had left behind, at Meridiana's request. A few days later, Dudon returns with the giant and an army of 40,000 men, led by Meridiana herself (46–62). In Danismarche Faburro and 4,000 of his men join forces with the paladins and Meridiana's troops (63–68). Meanwhile in France, Gano approaches Lionfant with a new plot against his people. The Saracen, appalled by the man's treacherous nature, jails him. Astolfo, however, whom Lionfant has informed of Gano's treason, is compelled, for political reasons, to ask for the Lord of Maganza's safe return to Paris (69–83). Erminion, having learned of Fieramonte's death and the fall of Danismarche, pledges to take his revenge on the Christian knights he is holding prisoner (84–93).

2, 5. For the "laurel tree" mentioned in this line, see III, 17, 6–7.
2, 6. Taurus, whose time falls between April and May, is the second sign of the zodiac. Taurus (Latin for bull) is also the name the Romans gave to Zeus, who was believed to take on the form of a bull to perform his amorous exploits.
4, 5–8. An ironical allusion to Astolfo's tendency to fall when fighting on horseback, as we will see in stanza 58 of canto XXI.

5, 3–4. In these verses Pulci provides, as Angelo Gianni notes (173), "one of the most vivid and salient portraits of Gano."

6, 3. The proverbial sentence expressed in this line with reference to Rinaldo emphasizes by contrast Charlemagne's extreme gullibility.

10–12. In these stanzas, Oliver responds to the eloquent and moving request of Meridiana to take her with him by promising to speedily return and assuring her of his undying love. Interestingly, in lines 2 and 3 of the following stanza, Pulci intervenes directly in the story, first to explain that the marquis has left Meridiana "surely with many sighs and many tears," and secondly to declare the futility of Meridiana's hope of seeing Oliver again. With regard to this episode, it must be noted that, when comparing it with the events told in stanzas 89–90 of canto IV, one cannot but form the impression that it was far more painful for Oliver to leave Forisena than it is for him to leave the pregnant Meridiana. In our opinion, the poet's comment in line 3 of stanza 13 is not, however, as puzzling as it may appear to be. Noting that Meridiana and Oliver do meet again later in the canto, Ageno considers Pulci's comment possible proof of the author's occasional lack of a clear idea about the direction his poem is going to take next (207). Getto, instead, sees in it the witty nature and the winking smile of the poet himself (80). Though it is true that there are occasional inconsistencies in *Morgante,* Ageno's explanation would surely assign Pulci a very short memory had the poet forgotten in stanza 63 what he had stated fifty-one stanzas earlier. More convincing is Getto's interpretation, though it needs elaboration and clarification. We see, in fact, in Pulci's comment something more than a simple desire to be witty by poking fun at Oliver. The poet's words reflect, instead, his personal involvement with the story. Pulci's further stressing of the instability of Oliver's character in romantic matters is not at all inconsistent with what takes place in the second part of the canto. If, in fact, Meridiana's hope materializes and she is again united with her lover, the cause for this reunion rests solely with her; Oliver has little or nothing to do with it, no matter what he says in lines 5–8 of stanza 63.

20–21 and 22, 1–5. The desire of a number of warriors to gain possession of Rinaldo's horse, Baiardo, is the cause of several of the paladins' duels. In this instance, as again in canto XIII, the duel is preceded by an amusing fable, with animals as protagonists. It is told by the clever Rinaldo more to make fun of his adversary than to illustrate a point. It must be noted that the fable in question, which follows that of the ant in canto II, 55–57, is also to be found in canto XIV of *Orlando.* In telling the story of the fox and the rooster, however, Pulci is able to inject a comic wisdom that is lacking in the fable narrated in the anonymous *cantare popolare.* Giovanni Getto, who considers the Florentine poet a "great portraitist of animals," writes that in these stanzas the poet succeeds in representing animals as human, without, however, depriving them of their natural qualities and features as animals (57).

25, 6–8; and 26–27. This episode shows once more Rinaldo's inclination to fly into a mortal rage whenever his honor is, directly or indirectly, questioned. In a sudden change of mood, the "madly fuming" paladin challenges Fieramonte to a duel, without, however, revealing his true identity. By declaring to fight on behalf of Rinaldo, whom the Saracen has falsely accused of treason, Rinaldo achieves a double goal: punishing the arrogant Fieramonte for his insulting lie, and keeping secret the fact that he and his companions are Christians. Ironically, the pagan dies without knowing that the "demon" who has killed him is none other than Rinaldo himself. In these stanzas, as well as in lines 2–7 of stanza 34, we find additional evidence of Rinaldo's political shrewdness as well as his basically realistic nature. Even in the heat of passion, the paladin never loses total control of his emotions.

36–37. We learn here that Morgante had been left behind at the request of Meridiana as a "pledge" of Oliver's love for her. In reality the marquis had consented to his lover's wishes mostly because he wanted the giant to protect the life of his soon-to-be-born child. Shouldn't Oliver's fear of Caradoro's wrath have been sufficient reason for his taking Meridiana along with him when he and his companions left Caradoro's court earlier in the canto? Since Meridiana had valiantly fought beside Orlando, Oliver, Dudon, and Morgante, greatly contributing to Manfredonio's final defeat (stanzas 57–86 of canto VII), the king could hardly have objected to his daughter's joining forces with his new Christian friends and allies. In stanzas 54–55, in fact, Meridiana will promptly obtain Caradoro's permission to lead an army of 40,000 of his subjects to the aid of Rinaldo and his men.

44–45. The rapid, matter-of-fact conversion of Faburro and the people of Danismarche is clearly conventional. The event is also found in canto XIV of *Orlando,* where, however, it takes up two stanzas (30 and 31, p. 63) and is narrated in the form of a dialogue. Though the two conversions are similar in their conventionality, they do differ in color and tone. The author of *Orlando,* in fact, seems eager to emphasize the conversion of Faburro, his sister, and the entire population of Danismarche for the religious edification of his audience. Pulci, who dedicates only a few lines to the same conversion, stresses instead the reasons that have motivated it: the unconstrained, almost joyful slaying of Erminion's wife and their children by an enthusiastic Rinaldo disguised as Fieramonte. Certainly this conversion elicits more laughter than devotion.

46, 6. See note, VIII, 38, 6.

49–59. Meridiana's passionate love for Oliver constitutes one of the best-developed and most charming love stories in the poem. Pulci depicts the girl's emotions and actions with great delight and an obviously joyful participation. Oliver is always in Meridiana's heart and mind. She is the first to run to embrace Dudon and, unheard by her father, is able to obtain news of her lover. Then, encouraged by Orlando's request for military assistance, she begs Caradoro to let her lead the troops that she hopes her father will dispatch to Rinaldo's aid. Only after she is sure that she will soon be able to be reunited with Oliver does Meridiana rejoice, engaging in an amusing verbal game with Morgante, in which both players state the obvious (57, 1–6) but make it sound as if it were out of the ordinary. Meridiana's happy mood is shared by the giant. Far from being a simpleton, Morgante takes pleasure in teasing Meridiana (58, 3–6) for saying one thing but meaning another (57, 7–8 and 58, 1–2). Meridiana's seemingly serious reply closes their brief dialogue.

66,8. As noted by Ageno (221), Faburro is quoting an old Tuscan proverb.

69, 3–8; and 70–73. Here, and again in stanza 92, 5–8, Charlemagne is depicted as a weeping and crazy old man whose main reason for being is, as Gianni writes (32), "listening to Gano's rumors and innuendos against his paladins." As always, the emperor's laments give Gano the opportunity to spring into action devising a new scheme. In this instance, however, it will be doomed to failure because of Lionfant's honest and generous nature.

73–76. According to Ageno (222), the fable of the fox, the wolf, and the dog, which is not in *Orlando,* is probably a contamination of Hervieux's *Fabulistes latins* and Aesop's *Fables.* With regard to this story, the third one in the poem, Momigliano writes that "the fraud of the fox, and particularly its mocking reply to the wolf, shows a refined humor worthy of the most scoffing pages in the *Decameron*" (208). Giovanni Getto, who maintains that Pulci's fables have little or nothing to do with the fables contained in medieval literary texts, sees in these stanzas "a light of wisdom" and a "savory mixture of things and morality." For this critic, the rhythmic and tonal elegance of some of these verses may foretell the poetry of La Fontaine and of Ariosto (60–61).

84, 1–2. As correctly pointed out by Ageno (225), there is an obvious inconsistency here. In fact, in canto VIII, 38, 1–2, the reader is told that Erminion, having dispatched Lionfant to Montalban, had set up camp just outside Paris.

87, 7–8; and 88, 1–6. Erminion, like Lionetto in canto II, 76–77, feels no compunction about cursing and denying Mohammed, whom he considers responsible for the death of his family members and the fall of Danismarche. Together with Arpalista (canto XXII) and King Marsilius (canto XXVI), Erminion is one of the poem's major blasphemous figures.

C A N T O   X

SUMMARY: Invocation (1). The first to reach Paris, Faburro duels with Gano, promptly unhorsing him. Upon their arrival in the city, Orlando, Rinaldo, Oliver, Meridiana, and Morgante are joyfully received by Charlemagne. Gano, who has run away, unsuccessfully incites the people of Paris to rebellion against the emperor (2–20). Rinaldo, Orlando, Oliver, Meridiana, Morgante, and Faburro decide to go and free the Christian knights held prisoner in the Saracen camp (21–24). Meridiana obtains Orlando's permission to make a quick raid into the enemy's camp, accompanied only by Morgante. When, however, the two are totally surrounded by Salincorno and his troops, Orlando, Rinaldo, and Oliver run to their defense, and the Lord of Montalban kills Salincorno (25–53). Erminion challenges Rinaldo to a duel. Having lost the match, the Saracen, as previously agreed with Rinaldo, releases all his prisoners. The paladins and their freed companions return immediately to Paris (54–74).

As the result of a hoax that Malagigi has played on Rinaldo, who is headed for Montalban, Rinaldo and Orlando decide to face each other on the battlefield (75–90). While the entire French court and even the Saracens blame the emperor for allowing this duel, Charlemagne and Gano rejoice (91–100). Orlando, followed by Charlemagne and Erminion, who has asked to be permitted to witness the event, ride on to Montalban, where Rinaldo is waiting. Just when the two cousins are about to start their fight, the duel is interrupted by the sudden appearance of a lion, which hands Orlando a letter addressed to him by Malagigi (101–115). Erminion, appalled by what he has seen, decides to embrace Christianity (116–120). Gano reacts to all this by dispatching a letter to Caradoro informing him of Meridiana's pregnancy and accusing her of being Oliver's whore (121–124). The last part of the canto (125–154) narrates the fight between Morgante and Vegurto, the formidable giant whom Caradoro has sent to Paris to bring Meridiana back home with him. At the end, Morgante kills his opponent.

12, 3–8. Morgante is here again depicted kneeling before Charlemagne, as he did earlier before Rinaldo and Oliver. Einhardt, Charlemagne's biographer, notes that the emperor himself was considered a "giant" among men. Modern scholars, in fact, estimate him at 6'6" in a society where 5'4" might have been normal. The fact that Morgante, though kneeling, towers over Charlemagne is an additional indication of the giant's truly phenomenal stature (see note, VII, 10, 7–8).

16, 7–8. Oliver's new attempt to distinguish himself in front of Meridiana calls to mind a similar scene in canto VI, 31, 2–5.

17, 8. Another recurrent gastronomic metaphor.

20, 3–4. The crown in question is also mentioned in *Orlando* (XII, 7, 1–2, p. 50), where Rinaldo removes it from Manfredonio's pavilion for the express purpose of donating it to Alda the Fair. While the *canterino* refers to this object only as "a crown with shining stones," Pulci, who has a penchant for rich jewels and precious clothes, describes it in more detail, emphasizing the crown's rare beauty and great value (see also XI, 27, 4–5).

21, 5–8 and 22, 1–6. Rinaldo's question to Charlemagne reveals, more than an outright lack of respect, an open tone of joking familiarity. To be sure, Charlemagne's reply to Rinaldo, a nephew he highly dislikes (94, 1–4), does not disclose the emperor's true inner feelings for the paladin.

25, 6–8; and 26. These stanzas reinforce our previous assessment of Erminion (VIII, 23–28) as a basically practical man. His avowed desire to avenge the deaths of his family members with those of the paladins he holds prisoner is readily put aside when he sees the harsh reality of Orlando's terrible reprisal.

27, 4. Cats, crickets, and falcons were the names given to various devices used during sieges (in this instance that of Montalban) for battering and crushing fortified walls (see Ageno, 236).

28–53. Meridiana's raid into the Saracen camp escorted only by Morgante, her ensuing encounter with Salincorno, and her subsequent delivery by Rinaldo constitute one of the canto's outstanding episodes. Meridiana, presented in canto III as ready to measure herself against Orlando (17–18), is again assigned here a significantly distinctive role both as a warrior and as a woman. Always determined to seize the opportunity to demonstrate her military skills (as she did fighting against Manfredonio in canto VII), she bravely faces Salincorno and, when hit by his spears, readily accuses him of cowardice for having violated a basic tenet of the chivalric code. To be sure, Salincorno does not appear to be having a good day. His feeble excuses after he has mistakenly decapitated his opponent's horse, and then his shameful failure to land a single blow of his sword on Meridiana in answer to her sarcastic challenge, impress him in our mind as a rather comic figure. That this was Pulci's intention is evinced by the obvious contrast between Salincorno's initial presentation as a "gentle, wise, and kind young man" (31, 7) and his actual behavior on the field of battle, where he demonstrates that he is neither wise nor kind, and least of all honorable.

Interestingly, in this episode Oliver does not appear to fare much better than Salincorno. In fact, even though Pulci has depicted Oliver as a man fighting desperately hard to reach Meridiana (43–44), the honor of bringing her to safety is reserved not to her lover but to Rinaldo (50–51), who also accomplishes, almost effortlessly, another feat: the killing of Salincorno (52, 5–8). Evidently Pulci, hardly a romantic, takes pleasure in making Oliver's efforts meet with ridiculous failure whenever he happens to fight either at Meridiana's side or on her behalf. Clearly the few words that Oliver finally manages to utter to Meridiana in stanza 53 must sound to her more like a poor excuse than the reporting of the truth.

43, 6. Ageno (240) explains that "to make the Agnus Dei" is a fifteenth-century proverbial expression meaning "to look behind oneself." *Agnus Dei* is Latin for "Lamb of God."

44, 7. Altachiara (Halteclere) is the name given to Oliver's sword.

51, 2. Pulci is particularly fond of the expression "to leap as fast as a cat." It is also found in one of the poet's most famous letters, addressed to Lorenzo de' Medici (see Letter XXIII in *Morgante e Lettere,* 977).

61, 7–8; and 62, 1–4. In these lines Erminion becomes almost a caricature of himself.

66, 3–8; and 67–68. Erminion, always the pragmatist, readily accepts defeat and ironically affirms that a man who risks shame seeking revenge is indeed a fool. When he singles out his wife and his faith in fortune as the causes for his personal failures, however, he is guilty of self-deceit. Stanza 16 of canto VIII shows, in fact, that he did not at all heed Lady Clemency's advice, as he allegedly states. His attempt to place the blame on his dead wife, based on the belief that to follow a woman's counsel invariably spells doom, is unquestionable proof of gender prejudice.

75, 5. In *Orlando* and *Morgante,* the bride of Rinaldo is Clarice, daughter of Ivone, the king of Bordella. Kidnapped by Mambrino after he laid siege to Bordella, Clarice was subsequently freed by Rinaldo (Ageno, 67 and 249).

77, 7–8. In Pulci's poem, where heavy drinking is hardly condemned or viewed as a weakness, great drinkers abound. Imbibing anything but water is definitely one of Rinaldo's great passions. He performs this act with unrestrained enthusiasm and outward pleasure. The paladin's love for beer and wine is no secret. It is Orlando's knowledge of this fact that makes the count believe that Rinaldo performed the exchange of horses and swords under the influence of excessive wine (87, 1–4). It is also probable that Malagigi, well acquainted with all aspects of Rinaldo's character, counted on his cousin's thirst to make sure that he would promptly drink his beer-tasting potion.

76, 4–8 through 114. Malagigi now stages his second entrance in the poem. He has again chosen to appear to Rinaldo disguised as an old man, though in this instance both Rinaldo and Orlando are the immediate victims of this new prank. In spite of Rinaldo's awareness of Malagigi's penchant for similar deeds (V, 30, 1), he fails once more to recognize the wizard or to suspect that anything is wrong. When these stanzas are examined vis-à-vis stanzas 22–30 of canto V, some important differences come to the fore. In canto V, Rinaldo's attention, like that of the audience, is immediately drawn to Malagigi's physical aspect and the air of mystery that surrounds him. Malagigi is unquestionably at the center of the scene, while his prank, the stealing of Baiardo, is secondary. In canto X, instead, the focus of the entire story is not on the person of Malagigi, who is simply and briefly presented here as "a white-haired, sweet old man," but on the prank itself and its potentially melodramatic consequences. The *vis comica* energizing this entire episode springs from the contrast between the essentially harmless prank of Malagigi and the unreasonable, stubbornly childish reaction it provokes in both Rinaldo and Orlando. Blinded by pride and oblivious of their close kinship, the two cousins are utterly mindless of the ill consequences that even the death of one of them could have for their people and their faith. (Note that a similar, but shorter and much less rapid, version of this story is told in cantos XVII, 22–XVIII, 25, pp. 75–80 of *Orlando.*) No less farcical is Charlemagne's hypocritical behavior (94–95). Though the old emperor nourishes an almost visceral hatred of Rinaldo, he tries to conceal his true feelings for the Count of Montalban, hoping that Orlando may soon rid him of his troublesome nephew. So while outwardly he declares his unhappines over the duel he did not oppose, deep within he cannot but rejoice (108, 7–8). Concerning stanzas 94–95, Ageno (254) clarifies that in earlier popular epics, Rinaldo is usually portrayed as a rebel and an enemy of Charlemagne. She also states that in Italian romances, Rinaldo and his younger brothers are said to have been sent by their mother, Clarice, to the court in Paris, where they were cordially received. It appears that in these romances, and presumably also in *Morgante,* Rinaldo has retained some of his earlier rebellious nature.

112, 4. The river in question is the Gironde; on its banks is located Rinaldo's castle, built by Malagigi's magic (XXVIII, 65, 7–8) after Rinaldo's slaying of Mambrino (concerning Mambrino, see note, III, 32, 8 and VIII, 15, 6).

115–120. Erminion's sudden but not illogical or surprising conversion takes place in an atmosphere of great wonder and general thanksgiving, caused by the last-minute resolution of the dispute between the two Christian champions. The scene that Erminion has just witnessed, coupled with the recent misfortunes that have considerably shaken his faith in Mohammed, is enough to convince him of the superiority of the Christian god. Nevertheless, what makes the spiritual crisis of this professional blasphemer amusing is the fact that it is brought about by the prodigious appearance of a letter-carrying lion, the product of Malagigi's magic. Apparently moved by Erminion's conversion, Charlemagne promptly embraces his former enemy and takes him to a nearby river, where he baptizes him. Commenting upon this event, Momigliano rather cynically suggests that Charlemagne's emotional state, rather than being a manifestation of his religious fervor, is probably caused by the emperor's disappointment over the unexpected cancellation of a duel he wanted and from which he hoped to be freed of Rinaldo (215). In *Orlando,* the conversion of Erminion takes place in stanzas 26–29 of canto XVII, p. 80. Though it is essentially brought about by the same reasons, the way in which the *canterino* portrays the two kings (the repentant but dry-eyed Erminion, and the less talkative and more dignified Charlemagne) is again emblematic of the different attitudes of the two poets with regard to religious matters.

121–124. It seems ironic that Gano does not promptly realize that the secret love affair between Oliver and Meridiana, if adequately exploited, could provide him with an excellent weapon against Charlemagne. Perhaps the Lord of Maganza's constant preoccupation with devising new, elaborate schemes prevents him from grasping the obvious. Note that line 2 of stanza 122 contains an old proverbial expression stating that when things keep turning bad no matter what, the devil has had a hand (literally "his tail") in them.

125, 5–8; and 126–127. With the simple, pathetic, and yet poignantly truthful words of Caradoro's wife, Pulci has masterfully rendered the shock and grief felt by Meridiana's parents as a result of Gano's slanderous letter.

130, 4. When one recalls that the horse that Clairmont had given to Morgante was almost instantly crushed by the giant's weight (I, 68 and 69, 1–3), one wonders how Vegurto's Arab horse can survive carrying a much heavier rider than Morgante (131, 3–4).

131, 4–8; and 132–135, 1–4. Rather than being "a puppet," as Getto maintains (72–73), Vegurto is one of the minor characters that Pulci has depicted with particular care. Contrasting with Morgante, who on occasion can be witty, thoughtful, respectful, and even gentle, Vegurto is totally crude and insensitive. He trusts only his formidable physical strength and shows no acquaintance with, or understanding of, the most elementary rules of social behavior. In this way, Vegurto appears somewhat related to the large family of grotesque figures, such as the "giant of the deer" (canto IV, 26–33), that abound in the poem.

If Vegurto's first appearance on the scene generates considerable bewilderment, the words of salutation he addresses to Charlemagne are, to say the least, shocking because of their derisive and disparaging confidentiality. What greatly astonishes the paladins who surround the emperor is not really Vegurto's litany of accusations per se—they know that some are, to a certain extent, true—but the extremely arrogant, highly threatening, and unacceptable tone with which these accusations are voiced. This generates the immediate outraged reaction of Oliver, Ugier the Dane, Rinaldo, and Meridiana, a reaction that sharply underlines the contrast with the overly meek and civilized reply of the emperor (it would be wrong to see in Charlemagne the role of reason as opposed to that of brute ignorance personified by Vegurto). With regard to Meridiana's words in her own defense, it is significant to point out that she does not categorically deny or admit anything. She says only that she considers her father's behavior foolish and forcefully declares—which is probably true—that since she has been at Charlemagne's court, Oliver has treated her "like a queen" (138).

139, 3–8; and 141–142. This is a lively and humorous scene in which a caution-preaching Namo—prudence and formal respect for the rules are his main concerns (as in 143, 4–5)—succeeds, apparently without much effort, in disarming Oliver, who is about to fling himself against Vegurto. Since patience is not one of the giant's virtues, he attacks the marquis, who, in warding off a mortal blow from Vegurto's ax, hits Charlemagne, making him fall off his chair. Fortunately for Oliver, Morgante intervenes in the fight, throwing his opponent to the ground.

144, 1–5. As shown here, Oliver also likes to show off his knowledge of classical culture. Briareus, the son of Uranus and Earth, was a giant who had one hundred hands and one hundred heads. When he sided with the Titans during their war against the gods, he was killed by Jove. A similar fate was met by another giant, Ephialtes, who was also guilty of having opposed the gods. First wounded by Apollo, he was then killed by Heracles, who shot an arrow into his right eye. Capaneus, instead, was one of the seven kings who, having scaled the walls of Thebes, dared to challenge Jove to come and defend the city. For his arrogance he was thunderstruck by the irate god. Antaeus, son of Poseidon and Earth, was a giant who ruled over Libya, and who used to force all those who passed through his lands to wrestle with him. But no one could defeat him, since every time he touched the ground, which had generated him, he regained all his strength. However, Hercules finally succeded in killing him by lifting him up in the air while crushing him to death between his powerful arms (see *The Meridian Book of Classical Mythology,* 52–53, 137, 149, 224, and Ageno, 267).

145, 1–8; and 149, 1–6. Pulci's laughing remark is clearly aimed at poking fun at Oliver, who is always tirelessly trying to shine in front of his lady. Fortunately, however, while the marquis goes to arm himself fully (obviously Altachiara alone would not do the job), Morgante, without waiting for Charlemagne's consent, resumes his fight with Vegurto. Thus Oliver is probably spared another embarrassing failure, or maybe even death. It is hilarious to note how fast our hero loses his desire to face Vegurto and keeps himself at a safe distance when, upon his return, he sees the two giants engaged in mortal hand-to-hand combat. Oliver, who is not smiling now, as he was in stanza 143, 3, will be happy again only when Vegurto, hit by Morgante's huge clapper, finally falls dead to the ground.

C A N T O   X I

SUMMARY: Invocation (1). Gano writes to Charlemagne, who welcomes him back to Paris (2–7). While playing chess, Oliver and Rinaldo get into a heated argument. Accused by Charlemagne of being a troublemaker, Rinaldo calls the emperor a liar; he then, at Orlando's urging, departs for Montalban (8–13). Charlemagne calls a meeting of the Council, which banishes Rinaldo from Paris. Astolfo, who has unsuccessfully opposed its decision, joins Rinaldo in Montalban (14–18). Having decided to become highway bandits, Rinaldo, Astolfo, and Ricciardetto rob and pillage the countryside (19–23). At Gano's suggestion, Charlemagne announces a joust, promising a magnificent diamond ring as a reward to the winner (24–27). Rinaldo, Astolfo, and Ricciardetto, in disguise, go to Paris to take part in the joust. At the end of the day, Rinaldo, who has covered himself with glory, is declared the winner (28–40).

Rinaldo and his companions, while resting at an inn outside the city, are suddenly attacked by Gano and his men. The Maganzans succeed in capturing only Astolfo, who is taken before the emperor and jailed (41–46). Orlando, who had left Paris before the joust began, arrives at Montalban, where his cousin informs him of Astolfo's fate. Determined to save Astolfo's life, the count, Rinaldo, and Ricciardetto leave for Paris (47–55). Unmoved by his people's pleas for mercy, Charlemagne orders Astolfo to be hanged, trusting that the sentence will be carried out by Gano (56–69). However, just when Astolfo is about to be hanged, he is saved by Orlando, Rinaldo, and Ricciardetto. Aided by Astolfo, who has armed himself, Orlando and Rinaldo kill many of Gano's men while, pursued by Ricciardetto, the Lord of Maganza runs for his life (70–108). When the enraged Rinaldo reaches the court, he vows to kill both the emperor and Gano. In the meantime, Gano surrenders to Orlando, and Charlemagne is hidden away by Alda the Fair in Orlando's palace (109–116). In the last stanzas of the canto, Orlando succeeds in convincing Rinaldo to forgive the emperor. Sitting again on his throne, Charlemagne forgives Astolfo and is forgiven by him (117–133).

1, 1–3. Ageno explains (271) that the pelican was believed to be able to revive its chicks that had been killed by a viper's poisonous bite by feeding them the blood of its chest. This belief is the reason why in medieval bestiaries the pelican came to symbolize Christ, who gave His life to save man.

6, 1. As previously noted, "Carlo," Italian for Charles, is often used with reference to Charlemagne.

7. In the *Chanson de Roland* (Digby 23) there is reference to a previous conflict between Roland and Ganelon, an alleged offense that Ganelon uses as justification for his hostility toward Roland. In this canto we are enabled to see an episode created by the tradition to respond to this otherwise unknown conflict. A disguised Gano assaults Orlando, who later thwarts his plans to hang Astolfo.

12–15. Charlemagne's covert hostility toward Rinaldo (X, 94, 1–4) is openly expressed here. To be sure, the emperor's easily triggered anger at his paladins is continually fed by Gano, whose slanderous accusations spare no one and are believed even when they concern Orlando (I, 11–15). Momigliano (260–263), for whom Charlemagne is "the first good portrait of a character we find in *Morgante*," states that Pulci has depicted the emperor as a much more comical figure than the one portrayed in traditional chivalric poetry, such as *Orlando,* where Charlemagne acts in a more dignified and less ridiculous manner. Commenting, then, upon the emperor's unwavering trust in Gano's loyalty, the critic convincingly argues that "no one is more attached to his own ways than an old man." It is natural, therefore, that the emperor cannot cease to believe Gano until the moment he has given him "irrefutably terrible proof of his treachery and wickedness." For Angelo Gianni (31–32), instead, Charlemagne appears to be like a statue that has become one with the throne on which it is seated. The emperor's main reason for being would be to lend a trustful ear to Gano's malicious insinuations against the paladins.

Note that in stanzas 13, 14, and 15 there is a patterned reminiscence of the Roncevaux councils. Here Orlando speaks in favor of sparing Rinaldo, a fact confirmed by Namo, the wise counselor whose final word always determines the future course of events. As in the *Chanson de Roland,* Namo's advice turns out not to have been wise. Moreover, there is a purposeful presentation here of Orlando as a wise and measured counselor. One should recall the famous verses *Roland est preux et Olivier est sage / Ambedui ont merveillous vasselage.* These lines are frequently misinterpreted by modern critics as presenting Roland and Olivier as two different types, Fortitudo and Sapientia, as if the conjunctive *et* (and) were an adversative *mais* (but). This interpretation also neglects the fact that the first meaning of *preux* in the twelfth century was *sage* (wise), and that the two lines are really stressing the equality of the two knights: *Ambedui,* etc. Although a couple of manuscripts of the *Chanson de Roland* omit these lines, while others change the words *preux* and *sage,* all manuscripts that have the two lines in some form stress the equality in the second verse. It is most interesting to note that Pulci gives Orlando the humane and wise choice of waiting until the youthful, hotheaded Rinaldo has had time to cool down.

19–21. What makes this brief, roguish dialogue distinctly amusing is not really Rinaldo's sudden proposal to lead a life of crime (a fact which is stated also in *Orlando* [XIX, 41 and XX, 3–4, pp. 86–87]), but the joyfully bold and irreverent enthusiasm that pervades his words—an enthusiasm immediately shared by Astolfo, who answers him accordingly.

21, 2–3. See note, I, 2, 4.

27, 3–4. See note, X, 20, 3–4.

29, 6. See note, III, 31, 1.

30, 1–3. These three verses seem to have been taken almost verbatim from *Orlando* (XX, 15, 1–3), where we read: "All those French barons used to dismount at Gualtieri's inn, better known, according to custom, as Don Simon." Gualtieri of Mulion (I, 10, 4; VIII, 93, 6; and XII, 35, 5) is a loyal friend of the paladins. He will fight and die in the Battle of Roncesvalles.

30, 8. As Getto notes (45), "The figure of the innkeeper is a richly suggestive, constant element in Pulci's world."

31, 1. Ricciardo and Ricciardetto are one and the same.

35–36. Oliver, presented in 33, 8 as a man "eager to use his spear and show its might," is again the object of Pulci's irony. Even though the poet tells the reader that neither Rinaldo nor Oliver was hurt significantly in the duel, there is no question as to who is the stronger of the two knights. In fact, while Oliver, who has fallen from his horse, rises "bewildered still and pale," Rinaldo, steadily riding his Baiardo, grabs a new spear and resumes jousting.

39, 7. Gallerana is the wise and highly respected wife of Charlemagne. In canto XII (15, 4–6; 18, 5–8; and 19, 1–6) the queen tries unsuccessfully to persuade her husband to spare and free Ricciardetto and not to trust Gano so much.

47, 7. The castle of Agrismont belongs to Buovo of Agrismont, father of Malagigi and of Viviano. (Concerning Buovo, see note, III, 31, 8.)

50, 4. See note, VIII, 6. The same for 94, 3 and 97, 8.

50, 6. Terigi is Orlando's brave and faithful squire. He makes his appearance in several cantos of the poem, either with his master or alone. Terigi will be charged by Rinaldo with bringing to Charlemagne the news of the death of Orlando and almost all of his companions at Roncesvalles. He will die immediately thereafter because of his wounds (XXVII, 178–185).

62, 1–4. For the critics Gianni (6) and Getto (90), these verses are yet another instance of the emergence in the poem of a pathetic vein, particularly where parental or family love is concerned.

63, 6. Ageno (287) notes that Longinus is the name given in the apocryphal Gospels to the thief forgiven by Christ on the cross. According to the *Oxford Dictionary of the Christian Church* (F. L. Cross, ed. [London: Oxford University Press, 1974], 835), which gives as its sources the apocryphal "Acts of Pilate," Longinus was the name traditionally given to the Roman soldier who pierced Christ's side with his spear. This would explain the Roman name of the man, as well as Pulci's mention of him as forgiven by Christ (Longinus was said, in fact, to have been subsequently baptized by one of the Apostles). One should also note that the blood from Christ's wound was collected in a vessel by Joseph of Arimathea, who eventually—in the Arthurian legends—made his way to England and entrusted the "grail of blood" to the British ruler for protection.

64, 6–7. Gano is said to be a worse traitor than Judas and Trojan Sinon. The latter is the name given to the Greek soldier who was left behind by his comrades so that, once captured, he could persuade the Trojans to bring the wooden horse into their city (see Dante's *Inferno,* XXX, 98).

68–107. The capture of Astolfo (42–46) and, following Charlemagne's obstinate refusal to forgive him (59–68), Gano's attempted hanging of him (72–107) occupy a position of prominence in the canto. Concerning this episode, it must be pointed out that in cantos XIX and XX of *Orlando,* it is Ricciardetto, and not Astolfo, whom Gano, aided by the emperor himself, first captures and later fails to hang. Astolfo's tragicomic presence in canto XI of *Morgante* is due, therefore, solely to Pulci's creative imagination. Angelo Gianni (225–283) states that while there are structural similarities between cantos XIX and XX of *Orlando* and canto XII of *Morgante,* both of which narrate Ricciardetto's capture and his attempted hanging, the story of Astolfo is, because of its many, varied aspects, "one of the greatest original additions" Pulci made to his poem.

71, 6. As noted by Ageno (289), Pulci uses here a proverbial expression meaning "to arrive at the right moment." It derives from the custom of serving roasted meat toward the end of a meal.

72, 5–6. This lively simile is further proof that Pulci, as Getto maintains (56), was "one of the first and most skillful illustrators of the animal kingdom."

73, 1–8; and 85–92. The scenes described in these stanzas contain several details taken from the Crucifixion of Christ as told in the Gospels (Ageno, 290). Commenting upon the English knight's attempted hanging, De Robertis (408) writes that the paladin's laments, which recall the insults inflicted upon the Son of God in the liturgy of the Passion of Christ, "are the stations of Astolfo's own *Via Crucis.*" In partial agreement with De Robertis, Remo Ceserani also perceives, interwined with the theme of the *Via Crucis,* the "old motif (dear to Pulci) of the gallows, as the symbol of a lawless world, inhabited by thieves, criminals, vagabonds, which is in its own way a 'travesty' of the real world" (see "Studi sul Pulci," *Giornale storico della letteratura italiana* 146 [1969]: 429).

74, 6. Judecca, so called after the traitor Judas, is the area in Dante's *Inferno* (XXXIV) where those who betrayed their benefactors are punished. Among them, trapped and suffering in the ice of a frozen lake, is Lucifer, God's archtraitor. In stanzas 74–79, ingratitude, the most pernicious of all sins, is singled out as the main reason for Charlemagne's unwilliness to forgive Astolfo's transgressions.

75, 1–4. Reference is made here to the Roman general Scipio Africanus (235–183 B.C.), who in 202 defeated the Carthaginian general Hannibal at Zama, where the final battle of the Second Punic War took place. Consequently, as the poet remarks, Hannibal lost the reputation of invincibility he had gained with his victory over the Romans at Cannae (216 B.C.). Additional references to Scipio Africanus and Hannibal are found in several other cantos.

76, 5. This line contains a direct allusion to the destruction of Jerusalem announced by Christ (see Mark 13:2, Matthew 24:2, Luke 21:6, and John 11:48).

80–96. Earlier in the canto (44, 5), Pulci has portrayed Astolfo as a man so grief-stricken by his sudden capture by Gano as to be unable to utter a single word. A few stanzas later (62, 2–5 and 63–64), Astolfo, who first pleads for his life and then implores Charlemagne at least not to allow him to be hanged by Gano, is a figure who arouses in the reader a feeling of pity or compassion. The fear-stricken Astolfo depicted in stanzas 80–96 becomes, instead, a truly comical figure. Astolfo's "unrestrained weeping, his laments, his weak reluctance to climb up the gallows' steps, the Maganzans' mocking words, Gano's sarcastic exhortations to go forward, while he looks around bewildered, searching for someone to come and rescue him, are certainly not details which portray the dignified behavior of a paladin being taken to his death" (Momigliano, 205). The episode reaches its climax in stanza 91 (6–8), where Astolfo, in a fit of powerless rage, bangs his head against the ladder. In his "extremely ridiculous rage," writes Momigliano, Astolfo behaves here "like a child who, unable to give vent to his anger in any other way, stamps his feet." In representing Astolfo's personal and military worth being defeated by Gano's malice and deceit, Pulci has enhanced the *vis comica* of the episode. To quote Momigliano (206) again, the portrayal of "force conquered by cunning is often ridiculous."

86, 8. For the reference to Elijah, see Matthew 27:46–47: "And about the ninth hour Jesus cried with a loud voice, saying, *Eli, Eli, lama sabachthami?* That is to say, My God, my God, why hast thou forsaken me?"

93, 2. The proverbial expression used in this line derives from Job's legendary suffering.

103, 3–4 and 107, 1–4. Moments after he has finally accepted his ignominious fate, Astolfo is freed. The rapidity with which the paladin regains his lost strength and, once again on horseback, starts killing Maganzans is as amazing as it is ironically amusing.

109 and 114. By being more interested in saving his life than his royal dignity, Charlemagne gives another poor demonstration of his personal worth. Considering the character of the man, it is not surprising that in stanza 133 the emperor tries to excuse all his past actions by placing the blame on Gano. In the following canto, however, he will pardon Gano and continue to listen to him.

110–133. In a sharply humorous contrast with the terrible things he has vowed to inflict upon Charlemagne (52, 6; 71; 111; and 112, 1–3), Rinaldo, in stanzas 127–131, not only forgives the emperor, but wants him fully reinstated on his throne. The credit for Rinaldo's turnabout belongs to Orlando, who, knowing his cousin's nature only "too well" (121, 7), has waited for the right moment to reveal to him his cleverly concocted dream (122–126). It must be pointed out, however, that Rinaldo's respect and consideration for Charlemagne are of short duration (XIII, 23–24). One could say, in fact, that he forgets as easily as he forgives. Stanzas 128, 8; 130; and 131, 1–4 attest to Rinaldo's considerable knowledge of ancient Roman history. The Count of Montalban's "strange love for classical erudition" makes him, according to Momigliano, "the most learned individual in *Morgante*" as well as "the paladin on whom the influence of fifteenth-century civilization is more greatly felt" (268). The sources Pulci used in the above-mentioned stanzas are, according to Ageno (305–306), Cornelius, Livy, and Petrarch.

131, 3. The "high bird" mentioned here is the Roman eagle that Camillus took back from the Gauls who had occupied the Capitolium. See also note, XXII, 132, 1–2.

CANTO   XII

SUMMARY: Invocation (1). Pardoned by Charlemagne, Gano resumes plotting against Rinaldo with the emperor's knowledge and consent (2–9). Ricciardetto is ambushed and captured by Gano, who hands him over to Charlemagne to be hanged (10–11). In spite of Orlando's threats and the pleas for mercy by almost his entire court, the emperor orders that the gallows be put up (12–22). Having received Astolfo's letter informing him of Ricciardetto's imminent hanging, Rinaldo returns to Paris, frees his brother, kills many Maganzans, and even succeeds in wounding Gano, who is taken back to Maganza by his men (23–26). While Charlemagne flees Paris, Rinaldo sacks and burns the city; then, out of respect for Gallerana, he orders the burning to be stopped (27–31). The Lord of Montalban is crowned emperor, and many of the knights who had left the court to show their disapproval of Charlemagne's actions return to Paris (32–36).

Orlando, who, enraged with his king, had also left Paris, after a month-long trip arrives in Persia. Here he learns that the city ruled by the Admiral, father of the beautiful Chiariella, is besieged by the Sultan and a giant named Marcovaldo, both in love with the Sultan's daughter (37–42). Upon reaching Marcovaldo's pavilion, Orlando and Terigi kill several of the giant's men right in front of him (43–47). The ensuing duel between Orlando and Marcovaldo ends with the death of the giant, who, before expiring, asks Orlando to baptize him (48–71). Their identity unknown to all, Orlando and Terigi arrive at the Admiral's palace, where both the father and the daughter, elated at the news of Marcovaldo's death, welcome them most warmly (72–80). Having been told by a necromancer that Marcovaldo was slain by a Christian, the Sultan writes a letter to the Admiral pledging to avenge the giant's death and offering to make peace with him (80–84). Angry to find out that his two guests are Christians, the Admiral sends for the Sultan. As a result of their meeting,

Orlando and Terigi, captured while asleep, are thrown in a cell at the bottom of a tower (85–89).

3, 5. A proverbial expression meaning "to become daring again" (Ageno, 308).

6, 7. Latin for "Have mercy upon me, o Lord, because I have sinned" (Psalms 51:1–2).

8, 1–8. Torn between desiring to get rid of Rinaldo and not knowing how to make this wish a reality (5, 1–4), Charlemagne gladly accepts Gano's plan, thus becoming his accomplice. In stanza 8 the reader is amused by the emperor's ridiculously hypocritical performance (we have seen the first proof of his duplicity in canto X, 108, 7–8). It would appear as if, through his daily dealings with Gano, Charlemagne has assimilated some of the Lord of Maganza's deceiving nature (Momigliano, 265). Indeed, what makes Charlemagne's presence comical in this portion of the canto is his belief in his own shrewdness, when he is actually a foolish old man who lends Gano a hand in bringing about his own downfall.

10, 6. See note, X, 112, 4.

11, 1–8. Obviously Gano does not consider his second attempt at capturing Rinaldo a failure. Ricciardetto is in fact a better catch for him than Astolfo.

12, 5–8; and 13–15. It is evident that fear and expediency were the only reasons that motivated Charlemagne to forgive Astolfo at the end of canto XI. Not even Orlando's deadly threats can shake his faith in Gano.

20–21. Again, as in the preceding canto, many of Charlemagne's paladins and knights prefer to leave the court, as Orlando has done, rather than openly rebel against their king.

22, 5. Pontier is the name of the castle of Gano of Maganza.

23, 4. See note, II, 60, 4–5.

23, 8. The Vivian mentioned in this verse is Vivian of Pontier, who will be killed by Alardo in stanza 26, 1–4. The attribute "good" used with reference to this Maganzan knight ironically alludes to his skills as a hangman, not to his moral character. He must not be confused with Vivian, brother of Malagigi and one of Charlemagne's paladins.

27, 6. See notes, VI, 27, 1–5 and IX, 10–12.

28, 1–3. While it may be true, as Momigliano argues (266), that in these lines Charlemagne realizes the iniquity and the erroneousness of his actions, it is a fact that his so-called "realization" does not produce any lasting effect. The emperor's opinion of Gano will change only at the very end of the poem. It can be said, therefore, that in stanza 28 Charlemagne acts more like a frightened man than a repented soul.

28, 4–8; and 29–30. Giovanni Getto (96–97), for whom Rinaldo "is without a doubt the most surprisingly inconstant character" in *Morgante,* states that in these verses the Count of Montalban "appears on the scene wrapped in a roguishly plebeian light." Certainly Rinaldo's orders to kill and to sack and burn the city, shouted in rapid succession at the top of his lungs, do make him appear somewhat "plebeian" and less dignified a knight. As we have already noted, however (IX, 25–27), it is a peculiarity of Rinaldo's character to become madly furious when in combat. In this particular instance his rage appears justified since it has been caused by the unopposed attempted hanging of his brother Ricciardetto. Interestingly, when Rinaldo is begged by Gallerana, whom he highly respects, his fury rapidly subsides and the fighting stops.

32, 1–8. If Rinaldo's accession to Charlemagne's throne has taken place with the approval of all, the fear and awe that everyone feels for the paladin's mighty deeds have obviously contributed to this unanimity.

34, 1–8. Here Pulci mockingly argues with his sources and ironically comments upon human weakness (Rinaldo's mother's ardent desire to wear the empress's diadem).

35, 2–3. The Baldovin (also called Baldwin and Baldovino) mentioned here is the son of Ugier the Dane, also known as Scaglion's Lord. The other Baldovin mentioned in *Morgante* is Gano's son (see I, 10, 4).

35, 5. Otho, like his brothers Berlinghier, Avolio, and Avin, is one of Namo's sons (see note, I, 9–10). He must not be confused with the Otho who is king of England and father of Astolfo.

36, 1–8. Getto (54) singles out this stanza as one of those in which Pulci occasionally represents "lively animated scenes of collective merriment and entertainment."

39, 9. In *Morgante,* the Sultan is an Egyptian monarch and Babylon is an Egyptian city (see Ageno, 317).

40, 8 and 41–44, 1–2. It is love for Chiariella, Pulci warns the reader, that has transformed the once wise and brave giant Marcovaldo (the seventh giant we encounter in the poem) into a man who has "lost his wits." To be sure, neither his ridiculously illogical rage when he notices Orlando glancing admiringly at his pavilion, nor his ordering his men to throw Orlando and Terigi out of his camp in blatant disregard of all laws of hospitality is the action of a sane person. He seems, nevertheless, to come back to his senses (stanza 48) when he says that only the Count of Angrante could equal what the knight, whose identity he ignores, has done to his men.

48, 5. The Lord of Angrante is Orlando, who has inherited from his father, Milon, the castle of Angrante.

49 through 62, 1–4. Orlando's logical self-defensive reaction to the attack of Marcovaldo's men sharply contrasts with the giant's irrational behavior. The poet tells us that Orlando—usually a "gentle and discreet" knight, who becomes proud and scornful only when he loses his temper (X, 91, 1–3)—"laughs aloud" upon hearing Marcovaldo compare him to the Lord of Angrante (48, 7). The reader should be aware, however, that every time Orlando smiles or laughs (as in I, 78, 3 and in III, 18, 1 and 19, 3), he does so out of scorn or commiseration. As already noted, not even when laughing does the paladin appear to lose his usually serious countenance. If it is true that his answers, first to Terigi (51, 1–6) and then to Marcovaldo (57 and 59, 1–6), sound hilarious, it is also true that Orlando neither is aware nor intends to be such. He is simply stating things as he sees them: his sword can reach only as high as the giant's belly button; he looks like a frog next to Marcovaldo. The comic element is not in the words per se, but in the situation they portray. The comic figure in this episode is definitely Marcovaldo, who, guilty already of having violated chivalric rules (49), ironically appears to lie even when he is telling the truth (55, 5–8). There is some humorous contrast between what Marcovaldo self-deceivingly believes—that he is better at using the sword than the spear (56, 7–80), that Chiariella is proud of him, and that he can bring her Orlando's head as a gift (58)—and what the giant is actually capable of accomplishing. Notwithstanding all his boastful threats, not only is Marcovaldo easily defeated by a much cooler and superior Orlando (59, 7 and 61–62), but, proving how groundless his amorous hopes were, Chiariella seems hardly grieved at the news of his death (78, 6–7 and 79, 5–8).

69, 1–3. As the story is retold by Ovid, Pyramus is in love with Thisbe, his next-door neighbor. Because of their parents' opposition to their marriage, the two young people decide to leave their homes and meet at night under a big mulberry tree near a cool spring. Frightened by the sudden appearance of a lioness, Thisbe, who was the first to arrive at the established meeting place, seeks refuge in a cave, dropping her veil as she runs. Upon seeing the veil, which the lioness has mangled with her bloody jaws, Pyramus kills himself with his sword, convinced that his beloved has been devoured by a wild animal. Finding Pyramus lying dead under the mulberry tree and realizing what has happened, Thisbe throws herself on his sword and dies. By the will of the gods, the dark-red colored fruits of the mulberry tree are to be a reminder of the blood shed by the two young lovers (*Metamorphoses,* 83–86).

For Angelo Gianni (4–6), "the sad and solemn baptismal ceremony of the dying Marcovaldo, his silent burial, and Orlando's tears" constitute another of the more touching episodes in Pulci's poem (see also note, III, 21–24, 1–4). Of a similar opinion is Getto (91–92), who maintains that while Pulci frequently uses death as a pretext for laughter, in narrating Marcovaldo's demise and in expressing his last wish to be loved, he has composed "extremely beautiful verses." Even if one does not fully subscribe to Gianni's and Getto's opinions, it must be acknowledged that between the stanzas of the rapid, conventional conversion of Marcovaldo (62, 3–8 and 65, 1–6) and those of his death (containing a direct reminiscence of one of Petrarch's most famous songs), it is possible to perceive a definite change in tone. One could say that in dying, Marcovaldo has acquired a human and sentimental dimension that he lacked when alive.

73–79. In these stanzas we have the first close-up presentation of Chiariella, another significant female figure in the poem. The reader is told that this young lady, who has been admiring the Lord of Angrante from afar, has no compunction about telling her father that she would like him to be no other than the great Christian knight Orlando. It is at this point that Orlando, amused by Chiariella's words—her wish has become a reality—smiles once more (74, 6). A few verses later, Chiariella, unable to contain her feelings, runs to embrace the not at all displeased Orlando (78, 6–8). Her gesture provokes Orlando's ironic comment regarding his cousin Rinaldo's behavior were he to be in his place (79, 1–4). In stanza 69, 7–8 Pulci tells us that Orlando delivered "in due time and place" the giant's last message to Chiariella, thus keeping the promise made to Marcovaldo. Interestingly, no further mention of this matter is to be found, either in these stanzas or elsewhere in the poem.

C A N T O   X I I I

SUMMARY: Invocation (1). In love with Orlando, Chiariella becomes, with her father's consent, his jailer and succeeds in having Terigi released from prison (2–13). Upon reaching Paris, Terigi informs Rinaldo of his cousin's imprisonment in the Admiral's palace (14–19). Acting upon Namo's advice, Rinaldo recalls Charlemagne to Paris, gives him back his throne, and, accompanied only by Terigi, Oliver, and Ricciardetto, leaves the court to go and free Orlando (20–28). On the road to Spain, Rinaldo and his companions meet with King Marsilius, whom Rinaldo easily unhorses when the king challenges him to a duel for the possession of Baiardo (29–42). Though aware of Rinaldo's and his friends' true identity, Marsilius invites them all to his palace in Saragossa, where Rinaldo immediately falls in love with the king's beautiful daughter, Luciana (43–50). While at Marsilius's court, Rinaldo gives another demonstration of his great might by taming a huge horse that has been responsible for the deaths of hundreds of men (51–68). This feat accomplished, Rinaldo, Terigi, Oliver, and Ricciardetto take leave from Marsilius, who has promised Rinaldo an army of 20,000 soldiers, and from weeping Luciana (69–70). In a forest near the city of Arma, the paladins find a large number of grieving people and are told that the cause of their affliction is the cruel King Vergante. Having decided to enter Arma, Rinaldo and his companions stop for the night at an inn outside the city (71–76).

1, 4. Here Pulci paraphrases a line of the Lord's Prayer. For the word "manna," see note I, 27, 1–2.
2–14. While in the preceding canto (40, 1–4) Pulci has provided only a brief physical description of the poem's third female figure, in these stanzas he completes the picture by showing the other side of Chiariella's character. A spiritual sister of Meridiana, this young lady possesses as much mind and determination as she has beauty. She therefore does not hesitate to deceive her father to protect the knight she loves, whose deeds remind her of long-admired Orlando. When Chiariella discovers that the man of her dreams and the man she holds captive are one and the same (10–11, 1–3), she declares

herself ready to commit parricide rather than allow Orlando to be killed. She further shows (14, 1) much personal satisfaction in reporting to the count that the plan she devised is working.

22, 1. In medieval Italian city-states the *gonfaloniere* was a high magistrate, later becoming the head of the civilian government. The appointment of Astolfo to such a post would compensate him for the outrage he suffered in canto XII, and would also ensure some degree of protection against Gano's future treacherous plots.

23–25. The insulting tone of Rinaldo's letter leaves no doubt as to the paladin's true feelings toward the emperor. In *Orlando* (XXV, 17, 7–8 through stanza 21, 1–2), instead, Rinaldo, who does not address the emperor as a senile old man as he does here, uses a less disrespectful and more businesslike tone. In fact, after telling him that because of his past actions he deserves to be banished, the Lord of Montalban declares himself willing to forgive Charlemagne, provided that he accept three important conditions: not to wage war against him and his kin, to allow Astolfo to be gonfalonier of the kingdom until the return of Orlando, and to banish Gano for five years.

29, 7–8 through 35. The Spanish king Marsilius, briefly mentioned in canto VIII (32–33) in connection with Erminion, here becomes one of the poem's active characters. With regard to his request that Rinaldo give Baiardo to him, it must be pointed out that his demand is not as outlandish as it may seem. Pulci tells the reader that the Spanish ruler had dreamed about acquiring such a horse, and as Ageno also notes (338), early-morning dreams were deemed to be truthful. Rinaldo, however, who does not believe in such dreams, readily invents an amusing tale which makes fun of Marsilius's convenient pretext to gain his horse. Even though the same tale occurs also in *Orlando* (XXV, 29–35, 1–2), a careful reading of the two versions confirms Pulci's far superior stylistic and creative genius. Thus, what in the anonymous poem is recounted in a linguistically dull, syntactically awkward, and humorless fashion is expressed in *Morgante* with lively immediacy, dynamic style, and colorful humor.

37, 1–4. With regard to the amusing reference to Plato and Trismegistus uttered by Marsilius, Ageno (340) explains that in the Middle Ages the Egyptian god Thoth was to some extent identified with the Grecian Hermes Trismegistus (and his Roman equivalent, Mercury). To Hermes Trismegistus were ascribed various mystical, religious, and philosophical treatises, known today under the title *Corpus Hermeticum*. Beginning with the fourth century A.D., Hermes Trismegistus's doctrines became linked with those of Plato and Pythagoras. Paolo Orvieto (252) maintains that in these lines Pulci is unquestionably talking about Marsilio Ficino, who, before producing his own major philosophical writings, was famous for his translations of Plato and Hermes Trismegistus.

38, 3. Concerning Mount Aetna (*Mongibello* in the Italian text), see note, XVII, 26, 1–2.

41–47. The entire conversation between Marsilius and Rinaldo is marked by a subtly ironic exchange of chivalric courtesies. In this pleasantly amusing "duel of words," the two try to outdo each other.

48–50. Note that Luciana is Rinaldo's first love—a love as sudden as it is short-lived.

51–68. By having Rinaldo tame the wild steed, Pulci perhaps intended to give him (as he did for Oliver in earlier cantos) the opportunity to flaunt his valor before Luciana; yet the episode can hardly be considered out of the ordinary, particularly since so powerful a paladin as Rinaldo is at the center of the action. Indeed, what makes this episode memorable is the humor generated by the unconstrained, ridiculous fear of the page whom Marsilius has assigned to Rinaldo as a guide. His cowardice, already revealed by his actions and words and emphasized by Oliver's and Ricciardetto's comments, has its final, masterful depiction in lines 5–8 of stanza 66. By contrasting the timid behavior of Marsilius's page—whom Momigliano calls the poem's "most fearful pagan" (248)—with the easiness with which an unperturbed Rinaldo has just stunned the wild horse (64, 5–8), the poet has clearly achieved a noteworthy comical effect. In *Orlando* (XXVI, 7–21), the episode of the page told in stanzas 60–63 of Pulci's poem is totally absent. Here Marsilius appoints as Rinaldo's guide not a page, but the same knight who has brought him the news of the murderous horse. The entire event is narrated in an extremely serious fashion, and Rinaldo is presented as humbly asking for God's assistance before facing the devilish animal. The Gisberto who in *Morgante* is mentioned as the owner of the wild horse (51, 7) is identified in the anonymous *cantare popolare* with the nephew of Marsilius, who is killed by the horse in line 55, 2 of Pulci's poem. The Breusse, or *Breus sans pité,* named in stanza 54, 7 is, according to Ageno (345), a character appearing in the romances of the Breton cycle, as well as in Italian popular epics.

71, 5. In canto XIV, 21, 7, this vavasor is called Balante. Note that in the feudal system, a vavasor was a vassal ranking below a baron. The Italian term used by Pulci is *barbassoro,* deriving from the words *valvassore* (vassal) and *barba* (beard).

73, 3. For Trevigant, see note, II, 70, 5.

75–76. For the figure of the inkeeper, see note, XI, 30, 8. In this canto, as well as in cantos XIV and XV, there is no closing religious invocation.

C A N T O   X I V

SUMMARY: Invocation (1). After a restful night at the inn, Rinaldo and his companions enter Arma. Once inside the king's palace, Rinaldo first showers Vergante with insults, then snatches the crown off his head, tears off his royal clock, and finally throws him off one of the palace's balconies (2–11). After a brief sermon, Rinaldo proceeds to baptize Vergante's subjects, who are all rejoicing over the death of their despised tyrant. Among them is Balante, the bearded man Rinaldo met at the end of canto XIII (12–24). A few days later,

Rinaldo, who has declined to be crowned king of Arma, asks for the people's help in freeing Orlando (25–27). In answer to his call, in a month's time a 90,000-man army is assembled, with 10,000 more men led by the giants Corante and Liorgante (28–30). Having refused to follow Rinaldo, Liorgante is easily killed by the Lord of Montalban, who dispatches a messenger to Saragossa to remind Luciana of her promise (31–34). Accompanied by Balugante, Luciana leaves for Arma with 20,000 horsemen (35–39). Once she has joined Rinaldo in Arma, Luciana gives him a rich pavilion where are represented fire, air, sea, and earth, with all the animals that live on it (40–92).

1, 5–6. *Morgante* contains 3,763 stanzas, for a total of 30,104 lines. While cantos I–XIV number 1,305 stanzas (or 10,440 lines), cantos XV–XXVIII total 2,458 stanzas (or 19,664 verses). In view of the above data, Pulci's assertion that he is "midway" through his work (1, 5–6) is hardly accurate. The last fourteen cantos of the poem, in fact, contain 88 percent more stanzas than the first fourteen cantos (2,458 as opposed to 1,305). Since the comment expressed in lines 5–6 is also found in the first and second twenty-three-canto edition of *Morgante,* Ageno (353) argues that it is possible that when Pulci made this comment, he was not thinking of dividing his poem according to the number of cantos, but rather according to the number of stanzas (1,213 in cantos I–XIII and 1,444 in cantos XIV–XXIII). The plausibility of Ageno's thesis is supported by the fact that without the long episode of Margutte in cantos XVIII and XIX, which was not included in the first and second editions of the work, the number of stanzas contained in cantos I–XIII is about equal to that of cantos XIV–XXIII. It is quite possible that Pulci either forgot or did not bother to make any change with regard to this point in his final twenty-eight-canto version of *Morgante.*

7–10, 1–4. Getto, for whom these stanzas constitute "a true verbal orgy," identifies in them Pulci's penchant for choosing words capable of creating particular sounds (155–156). It must be noted that the paladin's contemptuous tirade against Vergante is absent in the corresponding stanzas of *Orlando* (XXVII, 3–XXVIII, 15).

9, 5. Reference is made here to the nymph Echo, whom the goddess Hera condemned never to be able to begin a conversation, but only to repeat the words of others. Having fallen in love with Narcissus, Echo was spurned by the beautiful youth and, her body consumed by grief, became only a voice to be heard among the mountains (see Ovid's *Metamorphoses,* "The Story of Echo and Narcissus," III, 67–69).

10, 7–8. It is hilarious that Vergante's subjects, though pagans, resort to a Christian motto to express their wholehearted agreement with Rinaldo's assessment of their king.

12–21, 1. The mass conversion of the people of Vergante is the most joyous, the noisiest, and, certainly for Rinaldo, the most strenuous catechistical effort. It takes place just outside the palace's main gate, where Rinaldo, standing as on a pulpit, faces a square filled with the dead tyrant's subjects.

The paladin's concluding exhortation to embrace Christianity (17, 7–8) is met by the shouted unanimous reply of the crowd (18, 3–8; 19, 1–4; and 20, 2–3). Indeed, the scene resembles a political rally.

When this canto of *Morgante* is compared with the previously mentioned cantos XXVII and XXVIII of *Orlando,* some important differences become evident. In the anonymous *cantare popolare,* the Count of Montalban's decision to enter Arma seems to be dependent upon the innkeeper's assurance that Vergante's subjects will not go to war for their king. Additionally, when Rinaldo and his companions near Vergante's palace, they first hear the sorrowful laments of the young ladies held captive in it, and then Rinaldo engages in a conversation with some of these girls who have appeared at the windows of their prison. Having received their assurance that they are ready to become Christians, Rinaldo promises to free them. Consequently he dispatches Oliver to Vergante to request the immediate release of all his prisoners. Irritated at Oliver's words, Vergante orders his barons to seize him. In the ensuing scuffle, Oliver kills two of Vergante's men, while, attracted by the commotion, Rinaldo and Ricciardetto enter the royal hall. Without uttering a word, the Count of Montalban grabs the king, lifts him up, and throws him down from a window. Vergante's followers immediately kneel before Rinaldo, pledging loyalty to him. The paladin urges them to embrace Christianity, since it has been demonstrated that "their Mahound is not worth a cent" (XXVII, 19, 4).

33, 7–8 and 34, 1. The ludicrous description of Liorgante's death is rendered clumsy by the striking contrast generated by the two hyperboles, the first of which compares the giant to "a small chicken" and the second to "a mighty tower" (Momigliano, 172).

38, 1. Balugante (also called Balugant) is a captain in Luciana's army.

40, 6–8. Concerning these two lines, Momigliano (234) acutely observes that Rinaldo's words sound more like a joking remark than the expression of passionate love.

43, 6. Athena (or Athene), born out of Zeus's head and better known as the goddess of war, was also the goddess of arts and crafts. Pulci's reference to Athena derives here from her fame as patroness of women engaged in spinning, embroidering, and weaving.

45–84. With regard to the stanzas which describe the elaborately decorated tent that Luciana has donated to Rinaldo, Ageno observes that the animals listed here are more or less those we find in the bestiaries of the time (see M. S. Garver and K. McKensie, "Il bestiario toscano secondo la lezione dei codici di Parigi e di Londra," *Studi Romanzi* VIII [1912]: 1–100, and Cecco d'Ascoli [Francesco Stabili], *Acerba,* Ridotta a miglior lezione dal prof. dott. A Crespi [Ascoli Piceno, 1927]). Ageno further adds that the "greater richness in Pulci's enumeration, with respect to medieval bestiaries ... derives from his direct and factual knowledge of the animal world" (364). Of the same opinion is John Raymond Shulters, author of *Luigi Pulci and the Animal Kingdom* (Baltimore: J. H. Furst Company, 1920), a work which Ageno was unable to see. Commenting upon the lack of a systematized study of Pulci's use of the animal kingdom in his poem, "either for the purpose of correlating it with fable and bestiary literature or of calling attention to its literary value, which in many cases is not small," Shulters declares that the poet's "acquaintance with the animal kingdom grew, doubtless, out of the hunts and fishing excursions of the Court and he must have exercised an immense observation and have felt a certain attraction towards the beasts and birds of his native forests" (3–4). Shulters further maintains that in *Morgante* "the literary worth of the beast episodes lies almost always in their humorous quality" (4), and he adds that in his poem Pulci has succeeded in rendering "ridiculous the story told as fact in the bestiaries" (5). (For a detailed discussion of Pulci's use of animals in this canto, where 315 of the 360 animals that appear in the poem are named, see Shulters's "The Padiglione Episode," 7–40.) It is interesting to note that in canto XXVIII of *Orlando,* the description of Luciana's pavilion ends with stanza 15; since stanzas 2 to 13 are missing, the anonymous poet dedicated only a few stanzas to this episode.

The stanzas about Luciana's pavilion have been more recently investigated by Paolo Orvieto, who, in his attempt to define the poet's originality and writing technique, has found close and "unexpected connections" between Pulci's masterpiece and such works as *Rinaldo da Montalbano, Uggieri il Danese, Falconetto, Il padiglione di Fierabraccio,* and *La Reina Ancroia* (see chapter IV of Orvieto's *Pulci medievale,* particularly pp. 133–142). Orvieto's findings are fully subscribed to by Maria Pia Ratti, who, while recognizing in the episode of Luciana's pavilion the poet's debt to the well-established tradition of the bestiaries in the *cantari popolari,* does not fail to point out, in the first part of the story of Rinaldo's encounter with the lion about to be killed by a dragon (IV, 7–16), Pulci's debt to the *Yvain* of Chrétien de Troyes (see "Avaler la tradition: sul bestiario del *Morgante,*" *Lettere Italiane* 42, 2 [aprile–giugno 1990]: 264–275). The literary value of this portion of canto XIV is acknowledged also by both Giovanni Getto (158–159) and Angelo Gianni (118–124), in whose opinion it would be a mistake to consider it simply a list.

45, 5–6. Pulci derives the expression "eternal love" from Dante's *Purgatorio* (III, 134) and *Paradiso* (VII, 33 and XXIX, 18). The phrase "fire of eternal love" reoccurs also in canto XXVII, 156, 3.

45, 7–8. Ageno (364–365) explains that according to an ancient tradition, the salamander, the chameleon, the anchovy, and the mole corresponded to the four elements—fire, air, water, and earth, respectively—in which these animals lived.

46, 3–6. Pulci's source for these verses was certainly Dante's *Inferno,* canto XIV, 52–57. The "twelve signs" are those of the zodiac.

47, 1–6. The story of the eagle is narrated in *Il bestiario toscano* and in *Acerba* (Ageno, 365).

47, 7–8. Information about the phoenix is contained in several works, such as *Acerba, Fabulistes latins,* and Lattanzio's *De ave phoenice* (Ageno, 366).

49, 1. It is a well-known fact that falcons were used for hunting as early as Roman times. Interestingly, in stanza 11, 1–4 of his *Uccellagione di starne* (also known as *Caccia col falcone*), Lorenzo de' Medici asks where Luigi Pulci, one of the hunters, has gone, since his voice is no longer heard (see *Opere,* ed. Luigi Cavalli [Napoli: Casa Editrice Fulvio Rossi, 1970], 61).

51, 1–2. See note, XI, 1, 1–3.

53, 2–5. In these lines Pulci briefly alludes to the Sienese fool who, having bought from a farmer a woodpecker that he believed to be a parrot, eventually donated it to Pope Pius II, during the pontiff's visit to his native Corsignano, near Siena, in the fall of 1462. This story was narrated by Pulci in a novella, written probably in 1471, which he dedicated to Madonna Ippolita Maria Sforza, wife of Alphonse of Aragon, the duke of Calabria. (For the text of this novella, see Luigi Pulci, *Opere Minori,* ed. Paolo Orvieto [Milano: Mursia, 1986], 125–131. For a discussion concerning its date of composition, its paternity, and its political implications, see Stefano Carrai, "La novella di Pulci," in *Le muse dei Pulci,* Studi su Luca e Luigi Pulci [Napoli: Guida editori, 1985, 53–74].) The comical and literary worth of this minor Pulci work is also debated by Momigliano (208–212), who considers it essentially a satire on the simplemindedness of the people of Siena.

54, 6. According to Genesis (8:6–8), the raven was the first bird to leave Noah's Ark at the end of the forty days.

55, 1–2. Citing the *Bestiario toscano,* Ageno (370) explains that the vain peacock is saddened when it looks down at its feet and sees how ugly they are.

56, 4–6. A direct reference to a legend dating back to classical times which maintains that white swans sing more melodiously when they are near death.

59, 4. Both the beccafico (a warbler) and the ortolan are small European birds.

61, 8. The griffon (or griffin) was a fabulous bird with the head and wings of an eagle and the body of a lion.

62, 1–8. Juno, wife of Jupiter, was the Roman counterpart of the Greek goddess Hera. Deiopeia was one of her most beautiful nymphs. Aeolus, keeper of the winds, was king of the Aeolian Islands, where he lived with his wife and family. He kept all the winds, among them Notus (the south wind) and Aquilon (the north wind), confined in a great cave, releasing them at will or when requested by another god. Orion, a giant-sized hunter related to Poseidon, was said to have been slain by mistake by Artemis, daughter of Zeus and sister of Apollo. To commemorate the demise of her hunting companion, Artemis placed Orion in the sky as a constellation.

63, 1–4. For the well-known story of Daedalus and Icarus, as well as the myth of Phaëthon, son of Helios and Clymene, see *Metamorphoses,* VIII, 187–189, and "The Story of Phaethon," II, 28–40.

64, 6–8. Ageno (374) remarks that this was probably a belief of popular origin, which is found neither in medieval bestiaries nor in Ovid's *Metamorphoses.*

65, 4–8. The crab's crafty behavior is recounted in *Acerba* (Ageno, 374).

69, 1–8. A direct reference to the myth of the Argonauts, who sailed the Black Sea in quest of the Golden Fleece, which was believed to be kept in the land of Cholchis. Tiphys was the young Greek steersman of the ship *Argo*. Once a beautiful virgin, Scylla was transformed by Glaucus into a monster who devoured any sailor venturing through the Straits of Messina. A minor sea goddess, Thetis was forced by Zeus to marry a mortal, Peleus, who fathered her a son, Achilles.

70, 1–8. Cymothoe and Triton are mentioned in Virgil's *Aeneid* (I, 142–145). Originally a fisherman, Glaucus was transformed into a minor sea god when he ate a prodigious herb. He became a favorite patron of sailors. According to Ovid, Aesacus, remorseful for having unwillingly caused the death of Hesperia, whom he loved, threw himself into the sea, but was changed into a diver bird by Tethis (see "Story of Aesacus and Hesperia," *Metamorphoses*, XI, 282–284). Polyphemus is the one-eyed cyclops blinded in Homer's *Odyssey* at the hands of Ulysses. He was in love with the beautiful sea nymph Galatea, who despised him.

71, 5. The sagittae were long, oar-propelled boats (Ageno, 377).

73, 1–2. By describing the elephant as "all one piece in front," Pulci obviously follows the belief expressed in medieval bestiaries. Being deprived of joints, the elephant was said to be forced to sleep leaning on a tree (Ageno, 378). This sleeping habit of elephants is stated in canto XVIII, 161, 1–2.

74, 1. Citing *Acerba* as her source, Ageno (378) writes that according to an ancient belief, the jackal would assist the lion in catching its prey, while the lion, in turn, would let the jackal eat the remainder of its meals.

74, 5–8. This peculiar habit of the beaver is outlined in the *Bestiario toscano* (Ageno, 378).

75, 3–8. A mythical animal, the unicorn eventually came to symbolize chastity and even Christ. Its penchant for falling asleep at the feet of a young virgin is also told in the *Bestiario toscano* (Ageno, 379).

76, 7–8. The belief that a deer could be put into a trance by a singing voice is found in *Acerba* (Ageno, 379).

81, 2–4 and 82, 1–2. The stories of the dragon crushed by the elephant it had killed, and the crocodile's curious habit of crying over the man it has just devoured are retold in *Acerba*, where the crocodile typifies hypocrisy (Ageno, 381).

82, 3–6. As explained by Ageno (381), this strange behavior of the asp is mentioned not only in ancient texts, but also in early Italian lyric and in medieval bestiaries.

82, 7–8. The legendary belief that this mythical creature could kill with its breath or look gave rise to several proverbial expressions. For a discussion of Pulci's sources with regard to this matter, see Ageno (382).

83, 1. The cerastes is one of the several types of snakes Pulci lists in his *Vocabolista* (Ageno, 382).

84, 5–7. The ancients believed that a great number of dreadful reptiles, generated by drops of blood fallen from Medusa's head, inhabited the Libyan desert. Among these were snakes called "chelydri," "jaculi," and "phareans" (see Lucan's *Pharsalia*, XI, 708–721, and "The Story of Perseus" in Ovid's *Metamorphoses*, IV, 101). The same reptiles are named in canto XXIV (85–87) of Dante's *Inferno*.

85, 4–8; and 86, 1. Persephone, Proserpina for the Romans, was the only child of Zeus and Demeter, whom the Romans worshiped as Ceres, goddess of agriculture. Kidnapped, with her father's consent, by Hades, Zeus's brother, called Pluto by the Romans, Persephone spent one-third of the year in the underworld with Hades, and the rest of the time with her mother.

87, 4. For Philomela, see note, I, 3, 1–4.

87, 5–8; and 88, 1–8. How much credence the reader should give to Rinaldo's overstated profession of love for Luciana is a question that will soon be resolved. Certainly, when Rinaldo's speech is compared with Luciana's simple yet eloquent words, the sincerity of her feelings far overshadows that of her inconstant lover.

C A N T O   X V

SUMMARY: Invocation (1). Rinaldo, Balante, and Luciana leave for Persia with an army of 120,000 men. Upon their arrival in the Admiral's lands, Rinaldo dispatches Ricciardetto to challenge the Admiral to a duel (2–10). Chiariella reveals to her father the real identity of his prisoner and suggests that he send Orlando to fight with Rinaldo. The Admiral promptly agrees, requesting Orlando's pledge to return to prison after the combat (11–13). Orlando, together with Chiariella and three hundred horsemen, leaves the city for Rinaldo's camp, where they are met by the Lord of Montalban, Luciana, and an equal number of armed men (14–20). Not recognizing each other, the two cousins fight a long, fierce duel, first on horseback and then on foot. When night falls, the duel is interrupted, and both parties agree to resume it in twenty days (21–36).

Rinaldo goes back to his camp with Luciana, and Orlando returns to the city with Chiariella (38–39). With five hundred of his best troops, the giant Corante slaughters many of the Admiral's men. Begged by Chiariella, Orlando prepares to face the giant (40–45). Seeing Corante waiting for them outside the city walls, Chiariella wants to be the first to fight with him, but the giant easily throws her from her horse (46–47). While Orlando exchanges heated words with Corante, Copardo, Chiariella's brother, attacks the giant, who unhorses him and takes him prisoner (48–51). Insulted by Orlando, Corante hurls himself at the count, who kills him (52–54). Having revealed to Rinaldo that Corante was killed by Orlando, Copardo promises the paladin to help him gain access to the city (55–60).

Released by Rinaldo, Copardo returns to his father's palace, where he and his sister decide to betray their father. Chiariella, ready to become a Christian, frees Orlando, who in turn sends a messenger to Rinaldo advising him to come to the city the following night (61–71). Having joined Orlando, Chiariella, and Copardo through an open gate, Rinaldo and his men storm the city. Awakened by the confusion, the Admiral mounts his horse, but is effortlessly killed by Oliver (72–75). While the giant Grandono unhorses both Oliver and Luciana, Orlando mistakenly unhorses Ricciardetto and Terigi (76–84). After a night of relentless fighting, the inhabitants of the city put down their arms (85–86). The Admiral is buried, Copardo is declared king and Chiariella queen, while Rinaldo rules the city and Orlando spends most of his time with Chiariella (87–89). Upon receiving news of the Admiral's demise, the Sultan, who arrogantly claims for himself the Admiral's lands (90–94), sends a messenger to Rinaldo. Rinaldo kills the messenger, and, adhering to his daughter Antea's request, the Sultan sends her as his envoy to Rinaldo (95–97). The last stanzas of the canto contain a description of Antea's beauty and her marvelous steed (98–112).

9, 1. In *Morgante* the cities of Carrara (see note, IV, 42, 8) and Arma are both located in Morocco.

11–18. Luciana's presence in this canto is perfunctory. Until Antea's appearance on the scene (stanzas 98–112), in fact, Chiariella is the canto's dominant female figure. She is a person who knows how to do the right thing at the right time. Seeing her father torn between indecision and fear, she seizes the opportunity to reveal to him the true identity of his prisoner, suggesting that Orlando could fight against his challenger. Then, to prevent any possible objection on his part, she explains that Orlando will do anything she asks of him because of his love for her. To be sure, the Admiral's illogical request (13, 1–4) is further proof of the cowardly and scheming nature of the man, who tries to hide his fears behind either a facade of raging arrogance (5–7, 1–6) or humble expressions of contrition (17). What matters to Chiariella the most— she has fallen in love with Orlando because of his fame as the greatest of knights (XII, 73–74)—is the count's well-being; thus she can be completely honest with Orlando while showing no compunction about deceiving and then betraying her own father. The Admiral, guilty also of having violated the almost sacred law of hospitality (XII, 87–88), hardly deserves his children's respect and affection.

24, 5–8. Through a direct intervention, Pulci ironically comments on his hyperbolic comparisons of Rinaldo and Orlando with Marcellus, the Roman conqueror of the city of Syracuse, and the Carthaginian general Hannibal, as well as the Greek warriors Hector and Achilles.

25–35. The duel between Orlando and Rinaldo, the second fought by the two cousins, each unaware of the other's identity, is as fierce as it is amusing. The paladins' exaggerated fury, Orlando's sudden fear and his calling to the Virgin for assistance, the incredible cutting blow of Rinaldo's Frusberta, and the ongoing conversation between two raging knights are vividly and comically portrayed.

42–49. Chiariella, whose gracious intervention has put a temporary end to Orlando's and Rinaldo's duel (stanza 36), again begs the count to come to the aid of her people against the giant Corante. Then she too, as Meridiana has often done, wants to prove her military worth (46–47). Chiariella is no match for Corante, and thus there is nothing comical about her being thrown off her horse, even when Orlando seriously tries to justify her fall by blaming her mount.

50. Note that in his sarcastic answer to Corante, Orlando too—as Oliver and Rinaldo did in canto IV with regard to Forisena—compares Chiariella to food.

56, 4–8. Momigliano (260–270) sees in these lines a further demonstration of Rinaldo's comic boasting.

63, 1–5. What the Admiral tells his son in these lines appears to justify Copardo's recent decision to help Rinaldo gain possession of his father's realm.

68–69. Orlando's reply to Chiariella's revelation (65–67) is indicative of the true nature of the count's feelings for the princess. His Petrarch-like addressing of Chiariella as his angel and his star, as well as his metaphorical pledge of eternal love, appears to be marked more by literary influences than by heartfelt emotion. If it is true that his words speak of love, and he seems to enjoy Chiariella's company greatly (89, 5), it is equally true that his actions tell a different story. In canto XVI, in fact, when he is about to leave for Babylon to free Oliver and Ricciardetto from the Sultan's prisons, Orlando will put an abrupt end to Chiariella's amorous hopes, ordering her to marry Balante (93)—hardly the behavior of a passionate lover.

70, 8. This line shows that Chiariella, Orlando's angelic woman, is, when necessary, a shrewd plotter.

71, 5. This expression, used metaphorically to indicate that someone has been hanged, occurs several times in *Morgante*.

73–75, 1–5. The Admiral's final appearance in the poem completes Pulci's portrait of the man. His inglorious death and Oliver's unhappy encounter with the giant Grandono just a few stanzas later (77–79, 1–4) are among the canto's most humorous episodes.

79, 6–8; and 80–84. It often happens that in the heat of battle, particularly when, as Pulci ironically remarks, "night and madness" rule (77, 8), pagans (Grandono) as well as Christians (Orlando) mistakenly hit their friends together with their enemies. In telling Terigi that darkness may cause such errors, Orlando does not intend to be funny; he simply recognizes one of the unfortunate accidents of war.

88, 4. Though presumably still taken by Luciana's charms, Rinaldo cannot refrain from enthusiastically expressing his admiration for beautiful Chiariella, a woman with whom he could easily fall in love.

90, 2. Bambillona (Babylon), a city famous for its beautiful buildings and its hanging gardens, was the center of a great civilization that flourished between 2800 and 1750 B.C. It was the capital of Babylonia, a region situated between the Euphrates and the Tigris rivers. In the year 538 B.C., Cyrus, king of Persia, annexed it to his empire.

93–95. The foolish arrogance and total lack of diplomatic skills of the vavasor indeed provoke Rinaldo's extreme reaction. In its rapidity, the scene acquires a remarkable *vis comica*. As Momigliano rightly acknowledges (190), "few poets can equal Pulci in portraying the comicity of details with the greatest possible simplicity of means."

96–104. Pulci, who has dedicated only twelve lines to Meridiana's physical description (VI, 17 and 18, 1–4), here uses nine stanzas to introduce Antea to the reader. It is, however, in the first two stanzas—96 and 97—that, in my opinion, Antea comes to life as a real character. Her succinct and yet most persuasive conversation with her father is, in fact, more revealing of her personality than our poet's lavish description of her physical beauty and personal qualities.

Commenting upon these stanzas, Getto (71) observes that Pulci's unusual physical description of Antea, with all its mythological references, resulted in the creation of "an elegant and happy doll," rather than the portrait of a real woman. Momigliano (235), for whom Rinaldo's passion for Antea is more amply treated than his love for Luciana, maintains that the hyperbolic physical description of the Sultan's daughter may provoke in the reader a smile rather than a feeling of admiration.

In his *Pulci medievale,* Paolo Orvieto dedicates two chapters (48–105) to Antea and the description of her horse. Examining some traditional *topoi,* such as those of feminine beauty and of the perfect steed, the critic discusses the changes worked by Pulci in dealing with them. By comparing the description of Antea with that of a young woman in Boccaccio's *Teseida* (XII, 53–56), Orvieto clearly shows the presence of the same matrix in the *topos* of beauty, not only as it occurs in the poetry of Pulci but also in that of Lorenzo the Magnificent and Poliziano. The difference, where it exists, is determined primarily by a question of choice and combination. According to Orvieto, the sources of the episode of Antea must be traced back to medieval romances and traditional lyric poetry. The same can be said with regard to the portrait of Antea's horse (stanzas 105–107), which reveals, in its repetition of the traditional pattern, a definite derivation from some of the better-known medieval texts, among them the numerous *De bestiis,* with which the Florentine poet was either directly or indirectly acquainted. Incidentally, Orvieto does not fail to observe that Pulci's more traditional description of the perfect horse differs considerably from the more poetic and individualistic ones we find in Lorenzo's and Poliziano's writings.

99, 1. For this reference to Daphne, see note, III, 17, 6–7.

99, 8. Pallas was a commonly used title for the goddess Athena (see note, XIV, 43, 6).

100, 8 and 101, 1. Regarding Proserpina and Deiopeia, see notes, XIV, 85, 4–8 and 62, 1–8.

102, 1–8. In this stanza, where Ageno (411–412) believes that Pulci continues the parody of love poetry he began in stanza 91, are references to Dante's *Paradiso,* Petrarch's *Rime,* Ovid's *Fasti* and *Metamorphoses,* as well as the first book of the Bible. The stories of Joseph (who rejected Potiphar's wife's request to make love to her) and Rachel (Laban's daughter, for whom Jacob served her father for seven years) are told in Genesis 39:6–12 and 29:15–20. For the story of Narcissus, see note, XIV, 9, 5.

105–107. While Meridiana's unusual horse was generated by the mating of an Arab mare with a serpent (IX, 6061, 1–3), there is nothing magical about Antea's perfect charger.

109, 1. Camilla, a fierce woman warrior, daughter of the king of the Volscians, is mentioned at the end of book VII of Virgil's *Aeneid.* An Amazon queen, Penthesileia, having become an ally of the Trojans, killed many Greeks and was then slain by Achilles, who fell in love with her corpse (see *The Meridian Handbook of Classical Antiquity,* 461).

109, 3–5. Antea's magic armor, forged in Damascus, a city famous for its arms and silks, is the reason why she will be able to come through Orlando's onslaught in canto XVI unharmed.

111, 5. Baal was the first, god-like king of the Assyrians. Ninus, Baal's son, was celebrated as the founder of the city of Nineveh.

C A N T O   X V I

SUMMARY: Invocation (1). Antea, most graciously received by Rinaldo, Orlando, Chiariella, and Luciana, delivers her message: the Admiral's land must be returned to her father, the Sultan. If her request is denied, Rinaldo must face her in combat. If she is defeated, she will leave immediately for Persia; but if she wins, the Sultan will regain possession of the Admiral's lands (2–17). Rinaldo accepts the challenge and, realizing that he is in love with Antea (as she is with him), asks her to spend a day as the paladins' honored guest before returning to her father (18–28). Stanzas 29 to 61 contain Rinaldo's lovesick laments and Orlando's exhortations to his cousin not to neglect his duties. When, however, Rinaldo comes face to face with Antea, he turns his horse around, refusing to fight (62–66). Oliver and Ricciardetto, who have taken up Rinaldo's fight, are easily unhorsed by Antea and become her prisoners (67–72). While Rinaldo looks on, hoping for the count's defeat, Orlando and Antea duel for an entire day with no success (73–82).

In the meantime Gano, meeting with the Sultan, persuades him to return to Persia, taking Oliver and Ricciardetto along with him (83–88). Consequently, Rinaldo and Orlando decide to follow the Sultan to Babylonia in order to gain Oliver's and Ricciardetto's freedom. Before leaving, however, they put Chiariella and Balante, who have been married on Orlando's order, in charge of the Admiral's lands, and send Luciana back to Saragossa (89–95).

On their way to Persia, Orlando and Rinaldo encounter five giants, kill two, and are separated (96–103). Having liberated King Costanzo's daughter from the giants, Orlando and the girl start searching for Rinaldo (104–105). While Rinaldo is asleep, his horse is stolen by a shepherd, who promptly sells it to the Sultan's hangman. The Lord of Montalban is thus forced to reach the city of Babylon on foot (106–117).

1, 4. See note, I, 2, 4.

3–4. Antea's intention to impress Rinaldo, Orlando, and all their companions with a remarkable demonstration of her outstanding military skills and exceptional equestrian mastery does obtain the desired effect. Clearly the Syrian princess is portrayed by Pulci as a woman whose bravery and intelligence perfectly match her beauty. This brief though important detail is not to be found in canto XXXI of *Orlando*, where the anonymous poet—during Antea's conversation with the Sultan (7–8) and at the moment of her appearance before the paladins (13)—mainly stresses the princess's proud reliance upon the irresistible effects that her beauty exerts on all men, be they pagans or Christians.

6–17. Note the abysmal difference between the vavasor's insolent message in canto XV, 93–94 and Antea's carefully constructed and masterfully delivered speech. It is a splendid diplomatic performance, in which the princess, having invoked God's assistance to all parties concerned, combines feminine grace with an appeal to reason, a justified expression of outrage, and the right measure of firmness. It develops in two distinct moments, of five stanzas each (6–10 and 13–17), only briefly interrupted by Antea's halfhearted condemnation of Chiariella and Copardo (11–12).

7, 3. See note, VIII, 38, 6.

12, 1–4. A further reference to Petrarch's *Rime* (Ageno, 419).

14, 5–6. The giants Chiariello and Brunamonte, Mambrino's brothers (see note, canto III, 32, 8), appear in the prose epic *Rinaldo da Montalbano*, where one reads that, having slain cruel Brunamonte, Rinaldo also kills Chiariello, even though the latter is helped by a lion. This is why Rinaldo bears the figure of a lion as insignia on his armor (Ageno, 419–420).

17–21. Commenting upon these stanzas, Angelo Gianni (23–24) maintains that, at least at the beginning, the sudden, mutual falling in love of Rinaldo and Antea is one of the poem's "most linear and moving" episodes. The critic, however, believes that when Pulci wishes to elevate the tone of the story with the addition of a rhetorical passage, "the suggestive quality of his stanzas is shattered." Rinaldo's nocturnal laments (30–45, 1–2) constitute just such a case for Gianni.

22–23. Here Rinaldo falls in love with Antea as quickly as he fell in love with Luciana in canto XIII (49–50). The Lord of Montalban, however, is so overtaken by this new love that he is unable to personally attend to Antea as he did to Luciana. Thus his request to Oliver to supervise the banquet he gives in her honor. The ironic quality of this comment by Oliver, who is hardly a paragon of fidelity, cannot escape the reader. Interestingly, Oliver's remark concerning Luciana's romantic misfortune—which is revealing of Luigi Pulci's constant mocking presence in the poem—is missing in *Orlando*, where Oliver's answer to Rinaldo's request is simply, "I will do what you asked" (XXXI, 23, 4).

25, 7. The cittern was a pear-shaped musical instrument consisting of a soundbox and numerous wire strings stretched over it. The decachord, as the name implies, was another ancient instrument, having no more than ten strings.

26, 2. Granada, the last Moorish stronghold in Spain, was conquered in 1492 by King Ferdinand. It is located in the western mountain region of Andalusia.

29, 2–8 through 41, 1–2. Barely able to control his tears upon Antea's departure (27, 3–8), Rinaldo, once alone in his room, gives vent to his inner feelings in a highly rhetorical, conventional fashion. To develop the concept that had Antea lived in ancient times, no man would have been able to love another woman, Pulci uses almost twelve stanzas, replete with numerous mythological references, mostly of Ovidian derivation.

31, 1–8. Having fallen in love with Europa, King Phoenix's beautiful daughter, Zeus transformed himself into a gentle white bull, and thus was able to carry her on his back to Crete, where she became the god's mistress. Struck by Ganymede's exceptional beauty, Zeus was also said to have abducted the youth to be his cupbearer in heaven (*The Meridian Handbook of Classical Mythology*, 239 and 248). For the references to Daphne and Phoebus, see note, III, 17, 6–7.

32, 1–4. Admetus, king of the Thessalian city of Pherae, treated with great respect and kindness Apollo, whom Zeus had condemned to spend a year in servitude to a mortal as punishment for killing the Cyclops who had assisted Zeus against Asclepius (*The Meridian Handbook of Classical Mythology*, 11–12). For the story of Jacob and Rachel, see note, XV, 102.

33, 1–6. Flying over Ethiopia carrying with him the head of Medusa, whom he had killed following Athena's instructions, Perseus, king of Mycenae, saw beautiful Andromeda chained to a rock by the sea. Having learned from her father, King Cepheus, that she had been placed there to placate a sea monster, Perseus asked for her hand in marriage in return for her rescue. During the nuptial banquet, Phineus, who had been promised Andromeda as a bride by his brother Cepheus, came with many armed men to claim her for himself. To save his life, Perseus was forced to take Medusa's head out of its pouch, thus instantly turning Phineus and his followers to stone (*The Meridian Handbook of Classical Mythology*, 465–468). Reference is made here to Hippolytus, whose tragic destiny is the topic of two famous plays, Euripides' *Hippolytus* and Seneca's *Phaedras*. Hippolytus, son of Theseus, king of Athens, having spurned his father's wife's love, was accused of rape by Phaedra before she hanged herself. For the story of Orpheus and Eurydice, see note, II, 38, 4.

Seeing Arethusa bathing in his river, Alpheius, god of the river of Elis, fell in love with the beautiful nymph and, in human form, pursued her. To escape the god, Arethusa was transformed by Diana, at her request, into a spring (*The Meridian Handbook of Classical Mythology*, 39).

34, 1–6. A virgin huntress who wanted to remain forever a maiden, Atalanta declared that she would marry only the man who could run faster than she. Where many young men had lost their heads in the attempt (all losers were decapitated), Hippomenes succeeded. He achieved this feat by dropping, one by one as he ran, the three golden apples that the goddess Aphrodite (Venus) had given him. When Atalanta, overconfident in her superior powers, stopped to pick up the third apple, which her suitor had thrown as far away as possible, she was unable to catch up with Hippomenes, who thus won the race and her hand (*The Meridian Handbook of Classical Mythology*, 100–111). According to Ovid's *Heroides,* Acontius, too poor to be able to ask for Cydippe's hand in marriage, managed one day to send her an apple on which he had written "I swear to belong forever to Acontius." Cydippe, by unknowingly reading aloud Acontius's words before Diana, was forced to marry him in spite of his poverty. Since it is stated in *Morgante* that the name written on the apple is that of Cydippe, Pulci, Ageno notes (425), was less than accurate in reporting this story.

34, 7–8; and 35. A reference to the golden apple which bore the inscription "For the Fairest." It eventually led to the Trojan War, after Paris adjudged it to Aphrodite, who had offered him as a reward the love of Helen, wife of Menelaus, king of Sparta (*The Meridian Handbook of Classical Mythology*, 446–448). For Narcissus, see note, XIV, 9, 5.

36, 1–8. In his *Heroides,* Ovid tells that every night Leander of Abydos swam across the Dardanelles to reach his beloved Ero, who would wait for him on the beach of Sestos holding a torch to guide him. One stormy night, however, the wind extinguished Ero's torch, and Leander, having lost all sense of direction as well as his strength, perished at sea. When Ero saw the body of her beloved lying lifeless on the beach the next morning, she plunged into the sea, where she drowned. Ageno (426) explains that Pulci probably derived the detail of the dolphin (line 3) from Boccaccio's *Elegia di Madonna Fiammetta.* For Polyphemus and Galatea, see note, XIV, 70, 1–8.

37, 1–7. Hippolyte, queen of the Amazons, often confused with her sister Antiope, was said to have been Theseus's wife. During his adventures in Crete, Theseus killed the Minotaur and, thanks to the ball of thread given him by Ariadne, was able to find his way out of Minos's Labyrinth. Having taken Ariadne with him, Theseus, according to a version Pulci followed, eventually abandoned her for love of Aegle, whom he later married. Ageno (427) believes instead that the woman for whom Theseus left Ariadne was her sister Phaedra (for the complete story of Theseus, see *The Meridian Handbook of Classical Mythology*, 562–672). Palaemon and Arcita, mentioned in line 5, are the protagonists of Boccaccio's *Teseida.* For the reference to Pyramus, see note, XII, 69, 1–3.

39, 6. According to Ovid, Peleus's spear had the prodigious property of healing the wounds it inflicted (Ageno, 427).

In his perceptive and stimulating analysis of Rinaldo's and Antea's love affair, Attilio Momigliano (236–243) writes that, moved to pity, Pulci wishes to console Rinaldo (29, 2–3), who, however, voices his feelings "with such over-elaborated phrases as to make us believe that his tears and moaning are nothing but a cheerful comedy." The critic, who claims not to be acquainted with a more humorous, longer amorous speech than that of Rinaldo, believes that in making the paladin show off an overwhelming knowledge of mythology, Pulci forgets who is actually doing the talking. The poet appears to have transformed Rinaldo the lover into Rinaldo the "lecturer." Thus the paladin's "mythological tirade" would have been introduced either "to obtain a comical effect" or "to make fun of Rinaldo, who is getting excited and branches off into a digression even when talking about his own love." For Momigliano, Pulci's comical intent becomes apparent in the last two lines of stanza 39, where Rinaldo's mind finally returns to Antea, the cause of all his mythological reminiscences. To be sure, love renders Rinaldo unbearably loquacious. (Note that in *Orlando* [XXXI, 33–34], Rinaldo's laments take only two stanzas and end with the paladin's request that Love make Antea suffer at least as much as he.)

41, 3–8 through 52. Rinaldo's pitiful attempt at deceiving his cousin provokes the immediate ironic reaction of the usually serious-minded but perceptive Orlando, who makes fun of him, first relating the amusing tale of the two monks, and then mockingly repeating the tone of Rinaldo's laments. Note that the joking reference to "Mistress Moon" derives from a game played by Florentine children (Ageno, 429).

In the corresponding stanzas of *Orlando* (XXXI, 35–40), Orlando's reaction to Rinaldo's confession sharply contrasts with the count's behavior in *Morgante*. Not only is the tale of the two monks missing in the anonymous poem, but Orlando's words reveal a sincere concern and a friendly commiseration, rather than a stinging irony or a burlesque intention.

57, 5–6 and 58, 3–8. If it is true that Orlando's knowledge of women and the nature of love may be limited (as blatantly stated by Rinaldo in 56, 5–6), he is nevertheless a good judge of the modes of behavior of his male friends, as his wise comments directed to Rinaldo and Oliver attest.

58. Here Pulci is briefly retelling one of Boccaccio's better-known novellas (see *Decameron*, IX, 2).

62, 6–7. Orlando's great expertise in sounding the paladins' ivory horn, called the "oliphant," derives from the *Chanson de Roland*. Rinaldo's request that Orlando perform such a task is for Momigliano (240) "a specious excuse." Troubled by anxiety and lovesick, the paladin would not have had enough breath in his body to sound the horn. (In *Orlando* [XXXII, 8, 2] there is no mention of Rinaldo's request; Orlando simply sounds the horn.)

Clearly this passage burlesques one of the most famous scenes in *chanson de geste* history. As the Franks return from Roncevaux, the army is stopped in its tracks by the sound of Roland's horn. The traitor, Ganelon, fearful lest Charlemagne return in time to save Roland and the rear guard, tries to pretend that Roland might well be blowing his horn in jest. What is important here is how uncharacteristic of Roland's personality such levity would be. Certainly Roland does not "commonly" blow the horn. When Charlemagne hears the third blast, he states that Roland would sound the horn only if he were in desperate straits. In fact, Ganelon's suggestion is so false that it causes his immediate arrest for treason. The power of Roland's blast is legendary. Not only does it reach the distant troops of the emperor, but it is the sole cause of his death, as he remains unscathed by Saracen weapons. In *Morgante* the humor plays on Roland's alleged expertise and the strength of his sound. Ironically, it is the weakness of Roland's third effort that signals his dying condition. For further discussion of the horn scene and its relation to Ganelon's treason, see Emanuel J. Mickel, *Ganelon, Treason and the "Chanson de Roland"* (University Park: Pennsylvania State University Press, 1989).

66–82. As Momigliano further points out (240), stanza 66 contains some amusing contrasts: Antea calls "darling" the man she has challenged to fight against her; likewise, Rinaldo, while declaring himself ready to duel with her, would prefer to use a weapon "that did not cut." The paladin's subsequent refusal to face the princess on the field, his silence when he is sternly rebuked by Orlando, the rapid unhorsing of both Oliver and Ricciardetto, and Pulci's own ironic considerations (79) further contribute to the burlesque quality of this entire episode. Interestingly, Antea seems to behave in a more dignified manner than all her male counterparts, Orlando included, who, having pledged to kill the Syrian princess (74), fights a long and bloodless duel with her. Note that line 8 of stanza 78 renders the Italian verse *dice l'orazione della bertuccia* ("he says the prayer of the monkey"). The expression derives from the Barbary apes' peculiar habit of rapidly moving their lips in fear or anger (Ageno, 439). A similar expression, *dire il paternostro della scimia,* is again used by Pulci (89, 9).

94. Luciana, mentioned at the beginning of the canto together with Chiariella, now shares the fate of the Admiral's daughter. Aware, as Oliver had anticipated (23, 5–7), that Rinaldo has forgotten her, she leaves for Spain without outwardly lamenting her lover's abandonment. In so doing, she shows great dignity and practicality.

106–109. It is ironic that Rinaldo, who has successfully prevented the giants from taking Baiardo away from him, ends up having his horse stolen by a shepherd whose miserable meal he has shared. If it is true that the greedy shepherd's ineptitude at riding Baiardo costs him two broken ribs, it also earns him a huge sum of money. The scene outlines, by contrast, the good nature of the amused hangman, who, surprisingly, pays the shepherd the amount he had requested. Note that a doubloon was a gold coin, equal to two *escudos,* originally issued in the Spanish kingdom of Castile.

112–113. The heedless pagan that Rinaldo meets in Babylonia is not as lucky as the shepherd. Rinaldo may act like a fool when in love, but he is extremely dangerous when made fun of by anyone else, as this humorous scene demonstrates.

CANTO XVII

SUMMARY: Invocation (1). Before meeting with Rinaldo, who is waiting for her outside Babylon, Antea informs her father of the paladin's arrival. Acting upon Gano's advice, the Sultan tells his daughter to persuade Rinaldo to kill the Old Man of the Mountain in exchange for Oliver's and Ricciardetto's freedom (2–18). When the Sultan learns that Rinaldo has accepted his proposal, he convinces Antea to lead an army against Rinaldo's homeland. Eager to attain great military glory, Antea leaves for Montalban accompanied by Gano (19–31). After a fierce duel, Rinaldo defeats the Old Man of the Mountain, who invites him to his home and becomes his traveling companion (32–49). Meanwhile Antea, having laid siege to Montalban, successfully duels with Guicciardo and Alardo, who become her prisoners. Gano, who has suggested that they be killed, is given a good beating by four of Antea's men. Guicciardo and Alardo give Antea the key to the city, where they all await Rinaldo's return (50–72).

The second half of the canto retells the adventures of Orlando, who is searching for Rinaldo together with Terigi and Uliva, King Costanzo's daughter (73–82). To defend the girl he has saved from the giants, Orlando is forced to kill Calandro, a nephew of King Falcon, who honors the count and his companions in his palace (83–90). Then, to save Uliva from Salincorno, Orlando fights against the giant Don Bruno, whose life he spares on the condition that he and his brother Salincorno cease to exact their yearly tribute from the king (91–106). Refusing to honor his brother's promise, Salincorno engages in an unsuccessful duel with Orlando. The confrontation ends with the giant's solemn pledge not to make any more demands upon the king and his people (107–131). Having taken leave from King Falcon, Orlando delivers to King Costanzo and his wife the daughter they had believed lost forever (132–137). The canto ends with the Sultan's invitation to King Costanzo to be present at Oliver's and Ricciardetto's execution (138–139).

8, 1. In 1090 a certain Hasan-i Sâbbah conquered the rock fortress at Alamut in the Persian province of Mazandaran at the center of the Elbruz chain of mountains south of the Caspian Sea. Hasan and his zealous religious followers formed part of the Ismâ 'îlîs, a sect of the part of Islam known as the Shi'â. When the Fatimid dynasty fell, the Shi'â attempted to overthrow the powerful Seljuk Turks. Hasan's sect became known as the Assassins and acquired fame for killing great military leaders, viziers, and occasionally sultans.

In this way the fanatical religious sect grew to be a strong political force in the twelfth and thirteenth centuries, until their destruction by the Mongols. Such was the fanaticism of this heretical sect that it was alleged that Sheikh Hasan, known as the Old Man of the Mountain, used drugs and promises of a mystical paradise to gain the suicidal and fanatical loyalty of his followers. William of Tyre says that the Saracens call them Assassins, but he does not know whence the name comes (Guillaume de Tyre, *Histoire des Croisades. Collection des Mémoires relatifs à l'histoire de France,* ed. M. Guizot, XVIII [1832–1835], 297). It is difficult to say when the term, deriving from the Arabic word *hashîshiyya,* first came to be used generically for someone committing a political murder. Dante's use of the word "assassin" in the *Divina Commedia* is the first known general use of the term in Europe. (For more on the Assassins, see M. G. S. Hodgson, *The Order of the Assassins* [The Hague, 1955].) The story of the Old Man of the Mountain is narrated also in *I viaggi di Marco Polo veneziano. Descritti da Rusticano da Pisa* (Padova: Signum Edizioni, 1983), 33–35. For a discussion of possible links between the works of Polo and Pulci, see Ruggero M. Ruggieri's article "Affinità di tematiche e di personaggi tra *Il Milione* e il *Morgante,*" in *Symposium in honorem Prof. M. De Riquer* (Universitat de Barcelona, Quaderns Crema, 1984), 349–362. Pulci uses the well-known figure of the Old Man to characterize Saracen relations. The sect's leader had become famous during the Crusades and even tried to have the French king Louis IX (Saint Louis) assassinated.

11, 4. This line clearly derives from Petrarch, who, in one of his sonnets (*Rime,* CCXXV, 2), refers to Laura as a sun surrounded by twelve stars.

13, 3–6. For the reference to Thisbe and the mulberry tree, see note, XII, 69, 1–3. As Ageno clarifies (453), Pulci seems to confuse the city of Babylon located in Mesopotamia, and the one referred to by Ovid (see note, XV, 90, 2), with the Egyptian Babylon. Pulci's error was shared by Dante and other writers.

17, 6. Slaves of Turkish origin, the Mamelukes became the personal guard of the Sultan of Egypt, gaining a great amount of political and military power particularly between the thirteenth and the sixteenth centuries. Napoleon defeated the Mamelukes during his 1798 Egyptian campaign.

22–25. In spite of her reiterated declarations of love for Rinaldo and her stated intention to remain true to her word, Antea offers only mild resistance to her father's utilitarian and persuasive plan. A desire for easily gained glory, in addition to Rinaldo's love (28, 7–8 and 29, 1–8), seems here to overcome all sentimental and moral scruples the princess may have.

26, 1–2. The Roman counterpart of the Greek god Hephaestus, Vulcan, a legendary god of fire, had his smithy, manned by the Cyclopes, on Mount Aetna, Europe's highest volcano, and still active today. A reference to Mount Aetna as the place of Vulcan's activities is also found in XIII, 38, 3.

28, 4. See note, VIII, 38, 6.

34–50. With regard to Rinaldo's encounter with the Old Man of the

Mountain, particularly noteworthy is the shift in tone—from grave and ominous to comical and hilarious—characterizing these stanzas. The episode, which begins with the threatening appearance of the much-feared Old Man, depicted at the center of a dark and remote forest, ends in a convivial atmosphere, with Rinaldo's foe becoming his companion. Contrasting with his past braggadocio, the sudden fear of the Old Man upon hearing the name of his opponent is as comical as it is unexpected.

45, 3. The gorget was a piece of armor, made of steel, worn to protect one's throat.

53, 1–2. I believe that Antea's smile is not caused as much by Guicciardo's intentionally ironic reply to her challenge (52, 5–8) as by the princess's confidence in her superior military prowess. By agreeing to duel with her, Guicciardo assures Antea of a speedy and essentially bloodless conquest of Montalban. Note that in stanzas 54–67, 1–6 Pulci gives the reader an exemplary demonstration of the exquisite application of the rules of chivalric etiquette by Antea and Rinaldo's brothers.

64, 3–4. Antea's question to Gano—aware of the Maganzan's treacherous nature, she could not have expected a different reply—gives the impression that the princess is playing a game with him. Having reassured Guicciardo and Alardo that no harm will come to them because of her love for Rinaldo, she then gives Gano the punishment he deserves. Contrasting with the tone of gentility and mutual courtesy which marks the preceding stanzas, the scene portrayed in stanza 68 appears even more amusingly comical. Antea's ironic explicatory comment to Gano (69, 7–8) expresses not only a general view (and that of the poet himself), but also her own personal opinion. Her actions, in fact, clearly demonstrate that if it is true that she despises the traitor, it is equally true that she makes use of his advice as long as it is beneficial to her. In *Orlando* (XXXVI, 1–21), where Antea's comment is missing, the episode is recounted in a pedestrian manner and is lacking in *vis comica*. Angrily reacting to Gano's suggestion that she hang both Guicciardo and Alardo, Antea calls him a traitor and orders that he be flogged in Mahound's name. Only after Gano has loudly lamented his misfortune (stanza 12) does Antea reveal to the two brothers her true identity and her love for Rinaldo. With regard to the expression "nasserì bizeffe" (68, 8), *nasserì* was the name given to a silver Arabian coin; the term *bizeffe* (*a bizzeffe* in modern Italian) means "in great quantity."

74–75. Curses (as well as blessings, invocations, laments, and interrogations) in which the initial phrase is repeated in each line are a conventional ingredient in popular poetry. In *Morgante,* as we have seen in canto XVI, they often extend for more than one stanza. The same can be said for stanzas 80, 123, and 136.

78 through 81, 1–4. Orlando's request for God's help is immediately granted. The count hears the reassuring voice of the Lord, just as Rinaldo heard it in stanza 12, 1–6 of canto IV. Of all the Christian characters in the poem, except for Charlemagne, whom the Almighty showers with numerous miracles (XXVII), Orlando and Rinaldo are the preferred recipients of God's benevolence. For the reference to Raphael and Tobias (79, 6), see note, IV, 5, 4. In stanza 80 Pulci alludes to Abraham's willingness to offer his son Isaac's life to God (Genesis 22:2–12); concerning Joseph of Galilee and Joachim, see note, V, 1, 7. Zacharias was the father of John the Baptist (Luke 1:57–63).

79, 1–2. See note, I, 2, 4.

82, 1–2. These two lines, in which God tells Orlando that he will find Rinaldo's horse, which is now in the hands of a giant, clearly contradict both stanzas 107–110 of canto XVI (Baiardo has been sold to the Sultan's hangman by the shepherd who stole it from Rinaldo) and stanzas 12–14 of canto XVIII (it is Rinaldo, not Orlando, who regains possession of the steed following the killing of the Sultan's hangman). This inconsistency—not the first one we have encountered in the poem (see note, IX, 10–12)—is explained by Ageno (472) as the result of Pulci's incorrect reading of stanza 33, 1–3 of canto XXXVI of *Orlando*. In his *Storia del Morgante* (31), Domenico De Robertis, commenting upon these lines, maintains that Pulci did not make an error of interpretation as serious as Ageno seems to believe. For De Robertis, this inconsistency, like others in Pulci's poem, stems essentially from the Florentine poet's "lack of attention and insufficiently careful revision of his own text." Whatever the reason for Pulci's so-called "inconsistency," it is amusing to note that in canto XVII not even God is a very reliable prophet.

89, 3–4. Pulci's admiring comment regarding King Falcon serves to emphasize, by contrast, Don Bruno's radically opposite behavior.

96, 3. Salincorno the giant is not to be confused with Erminion's brother Salincorno, who was killed by Rinaldo (X, 53, 1).

101, 2–3. See note, XII, 34, 1–8.

102, 2 through 105. This episode is also found in *Orlando* (XXXVII, 28–31). However, even a cursory comparison of the two texts attests to Pulci's superior artistic genius. While the *canterino* states only that Don Bruno's face is covered with blood because Orlando has broken three of his teeth, Pulci vividly and comically depicts Don Bruno in the act of uselessly searching for his "fangs" as he insults his god. In *Morgante* the more appropriate *zanne* (fangs) replaces the word *denti* (teeth) used in *Orlando*. The word *Gramolazzo* in stanza 105, 8 appears for the first time in one of Pulci's earlier minor works, as the name of a person whose *chiappe* (buttocks) were made of iron. According to Ageno (479), Gramolazzo was probably a figure, partially or completely made of iron, which decorated a public building in Pulci's time. (For the reference to Gramolazzo, see *Ciriffo Calvaneo,* Parte III, LII, 1–2, 24.)

109, 2–4. Don Bruno's comparison of Orlando to a "good herbalist" derives from the fact that wandering salesmen of medicinal herbs also extracted teeth when necessary.

114, 7–8. Lines 7–8 of the original Italian text (*quel ch'io gli ho fatto mi pare una zacchera; / tanto è che preso non fia più a mazzacchera*), in which the word *zacchera* (a term used with reference to somehing of no value) rhymes with *mazzacchera* (the name of a tool used to catch eels and frogs), present a remarkable challenge to any translator. As Ageno notes (481), by telling Salincorno that what he has done to his brother is little or nothing, and that Don Bruno will again not be taken by bait (literally, be caught with a *mazzacchera*), Orlando is ironically intimating that Don Bruno will no longer make the mistake of trying to exact a tribute from King Falcon. To solve the problem presented by these two lines, Tusiani, usually quite faithful to the text of the original, is forced here to interpret them in his own creative way.

117–118, 1–4. See XVI, 96–101.

119–131. No less amusing than Orlando's duel with Don Bruno is the count's armed encounter with Salincorno, when the bragging and raging giant comes face to face with the much more poised and chivalrous paladin. Salincorno's surprise at being hit by Orlando's spear (120, 1–2), his comical attempt to attribute his fall to his mount (121, 4–8), and Orlando's mocking reply (122, 1–3) cannot but elicit the reader's smile. Equally humorous is the fact that it is the giant's huge size that provokes his second fall and ends, to all effects, the duel. Though fear-stricken when he hears the name of his opponent (127)—as happened earlier in the canto to the Old Man of the Mountain—Salincorno cannot overcome his tendency to brag, and pledges to kill Rinaldo in order to avenge himself and his people (128, 3–8 through 129). Orlando's matter-of-fact reply (130, 7–8)—Salincorno's threat does not appear to worry the count—underscores again the burlesque tone of the entire episode.

Lines 1 and 3 of stanza 123 refer to the sounding of the bells announcing daily religious services: at three o' clock in the afternoon (nones), at six in the evening (vespers), and at three in the morning (matins). Other prayers are recited at daybreak (prime), at nine in the morning (tierce), at noon (sext), and at nine in the evening (complin), the last of the seven canonical hours. Note that line 2 of 123 reproduces almost verbatim one of Dante's most famous tercets (see *Inferno,* V, 25). For line 2 of stanza 128, see XVI, 80, 7–8. Orlando's invulnerability is restated in XXV, 103, 3–8. For Mambrin(o) of Ulivant, see note, III, 32, 8.

In line 4 of stanza 129, Salincorno declares that "Salinferno blood" runs in his veins. Puccini (600) suggests that Pulci may have invented this word to make it rhyme with *sempinterno* in line 2 of the original Italian text.

CANTO XVIII

SUMMARY: Invocation (1). King Costanzo shows Orlando the Sultan's letter; then he, his daughter, the count, and 100,000 men all leave for Babylon (2–7). Suspicious about the size of King Costanzo's army, the Sultan sends for Salincorno, who promptly arrives with 10,000 warriors (8–9). On his way to Babylon together with the Old Man of the Mountain and Antea's Mamelukes, Rinaldo encounters the Sultan's hangman mounted on Baiardo. The Old

Man kills the hangman, and Rinaldo regains possession of his horse (10–20). With the Sultan's permission, Orlando, Spinellon, and Costanzo visit Oliver and Ricciardetto in their cell (21–28). When the Sultan tries to remove Orlando's helmet in order to uncover the paladin's face, the count slaps him hard on the cheek (29–34). Pressed by Salincorno and encouraged by the arrival of Mariotto and his men, the Sultan orders the immediate execution of Oliver and Ricciardetto (35–43).

Informed by a spy that the hanging procession is about to start, Orlando and Spinellon rally their men, while Oliver and Ricciardetto still hope to be rescued (44–47). Mariotto, heading the procession, challenges Spinellon, who kills him. Orlando and King Costanzo join Spinellon in fighting the Sultan's troops (48–55). Having arrived at the battlefield, Rinaldo and the Old Man meet by chance with Spinellon, who takes them where Orlando is fighting (56–62). Happily reunited, Rinaldo and Orlando, escorted by Spinellon and the Old Man of the Mountain, move to attack the Sultan, whom the Old Man succeeds in killing (63–68). While Rinaldo is engaged in freeing Ricciardetto and Oliver (69–74), Salincorno slays both King Costanzo and Spinellon, the latter of whom is baptized by Orlando before he dies (75–86). Rinaldo and Salincorno decide to meet on the battlefield the following morning (87–94). While the Lord of Montalban is asleep in his tent, Salincorno leaves Babylon to attack Rinaldo by surprise. He is intercepted, however, by the always vigilant Old Man of the Mountain (95–96). Awakened by the commotion, Rinaldo faces Salincorno and, after a fierce duel, kills him as the Sultan's men seek refuge in Babylon (97–109).

In the meantime, in Paris, Charlemagne sends Meridiana back to her father Caradoro, entrusting her safety to Morgante (110–111). Mission accomplished, Morgante, on his way to Syria to rejoin Orlando, meets the half-giant Margutte and hears his profession of faith (112–144). Margutte accepts Morgante's invitation to be his traveling companion, and the two stop at an inn, where they eat and drink all that the innkeeper has to offer and more. Then, while the innkeeper sleeps, Margutte, who has stolen everything he can find, sets fire to the inn and leaves with Morgante (145–179). On the third day of their voyage, the two famished giants see a unicorn, which Morgante promptly kills and Margutte cooks. When the two companions are ready to eat, Morgante devours most of the unicorn, leaving the disappointed Margutte only a few mouthfuls (180–200).

1, 1–2. As noted by Ageno (489), these two lines are a "strange travesty" of Mary's prayer, known as the Magnificat (see Luke 1:46–47.

4, 3. The legendary exploits of the Knights of the Round Table, whose leader was Arthur, king of ancient Britain, are recounted in the twelfth-century romances of Chrétien de Troyes (see note, IV, 7–22).

15, 5. This is the same Mameluke who was ordered by Antea to serve as Rinaldo's guide in canto XVII, 17, 6–8; 32, 3 through 33, 5.

19, 6. For the reference to Nebuchadnezzar, king of Babylonia, who invaded Judea, see 2 Kings 24:10–11.

23, 4. No matter how dreadful the situation in which Oliver finds himself, he can never refrain from making a gastronomic comparison.

24, 5. Note that a similar expression is used in canto XV, 71, 5.

33, 5–8. Antea's father, the Sultan, is definitely a more complex and better delineated character than Chiariella's father, the Admiral. A shrewd and unscrupulous ruler who has demonstrated that he fully appreciates the political value of Gano's treacherous plan (XVII, 6–9), in these lines the Sultan seems to behave in a rather cowardly manner. Indeed, his ridiculous momentary fear is caused by the realization of his helplessness before Orlando's and Spinellon's raging fury. Nevertheless, when his fear subsides, his assessment of the perilous military situation he faces is indeed correct (36–37), as is his desire to adopt a wait-and-see policy (38). However, he gives in to Salincorno's pressure and decides to alter his wise policy, encouraged by the arrival of Mariotto and his army. By hastening Ricciardetto's and Oliver's execution (39–42), he makes a mistake that will bring about his downfall. While it is true that it is ludicrous for a man such as he to have the audacity to address Ricciardetto and Oliver as "traitors" (46, 6)—an insult which prompts Ricciardetto's sharp retort (46, 8 through 47, 1–5)—it is also true that the Sultan, though by no means a hero, ultimately faces his fated death with dignity (54, 7–8 and 65–88, 1–5).

45, 1–2. The two knights mentioned here are Oliver and Ricciardetto.

48, 6. As the reader is told in canto XX, 58, Mariotto is the son of the emperor of the city of Mezza and the seaport of Monaca.

51, 5. The giant Burrato is a figure encountered in the Italian romance *Uggieri il Danese* (see Ageno, 503).

63, 3–6. As has been seen in canto XV, 56, 4–8, this is another comical outburst of Rinaldo's rage.

67, 1–2. See canto XVII, 37, 1–7.

71, 6–8; 72–73. Here Rinaldo's behavior is a carbon copy of Orlando's in stanzas 23–27. The same can be said for stanzas 32–36 of canto XXXIX and stanzas 14–19 of canto XLI of *Orlando.* In reading both versions of this episode, one has the impression that by not immediately revealing their identities to Oliver and Ricciardetto, Orlando and Rinaldo enjoy prolonging the anguish of their fellow paladins. That the anonymous author of *Orlando* clearly intended to reinforce this impression is attested by lines 1–2 of stanza 19 of canto XLI, where he has Ricciardetto tell Rinaldo, who has lifted his helmet to reveal his face, "Why do you deride me, brother? Don't you think we have suffered enough?" In spite of the similarity of the two texts, one notices a small but rather significant difference. The fact that in *Morgante* Ricciardetto does not question his brother, thus forcing the reader to speculate about the reasons for Orlando's and Rinaldo's actions, constitutes, I believe, a further measure of Pulci's superior artistic capabilities.

77–85. Mortally wounded by Salincorno, Spinellon has a prodigious vision of Paradise just before breathing his last breath. Thus, Spinellon's questions and Orlando's answers initiate what, making use of a more contemporary term, we could call an "audio-visual" lesson of Christian catechism. If we compare these stanzas with the corresponding lines in *Orlando* (XLI, 24–35), we can clearly detect an underlying tone of joking familiarity, which has the effect of depriving the doctrinal explanation of any persuasive force. The outwardly simple and apparently devout manner in which Orlando explains to Spinellon his vision of Paradise reveals an amusingly superficial concept of matters of faith. For the Lord of Angrante, Christ is He "Who feeds on happiness and hope all men on earth" (77, 5–6), as if Christian religion were nothing but a continuous party; the Apostles are cheerfully referred to as "this little company" (79, 3); the usually sternly portrayed figure of John the Baptist is presented as a man "who holds a lovely cross and most intently seems to gaze on Jesus" (79, 5–6); Adam is seen looking at God with a puzzling question in his eyes (80, 5–6); dear old Saint Joseph is happily singing Hosanna at Mary's feet (81, 1–3); and the description of legions of martyrs, confessors, prophets, angels, and saints seems a parody of Dante as well as of the liturgy of the Catholic Church.

The text of *Orlando* (where Spinellon is identified as Costanzo's twenty-four-year-old son, who in canto XXXIX, 8 is said to be eager to embrace Christianity because of his love for Orlando) presents a number of notable differences from Spinellon's conversion in *Morgante*. Urged by Orlando to renounce his false god, the dying Saracen declares himself ready to do so, provided that the count pledge to avenge his death and protect his sister Uliva (25–26). When Rinaldo arrives with the Old Man of the Mountain, Orlando asks his cousin to send his squire to fetch some water so that he can baptize Spinellon. Spinellon's miraculous vision, which God allows Orlando to experience too (27–31), occurs as he is being baptized. More important, Spinellon's indoctrination—which extends for nine full stanzas in *Morgante*—occupies only thirty-two lines in the anonymous poem (32–35). Spinellon asks Orlando only two questions (as opposed to the thirteen he formulates in *Morgante*). Answering them, the paladin points out to him Jesus Christ, His mother Mary, Mary Magdalene, Martha, the angels, archangels, thrones, cherubim, and seraphim, the twelve crowned Apostles, and the legions of saints and blessed souls who surround Christ.

The conventional nature of religious conversions such as that of Spinellon in both *Morgante* and *Orlando* is a fact recognized by many scholars. It must be pointed out, however, that the author of *Orlando* has at least attempted to prepare and justify the event, first by informing the reader of Spinellon's love for Orlando, and then by exacting from him the promise to avenge his death and protect his sister in exchange for his becoming a Christian. This form of *do ut des* makes Spinellon's conversion somewhat more logical, and hence more acceptable to an audience, than the Saracen's totally unexpected conversion in Pulci's poem. As noted with regard to the conversions we have previously encountered, the particular tone and length of the religious discussion taking place in *Morgante,* between a suddenly devout Spinellon and a zealous Orlando (XVIII, 77–85), may be a further indication of Luigi Pulci's parodic intentions.

Commenting upon Spinellon's conversion, Giovanni Getto maintains instead that the religious motif interests Pulci the poet only as a pretext for exercising his artistic capabilities. "Deprived of any logical and ethical content," religion becomes naturally "reduced to a mere scenario, to a mythology and a liturgy capable of the most unexpected disguises and the most changing lights" (99). Spinellon's vision should be interpreted, therefore, from a liturgical and mythological perspective. Particularly significant for the Italian critic is stanza 79 of canto XVIII, where the twelve Apostles are referred to as "this little company" and John the Baptist as "His dear cousin." According to Getto, these two figures are represented by Pulci immersed in "that climate of middle-class affability" which "extends also to religious matters and determines its prevailing tone" (99–100).

80, 2. One of the "three Marys" is the Virgin Mary, while the other two are Mary Magdalene and Mary, mother of James (see Mark 16:1–2).

81, 1. The "dear old man" is obviously Saint Joseph.

81, 6–7. See note, V, 1, 7.

82, 6. The prophet Jeremiah, already mentioned in canto XVII, 80, 7.

84–85. The classification of the nine celestial orders (seraphim, cherubim, thrones, dominations, virtues, powers, principalities, archangels, and angels) is taken directly from Dante.

87, 4. For this reference to Paul, see 2 Corinthians 12:2–4.

91, 2. See note, XVI, 14, 5–6.

91, 7. Costantino too appears in the Italian epics that recount the adventures of Ammon's four sons. He falls victim to Rinaldo's sword after the Lord of Montalban has killed Mambrino, Costantino's and Salincorno's brother.

103, 8. Beginning with the second half of the fourteenth century, the hilt of a sword was connected, by means of a hanging silver chain, to the upper part of a knight's armor (Ageno, 517).

112. Though Margutte has a rather short life in the poem (he dies, in fact, in stanza 149 of canto XIX), he is undoubtedly one of the most original and unforgettable figures that Pulci created. To quote Attilio Momigliano, "Everything in this character has been wonderfully well conceived: his size and clothes, the way he makes his appearance on stage and his personality, his deeds and his death" (286). In stanzas 115–145 he will swiftly succeed in conquering, with all the charm of his perverse and pervasive wickedness, the esteem and respect of the much stronger but less intellectually gifted Morgante.

The sources that critics have most frequently suggested for this famous figure are the pseudo-Homeric poem *Margite* and the *Driadeo d'Amore* by

Luca Pulci. With regard to the *Driadeo d'Amore* (a poem consisting of 441 stanzas), it must be pointed out that several of its episodes have been attributed to Luigi Pulci's pen. Among them are the stanzas recounting the adventures of Sosia, a character somewhat resembling Margutte (see Parte II, stanzas 6–61 in *Il Driadeo di Luca Pulci al Magnifico Lorenzo de' Medici* [Napoli: Tipografia Trani, 1881], 55–69). (On this point, see Mark Davie's article "Pulci's Margutte Episode Re-examined," *Italian Studies: An Annual Review* 33 [1978]: 29–55.) Discussing other possible sources, Carlo Pellegrini maintains that no matter where Pulci may have gotten his inspiration, the fact has "no critical value," since Margutte is essentially and foremost a product of Luigi Pulci's creative mind (109–110).

With regard to the name Margutte, Ageno (520) interestingly observes that this name was commonly given in medieval times to life-size wooden figures of Saracen warriors used by Christian knights to show off their military skills during tournaments.

Certainly the moment Margutte makes his appearance in the poem, both Morgante and the reader realize that they are in the presence of a new, impressive personality. Asked by Morgante to reveal his name, the wayfarer promptly and happily complies, cleverly explaining the reason for his being as tall as he is (stanza 113, 6–8). As Momigliano acutely notes (287), Margutte is too intelligent to be a giant, and he has too formidable an appetite to be a man. He can only be, therefore, a "half-giant." After this brief physical description of himself, Margutte voices, with an obviously sincere satisfaction, his famous materialistic profession of faith. Stanzas 115–117 constitute a joyfully impudent parody of the Christian concept of the Trinity and end by equating faith to itching, which some feel and others do not. It is immediately followed by a detailed inner self-portrait (stanzas 118–122), the celebration of his extraordinarily refined knowledge of culinary art (stanzas 123–128), the boastful enumeration of all his "cardinal" and "theological" virtues, and, finally, the surprising revelation that he has never committed an act of treason (129–142).

The recently converted Morgante, whose atavistic tendencies to violence and to a life of material pleasures appear to have been reawakened by the wayfarer's confession, promptly tells him that they can be "bosom friends" as long as Margutte believes in the power of Morgante's clapper (143–145).

For Illidio Bussani, the Margutte-Morgante episode illustrates one of the strangest friendships ever narrated, since it involves two individuals who are, physically as well as morally, poles apart. Having stated that "Morgante is good and a believer, while Margutte is wicked and an atheist," Bussani wonders how two such persons, one the antithesis of the other, can become friends. The critic speculates that their friendship is made possible by the one quality they have in common: gluttony. Margutte's gastronomic credo and the description of his culinary expertise are the reason for Morgante's desire to form with him an "association of mutual gastronomic assistance" (*Il romanzo cavalleresco in Luigi Pulci,* 20–30).

On the question of Margutte's confession, Momigliano argues that Margutte, lacking any notion of the nature of evil, and ignorant of why evil must not be perpetrated, "is not only a materialistic atheist, but a real amoral spirit," who at best "believes in the destinies of gastronomy" (288). The "first clear proof of Margutte's amorality" is the totally unaffected manner in which he announces the murder of his father, a statement that prompts Momigliano to add: "If he is not moral, he is nevertheless sincere; and he is sincere because he is amoral" (290). What makes Margutte—"the personification of com-icity"—appealing is the feeling that "we are facing a person who elicits laughter from anything, even from those things which others consider to be tragic and immoral; instead of moral principles, nature has given him cheerfulness" (290–291).

Of essentially the same opinion is Carlo Pellegrini, who maintains that Margutte's spirited confession of his sins is the best proof of his amorality. For this critic, Margutte is substantially "an artist of crime," who derives pleasure from committing criminal acts and boasting about them. The comical merriment with which this character presents himself is, for Pellegrini, what renders Margutte likable to the reader (112–113). Momigliano's thesis is followed also by Umberto Biscottini, for whom Margutte is "evil because he is not good" and cannot be immoral "because he is not capable of morality" (48).

As Stendhal (*Roma* [Roma e Torino: Roux e Viarengo, 1906], 76) and others have also suggested, it may be possible to perceive instead, behind the mask of Margutte's whimsically hyperbolic pronouncements, Luigi Pulci's skeptical smile. The poet—who in his *Io vo' dire una frottola* states that wise are those who behave like Thomas (see *Le frottole di Luigi Pulci,* rivedute nel testo e annotate da GuglielmoVolpi [Firenze:Tipografia Galileiana, 1912], lines 14–15)—here may have used Margutte as a spokesman for his own religious feelings. Even if we choose not to see in the words of this strange new character a polemic intention on the part of his creator (the vibrantly sincere tone of Margutte's credo could be interpreted as vindication for Pulci's cold and conventional *Confessione*), it is not clear why Margutte would boast of having killed his father and having committed so many crimes if he did not consider them morally offensive. If he had no knowledge of what evil and good are, as Momigliano and Pellegrini maintain, why did he so enthusiasti-cally proclaim to be the perpetrator of acts which, conceived outside any possibility of a moral choice, should be either indifferent or natural for him? Moreover, doesn't his use of words such as "sins," "vices," and "virtues" reveal that he—the son of a nun and a priest—may have known their true meaning? Otherwise, why such pride in possessing qualities that are in direct opposition to what morality considers virtues? Margutte's great satisfaction in having violated all natural and divine laws is perhaps a manifestation of his immorality, rather than his amorality. While it may be true that Margutte's final proclama-tion of his only true moral virtue—never having betrayed anyone—could lend support to the thesis of his amorality (given the fact that he seems to boast indifferently both his bad and good deeds), it is equally true that Pulci could have injected a personal note into Margutte's confession. In a subtle reference to his no longer warm relationship with the Magnificent, Luigi Pulci perhaps wished to reaffirm at this point his loyalty to his august friend (interestingly, in lines 34–52 of his previously cited *Io vo' dire una frottola,* the poet alludes to a friendship that has been betrayed, as well as to his inability to select his friends carefully).

In conclusion, the critics who refuse to even consider the possibility of recognizing in the words of our half-giant the voice of the author, thus denying any autobiographical value to this episode, single out as the *causa prima* for Margutte's presence in *Morgante* either Pulci's cheerful disposition or his rebellion against conformism (see Norbert Jonard's article "La nature du comique dans le *Morgante* de Pulci," in *Culture et société en Italie du Moyen-Âge à la Renaissance,* Hommage à André Rochon [Paris: Université de La Sorbonne Nouvelle, 1985], 92–93).

With regard to Morgante and Margutte, Paolo Orvieto (171–205) points out that Benedetto Dei, a personal friend of Luigi Pulci, transcribed the beginning verses of the famous thirty-seven stanzas of Margutte's confession (112–151) in one of his letters, giving Morgante and Margutte the names Bernardo and Antonio respectively. Orvieto argues that the author of this singular change was Pulci himself, who wanted to make fun of two well-known members of the Medici clan, the poets Bernardo Bellincioni and Antonio di Guido (whom he recalls as personal friends in canto XXVIII, 143, 2 and 144, 1). The latter, a prolific popular poet and author of several *canzoni* where all types of vices are listed and condemned, did not, however, enjoy the reputation of being a particularly virtuous individual. In fact, some aspects of his personality, as well as some events in his life (he owned a tavern and was a culinary expert), present several points in common with Margutte. According to Orvieto, Margutte's confession, a joyful celebration of the vices that Antonio di Guido had condemned in his *canzoni,* appears to be in direct opposition to Antonio's poetical writings; hence Pulci's intention to poke fun at him by changing Margutte's name to Antonio. (With regard to Orvieto's identification of Margutte with the poet Antonio di Guido, Lorenz Beninger rejects it as "very implausible." Referring only to secondary sources, Beninger maintains that one of the main texts Orvieto used to support his thesis of di Guido's depravity is unreliable since it contains the slanderous charges of an envious author [see "Notes on the Last Years of Luigi Pulci (1477–1484)," *Rivista dell'Istituto Nazionale di Studi sul Rinascimento* XXVII (1987): 261].) Certainly many of the characters in *Morgante* are based to some extent on Luigi Pulci's contemporaries, even though it is no longer possible to identify them.

Margutte's extended confession (where Pulci clearly employs the technique Boccaccio uses in presenting Ser Ciappelletto in the first story of the

Decameron) is, according to Orvieto, an "undeniable anti-prototype of the numberless illustrations of perfect confessions, in which a sinner/guinea pig would confess all existing sins according to an archetypal progression and distribution" (189). While the poet's own *Confessione* and that of Orlando in *Morgante* are "positive confessions" since they follow long-established rules, Margutte's "monologue," patterned on medieval acknowledgments of sins, becomes instead a negative confession, a parodic deformation of its prototype. If I am interpreting Orvieto well, he believes that "it is absurd to think that the composition of the character of Margutte implied for Pulci a preliminary moral choice," just as it is not possible to determine an "*a priori* reason for the poet's own *Confessione*" (196).

At the beginning of his recent study *L'ombra dell'eroe. 'Il Morgante'* (Urbino: Edizioni QuattroVenti, 1986), Andrea Gareffi rightly observes that Pulci's poem marks the fall of the myth of the hero, traditionally represented as the upholder of the faith and the repository of all spiritual and moral virtues. Focusing his attention on the Morgante and Margutte episodes in canto XVIII, he defines Margutte as "a living contradiction of the heroic ideal" and concludes his stimulating analysis by stating that with Margutte, "the myth of the hero becomes a myth of the self." If it is true that by questioning the traditional image of the hero, Pulci has built "a poetic system which goes against the course of Christian history and culture," it is also true that the poet, by so congenially portraying the character of his half-giant, has rendered himself, as well as the reader, an accomplice in Margutte's evil deeds (pp. 27–42).

113, 8. In the original Italian text, Margutte says that he is exactly "*sette braccia*" tall. Since one *braccio* corresponds to 460 centimeters, he is 4 meters and 20 centimeters tall, or well over 13 feet.

114, 2. The thirsty Morgante jokingly compares Margutte, whose height is but a fraction of his, to a "flask."

115, 1–2. Margutte, as conveyed by the proverbial expressions he uses, starts his parodic confession by claiming to believe in nothing.

115, 7–8. These two lines contain, according to Angelo Gianni (15), "the most innocent heresy in the world." For this critic, the question of whether we can identify in Margutte's confession Luigi Pulci's heterodox opinions "no longer has any weight for the modern reader." Gianni, for whom "the history of religious *vituperium* is ancient as medieval history," maintains, in fact, that the parody of sacred writs was not substantially irreverent or intentionally blasphemous (302).

116, 1–6. These lines contain irreverent allusions to the Virgin Mary, Christ, and the mystery of the Trinity. In his commentary to Pulci's *Morgante,* Davide Puccini (644) notes that "in order to fully understand the famous parody of the *Credo,* one must keep in mind that such comical professions of faith were a literary genre rather widespread in the sixteen century." For Puccini, Pulci's verses are therefore "less blasphemous than they may seem at first."

116, 6–8 through 117, 1–2. The Koran forbids the drinking of alcoholic beverages; hence Margutte's rejection of the Muslim religion and the definition of Mohammed, Apollin, and Trivigant as a sort of nightmarish dream.

118, 4. The Italian word *papasso,* rendered in English as "holy pope," indicates, according to Ageno (522), a Muslim cleric and not a priest of the Eastern Orthodox Church. Bursia (today Bursa), a former Ottoman capital, is a city located in northwest Turkey.

121, 7. The Italian proverb *giocarsi perfino i peli della barba* ("to gamble even the hair of one's beard") means "to lose everything one possesses."

122, 1–4. Addressing Morgante, and thus also the reader, Margutte uses expressions that pertain to the game of dice.

122, 5–7. The original Italian text contains some slang words and expressions that Pulci lists in his *Vocabolarietto della lingua furbesca.*

124, 4. The *migliaccio,* or blood pudding, is made using the blood of a recently butchered pig as one of its ingredients.

126, 4–6. As Margutte knows well, overcooked liver easily hardens.

127, 5. An eel-like marine or freshwater fish, the lamprey was a much-requested fish at fourteenth- and fifteenth-century Florentine markets.

127, 7. According to Margutte, gluttony can be satisfied only by paying attention to an almost infinite number of details.

128, 5. Aegina is the name of an island and a seaport in the Saronic Gulf along the southeast coast of Greece.

129, 3–6. The proverbial expression used here means, as Ageno explains (526), "to behave against nature." Margutte clearly recognizes that he has often deserved to be imprisoned and to be sent to the stake.

129, 7–8. According to Carlo Pellegrini (112), these two lines "contain the essence" of Margutte's personality.

130, 8. The words "extra rhymes," translating the Italian *mille novellette,* stand for "fabricated details."

131, 1. Another proverbial expression used by Margutte to reveal that he was also a pimp.

132, 4. The proverbial expression means "and you will learn all other secrets."

132, 5–8. Margutte's passion for stealing often caused him to be paraded around town wearing the shameful insignia of a convicted criminal. Ageno explains (527) that individuals condemned to public scorn wore a headpiece similar to a papal miter and had two brooms in the form of a cross tied behind their backs.

134, 3. In their zeal to place a debtor's property under restraints, town hall clerks even sequestered a farmer's kitchen pot.

135, 5. The "twig" mentioned here (in Italian, *il maio*) is the wreath previously mentioned in canto IV, 19, 8.

137, 6–8. Titles were called "rubrics" (from the Latin *ruber*) because they were written or printed in red. A corner at the bottom of the first page of each *quaternum* (or section of a manuscript or book) was marked with a (small) letter of the alphabet, while Roman numerals were used to mark individual pages (Ageno, 529).

138, 3. The figs mentioned in this line ripen close to Saint Peter's Day (end of June), hence their name of *fichi sampieri* (Saint Peter's figs).

139, 2–4 and 142, 6. Margutte uses here two more common proverbial expressions.

142, 8. With this, his only positive quality, ends Margutte's confession, which, to quote Giovanni Getto (120), is uttered in a series of stanzas reproducing "a masterful mixture of visual, olfactory, tactile, and gustatory impressions."

144, 8. This line renders the well-known proverb *co' santi in chiesa e co' ghiotti in taverna,* which is reproduced almost verbatim in Dante's *Inferno (*XXI, 14–15).

146, 8. The meaning of line 8 in the original Italian text is "I would try to catch with a net [used for hunting birds] even a fake penny."

143–148. Morgante, who has listened attentively to Margutte's dissertation, is duly impressed and attracted by the cheerful perversity of the half-giant, and even more by the prospects of accomplishing great culinary feats with his help. These stanzas, like those which describe their adventures at the end of this canto and in canto XIX, clearly indicate that Morgante and Margutte complement each other. As Pellegrini writes (113): "one has found in the other a part of himself."

With regard to the newly established friendship of Morgante and Margutte, Vittorio Gajetti underlines the fact that it is mostly based on Margutte's immediate willingness to place his cunning at the service of Morgante's formidable voracity. As the critic points out, the stanzas that follow the episode at the inn of il Dormi (Sleep) show the increasingly precarious nature of this relationship. Margutte, whose shrewdness cannot protect him against the giant's repeated hoaxes and deceits, reveals, in fact, a growing angry vexation. According to Gajetti, Margutte, made by Morgante to suffer from thirst and hunger, gets thereby a much-deserved punishment "for all his evil doings and his innate malice" ("Tematica della gola e morte di Margutte," in *L'arte dell'interpretare: studi critici offerti a Giovanni Getto* [Cuneo: Arciere, 1984], 165–178).

154, 3. Note that a quite similar expression is used in canto XIX, 127, 2.

155, 2. "Three basketsful of bread" translates *tre staia di pane.* The *staio,* a wooden cylindrical vessel used in Florence to measure cereals and forage, held twenty-five liters (Ageno, 535). Thus three *staia* corresponded to well over nineteen gallons.

155, 7–8. The one who makes this comment is obviously the author himself, not Margutte.

156, 1–4. Pulci says that the cheese weighed *sei libbre.* Since a Florentine *libbra* corresponds to 350 grams today, the total weight of the cheese was a mere 2,100 grams, or a little more than 2 kilos (4 pounds 8 ounces).

157, 1. A Florentine ounce was one-twelfth of a *libbra* and was the equivalent of 28 grams. The ounce was used mostly as a unit of weight in chemists' and spice shops (Ageno, 536).

161, 1–2. Morgante sleeps here like an elephant (see note, XIV, 161, 1–2).

162, 5. A proverbial expression used to transmit one's desire for an additional drink or nightcap.

170, 4. See note, XVI, 106–109.

170, 7. The ducat was an old coin made of gold or silver. The most famous was the large Venetian silver ducat (Ageno, 540).

172, 3. The names Pulci has chosen for the innkeeper (il Dormi, "Sleep") and Margutte (il Graffigna, "Pilfer") masterfully reflect the personalities of the two men. Note that the Italian verb *sgraffignare* means "to steal with great ability and rapidity."

The figure and role of the innkeeper in Pulci's poem have been the topic of a recent article by Maria Grazia Di Paolo, in which, focusing her attention on il Dormi and Chiarione, the innkeeper in cantos XX and XXI, the critic points out that these two lively characters "acquire a prominent position because, thanks to them, the inn is no longer a mere background, but becomes a dynamic element in the events of which it is a part." Particularly stimulating is Di Paolo's interpretation of Margutte's mockingly deceiving and yet surprisingly gentle behavior with il Dormi. By making sure that Sleep is not around while he is busy stealing, Margutte avoids being forced to kill him as he did his own father. This fact may reveal that the half-giant had no real intention to physically harm the poor innkeeper, who is as naive as Margutte is clever. According to Di Paolo, "This is only a thin thread of light, but in it one can perceive, in the same moment in which it disappears, a different Margutte, a Margutte who believes in something else, besides the cake and pie" (see "Osti e osterie nel *Morgante* del Pulci," *Forum Italicum* 24, 1 [Spring 1990]: 80–93).

175, 5. It reveals Pulci's own pleased commentary on Margutte's actions.

178, 4–5. The derogatory Italian word used by Pulci is *birri* (*sbirri* in modern Italian), corresponding to the English slang word "coppers." Pulci makes a direct allusion here to the proverbial greed of the policemen of his day.

184, 8. Yellow and red are the color of bruises. Or it may be a play on words, as with the "black or blue" mentioned in stanza 115, 2.

185, 5–8. Margutte's prompt reply may have been determined by the innkeeper's words in stanza 170, 5 (see Puccini, 674).

192, 4–6. In courtly and stilnovist poetry, "tinder and flint" are the symbols of the fire of love, things which Margutte cannot carry upon his person (Ageno, 546).

196, 1–2. As noted by Gianni and other critics, in Pulci's poem "hunger is something tangible, an oppressive and dark cloud" (48).

199, 7. Surely the irony of Morgante's quoting from Dante's *Inferno* (IV, 131) cannot escape the reader.

150–200. Having just delivered a most joyful and self-congratulory oral report on his "cardinal and theological virtues," Margutte provides here an impressive and most amusing demonstration of what his mind is capable of concocting. He does, in fact, succeed in bringing food to the table where Morgante's brute force (his clapper) has failed. Moreover, once Morgante leaves the scene, our half-giant completely takes over, conceiving and carrying out a hoax worthy of the craftiest minds in Boccaccio's *Decameron*. Indeed, the masterful way in which Margutte first erases the innkeeper's distrust and fears (162–171) and then, spurred on by his obtuse and gullible nature, devises with the man's help his ruin (172–176) is, as Carlo Pellegrini writes (114), "a true masterpiece of psychological shrewdness and comical force." In this episode, as Pellegrini further states, Margutte displays "two qualities not easily found together: a great meditative power, which allows him to conceive a plan even in its smallest details, and a prodigious immediacy of execution" (116).

C A N T O   X I X

SUMMARY: Invocation (1). Guided by a lamenting cry, Morgante and Margutte find a beautiful young maiden chained to a rock. Morgante kills the lion that is guarding her and asks her to tell her story (2–7). The girl, whose name is Florinetta, recounts how one day, while picking flowers in a field near her father's castle, she was kidnapped by a giant, Beltramo, who, with his brother Sperante, has been holding her prisoner for seven years (8–32). Before Morgante, moved to pity, can start to comfort poor Florinetta, Beltramo and Sperante suddenly appear (33–34). Stanzas 35–53 describe the fights of Morgante with Sperante and Margutte with Beltramo, which result in the deaths of the two brothers and in Morgante's pledge to take Florinetta back to her parents.

As the three travel together, Morgante kills a huge turtle, which Margutte puts on a spit to roast; while the turtle is cooking, the half-giant goes looking for something to drink, soon returning with two barrels of wine. Once they start eating, Morgante drinks all the wine, leaving none for Margutte, who, annoyed, declares that he will soon part company (54–64). The following day Morgante slays a basilisk, which is speedily roasted and consumed by all before nightfall (65–70). After another day and a night spent walking, the three famished and thirsty travelers spot a huge elephant leaning against a tree asleep; the animal is promptly killed by Morgante, who devours it all by himself while Margutte is gone to fetch water (71–85). Florinetta convinces Margutte not to abandon them, promising him great culinary rewards once she has been reunited with her parents (86–90).

Several days later they arrive at a village, where Margutte roasts the camel stolen from Sleep, and where they learn that they are now in the kingdom of Belfior, ruled by Florinetta's father (91–107). Walking along the river Nile, Morgante kills a crocodile that has attacked him (108–110). Having entered the city of Belfior, Florinetta is recognized by her parents and her people, to whom she retells the story of her kidnapping and subsequent liberation by Morgante (111–125). Morgante accepts Florinetta's invitation to rest for a while in her father's castle, while Margutte spends all his time in the kitchen (126–138). A few days later Morgante, anxious to rejoin Orlando, leaves Belfior with Margutte, who shortly thereafter dies of laughter (139–155). Having arrived near the city of Babylon, Morgante is finally reunited with Orlando. With the giant's help, the Christian troops succeed in conquering Babylon (156–181).

1, 1–2. See Psalms 112:1. As noted by Ageno (550), the content of this entire canto is the product of Pulci's creative imagination. It centers on the adventures of the perennially famished Morgante and Margutte and the story of gentle Florinetta, whom they free from captivity and return to her parents. Critics consider this canto—in which all the major themes of popular epic poetry blend together in a succession of grotesque, pathetic, elegiac, fabulous, and comical situations—one of the very best in the poem.

5, 4–8. In his previously cited article (see note, XVIII, 112), Norbert Jonard considers the scene depicted in these lines "the most erotic in the poem" (98).

7, 1–2. The reader should be aware that in canto XX Morgante, after successfully killing a huge whale, dies of the bite of a crab (stanzas 50–51). By making his giant utter in line 2 a proverbial expression that denies the probability of such an event's ever taking place, Pulci gives Morgante's words a clearly ironic twist.

8–32. Though Florinetta's story begins in stanza 8, her presence in the poem materializes the moment the two traveling companions hear her laments in stanza 3. The initial atmosphere of the canto is one of solitude, silence, and darkness (2, 2–5), and this fact intensifies the effect that Florinetta's voice exerts first on Morgante and, more surprisingly, also on Margutte (3, 1–6).

Domenico De Robertis, in his brillant analysis of the Florinetta episode (412–420), points out that in stanzas 8–32, "Florinetta lives exclusively in the elegiac narration of her adventures, in the image she gives us of herself, in that long, sorrowful recollection of her past happiness." For the critic, in stanzas 33–53 and, though to a lesser degree, also in stanzas 54–104, Florinetta is only a "minor figure." The fight between Morgante and Sperante, occurring while Margutte is forced to face the much bigger but less clever Beltramo, places at center stage "the violent and noisy nature" of the contenders. It constitutes, to be sure, "the most spectacular bloody brawl in the entire poem, and it offers Pulci an unfailing occasion for amusement and comical interpretation." According to De Robertis, the character of Florinetta regains poetic vitality and color in stanza 105, and increasingly in stanzas 111–112, where "she again comes in contact with her own reality," that reality she created in her fairy-like tale and "in which she has found, like a new Proserpina, the strength to survive." Commenting further upon the literary reminiscences encountered in this canto—Ovid, Dante, Petrarch, and Poliziano—as well as the several mythological references, the critic considers them definitely in keeping with the tone and the suggestive quality of the episode.

While we believe that De Robertis's keen interpretation of Florinetta's role in the canto is essentially correct (the fairy-like, poetic quality of Florinetta's initial stanzas is recognized also by Giovanni Getto [68–69 and 123–124]), we also deem Attilio Momigliano's opinion of this female character to be unjustly negative and critically questionable. Momigliano writes that Florinetta is guilty of praising "a bit too naively her beauty," of lamenting her lost happiness in a somewhat "ridiculously rhetorical fashion," of "speaking in an affected tone comically contrasting with the sad condition in which she finds herself," and of saying (as in stanza 113) "incredibly foolish things" at times (248).

De Robertis's thesis is partially accepted by Angelo Gianni (297–370), who maintains that those who believe Florinetta to be a poetic character only when she is telling her story and repute her to be a secondary figure elsewhere "have killed Florinetta, have inhibited themselves from the possibility of savoring one of Pulci's central creations" (p. 328). According to Gianni, Florinetta, who during the hand-to-hand combat between the four giants has only briefly assumed the role of a spectator, in stanza 54 resumes her role as one of the protagonists of canto XIX. To be sure, Gianni's overly enthusiastic, though not always convincing, evaluation of this female character is consistent with a statement he makes on page 324: "Of all the female figures in the poem, each so similar to the other and almost devoid of distinguishing features, that of Florinetta, light, almost weightless, in some aspects a Poliziano-like figure, and yet a good pal of Margutte . . . is the only one . . . that remains in our memory as one of the symbols of the poem, the typical woman of *Morgante.*" For Ageno, Florinetta's liberation by Morgante and Margutte is "a true parody of noble and gentle deeds" (see "Scelta linguistica e reazione antiletteraria nel *Morgante,*" *Lettere Italiane* VII [1955]: 116).

9, 4–8. In these lines critics see a direct reference to Proserpina's kidnapping. For the myth of Proserpina, see note, XIV, 85, 4–8 and 86, 1.

10, 7. For the mythical Philomela, see note, I, 3, 1–4.

14, 8. For the story of the nymph Echo, see note, XIV, 9, 5.

15, 4. In 2 Samuel 18:9 we read that the mule on which Absalom was riding went under the thick boughs of a large oak tree, and the rider's head became entangled in the branches of the tree.

20–21. As noted by Getto (91), through Florinetta's disconsolate words, Pulci is able to evoke "with an extreme simplicity of means . . . the nostalgic song of parting and the lost sweetness of family love." We also find in these stanzas a clear Petrarchian reminiscence (see *Rime,* CXXVIII, 81–83).

27, 2. For the reference to Job, see note, XI, 93, 2.

28–29. Mercilessly beaten with an iron chain for no apparent reason and forced to eat the meat of "snakes and vipers," the unfortunate maiden is grotesquely expected to play with some "newborn serpents" and "little bears" brought to her by Beltramo and his brother. Angelo Gianni argues that when Beltramo strikes Florinetta, he does so because of his "evil and gigantic nature," and that he feeds her either instinctively or in order to nourish her; when instead he brings her small animals to play with as toys, the giant reveals "under his ferocious appearance the soul of a child" (334). In representing Beltramo (and Sperante) as an irrational and unpredictable mixture of brute strength, wild cruelty, and deranged childish behavior, Pulci has created a powerfully bizarre and nightmarish figure worthy of a contemporary horror movie.

30, 3. For Burrato, see note, XVIII, 51, 5.

35–50, 1–3. Morgante's initially respectful dealings with the two brothers indicate that he is not looking for a fight; in fact, he even tries to appeal to a certain kinship with them. If it is true that his stating that he and Margutte are wandering knights ready to fight for love may make us smile or seem somewhat ridiculous, it is equally true that Morgante seriously believes in what he says, as his behavior first with Meridiana and now with Florinetta clearly confirms. Since he became a Christian, his attitude toward the fairer sex has been better than that of the paladins, except maybe for Orlando. Interestingly, however, when Sperante suddenly hits him with the dragon, Morgante—who had previously told Beltramo to be ready to use his clapper against his opponent's mace—throws away his formidable weapon just when it would appear that he needs it the most. Thus he engages Sperante in one of the poem's most memorable hand-to-hand battles, in which the immense strength and savagery of the two contenders are depicted in an almost epic fashion. In representing instead the fight between Margutte and Beltramo, Pulci focuses the attention of the reader/spectator on his half-giant, who, maybe for the first time in his life, is in real danger of being killed. The winner of this lively and amusing confrontation is Margutte, who owes his success to his superior physical agility and the masterful use of his spurs. By comparing Margutte, who triumphantly jumps on top of Beltramo's dead body, to a rooster, Pulci concludes this encounter in a way which is most appropriate to the nature of this most bizarre character.

43, 7–8. For "nones" and "vespers," see note, XVII, 119–131.

50, 4–8 through 52. In consoling Florinetta, Morgante displays a tender, paternal attitude. Note that line 5 of stanza 52 contains another instance of what can be called "artistic irrationality" (a forty-meter-tall giant walking hand in hand with a girl). For Gianni (339), Pulci's use there of the adverb "always" "anticipates the rest of the canto . . . and humanizes the big brute as does no other word in the entire episode."

53, 5–8. Momigliano (279) maintains that Morgante is "a merry good fellow" and considers him a witty character. For the critic, however, Morgante's humor is substantially different from that of an ordinary man, because, since he is a giant, his humor is by nature "grotesque." In lines 5–8 of this stanza we have one of several instances in which Margutte becomes the target of Morgante's witty disposition.

56–59. While Florinetta looks on rejoicingly, the clapper that Morgante has failed to use against Sperante is put to work here to kill the turtle and to start a fire. Though they may seem a partial repetition of what has been described in stanzas 190–194 of the preceding canto, these lively, amusing stanzas serve to stress the different functions that Morgante and Margutte usually perform in the story: while the former provides the food, the latter cooks it, also making sure that there is wine or water on the table.

60–64. In this humorous scene, Morgante, quite pleased with himself for leaving no wine for his thirsty companion (the giant's laughter in line 7 of stanza 58 should have served him as a warning), immediately provokes Margutte's loud resentment, which is highly comical in its total uselessness (he has too much respect for Morgante's clapper). It is revealing of Margutte's roguish personality, however, that while outwardly laughing at Florinetta's mocking words, in his mind he is making plans for her (the ambiguous reference to the "many a luscious pear" he has had in the past leaves no doubt as to the nature of his intentions).

66, 5 through 70. Ironically, it is the maiden "with a heavenly face" who helps to dispel the unusually strange doubts of her companions. Evidently her lengthy experience as a captive and her recent familiarity with Morgante and Margutte are influencing both her thinking and her actions (as her clangorous burst of laughter in lines 7–8 of stanza 70 illustrates). Note that a basilisk (line 6, stanza 66) is a greenish tropical snake with black stripes. In Greek-Roman mythology it was believed to be a monster possessing great evil powers.

71–90. It is interesting to note that in this third eating episode, Margutte seems to have forgotten that in stanza 70 he declared that Morgante cannot be left alone with food. In all fairness to his half-giant, however, Pulci explains the reasons for Margutte's apparent lack of consistency. As the half-giant repeatedly states in stanzas 74 (line 4) and 76 (lines 7–8), and confidently reaffirms in stanza 80 (lines 7–8), he is sure that the elephant is too big for Morgante to consume all by himself. The giant's promise that this time he will wait for him (stanza 81, 1–3)—a promise that Morgante has no intention of keeping—is believed not because Margutte trusts Morgante, but rather because he doesn't consider him capable of eating such a huge beast. In the ensuing stanzas, Margutte appears so bewildered by what has happened (Florinetta's intervention has almost no effect on him) as to be momentarily unable to react to Morgante's openly making fun of his failure to understand his play on words (84, 7–8 and 85, 1–2). (Incidentally, here Morgante gives another demonstration of his humorous temperament.) When Margutte finally realizes that he has misjudged his companion's eating capabilities (he must consider himself lucky that Margutte did not eat him too), he expresses again his strong disappointment and renews his determination to part company.

Everything considered, however, his words are rather subdued in tone. Indeed, they do not seem to upset the giant; on the contrary, they make him laugh even louder (87, 4). Conversely, in spite of what Margutte declares to feel in stanza 89, Florinetta's promise of great culinary feats suffices to calm him down and make him change his mind.

As we have already noted, Morgante, who has elected himself protector of Florinetta, never fails to give the girl her portion of food and drink (61, 2–4 and 82, 7). It must be pointed out also that in line 4 of stanza 77, Florinetta, in order to express her hunger, uses the same image previously voiced by Morgante in canto XVIII (196, 1–2). In our opinion, the repetition of this beautiful image here is purely mechanical. According to Gianni (348), stanza 79, 1–5 "is the most felicitous in the canto, if not in the entire poem."

94, 5 through 102, 1–4. After making sure that Morgante's voracity doesn't deprive him again of his portion of the camel (96), Margutte gives an amusing show of his libertine tendencies at the expense of innocent Florinetta (97, 2–3). Harshly insulted and reprimanded by Morgante (98), he can promise only to do worse next time (100, 5–8). Then, when Morgante threatens to use his clapper on him (101, 1–2), the perverse half-giant, making an obscene allusion, declares that perhaps he will use his clapper before Morgante uses his.

114, 7–8. Gianni (355) states that in these lines Margutte appears momentarily "moved by the pathetic element" that pervades stanzas 111–114. On the basis of what we know of Margutte's nature, his sincerity here is questionable, to say the least.

115–124. Commenting upon these stanzas, which he considers to be "the essential stanzas in the canto," Gianni (356–359) contends that Pulci, "aware that he is giving his readers one of the most extraordinary reunions" in the poem, can hardly refrain from showing his joyful participation in the event (as line 6 of stanza 115 and lines 1–2 of stanza 118 would clearly indicate).

During the moving scene in which Florinetta is recognized by her father (stanzas 116–117), the dramatic tension of the moment is expressed by the sound of only one voice, that of Filomeno. Here, as elsewhere in *Morgante,* the characters are revealed through their actions (De Robertis, 519).

126, 7–8 through 133. As Giovanni Getto writes (121), Margutte's "gastronomic voyage ends with his arrival at Filomeno's court" and his appointment as kitchen supervisor, a most appropriate and welcome task which authorizes him not only to eat and steal as much as he can, but also to commit all sorts of perverse deeds. In this section of the canto, where Margutte makes his last appearance before his death, "the epos of gluttony is intertwined with he epos of rascality" (Getto, 122).

131, 5. Note that the expression used in this verse has a definite obscene meaning.

145–151. It is a commonly held opinion that Margutte's sudden death— one of the best-known and most widely read episodes in the poem—reflects

Pulci's desire to reunite Morgante with the count and take up again the matter narrated in *Orlando*. For Gianni (363), the death of the half-giant is essentially a "gag," a "humorous device" adopted by Pulci to skillfully rid himself of a character in which he had lost interest and which he no longer intended to use. For whatever reasons Pulci decided that it was time for Margutte to exit his poem, he certainly chose the way that best suited the personality of our half-giant. It is appropriate to mention at this point that Margutte makes his indirect reappearance on the stage of *Morgante* in stanzas 139–140 of canto XXVII. Here the Angel Gabriel, having told the dying Orlando that his beloved Morgante is saved in heaven, also reveals to him that Margutte is in hell, where "he is still laughing, and will laugh forever." Margutte is undoubtedly the poem's most consistent character.

For Domenico De Robertis, who defines Margutte as "a colossal hyperbole . . . the rhetorical transposition of an essentially verbal and metaphorical inspiration" (363), the death of the half-giant, "a victim of his own laughter, seems to acquire a symbolic meaning [the story ends with him and in the same way]" (364). The critic adds that as a character, Margutte "is never more completely himself than in his self-presentation; his extraordinariness and enormity are those of his intentions" (411). It is De Robertis's contention that what Margutte does after his so-called profession of faith is of relative importance, since all his actions, which end with his gastronomic "vacation" at Filomeno's court, are nothing but the logical outcome of the portrait he has made of himself (411).

Concerning the manner of Margutte's death, Gajetti, in his previously cited "Tematica della gola e morte di Margutte," acutely observes (174) that it would have been "a too obvious and banal solution" for Pulci to make Margutte die of indigestion. Our half-giant dies instead of laughter, caused by the last prank Morgante has played on him, a prank that Margutte himself could have conceived. In his article "Gli stivali di Margutte," Franco Martinelli points out that Margutte's feet, with which he has shamelessly tickled Florinetta's foot (97, 2–3), are finally the cause of his demise. According to Martinelli, in Margutte's death Pulci "acknowledges the result of a just will" (see *Annali d'Italianistica* 1 [1983]: 49–54).

149, 3–8 through 151. Margutte's totally unexpected death, a death he has unwillingly caused, makes the astonished and dismayed Morgante think that, having lost his friend, "nothing he would do would matter now" (lines 2–3 of stanza 150). Gianni (p. 363) may be right in interpreting these verses as a first clue to Pulci's intention to terminate Morgante's life soon as well (indeed, the giant's "untimely" demise, announced in line 5 of stanza 152, will take place in canto XX).

152–153. Note that in these two stanzas Pulci identifies as the primary literary source for his *Morgante* a poem he calls *Cantare d'Orlando* (Orlando's Song), which is not necessarily Rajna's *Orlando,* as Paolo Orvieto maintains (see introductory note to canto I). Pulci further explains from what other work he has derived the character of Margutte. It goes without saying that both the title of this book, *Statuti delle Donne,* and its author, a certain Alfamennone, are purely imaginary.

154, 7. Mentioned in the Old Testament (Genesis 10:8–10) as a mighty hunter and the first king of Babylonia, Nimrod is considered in patristic tradition to be greatly responsible for the construction of the Tower of Babel. It is possible that this belief, followed also by Dante, originated from the *Antiquities of the Jews* of Josephus, where Nimrod is presented as the proud leader in the line of Ham who led the Jews in adopting a rebellious attitude toward God. For the reference to the Tower of Babel, see Genesis 11:1–9.

157, 3. A further allusion to Morgante's height.

157, 5–8. As previously explained, the clapper is such an integral part of Morgante that upon seeing it, Orlando can more easily recognize his old friend. Note that in line 6 Orlando invokes the "god Mahound"; he may do so either to conceal his Christian identity or because he has been living too long among Saracens.

158. Calling Morgante "a good devil," Carlo Pellegrini recognizes that the giant harbors a sincere devotion and strong loyalty to Orlando, whose "moral influence" he obviously feels, since when he is in his company Morgante behaves in a much better and dignified manner (105). In lines 7–8 Pulci has colorfully and appropriately expressed the giant's overwhelming joy in being finally reunited with Orlando.

159–160. In reading these two stanzas depicting a joyful and moving occasion, one almost forgets that Morgante, though kneeling before Orlando, is still towering over him. To be sure, art renders realistic considerations irrelevant.

161, 1–2. Alexander the Great (356–323 B.C.), king of Macedonia, conquered the Greek city-states and ruled over the entire Persian empire. For the references to Hannibal, Caesar, and Marcellus, see notes XI, 75, 1–4; VII, 55, 7–8; and XV, 24, 5–8.

162, 1. Arnald of Bellanda, first-born son of Gherardo da Fratta, is a major character in the poems *Aspramonte* and *La Spagna.*

171, 6. For the story of Samson, see Judges 14–16.

172–173. The gastronomic comparison in line 8 of stanza 173 constitutes a perfect closing to these two colorful stanzas, where actions and images follow each other in rapid succession.

C A N T O   X X

SUMMARY: Invocation (1–2). Gano writes to Malagigi, who obtains the Maganzan's freedom from Antea (3–4). While traveling through Pagandom, Gano finds and hangs the shepherd who stole and sold Rinaldo's horse (5–12). Soon after, he encounters some of Salincorno's brothers. He kills one but is overcome by them, and he avoids immediate torture and death by confessing his mortal hate for Rinaldo (13–17). The giants take Gano to the castle of their mother, Creonta, where he is to be imprisoned. In the meantime, the shepherd who provided Gano with the hanging rope at the beginning of the canto secretly tells the Lord of Maganza that he is going to Babylon to inform Orlando of what has happened to him (18–20). Upon reaching the city, the shepherd is well received by Orlando and Rinaldo, who send him back to reassure Gano that they are going to rescue him (21–24).

Orlando, Rinaldo, Morgante, Oliver, Ricciardetto, and the Old Man of the Mountain board a ship owned by two pagans named Scirocco and Greco (25–30). On the high seas, a violent storm shakes the boat, causing great fear in everyone. During the storm Rinaldo throws Scirocco overboard, while Morgante saves the ship twice, first by using his body as a foremast and then by killing a huge whale which has threatened to capsize the vessel (31–48). Upon coming ashore, Morgante, who took off his boots to fight the whale, is bitten on the foot by a crab, and as a result of this bite he shortly dies. The giant's death is greatly lamented by Orlando and his companions, who have Morgante's body embalmed and sent to Babylon for burial (49–57).

Chiarione, owner of the Monaca inn where Orlando and his companions are temporarily lodged, informs his guests that the Emperor of Mezza, grief-stricken over his son Mariotto's death, has pledged to take revenge upon Rinaldo, Orlando, and his men (58–59). While professing to be Persian knights resting at the inn, the paladins are attacked by some of the emperor's men, several of whom they kill (60–67). The emperor himself goes to the inn and, greatly impressed with Orlando, invites the count to join him in his castle together with his companions (68–78). Leopante, the Admiral of Cavery, goes to Chiarione's inn, duels with Orlando, and is killed by him (79–91). To avenge Leopante's death, a young pagan warrior, Aldighieri, challenges Orlando, who, however, asks Ricciardetto to take his place. Aldighieri defeats both Ricciardetto and Oliver and kills the Old Man of the Mountain (92–96). Enraged at the Old Man's death, Rinaldo fights with Aldighieri, finally knocking him to the ground with a blow of his sword (97–99). When Aldighieri regains consciousness, he is questioned by Orlando and is consequently recognized by the count and Rinaldo as their own cousin (100–115).

1–2. Cantos XVIII and XIX (containing 200 and 181 stanzas respectively) are the longest that Pulci has written up to this point. In lines 1–3 of stanza 2, the poet seems to apologize for having gone beyond the limits he has previously observed. According to Ageno (602), the "error" that Pulci is referring to in line 4 of stanza 2 is "without a doubt that of having begun canto XVIII with a curious travesty of Mary's prayer" (see note, XVIII, 1, 1–2). Indeed, in lines 1–6 of the opening stanza of this canto, the poet offers a more appropriate interpretation of Mary's prayer.

3, 3–4. Gano, forced to leave Charlemagne's court and seek refuge in Pontiers (XII, 33, 1–3), was then banished from Paris by Rinaldo in canto XIII (22, 4 and 25, 6).

3, 5. Gano is surely correct in stating that Rinaldo is "at war." It was, in fact, at his suggestion that the Sultan asked the Lord of Montalban to kill the Old Man of the Mountain (XVII, 7–14). His alleged concern for the welfare of Rinaldo—whom he, a few stanzas later, recognizes to be a mortal enemy of his—further demonstrates the man's constant duplicity.

5, 8. For the reference to Spinellon's sister, see note, XVIII, 77–85.

8–9. See canto XVI, 106–110, 1.

11, 1–4. The shepherd's ironically amusing retort attests to Gano's ill repute as a traitor. The shepherd is unquestionably a thief and a liar, but he is a long way from being the artist of deceit that Gano is.

17–18. In spite of the giants' awareness of Gano's many treacherous actions, the Maganzan once again succeeds in disentangling himself from a very perilous situation.

19, 5–8 through 24. Though only a shepherd, the man portrayed in these stanzas could be Gano's spiritual brother. His clever plan and his eloquent speech could have been devised and delivered by Gano himself. In *Orlando* (XLIII, 28–30 and 35–38), by contrast, the shepherd is depicted as an individual without a mind of his own, whose only *raison d'être* is delivering to Rinaldo, following Gano's instructions, the Maganzan's request for help.

27, 1–4. It must be pointed out that *scirocco* and *greco* are also the names given to two major winds that blow over the Mediterranean Sea. The former, also called *scilocco,* is a warm and humid southeast wind originating in Africa; the latter, more commonly known as *grecale,* is a strong northeast wind active mainly during the winter months. The fact that in both *Morgante* and *Orlando* (XLIV, 4, 1–4) the man bearing the name of the African wind is depicted as crude and evil, while his partner, whose name calls to mind ancient Greece, is said to be a kind and refined individual, clearly indicates that this was not a casual choice of names. By adopting the same names used by the *canterino,* Pulci obviously intended to stress, for the benefit of his audience, the fundamental distinction between the pagan and the "civilized" world. A further reference to *greco* and *scirocco,* but only as winds, can be found in stanza 12, line 6 of canto XXI (such a reference is absent, however, in the corresponding stanzas of canto XLVI of *Orlando*).

28, 1. *Salvum me fac* is an imperative Latin expression, deriving from the Gospel as well as from juridical language; it literally means "save me." According to Ageno (610), it is used here to mean "to be paid in advance." In the original Italian version, the Latin imperative *fac* becomes *facche* to reflect the Tuscan pronunciation of such a verbal form.

28, 6. "Mister Goody-Goody" is the English rendition of the Italian *Pagol Benino,* an old fictitious character famous for his simplemindedness.

29–57. Though Pulci's epic is titled after Morgante, the giant appears in only ten of the first twenty cantos of the poem (I, II, III, VI, VII, IX, X, and then XVIII, XIX, and XX). As already noted, after Margutte's death, Morgante's days are numbered. Stanzas 29–57 of canto XX include the giant's last formidable deeds prior to his bizarre disappearance from the poem.

It must be pointed out that Morgante's role in Pulci's poem is far more significant and poetically meaningful than that of his namesake in the anonymous poem. To be sure, the similarities between the two characters concern mostly their physical attributes. In *Orlando,* while Morgante appears somewhat frequently in cantos I, II, III, IV, V, and X, he is only briefly mentioned in cantos XII, XIV, XV, and XVI. If I am not mistaken, he returns for the last time in the poem in stanza 5 of canto XVII, where the reader is told that Morgante runs to give assistance to Meridiana, whose horse has been killed by Salincorno. Morgante's presence aboard Greco's and Scirocco's ship, his saving it from sinking, as well as from the whale, and finally the scene of his death are nowhere to be found in *Orlando.* The fact that the *canterino* does not care to give his audience further news about Morgante clearly implies that he considers him only a secondary character.

Domenico De Robertis (39) is of the opinion that even if Pulci somehow knew the content of the lost closing cantos of the anonymous poem (the manuscript of *Orlando* ends abruptly with stanza 12 of canto LXI), it is quite probable that this last section made no mention of Morgante's death. With regard to this matter, the critic further suggests that "it cannot be excluded that the entire episode of canto XX, 45–57 was added by our poet at a later date in order to gratify the legitimate curiosity of the readers, which the anonymous poet had left unsatisfied." De Robertis is also correct in believing that Morgante's presence in canto XX not only gave Pulci the opportunity to create a most amusing scene, but also offered him the perfect chance to eliminate from the poem, thanks to the bite of a small crab, "that dear, cumbersome giant . . . about whom the anonymous poet was saying nothing anymore." Let us now compare stanzas 29–57 of canto XX of *Morgante* with the corresponding stanzas of canto XLIV of *Orlando.* While Pulci dedicates five masterful stanzas of his poem (31–33 and 35–36) to depicting the increasingly raging violence of the storm and the destructive effects it has on the ship, the anonymous poet merely informs his audience that a storm is taking place (7, 7–8 and 8, 3–8). In *Orlando* the entire episode, from the breaking of the storm to Rinaldo's throwing Scirocco overboard, occupies only six monotonous stanzas (7–11); Pulci, instead, narrates it in twelve rousing, lively, and delightfully amusing stanzas (31–42). Even if Pulci did pattern his poem on the text of *Orlando,* he so much improved on it as to make this episode entirely his own.

In his analysis of the character of Morgante, Paul Larivaille offers some interesting, if somewhat questionable, observations with regard to the giant's role in Pulci's poem. Noting that Morgante's decision to become a Christian (I, 39–46) is the result of a vision he has just had and not of a fight he has lost, the critic believes that the giant's initial conversion is a "device" which serves to establish Morgante's invincibility throughout the poem. With regard to this point, I would like to observe that Larivaille, who states that Pulci's masterpiece must be read in comparison with *Orlando,* though "without chronological implications of any kind," fails to explain whether Morgante's conversion in the anonymous poem, which is caused by the same vision, can also be considered a clever device, particularly in view of Morgante's marginal as well as lackluster performance in the *cantare popolare*. The critic further states that if Morgante's death, caused by the bite of a small crab, seems ridiculous, it nevertheless is "anything but comical and does not in the least infringe upon his already tested titanic strength."

Larivaille also maintains, in what is the most convincing section of his article, that in the personality of Pulci's main giant we can single out "a genuine chivalrous dimension" (not to be found in *Orlando*'s Morgante), thanks to which the giant is able to attain the "status of a paladin." For the critic, in fact, a close reading of the Morgante, Margutte, and Florinetta episode provides repeated and clear proof of Morgante's "definitive transformation into a perfect knight." Having recognized that gentle and delicate feelings coexist in Morgante with "excesses of barbarian fury," Larivaille points out that such "excesses" are not peculiar only to giants, but can also be found to a remarkable extent in paladins such as Orlando and Rinaldo (see "Morgante da 'fiero' a 'gentil gigante': Carnevalizzazione della materia cavalleresca e ricupero cavalleresco di tradizioni carnevalesche," in *Culture et société en Italie di Moyen-Âge à la Renaissance,* Hommage à André Rochon [Paris: Université de la Sorbonne Nouvelle, 1985], 103–115).

33, 4. Saint Erasmus was the patron saint of sailors and seafarers. A holy bishop and a native of Syria, he was tortured during one of Diocletian's persecutions. He was said to have been taken by an angel to the shores of Lake Lucrino in Italy, where he was again tortured. It is believed that he died in Formia in the year A.D. 303. The small flames which can be seen atop shipmasts at night during electrical storms are called "Saint Erasmus's fires" because they are attributed to this saint (Ageno, 612).

47, 5. As we have noted, Pulci often carries his portrayal of Rinaldo's rage to excess. He does likewise when he wishes to describe the Lord of Montalban's physical strength. Here we are told that Rinaldo hands Morgante his clapper as if it were a spear and not something weighing more than several hundred pounds.

50–51. In canto XIX, Morgante, after being attacked by a lion, compared this beast to a crab and himself to a whale (see note, 7, 1–2). The fact that our giant, who has just killed a huge whale, dies now because of the bite of that same small animal he has previously made fun of, attests to the poet's humorous intention. Morgante is mentioned again in the last two cantos of the poem: first in canto XXVII together with Margutte (see note, XIX, 145–151), and then in canto XXVIII, when in his closing stanzas the poet, who has placed Morgante in heaven, states that his giant will surely use his clapper against all who speak ill of his creator (136, 5–8).

53, 6. Dudon and Dudone are one and the same.

54, 7–8. According to Ovid's *Metamorphoses* (V, 313–340), when the giants climbed Mount Olympus, the gods, frightened by Typhoeus, ran from their heavenly home and eventually found refuge in Egypt, where they hid themselves in a variety of disguises.

61–62. The usually easily provoked Rinaldo seems surprisingly calm here at Can di Gattaia's insulting reply. The reason for Rinaldo's momentary lack of response is that he is busy once more courting a woman, the mistress of the inn, who is flirting with him. Obviously the paladin does not display a discriminatory attitude toward the fairer sex; a woman's social station means little to him as long as she is young and beautiful. A few stanzas later (79, 1–4), in fact, he even pledges to marry Chiarione's daughter, who has been dressing his wounds. Canto XXI, 16–17 will clearly show how reliable his promises are.

70, 2–4. A further instance in which circumstances contribute to render the count's presence in the poem either comical or ridiculous. As Momigliano writes (251), here Orlando's "squinting eyes give his gaze a mechanical and stern look."

79, 8. For the reference to Minos, see Dante's *Inferno,* V, 4.

85, 4. With regard to the custom of transporting mad people on carts, see note, VIII, 57–95.

91, 8. As noted by Ageno (629), this line contains an old Tuscan proverbial expression.

93, 1–6. Orlando's gallant behavior reveals his admiration for the courageous, and still unknown, young knight.

105, 8. Gerard (Gherardo) of Rossiglione is one of the sons of Bernard of Clairmont, brother of both Milo and Ammon, so Aldighieri is therefore Orlando's and Rinaldo's cousin. See note, I, 8–10.

111, 3. For the reference to Ugier's conversion, see note, IV, 94, 4.

C A N T O   X X I

SUMMARY: Invocation (1). Attacked by the emperor's men, Rinaldo kills Can di Gattaia and the emperor, then he and his companions take possession of the city of Monaca (2–12). Aldighieri is baptized and named emperor; also baptized are Chiarione and Greco, to whom Rinaldo gives Chiarione's daughter in marriage (13–18). Having appointed Chiarione governor of the kingdom, Orlando, Rinaldo, Oliver, Ricciardetto, Aldighieri, and the latter's squire, Rinieri, leave Monaca to free Gano (19–21). Upon reaching Castelfalcone, the paladins learn from two shepherds that Gano is imprisoned in Creonta's castle, and that the castle has six gates, each guarded by a lion (22–25). After they kill two of these beasts, the paladins enter the castle, where Rinaldo, Aldighieri, Oliver, and Orlando each slay one of Creonta's four sons. They all remain prisoners of the sorceress, however, whom they fail to kill, no matter how hard they try (26–52). In the meantime, Malagigi, desiring to rescue Rinaldo and his companions, sets out from Montalban with Astolfo, Guicciardo, Alardo, and Antea. Along the way, Astolfo is unhorsed by a Saracen knight, Liombrun, who is then confronted and killed by Alardo (53–64). Upon their arrival in Castelfalcone, Malagigi, with Rinaldo's assistance, succeeds in causing Creonta's death, thus lifting her spell from the castle (65–78).

During the night Astolfo, offended by Rinaldo's mockery, departs from the castle, leaving Malagigi and the other paladins behind (79–82). Wandering through a desert, the English lord finds lodging with three hermits. During the night a band of Saracen highwaymen enter the hermitage, gag the hermits, and make off with everything they can find, Astolfo's horse included. When the knight awakes and discovers that his steed has been stolen, he immediately runs after the bandits, kills four of them, and forces the hermits to hang the other six he has taken prisoner (83–92). Orlando leaves Creonta's castle in search of Astolfo, while Rinaldo and his companions, Gano among them, accompany Antea to Babylon. After a few days in Babylon, they resume their trip, eventually returning to Monaca (93–99).

Astolfo arrives in the city of Corniglia, which is ruled by the cruel giant Chiaristante, who makes his subjects worship him and his wife Filiberta as gods (100–103). Orlando stops at the hermitage previously visited by Astolfo. Here he is told by an angel that he will soon find Astolfo. Upon resuming his journey, the count frees a griffin from the mortal coils of a serpent. Then, while he is being attacked by four huge lions, the griffin comes to Orlando's aid, blinding one lion and killing another. Shortly thereafter, Orlando reaches Corniglia (104–116). In the meantime, the owner of the inn just outside Corniglia where Astolfo is staying reveals to the paladin that he would rather kill his daughter and then himself than hand her to Chiaristante as he has been ordered. Astolfo, determined to champion the innkeeper's cause, challenges Chiaristante to a duel, which takes place in the city's main square. Astolfo, who goes by the name of Galliano, succeeds in knocking Chiaristante off his horse. The giant is finally killed by Orlando, who, unrecognized by his cousin, has witnessed Astolfo's encounter with Chiaristante. Before dying, the giant reveals to the count that Greco is Corniglia's rightful king (117–144). At Orlando's prompting, Galliano is declared ruler of Corniglia; Orlando takes off his helmet and is recognized by Astolfo, and the two cousins happily embrace (145–154). Filiberta, acting upon the advice of two pilgrims, goes to Monaca to ask for Rinaldo's help in regaining her throne from Galliano (155–161). Upon seeing Filiberta, Greco announces that he is the dethroned king of Corniglia. Rinaldo, his companions, and a thousand horsemen leave immediately for Corniglia to reclaim the city from Galliano (162–172).

1, 1–3. In these verses Pulci paraphrases the beginning lines of the "Hail Mary."

4 through 7, 1–5. Though young Can di Gattaia's presence in the poem (he was first introduced in stanzas 60–61 of canto XX) lasts only a few stanzas, he is one of the many minor figures that the author of *Morgante* has rendered particularly noteworthy. Indeed, the *vis comica* of the episode is generated by the contrast between the shouted threats of the Saracen, reinforced by Pulci's own ironic remarks in lines 5–8 of stanza 4, and the cool ease with which

Rinaldo disposes of his blatantly arrogant adversary. The critic Ruggero M. Ruggeri, commenting upon the name Can di Gattaia given to the Saracen knight (in Italian *can[e]* means "dog," while *gattaia* derives from *gatto,* "cat"), suggests (355) that the poet might have chosen this name to amuse his readers. The "clever and humorous" mixing of the words *cane* and *gatto* would have the effect of ridiculing the Saracen, implying that he belongs to "a land of cats even though he is a dog" (see "Affinità di tematiche e di personaggi tra il *Milione* e il *Morgante,"* 349–362).

16–17. With the same facility with which, in the preceding canto, Rinaldo promised to marry the young lady who had momentarily charmed him (we are told here that she is Chiarione's daughter), he now tells her that he cannot keep his word because he is already married. He is lying, of course, to conceal the fact that he has lost interest in the girl. As Momigliano writes (244), this fact makes Rinaldo appear "a suitor in bad faith and an adulterer, in his intentions at least." The joyful willingness with which Chiarione's daughter accepts Rinaldo's decision to have Greco take his place as her husband—a solution Rinaldo has proposed to make amends for his "betrayal"—reveals once more that in *Morgante* love is rarely treated as a serious or tragic matter.

18, 5–8. For the old Tuscan proverb reproduced in these lines, see Ageno (641).

20, 1–2. The "good captain" and the "fair maiden" mentioned in these lines are Greco and his new bride.

21, 1–8. Pulci's ironically polemic discussion as to who was really appointed governor of Monaca stems from the fact that in *Orlando* (XLVI, 39, 3–4 and 41, 1), Greco and not Chiarione is named ruler of that city. Commenting upon this negligible detail, Puccini, in a note to his edition of *Morgante* (792), maintains that Pulci may have introduced the change because it simply made sense (as the poet himself explains in the last two lines of this stanza).

24, 5–6. This is another proverbial expression of Tuscan origin.

26, 1–8. Note that within the vividly horrid physical description of Creonta, Pulci has captured in the words "squint-eyed" and "malicious" the essence of the monster's character.

27, 4. See note, II, 39, 5–6.

28, 4. This proverbial expression, still in use today, appropriately renders Rinaldo's instinctive desire to fight.

29, 8. First mentioned in line 5 of stanza 13, Rinieri is Aldighieri's squire.

33, 5. The giant now talking is the one who had his nose cut by Gano in stanza 15 of canto XX.

34, 3–5 through 36, 7. The noseless, long-bearded, bald-headed giant is only another in the colorful gallery of grotesque creatures that populate *Morgante.* Note that the metaphor "hardest pear" is used in line 6 of stanza 35 with reference to the giant's head, which has been split in two by a quick blow of Rinaldo's sword. Likewise, in line 7 of stanza 36, "melon" is a metaphor for the arm that Aldighieri amputates from the giant he finally kills. Most of the poem's armed encounters, be they fought among knights or by humans against giants and/or monsters, are characterized by rapidity. In fact, as Momigliano writes (191), "Pulci leaves to Ariosto the long and uncertain exchanging of blows; his duels, usually extremely swift, lack in epic dignity."

40, 6–8 and 41. Here, as in stanza 89, 1–4 of the preceding canto, Rinaldo's taunting words have the effect of increasing Orlando's anger and his resolve to bring the fight to a speedy conclusion.

43, 5. For the reference to the sorceress Erichto, see again note, II, 39, 5–6.

46, 8 through 49. In spite of his religious upbringing (Luigi's younger brother Berardo and Berardo's wife, Antonia, both wrote sacred plays), Pulci soon abandoned the observance of Catholic practices to dedicate himself, for a period that lasted at least twenty years, to the study of the occult sciences, which experienced a remarkable revival in Florence toward the second half of the fifteenth century. In these stanzas, as Guglielmo Volpi points out, the poet wants to show that "he is familiar with demons and that he knows their qualities" (see "Luigi Pulci. Studio Biografico," 30–34). With regard to the infernal spirit Smahel, Puccini (800) suggests that he could also be the biblical Ishmael, son of Nethaniah, the ferocious killer of many Jews (Jeremiah 41:1– 3). Salayè, a word of possibly Arabic derivation (Ageno, 649), is the name of an evil spirit, perhaps a fallen angel, whom Pulci further mentions in three letters—III, VI, and VIII—all addressed to Lorenzo de' Medici and written before 1467 (Luigi Pulci, *Morgante e Lettere,* 942, 950, and 952). Niello, Squarciaferro (who reappears in canto XXV, 265, 5 as Squarciafer), Bocco, Nillo, Sottìn, Obysìn, and Rugiadan are the names of other devils, possibly invented by Pulci. It is difficult for the modern reader to grasp the true meaning of some of the references we find in stanzas 48–49. As Giuliano Dego, editor of the most recent edition of *Morgante* (Milano: Biblioteca Universale Rizzoli, 1992), notes (728), the reference to the jewels (or rings, bearing magic inscriptions) stolen by Rugiadan "has remained incomprehensible to all of Pulci's commentators." Berith, an idol worshiped in the ancient Palestinian town of Shechem or Sychem, today Nablus, was believed to be able to transform all types of metals into gold, and to make a person's voice more easily understood (Ageno, 649).

Ageno further explains (650) that, according to the *Liber Bileth,* Bileth was the most powerful of evil spirits and that "almandal" was the Arabic name given to the magic square used to conjure up all sorts of devils. The "certain snails" mentioned in stanza 49, 2 refer to rolled-up green, white, red, and yellow silk drapes attached to the four iron bars that were placed at the corners of the almandal. In Judges 2:13 it is written that the children of Israel "forsook the Lord, and served . . . Ashtaroth." Pulci transforms the Egyptian god into a devil; he will appear in canto XXV conjured up by Malagigi (119, 1–5). The fact that Pulci mentions Astaroth here in reference to Rinaldo's horse, which this devil will eventually enter by order of Malagigi (XXV, 133, 2), either proves (Ageno, 650) or leads us to believe (Puccini, 801) that Pulci had already conceived, even before completing canto XXIII, the last five cantos of *Morgante*. The "fool" mentioned in line 4 of stanza 49 perhaps is the Sienese citizen previously alluded to in canto XIV (see note, 53, 2–5). Quite obscure also are the references to Oratas (an evil spirit listed in the *Liber Bileth*) and the "doves" (stanza 49, 5).

56–64. After the tragicomic portrayal of Astolfo that Pulci has given in canto XI (68–107), here the English lord once more becomes the target of the poet's smiling mockery. Confirming—as previously stated in canto IX, 4, 5–8—his tendency to fall from his horse on the battlefield, Astolfo is shamefully thrown to the ground by the very man he so fiercely challenged just a few moments before. Commenting upon the paladin's behavior, Momigliano (256) calls him a "clown." Clearly Astolfo covers himself with ridicule when, even more distressed because of Antea's presence, he tries to blame his poor performance on his horse. Antea's biting reply, though expressed in an ironically consolatory tone, recalls Meridiana's mocking words to Oliver in canto VII (see note, 57–69). Astolfo is unhorsed in *Orlando* (XLVIII, 15–21) as well, where, however, Antea, though present at the duel, remains silent. In comparing the two versions of this episode, the reader cannot but agree with Momigliano (257), who affirms that in the anonymous poem Astolfo is portrayed in a "more dignified manner."

65, 5. Here and in several other stanzas in the poem, Malagigi is spelled Malgigi, as in the Italian text.

67, 5–8. Note that in this particular instance Antea, her face flushed, and holding hands with Rinaldo, appears to be genuinely in love with the Lord of Montalban.

68, 2–4. These lines are an amusing amplification of verse 3, stanza 41 of Part IV of *Ciriffo Calvaneo*, where reference is made to "the one who shod geese in Ormignacca." The buttrice (or butteries) is a sharp tool used by the blacksmith in shoeing horses or oxen.

74, 2 through 78, 2. In the description of Malagigi's actions and of Creonta's death, as in other pages of *Morgante,* Pulci reveals his particular fondness for magic. However, as Getto perceptively observes (106–107), the poet is not attracted to magic as a means of escape from the reality of everyday life; nor does he use it as a natural or necessary ingredient in the construction of a fairy tale. According to Getto, who states that "magic places itself at the center of the poet's curiosity," Pulci appears to be more interested in the technical and visual aspects of this mysterious art (as shown in stanza 76) than in the powerful suggestions it is capable of creating.

77, 8. Meleager, son of Althea, queen of Calydon, donated to beautiful Atalante the teeth of the great boar he had hunted, then killed his two uncles who had taken his gift away from the girl. To avenge the death of her two brothers, Althea then threw into a fire the half-burned log associated, by will of the Fates, with her son's life. As the log burned into ashes, Meleager, burning with fever, died a painful death. (For the story of Meleager, see Book VIII, 406–530 of Ovid's *Metamorphoses*.)

79–81. Enraged by Rinaldo's scornful reproaches, Astolfo totally loses his temper (as he did in VIII, 39–40) and reveals his extreme touchiness, while Rinaldo, able to remain cool, shows greater wisdom.

82, 1–8. In these considerations on fortune (they occupy an entire stanza in *Morgante* and are absent in the corresponding canto of *Orlando* [XLVIII, 36–40]), it is difficult not to perceive a personal note on Pulci's part. Indeed, stanza 82 has little or no connection with the stanzas that immediately precede and follow it. If it is true that fortune is often mentioned and that remarks about her interventions recur here and there in the poem (as in cantos I, 11, 1–2; XX, 45, 1; and XXI, 168–169), it is also true that they are a conventional *topos* in epic poetry and are usually motivated by the author's desire to comment on the story or to introduce a new development and/or character. Significantly, Angelo Gianni (135) considers stanza 82 "a parenthesis" in the plot of Astolfo's adventures.

83–92. In these stanzas Astolfo happens to meet three "holy hermits," who are no less fearful and cowardly than Abbot Clairmont's monks in cantos I and II. The English lord's conversation and subsequent confrontation with these friars constitute one of *Morgante*'s most humorous scenes, and it is portrayed by Pulci with colorful immediacy and unquestionable irony. The poet openly makes fun of these hypocritical and sly hermits who, desiring to lead a quiet life, endure many vexations and constant lootings, while claiming that their slothful lack of resistance is motivated by religious scruples. In reality, their actions appear uniquely dictated by their desire to avoid trouble at any cost. If in the past the fear of the Saracen highwaymen prevented them from defending themselves, now the pain inflicted upon them by Astolfo's furious beatings quickly transforms them into expert hangmen.

The episode is also important because it gives the reader deeper insight into the true quality of the faith of Astolfo, a character Momigliano (225) defines as "the poem's most impious paladin." To be sure, Astolfo does not openly deny God, but to a possible divine justice (the one invoked by the frightened hermits), he much prefers his own personal type of justice, one more immediate and certain. Astolfo relies only upon his own physical strength and does not appear to feel any need for God. We could say that Pulci portrays him as a very practical and skeptical individual who cares little about divine reward or punishment. In his previously cited work *Io vo' dire una frottola* (lines 164–171), Pulci asserts that he trusts "little, not at all, or seldom" six things; of these, the one he trusts the least is *fè di cherica rasa*, "the faith of a cleric." The monks and the hermits we encounter in *Morgante* seem to belong to this last category.

99, 2. The maiden mentioned here is obviously Chiarione's daughter and Greco's wife.

100, 5–8. See note, IX, 20–21 and 22, 1–5.

101, 2. For the reference to Barbary, see note, II, 50, 5.

103, 4–5. See note, XI, 30, 8.

104, 4. The "someone" alluded to here is the Saracen highwaymen hanged by the hermits.

114–115. As noted by Ageno (668), in these stanzas Pulci gives a brief moralizing speech containing allusions to well-known Aesopian fables and equally well-known collections of proverbs and sayings taken from the classics and Christian authors. Certainly line 5 of stanza 114 derives from the famous words "Some fell upon stony places. . . . And some fell among thorns" (Matthew 13:5–7). The Aesop's fable that Pulci is referring to in lines 7–8 of stanza 114 tells how a small mouse was able to free a lion, which had previously saved its life, by gnawing away at the ropes of the hunter's net into which the lion had fallen. The *Detti de' morali,* mentioned in line 3 of stanza 115, is believed by Ageno (669) to be a collection of sentences attributed to Guillaume de Conches, the title of which is *Moralium dogma philosophorum.*

116, 7. The story that Pulci wishes to shorten here is the one told in the anonymous *Orlando.*

117, 1. See note, 103, 4–5.

123, 1. Pulci uses the expression "like a burned cat" to indicate the extreme speed with which the messenger returned to his king.

129–135, 4. The sight of Orlando, who, accustomed to paying for his lodging with either a club or his sword when out of money, appears now to accept the innkeeper's willingness to give him credit and, because of his emaciated appearance, becomes, with his horse, the object of insults and ridicule, is a good example of the deterioration in the representation of Charlemagne and his knights which had gradually been taking place in chivalric literature (see note, III, 26–30). Concerning Orlando's appearance in these stanzas, Giovanni Getto (95–96) writes that "Pulci can hardly renounce plunging him into that pungent and smoky atmosphere of the picaresque genre." To understand the full meaning of line 1 of stanza 132, one must keep in mind that on May first (*Calendimaggio*), Florentines celebrated spring and did not have to work.

137, 3–4. Chiaristante's ridiculous attempt to justify his fall from his horse is not much different from the excuse given by Astolfo in stanza 63. It may be that, recognizing this fact, Astolfo, though not fully accepting Chiaristante's explanation, declines to make fun of his challenger and is even willing to accept the verdict of a bystander (Orlando).

138, 3–5. Germans were proverbially represented as drunkards and guzzlers. A reference to Germany as "the land of drunken Germans" can also be found in Dante's *Inferno,* XVII, 21.

138, 6–7 and 139, 7. See note, XX, 70, 2–4.

142, 7. Ageno (677) explains that the reason the giraffe, a wild but certainly not ferocious animal, is mentioned here as a formidable adversary is probably that the poet, never having seen one, imagined it to be much bigger and very dangerous.

142, 8. Note Pulci's ironic comment concerning the stirrup, previously mentioned in stanza 139, 3.

146, 1–4. The vividly realistic scene depicted in these lines attests to Pulci's careful observation of animal behavior.

147 through 150, 1–2. Pulci's skeptical considerations on the wisdom of Chiaristante's former subjects is eloquently and bitterly expressed here. The mood of the masses can change from one moment to the next, and today's respected ruler can become tomorrow's despised tyrant.

151 through 153, 4. As we have seen, paladins occasionally like to play a practical joke on their fellow knights. Orlando is no exception. Once again angry words are followed by tears, hugs, and kisses.

159, 1–2. The advice that the two mysterious pilgrims—the reader is left unsure also of their religious faith—give to Filiberta in order to help her regain her throne is, to say the least, amusingly cynical. There is, by contrast, no sense of mystery or ambiguity in *Orlando* (LXI, 33–37), where one of the two pilgrims, said to be a wise and holy man, strongly urges Filiberta to renounce Mahound immediately and believe in Christ. Significantly, it is only after the queen has agreed to convert that the two men tell her to seek Rinaldo's help in Monaca.

159, 8. *Salamelecca* (*salamelecche* in the Italian text) derives from the Arabic *as-salam 'alaik* (peace be with you).

160, 8. Another proverbial expression of Tuscan origin.

161, 1–3. These lines contain an almost verbatim translation of the well-known Latin proverb *Audaces fortuna iuvat, timidosque repellit*.

164, 1. For Baal, see note, XV, 111, 5.

164, 4. Reference is made here to the myth of Prometheus, who gave men the fire he stole from heaven. For this he was punished by Jove, who had him chained to Mount Caucasus; he was eventually freed by Hercules.

164, 6. For Capaneus, see note, X, 144, 1–5.

165, 4–8. Maybe also in Greco's somber remarks about the fickleness of fortune we can detect, though to a lesser extent than in stanza 82, the author's own voice.

171, 1. Note that the words "et cetera" in this line also refer to *Orlando* (see note, 116, 8).

C A N T O   X X I I

SUMMARY: Invocation (1). Astolfo and Orlando meet Rinaldo and his companions, who are camped outside Corniglia. Orlando challenges Rinaldo, but the duel is interrupted when the count reveals himself to his cousin. Astolfo and Orlando return to the city together with Rinaldo, Alardo, Oliver, Guicciardo, Malagigi, Greco, and Gano (2–14). A few days later they learn from Dudon, who has reached Corniglia, that Calavrion has arrived in France with an army of 140,000 men to avenge the death of the Old Man of the Mountain, his brother. Dudon also tells them that equally in danger is

Montalban, which has been besieged by 60,000 Maganzans. This last news immediately provokes Gano's protestations of innocence as well as Rinaldo's and Astolfo's accusations (14–33).

After Rinaldo has named Filiberta queen of Monaca and Greco her successor, the Christian knights, Gano and Greco among them, leave for Paris. Along the way they stop in Villafranca, whose ruler, Diliante, a nephew of the Old Man of the Mountain, invites them to dine with him (34–41). While eating, Rinaldo kills a young clown who has been stealing food from his plate. This fact enrages Diliante, whom Rinaldo challenges to a duel. Amazed by Rinaldo's military might, Diliante asks him to tell him his name. Rinaldo kindly obliges, revealing also the identity of all but one of his companions. To Diliante, who believes that Rinaldo has killed the Old Man of the Mountain, the Lord of Montalban replies that the Old Man was his friend, that he baptized him and then killed the giant who had slain him. Diliante, who has just started talking about Calavrion's reasons for invading France, is suddenly interrupted by the roar of a huge white lion that has been terrorizing his subjects. When Rinaldo, who has gone to a nearby forest to kill the lion, returns to Villafranca, he is worshiped like a god by the townspeople (42–64). A grateful Diliante pledges military assistance against Calavrion, and states that Uliva, King Costanzo's daughter, may also be willing to hire, with his financial support, an army of 100,000 men. Orlando promptly approves Diliante's proposal.

Rinaldo, with Ricciardetto, Guicciardo, and Alardo, departs immediately by sea to contact Uliva in Babylon (65–73). Soon after Rinaldo's departure, and while Orlando is momentarily away from the palace, Gano reveals to Diliante that the Old Man of the Mountain was killed by Aldighieri. Replying to Diliante's insulting charges, Aldighieri challenges him to a duel and succeeds in killing him (74–108). Orlando and his companions, accompanied by Diliante's men, who are happy to have been freed from the lion and their cruel king, leave Villafranca for Paris, where they are joyfully received by Charlemagne (109–115). Queried by the emperor as to Gano's whereabouts, Orlando informs him that the Maganzan has gone to Montalban to see Grifonetto. While Calavrion and Archilagio are deeply disturbed because of Orlando's return to Paris, the count suggests that Aldighieri leave with 10,000 horsemen for Montalban, where his father, Gherardo, happens to be (116–123). While attempting to take Montalban, Gano is confronted by Aldighieri. Aided by Beltramo and Pulidor, Gano succeeds in gravely wounding the young knight. Berlinghieri, who has valiantly fought alone against the Maganzans, is soon joined by Gherardo, the Dane, Vivian, and 3,000 horsemen. Their arrival causes the retreat of Gano and his troops (123–138). Shortly after Aldighieri has met his father, he dies. His body is then taken to Paris, where his funeral is to take place (139–146). Upon learning of Aldighieri's death, Calavrion obtains Charlemagne's permission to attend the former Saracen knight's funeral and subsequently, with his troops, joins the emperor in laying siege to Pontier, where Gano has gone, taking with him Grifonetto and his men (147–155).

Rinaldo, Guicciardo, Alardo, and Ricciardetto arrive by sea near Saliscaglia, which is ruled by Arpalista and defended by some brave female warriors. Rinaldo enters the city with a couple of seamen and steals food and wine. When he later returns to Saliscaglia with his brothers, they kill all the female warriors that Arpalista has sent against them (156–170). Rinaldo first slays Arpalista's cousin, Archilesse, then duels with Arpalista, who surrenders. The Lord of Montalban orders him to go and offer submission to Orlando (171–189). Unable to find Orlando in Paris, Arpalista goes to Pontier, where Gano, accusing him of being a spy, challenges him to a duel. Arpalista easily unhorses the Maganzan, who, changing tactics, invites him to his palace. Here Gano succeeds in convincing the Saracen to go and see Charlemagne in order to obtain the emperor's pardon on his behalf (190–205). Arpalista's mission is successful; it is agreed, however, that Gano's pardon must also be approved by Rinaldo. Gano meets with Charlemagne and pledges to go looking for Rinaldo. Angered by this pact, Calavrion confronts Arpalista, and in the ensuing duel, the two Saracens manage to kill each other (205–215).

In the meantime Rinaldo, having baptized the people of Saliscaglia, leaves the city alone to go and free the way to the Holy Sepulcher from the bandit Fuligatto. After he and some pilgrims who are traveling with him have landed, they enter a nearby city. Here Rinaldo wins a joust fighting on behalf of Brunetta, one of the two daughters of the admiral who rules over the city (216–238). Then, while crossing a desert, he meets up with Gano and forgives him (239–241). When the Lord of Montalban and the pilgrims reach Sardonia, a city whose male inhabitants have all been killed by Fuligatto, they are cordially received by Queen Filisetta. Shortly thereafter, Rinaldo departs alone in search of Fuligatto (241–262).

1, 1–3. In these lines we find a further demonstration of Pulci's lack of accuracy with regard to religious matters. The poet, in fact, attributes the creation of the universe to the "Son of Israel" and states that Christ sent the Angel Gabriel to announce Jesus' birth to Mary. Concerning Gabriel, see note, I, 2, 4.

3, 1–8. In feigning anger (2, 5–7), Astolfo shows that he too likes making fun of his friends. This time the joke is on Rinaldo, who is perhaps the poem's major prankster. Interestingly, the usually serious Orlando immediately joins in with Astolfo. Clearly both knights, by making overt allusions to Rinaldo's well-known weakness for the fairer sex, fully enjoy provoking the irate paladin's humorous, though short-lived, reaction.

4, 4. Vegliantino's dreadful physical condition is described in canto XXI (130, 5; 131, 5; 132, 1–2; and 140, 1–2). Obviously Orlando's horse has not yet had time to regain its former strength.

6, 7. The "man" Rinaldo is referring to is Greco, Corniglia's rightful ruler.

18, 5. Vivian (or Viviano), a paladin, is Malagigi's brother (see note, XII, 23, 8).

18, 6. Ricciardetto cannot be in Montalban because he is in Corniglia with his brothers Rinaldo, Alardo, and Guicciardo.

19, 2. If it is technically true that in this instance Gano cannot be held directly responsible for the attack that one of his captains has led against Montalban, it is also true that the Lord of Maganza has been plotting, at least since canto XVII, to gain possession of Rinaldo's fortified city. Gano's actions later in the canto prove that Rinaldo and Astolfo are indeed right not to believe a word that he says.

20, 4. Grifon, also called Grifonetto, must not be confused with another Maganzan, Grifon of Altafoglia, mentioned in canto XI, 25, 8.

21–24. Orlando's reply to his cousin suggesting fairness in judging the Lord of Maganza prompts Gano's protestations of friendship for Rinaldo, whose behavior toward him he declares difficult to understand, since Rinaldo was among those who left Monaca to go and free him from Creonta's castle (canto XXI). Not only does he pledge to punish Grifonetto, but in a frenzy of hypocritical enthusiasm he even declares himself to be a totally changed man, ready to make amends for his past sins and to spend the rest of his life making pilgrimages to the Holy Land and other shrines. The overstated tone of this sudden contrition has the effect of making his alleged change of heart as incredible as it is comical. With regard to line 3 of stanza 24, note that the body of the Apostle James was believed to be buried in Santiago de Compostela, in Galicia, Spain.

25–26. In his highly ironic answer to Gano, Rinaldo first states that the Lord of Montalban cannot fool him into believing that he feels shame for his past transgressions, since he has no shame at all. Then, recognizing that Gano has more vices than the alphabet has letters, he compares him to a charlatan who tries to sell vases filled with useless ointments. With regard to stanza 26, it must be noted that the original Italian text contains a number of colorful idiomatic and slang expressions which are difficult to render in English. The "mandrake root" (in Italian *mandragola*) mentioned in line 6 of stanza 26 is a plant belonging to the Solanaceae or nightshade family. In ancient times, as we are told in Niccolò Machiavelli's famous play *La Mandragola,* the mandrake root was believed to have magical powers. With reference to line 7 of the same stanza, Ageno (694) notes that charlatans were also deemed capable of taming snakes.

27–33, 1–6. Compared with Rinaldo's brief sardonic remarks in stanzas 26–27, Astolfo's repetitive tirade proves definitely less biting. Indeed, the English lord's denunciation of Gano's constant deceitfulness has no adverse effect on Orlando, who seems to consider it little more than a childish outburst. Worthy of note are, however, Astolfo's contemptuous words for Charlemagne (stanza 29, 2–8), which are once again indicative of the terribly low esteem in which the emperor is held by his own paladins.

If one considers the context of Pulci's *Morgante,* one cannot but notice that Astolfo's diatribe reflects on the foolishness of the French to believe the ever-deceitful Gano in the *Chanson de Roland*. One might also point out, with regard to Pulci's intertextual references to the Roland tradition, that the indication of an earlier quarrel between Roland and Ganelon reads as if he were supplying an answer to this old-age accusation by Ganelon in the *Chanson de Roland*. No one knows of such a previous quarrel. The comments of Astolfo surely emphasize the foolishness—here attributed to Charlemagne's advanced age—that the emperor displays in not seeing through Ganelon. Ultimately it will cost him everything, as Roland ends up being the bait in the trap. For the references to Joseph and Job made in lines 1 and 4 of stanza 28, see notes, XV, 102, 1–8 and XI, 93, 2.

36, 3–6. For these verses, as well as for lines 6–8 of stanza 200 and 1–3 of 201, see note, 20–21 and 22, 1–5.

37, 7. The Italian expression *buon tre volte* ("good three times") means "very foolish."

38, 5–8. Divine justice, according to Malagigi, will finally make Gano pay for all his sins.

40, 2. Note Rinaldo's promptness in accepting Diliante's offer. It would definitely be against the Lord of Montalban's nature to turn down a dinner invitation.

42 through 45, 1–6. Here Rinaldo's behavior is similar to that which he displays in stanzas 46–51 of canto III. For the reference to the Germans in line 7 of stanza 43, see note, XXI, 138, 1–5.

47, 8. Ageno explains (701) that sugar-coated pears that had been poached in wine were customarily served at the end of a meal. The proverbial expression *aspettar le pere guaste* ("to wait for a rotten pear") meant "to remain at a table longer than is proper."

52, 5–6. These lines clearly derive from Matthew 5:39. The fact that Diliante, a pagan, utters them does not necessarily imply a resort to irony on Pulci's part. It rather attests to the proverbial significance that this biblical verse had acquired in Pulci's time.

55, 6–7. Here Rinaldo is brazenly lying to Diliante; the Old Man of the Mountain was, in fact, killed by Aldighieri in canto XX, 95, 2–8.

60, 4. According to Luke 19:1–4, Zacchaeus, a rich but short inhabitant of Jericho, climbed a sycamore tree in order to catch a better view of Jesus passing through his city.

62, 6–8. Giovanni Getto (74) calls this memorable scene, where men are suddenly seen as birds, "a grotesque and essential xylography."

70, 1–8. For the story of Uliva, King Costanzo's daughter who was saved by Rinaldo and Orlando from the giants who were holding her captive, see XVI, 96–101, 104–105 and XVII, 83–135.

72, 4–5. Here Orlando (or, even better, Pulci himself) is less than accurate; it is, in fact, Rinaldo who has slain Salincorno, thus avenging the deaths of both King Costanzo and Spinellone (XVIII, 99–107).

74, 7–8 through 85. Attilio Momigliano, who defines Gano as "an artist of the word, if not of action," states that the Lord of Maganza's entire life consists of "unctuous manners, crafty sentences, and perfidious advice" (310). Indeed, in this canto Gano gives another brilliant performance of his consummate mastery of deceit. Though the idea for a new treason has been in his mind for some time (54, 5–6), he has been patiently waiting for the right moment to act on it. Once the shrewd and smooth-talking Gano has obtained Diliante's pledge to secrecy, he reveals that Rinaldo has deceived him, inasmuch as it was Aldighieri who killed the Old Man of the Mountain. The facts the Maganzan relates, in a reasonable and convincing tone, are only partially true (77–80); in reality, what prompts him to speak is the desire to bring great harm to his fellow Christian knights by presenting the death of the Old Man not as an accident of war but as the result of premeditated murder (81–84).

86, 7. This line contains a proverbial expression commonly used in Pulci's time. As noted by Ageno (712), it has the same meaning as the expression "to catch a mouse with a trap."

87 through 91, 1–4. The manner in which Diliante approaches the matter of the Old Man's death, as well as the tone he uses throughout his confrontation with an initially stunned Orlando, indicates not only that Gano has made quite an impression on him, but that he has also learned a great lesson from such a teacher. If it is true that in order to conceal his source the Saracen must accuse Gano, too, it is also possible that in reaffirming the Christian lord's treacherous nature, the pagan ruler expresses a certain degree of ironic satisfaction. To be sure, Diliante's clever performance elicits Pulci's congratulatory remark in lines 5–6 of stanza 91. With regard to the meaning of lines 3–4 of stanza 91, it must be pointed out that Pulci, using an old Tuscan proverb, compares Gano to a cat that, having finally been caught in the act of stealing a piece of lard, gets the punishment it deserves.

94–97. Resuming the role of moderator that he previously played in the canto, Orlando intervenes in the discussion to express his full approval of Aldighieri's challenge, and to proclaim his companions' consistently honorable behavior and also his own. Having stated that "treason is not a common thing in France" (97, 1), Orlando in all fairness clears Gano of any responsibility in the death of the Old Man of the Mountain.

98, 6–8 and 99, 1–4. Note that Gano's attempt to keep up the comedy by threatening Diliante—who once again seems to be pleased to call him a traitor—provokes Pulci's further appreciative comment.

100, 4 and 7. Two frequently used proverbial expressions are contained in these lines.

101, 1. In the Italian text Astolfo's reply to Orlando is *"Tanti billi billi!"* (translated as "Why such mystery?"). Ageno notes (716) that while the popular expression *fare billi billi* literally means "to call the chickens" (at feeding time), used figuratively it means "to make covert allusions." Commenting upon the first few lines of stanza 101, De Robertis (318) rightly observes that in replying to Orlando, Astolfo expresses his feelings by resorting to "most colorful language," which greatly contrasts with the more diplomatic and metaphorical language uttered by the count.

101, 8. Ageno (717) explains that the expression "to make a hare come out into the open" contained in this line derives from the language of hunters and means "to reveal a secret."

102, 1–8. Giovanni Getto (106–107) maintains that Pulci does not resort to magic as a means to escape from the limits of reality, nor is he attracted to it because of its functional value as a determining ingredient in a fabulous tale. For Getto, Pulci usually appears more interested in the technical aspects of magic than in the atmosphere of mystery that magic creates. Stanza 102 clearly supports Getto's thesis. Note that the "pentacle" was a five-cornered object made of stone, metal, or parchment paper on which magical signs were drawn; the "seals" were magical letters or symbols; the "tapers" were very slender candles used with the magic square or "almandal" needed to conjure up devils; in the "pots," special terra-cotta vessels, were placed carbonized pieces of aromatic wood (Ageno, 717). See also note, XXI, 46–49.

104, 2. Davide Puccini (883) offers a different interpretation of this line. He maintains that Pulci, recalling Dante's *Inferno* (XXXII, 60), says that everyone would have liked to plunge Gano into the icy section of hell [*in gelatina*], where traitors are punished.

109, 6. A direct reference to the Israelites' exodus from Egypt.

110, 3. This is a poet's oversight. According to XX, 26, 2, the flags that the Christian knights have been carrying from Babylon portray "a lion . . . in a black field."

114, 4–6. The author here bitterly comments upon the inconstant behavior of the Jewish people who, after having triumphantly received Christ in Jerusalem (Matthew 21:8–11), allowed His crucifixion. A somewhat similar consideration is expressed in canto XXI (see note 147–150).

117, 3–8. Once more Astolfo's behavior toward the emperor greatly contrasts with Orlando's. The English lord, like his cousin Rinaldo, has no compunction about voicing (as he did in 29, 3–8)—this time, however, to Charlemagne's face—his derision for the emperor's loyalty to Gano. It must be noted that Astolfo's disrespectful words elicit no response from Charlemagne. Orlando is unusually silent as well. While the emperor's lack of reaction may be due to the fact that the old king has become deaf to any criticism concerning Gano, Orlando's silence may indicate his agreement with Astolfo's assessment of the situation, even though he may object to the form in which it is expressed. As lines 7–8 of stanza 91 attest, Orlando is not unaware of Gano's true nature.

121, 7–8. A proverbial expression meaning "the person who boasts of being courageous when not in danger, has no courage at all when he must face danger" (Ageno, 722).

124, 2–3. Both Beltramo of Maganza and Count Pulidor of Lausanne appear only in this canto of *Morgante*. The latter is killed by Berlinghieri in stanza 129, and the former by Aldighieri in stanza 130.

124, 7. The falcon's emblem belongs to the House of Maganza.

126, 6. Ageno remarks (724) that the expression *fare le mummie* means "to try to make oneself disappear."

130, 4–8 through 135. With these stanzas begins the amusingly hyperbolic rehabilitation process of Berlinghieri, who, as Pulci jokingly remarks in stanzas 73–88 of canto VIII, had hardly given a shining demonstration of his military worth.

132, 1–2. For the reference to Marcellus, see note XV, 24, 5–8. The African is Publius Cornelius Scipio Africanus, victor over Hannibal in the Battle of Zama (202 B.C.). Paulus is Lucius Emilius Paulus, the Roman consul who in 168 B.C. defeated Perseus, the king of Macedonia. Camillus is the Roman general Marcus Furius Camillus; he conquered and destroyed the ancient Etruscan city of Veii, freed Rome from the Gauls, and died in 365 B.C.

134, 7–8. As previously noted, Pulci makes frequent use of metaphors, which he derives from the animal kingdom, and in this particular case from one of Aesop's fables (Ageno, 726).

135, 1. Horatius is Publius Horatius Cocles, the Roman soldier who, according to legend, fought alone against the Etruscan troops of King Porsenna at the head of the Sublicius Bridge in the year 507 B.C.

135, 5–8. Giovanni Getto (185–186) writes that *Morgante* "offers spaces and corners in which the author loves to seek refuge in order to confess his artistic credo to himself and others." Lines 5–8 of stanza 135 constitute for Getto one of those occasional moments in which Pulci expresses his own feelings, revealing, as he does in this particular instance, his pervasive enjoyment "in losing himself in the pure pleasure of a dream and of an adventure, [and] in constantly enriching with details the beautiful deeds of a paladin."

140–141. Aldighieri's "extraordinary end" is for Angelo Gianni (7) one of the poem's most pathetic moments. Attilio Momigliano, who maintains that only when Pulci ceases to be an artist and remembers that he is a man is he "capable of finding an expression of compassion for the vanquished" (184), also recognizes the episode of Aldighieri's death as "exceptionally moving."

146, 3. Douai (from medieval Latin *Doasium*), in the French section of Flanders, gave its name to the precious fabrics made in that city.

149, 6. Riccieri, son of Rambaldo, the duke of Risa (Reggio Calabria), is a character in Andrea da Barberino's *Aspramonte,* where he is proclaimed to be the world's bravest knight. As Davide Puccini observes (899), Pulci's remark has a decisively ironic meaning.

150, 4–5. Two proverbial expressions, still in use today, though with a facetious implication.

153, 1. The "orator" in question is Marcus Tullius Cicero, who was born in Arpino in 106 and died in Formia in 43 B.C.

155, 5–8. For the metaphors contained in these lines, see note, 101, 8.

158–164. The captain's description of the warrior women (lines 5–8 of stanza 158) has definitely awakened Rinaldo's interest in anything that is unusual or weird. It is therefore with great, defiant enthusiasm that he hurls himself into a new adventure, thus again demonstrating that he is a rascal, a voracious eater, and a drunkard. Visually suggestive are lines 7–8 of stanza 164, which, Momigliano writes (181), "give visible form to the effects that drunkenness was bound to produce in Rinaldo's brain."

165–170. Commenting upon these stanzas, Angelo Gianni (164) maintains that "the battle ... has transformed itself into a close succession of obscene allusions, into a carnal combat of bold young men with hairy women, who are quite suitable for a different type of fight." Ageno explains (736) that Pulci's amusing observation that everyone was fighting in the dark because all the gates of the city were closed (168, 1–2) "emphasizes the numerous double meanings contained in the preceding and following lines."

The paladins' encounter with the female warriors is recounted also in *Orlando* (canto LVI, 5–26). In this poem, the female warriors, rather than being ugly and hairy, are presented as brave, strong, and beautiful. The confrontation of Rinaldo's brothers with these "Amazons" takes place as soon as the paladins, having landed, arrive before the gates of Saliscaglia. Repelled by Arpalista's women during their first attempt to enter the city, Ricciardetto, Guicciardo, and Alardo, having been harshly scolded by Rinaldo, finally succeed in overpowering them. There is no mention in *Orlando* of Rinaldo's food raid into the city, nor of his being drunk. As a matter of fact, the gastronomic element, which is the main reason for the entire episode in *Morgante,* has a purely marginal role in *Orlando.* Only after the paladins have routed the female warriors does Rinaldo worry about food, which he obtains from the captain of the ship (stanzas 25–26).

In his previously cited article "Sul rapporto *Morgante-Orlando Laurenziano*" (see introductory note to canto I), Paolo Orvieto reports that Rajna finds Rinaldo's mockery of his victorious brothers in *Morgante* (169, 1–3) inexplicable, whereas he considers it to be justified in *Orlando.* With regard to this important point, Orvieto explains that "Rajna failed to realize that Pulci is totally uninterested in proclaiming the traditional military valor attributed to the Amazons; nor is Rinaldo's derision intended to express any evaluation whatsoever of the outcome of the fight"; according to Orvieto, Rajna "did not understand that [in these stanzas] Pulci engages in a very amusing polysemous exploit of an erotic and sexual nature, all traces of which are erased by the extremely religious author of *Orlando*" (151).

171, 8. The poet resorts here to an amusing play on words to tell how Guicciardo found himself thrown "from the top" (his horse, but also Saliscaglia, located on a mountaintop [161, 1–2]) down "in the plain" (onto the ground).

172, 3–8 through 174. In *Orlando,* Rinaldo's duel with Archilesse (who, aided by one hundred pagans, has been fighting for a while with Alardo, Guicciardo, and Ricciardetto) takes place in cantos LVI, 38–40 and LVII, 3–7. It is only when this armed confrontation ends (8–11) that a famished Rinaldo can share with his brothers the food and drink that he and the captain have brought back from the ship.

176, 1–8; 177, 1–2; and 179, 2–6. Rinaldo, who is making fun of

Arpalista, his god, and his spear, demonstrates that he is also "a witty and mocking speaker" (Momigliano, 274). Being a practical man, however, he does not hesitate to arm himself with as enormous a spear as that of his adversary.

180–188. The duel between Rinaldo and Arpalista is also narrated in *Orlando* (LVII, 17–39). In the anonymous poem, however, the entire episode is marked by a particularly serious and solemn tone. The *canterino,* who dedicates at least fifteen lines to describing Arpalista's preparation for battle, clearly intends to create an atmosphere of impending danger. Arpalista's appearance on stage causes Ricciardetto's fear for his brother's life as well as Rinaldo's reassuring reply. The two contenders do not exchange insulting threats, but only polite words of challenge. While Pulci's Arpalista reacts to his defeat with a series of insults against his own god—for which he has been called "pagandom's most vigorous blasphemer" (Momigliano, 248)—*Orlando's* Arpalista blames mostly himself, only once accusing Mahound of having betrayed him (39, 4).

195–205. Gano's speech to Arpalista is a masterful mixture of obvious truths, half-truths, and blatant lies, uttered, however, in a crescendo of convincing eloquence, aimed at presenting the speaker as the innocent victim of his enemies' envy and ill will.

In Gano's laments concerning Charlemagne's lack of gratitude for the many services he has rendered the emperor (197), Angelo Gianni (133) recognizes a personal note on Pulci's part. The critic further adds that it is difficult not to identify, behind the "chatterboxes" and "flattering nincompoops" mentioned in line 5 of stanza 197, the "profile of the priest Matteo Franco," the poet's old rival at Lorenzo de' Medici's court.

207, 5. This is the first and only time in the poem that Gano refers to himself as Orlando's stepfather. Both Ageno (747) and Puccini (919) observe that such a kinship between Gano and Orlando is first mentioned in the *Chanson de Roland.*

207, 6. Note that this is the second time in the canto (99, 4) that Pulci feels the need to comment upon Gano's resourceful astuteness.

208, 6. "Evil Claws" probably derives from *Malebranche,* the name given by Dante to the fifth ditch of the eighth circle of hell, guarded by clawed devils (*Inferno,* XXI, 37).

220, 6–7. A kiss on the lips was given to formally seal a promise (Ageno, 751).

221, 6. See note, II, 50, 5.

222, 7. Chunks of pitch-coated tow were inserted between a ship's wooden boards in order to make its bridges and plankings waterproof.

224–238, 1–6. The episode of Rinaldo's and the Admiral's blonde and brunette daughters is also narrated in *Orlando* (LIX, 32–34 and LX, 3–29), where the two girls are called Bianca and Bruna. Their story also appears in other chivalric romances (Ageno, 752). This is the last time in *Morgante* that, answering Brunetta's request, Rinaldo shows his willingness to be of service to a member of the fairer sex. Not only does he fight and win for her, but he even proclaims Brunetta, to whom, as readily as usual, he has given his heart, to be the more beautiful (even though her sister is said to be the fairer of the two). Consequently, the Admiral's blonde daughter, who has also fallen in love with Rinaldo (235, 6–8), overcome with disappointment and grief, hangs herself. Her suicide (which is not mentioned in *Orlando*—canto LX appears to be without its closing stanzas), the second in Pulci's poem, has none of the dramatic impact of Forisena's suicide in canto V. The blonde girl's sudden death seems to provide, as Momigliano writes (244), a "tragicomic ending" to the episode.

225, 6–7. The meaning of these lines is "No one is willing to fight for you, not even with a spear as light as a stump of fennel."

227, 7. "Lady Prudish," *mona Onesta de Campi* in the Italian text, is a fictitious character who came to personify hypocrisy (Ageno, 753).

228, 1. Another metaphor derived from the language of hunters. Here it has the meaning of alluring, drawing someone close.

233, 5. See note, XIII, 29, 7–8 through 35.

244, 1–2. Pulci transcribes, almost verbatim, one of Dante's most famous lines (*Inferno,* V, 142).

244, 2. It appears here that Rinaldo (and perhaps also Pulci) has forgotten that in the dream he had earlier (stanza 217), the angel told him "to go on foot from hill to hill" until he found Fuligatto.

CANTO XXIII

SUMMARY: Invocation (1). Having finally found Fuligatto, Rinaldo successfully fights with him. The defeated bandit burns down his own home and becomes his victor's traveling companion (2–15). While riding on, the two are attacked by Spinardo, a half-man, half-horse monster who, from the cave in which he is hiding, pierces one of Fuligatto's arms with an arrow, causing him to fall almost senseless to the ground. In a fit of anger, Rinaldo kills the monster, then heals Fuligatto's wound with some special herbs, and baptizes him (16–28). Soon after, they encounter a large group of fierce-looking pagans. Pilagi d'Ulivant, their leader, tells the Lord of Montalban that he is headed for Saliscaglia to wage war against Rinaldo and his friends. The paladin and Pilagi decide to prove their worth on the battlefield; however, the moment Rinaldo turns his mount toward his adversary, the horse falls to the ground, bringing his rider down with him. While a raging Rinaldo kills the animal with a blow of his fist, Fuligatto slays Pilagi, whose men are then either slaughtered or routed by Rinaldo, aided by Fuligatto (29–40). Having resumed their trip, the two famished companions arrive at a hermitage, where they find food and lodging (41–47). The last stanzas of the canto contain the announcement of the continuation of the poem (48–54).

1, 1. See Psalms 69:1.

4, 4–8 through 14. Fuligatto's initial boasting, his duel with Rinaldo, and his consequently becoming the paladin's traveling companion call to mind the episode of the Old Man of the Mountain in canto XVII (40–48). When Fuligatto, intending to insult his adversary, identifies him with the snake in his dream, the Lord of Montalban wittily retorts by retelling the fable of the hedgehog, in which, as Momigliano writes (274), "the shame of that metamorphosis" is placed squarely on Fuligatto.

5, 1–8. Noting that the fable of the hedgehog and the snake is not to be found in any medieval collections, Ageno (765) states that it is difficult to establish the source that Pulci might have used.

6, 8. By raising the marshy fields of Fucecchio (located in the province of Florence, Tuscany) to the status of a lake, Pulci vividly represents the hyperbolic effects of Rinaldo's blow.

12, 3. Concerning Fieramont(e), Erminion's brother, see note, IX, 25–27.

12, 5. For the family relationship between Buovo d'Agrismonte (also called Buovo of Agrismont) and Orlando and Rinaldo, see note, III, 31, 8. Buovo, father of Malagigi and Vivian(o), is also mentioned in XI, 47, 7.

19, 4–8. Commenting upon Rinaldo's ready acceptance of Fuligatto's proposal, Gianni (65) states that Pulci's paladins "appear no more attached to their own faith" than the Saracen warriors, such as Arpalista and King Marsilius.

20, 6. Note that in the Italian text Pulci, playing on words, uses the word *Bellosguardo,* the name of a locality near Florence from which one can see the city and the surrounding countryside. It has the same meaning as Belvedere (literally, "a fine vista"), another Italian word used in English with reference to a building or a place designed to look out upon a pleasant view.

22, 2. An amusing reference to Solomon's proverbial wisdom, uttered by a Rinaldo who is just as madly enraged as Spinardo.

22, 6–8. A similar comparison can be found in VIII, 82, 1–2, where Mattafol is referred to as a falcon and Berlinghier as a pigeon.

26–29. Fuligatto's conversion, the expected outcome of the pact he has previously made with Rinaldo, is a purely conventional act. It is also the last conversion we encounter in the poem. It appears that with the useless brief sermon which Rinaldo, suddenly possessed by a comical religious zeal, delivers for Fuligatto's benefit, Pulci intends to make fun once more of the resounding eloquence of theologians and preaching friars. As Carlo Curto maintains, this sermon reveals the poet's smile at religious tradition (*Le tradizioni popolari nel 'Morgante' di Luigi Pulci* [Casale: Tipografia Cooperativa Bellatore and Co., 1918], 142). Indeed, the author's tongue-in-cheek remarks in lines 2–8 of stanza 28 provide further evidence of Pulci's lighthearted attitude toward spiritual matters. Note also that in lines 1–2 of stanza 27, Rinaldo seems to confuse the "Word" (Christ) with the Holy Spirit. Astaroth will do the same in XXV, 152, 1.

32, 1–8. Giovanni Getto (154) singles out this stanza as one of the numerous instances in which Pulci reveals his "irresistible inclination" to replace narrative discourse with the more immediate and dramatically effective use of direct speech. For the Italian critic, this is among the "most vital and picturesque proof" of the poet's dialogue techniques.

33, 1. The man Pilagi is accusing of being a traitor is Rinaldo.

34, 1 and 3. These two lines may need some clarification, since they try to convey the meaning of two colorful Italian proverbial expressions: *pigliar lucciole* (literally "to catch fireflies") in line 1 and *dare succiole* ("to give someone boiled chestnuts") in line 3. The meaning of line 1 is that Rinaldo did not lose any time; line 3 means, instead, "to deal the Saracen very heavy blows."

38, 8. As Getto points out (46), duels and, particularly, scenes of battle "offer to Pulci's fantasy the most unexpected series of gastronomic images." See also VII, 56, 5.

41, 5. See note, XVIII, 196, 1–2. Concerning this line, Puccini (953) keenly remarks that while it is possible that hunger, which in canto XVIII appears to Morgante as a dark cloud full of rain, may illustrate the rumbling of the giant's empty stomach, compared now to a rainbow it may signify the hope of filling it.

41, 8. For religious festivities, churches used to be decorated with laurel branches.

42, 6–8 through 46. In this episode we find that gastronomy is amusingly, if irreverently, mixed with the miraculous element. To satisfy Rinaldo's hunger, an angel, perhaps the same one that has spoken to him in a dream in canto XXII (216, 5–8 and 217), is sent from heaven to bring God's food to the paladin. It is strange, to say the least—and Pulci's undoubtedly ironic comment in line 6 of stanza 46 alerts the reader to this point—that a man who has declared himself willing to renounce God (19, 4–8), and to be ready to praise Christ's mother only if he can have something to eat, should be so privileged by God. In these stanzas Pulci provides a rather crude testimonial of his character's spiritual life.

47, 1–8. This stanza, consisting almost entirely of *bisticci* (words having similar sounds but different meanings), is called by Gianni (113) "the poem's most twisted stanza."

48, 5–8. By mentioning the horn that Orlando will sound in stanza 69 of canto XXVII, Pulci announces the continuation of his poem through cantos XXIV–XXVIII. Note that line 8 is a direct quotation from Dante's *Inferno*, V, 25.

49, 1. According to canto XXII (218, 8), Ricciardetto should still be in Saliscaglia with his brothers Guicciardo and Alardo.

49, 2–8. The portentous facts alluded to here—a forewarning of Orlando's death—are narrated in canto XXV. Ageno (778) points out that the seven-headed serpent, most probably a reminiscence from Apocalypse 13:1, symbolizes Gano's treason and the massacre at Roncesvalles.

50, 1–5. The descendant of the Old Man of the Mountain is Buiaforte, his son. He makes his first appearance in the poem in stanzas 6–7 of canto XIV. As the reader will note, Buiaforte's brief participation in the events narrated in cantos XXV, XXVI, and XXVII hardly corresponds to what Pulci says of him in these lines. This fact may mean either that the poet changed his mind with regard to Buiaforte's role in the poem or, as maintained by Ageno (778), that what takes place after stanza 143 of canto XXVI had not yet been written or clearly thought out. According to Puccini (956–957), the introduction of Buiaforte—against whom Antea will try to avenge the death of the Sultan, her father, killed by the Old Man—may have been conceived initially as a way of binding together the first part of the poem with its last five cantos. The critic, however, believes that this rather "weak bond" was "later abandoned by Pulci."

51, 1–8. In line 1 the sound of Orlando's horn is compared to that of the trumpet announcing the Last Judgment (see note, I, 6, 7–8, and also Matthew 24:31). Lines 6–7 contain a reference to the destruction of Saragossa, which will take place in canto XXVII. Both Ageno (779) and Puccini (957) rightly speak of the seemingly prophetic tone of this stanza, achieved by the use of phrases taken from Matthew (24:2), Mark (13:2), and Luke (21:6).

52, 1–8. The ferocious animals mentioned here probably stand for the Saracens and the Christians fighting at Roncesvalles. For the reference to the "demons" in line 5, see XXVI (89–90) and XXVII (51–55).

53, 1–8. While in the first five lines of this stanza the poet introduces the topic he will sing in the next canto (the military expedition of Antea and Marsilius against France), in lines 7–8, with a renewed biblical tone, he announces a new earthquake.

54, 1–2. See XXVII, 171–176.

54, 7–8. As Ageno notes (780), in the 1482 twenty-three-canto edition of *Morgante,* Pulci ended his poem with these lines: "We will say what followed in the other world. May Christ save you from the infernal abyss" (Italian text: *Diren quel che seguì nell'altro mondo. / Cristo vi scampi dallo infernal fondo*). In the 1483 twenty-eight-canto edition, the above-mentioned two lines were changed in order to better bind together canto XXIII and canto XXIV.

C A N T O   X X I V

SUMMARY: Invocation (1). Having stated that Rinaldo and his brothers will one day return to Montalban, the poet first declares his intention to resume narrating the story of Charlemagne and of Gano's punishment, then tells the reader that Buiaforte—whom Antea hates for being the son of the Old Man of the Mountain—is an honored guest at the court of King Marsilius (2–7). Desiring to avenge her father's death, Antea, prompted by Gano's letters, proposes that King Marsilius join forces with her for the invasion of France. Marsilius welcomes her suggestion and immediately recalls King Bianciardino, whom he had sent to Paris as his ambassador to discuss a peace treaty with Charlemagne (8–13). Advised by Bianciardino against waging a war at this particular time, Marsilius communicates his decision to Antea, who in turn writes to Gano requesting his assistance in the matter (14–18).

Alerted by Gano's artful letter to Marsilius, the king forwards to Antea that very message, notifying the queen that he has changed his mind and that an army of 100,000, led by Balugante, is ready to move against the French. Welcoming the news and oblivious of her past love for Rinaldo, Antea readies her troops and pledges to hang treacherous Gano one day (19–32). When the news that Marsilius is preparing for war reaches Paris, the emperor convenes the Council. During the meeting, all major Christian leaders accuse the Maganzan, who, while attempting to defend himself, is slapped on the face by Oliver, who is urged in turn by Orlando to leave the room so as to escape Charlemagne's wrath (33–52). Upon learning that Antea has amassed an army of 300,000 men in Babylon, Charlemagne reconvenes the Council, which decides to send Ugier the Dane to Spain as envoy, accompanied by Astolfo, Berlinghieri, and Sansonetto. Orlando orders the entire country to prepare itself for war (53–56).

In the meantime the pagan troops, led by Antea and by the giants Cattabriga and Fallalbacchio, camp a few miles away from Paris, killing and destroying everything in their path (57–62). Orlando asks Malagigi, who has returned to Paris from Montalban, to get rid of the two giants with his magic. Oliver, whom Orlando has sent to Antea to learn the reasons for her invasion, is warmly welcomed by the queen. She tells him that she wishes to duel with Orlando in order to avenge the death of the Sultan, her father (63–83). Thanks to Malagigi's magic and the antics of Marguttino, a giant the wizard has made suddenly appear on the scene, Cattabriga and Fallalbacchio perish in a forest fire (84–113).

Antea and Orlando meet and decide to fight. The count pledges to give France to Antea if she is the victor; Antea promises to return to Babylon with her troops if she is the loser. While Orlando and the queen are dueling with no result, the pagan troops, led by Sicumore, inflict great losses on the Christians. When Charlemagne is thrown from his horse, Baldovino urges Orlando to come and rescue the emperor. Orlando's intervention changes the outcome of the battle, and when evening falls, Antea requests a twenty-day truce in order to bury her dead (114–146). In Spain, Marsilius, following the arrival of the Dane, sends Falseron as his ambassador to Charlemagne, trying once more to make peace (147–170). Falseron reveals to Orlando that he wishes to see Antea before returning home. As a result of the queen's meeting with Marsilius's envoy, Antea makes peace with Charlemagne and leaves France with all her troops (171–179).

1, 1–2. See Matthew 10:22 and 24:13.

2, 1–8. Proclaiming the necessity to be faithful to one's sources, Pulci states that in telling the stories of Ulysses and Achilles, Homer was far from truthful; the wise reader must be capable, therefore, of distinguishing a character's true glory from poetic exaggerations. In light of the freedom that Pulci has previously exercised in the use of his sources, and the fact that he invents as he goes (as he himself states in line 3 of stanza 3), the above-mentioned pronouncement is surprising, to say the least. It may be an indication of the fact that in this second part of *Morgante* the discussion of sources becomes, as remarked by Davide Puccini (980), "a serious matter" for Pulci (see note, 52, 1–8).

4, 3–4. The story of Charlemagne, which, according to Pulci, was "badly understood and written worse" (I, 4, 7–8), is the main topic of the poem's last five cantos. As Ageno notes (782), while cantos XXVIII–XL of *La Spagna* are the primary source for this canto of *Morgante,* Antea's presence here is one of Pulci's inventions.

7, 7–8. The reason why Buiaforte is said to be "very dear" to King Marsilius is given neither here nor in the following cantos of the poem, where this character briefly reappears (XXV, 179, 4; XXVI, 128, 6–8; 144–152; and XXVII, 24–25).

8, 4. Semiramis was a beautiful, brave legendary Assyrian queen, believed to be the founder of Babylon. As previously pointed out (see notes, XV, 90, 2 and XVII, 13, 3–6), Pulci again confuses the city of Babylon in Egypt with the Mesopotamian Babylon.

9, 1–4. According to Ageno (783), the specific mention of the bread placed upside down before Antea in order to remind her of the still-unavenged death of her father derives from an anecdote of Darius (*Herodotus,* V, 105). It tells that before each meal, the Persian king had a slave remind him in this way of the insult the Athenians had inflicted upon him by burning the city of Sardis; hence the popular belief that bread placed upside down on a table brings bad luck. Ageno further adds that Pulci might have read Herodotus's historical work thanks to Lorenzo Valla's translation, which Iacobus Rubeus had printed in Venice in 1474.

10, 1. Gano, forgiven by Rinaldo (XXII, 241, 1–2) for his role in the killing of Aldighieri, has returned to Paris, where he is not idle but is busy as always devising new treacherous plans. For this reason, he is certainly the most static character in the poem.

16, 1–6. Charlemagne's planned coronation of Orlando as king of Spain is first announced in stanzas 9–10 of canto I of *La Spagna,* where the emperor, lamenting the fact that he has no sons to succeed him, declares that when Orlando betrothed Alda the Fair, he pledged to crown him king of all Spain.

Note that Pulci mentions here the death of Ferraù, who was killed by Orlando on a bridge, as a well-known fact (it will be recalled also by Falseron, Ferraù's father, in 158, 3–8). The duel between Ferraù and Orlando, alluded to by Pulci, is narrated in *La Spagna;* it lasts three days and extends for at least seventy-nine stanzas (III, 34–48; IV, 1–9 and 24–45; and V, 9–40). A somewhat similar though much longer version of this episode, also ending with Feragu's being killed on a bridge by Roland, is to be found in an earlier Franco-Venetian poem entitled *L'Entrée d'Espagne* (it begins with line 2436 and ends with Roland's prayer after Feragu's demise in line 4144). Composed about 1320 by an anonymous writer from the northern Italian city of Padua, the *cantare* originally consisted of more than 20,000 verses, of which fewer than

16,000 have come down to us. The published text of *L'Entrée* was edited by the French scholar Antoine Thomas and was printed in Paris in 1913 under the sponsorship of the Société des anciens textes français. Pulci may also have known this poem.

17, 6. As noted by Ageno (786), Pulci's reference to Turnus is not entirely correct. In Virgil's *Aeneid* (XI, 279–80), in fact, Diomedes does not address Turnus, but gives his answer to the ambassadors of King Latinus, who has sought his help against Aeneas. Turnus, the mythical king of the Rutili, is killed in combat by Aeneas in canto XII of the *Aeneid*.

22, 2. The Duke of Brittany is Salamon (I, 10, 3).

23, 4. The flag mentioned in this line is the oriflamme, the red banner of Saint Denis which the early kings of France used as a military ensign. According to Andrea da Barberino's *I reali di Francia* (I, 9–10), the oriflamme was given to Fiovus, Costantine's son, by the hermit Sansone, his maternal uncle, who had received it from one of God's angels.

26, 6–8. The pagan army's arrival in Paris is compared here to Hannibal's siege of Rome as told by Livy.

27, 2–4. Charlemagne t is Tusiani's rendition of *Mainetto*, the name used in the Italian text. In *I Reali di Francia* (V, 19–31), Charlemagne appears as Mainetto, the name he gave himself when, as a young man, he sought refuge in Spain at King Galafro's court. Charlemagne eventually married Gallerana, Galafro's daughter and King Marsilius's sister. Charlemagne's story is told by Pulci in XXVIII, 54–129.

27, 7. The "savage and voracious lion" mentioned in this line is Charlemagne's army.

30, 7. This is the third time that Balugante appears in the poem. He first accompanied Luciana to Arma (XIV, 38), then was sent back to Saragossa with Luciana (XVI, 93).

32, 2. For the reference to Rinaldo's getting old, see also 3, 1–4. For Davide Puccini (972), this line indicates that "a long period of time elapses between the first and the second poem" (I–XXXIII and XXIV–XXVIII). Clearly Antea's passionate love for Rinaldo, like that of Rinaldo for the queen, has withered as rapidly as it flourished.

34, 4–5. Another of the many Tuscan proverbs quoted by Pulci.

35, 1–4. These lines, in which the emperor is portrayed as an old and gray-haired man, but no longer as the dotard depicted in the preceding twenty-three cantos—particularly stanzas 128–129, where for the first and last time in the poem Carlo's body is said to be covered with the blood of the enemies he has slain with his sword—constitute, according to Mark Davie, the first clue to Pulci's intention of beginning Charlemagne's rehabilitation process ("Biography and Romance: The *Vita Caroli Magni* of Donato Acciaiuoli and Luigi Pulci's *Morgante*," in *The Spirit of the Court*, Selected Proceedings of the Fourth Annual Congress of the International Courtly Literature Society [Toronto, 1983], ed. G. S. Burgess and R. A. Taylor [Dover, N.H.: D. S. Brewer, 1985], 137–52).

38, 8. Another Tuscan proverb, popular today in its more modern form *le bugie hanno le gambe corte* ("lies have short legs").

39, 3. Ermine is white and is a symbol of purity. In Gano's case, however, ermine is black because he professes to be innocent, whereas his actions prove him guilty.

39, 4–5. Here Orlando seems to quote from Matthew 26:24 and Mark 14:21.

42, 1–8. This stanza calls to mind Judas's betrayal of Christ in Gethsemane (Mark 14:43–46, Luke 22:47, and John 18:3).

43–46. Though Gano's brief speech in self-defense is unsuccessful, he does play the role of the wrongly accused innocent victim with great cleverness.

48, 1–8. Having announced Oliver's death in Roncesvalles (lines 1–2), Pulci states that it is on this very day that Gano, provoked by Oliver's slap, decides to betray Charlemagne, just as Judas decided to betray Christ when he saw Mary Magdalene wet "with precious ointment Jesus' feet" (line 4). Davide Puccini (979) explains that while Matthew (26:7–16) and Mark (14:3–11) speak only in general terms of a woman, identified by tradition as Mary Magdalene, who is said to have anointed Christ's head and not his feet, John (11:2 and 12:3–6) asserts instead that this woman was Lazarus's sister, Mary, and that she washed Jesus' feet.

50, 1–6. Though it is not the first time that Charlemagne is spoken to so insultingly by one of his paladins, it is interesting that in this instance the emperor's reaction is immediate and much more forceful than in the preceding cantos.

52, 1–8. In canto XXIX of *La Spagna* we read that Bianciardino, whom Marsilius has sent, together with several other African kings, to France as his ambassador (3–4), tells Charlemagne that upon leaving Spain, King Marsilius will personally go to Paris to be baptized and pay the French a very rich tribute in gold (11). After some discussion regarding Marsilius's good faith (13–23), Orlando suggests that Gano accompany Bianciardino to Saragossa in order to find out if Marsilius is really disposed to hand over the promised tribute (24–24). It is at this point that Oliver slaps Gano because of the latter's expressed reluctance to accept the proposed mission (26–27, 1–6). Commenting upon the "authors" who report this fact, Pulci rightly argues that they must have mistaken King Bianciardino for Falseron (in XXV, 3–5, Falseron replaces Bianciardino as Marsilius's envoy; Gano will accompany him to Saragossa at Charlemagne's request but against the paladins' advice). It would make little sense, in fact, for Orlando, who is fully aware of Gano's treacherous nature, to propose that the Maganzan, slapped by Oliver, be sent to Spain with Bianciardino (on this point, see note, 2, 1–8).

53, 3–4. The Church requires that fasting be observed on the eve of a religious holiday; the "sad holiday" mentioned here, and for which there is no fasting, is the war for which Antea is making preparations.

54, 4–8. Like Ugier the Dane (see note, I, 9–10), Sansonet(to), the son of the Sultan of Mecca, is a former Saracen warrior who has converted to Christianity because of his friendship with Orlando, with whom he will die at Roncesvalles. This is the first time Sansonet is mentioned in the poem.

55, 8. Saint Denis's Day is October 9.

56, 2. A historic region in northern France, today a province, the capital of which is Rouen.

56, 3. The Italian nouns *Ilanda* and *Silanda* are translated here as Holland and Seeland. Ageno (1088) tentatively identifies *Ilanda* as Holland and *Silanda* as Seeland in the North Sea. For Puccini (982), instead, *Silanda* is Zeeland (a province in the southwestern Netherlands, consisting mostly of islands), and *Ilanda* is the Danish peninsula of Jutland.

56, 4. Rossiglion (Roussillon) is a historic province in southern France. It belonged first to the Spanish kingdom of Aragon, then was annexed in 1659 to the kingdom of France. Navarra, today a province of Spain with Pamplona as its capital, was formerly a kingdom located in southwestern France and northern Spain. Piccardy is a region in northern France with its capital at Amiens.

58–59, 1–2. Of the two giants Cattabriga (in English, "Wrangler") and Fallalbacchio ("Bungler"), Pulci provides, as Momigliano writes (173), "the most complete, nay a bit excessive," of all descriptions of giants in *Morgante*. Certainly their appearance not only makes Charlemagne wish to be back in Paris (90, 1–2), but even causes the bewildered Orlando to ask for Malagigi's assistance in getting rid of them (65, 1–4).

63, 1–4. Even more ominous signs appear in XXV, 73–74.

67–68. For Momigliano (243), these stanzas provide further proof of Antea's fickleness in matters of the heart. The critic asserts that here Antea "seems to be in love with Oliver."

68, 3–4. Defeated by Antea just before the queen's first duel with Orlando (XVI, 71–72), Oliver was then taken prisoner to Babylon, where the Sultan was planning to execute him (XVII, 66 and 138).

68, 8. Antea is referring here to Morgante's actions in canto XIX, 167–77.

69, 7. See note, 8, 4.

70, 7–8. Remembering that Rinaldo threw his spear away, refusing to fight against her (XVI, 66), Antea believes that the Lord of Montalban, who no longer loves her, would now perhaps duel with her.

73, 1–5. For both Ageno (802) and Puccini (988), Antea's remark that her troops speak many different languages may be a reminiscence of what Livy writes about Hannibal's army (XXX, 33, 8).

74–76. It must be noted that, in total contrast to Charlemagne's and even Orlando's reaction, Oliver's response to Cattabriga and Fallalbacchio is more surprised though controlled amusement than actual fear. Surely his smile and his ironic utterances (75, 7–8 and 76, 1–4) seem to indicate just that. For the reference to Nimrod, see note, XIX, 154, 7.

77–81. Here Oliver delivers a concise and eloquent speech, thus revealing himself to be, to use Momigliano's definition (258), a "humorous philosopher." The story to which Oliver is referring (79, 1–4), about the giant Marcovaldo in love with Chiariella, and Orlando's capture and imprisonment by Chiariella's father, is told in XII, 40–89. For lines 5–6 of stanza 80, see XVIII, 67–68.

86, 2. The two giants will be caught in Malagigi's "special glue" (65, 7–8) like birds in birdlime.

87, 1. The "field" of Saint Denis is where the Church of Saint Denis is located, outside the Paris city walls (see note, I, 9–10, and also VIII, 57, 8).

87, 5–8 through 89. Commenting on these stanzas, Momigliano (173–174) observes that while Charlemagne's reaction at first expresses "a comic astonishment not devoid of a certain fear," lines 3–4 of stanza 89 beautifully portray the state of mind of Charlemagne, who is bewildered and frightened in contemplating the enormous frames of Cattabriga and Fallalbacchio.

88, 7–8. The meaning of these lines is that no one could withstand Cattabriga's and Fallalbacchio's blows, even if he were as tall and large as a mountain. According to Greek mythology, Atlas, a Titan, was condemned to support the sky on his shoulders. In a later tradition, Atlas was identified with a mountain range in northwestern Africa, called "the pillars of the sky." It is believed (Puccini, 993) that Pulci derived this notion from Ovid's *Metamorphoses*. Tambernic (in Italian, *Stambernicchi*) is the name of a mountain we find in Dante's *Inferno* (XXXII, 28). Dante scholars believe it to be Mount Tambura in Tuscany, mentioned in ancient texts as *Stamberlicche*.

92–99. In the scene depicted here, the almost supernatural brute strength of the giants Cattabriga and Fallalbacchio is tamed by Malagigi's cunning use of his magic. As Momigliano suggests (219–220), the burlesque element of this episode—which is "one of Pulci's most powerfully grotesque inventions"—is generated by the excessive disproportion of the contenders. This fact has the effect of making the reader forget Malagigi's magic, since the scene emphasizes the gigantic aspect rather than the diabolic one. The sudden, rollicking appearance of Marguttino ("little Margutte") constitutes for De Robertis (189–90) "one of the happy moments in *Morgante*, where words, images, and verses sparkle with intelligence, and laughter is like a young and light wine." Of fundamentally the same opinion is Getto (104), for whom "Marguttino is the subject of a joyful, strange dance, happily conceived by the creative mind of the poet, eager for surprises and adventures." For Davide Puccini, however (995), Marguttino is an "almost pathetic" character; it is "Pulci's attempt to revive Margutte briefly, that is to say a carefree way of writing poetry which he contemplates with regret."

92, 8. Fracurrado was a legless finger puppet made of either wood or cloth; it derived its name (Brother Conrad) from the fact that it originally wore a monk's habit. Arrigobel was the name given to a clown who danced and played music while inviting the people to play games (see Ageno, 807, and Puccini, 994–95).

95, 1–3. See note, IX, 20–21 and 22, 1–5.

97, 4–8. To catch all types of birds, hunters used to build a small fake wood made of trees, the branches of which were covered with birdlime. To attract birds, the hunters kept a thrush in a cage, making it screech in fear by showing it an owl. The whistle mentioned in line 8 was an instrument used to imitate the warbling of birds.

103, 2–5. The story of the Jewish men Shadrach and Meshach (and Abednego), who emerged unscathed from the fiery furnace into which they had been thrown for refusing to worship the golden image of Nebuchadnezzar, is told in Daniel 3:8–26. Note that stanzas 103–113 contain Pulci's solemn protestation of veracity as well as his seemingly serious and yet finely ironic discussion of magic.

104, 2–5. The "Poet" whom Pulci somewhat freely quotes here is Dante (*Inferno,* XVI, 124–126).

104, 6. Reference is made here to Cassandra, who, after receiving from Apollo the gift of prophecy, rejected the god's love and, as punishment, was no longer believed.

107, 8. From Luke 1:51.

108, 1. Note that here Pulci replaces Paul's words *arcana verba* (2 Corinthians 12:3–4) with *arcana Dei* (Latin for "the mysteries of God").

109, 1–4. These "spirit elves" are the souls mentioned in Dante's *Inferno,* III, 34–9.

109, 5–8. In his poem *Città di Vita,* the Florentine writer and Pulci's contemporary Matteo Palmieri (1406–1475) expresses the belief that the spirits who remained neutral during Lucifer's rebellion against God were destined to be incarnated in human bodies. Modern scholarship has established that Palmieri did not adhere to the doctrine of metempsychosis, which was attributed to Pythagoras (who lived in the 5th century B.C.), and which maintained that a soul after death can migrate from a human or animal to some other human or animal body. From stanza 109 it is not clear whether Pulci considered Palmieri to be a proponent of this doctrine. With regard to Pythagoras, who is mentioned in line 8, Ageno (813) explains that Pulci may have learned of Pythagoras's assertion that his soul had previously inhabited other bodies, such as that of the Trojan hero Euphorbius, from Ambrogio Traversari's translation of Diogene Laerzio's *Vitae Philosophorum,* printed in Venice in 1475.

110, 1. The life of the quasi-legendary Pythagorean philosopher Thyaneus, also known as Apollonius of Tiana, who lived in the first century A.D., is narrated by the third-century A.D. Athenian writer Filostrato. In Filostrato's book it is said that Apollonius remembered having once lived as a helmsman, and that some pirates offered him a great reward if he would agree to steer the ship in the direction they would designate. Pulci's reference to Apollonius as a pirate, however, is not clear, and must refer to another episode in his life (Ageno, 813). Puccini (1002) believes that Pulci may have used a different source.

110, 5. Asmodeus is the demon who is said to have entered the body of Sarah and to have killed her seven husbands (Tobias 3:8).

112–114. In this stanza and the two that follow, Pulci, though trying to minimize the fact, is actually confessing his past fondness for the occult sciences. The visit to the cave of the Sibyl of Norcia, mentioned in 112, 4, took place in late December 1470 or soon thereafter. In a letter to Lorenzo De' Medici dated December 4, 1470, and written while the poet was in Foligno, he promises the Magnificent to send him more fresh truffles after his return from Norcia, where he is about to go in order to visit the sibyl (*Morgante e Lettere,* Lettera XVI, 963).

112, 8. A contemporary of Andrea da Barberino, Cecco d'Ascoli (whose real name was Francesco Stabili) was born near Ascoli, in the Marche region, in 1269. A professor of astrology at the University of Bologna, a city he was forced to leave in 1324, he eventually moved to Florence, where he was tried and burned alive as a heretic in 1327. His major work is an unfinished pseudo-scientific poem entitled *Acerba,* for a long time considered to be an important text by all those interested in magic. Cecco d'Ascoli is today best remembered as one of Dante's fiercest enemies.

113, 1–3. As Puccini notes (1003), Cecco d'Ascoli in his *Acerba* tells how the demons Moco, Scarbo, and Marmores can be evoked. He also explains that a "bifurcate bone" taken fron the breast of a rooster that has been be-witched and placed in a fire can answer a wizard's questions by opening or closing itself.

113, 4. Parnassus, a mountain in central Greece, was in ancient times considered sacred to Apollo and the Muses.

113, 6. For Minos, see note, XX, 79, 8.

113, 8. Pyromancers were believed capable of divining the future by observing forms appearing in fire; hydromancers could tell the future by examining signs in water; and geomancers could predict the future by analyzing a figure or figures made by throwing a handful of earth on the ground.

117, 2. For the reference to the Archangel Michael's fight with the devil, see Jude 9.

119, 1–8. It should be noted that the events Orlando recalls in this stanza are narrated in XXI, 94–97, where, however, it is Rinaldo, and not the count, who has accompanied Antea back to Babylon, placing her on the throne that belonged to her father. Since, as Rinaldo states at the end of stanza 96, he is doing what Orlando himself would do, Orlando (and Pulci) may feel justi-fied in attributing his cousin's actions to himself.

123–124. This duel—which is considerably shorter and is less vehe-mently fought than the one narrated in XVI (76–81)—also ends with neither of the contenders emerging as the victor (they are, after all, protected by magic armor and weapons). One is under the impression that both Antea and Orlando are no longer what they used to be (123, 1–2), and Pulci tries to make up for their diminished fiery strength by hyperbolically comparing Orlando to Achilles and Antea to the Trojan hero Hector. Ruedi Ankli, who also maintains that Orlando and Antea appear to be "tired and without vivacity," writes that "the rhythm of the battle . . . seems to become the true object of these stanzas, and not the actions of Charlemagne's individual paladins." For the Swiss scholar, for whom canto XXIV serves as a "bridge" between the two parts of the poem, the "great stylistic and thematic turning point of the *Rout of Roncesvalles* [XXIV–XXVIII] consists in the dissolution of the valor of the individual fighter into a general battle" (*Morgante Iperbolico, L'iperbole nel Morgante di Luigi Pulci* [Firenze: Olschki, 1993], 316–317).

126, 4. Another ironic comment on Oliver's tendency to fall from his horse. Unhorsed by King Manfredonio in VII (57) and thrown to the ground by Antea in XVI (72), the marquis prudently decides to quit while he is ahead.

128, 4. "Gioiosa," Charlemagne's sword, is mentioned several times in *La Spagna;* it appears for the first time in the *Chanson de Roland* as "joiuse" (2501–2508). (See *La Chanson de Roland,* Edition critique et traduction de Ian Short, Le livre de poche [Librairie Générale Française, 1990], and *The Song of Roland,* translated with an introduction by Patricia Terry [New York: Macmillan, 1992].)

129, 7. Lucan (Marcus Annaeus Lucanus), born in Cordoba, Spain, died in Rome in A.D. 65. He lived at Nero's court, where he committed suicide after taking part in a conspiracy against the emperor. His major work is *Bellum Civile* (also known as *Pharsalia*), a poem that tells of the war between Caesar and Pompeii. He is mentioned in Dante's *Inferno* (IV, 90) as one of the great poets of antiquity.

130, 6–8. This is the second time in the poem that we see Turpin engaged in a military action. While he is now quite successful at killing Antea's men, in VIII (93, 6–8) he was easily defeated and taken prisoner by Mattafol. Commenting upon these lines, Puccini (1009) asks himself: "Does Pulci wish to suggest perhaps that one can inflict more harm with a pastoral than with a sword?"

132, 1–8. See note, III, 46, 1–8.

136–137. Here Baldwin, Gano's son (also called Baldovino), makes his formal appearance on the stage of *Morgante*. He is a brave and loyal friend of Orlando, as his father tells Marsilius in XXV (109, 2–4).

139, 6. For Zacchaeus, see note, XXII, 60, 4.

140, 1. Concerning the giants' rebellion against the gods, see note, XX, 54, 7–8.

141, 2. See note, XVII, 17, 6.

141, 6. The river Serchio, mentioned in Dante's *Inferno* (XXI, 49), runs near the city of Lucca, then flows into the Tyrrhenian Sea.

149, 5. This is the same Falseron that Pulci mentioned in stanza 52, 8.

152, 1–8. Falseron's speech is clear proof of the sharpness of his mind and of his remarkable eloquence. As Puccini (1017) notes, to avoid having to answer embarrassing questions concerning Bianciardino's sudden departure from Paris, he resorts to the skillful use of some abstruse philosophical concepts.

153, 5. Here Falseron repeats the words of Pilate's reply to the chief priests: "What I have written I have written" (John 19:19–22).

154, 4. With regard to Ida's Woods, whose derivation Ageno (826) has not been able to identify, Puccini (1018) has found it listed in Pulci's mythological catalogue as "Ida: a wood in Crete where Jove was reared."

158, 5–8. Concerning Falseron's son Ferraù, see note, 16, 1–6.

159, 4–6. Though at this point the poet chooses to withhold judgment regarding the sincerity of Falseron's tears, he nevertheless underscores the fact that the Saracen's body language (his gestures) fully complements his oral delivery; all in all, it is a splendid performance.

165, 4–5. In *La Spagna* (VI, 3, 1–8) we read that Charlemagne, upon seeing Ferraù's soul being carried toward heaven by two angels (a number that is greatly increased in *Morgante*), believed it to be that of his nephew Orlando.

166, 6–8. With this comment, addressed to Charlemagne, Pulci clearly answers the question he left unanswered in line 4 of stanza 159. For Christ's words to Judas—"Friend, wherefore art thou come?"—see Matthew 26:50. The Latin phrase in line 8, which means "You entrusted the sheep to the wolf," is taken from Terence's play *Eunuchus* (Ageno, 829).

169, 3–4. In the original Italian text, Pulci makes an obvious play on the sound of the words *Carlo matto* (Charle-mad) and *Carlo Mano* (Charlemagne).

169, 8. Concerning Cassandra, see note, 104, 6.

174, 3. Note the further play on words which is obtained by attributing the adjective "false" (*falso*) to Falseron, a name in which the same adjective appears.

174, 3–8; 175. As the poet himself recognizes in stanza 176, Falseron again succeeds in saying things in such a way that they lend themselves to a quite different interpretation.

179, 1–2. Not only does Antea leave Paris "forever," but she also exits *Morgante,* never to be mentioned again.

179, 3–4. According to Paolo Orvieto (*Pulci medievale,* 252), in these lines Pulci clearly announces the necessity for an allegorical reading of the last five cantos of *Morgante.*

CANTO XXV

SUMMARY: Invocation (1). Against his paladins' advice, Charlemagne decides to send Gano to Saragossa as his ambassador in order to discuss a peace treaty with Marsilius (2–11). Falseron immediately informs the king by letter of their imminent arrival (12–14). Marsilius and his entire court greatly honor Gano by meeting him several miles outside the city, where the Maganzan is later escorted to take lodging in Bianciardino's palace (15–25). The following morning, before Marsilius and all his subjects, Gano publicly delivers Charlemagne's message of peace, which he concludes by urging Marsilius to become a Christian, and to which the king replies by retelling the fable of the six columns (26–46). When, after much partying, Gano and the king are alone, the Maganzan, spurred on by Marsilius's shrewd words, finally reveals his plan for bringing about Orlando's death at Roncesvalles (47–71). As Gano ends his speech, the chair in which Marsilius is seated suddenly overturns, a mishap followed by several other portentous signs (72–80), for which the sage men immediately convened by Marsilius offer different, though favorable, interpretations (81–86).

Gano writes to Charlemagne informing him that peace has been arranged, that Orlando must go to Roncesvalles to receive Marsilius's tribute, and that the emperor himself should also leave for Piè di Porto, where King Marsilius will meet him. His letter also mentions all the precious gifts that Marsilius is sending to Charlemagne and his paladins as a token of friendship (87–94). Upon receiving Gano's letter, a rejoicing Charlemagne writes first to Orlando, ordering him to go to Roncesvalles, and then to Gano (95–101). Having outlined his treacherous plan to Marsilius, recommending that he spare the life of Gano's son Baldwin, who is serving in Orlando's army, Gano returns to Paris, where he is most joyfully received by Charlemagne (102–114). Malagigi evokes the devil Astaroth; after learning from him that Rinaldo is in Egypt, he orders the devil to go there immediately and take Rinaldo and Ricciardetto to Roncesvalles within three days (115–133). Questioned by Malagigi about his knowledge of the future, Astaroth replies by launching into a long pseudo-theological discussion (134–161). Having then told the wizard that Marsilius is in Saragossa working on a deceitful plan, Astaroth takes leave, pledging that both Rinaldo and Ricciardetto will arrive safely in Roncesvalles; he will accomplish this by entering into Baiardo while the devil Farferello enters Ricciardetto's horse (162–167).

As Charlemagne awaits in Piè di Porto, and Orlando in Roncesvalles, Marsilius, having sent Bianciardino to Orlando to assure him of the king's peaceful intentions, speaks to his troops, proclaiming a holy war. He then divides his army into three formations and sets out toward Roncesvalles (168–200). Having reached Rinaldo and his three brothers in Egypt, Astaroth gives Malagigi's letter to the Lord of Montalban. While Guicciardo and Alardo set out to return home, Astaroth and Farferello, having entered into Rinaldo's and Ricciardetto's horses, unseen by all, start transporting the two paladins toward Roncesvalles, flying over land and water. Along the way Rinaldo and Astaroth engage in a theological discussion. They stop to rest and eat. Once they are in the proximity of Toledo, they are challenged by a Saracen necromancer, who tries to abort their trip (201–288). On the last leg of their voyage, while flying over Saragossa, Rinaldo and Ricciardetto decide to participate in Queen Blanda's dinner. During the great confusion provoked by the two invisible and famished paladins, Rinaldo hugs and kisses a bewildered Luciana (289–304). After they resume their trip, Rinaldo mentions the ornate pavilion that Luciana has given him; this prompts Astaroth to list all the animals that are not represented in Luciana's pavilion (305–332).

1, 2–3. A reference to Ariadne's thread, which she gave to Theseus and which he used to find his way out of the labyrinth after he killed the Minotaur.

2, 1. In this canto, as elsewhere in the poem, the emperor is often called Carlo instead of Charles or Charlemagne.

2, 1–8. Addressing himself to Charlemagne, Pulci blames the emperor for having decided to send Gano to King Marsilius together with Falseron. Interestingly, it is only a few stanzas later that the poet gives Charlemagne's reasons for selecting Gano over Orlando as his ambassador (7), and reports Gano's attempt to back out of the mission, with a suggestion that the emperor send Orlando instead (8). This is clearly a case in which an action (Charlemagne's decision to send Gano) precedes the explanation of the reason or reasons for that action. Commenting upon this fact, Gianni states that in the last five cantos of the poem, Pulci no longer tells his story "stanza by stanza" but reveals, instead, that his mind "is engaged in the weaving of a plot." The comments interspersed in the last part of *Morgante,* in which the poet tells beforehand what is going to happen later on in the poem (as with the remark addressed to Oliver in XXIV, 48, 1–2), are considered by Gianni proof of Pulci's new way of conceiving his story, now that he can no longer use *Orlando* as his main source of inspiration (385–386).

As noted by Ageno (833), Gano's trip to Saragossa (together with Bianciardino, not Falseron) and the pact he makes with Marsilius, as well as the latter's speech to his people, are narrated also in *La Spagna* (XXIX, 31 through XXX, 38).

3, 7–8. In these lines Charlemagne, using similar words, expresses a concept previously voiced by Gano in XXII, 206, 6–7. Elaborating upon the emperor's continued trust in Gano, Momigliano (264) states that Charlemagne and Shakespeare's King Lear share more or less the same "weakness." The two kings, the critic explains, "need to be flattered or, even better, need to be deceived. Charlemagne despises the paladins for the same reasons that King Lear despises Cordelia," who is incapable, as are the Christian knights, of adulating her king. It is a weakness that brings about the tragedy of Roncesvalles just as it leads King Lear to madness. As Momigliano points out, "In the blindness of these two kings there is the same sad humor."

5, 2. Note that in the original Italian text Pulci uses the word *rabi* (rabbi), which he lists in his *Vocabolista* as the Jewish term corresponding to the Italian *maestro* (teacher). Calling to mind Judas's betrayal of Christ in Gethsemane (Matthew 26:49 and Mark 14:45), Oliver is here comparing Gano to Judas, just as Ugier has done in XXIV, 42, 1–8. On this point Davide Puccini (1029) notes that "the identification of Gano with Judas . . . constantly recurs in the second part of the poem."

7, 3–4. It is clear from these lines that Charlemagne is perfectly aware of Gano's treacherous nature. Yet he refuses to entertain the idea that the Maganzan may betray him too.

8, 5–8. Here, as Pulci occasionally does in the poem, we find a metaphor derived from the sport of bird hunting. With reference to these lines, see note, XXIV, 97, 4–8.

10, 4. The death of Serpentìn, Marsilius's nephew, is narrated in *La Spagna,* XXVIII, 1–30. For the reference to Ferraù, see note, XXIV, 16, 1–6.

12, 7. The Bacchiglione River, here "Bacchillòn," runs through the northern Italian cities of Vicenza and Padua. Dante mentions it, in conjunction with the Arno River, in *Inferno,* XV, 113. From this Dantesque line, as Ageno observes (837), derives the proverbial expression "to jump from the Arno into the Bacchillone" (to jump from one subject to another). In the Italian text, Pulci makes an amusing play on words by using *Bacchillone,* the name of a river, together with *bacchillone,* a common noun meaning "simpleton."

20, 5. See XXII, 25, 8.

23. This stanza, as Getto keenly points out (54–55), constitutes another instance revealing the poet's ability to depict "lively scenes of festive collective merriment." For the critic, stanzas such as this one "celebrate and exalt" Pulci's peculiar taste for representing "that wheel of colors, sounds, gestures, and movements in which he expresses the elation and the joyfulness of a crowd."

23, 8. "Montjoie," the name of the flag and war cry of the French (see *La Chanson de Roland,* 3092–3095), derives from the Latin *Mons gaudii,* the Vatican hill where, according to tradition, Pope Leo III gave Charlemagne the Roman flag. Saint Denis is Paris's patron saint (see note, I, 9–10).

24, 1. For Furius Marcus Camillus, see note, XXII, 132, 1–2.

24, 5–8. See note, 2, 1–8.

27, 2–4. As already remarked (XIV, 38, 1), Balugant is a captain in Luciana's army. First mentioned in the *Chanson de Roland* as Balaguez (894), in *La Spagna* (I, 28, 2) Balugant is king of Portugal and a brother of Marsilius and Falseron. Galleran (also called Gallerano) is a captain in Marsilius's army and will be seriously wounded by Rinaldo in XXVII, 91. Arcaliffa (also called Arcalif), the caliph of Bagdad and King Marsilius's uncle, is a character appearing both in the *Chanson de Roland* (453) and in *La Spagna* (where he is called Argaliffo or Argalifa; II, 3, 3).

28, 4. Gano here shares the belief of some theologians who maintained that God created man in the Plain of Damascus. The free will that God gave Adam induced Eve to transgress the divine law, thus damning the entire human race.

30, 1–3. Some commentators on the Bible maintain that the Saracens derived their name from Abraham's wife Sarah (Sarah is mentioned in Genesis 11:29). As Puccini clarifies (1039), "Muslims believe that revelation manifested itself also through the Jewish Bible and the Gospel of Jesus, about which the Koran speaks with profound respect."

31, 6–8. As noted by Ageno (842), Pulci derives this notion from the *Aspramonte* (III, 157).

32, 1–8. See note, XXIV, 27, 2–4.

34, 2–5. The fact that the English theologian and scholar Alcuin of York (735–804), founder of the Palatine Academy in Paris, was a teacher and adviser of Charlemagne prompts Pulci to state that the emperor was well acquainted with both Latin and Greek. Pulci's notion is confirmed by Einhard, who in chapter 25 of his *Vita Caroli Magni* writes that Charlemagne was fluent and had the gift of eloquence in speech. Not content merely to speak his native language (Frankish), Charlemagne mastered the Latin language and could speak it as well as his own. According to Einhard, the emperor understood Greek better than he could speak it. Charlemagne cultivated the liberal arts personally and promoted them at court. Einhard further comments that the emperor had little success in learning to write because he began too late in life, this despite keeping his writing tablet under his pillow at night for use in his leisure time.

35, 1. Scipio Nasica, Roman consul between 162 and 155 B.C., not to be confused with Scipio Africanus ("Scipio the Elder"), who defeated Hannibal, and Scipio Emilianus ("Scipio the Younger"), who destroyed Carthage.

38, 7. Here Pulci transcribes—making a small change for reason of rhyme (*portando* replaces *portate* of the original Latin)—a phrase of Paul's Letter to the Galatians 6:2, the meaning of which is "Bear ye one another's burdens."

40, 4. Malebranche (literally, "Evil Claws") is the name Dante coined for the devils that oversee the souls punished in the fifth circle of hell (*Inferno*, XXI, 37). In the Italian text Pulci uses the singular form *Malabranca,* referring specifically to Satan.

42–45. Marsilius's fable of the six columns calls to mind the famous tale of the three rings told by the Jewish banker Melchisedech to the Saladin in Boccaccio's *Decameron* (I, 3). It is believed that the six columns in Marsilius's fable symbolize the Jewish, Christian, Muslim, Egyptian, Greek, and Chaldaic religions. In the Middle Ages, the Spanish city of Toledo was a well-known center for the study of occult sciences. When, driven by his own eloquence and flattered by the effect of his words on the audience, Gano concludes his speech by urging Marsilius to embrace Christianity (40, 1–8), the Saracen king replies by narrating the tale of the six columns. He does not, however, provide an answer as to which of the six columns represents the real faith. Marsilius, well aware of Gano's deceitfulness (41, 6 and 46, 1–8), is not fooled by the Maganzan's words. Gano's faked attempt to convert the king, and Marsilius's seemingly tolerant attitude toward religious beliefs do not express what the two men really feel and think. As Momigliano correctly observes (318), only the people of Saragossa, who are hoping for peace, take their words seriously and are duped by them.

46, 4. A proverbial expression that we find in Dante's *Inferno,* XXXIII, 120. Here it means that Gano cannot be easily fooled, just as dates cannot be mistaken for the cheaper figs.

48–114. In the first part of this canto, which is the longest in *Morgante,* most of the action is centered on Gano, whom we see engaged, particularly in stanzas 48–69, in a subtle and fascinating game with Marsilius, an interlocutor unquestionably worthy of him. It is in fact the Maganzan's continued reluctance to reveal openly what his guarded words and actions have already implied that forces Marsilius, confident in Gano's past track record, to take him aside for a one-on-one talk. If it is true that stanzas 53–59 demonstrate that the Saracen king is a most capable chess player, he is nevertheless checkmated by Gano. It is in fact the Maganzan's engaging silence that finally prompts Marsilius to state what Gano has been thinking all along, but has been reluctant to say. By agreeing with Marsilius—whom he calls a "tempter wise and sly" (61, 6)—that Orlando must die, Gano actually shares with the king the responsibility for the count's death, which a few lines later he tries to justify by declaring it to be an act of revenge and not of treason (65, 6–8).

In these stanzas Pulci provides a masterful psychological profile of the Lord of Maganza. Commenting on stanza 48, Davide Puccini (1046) writes that here "Gano's figure redeems itself poetically from the role of a caricature capable only of plotting treason after treason." In his cogent reading of this episode, Momigliano (316) maintains that these stanzas are of primary importance in the portrayal of Gano's personality, since "what goes through the Maganzan's mind is hinted at so skillfully and with such humor as to make this point one of the most remarkable in the poem." Giovanni Getto (85) keenly points out that the excessive demonstrations of welcome and the distrustful kindness which characterize the meeting between Gano and Marsilius "create an atmosphere which is conducive and favorable to treason."

53, 5–6. Another old Tuscan proverb.

55, 6. The name of the Sicilian volcano is used metaphorically to mean "ardent love."

56, 2. Zambugeri (also called Zambuger) is Marsilius's son. He will die by Orlando's hand during the Battle of Roncesvalles (XXVII, 36–37). Note that in the *Chanson de Roland,* Marsilius's son is named Jurfaleu le Blund. In that poem, a blow of Orlando's sword severs both Marsilius's right hand and Jurfaleu's head (1903–1904).

61, 8. The meaning of this proverbial expression is "We are two clever fellows bound together by a common interest."

62, 2–3. See XXIV, 47, 7–8.

64, 3. The crow to which Gano is referring is the first animal Noah sent out of the Ark when the flood ceased (Genesis 8:6–7).

64, 4. The bird mentioned here is both the crow of line 3 and, figuratively, Orlando.

65, 2. A reference to the thirty pieces of silver promised to Judas by the high priests as a reward for his betrayal of Christ (Matthew 26:15).

66, 1–4. Now that Marsilius is sure of Gano's intentions, leaving all precautions aside, he decides that they should proceed full speed ahead with their plan. Note that the Latin oars were a nautical instrument formed by two long shafts with a broad plate at each end. One shaft was placed on the left and the other on the right side of the stern. The oarsman steered the ship to the left by dipping the left shaft into the water and vice versa (Ageno, 852).

67, 7–8. There is a striking similarity between Gano's words and Ser Ciappelletto's reply to the two Florentine usurers in whose home he is lodging: "I have committed so many offenses against God in the course of my life, that one more in the hour of my death will make no difference at all" (Boccaccio's *Decameron,* I, 1).

69, 8. A popular proverbial expression. Gano says that his death means nothing because it is like the death of a fly in Apulia, where flies were plentiful.

70, 5. Piè di Porto, called also Port of Saint John (170, 6), in the region of Navarre in southwest France.

71, 4–5. Gano, as the Abbot Clairmont did in canto III (80, 3), quotes from Luke 2:29.

72, 5. The reference to Friar Alberigo and his tribute derives from Dante's *Inferno,* XXXIII, 118–119. Marsilius's tribute, like that of Friar Alberigo, will bring to Charlemagne only betrayal and death. In May 1285, Alberigo Ugolino dei Manfredi, a native of Faenza and a Guelph leader, invited to a "reconciliation" dinner two relatives of his, Manfredo and his son Alberghetto, both of whom he hated, the latter for having slapped him during an argument. At the end of the dinner, when Alberigo called for the fruit to be brought to the table, a group of armed men entered the room and murdered the two unsuspecting guests. Hence the proverbial expression "to receive Friar Alberigo's fruits," used to indicate betrayal and death.

72, 6–8 and 73, 1. Pulci's commentators note that the incident of Marsilius's fallen chair is narrated also in *La Spagna* (XXX, 3, 1–4), where it is called a "miracle"—which, however, does not deter Gano from going ahead with his treacherous plan. According to Ageno (854), it is possible that Pulci, recalling the text of *La Spagna,* in line 1 of stanza 73 wishes to clarify that what has happened to Marsilius's chair must be considered not a miracle but a divine warning to Gano.

73, 2–8. See XXIV, 63, 1–4.

74, 3–8. "That golden leafage" refers to the long-haired nymph Daphne (see note, III, 17, 6–7). The ancients believed that the laurel tree could not be struck by lightning.

75, 5. In the Italian text Pulci uses the words *tremuoto rubesto,* deriving them from a line in Dante's *Inferno,* XXXI, 106. The earthquake mentioned in line 5 of stanza 75 calls to mind the one that shook the earth the moment Christ expired on the cross (Matthew 27:51).

77, 1–2. The notion that Judas hanged himself from a carob tree is not found in the New Testament. It is a traditional popular belief. Referring to Judas's death, Matthew says only that "he cast down the pieces of silver in the temple, and departed, and went and hanged himself" (Matthew 27:5).

77, 7–8. While it appears that all the portentous events listed in stanzas 72–76 have had little or no effect on Gano, the Maganzan is overwhelmed with fear the moment his head is hit by a fruit of the carob tree. To be sure, this scene combines elements of both tragedy (Gano's betrayal of Charlemagne is related to Judas's betrayal of Christ) and comedy (the visually spectacular result caused by the falling of such a small fruit on Gano's head).

80, 5–8 and 81, 1–2. Clearly Gano knows the correct interpretation of the portentous events narrated in the preceding stanzas, but he is unwilling or, better, unable (as Pulci has stated in stanzas 48, 6–8 and 69, 1–8) to change his nature and the course of events.

82, 8. For the story of Nebuchadnezzar's dream and Daniel's interpretation of it, see Daniel 2:1–45.

89, 3. For the reference to the salamander, see note, XIV, 45, 7–8.

90, 4. See note, XXI, 142, 7.

91, 6. Darius I (the Great) was king of Persia from 521 to 485 B.C.

92, 1–4. Farès and Floro are mentioned only in this stanza. Interestingly, in stanzas 161–162, Astaroth, as a warning to Rinaldo, expresses quite a different opinion concerning all types of spirit elves.

93, 3. The word *seraffo* is the Italian rendition of the name of an old golden Persian coin. We find it also in one of Pulci's sonnets (Puccini, 1062).

96, 2. The Duke of Burgundy is Oliver.

98, 1–3. The story of the alleged conquest of Jerusalem by Orlando, accompanied by Sansonetto and an army of 60,000 horsemen, is narrated in *La Spagna*. In this poem we also read that Orlando, having entrusted the defense of the Holy Sepulcher to Ansuigi and 20,000 men, leaves Jerusalem to resume fighting against the Saracens (*La Spagna,* XVIII, 31–36; XIX, 14–45; and XX, 1–24). Pulci again mentions Orlando's liberation of the Holy Land in XXVII, 192, 1–6.

98, 8 and 99, 1–3. Very briefly mentioned in XXVI, 76 and 134 as a participant in the Battle of Roncesvalles, Count Anselmo (also called Anselm) dies in XXVII, 93, killed by Mattafirro. Pulci devotes to this character and his deeds no more than nineteen lines.

100, 3–8. Note Pulci's direct intervention in the story and his mocking remark concerning the questionable presence of the Angel Raphael at Orlando's side at Roncesvalles. With regard to the Angel Raphael as a traveling companion of Tobias, see note, IV, 5, 4.

102, 7–8 and 103, 4–8. In Andrea da Barberino's *Aspramonte* (III, 73), Orlando is said to have been granted invulnerability by three saints, the most important of whom was Saint George. The same poem also provides the notion that no one can face up to Orlando during the third day of battle (Ageno, 862–63). The Saracen king of Africa, Agolant(e), and his son, King Almont(e), are characters Pulci derives from the above-mentioned Barberino poem. See note, I, 13, 1–8.

104, 1–8. In fourteenth-century poems and romances, Michael is never mentioned among Orlando's patron saints. By assigning to the Archangel Michael the role which was commonly performed by Saint George during Orlando's investiture as a knight, Pulci intended to ironically underline, as

Davide Puccini notes (1065), "the scarce reliability of a tradition which . . . runs the risk of rendering even the truth unbelievable." The Italian expression *più dolce che miele* ("sweeter than honey") characterizes as "foolish" those who "affirm that it was Saint George or Fata Morgana." Note that "Fata Morgana" is the Italian equivalent of Morgan le Fay. This figure appears in Celtic and Arthurian legend as the fairy sister of King Arthur.

106, 7–8; and 107. In this canto of *Morgante,* Gano's suggestion that wine must be used in order to help defeat Orlando and his men (just as smoke is used to catch bees or to make them leave the hive [as stated in VII, 32, 60]) derives possibly from *La Spagna.* In canto XXX, 37–38 of that poem, Marsilius orders Bianciardino to bring to Orlando "a thousand loads" of food and wine, stating that once the Christians are satiated and inebriated, he and his men will attack them. In stanzas 39–40, 1–3, we are told that Bianciardino delivered his goods to Orlando. As a result, many Christians got drunk that night. It appears, however, that Pulci decided not (or possibly forgot) to elaborate on this detail; in stanza 183, 1–5, in fact, the poet states only that Bianciardino arrives at Roncesvalles bringing Orlando "camels with wine and ample food." He makes no mention of any of Orlando's men getting drunk.

108, 4. The meaning of this line is "they will pay (with their death) for all they have eaten and drunk."

108, 6. The word "kites" translates the Italian *nibbi.* As Ageno explains (864), the name of this small bird was used metaphorically to indicate a foolish person.

109, 2. For Baldwin, mentioned here and again in stanzas 172, 5–8 and 173, see notes, I, 10, 4–5 and XXIV, 136–137.

114, 3. Latin version of the question Jesus asked Judas: "[Friend], wherefore art thou come?" (Matthew 26:50).

114, 4. Here Pulci ironically remarks on Charlemagne's constant readiness to believe Gano's words as the gospel truth (just as the emperor did in VIII, 56, 8).

114, 6. *Dirupisti* is the past tense of a Latin verb, the meaning of which is "You caused the ruin of everything." According to Davide Puccini (1069), the expression derives from Psalms 73:15 and 115:7, but Pulci uses it here totally out of context, possibly for the purpose of rhyming with *evangelisti* and lending the line a biblical tone.

115, 4–5. The "Angel" to whom Pulci is referring here is Agnolo Ambrogini, who was born in Montepulciano, near Florence, in 1454, and died in Florence in 1494. Universally known as Angelo Poliziano (from the Latin name of his birthplace, *Mons Politianus*), he was the most refined poet and the greatest humanist of his time, the only one that Pulci highly admired and respected, together with two minor poets, Bernardo Bellincioni and Antonio di Guido, who were personal friends of his. Poliziano is again mentioned, as "Angiolino," in stanza 169, 1–8 and in XXVIII, 145, 7–8. Note that Arnald(o)'s text, which the poet indicates as one of his sources (see also stanza 168, 6), is considered to be the product of Pulci's imagination.

116–117. The polemic tone of these two stanzas attests to Pulci's more openly expressed desire to defend his work and cultural formation against those who had criticized the first twenty-three cantos of his *Morgante*. By declaring that nature alone has been his teacher, and therefore he is free from the impositions or rules of any school, he clearly spurns the teaching of Marsilio Ficino's Florentine Academy.

119–121. First mentioned in XXI, 49, 3 (see note, XXI, 46, 8 through 49), Astaroth here makes his formal entrance in the poem. He is described as "a very wise yet fierce and savage" spirit who, having unsuccessfully tried to intimidate Malagigi, kindly agrees to follow his exorciser's orders. He proves not only to be well acquainted with Rinaldo's adventures, but also to possess a remarkable classical erudition. Since the tone of his words is ever restrained, calm, and cultured, one could almost forget that he is a creature of hell, were it not for some expressions from which his true demonic nature transpires. As the poet himself ironically remarks, Astaroth refuses to mention Christ by name, resorting instead to such circumlocutions as "the tomb of Calvary" for Christ's sepulcher (127, 1), and "Thomas's faith" for Christianity (129, 3). It is interesting that the reference to Saint Thomas in Astaroth's latter periphrasis calls to mind lines 13–14 of Pulci's *Frottola II,* where it is stated that only he who, like Thomas, needs to touch in order to believe, is to be considered wise and reasonable (*Chi, come Tomma palpa / Mi par savio e discreto*). Why does Pulci make Astaroth say that the Christian religion is the faith of Thomas—the most recalcitrant of the Apostles to believe in the Resurrection of Christ (as it is stated in John 20:24–25)—and not the faith of Peter or, even better, of Paul? Certainly Pulci's liking for Thomas—for whom the attribute "wise," also assigned to Astaroth, is used—derives from the inclination to skepticism that the poet shares with the Apostle.

128, 6–7. Mount Tabor is located in today's Israel, east of the city of Nazareth. Prester John, from the French *Preste Jean,* is a legendary figure associated during the Middle Ages with fabulous travels. While in French chivalric literature and in Marco Polo's book of travels Prester John is an eastern monarch, in Italian romances he appears instead as the king of the ancient African country of Numidia (today's Algeria).

In Pulci's description of Rinaldo's and his companions' trip toward the Orient, the dangers they encounter and overcome, the cities they visit, and the mountains and rivers they cross (stanzas 126–129), the critic Ruggero Ruggieri notices several similarities to the descriptions of events that took place during a "pilgrimage to the Holy Places" (353). According to this Italian scholar, the several connections that can be found between *Morgante* and Marco Polo's book, particularly with regard to some male and female characters (such as the Old Man of the Mountain, Antea, Prester John, and others), allow us to perceive in Pulci's masterpiece "a mysterious and subtle (even though at times nebulous) Euro-Asian atmosphere" (356) (see "Affinità di tematiche e di personaggi tra il *Milione* e il *Morgante,*" 349–362). For the reference to Atlas (129, 6), see note, XXIV, 88, 7–8. Lines 7–8 of stanza 130 derive from the famous story of Ulysses' travels and death, told in Dante's *Inferno,* XXVI, 90–142.

135–136. In these and the following stanzas, Astaroth reveals even more of himself: in addition to being an expert on Holy Scriptures, he is also a fine, though somewhat unorthodox, theologian and possesses a well-rounded knowledge of astrology and the theories concerning the influence of the stars (137–139). Questioned here by Malagigi concerning Gano's betrayal of Orlando at Roncesvalles, he answers that not even if he thought about it for an entire night could he give him a more precise answer. Like any other infernal spirit, he can foresee the future, but just as astrologers and learned men can. Astaroth's foresight, therefore, is limited; were it not so, no one could escape from the devil's domination. If Astaroth is acquainted with the past, only God—referred to here as "the First" (136, 4) (the devil never directly names God or Christ)—knows everything about the past, the present, and the future (136, 4–7). According to Astaroth, however, God the Father's omni-science is not equally shared by God the Son (136, 8). In subscribing to this heretical belief, which originated with some Fathers of the Greek Church and subsequently spread to Tuscany and Italy as result of the renewed interest in Greek studies and Neoplatonism (Ageno, 872 and Puccini, 1077), Astaroth again shows his lineage in Thomas.

137, 4. The astrolabe is an ancient astronomical instrument used by the Greeks for determining the position of the sun and the stars.

137, 6–8 and 138, 1–4. What is being said here is that since the position of Mars in the sky, within the constellation of Scorpius, is in ascending conjunction with Saturn, the motions of the stars are going to exert (on events soon to take place at Roncesvalles) a much more woeful influence than they exerted on the war between Turnus and Aeneas. For the reference to Turnus, see note, XXIV, 17, 6.

139, 3. *Veru* and *Dominus Ascone* are the names of two of the nine comets listed by astrologers in Pulci's time. Davide Puccini (1078) mentions as Pulci's possible source Lorenzo Bonincontri, who lectured at the Platonic Academy between 1475 and 1477.

141–144. Note that Astaroth, requested by Malagigi to explain his previous pronouncement on the inferiority of the Son with regard to the Father (141, 7–8), replies to him by quoting, almost verbatim, from Mark 13:32. In addition, eager to dispel any further doubts that Malagigi may have, he launches into a discussion on the nature of the Trinity, challenging theologians to disprove his "solution" and concluding that only God (whom he calls "that Father" and "that ancient Sire") is all-knowing.

145–146. For Astaroth, the reason for the damnation of Lucifer and of the fallen angels resides in their not having been able to foresee the future. For the reference to Lucifer and Judecca, see note, XI, 74, 6. The source for Asta-roth's mention of Satan's temptations of Christ (referred to as "the mightiest Saint of all Saints" [146, 5–8]) is again the Gospel, particularly Mark 4:5–6.

148–153. To Malagigi—who wonders whether God is responsible for the damnation of Lucifer and the angels who followed him, since the Lord had foreknowledge of their rebellion—Astaroth replies that it is free will that has damned both Lucifer and all other fallen angels. The reason for Astaroth's sudden anger (150, 1) may be that Malagigi has hit his sore spot. He, like Lucifer, is guilty of his own sin through bad judgment. He was free to choose and thus responsible. Then, in a discussion considered by some to be a parody of the many disputes among doctors and theologians attempting to reconcile the doctrine of divine prescience with the question of free will (note in line 2 of stanza 150 the use of the Hebrew word "Sabaoth" for God), Astaroth states that God is right in punishing the fallen angels, who, however, cannot repent. This is because God does not grant repentance when a sin is the result of a free decision of the will. Only those who, like Adam, are unaware of sinning can be forgiven. God, in fact, is merciful toward those who commit sin yielding to temptation. Even Judas, who repented, could have saved himself had he not lacked hope, without which "no man can e'er be saved."

Just as Rinaldo did in canto XXIII (see note, 26–29), Astaroth too (152, 1–2) confuses the "Word" (Christ) with the Holy Spirit. With regard to the meeting of Christ ("that Sage") with Pilate (154, 5–8), Astaroth points out that if the Roman's initial ignorance of the truth (Christ's innocence) was not a sin, when Pilate, who had declared Christ to be "a just person," washed his hands of him (Matthew 27:24), he then committed a sin.

155, 6. Origen was a Christian theologian and a doctor of the Greek Church who lived between A.D. 185 and 254. In his book *De principiis,* he maintains that evil will be gradually defeated, and that at the end of time there will no longer be devils and sinners.

155, 8. The meaning of this Latin phrase is "In those days shall Judas be saved" (Jeremiah 33:16). As Pulci's commentators point out, here the name of Judas probably stands for the entire Jewish people.

157, 6–8 through 160. Answering Malagigi's previously posited question—Why did God create the angels knowing that some of them would be destined to damnation?—Astaroth candidly declares his total ignorance on the matter. He then lashes out against "poets, philosophers, and theologians" who arrogantly pretend to explain every mystery by resorting to questionable arguments and mental acrobatics.

In Pulci's time the sources of the Nile (158, 5) were unknown. Line 8 of stanza 158 clearly derives from Psalms 145:17: "The Lord is righteous in all his ways, and holy in all his works." The Dionysius and the Gregory mentioned in line 7 of stanza 159 are Saint Dionysius, first bishop of Athens and a martyr believed to have authored several works of Neoplatonic inspiration; and Saint Gregory the Great, pope from A.D. 590 to 604, reformer of church liturgy, and the founder of Gregorian chant. According to Ageno (879) and Puccini (1086), Pulci derives the reference to both Dionysius and Gregory from Dante's *Paradiso,* XXVIII, 130–139. Concerning the "spirit elves" (160–

161), see note, 92, 1–4. It is quite probable, as Davide Puccini also suggests (1086), that the term "spirit elves" is here mockingly used with reference to real people who were Pulci's contemporaries.

165, 1–2. Rubicante, named along with Farferello (also called Farferel), is another of Dante's devils (see note, II, 31, 3–4).

165, 7. For the reference to Beelzebub, see note, II, 39, 7.

168, 6 and 169, 1–4. See note, 115, 4–5.

161, 1. See note, 115, 4–5.

169, 6. See note, 34, 2–5. Pulci wrongly attributes to Alcuin of York the paternity of Einhard's *Vita Karoli*.

170, 6 and 171, 3. See note, 70, 5.

172, 5–8; and 173. See note, 109, 2.

174, 5 (and again 176, 7–8). The Syrian king Arlotto has a brief life in the poem; he falls victim to Astolfo's spear in XXVI, 50, 5–8 through 53, 1–6.

176, 4. In ancient times, the satraps were the military governors of the various provinces of the Persian empire.

177, 1–8. Of the five Saracens mentioned in these lines, three—Turchion, Finadust, the poem's last giant, and King Malprimo—are killed in canto XXVI, while the other two—Fidasso and Maldue of Frasse—are slain by Rinaldo in canto XXVII.

178, 2 and 180, 1. For Pulci's reference to Turpin as one of his most reliable historical sources, see note, I, 5, 3.

179, 1–8. Except for King Fiorello, who is killed in canto XXVI, all the other pagan warriors mentioned in this stanza (Kings Chiariello and Margheriton included) meet their death in canto XXVII. Note that the Fieramonte mentioned in line 3 is Fieramont(e) of Balzia, not to be confused with King Erminion's brother Fieramonte, who was slain by Rinaldo in canto IX. For Buiafort(e), son of the Old Man of the Mountain and Orlando's admirer, see note, canto XXIV, 7, 8. Regarding King Balugant(e), see note, 27, 2–4.

180, 3. Both the Arcalif (see note, 27, 2–4) and the Saracen king Grandonio (also called Grandonius) are killed in canto XXVII.

182, 1–6. See note, XXIV, 54, 4–8. In *La Spagna,* where he appears quite frequently (XV–XXXVI), Sansonetto is befriended by Orlando, converts to Christianity, and bravely fights against the Saracen army. He is killed at Roncesvalles by Marsilius (XXXVI, 13). In *Morgante,* Sansonetto, only one of the many minor Pulci characters, is slain instead by Grandonius while fighting alongside Orlando (XXVII, 10, 1–5).

183. See note, 106, 7–8 and 107.

184, 3. A reference to the Magi, who, warned by God in a dream not to return to Herod, went back home by another route (Matthew 2:12).

189, 1. The Latin term *iusiurandum* (oath) is used here in its dative (or ablative) case to rhyme it with *quando* in line 3 of the Italian text. Ageno (887) explains that this word is part of a sentence attributed to Caesar in Cicero's *De officiis* (III, 21, 82).

189, 6–8. The "little widow" mentioned in these lines is Judith, Manasse's widow, who beheaded Holophernes, thus freeing the city of Betulia from a pending Assyrian invasion (see Judith 8–13 in the Catholic Bible).

190, 2, 4, and 6. "Mec" stands for Mecca (the spiritual center of Islam), which Pulci has amusingly shortened to make it rhyme with the other two words ending in "ec"; "alec" is an abbreviated form of *Salam-alec,* the Arabic greeting *as-salam 'alaik* (peace be with you).

190, 7. For Puccini (1096), the "holy ark" is the iron sarcophagus which contains Mohammed's mortal remains in Medina. Ageno (888) maintains instead that this ark is perhaps the *Kaaba,* a small cubic temple erected in the courtyard of Mecca's Great Mosque which serves as the repository for a sacred black stone.

197, 7. For the reference to Belfagor, see note, IV, 97, 3.

201, 6. See note, 165, 1–2.

202, 1–8. It is believed that Pulci derives the names of the four pharaohs mentioned in this stanza from Poggio Bracciolini's Latin translation, titled *Bibliotheca,* of the Greek historian Diodorus Siculus's work (Ageno, 891). Born in Sicily, Diodorus Siculus wrote a history of the world, which goes as far as the year 58 B.C. Of the forty volumes he authored, only fifteen have come down to us.

204, 4. While any plant that turns toward the sun can be called a heliotrope, this is also the name given to a variety of red-spotted dark green jasper. As Pulci states in lines 5–6, ancients believed that this stone could render invisible those who carried it on their person (see Boccaccio's *Decameron,* VIII, 3).

207, 2 and 5–6. As previously noted, Beelzebub and Lucifer are one and the same (see note, canto II, 39, 7).

210, 1. Note that "Milùs" stands for "Milusse" (see 205, 2).

210, 3. The land that Astaroth has previously referred to as "Ethiopia" (204, 2) is now called "the Antipodes," the name given to that part of the world located on the other side of the globe.

211, 2. In no other canto of the poem does Pulci tell of Baiardo's having experienced a similar "occupation" by a devil. It must be, as Puccini remarks (1103), "an extemporaneous statement" of the poet.

212, 2. It is believed that Pulci derives the information regarding the marsh/lake of Moeris, located west of the river Nile, not from Diodorus Siculus but from a first-century Latin writer, Pomponius Mela, author of the geographical treatise *De situ orbis,* used by Pliny the Elder as one of his sources (Ageno, 894).

213, 2–3. Triton is a river in North Africa which, before flowing into the sea, forms a marsh. It takes its name from the sea god Triton, and not, as Pulci incorrectly states, from Tritonia, a descriptive name for the goddess Minerva (Ageno, 894).

213, 5. The Mejerdah is a river that flows into the sea near Tunis. In the Italian text, Pulci calls this river by its old name, Bagrade (Ageno, 894). The anecdote about the Roman general Marcus Atilius Regulus and the 120-foot-long snake he killed and sent to Rome is taken from Pliny's *Naturalis Historia*.

214, 1–8. In spite of the more somber tone of this last part of the poem, here, as in stanzas 220, 1–5 and 304, Rinaldo does not seem to be much different from the man Pulci has portrayed in the preceding cantos. Interestingly, Astaroth, like Malagigi, appears to be well acquainted with the paladin's gluttonous voracity and his strong roguish inclination.

216, 4–8; and 217. For warblers and ortolans, see note, XIV, 59, 4. Pulci states that the people of Tuscany believe that ortolans do not exist anywhere else in the world; thus, these birds are deemed to be a food worthy of the gods. Prato (217, 2), today one of Europe's leading wool-manufacturing centers, is a city in central Italy, located only a few miles northwest of Florence. Ambrosia and nectar (216, 8) were thought to be foods of the gods. "Pastor Arlotto" (217, 3) is Arlotto Mainardi (1396–1484), a Tuscan cleric famous for his humorous sayings and witty remarks, which were collected and published by a friend after his death (see *Motti e facezie del piovano Arlotto,* a. c. di G. Folena [Milano-Napoli: Ricciardi, 1953]). According to Pulci, Pastor Arlotto explains the mystery surrounding these delicious birds by asserting (217, 7–8) that when the resurrected Christ appeared to Mary Magdalene, he did so disguised as an ortolan. (In John 20:15 we read, instead, that Mary Magdalene spoke to Jesus "supposing him to be the gardener.") Given the fact that the Italian word *ortolano* means both "bird" and "gardener," the use of this term in this particular instance constitutes an amusing play on words (Ageno, 895).

218, 7–8. From Matthew 17:2–4, we read that after Christ's transfiguration on the mountain, Peter asked him to let the Apostles build three tabernacles. In a comical burst of joy over the sumptuous banquet that Astaroth has miraculously prepared for them, Rinaldo proposes to immortalize the event by erecting not three but six tabernacles.

221, 1–4. These lines may allude to what the poet has stated in 107 (1–2) and 183 (1–2).

226, 4. See note, XIV, 63, 1–4.

227, 3–4. Calpe (on the African coast) and Abila (on the European coast) are the ancient names of the two mountains known as the Pillars of Hercules.

228–244. More precise, but not necessarily orthodox, are Astaroth's ideas concerning the destiny of man and the future of the Christian religion. Anticipating by several years Columbus's voyages of discovery, our devil-theologian first asserts that it is possible to travel beyond Hercules' Pillars (a notion Pulci likely derived from Lorenzo Bonincontri's lectures [see note, 139, 3]); then to Rinaldo, who is questioning him regarding the possibility of salvation for the inhabitants of the Antipodes, he expresses some very liberal views (233, 5–8; and 234–239) which Dante would have deemed totally unacceptable.

Since, according to Astaroth, religion differentiates "beasts from men," the Romans, though honoring false gods, did not displease God. Likewise, the people of the Antipodes, who when adoring the planets believe in worshiping correctly, will find justice with God, as do all those "who observe their own religious laws." Though recognizing that Christianity is the only true faith, Astaroth declares that anyone who has a faith can be saved, except the Jews and Muslims, unless, inspired by God, they come to acknowledge in Christ the true Messiah, whose coming has been announced by the prophets, many sibyls, and the great poets of antiquity. In other words, Jews and Muslims cannot claim ignorance for their refusal to recognize and accept the "Word," as do pious pagans (before Christ) and the inhabitants of the Antipodes, who follow their own faith. God is omniscient and would have seen that these people would never know Christ; hence to create them for damnation is not reasonable.

Astaroth's long theological discussion ends with stanza 244, where he justifies the heretical pronouncement made in stanza 136, 7–8, explicating that Christ as a man is inferior in knowledge to God, but "when His divine nature is conjoined," He "can all things know."

The Latin phrase that Astaroth quotes in line 6 of stanza 237 comes from the Book of Psalms (36:3): "He hath left off to be wise, and to do good." Note also that God is again referred to as "Heaven" (234, 7), "First Father" (238, 5), "Highest Jove" (239, 4), "High Emmanuel" (241, 2), and "Highest Mind" (244, 7). Eritrea (241, 7) is the name given to the sibyl who was best known during the Middle Ages (Ageno, 902). For lines 4–5 of stanza 242, see John 11:43 and Matthew 9:2–7. The Greek word "Tetragrammaton" (242, 8) was used to represent the Hebrew word for God, formed by the four letters *yod, he, vav,* and *he.* For the reference to Elijah's miracles, witnessed by Elisha and alluded to in lines 1–2 of stanza 243, see 2 Kings 2:1–22. The Latin words *ab initio* (244, 8) mean "from the beginning." Stanza 230 is considered by Giovanni Getto (109) to be "one of Pulci's more spellbinding stanzas."

To be sure, the profession of faith by Astaroth—a character the leading nineteenth-century Italian literary historian Francesco De Sanctis labeled a "free thinker," identifying in him the new spirit that was emerging in late-fifteenth-century Florence (*Storia della letteratura italiana,* vol. I, a cura di Benedetto Croce [Bari: Laterza, 1925], 369)—consists of an intelligent mixture of orthodox tenets and heretical pronouncements. Believing in predestination (as do Gano, the Old Man of the Mountain, King Marsilius, and many others), Astaroth denies the usefulness of repentance, recognizing at the same time that man can save himself provided that one sins ignorant of sinning.

He first categorically proclaims that God the Son is less omniscient than God the Father, then tries to clarify his assertion by resorting to an explanation which appears to be lacking in conviction to some critics, and to be a mere afterthought to others. If with regard to problems of a religious nature, and particularly the fate of non-Christians, he posits opinions that call to mind in their tolerance those expressed by Marsilius (42–46), on the fundamental question of the creation and the damnation of souls, he prefers to remain silent.

Though he states that the Christian religion is the only true faith, Astaroth also maintains that one needs only to have a faith, whatever it may be, in order to be saved (except, of course, for those who know Christ and consciously reject him). On this point, the devil-theologian shows a clear affinity with Margutte, who believes that "faith is just as man has fashioned it" (XVIII, 118, 1). If it is true that we cannot find in this canto the coarse laughter that permeates Margutte's episode, it is also true that Astaroth's conciliatory and accommodating theology may be perceived as a more dangerous doctrine than Margutte's systematic materialism.

Carlo Pellegrini believes that in Astaroth's voice one can recognize, to a certain extent, the voice of the poet. Writing in support of his thesis of Pulci's sincere religiosity, the critic states (122): "We must believe, particularly because of the heartfelt conviction with which Astaroth states his ideas, that these are the same as those professed by the author." We believe that it would be a mistake to consider Astaroth a believer, a fallen spirit who feels a certain nostalgia for his past celestial status, as it is wrong to assume that he brings Rinaldo to Roncesvalles mainly to help the Christian cause. The truth of the matter is that Rinaldo's presence at Roncesvalles will result in the deaths of many pagans, whose souls are going to fill the city of the damned. (Astaroth's true diabolic nature further transpires in stanzas 270–273 and in stanza 89 of canto XXVI.)

Attilio Momigliano (336) considers Astaroth—whom he calls "the most hypocritical devil that has ever existed"—to be more perverse than Gano because, "while the Maganzan's lies are easily discovered, Astaroth feigns a tone of sincerity so well that those who observe him only when he talks of theology are inclined to believe that a devil has miraculously become a true hermit." For Momigliano (337), it is possible to see in the black angel's "mocking and hypocritical disposition" a reflection of the humanists of the fifteenth century who, while they "do not dare as yet to operate as atheists, behave nevertheless as misbelievers, though still speaking devoutly about religion."

Angelo Gianni maintains instead that Astaroth's theological discussion is prompted more by "conspicuous and external intellectual motives" than by "a sincere impulse of Pulci's creative imagination" (393). The presence in *Morgante* of this syllogizing devil is explained as due partly to the author's "unconventional sense of humor," and partly to Pulci's desire "to reassure Lorenzo's entourage, and to convince [everyone] that the old lover of occult sciences and author of the incriminating sonnets [Pulci] has returned to the fold" (395). Gianni further states that the stanzas in which Astaroth talks about the creation of the angels and utters his doctrine on the inhabitants of the Antipodes are "twelve stanzas of sheer theology" and treat questions that "were debated at length in Ficino's *De Christiana religione* and are therefore in full agreement with the Platonism of the second half of the fifteenth century" (396). Concerning Astaroth's role in the poem, the critic in his conclusive remarks states that, everything considered, Astolfo's words and actions in the famous episode of canto XXI are "much more daring and roguish" than all the "heterodox statements attributed to [this] new character" (398).

For Giovanni Getto, one can refer to Astaroth as a character only "in the sense that he constitutes an aesthetic unity"; his presence in the poem originates, therefore, from Pulci's desire to create an atmosphere in which the "colors and themes" that are so dear to our poet can be expressed and developed. The Astaroth episode, from which exudes "a joyful doctrinal curiosity," reveals Pulci's constant eagerness to touch upon and discuss the most important points of contemporary knowledge, making "the most unforeseen excursions through theologiocal, magical, geographic, and zoological doctrines" (108).

Paolo Orvieto, in a chapter devoted to a close and stimulating analysis of cantos XXIV–XXVIII of *Morgante* (244–283), subtly observes that while the events narrated in the first twenty-three cantos of the poem constitute a most skillful "collage" and need no "connecting superstructure of historical order" (245), the structure of the narrative and the dramatic organization of the last five cantos clearly manifest Pulci's return to the *Chanson de Roland* as well as his deliberate attempt to adhere more closely to those texts traditionally held as "genuine documents of Carolingian historiography" (246–247). To be sure, in this last part of the poem, Pulci's "protestations of historical veracity" become more and more pressing (a fact attested by the poet's personal interventions in cantos XXIV, 2; XXV, 115–116, 168, 5–8 through 169, 178, 1–5, and 180, 1–2; and, subsequently, in canto XXVIII).

According to Paolo Orvieto (250), in order to understand and justify Pulci's intention to elevate the tone of his poem with supporting historical, religious, and astrological references, a scholar ought to "postulate" an "enigmatic reading" of the text, taking into serious consideration the contemporary personal experiences of the poet, particularly his fierce dispute with Marsilio Ficino. This dispute should not be explained as due only to ideological differences, but also as caused by the clash of two diametrically opposed cultural beliefs: the revolutionary, Neoplatonic, and essentially elitist one advocated by Ficino (and eventually embraced by the Medicis), and the conservative and allegorical one, deeply rooted in medieval poetical tradition, strongly advocated by Pulci. Consequently, a correct reading of cantos XXIV–XXVIII implies a definite distinction between the material Pulci wrote before his polemic with Ficino and the material he wrote or changed after it. The presence in several stanzas of the last five cantos of *Morgante* of modifications of an allegorical-polemic nature—superimposed on the already established plot—complicates the task of the scholar, who is presented with difficult philological and interpretative problems. These allegorical changes make it possible for the scholar to conduct an "enigmatic reading" of the text, as a result of which Orvieto feels authorized to say that while the poet "hides Ficino behind King Marsilius, he will at times hide himself behind Orlando, the innocent lamb sent to slaughter" (254).

With regard to Astaroth's doctrinal, astrological, and philosophical disqui-
sitions, the critic is of the opinion that they acquire a "historical reason" only
if they are considered within the context of the Pulci/Ficino dispute.
Astaroth's presence in the poem testifies to the acculturation process that was
imposed on the Florentine poet, and of which "Pulci, disguised as Astaroth, in
his attempt to surpass the skills of philosophers and astrologers, makes a willing
or unwilling parody." The poet, explains Orvieto, having introduced the black
angel mainly for "comical and structural motives" (he must take Rinaldo to
Roncesvalles), uses Astaroth in order to contrast the devil's wisdom and
religious knowledge with a culture and a religion which were becoming "ever
more elitist and incomprehensible to the people" (259).

246, 8. Latin for "Into thine hand I commit my spirit" (Psalms 31:5).

248, 6. See note, XIV, 63, 1–4.

250, 6. The zodiac is an imaginary belt of the heavens containing the
apparent annual paths of the sun. The zodiac is divided into twelve con-
stellations and signs (see note, XIV, 46, 3–6).

252, 1–8. Ricciardetto's great fear (248–252), the cause of Farferel's
mocking neigh, is, according to Momigliano (217), not only comical and
unbecoming a knight of his reputation, but also unjustified by the circum-
stances.

253, 3. In Roman times, the land crossed by the river Baetis (now
Guadalquivir) was called "Baetica." It is known today as Andalusia (Ageno,
906).

254, 2–6. Avicenna (A.D. 980–1037) was an Arab philosopher and phys-
ician, author of commentaries on Galen and Aristotle. Born in Spain, Aver-
roës (A.D. 1126–1198) was an Arab philosopher who wrote a celebrated
commentary on Aristotle. The works of these men, whom Dante mentions
several times in *Inferno* and the *Convivio,* were widely known in the Middle
Ages. Ageno (906) and Puccini (1120) note that Avicenna was not born in
Cordoba, Spain, as believed by Pulci, but in Afsenna, in the Middle Eastern
region of Bokhara.

255, 2–4. "Guadian land" derives from the Guadiana River, which in
ancient times was called Anas. The Anas River is also mentioned in Pom-
ponius Mela's work (see note, 212, 2).

255, 5. Note that the Latin name of Cazlona was Castulo, from which
comes the word "Castulon" used by Pulci in the Italian text.

255, 7. The Tagus (*Tajo* in Spanish and *Tejo* in Portuguese) is a 566-mile-
long river flowing west through central Spain and Portugal until it reaches the
Atlantic at Lisbon.

259, 1–8. For this stanza, see notes, XXIV, 113, 1–3 and 113, 8. With
regard to line 8, Ageno (908) points out that Cecco d'Ascoli in his *Acerba*
writes that frequent "flickering of eyes is a certain sign of impending events."

263, 1. The saint in question is the Apostle James; he is believed to be
buried in Santiago de Compostela, in Galicia (he is first mentioned in XXII,
24, 3).

265, 5. For Squarciafer(ro), see note, XXI, 46, 8 through 49.

265, 8. The popular Tuscan expression given in this line is *tentar non nuoce* ("it doesn't hurt to try").

266, 1–4. To keep a stitch from coming undone, a tailor makes a knot. By telling Rubicant to "close the stitch," the necromancer is metaphorically warning him to be careful in his dealings with Astaroth.

266, 7–8. The meaning of the Tuscan proverbial expression about the "two graters" is that a scoundrel (in this case Squarciaferro, the first grater) cannot easily fool another scoundrel (Astaroth, the other grater); the necromancer would therefore advise Rubicant to resort to a better plan ("a different cheese").

271, 3–8. Attilio Momigliano (164–165) remarks that though this devil, disguised as a saintly old hermit, is depicted with details that highlight more his soul than his physical aspect, "as a whole he appears before our eyes as a lively and comical [character]." In lines 7–8 Pulci commentators see a reference to Matthew 7:17: "Beware of false prophets, which come to you in sheep's clothing, but inwardly they are ravenous wolves."

272, 3. In Catholic liturgy, the Miserere (see Psalms 51:1) is a prayer which is recited mainly during Lent, Holy Week, and funeral services.

273, 5. "Brother Clever Simpleton" is the English version of *frate Ciullo Biondo,* an amusing name invented by Pulci.

274, 1–4. As in 256, 1–3, Pulci is again addressing the reader. Here, and particularly in 276–277, 1–4, however, his considerations acquire a more serious, heartfelt tone.

276, 7. The "Poet" that Pulci is freely quoting here is Dante (see *Paradiso,* XIII, 136–138).

278, 7. The words "mighty snow" stand for the souls of the Saracens killed at Roncesvalles.

279, 7. This proverbial expression ("It is hard for two rascals to deceive each other") is similar in meaning to the one in line 7 of stanza 266.

283, 4–8. Interestingly, in commenting upon his use of a line from Petrarch's *Trionfo d'Amore* (II, 98), the paternity of which he farcically attributes to Rinaldo, Pulci humorously restates an author's right to borrow from fellow poets.

284, 4–8. What Astaroth says concerning how easy it is for Christians to save themselves does not substantially differ from what Turpin tells Orlando in stanzas 2–3 of canto XXVII.

284, 6. Latin for "Against thee, thee only, have I sinned" Psalms 51:4. See also note, 272, 3.

286, 1. Note Rinaldo's irony in addressing the devil Squarciaferro as "holy father."

289, 2. "Iber" is the river Ebro, flowing southeast from northern Spain to the Mediterranean.

289, 4–5 through 290, 5. Once the thought of Luciana has entered Rinaldo's mind, he immediately finds a plausible excuse to make a detour and stop in Saragossa. Then, his resolve fortified by Astaroth's mention of food, the true Rinaldo we have come to know in the poem's first twenty-three cantos comes to life again.

294, 1. "Bagdad's arch-braggart" is the amusing and yet powerful-sounding name of a nonexistent Muslim dignitary invented by Farferello to intimidate the saucy footman.

298, 5–8. Angelo Gianni (400) calls these lines "a whimsical ballet of images."

299, 8. See note, XVI, 14, 5–6.

302, 1. In the Italian text, Pulci uses the scientific Latin word *musa* for "banana" (Ageno, 920).

304, 8. See note, VI, 9, 2. Rinaldo's roguish kiss stands as a perfect conclusion to the lively and comical scene narrated in stanzas 295–304, which critics consider to be among Pulci's finest.

With regard to Rinaldo's and Ricciardetto's invisible participation at Queen Blanda's table, Rossella Bessi has identified striking similarities between this Pulcian episode and the concluding section of the popular poem *Liombruno.* However, since the question of the dating of the latter is still unsolved, it is not possible to consider *Liombruno* a possible source for Pulci's *Morgante* ("Il *Morgante* e il *Liombruno,*" *Interpres* IX [1989]: 267–274).

306, 7–8. What Pulci states here is not precisely correct. In stanzas 35–41 of canto XIV we read, in fact, that Luciana, answering Rinaldo's request for assistance, joins the Lord of Montalban in the Moroccan city of Arma, and not in Persia.

307, 1–8. For the description of Luciana's pavilion, see XIV, 42–86.

311, 1. Astaroth begins here what is commonly referred to as the poem's "second bestiary." In her commentary on the last section of this canto, Franca Ageno explains (922–923) that stanzas 311 through 322, 4 include information that Pulci derives from book VIII of Pliny's *Historia naturalis;* stanzas 322, 7 through 323, 8 contain the transcription of lines 696–733 from book IX of Lucan's *Pharsalia,* while stanzas 323 through 331 are related to books XXV and XXIII of Albertus Magnus' *De animalibus.*

311, 3. The amphisbaena is a mythological snake having two heads at each end of its body.

311, 7. Manticores (mantichorae) are fabulous Indian animals.

312, 1. The fountain mentioned in this line is the Spring of Hippocrene, which the mythical winged horse Pegasus opened with a stroke of his hoof.

312, 7. The rufium is an animal belonging to the leopard family.

312, 8 and 313, 1. While the crocuta is a beast found in Ethiopia (from the description it could be the hyena), the leucrocuta lives in India.

313, 7. Native also to India is the axis, which may be the animal that the Swedish botanist Linnaeus calls *cervus axis.*

314, 1. For Pulci the catoblepas (here *catoblepe*) is a serpent having the same peculiar powers (lines 4–8) that Pliny attributes to the basilisk. Latin dictionaries, however, list the catoblepas as a type of Ethiopian bull which always walks with its head down.

315, 1. The ichneumon, or Egyptian mongoose, feeds on crocodile eggs and is noted for killing venomous snakes.

315, 8. The wren is a small and very active passerine bird. Pliny writes that by hopping around in front of a crocodile, the wren causes it to open its mouth wide. The bird then picks at the crocodile's teeth, making the animal fall asleep in dead pleasure (Ageno, 924–25).

316, 1. The eale is another Ethiopian wild animal listed by Pliny.

318, 8. As Ageno clarifies (926), the reference to the hippopotamus's "bifid tongue" is due to the poet's incorrect reading of Pliny's text.

319, 3. The "tragelaphus" is probably a steinbok.

322, 8. According to Lucan's *Pharsalia* (IX, 696–699), when the drops of blood from Medusa's head sank into the earth, they generated several types of poisonous snakes (Ageno, 928).

323, 1–3. Celidri are amphibious reptiles mentioned by such poets as Virgil and Dante; the dipsas is a desert viper, the bite of which was believed to provoke a burning thirst; the snake called haemorrhois was thought to suck all the blood of its victims (Puccini, 1146).

324, 1–8. As previously noted, the information concerning the reptiles that Pulci lists in this stanza is taken from Albertus Magnus's treatise. Dracopedes are dragons with childlike faces; armena take their name from Armenia, the region where they originate; calcatrix is another name for the crocodile; because of its color, the irundo snake derives its name from a bird, the swallow (called *hirundo* in Latin); the alsordius, arachs, and altynanyti are small but dangerous snakes; the centupeda is a fabulous reptile with several short legs; the cornuta is a horned snake; the rimatrix is a reptile that contaminates any food it touches; the naderos is a relatively large and extremely poisonous snake found in Germany; the berus, boa, natrix, andrius, and possibly phareas are all water snakes; the ahedysymon and the alhartraf are large, long serpents.

325, 1–8. The ibis is a large wading bird, related to herons and storks. According to Albertus Magnus (Ageno, 930), the Greek physician Galen got the idea for a human enema by observing these birds' behavior.

326–331. The information concerning the birds listed in these stanza derives also from Albertus Magnus's *De animalibus*. The caprimulgus (known as agothylex in Greek) is a nocturnal bird of the bat family; the cynamulgus, a native of Ethiopia, makes its nest on the tallest branches of the cinnamon tree. According to a classical legend, the memnonides (stilt-birds) were generated from the smoke rising out of the funeral pyre of the Ethiopian prince Memnon, who, having become an ally of the Trojans against the Greeks, was then slain by Achilles. It was also believed that every year flocks of these birds returned to sprinkle water on Memnon's grave after wetting their wings in the Aesepus River. Following Albertus Magnus's text, Pulci identifies the Ethiopian prince with the Pythagorean philosopher Memnon, who was thought to be buried in Troy. As Ageno explains (931), the belief, shared also by Albertus Magnus, that the coredula (skylark) feeds only on the heart of its victims was due to a wrong interpretation of this bird's name. Choretes are possibly birds of prey, while the bistarda is perhaps a type of stilt-bird. The caladrius is a plover or a type of shore bird; the ibor is a bird originating in the Orient; the incendula (firebird) was thought by the ancients to be a bird of ill omen; the porfirion is an aquatic bird, most probably a coot, found in both Europe and in North America.

332, 3–4. See note, 69, 8.

332, 8. The name of Christ, which Astaroth has consistently avoided or has only metaphoriocally mentioned, is uttered here by the poet as he again closes the canto with a religious invocation.

C A N T O   X X V I

SUMMARY: Invocation (1). Oliver, who from a mountaintop has sighted Marsilius's army descending toward Roncesvalles, runs back to the Christian camp (2–11). Stunned at the realization of Marsilius's betrayal, Orlando proudly refuses his companions' request to sound the oliphant; then, after meekly listening to Oliver remind him that he should have heeded his warnings, the count addresses his men, urging them to fight bravely and die, if necessary, trusting in God's eternal reward (12–39). While Orlando jumps on his horse, Archbishop Turpin blesses the troops (40–42). Speaking briefly to his men, Falseron claims the right to kill Orlando in order to avenge Ferraù's death, and as soon as the shouting pagan army confronts the Christian troops, the battle begins (43–49). The first Christian knight to engage the enemy is Astolfo, who kills the Syrian king Arlotto (50–53). Astolfo is followed by Angiolin of Bayonne and by Avin, who fight bravely, but unsuccessfully, with Kings Malducco and Mazzarigi respectively (54–57). More fortunate is Oliver, who slays King Malprimo (58–61), whose death Turchion is unable to avenge as Turpin's spear mortally pierces him (62–63). While Orlando's mighty brigade creates havoc among the enemy lines, the count kills Falseron, whose body portentously disappears as it hits the ground (64–71). Berlinghier wounds the giant Finadusto in the chest, while Oliver, who has recovered from a blow inflicted upon him by the now-dead King Malprimo, rejoins Orlando and his paladins, who have suffered only one casualty: Angiolin of Bordeaux (72–78).

The moment Rinaldo and Ricciardetto, who from high above have beheld the scene of the battle, touch ground near Roncesvalles, they become visible again; however, before the Lord of Montalban and his brother go and fight King Bianciardino's men, Rinaldo bids farewell to Astaroth, who promptly vanishes. Astaroth is then seen on the bell tower of a nearby church, catching, with Squarciafer's assistance, the passing souls of the Saracens killed at Roncesvalles (79–91). Rinaldo attacks Bianciardino's troops, killing many, while Marsilius, unaware of the presence of the two paladins on the battlefield, thinks that Gano may have betrayed him (92–96). Rinaldo and Ricciardetto leave Bianciardino to join Orlando, who greatly rejoices upon seeing his two cousins (97–110). Informed by Bianciardino of the exploits of the two mysterious knights, Marsilius believes them to be some of Malagigi's demons (111–114). However, when Mazzarigi informs him of Falseron's death and of the arrival of Rinaldo and Ricciardetto, the king bursts out in a vehement invective against his god in great dismay for the losses suffered by his army (115–125). As the battle continues to rage, the Christian knights, especially Berlinghier, who succeeds in killing Finadusto, give further demonstrations of their valor (126–143). Having been told by Buiaforte that Gano and Marsilius have betrayed him, Orlando gladly spares the life of the son of the Old Man of the Mountain, warning him, however, to keep away from Rinaldo (126–152).

1, 3. The archangel mentioned here is Michael (see also XXVII, 77, 1).

3, 1. "The one" referred to in this line is the sun. For the myth of Prometheus, see note, XXI, 164, 4.

3, 3. The name of this Indian river is used by Pulci, as it was previously used by Dante in his poem (*Purgatorio,* II, 5), to indicate the East, where the sun is born.

5, 1. In *Morgante,* Guottibuoffi (called also Guottibuoff) is a Burgundian knight who fights with Orlando and dies in XXVII, 82, 2. As Davide Puccini notes (1152), this character, named Gottebuof or Gottebouf, appears both in Andrea da Barberino's *I Reali di Francia,* where he is said to be the king of Frigia and one of Charlemagne's counselors, and in the poem *Aspramonte,* where he is identified as the king of Bohemia.

6, 1–8. As we have noted in canto XXV, several events and characters mentioned in this canto of *Morgante* are also found in cantos XXXI–XXXIV of *La Spagna* (where, however, no mention is made of Rinaldo's, Ricciardetto's, and Buiafort's participation in the Battle of Roncesvalles). Aside from the far superior artistry of the author of *Morgante,* the most striking difference between the texts of the two poems is the atmosphere of solemnity and impending tragedy that, in spite of a few occasional ironic and amusing remarks, pervades this canto.

In this stanza we read that Orlando attributes Oliver's dream to his intoxication. The count makes the same accusation in *La Spagna* (XXXI, 7–10), but only after Oliver awakes him with the news that a great Saracen army is about to attack. For the reference to Daniel's interpretation of Nebuchadnezzar's dream, see Daniel 4:8–27.

10, 1. Malagigi's prophecies are expressed in canto XXIV, 169, 1–5.

12–15. Commenting upon the predominantly somber spirit that is peculiar to the last cantos of the poem, Gianni (379) perceives in Orlando's words in stanza 13, 5–8 "an undeniable sense of fatalism and defeat."

15, 1–4. These lines repeat the names of famous men previously mentioned by the poet. For Scipio and Hannibal, see note, XI, 75, 1–4. For Caesar, see note, VII, 55, 7–8. Regarding Marcellus and Nebuchadnezzar, see notes, XV, 24, 5–8 and XVIII, 19, 6. For Alexander, also mentioned in stanza 48, 8, see note, XIX, 161, 1–2. For Darius, see note, XXV, 91, 6. Xerxes, son of King Darius, ruled over the Persian empire from 485 to 465 B.C. Both Darius and Xerxes are mentioned again in stanza 110, 7.

17, 8. For the reference to the valley of Jehoshaphat, see note, I, 6, 7–8.

20, 7. As Ageno explains (939), the idiomatic expression *aspettare le mummie* used here by Pulci means "to wait for something that will never happen." Charlemagne is vainly waiting for "his mummies," since Orlando and his knights will all die at Roncesvalles. Oliver's harsh words against Marsilius (20, 3–8 and 21, 3–8) are discussed in a note to stanzas 118–119.

24. Orlando's speech to his troops, lasting almost sixteen stanzas (24–40, 1–3), is totally missing in *La Spagna*.

26, 1–6. In these lines Marsilius is ironically compared to Melchizedek, the loyal king of Salem, who offered bread and wine to Abraham and blessed him (Genesis 14:18–20). He is said to be a man capable of speaking many languages (consequently one who should not be trusted), and worthy as well of the Arab greeting *Salam-alec* ("Peace be with you"). Interestingly, Pulci writes *Alec-salam Salam-alec,* placing the answer to the Koran-prescribed greeting before the greeting itself. According to Davide Puccini (1159), the poet may have intentionally inverted the order to state ironically that Marsilius deserves to be trusted because he answers a man's greeting even before he has been greeted. Note that according to Jewish tradition, Lamech was believed to have killed Cain for slaying Abel (Ageno, 941).

26, 7–8. In these lines Marsilius is further compared to Ahithophel and Marsyas. Ahithophel, King David's counselor, hanged himself after having sided with Absalom in his conspiracy against David (2 Samuel 15:12 and 17:23). Having found the flute that Minerva had invented and had thrown away in a moment of rage, Marsyas dared to challenge Apollo to a musical contest. The god easily won it and punished the arrogant Marsyas by flaying him alive.

28, 1. The Greek leader is Leonida, the king of Sparta, whom the Persians killed with all his men at the Battle of the Thermopylae in 480 B.C. Ageno (941) notes that Pulci is quoting from Cicero (*Tusc.,* 1, 42, 101).

29, 2. Orlando compares himself to Isaac, whose father, Abraham, was prepared to offer him as a sacrifice to God as he had been ordered (Genesis 22:2–13). Note the importance of this comparison for understanding the battle.

29, 7. The meaning of this Latin sentence is "Come, ye blessed of my Father" (Matthew 25:34).

31, 5–8. It seems that in these lines Orlando, considering Christianity a merely human institution, foretells its end.

35, 8. A reference to the story of Daniel, who came out unharmed from the lions' den into which he had been thrown on Darius's order (Daniel 6:16–23).

36, 1. The Greek philosopher Thales was born in Miletus circa 640 B.C. and died in 546 B.C.

37, 1. Pulci's commentators (Ageno, 944, and Puccini, 1163–1164) argue that the poet refers here to two, possibly three, members—father, son, and grandson—of the Roman family of the Decii, all bearing the name P. Decius Mure. According to tradition, they all died fighting in different wars (340, 295, and 279 B.C.) in defense of Rome. Dante mentions them, together with the Fabii, another famous Roman family (see *Paradiso*, VI, 47).

38, 2. The legendary Roman soldier Publius Horatius Cocles in 507 B.C. faced King Porsenna's troops alone in order to give his fellow citizens enough time to destroy the Sublicius Bridge behind him. The Roman aristocrat Marcus Curtius, according to legend, in 362 B.C. threw himself fully armed and on horseback into a chasm which had suddenly opened on the floor of the Forum, believing that his sacrifice would appease the gods.

42, 7–8. See note, I, 13, 1–8. For Orlando's victory over King Almont, see also XXVIII, 56, 6–8.

45, 8. For Alexander, see note, XIX, 161, 1–2.

46, 6. Concerning Scylla, see note, XIV, 69, 1–8. Almost always mentioned together with Scylla, Charybdis is a mythological sea monster believed to inhabit a rock in the Straits of Messina.

47, 5. See note, II, 50, 5.

47, 6. For Alcuin, see notes, XXV, 34, 2–5 and 169, 6.

48, 5–8. With regard to these lines, noting the poet's "whimsical and brilliant intervention" in the poem, Getto (81) writes that here "the limits between characters and prompter, between stage and audience, are joyfully and lightheartedly confused."

50–52. In *La Spagna,* too, Astolfo is the first Christian knight who engages the enemy. In the *cantare popolare,* however, the English lord, using his spear and then his sword, effortlessly kills first King Ardalotto and then two other Saracen warriors (XXXII, 6–9). Missing in *La Spagna* are the narrator's ironic exhortation to Astolfo not to let himself be thrown from his horse; Oliver's mocking remark to Orlando, and the amusing concluding comment on lines 7–8 of stanza 53.

54, 1. Previously mentioned in I, 9, 7 and in VIII, 94, 4–6, Angiolin of Bayonne is the second paladin to face the enemy with uncertain success. In *La Spagna,* where he is called Angiolier (XXXII, 25, 1), he is instead preceded in combat by Avino, Orlando, Sansonetto, Oliver, and Angiolin of Bordeaux. After a brief reappearance in stanza 143, 1, Angiolin of Bayonne is slain by Marsilius in XXVII, 13, 1–3.

54, 6. King Malducco, already mentioned as Maldue of Frasse (XXV, 177, 7), bears some similarity to Ulimandocco, a seven-foot-tall Saracen, the king of Trasse, who in *La Spagna* kills Mark and Matthew of Saint Michael's Plain, and is immediately thereafter slain by Orlando (XXXII, 33–35, 1–6). It is possible that the name Malducco (or Maldue) derives from the *Chanson de Roland* (642), where we find a certain Malduit, said to be Marsilius's treasurer. Mark and Matthew of Saint Michael's Plain are mentioned together in this canto (78, 1–2) and again in XXVII (43, 4–5), where they are both killed by a terrible blow of Syrion's club.

56, 5–8. When one remembers the poor proof that Avin has given of his military prowess during his duel with Mattafol (VIII, 92, 7–8 and 93, 1), Momigliano's definition of Avin's challenge as "the briefest, loudest, most affected, and most comical in the whole poem" (197) does have some merit.

57, 2. In *La Spagna* we read that, having been defeated by Orlando, Mazarigi, the king of Pamplona and Marsilius's brother-in-law, saves his own life by agreeing to be baptized. Then, that same night, he secretly leaves Pamplona and finds refuge in Saragossa (XXV, 34–48 and XXVI, 2). While in Pulci's poem he is killed by Baldwin of Maganza, in *La Spagna* the apostate is slain by Orlando (XXXVI, 24, 5–8).

58, 3. Malprimo, too, is a character presented in *La Spagna,* where, however, he has quite a different story. Having loudly requested that Marsilius grant him the honor of killing Orlando (XXX, 31 and 32, 7–8), he does fight at Roncesvalles, but does not duel either with the count or with Oliver. From stanza 24 of canto XXXIII we learn, in fact, that shortly after noon on the first day of battle, King Malprimo, the lone survivor of the first 100,000–strong Saracen army, returns to Saragossa to deliver to Marsilius the news that the attack has been repelled by Orlando and his 19,600 men. Then, having made his report, Malprimo falls dead to the ground.

62, 6. In *La Spagna* (XXXII, 18–19, 1–4), Turchione, king of Toulouse, is killed not by Turpin but by Sansonet(to). Regarding Sansonet, see note, XXV, 182, 1–6.

64, 2–6. Mentioned only twice before (I, 10, 2 and VIII, 94, 1–3), Richard, the duke of Normandy, is just one of the numerous characters who make a fleeting appearance on the stage of *Morgante.* His death, like those of Guottibuoffi and Duke Egibard, is not narrated but is merely announced by the poet in XXVII, 82, 1–3. For Count Anselmo, see note, XXV, 98, 8 through 99, 1–3.

66–70. Falseron's sudden fear as he finally finds himself face to face with Orlando, whom he has repeatedly vowed to kill, lends an initial comical tone to the scene. This rapidly dissolves, however, as an atmosphere of wonderment, generated by the portentous disappearance of the body of the dead Saracen, sets in. It must be noted that in *La Spagna* Falseron's death is not much different from or less predictable than the demise of so many of his fellow soldiers. In the *cantare popolare,* having killed three French knights and caused havoc among the Christian troops (XXXIII, 6–7), Falseron is wounded in the shoulder by Orlando (8, 3–4); a few stanzas later he is more seriously wounded, this time in the hip, by Oliver (20). He is finally dispatched by Orlando (21, 3–6).

73–75. The extreme rapidity of Finadusto's flight cannot but make the reader smile when contrasted with the quite detailed description of the giant's immense physical strength and the terrible losses he is said to be capable of inflicting upon his enemies (see XXV, 177, 5: "one cemetery a day was not enough" for him).

77, 6. By comparing men to broccoli, Pulci clearly shows that not even in the last cantos of his poem does he renounce the use of gastronomic and/or food images. See also 137, 8 and 138, 5–6.

77, 7. Angiolin of Belland must not be confused with Angiolin of Bayonne or with Angiolin of Bordeaux. In canto XXVII, after being thrown from his horse by Balsamin (18, 1–4), Angiolin of Belland is killed by a blow of Syrion's club (43, 3).

78, 1–2. See note, 54, 6. As Ageno points out (955), the reason for Pulci's preferring to use the name "Saint Michael's Mount" instead of Saint Michael's Plain is that Mont Saint Michel was a well-known locality. In line 1428 of the *Chanson de Roland,* we find, in fact, a reference to the abbey of "Seint Michel del Peril."

78, 7. Angiolin of Bordeaux is the first paladin killed at Roncesvalles. In *La Spagna,* as we have already noted, the first to die is Matthew of Saint Michael's Plain.

80, 8. See XXV, 204–205 and 210.

82, 7. The meaning of the Latin words in this line is "I speak because I have been asked to do so" (in this instance, by Squarciafer). *Rogatus rogo* is a legal formula used in documents drawn up by a public official.

84–85. In these stanzas, Getto (113–114) perceives neither a smile nor a humorous intention, but rather "a note of affectionate and tender kindness." The moving quality of this scene is recognized by other scholars as well, Gianni (399) among them.

90, 1–4. Because of the love for justice they both had shown when alive, Aeacus (son of Zeus and Aegina) and Rhadamanthys (son of Zeus and Europa) were made judges in Hades after their deaths. For the third judge, Minos, see note, II, 38, 7–8. Regarding Charon, see note, II, 39, 1.

91, 1–2. In this stanza, where the biblical manna (see note, I, 27, 1–2) is associated with ambrosia and nectar, foods of the gods, Pulci portrays Saint Peter, ever busy in welcoming to heaven the souls of the dead Christian soldiers, with the same affectionate familiarity traditionally shown by simple people for their preferred saints.

98, 1–8. Comparing Pulci's duels with the much longer duels we read in Ariosto's *Orlando Furioso,* Momigliano (191) considers the former to be usually "too swift," and therefore "lacking in epic dignity." Rinaldo's exploits in this stanza are emblematic of this point.

100–102. Orlando's and, particularly, Oliver's ecstatic surprise upon seeing Rinaldo and Ricciardetto is depicted by Pulci with a humorous pictorial mastery. Note in line 8 of stanza 102 the amusing reference to the Gospel of John (11:44).

106, 5–8 through 110. Once again in these stanzas the practical side of Rinaldo's personality clearly contrasts with that of his more seriously minded, self-commiserating, and definitely fatalistic cousin. As Ageno explains (964), Orlando's killing of Charlemagne's enemy Don Chiaro (109, 1) is narrated in Andrea da Barberino's poem *Aspramonte.* (A nephew of Gherardo of Fratta, Don Chiaro had been sent by his uncle, who was then at odds with Charlemagne, to fight against the count.)

116, 6–8 through 117. Marsilius's blustering invective against his own god is undoubtedly one of the most colorful, lengthiest, and most varied in the poem. For the reference to Tobias in 117, 5, see IV, 5, 4.

118–119. In these stanzas Pulci declares that Marsilius, already accused of treachery by Oliver (20–21), is nothing but a blasphemer, a hypocrite, and a traitor. Then, recalling his earlier definition of the Saracen king as "a wise, generous man" (XIII, 43, 1), the poet tries to explain the sudden change that has taken place in Marsilius's personality, ascribing it to the fact that "one virtue does not change an evil trait" (118, 8).

As has been previously noted (XXV, 228–244), Paolo Orvieto writes that in the last part of *Morgante,* Pulci "hides Ficino behind King Marsilius" (254). According to Orvieto, while in the cantos written before his polemic with the philosopher Marsilio Ficino, King Marsilius is depicted as a noble, dignified, and wise monarch, it is only in the cantos composed after that "virulent" dispute that the Saracen king's moral fiber abruptly changes (as Oliver's words in stanzas 20–21 already attest). By means of a highly informed and stimulating textual analysis of the lines contained in stanzas 118–119, Orvieto (255–257) argues convincingly that the stanzas in question were written by Pulci for the purpose of attacking the head of the Platonic Academy, whom the poet considered a receptacle for all the vices he covertly attributed to King Marsilius.

Orvieto's thesis is espoused also by Davide Puccini (1192), who sees in the sudden identification of King Marsilius with Gano and Judas the poet's intention "to give vent to his resentment against Ficino, whose first name is Marsilio."

121, 1–8. The event alluded to here is narrated in XXV, 79, 7 through 80, 4.

123, 6. The Ebro is a 470-mile-long river flowing southeast from northern Spain to the Mediterranean Sea (see note, XXV, 289, 2).

127, 7. The meaning of this line is "The Saracens will also teach the French the song of torture with the rope" (here "song" stands for the lament and the crying of the wounded). As Ageno explains (969), "sol" and "fa" are the two musical notes which in the ancient musical system constituted the basis of two hexachords.

128–130. Chiariello of Portugal—first mentioned with Margheriton,

Balsamin, Fieramonte, Fiorello, Buiaforte, Syrion, Balugante, the Arcalif, and Grandonio in XXV, 179–180—is killed by Orlando in XXVII, 19, 1. He appears also in *La Spagna* (XXXII, 35–36), where he is slain by the count. In both poems his role is reserved to that of a "walk-on." Fieramont of Balzia, whom Orlando kills immediately after he has slain Chiariello (XXVII, 19, 3), is mentioned twice in *La Spagna* as a participant in the Battle of Roncesvalles (XXVI, 30, 3 and XXX, 35, 1). Equally brief is Fiorello's appearance both in *Morgante*, where he is killed by Matthew of Saint Michael's Mount (139, 1–4), and in *La Spagna*, where he is mortally wounded by Oliver (XXXIV, 31, 1–2). Pulci has assigned a more important role to Balsamin, who, after having killed Astolfo (XXVII, 17) and Angiolin of Belland (18), is wounded by Orlando (21) and is then decapitated by Avin (23). The name Balsamin may derive from Balsimino, who is mentioned only once in *La Spagna* (XXX, 30, 2), as Grandonio's brother. For Buiaforte, see note, XXIV, 7, 7. Margheriton, first encountered as Margariz de Sibilie in the *Chanson de Roland* (line 955), is killed by Rinaldo as soon as the Lord of Montalban has slain Syrion, killer of Angiolin of Bellanda and of both Mark and Matthew of Saint Michael's Mount (XXVII, 42–45). In *La Spagna*, Margaritone is king of Seville and a member of Marsilius's council. At Roncesvalles he fights alongside King Fiorello (XXXIV, 29, 1–5), then is wounded and thrown from his horse by Angiolin of Bordeaux (XXXIV, 32, 5–8). The Saracen kings Brusbacca, who is killed by Oliver (XXVII, 59, 1–3), and Mattafirro, who slays Anselmo and is shortly thereafter killed by Rinaldo (XXVII, 93–94), are characters not to be found in *La Spagna*. Neither is the club-swinging Syrion, whose head is split in half like a melon by Rinaldo (XXVII, 42). A famous hunter, Actaeon (129, 4), having inadvertently seen Artemis while she was bathing, as a punishment for this crime was transformed into a stag and was torn to pieces by his own hounds.

130, 3. For the already mentioned Balugant and Arcaliffa, see note, XXV, 27, 2–4.

130, 5. For Zambuger, see note, XXV, 56, 2. While in *La Rotta di Roncisvalle* (V, 33, 6–8 and 34, 1–4) Marsilius's son, called Zabuer(i), is described as a young and inexperienced fighter who tries to shield his father from Orlando's sword—as Zambuger does in *Morgante*—in *La Spagna*, Marsilius's "infant son" (who is not mentioned by name) is held in his father's left arm. Orlando's sword hits the king on his left shoulder, severing his arm and mortally wounding the child (XXXVI, 22–23).

131, 5. Pulci refers here to Livy, who wrote an account of the bloody Trasimene and Cannae battles won by Hannibal against the Romans.

131, 6–8. See note, XX, 54, 7–8.

132, 1–8. Linking this stanza to stanza 119, Orvieto (257) writes that it could be considered a parody of the philosophical activities of Ficino, who "must have appeared to Pulci's eyes as a denier of every divine entity, be it Christian or pagan."

134, 1. For Anselmo, see note, XXV, 98, 8 and 99, 1–3.

135, 7 and 136, 1. In chivalric poems Oliver is often referred to as the Viennese marquis, just as Astolfo is called the English duke.

137, 1–8. For the rapidity of the duels in *Morgante,* see note, 98, 1–8. On Pulci's use of gastronomic and/or food images, see note, 77, 6. The same can be said also for lines 5–6 of stanza 138.

139, 5. For the reference to Antaeus, see note, X, 144, 1–5.

144, 4–8 through 151. The events narrated in these stanzas—Buiaforte's encounter with Orlando, his confirmation of Gano's treason, and the revelation of Baldwin's strange invulnerability—are not to be found in *La Spagna* or in *La Rotta di Roncisvalle.* For Buiaforte, who is first mentioned in canto XXIV, see note, XXIV, 7, 7–8.

151, 8. Argus is a mythical monster who was said to possess one hundred eyes placed all over his body. Aware of Zeus's interest in a young girl, called Io, Hera, Zeus's wife, transformed her into a cow and entrusted her custody to Argus. Only after various failures was Hermes, using a disguise, able to get closer to Argus and kill him, thus freeing Io.

CANTO   XXVII

SUMMARY: Invocation (1). In spite of Rinaldo's participation in the battle, the poet greatly fears for the fate of Orlando and his troops (2–3). Orlando reveals to Baldwin the reason for his not being attacked by the enemy. Offended by the count's lack of trust in his loyalty, the young Maganzan knight throws himself into the midst of the fight, immediately killing King Mazzarigi (4–8). Leading a Saracen army, Grandonius slays Sansonetto and seriously wounds Walter of Mulion, while Oliver unsuccessfully hits the pagan with his sword (9–11). King Marsilius pierces Angiolin of Bayonne in the abdomen, killing him. Looking for Sansonetto, Orlando finds him dead near Oliver, who is surrounded by Marsilius, Zambuger, and the Arcalif. While the pagans flee before him, Orlando orders Terigi to take Sansonetto's body to his tent (12–16). In the meantime King Balsamin kills Astolfo, then gravely wounds Angiolin of Belland, who is later rescued by Ricciardetto (17–18). Astolfo's death is avenged by a raging Orlando, who, after killing Chiariello and Fieramonte, severs all but one of Balsamin's fingers; the pagan king is then finished off by Avin, who cuts off his head (19–23). Rinaldo slays Buiaforte, while Ricciardetto and Turpin fight bravely beside him (24–26).

Orlando avenges Sansonetto's death by splitting in two the skull and the entire upper body of the club-swinging Grandonius (27–34). Then, having sighted Marsilius, the count runs to attack him, but his Durlindana, instead of hitting the king, mortally wounds his young son Zambuger, who had thrown himself in front of Marsilius to shield him (35–37). There are some remarks here by the poet (38–41). Rinaldo kills both Kings Margheriton and Syrion, thus avenging the deaths of Angiolin of Belland and of the brothers Mark and

Matthew of Saint Michael's Mount (42–45). As Bianciardino and his troops push on, Baldwin, whose chest has been pierced by two spears, dies, proclaiming again his innocence to Orlando. Saddened by Baldwin's demise, Orlando resumes fighting alongside Rinaldo and the other surviving paladins (46–49).

Description of the scene of the battle (50–57). King Maldue, who has killed Otho and Berlinghier, is in turn slain by Orlando (58). Having killed King Brusbacca, Oliver is then attacked by the Arcalif of Bagdad, who plunges his sword into the marquis's side. Though mortally wounded, Oliver succeeds in killing him and, in a delirious, blind rage, even hits Orlando on his helmet. At Oliver's request, Orlando guides his cousin into the midst of the fight, where the two kill many Saracens. Then, having reached their tents, Oliver breathes his last (59–68). Orlando sounds the oliphant (69). Rinaldo and Ricciardetto continue slaughtering the routed Saracens, helped by Saint Michael, as reported by some authoritative authors (70–80). Duke Egibard, Guottibuoff, Avin, Avolius, Richard of Normandy, and Walter of Mulion having all been killed, the only paladins still able to fight are Anselm, Ricciardetto, Turpin, and Rinaldo. Rinaldo kills Galleran and King Mattafirro, avenging the death of Anselm, whom Mattafirro has just slain. Orlando, Rinaldo, Ricciardetto, and Turpin succeed in routing Kings Bianciardino, Marsilius, and Balugant and all their remaining troops (81–98). Terigi is on the ground with one foot caught in something. Blinded by his own blood, the count cannot see and help his faithful squire (99). Vegliantino dies, and Orlando takes leave of his horse and his sword (100–109). The battle having ended, Rinaldo, Turpin, and Ricciardetto rejoin Orlando (110–111). Considerations by the poet (112–115). Stanzas 116–159 contain Orlando's confession, Turpin's absolution, the count's long prayer (answered by the equally long reply of the Angel Gabriel), Orlando's final words, and a description of the portentous events that follow his death.

After a brief rest, Terigi leaves to inform Charlemagne of what has taken place at Roncesvalles (160). In the meantime, convinced of Gano's treason by the third sounding of the oliphant, the emperor orders that the Lord of Maganza be imprisoned. He then leaves Paris for Spain with his army. On the way to Roncesvalles he meets Terigi, who, having relayed his message to the emperor, falls dead at his feet (161–185). Saddened by the terrible news of Orlando's death, but comforted by Namo and the Dane, Charlemagne and his men resume marching toward Roncesvalles. Before arriving there, however, the emperor meets young Ansuigi, who relates to him that the Saracens have seized Jerusalem (186–196). In Roncesvalles Charlemagne embraces the dead body of Orlando, asking him to give his Durlindana back to him. By God's will, the dead Orlando rises to his knees and, smiling, hands his sword over to the emperor (197–208). While the majority of the fallen Christian soldiers are buried at Roncesvalles, the embalmed bodies of the paladins, among them those of Oliver and Orlando, are sent back to France, where they are received by a tearful Alda the Fair (209–223). Having returned to the battlefield, Balugant is recognized by Rinaldo and killed by Charlemagne (224–233).

The Christians follow the fleeing Saracens into Saragossa, slaughtering men, women, and children, except for Queen Blanda and Luciana, whose lives are spared at Rinaldo's request (234–265). After the captured kings Bianciardino and Marsilius are hanged by Turpin, victorious Charlemagne sends Queen Blanda back to Granada and then leaves Saragossa to return to France (266–288).

1, 8 and 2, 2. The words "tragedy" and "comedy" are used in their medieval meaning: the former, a tale which has a painful, sad ending; the latter, a tale that ends well (as in Dante's *Divine Comedy*).

2, 3. For Alcuin, see note, XXV, 34, 2–5.

3, 1. As already observed, Ricciardo and Ricciardetto are one and the same.

6–8. In the episode about Baldwin, who seeks death (stanzas 6–8 and 47) to wash away his father's ignominious behavior and to demonstrate his loyalty to Orlando, Pulci has given us, as Getto puts it (93), a touching and delicate portrait of Gano's adolescent son. In this episode, as well as in a few other instances in the very last cantos of the poem, Gianni (381–882) recognizes the presence of "a deeper voice," of a distinctly "authentic epic tone," of "an internal emotion which is entirely Pulcian." The correctness of Getto's and Gianni's critical evaluations of this episode is clearly demonstrated by a contrasting reading of stanzas 9–13 of canto XXXIV of *La Spagna*, where the same circumstances of Baldwin's death are also narrated, without, however, the moving, elegiac qualities of Pulci's poetry.

8, 5. Here "Patarine" means heretic. Patarines were the followers of a religious movement formed in Milan in the second half of the eleventh century for the purpose of combating the corruption of the clergy. As time went by, the Patarines become confused with the Catari, the members of a religious sect of eastern origin which preached the renunciation of all wordly goods. Condemned by the Tribunal of the Inquisition as heretics, the Catari were all extinguished before the end of the fourteenth century.

8, 6. Styx is a mythical river flowing through the deepest section of the world of the dead.

10, 1. For Sansonetto, see XXIV, 54, 4–8.

10, 4. See note, XXVI, 77, 6.

11, 7. A son of Vulcan, Caucus was a fire-breathing giant who was killed by Hercules (Heracles) for having stolen some cattle entrusted to his care.

22, 1. A centaur, Cheiron was reputed to be one of the wisest and most learned of living beings. Among the many pupils he taught were said to be Asclepius and Achilles.

22, 8. In the eleventh century, the musical scale was represented by an open hand. The first note, called *ut* (sol), fell on the thumb.

24–25. Buiaforte's failure to heed Orlando's warning is the cause of his death. See note, XXVI, 144, 4–8 through 151.

25, 7. See note, IV, 97, 3.

27–33. First mentioned in XXX, 25–27 of *La Spagna,* where he is ordered by Marsilius to engage the enemy, Grandonio is depicted as a "valiant" warrior who, armed with spear and sword, kills four of Namo's sons—Avin, Avolio, Berlinghier, and Otho (XXXIV, 21–23)—to then be killed by Orlando (33–35). (Note that in canto XXXVII, 42, 3 of *La Spagna,* Namo has a fifth son, Beltramo, appointed a peer by Charlemagne.) Though overtaken by fear when facing the count, the Saracen still manages to deliver a tremendous sword blow to Orlando's helmet. If it is true that in *Morgante* the club-carrying giant Grandonius is depicted, at least initially, as a formidable adversary (he kills many Christians, among them Sansonetto), it is equally true that his sudden flight and subsequent total lack of resistance when a colorfully insulting Orlando hurls himself at him are as surprising as they are humorous. The lively comic flavor of the episode is further emphasized by the following details: the fact that Durlindana remains stuck in the ground, thus bringing Vegliantino to his knees; the question the count posits to his steed and the horse's reaction to his words; and, last but not least, the poet's ironic comment in lines 5–8 of stanza 33 (needless to say, all these things are not to be found in the *cantare popolare*). (Note that Grandonie is a character in the Digby 23 manuscript of the *Chanson de Roland.*)

38, 4. Pulci's comment in this line lends itself to different interpretations. It has been suggested, on one hand, that it is an indication of the poet's intention to poke fun at the Catholic veneration of relics. On the other hand, as Davide Puccini (1217) maintains, its purpose could be to focus the attention of the reader on the fact that Marsilius, "instead of crying over his son's death, is already thinking how he can profit from it."

38, 7. For Belfagor, see note, IV, 97, 3.

39, 5. Thraso (a braggart soldier) and Gnatho (a slandering informer) are characters found in Terence's comedy *Eunuchus.*

40–41. With regard to the rather obscure meaning of these two stanzas, Paolo Orvieto maintains (253) that "they first denounce a precise intention of a textual polysemy, and then they define that distinctive polysemous quality by means of what it is not and it does not want to be." For the critic, it is not a question of a "Scholastic-type allegory," nor of "an edifying Dantean allegory, but more simply of an 'enigmatic' allegory: between the lines of the text are hidden 'powerful men' and polemic accusations of a personal nature." Orvieto's interpretation, which is shared by other Pulci scholars, is supported by the inclusion in line 1 of stanza 41 of the word "cicadas," which is used here in reference to the philosopher Marsilio Ficino and his colleagues. It must be noted that it is not unusual for Pulci to address the members of the Platonic Academy as *cicale* (cicadas). Sonnet XXIII, which Pulci wrote against the priest Matteo Franco, begins with the line *I' ho tanto grattato le cicale* ("I scratched cicadas for so long"). More important, in sonnet XCVI—which starts with the line *Se Dio ti guardi brutto ceffolino* ("May God watch over you, you ugly face"), and which Pulci scholars agree is addressed to Marsilio Ficino—the head of the Platonic Academy is called *lo Dio delle cicale* ("the god of the cicadas"). Matteo Franco, in a sonnet written to Lorenzo De Medici (LXII, line 14) referring to the eloquence of the Neoplatonists, also uses the term *cicale*.

40, 7–8. The Lethe is a mythical river flowing through the underworld. The souls of the dead were believed to dive into it in order to lose all memory of their past life. The Misenus Coast, better known as Cape Misenus, is located a few miles south of Naples. It was named after Misenus, son of the god of winds, who spurred the Trojans on to battle with the sound of his trumpet. After Hector's death, he followed Aeneas to Italy. Having drowned during the sea voyage, the dead trumpeter was buried by Aeneas in the land where he was found (see Virgil's *Aeneid*, VI, 241–260).

43, 3; 44, 7; and 45, 4. See note, XXVI, 77, 6.

50, 8. Regarding Echo, see note, XIV, 9, 5.

53–55. In Momigliano's opinion (176), on the day of the Battle of Roncesvalles, Lucifer and Death "celebrate their biggest and most gruesome banquet." Though Lucifer is still sneering, as he does in medieval paintings, where he is portrayed in the act of taking possession of the souls of the damned, here his sneer "is no longer as terrible as it once was; it is the laughter of a glutton, not of a spirit who delights in evil." Grotesque also is the poet's more "plebeian" representation of Death, the cause of hell's great ball. In treating Death, however, Pulci shows no fear of her; rather, "he jokes with her as if she were a despicable and ugly old woman."

53, 3. See note, XXVI, 77, 6.

55, 1. The name of a round country dance that originated in the Austrian province of Carinthia.

55, 4. Note that the expression "afterer-and-afterest" was coined by the translator in his rendition of *poscrai e proscrigno e posquacchera* in the Italian text.

55, 5. This line contains a reference to Roman festivities at harvest time.

56. "The gastronomic interpretation of the battlefields"—present, as we have already noted, in stanzas 43 (3), 44 (7), 45 (4), and 53 (3)—"explodes," as Gianni (49) writes, in this stanza, one of the most famous in *Morgante*. Commenting upon stanza 56, Momigliano (187), though recognizing that the last cantos are the most serious in the poem, sustains that nowhere else in his work has Pulci found "an image more grandiosely and comically macabre than this one." In total disagreement with Momigliano and the critics who propose a satirical reading of this stanza, Gianni (408) maintains that in spite of its "coarse and grotesque images, strange and vulgar expressions, and bizarre confusion of sounds," the lines in stanza 56 denote "neither the accent nor the spirit of the so-called mock-heroic poems." On the contrary, for Gianni the "description of the Battle of Roncesvalles as a 'saucepan' is not a comic but an epic page, even though a typically Pulcian one."

56, 6. For the reference to Nessus, see note, I, 72, 2.

59–70. The circumstances of Oliver's death are very similar to those narrated in stanzas 14–21 of canto XXXVI of *La Spagna*. In comparing the two texts, however, one notices that in Pulci's version of these events there are two small yet significant differences.

In *La Spagna* the marquis, wounded by the Arcalif of Bagdad in a fair fight, succeeds in killing the pagan and, guided by Orlando, returns to the battlefield, where he slays more than thirty Saracens. Oliver's horse then carries Oliver back to his tent, where he dies alone. It is only when the count sees Oliver's riderless steed kicking and biting the enemy soldiers that he realizes that his brother-in-law is dead.

In *Morgante,* instead, Oliver falls victim to the Arcalif's assault, as the marquis is busy dueling with King Brusbacca. After slaying the Arcalif, Orlando and his brother-in-law fight side by side and return together to their tents, where Oliver dies as Orlando tells him that he is now ready to sound the horn.

The changes pointed out above are, we believe, indicative of Pulci's intention in this last part of his poem to celebrate both the military prowess of Oliver, a knight who could be vanquished only as the result of a treacherous act, and the profound, almost tender bond of friendship that unites the two paladins. Though the unchivalrous behavior of the Arcalif of Bagdad can be traced back to the *Chanson de Roland* (1943–1947) (where we read that the caliph "land[s] his spear deep in Oliver's back"), it appears that Pulci is following the text of the *cantare popolare* more closely than that of the French epic. In the *Chanson de Roland,* in fact, we read that because of his wounds, Roland faints twice and opens his eyes only when Oliver strikes him on his helmet. Soon after, the marquis dismounts from his horse, asks God's forgiveness for his sins, blesses Charles and Roland, and then dies (1947–2023). Moreover, the *chanson* makes no mention of Oliver's horse charging the Saracens to avenge the death of his master. It is interesting to note also that while in the *Chanson de Roland* blood pours out of Orlando's mouth as he sounds the oliphant (1763), in *La Spagna* (XXXVI, 35, 5–6) the force with which the count sounds the horn causes him to bleed conspicuously. In lines 5–8 of stanza 69, Pulci combines the information given in his two sources (Orlando blows the horn so hard that it makes blood pour out of his mouth and ears), and also introduces an additional detail—that "the horn cracked and split"—which he attributes to Turpin. (This last detail is to be found, according to Gianni [407], in the work known as the *Pseudo-Turpin* [see note, I, 5, 3]). Indeed, in the *Chanson de Roland* (2287–2298) as well, the count cracks the oliphant, but not by blowing in it; rather, he uses it as a weapon on the head of a Saracen soldier who, taking advantage of his having once more lost consciousness, tries to steal his Durendal away from him.

74, 4–5. See note, XXIII, 38, 8.

74, 6. The tigers from Hyrcania (an ancient land located southeast of the Caspian Sea) were considered by poets to be the most ferocious of all such animals.

74, 8. After the fall of Troy, Hecuba, the wife of the Trojan king Priam, became a Greek slave. When she found out that her son Polydorus had been treacherously murdered by Polymestor, a former Trojan ally, in a cold, mad rage she blinded Polymestor by digging his eyeballs out of their sockets with her fingers. Though the story of Hecuba is narrated in Ovid's *Metamorphoses* (XIII, 399–575), it is believed that Pulci derives it from a line in Dante's *Inferno* (XXX, 20), where we read that Hecuba, "now gone quite mad, went barking like a dog."

77, 1–4. According to Pulci commentators, the poet is referring here to the destruction near Jerusalem of the Assyrian army of King Sennacherib by the Archangel Michael (see 2 Kings 19: 35–36). The letter *M* stands for the Italian word *mille* (one thousand, here rendered with the word "myriad") and indicates the number of men killed by Michael with each blow of his sword. Pulci derives the use of this letter from Dante's *Paradiso* (XIX, 129), where it is said that King Charles of Naples had only one virtue but one thousand vices.

78, 2–3. Pulci has doubled the size of the Saracen army, which in *La Spagna* (XXX, 9–10 and 34–35) totals 300,000, divided into three formations, each composed of 100,000 men led by Falseron, Grandonius, and Marsilius, respectively. The size of Orlando's Christian army, however is unchanged: 20,600 (see *La Spagna, XXX*, 26, 1).

78, 7. For the reference to Turpin and Urman, see note, I, 5, 3.

79, 1–5. Pulci spares Turpin's life at Roncesvalles because, as previously noted, he attributes to him the paternity of the *Historia Karoli Magni et Rotholandi*. In *La Spagna* (XXXVI, 29, 1–8), instead, having most valiantly fought the enemy, the soul of Turpin, the last of Orlando's companions to die, is taken to heaven by a legion of angels.

79, 6. For Alcuin, see note, XXV, 34, 2–5 and 169, 6. Alcuin is mentioned several times also in canto XXVIII.

80, 1. Regarding Arnald, see note, XXV, 115, 4–5.

85, 3–6. Note the further use of gastronomic images: the riddled bellies of the dead Saracens are compared to either a cheese grater or a pan used to roast chestnuts.

87, 2. See note, XXVI, 131, 5.

88, 6. The fierceness of Turkish troops was proverbial in Europe.

90, 1–8. For the representation of Death, see note, 53–55.

92, 2. An indirect reference to Samson's massacre of the Philistines (see Judges 16:27–30).

92, 6–8. A chronicler, a merchant, and a political informer, Benedetto Dei was born in Florence in 1417 and died there in 1492. After a period of service as a public official, he was forced to leave Florence because of his implication in a conspiracy against a member of one of the city's oldest and most influential families. He traveled extensively in Asia and Africa, and also resided for some time in Constantinople. His *Cronica* contains interesting and valuable information on his travels and his personal observations on the Ottoman

Empire. He was a close friend of Luigi Pulci, with whom he corresponded and exchanged sonnets. In a letter (XLVIII) addressed to Benedetto Dei in Milan, and which was probably written in August of 1481 (see De Robertis's edition of *Morgante e Lettere,* 1076), Pulci, referring to Francesco Filelfo's recent death, writes that the humanist, who had just returned to Florence after many years of banishment from that city, "andò a sentire nascere il grano o 'l miglio" (went to hear the lowest sprouting of the wheat). The proverbial expression "to hear the lowest sprouting of the wheat (or millet)" means "to die and be buried." Pulci also addressed to Benedetto Dei one of his most "irreverent" sonnets (CXLIV), in which he makes fun of the pilgrims going to Rome on the occasion of the Holy Year.

94, 5. Pyrrhus, king of Epirus (318–272 B.C.), after having fought successfully against the Romans, was defeated at Benevento in 275 and forced to leave Italy and return to his kingdom in northwestern Greece. For Marcellus, see note, XV, 24, 5–8. Ageno (1003) suggests that Marcellus is remembered here as a traitor because of the stratagem he is reported to have concocted in order to gain access to the city of Syracuse during the Second Punic War.

95, 6. The Libyan dragon mentioned here is the snake called amphisbaena in canto XXV (see note, 311, 3).

99, 1–8. By focusing the reader's attention on the particularly grotesque situation in which Terigi finds himself—he is being compared to a squirming fish—Pulci creates, in Momigliano's opinion (166), a sort of caricature of Orlando's faithful squire.

101–102. Giovanni Getto perceives here, as elsewhere in the poem, a delicate tone of trepidation and melancholy. These lines, which express with a feeling of heartfelt participation the theme of death as the terminator of life, are considered by Getto to be "of a diaphanous beauty" (92). Orlando's sorrowful leavetaking of his faithful charger is not found in either the *Chanson de Roland* or *La Spagna.* In the former, Veillantif, who has received more than thirty wounds, falls dead to the ground, thus leaving Roland to fight on foot (2160–2161). In the latter, where Orlando's horse is not even mentioned by name, we are told only that it dies while running, and that Orlando immediately mounts Oliver's charger, which, riderless, has been kicking and biting the enemy by his side (XXXVI, 26, 6–8 and 27, 1–2).

In total disagreement with Getto is Momigliano (220–226), who perceives in the miracles of Roncesvalles "a less creative force, but a more subtle comic refinement" (220). The critic believes that Orlando's steed, kneeling before his master as if to ask his permission to leave, gives the impression of being more a well-trained horse than a miraculous animal. Even more curious are Orlando's asking his dead mount for forgiveness and Vegliantino's reopening his eyes as if to express his assent. The fact that Pulci again calls on the authority of Turpin constitutes for Momigliano further proof of the author's mocking intention (221).

103, 7–8. For the story of Pyramus and Thisbe—here compared to Orlando and his horse—see note, XII, 69, 1–3.

105, 1. A line from Book One of Virgil's *Aeneid,* the meaning of which is "Thrice and four times happy those." These words are pronounced by Aeneas, who, stricken by a furious storm while at sea, calls happy those who have died at Troy.

106, 1. For Malagigi's prediction of Gano's treason, see XXIV, 169.

106, 5. For Saint Denis, see note, I, 9–10.

107, 2. Regarding Terigi's comparison to a thrush, see note, XXIV, 97, 4–8. In *La Spagna* Terigi suddenly appears before Orlando at Roncesvalles (XXXVI, 32, 7–8) and is charged by the count with bringing to the emperor the news of Gano's treason (39–40), a mission the squire promptly accomplishes after embracing the body of his dead master (42–55). In canto XL, Terigi duels with Pinabello, kills him (36), and is never mentioned again. Terigi probably derives from Thierry of Anjou, who slays Pinabel in the *Chanson de Roland*'s final duel (see note, XXVIII, 8–15).

108–109. Orlando's unsuccessful attempts to break his sword, as well as the brief speech that he addresses to Durlindana, derive from the *Chanson de Roland,* where, however, the episode is considerably longer (2300–2354). In *La Spagna,* Orlando, followed by Terigi, climbs over the top of a hill, where he tries to destroy his sword by smashing it against a great rock. It is only at this point that the count, realizing the futility of his efforts, decides to sound the oliphant for the first time (XXXVI, 33, 2 through 35, 1–6).

110. As already noted, the presence of Rinaldo (and of his younger brother Ricciardetto) at Roncesvalles is a Pulci invention. Together with Turpin and Terigi, they are the only Christians to survive the massacre.

111, 6–8 through 115, 8. Pulci states that the battle took place on Saint Michael's feast day, that is, on May 8, 806. As noted by Pulci commentators, both the month and the year are wrong, since the battle occurred on August 15, 778. The year of the Battle of Roncesvalles was a half-leap year; on the day the battle was fought, in fact, the sun shone for twelve additional hours—a miracle granted by Christ at Charles's request (172).

The expression "white ink is not good here" (112, 8) means that things written with this type of ink are false and therefore not destined to last. According to Davide Puccini (1243), Pulci's facetious clarification may imply "a veiled polemic against ill-disposed critics: Pulci pretends to explain scientifically, for love of the truth, the prodigious or fabulous event peculiar to chivalric romances." For Pulci, the participation in the battle of the Archangel Michael explains, at least in part, the presence of so many dead Saracen soldiers (113). Nor can one question that May was the month in which the rout occurred.

Interpreting the somewhat obscure meaning of stanza 114, Franca Ageno (1008) explains that the proverbial expression "We are not of May" derives from a story in which a man, in order to make sure he has clearly understood and will not forget all the things that another man has been telling him, asks this man to repeat everything once more. The interlocutor's reply is: "We are not of May ... because in May donkeys bray." Even though he has twice repeated that the battle occurred in May (111, 8 and 113, 8), Pulci, Ageno concludes, "observes that it is helpful to state it again, because the proverb teaches that while one must not repeat things during all other months, one must do so in May." Lines 7–8 of stanza 114 contain another extremely popular proverbial expression, *A tavola non s'invecchia,* which is commonly used even today.

116, 1. This line is a verbatim transcription of a famous verse from Dante's *Inferno,* V, 25.

117. While in the *Chanson de Roland* Orlando confesses his sins directly to God (Turpin has already died), and his confession lasts only four lines (2369–2372), in *Morgante* he makes his confession to Turpin, a character often depicted in chivalric poems more as a warrior than as a priest (according to Momigliano [260], he performs his military duties "with the same ease with which he fulfills his ecclesiastical functions").

117, 2–3. Orlando confesses to having uttered insulting words against the emperor; he has, therefore, committed the sin of lese majesty. The use of the Latin expressions reported in these lines testifies to Pulci's observance of the legal terminology so dear to public officials (see note, XXVI, 82, 7).

117, 4–6. See note, XXV, 31, 6–8.

117, 8. Regarding Don Chiaro, see note, XXVI, 106, 5–8 through 110.

120. Revealing himself to be a most indulgent confessor, the archbishop simply tells Orlando to recite as a penance the Lord's Prayer and the Miserere (see note, XXV, 272, 3 and 284, 6) up to the word *Peccavi* ("I sinned"), which is in line 6 of that psalm.

120, 5. Cephas (stone = Peter) is the name Christ gave to Simon, the son of Jonah (John 1:42).

121–130. In the prayer of the dying Orlando and in his death filled with compunction, even Momigliano (98) perceives "an affectionate and elegiac tone."

121, 4. This line is taken from Dante's *Paradiso* (IX, 138). For Gabriel, see also note, I, 2, 1–4.

122, 8. See Matthew 20:16 ("for many be called, but few chosen").

124, 3. For the pelican, see note, XI, 1, 1–3.

124, 6. With these Latin words begins line 2 of Ecclesiastes 1.

125, 4. See note, XXVI, 106, 5–8 through 110.

127, 3. Another line that Pulci derives from Dante's *Paradiso,* XXX, 5–6.

129, 1–3. From Psalms 143:2, "And enter not into judgment with thy servant: for in thy sight shall no man living be justified."

131, 3–4. These lines appear to contain a reminiscence from Dante's *Paradiso,* XXXIII, 116–119.

131, 8. Saint Francis of Assisi, who received Christ's stigmata.

132, 6. The same line is found in I, 2, 4. Gabriel is the angel in question. He has been charged by God with taking Orlando's soul to heaven. In the

Chanson de Roland this task is entrusted to the angels Cherubin, Michael, and Gabriel (2390–2396). In *La Spagna* no angel appears to Orlando, but in reply to the paladin who has asked the Lord to let him die, he sees a shining light and hears a voice that promises him what he has asked (XXXVI, 30–32, 1–3); then, after his death, a legion of angels carry his soul to Paradise.

132, 8. The Latin *O Viri Galilei* ("Ye men of Galilee") are the words with which the angels greet the disciples after Christ's Ascension to heaven (see Acts 1:11).

134, 7. Here the title of archimandrite, usually reserved for the superior of a monastery or a very prominent religious figure, is used with reference to Orlando.

136, 1. Sutri was, according to *I Reali di Francia* (VI, 52–53), Orlando's city of birth.

136, 6. For Sansonetto, see note, XXIV, 54, 4–8.

137, 2–6. Regarding Charlemagne's siege of Pamplona and Macarius's betrayal, see notes, XXVIII, 58, 4–6 and 60, 3.

138, 1. Ageno (1015) observes that Troiano and Pantalisse are characters appearing in Andrea da Barberino's *Aspramonte*. The son of Agolante and Almont's brother, Troiano is killed by Orlando (III, 115–117); the Saracen king Pantalisse, Troiano's friend, is also killed by Orlando.

138, 3–4. See note, XXV, 10, 4. Puccini (1253) suggests that Adastro may be a Saracen king, as his name, which derives from the legendary king of Argo, Adrasto, leads us to believe.

138, 5–6. Orlando's exploits in Egypt are narrated in the first part of canto XVIII and in the last thirty stanzas of the following canto.

139, 7. This is the last time the poet mentions Margutte together with Morgante. The good giant is again remembered in canto XXVIII, 136, 5–8 and 142, 1.

141–142. For the story of Job, and the Latin phrases transcribed in stanzas 142, see Job 1:1–22 and 2:9–10. The meaning of the Latin sentence *sicut Domino placuit, in ea factum est* is "So it happened as it pleased the Lord." In this sentence Pulci replaces the original Latin *ita* with *in ea,* possibly, as Ageno suggests (1016), to make this word rhyme with the verb *avea* in line 3 of the Italian text.

143–144. Gabriel seems to reply here to a request that Orlando has not voiced in his prayer to God (121–130). To be sure, the request is clearly expressed in *La Spagna* (XXXVI, 31–32), where, refusing God's offer to send him fresh troops, Orlando asks instead that his dead companions be allowed to come back to life. The answer Orlando receives in *La Spagna* is quite similar to the angel's reply in stanza 144.

145, 3. The "holy bride" is Saint Catherine of Alexandria.

145, 6. Aries, the first sign of the zodiac, stands here for the sun; Flora is the goddess of springtime flowers.

146, 1–3. Dante is clearly the source for Pulci's placing of Charles "in the corner of the Cross." In *Paradiso,* XVIII, 34, Cacciaguida prompts the pilgrim to look up and observe the arms of the Cross, which are formed by the spirits of those warriors who fought for the Faith. Among them (37–39) Dante sees Joshua, Moses' successor and the conqueror of Canaan, and, a few lines later (43), Roland and Charlemagne.

147, 8 through 148, 1–2. In *I Reali di Francia* (IV, 4) we read that when Duodo of Maganza orders that Guidone of Antona be killed in order to avenge the death of Duodo's father, the old duke falls on his knees, picks up a bit of earth, takes communion with it, and commends his soul to God. Pulci probably derives this notion from Andrea da Barberino's work.

149, 7. Saint Jerome, a Church father and translator of the Bible, is famous for the harsh physical punishments he inflicted upon his body for the remission of his sins.

150, 2. See note, III, 80, 3.

152, 8. See note, XI, 86, 8.

153. The portentous events that follow Orlando's death do not occur in *La Spagna*. In this and the following stanzas, Pulci's main sources of inspiration are Dante and the Bible.

153, 7–8. See note, 147, 8 and 148, 1–2.

154, 6–7. For the Latin sentence quoted in these lines ("When Israel went out of Egypt"), see Psalms 114:1.

155, 2–5. See Dante's *Paradiso,* XXI, 136–138.

156, 3. See note, XIV, 45, 5–6.

157, 4–5. For these two lines, see Dante's *Inferno* (XXVI, 34–39), where it is said that the prophet Elisha saw Elijah carried up to heaven on a chariot.

157, 6–8. This event in the life of Moses is retold in Exodus 3:2.

158–159. The fact that a white dove—considered a symbol of the Holy Spirit (Matthew 3:16)—enters Orlando's mouth, feathers and all, does lend to the episode a somewhat comic resonance. This opinion is shared by, among others, Puccini (1260) and Getto, who indicates this stanza as among those having an almost puppet-show quality (98), while Momigliano deems this scene "an unbecoming blunder" (214).

160, 5–8. In *La Spagna,* after Orlando's soul has been taken to heaven by a legion of angels, a most sorrowful Terigi laments his master's death, then leaves for France (XXXVI, 41–42). At this point, the *canterino* turns his attention, as Pulci does in stanza 161, to Charles by describing the emperor's reaction to the sound of the oliphant.

163, 6. Regarding Agrismont, see note, XI, 47, 7.

165, 7–8. The emperor's words are reminiscent of those Christ addressed to His disciples on the evening of the Last Supper (John 13:10)."Ye are clean, but not all."

166, 2. The same words Christ told Judas: "Good were it for that man if he had never been born" (Mark 14:21).

167, 5. See XXV, 4–5.

168, 8. The cry "Crucify" is repeated in stanza 267, 2, this time, however, in reference to Marsilius.

169. Also in *La Spagna* (XXXVI, 46), Charlemagne orders that Gano be tied up and imprisoned in a tower guarded by five hundred armed men.

172–174, 7. The miracle of the sun occurs first, in answer to Charlemagne's prayer, in the *Chanson de Roland* (2447–2469). In *La Spagna* (XXXVI, 48) the emperor asks God for two miracles: to stop the course of the sun in the sky, and to level all the mountains his army would have to climb before getting to Roncesvalles. Clearly Pulci derives both miracles from *La Spagna*. For the biblical reference to the miracle of the sun (Joshua is mentioned in 173, 2), see Joshua 10:12.

175–176. Our poet, who hardly believes in miracles (Puccini [1266] writes that "for the bourgeois Pulci, a miracle is a challenge to his common sense"), cannot refrain from making some appropriately witty remarks, which, however, are directed not so much to the miracles themselves, a necessary ingredient of traditional chivalric epic, as to his plausible critics. Concerning Marsyas (175, 8), see note, XXVI, 26, 7–8.

177. In *La Spagna*, too, Charlemagne meets Terigi while he is riding with his army toward Roncesvalles (XXXVI, 50, 6–8). In this poem, Terigi's report of the battle takes less than four stanzas (52–55, 1–6); he tells the emperor that Orlando, Astolfo, Sansonetto, Oliver, Turpin, Avino, Avolio, Otho, Berlinghieri, Angiolin of Bordeaux and Angiolin of Bayonne, Ugone, Walter of Mulion, and Mark and Matthew of Saint Michael's Mount are all dead because of Gano's and Marsilius's treacherous pact. In *Morgante,* by contrast, the space that Pulci devotes to Terigi's eloquent speech is more than doubled.

178, 2. The meaning of the Latin phrase in this line is "you arrived too late."

179, 8. See note, I, 2, 1–4.

181, 8. The three paladins in question are Angiolin of Bayonne, Angiolin of Bordeaux, and Angiolin of Belland.

185, 8. As I have already mentioned, in *La Spagna* Terigi does not die, but goes on to challenge the Maganzan Pinabello, whom he kills after a long, fierce duel (XL, 28, 7–8 through 36).

187, 3. The adage that Pulci refers to here probably derives from Dante's famous line *Amor, ch'a nullo amato amar perdona*—"Love, that excuses no one loved from loving" (*Inferno,* V, 103).

190, 6. Namo's dead sons are Avin, Avolio, Otho, and Berlinghier(i). In *La Spagna,* too (XXXVII, 11–14), Namo puts a stop to Charlemagne's laments, reminding him that he has lost four sons and that crying is useless. Namo's intervention, however, takes place only after the dead Orlando, by will of the Holy Spirit, miraculously gets up, smilingly hands his sword to the weeping Charles, and then falls dead again onto the ground (XXXVII, 4–10).

192–194. Note that in *La Spagna* (XXXVII, 25–33) the meeting with Ansuigi takes place the morning after Charlemagne's arrival, on the battlefield of Roncesvalles as the French army is about to march toward Spain. In *Morgante* the encounter occurs before Charles and his troops reach Roncesvalles. The conquest of Jerusalem, which Pulci attributes to Orlando (192, 1–

3), is narrated in *La Spagna* (XVIII, 34–37, 1–2; XIX, 11 through XX, 23), where we learn that the count has left his cousin Ansuigi (see note, I, 9–10) to guard that city in his name. The loss of Jerusalem is announced in both poems. In La *Spagna* (XXXVII, 37–38), Ansuigi informs the emperor that he could no longer defend Jerusalem against King Balugant, whose army of 200,000 men is at this moment no more than six miles from Roncesvalles. For the words *Salamalec* and *Melchizedek* (194, 4 and 6), see note, XXVI, 26, 1–6.

195, 5. For Hecuba, see note, 74, 8.

196, 1. For Job, see note, 141–142.

197, 1 and 3. By using the first-person plural of the verb ("we want . . . let's go"), it seems that the poet wishes to join Charles and his troops on the last leg of their march to Roncesvalles.

198, 8. The facetious tone we have noted elsewhere in the canto is heard here once more. It could also reflect the poet's practical inclination.

201. A very similar curse is uttered by Charlemagne in *La Spagna* (XXXVII, 21).

201, 8. In Dante's *Inferno,* the first of the four *gironi* (circles) that divide the lowest part of hell is called Caina. In this circle—or "bolgia," as Pulci calls it— are tormented the souls of those who have treacherously betrayed their kin.

202, 6–8 through 208. In the *Chanson de Roland,* when Charles finds his dead nephew, he dismounts from his horse, holds him in his arms, and then, overcome by grief, falls unconscious to the ground. Once he recovers, having spoken only a few disconsolate words, the emperor faints for a second time (2879–2891). When he regains consciousness, he tells Roland, in the thirty-nine lines of his address, that he is responsible for the death of Christianity's greatest champion, that he no longer has a friend in the world, that he will have to bring the sad news of Roland's death back to Aix-la-Chapelle, that his enemies will rise again against France, and that his sorrow is so great that he prays that God will let him die and be buried near his nephew and his men (2898–2905; 2909–2929; 2933–2942).

In *La Spagna* as well (XXXVII, 4–6; and 7, 5–8 through 11), Charlemagne laments Orlando's death and expresses similar sentiments; however, more than half of the fifty-two lines the *canterino* devotes to this episode are taken up by the introduction into the story of a new detail. When in his lamentations Charles reminds his nephew that he promised to give him Durlindana—the sword Orlando had taken from Almont, whom he had killed in a duel—the paladin gets up, hands Durlindana over to his uncle, smilingly tells him: "King Charlemagne, I give your sword back to you," and then falls dead again to the ground.

In stanzas 202–208, Pulci's debt to *La Spagna* is beyond dispute. It is also clear that by adding to the text of the *Chanson de Roland* the episode of Orlando's momentary resurrection, both the *canterino* and Pulci intended to create something new, emphasizing at the same time the occurrence of the supernatural in their story. In comparing the text of *La Spagna* with that of *Morgante,* however, one realizes the considerable difference with respect to the mood of the two episodes: the former subdued and wonder-stricken, the latter amused, though seemingly edifying. Note that the facts to which Charlemagne is referring in 205, 6–8 are narrated in Andrea da Barberino's *Aspramonte*.

210–211. This miracle, too, is narrated in *La Spagna* (XXXVII, 17–18).

213, 3–5. Concerning the pelican, see note, XI, 1, 1–3.

215. For line 1, see note, XXV, 210, 3. It has been suggested that in this stanza Pulci may refer to the doctrine of the fifth-century B.C. Greek philosopher Empedocles, according to which all things derive from the union (love) or the separation (hate) of the four basic and eternal elements: earth, air, fire, and water.

216, 3. For the reference to Phaëthon, see note, I, 3, 5–6.

216, 8. The Belgian city of Aachen (Aquisgrana in Italian), located near the French border, is famous since Roman times for its thermal water. It is mentioned again in XXVIII, 48, 7.

217–220. The author of the *Chanson de Roland* quite graphically describes the preparation of the bodies of Roland, Oliver, and Turpin before they are placed in marble coffins covered with "palls of silk brocade" (2962–2973). Brought back to France, the three are buried in the Church of Saint-Romain in Blaye (3689–3693).

In *La Spagna* (XXXVII, 22–23) Charlemagne orders that fourteen wooden coffins be immediately built; in these coffins, covered with a dark cloth bearing the coat of arms of each knight, are then placed the bodies of Orlando and those of his paladins. In canto XL we learn that once they have reached Paris, they are taken for burial in the Basilica of Notre Dame amid great demonstrations of sorrow on the part of the populace (8). It is at this point that the *canterino* adds another twist to the story (10–20). The emperor summons Alda the Fair to the court, telling her that Orlando and Oliver have returned home. When Alda arrives in Paris expecting to see her spouse and brother alive, Charlemagne is forced to tell her the terrible truth: Orlando and Oliver now reside in Notre Dame! Weeping over the tombs of both men, Alda asks God to allow one of them to speak to her. When Oliver tells her that he is resting in peace in the glory of God, Alda dies of grief between the coffins of Orlando and her brother, with whom she is later buried.

It is not clear why Pulci, who in so many instances adhered to his sources as well as to tradition, decided to have Orlando buried in Aachen (219, 6 and 220, 2) instead of in Blaye or in Paris. Certainly the desperation of Alda the Fair is more dramatically depicted in *La Spagna* than in *Morgante,* where she is also compared to Dido. Since Dido, who had pledged to remain faithful to her dead husband, Sichaeus, does later on fall in love with Aeneas, the example is, according to Davide Puccini (1280), "either unfortunate or malicious." Note further that in line 8 of 217, Pulci is possibly referring to the destruction of Corinth and Carthage. For 220, 5, see note, 116, 1.

221, 7. Pericles (493–429 B.C.), one of Greece's most eminent political figures, ruled Athens for more than thirty years, giving it a more democratic constitution and expanding its supremacy in Greece and Egypt. He was also a great orator and a protector of culture and the arts.

224, 7. In the *Chanson de Roland* (2639–2844), the great Emir Baligant, unaware of what has happened at Roncesvalles, lands in Saragossa's harbor with a huge army, seventeen kings, and more than four thousand vessels. He immediately sends messengers to King Marsilius, declaring himself ready to fight Charlemagne in France. Marsilius promptly replies that the emir can indeed have his kingdom, provided that he lead his army against Charles and his troops, who are camped only seven leagues from Saragossa. After a brief meeting with Marsilius in Saragossa, Baligant leaves the city with his thirty divisions to face Charlemagne on the battlefield (2639–2844). Informed of Baligant's imminent arrival, Charlemagne, who is about to return to France with his dead paladins, readies his 300,000-man army, made up of French, Bavarians, Germans, Normands, Bretons, Flemish, Burgundians, and others. The clash between the two opposing armies ends with the death of Baligant, whom Charlemagne, assisted by Saint Gabriel, is finally able to kill. Only a handful of pagans manage to escape (2974–3632).

In *La Spagna*, warned by Ansuigi that Balugante is approaching with an army of 200,000 pagans, Charlemagne orders his troops to get ready for war. At Namo's suggestion, twelve new "peers" are appointed, six selected among the younger and six among the oldest knights (XXXVII, 38–44). The battle between the pagan army and the three divisions of Charlemagne, each consisting of 20,000 soldiers, takes place in canto XXXVIII, at the end of which (37–43) Balugante's head is split in two by a blow of the sword of Charlemagne, who in this poem as well is encouraged to action by a heavenly voice that promises him God's assistance. After Balugante's demise, the surviving Saracens flee into Saragossa, pursued by the Christians (XXXIX, 1–7).

227, 1. See note, 259, 1–5.

230, 5. Malchus is the servant of the high priest whose right ear was cut off by a blow of Simon Peter's sword (see John 18:10).

231. Here Charlemagne kills Balugante without any outside assistance (he hears no heavenly voice, nor is the Angel Gabriel beside him).

232, 1–4. The "Testaccio" was a hill erected in Rome with stones piled one on top of the other, from the city's earliest times. At carnival time and other festive occasions, the Romans held bullfights and fairs there (Ageno, 1041). Pulci refers to the festival that took place on this hill as the "Testaccia Feast."

233, 4. Arnaldo of Belland, mentioned here for the first time, is a Christian knight, appointed a paladin at Roncesvalles by Charlemagne (see *La Spagna*, XXXVII, 41, 6). Having fought against Balugante's army, he accepts for one of his sons the governorship of the former Saracen city of Nerbona (XXXIX, 47–49).

233, 6. Capernaum was an ancient city in Palestine, whose inhabitants, in spite of Jesus' miracles, did not repent (see Matthew 11:23). Puccini notes (1285) that Pulci obviously considers this city a sort of "antechamber of hell."

234–240. From these stanzas, in which Pulci vividly and graphically depicts the terrible slaughter taking place in Saragossa so that Charlemagne's revenge may be accomplished, transpires an almost epic tone of gloom and despair not to be found in the *cantari popolari* written before *Morgante.*

244, 7. For the reference to Horatius, see note, XXII, 135, 1.

248. While in stanza 42, 1–4 of the preceding canto we have seen the archbishop perform his priestly duties, we see him here in action as a man of arms, and a formidable one at that! Pulci completes his portrait of Turpin in stanza 268, 5–8, where the overly enthusiastic archbishop doubles as an expert hangman.

249–253. In *La Spagna,* Marsile's wife, called Branda, appears briefly only in canto XXX: the first time in stanza 4, 5–8 together with her husband, and the second time in stanza 15, where she hands Gano a purse decorated with five precious stones, which she asks the Maganzan to give to his wife.

In the *Chanson de Roland,* Queen Bramimonde, Marsilius's wife, has a slightly bigger role: she weeps in grief for the king, who has fainted before her (2576–2577); she sadly laments the fact that the gods have abandoned the Saracen cause (2598–2608); and after the conquest of Saragossa, she is said to have been captured and taken to "sweet France to be converted by love, as Charles commands" (3660–3674).

Pulci's Blanda, instead, possesses the bearing of a true queen and shows, even in the extremely difficult situation in which she finds herself, a great sense of dignity. She certainly deserves a better fortune than Bramimonde or Branda, and the one responsible for her good fortune is Rinaldo, the most gallant of Charlemagne's paladins. Upon seeing Luciana forcefully dragged along with the queen by some knights, the Lord of Montalban intervenes in an immediate and most effective way. Charlemagne, who knows his weakness for the gentler sex, agrees to release the two women in his custody. A few stanzas later (286), the reader learns that Blanda has been sent back to her father's home in Granada. An even happier ending awaits Luciana. Taken to Paris, she converts to Christianity and becomes Ansuigi's bride (XXVIII, 27).

250, 1. For Erichto, see note, II, 39, 5–6.

250, 8. In Statius's *Thebaid* it is stated that Jocasta, the queen of Thebes, hangs herself when she finds out that Oedipus, her second husband, is also her son. Puccini (1290) argues that Pulci might have known about Jocasta more from Dante (*Purgatorio,* XXII, 56) than from Statius.

251, 3–4. These lines allude to an episode in Book II of Virgil's *Aeneid,* which tells the story of Coroebus, who became furious when he saw the Trojan prophetess Cassandra, whom he loved, being taken away by Greek soldiers on the night of Troy's fall. He is believed to have been killed by either Neoptolemus or Diomedes.

254, 1. The destruction of these two cities is narrated in Genesis 19: 24–25.

255, 1–3. The Thebans in question are Eteocles and Polynices, twin sons of Jocasta and Oedipus (see note, 250, 8), who were said to have killed each other during the War of the Seven against Thebes. In his *Thebaid,* Statius writes that as soon as their dead bodies were placed together on the funeral pyre, the flame split. This fact is mentioned also by Dante in his *Inferno* (XXVI, 52–54), where the two-pointed flame containing the souls of Ulysses and Diomedes is compared to the flame engulfing the bodies of the two Theban brothers.

255, 6–7. See note, II, 39, 5–6.

256, 3. As Ageno notes (1047), here Pulci appears to "translate" the words that Jesus addressed to His disciples as He departed from the temple of Jerusalem: "There shall not be left here one stone upon another" (Matthew 24:2).

257, 5. For the Iber River, see note, XXV, 289, 2.

258, 8. See note, XI, 64, 6–7.

259, 1–5. Here Pulci recalls the annihilation of the cities of Jerusalem, Sagunto, and Carthage. Besieged first by Vespasian, Jerusalem was then razed by his son Titus in A.D. 70. Having entered into an alliance with Rome, the ancient seaport city of Sagunto, in Spain, was destroyed by Hannibal in 219 B.C. Carthage, Hannibal's native city, was eradicated by Scipio the Younger in 146 B.C. (see note, XXV, 35, 1).

260, 5–6. The unexpected cowardly fear that Bianciardino displays in the last stanzas of this canto (a fear which Marsilius, aware of his hiding place, promptly acknowledges [246, 6–8]) not only deprives the Saracen king of any dignity he might have left, but also renders him a pitiful caricature of the arrogant and valiant man he once was.

262. Pulci, whose *Ciriffo Calvaneo* contains several giants who feed on grown men as well as children, introduces at this point in the poem a new, grotesquely merry character, Orco, *Morgante's* only unforgettable man-eating creature, whose cannibalistic exploits—as the poet slyly remarks in 264, 8—are totally unknown to Charles.

263, 1. Born in Priene in the sixth century B.C., the ancient philosopher Biantes was considered to be one of the Seven Wise Men of Greece. When he was sent into exile, the only possession he took with him was his life.

263, 6. This Greek word means "beautiful."

266. What Pulci says of Chiron in this stanza derives from cantos XXVI and XXVII of *La Spagna.* In this poem Ghione (Pulci's Chiron), the son of Salamon of Brittany, is sent, at Gano's suggestion, as Charlemagne's envoy to King Marsilius. Having delivered his message, upon leaving Saragossa he is ambushed by Marsilius's men, but succeeds in getting away, though he is very seriously wounded (XXVI, 16–50). Once Ghione has reached Pamplona and has related Marsilius's negative reply to Charlemagne, he dies (XXVII, 1–10 and 13–17). The Anselm mentioned in line 2 is Anselm of Flanders, not to be confused with Count Anselm(o) (see note, XXV, 98, 8 and 99, 1–3).

266, 6–8. See note, 256, 3.

267, 7–8. See note, XXV, 77, 1–2.

269–270. For the park, the fountain, and the laurel tree recalled here by Charlemagne, see canto XXV, 54–74. For the reference to Curtius (270, 8), see note, XXVI, 38, 2.

271, 8. See Matthew 10:26: "There is nothing covered, that shall not be revealed."

272, 5–8. See XXIV, 159.

273, 7. See note, XV, 71, 5.

274. Pulci seems to forget here that in XXV, 84, 5–8 he states that the necromancer, finding the carob's case so strange, leaves its interpretation entirely to Gano.

275. During his conversation with Diliante in canto XXII, Gano tells him that Rinaldo could not have killed his uncle, the Old Man of the Mountain, who had expressed his desire to become a Christian, because "Our law does not allow by any means / to kill a man who makes it known to us / that he would like to be by us baptized" (84, 1–3). This is why both Turpin and Rinaldo laugh at Marsilius's request to convert; knowing the true nature of the man, they believe it to be nothing but a last-minute trick to save his neck.

276. The expression in line 2 refers to a most common proverbial expression, *Chi lava la testa all'asino, perde il ranno e il sapone* ("He who washes a donkey's head wastes lye and soap"); for the reference to German gluttony in lines 5–6, see note, XXI, 138, 3–5.

278–279, 1–4. Gano's last treason has had the effect of rendering Charlemagne sane again. As Momigliano writes (267), in this stanza Charles "appears to be a respectable, wise, and even sarcastic emperor." For the Italian critic, the reason for this drastic change is that the old monarch no longer feels in his heart the same love for Gano that had made him think and act like a fool. For Charon (278, 3), see note, II, 39, 1. Concerning what Marsilius says in lines 5–8 of 279, see note, 274.

281–283. See XXVIII, 54, 1 through 55, 2.

284–285. Marsilius's request that his wife's life be spared, and his calm, resigned, and fatalistic last words greatly contrast with the undignified behavior of a merciless Turpin, who in his unrestrained enthusiasm to perform his hanging duties is forced to pull up his priestly robe to gain more freedom of movement. (One wonders whether Pulci intended to portray in Turpin the personal qualities of a cleric he despised.) By having Marsilius end up hanged by the archbishop, Pulci has chosen for him quite a different death from the one reserved for him by the authors of the *Chanson de Roland* and *La Spagna*.

In the *Chanson de Roland,* upon hearing his wife, Bramimonde, shout that Balugante has been killed and that the Saracen troops have fled the field, King Marsile, his eyes filled with tears and his head bent down, suddenly dies of grief, as demons come and take his "sinful soul" away (3643–3647).

In canto XXXIX of *La Spagna,* when the French troops enter Saragossa, Marsilius, in great pain from the wound he has received in his left shoulder, is alone in his palace. Upon learning from some fleeing soldiers that Charles is taking possession of his city, the Saracen king insults the gods for having let him down, curses Gano, laments his adverse destiny, and then jumps headfirst from a window, to die on the ground below (10, 7–8 through 17).

CANTO XXVIII

SUMMARY: Invocation (1–3). After Charlemagne and his troops have returned to Saint John of Port, Gano is finally executed (4–14). Pulci's considerations on Charlemagne's friendship with Gano and on the emperor's deeds (15–41). Pulci's self-defense (42–46). Charlemagne's death (47–52). Charlemagne's legendary exploits, as told by Lactantius (53–66). Alcuin of York's alleged historical account of Charlemagne's life (67–104). Charlemagne's funeral (105–111). The emperor's last will and testament (112–118). Pulci's portrait of Charlemagne (119–128). Pulci's praise of Lucrezia Tornabuoni (129–136) and Angelo Poliziano (136–152) and his closing prayer to the Virgin Mary (1–3).

2, 1–4. The "lady" in question is Lucrezia Tornabuoni, wife of Piero de' Medici and mother of Lorenzo the Magnificent. She gave birth also to another son, Giuliano, who was to fall victim to a conspiracy, and to three daughters. Born in 1425 to an old and distinguished Florentine family, she died on March 25, 1482. A gifted and deeply religious woman, she was highly respected by the men of letters who frequented Lorenzo's court, and particularly by the poets Angelo Poliziano and Luigi Pulci, who revered her as their benefactress. A poet herself, she wrote religious hymns, called *Laude,* and produced a number of writings dealing with the lives of the saints. Until the day she died, Lucrezia never interfered or got involved in Florentine politics. See also note, I, 4, 1–3.

3, 2. For Parnassus, see note, XXIV, 113, 4.

3, 3–4. Calliope and Clio, daughters of Zeus and Mnemosyne, were two of the nine Muses; while the former was the Muse of epic and elegiac poetry, the latter presided over history. Calliope and Clio are called Pegasus's sisters because they lived near the fountain Hippocrene, which Pegasus had created on Mount Helicon with a stamp of his foot. See note, XXV, 312, 1.

4, 6–8. See XXVII, 236, 8.

6, 1–6. Pulci refers here to stanzas 21–27 of canto XXXIX of *La Spagna,* where we read that Gano, having killed the naive young jailer whom he had invited to eat with him, escapes on horseback from the tower in which he has been imprisoned. By God's will, however, the sky turns from clear and starry to dark and misty, so that the Maganzan wanders all night long around the tower, covering no more than a mile's distance. At the break of dawn, having discovered his escape, the guards search and find a thoroughly confused Gano in the nearby fields.

7, 7–8. See note, XVIII, 132, 5–8.

8, 4. For the meaning of the word "pharisees," see note, IV, 97, 3.

8–15. Pulci's masterful depiction of Gano's punishment is considerably shorter than and also strikingly different from the episodes of Gano's execution we read in the *Chanson de Roland* and *La Spagna*. A brief analysis of the episodes narrated in these two earlier poems illustrates how Pulci's text differs from his sources.

In the *Chanson de Roland,* after Aude (Alda the Fair) has died of grief after being told by Charles of Roland's death (3705–3722), the emperor orders all his vassals to convene in Aix-la-Chapelle to attend Ganelon's trial. As the trial begins, Ganelon asks Pinabel, the mightiest of the thirty members of his family who are also present, to defend him. Trusting in his military prowess, Pinabel pledges to kill whoever wants to hang the Lord of Maganza (3747–3792). Asked by his vassals to spare Ganelon's life, since killing him would not bring back Roland, an enraged emperor replies by calling them "traitors" (3793–3814). It is at this point that a young French knight, the chevalier Thierry of Anjou, comes forward, proclaims that Ganelon is guilty of treason, and challenges any of his kin to fight with him (3818–3844). The ensuing encounter between Thierry and Pinabel takes place in a meadow below Aix-la-Chapelle. Though Pinabel appears to be the stronger fighter, Thierry, aided by God, succeeds in splitting his opponent's skull in two, while the rejoicing Frenchmen proclaim that a miracle has taken place (3873–3931). As a result of the duel, all the Maganzans are hanged, and Ganelon, his hands and feet tied to four warhorses, all set galloping in different directions, dies a most horrible death (3932–3973).

In *La Spagna* (XL, 21–39), after the paladins' burial, while Charlemagne is thinking of bringing Gano to justice, Bertha, his sister and Gano's second wife, begs the emperor not to kill her husband, both because she believes him to be innocent and because she does not want to be left a widow for a second time. Charlemagne calls a meeting of the Council, during which he reveals that he is still not convinced of Gano's treason. A Maganzan knight, Pinabello, challenges to a duel any and all of his uncle's accusers. Terigi accepts Pinabello's challenge, and the duel takes place in a square, with the entire court in attendance, Gano included. While Terigi and Pinabello face one another, Gano arrogantly threatens to take his revenge upon Salamon should Pinabello be the victor. The long and fierce duel ends, however, with Pinabello's death. When Charles asks Gano what type of death he prefers, the impudent Maganzan, confident that the emperor will spare him such a death, chooses the punishment commonly reserved to traitors: death by quartering. Gano's wish is promptly carried out, and his remains are burned and the ashes dispersed to the wind.

Comparing Pulci's text with those of the *Chanson de Roland* and *La Spagna,* it is clear that while in the latter two poems Gano's execution is merely the last in a series of chronologically described events, in *Morgante* it is Gano's last tormented hour that becomes the focus of the narrative. In Pulci's few fast-moving, action-filled, and visually powerful stanzas, no mention is made of several specific details—such as Charlemagne's convening the Council in order to try Gano; the Lord of Maganza's asking Pinabel to defend him against his accusers and Pinabel's ensuing duel with Thierry of Anjou; Bertha's request that Charlemagne spare her husband's life; and Terigi's final victory over Pinabello—which occur prior to Gano's death and constitute the bulk of the narratives in both the *Chanson de Roland* and *La Spagna*. Obviously in Pulci's version, Gano's death sentence is not determined by a deliberation of the Council, but is requested by the thunderous shouting of the members of Charles's court. When the Maganzan is brought before the emperor, the ever-shrewd Rinaldo hands him to the raging mob before the condemned man can utter a single word in his defense. Deprived of the power of speech, which he had mastered so well, the Lord of Maganza is doomed.

Indeed, in describing Gano's punishment, Pulci has portrayed not an execution scene (as is the case for the *Chanson de Roland* and *La Spagna*) but an uncontrollably wild lynching. The fact that even in *Morgante* Gano is finally quartered is of secondary importance, since when he is tied to the four horses he must be dead already. No one, in fact, could have survived such a lynching. It is curious that Pulci's account reflects a reality in early medieval treason: traitors recognized by everyone as guilty often did not have what moderns call a trial. When guilt was "known," only the sentence needed to be declared. However, Pulci's description of Gano's torture has nothing to do with medieval law. He may have taken this idea from the beating Gano receives from the cooks in the *Chanson de Roland*. For a reading of Ganelon's trial, consult the previously quoted study by Emanuel J. Mickel (see note, XVI, 62–67).

In accordance with Rinaldo's order, Gano's quartered remains are not burned, as in *La Spagna,* but are scattered as food for wolves and dogs. By adding this final detail, Pulci has provided a befitting conclusion to Gano's treacherous existence. It must also be noted that in these stanzas of *Morgante*, contrary to what is stated in *La Spagna,* Charlemagne does not show any sign of relenting in his resolve to punish Gano for his crimes. Interestingly, it is at this point that Pulci offers the only possible explanation for the emperor's extreme gullibility, remarking ironically that "it was preordained" that Gano's role in life was to betray, and Charles's was to believe (15, 6–8).

16, 3. For Alcuin of York, see note, XXV, 34, 2–5.

21, 7–8. See XXV, 68–69.

22, 1–4. The event mentioned here takes place in canto XXIV, 47–48.

22, 5. On December 26, 1476, the Milanese nobleman Giovanni Andrea Lampognano (also called Lampugnani), conspiring with other Milanese young men, killed, possibly to avenge a personal offense, Gian Galeazzo Sforza, the despotic and cruel ruler of Milan.

24, 4. The "steersman" to whom the poet is referring is Lucrezia Tornabuoni (see note, 2, 1–4).

25, 1. As previously noted, in *Morgante* Turpin survived the Battle of Roncesvalles; however, since, according to Pulci, the archbishop died before Charlemagne, the poet can no longer rely on him as a source of information.

26, 1. For Arnaldo as Pulci's new source, see note, XXV, 115, 4–5.

26, 5–8. Rinaldo's comparison to a bird of prey most adequately portrays the paladin's exultation over Gano's death.

28, 4. The present that Rinaldo gives back to Luciana is the pavilion she gave him in canto XIV, 42, 4–8.

31–32. It appears from these stanzas that Pulci intended to compose a poem dedicated to the retelling of Rinaldo's deeds after Roncesvalles, which, however, he never wrote. In a letter (XVI) dated December 4, 1470, and addressed to Lorenzo de' Medici from Foligno, Luigi, while asking the Magnificent to remember him to Lucrezia Tornabuoni, states that upon his return to Florence he will write "marvelous things about the Dane and Rinaldo."

33, 5–8. See XXV, 229–336.

34, 2. For the Angel Gabriel's words to Mary, see Luke 1:37.

34, 8. Ageno (1068) notes that in the present context, this proverbial Tuscan expression means "he who fancies himself to be a learned man is not inclined to believe in miracles." For Davide Puccini (1317), who perceives a possible ambiguous intention in this line, the true meaning of the proverb is instead "the more learned one is, the less gullible."

35, 1. According to an old folktale, it was believed that Saint John the Evangelist would not die until the end of the world.

36, 1–6. The legend of Ugier the Dane's survival can be found in a thirteenth-century French poem in Alexandrines and in a French prose romance of the same period, both based on the *Chevalerie Ogier;* these works subsequently became known in Italy as well (see Ageno, 1068–1069).

38, 7. Latin for "Therefore, Charles, you arrived at the right time." The use of Latin gives these words the solemn tone of a theological discussion (Ageno, 1069).

39, 2. Francis and Dominic are obviously Saint Francis of Assisi (1182–1226), founder of the Order of the Minor Friars, and Saint Dominic of Guzmán (Calaruega, Spain, 1170–Bologna, 1221), founder of the Dominican Order.

40, 1. See note, I, 8, 7–8.

40, 7. The celebrated Roman historian Sallust (Caius Crispus Sallustius), author of *De coniuratione Catilinae* and of *Bellum Iugurthinum,* lived between 86 and 35 B.C. The historian Justin (M. Iunianus Iustinus), who lived between the second and third centuries A.D., was known during the Middle Ages for his compilation of the *Historiae Philippicae et totius mundi origines et terrae situs,* a lost work by the first-century Latin historian Pompeius Trogus.

42, 1. With this bitter personal observation, Pulci begins his famous self-defense against the accusations of irreligiousness, and even heresy, caused by the appearance in 1475 of a sonnet (CXLIV) in which he makes fun of the pilgrims going to Rome on the occasion of the Holy Year (this entire matter is discussed in the Introduction).

42, 4. Note the poet's further allusion to the proverbial gluttony of monks and friars, who love to eat just as much as they delight in spreading slanderous rumors.

42, 8. This is the beginning line of sonnet CXLIV ("In principio era bujo, e bujo fia"), addressed by Pulci to his friend Benedetto Dei.

43, 1–3. See Genesis 1:1–2.

43, 7–8. Pulci states that the "futile things" he wrote (among them the above-mentioned sonnet) were directed "against hypocrites, and not against you, God." Also in this particular instance, the use of Latin emphasizes the confessional tone of the poet's words (see note, 38, 7).

44, 1–2. The poet declares that the appropriate place for a sinner to be reprimanded is the confessional and not the pulpit. Recognizing in these lines, as most Pulci scholars do, the presence of a personal polemic tone, Stefano Carrai convincingly argues that Pulci is referring to the preaching of a specific monk, the Dominican Gerolamo Savonarola. Born in Ferrara in 1452, Savonarola was tortured and hanged in Florence in 1498 (see *Le muse dei Pulci*, 173–187).

44, 6. The other Pulci credo is his *Confessione* (see note, I, 2, 1–4).

44, 8. Augustin is obviously Saint Augustine.

45, 2. For this further reference to Saint Thomas, see note, XXV, 119–121.

45, 6–7. The monochord is an ancient musical instrument, possibly of Egyptian origin, consisting of a single string stretched over a sounding board, and a movable bridge set on a graduated scale. As previously pointed out, "sol" and "fa" are the two musical notes which in the ancient musical system constituted the basis of two hexachords. Pulci metaphorically threatens to use invective and satire as weapons against all kinds of friars and monks.

46, 1–6. In this stanza the poet declares that his learned detractors' fallacious and captious reasoning will not succeed in sweetening his sharp rebukes, which he will express in clearly understandable language (Florentine).

48, 7. The fact that Charles is said to have established his court in Aachen, while Italian chivalric tradition locates it in Paris, is, according to Ageno (1073–1074), "the first approximately precise historical information that Pulci utilizes in this canto."

49, 3. Born in 742, Charles became king in 768; he abdicated the throne in 813 in favor of his son Louis I the Pious, and died in Aachen on January 28 of 814. Repeating a computing mistake made by historian Donato Acciaiuoli, Pulci states that Charlemagne was king for forty-seven years (see notes, 70–104, 104–108, and 110, 1–8).

50, 2–3. For Urman of Paris, Charlemagne's alleged chronicler, see note, I, 5, 3. As Ageno points out (1074), Alcuin died in 804, while Einhard's *Vita*

Caroli Magni, a work that Pulci attributes to Alcuin, was written between 814 and 828 (see also note, XXV, 34, 2–5).

52, 1–5. One of the Cyclades islands in the Aegean Sea, Delos was famous for a temple to Apollo located in Delphi, as well as for being Apollo's and Artemis's birthplace. Cynthus is the name of a mountain on the island of Delos. In Ovid's *Metamorphoses* we read that Hyacinth, a beautiful young Spartan prince, was much loved by the god Apollo. One day while the two friends were practicing discus throwing, the discus cast by Apollo accidentally hit the handsome prince in the head, killing him. From the earth drenched with Hyacinth's blood sprang a marvelous flower that bore the young Spartan's name. For Daphne, see note, III, 17, 6–7. Quoting from Pulci's *Vocabulista,* Puccini (1325) notes: "Ismara: a Thracian mountain, where Orpheus often sang"; "Cyrrha: a hill near Mount Parnassus, consecrated to Apollo"; "Pindus: a mountain visited by famous ancient shepherds"; "Aracynthus: a place where Amphion [who with Zethus amicably ruled the city of Thebes] often played his lyre."

52, 6–7. For Marsyas, see note, XXVI, 26, 7–8. Thamyris was a famous and very proud Thracian poet and singer who dared to challenge the Muses to a contest. Having been defeated, he was blinded and deprived of his voice.

54–55. Though Pulci claims that Lactantius is the author of a book on Charlemagne's earlier years, in reality he derives the content of these two stanzas from section VI, 1–51 of Andrea da Barberino's *I Reali di Francia.* Regarding "Charlemagnet," see note, XXIV, 27, 2–4.

56, 1 through 57, 2. As Ageno notes (1076), Pulci's source for these lines is another of Andrea da Barberino's works, *Aspramonte,* where (I, 1–4) we read that Agolant, the Saracen king of Africa, was induced to go to France with a great army because he had been told that Charlemagne was a more magnificent and nobler monarch than he. As the story goes (III, 26–37), when Charlemagne, who had left his camp in pursuit of Agolant's son Almont, found himself in danger of being defeated by his adversary, he was saved by a still-adolescent Orlando, who succeeded in slaying Almont (see also note, I, 13, 1–8). For Gerard (Gherardo of Fratta), see note, I, 13, 1–8. Don Buoso and Don Chiaro are the nephews of Gherardo of Fratta. For Don Chiaro, see note, XXVI, 106, 5–8 through 110. In *Aspramonte* (I, 42), Riccier di Risa, a valiant Christian knight, is treacherously murdered by Almont.

57, 3. From this line on, *La Spagna* is Pulci's main source.

57, 7–8. Regarding Ferraù's death, see note, XXIV, 16, 1–6.

The conquest of the Saracen city of Lazzera (Lazera) is narrated in cantos VI and VII of *La Spagna.* It is made possible by Orlando, who, wearing Ferraù's armor, succeeds in entering the city. Here Orlando, following Ferraù's instructions, kills the Saracen's mother, frees the Christian knights held captive therein, and, with their help, engages the enemy in a street-by-street fight. When, outside the city walls, Charlemagne sees Orlando's banner flying high above a tower, he orders his troops to attack. After a brief struggle, the Saracen garrison surrenders, Lazera's citizens embrace the Christian faith, and Ferraù, whom Orlando has slain and baptized *in extremis,* is buried at the end of a solemn funeral ceremony (VII, 31–34, 1–2).

58, 1–3. Concerning Serpentino and the city of Stella, see note, XXV, 10, 4.

58, 4–6. Pulci's chronology of these events is incorrect. In *La Spagna,* in fact, the siege of Pamplona, which was ruled by Mazarigi and defended by his son Isolieri, King Marsilius's nephew, occurs long before Serpentino's death. The story of this seven-year-long siege, which starts when Charlemagne, after a two-month stay in Lazera, decides to depart for Spain (VIII, 35), is interrupted (XII, 38) when, upon the arrival of a messenger, Orlando leaves the Christian camp to go and conquer Nobile (XII, 39 through XIV, 37). Eventually Orlando returns to Spain, just in time to prevent Charlemagne's army from raising the siege from Pamplona (XX, 30 through XXI, 35).

59, 1–2. Holding Orlando responsible for the death of Samson of Piccardy during the battle for the conquest of Nobile (*La Spagna,* X, 33–34, 1–2), Charlemagne slaps his nephew in the face with his iron glove (XIV, 11, 5–8). This is the cause for the paladin's "anger and disdain" and his subsequent departure for the Orient (XIV, 14–33)

59, 3 through 62, 2. Again all the facts mentioned in these lines are derived from *La Spagna.* While traveling in the Orient, Orlando reaches the Persian city of Lamech (Mecca), which is surrounded by the troops of Machidante, the Saracen king of Jerusalem. Having offered his services to the Sultan of Lamech, who declines them, the count is instead most kindly received by Sansonetto, the sultan's son. When the sultan's young daughter, requested in marriage by the much older Machidante, refuses to marry him, Machidante's nephew, the admiral, threatens to have her tortured. Intervening in defense of the young princess, Orlando challenges the admiral to a duel, which results in the Saracen's death. Pledging to avenge his nephew's demise, Machidante leaves for Jerusalem. In the meantime the sultan appoints Orlando, whom everyone knows as Lionagio, to lead the Persian army. During the battle that takes place after Machidante returns to Lamech together with the admiral's brother, Polinoro, and a huge army, not only does Orlando save Sansonetto's life, but he also prevents the sultan and his daughter from being captured by Polinoro, whom he kills, while Machidante flees by sea toward Jerusalem. In pursuit of Machidante, Orlando, Sansonetto, and the sultan lay siege to Jerusalem (XIV, 38 through XVIII, 36).

In the meantime in Paris, Ugone and Ansuigi, ordered by Charlemagne's wife to go and search for Orlando, leave France with an army of 10,000 horsemen. Upon their arrival in Betania, which is in Christian hands, they meet Pilagi, Machidante's son, who, in exchange for their military assistance, cedes half of the city of Jerusalem to them. During the ensuing battle, Sansonetto, dueling with Ugone, is forced to call on Orlando for help. Orlando reveals his true identity to Ugone, whom he warns not to trust Machidante. That same night, in fact, Pilagi, who does not wish to stain his honor, reveals to Ugone and Ansuigi that his father is planning to attack them. Ugone kills

Machidante and, together with Orlando, takes possession of the entire city. Sansonetto, the sultan, his daughter, Pilagi, and all the other Saracens are baptized. Ansuigi, who has been given the sultan's daughter in marriage, is left in charge of the Holy City, as Orlando, Sansonetto, and Ugone sail for Spain to return to Pamplona (XVIII, 37 through XX, 30, 4).

60, 3 through 61, 2. The episode of Charlemagne's return to France, transported on the back of the devil Macabel (Malachel in *Morgante*), as well as the killing of the usurper Macarius just when he is about to marry Charlemagne's wife, is also narrated in *La Spagna* (XXI, 38, 4 through XXIII, 30). In this poem Macarius, one of Gano's nephews, is slain by the queen's faithful squire Ghione, son of Salomon, the king of Brittany (called Chiron in *Morgante*). It must be further noted that the devil Macabel is conjured by Orlando using a book donated to him by the Sultan of Lamech.

61, 3. The conquest of Pamplona is finally accomplished with the arrival in Spain of King Desiderius and his Italian army. The Italians build a variety of wooden contraptions which enable the Christians to storm the walls and take possession of the city (XXV, 5–41). Concerning Chiron (61, 6), see note, XXVII, 266.

63, 1–2. Pulci is referring here to the content of the first twenty-three cantos of his poem.

64, 1–8. It is believed that the information given in this stanza is taken from a prose version of Ugier the Dane's adventures contained in the mss. laurenziani XLII, 37 and LXXXXIX, 64 (see Ageno, 1079). Durafort is the name of Ugier's horse, elsewhere called also Broiafort. Ugier's killing of Charlemagne's son Carlotto is again caused by Gano's evil machinations. Envious of Ugier's growing military fame and power, the Maganzan tells Carlotto that the emperor is planning to pass his throne on to Ugier's son Baldovino, and that he should therefore eliminate his potential rival, using a joust as the occasion. Overcome with rage upon learning of his son's death, Ugier slays Carlotto, a killing for which he spends the next fourteen years in prison. In the meantime Bravieri, the terrifying king of Nubia, attacks Paris and captures Charlemagne and all his paladins. Released from prison following his wife Armellina's appeal to the pope, Ugier eventually kills Bravieri, brings Charlemagne and his paladins back to Paris, and, recognized by the emperor, is forgiven and reinstated in his position (Ageno, 1079–1080). Note that "the March" mentioned in line 7 is the *Marca Trevigiana,* a region in northern Italy which Ugier has gained by defeating Massimone, the king of Verona.

65, 1–6. Concerning the sources for Rinaldo's earlier years, see Ageno, 1080, and also note, X, 76, 4–8 through 114.

65, 7–8. See note, X, 112, 4.

68, 7. For Philomel(a), see note, I, 3, 1–4.

70–104. Pulci scholars have established that the historical account of Charlemagne's life is based on Donato Acciaiuoli's *Vita Caroli Magni.* A Florentine nobleman born in 1429, Acciaiuoli was a distinguished public official and a highly respected orator and scholar who, in addition to his *Vita Caroli Magni* (composed in 1461), wrote biographical accounts of Hannibal and Scipio and translated into Italian some of Plutarch's *Lives* and Leonardo Bruni's *History of Florence*. He died in Milan in 1478. (For additional information and partial transcriptions of Acciaiuoli's original Latin text, see Ageno, 1081–1104.)

In his previously mentioned article on Acciaiuoli's *Vita* and Pulci's *Morgante* (see note, XXIV, 35, 1–4), Mark Davie points out that while Acciaiuoli "produces a portrait of the emperor which has to reconcile . . . the monarchist ideal of the Holy Roman Empire with the Florentines' jealousy of their liberties," Pulci begins to recount Charlemagne's life "in the terms prescribed by Lucrezia and announced in his opening stanzas" only in the very last part of his poem. When he does so, the poet turns to the work of the Florentine historian, "as if guiltily aware that Acciaiuoli had succeeded in fulfilling the commission which he had neglected" (142). If it is true that the celebration of Charlemagne's life and deeds in canto XXVIII is to be considered the poet's final attempt to make up for his previous unflattering picture of the emperor, it is equally true that the poem's last cantos reflect, to a certain extent, the cultural changes which had occurred in Florence between 1465 and 1480. After making a specific reference to lines 5–8 of stanza 136, where the poet declares that he may turn to Morgante's clapper for help, Davie concludes that "for all his attempts at writing a serious historical epic in his second poem, he [Pulci] was right to reassert at the end that the good-natured giant Morgante was still his presiding genius" (151–152).

With regard to Pulci's praise of Charlemagne, Momigliano considers it to be "nothing more than an awkward panegyric, but detached from the rest of the poem: after Gano's death, Charles no longer operates" (267). Angelo Gianni, who calls these same stanzas Pulci's "Carleide" and deems them "the least felicitous ones" in the poem's last five cantos, believes that they represent Pulci's last unsuccessful attempt to regain the favor of the Magnificent, his last hope "to reestablish an intellectual relationship which was no longer possible" in Florence's new cultural climate (377–378).

72, 1–2. The Aquitanians inhabited Aquitania, a Roman division of western Gaul, a land bordered by the Garonne River, the Pyrenees, and the Atlantic Ocean. The ancient southwestern province of Guyenne has the city of Bordeaux as its capital.

72, 6. The "other pens" mentioned here refer to Donato Acciaiuoli, from whose text Pulci is quoting, but as if Alcuin had written it.

74, 1. The Hesperian land is Italy. This was a name given to the Italian peninsula by the Greeks.

74, 2–3. The Lombards (Longobards) were an ancient German people, so called because they wore long beards and long hair. In 568, Albuinus, their king, decided to move his people south (see note, 75, 1–3). The kingdom that he established in northern Italy ended in 773 when Charlemagne, answering Pope Hadrian's call for help, descended upon Italy, defeated the Lombards, and dispossessed King Desiderius, his former father-in-law, of his throne. (Desiderius's daughter, Ermengarda, was Charlemagne's first wife; after he repudiated her—the reasons are unknown—he married a Swedish princess, Hildegarde.)

75, 1–3. Narses, one of Justinian I's great generals, lived between 478 and 568. He successfully fought against the Goths, the Franks, and the Alemanni and for fifteen years ruled over the Italian peninsula as the Byzantine emperor's exarch in Ravenna. According to Acciaiuoli's *Vita Caroli Magni,* it was Narses who invited Albuinus and his Lombards to leave Germany for Italy (*"Inde Albuinus eorum rex accersitus ab Narsete eunuco . . . in Italiam venit"* [Ageno, 1083]).

75, 8. Charles Martel, the son of Pepin II of Heristal, lived between 689 and 741. In 732 at Poitiers he registered a resounding victory over the Arabs, thus putting an end to Muslim penetration into western Europe. Charles Martel was succeeded by his son Pepin III, known as Pepin the Short, who in 751 was crowned king of the Franks. In 754, on the occasion of Pope Stephanus II's solemn recognition of his title in the Church of Saint Denis, Pepin pledged the support of the Carolingian dynasty to the Roman pontiff against the Lombard king Astolph. Keeping his word, Pepin sent two military expeditions to Italy, as a result of which Astolph was forced to cede the territory of Ravenna and the cities of Rimini, Pesaro, Fano, Senigallia, and Ancona to the pope. Together with the Duchy of Rome, these cities constituted the State of the Church, thus giving birth to the temporal power of the popes.

76, 4–8. The Carthaginians are called "Barcans," probably because Barca was Hannibal's family name. As the commentators of *Morgante* point out, Pulci's reading of Acciaiuoli's text is not precisely correct. Hannibal and Charlemagne, in fact, did not follow the same route. While Hannibal climbed over the Alps through the Monginevro Pass, part of Charlemagne's army reached Italy through the Moncenisio Pass, and part through the Pass of the Great Saint Bernard. Note that the word "Apennines" here stands for the Alps.

78, 2. Vercelli is a city located in the northern region of Piedmont. At the time of Charlemagne's expedition to Italy, Vercelli, with its surrounding territory, was a northern Lombard duchy.

78, 4. Pavia, one of northern Italy's oldest cities, was founded by the Romans, who called it Ticinum. Chosen by Theodoricus, king of the Ostrogoths, as his capital, it later became the capital of Albuinus's Lombard kingdom.

79, 4. Benevento, in the southern region of Campania, had been a Lombard duchy since 571. The considerably smaller city of Spoleto, also a Lombard duchy, is located in the central region of Umbria, not far from Perugia.

80, 8. This confusing reference to Desiderius's sons (Ageno considers it to be almost "incomprehensible" [1086]) shows that Pulci once more misinterprets Acciaiuoli's words. The conflict between the Lombard king and Pope

Hadrian was outwardly caused by the pontiff's refusal to grant Desiderius's request that he anoint the two adolescent sons of Carloman (Pepin the Short's younger son). After their father's death, Charlemagne having dispossessed them of their rights to the throne, the two princes and their mother, Gerberga, sought asylum in Pavia at King Desiderius's court. When, after a long siege, Pavia surrendered, Desiderius, delivered to Charlemagne by his own men, was taken to France and imprisoned in the monastery of Corbie, where he died. In the meantime, Charlemagne moved against Verona, where Adelchi, Desiderius's son, had gone together with Gerberga and her two sons. As the enemy army approached Verona, Gerberga and her children ran out of the city and placed themselves under the protection of Charlemagne. When Verona, too, fell, Adelchi fled south, eventually landing in Constantinople. After several years, Adelchi, having returned to Italy at the head of some Greek troops, again fought against the Franks and was killed. It is clear that the "sons" Pulci mentions in line 8 are not Desiderius's children but, as stated in 81, 8, Carloman's.

81, 3. While the Goths (divided into Visigoths and Ostrogoths), the Vandals, and the Heruli all shared a common German origin, the Huns were a fierce nomadic Mongolian tribe. The Huns' power in central and eastern Europe was terminated with Attila's death in 453.

82, 5–8. Following Guglielmo Volpi, Ageno (1087) suggests that in these lines Pulci alludes to Ugolino Verino's *Carliade,* a Latin poem this Florentine humanist, who was a friend of both Poliziano and Pulci, wrote to celebrate Charlemagne's historical role as defender of the faith. Verino, who was born in Florence in 1438 and died there in 1516, in 1493 sent his poem to Charles VIII of France. The *Carliade,* however, was terminated in 1480, when Verino sent it to Poliziano for his comments and revision.

86, 5. See note, XXIV, 56, 3.

87, 1. See note, XXVII, 120, 5.

87, 5. Lucius Papirius Cursor, a Roman consul and twice a dictator, in 325, 320, and again in 309 B.C. successfully fought against the Samnites, an ancient central Italian people. He represented Roman courage, steadfastness, and uncompromising principle.

88, 2. See note, IV, 97, 2.

91, 1. Concerning Anselmo, see note, XXV, 98, 8 and 99, 1–3.

92, 6–8. In 787, after the annexation of Desiderius's kingdom to his own, Charlemagne waged war against Araysus, head of the Lombard duchy of Benevento. Though Charlemagne was victorious, he gained complete control of this rebellious province only in 812.

94, 1. For Camillus, see note, XXII, 132, 1–2.

94, 3–8 through 95. Though he had renewed his oath of vassalage to Charlemagne and had therefore been pardoned, the Duke of Bavaria was subsequently accused of treason, removed from office, and confined in a monastery.

96, 1. The Velatabi lived in the regions situated on the Baltic Sea; the

Abroditi inhabited the German lands located between the Elbe and Oder rivers.

96–97. The people that Pulci calls Hungarians are actually the Avars, a people of Mongolian stock who emigrated to central Europe together with the Huns. The Avars took up residence in Pannonia (today's Hungary), an ancient Roman province situated between the Alps, Germany, Dacia, and Illyria. Only in 896 was the region occupied by the Hungarians. Charlemagne's campaign against the Avars, which he began in 791, lasted several years.

98, 4. Carlo (called Carlotto in 64, 3) was Charlemagne's oldest son. Both Carlo and Pepin, his second-born son, died before their father. Charlemagne's only surviving son was Louis I the Pious, who was king of France from 814 to 840.

98, 5–8 through 99. The sequence of events is as follows: In 799, Pope Leo III, successor of Hadrian I, having been expelled from the Eternal City as the result of a conspiracy, joins Charlemagne in Paderborn. In 800, Charlemagne goes to Rome. On December 23, the pontiff solemnly swears that the accusations leveled against him by his enemies are false. Then on December 25, during a Christmas Mass in Saint Peter's Basilica, Leo crowns Charlemagne emperor of the Holy Roman Empire.

100, 4. The eagle was considered a symbol of Jove because it was believed to carry the god's thunderbolts.

100, 7–8. See note, I, 7, 1–8.

104–108. In the Treaty of Aachen of 812, the Byzantine emperor Michael I gives Charlemagne the title of emperor, and in exchange Charlemagne renounces any claims he might have over Venice and the Dalmatian coasts. In 813, the emperor proclaims his only son Louis as his colleague and successor. On January 28 of the following year, Charlemagne dies, and his mortal remains are buried in Aachen's cathedral.

110, 1–8. As noted above, Charlemagne died on January 28, 814. Misinterpreting Acciaiuoli's text, Pulci first gives January 24 as the day of Charlemagne's death, then, repeating the computing mistake made by Acciaiuoli (Ageno, 1097), states that the year was 815.

111–119. All the facts reported in these stanzas are also taken directly from Acciaiuoli's *Vita Caroli Magni*. According to Acciaiuoli, Charlemagne made his last will and testament three years before his passing (see Ageno, 1098–1099).

118, 1–4. The work Pulci announces that he is working on is the *Ciriffo Calvaneo,* an unfinished poem which narrates events that occurred during the life of Charlemagne's son Louis the Pious but that are dated to have happened about a century later. Concerning the still-debated question of the paternity of this poem, Laura Mattioli maintains that the *Ciriffo Calvaneo* was composed "by the two brothers [Luca and Luigi Pulci] in two subsequent phases" (*Luigi Pulci e il 'Ciriffo Calvaneo'* [Padova: Sanavio e Pizzati, 1900]), a thesis which is basically shared by Italiano Marchetti, for whom the poem is "the product of a two-person collaboration" ("Collaborazione di poeti in un poema quattro-centesco," *Lettere Italiane* 4 [1953]: 105–120). More recently, Ruedi Ankli, convinced that an intertextual analysis of the style and narrative technique of *Morgante* and *Ciriffo* could help solve the question of the latter's authorship, demonstrates in his well-documented article that a "rhetorical and stylistic analysis" provides a "further means for attributing the greatest part of the *Ciriffo* . . . to Luigi rather than to Luca" ("Un problema di attribuzione sempre aperto: Il *Ciriffo Calvaneo,*" *L'attribuzione: teoria e pratica,* Atti del Seminario di Ascona, 30 settembre–5 ottobre 1992, a c. di O. Besomi e C. Caruso [Basel: Birkhäuser, 1994], 259–304).

119. Here Pulci begins the physical description of Charles, which is followed by a sort of review of the emperor's moral qualities. In stanzas 119–128, the poet again greatly relies upon Acciaiuoli's *Vita* (Ageno, 1100–1104).

121, 8. See note, I, 7, 1–8.

122, 2. This bridge, located near Mainz, was destroyed by fire before Charlemagne's death (Puccini, 1349).

124, 1. As previously noted, Aachen was famous for its thermal waters, known already to the Romans.

125, 5. Concerning Baal, see note, XV, 111, 5.

126, 1–4. See note, XXV, 34, 2–5.

127, 1–6. Acciaiuoli errs in stating that Bertha, mother of Charlemagne, is the daughter of the Byzantine emperor Heraclius. As Puccini remarks (1351), the fact is historically impossible, because Heraclius ruled his empire from 610 to 640, while his alleged son-in-law, Pepin the Short, Charlemagne's father, was crowned in 751. In *I Reali di Francia* (V, 13–18), Bertha is said to be, instead, the daughter of King Pepin of Hungary. Furthermore, in this chival-ric romance, Charlemagne is barely a teenager when Bertha dies of poisoning. A year later, the king, her husband, is also poisoned, while Charlemagne avoids his parents' gruesome end by secretly leaving the court.

128, 5–6. The poet feels the call to turn his attention to the composition of a new work (the *Ciriffo Calvaneo,* already announced in stanza 118). He reveals the title of this work in stanza 129, 7.

130. The allegorical meaning of this stanza is that now that the poet has completed his trip (*Morgante*), he is reluctant as yet to initiate another, equally long and uncertain voyage (a new poem), particularly when present circum-stances do not seem to be too favorable (the attacks made against him), unless he is given a sign that things have changed (the return of the "raven," which, according to some critics, may be Lorenzo de' Medici).

131, 3–8. The name of the lady mentioned in this line is given in stanza 132, 4, where the poet purposely spells Lucrezia's family name Torna-*buona,* instead of Tornabuoni, in order to declare that she has turned out to be not only good but perfect.

133, 1–8. According to Pulci, in addition to published religious poetry dealing with Esdras, Tobias, Judith, and John the Evangelist, Lucrezia also wrote a *Vita di Maria* (Life of Mary), of which no copy has yet been found

(Ageno, 1106). (On Lucrezia's writings, see Fulvio Pezzarossa's study *I poemetti sacri di Lucrezia Tornabuoni* [Firenze: Olschki, 1978].)

136, 5–8. It seems that with the mere mention of his beloved giant—the theraupetic functions of whose clapper the poet paradoxically invokes as a protection against his enemies—Pulci finds once more that caustic and bemused spirit which characterizes so many of his earlier cantos.

137, 1–3. Here Pulci metaphorically warns his detractors that he will harm them just as the hawk harmed the geese of Mount Taurus. According to Ageno (1107), Pulci's source for these lines is the Latin historian Ammianus Marcellinus (330–400), author of *Rerum Gestarum Libri XXXI,* written as a continuation of Tacitus's *Historiae.*

137, 6. Pulci's words, as Puccini correctly notes (1355), could have been uttered by Margutte himself.

138, 4. Aganippe is the name of a fountain located on Mount Helicon, in the ancient Greek district of Boeotia. Both the fountain and the mountain were sacred to the gods.

138, 7. Damoetas and Thyrsis are well-known ancient shepherds.

139, 2. The citharist and the satyr mentioned in these lines are Marsyas (see note, XXVI, 26, 7–8) and Thamyris (see note, 52, 6–7).

139, 4. Note the author's ironic remark about his own physical appearance. Aware of the disparaging words that had been written concerning his not particularly attractive features (it is enough to think of the extremely pungent comments expressed in Matteo Franco's sonnets IX, XXXIV, XXXVII, and XLVIII), Luigi shows that he is also capable of poking fun at himself.

139, 5–8. We know that the cultural revolution that occurred in Florence in the mid-1470s brought about substantial changes from which even official courtly poets were not immune. Paolo Orvieto (283) considers lines 5–8— where "Pulci declares his total defeat and his inability to adapt himself to the circumstances"—as well as most of canto XXVIII to be a clear indication that "a true and actual transfer of the highest literary powers" has taken place (283).

141, 4. Concerning the Sibyl and Parnassus, see notes, XXIV, 112–114 and 113, 4.

141–142. Addressing his readers with a seemingly lighthearted tone of confession, Pulci puts forward, as a justification for *Morgante,* his desire to please all by offering in his poem a variety of topics which, he believes, should appeal to people of different tastes. Though occasional comments of a personal nature can also be found in other cantos, it is here and in the preceding stanzas—where "the private voice of the poet appears . . . to find a perfect harmony with the voice of his poetry" (Getto, 189)—that Pulci more meaningfully and openly reveals what can be construed as his poetic canon.

142, 7. The "different clapper" is obviously Pulci's pen.

143, 1. Ruphus Varius is the Latin poet who, assisted by Tucca, edited and published, at Augustus's urging, Virgil's *Aeneid* after the poet's death.

143, 2–3. Born in Florence in 1452, the poet Bernardo Bellincioni spent his earlier years as a member of Lorenzo de' Medici's court. In 1480, because of financial problems, he left Florence for Mantua, moving in 1485 to Milan when he entered the service of Duke Ludovico Sforza. Bellincioni, who died in Milan in 1492, wrote sonnets, love poems, and also political and satirical poetry. Bernardo was one of Pulci's friends. Not only did Bernardo insert two lines from Pulci's *Confessione* into his poem *La Visione,* but he also expressed high praise for his friend's poem in a sonnet entitled "In Laude di Luigi Pulci per l'opera del Morgante e Margutte da lui composta" (see sonnet LI in Bernardo Bellincioni, *Le Rime,* I, redatte e annotate da Pietro Fanfani [Bologna: Presso Gaetano Romagnoli, 1876]).

143, 5–6. The proverbial expression "to go into the water carrying a pumpkin fastened on one's back in order to remain afloat" means "to proceed with great caution" (Ageno, 1110).

144, 1. Another good friend of Luigi Pulci, Antonio di Guido, wrote sacred and secular verse, which earned him the reputation of Florence's greatest *improvvisatore*. In 1459 he sang with his lyre a short poem in praise of Francesco Maria Sforza, the duke of Milan, in the Medicean villa of Careggi, the seat of the Platonic Academy of Florence (which, according to Ageno [1110], is the event referred to in lines 2–3). Also note that the word "Ausonian," used mostly in poetry, means "Italian" (line 3). Vallombrosa, where Antonio di Guido (who died in 1486) was residing, is located east of Florence, on a mountaintop of the Tuscan Apennines.

145, 1–8. Pulci, who does not expect to be treated with all the honors reserved to a great poet, does not wish to emphasize the importance of his work with external gimmicks (printing the names in red), as is done for books of no literary value. This will be achieved, instead, with the poetic assistance of Angelo Poliziano, true glory of his native Montepulciano. Ageno (1111) identifies the "Serafin" in line 5 with the friar Mariano da Gennazzano, whom Pulci, in his *Confessione,* credits with his return to religious practices. Observing that in canto XXV, 169, 1–3 Pulci calls Poliziano both "cherub" and "seraphim," Davide Puccini (1353) is of the opinion that "Serafin" and "Angiolino" are one and the same.

146, 1–8. The lyric poet Alcaeus, who lived between the seventh and sixth centuries B.C., authored ten books of poetry, of which about one hundred fragments have come down to us. The mythical son of Zeus, Amphion, was believed to have built the walls around Thebes with the sound of his lyre. He died of despair when all his children were killed. Musaeus, a mythical Thracian poet, was credited with having introduced poetry in Greece. Regarding Orpheus, see note, II, 38, 4. The "laurel tree" mentioned in line 4 is Lorenzo de' Medici, a name given to him by the Florentine poets.

147, 1–4. Pallas is the young son of Evander, Aeneas's ally, who is slain by Turnus (*Aeneid,* VIII). Ageno (1111) asserts that this character represents Lorenzo's oldest son Piero, who in 1482 was twelve years old. Puccini (1360), though not entirely rejecting Ageno's thesis, admits nevertheless the possibility, supported also by other critics, that Pallas may be the Magnificent himself.

147, 5–8. Commenting upon these lines, Puccini (1360) remarks that Pulci's wish to die together with Poliziano, who is twenty years his junior, is purely hypothetical. It is possible that Pulci derives the image of the flame from the myth of Eteocles and Polynices (see note, XXVII, 255, 1–3), but with the notable difference that here Luigi and Angelo are united by love in only one flame, while the flame that envelops the twin sons of Jocasta and Oedipus is split by their hate.

148, 1–8. The river Eurote flows in the Peloponnesus, Greece's largest peninsula. For Cynthus, Pindus, Aracynthus, Delphi, and Delos, see note, 52, 1–5. Quirinus is the name given to Rome's first king, Romulus, after he ascended to heaven as a god.

149, 1–2. Caius Asinius Pollio (76 B.C.–A.D. 5) was a Roman writer and politician, credited with having founded the first public library in Rome. He is believed to have inspired Virgil's *Bucolics*. C. Cilnius Maecenas was a first-century B.C. Roman aristocrat and politican, who became Augustus's friend. He used his great riches as a patron of artists and writers, among them Propertius, Horace, and Virgil, whose *Georgics* he is said to have inspired.

150, 1–8. The three Graces (Euphrosyne, Aglaea, and Thalia), all the nymphs, and Pallas, the goddess of knowledge, come together to sing Poliziano's praises, because a poet's creative fantasy can change what the stars have preordained.

151, 1–8. The "boughs and twigs" in line 2 are probably Lorenzo's (the laurel tree) younger sons, Giovanni and Giuliano. Indus and Maurus are the Indian and Atlantic oceans, respectively. With the words "Mercuries" (Mercury was the god of science) and "Apollos" (Apollo was the god of poetry), the poet is referring to the new men of science and the poets who will bring back the golden age that humanity enjoyed under the reign of Saturn. (This ancient Roman god of fertility and agriculture, having been thrown out of Olympus by Jove, took up residence in Latium, where he introduced the agricultural arts, thus bringing a great civilization to Italy.)

152, 5. This line, where the pastoral poet Gallus represents all poets, is a faithful translation of Virgil's verse "Neget quis carmina Gallo?" (*Eclogues,* X, 3).

Constance Jordan, in her article "The Ending of Pulci's *Morgante:* The Poet as Virgil's Gallus" (*Romanic Review* 75, 4 [November 1984]: 399–413), declares that a careful examination of stanzas 130–152 "signals [Pulci's] disbelief in the possibility of a history celebrating the emperor Charlemagne, testifies to his interest in entertaining a notion of pastoral, and finally reveals that he rejects even his modest vision of the nature of his work."

In the part of her article that deals with lines 7–8 of stanza 151 and 6–7 of stanza 152, Jordan writes that Pulci "has failed to clearly identify himself ... either with Virgil's pastoral poet, ... or with Gallus himself." Even assuming that it is possible to recognize Lorenzo de' Medici in the person of Gallus, or to read the last stanzas of *Morgante* as "a sophisticated imitation of Virgil's *Eclogues,*" Jordan suggests that Pulci "colors his proposal with the ambivalence that in Virgil's poem allows one to question, with Gallus, the enterprise of writing pastoral at the very moment it is being proposed." For Jordan, Pulci's intention to dedicate himself to the writing of pastoral poetry must be perceived, therefore, as the poet's awareness of his failure as the author of an epic romance, written to exalt Charlemagne's achievements and capable of promoting the return of the age of chivalry in the Florence of his time. Her previous statement concerning Pulci's failure notwithstanding, the critic believes that Pulci's imitation of Virgil's *Eclogues* does "lend support to an interpretation of the poet's as Virgil's Gallus, voicing, however indirectly, his despair." (With regard to Professor Jordan's book *Pulci's "Morgante": Poetry and History in Fifteenth-Century Florence* [Washington, D.C.: The Folger Shakespeare Library; London: Associated University Presses, 1986], the first [but in many aspects disappointing] full-length study in English on the work of the Florentine poet, see my bibliographical review "Un decennio di studi pulciani: 1984–1994," in *Annali d'Italianistica: The Italian Epic & Its International Context,* ed. Dino S. Cervigni, vol. 12 [1994], 233–265.)

152, 6. Note that also in this concluding line, Pulci resorts to Latin to express emphatically that what he has written is not enough, compared to the importance of the subject treated and his initial desire.

In the final three unnumbered stanzas, Pulci inserts the "Salve Regina" prayer which he had originally placed at the end of canto XXIII. It contains many of the metaphors and the invocations to Mary that we find in the poem's first twenty-three cantos, and adds nothing new to what we have already said about Luigi's religious feelings. Commenting upon the few minor changes in stanza 3 prompted by Lucrezia's death in 1482, Ageno (1114) finds it "strange," and rightly so, that Pulci, who in stanza 135 has proclaimed Lorenzo's mother to be among the blessed souls in heaven, now begs Mary to keep Lucrezia in her grace.

BIBLIOGRAPHY

Ageno, Franca. "Scelta linguistica e reazione antiletteraria nel *Morgante*." *Lettere Italiane* VII (1955): 113–129.
———. "Le tre redazioni del *Morgante*." *Studi di filologia italiana* 9 (1951): 5–37.
Alighieri, Dante. *Inferno*. Translated by Mark Musa. Bloomington: Indiana University Press, 1971.
Ankli, Ruedi. *Morgante Iperbolico*. L'iperbole nel *Morgante* di Luigi Pulci. Firenze: Olschki, 1993.
———. "Un problema di attribuzione sempre aperto: Il *Ciriffo Calvaneo*." In *L'attribuzione: teoria e pratica*, Atti del Seminario di Ascona, 30 settembre–5 ottobre 1992, 259–304. A c. di O. Besomi e C. Caruso. Basel: Birkhäuser, 1994.
Atchity, Kenneth John. "Renaissance Epic in English." *Italica* 50, 3 (Autumn 1973): 435–439.
Baccini, P. G. "I poeti fratelli Pulci in Mugello e il *Driadeo d'Amore*." *Giotto* 2 (1903): 352–363, 371–382, and *Giotto* 3 (1904): 401–411.
Bart, B. F. "Aspects of the Comic in Pulci and Rabelais." *Modern Language Quarterly* 11 (1951): 156–163.
Bellincioni, Bernardo. *Le Rime*. I. Redatte e annotate da Pietro Fanfani. Bologna: Presso Gaetano Romagnoli, 1876.
Bessi, Rossella. "Il *Morgante* e il *Liombruno*." *Interpres* IX (1989): 267–274.
Biscottini, Umberto. *L'anima e l'arte del 'Morgante.'* Livorno: Giusti, 1932.
Boni, Marco. "A proposito di un personaggio del *Morgante* ('Dodone, il figliol del Danese')." In *Atti dell'Accademia delle Scienze dell'Istituto di Bologna. Rendiconti*, vol. LXXIII (1984–85), 97–113. Bologna: Tipografia Compositori, 1986.
Boninger, Lorenz. "Notes on the Last Years of Luigi Pulci (1477–1484)." *Rivista dell'Istituto Nazionale di Studi sul Rinascimento* XXVII (1987): 259–271.
Bussani, Illidio. *Il romanzo cavalleresco in Luigi Pulci*. Torino: Fratelli Bocca Editori, 1933.
Carducci, Giosuè. *Discorsi letterari e storici*. Edizione Nazionale delle opere, vol. VII. Bologna: Zanichelli, 1945.
Carnesecchi, Carlo. "Per la biografia di Luigi Pulci." *Archivio storico italiano* XVII (1896): 371–379.
Carrai, Stefano. *Le muse dei Pulci*. Studi su Luca e Luigi Pulci. Napoli: Guida editori, 1985.
Carrara, Enrico. *Da Rolando a Morgante*. Torino: Erma, 1932.
Ceserani, Remo. "L'allegra fantasia di Luigi Pulci e il rifacimento dell'*Orlando*." *Giornale storico della letteratura italiana* 135 (1958): 171–214.
———. "Studi sul Pulci." *Giornale storico della letteratura italiana* 146 (1969): 412–35.
La Chanson de Roland. Edition critique et traduction de Ian Short. Le livre de poche. Librairie Générale Française, 1990.

Ciriffo Calvaneo. Composto per Luca De' Pulci a petizione del Magnifico Lorenzo De' Medici. Con Osservazioni Bibliografico-Letterarie di S.L.G.E. Audin. Firenze: Tipografia Arcivescovile, 1834.

Crescimbeni, Mario Giovanni. *L'istoria della volgar poesia.* Roma, 1968.

Croce, Benedetto. *Ariosto, Shakespeare, Corneille.* Bari: Laterza, 1961.

————. *Conversazioni critiche.* Bari: Laterza, 1932.

————. *La letteratura italiana per saggi storicamente disposti.* Edited by Mario Sansone. Vol. I. Bari: Laterza, 1957.

Curto, Carlo. "Gli studi sul Pulci nel dopoguerra: 1918–1932." *Rivista di sintesi letteraria* I (1934): 102–119.

————. *Pulci.* Torino: Paravia, 1932.

————. *Le tradizioni popolari nel 'Morgante' di Luigi Pulci.* Casale: Tipografia Cooperativa Bellatore and Co., 1918.

da Barberino, Andrea. *I Reali di Francia.* Firenze: Salani, 1915.

d'Ascoli, Cecco (Stabili, Francesco). *Acerba.* Ridotta a miglior lezione dal prof. dott. A. Crespi. Ascoli Piceno, 1927.

Davie, Mark. "Biography and Romance: The *Vita Caroli Magni* of Donato Acciaiuoli and Luigi Pulci's *Morgante.*" In *The Spirit of the Court,* ed. G. S. Burgess and R. A. Taylor, 137–152. Selected Proceedings of the Fourth Annual Congress of the International Courtly Literature Society (Toronto 1983). Dover, N.H.: D. S. Brewer, 1985.

————. "Luigi Pulci's *Stanze per la Giostra:* Verse and Prose Accounts of a Florentine Joust of 1469." *Italian Studies* 44 (1989): 41–58.

————. "Pulci's Margutte Episode Re-examined." *Italian Studies: An Annual Review* 33 (1978): 29–55.

della Torre, Arnaldo. *Storia dell'Accademia Platonica di Firenze.* Firenze: Carnesecchi, 1902.

de' Medici, Lorenzo. *Opere.* Edited by Luigi Cavalli. Napoli: Casa Editrice Fulvio Rossi, 1970.

De Robertis, Domenico. *Storia del Morgante.* Firenze: Le Monnier, 1958.

De Sanctis, Francesco. *Storia della letteratura italiana.* Vol. I. Edited by Benedetto Croce. Bari: Laterza, 1925.

de Tyre, Guillaume. *Histoire des Croisades. Collection des Mémoires relatifs à l'histoire de France.* Edited by M. Guizot. Vol. XVIII. 1832–1835.

Di Paolo, Maria Grazia. "Osti e osterie nel *Morgante* del Pulci." *Forum Italicum* 24, 1 (Spring 1990): 80–93.

di Pino, Guido. "Novità del Morgante." In *Linguaggio della tragedia alfieriana e altri studi,* 51–59. Firenze: La Nuova Italia, 1952.

————. *Saggio sul 'Morgante.'* Bologna: Zanichelli, 1934.

Il Driadeo di Luca Pulci al Magnifico Lorenzo de' Medici. Napoli: Tipografia Trani, 1881.

Elogj degli uomini illustri toscani. Tomo II. Lucca, 1772.

L'Entrée d'Espagne. Edited by Antoine Thomas. Paris: Société des anciens textes français, 1913.

Fatini, Giuseppe. "Rassegna della bibliografia pulciana (1811–1952)." *Atti e memorie dell'accademia toscana di scienze e lettere "La Colombaria"* 17, n.s. 3 (1951–52): 207–266. Firenze: Olschki, 1952.

Ficino, Marsilio. *Opera ommia.* Vol. I, pt. 2. Riproduzione in fototipia dell'edizione di Basilea del 1576. A c. di M. Sancipriano, con presentazione di Paul Oscar Kristeller. Torino: Bottega d'Erasmo, 1959.

Flamini, Francesco. *La lirica toscana del Rinascimento anteriore ai tempi del Magnifico.* Pisa: Nistri, 1891.

Frappier, Jean. *Les Chansons de Geste du Cycle de Guillaume d'Orange.* Paris: Société d'édition d'enseignement supérieur, 1955.

Gajetti, Vittorio. "Tematica della gola e morte di Margutte." In *L'arte dell'interpretare: studi critici offerti a Giovanni Getto,* 165–178. Cuneo: Arciere, 1984.

Gareffi, Andrea. *L'ombra dell'eroe. Il 'Morgante.'* Urbino: Edizioni Quattroventi, 1986.

Garver, M. S., and K. McKensie. "Il bestiario toscano secondo la lezione dei codici di Parigi e di Londra." *Studi Romanzi* VIII (1912): 1–100.

Getto, Giovanni. *Studio sul 'Morgante.'* Firenze: Olschki, 1967.

Gianni, Angelo. *Pulci uno e due.* Firenze: La Nuova Italia, 1967.

Gravina, Gian Vincenzo. *Della ragion poetica.* Libro II. Venezia: Presso Angiolo Geremia, 1731.

Harris, Julian. "The Role of the Lion in Chrétien de Troyes' *Yvain*." *PMLA* 64 (1949): 1143–1163.

Hartley, K. H. "Rabelais and Pulci." *Australasian Universities Modern Language Association* 9 (November 1958): 71–78.

Historia Karoli Magni et Rotholandi ou Chronique du Pseudo-Turpin. Edited by C. Meredith-Jones. Paris: E. Nizet, 1936.

Hodgson, M. G. S. *The Order of the Assassins.* The Hague, 1955.

Hübscher, Johannes. *Ausgaben und Abhandlungen aus dem Gebeite der Romanischen Philologie LX. "Orlando" Die Vorlage zu Pulci's "Morgante,"* 1–264. Marburg: N. G. Elwert'sche Verlagsbuchhandlung, 1886.

Jonard, Norbert. "La nature du comique dans le *Morgante* de Pulci." In *Culture et société en Italie du Moyen-Âge à la Renaissance,* Hommage à André Rochon, 83–101. Paris: Université de la Sorbonne Nouvelle, 1985.

Jordan, Constance. "The Ending of Pulci's *Morgante*: The Poet as Virgil's Gallus." *Romanic Review* 75, 4 (November 1984): 399–413.

———. *Pulci's 'Morgante': Poetry and History in Fifteenth-Century Florence.* Washington, D.C.: The Folger Shakespeare Library; London and Toronto: Associated University Presses, 1986.

Jovine, Vincenzo. "L'Astarotte di Luigi Pulci e il Mefistofele di W. Goethe." *Rendiconti della R. Accademia dei Lincei* 18 (1908): 482–517.

Kristeller, Paul Oscar. *Supplementum Ficiniamnum.* Vol. II, 287–289. Firenze: 1937.

Larivaille, Paul. "Morgante da 'fiero' a 'gentil gigante': Carnevalizzazzione della materia cavalleresca e ricupero cavalleresco di tradizioni carnevalesche." In *Culture et société en Italie du Moyen-Âge à la Renaissance,* Hommage à André Rochon, 103–115. Paris: Université de la Sorbonne Nouvelle, 1985.

Lèbano, Edoardo A. "Cent'anni di bibliografia pulciana: 1883–1993." *Pulci and Boiardo. Annali d'Italianistica* 1 (1983): 55–79.

———. "Un decennio di studi pulciani: 1984–1994." *The Italian Epic and Its International Context. Annali d'Italianistica* 12 (1994): 233–265.

———. "Due esempi di satira antifratesca nel *Morgante*." In *Studies in Honor of Tatiana Fotich,* 203–209. Washington, D.C.: The Catholic University of America Press, 1972.

———. "Luigi Pulci and Late Fifteenth-Century Humanism in Florence." *The Renaissance Quarterly* 27, 4 (1974): 489–498.

Lèbano, Edoardo A., and Paolo Orvieto. "Il 'Tractato del prete colle monache.'" *Interpres* II (1979): 282–294.

Leo, Ulrich. "Luigi Pulci e il Diavolo." *Der Vergleich Literatur- und Sprachwissenschaftliche Interpretationen. Festgabe für Hellmuth Petriconi zum 1 April 1955.* Edited by Rudolf Grassmann, Walter Pabst, and Edmund Schramon. Vol. 42 (1955): 123–143.

Mancini, Albert N. "The English Face of Pulci." A Foreword to Joseph Tusiani's *From Pulci's "Morgante."* *Forum Italicum* 18, 1 (Spring 1984): 117–122.

Marchetti, Italiano. "Collaborazione di poeti in un poema quattrocentesco." *Lettere Italiane* 4 (1953): 105–120.

Mariani, Gaetano. *Il Morgante e i cantari trecenteschi.* Firenze: Le Monnier, 1953.

Martinelli, Franco. "Gli stivali di Margutte." *Annali d'Italianistica* 1 (1983): 49–54.

Mattioli, Laura. *Luigi Pulci e il 'Ciriffo Calvaneo.'* Padova: Sanavio e Pizzati, 1900.

Mickel, Emanuel J. *Ganelon, Treason and the "Chanson de Roland."* University Park: Pennsylvania State University Press, 1989.

Momigliano, Attilio. *L'indole e il riso di Luigi Pulci.* Rocca San Casciano: Cappelli, 1907.

Morpurgo, Giuseppe. "Tre amici (Lorenzo de' Medici, Luigi Pulci, Angiolo Poliziano)." *Rivista d'Italia* XVII 1 (Gennaio 1914): 40–54.

Motti e facezie del piovano Arlotto. Edited by G. Folena. Milano-Napoli: Ricciardi, 1953.

Nigro, Salvatore. *Pulci e la cultura medicea.* Bari: Editori Laterza, 1972.

Orvieto, Paolo. *Pulci medievale.* Roma: Salerno Editrice, 1978.

———. "Sul rapporto *Morgante-Orlando Laurenziano.*" *Die Ritterepik der Renaissance.* Akten des Deutsch-Italienischen Kolloquiums, Berlin, 30.3.–2.4.1987, 145–153. A c. di Klaus W. Hempfer. Stuttgart: Franz Steiner Verlag, 1989.

The Other Bible. Edited by Willis Barnstone. San Francisco: Harper Collins Publishers, 1992.

Ovid. *Metamorphoses.* Translated by Rolfe Humphries. Bloomington: Indiana University Press, 1957.

Oxford Dictionary of the Christian Church. Edited by F. L. Cross. London: Oxford University Press, 1974.

Pellegrini, Carlo. *Luigi Pulci: l'uomo e l'artista.* Pisa: Nistri, 1912.

Pezzarossa, Fulvio. *I poemetti di Lucrezia Tornabuoni.* Firenze: Olschki, 1978.

Poemi Cavallereschi del Trecento. Edited by Giuseppe Guido Ferrero. Torino: UTET, 1965.

Pulci, Antonia. *Florentine Drama for Convent and Festival: Seven Sacred Plays.* Translated by James Wyatt Cook. Edited by James Wyatt Cook and Barbara Collier Cook. Chicago: University of Chicago Press, 1996.

Pulci, Luigi. *Le frottole di Luigi Pulci.* Rivedute nel testo e annotate da Guglielmo Volpi. Firenze: Tipografia Galileiana, 1912.

———. *Lettere di Luigi Pulci a Lorenzo il Magnifico e ad altri.* Nuova edizione corretta e accresciuta a c. di Salvatore Bongi. Lucca: Giusti, 1886.

———. *Morgante.* Edited by Franca Ageno. Milano-Napoli: Ricciardi, 1955.

———. *Morgante.* Edited by Giuliano Dego. Milano: Biblioteca Universale Rizzoli, 1992.

———. *Morgante.* Edited by Giuseppe Fatini. Torino: UTET, 1927. (Last reprints, 1984.)

———. *Morgante.* Edited by Davide Puccini. Firenze: Garzanti, 1989.

———. *Morgante.* Edited by Gugliemo Volpi. Firenze: Sansoni, 1900–1904.

———. *'Morgante' e 'Lettere.'* Edited by Giuseppe De Robertis. Firenze: Sansoni, 1962.

———. *Opere minori.* Edited by Paolo Orvieto. Milano: Mursia, 1986.

———. *Strambotti di Luigi Pulci fiorentino.* Edited by Albino Zenatti. Firenze: Libreria Dante, 1887.

Quadrio, Gian Battista. *Della storia e ragione di ogni poesia.* Tomo IV, Libro II. Milano, 1749.

Rajna, Pio. "La materia del *Morgante* in un ignoto poema cavalleresco del secolo XV." *Il Propugnatore* 2, 1 (1869): 7–35, 220–252, 353–384.

Ramat, Raffaello. "Storia di Luigi Pulci." In *Antologia della critica letteraria,* vol. II, 252–270. A c. di Giuseppe Petronio. Bari: Laterza, 1964.

Ratti, Maria Pia. "Avaler la tradition: sul bestiario del *Morgante.*" *Lettere Italiane* 42, 2 (aprile–giugno 1990): 264–75.

Raymond, Marcel. *Marsile Ficin.* Paris: Société d'Edition "Les Belles Lettres," 1958.

Ruggieri, Ruggero M. "Affinità di tematiche e di personaggi tra *Il Milione* e il *Morgante.*" In *Symposium in honorem Prof. M. De Riquer,* Universitat de Barcelona, 349–362. Quaderns Crema, 1984.

————. "La serietà del *Morgante*" and "La polemica del *Morgante*." In *L'umanesimo cavalleresco italiano: da Dante al Pulci,* 199–223 and 225–251. Roma: Edizioni dell'Ateneo, 1962.

Sacchetti, Franco. *Il trecento novelle.* Edited by Antonio Lanza. Firenze: Sansoni, 1984.

Santini, Emilio. "All'ombra del Magnifico." *Rivista d'Italia* XVI (1913): 515–553.

Scardeone, Bernardino. *De antiquitate urbis Patavii.* Basileae, 1560.

Scrivano, Riccardo. "Luigi Pulci nella storia della critica." *Rassegna della letteratura Italiana* 59, 4 (1955): 232–258.

Shulters, John Raymond. *Luigi Pulci and the Animal Kingdom.* Baltimore: J. H. Furst Co., 1920.

Solmi, Edmondo. "Nuovi contributi alle fonti dei manoscritti di Leonardo da Vinci." *Giornale storico della letteratura italiana* LVIII (1911): 328–252.

Sonetti di Matteo Franco e di Luigi Pulci, insieme con la Confessione. Stanze in lode della Beca ed altre rime del medesimo Pulci. Lucca, 1759.

The Song of Roland. Translated with an introduction by Patricia Terry. New York: Macmillan, 1992.

La Spagna. Poema cavalleresco del secolo XIV. Edito e illustrato da Michele Catalano, vols. I–III. Bologna: Commissione per i testi di lingua, 1939.

Stendhal. *Roma.* Roma and Torino: Roux e Viarengo, 1906.

Tancredi, Giovanni. "Il Margutte del Pulci, il Cingar del Folengo e il Panurgo del Rabelais." *Atti del congresso internazionale di scienze storiche* (Roma) IV (1904): 227–239.

Tetel, Marcel. "Pulci and Rabelais: A Revaluation." *Studi francesi* 9 (1965): 89–93.

Tiraboschi, Girolano. *Storia della letteratura italiana.* Tomo VI, Libro III. Napoli, 1781.

Tripp, Edward. *The Meridian Handbook of Classical Mythology.* New York: New American Library, 1970.

Vallese, Giulio. "Il *Morgante* e l'antiumanesimo del Pulci." *Italica* 30 (1953): 81–85.

I viaggi di Marco Polo veneziano. Descritti da Rusticano da Pisa. Padova: Signum Edizioni, 1983.

Volpi, Guglielmo. "Un cortigiano di Lorenzo il Magnifico (Matteo Franco) e alcune sue lettere." *Giornale storico della letteratura italiana* XVII (1891): 239.

————. "La *Divina Commedia* nel *Morgante* di Luigi Pulci." *Giornale Dantesco* XII (1903): 170–74.

————. "Luigi Pulci. Studio Biografico." *Giornale storico della letteratura italiana* XXII, 64–65 (1893): 1–55.

Walser, Ernst. *Lebens- und Glaubensprobleme aus dem Zeitalter der Renaissance: Die Religion des Luigi Pulci, ihre Quellen und ihre Bedeutung.* Marburg: a. n. Lahme Envert, 1926.

Wilkins, Ernest H. "On the Dates of Composition of the *Morgante* of Luigi Pulci." *PMLA* 66 (1951): 244–250.

INDEX OF NAMES

Mythological, classical, biblical, and well-known historical and geographical names are not included in this index (they are, however, noted in the commentary). The first occurrence of each name in the poem is indicated by both canto and stanza number; subsequent occurrences are noted by canto number only.

Note: Some characters' names appear in more than one version in the poem. In addition, names sometimes appear with accents added to show rhythmic stress.

Arpalista (Lord of Saliscaglia): XXII, 157, and following stanzas
Astaroth (a devil): XXI, 49; XXV, XXVI, XXVII, XXVIII
Astolfo (duke; son of Otho, King of England; and Orlando's and Rinaldo's cousin): I, 9; II, III, VIII, IX–XIII, XV–XVII, XIX, XXI–XXII, XXIV–XXVII
Avin(o) (Namo's son): I, 10; III, VIII, XI, XII, XIX, XXIV, XXVI, XXVII
Avolio (Namo's son): I, 10; III, VIII, XI, XII, XIX, XXIV, XXVI, XXVII

Baal (first king of the Assyrians): XV, 111
Baetica, XXV, 253
Baetis (the Guadalquivir River): XXV, 254
Bacchillòn (an Italian river): XXV, 12
Bagdad (city ruled by Arcaliffa): XXV, 294; XXVII
Baiard(o) (Rinaldo's horse): III, 46; IV–VII, IX–XIV, XVI–XVIII, XX–XXVII
Balante (Chiariella's future husband): XIII, 71–73; XIV–XVI
Baldovin(o) (son of Ugier the Dane): XII, 21; XIII
Baldwin (son of Gano, Lord of Maganza): I, 10; XXIV–XXVII
Balsamin (a Saracen king): XXV, 179; XXVI, XXVII
Balugant(e): XIV, 38; XVI, XXV, XXVI, XXVII
Bambillona (Babylon) (capital of Babylonia): XV, 90; XVII–XXV
Barbary (a northwestern African region): II, 50; III, XV, XVII, XXI, XXII, XXVI
Bartholomew (an innkeeper): XI, 30
Beatrice (Rinaldo's mother): XII, 34
Beelzebub: II, 39; V, XIV, XV
Belfagor (a devil): IV, 97; XV, XXVII
Belfior (name of the castle of Filomeno, Florinetta's father): XIX, 9, and following stanzas
Bellamarina (a land ruled by King Costanzo): XVI, 97; XVII
Beltramo (a giant): XIX, 12, and following stanzas
Beltramo (of Maganza): XXII, 124–129
Benevento (a city in southern Italy): XXVIII, 79, 92
Berith (a devil): XXI, 48
Berlinghier(i) (son of Namo): I, 9; II, III, VIII, X–XIII, XIX, XXII, XXIV–XXVII
Bernard of Pontier: III, 27
Bertha (Charlemagne's mother): XXVIII, 127
Bianciardin(o) (Marsilius's ambassador to France): XXIV, 13; XXV–XXVII
Bileth (a devil): XXI, 49
Blanda (Queen of Spain): XXV, 113; XXVII
Bocco (a devil): XXI, 48
Brava (Orlando's castle): I, 17

Bravieri (King of Nubia): XXVIII, 64
Breusse: XIII, 54
Brunamonte (a giant): XVI, 14; XVIII
Brunetta: XXII, 224–238
Brunoro (a giant): III, 33, and following stanzas
Brunoro (a name adopted by Orlando): II, 69; III, VI, VII
Brusbacca (a Saracen king): XXVI, 129; XXVII
Buiafort(e) (son of the Old Man of the Mountain): XXIV, 6–7; XXV–XXVII
Buovo of Agrismont (Ammon's and Milo's brother): III, 77; XI, XXIII
Burrato (a giant): XVIII, 51; XIX

Cagnazzo (a devil): II, 31
Calandro (King Falcon's nephew): XVII, 83–87
Calavrion(e) (brother of the Old Man of the Mountain): XXII, 26, and following stanzas
Can di Gattaia: XX, 60; XXI
Caradoro (a pagan king, father of Meridiana): II, 12; III, V–X
Carlo (also called Carlotto) (first-born son of Charlemagne): XXVIII, 64, 98, 114
Carloman (Charlemagne's brother): XXVIII, 71
Carrara (a Saracen city): IV, 42
Castelfalcone (Creonta's castle): XXI, 22
Cattabriga (a giant): XXIV, 59, and following stanzas
Cazlona (a Spanish city): XXV, 255
Cecco d'Ascoli (a writer, contemporary of Dante): XXIV, 112
Charlemagne (also Carlo, Charles, Charlie, Pepin's son): I, 4; except for cantos V, VII, XIV, and XXI, the French emperor is either mentioned or appears in all other cantos, particularly XXIV–XXVIII
Cheiron (a centaur): XXVII, 22
Chemmis (Egyptian pharaoh): XXV, 202
Chiariella (daughter of the Admiral of Persia): XII, 40; XIII, XV–XVI
Chiariello (a giant): XVI, 14; XVIII
Chiariello (King of Portugal): XXVI, 128; XXVII
Chiarione (innkeeper): XX, 63; XXI
Chiaristante (King of Corniglia): XXI, 101; XXII
Chimento (Rinaldo's messenger): II, 41; III
Chiron (son of Salamon of Brittany): XXVII, 266; XXVIII
Clairmont (Abbot of Clairmont): I, 20; II, III, IV
Clemency (Lady Clemency) (Erminion's wife): VIII, 15; IX, X
Constantine (Greek emperor): XXVIII, 104

Copardo (Chiariella's brother): XV, 45; XVI
Corante (a giant): XIV, 30; XV
Corbante (a Saracen king): IV, 41;V, VI
Corsignano (a small Tuscan town): XIV, 53
Cortana (Ugier the Dane's sword): I, 17; II,
   VI,VII, X
Costantino (a giant): XVIII, 91
Costanzo (King of Bellamarina): XVI, 97;
   XVII, XVIII, XX, XXII
Creonta (a sorceress): XX, 19; XXI

Dane (the). *See* Ugier the Dane
Danismarche (Erminion's kingdom): IX,16; X
Desiderius (King of the Longobards):
   XXVIII, 61, and following stanzas
Diliante (King of Villafranca and a nephew
   of the Old Man of the Mountain):
   XXII, 39–46, and following stanzas
Don Bruno (a giant): XVII, 90–116
Don Buoso (a nephew of Gerard of Fratta):
   XXVIII, 57
Don Chiaro (a nephew of Gerard of Fratta):
   XXVI, 109; XXVII, XXVIII
Dudon (also Dudòn) (Ugier's second-born
   son): III, 30; IV–IX, XX, XXII
Durafort (Ugier's horse): XXVIII, 64
Durlindana (Orlando's sword): I, 16; III–IV,
   VII, X, XII, XXVIII

Egibard, Duke: XXVI, 64; XXVII
Ermellina (Namo's daughter and Ugier's
   wife): I, 17
Erminion(e) (King of Danismarche and
   Fieramonte's brother): VIII, 15; IX–
   XII, XX
Eviltail (a devil): II, 31

Faburro: IX, 28; X
Falcon (a king): XVII, 83, and following
   stanzas
Fallalbacchio (a giant friend of Cattabriga):
   XXIV, 58, and following stanzas
Falseron (Marsilius's envoy to Charlemagne):
   XXIV, 150; XXV, XXVI, XXVII
Farès (an evil spirit): XXV, 92
Farferello (also Farferel) (a devil): II, 31;
   XXV, XXVI, XXVII
Ferraù (a Saracen warrior): XXIV, 16; XXV–
   XXVIII
Fidasso: XXV, 177; XXVI–XXVII
Fieramont (Erminion's brother): VIII, 25–
   26; IX, X, XXIII
Fieramonte of Balzia: XXV, 179; XXVI,
   XXVII
Filiberta (Chiaristante's wife): XXI, 102;
   XXII
Filisetta (Queen of Sardonia); XXII, 255,
   and following stanzas
Filomeno (Florinetta's father): XIX, 9, and
   following stanzas

Finadust (the poem's last giant): XXV, 177;
   XXVI
Fiorello (a Saracen king): XXV, 179; XXVI
Fiovus (Emperor Constantine's son): XXIV,
   23
Florinetta: XIX, 5, and following stanzas
Floro (an evil spirit): XXV, 92
Forisena (King Corbante's daughter): IV, 41;
   V;VI,VIII, XVI
Frasmondo (a Maganzan knight): XI, 36
Frusberta (Rinaldo's sword): III, 55; IV–VII,
   IX–XII, XIV–XVIII, XX–XXIII,
   XXVII
Fucecchio (a lake in Tuscany): XXIII, 6
Fuligat(to) (a bandit): XXII, 217; XXIII,
   XXIV, XXV

Galafro (Marsilius's father): XXVII, 281;
   XXVIII
Galigante (Galigant) (a Saracen king): XXII,
   254 and 257
Galicia: XXV, 263, 266; XXVII
Gallerana (Charlemagne's wife): XI, 30; XII,
   XIII, XXV, XXVII, XXVIII
Gallerano (a Saracen king): XXV, 27; XXVI,
   XXVIII
Galliano (a name adopted by Astolfo): XXI,
   125; XXII
Gan(o) of Pontier (also known as Ganelon
   and Lord of Maganza): I, 8; II, IV, VI–
   XIII, XVI–XXII, XXIV–XXVIII
Gerard (also Gherardo) of Fratta (Marquis of
   Vienna, in Burgundy, and Oliver's
   uncle): I, 13; XXVIII
Gerard (Gherardo) of Rossiglione: XX, 105;
   XXII
Gioiosa (Charlemagne's sword): XXIV, 128
Gisberto (Marsilius's nephew): XIII, 51
Goths: XXVIII, 81
Gramolazzo: XVII, 105
Grandonio (a Saracen king): XXV, 180;
   XXV, XXVII
Grandono (a giant): XV, 76–79
Greco (a ship captain): XX, 27; XXI, XXII
Gregory, Pope: XXV, 159
Grifon of Altafoglia (a Maganzan): XI, 25–
   27, 36
Grifonetto (a Maganzan): XXII, 18, and fol-
   lowing stanzas
Guadian land. See note, XXV, 255, 2–4
Gualtieri (a Saracen): XVI, 116–117; XVII
Guicciardo (Rinaldo's brother): III, 31;VIII,
   XVII, XXII, XXV, XXVIII
Guottibuoffi (Guottibuoff): XXVI, 5; XXVII

Hadrian, Pope: XXVIII, 75
Heraclius (a Byzantine emperor): XXVIII,
   127
Heruli: XXVIII, 81
Hungarians: XXVIII, 96

Hunold: XXVIII, 73
Huns: XXVIII, 81

Iber (the River Ebro): XXV, 289; XXVI, XXVII

Lactantius: XXVIII, 53–56, 68
Lazzera (a Saracen city): XXVIII, 57
Leo, Pope: III, 77; XXVIII
Leopantè: XX, 80, and following stanzas
Liombrun(o) (Marsilius's nephew): XXI, 56, and following stanzas
Lionetto (Meridiana's brother): II, 67; III
Lionfant(e) (Erminion's admiral): VIII, 24; IX–XII
Liorgante (a giant): XIV, 30–33
Luciana (King Marsilius's daughter): XIII, 48; XIV–XVI, XXV, XXVII, XXVIII
Lucifer: XI, 74; XIX, XXIII, XXV–XXVIII
Ludwig (Charlemagne's third son and successor): XXVIII, 114, 116
Lupus (Duke of Gascony): XXVIII, 73
Lustycock: a devil, II, 31

Macarius: XXVII, 137; XXVIII
Machidant: XXVIII, 59
Magagna: IX, 71; X
Mahomet and/or Mahound (see note, I, 35, 6): found in all cantos of the poem except XI and XVI
Malabranca (Satan): XXV, 40
Malachel (a devil): XXVIII, 60
Malagigi (Malgigi) (Orlando's and Rinaldo's first cousin): III, 31; V, X–XII, XVII, XIX–XXVIII
Maldue (King of Frasse): XXV, 177; XXVI, XXVII
Malprimo (a Saracen king): XXV, 177; XXVI
Mambrin(o) of Ulivant: III, 32; VIII, IX, X, XVII, XVIII
Manfredonio: II, 14; III, V–VIII, XX
Marcovaldo (a giant): XII, 40; XIII, XVI, XXIV
Margheriton (a Saracen king): XXV, 179; XXVI, XXVII
Margutte: XVIII, 120–200; XIX, XXIV, XXVII
Marguttino: XXIV, 92–98
Mariotto (son of the Emperor of Mezza): XVIII, 41; XX, XXII
Mark of Saint Michael's Mount: XXVI, 78; XXVII
Marmores (a demon): XXIV, 113
Marsilius (King of Spain): VIII, 32; XIII, XIV, XVI, XXI, XXIV–XXVIII
Martel (Charles Martel, Pepin's father): XXVIII, 75
Mattafellon(e) (Gano's horse): XI, 38; XX, XXII

Mattafirro (an African king): XXVI, 129; XXVII
Mattafol(le) (Erminion's ambassador to France): VIII, 39; IX, XII
Matthew of Saint Michael's Mount: XXVI, 78; XXVII
Mazzarigi: XXVI, 57; XXVII
Menappello (Manoppello): I, 6 (see note, I, 6, 1–3)
Meridiana (King Caradoro's daughter): II, 67; III, V–XII, XVI, XVIII, XX
Milo(n) of Anglante (Orlando's father): I, 85; II–IV, X, XII, XV, XVII, XVIII, XXI, XXIV–XXVII
Milusse (a devil): XXV, 205; XXVI
Monaca, city of: XX, 58; XXI, XXII
Moco (an evil spirit): XXIV, 113
Montalban (Rinaldo's castle): II, 43; III–XXV, XXVIII
Morando: XXVIII, 54
Morgana: XXV, 104
Morgante: I, 20; II, III, VI–XII, XVIII–XX, XXIV, XXVII, XXVIII

Namo (Duke of Bavaria): I, 10; II, III, VIII, X–XIII, XIX, XXII, XXIV, XXV, XXVII
Narses: XXVIII, 75
Niello (a devil): XXI, 48
Nillo (a devil): XXI, 48
Ninus (a son of Baal): XV, 111

Obysìn (a devil): XXI, 48
Old Man of the Mountain: XVII, 8; XVIII–XX, XXII–XXIV, XXVI, XXVII
Oldorigi: XXVIII, 55
Oliver of Burgundy ("the marquis") (Alda's brother): I, 9; his name appears in all cantos except XXIII
Oratas (an evil spirit): XXI, 49
Orco (Charlemagne's slave): XXVII, 262
Orlando (Lord of Anglante, "the count," "the Roman senator"): beginning with I, 8, appears in all cantos
Otho (Namo's son): I, 10; VIII, XII, XIX, XXIV–XXVII
Otho (King of England): III, 77; VIII, XI, XXVII

Pannonia: XXVIII, 96
Pantalisse: XXVII, 138
Passamonte (Alabaster's and Morgante's brother): I, 20; III
Pepin (Charlemagne's father): I, 10; VIII–XI, XXIV, XXV, XXVIII
Pepin (Charlemagne's son): XXVIII, 114
Piè di Porto (of Saint John): XXV, 70; XXVI–XXVIII
Pietrapana (a mountain in Tuscany): VII, 18

Pilagi d'Ulivant: XXIII, 31, and following stanzas
Pilfer: XVIII, 172
Pontier (Gano's castle): XIII, 16; XXII
Prester John: XXV, 128
Pulidor (Count of Lausanne): XXII, 124

Ricciardetto (Rinaldo's brother): III, 31; VIII–XIII, XV–XXVIII
Riccieri of Risa: XXII, 149; XXVIII
Richard of Normandy: XXVI, 64
Rinaldo (Lord of Montalban and Ammon's son): II, 3, and all cantos thereafter
Rinieri (Rinaldo's squire): XXI, 13, and following stanzas
Rondel (Ugier's horse): I, 17; II, III, IV, VII, IX, X, XX, XXIV, XXVI, XXVII
Rosaspina (Aldighieri's mother): XX, 105
Rubicante (a devil): XXV, 165, and following stanzas
Rugiadan (a devil): XXI, 48
Ruinatto (Orlando's squire): X, 76; XII

Saint Denis (Church of): VIII, 38; IX, XI, XVI, XVII, XXIV, XXV, XXVII, XXVIII
Saint Liberator (Abbey of): I, 6
Salamon (Salomon) (King of Brittany): I, 10; II, III, VIII, IX, XI–XIII, XIX, XXIV, XXV, XXVII
Salayè (a devil): XXI, 47
Salincorno (a giant): XVII, 96; XVIII, XXII
Salincorno (Erminion's brother): VIII, 25; IX, X
Saliscaglia, city of: XXII, 158, and following stanzas
Salyass (an evil spirit): XXI, 48
Sansonet(to): XXIV, 54; XXV–XXVIII
Saragossa, city of: XIII, 44; XIV–XVI, XXIV, XXVI–XXVIII
Sardonia, city of: XXII, 244, and following stanzas
Satan: II, 29; IV, V, IX, XXI, XXIV, XXV–XXVII
Scarbo (a demon): XXIV, 113
Scirocco (a ship master): XX, 27, and following stanzas
Scythians: XXVIII, 96
Seeland: XXIV, 56
Serchio (a Tuscan river): XXIV, 141
Serpentin: XXV, 10
Sibyl of Norcia: XXIV, 112; XXVIII
Sicumoro: XXIV, 62, and following stanzas
Sleep (the innkeeper): XVIII, 169, and following stanzas
Smahèl: XXI, 46
Sottìn (a devil): XXI, 48
Sperante (a giant): XIX, 28, and following stanzas

Spinardo (a centaur): XXIII, 16–24
Spinellon (also Spinellone, Ispinellón): XVIII, 21; XX, XXII
Squarciafer(ro) (a devil): XXI, 48; XXV–XXVII
Stella, city of: XXVIII, 58
Sultan of Babylon (Antea's father): III, 38; X, XII, XIII, XV–XVIII, XX, XXII, XXIV, XXV, XXVIII
Sutri, city of: XXVII, 136
Syrion: XXV, 179; XXVI, XXVII

Tagus (the Spanish river Tajo): XXV, 255
Tambernic (Stambernicchi) (a mountain): XXIV, 88
Taxillo (a Bavarian duke): XXVIII, 94–95
Terigi (Orlando's squire): X, 76; XI–XIII, XV–XVII, XXIV, XXVI, XXVII
Tesoretto (Rinaldo's squire): X, 89, and following stanzas
Trasimene (an Italian lake): XXVI, 131
Trevigant (also Trivigant): II, 70; III, IV, XIII, XIV, XV, XVII, XVIII, XXI, XXII, XXV
Troiano: XXVII, 138
Turchion: XXV, 177; XXVI
Turpin, Archbishop: I, 5; VIII, XI, XII, XXIV–XXVIII

Ugier the Dane: I, 9; II–IV, VII–XIII, XV, XVII, XIX, XX, XXII, XXIV, XXV, XXVII, XXVIII
Ugone (Ugon): XXVIII, 59
Uliva (King Costanzo's daughter): XVI, 96; XVII, XX, XXII
Urman of Paris: I, 5; XXVII, XXVIII

Vandals: XXVIII, 81
Vegliantin (also Vegliantino, Vegliantìn) (Orlando's horse): III, 4; IV–VII, X–XIV, XVI–XXII, XXIV, XXVI, XXVII
Vegurto (a giant): X, 128; XI
Velatabi: XXVIII, 96
Vergante (King of Arma): XIII, 73; XIV, XV
Villafranca, city of: XXII, 39, and following stanzas
Vivian of Maganza: XII, 20, 23, 26
Vivian (a Christian knight): XXII, 18 and following stanzas

Walter of Mont Leon (also known as Don Simon): I, 10; VIII, XI, XII, XXVI, XXVII

Zambuger(i) (Marsilius's son): XXV, 56; XXVI, XXVII

Joseph Tusiani, Distinguished Service Professor,
retired from City University of New York in 1983. His
other translations include *The Complete Poems of Michelangelo,*
Tasso's *Jerusalem Delivered* and *Creation of the World,* Boccaccio's
Nymphs of Fiesole, Leopardi's *Canti,* and Dante's *Lyric Poems.* A
poet in his own right, Tusiani is the author of *Rind and All,*
The Fifth Season, and *Gente Mia and Other Poems.* He has
also published four collections of verse in Latin, the last
of which, *Confinia Lucis et Umbrae,*
appeared in 1989.

Edoardo A. Lèbano, Professor of French and Italian
at Indiana University, has published several articles dealing
with Luigi Pulci's culture and works.